Advanced Accounting

Eleventh Edition

Joe B. Hoyle

Associate Professor of Accounting
Robins School of Business
University of Richmond

Thomas F. Schaefer

KPMG Professor of Accountancy
Mendoza College of Business
University of Notre Dame

Timothy S. Doupnik

Professor of Accounting
Darla Moore School of Business
University of South Carolina

The McGraw-Hill Companies

ADVANCED ACCOUNTING
International Edition 2013

Exclusive rights by McGraw-Hill Education (Asia), for manufacture and export. This book cannot be re-exported from the country to which it is sold by McGraw-Hill. This International Edition is not to be sold or purchased in North America and contains content that is different from its North American version.

Published by McGraw-Hill/Irwin, a business unit of The McGraw-Hill Companies, Inc., 1221 Avenue of the Americas, New York, NY 10020.

10 09 08 07 06 05 04 03 02 01
20 15 14 13
CTP MPM

When ordering this title, use ISBN 978-1-259-07172-0 or MHID 1-259-07172-3

Printed in Singapore

www.mhhe.com

To our families

The real purpose of books is to trap the mind into doing its own thinking.

—Christopher Morley

About the Authors

Joe B. Hoyle, *University of Richmond*

Joe B. Hoyle is Associate Professor of Accounting at the Robins School of Business at the University of Richmond, where he teaches Intermediate Accounting and Advanced Accounting. In 2009, he was named one of the 100 most influential people in the accounting profession by *Accounting Today.* He was named the 2007 Virginia Professor of the Year by the Carnegie Foundation for the Advancement of Teaching and the Center for Advancement and Support of Education. He has been named a Distinguished Educator five times at the University of Richmond and Professor of the Year on two occasions. Joe recently authored a book of essays titled *Tips and Thoughts on Improving the Teaching Process in College,* which is available without charge at http://oncampus.richmond.edu/~jhoyle/.

Thomas F. Schaefer, *University of Notre Dame*

Thomas F. Schaefer is the KPMG Professor of Accounting at the University of Notre Dame. He has written a number of articles in scholarly journals such as *The Accounting Review, Journal of Accounting Research, Journal of Accounting & Economics, Accounting Horizons,* and others. His primary teaching and research interests are in financial accounting and reporting. Tom is active with the Association for the Advancement of Collegiate Schools of Business International and is a past president of the American Accounting Association's Accounting Program Leadership Group. Tom received the 2007 Joseph A. Silvoso Faculty Merit Award from the Federation of Schools of Accountancy.

Timothy S. Doupnik, *University of South Carolina*

Timothy S. Doupnik is Vice Provost and Professor of Accounting at the University of South Carolina, where he teaches Financial and International Accounting. Tim has published extensively in the area of international accounting in journals such as *The Accounting Review; Accounting, Organizations, and Society; Abacus; International Journal of Accounting;* and *Journal of International Business Studies.* Tim is a past president of the American Accounting Association's International Accounting Section, and he received the section's Outstanding International Accounting Educator Award in 2008.

Students Solve the Accounting Puzzle

The approach used by Hoyle, Schaefer, and Doupnik allows students to think critically about accounting, just as they will in their careers and as they prepare for the CPA exam. Read on to understand how students will succeed as accounting majors and as future CPAs by using *Advanced Accounting, 11e.*

Thinking Critically

With this text, students gain a well-balanced appreciation of the accounting profession. As *Hoyle 11e* introduces them to the field's many aspects, it often focuses on past controversies and present resolutions. The text shows the development of financial reporting as a product of intense and considered debate that continues today and will in the future.

Readability

The writing style of the 10 previous editions has been highly praised. **Students easily comprehend** chapter concepts because of the conversational tone used throughout the book. The authors have made every effort to ensure that the writing style remains engaging, lively, and consistent.

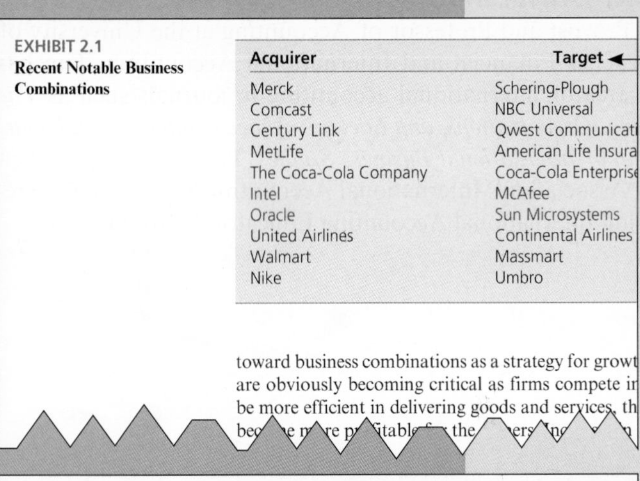

EXHIBIT 2.1
Recent Notable Business Combinations

Acquirer	Target
Merck	Schering-Plough
Comcast	NBC Universal
Century Link	Qwest Communicati
MetLife	American Life Insura
The Coca-Cola Company	Coca-Cola Enterpris
Intel	McAfee
Oracle	Sun Microsystems
United Airlines	Continental Airlines
Walmart	Massmart
Nike	Umbro

toward business combinations as a strategy for growt
are obviously becoming critical as firms compete ir
be more efficient in delivering goods and services, th

Real-World Examples

Students are better able to relate what they learn to what they will encounter in the business world after reading these frequent examples. Quotations, articles, and illustrations from *Forbes, The Wall Street Journal, Time,* and *BusinessWeek* are incorporated throughout the text. Data have been pulled from business, not-for-profit, and government financial statements as well as official pronouncements.

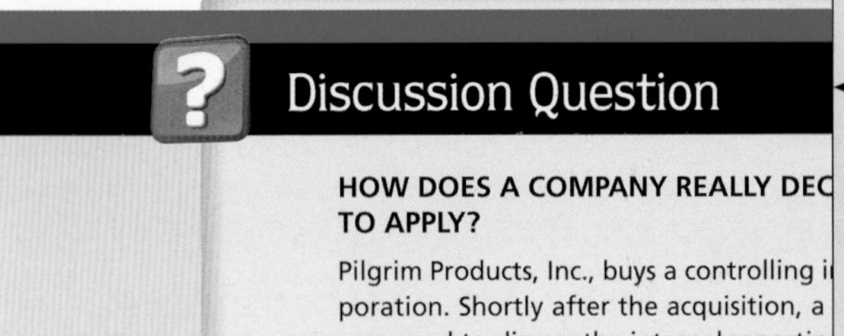

Discussion Question

HOW DOES A COMPANY REALLY DEC
TO APPLY?

Pilgrim Products, Inc., buys a controlling i
poration. Shortly after the acquisition, a
convened to discuss the internal reportin
subsidiary. Each member of the staff ha
method, initial value method, or partial e

Discussion Questions

This feature **facilitates student understanding** of the underlying accounting principles at work in particular reporting situations. Similar to minicases, these questions help explain the issues at hand in practical terms. Many times, these cases are designed to demonstrate to students why a topic is problematic and worth considering.

CPA Simulations

Hoyle et al.'s CPA Simulations, powered by Kaplan, are found in Chapters 1, 2, and 10 of the 11th edition and have been updated in this edition to reflect the task-based approach of the CPA exam. Simulations are set up in the text and completed online at the 11th edition website (mhhe.com/hoyle11e). This allows students to practice advanced accounting concepts in a web-based interface identical to that used in the actual CPA exam. There will be no hesitation or confusion when students sit for the real exam; they will know exactly how to maneuver through the computerized test.

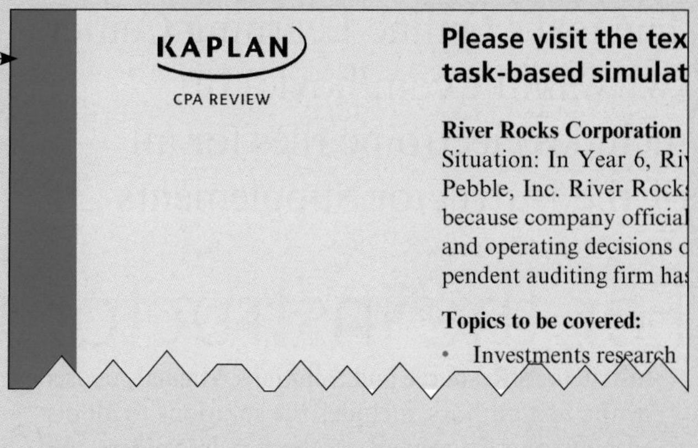

KAPLAN
CPA REVIEW
Please visit the tex
task-based simulat
River Rocks Corporation
Situation: In Year 6, Ri
Pebble, Inc. River Rock
because company officia
and operating decisions
pendent auditing firm ha
Topics to be covered:
• Investments research

End-of-Chapter Materials

As in previous editions, the end-of-chapter material remains a strength of the text. The sheer number of questions, problems, and Internet assignments tests, and therefore **expands, the students' knowledge** of chapter concepts.

Excel Spreadsheet Assignments extend specific problems and are located on the 11th edition website at mhhe.com/hoyle11e. An Excel icon appears next to those problems that have corresponding spreadsheet assignments.

"Develop Your Skills" asks questions that address the four skills students need to master to pass the CPA exam: Research, Analysis, Spreadsheet, and Communication. An icon indicates when these skills are tested.

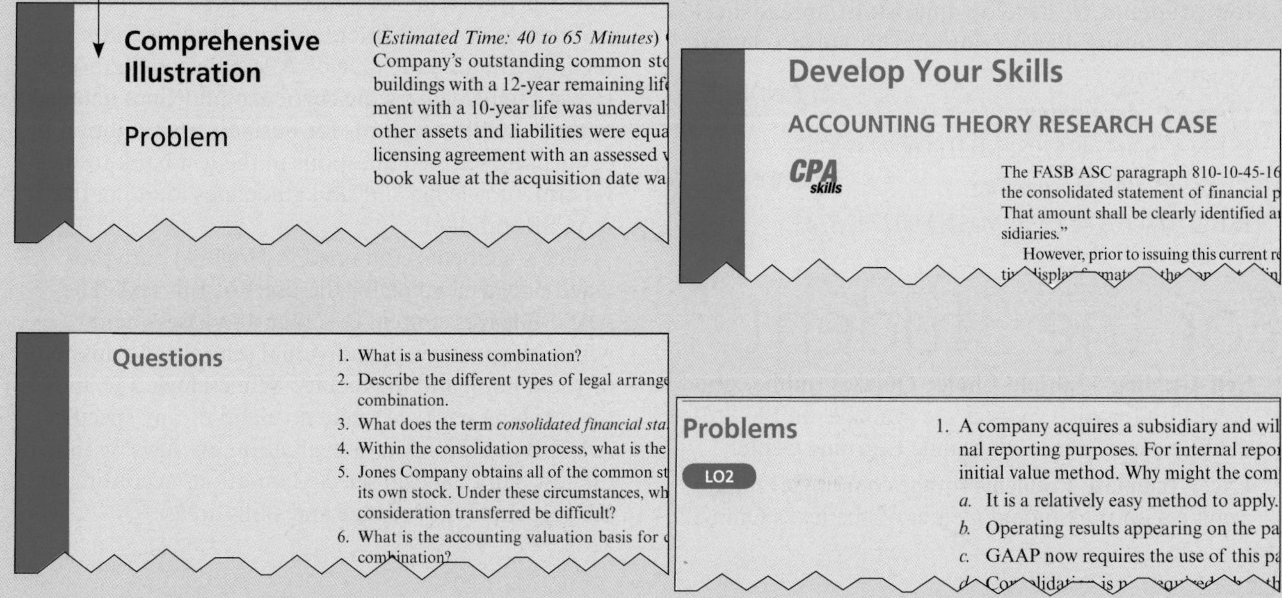

Comprehensive Illustration
Problem
(Estimated Time: 40 to 65 Minutes)
Company's outstanding common st
buildings with a 12-year remaining lif
ment with a 10-year life was underval
other assets and liabilities were equa
licensing agreement with an assessed
book value at the acquisition date wa
Develop Your Skills
ACCOUNTING THEORY RESEARCH CASE
CPA skills
The FASB ASC paragraph 810-10-45-16
the consolidated statement of financial p
That amount shall be clearly identified a
sidiaries."
However, prior to issuing this current r
Questions
1. What is a business combination?
2. Describe the different types of legal arrang
combination.
3. What does the term consolidated financial sta
4. Within the consolidation process, what is the
5. Jones Company obtains all of the common s
its own stock. Under these circumstances, w
consideration transferred be difficult?
6. What is the accounting valuation basis for
Problems
LO2
1. A company acquires a subsidiary and wi
nal reporting purposes. For internal repo
initial value method. Why might the com
a. It is a relatively easy method to apply.
b. Operating results appearing on the pa
c. GAAP now requires the use of this p

The text's Online Learning Center (www.mhhe.com/hoyle11e) includes electronic files for all of the Instructor Supplements

For the Instructor

- **Instructor's Resource and Solutions Manual,** revised by the text authors, includes the solutions to all discussion questions, end-of-chapter questions, and problems. It provides chapter outlines to assist instructors in preparing for class.
- **Test Bank,** revised by Stephen Shanklin, University of Southern Indiana, has been significantly updated.
- **EZ Test Computerized Test Bank** can be used to make different versions of the same test, change the answer order, edit and add questions, and conduct online testing. Technical support for this software is available at (800) 331-5094 or visit www.mhhe.com/eztest.
- **PowerPoint® Presentations,** revised by Anna Lusher, Slippery Rock University, deliver a complete set of slides covering many of the key concepts presented in each chapter.
- **Excel Template Problems and Solutions,** revised by Jack Terry of ComSource Associates, Inc., allow students to develop important spreadsheet skills by using Excel templates to solve selected assignments.
- ***Connect® Accounting*** (connect ACCOUNTING)
  ISBN 9780077425708; MHID 0077425707.
- ***Connect® Plus Accounting*** (connect plus+ ACCOUNTING)
  ISBN 9780077425722; MHID 0077425723.

For the Student

- **Self-Grading Multiple-Choice Quizzes** (mhhe.com/hoyle11e) for each chapter are available on the Student Center of the text's Online Learning Center.
- **Excel Template Problems** (mhhe.com/hoyle11e) are available on the Student Center of the text's Online Learning Center. The software includes innovatively designed Excel templates that may be used to solve many complicated problems found in the book. These problems are identified by a logo in the margin.
- **PowerPoint Presentations** (mhhe.com/hoyle11e) are available on the Student Center of the text's Online Learning Center. These presentations accompany each chapter of the text and contain the same slides that are available to the instructor.

Assurance of Learning Ready

Many educational institutions today are focused on the notion of assurance of learning, an important element of some accreditation standards. Hoyle 11e is designed specifically to support your assurance of learning initiatives with a simple, yet powerful solution.

Each test bank question for Hoyle 11e maps to a specific chapter learning outcome/objective listed in the text. You can use our test bank software, EZ Test, to easily query for learning outcomes/objectives that directly relate to the learning objectives for your course. You can then use the reporting features of EZ Test to aggregate student results in a similar fashion, making the collection and presentation of assurance of learning data simple and easy.

AACSB Statement

The McGraw-Hill Companies is a proud corporate member of AACSB International. Understanding the importance and value of AACSB accreditation, Hoyle 11e recognizes the curricula guidelines detailed in the AACSB standards for business accreditation by connecting selected questions in the test bank to the general knowledge and skill guidelines found in the AACSB standards.

The statements contained in Hoyle 11e are provided only as a guide for the users of this text. The AACSB leaves content coverage and assessment within the purview of individual schools, the mission of the school, and the faculty. While Hoyle 11e and the teaching package make no claim of any specific AACSB qualification or evaluation, we have, within the test bank, labeled selected questions according to the six general knowledge and skills areas.

McGraw-Hill *Connect®* *Accounting*

Less Managing. More Teaching. Greater Learning.

McGraw-Hill *Connect Accounting* is an online assignment and assessment solution that connects students with the tools and resources they'll need to achieve success. McGraw-Hill *Connect Accounting* helps prepare students for their future by enabling faster learning, more efficient studying, and higher retention of knowledge. *Connect Accounting* offers a number of powerful tools and features to make managing assignments easier, so faculty can spend more time teaching. With *Connect Accounting,* students can engage with their coursework anytime and anywhere, making the learning process more accessible and efficient. *Connect Accounting* offers you the features described below.

Simple assignment management

With McGraw-Hill's *Connect Accounting,* creating assignments is easier than ever, so you can spend more time teaching and less time managing. *Connect Accounting* enables you to:

- Create and deliver assignments easily with selectable end-of-chapter questions and test bank items.
- Streamline lesson planning, student progress reporting, and assignment grading to make classroom management more efficient than ever.
- Go paperless with the eBook and online submission and grading of student assignments.

Smart grading

When it comes to studying, time is precious. *Connect Accounting* helps students learn more efficiently by providing feedback and practice material when they need it, where they need it. The grading function enables you to:

- Have assignments scored automatically, giving students immediate feedback on their work and side-by-side comparisons with correct answers.
- Access and review each response; manually change grades or leave comments for students to review.
- Reinforce classroom concepts with practice tests and instant quizzes.

Student progress tracking

McGraw-Hill's *Connect Accounting* keeps instructors informed about how each student, section, and class is performing, allowing for more productive use of lecture and office hours. The reports tab enables you to:

- View scored work immediately and track individual or group performance with assignment and grade reports.
- Access an instant view of student or class performance relative to learning objectives.
- Collect data and generate reports required by many accreditation organizations, such as AACSB and AICPA.

McGraw-Hill *Connect® Plus Accounting*

McGraw-Hill reinvents the textbook learning experience for the modern student with *Connect Plus Accounting.* A seamless integration of an eBook and *Connect Accounting, Connect Plus Accounting* provides all of the *Connect Accounting* features plus an integrated eBook, allowing for anytime, anywhere access to the textbook; dynamic links between the problems or questions you assign to your students and the location in the eBook where that problem or question is covered; and a powerful search function to pinpoint and connect key concepts in a snap.

For more information about *Connect,* go to **www.mcgrawhillconnect.com,** or contact your local McGraw-Hill sales representative.

CPA Simulations

CPA REVIEW

The McGraw-Hill Companies and Kaplan have teamed up to bring students CPA simulations to test their knowledge of the concepts discussed in various chapters, practice critical professional skills necessary for career success, and prepare for the computer-based CPA exam. Kaplan CPA Review provides a broad selection of web-based simulations that were modeled after the AICPA format. Exam candidates become familiar with the item format, the research database, and the spreadsheet and word processing software used exclusively on the CPA exam (not Excel or Word), as well as the functionality of the simulations, including the tabs, icons, screens, and tools used on the exam. CPA simulations are found in the end-of-chapter material after the very last cases in Chapters 1, 2, and 10 and have been updated in this edition to reflect the task-based approach of the CPA exam.

Online Learning Center

www.mhhe.com/hoyle11e For instructors, the book's website contains the Instructor's Resource and Solutions Manual, PowerPoint slides, Excel templates and solutions, Interactive Activities, Text and Supplement Updates, and links to professional resources. The student section of the site features online multiple-choice quizzes, PowerPoint presentations, Check Figures, and Excel template exercises.

ALEKS® for Financial Accounting

ALEKS (Assessment and Learning in Knowledge Spaces) delivers precise, qualitative diagnostic assessments of students' knowledge, guides them in selecting appropriate new study material, and records their progress toward mastery of curricular goals in a robust classroom management system. ALEKS interacts with the student much as a skilled human tutor would, moving between explanation and practice as needed, correcting and analyzing errors, defining terms, and changing topics on request.

CourseSmart

CourseSmart is a new way to find and buy eTextbooks. At CourseSmart you can save up to 55% off the cost of a print textbook, reduce your impact on the environment, and gain access to powerful web tools for learning. Go to **www.coursesmart.com** to learn more.

Tegrity Campus: Lectures 24/7

Tegrity Campus, a new McGraw-Hill company, provides a service that makes class time available 24/7 by automatically capturing every lecture. With a simple one-click start-and-stop process, you capture all computer screens and corresponding audio in a format that is easily searchable, frame by frame. Students can replay any part of any class with easy-to-use browser-based viewing on a PC or Mac, an iPod, or other mobile device.

Educators know that the more students can see, hear, and experience class resources, the better they learn. In fact, studies prove it. Tegrity Campus's unique search feature helps students efficiently find what they need, when they need it, across an entire semester of class recordings. Help turn your students' study time into learning moments immediately supported by your lecture. With Tegrity Campus, you also increase intent listening and class participation by easing students' concerns about note-taking. Lecture Capture will make it more likely you will see students' faces, not the tops of their heads.

To learn more about Tegrity, watch a 2-minute Flash demo at **http://tegritycampus.mhhe.com**.

Online Course Management

McGraw-Hill Higher Education and Blackboard have teamed up. What does this mean for you?

1. **Your life, simplified.** Now you and your students can access McGraw-Hill's *Connect*® and Create™ right from within your Blackboard course—all with one single sign-on. Say goodbye to the days of logging in to multiple applications.
2. **Deep integration of content and tools.** Not only do you get single sign-on with *Connect* and Create, you also get deep integration of McGraw-Hill content and content engines right in Blackboard. Whether you're choosing a book for your course or building *Connect* assignments, all the tools you need are right where you want them—inside of Blackboard.
3. **Seamless grade books.** Are you tired of keeping multiple grade books and manually synchronizing grades into Blackboard? We thought so. When a student completes an integrated *Connect* assignment, the grade for that assignment automatically (and instantly) feeds your Blackboard grade center.
4. **A solution for everyone.** Whether your institution is already using Blackboard or you just want to try Blackboard on your own, we have a solution for you. McGraw-Hill and Blackboard can now offer you easy access to industry leading technology and content, whether your campus hosts it, or we do. Be sure to ask your local McGraw-Hill representative for details.

In addition to Blackboard integration, course cartridges for whatever online course management system you use (e.g., WebCT or eCollege) are available for Hoyle 11e. Our cartridges are specifically designed to make it easy to navigate and access content online. They are easier than ever to install on the latest version of the course management system available today.

McGraw-Hill/Irwin CARES

At McGraw-Hill/Irwin, we understand that getting the most from new technology can be challenging. That's why our services don't stop after you purchase our book. You can e-mail our product specialists 24 hours a day, get product training online, or search our knowledge bank of Frequently Asked Questions on our support website. For customer support, call 800-331-5094 or visit **www.mhhe.com/support**. One of our technical support analysts will assist you in a timely fashion.

Overall—this edition of the text provides relevant and up-to-date accounting standards references to the Financial Accounting Standards Board (FASB) *Accounting Standards Codification* (ASC).

Chapter Changes for *Advanced Accounting,* 11th Edition:

Chapter 1

- Modified the structure by moving coverage of excess purchase price amortizations to immediately follow the basics of equity method accounting.
- Updated real-world references.
- Included a new Chapter 1 problem 14 that provides basic coverage of an investor's accounting for an investee's reported other comprehensive income.
- Updated the end-of-chapter analysis case on Coca-Cola's equity method investees in light of Coca-Cola's acquisition of a controlling interest in Coca-Cola Enterprises (CCE).
- Added two new CPA exam style simulations.

Chapter 2

- Added new descriptive coverage of three recent business combinations—United and Continental Airlines, Merck and Schering-Plough, and Nike and Umbro. These combinations provide real-world examples of motivations to combine, the financial magnitudes that often characterize acquisitions, and the underlying risks that accompany business combinations.
- Updated other chapter real-world references including the latest efforts by the FASB and IASB to define control.
- Added six new end-of-chapter problems and two new cases. The first new case is an ASC research case involving accounting for a defensive intangible asset acquired in a business combination. The second new case asks students to research Abbot Labs's recent acquisition of Solvay Pharmaceuticals.
- Added CPA exam style simulation.
- Moved coverage of the legacy purchase and pooling of interests methods into an appendix given the time elapsed since the ASC requirements for the acquisition method.
- Added a new end-of-chapter problem briefly reviewing the main points of the legacy methods.

Chapter 3

- Updated material on goodwill impairment to reflect a 2011 amendment to FASB ASC Topic 305 that allows an entity the option to first assess qualitative factors to determine whether it is more likely than not that a reporting unit's fair value is less than its carrying amount.
- Added four new end-of-chapter problems and a new research case that compares goodwill impairment testing procedures across IFRS and U.S. GAAP.

Chapter 4

- Updated real-world references throughout Chapter 4.
- Added five new end-of-chapter problems.
- Added two new research cases. The first covers Coca-Cola's acquisition of Coca-Cola Enterprises (CCE) and focuses on accounting for employee replacement awards issued in conjunction with the business combination. The second new case asks students to research the Accounting Standards Codification (ASC) regarding basic financial reporting issues for business combinations. Next two additional questions require research into the differences between IFRS and U.S. GAAP concerning acquisition-date noncontrolling interest valuation alternatives.
- Discontinued coverage of post-acquisition financial statement preparation under the legacy purchase and pooling methods given current requirements for the acquisition method. Chapter 2, however, continues coverage of the legacy methods in an appendix.

Chapter 5

- Changed the text presentation order for the consolidation processes for intra-entity inventory transfers first using an example where the parent employs the equity method, followed by the initial value method and discussion of the partial equity method.
- Consolidation worksheet entries now debit the Investment in Subsidiary account instead of Equity in Subsidiary Earnings for intra-entity beginning inventory profits from downstream sales when the parent uses the equity method. A revised footnote presents and discusses the equivalence of a debit to the Equity in Subsidiary Earnings account for beginning inventory intra-entity profit recognition.
- Modified end-of-chapter problem 18 to increase its focus on consolidated net income determination and allocation to the controlling and noncontrolling interests.

Chapter 6

- Updated real-world references throughout the chapter, including discussion of the new International Accounting Standards, *IFRS 10* and *IFRS 12,* on consolidations and related disclosures.
- Added a new problem 25 to provide an assignment covering the preparation of acquisition-date consolidated financial statements for a parent and its variable interest entity (VIE).
- Edited the text example for consolidating VIEs to include separate calculations for acquisition-date valuation.
- Modified the intra-entity bond text example (and related end-of-chapter problems) to include (1) separate consolidation worksheet entries for bond premiums and discounts, and (2) worksheet entries to recognize subsequent year effects from effective bond retirements when the equity method is employed by the parent.
- Streamlined the coverage of intra-entity bonds in the presence of a noncontrolling interest to allow a better focus on the basic issue of parent-only allocation of income effects.

Chapter 7

- Rewrote several areas of the chapter to enhance clarity and conciseness.
- Revised several end-of-chapter problems including the deferred tax case at the end of the chapter. The case includes coverage of Coca-Cola's acquisition of Coca-Cola Enterprises (CCE) and its impact on Coca-Cola's deferred taxes.

Chapter 8

- Updated all annual report excerpts and examples.
- Added a flowchart for determining reportable operating segments.

Chapter 9

- Added a table summarizing the accounting for hedges of foreign exchange risk.
- Provided additional explanation of the journal entries in the examples demonstrating the accounting for hedges of foreign currency denominated assets and liabilities and foreign currency firm commitments.
- Added discussion of the IASB's exposure draft on hedge accounting issued in 2011.
- Updated annual report excerpts and examples and end-of-chapter cases requiring the use of actual exchange rates.

Chapter 10

- Updated references to international mergers and acquisitions.
- Added discussion of countries recently designated as highly inflationary economies.
- Added discussion of the appropriate exchange rate to use for translation in those countries in which there is more than one rate at which local currency amounts can be converted into foreign currency.
- Added an example for the translation of nonlocal currency balances.

Chapter 11

- Updated all annual report excerpts and discussion related to them.
- Updated tables on IFRS and the worldwide use of IFRS in preparing consolidated financial statements.

- Added discussion of the two primary methods used by countries to incorporate IFRS into their financial reporting requirements.
- Deleted much of the detail provided on the IASB-FASB convergence process.
- Added a summary of the SEC staff discussion paper issued in 2011 that suggests a probable framework for incorporating IFRS into the U.S. financial reporting system.

Chapter 12

- Added reference to and brief description of the Dodd-Frank Wall Street Reform and Consumer Protection Act.
- Updated various SEC statistics.
- Clarified SEC division information.
- Rechecked web links used in footnotes and updated as necessary/appropriate.
- Supplemented web link footnotes/added additional footnotes.
- Made minor revisions to the end of the chapter problems and Solutions Manual.

Chapter 13

- Updated all statistics about the size and number of bankruptcies occurring in the United States.
- Extended the coverage of prearranged bankruptcies as they have become more prevalent.
- Updated various monetary limitations used in the bankruptcy laws that automatically change every three years based on inflation.
- Included a discussion of the method by which General Motors determined its reorganization value as it exited from bankruptcy.
- Added a discussion of analyzing a business to determine its risk of failure.
- Added numerous quotes about recent bankruptcies involving companies such as Borders and Lehman Brothers.

Chapter 14

- Updated for change in the tax code and other references.
- Added new end-of-chapter problems, including an application of the hybrid method to account for a partner withdrawal.

Chapter 15

- Updated the end-of-chapter analysis case.

Chapter 16

- Updated references to financial information as reported by state and local governments across the United States.
- Updated end-of-chapter material.

Chapter 17

- Updated the rule for blending component units.
- Added a discussion of the GASB's codification of its standards, including GASB Codification of Governmental Accounting and Financial Reporting Standards.
- Updated end-of-chapter material.

Chapter 18

- Added discussion about the tax status and tax reporting of not-for-profit organizations.
- Included a new discussion on the inclusion of performance indicators to help readers of financial information make better evaluations of an organization's efficiency.
- Updated end-of-chapter material.

Chapter 19

- Updated rates, exemptions, and calculations to reflect the 2011 and 2012 tax law changes.
- Rechecked Internal Revenue Code citations and web links used in footnotes and updated as necessary/appropriate.
- Supplemented web link footnotes/added additional footnotes and/or updated footnotes to reflect tax law changes.
- Updated charts, tables, and problems to reflect the 2011 and 2012 tax law changes—where the changes have already been enacted into law.
- Revised problems in the text to reflect the tax law changes to rates, brackets, and exemptions.
- Updated all problems to reflect current dates, tax rates, and laws.

Acknowledgments

We could not produce a textbook of the quality and scope of *Advanced Accounting* without the help of a great number of people. Special thanks go to James O'Brien of the University of Notre Dame for his contribution to Chapters 12 and 19 and corresponding Solutions Manual files and to Gregory Schaefer for his Chapter 2 descriptions of recent business combinations. Additionally we would like to thank Steve Shanklin of University of Southern Indiana for revising and adding new material to the Test Bank and online student quizzes; Anna Lusher of Slippery Rock University, for updating and revising the PowerPoint presentations; Jack Terry of ComSource Associates for updating the Excel Template Exercises for students to use as they work the select end-of-chapter material; Ilene Leopold Persoff of CW Post Campus/Long Island University and Beth Woods of Accuracy Counts for checking the text and Solutions Manual for accuracy; Beth Woods for checking the Test Bank for accuracy; Barbara Gershman of Northern Virginia Community College for checking the PowerPoints; and Penny Clayton of Drury University for checking the quizzes for accuracy.

We also want to thank the many people who completed questionnaires and reviewed the book. Our sincerest thanks to them all:

Benjamin Bae
California State University, Bakersfield

John S. Bildersee
New York University

Kristine Brands
Regis University

Jim DeSimpelare
University of Michigan

Wei (Vivian) Fang
Rutgers, The State University of New Jersey

Becky Kerr
University of South Carolina

J. Edward Ketz
Pennsylvania State University

Stephani Mason
Hunter College

Mike Metzcar
Indiana Wesleyan University

David O'Bryan
Pittsburg State University (Kansas)

William Ruland
Baruch College, CUNY

Richard W. Schrader
Bellarmine University

Dan Sevall
Lincoln University

Stephen B. Shanklin
University of Southern Indiana

Kendall L. Simmonds
University of Southern California

Nathan Slavin
Hofstra University

Kathleen Sobieralski
University of Maryland University College

Randall Zhaohui Xu
University of Houston—Clear Lake

We also pass along a word of thanks to all the people at McGraw-Hill/Irwin who participated in the creation of this edition. In particular, Diane Nowaczyk, Senior Project Manager; Carol Bielski, Production Supervisor; Pam Verros, Designer; Danielle Andries, Editorial Coordinator; Dana Woo, Senior Sponsoring Editor; Tim Vertovec, Publisher; Bruce Gin and Joyce Chappetto, Media Project Managers; and Kathleen Klehr, Marketing Manager, all contributed significantly to the project, and we appreciate their efforts.

Brief Contents

Contents

Chapter Ten
Translation of Foreign Currency Financial Statements 449

Chapter Eleven
Worldwide Accounting Diversity and International Standards 505

chapter

1

The Equity Method of Accounting for Investments

The first several chapters of this text present the accounting and reporting for investment activities of businesses. The focus is on investments when one firm possesses either significant influence or control over another through ownership of voting shares. When one firm owns enough voting shares to be able to affect the decisions of another, accounting for the investment can become challenging and complex. The source of such complexities typically stems from the fact that transactions among the firms affiliated through ownership cannot be considered independent, arm's-length transactions. As in many matters relating to financial reporting, we look to transactions with *outside parties* to provide a basis for accounting valuation. When firms are affiliated through a common set of owners, measurements that recognize the relationships among the firms help to provide objectivity in financial reporting.

Learning Objectives

After studying this chapter, you should be able to:

- LO1 Describe in general the various methods of accounting for an investment in equity shares of another company.
- LO2 Identify the sole criterion for applying the equity method of accounting and guidance in assessing whether the criterion is met.
- LO3 Prepare basic equity method journal entries for an investor and describe the financial reporting for equity method investments.
- LO4 Allocate the cost of an equity method investment and compute amortization expense to match revenues recognized from the investment to the excess of investor cost over investee book value.
- LO5 Record the sale of an equity investment and identify the accounting method to be applied to any remaining shares that are subsequently held.
- LO6 Describe the rationale and computations to defer unrealized gross profits on intra-entity transfers until the goods are either consumed or sold to outside parties.
- LO7 Explain the rationale and reporting implications of the fair-value option for investments otherwise accounted for by the equity method.

The Reporting of Investments in Corporate Equity Securities

In its recent annual report, The Coca-Cola Company describes its 32 percent investment in Coca-Cola FEMSA, a Mexican bottling company with operations throughout much of Latin America. The Coca-Cola Company uses the equity method to account for several of its bottling company investments, including Coca-Cola FEMSA. The Coca-Cola Company states that its

> consolidated net income includes the Company's proportionate share of the net income or loss of these companies. The carrying values of our equity method investments are increased or decreased by our proportionate share of the net income or loss and other comprehensive income (loss) ("OCI") of these companies. The carrying values of our equity method investments are also decreased by dividends we receive from the investees.

Such information is hardly unusual in the business world; corporate investors frequently acquire ownership shares of both domestic and foreign businesses. These investments can range from the purchase of a few shares to the acquisition of 100 percent control. Although purchases of corporate equity securities (such as the one made by Coca-Cola) are not uncommon, they pose a considerable number of financial reporting issues because a close relationship has been established without the investor gaining actual control. These issues are currently addressed by the *equity method.* This chapter deals with accounting for stock investments that fall under the application of this method.

LO1

Describe in general the various methods of accounting for an investment in equity shares of another company.

At present, generally accepted accounting principles (GAAP) recognize three different approaches to the financial reporting of investments in corporate equity securities:

- The fair-value method.
- The consolidation of financial statements.
- The equity method.

The financial statement reporting for a particular investment depends primarily on the degree of influence that the investor (stockholder) has over the investee, a factor typically indicated by the relative size of ownership.[1] Because voting power typically accompanies ownership of equity shares, influence increases with the relative size of ownership. The resulting influence can be very little, a significant amount, or, in some cases, complete control.

Fair-Value Method

In many instances, an investor possesses only a small percentage of an investee company's outstanding stock, perhaps only a few shares. Because of the limited level of ownership, the investor cannot expect to significantly affect the investee's operations or decision making. These shares are bought in anticipation of cash dividends or in appreciation of stock market values. Such investments are recorded at cost and periodically adjusted to fair value according to the Financial Accounting Standards Board (FASB) Accounting Standards Codification (ASC) Topic 320, Investments—Debt and Equity Securities.

Because a full coverage of limited ownership investments in equity securities is presented in intermediate accounting textbooks, only the following basic principles are noted here.

- Initial investments in equity securities are recorded at cost and subsequently adjusted to fair value if fair value is readily determinable (typically by reference to market value); otherwise, the investment remains at cost.[2]
- Equity securities held for sale in the short term are classified as *trading securities* and reported at fair value, with unrealized gains and losses included in earnings.
- Equity securities not classified as trading securities are classified as *available-for-sale securities* and reported at fair value with unrealized gains and losses excluded from earnings and reported in a separate component of shareholders' equity as part of *other comprehensive income.*
- Dividends received are recognized as income for both trading and available-for-sale securities.

The above procedures are typically followed for equity security investments when neither significant influence nor control is present. However, as observed at the end of this chapter, FASB ASC Topic 825, Financial Instruments, allows a special fair-value reporting option for available-for-sale securities. Although the balance sheet amounts for the investments remain at fair value under this option, changes in fair values over time are recognized in the income statement (as opposed to other comprehensive income) as they occur.

Consolidation of Financial Statements

Many corporate investors acquire enough shares to gain actual control over an investee's operation. In financial accounting, such control is recognized whenever a stockholder accumulates more than 50 percent of an organization's outstanding voting stock.

[1] The relative size of ownership is most often the key factor in assessing one company's degree of influence over another. However, other factors (e.g., contractual relationships between firms) can also provide influence or control over firms regardless of the percentage of shares owned.

[2] The FASB ASC (para. 325-20-35-1 and 2) notes two exceptions to the cost basis for reporting investments:

1. Dividends received in excess of earnings subsequent to the date of investment are considered returns of the investment and are recorded as reductions of cost of the investment.
2. A series of an investee's operating losses or other factors can indicate a decrease in value of the investment has occurred that is other than temporary and should be recognized accordingly.

At that point, rather than simply influencing the investee's decisions, the investor clearly can direct the entire decision-making process. A review of the financial statements of America's largest organizations indicates that legal control of one or more subsidiary companies is an almost universal practice. PepsiCo, Inc., as just one example, holds a majority interest in the voting stock of literally hundreds of corporations.

Investor control over an investee presents a special accounting challenge. Normally, when a majority of voting stock is held, the investor-investee relationship is so closely connected that the two corporations are viewed as a single entity for reporting purposes. Hence, an entirely different set of accounting procedures is applicable. Control generally requires the consolidation of the accounting information produced by the individual companies. Thus, a single set of financial statements is created for external reporting purposes with all assets, liabilities, revenues, and expenses brought together.[3] The various procedures applied within this consolidation process are examined in subsequent chapters of this textbook.

The FASB ASC Section 810-10-05 on variable interest entities expands the use of consolidated financial statements to include entities that are financially controlled through special contractual arrangements rather than through voting stock interests. Prior to the accounting requirements for variable interest entities, many firms (e.g., Enron) avoided consolidation of entities in which they owned little or no voting stock but otherwise were controlled through special contracts. These entities were frequently referred to as "special purpose entities (SPEs)" and provided vehicles for some firms to keep large amounts of assets and liabilities off their consolidated financial statements. Accounting for these entities is discussed in Chapters 2 and 6.

Equity Method

Another investment relationship is appropriately accounted for using the equity method. In many investments, although control is not achieved, the degree of ownership indicates the ability for the investor to exercise *significant influence* over the investee. Recall Coca-Cola's 32 percent investment in Coca-Cola FEMSA's voting stock. Through its ownership, Coca-Cola can undoubtedly influence Coca-Cola FEMSA's decisions and operations.

To provide objective reporting for investments with significant influence, the FASB ASC Topic 323, Investments—Equity Method and Joint Ventures, describes the use of the equity method. The equity method employs the accrual basis for recognizing the investor's share of investee income. Accordingly, the investor recognizes income as it is earned by the investee. As noted in FASB ASC (para. 323-10-05-5), because of its significant influence over the investee, the investor

> . . . has a degree of responsibility for the return on its investment and it is appropriate to include in the results of operations of the investor its share of the earnings or losses of the investee.

Furthermore, under the equity method, dividends received from an investee are recorded as decreases in the investment account, not as income.

In today's business world, many corporations hold significant ownership interests in other companies without having actual control. The Coca-Cola Company, for example, owns between 20 and 50 percent of several bottling companies, both domestic and international. Many other investments represent joint ventures in which two or more companies form a new enterprise to carry out a specified operating purpose. For example, Microsoft and NBC formed MSNBC, a cable channel and online site to go with NBC's broadcast network. Each partner owns 50 percent of the joint venture. For each of these investments, the investors do not possess absolute control because they hold less than a majority of the voting stock. Thus, the preparation of consolidated financial statements is inappropriate. However, the large percentage of ownership indicates that each investor possesses some ability to affect the investee's decision-making process.

[3] As is discussed in the next chapter, owning a majority of the voting shares of an investee does not always lead to consolidated financial statements.

Discussion Question

DID THE COST METHOD INVITE EARNINGS MANIPULATION?

Prior to GAAP for equity method investments, firms often used the cost method to account for their unconsolidated investments in common stock regardless of the presence of significant influence. The cost method employed the cash basis of income recognition. When the investee declared a dividend, the investor recorded "dividend income." The investment account typically remained at its original cost—hence the term *cost method*.

Many firms' compensation plans reward managers based on reported annual income. How might the use of the cost method of accounting for significant influence investments have resulted in unintended wealth transfers from owners to managers? Do the equity or fair-value methods provide similar incentives?

Finally, as discussed at the end of this chapter, firms are now allowed a fair-value option in their financial reporting for certain financial assets and financial liabilities. Among the qualifying financial assets for fair-value reporting are significant influence investments otherwise accounted for by the equity method.

International Accounting Standard 28—Investments in Associates

The International Accounting Standards Board (IASB), similar to the FASB, recognizes the need to take into account the significant influence that can occur when one firm holds a certain amount of voting shares of another. The IASB defines significant influence as the power to participate in the financial and operating policy decisions of the investee, but it is not control or joint control over those policies. The following describes the basics of the equity method in International Accounting Standard (IAS) 28:[4]

> If an investor holds, directly or indirectly (e.g., through subsidiaries), 20 per cent or more of the voting power of the investee, it is presumed that the investor has significant influence, unless it can be clearly demonstrated that this is not the case. Conversely, if the investor holds, directly or indirectly (e.g., through subsidiaries), less than 20 per cent of the voting power of the investee, it is presumed that the investor does not have significant influence, unless such influence can be clearly demonstrated. A substantial or majority ownership by another investor does not necessarily preclude an investor from having significant influence.
>
> Under the equity method, the investment in an associate is initially recognised at cost and the carrying amount is increased or decreased to recognise the investor's share of the profit or loss of the investee after the date of acquisition. The investor's share of the profit or loss of the investee is recognised in the investor's profit or loss. Distributions received from an investee reduce the carrying amount of the investment.

As seen from the above excerpt from *IAS 28,* the equity method concepts and applications described are virtually identical to those prescribed by the FASB ASC.

[4] International Accounting Standards Board, *IAS 28 Investments in Associates*, Technical Summary (www.iasb.org).

Application of the Equity Method

An understanding of the equity method is best gained by initially examining the FASB's treatment of two questions:

1. What parameters identify the area of ownership for which the equity method is applicable?
2. How should the investor report this investment and the income generated by it to reflect the relationship between the two companies?

Criteria for Utilizing the Equity Method

LO2

Identify the sole criterion for applying the equity method of accounting and guidance in assessing whether the criterion is met.

The rationale underlying the equity method is that an investor begins to gain the ability to influence the decision-making process of an investee as the level of ownership rises. According to FASB ASC Topic 323 on equity method investments, achieving this "ability to exercise significant influence over operating and financial policies of an investee even though the investor holds 50 percent or less of the voting stock" is the sole criterion for requiring application of the equity method [FASB ASC (para. 323-10-15-3)].

Clearly, a term such as *the ability to exercise significant influence* is nebulous and subject to a variety of judgments and interpretations in practice. At what point does the acquisition of one additional share of stock give an owner the ability to exercise significant influence? This decision becomes even more difficult in that only the *ability* to exercise significant influence need be present. There is no requirement that any actual influence must have ever been applied.

FASB ASC Topic 323 provides guidance to the accountant by listing several conditions that indicate the presence of this degree of influence:

- Investor representation on the board of directors of the investee.
- Investor participation in the policymaking process of the investee.
- Material intra-entity transactions.
- Interchange of managerial personnel.
- Technological dependency.
- Extent of ownership by the investor in relation to the size and concentration of other ownership interests in the investee.

No single one of these guides should be used exclusively in assessing the applicability of the equity method. Instead, all are evaluated together to determine the presence or absence of the sole criterion: the ability to exercise significant influence over the investee.

These guidelines alone do not eliminate the leeway available to each investor when deciding whether the use of the equity method is appropriate. To provide a degree of consistency in applying this standard, the FASB provides a general ownership test: *If an investor holds between 20 and 50 percent of the voting stock of the investee, significant influence is normally assumed and the equity method is applied.*

> An investment (direct or indirect) of 20 percent or more of the voting stock of an investee should lead to a presumption that in the absence of evidence to the contrary an investor has the ability to exercise significant influence over an investee. Conversely, an investment of less than 20 percent of the voting stock of an investee should lead to a presumption that an investor does not have the ability to exercise significant influence unless such ability can be demonstrated.[5]

Limitations of Equity Method Applicability

At first, the 20 to 50 percent rule may appear to be an arbitrarily chosen boundary range established merely to provide a consistent method of reporting for investments. However, the essential criterion is still the ability to significantly influence (but not

[5] FASB ASC (para. 323-10-15-8).

control) the investee, rather than 20 to 50 percent ownership. If the absence of this ability is proven (or control exists), the equity method should not be applied regardless of the percentage of shares held.

For example, the equity method is not appropriate for investments that demonstrate any of the following characteristics regardless of the investor's degree of ownership:[6]

- An agreement exists between investor and investee by which the investor surrenders significant rights as a shareholder.
- A concentration of ownership operates the investee without regard for the views of the investor.
- The investor attempts but fails to obtain representation on the investee's board of directors.

In each of these situations, because the investor is unable to exercise significant influence over its investee, the equity method is not applied.

Alternatively, if an entity can exercise *control* over its investee, regardless of its ownership level, consolidation (rather than the equity method) is appropriate. FASB ASC (para. 810-10-05-8) limits the use of the equity method by expanding the definition of a controlling financial interest and addresses situations in which financial control exists absent majority ownership interest. In these situations, control is achieved through contractual and other arrangements called *variable interests.*

To illustrate, one firm may create a separate legal entity in which it holds less than 50 percent of the voting interests but nonetheless controls that entity through governance document provisions and/or contracts that specify decision-making power and the distribution of profits and losses. Entities controlled in this fashion are typically designated as *variable interest entities,* and their sponsoring firm may be required to include them in consolidated reports despite the fact that ownership is less than 50 percent. Many firms (e.g., The Walt Disney Company and Mills Corporation) reclassified former equity method investees as variable interest entities and now consolidate these investments.[7]

Extensions of Equity Method Applicability

For some investments that either fall short of or exceed 20 to 50 percent ownership, the equity method is nonetheless appropriately used for financial reporting. As an example, AT&T, Inc., disclosed that it uses the equity method to account for its 9 percent investment in América Móvil, a wireless provider in Mexico with telecommunications investments in the United States and Latin America. In its annual report, AT&T notes that it is a member of a consortium that holds voting control of the company, thus providing it significant influence.

Conditions can also exist where the equity method is appropriate despite a majority ownership interest. In some instances approval or veto rights granted to noncontrolling shareholders restrict the powers of the majority shareholder. Such rights may include approval over compensation, hiring, termination, and other critical operating and capital spending decisions of an entity. If the noncontrolling rights are so restrictive as to call into question whether control rests with the majority owner, the equity method is employed for financial reporting rather than consolidation. For example, prior to its acquisition of BellSouth, AT&T, Inc., stated in its financial reports "we account for our 60 percent economic investment in Cingular under the equity method of accounting because we share control equally with our 40 percent partner BellSouth."

To summarize, the following table indicates the method of accounting that is typically applicable to various stock investments:

[6] FASB ASC (para. 323-10-15-10). This paragraph deals specifically with limits to using the equity method for investments in which the owner holds 20 to 50 percent of the outstanding shares.

[7] Chapters 2 and 6 provide further discussions of variable interest entities.

Criterion	Normal Ownership Level	Applicable Accounting Method
Inability to significantly influence	Less than 20%	Fair value or cost
Ability to significantly influence	20%–50%	Equity method or fair value
Control through voting interests	More than 50%	Consolidated financial statements
Control through variable interests (governance documents, contracts)	Primary beneficiary status (no ownership required)	Consolidated financial statements

Accounting for an Investment—The Equity Method

Now that the criteria leading to the application of the equity method have been identified, a review of its reporting procedures is appropriate. Knowledge of this accounting process is especially important to users of the investor's financial statements because the equity method affects both the timing of income recognition as well as the carrying value of the investment account.

In applying the equity method, the accounting objective is to report the investor's investment and investment income reflecting the close relationship between the companies. After recording the cost of the acquisition, two equity method entries periodically record the investment's impact:

1. The investor's investment account *increases as the investee earns and reports income*. Also, the investor recognizes investment income using the accrual method—that is, in the same time period as the investee earns it. If an investee reports income of $100,000, a 30 percent owner should immediately increase its own income by $30,000. This earnings accrual reflects the essence of the equity method by emphasizing the connection between the two companies; as the owners' equity of the investee increases through the earnings process, the investment account also increases. Although the investor initially records the acquisition at cost, upward adjustments in the asset balance are recorded as soon as the investee makes a profit. A reduction is necessary if a loss is reported.

2. The investor's investment account is *decreased whenever a dividend is collected*. Because distribution of cash dividends reduces the carrying value of the investee company, the investor mirrors this change by recording the receipt as a decrease in the carrying value of the investment rather than as revenue. Once again, a parallel is established between the investment account and the underlying activities of the investee: The reduction in the investee's owners' equity creates a decrease in the investment. Furthermore, because the investor immediately recognizes income when the investee earns it, double counting would occur if the investor also recorded subsequent dividend collections as revenue. Importantly, the collection of a cash dividend is not an appropriate point for income recognition. Because the investor can influence the timing of investee dividend distributions, the receipt of a dividend is not an objective measure of the income generated from the investment.

Application of Equity Method	
Investee Event	**Investor Accounting**
Income is earned.	Proportionate share of income is recognized.
Dividends are distributed.	Investor's share of investee dividends reduce the investment account.

Application of the equity method causes the investment account on the investor's balance sheet to vary directly with changes in the investee's equity. As an illustration, assume that an investor acquires a 40 percent interest in a business enterprise. If the

EXHIBIT 1.1 Comparison of Fair-Value Method (ASC 320) and Equity Method (ASC 323)

			Accounting by Big Company When Influence Is Not Significant (available-for-sale security)			Accounting by Big Company When Influence Is Significant (equity method)	
Year	Income of Little Company	Dividends Paid by Little Company	Dividend Income	Carrying Value of Investment	Fair-Value Adjustment to Stockholders' Equity	Equity in Investee Income	Carrying Value of Investment
2012	$200,000	$ 50,000	$10,000	$235,000	$ 35,000	$ 40,000*	$230,000†
2013	300,000	100,000	20,000	255,000	55,000	60,000*	270,000†
2014	400,000	200,000	40,000	320,000	120,000	80,000*	310,000†
Total income recognized			$70,000			$180,000	

*Equity in investee income is 20 percent of the current year income reported by Little Company.
†The carrying value of an investment under the equity method is the original cost plus income recognized less dividends received. For 2012, as an example, the $230,000 reported balance is the $200,000 cost plus $40,000 equity income less $10,000 in dividends received.

investor has the ability to significantly influence the investee, the equity method may be utilized. If the investee subsequently reports net income of $50,000, the investor increases the investment account (and its own net income) by $20,000 in recognition of a 40 percent share of these earnings. Conversely, a $20,000 dividend paid by the investee necessitates a reduction of $8,000 in this same asset account (40 percent of the total payout).

In contrast, the fair-value method reports investments at fair value if it is readily determinable. Also, income is recognized only upon receipt of dividends. Consequently, financial reports can vary depending on whether the equity method or fair-value method is appropriate.

To illustrate, assume that Big Company owns a 20 percent interest in Little Company purchased on January 1, 2012, for $200,000. Little then reports net income of $200,000, $300,000, and $400,000, respectively, in the next three years while paying dividends of $50,000, $100,000, and $200,000. The fair values of Big's investment in Little, as determined by market prices, were $235,000, $255,000, and $320,000 at the end of 2012, 2013, and 2014, respectively.

Exhibit 1.1 compares the accounting for Big's investment in Little across the two methods. The fair-value method carries the investment at its market values, presumed to be readily available in this example. Because the investment is classified as an *available-for-sale security,* the excess of fair value over cost is reported as a separate component of stockholders' equity.[8] Income is recognized as dividends are received.

In contrast, under the equity method, Big recognizes income as it is earned by Little. As shown in Exhibit 1.1, Big recognizes $180,000 in income over the three years, and the carrying value of the investment is adjusted upward to $310,000. Dividends received are not an appropriate measure of income because of the assumed significant influence over the investee. Big's ability to influence Little's decisions applies to the timing of dividend distributions. Therefore, dividends received do not objectively measure Big's income from its investment in Little. As Little earns income, however, under the equity method Big recognizes its share (20 percent) of the income and increases the investment account. The equity method reflects the accrual model: Income is recognized as it is earned, not when cash (dividend) is received.

Exhibit 1.1 shows that the carrying value of the investment fluctuates each year under the equity method. This recording parallels the changes occurring in the net asset figures reported by the investee. If the owners' equity of the investee rises through income, an increase is made in the investment account; decreases such as losses and dividends cause reductions to be recorded. Thus, the equity method conveys information that describes the relationship created by the investor's ability to significantly influence the investee.

[8] Fluctuations in the market values of *trading securities* are recognized in income in the period in which they occur.

LO3

Prepare basic equity method journal entries for an investor and describe the financial reporting for equity method investments.

Equity Method Accounting Procedures

Once guidelines for the application of the equity method have been established, the mechanical process necessary for recording basic transactions is quite straightforward. The investor accrues its percentage of the earnings reported by the investee each period. Dividend declarations reduce the investment balance to reflect the decrease in the investee's book value.

Referring again to the information presented in Exhibit 1.1, Little Company reported a net income of $200,000 during 2012 and paid cash dividends of $50,000. These figures indicate that Little's net assets have increased by $150,000 during the year. Therefore, in its financial records, Big Company records the following journal entries to apply the equity method:

	Debit	Credit
Investment in Little Company	40,000	
Equity in Investee Income		40,000
To accrue earnings of a 20 percent owned investee ($200,000 × 20%).		
Cash	10,000	
Investment in Little Company		10,000
To record receipt of cash dividend from Little Company ($50,000 × 20%).		

In the first entry, Big accrues income based on the investee's reported earnings even though this amount greatly exceeds the cash dividend. The second entry reflects the actual receipt of the dividend and the related reduction in Little's net assets. The $30,000 net increment recorded here in Big's investment account ($40,000 − $10,000) represents 20 percent of the $150,000 increase in Little's book value that occurred during the year.

LO4

Allocate the cost of an equity method investment and compute amortization expense to match revenues recognized from the investment to the excess of investor cost over investee book value.

Excess of Investment Cost Over Book Value Acquired

After the basic concepts and procedures of the equity method are mastered, more complex accounting issues can be introduced. Surely one of the most common problems encountered in applying the equity method concerns investment costs that exceed the proportionate book value of the investee company.[9]

Unless the investor acquires its ownership at the time of the investee's conception, paying an amount equal to book value is rare. A number of possible reasons exist for a difference between the book value of a company and the price of its stock. A company's value at any time is based on a multitude of factors such as company profitability, the introduction of a new product, expected dividend payments, projected operating results, and general economic conditions. Furthermore, stock prices are based, at least partially, on the perceived worth of a company's net assets, amounts that often vary dramatically from underlying book values. Asset and liability accounts shown on a balance sheet tend to measure historical costs rather than current value. In addition, these reported figures are affected by the specific accounting methods adopted by a company. Inventory costing methods such as LIFO and FIFO, for example, obviously lead to different book values as does each of the acceptable depreciation methods.

If an investment is acquired at a price in excess of book value, logical reasons should explain the additional cost incurred by the investor. The source of the excess of cost over book value is important. Income recognition requires matching the income generated from the investment with its cost. Excess costs allocated to fixed assets will likely be expensed over longer periods than costs allocated to inventory. In applying the equity method, the cause of such an excess payment can be divided into two general categories:

1. Specific investee assets and liabilities can have fair values that differ from their present book values. The excess payment can be identified directly with individual accounts such as inventory, equipment, franchise rights, and so on.

[9] Although encountered less frequently, investments can be purchased at a cost that is less than the underlying book value of the investee. Accounting for this possibility is explored in later chapters.

Discussion Question

DOES THE EQUITY METHOD REALLY APPLY HERE?

Abraham, Inc., a New Jersey corporation, operates 57 bakeries throughout the northeastern section of the United States. In the past, its founder, James Abraham, owned all the company's entire outstanding common stock. However, during the early part of this year, the corporation suffered a severe cash flow problem brought on by rapid expansion. To avoid bankruptcy, Abraham sought additional investment capital from a friend, Dennis Bostitch, who owns Highland Laboratories. Subsequently, Highland paid $700,000 cash to Abraham, Inc., to acquire enough newly issued shares of common stock for a one-third ownership interest.

At the end of this year, the accountants for Highland Laboratories are discussing the proper method of reporting this investment. One argues for maintaining the asset at its original cost: "This purchase is no more than a loan to bail out the bakeries. Mr. Abraham will continue to run the organization with little or no attention paid to us. After all, what does anyone in our company know about baking bread? I would be surprised if Abraham does not reacquire these shares as soon as the bakery business is profitable again."

One of the other accountants disagrees, stating that the equity method is appropriate. "I realize that our company is not capable of running a bakery. However, the official rules state that we must have only the *ability* to exert significant influence. With one-third of the common stock in our possession, we certainly have that ability. Whether we use it or not, this ability means that we are required to apply the equity method."

How should Highland Laboratories account for its investment in Abraham, Inc.?

2. The investor could be willing to pay an extra amount because future benefits are expected to accrue from the investment. Such benefits could be anticipated as the result of factors such as the estimated profitability of the investee or the relationship being established between the two companies. In this case, the additional payment is attributed to an intangible future value generally referred to as *goodwill* rather than to any specific investee asset or liability. For example, in its 2010 annual report, ebay Inc. disclosed that goodwill related to its equity method investments was approximately $27.4 million.

As an illustration, assume that Grande Company is negotiating the acquisition of 30 percent of the outstanding shares of Chico Company. Chico's balance sheet reports assets of $500,000 and liabilities of $300,000 for a net book value of $200,000. After investigation, Grande determines that Chico's equipment is undervalued in the company's financial records by $60,000. One of its patents is also undervalued, but only by $40,000. By adding these valuation adjustments to Chico's book value, Grande arrives at an estimated $300,000 worth for the company's net assets. Based on this computation, Grande offers $90,000 for a 30 percent share of the investee's outstanding stock.

Book value of Chico Company (assets minus liabilities [or stockholders' equity])	$200,000
Undervaluation of equipment	60,000
Undervaluation of patent	40,000
Value of net assets	$300,000
Portion being acquired	30%
Purchase price	$ 90,000

Although Grande's purchase price is in excess of the proportionate share of Chico's book value, this additional amount can be attributed to two specific accounts: Equipment and Patents. No part of the extra payment is traceable to any other projected future benefit. Thus, the cost of Grande's investment is allocated as follows:

Payment by investor		$90,000
Percentage of book value acquired ($200,000 × 30%)		60,000
Payment in excess of book value		30,000
Excess payment identified with specific assets:		
Equipment ($60,000 undervaluation × 30%)	$18,000	
Patent ($40,000 undervaluation × 30%)	12,000	30,000
Excess payment not identified with specific assets—goodwill		–0–

Of the $30,000 excess payment made by the investor, $18,000 is assigned to the equipment whereas $12,000 is traced to a patent and its undervaluation. No amount of the purchase price is allocated to goodwill.

To take this example one step further, assume that Chico's owners reject Grande's proposed $90,000 price. They believe that the value of the company as a going concern is higher than the fair value of its net assets. Because the management of Grande believes that valuable synergies will be created through this purchase, the bid price is raised to $125,000 and accepted. This new acquisition price is allocated as follows:

Payment by investor		$125,000
Percentage of book value acquired ($200,000 × 30%)		60,000
Payment in excess of book value		65,000
Excess payment identified with specific assets:		
Equipment ($60,000 undervaluation × 30%)	$18,000	
Patent ($40,000 undervaluation × 30%)	12,000	30,000
Excess payment not identified with specific assets—goodwill		$ 35,000

As this example indicates, *any extra payment that cannot be attributed to a specific asset or liability is assigned to the intangible asset goodwill.* Although the actual purchase price can be computed by a number of different techniques or simply result from negotiations, goodwill is always the excess amount not allocated to identifiable asset or liability accounts.

Under the equity method, the investor enters total cost in a single investment account regardless of the allocation of any excess purchase price. If all parties accept Grande's bid of $125,000, the acquisition is initially recorded at that amount despite the internal assignments made to equipment, patents, and goodwill. The entire $125,000 was paid to acquire this investment, and it is recorded as such.

The Amortization Process

The preceding extra payments were made in connection with specific assets (equipment, patents, and goodwill). Even though the actual dollar amounts are recorded within the investment account, a definite historical cost can be attributed to these assets. With a cost to the investor as well as a specified life, the payment relating to each asset (except land, goodwill, and other indefinite life intangibles) should be amortized over an appropriate time period.

Historically, goodwill implicit in equity method investments had been amortized over periods less than or equal to 40 years. However, in June 2001, a major and fundamental change in GAAP occurred for goodwill. The useful life for goodwill is now considered indefinite. Therefore, goodwill amortization expense no longer exists in financial reporting.[10] Any implicit goodwill is carried forward without adjustment until the investment is sold or a permanent decline in value occurs.

Goodwill can maintain its value and theoretically may even increase over time. The notion of an indefinite life for goodwill recognizes the argument that amortization of goodwill over an arbitrary period fails to reflect economic reality and therefore does not provide useful information. A primary reason for the presumption of an indefinite life for goodwill relates to the accounting for business combinations (covered in Chapters 2 through 7). Goodwill associated with equity method investments, for the most part, is accounted for in the same manner as goodwill arising from a business combination. One difference is that goodwill arising from a business combination is subject to annual impairment reviews, whereas goodwill implicit in equity investments is not. Equity method investments are tested in their entirety for permanent declines in value.[11]

Assume, for illustrative purposes, that the equipment has a 10-year remaining life, the patent a 5-year life, and the goodwill an indefinite life. If the straight-line method is used with no salvage value, *the investor's cost* should be amortized initially as follows:[12]

Account	Cost Assigned	Useful Life	Annual Amortization
Equipment	$18,000	10 years	$1,800
Patent	12,000	5 years	2,400
Goodwill	35,000	Indefinite	−0−
Annual expense (for five years until patent cost is completely amortized)			$4,200

In recording this annual expense, Grande reduces the investment balance in the same way it would amortize the cost of any other asset that had a limited life. Therefore, at the end of the first year, the investor records the following journal entry under the equity method:

Equity in Investee Income	4,200	
Investment in Chico Company		4,200
To record amortization of excess payment allocated to equipment and patent.		

Because this amortization relates to investee assets, the investor does not establish a specific expense account. Instead, as in the previous entry, the expense is recognized by decreasing the equity income accruing from the investee company.

To illustrate this entire process, assume that Tall Company purchases 20 percent of Short Company for $200,000. Tall can exercise significant influence over the investee; thus, the equity method is appropriately applied. The acquisition is made on January 1, 2013, when Short holds net assets with a book value of $700,000. Tall believes that the investee's building (10-year life) is undervalued within the financial records by $80,000 and equipment with a 5-year life is undervalued by $120,000. Any goodwill established by this purchase is considered to have an indefinite life. During 2013, Short reports a net income of $150,000 and pays a cash dividend at year's end of $60,000.

[10] Other intangibles (such as certain licenses, trademarks) also can be considered to have indefinite lives and thus are not amortized unless and until their lives are determined to be limited. Further discussion of intangibles with indefinite lives appears in Chapter 3.

[11] Because equity method goodwill is not separable from the related investment, goodwill should not be separately tested for impairment. See also FASB ASC para. 350-20-35-59.

[12] Unless otherwise stated, all amortization computations are based on the straight-line method with no salvage value.

Tall's three basic journal entries for 2013 pose little problem:

January 1, 2013		
Investment in Short Company	200,000	
Cash		200,000
To record acquisition of 20 percent of the outstanding shares of Short Company.		

December 31, 2013		
Investment in Short Company	30,000	
Equity in Investee Income		30,000
To accrue 20 percent of the 2013 reported earnings of investee ($150,000 × 20%).		
Cash	12,000	
Investment in Short Company		12,000
To record receipt of 2013 cash dividend ($60,000 × 20%).		

An allocation of Tall's $200,000 purchase price must be made to determine whether an additional adjusting entry is necessary to recognize annual amortization associated with the extra payment:

Payment by investor		$200,000
Percentage of 1/1/13 book value ($700,000 × 20%)		140,000
Payment in excess of book value		60,000
Excess payment identified with specific assets:		
Building ($80,000 × 20%)	$16,000	
Equipment ($120,000 × 20%)	24,000	40,000
Excess payment not identified with specific assets—goodwill		$ 20,000

As can be seen, $16,000 of the purchase price is assigned to a building and $24,000 to equipment, with the remaining $20,000 attributed to goodwill. For each asset with a definite useful life, periodic amortization is required.

Asset	Attributed Cost	Useful Life	Annual Amortization
Building	$16,000	10 years	$1,600
Equipment	24,000	5 years	4,800
Goodwill	20,000	Indefinite	–0–
Total for 2013			$6,400

At the end of 2013, Tall must also record the following adjustment in connection with these cost allocations:

Equity in Investee Income	6,400	
Investment in Short Company		6,400
To record 2013 amortization of excess payment allocated to building ($1,600) and equipment ($4,800).		

Although these entries are shown separately here for better explanation, Tall would probably net the income accrual for the year ($30,000) and the amortization ($6,400) to create a single entry increasing the investment and recognizing equity income of $23,600. Thus, the first-year return on Tall Company's beginning investment balance (defined as equity earnings/beginning investment balance) is equal to 11.80 percent ($23,600/$200,000).

Equity Method—Additional Issues

The previous sections on equity income accruals and excess cost amortizations provide the basics for applying the equity method. However, several other nonroutine issues can arise during the life of an equity method investment. More specifically, special procedures are required in accounting for each of the following:

1. Reporting a change to the equity method.
2. Reporting investee income from sources other than continuing operations.
3. Reporting investee losses.
4. Reporting the sale of an equity investment.

Reporting a Change to the Equity Method

In many instances, an investor's ability to significantly influence an investee is not achieved through a single stock acquisition. The investor could possess only a minor ownership for some years before purchasing enough additional shares to require conversion to the equity method. Before the investor achieves significant influence, any investment should be reported by the fair-value method. After the investment reaches the point at which the equity method becomes applicable, a technical question arises about the appropriate means of changing from one method to the other.[13]

FASB ASC (para. 323-10-35-33) addresses this concern by stating that "The investment, results of operations (current and prior periods presented), and retained earnings of the investor shall be adjusted retroactively. . . ." *Thus, all accounts are restated so that the investor's financial statements appear as if the equity method had been applied from the date of the first acquisition.* By mandating retrospective treatment, the FASB attempts to ensure comparability from year to year in the financial reporting of the investor company.

To illustrate this restatement procedure, assume that Giant Company acquires a 10 percent ownership in Small Company on January 1, 2012. Officials of Giant do not believe that their company has gained the ability to exert significant influence over Small. Giant properly records the investment by using the fair-value method as an available-for-sale security. Subsequently, on January 1, 2014, Giant purchases an additional 30 percent of Small's outstanding voting stock, thereby achieving the ability to significantly influence the investee's decision making. From 2012 through 2014, Small reports net income, pays cash dividends, and has fair values at January 1 of each year as follows:

Year	Net Income	Cash Dividends	Fair Value at January 1
2012	$ 70,000	$20,000	$800,000
2013	110,000	40,000	840,000
2014	130,000	50,000	930,000

In Giant's 2012 and 2013 financial statements, as originally reported, dividend revenue of $2,000 and $4,000, respectively, would be recognized based on receiving 10 percent of these distributions. The investment account is maintained at fair value because it is readily determinable. Also, the change in the investment's fair value results in a credit to an unrealized cumulative holding gain of $4,000 in 2012 and an additional credit of $9,000 in 2013 for a cumulative amount of $13,000 reported in Giant's 2013 stockholders' equity section. However, after changing to the equity method on January 1, 2014, Giant must restate these prior years to present the investment as if the equity method

[13] A switch to the equity method also can be required if the investee purchases a portion of its own shares as treasury stock. This transaction can increase the investor's percentage of outstanding stock.

had always been applied. Assuming any excess of Giant's investment costs over its share of Small's book value was attributable to goodwill (and thus no amortization), Giant's comparative income statements would show equity income of $7,000 in 2012 and $11,000 in 2013 based on a 10 percent accrual of Small's income for each year.

The income restatement for these earlier years can be computed as follows:

Year	Equity in Investee Income (10%)	Income Reported from Dividends	Retrospective Adjustment
2012	$ 7,000	$2,000	$ 5,000
2013	11,000	4,000	7,000
Total adjustment to Retained Earnings			$12,000

Giant's reported earnings for 2012 will increase by $5,000 with a $7,000 increment needed for 2013. To bring about this retrospective change to the equity method, Giant prepares the following journal entry on January 1, 2014:

	Debit	Credit
Investment in Small Company	12,000	
Retained Earnings—Prior Period Adjustment— Equity in Investee Income		12,000
To adjust 2012 and 2013 records so that investment is accounted for using the equity method in a consistent manner.		
Unrealized Holding Gain—Shareholders' Equity.	13,000	
Fair Value Adjustment (Available-for-Sale)		13,000
To remove the investor's percentage of the increase in fair value (10% × $130,000) from stockholders' equity and the available-for-sale portfolio valuation account.		

The $13,000 adjustment removes the valuation accounts that pertain to the investment prior to obtaining significant influence. Because the investment is no longer part of the available-for-sale portfolio, it is carried under the equity method rather than at fair value. Accordingly, the fair-value adjustment accounts are reduced as part of the reclassification.

Continuing with this example, Giant makes two other journal entries at the end of 2014, but they relate solely to the operations and distributions of that period.

	Debit	Credit
Investment in Small Company	52,000	
Equity in Investee Income.		52,000
To accrue 40 percent of the year 2014 income reported by Small Company ($130,000 × 40%).		
Cash	20,000	
Investment in Small Company		20,000
To record receipt of year 2014 cash dividend from Small Company ($50,000 × 40%).		

Reporting Investee Income from Sources Other Than Continuing Operations

Traditionally, certain elements of income are presented separately within a set of financial statements. Examples include extraordinary items, discontinued operations, and other comprehensive income. A concern that arises in applying the equity method is whether items appearing separately in the investee's financial statements require similar treatment by the investor.

To examine this issue, assume that Large Company owns 40 percent of the voting stock of Tiny Company and accounts for this investment by means of the equity method. No excess amortization resulted from this investment. In 2012, Tiny reports net income of $200,000, a figure composed of $250,000 in income from continuing operations and a $50,000 extraordinary loss. Large Company accrues earnings of $80,000 based on 40 percent of the $200,000 net figure. However, for proper disclosure, the extraordinary loss incurred by the investee must also be reported separately on the financial statements of the investor. This handling is intended, once again, to mirror the close relationship between the two companies.

Based on the level of ownership, Large recognizes $100,000 as a component of operating income (40 percent of Tiny Company's $250,000 income from continuing operations) along with a $20,000 extraordinary loss (40 percent of $50,000). The overall effect is still an $80,000 net increment in Large's earnings, but this amount has been appropriately allocated between income from continuing operations and extraordinary items.

The journal entry to record Large's equity interest in the income of Tiny follows:

Investment in Tiny Company	80,000	
Extraordinary Loss of Investee	20,000	
Equity in Investee Income.		100,000
To accrue operating income and extraordinary loss from equity investment.		

One additional aspect of this accounting should be noted. Even though the investee has already judged this loss as extraordinary, Large does not report its $20,000 share as a separate item unless it is material with respect to the investor's own operations.

Other comprehensive income (OCI) represents another source of change in investee company net assets that is recognized under the equity method.[14] OCI includes items such as foreign currency translation adjustments, unrealized holding gains and losses on available-for-sale securities, and certain pension adjustments. When the investee reports a current year component of other comprehensive income, the investor company likewise adjusts its investment account for the change in investee equity. The investor also adjusts its OCI for its share of the investee's currently reported OCI item.

Reporting Investee Losses

Although most of the previous illustrations are based on the recording of profits, accounting for losses incurred by the investee is handled in a similar manner. The investor recognizes the appropriate percentage of each loss and reduces the carrying value of the investment account. Even though these procedures are consistent with the concept of the equity method, they fail to take into account all possible loss situations.

Permanent Losses in Value

Investments can suffer permanent losses in fair value that are not evident through equity method accounting. Such declines can be caused by the loss of major customers, changes in economic conditions, loss of a significant patent or other legal right, damage to the company's reputation, and the like. Permanent reductions in fair value resulting from such adverse events might not be reported immediately by the investor through the normal equity entries discussed previously. The FASB ASC (para. 323-10-35-32) provides the following guidance:

> A loss in value of an investment which is other than a temporary decline should be recognized the same as a loss in value of other long-term assets. Evidence of a loss in value might include, but would not necessarily be limited to, absence of an ability to recover the carrying amount of the investment or inability of the investee to sustain an earnings capacity which would justify the carrying amount of the investment.

[14] OCI is defined as revenues, expenses, gains, and losses that under generally accepted accounting principles are included in comprehensive income but excluded from net income. OCI is accumulated and reported in stockholders' equity.

Thus, when a permanent decline in an equity method investment's value occurs, the investor must recognize an impairment loss and reduce the asset to fair value. However, this loss must be permanent before such recognition becomes necessary. Under the equity method, a temporary drop in the fair value of an investment is simply ignored.

For example, Novelis Corporation noted the following in its 2010 annual report:

> We review equity investments for impairment whenever certain indicators are present suggesting that the carrying value of an investment is not recoverable. This analysis requires a significant amount of judgment to identify events or circumstances indicating that an equity investment may be impaired. Once an impairment indicator is identified, we must determine if an impairment exists, and if so, whether the impairment is other than temporary, in which case the equity investment would be written down to its estimated fair value.

Investment Reduced to Zero

Through the recognition of reported losses as well as any permanent drops in fair value, the investment account can eventually be reduced to a zero balance. This condition is most likely to occur if the investee has suffered extreme losses or if the original purchase was made at a low, bargain price. Regardless of the reason, the carrying value of the investment account is sometimes eliminated in total.

When an investment account is reduced to zero, the investor should discontinue using the equity method rather than establish a negative balance. The investment retains a zero balance until subsequent investee profits eliminate all unrecognized losses. Once the original cost of the investment has been eliminated, no additional losses can accrue to the investor (since the entire cost has been written off).

Abakan, Inc., for example, explains in its 2010 financial statements:

> When the Company's carrying value in an equity method investee company is reduced to zero, no further losses are recorded in the Company's financial statements. . . . When the investee company subsequently reports income, the Company will not record its share of such income until it equals the amount of its share of losses not previously recognized.

LO5

Record the sale of an equity investment and identify the accounting method to be applied to any remaining shares that are subsequently held.

Reporting the Sale of an Equity Investment

At any time, the investor can choose to sell part or all of its holdings in the investee company. If a sale occurs, the equity method continues to be applied until the transaction date, thus establishing an appropriate carrying value for the investment. The investor then reduces this balance by the percentage of shares being sold.

As an example, assume that Top Company owns 40 percent of the 100,000 outstanding shares of Bottom Company, an investment accounted for by the equity method. Any excess investment cost over Top's share of Bottom's book value is considered goodwill. Although these 40,000 shares were acquired some years ago for $200,000, application of the equity method has increased the asset balance to $320,000 as of January 1, 2013. On July 1, 2013, Top elects to sell 10,000 of these shares (one-fourth of its investment) for $110,000 in cash, thereby reducing ownership in Bottom from 40 percent to 30 percent. Bottom Company reports income of $70,000 during the first six months of 2013 and distributes cash dividends of $30,000.

Top, as the investor, initially makes the following journal entries on July 1, 2013, to accrue the proper income and establish the correct investment balance:

Investment in Bottom Company	28,000	
Equity in Investee Income.		28,000
To accrue equity income for first six months of 2013 ($70,000 × 40%).		
Cash.	12,000	
Investment in Bottom Company.		12,000
To record receipt of cash dividends from January through June 2013 ($30,000 × 40%).		

These two entries increase the carrying value of Top's investment by $16,000, creating a balance of $336,000 as of July 1, 2013. The sale of one-fourth of these shares can then be recorded as follows:

Cash	110,000	
Investment in Bottom Company		84,000
Gain on Sale of Investment		26,000
To record sale of one-fourth of investment in Bottom Company (1/4 × $336,000 = $84,000).		

After the sale is completed, Top continues to apply the equity method to this investment based on 30 percent ownership rather than 40 percent. However, if the sale had been of sufficient magnitude to cause Top to lose its ability to exercise significant influence over Bottom, the equity method would cease to be applicable. For example, if Top Company's holdings were reduced from 40 percent to 15 percent, the equity method might no longer be appropriate after the sale. The shares still being held are reported according to the fair-value method with the remaining book value becoming the new *cost* figure for the investment rather than the amount originally paid.

If an investor is required to change from the equity method to the fair-value method, no retrospective adjustment is made. Although, as previously demonstrated, a change to the equity method mandates a restatement of prior periods, the treatment is not the same when the investor's change is to the fair-value method.

Deferral of Unrealized Profits in Inventory[15]

LO6

Describe the rationale and computations to defer unrealized gross profits on intra-entity transfers until the goods are either consumed or sold to outside parties.

Many equity acquisitions establish ties between companies to facilitate the direct purchase and sale of inventory items. Such intra-entity transactions can occur either on a regular basis or only sporadically. For example, The Coca-Cola Company recently disclosed that it sold $6.2 billion of syrup, concentrate, and other finished products to its equity method investees.

Regardless of their frequency, inventory sales between investor and investee necessitate special accounting procedures to ensure proper timing of revenue recognition. An underlying principle of accounting is that "revenues are not recognized until earned . . . and revenues are considered to have been earned when the entity has substantially accomplished what it must do to be entitled to the benefits represented by the revenues."[16] In the sale of inventory to an unrelated party, recognition of revenue is normally not in question; substantial accomplishment is achieved when the exchange takes place unless special terms are included in the contract.

Unfortunately, the earning process is not so clearly delineated in sales made between related parties. *Because of the relationship between investor and investee, the seller of the goods is said to retain a partial stake in the inventory for as long as the buyer holds it.* Thus, the earning process is not considered complete at the time of the original sale. For proper accounting, income recognition must be deferred until substantial accomplishment is proven. Consequently, when the investor applies the equity method, reporting of the related profit on intra-entity transfers is delayed until the buyer's ultimate disposition of the goods. When the inventory is eventually consumed within operations or resold to an unrelated party, the original sale is culminated and the gross profit is fully recognized.

In accounting, transactions between related companies are identified as either *downstream* or *upstream. Downstream transfers* refer to the investor's sale of an item to the

[15] Unrealized gains can involve the sale of items other than inventory. The intra-entity transfer of depreciable fixed assets and land is discussed in a later chapter.

[16] FASB, *Statement of Financial Accounting Concepts No. 6,* "Recognition and Measurement in Financial Statements of Business Enterprises" (Stamford, CT: December 1984), para. 83.

EXHIBIT 1.2
Downstream and Upstream Sales

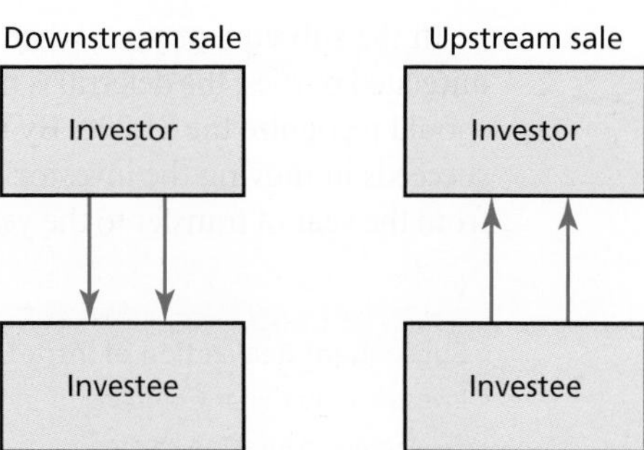

investee. Conversely, an *upstream sale* describes one that the investee makes to the investor (see Exhibit 1.2). *Although the direction of intra-entity sales does not affect reported equity method balances for investments when significant influence exists, it has definite consequences when financial control requires the consolidation of financial statements, as discussed in Chapter 5.* Therefore, these two types of intra-entity sales are examined separately even at this introductory stage.

Downstream Sales of Inventory

Assume that Major Company owns a 40 percent share of Minor Company and accounts for this investment through the equity method. In 2013, Major sells inventory to Minor at a price of $50,000. This figure includes a gross profit of 30 percent, or $15,000. By the end of 2013, Minor has sold $40,000 of these goods to outside parties while retaining $10,000 in inventory for sale during the subsequent year.

The investor has made downstream sales to the investee. In applying the equity method, recognition of the related profit must be delayed until the buyer disposes of these goods. Although total intra-entity transfers amounted to $50,000 in 2013, $40,000 of this merchandise has already been resold to outsiders, thereby justifying the normal reporting of profits. For the $10,000 still in the investee's inventory, the earning process is not finished. In computing equity income, this portion of the intra-entity profit must be deferred until Minor disposes of the goods.

The gross profit on the original sale was 30 percent of the transfer price; therefore, Major's profit associated with these remaining items is $3,000 ($10,000 × 30%). *However, because only 40 percent of the investee's stock is held, just $1,200 ($3,000 × 40%) of this profit is unearned.* Major's ownership percentage reflects the intra-entity portion of the profit. The total $3,000 gross profit within the ending inventory balance is not the amount deferred. Rather, 40 percent of that gross profit is viewed as the currently unrealized figure.

Remaining Ending Inventory	Gross Profit Percentage	Gross Profit in Ending Inventory	Investor Ownership Percentage	Unrealized Intra-Entity Gross Profit
$10,000	30%	$3,000	40%	$1,200

After calculating the appropriate deferral, the investor decreases current equity income by $1,200 to reflect the unearned portion of the intra-entity profit. This procedure temporarily removes this portion of the profit from the investor's books in 2013 until the investee disposes of the inventory in 2014. Major accomplishes the actual deferral through the following year-end journal entry:

Deferral of Unrealized Gross Profit		
Equity in Investee Income	1,200	
Investment in Minor Company.		1,200
To defer unrealized gross profit on sale of inventory to Minor Company.		

In the subsequent year, when this inventory is eventually consumed by Minor or sold to unrelated parties, the deferral is no longer needed. The earning process is complete, and Major should recognize the $1,200. By merely reversing the preceding deferral entry, the accountant succeeds in moving the investor's profit into the appropriate time period. Recognition shifts from the year of transfer to the year in which the earning process is substantially accomplished.

Subsequent Realization of Intra-Entity Gross Profit		
Investment in Minor Company	1,200	
Equity in Investee Income.		1,200
To recognize income on intra-entity sale that has now been earned through sales to outsiders.		

Upstream Sales of Inventory

Unlike consolidated financial statements (see Chapter 5), the equity method reports upstream sales of inventory in the same manner as downstream sales. Hence, unrealized profits remaining in ending inventory are deferred until the items are used or sold to unrelated parties. To illustrate, assume that Major Company once again owns 40 percent of Minor Company. During the current year, Minor sells merchandise costing $40,000 to Major for $60,000. At the end of the fiscal period, Major still retains $15,000 of these goods. Minor reports net income of $120,000 for the year.

To reflect the basic accrual of the investee's earnings, Major records the following journal entry at the end of this year:

Income Accrual		
Investment in Minor Company	48,000	
Equity in Investee Income.		48,000
To accrue income from 40 percent owned investee ($120,000 × 40%).		

The amount of the gross profit remaining unrealized at year-end is computed using the 33⅓ gross profit percentage of the sales price ($20,000/$60,000):

Remaining Ending Inventory	Gross Profit Percentage	Gross Profit in Ending Inventory	Investor Ownership Percentage	Unrealized Intra-Entity Gross Profit
$15,000	33⅓%	$5,000	40%	$2,000

Based on this calculation, a second entry is required of the investor at year-end. Once again, a deferral of the unrealized gross profit created by the intra-entity transfer is necessary for proper timing of income recognition. *Under the equity method for investments with significant influence, the direction of the sale between the investor and investee (upstream or downstream) has no effect on the final amounts reported in the financial statements.*

Deferral of Unrealized Gross Profit		
Equity in Investee Income	2,000	
Investment in Minor Company.		2,000
To defer recognition of intra-entity unrealized gross profit until inventory is used or sold to unrelated parties.		

After the adjustment, Major, the investor, reports earnings from this equity investment of $46,000 ($48,000 − $2,000). The income accrual is reduced because a portion of the intra-entity gross profit is considered unrealized. When the investor eventually consumes or sells the $15,000 in merchandise, the preceding journal entry is reversed. In this way, the effects of the transfer are reported in the proper accounting period when the profit is earned by sales to an outside party.

In an upstream sale, the investor's own inventory account contains the unrealized profit. The previous entry, though, defers recognition of this profit by decreasing Major's investment account rather than the inventory balance. An alternative treatment would be the direct reduction of the investor's inventory balance as a means of accounting for this unrealized amount. Although this alternative is acceptable, decreasing the investment remains the traditional approach for deferring unrealized gross profits, even for upstream sales.

Whether upstream or downstream, the investor's sales and purchases are still reported as if the transactions were conducted with outside parties. Only the unrealized gross profit is deferred, and that amount is adjusted solely through the equity income account. Furthermore, because the companies are not consolidated, the investee's reported balances are not altered at all to reflect the nature of these sales/purchases. Obviously, readers of the financial statements need to be made aware of the inclusion of these amounts in the income statement. Thus, reporting companies must disclose certain information about related-party transactions. These disclosures include the nature of the relationship, a description of the transactions, the dollar amounts of the transactions, and amounts due to or from any related parties at year-end.

Financial Reporting Effects and Equity Method Criticisms

Equity Method Reporting Effects

It is important to realize that business decisions, including equity investments, typically involve the assessment of a wide range of consequences. For example, managers frequently are very interested in how financial statements report the effects of their decisions. This attention to financial reporting effects of business decisions arises because measurements of financial performance often affect the following:

- The firm's ability to raise capital.
- Managerial compensation.
- The ability to meet debt covenants and future interest rates.
- Managers' reputations.

Managers are also keenly aware that measures of earnings per share can strongly affect investors' perceptions of the underlying value of their firms' publicly traded stock. Consequently, prior to making investment decisions, firms will study and assess the prospective effects of applying the equity method on the income reported in financial statements. Additionally, such analyses of prospective reported income effects can influence firms regarding the degree of influence they wish to have or even on the decision of whether to invest. For example, managers could have a required projected rate of return on an initial investment. In such cases, an analysis of projected income will be made to assist in setting an offer price.

For example, Investmor Co. is examining a potential 25 percent equity investment in Marco, Inc., that will provide a significant level of influence. Marco projects an annual income of $300,000 for the near future. Marco's book value is $450,000, and it has an unrecorded newly developed technology appraised at $200,000 with an estimated useful life of 10 years. In considering offer prices for the 25 percent investment in Marco, Investmor projects equity earnings as follows:

Projected income (25% × $300,000)	$75,000
Excess unpatented technology amortization ([25% × 200,000]/10 years)	(5,000)
Annual expected equity in Marco earnings	$70,000

Investmor's required first-year rate of return (before tax) on these types of investments is 20 percent. Therefore, to meet the first-year rate of return requirement involves a maximum price of $350,000 ($70,000/20% = $350,000). If the shares are publicly traded (leaving the firm a "price taker"), such income projections can assist the company in making a recommendation to wait for share prices to move to make the investment attractive.

Criticisms of the Equity Method

Over the past several decades, thousands of business firms have accounted for their investments using the equity method. Recently, however, the equity method has come under criticism for the following:

- Emphasizing the 20–50 percent of voting stock in determining significant influence versus control.
- Allowing off-balance sheet financing.
- Potentially biasing performance ratios.

The guidelines for the equity method suggest that a 20–50 percent ownership of voting shares indicates significant influence that falls short of control. But can one firm exert "control" over another firm absent an interest of more than 50 percent? Clearly, if one firm controls another, consolidation is the appropriate financial reporting technique. However, over the years, firms have learned ways to control other firms despite owning less than 50 percent of voting shares. For example, contracts across companies can limit one firm's ability to act without permission of the other. Such contractual control can be seen in debt arrangements, long-term sales and purchase agreements, and agreements concerning board membership. As a result, control is exerted through a variety of contractual arrangements. For financial reporting purposes, however, if ownership is 50 percent or less, a firm can argue that control technically does not exist.

In contrast to consolidated financial reports, when applying the equity method, the investee's assets and liabilities are not combined with the investor's amounts. Instead, the investor's balance sheet reports a single amount for the investment and the income statement reports a single amount for its equity in the earnings of the investee. If consolidated, the assets, liabilities, revenues, and expenses of the investee are combined and reported in the body of the investor's financial statements.

Thus, for those companies wishing to actively manage their reported balance sheet numbers, the equity method provides an effective means. By keeping its ownership of voting shares below 50 percent, a company can technically meet the rules for applying the equity method for its investments and at the same time report investee assets and liabilities "off balance sheet." As a result, relative to consolidation, a firm employing the equity method will report smaller values for assets and liabilities. Consequently, higher rates of return for its assets and sales, as well as lower debt-to-equity ratios, could result.

On the surface, it appears that firms can avoid balance sheet disclosure of debts by maintaining investments at less than 50 percent ownership. However, the equity method requires summarized information as to assets, liabilities, and results of operations of the investees to be presented in the notes or in separate statements. Therefore, supplementary information could be available under the equity method that would not be separately identified in consolidation. Nonetheless, some companies have contractual provisions (e.g., debt covenants, managerial compensation agreements) based on ratios in the main body of the financial statements. Meeting the provisions of such contracts could provide managers strong incentives to maintain technical eligibility to use the equity method rather than full consolidation.

Fair-Value Reporting Option for Equity Method Investments

LO7

Explain the rationale and reporting implications of the fair-value option for investments otherwise accounted for by the equity method.

In 2007, the FASB introduced a fair-value option under which an entity may irrevocably elect fair value as the initial and subsequent measurement attribute for certain financial assets and financial liabilities. Under the fair-value option, changes in the fair value of the elected financial items are included in earnings. Among the many financial assets available for the fair-value option are investments accounted for under the equity method.

For example, Citigroup now reports at fair value certain of its investments that previously were reported using the equity method. In its 2010 annual report Citigroup noted that: "Certain investments in non-marketable equity securities and certain investments that would otherwise have been accounted for using the equity method are carried at fair value, since the Company has elected to apply fair value accounting. Changes in fair value of such investments are recorded in earnings." Many other firms, however, have been reluctant to elect the fair-value option for their equity method investments.

Typically, the election date for the fair-value option is the date an investment first qualifies for equity method treatment—in other words, once significant influence is present.[17] However, such an election is irrevocable, leaving the firm no future option to apply the equity method for the investment. Any initial effect of the fair-value option election (e.g., adjusting an investment previously reported at cost or using a fair-value adjustment account) is reported as a cumulative-effect adjustment to the opening balance of retained earnings.

Under the fair-value option, firms simply report the investment's fair value as an asset and changes in fair value as earnings. As such, firms neither compute excess cost amortizations nor adjust earnings for intra-entity profits. Dividends received from an investee are included in earnings under the fair-value option. Because dividends typically reduce an investment's fair value, an increase in earnings from dividends received would be offset by a decrease in earnings from the decline in an investment's fair value.

To illustrate application of the fair-value option, on January 1, 2012, Westwind Co. pays $722,000 in exchange for 40,000 common shares of Armco, Inc. Armco has 100,000 common shares outstanding, the majority of which continue to trade on the New York Stock Exchange. During the next two years, Armco reports the following information:

Year	Net Income	Cash Dividends	Common Shares Total Fair Value at December 31
2012	$158,000	$25,000	$1,900,000
2013	125,000	25,000	1,870,000

Westwind elects to adopt the fair-value reporting option and accordingly makes the following journal entries for its investment in Armco over the next two years.

Account	Debit	Credit
Investment in Armco, Inc.	722,000	
Cash		722,000
To record Westwind's initial 40 percent investment in Armco, Inc.		
Cash	10,000	
Dividend Income		10,000
To recognize 2012 dividends received (40%) as investment income.		
Investment in Armco, Inc.	38,000	
Investment Income		38,000
To recognize Westwind's 40 percent of the 2012 change in Armco's fair value ([$1,900,000 × 40%] − $722,000).		
Cash	10,000	
Dividend Income		10,000
To recognize 2013 dividends received (40%) as investment income.		
Investment Loss	12,000	
Investment in Armco, Inc.		12,000
To recognize Westwind's 40 percent of the 2013 change in Armco's fair value (40% × [$1,870,000 − $1,900,000]).		

[17] Firms also had the opportunity to elect fair-value treatment for equity method investments existing in 2008 the first effective year for the fair-value option.

Discussion Question

SHOULD INVESTOR-INVESTEE RELATIONS DETERMINE INVESTOR ACCOUNTING FOR INVESTEE?

As part of its *Accounting for Financial Instruments* joint project with the IASB, the FASB is considering changes to its requirements for equity method accounting. Although all board decisions are tentative prior to extensive due process and final approval, the FASB reported the following in 2010:

> The Board decided that an investor should apply the equity method of accounting if the investor has significant influence over the investee and the investment is considered related to the investor's consolidated businesses. Otherwise, the investment would be measured at fair value with changes included in earnings. The Board directed the staff to develop the criteria for determining whether an investee is related to the investor's consolidated businesses.
>
> The Board decided that an entity may not elect the fair value option for equity investments that would be accounted for under the equity method under the decision reached above.

This tentative decision would add to the equity method a criterion that "the investment is considered related to the investor's consolidated businesses." Without such a relationship, the investment valuation for financial reporting would be fair value, even when ability to significantly influence the investee is present.

How would the FASB's decision affect firms' future election of the fair-value option? Do you think the addition of a relationship criterion for equity method use would increase the relevance of financial reporting for investments?

In its December 31, 2013, balance sheet, Westwind thus reports its Investment in Armco account at $748,000, equal to 40 percent of Armco's total fair value (or $722,000 initial cost adjusted for 2012–2013 fair-value changes of $38,000 less $12,000).

In addition to the increasing emphasis on fair values in financial reporting, the fair-value option also is motivated by a perceived need for consistency across various balance sheet items. In particular, the fair-value option is designed to limit volatility in earnings that occurs when some financial items are measured using cost-based attributes and others at fair value. As FASB ASC (para. 825-10-10-1) observes, the objective of the fair value option is

> . . . to improve financial reporting by providing entities with the opportunity to mitigate volatility in reported earnings caused by measuring related assets and liabilities differently without having to apply complex hedge accounting provisions.

The fair-value reporting option is also available for available-for-sale and held-to-maturity securities. However, consolidated investments are specifically excluded from the standard's scope.

Summary

1. The equity method of accounting for an investment reflects the close relationship that could exist between an investor and an investee. More specifically, this approach is available when the owner achieves the ability to apply significant influence to the investee's operating and financial decisions. Significant influence is presumed to exist at the 20 to 50 percent ownership level. However, the accountant must evaluate each situation, regardless of the percentage of ownership, to determine whether this ability is actually present.

2. To mirror the relationship between the companies, the equity method requires the investor to accrue income when the investee earns it. In recording this profit or loss, the investor separately reports items such as extraordinary gains and losses, as well as other comprehensive income and discontinued operations, to highlight their special nature. Dividend payments decrease the owners' equity of the investee company; therefore, the investor reduces the investment account when collected.
3. When acquiring capital stock, an investor often pays an amount that exceeds the investee company's underlying book value. For accounting purposes, such excess payments must be either identified with specific assets and liabilities (such as land or buildings) or allocated to an intangible asset referred to as *goodwill.* The investor then amortizes each assigned cost (except for any amount attributed to land, goodwill, or other indefinite life assets) over the expected useful lives of the assets and liabilities. This amortization reduces the amount of equity income being reported.
4. If the investor sells the entire investment or any portion of it, the equity method is applied until the date of disposal. A gain or loss is computed based on the adjusted book value at that time. Remaining shares are accounted for by means of either the equity method or the fair-value method, depending on the investor's subsequent ability to significantly influence the investee.
5. Inventory (or other assets) can be transferred between investor and investee. Because of the relationship between the two companies, the equity income accrual should be reduced to defer the intra-entity portion of any gross profit included on these transfers until the items are either sold to outsiders or consumed. Thus, the amount of intra-entity gross profit in ending inventory decreases the amount of equity income being recognized in the current period although this effect is subsequently reversed.
6. Since 2008, firms may elect to report significant influence investments at fair value with changes in fair value as earnings. Under the fair-value option, firms simply report the investment's fair value as an asset and changes in fair value as earnings.

Comprehensive Illustration

(*Estimated Time: 30 to 50 Minutes*) Every chapter in this textbook concludes with an illustration designed to assist students in tying together the essential elements of the material presented. After a careful reading of each chapter, attempt to work through the comprehensive problem. Then review the solution that follows the problem, noting the handling of each significant accounting issue.

Problem

Part A

On January 1, 2012, Big Company pays $70,000 for a 10 percent interest in Little Company. On that date, Little has a book value of $600,000, although equipment, which has a five-year life, is undervalued by $100,000 on its books. Little Company's stock is closely held by a few investors and is traded only infrequently. Because fair values are not readily available on a continuing basis, the investment account is appropriately maintained at cost.

On January 1, 2013, Big acquires an additional 30 percent of Little Company for $264,000. This second purchase provides Big the ability to exert significant influence over Little and Big will now apply the equity method. At the time of this transaction, Little's equipment with a four-year life was undervalued by only $80,000.

During these two years, Little reported the following operational results:

Year	Net Income	Cash Dividends Paid
2012	$210,000	$110,000
2013	250,000	100,000

Additional Information

- Cash dividends are always paid on July 1 of each year.
- Any goodwill is considered to have an indefinite life.

Required

a. What income did Big originally report for 2012 in connection with this investment?

b. On comparative financial statements for 2012 and 2013, what figures should Big report in connection with this investment?

Part B (Continuation of Part A)

In 2014, Little Company reports $400,000 in income from continuing operations plus a $60,000 extraordinary gain. The company pays a $120,000 cash dividend. During this fiscal year, Big sells inventory costing $80,000 to Little for $100,000. Little continues to hold 30 percent of this merchandise at the end of 2014. Big maintains 40 percent ownership of Little throughout the period.

Required

Prepare all necessary journal entries for Big for the year 2014.

Solution

Part A

a. Big Company accounts for its investment in Little Company at cost during 2012. Because Big held only 10 percent of the outstanding shares, significant influence was apparently not present. Because the stock is not actively traded, fair values are not available and the investment remains at cost. Therefore, the investor records only the $11,000 ($110,000 × 10%) received in dividends as income in the original financial reporting for that year.

b. To make comparative reports consistent, a change to the equity method is recorded retrospectively. Therefore, when the ability to exert significant influence over the operations of Little is established on January 1, 2013, both Big's 2012 and 2013 financial statements will reflect the equity method.

Big first evaluates the initial purchase of Little's stock to determine whether either goodwill or incremental asset values need to be reflected within the equity method procedures.

Purchase of 10 Percent of Voting Stock on January 1, 2012

Payment by investor	$70,000
Percentage of book value acquired ($600,000 × 10%)	60,000
Payment in excess of book value	10,000
Excess payment identified with specific assets:	
Equipment ($100,000 × 10%)	10,000
Excess payment not identified with specific assets—goodwill	–0–

As shown here, the $10,000 excess payment was made to recognize the undervaluation of Little's equipment. This asset had a useful life at that time of five years; thus, the investor records amortization expense of $2,000 each year.

A similar calculation must be carried out for Big's second stock purchase:

Purchase of 30 Percent of Voting Stock on January 1, 2013

Payment by investor	$264,000
Percentage of book value* acquired ($700,000 × 30%)	210,000
Payment in excess of book value	54,000
Excess payment identified with specific assets:	
Equipment ($80,000 × 30%)	24,000
Excess payment not identified with specific assets—goodwill	$ 30,000

*Little's book value on January 1, 2013, is computed by adding the 2012 net income of $210,000 less dividends paid of $110,000 to the previous book value of $600,000.

In this second acquisition, $24,000 of the payment is attributable to the undervalued equipment with $30,000 assigned to goodwill. Because the equipment now has only a four-year remaining life, annual amortization of $6,000 is appropriate ($24,000/4).

After the additional shares are acquired on January 1, 2013, Big's financial records for 2012 must be retrospectively restated as if the equity method had been applied from the date of the initial investment.

Financial Reporting—2012

Equity in Investee Income (income statement)	
Income reported by Little	$210,000
Big's ownership	10%
Accrual for 2012	$ 21,000
Less: Equipment amortization (first purchase)	(2,000)
Equity in investee income—2012	$ 19,000
Investment in Little (balance sheet)	
Cost of first acquisition	$ 70,000
2012 Equity in investee income (above)	19,000
Less: Dividends received ($110,000 × 10%)	(11,000)
Investment in Little—12/31/12	$ 78,000

Financial Reporting—2013

Equity in Investee Income (income statement)	
Income reported by Little	$250,000
Big's ownership	40%
Big's share of Little's reported income	$100,000
Less: Amortization expense:	
Equipment (first purchase)	(2,000)
Equipment (second purchase)	(6,000)
Equity in investee income—2013	$ 92,000
Investment in Little (balance sheet)	
Book value—12/31/12 (above)	$ 78,000
Cost of 2013 acquisition	264,000
Equity in investee income (above)	92,000
Less: Dividends received ($100,000 × 40%)	(40,000)
Investment in Little—12/31/13	$394,000

Part B

On July 1, 2014, Big receives a $48,000 cash dividend from Little (40% × $120,000). According to the equity method, receipt of this dividend reduces the carrying value of the investment account:

Cash	48,000	
Investment in Little Company		48,000
To record receipt of 2014 dividend from investee.		

Big records no other journal entries in connection with this investment until the end of 2014. At that time, the annual accrual of income as well as the adjustment to record amortization is made (see Part A for computation of expense). The investee's continuing income is reported separately from the extraordinary item.

Investment in Little Company	184,000	
Equity in Investee Income		160,000
Extraordinary Gain of Investee		24,000
To recognize reported income of investee based on a 40 percent ownership level of $400,000 operating income and $60,000 extraordinary gain.		
Equity in Investee Income	8,000	
Investment in Little Company		8,000
To record annual amortization on excess payment made in relation to equipment ($2,000 from first purchase and $6,000 from second).		

Big needs to make only one other equity entry during 2014. Intra-entity sales have occurred and Little continues to hold a portion of the inventory. Therefore, an unrealized profit exists that must be deferred. The gross profit rate from the sale was 20 percent ($20,000/$100,000). Because the investee still possesses $30,000 of this merchandise, the related gross profit is $6,000 ($30,000 × 20%). However, Big owns only 40 percent of Little's outstanding stock; thus, the unrealized intra-entity gross profit at year's end is $2,400 ($6,000 × 40%). That amount must be deferred until Little consumes or sells the inventory to unrelated parties in subsequent years.

Equity in Investee Company	2,400	
Investment in Little Company		2,400
To defer unrealized gross profit on intra-entity sale.		

Questions

1. A company acquires a rather large investment in another corporation. What criteria determine whether the investor should apply the equity method of accounting to this investment?
2. What indicates an investor's ability to significantly influence the decision-making process of an investee?
3. Why does the equity method record dividends received from an investee as a reduction in the investment account, not as dividend income?
4. Jones Company possesses a 25 percent interest in the outstanding voting shares of Sandridge Company. Under what circumstances might Jones decide that the equity method would not be appropriate to account for this investment?
5. Smith, Inc., has maintained an ownership interest in Watts Corporation for a number of years. This investment has been accounted for using the equity method. What transactions or events create changes in the Investment in Watts Corporation account being recorded by Smith?
6. Although the equity method is a generally accepted accounting principle (GAAP), recognition of equity income has been criticized. What theoretical problems can opponents of the equity method identify? What managerial incentives exist that could influence a firm's percentage ownership interest in another firm?
7. Because of the acquisition of additional investee shares, an investor can choose to change from the fair-value method to the equity method. Which procedures are applied to effect this accounting change?
8. Riggins Company accounts for its investment in Bostic Company using the equity method. During the past fiscal year, Bostic reported an extraordinary gain on its income statement. How would this extraordinary item affect the investor's financial records?
9. During the current year, Davis Company's common stock suffers a permanent drop in market value. In the past, Davis has made a significant portion of its sales to one customer. This buyer recently announced its decision to make no further purchases from Davis Company, an action that led to the loss of market value. Hawkins, Inc., owns 35 percent of the outstanding shares of Davis, an investment that is recorded according to the equity method. How would the loss in value affect this investor's financial reporting?
10. Wilson Company acquired 40 percent of Andrews Company at a bargain price because of losses expected to result from Andrews's failure in marketing several new products. Wilson paid only $100,000, although Andrews's corresponding book value was much higher. In the first year after acquisition, Andrews lost $300,000. In applying the equity method, how should Wilson account for this loss?
11. In a stock acquisition accounted for by the equity method, a portion of the purchase price often is attributed to goodwill or to specific assets or liabilities. How are these amounts determined at acquisition? How are these amounts accounted for in subsequent periods?
12. Princeton Company holds a 40 percent interest in the outstanding voting stock of Yale Company. On June 19 of the current year, Princeton sells part of this investment. What accounting should Princeton make on June 19? What accounting will Princeton make for the remainder of the current year?
13. What is the difference between downstream and upstream sales? How does this difference impact application of the equity method?
14. How is the unrealized gross profit on intra-entity sales calculated? What effect does an unrealized gross profit have on the recording of an investment if the equity method is applied?

15. How are intra-entity transfers reported in an investee's separate financial statements if the investor is using the equity method?
16. What is the fair-value option for reporting equity method investments? How do the equity method and the fair-value option differ in recognizing income from an investee?

Problems

LO3

1. When an investor uses the equity method to account for investments in common stock, cash dividends received by the investor from the investee should be recorded as
   a. A deduction from the investor's share of the investee's profits.
   b. Dividend income.
   c. A deduction from the stockholders' equity account, Dividends to Stockholders.
   d. A deduction from the investment account.
   (AICPA adapted)

LO2

2. Which of the following does not indicate an investor company's ability to significantly influence an investee?
   a. Material intra-entity transactions.
   b. The investor owns 30 percent of the investee but another owner holds the remaining 70 percent.
   c. Interchange of personnel.
   d. Technological dependency.

LO3

3. Sisk Company has owned 10 percent of Maust, Inc., for the past several years. This ownership did not allow Sisk to have significant influence over Maust. Recently, Sisk acquired an additional 30 percent of Maust and now will use the equity method. How will the investor report this change?
   a. A cumulative effect of an accounting change is shown in the current income statement.
   b. No change is recorded; the equity method is used from the date of the new acquisition.
   c. A retrospective adjustment is made to restate all prior years presented using the equity method.
   d. Sisk will report the change as a component of accumulated other comprehensive income.

LO7

4. Under the fair-value option, which of the following affects the income the investor recognizes from its ownership of the investee?
   a. The investee's reported income adjusted for excess cost over book value amortizations.
   b. Changes in the fair value of the investor's ownership shares of the investee.
   c. Intra-entity profits from upstream sales.
   d. Extraordinary items reported by the investee.

LO7

5. When an investor elects the fair-value option for a significant influence investment, cash dividends received by the investor from the investee should be recorded as
   a. A deduction from the investor's share of the investee's reported income.
   b. A deduction from the investment account.
   c. A reduction from accumulated other comprehensive income reported in stockholders' equity.
   d. Dividend income.

LO3

6. On January 1, Puckett Company paid $1.6 million for 50,000 shares of Harrison's voting common stock, which represents a 40 percent investment. No allocation to goodwill or other specific account was made. Significant influence over Harrison is achieved by this acquisition and so Puckett applies the equity method. Harrison distributed a dividend of $2 per share during the year and reported net income of $560,000. What is the balance in the Investment in Harrison account found in Puckett's financial records as of December 31?
   a. $1,724,000.
   b. $1,784,000.
   c. $1,844,000.
   d. $1,884,000.

LO3, LO4

7. In January 2012, Wilkinson, Inc., acquired 20 percent of the outstanding common stock of Bremm, Inc., for $700,000. This investment gave Wilkinson the ability to exercise significant influence over Bremm. Bremm's assets on that date were recorded at $3,900,000 with liabilities of $900,000. Any excess of cost over book value of the investment was attributed to a patent having a remaining useful life of 10 years.

In 2012, Bremm reported net income of $170,000. In 2013, Bremm reported net income of $210,000. Dividends of $70,000 were paid in each of these two years. What is the equity method balance of Wilkinson's Investment in Bremm, Inc., at December 31, 2013?

a. $728,000.
b. $748,000.
c. $756,000.
d. $776,000.

LO3, LO4

8. Ace purchases 40 percent of Baskett Company on January 1 for $500,000. Although Ace did not use it, this acquisition gave Ace the ability to apply significant influence to Baskett's operating and financing policies. Baskett reports assets on that date of $1,400,000 with liabilities of $500,000. One building with a seven-year life is undervalued on Baskett's books by $140,000. Also, Baskett's book value for its trademark (10-year life) is undervalued by $210,000. During the year, Baskett reports net income of $90,000 while paying dividends of $30,000. What is the Investment in Baskett Company balance (equity method) in Ace's financial records as of December 31?

a. $504,000.
b. $507,600.
c. $513,900.
d. $516,000.

LO3, LO4

9. Goldman Company reports net income of $140,000 each year and pays an annual cash dividend of $50,000. The company holds net assets of $1,200,000 on January 1, 2012. On that date, Wallace purchases 40 percent of the outstanding stock for $600,000, which gives it the ability to significantly influence Goldman. At the purchase date, the excess of Wallace's cost over its proportionate share of Goldman's book value was assigned to goodwill. On December 31, 2014, what is the Investment in Goldman Company balance (equity method) in Wallace's financial records?

a. $600,000.
b. $660,000.
c. $690,000.
d. $708,000.

LO6

10. Perez, Inc., applies the equity method for its 25 percent investment in Senior, Inc. During 2013, Perez sold goods with a 40 percent gross profit to Senior. Senior sold all of these goods in 2013. How should Perez report the effect of the intra-entity sale on its 2013 income statement?

a. Sales and cost of goods sold should be reduced by the amount of intra-entity sales.
b. Sales and cost of goods sold should be reduced by 25 percent of the amount of intra-entity sales.
c. Investment income should be reduced by 25 percent of the gross profit on the amount of intra-entity sales.
d. No adjustment is necessary.

LO6

11. Panner, Inc., owns 30 percent of Watkins and applies the equity method. During the current year, Panner buys inventory costing $54,000 and then sells it to Watkins for $90,000. At the end of the year, Watkins still holds only $20,000 of merchandise. What amount of unrealized gross profit must Panner defer in reporting this investment using the equity method?

a. $2,400.
b. $4,800.
c. $8,000.
d. $10,800.

LO3, LO4, LO6

12. Alex, Inc., buys 40 percent of Steinbart Company on January 1, 2012, for $530,000. The equity method of accounting is to be used. Steinbart's net assets on that date were $1.2 million. Any excess of cost over book value is attributable to a trade name with a 20-year remaining life. Steinbart immediately begins supplying inventory to Alex as follows:

Year	Cost to Steinbart	Transfer Price	Amount Held by Alex at Year-End (at transfer price)
2012	$70,000	$100,000	$25,000
2013	96,000	150,000	45,000

Inventory held at the end of one year by Alex is sold at the beginning of the next.

Steinbart reports net income of $80,000 in 2012 and $110,000 in 2013 while paying $30,000 in dividends each year. What is the equity income in Steinbart to be reported by Alex in 2013?

a. $34,050.

b. $38,020.

c. $46,230.

d. $51,450.

LO3, LO4

13. On January 3, 2013, Matteson Corporation acquired 40 percent of the outstanding common stock of O'Toole Company for $1,160,000. This acquisition gave Matteson the ability to exercise significant influence over the investee. The book value of the acquired shares was $820,000. Any excess cost over the underlying book value was assigned to a copyright that was undervalued on balance sheet. This copyright has a remaining useful life of 10 years. For the year ended December 31, 2013, O'Toole reported net income of $260,000 and paid cash dividends of $50,000. At December 31, 2013, what should Matteson report as its investment in O'Toole under the equity method?

LO3

14. On January 1, 2013, Fisher Corporation paid $2,290,000 for 35 percent of the outstanding voting stock of Steel, Inc., and appropriately applies the equity method for its investment. Any excess of cost over Steel's book value was attributed to goodwill. During 2013, Steel reports $720,000 in net income and a $100,000 other comprehensive income loss. Steel also declares and pays $20,000 in dividends.

a. What amount should Fisher report as its Investment in Steel on its December 31, 2013, balance sheet?

b. What amount should Fisher report as Equity in Earnings of Steel on its 2013 income statement?

LO3, LO4, LO7

15. On January 1, 2012, Alison, Inc., paid $60,000 for a 40 percent interest in Holister Corporation's common stock. This investee had assets with a book value of $200,000 and liabilities of $75,000. A patent held by Holister having a $5,000 book value was actually worth $20,000. This patent had a six-year remaining life. Any further excess cost associated with this acquisition was attributed to goodwill. During 2012, Holister earned income of $30,000 and paid dividends of $10,000. In 2013, it had income of $50,000 and dividends of $15,000. During 2013, the fair value of Allison's investment in Holister had risen from $68,000 to $75,000.

a. Assuming Alison uses the equity method, what balance should appear in the Investment in Holister account as of December 31, 2013?

b. Assuming Alison uses the fair-value option, what income from the investment in Holister should be reported for 2013?

LO6

16. On January 1, 2013, Ruark Corporation acquired a 40 percent interest in Batson, Inc., for $210,000. On that date, Batson's balance sheet disclosed net assets with both a fair and book value of $360,000. During 2013, Batson reported net income of $80,000 and paid cash dividends of $25,000. Ruark sold inventory costing $30,000 to Batson during 2013 for $40,000. Batson used all of this merchandise in its operations during 2013. Prepare all of Ruark's 2013 journal entries to apply the equity method to this investment.

LO1, LO2, LO3, LO4

17. Waters, Inc., acquired 10 percent of Denton Corporation on January 1, 2012, for $210,000 although Denton's book value on that date was $1,700,000. Denton held land that was undervalued by $100,000 on its accounting records. During 2012, Denton earned a net income of $240,000 while paying cash dividends of $90,000. On January 1, 2013, Waters purchased an additional 30 percent of Denton for $600,000. Denton's land is still undervalued on that date, but then by $120,000. Any additional excess cost was attributable to a trademark with a 10-year life for the first purchase and a 9-year life for the second. The initial 10 percent investment had been maintained at cost because fair values were not readily available. The equity method will now be applied. During 2013, Denton reported income of $300,000 and distributed dividends of $110,000. Prepare all of the 2013 journal entries for Waters.

LO6

18. Tiberend, Inc., sold $150,000 in inventory to Schilling Company during 2012 for $225,000. Schilling resold $105,000 of this merchandise in 2012 with the remainder to be disposed of during 2013. Assuming that Tiberend owns 25 percent of Schilling and applies the equity method, what journal entry is recorded at the end of 2012 to defer the unrealized gross profit?

LO3, LO4, LO6

19. BuyCo holds 25 percent of the outstanding shares of Marqueen and appropriately applies the equity method of accounting. Excess cost amortization (related to a patent) associated with this investment amounts to $10,000 per year. For 2012, Marqueen reported earnings of

$100,000 and pays cash dividends of $30,000. During that year, Marqueen acquired inventory for $50,000, which it then sold to BuyCo for $80,000. At the end of 2012, BuyCo continued to hold merchandise with a transfer price of $32,000.

a. What Equity in Investee Income should BuyCo report for 2012?

b. How will the intra-entity transfer affect BuyCo's reporting in 2013?

c. If BuyCo had sold the inventory to Marqueen, how would the answers to (*a*) and (*b*) have changed?

LO1, LO2, LO3

20. On January 1, 2011, Monroe, Inc., purchased 10,000 shares of Brown Company for $250,000, giving Monroe 10 percent ownership of Brown. On January 1, 2012, Monroe purchased an additional 20,000 shares (20 percent) for $590,000. This latest purchase gave Monroe the ability to apply significant influence over Brown. The original 10 percent investment was categorized as an available-for-sale security. Any excess of cost over book value acquired for either investment was attributed solely to goodwill.

Brown reports net income and dividends as follows. These amounts are assumed to have occurred evenly throughout these years.

	Net Income	Cash Dividends (paid quarterly)
2011	$350,000	$100,000
2012	480,000	110,000
2013	500,000	120,000

On July 1, 2013, Monroe sells 2,000 shares of this investment for $46 per share, thus reducing its interest from 30 to 28 percent. However, the company retains the ability to significantly influence Brown. Using the equity method, what amounts appear in Monroe's 2013 income statement?

LO1, LO2, LO3

21. Collins, Inc., purchased 10 percent of Merton Corporation on January 1, 2012, for $345,000 and classified the investment as an available-for-sale security. Collins acquires an additional 15 percent of Merton on January 1, 2013, for $580,000. The equity method of accounting is now appropriate for this investment. No intra-entity sales have occurred.

a. How does Collins initially determine the income to be reported in 2012 in connection with its ownership of Merton?

b. What factors should have influenced Collins in its decision to apply the equity method in 2013?

c. What factors could have prevented Collins from adopting the equity method after this second purchase?

d. What is the objective of the equity method of accounting?

e. What criticisms have been leveled at the equity method?

f. In comparative statements for 2012 and 2013, how would Collins determine the income to be reported in 2012 in connection with its ownership of Merton? Why is this accounting appropriate?

g. How is the allocation of Collins's acquisition made?

h. If Merton pays a cash dividend, what impact does it have on Collins's financial records under the equity method? Why is this accounting appropriate?

i. On financial statements for 2013, what amounts are included in Collins's Investment in Merton account? What amounts are included in Collins's Equity in Income of Merton account?

LO3, LO6

22. Parrot Corporation holds a 42 percent ownership of Sunrise, Inc. The equity method is being applied. Parrot assigned the entire original excess purchase price over book value to goodwill. During 2012, the two companies made intra-entity inventory transfers. A portion of this merchandise was not resold until 2013. During 2013, additional transfers were made.

a. What is the difference between upstream transfers and downstream transfers?

b. How does the direction of an intra-entity transfer (upstream versus downstream) affect the application of the equity method?

c. How is the intra-entity unrealized gross profit computed in applying the equity method?

d. How should Parrot compute the amount of equity income to be recognized in 2012? What entry is made to record this income?

e. How should Parrot compute the amount of equity income to be recognized in 2013?

f. If none of the transferred inventory had remained at the end of 2012, how would these transfers have affected the application of the equity method?

g. How do these intra-entity transfers affect Sunrise's financial reporting?

LO1, LO5

23. Several years ago, Einstein, Inc., bought 40 percent of the outstanding voting stock of Brooks Company. The equity method is appropriately applied. On August 1 of the current year, Einstein sold a portion of these shares.

a. How does Einstein compute the book value of this investment on August 1 to determine its gain or loss on the sale?

b. How should Einstein account for this investment after August 1?

c. If Einstein retains only a 2 percent interest in Brooks so that it holds virtually no influence over Brooks, what figures appear in the investor's income statement for the current year?

d. If Einstein retains only a 2 percent interest in Brooks so that virtually no influence is held, does the investor have to retroactively adjust any previously reported figures?

LO3, LO4, LO6

24. Russell owns 30 percent of the outstanding stock of Thacker and has the ability to significantly influence the investee's operations and decision making. On January 1, 2013, the balance in the Investment in Thacker account is $335,000. Amortization associated with this acquisition is $9,000 per year. In 2013, Thacker earns an income of $90,000 and pays cash dividends of $30,000. Previously, in 2012, Thacker had sold inventory costing $24,000 to Russell for $40,000. Russell consumed all but 25 percent of this merchandise during 2012 and used the rest during 2013. Thacker sold additional inventory costing $28,000 to Russell for $50,000 in 2013. Russell did not consume 40 percent of these 2013 purchases from Thacker until 2014.

a. What amount of equity method income would Russell recognize in 2013 from its ownership interest in Thacker?

b. What is the equity method balance in the Investment in Thacker account at the end of 2013?

LO1, LO3, LO7

25. On January 1, 2012, Allan acquires 15 percent of Bellevue's outstanding common stock for $62,000. Allan classifies the investment as an available-for-sale security and records any unrealized holding gains or losses directly in owners' equity. On January 1, 2013, Allan buys an additional 10 percent of Bellevue for $43,800, providing Allan the ability to significantly influence Bellevue's decisions.

During the next two years, the following information is available for Bellevue:

	Income	Dividends	Common Stock Fair Value (12/31)
2012	$ 80,000	$30,000	$438,000
2013	100,000	40,000	468,000

In each purchase, Allan attributes any excess of cost over book value to Bellevue's franchise agreements that had a remaining life of 10 years at January 1, 2012. Also at January 1, 2012, Bellevue reports a net book value of $280,000.

a. Assume Allan applies the equity method to its Investment in Bellevue account:

1. On Allan's December 31, 2013, balance sheet, what amount is reported for the Investment in Bellevue account?
2. What amount of equity income should Allan report for 2013?
3. Prepare the January 1, 2013, journal entry to retrospectively adjust the Investment in Bellevue account to the equity method.

b. Assume Allan elects the fair-value reporting option for its investment in Bellevue:

1. On Allan's December 31, 2013, balance sheet, what amount is reported for the Investment in Bellevue account?
2. What amount of income from its investment in Bellevue should Allan report for 2013?

LO1, LO3, LO4, LO5, LO6

26. Anderson acquires 10 percent of the outstanding voting shares of Barringer on January 1, 2011, for $92,000 and categorizes the investment as an available-for-sale security. An additional 20 percent of the stock is purchased on January 1, 2012, for $210,000, which gives Anderson the ability to significantly influence Barringer. Barringer has a book value of $800,000 at January 1, 2011, and records net income of $180,000 for that year. Barringer paid dividends of $80,000 during 2011. The book values of Barringer's asset and liability

accounts are considered as equal to fair values except for a copyright whose value accounted for Anderson's excess cost in each purchase. The copyright had a remaining life of 16 years at January 1, 2011.

Barringer reported $210,000 of net income during 2012 and $230,000 in 2013. Dividends of $100,000 are paid in each of these years. Anderson uses the equity method.

a. On comparative income statements issued in 2013 by Anderson for 2011 and 2012, what amounts of income would be reported in connection with the company's investment in Barringer?

b. If Anderson sells its entire investment in Barringer on January 1, 2014, for $400,000 cash, what is the impact on Anderson's income?

c. Assume that Anderson sells inventory to Barringer during 2012 and 2013 as follows:

Year	Cost to Anderson	Price to Barringer	Year-End Balance (at transfer price)
2012	$35,000	$50,000	$20,000 (sold in following year)
2013	33,000	60,000	40,000 (sold in following year)

What amount of equity income should Anderson recognize for the year 2013?

LO3, LO4

27. Smith purchased 5 percent of Barker's outstanding stock on October 1, 2011, for $7,475 and acquired an additional 10 percent of Barker for $14,900 on July 1, 2012. Both of these purchases were accounted for as available-for-sale investments. Smith purchases a final 20 percent on December 31, 2013, for $34,200. With this final acquisition, Smith achieves the ability to significantly influence Barker's decision-making process and employs the equity method.

Barker has a book value of $100,000 as of January 1, 2011. Information follows concerning the operations of this company for the 2011–2013 period. Assume that all income was earned uniformly in each year. Assume also that one-fourth of the total annual dividends are paid at the end of each calendar quarter.

Year	Reported Income	Dividends
2011	$20,000	$ 8,000
2012	30,000	16,000
2013	24,000	9,000

On Barker's financial records, the book values of all assets and liabilities are the same as their fair values. Any excess cost from either purchase relates to identifiable intangible assets. For each purchase, the excess cost is amortized over 15 years. Amortization for a portion of a year should be based on months.

a. On comparative income statements issued in 2014 for the years of 2011, 2012, and 2013, what would Smith report as its income derived from this investment in Barker?

b. On a balance sheet as of December 31, 2013, what should Smith report as its investment in Barker?

LO3, LO4, LO6

28. Hobson acquires 40 percent of the outstanding voting stock of Stokes Company on January 1, 2012, for $210,000 in cash. The book value of Stokes's net assets on that date was $400,000, although one of the company's buildings, with a $60,000 carrying value, was actually worth $100,000. This building had a 10-year remaining life. Stokes owned a royalty agreement with a 20-year remaining life that was undervalued by $85,000.

Stokes sold inventory with an original cost of $60,000 to Hobson during 2012 at a price of $90,000. Hobson still held $15,000 (transfer price) of this amount in inventory as of December 31, 2012. These goods are to be sold to outside parties during 2013.

Stokes reported a loss of $60,000 for 2012, $40,000 from continuing operations and $20,000 from an extraordinary loss. The company still manages to pay a $10,000 cash dividend during the year.

During 2013, Stokes reported a $40,000 net income and distributed a cash dividend of $12,000. It made additional inventory sales of $80,000 to Hobson during the period. The original cost of the merchandise was $50,000. All but 30 percent of this inventory had been resold to outside parties by the end of the 2013 fiscal year.

Prepare all journal entries for Hobson for 2012 and 2013 in connection with this investment. Assume that the equity method is applied.

LO3, LO4, LO5, LO6

29. Penston Company owns 40 percent (40,000 shares) of Scranton, Inc., which it purchased several years ago for $182,000. Since the date of acquisition, the equity method has been properly applied, and the book value of the investment account as of January 1, 2013, is $248,000. Excess patent cost amortization of $12,000 is still being recognized each year. During 2013, Scranton reports net income of $200,000; $320,000 in operating income earned evenly throughout the year, and a $120,000 extraordinary loss incurred on October 1. No dividends were paid during the year. Penston sold 8,000 shares of Scranton on August 1, 2013, for $94,000 in cash. However, Penston retains the ability to significantly influence the investee.

During the last quarter of 2012, Penston sold $50,000 in inventory (which it had originally purchased for only $30,000) to Scranton. At the end of that fiscal year, Scranton's inventory retained $9,000 (at sales price) of this merchandise, which was subsequently sold in the first quarter of 2013.

On Penston's financial statements for the year ended December 31, 2013, what income effects would be reported from its ownership in Scranton?

LO3, LO4, LO6

30. On July 1, 2011, Gibson Company acquired 75,000 of the outstanding shares of Miller Company for $12 per share. This acquisition gave Gibson a 35 percent ownership of Miller and allowed Gibson to significantly influence the investee's decisions.

As of July 1, 2011, the investee had assets with a book value of $2 million and liabilities of $400,000. At the time, Miller held equipment appraised at $150,000 above book value; it was considered to have a seven-year remaining life with no salvage value. Miller also held a copyright with a five-year remaining life on its books that was undervalued by $650,000. Any remaining excess cost was attributable to goodwill. Depreciation and amortization are computed using the straight-line method. Gibson applies the equity method for its investment in Miller.

Miller's policy is to pay a $1 per share cash dividend every April 1 and October 1. Miller's income, earned evenly throughout each year, was $550,000 in 2011, $575,000 in 2012, and $620,000 in 2013.

In addition, Gibson sold inventory costing $90,000 to Miller for $150,000 during 2012. Miller resold $80,000 of this inventory during 2012 and the remaining $70,000 during 2013.

a. Prepare a schedule computing the equity income to be recognized by Gibson during each of these years.

b. Compute Gibson's investment in Miller Company's balance as of December 31, 2013.

LO3, LO4, LO5

31. On January 1, 2011, Plano Company acquired 8 percent (16,000 shares) of the outstanding voting shares of the Sumter Company for $192,000, an amount equal to Sumter's underlying book and fair value. Sumter pays a cash dividend to its stockholders each year of $100,000 on September 15. Sumter reported net income of $300,000 in 2011, $360,000 in 2012, $400,000 in 2013, and $380,000 in 2014. Each income figure can be assumed to have been earned evenly throughout its respective year. In addition, the fair value of these 16,000 shares was indeterminate, and therefore the investment account remained at cost.

On January 1, 2013, Plano purchased an additional 32 percent (64,000 shares) of Sumter for $965,750 in cash and began to use the equity method. This price represented a $50,550 payment in excess of the book value of Sumter's underlying net assets. Plano was willing to make this extra payment because of a recently developed patent held by Sumter with a 15-year remaining life. All other assets were considered appropriately valued on Sumter's books.

On July 1, 2014, Plano sold 10 percent (20,000 shares) of Sumter's outstanding shares for $425,000 in cash. Although it sold this interest, Plano maintained the ability to significantly influence Sumter's decision-making process. Assume that Plano uses a weighted average costing system.

Prepare the journal entries for Plano for the years of 2011 through 2014.

LO3, LO4, LO6

32. On January 1, 2012, Stream Company acquired 30 percent of the outstanding voting shares of Q-Video, Inc., for $770,000. Q-Video manufactures specialty cables for computer monitors. On that date, Q-Video reported assets and liabilities with book values of $1.9 million and $700,000, respectively. A customer list compiled by Q-Video had an appraised value of $300,000, although it was not recorded on its books. The expected remaining life of the customer list was five years with a straight-line depreciation deemed appropriate. Any remaining excess cost was not identifiable with any particular asset and thus was considered goodwill.

Q-Video generated net income of $250,000 in 2012 and a net loss of $100,000 in 2013. In each of these two years, Q-Video paid a cash dividend of $15,000 to its stockholders.

During 2012, Q-Video sold inventory that had an original cost of $100,000 to Stream for $160,000. Of this balance, $80,000 was resold to outsiders during 2012, and the remainder was sold during 2013. In 2013, Q-Video sold inventory to Stream for $175,000. This inventory had cost only $140,000. Stream resold $100,000 of the inventory during 2013 and the rest during 2014.

For 2012 and then for 2013, compute the amount that Stream should report as income from its investment in Q-Video in its external financial statements under the equity method.

Develop Your Skills

EXCEL CASE 1

On January 1, 2013, Acme Co. is considering purchasing a 40 percent ownership interest in PHC Co., a privately held enterprise, for $700,000. PHC predicts its profit will be $185,000 in 2013, projects a 10 percent annual increase in profits in each of the next four years, and expects to pay a steady annual dividend of $30,000 for the foreseeable future. Because PHC has on its books a patent that is undervalued by $375,000, Acme realizes that it will have an additional amortization expense of $15,000 per year over the next 10 years—the patent's estimated useful life. All of PHC's other assets and liabilities have book values that approximate market values. Acme uses the equity method for its investment in PHC.

Required

1. Using an Excel spreadsheet, set the following values in cells:
   - Acme's cost of investment in PHC.
   - Percentage acquired.
   - First-year PHC reported income.
   - Projected growth rate in income.
   - PHC annual dividends.
   - Annual excess patent amortization.
2. Referring to the values in (1), prepare the following schedules using columns for the years 2013 through 2017.
   - Acme's equity in PHC earnings with rows showing these:
     - Acme's share of PHC reported income.
     - Amortization expense.
     - Acme's equity in PHC earnings.
   - Acme's Investment in PHC balance with rows showing the following:
     - Beginning balance.
     - Equity earnings.
     - Dividends.
     - Ending balance.
   - Return on beginning investment balance = Equity earnings/Beginning investment balance in each year.
3. Given the preceding values, compute the average of the projected returns on beginning investment balances for the first five years of Acme's investment in PHC. What is the maximum Acme can pay for PHC if it wishes to earn at least a 10 percent average return on beginning investment balance? (*Hint:* Under Excel's Tools menu, use the Solver or Goal Seek capability to produce a 10 percent average return on beginning investment balance by changing the cell that contains Acme's cost of investment in PHC. Excel's Solver should produce an exact answer while Goal Seek should produce a close approximation. You may need to first add in the Solver capability under Excel's Tools menu.)

EXCEL CASE 2

On January 1, Intergen, Inc., invests $200,000 for a 40 percent interest in Ryan, a new joint venture with two other partners each investing $150,000 for 30 percent interests. Intergen plans to sell all of its production to Ryan, which will resell the inventory to retail outlets. The equity partners agree that Ryan will buy inventory only from Intergen. Also, Intergen plans to use the equity method for financial reporting.

During the year, Intergen expects to incur costs of $850,000 to produce goods with a final retail market value of $1,200,000. Ryan projects that, during this year, it will resell three-fourths of these goods for $900,000. It should sell the remainder in the following year.

The equity partners plan a meeting to set the price Intergen will charge Ryan for its production. One partner suggests a transfer price of $1,025,000 but is unsure whether it will result in an equitable return across the equity holders. Importantly, Intergen agrees that its total rate of return (including its own operations and its investment in Ryan) should be equal to that of the other investors' return on their investments in Ryan. All agree that Intergen's value including its investment in Ryan is $1,000,000.

Required

1. Create an Excel spreadsheet analysis showing the following:
   - Projected income statements for Intergen and Ryan. Formulate the statements to do the following:
     - Link Ryan's cost of goods sold to Intergen's sales (use a starting value of $1,025,000 for Intergen's sales).
     - Link Intergen's equity in Ryan's earnings to Ryan's net income (adjusted for Intergen's gross profit rate × Ryan's ending inventory × 40 percent ownership percentage).
     - Be able to change Intergen's sales and see the effects throughout the income statements of Ryan and Intergen. Note that the cost of goods sold for Intergen is fixed.
   - The rate of return for the two 30 percent equity partners on their investment in Ryan.
   - The total rate of return for Intergen based on its $1,000,000 value.
2. What transfer price will provide an equal rate of return for each of the investors in the first year of operation? (*Hint:* Under Excel's Tools menu, use the Goal Seek or Solver capability to produce a zero difference in rates of return across the equity partners by changing the cell that contains Intergen's sales.)

ANALYSIS CASE

Access The Coca-Cola Company's SEC 10-K filing at www.coca-cola.com and address the following:

1. What companies does Coca-Cola describe as significant equity method investments? How do these investments help Coca-Cola?
2. What criteria does Coca-Cola use in choosing to apply the equity method for these investments?
3. How does Coca-Cola describe its application of the equity method?
4. What amount of equity income did Coca-Cola report?
5. Coca-Cola reports the fair values of its publicly traded bottlers accounted for as equity method investments. List the book values and fair values for these equity method investments that have publically traded data. Discuss the relevance of each of these two values.

RESEARCH AND ANALYSIS CASE—IMPAIRMENT

Wolf Pack Transport Co. has a 25 percent equity investment in Maggie Valley Depot (MVD), Inc., which owns and operates a warehousing facility used for the collection and redistribution of various consumer goods. Wolf Pack paid $1,685,000 for its 25 percent interest in MVD several years ago, including a $300,000 allocation for goodwill as the only excess cost over book value acquired. Wolf Pack Transport has since appropriately applied the equity method to account for the investment. In its most recent balance sheet, because of recognized profits in excess of dividends since the acquisition, Wolf Pack reported a $2,350,000 amount for its Investment in Maggie Valley Depot, Inc., account.

However, competition in the transit warehousing industry has increased in the past 12 months. In the same area as the MVD facility, a competitor company opened two additional warehouses that are much more conveniently located near a major interstate highway. MVD's revenues declined 30 percent as customers shifted their business to the competitor's facilities and the prices for warehouse services declined. The market value of Wolf Pack's stock ownership in MVD fell to $1,700,000 from a high last year of $2,500,000. MVD's management is currently debating ways to respond to these events but has yet to formulate a firm plan.

Required

1. What guidance does the FASB ASC provide for equity method investment losses in value?
2. Should Wolf Pack recognize the decline in the value of its holdings in MVD in its current year financial statements?
3. Should Wolf Pack test for impairment of the value it had initially assigned to goodwill?

RESEARCH CASE—NONCONTROLLING SHAREHOLDER RIGHTS

Consolidated financial reporting is appropriate when one entity has a controlling financial interest in another entity. The usual condition for a controlling financial interest is ownership of a majority voting interest. But in some circumstances, control does not rest with the majority owner—especially when noncontrolling owners are contractually provided with approval or veto rights that can restrict the actions of the majority owner. In these cases, the majority owner employs the equity method rather than consolidation.

Required

Address the following by searching the FASB ASC Topic 810 on consolidation.

1. What are protective noncontrolling rights?
2. What are substantive participating noncontrolling rights?
3. What noncontrolling rights overcome the presumption that all majority-owned investees should be consolidated?
4. Zee Company buys 60 percent of the voting stock of Bee Company with the remaining 40 percent noncontrolling interest held by Bee's former owners, who negotiated the following noncontrolling rights:
   - Any new debt above $1,000,000 must be approved by the 40 percent noncontrolling shareholders.
   - Any dividends or other cash distributions to owners in excess of customary historical amounts must be approved by the 40 percent noncontrolling shareholders.

   According to the FASB ASC, what are the issues in determining whether Zee should consolidate Bee or report its investment in Bee under the equity method?

CPA REVIEW

Please visit the text website for the online Kaplan CPA simulation:

River Rocks Corporation

Situation: In Year 6, River Rocks Corporation bought 17 percent of the outstanding stock of Pebble, Inc. River Rocks wants to account for this investment by means of the equity method because company officials have demonstrated that significant influence is held over the financial and operating decisions of Pebble due to their representation on the board of directors. The independent auditing firm has asked you to document this assertion.

Topics to be covered:

- Investments research

Please visit the text website for the online Kaplan CPA simulation:

Topez

Situation: Topez owns 35 percent of the common stock of Estes Corporation. Topez has significant influence over Estes, thus it accounts for its investment in Estes using the equity method.

Topics to be covered:

- Investments
- Equity method: Initial and subsequent periods

chapter 2

Consolidation of Financial Information

Financial statements published and distributed to owners, creditors, and other interested parties appear to report the operations and financial position of a single company. In reality, these statements frequently represent a number of separate organizations tied together through common control (a *business combination*). When financial statements represent more than one corporation, we refer to them as *consolidated financial statements*.

Consolidated financial statements are typical in today's business world. Most major organizations, and many smaller ones, hold control over an array of organizations. For example, from 2000 through 2011, Cisco Systems, Inc., reported more than 70 business acquisitions that now are consolidated in its financial reports. PepsiCo, Inc., as another example, annually consolidates data from a multitude of companies into a single set of financial statements. By gaining control over these companies (often known as *subsidiaries*)—which include among others Pepsi Beverages Company, Tropicana Products, and Quaker Oats—PepsiCo (the *parent*) forms a single business combination and single reporting entity.

The consolidation of financial information as exemplified by Cisco Systems and PepsiCo is one of the most complex procedures in all of accounting. Comprehending this process completely requires understanding the theoretical logic that underlies the creation of a business combination. Furthermore, a variety of procedural steps must be mastered to ensure that proper accounting is achieved for this single reporting entity. The following coverage introduces both of these aspects of the consolidation process.

The FASB *Accounting Standards Codification* (ASC) contains the current accounting standards for business combinations under the following topics:

- Business Combinations (Topic 805).
- Consolidation (Topic 810).

Parent	Business combination
Subsidiary	

Learning Objectives

After studying this chapter, you should be able to:

- LO1 Discuss the motives for business combinations.
- LO2 Recognize when consolidation of financial information into a single set of statements is necessary.
- LO3 Define the term *business combination* and differentiate across various forms of business combinations.
- LO4 Describe the valuation principles of the acquisition method.
- LO5 Determine the total fair value of the consideration transferred for an acquisition and allocate that fair value to specific subsidiary assets acquired (including goodwill) and liabilities assumed or to a gain on bargain purchase.
- LO6 Prepare the journal entry to consolidate the accounts of a subsidiary if dissolution takes place.
- LO7 Prepare a worksheet to consolidate the accounts of two companies that form a business combination if dissolution does not take place.
- LO8 Describe the two criteria for recognizing intangible assets apart from goodwill in a business combination.
- LO9 Appendix: Identify the general characteristics of the legacy purchase and pooling of interest methods of accounting for past business combinations. Understand the effects that persist today in financial statements from the use of these legacy methods.

The Business Combinations topic provides guidance on the accounting and reporting for business combinations using the *acquisition method*. The acquisition method embraces a *fair value* measurement attribute. Adoption of this attribute reflects the FASB's increasing emphasis on fair value for measuring and assessing business activity. In the past, financial reporting standards embraced the cost principle to measure and report the financial effects of business combinations. This fundamental change from a cost-based to a fair-value model has transformed the way we account for and report business combinations in our society.

The Consolidation topic provides guidance on circumstances that require a firm to prepare consolidated financial reports and various other related reporting issues. Basically, consolidated financial reports must be prepared whenever one firm has a controlling financial interest in another. Although ownership of a majority voting interest is the usual condition for a controlling financial interest, the power to control may also exist with a lesser percentage of ownership through governance contracts, leases, or agreement with other stockholders.[1]

In this chapter, we first present expansion through corporate takeovers and present an overview of the consolidation process. Then we present the specifics of the acquisition method of accounting for business combinations where the acquirer obtains complete ownership of another firm. Later, beginning in Chapter 4, we introduce coverage of acquisitions with less than complete ownership.

Financial reporting for business combinations has experienced many changes over the past decade. Prior to the acquisition method requirement, accounting standards allowed either the purchase method or the earlier pooling of interests method of accounting for business combinations. Neither of these methods is now permitted for reporting the formation of new business combinations. However, because of the prospective application of the acquisition method beginning in 2009, legacy effects of these methods remain in many of today's financial statements. Therefore, an appendix to this chapter provides a review of the purchase and pooling of interests methods.

Expansion through Corporate Takeovers

Reasons for Firms to Combine

LO1

Discuss the motives for business combinations.

A frequent economic phenomenon is the combining of two or more businesses into a single entity under common management and control. During recent decades, the United States and the rest of the world have experienced an enormous number of corporate mergers and takeovers, transactions in which one company gains control over another. According to Thomson Reuters, the number of mergers and acquisitions globally in 2010 exceeded 40,000, with a total value of more than $2.4 trillion. Of these deals more than $773 billion involved a U.S. firm. As indicated by Exhibit 2.1, the magnitude of recent combinations continues to be large.

As with any other economic activity, business combinations can be part of an overall managerial strategy to maximize shareholder value. Shareholders—the owners of the firm—hire managers to direct resources so that the firm's value grows over time. In this way, owners receive a return on their investment. Successful firms receive substantial benefits through enhanced share value. Importantly, the managers of successful firms also receive substantial benefits in salaries, especially if their compensation contracts are partly based on stock market performance of the firm's shares.

If the goal of business activity is to maximize the firm's value, in what ways do business combinations help achieve that goal? Clearly, the business community is moving rapidly

[1] We discuss entities controlled through contractual means (known as variable interest entities) in Chapter 6.

EXHIBIT 2.1
Recent Notable Business Combinations

Acquirer	Target	Deal Value
Merck	Schering-Plough	$41.1 billion
Comcast	NBC Universal	24.1 billion
Century Link	Qwest Communications	22.1 billion
MetLife	American Life Insurance	16.0 billion
The Coca-Cola Company	Coca-Cola Enterprises	13.1 billion
Intel	McAfee	7.7 billion
Oracle	Sun Microsystems	7.4 billion
United Airlines	Continental Airlines	7.0 billion
Walmart	Massmart	2.3 billion
Nike	Umbro	565 million

toward business combinations as a strategy for growth and competitiveness. Size and scale are obviously becoming critical as firms compete in today's markets. If large firms can be more efficient in delivering goods and services, they gain a competitive advantage and become more profitable for the owners. Increases in scale can produce larger profits from enhanced sales volume despite smaller (more competitive) profit margins. For example, if a combination can integrate successive stages of production and distribution of products, coordinating raw material purchases, manufacturing, and delivery can result in substantial savings. As an example, Oracle's acquisition of Sun Microsystems enables Oracle to closely integrate its software product lines with hardware specifications. The acquisition allows Oracle to offer complete systems made of chips, computers, storage devices, and software with an aim toward increased efficiency and quality.[2] Other cost savings resulting from elimination of duplicate efforts, such as data processing and marketing, can make a single entity more profitable than the separate parent and subsidiary had been in the past.

Although no two business combinations are exactly alike, many share one or more of the following characteristics that potentially enhance profitability:

- Vertical integration of one firm's output and another firm's distribution or further processing.
- Cost savings through elimination of duplicate facilities and staff.
- Quick entry for new and existing products into domestic and foreign markets.
- Economies of scale allowing greater efficiency and negotiating power.
- The ability to access financing at more attractive rates. As firm size increases, negotiating power with financial institutions can increase also.
- Diversification of business risk.

Business combinations also occur because many firms seek the continuous expansion of their organizations, often into diversified areas. Acquiring control over a vast network of different businesses has been a strategy utilized by a number of companies (sometimes known as *conglomerates*) for decades. Entry into new industries is immediately available to the parent without having to construct facilities, develop products, train management, or create market recognition. Many corporations have successfully employed this strategy to produce huge, highly profitable organizations. Unfortunately, others discovered that the task of managing a widely diverse group of businesses can be a costly learning experience. Even combinations that are designed to take advantage of operating synergies and cost savings will fail if the integration is not managed carefully.

Overall, the primary motivations for many business combinations can be traced to an increasingly competitive environment. Three recent business combinations provide interesting examples of distinct motivations to combine: United Airlines and Continental Airlines, Merck and Schering-Plough, and Nike and Umbro. Each is discussed briefly in turn.

[2] Ben Worthen, Cari Tuna, and Justin Scheck, "Companies More Prone to Go 'Vertical,'" *The Wall Street Journal*, November 30, 2009.

United Airlines and Continental Airlines

On September 17, 2010, shareholders approved the business combination of U.S. airline giants United and Continental. The agreement created United Continental Holdings, Inc., which replaced Delta as the world's largest airline. The deal, valued at $7 billion, was completed through an exchange of stock. United shareholders received approximately 55 percent of the equity of the combined company and Continental shareholders received approximately 45 percent. The airline maintained the "United" name while the new logo combined the features of each company's design.[3]

At the time of the merger, United and Continental were the third and fourth largest airlines in the United States, respectively, each servicing over 2,700 daily flights to more than 230 destinations around the world. Despite the vast number of routes and destinations, there was minimal overlap between these two airlines. Domestically, the companies did not share a hub in any city, which made for very few shared routes. Outside the United States, the airlines had no overlap at all. Continental had an extensive network throughout Latin America and Europe, while United was stronger in Asia.[4] The surprising absence of duplicate routes made the two companies a great fit, according to United's CEO.[5]

The merger is expected to generate annual net synergies of $1.0 to $1.2 billion starting in 2013—composed of $800 to $900 million in estimated additional revenue, and $200 to $300 million in cost reductions. The combined network of hubs and destinations is expected to generate revenue from new international routes, while providing improved options for customers on existing routes. The cost savings are expected to come through streamlining of corporate functions and elimination of duplicate jobs and marketing expenses. Additionally, the combined fleet of airplanes should allow the company to operate its routes more efficiently. With a greater number of planes and plane sizes to select from, the new company should be able to better match demand and reduce the number of empty seats on its flights.[6]

The erratic circumstances faced by the airline industry in 2010 also likely served as a motivation for the merger. Both companies had reported significant losses in 2009 and were rebounding from a decade of terrorism fears, volatile oil prices, and the 2008 economic crisis. Faced with uncertain industry conditions, United and Continental determined that they could better handle these challenges as a combined entity.

Merck and Schering-Plough

On November 3, 2009, U.S. pharmaceutical firm Merck completed its acquisition of rival Schering-Plough in a deal valued at $41.1 billion. For each share held, Schering-Plough shareholders received a combination of cash and 0.5767 shares in the new company, giving them an approximate 32 percent stake. The deal makes Merck the world's second largest pharmaceutical firm (behind Pfizer), with annual sales of $46.9 billion in 140 countries.[7]

The acquisition was part of a general movement toward consolidation in the drug industry. Large pharmaceutical firms that had traditionally centered their businesses on drug development were looking to diversify as heightened FDA regulations, patent expirations, and the ongoing recession all threatened their core earnings.[8] To protect against these risks, larger firms in the industry like Pfizer and Roche turned to acquisitions to expand their portfolios. Pfizer acquired Wyeth for $68 billion in January 2009, and Swiss pharmaceutical giant Roche followed suit by purchasing Genentech for $48.6 billion in March 2009.

Like its rivals Pfizer and Roche, Merck was in a position to benefit significantly from an expanded product portfolio, facing several patent expirations on key drugs such as Singulair and Cozaar. Schering-Plough added nine drugs in the later stages of FDA approval to Merck's portfolio, doubling Merck's current pipeline. Schering-Plough also

[3] United Airlines press release, March 3, 2010.

[4] Surojit Chatterjee, "Continental merger to create synergies, cut costs," *International Business Times,* May 3, 2010.

[5] "UAL-Continental Shareholders Approve Merger," Reuters, September 17, 2010.

[6] Susan Carey, "UAL-Continental Merger Takes Off," *The Wall Street Journal,* September 18, 2010.

[7] Jonathan D. Rockoff, "Merck to Buy Rival for $41 Billion," *The Wall Street Journal,* March 10, 2009.

[8] Natasha Singer, "Merck to Buy Schering-Plough for $41.1 Billion," *The New York Times,* March 10, 2009.

provided Merck with established consumer products like Coppertone and Dr. Scholl's, thus reducing its reliance on drug production.[9] Along with the new sources of revenue from the acquisition, Merck expects significant cost savings. Analysts predicted annual cost synergies of $3.5 billion starting in 2012, resulting primarily from a 15 percent reduction in the combined companies' workforce.[10]

Nike and Umbro

On March 4, 2008, Nike completed its acquisition of Umbro, an England-based sportswear supplier, for GBP 285 million (approximately $565 million), thus increasing its presence in the international soccer market. Under the terms of the deal, Umbro maintained its brand name and headquarters in England while operating as a wholly owned subsidiary of Nike.[11] Umbro had a strong relationship with Europe's Football Association and supplied soccer equipment to large-market teams throughout Northern Europe. Umbro also had strong international market exposure, with sales in 90 countries.[12]

The deal was attractive from Umbro's standpoint as well. To Umbro, the buyout offered an opportunity to grow its brand by leveraging Nike's unparalleled global resources. Umbro hoped to achieve similar results as U.S. basketball brand Converse had when it was bought out by Nike in 2003. With the help of Nike's brand management strategies, Converse was able to rebound from near bankruptcy to a position of strength, achieving a growth rate of 22 percent by 2007. Given Nike's position atop the sports apparel industry and track record of successfully growing the brands of smaller acquired companies, Umbro gladly accepted the takeover bid.[13]

The timing of the deal proved to be less than ideal for Nike and demonstrates the risks inherent in any business combination, despite the promise, excitement, and optimistic projections surrounding the acquisition. The 2008 financial crisis hit almost immediately after the acquisition and sales in all of Nike's sectors suffered as a result. In its third quarter 2009, Nike reduced its carrying amount of Umbro by over one-third, recognizing a $199.3 million goodwill impairment charge. The impairment recognized the decline in Umbro's fair value in the brief time since the acquisition.

The Consolidation Process

LO2

Recognize when consolidation of financial information into a single set of statements is necessary.

The consolidation of financial information into a single set of statements becomes necessary when the business combination of two or more companies creates a single economic entity. As stated in FASB ASC (para. 810-10-10-1): "There is a presumption that consolidated financial statements are more meaningful than separate financial statements and that they are usually necessary for a fair presentation when one of the entities in the consolidated group directly or indirectly has a controlling financial interest in the other entities."

Thus, in producing financial statements for external distribution, the reporting entity transcends the boundaries of incorporation to encompass (i.e., consolidate) all companies for which control is present. Even though the various companies may retain their legal identities as separate corporations, the resulting information is more meaningful to outside parties when consolidated into a single set of financial statements.

To explain the process of preparing consolidated financial statements for a business combination, we address three questions:

- How is a business combination formed?
- What constitutes a controlling financial interest?
- How is the consolidation process carried out?

[9] Shannon Pettypiece, "Merck to Buy Schering-Plough for $41 Billion," *Bloomberg,* March 9, 2009.

[10] Hiedi N. Moore, "Merck & Schering-Plough: Analysts See a Win-Win Deal for Holders," *The Wall Street Journal,* March 9, 2009.

[11] Nike Press Release, December 21, 2007.

[12] Vidya Ram, "Goal! Nike Buys Umbro," *Forbes,* October 23, 2007.

[13] John Hoke, "Converse's All-Star Image," *Bloomberg Businessweek,* April 25, 2008.

LO3

Define the term *business combination* and differentiate across various forms of business combinations.

Business Combinations—Creating a Single Economic Entity

A business combination refers to a transaction or other event in which an acquirer obtains control over one or more businesses.

Business combinations are formed by a wide variety of transactions or events with various formats. For example, each of the following is identified as a business combination although it differs widely in legal form. In every case, two or more enterprises are being united into a single economic entity so that consolidated financial statements are required.

1. One company obtains the assets, and often the liabilities, of another company in exchange for cash, other assets, liabilities, stock, or a combination of these. The second organization normally dissolves itself as a legal corporation. Thus, only the acquiring company remains in existence, having absorbed the acquired net assets directly into its own operations. Any business combination in which only one of the original companies continues to exist is referred to in legal terms as a *statutory merger*.

2. One company obtains all of the capital stock of another in exchange for cash, other assets, liabilities, stock, or a combination of these. After gaining control, the acquiring company can decide to transfer all assets and liabilities to its own financial records with the second company being dissolved as a separate corporation.[14] The business combination is, once again, a statutory merger because only one of the companies maintains legal existence. This statutory merger, however, is achieved by obtaining equity securities rather than by buying the target company's assets. Because stock is obtained, the acquiring company must gain 100 percent control of all shares before legally dissolving the subsidiary.

3. Two or more companies transfer either their assets or their capital stock to a newly formed corporation. Both original companies are dissolved, leaving only the new organization in existence. A business combination effected in this manner is a *statutory consolidation*. The use here of the term *consolidation* should not be confused with the accounting meaning of that same word. In accounting, *consolidation* refers to the mechanical process of bringing together the financial records of two or more organizations to form a single set of statements. A statutory consolidation denotes a specific type of business combination that has united two or more existing companies under the ownership of a newly created company.

4. One company achieves legal control over another by acquiring a majority of voting stock. *Although control is present, no dissolution takes place; each company remains in existence as an incorporated operation.* NBC Universal, as an example, continues to retain its legal status as a corporation after being acquired by Comcast Corporation. Separate incorporation is frequently preferred to take full advantage of any intangible benefits accruing to the acquired company as a going concern. Better utilization of such factors as licenses, trade names, employee loyalty, and the company's reputation can be possible when the subsidiary maintains its own legal identity. Moreover, maintaining an independent information system for a subsidiary often enhances its market value for an eventual sale or initial public offering as a stand-alone entity.

Because the asset and liability account balances are not physically combined as in statutory mergers and consolidations, each company continues to maintain an independent accounting system. To reflect the combination, the acquiring company enters the takeover transaction into its own records by establishing a single investment asset account. However, the newly acquired subsidiary omits any recording of this event; its stock is simply transferred to the parent from the subsidiary's shareholders. Thus, the subsidiary's financial records are not directly affected by a takeover.

5. A final vehicle for control of another business entity does not involve a majority voting stock interest or direct ownership of assets. Control of a variable interest entity (VIE)

[14] Although the acquired company has been legally dissolved, it frequently continues to operate as a separate division within the surviving company's organization.

EXHIBIT 2.2
Business Combinations

Type of Combination	Action of Acquiring Company	Action of Acquired Company
Statutory merger through asset acquisition.	Acquires assets and often liabilities.	Dissolves and goes out of business.
Statutory merger through capital stock acquisition.	Acquires all stock and then transfers assets and liabilities to its own books.	Dissolves as a separate corporation, often remaining as a division of the acquiring company.
Statutory consolidation through capital stock or asset acquisition.	Newly created to receive assets or capital stock of original companies.	Original companies may dissolve while remaining as separate divisions of newly created company.
Acquisition of more than 50 percent of the voting stock.	Acquires stock that is recorded as an investment; controls decision making of acquired company.	Remains in existence as legal corporation, although now a subsidiary of the acquiring company.
Control through ownership of variable interests (see Chapter 6). Risks and rewards often flow to a sponsoring firm rather than the equity holders.	Establishes contractual control over a variable interest entity to engage in a specific activity.	Remains in existence as a separate legal entity—often a trust or partnership.

by design often does not rest with its equity holders. Instead, control is exercised through contractual arrangements with a sponsoring firm that, although it technically may not own the VIE, becomes its "primary beneficiary" with rights to its residual profits. These contracts can take the form of leases, participation rights, guarantees, or other interests. Past use of VIEs was criticized because these structures provided sponsoring firms with off-balance sheet financing and sometimes questionable profits on sales to their VIEs. Prior to 2004, many sponsoring entities of VIEs did not technically meet the definition of a controlling financial interest (i.e., majority voting stock ownership) and thus did not consolidate their VIEs. Current GAAP, however, expands the notion of control and thus requires consolidation of VIEs by their primary beneficiary.

As you can see, business combinations are created in many distinct forms. Because the specific format is a critical factor in the subsequent consolidation of financial information, Exhibit 2.2 provides an overview of the various combinations.

Control—An Elusive Quality

The definition of control is central to determining when two or more entities become one economic entity and therefore one reporting entity. Control of one firm by another is most often achieved through the acquisition of voting shares. By exercising majority voting power, one firm can literally dictate the financing and operating activities of another firm. Accordingly, U.S. GAAP traditionally has pointed to a majority voting share ownership as a controlling financial interest that requires consolidation.

The FASB continues its efforts to develop comprehensive guidance on accounting for affiliations between entities, including a definition of control. The following control model has been proposed by the FASB:[15]

> *The Control Model:* A reporting entity has the power to direct the activities of another entity when it has the current ability to direct the activities of the entity that significantly affect the entity's returns.

[15] FASB, Consolidation: Policy and Procedures—Joint Project of the IASB and FASB, March 15, 2011, Project Update.

Note that this proposed definition focuses on the "power to direct" the activities of another entity. The power criterion defines control both operationally through majority voting shares and conceptually through contractual rights. The definition is thus much more expansive, and it explicitly recognizes that voting interests provide but one among several potential vehicles for controlling another firm. As the complexity of arrangements between companies increases, defining when one firm controls another firm remains a continuing challenge for financial reporting standard setters.

Nonetheless, the primary way U.S. firms exercise control remains through the acquisition of a majority of another firm's voting shares. Consequently, in this text, we largely focus on control relationships established through voting interests. In Chapter 6, however, we expand our coverage to include the consolidation of firms where control is exercised through variable interests.

Consolidation of Financial Information

When one company gains control over another, a business combination is established. Financial data gathered from the individual companies are then brought together to form a single set of consolidated statements. Although this process can be complicated, the objectives of a consolidation are straightforward—to report the financial position, results of operations, and cash flows for the combined entity. As a part of this process, reciprocal accounts and intra-entity transactions must be adjusted or eliminated to ensure that all reported balances truly represent the single entity.

Applicable consolidation procedures vary significantly depending on the legal format employed in creating a business combination. *For a statutory merger or a statutory consolidation, when the acquired company (or companies) is (are) legally dissolved, only one accounting consolidation ever occurs.* On the date of the combination, the surviving company simply records the various account balances from each of the dissolving companies. Because the accounts are brought together permanently in this manner, no further consolidation procedures are necessary. After the balances have been transferred to the survivor, the financial records of the acquired companies are closed out as part of the dissolution.

Conversely, in a combination when all companies retain incorporation, a different set of consolidation procedures is appropriate. Because the companies preserve their legal identities, each continues to maintain its own independent accounting records. *Thus, no permanent consolidation of the account balances is ever made. Rather, the consolidation process must be carried out anew each time the reporting entity prepares financial statements for external reporting purposes.*

When separate record-keeping is maintained, the accountant faces a unique problem: The financial information must be brought together periodically without disturbing the accounting systems of the individual companies. Because these consolidations are produced outside the financial records, worksheets traditionally are used to expedite the process. Worksheets are a part of neither company's accounting records nor the resulting financial statements. Instead, they are an efficient structure for organizing and adjusting the information used to prepare externally reported consolidated statements.

Consequently, the legal characteristics of a business combination have a significant impact on the approach taken to the consolidation process:

What is to be consolidated?

- If dissolution takes place, appropriate account balances are physically consolidated in the surviving company's financial records.
- If separate incorporation is maintained, only the financial statement information (not the actual records) is consolidated.

When does the consolidation take place?

- If dissolution takes place, a permanent consolidation occurs at the date of the combination.

- If separate incorporation is maintained, the consolidation process is carried out at regular intervals whenever financial statements are to be prepared.

How are the accounting records affected?

- If dissolution takes place, the surviving company's accounts are adjusted to include appropriate balances of the dissolved company. The dissolved company's records are closed out.
- If separate incorporation is maintained, each company continues to retain its own records. Using worksheets facilitates the periodic consolidation process without disturbing the individual accounting systems.

Financial Reporting for Business Combinations

LO4

Describe the valuation principles of the acquisition method.

The Acquisition Method

Current financial reporting standards require the acquisition method to account for business combinations. Applying the acquisition method typically involves recognizing and measuring

- the consideration transferred for the acquired business and any noncontrolling interest.
- the separately identified assets acquired and liabilities assumed.
- goodwill, or a gain from a bargain purchase.

Fair value is the measurement attribute used to recognize these and other aspects of a business combination. Therefore, prior to examining specific applications of the acquisition method, we present a brief discussion of the fair-value concept as applied to business combinations.

Consideration Transferred for the Acquired Business

The fair value of the consideration transferred to acquire a business from its former owners is the starting point in valuing and recording a business combination. In describing the acquisition method, the FASB ASC states

> The consideration transferred in a business combination shall be measured at fair value, which shall be calculated as the sum of the acquisition-date fair values of the assets transferred by the acquirer, the liabilities incurred by the acquirer to former owners of the acquiree, and the equity interests issued by the acquirer. (FASB ASC para. 805-30-30-7)

The acquisition method thus embraces the fair value of the consideration transferred in measuring the acquirer's interest in the acquired business.[16] Fair value is defined as the price that would be received to sell an asset or paid to transfer a liability in an orderly transaction between market participants at the measurement date. Thus, market values are often the best source of evidence of the fair value of consideration transferred in a business combination. Items of consideration transferred can include cash, securities (either stocks or debt), and other property or obligations.

Contingent consideration, when present in a business combination, is an additional element of consideration transferred. Contingent consideration can be useful in negotiations when two parties disagree with each other's estimates of future cash flows for the target firm or when valuation uncertainty is high.[17] Acquisition agreements often contain provisions to pay former owners upon achievement of specified future performance measures. For example, GT Solar International disclosed in its 2011 annual report its

[16] An occasional exception occurs in a bargain purchase in which the fair value of the net assets acquired serves as the valuation basis for the acquired firm. Other exceptions include situations in which control is achieved without a transfer of consideration or determination of the fair value of the consideration transferred is less reliable than other measures of the business fair value.

[17] Cain, Denis, and Denis, 2011. "Earnouts: A study of financial contracting in acquisition agreements," *Journal of Accounting and Economics* 51, 151–170.

acquisition of 100 percent of the outstanding shares of common stock of privately held Crystal Systems. GT Solar International's agreement with the former owners of Crystal Systems provided for

> a potential additional $18.7 million of contingent consideration based on the attainment of certain financial and technical targets through the period ending March 31, 2012. The fair value of the contingent consideration was $12.5 million at the date of acquisition.

GT Solar International included the fair value of the contingent consideration as a component of the fair value of the consideration transferred for Crystal Systems.

The acquisition method treats contingent consideration obligations as a negotiated component of the fair value of the consideration transferred. Determining the fair value of contingent future payments typically involves probability and risk assessments based on circumstances existing on the acquisition date.

In Chapters 2 and 3, we focus exclusively on combinations that result in complete ownership by the acquirer (i.e., no noncontrolling interest in the acquired firm). As described in Chapter 4, in a less-than-100-percent acquisition, the noncontrolling interest also is measured initially at its fair value. Then, the combined fair values of the parent's consideration transferred and the noncontrolling interest comprise the valuation basis for the acquired firm in consolidated financial reports.

Assets Acquired and Liabilities Assumed

A fundamental principle of the acquisition method is that an acquirer must identify the assets acquired and the liabilities assumed in the business combination. Further, once these have been identified, the acquirer measures the assets acquired and the liabilities assumed at their acquisition-date fair values, with only a few exceptions.[18] As demonstrated in subsequent examples, the principle of recognizing and measuring assets acquired and liabilities assumed at fair value applies across all business combinations.

Fair value, as defined by GAAP, is the price that would be received from selling an asset or paid for transferring a liability in an orderly transaction between market participants at the measurement date. However, determining the acquisition-date fair values of the individual assets acquired and liabilities assumed can prove challenging. To estimate fair values, three sets of valuation techniques are typically employed: the market approach, the income approach, and the cost approach.

Market Approach The market approach recognizes that fair values can be estimated using other market transactions involving similar assets or liabilities. In a business combination, assets acquired such as marketable securities and some tangible assets may have established markets that can provide comparable market values for estimating fair values. Similarly, the fair values of many liabilities assumed can be determined by reference to market trades for similar debt instruments.

Income Approach The income approach relies on multiperiod estimates of future cash flows projected to be generated by an asset. These projected cash flows are then discounted at a required rate of return that reflects the time value of money and the risk associated with realizing the future estimated cash flows. The multiperiod income approach is often useful for obtaining fair-value estimates of intangible assets and acquired in-process research and development.

Cost Approach The cost approach estimates fair values by reference to the current cost of replacing an asset with another of comparable economic utility. Used assets can present a particular valuation challenge if active markets only exist for newer versions of the asset. Thus, the cost to replace a particular asset reflects both its estimated replacement cost and the effects of obsolescence. In this sense obsolescence is meant to capture economic declines in value including both technological obsolescence and physical deterioration. The cost approach is widely used to estimate fair values for many tangible assets acquired in business combinations such as property, plant, and equipment.

[18] Exceptions to the fair-value measurement principle include deferred taxes, certain employee benefits, indemnification assets, reacquired rights, share-based awards, and assets held for sale.

Goodwill, and Gains on Bargain Purchases

In a business combination, the parent records both the consideration transferred and the individual amounts of the identified assets acquired and liabilities assumed at their acquisition-date fair values. However, in many cases the respective collective amounts of these two values will differ. Current GAAP requires an asymmetrical accounting for the difference—in one situation the acquirer recognizes an asset, in the other a gain.

For combinations resulting in complete ownership by the acquirer, the acquirer recognizes the asset goodwill as the excess of the consideration transferred over the collective fair values of the net identified assets acquired and liabilities assumed. Goodwill is defined as an asset representing the future economic benefits arising in a business combination that are not individually identified and separately recognized. Essentially, goodwill embodies the expected synergies that the acquirer expects to achieve through control of the acquired firm's assets.

Conversely, if the collective fair value of the net identified assets acquired and liabilities assumed exceeds the consideration transferred, the acquirer recognizes a "gain on bargain purchase." In such cases, the fair value of the net assets acquired replaces the consideration transferred as the valuation basis for the acquired firm. Bargain purchases can result from business divestitures forced by regulatory agencies or other types of distress sales. Before recognizing a gain on bargain purchase, however, the acquirer must reassess whether it has correctly identified and measured all of the acquired assets and liabilities. Illustrations and further discussions of goodwill and of bargain purchase gains follow in the next section.

Procedures for Consolidating Financial Information

Legal as well as accounting distinctions divide business combinations into several separate categories. To facilitate the introduction of consolidation accounting, we present the various procedures utilized in this process according to the following sequence:

1. Acquisition method when dissolution takes place.
2. Acquisition method when separate incorporation is maintained.

As a basis for this coverage, assume that Smallport Company owns computers, telecommunications equipment, and software that allow its customers to implement billing and ordering systems through the Internet. Although the computers and equipment have a book value of $400,000, they have a current fair value of $600,000. The software developed by Smallport has only a $100,000 value on its books; the costs of developing it were primarily expensed as incurred. The software's observable fair value, however, is $1,200,000. Similarly, although not reflected in its financial records, Smallport has several large ongoing customer contracts. BigNet estimates the fair value of the customer contracts at $700,000. Smallport also has a $200,000 note payable incurred to help finance the software development. Because interest rates are currently low, this liability (incurred at a higher rate of interest) has a present value of $250,000.

BigNet Company owns Internet communications equipment and other business software applications that complement those of Smallport. BigNet wants to expand its operations and plans to acquire Smallport on December 31. Exhibit 2.3 lists the accounts reported by both BigNet and Smallport on that date. In addition, the estimated fair values of Smallport's assets and liabilities are included.

Smallport's net assets (assets less liabilities) have a book value of $600,000 but a fair value of $2,550,000. Only the assets and liabilities have been appraised here; the capital stock, retained earnings, dividend, revenue, and expense accounts represent historical measurements rather than any type of future values. Although these equity and income accounts can give some indication of the organization's overall worth, they are not property and thus not transferred in the combination.

EXHIBIT 2.3 Basic Consolidation Information

	BigNet Company Book Values December 31	Smallport Company Book Values December 31	Smallport Company Fair Values December 31
Current assets	$ 1,100,000	$ 300,000	$ 300,000
Computers and equipment (net)	1,300,000	400,000	600,000
Capitalized software (net)	500,000	100,000	1,200,000
Customer contracts	–0–	–0–	700,000
Notes payable	(300,000)	(200,000)	(250,000)
Net assets	**$ 2,600,000**	**$ 600,000**	**$2,550,000**
Common stock—$10 par value	$(1,600,000)		
Common stock—$5 par value		$(100,000)	
Additional paid-in capital	(40,000)	(20,000)	
Retained earnings, 1/1	(870,000)	(370,000)	
Dividends paid	110,000	10,000	
Revenues	(1,000,000)	(500,000)	
Expenses	800,000	380,000	
Owners' equity 12/31	**$(2,600,000)**	**$(600,000)**	
Retained earnings, 12/31	(960,000)*	(480,000)*	

*Retained earnings balance after closing out revenues, expenses, and dividends paid.
Note: Parentheses indicate a credit balance.

LO5

Determine the total fair value of the consideration transferred for an acquisition and allocate that fair value to specific subsidiary assets acquired (including goodwill) and liabilities assumed or to a gain on bargain purchase.

LO6

Prepare the journal entry to consolidate the accounts of a subsidiary if dissolution takes place.

Acquisition Method When Dissolution Takes Place

At the date control is obtained with complete ownership, the acquisition method typically records the combination recognizing

- the fair value of the consideration transferred by the acquiring firm to the former owners of the acquiree and
- the identified assets acquired and liabilities assumed at their individual fair values.

However, the entry to record the combination further depends on the relation between the consideration transferred and the net amount of the fair values assigned to the identified assets acquired and liabilities assumed. Therefore, we initially provide three illustrations that demonstrate the procedures to record a business combination, each with different amounts of consideration transferred relative to the acquired asset and liability fair values. Each example assumes a merger takes place and, therefore, the acquired firm is dissolved.

Consideration Transferred Equals Net Fair Values of Identified Assets Acquired and Liabilities Assumed

Assume that after negotiations with the owners of Smallport, BigNet agrees to pay $2,550,000 (cash of $550,000 and 20,000 unissued shares of its $10 par value common stock that is currently selling for $100 per share) for all of Smallport's assets and liabilities. Smallport then dissolves itself as a legal entity. As is typical, the $2,550,000 fair value of the consideration transferred by BigNet represents the fair value of the acquired Smallport business.

The $2,550,000 consideration transferred will serve as the basis for recording the combination in total. BigNet also must record all of Smallport's identified assets and liabilities at their individual fair values. These two valuations present no difficulties because BigNet's consideration transferred exactly equals the $2,550,000 collective net fair values of the individual assets and liabilities acquired.

Because Smallport Company will be dissolved, BigNet (the surviving company) directly records a consolidation entry in its financial records. Under the acquisition method, BigNet records Smallport's assets and liabilities at fair value ignoring original book values. Revenue, expense, dividend, and equity accounts cannot be transferred to a parent and are omitted in recording the business combination.

Acquisition Method: Consideration Transferred Equals Net Identified Asset Fair Values—Subsidiary Dissolved

BigNet Company's Financial Records—December 31		
Current Assets	300,000	
Computers and Equipment	600,000	
Capitalized Software	1,200,000	
Customer Contracts	700,000	
Notes Payable		250,000
Cash (paid by BigNet)		550,000
Common Stock (20,000 shares issued by BigNet at $10 par value)		200,000
Additional Paid-In Capital		1,800,000
To record acquisition of Smallport Company. Assets acquired and liabilities assumed are recorded at fair value.		

BigNet's financial records now show $1,900,000 in the Computers and Equipment account ($1,300,000 former balance + $600,000 acquired), $1,700,000 in Capitalized Software ($500,000 + $1,200,000), and so forth. Note that the customer contracts, despite being unrecorded on Smallport's books, are nonetheless identified and recognized on BigNet's financial records as part of the assets acquired in the combination. These items have been added into BigNet's balances (see Exhibit 2.3) at their fair values. Conversely, BigNet's revenue balance continues to report the company's own $1,000,000 with expenses remaining at $800,000 and dividends of $110,000. Under the acquisition method, only the subsidiary's revenues, expenses, dividends, and equity transactions that occur subsequent to the takeover affect the business combination.

Consideration Transferred Exceeds Net Amount of Fair Values of Identified Assets Acquired and Liabilities Assumed

In this next illustration BigNet agrees to pay $3,000,000 in exchange for all of Smallport's assets and liabilities. BigNet transfers to the former owners of Smallport consideration of $1,000,000 in cash plus 20,000 shares of common stock with a fair value of $100 per share. The resulting consideration paid is $450,000 more than the $2,550,000 fair value of Smallport's net assets.

Several factors may have affected BigNet's $3,000,000 acquisition offer. First, BigNet may expect its assets to act in concert with those of Smallport, thus creating synergies that will produce profits beyond the total expected for the separate companies. In our earlier examples, Merck, United Airlines, and Nike all clearly anticipated substantial synergies from their acquisitions. Other factors such as Smallport's history of profitability, its reputation, the quality of its personnel, and the economic condition of the industry in which it operates may also enter into acquisition offers. In general, if a target company is projected to generate unusually high profits relative to its asset base, acquirers are frequently willing to pay a premium price.

When the consideration transferred in an acquisition exceeds total net fair value of the identified assets and liabilities, the excess is allocated to an unidentifiable asset known as goodwill.[19] Unlike other assets, we consider goodwill as unidentifiable because we presume it emerges from several other assets acting together to produce an expectation of enhanced profitability. Goodwill essentially captures all sources of profitability beyond what can be expected from simply summing the fair values of the acquired firm's assets and liabilities.

[19] In business combinations, such excess payments are not unusual and can be quite large. When Oracle acquired PeopleSoft, it initially assigned $4.5 billion of its $11 billion purchase price to the fair value of the acquired identified net assets. It assigned the remaining $6.5 billion to goodwill.

Acquisition Method: Consideration Transferred Exceeds Net Identified Asset Fair Values—Subsidiary Dissolved

Returning to BigNet's $3,000,000 consideration, $450,000 is in excess of the fair value of Smallport's net assets. Thus, goodwill of that amount is entered into BigNet's accounting system along with the fair value of each individual asset and liability. BigNet makes the following journal entry at the date of acquisition:

BigNet Company's Financial Records—December 31		
Current Assets	300,000	
Computers and Equipment	600,000	
Capitalized Software	1,200,000	
Customer Contracts	700,000	
Goodwill	450,000	
Notes Payable		250,000
Cash (paid by BigNet)		1,000,000
Common Stock (20,000 shares issued by BigNet at $10 par value)		200,000
Additional Paid-In Capital		1,800,000
To record acquisition of Smallport Company. Assets acquired and liabilities assumed are recorded at individual fair values with excess fair value attributed to goodwill.		

Once again, BigNet's financial records now show $1,900,000 in the Computers and Equipment account ($1,300,000 former balance + $600,000 acquired), $1,700,000 in Capitalized Software ($500,000 + $1,200,000), and so forth. As the only change, BigNet records goodwill of $450,000 for the excess consideration paid over the net identified asset fair values.[20]

Bargain Purchase—Consideration Transferred Is Less Than Net Amount of Fair Values of Identified Assets Acquired and Liabilities Assumed

Occasionally, the fair value received in an acquisition will exceed the fair value of the consideration transferred by the acquirer. Such bargain purchases typically are considered anomalous. Businesses generally do not sell assets or businesses at prices below their fair values. Nonetheless, bargain purchases do occur—most often in forced or distressed sales.

For example, Westamerica Bank's acquisition of County Bank (California) from the FDIC resulted in a $48.8 million "bargain purchase" gain. The FDIC sold the failed County Bank to Westamerica for $0 and additional guarantees. As a result, Westamerica recorded the combination at the estimated fair value of the net assets acquired and recognized a gain of $48.8 million. This gain treatment is consistent with the view that the acquiring firm is immediately better off by the amount that the fair value acquired in the business combination exceeds the consideration transferred.

To demonstrate accounting for a bargain purchase, our third illustration begins with BigNet transferring consideration of $2,000,000 to the owners of Smallport in exchange for their business. BigNet conveys no cash and issues 20,000 shares of common stock having a $100 per share fair value.

In accounting for this acquisition, at least two competing fair values are present. First, the $2,000,000 consideration transferred for Smallport represents a negotiated transaction value for the business. Second, the net amount of fair values individually assigned to the identified assets acquired and liabilities assumed produces $2,550,000. Additionally, based on expected synergies with Smallport, BigNet's management may believe that the fair value of the business exceeds the net asset fair value. Nonetheless, because the consideration transferred is less than the net asset fair value, a bargain purchase has occurred.

[20] As discussed in Chapter 3, the assets and liabilities (including goodwill) acquired in a business combination are assigned to reporting units of the combined entity. A reporting unit is simply a line of business (often a segment) in which an acquired asset or liability will be employed. The objective of assigning acquired assets and liabilities to reporting units is to facilitate periodic goodwill impairment testing.

The acquisition method records the identified assets acquired and liabilities assumed at their individual fair values. In a bargain purchase situation, this net asset fair value effectively replaces the consideration transferred as the acquired firm's valuation basis for financial reporting. The consideration transferred serves as the acquired firm's valuation basis only if the consideration equals or exceeds the net amount of fair values for the assets acquired and liabilities assumed (as in the first two examples). In this case, however, the $2,000,000 consideration paid is less than the $2,550,000 net asset fair value, indicating a bargain purchase. Thus, the $2,550,000 net asset fair value serves as the valuation basis for the combination. A $550,000 *gain on bargain purchase* results because the $2,550,000 recorded value is accompanied by a payment of only $2,000,000. The acquirer recognizes this gain on its income statement in the period the acquisition takes place.

Acquisition Method: Consideration Transferred Is Less Than Net Identified Asset Fair Values, Subsidiary Dissolved

BigNet Company's Financial Records—December 31		
Current Assets	300,000	
Computers and Equipment	600,000	
Capitalized Software	1,200,000	
Customer Contracts	700,000	
Notes Payable		250,000
Common Stock (20,000 shares issued by BigNet at $10 par value)		200,000
Additional Paid-In Capital		1,800,000
Gain on Bargain Purchase		550,000
To record acquisition of Smallport Company. Assets acquired and liabilities assumed are each recorded at fair value. Excess net asset fair value is attributed to a gain on bargain purchase.		

A consequence of implementing a fair-value concept to acquisition accounting is the recognition of an unrealized gain on the bargain purchase. A criticism of the gain recognition is that the acquirer recognizes profit from a buying activity that occurs prior to traditional accrual measures of earned income (i.e., selling activity). Nonetheless, an exception to the general rule of recording business acquisitions at fair value of the consideration transferred occurs in the rare circumstance of a bargain purchase. Thus, in a bargain purchase, the fair values of the assets received and all liabilities assumed in a business combination are considered more relevant for asset valuation than the consideration transferred.

Related Costs of Business Combinations

Three additional categories of costs typically accompany business combinations, regardless of whether dissolution takes place. First, firms often engage attorneys, accountants, investment bankers, and other professionals for combination-related services. The acquisition method does not consider such expenditures as part of the fair value received by the acquirer. Therefore, professional service fees are expensed in the period incurred. The second category concerns an acquiring firm's internal costs. Examples include secretarial and management time allocated to the acquisition activity. Such indirect costs are reported as current year expenses, too. Finally, amounts incurred to register and issue securities in connection with a business combination simply reduce the otherwise determinable fair value of the securities. Exhibit 2.4 summarizes the three categories of related payments that accompany a business combination and their respective accounting treatments.

To illustrate the accounting treatment of these costs that frequently accompany business combinations, assume the following in connection with BigNet's acquisition of Smallport (also see Exhibit 2.3).

- BigNet issues 20,000 shares of its $10 par common stock with a fair value of $2,600,000 in exchange for all of Smallport's assets and liabilities.
- BigNet pays an additional $100,000 in accounting and attorney fees.

EXHIBIT 2.4
Acquisition Method—Accounting for Costs Frequently Associated with Business Combinations

Types of Combination Costs	Acquisition Accounting
Direct combination costs (e.g., accounting, legal, investment banking, appraisal fees, etc.)	Expense as incurred
Indirect combination costs (e.g., internal costs such as allocated secretarial or managerial time)	Expense as incurred
Amounts incurred to register and issue securities	Reduce the value assigned to the fair value of the securities issued (typically a debit to additional paid-in capital)

- Internal secretarial and administrative costs of $75,000 are indirectly attributable to BigNet's combination with Smallport
- Costs to register and issue BigNet's securities issued in the combination total $20,000.

Following the acquisition method, BigNet would record these transactions as follows:

BigNet Company's Financial Records		
Current Assets	300,000	
Computers and Equipment	600,000	
Capitalized Software	1,200,000	
Customer Contracts	700,000	
Goodwill	50,000	
Notes Payable		250,000
Common Stock (20,000 shares issued by BigNet at $10 par value)		200,000
Additional Paid-In Capital		2,400,000
To record Smallport acquisition for $2,600,000 consideration transferred.		
Professional Services Expense	100,000	
Cash		100,000
To record as expenses of the current period any direct combination costs.		
Salaries and Administrative Expenses	75,000	
Accounts Payable (or Cash)		75,000
To record as expenses of the current period any indirect combination costs.		
Additional Paid-In Capital	20,000	
Cash		20,000
To record costs to register and issue stock in connection with the Smallport acquisition.		

Summary of the Acquisition Method

For combinations resulting in complete ownership, the fair value of the consideration transferred by the acquiring firm provides the starting point for recording a business combination at the date of acquisition. With few exceptions, the separately identified assets acquired and liabilities assumed are recorded at their individual fair values. Goodwill is recognized if the fair value of the consideration transferred exceeds the net identified asset fair value. If the net identified asset fair value of the business acquired exceeds the consideration transferred, a gain on a bargain purchase is recognized and reported in current income of the combined entity. Exhibit 2.5 summarizes possible allocations using the acquisition method.

LO7

Prepare a worksheet to consolidate the accounts of two companies that form a business combination if dissolution does not take place.

The Acquisition Method When Separate Incorporation Is Maintained

When each company retains separate incorporation in a business combination, many aspects of the consolidation process are identical to those demonstrated in the previous section. Fair value, for example, remains the basis for initially consolidating the subsidiary's assets and liabilities.

EXHIBIT 2.5
Consolidation Values—The Acquisition Method

Consolidation Values	Acquisition Accounting
Consideration transferred equals the fair values of net identified assets acquired.	Identified assets acquired and liabilities assumed are recorded at their fair values.
Consideration transferred is greater than the fair values of net identified assets acquired.	Identified assets acquired and liabilities assumed are recorded at their fair values. The excess consideration transferred over the net identified asset fair value is recorded as goodwill.
Bargain purchase—consideration transferred is less than the fair values of net identified assets acquired. The total of the individual fair values of the net identified assets acquired effectively becomes the acquired business fair value.	Identified assets acquired and liabilities assumed are recorded at their fair values. The excess amount of net identified asset fair value over the consideration transferred is recorded as a gain on bargain purchase.

However, several significant differences are evident in combinations in which each company remains a legally incorporated separate entity. Most noticeably, the consolidation of the financial information is only simulated; the acquiring company does not physically record the acquired assets and liabilities. Because dissolution does not occur, each company maintains independent record-keeping. To facilitate the preparation of consolidated financial statements, a worksheet and consolidation entries are employed using data gathered from these separate companies.

A worksheet provides the structure for generating financial reports for the single economic entity. An integral part of this process involves consolidation worksheet entries. *These adjustments and eliminations are entered on the worksheet and represent alterations that would be required if the financial records were physically united.* Because no actual union occurs, neither company ever records consolidation entries in its journals. Instead, they appear solely on the worksheet to derive consolidated balances for financial reporting purposes.

To illustrate using the Exhibit 2.3 information, assume that BigNet acquires Smallport Company on December 31 by issuing 26,000 shares of $10 par value common stock valued at $100 per share (or $2,600,000 in total). BigNet pays fees of $40,000 to a third party for its assistance in arranging the transaction. Then to settle a difference of opinion regarding Smallport's fair value, BigNet promises to pay an additional $83,200 to the former owners if Smallport's earnings exceed $300,000 during the next annual period. BigNet estimates a 25 percent probability that the $83,200 contingent payment will be required. A discount rate of 4 percent (to represent the time value of money) yields an expected present value of $20,000 for the contingent liability ($83,200 × 25% × 0.961538). The fair-value approach of the acquisition method views such contingent payments as part of the consideration transferred. According to this view, contingencies have value to those who receive the consideration and represent measurable obligations of the acquirer. Therefore, the fair value of the consideration transferred in this example consists of the following two elements:

Fair value of securities issued by BigNet	$2,600,000
Fair value of contingent performance liability	20,000
Total fair value of consideration transferred	$2,620,000

To facilitate a possible future spinoff, BigNet maintains Smallport as a separate corporation with its independent accounting information system intact. Therefore, whenever financial statements for the combined entity are prepared, BigNet utilizes a worksheet in simulating the consolidation of these two companies. Although the assets and liabilities are not transferred, BigNet must still record the payment made to Smallport's owners. When the subsidiary remains separate, the parent establishes an investment account that initially reflects the acquired firm's acquisition-date fair value. Because Smallport maintains its separate identity, BigNet prepares the following journal entries on its books to record the business combination.

Acquisition Method—Subsidiary Is Not Dissolved

BigNet Company's Financial Records—December 31		
Investment in Smallport Company (consideration transferred)	2,620,000	
Contingent Performance Liability		20,000
Common Stock (26,000 shares issued by BigNet at $10 par value)		260,000
Additional Paid-In Capital (value of shares in excess of par value)		2,340,000
To record acquisition of Smallport Company, which maintains its separate legal identity.		
Professional Services Expense	40,000	
Cash (paid for third-party fees)		40,000
To record combination costs.		

As Exhibit 2.6 demonstrates, a worksheet can be prepared on the date of acquisition to arrive at consolidated totals for this combination. The entire process consists of seven steps.

EXHIBIT 2.6 Acquisition Method—Date of Acquisition

			Consolidation Entries		
Accounts	**BigNet**	**Smallport**	**Debits**	**Credits**	**Consolidated Totals**
Income Statement					
Revenues	(1,000,000)				(1,000,000)
Expenses	840,000*				840,000
Net income	(160,000)				(160,000)
Statement of Retained Earnings					
Retained earnings, 1/1	(870,000)				(870,000)
Net income (above)	(160,000)*				(160,000)
Dividends paid	110,000				110,000
Retained earnings, 12/31	(920,000)				(920,000)
Balance Sheet					
Current assets	1,060,000*	300,000			1,360,000
Investment in Smallport Company	2,620,000*	–0–		(S) 600,000 (A) 2,020,000	–0–
Computers and equipment	1,300,000	400,000	(A) 200,000		1,900,000
Capitalized software	500,000	100,000	(A) 1,100,000		1,700,000
Customer contracts	–0–	–0–	(A) 700,000		700,000
Goodwill	–0–	–0–	(A) 70,000		70,000
Total assets	5,480,000	800,000			5,730,000
Note payable	(300,000)	(200,000)		(A) 50,000	(550,000)
Contingent performance liability	(20,000)*				(20,000)
Common stock	(1,860,000)*	(100,000)	(S) 100,000		(1,860,000)
Additional paid-in capital	(2,380,000)*	(20,000)	(S) 20,000		(2,380,000)
Retained earnings, 12/31 (above)	(920,000)	(480,000)	(S) 480,000		(920,000)
Total liabilities and equities	(5,480,000)	(800,000)	2,670,000	2,670,000	(5,730,000)

Note: Parentheses indicate a credit balance.
*Balances have been adjusted for consideration transferred and payment of direct acquisition costs. Also note follow-through effects to net income and retained earnings from the expensing of the direct acquisition costs.
(S) Elimination of Smallport's stockholders' equity accounts as of December 31 and book value portion of the investment account.
(A) Allocation of BigNet's consideration fair value in excess of book value.

Step 1

Prior to constructing a worksheet, the parent prepares a formal allocation of the acquisition-date fair value similar to the equity method procedures presented in Chapter 1.[21] Thus, the following schedule is appropriate for BigNet's acquisition of Smallport:

Acquisition-Date Fair Value Allocation Schedule

Fair value of consideration transferred by BigNet.		$2,620,000
Book value of Smallport (see Exhibit 2.3).		600,000
Excess of fair value over book value		$2,020,000
Allocations made to specific accounts based on acquisition-date fair and book value differences:		
Computers and equipment ($600,000 − $400,000)	$ 200,000	
Capitalized software ($1,200,000 − $100,000).	1,100,000	
Customer contracts ($700,000 − 0)	700,000	
Notes payable ($250,000 − $200,000)	(50,000)	1,950,000
Excess fair value not identified with specific items—Goodwill		$ 70,000

Note that this schedule initially subtracts Smallport's acquisition-date book value. The resulting $2,020,000 difference represents the total amount needed on the Exhibit 2.6 worksheet to adjust Smallport's individual assets and liabilities from book value to fair value (and to recognize goodwill). Next, the schedule shows how this $2,020,000 total is allocated to adjust each individual item to fair value. The fair-value allocation schedule thus effectively serves as a convenient supporting schedule for the Exhibit 2.6 worksheet and is routinely prepared for every consolidation.

No part of the $2,020,000 excess fair value is attributed to the current assets because their book values equal their fair values. The Notes Payable account shows a negative allocation because the debt's present value exceeds its book value. An increase in debt decreases the fair value of the company's net assets.

Step 2

The first two columns of the worksheet (see Exhibit 2.6) show the separate companies' acquisition-date financial figures (see Exhibit 2.3). BigNet's accounts have been adjusted for the investment entry recorded earlier. As another preliminary step, Smallport's revenue, expense, and dividend accounts have been closed into its Retained Earnings account. The subsidiary's operations prior to the December 31 takeover have no direct bearing on the operating results of the business combination. These activities occurred before Smallport was acquired; thus, the new owner should not include any precombination subsidiary revenues or expenses in the consolidated statements.

Step 3

Consolidation Entry S eliminates Smallport's stockholders' equity accounts (S is a reference to beginning subsidiary stockholders' equity). These balances (Common Stock, Additional Paid-In Capital, and Retained Earnings) represent ownership accounts held by the parent in their entirety and thus no longer are outstanding. By removing these accounts, only Smallport's assets and liabilities remain to be combined with the parent company figures.

Step 4

Consolidation Entry S also removes the $600,000 component of the Investment in Smallport Company account that equates to the book value of the subsidiary's net assets. For external reporting purposes, BigNet should include each of Smallport's assets and liabilities rather than a single investment balance. In effect, this portion of the Investment in

[21] This allocation procedure is helpful but not critical if dissolution occurs. The asset and liability accounts are simply added directly into the parent's books at their acquisition-date fair value with any excess assigned to goodwill as shown in the previous sections of this chapter.

Smallport Company account is deleted and replaced by the specific assets and liabilities that it represents.

Step 5

Entry A removes the $2,020,000 excess payment in the Investment in Smallport Company and assigns it to the specific accounts indicated by the fair-value allocation schedule. Consequently, Computers and Equipment is increased by $200,000 to agree with Smallport's fair value: $1,100,000 is attributed to Capitalized Software, $700,000 to Customer Contracts, and $50,000 to Notes Payable. The unidentified excess of $70,000 is allocated to Goodwill. This entry is labeled Entry A to indicate that it represents the Allocations made in connection with Smallport's acquisition-date fair value. It also completes the Investment in Smallport Company account balance elimination.

Step 6

All accounts are extended into the Consolidated Totals column. For accounts such as Current Assets, this process simply adds Smallport and BigNet book values. However, when applicable, this extension also includes any allocations to establish the acquisition-date fair values of Smallport's assets and liabilities. Computers and Equipment, for example, is increased by $200,000. By increasing the subsidiary's book value to fair value, the reported balances are the same as in the previous examples when dissolution occurred. The use of a worksheet does not alter the consolidated figures but only the method of deriving those numbers.

Step 7

We subtract consolidated expenses from revenues to arrive at a $160,000 net income. Note that because this is an acquisition-date worksheet, we consolidate no amounts for Smallport's revenues and expenses. Having just been acquired, Smallport has not yet earned any income for BigNet owners. Consolidated revenues, expenses, and net income are identical to BigNet's balances. Subsequent to acquisition, of course, Smallport's income accounts will be consolidated with BigNet's (coverage of this topic begins in Chapter 3).

Worksheet Mechanics

In general, totals (such as Net Income and ending Retained Earnings) are not directly consolidated across on the worksheet. Rather, the components (such as revenues and expenses) are extended across and then combined vertically to derive the appropriate figure. Net income is then carried down on the worksheet to the statement of retained earnings and used (along with beginning retained earnings and dividends paid) to compute the December 31 Retained Earnings balance. In the same manner, ending Retained Earnings of $920,000 is entered into the balance sheet to arrive at total liabilities and equities of $5,730,000, a number that reconciles with the total of consolidated assets.

The balances in the final column of Exhibit 2.6 are used to prepare consolidated financial statements for the business combination of BigNet Company and Smallport Company. The worksheet entries serve as a catalyst to bring together the two independent sets of financial information. The actual accounting records of both BigNet and Smallport remain unaltered by this consolidation process.

Acquisition-Date Fair-Value Allocations—Additional Issues

Intangibles

LO8

Describe the two criteria for recognizing intangible assets apart from goodwill in a business combination.

An important element of acquisition accounting is the acquirer's recognition and measurement of the assets acquired and liabilities assumed in the combination. In particular, the advent of the information age brings new measurement challenges for a host of intangible assets that provide value in generating future cash flows. Intangible assets often comprise the largest proportion of an acquired firm. For example, when AT&T acquired AT&T Broadband, it allocated approximately $19 billion of the $52 billion purchase price to franchise costs. These franchise costs form an intangible asset representing the value attributed to agreements with local authorities that allow access to homes.

Intangible assets include both current and noncurrent assets (not including financial instruments) that lack physical substance. In determining whether to recognize an intangible asset in a business combination, two specific criteria are essential.

1. Does the intangible asset arise from contractual or other legal rights?
2. Is the intangible asset capable of being sold or otherwise separated from the acquired enterprise?

Intangibles arising from contractual or legal rights are commonplace in business combinations. Often identified among the assets acquired are trademarks, patents, copyrights, franchise agreements, and a number of other intangibles that derive their value from governmental protection (or other contractual agreements) that allow a firm exclusive use of the asset. Most intangible assets recognized in business combinations meet the contractual-legal criterion.

Also seen in business combinations are intangible assets meeting the separability criterion. An acquired intangible asset is recognized if it is capable of being separated or divided from the acquiree and sold, transferred, licensed, rented, or exchanged individually or together with a related contract, identifiable asset, or liability. The acquirer is not required to have the intention to sell, license, or otherwise exchange the intangible in order to meet the separability criterion. For example, an acquiree may have developed internally a valuable customer list or other noncontractual customer relationships. Although the value of these items may not have arisen from a specific legal right, they nonetheless convey benefits to the acquirer that may be separable through sale, license, or exchange.

Exhibit 2.7 provides an extensive listing of intangible assets with indications of whether they typically meet the legal/contractual or separability criteria.

The FASB (Exposure Draft, *Business Combinations and Intangible Assets,* para. 271) recognized the inherent difficulties in estimating the separate fair values of many intangibles and stated that

> Difficulties may arise in assigning the acquisition cost to individual intangible assets acquired in a basket purchase such as a business combination. Measuring some of those assets is less difficult than measuring other assets, particularly if they are exchangeable and traded regularly in the marketplace. . . . Nonetheless, even those assets that cannot be measured on that basis may have more cash flow streams directly or indirectly associated with them than can be used as the basis for measuring them. While the resulting measures may lack the precision of other measures, they provide information that is more representationally faithful than would be the case if those assets were simply subsumed into goodwill on the grounds of measurement difficulties.

Undoubtedly, as our knowledge economy continues its rapid growth, asset allocations to items such as those identified in Exhibit 2.7 are expected to be frequent.

Preexisting Goodwill on Subsidiary's Books

In our examples of business combinations so far, the assets acquired and liabilities assumed have all been specifically identifiable (e.g., current assets, capitalized software, computers and equipment, customer contracts, and notes payable). However, in many cases, an acquired firm has an unidentifiable asset (i.e., goodwill recorded on its books in connection with a previous business combination of its own). A question arises as to the parent's treatment of this preexisting goodwill on the newly acquired subsidiary's books.

By its very nature, such preexisting goodwill is not considered identifiable by the parent. Therefore, the new owner simply ignores it in allocating the acquisition-date fair value. The logic is that the total business fair value is first allocated to the identified

EXHIBIT 2.7 Illustrative Examples of Intangible Assets That Meet the Criteria for Recognition Separately from Goodwill (FASB ASC paragraphs 805-20-55-11 through 45)

The following are examples of intangible assets that meet the criteria for recognition as an asset apart from goodwill. The following illustrative list is not intended to be all-inclusive; thus, an acquired intangible asset could meet the recognition criteria of this statement but not be included on that list. Assets designated by the symbol [(c)] are those that would generally be recognized separately from goodwill because they meet the contractual-legal criterion. Assets designated by the symbol [(s)] do not arise from contractual or other legal rights but should nonetheless be recognized separately from goodwill because they meet the separability criterion. The determination of whether a specific acquired intangible asset meets the criteria in this statement for recognition apart from goodwill should be based on the facts and circumstances of each individual business combination.*

Marketing-Related Intangible Assets

1. Trademarks, trade names.[c]
2. Service marks, collective marks, certification marks.[c]
3. Trade dress (unique color, shape, or package design).[c]
4. Newspaper mastheads.[c]
5. Internet domain names.[c]
6. Noncompetition agreements.[c]

Customer-Related Intangible Assets

1. Customer lists.[s]
2. Order or production backlog.[c]
3. Customer contracts and related customer relationships.[c]
4. Noncontractual customer relationships.[s]

Artistic-Related Intangible Assets

1. Plays, operas, and ballets.[c]
2. Books, magazines, newspapers, and other literary works.[c]
3. Musical works such as compositions, song lyrics, and advertising jingles.[c]
4. Pictures and photographs.[c]
5. Video and audiovisual material, including motion pictures, music videos, and television programs.[c]

Contract-Based Intangible Assets

1. Licensing, royalty, standstill agreements.[c]
2. Advertising, construction, management, service, or supply contracts.[c]
3. Lease agreements.[c]
4. Construction permits.[c]
5. Franchise agreements.[c]
6. Operating and broadcast rights.[c]
7. Use rights such as landing, drilling, water, air, mineral, timber cutting, and route authorities.[c]
8. Servicing contracts such as mortgage servicing contracts.[c]
9. Employment contracts.[c]

Technology-Based Intangible Assets

1. Patented technology.[c]
2. Computer software and mask works.[c]
3. Unpatented technology.[s]
4. Databases, including title plants.[s]
5. Trade secrets, including secret formulas, processes, and recipes.[c]

*The intangible assets designated by the symbol (c) also could meet the separability criterion. However, separability is not a necessary condition for an asset to meet the contractual-legal criterion.

assets and liabilities. Only if an excess amount remains after recognizing the fair values of the net identified assets is any goodwill recognized. Thus, in all business combinations, only goodwill reflected in the current acquisition is brought forward in the consolidated entity's financial reports.

Acquired In-Process Research and Development

The accounting for a business combination begins with the identification of the tangible and intangible assets acquired and liabilities assumed by the acquirer. The fair values of the individual assets and liabilities then provide the basis for financial statement valuations. Many firms—especially those in pharmaceutical and high-tech industries—have allocated significant portions of acquired businesses to in-process research and development (IPR&D).

In a marked departure from past practice, current standards now require that acquired IPR&D be measured at acquisition-date fair value and recognized in consolidated financial statements as an asset. In commenting on the nature of IPR&D as an asset, Pfizer in an October 28, 2005, comment letter to the FASB observed that

> Board members know that companies frame business strategies around IPR&D, negotiate for it, pay for it, fair value it, and nurture it and they view those seemingly rational actions as inconsistent with the notion that IPR&D has no probable future economic benefit.

For example, when ARCA Biopharma acquired a significant in-process research and development asset through a merger with Nuvelo, Inc., it disclosed in its financial statements:

> A valuation firm was engaged to assist ARCA in determining the estimated fair values of these (IPR&D) assets as of the acquisition date. Discounted cash flow models are typically used in these valuations, and the models require the use of significant estimates and assumptions including but not limited to:
>
> - Projecting regulatory approvals.
> - Estimating future cash flows from product sales resulting from completed products and in-process projects.
> - Developing appropriate discount rates and probability rates by project.

The IPR&D asset is initially considered an indefinite-lived intangible asset and is not subject to amortization. IPR&D is then tested for impairment annually or more frequently if events or changes in circumstances indicate that the asset might be impaired.

Recognizing acquired IPR&D as an asset is clearly consistent with the FASB's fair-value approach to acquisition accounting. Similar to costs that result in goodwill and other internally generated intangibles (e.g., customer lists, trade names, etc.), IPR&D costs are expensed as incurred in ongoing business activities. However, a business combination is considered a significant recognition event for which all fair values transferred in the transaction should be fully accounted for, including any values assigned to IPR&D. Moreover, because the acquirer paid for the IPR&D, an expectation of future economic benefit is assumed and, therefore, the amount is recognized as an asset.

To illustrate further, assume that ClearTone Company pays $2,300,000 in cash for all assets and liabilities of Newave, Inc., in a merger transaction. ClearTone manufactures components for cell phones. The primary motivation for the acquisition is a particularly attractive research and development project under way at Newave that will extend a cell phone's battery life by up to 50 percent. ClearTone hopes to combine the new technology with its manufacturing process and projects a resulting substantial revenue increase. ClearTone is optimistic that Newave will finish the project in the next two years. At the acquisition date, ClearTone prepares the following schedule that recognizes the items of value it expects to receive from the Newave acquisition:

Consideration transferred		$2,300,000
Receivables	$ 55,000	
Patents	220,000	
In-process research and development	1,900,000	
Accounts payable	(175,000)	
Fair value of identified net assets acquired		2,000,000
Goodwill		$ 300,000

ClearTone records the transaction as follows:

Receivables	55,000	
Patents	220,000	
Research and Development Asset	1,900,000	
Goodwill	300,000	
Accounts Payable		175,000
Cash		2,300,000

Research and development expenditures incurred subsequent to the date of acquisition will continue to be expensed. Acquired IPR&D assets initially should be considered indefinite-lived until the project is completed or abandoned. As with other indefinite-lived intangible assets, an acquired IPR&D asset is tested for impairment and is not amortized until its useful life is determined to be no longer indefinite.

Convergence between U.S. and International Accounting Standards

The FASB ASC Topics on Business Combinations (805) and Consolidation (810) represent outcomes of a joint project between the FASB and the International Accounting Standards Board (IASB). The primary objective of the project was stated as follows:

> to develop a single high-quality standard for business combinations that can be used for both domestic and cross-border financial reporting. The goal is to develop a standard that includes a common set of principles and related guidance that produces decision-useful information and minimizes exceptions to those principles. The standard should improve the completeness, relevance, and comparability of financial information about business combinations . . . (FASB Project Updates: *Business Combinations: Applying the Acquisition Method—Joint Project of the IASB and FASB:* October 25, 2007)

The IASB subsequently issued International Financial Reporting Standard 3 (*IFRS 3*) Revised (effective July 2009), which along with FASB ASC Topics 805, Business Combinations, and 810, Consolidation, effectively converged the accounting for business combinations internationally. The two standards are identical in most important aspects of accounting for business combinations although differences can result in noncontrolling interest valuation and some other limited applications.[22] The joint project on business combinations represents one of the first successful implementations of the agreement between the two standard-setting groups to coordinate efforts on future work with the goal of developing high-quality comparable standards for both domestic and cross-border financial accounting.

In 2011 the IASB issued two new standards that deal with consolidated statements and accompanying disclosures—*IFRS 10*, "Consolidated Financial Statements" and *IFRS 12*, "Disclosure of Interests in Other Entities." The new requirements will be effective beginning in 2013. The standards employ a new singular definition of control that focuses on the power to direct the activities of an entity, exposure to variable returns, and a linkage between power and returns. Unlike the FASB, which currently has separate control models for voting interest versus variable interest entities, the IASB definition is intended to govern any control situation, regardless of whether it derives from voting or other rights.[23]

Summary

1. Consolidation of financial information is required for external reporting purposes when one organization gains control of another, thus forming a single economic entity. In many combinations, all but one of the companies is dissolved as a separate legal corporation. Therefore, the consolidation process is carried out fully at the date of acquisition to bring together all accounts into a single set of financial records. In other combinations, the companies retain their identities as separate enterprises and continue to maintain their own separate accounting

[22] Chapter 4 of this text provides further discussion of noncontrolling interest accounting differences across U.S. GAAP and IFRS. Other differences are presented in chapters where the applicable topics are covered.

[23] See KPMG, *In The Headlines,* "Consolidation: a new single control model," May 2011. Also see Patrick Finnegan, IFRS May 2011 perspectives, "At long last—a single model for consolidation." Evaluation of the existence of control is a complex and evolving issue. This textbook emphasizes financial reporting for combined firms under the assumption that one company controls one or more other companies.

systems. For these cases, consolidation is a periodic process necessary whenever the parent produces external financial statements. This periodic procedure is frequently accomplished through the use of a worksheet and consolidation entries.

2. Current financial reporting standards require the acquisition method in accounting for business combinations. Under the acquisition method, the fair value of the consideration transferred provides the starting point for valuing the acquired firm. The fair value of the consideration transferred by the acquirer includes the fair value of any contingent consideration. The acquired company assets and liabilities are consolidated at their individual acquisition-date fair values. Direct combination costs are expensed as incurred because they are not part of the acquired business fair value. Also, the fair value of all acquired in-process research and development is recognized as an asset in business combinations and is subject to subsequent impairment reviews.
3. If the consideration transferred for an acquired firm exceeds the total fair value of the acquired firm's net assets, the residual amount is recognized in the consolidated financial statements as goodwill, an intangible asset. When a bargain purchase occurs, individual assets and liabilities acquired continue to be recorded at their fair values and a gain on bargain purchase is recognized.
4. Particular attention should be paid to the recognition of intangible assets in business combinations. An intangible asset must be recognized in an acquiring firm's financial statements if the asset arises from a legal or contractual right (e.g., trademarks, copyrights, artistic materials, royalty agreements). If the intangible asset does not represent a legal or contractual right, the intangible will still be recognized if it is capable of being separated from the firm (e.g., customer lists, noncontractual customer relationships, unpatented technology).

Comprehensive Illustration

(*Estimated Time: 45 to 65 Minutes*) Following are the account balances of Miller Company and Richmond Company as of December 31. The fair values of Richmond Company's assets and liabilities are also listed.

Problem

	Miller Company Book Values 12/31	Richmond Company Book Values 12/31	Richmond Company Fair Values 12/31
Cash	$ 600,000	$ 200,000	$ 200,000
Receivables	900,000	300,000	290,000
Inventory	1,100,000	600,000	820,000
Buildings and equipment (net)	9,000,000	800,000	900,000
Unpatented technology	–0–	–0–	500,000
In-process research and development	–0–	–0–	100,000
Accounts payable	(400,000)	(200,000)	(200,000)
Notes payable	(3,400,000)	(1,100,000)	(1,100,000)
Totals	$ 7,800,000	$ 600,000	$ 1,510,000
Common stock—$20 par value	$(2,000,000)		
Common stock—$5 par value		$ (220,000)	
Additional paid-in capital	(900,000)	(100,000)	
Retained earnings, 1/1	(2,300,000)	(130,000)	
Revenues	(6,000,000)	(900,000)	
Expenses	3,400,000	750,000	
Totals	$(7,800,000)	$ (600,000)	

Note: Parentheses indicate a credit balance.

Additional Information (not reflected in the preceding figures)

- On December 31, Miller issues 50,000 shares of its $20 par value common stock for all of the outstanding shares of Richmond Company.
- As part of the acquisition agreement, Miller agrees to pay the former owners of Richmond $250,000 if certain profit projections are realized over the next three years. Miller calculates the acquisition-date fair value of this contingency at $100,000.
- In creating this combination, Miller pays $10,000 in stock issue costs and $20,000 in accounting and legal fees.

Required

a. Miller's stock has a fair value of $32.00 per share. Using the acquisition method:

1. Prepare the necessary journal entries if Miller dissolves Richmond so it is no longer a separate legal entity.
2. Assume instead that Richmond will retain separate legal incorporation and maintain its own accounting systems. Prepare a worksheet to consolidate the accounts of the two companies.

b. If Miller's stock has a fair value of $26.00 per share, describe how the consolidated balances would differ from the results in requirement (*a*).

Solution

a. 1. In a business combination, the accountant first determines the total fair value of the consideration transferred. Because Miller's stock is valued at $32 per share, the 50,000 issued shares are worth $1,600,000 in total. Included in the consideration transferred is the $100,000 acquisition-date fair value of the contingent performance obligation.

This $1,700,000 total fair value is compared to the $1,510,000 fair value of Richmond's assets and liabilities (including the value of IPR&D). The $190,000 excess fair value ($1,700,000 − $1,510,000) is recognized as goodwill. Because dissolution will occur, Richmond's asset and liability accounts are transferred to Miller and entered at fair value with the excess recorded as goodwill.

The $10,000 stock issue cost reduces Additional Paid-In Capital. The $20,000 direct combination costs (accounting and legal fees) are expensed when incurred.

Miller Company's Financial Records—December 31

	Debit	Credit
Cash	200,000	
Receivables	290,000	
Inventory	820,000	
Buildings and Equipment	900,000	
Unpatented Technology	500,000	
Research and Development Asset	100,000	
Goodwill	190,000	
Accounts Payable		200,000
Notes Payable		1,100,000
Contingent Performance Obligation		100,000
Common Stock (Miller) (par value)		1,000,000
Additional Paid-In Capital (fair value in excess of par value)		600,000
To record acquisition of Richmond Company.		
Professional Services Expense	20,000	
Cash (paid for combination costs)		20,000
To record legal and accounting fees related to the combination.		
Additional Paid-In Capital	10,000	
Cash (stock issuance costs)		10,000
To record payment of stock issuance costs.		

2. Under this scenario, the acquisition fair value is equal to that computed in part (*a*1).

50,000 shares of stock at $32.00 each	$1,600,000
Contingent performance obligation	100,000
Acquisition-date fair value of consideration transferred	$1,700,000

Because the subsidiary is maintaining separate incorporation, Miller establishes an investment account to reflect the $1,700,000 acquisition consideration:

Miller's Financial Records—December 31

Investment in Richmond Company	1,700,000	
Contingent Performance Obligation		100,000
Common Stock (Miller) (par value)		1,000,000
Additional Paid-In Capital (fair value in excess of par value)		600,000
To record investment in Richmond Company.		
Professional Services Expense	20,000	
Cash (paid for combination costs)		20,000
To record legal and accounting fees related to the combination.		
Additional Paid-In Capital	10,000	
Cash (stock issuance costs)		10,000
To record payment of stock issuance costs.		

Because Richmond maintains separate incorporation and its own accounting system, Miller prepares a worksheet for consolidation. To prepare the worksheet, Miller first allocates Richmond's fair value to assets acquired and liabilities assumed based on their individual fair values:

Fair value of consideration transferred by Miller	$1,700,000
Book value of Richmond	600,000
Excess fair value over book value	$1,100,000

Allocations are made to specific accounts based on differences in fair values and book values:

Receivables ($290,000 − $300,000)	$ (10,000)	
Inventory ($820,000 − $600,000)	220,000	
Buildings and equipment ($900,000 − $800,000)	100,000	
Unpatented technology ($500,000 − 0)	500,000	
In-process research and development	100,000	910,000
Goodwill		$ 190,000

The following steps produce the consolidated financial statements total in Exhibit 2.8:

- Miller's balances have been updated on this worksheet to include the effects of both the newly issued shares of stock, the recognition of the contingent performance liability, and the combination expenses.
- Richmond's revenue and expense accounts have been closed to Retained Earnings. The acquisition method consolidates only postacquisition revenues and expenses.
- Worksheet Entry S eliminates the $600,000 book value component of the Investment in Richmond Company account along with the subsidiary's stockholders' equity accounts.

Entry A adjusts all of Richmond's assets and liabilities to fair value based on the allocations determined earlier.

b. If the fair value of Miller's stock is $26.00 per share, then the fair value of the consideration transferred in the Richmond acquisition is recomputed as follows:

Fair value of shares issued ($26 × 50,000 shares)	$1,300,000
Fair value of contingent consideration	100,000
Total consideration transferred at fair value	$1,400,000

Because the consideration transferred is $110,000 less than the $1,510,000 fair valu[illegible] assets received in the acquisition, a bargain purchase has occurred. In th[illegible]

EXHIBIT 2.8 Comprehensive Illustration—Solution—Acquisition Method

MILLER COMPANY AND RICHMOND COMPANY
Consolidation Worksheet
For Period Ending December 31

Accounts	Miller Company	Richmond Company	Consolidation Entries Debit	Consolidation Entries Credit	Consolidated Totals
Income Statement					
Revenues	(6,000,000)				(6,000,000)
Expenses	3,420,000*				3,420,000*
Net income	(2,580,000)				(2,580,000)
Statement of Retained Earnings					
Retained earnings, 1/1	(2,300,000)				(2,300,000)
Net income (above)	(2,580,000)				(2,580,000)
Retained earnings, 12/31	(4,880,000)				(4,880,000)
Balance Sheet					
Cash	570,000*	200,000			770,000
Receivables	900,000	300,000		(A) 10,000	1,190,000
Inventory	1,100,000	600,000	(A) 220,000		1,920,000
Investment in Richmond Company	1,700,000*	–0–		(A) 1,100,000 (S) 600,000	–0–
Buildings and equipment (net)	9,000,000	800,000	(A) 100,000		9,900,000
Goodwill	–0–	–0–	(A) 190,000		190,000
Unpatented technology	–0–	–0–	(A) 500,000		500,000
Research and development asset	–0–	–0–	(A) 100,000		100,000
Total assets	13,270,000	1,900,000			14,570,000
Accounts payable	(400,000)	(200,000)			(600,000)
Notes payable	(3,400,000)	(1,100,000)			(4,500,000)
Contingent performance obligation	(100,000)*	–0–			(100,000)
Common stock	(3,000,000)*	(220,000)	(S) 220,000		(3,000,000)
Additional paid-in capital	(1,490,000)*	(100,000)	(S) 100,000		(1,490,000)
Retained earnings, 12/31 (above)	(4,880,000)*	(280,000)†	(S) 280,000		(4,880,000)
Total liabilities and equities	(13,270,000)	(1,900,000)	1,710,000	1,710,000	(14,570,000)

Note: Parentheses indicate a credit balance.
*Balances have been adjusted for issuance of stock, payment of combination expenses, and recognition of contingent performance obligation.
†Beginning retained earnings plus revenues minus expenses.

continues to recognize each of the separately identified assets acquired and liabilities assumed at their fair values. Resulting differences in the consolidated balances relative to the requirement (*a*) solution are as follows:

- The $110,000 excess fair value recognized over the consideration transferred is recognized as a "gain on bargain purchase."
- Consolidated net income increases by the $110,000 gain to $2,690,000.
- No goodwill is recognized.
- Miller's additional paid-in capital decreases by $300,000 to $1,190,000.
- Consolidated retained earnings increase by the $110,000 gain to $4,990,000.

Also, because of the bargain purchase, the "Investment in Richmond Company" account balance on Miller's separate financial statements shows the $1,510,000 fair value of the net identified assets received. This valuation measure is an exception to the general rule of using the consideration transferred to provide the valuation basis for the acquired firm.

Appendix

LO9

Identify the general characteristics of the legacy purchase and pooling of interest methods of accounting for past business combinations. Understand the effects that persist today in financial statements from the use of these legacy methods.

Legacy Methods of Accounting For Business Combinations

The acquisition method provides the accounting for business combinations occurring in 2009 and thereafter. However, for decades, business combinations were accounted for using either the **purchase** or **pooling of interests** method. From 2002 through 2008, the purchase method was used exclusively for business combinations. Prior to 2002, financial reporting standards allowed two alternatives: the purchase method and the pooling of interests method. Because the FASB required prospective application of the acquisition method for 2009 and beyond, the purchase and pooling of interests methods continue to provide the basis for financial reporting for pre-2009 business combinations and thus will remain relevant for many years. Literally tens of thousands of past business combinations will continue to be reported in future statements under one of these legacy methods.

The Purchase Method: An Application of the Cost Principle

A basic principle of the purchase method was to record a business combination at the cost to the new owners. For example, several years ago MGM Grand, Inc., acquired Mirage Resorts, Inc., for approximately $6.4 billion. This purchase price continued to serve as the valuation basis for Mirage Resorts's assets and liabilities in the preparation of MGM Grand's consolidated financial statements.

Several elements of the purchase method reflect a strict application of the cost principle. The following items represent examples of how the cost-based purchase method differs from the fair-value-based acquisition method.

- Acquisition date allocations (including bargain purchases).
- Direct combination costs.
- Contingent consideration.
- In-process research and development.

We next briefly discuss the accounting treatment for these items across the current and previous financial reporting regimes.

Purchase-Date Cost Allocations (Including Bargain Purchases)

In pre-2009 business combinations the application of the cost principle often was complicated because literally hundreds of separate assets and liabilities were acquired. Accordingly, for asset valuation and future income determination, firms needed a basis to allocate the total cost among the various assets and liabilities received in the bargained exchange. Similar to the acquisition method, the purchase method based its cost allocations on the combination-date fair values of the acquired assets and liabilities. Also closely related to the acquisition method procedures, any excess of cost over the sum of the net identified asset fair values was attributed to goodwill.

But the purchase method stands in marked contrast to the acquisition method in bargain purchase situations. Under the purchase method, a bargain purchase occurred when the sum of the individual fair values of the acquired net assets exceeded the purchase cost. To record a bargain purchase at cost, however, the purchase method required that certain long-term assets be recorded at amounts below their assessed fair values.

For example, assume Adams Co. paid $520,000 for Brook Co. in 2008. Brook has the following assets with appraised fair values:

Accounts receivable	$ 15,000
Land	200,000
Building	400,000
Accounts payable	(5,000)
Total net fair value	$610,000

However, to record the combination at its $520,000 cost, Adams cannot use all of the above fair values. The purchase method solution was to require that Adams reduce the valuation assigned to the acquired long-term assets (land and building) proportionately by $90,000 ($610,000 − $520,000).

The total fair value of the long-term assets, in this case $600,000, provided the basis for allocating the reduction. Thus, Adams would reduce the acquired land by (2/6 × $90,000) = $30,000 and the building by (4/6 × $90,000) = $60,000. Adams's journal entry to record the combination using the purchase method would then be as follows:

Accounts Receivable	15,000	
Land ($200,000 − $30,000)	170,000	
Building ($400,000 − $60,000)	340,000	
Accounts Payable		5,000
Cash		520,000

Note that current assets and liabilities did not share in the proportionate reduction to cost. Long-term assets were subject to the reduction because their fair-value estimates were considered less reliable than current items and liabilities. Finally, in rare situations firms recognized an extraordinary gain on a purchase, but only in the very unusual case that the long-term assets were reduced to a zero valuation.

In contrast, the acquisition method embraces the fair-value concept and discards the consideration transferred as a valuation basis for the business acquired in a bargain purchase. Instead, the acquirer measures and recognizes the fair values of each of the assets acquired and liabilities assumed at the date of combination, regardless of the consideration transferred in the transaction. As a result, (1) no assets are recorded at amounts below their assessed fair values, as is the case with bargain purchases accounted for by the purchase method, and (2) a gain on bargain purchase is recognized at the acquisition date.

Direct Combination Costs

Almost all business combinations employ professional services to assist in various phases of the transaction. Examples include target identification, due diligence regarding the value of an acquisition, financing, tax planning, and preparation of formal legal documents. Prior to 2009, under the purchase method, the investment cost basis included direct combination costs. In contrast, the acquisition method considers these costs as payments for services received, not part of the fair value exchanged for the business. Thus, under the acquisition method, direct combination costs are expensed as incurred.

Contingent Consideration

Often business combination negotiations result in agreements to provide additional payments to former owners if they meet specified future performance measures. The purchase method accounted for such contingent consideration obligations as post-combination adjustments to the purchase cost (or stockholders' equity if the contingency involved the parent's equity share value) upon resolution of the contingency. The acquisition method treats contingent consideration obligations as a negotiated component of the fair value of the consideration transferred, consistent with the fair value measurement attribute.

In-Process Research and Development (IPR&D)

Prior to 2009, financial reporting standards required the immediate expensing of acquired IPR&D if the project had not yet reached technological feasibility and the assets had no future alternative uses. Expensing acquired IPR&D was consistent with the accounting treatment for a firm's ongoing research and development costs. The acquisition method, however, requires tangible and intangible assets acquired in a business combination to be used in a particular research and development activity, including those that may have no alternative future use, to be recognized and measured at fair value at the acquisition date. These capitalized research and development costs are reported as intangible assets with indefinite lives subject to periodic impairment reviews. Moreover, because the acquirer identified and paid for the IPR&D, the acquisition method assumes an expectation of future economic benefit and therefore recognizes an asset.

The Pooling of Interests Method: Continuity of Previous Ownership

Historically, former owners of separate firms would agree to combine for their mutual benefit and continue as owners of a combined firm. It was asserted that the assets and liabilities of the former firms were never really bought or sold; former owners merely exchanged ownership shares to become joint owners of the combined firm. Combinations characterized by exchange of voting shares and continuation of previous ownership became known as pooling of interests. Rather than an exchange transaction with one ownership group replacing another, a pooling of interests was characterized by a continuity of ownership interests before and after the business combination. Prior to its elimination, this method was applied to a significant number of business combinations.[24] To reflect the continuity of ownership, two important steps characterized the pooling of interests method:

1. The book values of the assets and liabilities of both companies became the book values reported by the combined entity.
2. The revenue and expense accounts were combined retrospectively as well as prospectively. The idea of continuity of ownership gave support for the recognition of income accruing to the owners both before and after the combination.

Therefore, in a pooling, reported income was typically higher than under the contemporaneous purchase accounting. Under pooling, not only did the firms retrospectively combine incomes, but also the smaller asset bases resulted in smaller depreciation and amortization expenses. Because net income reported in financial statements often is used in a variety of contracts, including managerial compensation, managers considered the pooling method an attractive alternative to purchase accounting.

Prior to 2002, accounting and reporting standards allowed both the purchase and pooling of interest methods for business combinations. However, standard setters established strict criteria for use of the pooling method. The criteria were designed to prevent managers from engaging in purchase transactions and then reporting them as poolings of interests. Business combinations that failed to meet the pooling criteria had to be accounted for by the purchase method.

These criteria had two overriding objectives. First, to ensure the complete fusion of the two organizations, one company had to obtain substantially all (90 percent or more) of the voting stock of the other. The second general objective of these criteria was to prevent purchase combinations from being disguised as poolings. Past experience had shown that combination transactions were frequently manipulated so that they would qualify for pooling of interests treatment (usually to increase reported earnings). However, subsequent events, often involving cash being paid or received by the parties, revealed the true nature of the combination: One company was purchasing the other in a bargained exchange. A number of qualifying criteria for pooling of interests treatment were designed to stop this practice.

Comparisons across the Pooling of Interests, Purchase, and Acquisition Methods

To illustrate some of the differences across the purchase, pooling of interests, and acquisition methods, assume that on January 1, Archer Inc. acquired Baker Company in exchange for 10,000 shares of its $1.00 par common stock having a fair value of $1,200,000 in a transaction structured as a merger. In connection with the acquisition, Archer paid $25,000 in legal and accounting fees. Also, Archer agreed to pay the former owners additional cash consideration contingent upon the completion of Baker's existing contracts at specified profit margins. The current fair value of the contingent obligation was estimated to be $150,000. Exhibit 2.9 provides Baker's combination-date book values and fair values.

EXHIBIT 2.9
Precombination Information for Baker Company

January 1	Book Values	Fair Values
Current assets	$ 30,000	$ 30,000
Internet domain name	160,000	300,000
Licensing agreements	0	500,000
In-process research and development	0	200,000
Notes payable	(25,000)	(25,000)
Total net assets	$165,000	$1,005,000

[24] Past prominent business combinations accounted for by the pooling of interests method include ExxonMobil, Pfizer-Warner Lambert, Yahoo!-Broadcast.com, and Pepsi-Quaker Oats, among thousands of others.

Purchase Method Applied

Archer's valuation basis for its purchase of Baker is computed and allocated as follows:

Fair value of shares issued		$1,200,000
Direct combination costs (legal and accounting fees)		25,000
Cost of the Baker purchase		$1,225,000
Cost allocation:		
Current assets	$ 30,000	
Internet domain name	300,000	
Licensing agreements	500,000	
Research and development expense	200,000	
Notes payable	(25,000)	
Total net fair value of items acquired		1,005,000
Goodwill		$ 220,000

Note the following characteristics of the purchase method from the above schedule.

- The valuation basis is cost and includes direct combination costs, but excludes the contingent consideration.
- The cost is allocated to the assets acquired and liabilities assumed based on their individual fair values (unless a bargain purchase occurs and then the long-term items may be recorded as amounts less than their fair values).
- Goodwill is the excess of cost over the fair values of the net assets purchased.
- Acquired in-process research and development is expensed immediately at the purchase date.

Pooling of Interests Method Applied

Because a purchase–sale was deemed not to occur, the pooling method relied on previously recorded values reflecting a continuation of previous ownership. Thus, the following asset would be recorded by Archer in a business combination accounted for as a pooling of interests.

	Values Assigned
Current assets	$ 30,000
Internet domain name	160,000
Licensing agreements	–0–
In-process research and development	–0–
Notes payable	(25,000)
Total value assigned within the combination	$165,000

Note the following characteristics of the pooling of interests method from the above schedule.

- Because a pooling of interests was predicated on a continuity of ownership, the accounting incorporated a continuation of previous book values and ignored fair values exchanged in a business combination.
- Previously unrecognized (typically internally developed) intangibles continue to be reported at a zero value post-combination.
- Because the pooling of interests method values an acquired firm at its previously recorded book value, no new amount for goodwill was ever recorded in a pooling.

Acquisition Method Applied

According to the acquisition method, Archer's valuation basis for its acquisition of Baker is computed as follows:

Fair value of shares issued		$1,200,000
Fair value of contingent performance obligation		150,000
Total consideration transferred for the Baker acquisition		$1,350,000
Cost allocation:		
Current assets	$ 30,000	
Internet domain name	300,000	

Licensing agreements	500,000	
Research and development asset	200,000	
Notes payable	(25,000)	
Total net fair value of items acquired		1,005,000
Goodwill		$ 345,000

Note the following characteristics of the acquisition method from the above entry.

- The valuation basis is fair value of consideration transferred and includes the contingent consideration, but excludes direct combination costs.
- The assets acquired and liabilities assumed are recorded at their individual fair values.
- Goodwill is the excess of the consideration transferred over the fair values of the net assets acquired.
- Acquired in-process research and development is recognized as an asset.
- Professional service fees to help accomplish the acquisition are expensed.

The following table compares the amounts from Baker that Archer would include in its combination-date consolidated financial statements under the pooling of interests method, the purchase method, and the acquisition method.

Values Incorporated in Archer's Consolidated Balance Sheet Resulting from the Baker Transaction

	Pooling of Interests Method	Purchase Method	Acquisition Method
Current assets	$ 30,000	$ 30,000	$ 30,000
Internet domain name	160,000	300,000	300,000
Licensing agreements	–0–	500,000	500,000
In-process research and development asset*	–0–	–0–	200,000
Goodwill	–0–	220,000	345,000
Notes payable	(25,000)	(25,000)	(25,000)
Contingent performance obligation	–0–	–0–	(150,000)
Total net assets recognized by Archer	$165,000	$1,025,000	$1,200,000

*Acquired in-process research and development was expensed under the purchase method and not recognized at all under the pooling of interests method.

Several comparisons should be noted across these methods of accounting for business combinations:

- In consolidating Baker's assets and liabilities, the purchase and acquisition methods record fair values. In contrast, the pooling method uses previous book values and ignores fair values. Consequently, although a fair value of $1,350,000 is exchanged, only a net value of $165,000 (assets less liabilities) is reported in the pooling.
- The pooling method, as reflected in the preceding example, typically shows smaller asset values and consequently lowers future depreciation and amortization expenses. Thus, higher future net income was usually reported under the pooling method compared to similar situations that employed the purchase method.
- Under pooling, financial ratios such as Net Income/Total Assets were dramatically inflated. Not only was this ratio's denominator understated through failure to recognize internally developed assets acquired (and fair values in general), but the numerator was overstated through smaller depreciation and amortization expenses.
- Although not shown, the pooling method retrospectively combined the acquired firm's revenues, expenses, dividends, and retained earnings. The purchase and acquisition methods incorporate only post-combination values for these operational items. Also all costs of the combination (direct and indirect acquisition costs and stock issue costs) were expensed in the period of combination under the pooling of interests method.

- Finally, with adoption of the acquisition method, the FASB has moved clearly in the direction of increased management accountability for the fair values of all assets acquired and liabilities assumed in a business combination.

Questions

1. What is a business combination?
2. Describe the different types of legal arrangements that can take place to create a business combination.
3. What does the term *consolidated financial statements* mean?
4. Within the consolidation process, what is the purpose of a worksheet?
5. Jones Company obtains all of the common stock of Hudson, Inc., by issuing 50,000 shares of its own stock. Under these circumstances, why might the determination of a fair value for the consideration transferred be difficult?
6. What is the accounting valuation basis for consolidating assets and liabilities in a business combination?
7. How should a parent consolidate its subsidiary's revenues and expenses?
8. Morgan Company acquires all of the outstanding shares of Jennings, Inc., for cash. Morgan transfers consideration more than the fair value of the company's net assets. How should the payment in excess of fair value be accounted for in the consolidation process?
9. Catron Corporation is having liquidity problems, and as a result, it sells all of its outstanding stock to Lambert, Inc., for cash. Because of Catron's problems, Lambert is able to acquire this stock at less than the fair value of the company's net assets. How is this reduction in price accounted for within the consolidation process?
10. Sloane, Inc., issues 25,000 shares of its own common stock in exchange for all of the outstanding shares of Benjamin Company. Benjamin will remain a separately incorporated operation. How does Sloane record the issuance of these shares?
11. To obtain all of the stock of Molly, Inc., Harrison Corporation issued its own common stock. Harrison had to pay $98,000 to lawyers, accountants, and a stock brokerage firm in connection with services rendered during the creation of this business combination. In addition, Harrison paid $56,000 in costs associated with the stock issuance. How will these two costs be recorded?

Problems

LO1

1. Which of the following does not represent a primary motivation for business combinations?
   a. Combinations as a vehicle for achieving rapid growth and competitiveness.
   b. Cost savings through elimination of duplicate facilities and staff.
   c. Quick entry for new and existing products into markets.
   d. Larger firms being less likely to fail.

LO2

2. Which of the following is the best theoretical justification for consolidated financial statements?
   a. In form the companies are one entity; in substance they are separate.
   b. In form the companies are separate; in substance they are one entity.
   c. In form and substance the companies are one entity.
   d. In form and substance the companies are separate.
   (AICPA)

LO3

3. What is a statutory merger?
   a. A merger approved by the Securities and Exchange Commission.
   b. An acquisition involving the purchase of both stock and assets.
   c. A takeover completed within one year of the initial tender offer.
   d. A business combination in which only one company continues to exist as a legal entity.

LO4

4. FASB ASC 805, *Business Combinations,* provides principles for allocating the fair value of an acquired business. When the collective fair values of the separately identified assets acquired and liabilities assumed exceed the fair value of the consideration transferred, the difference should be:
   a. Recognized as an ordinary gain from a bargain purchase.
   b. Treated as negative goodwill to be amortized over the period benefited, not to exceed 40 years.

c. Treated as goodwill and tested for impairment on an annual basis.

d. Applied pro rata to reduce, but not below zero, the amounts initially assigned to specific noncurrent assets of the acquired firm.

LO8

5. What is the appropriate accounting treatment for the value assigned to in-process research and development acquired in a business combination?

   a. Expense upon acquisition.

   b. Capitalize as an asset.

   c. Expense if there is no alternative use for the assets used in the research and development and technological feasibility has yet to be reached.

   d. Expense until future economic benefits become certain and then capitalize as an asset.

LO8

6. An acquired entity has a long-term operating lease for an office building used for central management. The terms of the lease are very favorable relative to current market rates. However, the lease prohibits subleasing or any other transfer of rights. In its financial statements, the acquiring firm should report the value assigned to the lease contract as

   a. An intangible asset under the contractual-legal criterion.

   b. A part of goodwill.

   c. An intangible asset under the separability criterion.

   d. A building.

LO4

7. When does gain recognition accompany a business combination?

   a. When a bargain purchase occurs.

   b. In a combination created in the middle of a fiscal year.

   c. In an acquisition when the value of all assets and liabilities cannot be determined.

   d. When the amount of a bargain purchase exceeds the value of the applicable noncurrent assets (other than certain exceptions) held by the acquired company.

LO4

8. According to the acquisition method of accounting for business combinations, costs paid to attorneys and accountants for services in arranging a merger should be

   a. Capitalized as part of the overall fair value acquired in the merger.

   b. Recorded as an expense in the period the merger takes place.

   c. Included in recognized goodwill.

   d. Written off over a five-year maximum useful life.

LO4

9. When negotiating a business acquisition, buyers sometimes agree to pay extra amounts to sellers in the future if performance metrics are achieved over specified time horizons. How should buyers account for such contingent consideration in recording an acquisition?

   a. The amount ultimately paid under the contingent consideration agreement is added to goodwill when and if the performance metrics are met.

   b. The fair value of the contingent consideration is expensed immediately at acquisition date.

   c. The fair value of the contingent consideration is included in the overall fair value of the consideration transferred, and a liability or additional owners' equity is recognized.

   d. The fair value of the contingent consideration is recorded as a reduction of the otherwise determinable fair value of the acquired firm.

LO5

10. On June 1, Cline Co. paid $800,000 cash for all of the issued and outstanding common stock of Renn Corp. The carrying values for Renn's assets and liabilities on June 1 follow:

Cash	$150,000
Accounts receivable	180,000
Capitalized software costs	320,000
Goodwill	100,000
Liabilities	(130,000)
Net assets	$620,000

On June 1, Renn's accounts receivable had a fair value of $140,000. Additionally, Renn's in-process research and development was estimated to have a fair value of $200,000. All other items were stated at their fair values. On Cline's June 1 consolidated balance sheet, how much is reported for goodwill?

a. $320,000.
b. $120,000.
c. $80,000.
d. $20,000.

Problems 11 and 12 relate to the following:
On May 1, Donovan Company reported the following account balances:

Current assets	$ 90,000
Buildings & equipment (net)	220,000
Total assets	$310,000
Liabilities	$ 60,000
Common stock	150,000
Retained earnings	100,000
Total liabilities and equities	$310,000

On May 1, Beasley paid $400,000 in stock (fair value) for all of the assets and liabilities of Donovan, which will cease to exist as a separate entity. In connection with the merger, Beasley incurred $15,000 in accounts payable for legal and accounting fees.

Beasley also agreed to pay $75,000 to the former owners of Donovan contingent on meeting certain revenue goals during the following year. Beasley estimated the present value of its probability adjusted expected payment for the contingency at $20,000. In determining its offer, Beasley noted the following:

- Donovan holds a building with a fair value $30,000 more than its book value.
- Donovan has developed unpatented technology appraised at $25,000, although is it not recorded in its financial records.
- Donovan has a research and development activity in process with an appraised fair value of $45,000. The project has not yet reached technological feasibility.
- Book values for Donovan's current assets and liabilities approximate fair values.

LO4, LO5

11. What should Beasley record as total liabilities incurred or assumed in connection with the Donovan merger?
    a. $15,000
    b. $75,000
    c. $95,000
    d. $150,000

LO5, LO8

12. How much should Beasley record as total assets acquired in the Donovan merger?
    a. $400,000
    b. $420,000
    c. $410,000
    d. $480,000

LO5

13. Prior to being united in a business combination, Atkins, Inc., and Waterson Corporation had the following stockholders' equity figures:

	Atkins	Waterson
Common stock ($1 par value)	$180,000	$ 45,000
Additional paid-in capital	90,000	20,000
Retained earnings	300,000	110,000

Atkins issues 51,000 new shares of its common stock valued at $3 per share for all of the outstanding stock of Waterson. Immediately afterward, what are consolidated Additional Paid-In Capital and Retained Earnings, respectively?

a. $104,000 and $300,000.
b. $110,000 and $410,000.

c. $192,000 and $300,000.

d. $212,000 and $410,000.

Problems 14 and 15 are based on the following information:
Hill, Inc., obtains control over Loring, Inc., on July 1. The book value and fair value of Loring's accounts on that date (prior to creating the combination) follow, along with the book value of Hill's accounts:

	Hill Book Values	Loring Book Values	Loring Fair Values
Revenues	$(250,000)	$(130,000)	
Expenses	170,000	80,000	
Retained earnings, 1/1	(130,000)	(150,000)	
Cash and receivables	140,000	60,000	$ 60,000
Inventory	190,000	145,000	175,000
Patented technology (net)	230,000	180,000	200,000
Land	400,000	200,000	225,000
Buildings and equipment (net)	100,000	75,000	75,000
Liabilities	(540,000)	(360,000)	(350,000)
Common stock	(300,000)	(70,000)	
Additional paid-in capital	(10,000)	(30,000)	

LO5

14. Assume that Hill issues 10,000 shares of common stock with a $5 par value and a $40 fair value to obtain all of Loring's outstanding stock. How much goodwill should be recognized?
    a. −0−.
    b. $15,000.
    c. $35,000.
    d. $100,000.

LO5

15. On its acquisition-date consolidated balance sheet, what amount should Hill report as patented technology (net)?
    a. $200,000
    b. $230,000
    c. $410,000
    d. $430,000

LO8

16. Prycal Co. merges with InterBuy, Inc., and acquires several different categories of intangible assets including trademarks, a customer list, copyrights on artistic materials, agreements to receive royalties on leased intellectual property, and unpatented technology.
    a. Describe the criteria for determining whether an intangible asset acquired in a business combination should be separately recognized apart from goodwill.
    b. For each of the acquired intangibles listed, identify which recognition criteria (separability and legal/contractual) may or may not apply in recognizing the intangible on the acquiring firm's financial statements.

LO6

17. The following book and fair values were available for Westmont Company as of March 1.

	Book Value	Fair Value
Inventory	$ 630,000	$ 600,000
Land	750,000	990,000
Buildings	1,700,000	2,000,000
Customer relationships	–0–	800,000
Accounts payable	(80,000)	(80,000)
Common stock	(2,000,000)	
Additional paid-in capital	(500,000)	
Retained earnings 1/1	(360,000)	
Revenues	(420,000)	
Expenses	280,000	

Arturo Company pays $4,000,000 cash and issues 20,000 shares of its $2 par value common stock (fair value of $50 per share) for all of Westmont's common stock in a merger, after which Westmont will cease to exist as a separate entity. Stock issue costs amount to $25,000 and Arturo pays $42,000 for legal fees to complete the transaction. Prepare Arturo's journal entry to record its acquisition of Westmont.

LO6

18. Use the same facts as in problem (17), but assume instead that Arturo pays cash of $4,200,000 to acquire Westmont. No stock is issued. Prepare Arturo's journal entry to record its acquisition of Westmont.

LO4, LO5, LO6, LO7

19. Following are preacquisition financial balances for Padre Company and Sol Company as of December 31. Also included are fair values for Sol Company accounts.

	Padre Company	Sol Company	
	Book Values 12/31	Book Values 12/31	Fair Values 12/31
Cash	$ 400,000	$ 120,000	$ 120,000
Receivables	220,000	300,000	300,000
Inventory	410,000	210,000	260,000
Land	600,000	130,000	110,000
Building and equipment (net)	600,000	270,000	330,000
Franchise agreements	220,000	190,000	220,000
Accounts payable	(300,000)	(120,000)	(120,000)
Accrued expenses	(90,000)	(30,000)	(30,000)
Long-term liabilities	(900,000)	(510,000)	(510,000)
Common stock—$20 par value	(660,000)		
Common stock—$5 par value		(210,000)	
Additional paid-in capital	(70,000)	(90,000)	
Retained earnings, 1/1	(390,000)	(240,000)	
Revenues	(960,000)	(330,000)	
Expenses	920,000	310,000	

Note: Parentheses indicate a credit balance.

On December 31, Padre acquires Sol's outstanding stock by paying $360,000 in cash and issuing 10,000 shares of its own common stock with a fair value of $40 per share. Padre paid legal and accounting fees of $20,000 as well as $5,000 in stock issuance costs.

Determine the value that would be shown in Padre and Sol's consolidated financial statements for each of the accounts listed.

Accounts

Inventory	Revenues
Land	Additional paid-in capital
Buildings and equipment	Expenses
Franchise agreements	Retained earnings, 1/1
Goodwill	

LO5, LO6

20. On May 1, Soriano Co. reported the following account balances along with their estimated fair values:

	Carrying Value	Fair Value
Receivables	$ 90,000	$ 90,000
Inventory	75,000	75,000
Copyrights	125,000	480,000
Patented technology	825,000	700,000
Total assets	$1,115,000	$1,345,000
Current liabilities	$ 160,000	$ 160,000
Long-term liabilities	645,000	635,000
Common stock	100,000	
Retained earnings	210,000	
Total liabilities and equities	$1,115,000	

On that day, Zambrano paid cash to acquire all of the assets and liabilities of Soriano, which will cease to exist as a separate entity. To facilitate the merger, Zambrano also paid $100,000 to an investment banking firm.

The following information was also available:

- Zambrano further agreed to pay an extra $70,000 to the former owners of Soriano only if they meet certain revenue goals during the next two years. Zambrano estimated the present value of its probability adjusted expected payment for this contingency at $35,000.
- Soriano has a research and development project in process with an appraised value of $200,000. However, the project has not yet reached technological feasibility and the project's assets have no alternative future use.

Prepare Zambrano's journal entries to record the Soriano acquisition assuming its initial cash payment to the former owners was

a. $700,000.

b. $800,000.

LO4, LO5, LO6, LO7

21. On June 30, 2013, Wisconsin, Inc., issued $300,000 in debt and 15,000 new shares of its $10 par value stock to Badger Company owners in exchange for all of the outstanding shares of that company. Wisconsin shares had a fair value of $40 per share. Prior to the combination, the financial statements for Wisconsin and Badger for the six-month period ending June 30, 2013, were as follows:

	Wisconsin	Badger
Revenues	$ (900,000)	$ (300,000)
Expenses	660,000	200,000
Net income	$ (240,000)	$ (100,000)
Retained earnings, 1/1	$ (800,000)	$ (200,000)
Net income	(240,000)	(100,000)
Dividends paid	90,000	–0–
Retained earnings, 6/30	$ (950,000)	$ (300,000)
Cash	$ 80,000	$ 110,000
Receivables and inventory	400,000	170,000
Patented technology (net)	900,000	300,000
Equipment (net)	700,000	600,000
Total assets	$ 2,080,000	$ 1,180,000
Liabilities	$ (500,000)	$ (410,000)
Common stock	(360,000)	(200,000)
Additional paid-in capital	(270,000)	(270,000)
Retained earnings	(950,000)	(300,000)
Total liabilities and equities	$(2,080,000)	$(1,180,000)

Wisconsin also paid $30,000 to a broker for arranging the transaction. In addition, Wisconsin paid $40,000 in stock issuance costs. Badger's equipment was actually worth $700,000, but its patented technology was valued at only $280,000.

What are the consolidated balances for the following accounts?

a. Net income.

b. Retained earnings, 1/1/13.

c. Patented technology.

d. Goodwill.

e. Liabilities.

f. Common stock.

g. Additional paid-in capital.

LO4, LO7

22. On January 1, 2013, Pinnacle Corporation exchanged $3,200,000 cash for 100 percent of the outstanding voting stock of Strata Corporation. Pinnacle plans to maintain Strata as a wholly owned subsidiary with separate legal status and accounting information systems.

At the acquisition date, Pinnacle prepared the following fair-value allocation schedule:

Fair value of Strata (consideration transferred)		$3,200,000
Carrying amount acquired		2,600,000
Excess fair value		$ 600,000
to buildings (undervalued)	$ 300,000	
to licensing agreements (overvalued)	(100,000)	200,000
to goodwill (indefinite life)		$ 400,000

Immediately after closing the transaction, Pinnacle and Strata prepared the following post-acquisition balance sheets from their separate financial records.

	Pinnacle	Strata
Cash	$ 433,000	$ 122,000
Accounts receivable	1,210,000	283,000
Inventory	1,235,000	350,000
Investment in Strata	3,200,000	–0–
Buildings (net)	5,572,000	1,845,000
Licensing agreements	–0–	3,000,000
Goodwill	350,000	–0–
Total assets	$ 12,000,000	$ 5,600,000
Accounts payable	(300,000)	(375,000)
Long-term debt	(2,700,000)	(2,625,000)
Common stock	(3,000,000)	(1,000,000)
Additional paid-in capital	–0–	(500,000)
Retained earnings	(6,000,000)	(1,100,000)
Total liabilities and equities	$(12,000,000)	$(5,600,000)

Prepare a January 1, 2013, consolidated balance sheet for Pinnacle Corporation and its subsidiary Strata Corporation.

LO4, LO5, LO7

23. On January 1, 2013, Marshall Company acquired 100 percent of the outstanding common stock of Tucker Company. To acquire these shares, Marshall issued $200,000 in long-term liabilities and 20,000 shares of common stock having a par value of $1 per share but a fair value of $10 per share. Marshall paid $30,000 to accountants, lawyers, and brokers for assistance in the acquisition and another $12,000 in connection with stock issuance costs.

Prior to these transactions, the balance sheets for the two companies were as follows:

	Marshall Company Book Value	Tucker Company Book Value
Cash	$ 60,000	$ 20,000
Receivables	270,000	90,000
Inventory	360,000	140,000
Land	200,000	180,000
Buildings (net)	420,000	220,000
Equipment (net)	160,000	50,000
Accounts payable	(150,000)	(40,000)
Long-term liabilities	(430,000)	(200,000)
Common stock—$1 par value	(110,000)	
Common stock—$20 par value		(120,000)
Additional paid-in capital	(360,000)	–0–
Retained earnings, 1/1/13	(420,000)	(340,000)

Note: Parentheses indicate a credit balance.

In Marshall's appraisal of Tucker, it deemed three accounts to be undervalued on the subsidiary's books: Inventory by $5,000, Land by $20,000, and Buildings by $30,000. Marshall plans to maintain Tucker's separate legal identity and to operate Tucker as a wholly owned subsidiary.

a. Determine the amounts that Marshall Company would report in its postacquisition balance sheet. In preparing the postacquisition balance sheet, any required adjustments to income accounts from the acquisition should be closed to Marshall's retained earnings.

b. To verify the answers found in part (*a*), prepare a worksheet to consolidate the balance sheets of these two companies as of January 1, 2013.

LO4, LO5, LO7, LO8

eXcel

24. Pratt Company acquired all of Spider, Inc.'s outstanding shares on December 31, 2013, for $495,000 cash. Pratt will operate Spider as a wholly owned subsidiary with a separate legal and accounting identity. Although many of Spider's book values approximate fair values, several of its accounts have fair values that differ from book values. In addition, Spider has internally developed assets that remain unrecorded on its books. In deriving the acquisition price, Pratt assessed Spider's fair and book value differences as follows:

	Book Values	Fair Values
Computer software	$ 20,000	$ 70,000
Equipment	40,000	30,000
Client contracts	–0–	100,000
In-process research and development	–0–	40,000
Notes payable	(60,000)	(65,000)

At December 31, 2013, the following financial information is available for consolidation:

	Pratt	Spider
Cash	$ 36,000	$ 18,000
Receivables	116,000	52,000
Inventory	140,000	90,000
Investment in Spider	495,000	–0–
Computer software	210,000	20,000
Buildings (net)	595,000	130,000
Equipment (net)	308,000	40,000
Client contracts	–0–	–0–
Goodwill	–0–	–0–
Total assets	$ 1,900,000	$ 350,000
Accounts payable	$ (88,000)	$ (25,000)
Notes payable	(510,000)	(60,000)
Common stock	(380,000)	(100,000)
Additional paid-in capital	(170,000)	(25,000)
Retained earnings	(752,000)	(140,000)
Total liabilities and equities	$(1,900,000)	$(350,000)

Prepare a consolidated balance sheet for Pratt and Spider as of December 31, 2013.

LO4, LO5, LO6

25. Allerton Company acquires all of Deluxe Company's assets and liabilities for cash on January 1, 2013, and subsequently formally dissolves Deluxe. At the acquisition date, the following book and fair values were available for the Deluxe Company accounts:

	Book Values	Fair Values
Current assets	$ 60,000	$ 60,000
Building	90,000	50,000
Land	10,000	20,000
Trademark	–0–	30,000
Goodwill	15,000	?
Liabilities	(40,000)	(40,000)
Common stock	(100,000)	
Retained earnings	(35,000)	

Prepare Allerton's entry to record its acquisition of Deluxe in its accounting records assuming the following cash exchange amounts:

(1) $145,000.

(2) $110,000.

LO4, LO6, LO9

26. On June 30, 2013, Sampras Company reported the following account balances:

Receivables	$ 80,000	Current liabilities	$ (10,000)
Inventory	70,000	Long-term liabilities	(50,000)
Buildings (net)	75,000	Common stock	(90,000)
Equipment (net)	25,000	Retained earnings	(100,000)
Total assets	$250,000	Total liabilities and equities	$(250,000)

On June 30, 2013, Pelham paid $300,000 cash for all assets and liabilities of Sampras, which will cease to exist as a separate entity. In connection with the acquisition, Pelham paid $10,000 in legal fees. Pelham also agreed to pay $50,000 to the former owners of Sampras contingent on meeting certain revenue goals during 2014. Pelham estimated the present value of its probability adjusted expected payment for the contingency at $15,000.

In determining its offer, Pelham noted the following pertaining to Sampras:

- It holds a building with a fair value $40,000 more than its book value.
- It has developed a customer list appraised at $22,000, although it is not recorded in its financial records.
- It has research and development activity in process with an appraised fair value of $30,000. However, the project has not yet reached technological feasibility and the assets used in the activity have no alternative future use.
- Book values for the receivables, inventory, equipment, and liabilities approximate fair values.

Prepare Pelham's accounting entry to record the combination with Sampras.

LO4, LO5

27. SafeData Corporation has the following account balances and respective fair values on June 30:

	Book Values	Fair Values
Receivables	$ 80,000	$ 80,000
Patented technology	100,000	700,000
Customer relationships	–0–	500,000
In-process research and development	–0–	300,000
Liabilities	(400,000)	(400,000)
Common stock	(100,000)	
Additional paid-in capital	(300,000)	
Retained earnings deficit, 1/1	700,000	
Revenues	(300,000)	
Expenses	220,000	

Privacy First, Inc., obtained all of the outstanding shares of SafeData on June 30 by issuing 20,000 shares of common stock having a $1 par value but a $75 fair value. Privacy First incurred $10,000 in stock issuance costs and paid $75,000 to an investment banking firm for its assistance in arranging the combination. In negotiating the final terms of the deal, Privacy First also agrees to pay $100,000 to SafeData's former owners if it achieves certain revenue goals in the next two years. Privacy First estimates the probability adjusted present value of this contingent performance obligation at $30,000.

a. What is the fair value of the consideration transferred in this combination?

b. How should the stock issuance costs appear in Privacy First's postcombination financial statements?

c. How should Privacy First account for the fee paid to the investment bank?

d. How does the issuance of these shares affect the stockholders' equity accounts of Privacy First, the parent?

e. How is the fair value of the consideration transferred in the combination allocated among the assets acquired and the liabilities assumed?

f. What is the effect of SafeData's revenues and expenses on consolidated totals? Why?

g. What is the effect of SafeData's Common Stock and Additional Paid-In Capital balances on consolidated totals?

h. If Privacy First's stock had been worth only $50 per share rather than $75, how would the consolidation of SafeData's assets and liabilities have been affected?

LO4, LO5, LO6, LO7, LO8

28. On January 1, 2013, NewTune Company exchanges 15,000 shares of its common stock for all of the outstanding shares of On-the-Go, Inc. Each of NewTune's shares has a $4 par value and a $50 fair value. The fair value of the stock exchanged in the acquisition was considered equal to On-the-Go's fair value. NewTune also paid $25,000 in stock registration and issuance costs in connection with the merger.

Several of On-the-Go's accounts have fair values that differ from their book values on this date:

	Book Values	Fair Values
Receivables	$ 65,000	$ 63,000
Trademarks	95,000	225,000
Record music catalog	60,000	180,000
In-process research and development	–0–	200,000
Notes payable	(50,000)	(45,000)

Precombination January 1, 2013, book values for the two companies are as follows:

	NewTune	On-the-Go
Cash	$ 60,000	$ 29,000
Receivables	150,000	65,000
Trademarks	400,000	95,000
Record music catalog	840,000	60,000
Equipment (net)	320,000	105,000
Totals	$ 1,770,000	$ 354,000
Accounts payable	$ (110,000)	$ (34,000)
Notes payable	(370,000)	(50,000)
Common stock	(400,000)	(50,000)
Additional paid-in capital	(30,000)	(30,000)
Retained earnings	(860,000)	(190,000)
Totals	$(1,770,000)	$(354,000)

a. Assume that this combination is a statutory merger so that On-the-Go's accounts will be transferred to the records of NewTune. On-the-Go will be dissolved and will no longer exist as a legal entity. Prepare a postcombination balance sheet for NewTune as of the acquisition date.

b. Assume that no dissolution takes place in connection with this combination. Rather, both companies retain their separate legal identities. Prepare a worksheet to consolidate the two companies as of the combination date.

c. How do the balance sheet accounts compare across parts (*a*) and (*b*)?

LO4, LO5, LO7

eXcel

29. On December 31, 2012, Pacifica, Inc., acquired 100 percent of the voting stock of Seguros Company. Pacifica will maintain Seguros as a wholly owned subsidiary with its own legal and accounting identity. The consideration transferred to the owner of Seguros included 50,000 newly issued Pacifica common shares ($20 market value, $5 par value) and an agreement to pay an additional $130,000 cash if Seguros meets certain project completion goals by December 31, 2013. Pacifica estimates a 50 percent probability that Seguros will be successful in meeting these goals and uses a 4 percent discount rate to represent the time value of money.

Immediately prior to the acquisition, the following data for both firms were available:

	Pacifica	Seguros Book Values	Seguros Fair Values
Revenues	$(1,200,000)		
Expenses	875,000		
Net income	$ (325,000)		
Retained earnings, 1/1/12	$ (950,000)		
Net income	(325,000)		
Dividends paid	90,000		
Retained earnings, 12/31/12	$(1,185,000)		

(*continued*)

	Pacifica	Seguros Book Values	Seguros Fair Values
Cash	$ 110,000	$ 85,000	$ 85,000
Receivables and inventory	750,000	190,000	180,000
Property, plant, and equipment	1,400,000	450,000	600,000
Trademarks	300,000	160,000	200,000
Total assets	$ 2,560,000	$ 885,000	
Liabilities	$ (500,000)	$(180,000)	$(180,000)
Common stock	(400,000)	(200,000)	
Additional paid-in capital	(475,000)	(70,000)	
Retained earnings	(1,185,000)	(435,000)	
Total liabilities and equities	$(2,560,000)	$(885,000)	

In addition, Pacifica assessed a research and development project under way at Seguros to have a fair value of $100,000. Although not yet recorded on its books, Pacifica paid legal fees of $15,000 in connection with the acquisition and $9,000 in stock issue costs.

Prepare the following:

a. Pacifica's entries to account for the consideration transferred to the former owners of Seguros, the direct combination costs, and the stock issue and registration costs. (Use a 0.961538 present value factor where applicable.)

b. A postacquisition column of accounts for Pacifica.

c. A worksheet to produce a consolidated balance sheet as of December 31, 2012.

Appendix Problems

LO9

30. In a pre-2009 business combination, Acme Company acquired all of Brem Company's assets and liabilities for cash. After the combination Acme formally dissolved Brem. At the acquisition date, the following book and fair values were available for the Brem Company accounts:

	Book Values	Fair Values
Current assets	$ 80,000	$ 80,000
Equipment	120,000	180,000
Trademark	–0–	320,000
Liabilities	(55,000)	(55,000)
Common stock	(100,000)	
Retained earnings	(45,000)	

In addition, Acme paid an investment bank $25,000 cash for assistance in arranging the combination.

a. Using the legacy purchase method for pre-2009 business combinations, prepare Acme's entry to record its acquisition of Brem in its accounting records assuming the following cash amounts were paid to the former owners of Brem:

1. $610,000
2. $425,000

b. How would these journal entries change if the acquisition occurred post-2009 and therefore Acme applied the acquisition method?

LO9

31. On February 1, Piscina Corporation completed a combination with Swimwear Company. At that date, Swimwear's account balances were as follows:

	Book Values	Fair Values
Inventory	$ 600,000	$ 650,000
Land	450,000	750,000
Buildings	900,000	1,000,000
Unpatented technology	–0–	1,500,000
Common stock ($10 par value)	(750,000)	
Retained earnings, 1/1	(1,100,000)	
Revenues	(600,000)	
Expenses	500,000	

Piscina issued 30,000 shares of its common stock with a par value of $25 and a fair value of $150 per share to the owners of Swimwear for all of their Swimwear shares. Upon completion of the combination, Swimwear Company was formally dissolved.

Prior to 2002, business combinations were accounted for using either purchase or pooling of interests accounting. The two methods often produced substantially different financial statement effects. For the scenario above,

a. What are the respective consolidated values for Swimwear's assets under the pooling method and the purchase method?

b. Under each of the following methods, how would Piscina account for Swimwear's current year, but prior to acquisition, revenues and expenses?

- Pooling of interests method
- Purchase method

c. Explain the alternative impact of pooling versus purchase accounting on performance ratios such as return on assets and earnings per share in periods subsequent to the combination.

Develop Your Skills

FASB ASC RESEARCH AND ANALYSIS CASE—CONSIDERATION OR COMPENSATION?

NaviNow Company agrees to pay $20 million in cash to the four former owners of TrafficEye for all of its assets and liabilities. These four owners of TrafficEye developed and patented a technology for real-time monitoring of traffic patterns on the nation's top 200 frequently congested highways. NaviNow plans to combine the new technology with its existing global positioning systems and projects a resulting substantial revenue increase.

As part of the acquisition contract, NaviNow also agrees to pay additional amounts to the former owners upon achievement of certain financial goals. NaviNow will pay $8 million to the four former owners of TrafficEye if revenues from the combined system exceed $100 million over the next three years. NaviNow estimates this contingent payment to have a probability adjusted present value of $4 million.

The four former owners have also been offered employment contracts with NaviNow to help with system integration and performance enhancement issues. The employment contracts are silent as to service periods, have nominal salaries similar to those of equivalent employees, and specify a profit-sharing component over the next three years (if the employees remain with the company) that NaviNow estimates to have a current fair value of $2 million. The four former owners of TrafficEye say they will stay on as employees of NaviNow for at least three years to help achieve the desired financial goals.

Should NaviNow account for the contingent payments promised to the former owners of TrafficEye as consideration transferred in the acquisition or as compensation expense to employees?

ASC RESEARCH CASE—DEFENSIVE INTANGIBLE ASSET

Ahorita Company manufactures wireless transponders for satellite applications. Ahorita has recently acquired Zelltech Company, which is primarily known for its software communications development but also manufactures a specialty transponder under the trade name "Z-Tech" that competes with one of Ahorita's products. Ahorita will now discontinue Z-Tech and projects that its own product line will see a market share increase. Nonetheless, Ahorita's management will maintain the rights to the Z-Tech trade name as a defensive intangible asset to prevent its use by competitors, despite the fact that its highest and best use would be to sell the trade name. Ahorita estimates that the trade name has an internal value of $1.5 million, but if sold would yield $2 million.

Answer the following with supporting citations from the FASB ASC:

a. How does the FASB ASC Glossary define a defensive intangible asset?

b. According to ASC Topic 805 Business Combinations, what is the measurement principle that an acquirer should follow in recording identifiable assets acquired in a business combination?

c. According to ASC Topic 820 Fair Value Measurement, what value premise (in-use or in-exchange) should Ahorita assign to the Z-Tech trade name in its consolidated financial statements?

d. According to ASC Topic 350 General Intangibles Other than Goodwill, how should Ahorita determine the estimated useful life of its defensive intangible asset?

RESEARCH CASE—ABBOTT'S ACQUISITION OF SOLVAY PHARMACEUTICALS

In February 2010, Abbott Laboratories acquired Solvay Pharmaceuticals in exchange for $6.1 billion in cash plus contingent consideration. Referring to Abbott's 2010 financial statements, answer the following questions related to Abbott's acquisition of Solvay Pharmaceuticals:

1. Why did Abbott acquire Solvay Pharmaceuticals?
2. What policies did Abbot follow in accounting for the acquisition?
3. What allocations did Abbott make to the assets acquired and liabilities assumed in the acquisition? Provide a calculation showing how Abbott determined the amount allocated to goodwill.
4. How did Abbott account for the contingent consideration portion of the deal?
5. How did Abbott account for the in-process research and development acquired in the combination?
6. How did Abbott account for its acquisition-related expenses?

FASB ASC RESEARCH CASE—THE DOW CHEMICAL COMPANY'S ACQUIRED CONTINGENCIES

On April 1, 2009, The Dow Chemical Company completed its acquisition of Rohm and Haas Company. Dow Chemical paid $15,681 million cash consideration to Rohm and Haas stockholders in exchange for their ownership shares. Rohm and Haas continued as a wholly owned subsidiary of Dow Chemical.

Refer to Dow Chemical's 2009 second-quarter report, as well as related GAAP, to answer the following questions:

1. Did Dow Chemical recognize any acquired contingencies for its acquisition of Rohm and Haas? If it did, how were they measured? If not, why not?
2. Under what circumstances should a firm recognize an asset acquired or a liability assumed in a business combination that arises from a contingency?
3. How should Dow Chemical account for its acquired contingencies in periods after the acquisition date?
4. What is the disclosure requirement for Dow Chemical's acquired contingencies?
5. What are some potential concerns with authoritative accounting literature for acquired contingencies?

CPA REVIEW

Please visit the text website for the online Kaplan CPA simulation:

Consolidation

Situation: For each parent-subsidiary relationship, determine the proper accounting treatment.

Topics to be covered:

- Consolidation requirements
- Consolidation exceptions

chapter 3

Consolidations—Subsequent to the Date of Acquisition

In 1996, Berkshire Hathaway, Inc., acquired all of the outstanding stock of Geico, Inc., an insurance company. Although this transaction involved well-known companies, it was not unique; mergers and acquisitions have long been common in the business world.

Berkshire Hathaway's current financial statements indicate that Geico is still a component of this economic entity. However, Geico, Inc., continues as a separate legally incorporated concern long after its purchase. As discussed in Chapter 2, a parent will often maintain separate legal status for a subsidiary corporation to better utilize its inherent value as a going concern.

For external reporting purposes, maintenance of incorporation creates an ongoing challenge for the accountant. In each subsequent period, consolidation must be simulated anew through the use of a worksheet and consolidation entries. Thus, for more than a decade, the financial data for Berkshire Hathaway and Geico (along with dozens of other subsidiaries) have been brought together periodically to provide figures for the financial statements that represent this business combination.

As also discussed in Chapter 2, the acquisition method governs the way we initially record a business combination. In periods subsequent to acquisition, the fair-value bases (established at the acquisition date) for subsidiary assets acquired and liabilities assumed will be amortized (or tested for possible impairment) for proper income recognition. Additionally, some combinations require accounting for the eventual disposition of contingent consideration, which, as presented later in this chapter, continues to follow a fair-value model.

In the next several sections of this chapter, we present the procedures to prepare consolidated financial statements in the years subsequent to acquisition. We start by analyzing the relation between the parent's internal accounting method for its subsidiary investment and the adjustments required in consolidation. We also examine the specific procedures for amortizing the acquisition-date fair-value adjustments to the subsidiary's assets and liabilities. We then cover testing for goodwill impairment, accounting for contingent consideration, and push-down accounting.

Consolidation—The Effects Created by the Passage of Time

In Chapter 2, consolidation accounting is analyzed at the date that a combination is created. The present chapter carries this process one step further by examining the consolidation procedures that must be

Learning Objectives

After studying this chapter, you should be able to:

LO1 Recognize the complexities in preparing consolidated financial reports that emerge from the passage of time.

LO2 Identify and describe the various methods available to a parent company in order to maintain its investment in subsidiary account in its internal records.

LO3 Understand that a parent's internal accounting method for its subsidiary investments has no effect on the resulting consolidated financial statements.

LO4 Prepare consolidated financial statements subsequent to acquisition when the parent has applied in its internal records:

a. The equity method.
b. The initial value method.
c. The partial equity method.

LO5 Discuss the rationale for the goodwill impairment testing approach.

LO6 Describe the procedures for conducting a goodwill impairment test.

LO7 Understand the accounting and reporting for contingent consideration subsequent to a business acquisition.

LO8 Understand in general the requirements of push-down accounting and when its use is appropriate.

LO1

Recognize the complexities in preparing consolidated financial reports that emerge from the passage of time.

followed in subsequent periods whenever separate incorporation of the subsidiary is maintained.

Despite complexities created by the passage of time, the basic objective of all consolidations remains the same: to combine asset, liability, revenue, expense, and equity accounts of a parent and its subsidiaries. From a mechanical perspective, a worksheet and consolidation entries continue to provide structure for the production of a single set of financial statements for the combined business entity.

For example, subsequent to an acquisition, the parent company must report consolidated net income. Consolidated income determination involves first combining the separately recorded revenues and expenses of the parent with those of the subsidiary on a consolidated worksheet. Because of separate record-keeping systems, however, the subsidiary's expenses typically are based on their original book values and not the acquisition-date values the parent must recognize. Consequently, adjustments are made that reflect the amortization of the excess of the parent's consideration transferred over the subsidiary book value. Additionally, the effects of any intra-entity transactions are removed.

The time factor introduces other complications into the consolidation process as well. For internal record-keeping purposes, the parent must select and apply an accounting method to monitor the relationship between the two companies. The investment balance recorded by the parent varies over time as a result of the method chosen, as does the income subsequently recognized. These differences affect the periodic consolidation process but not the figures to be reported by the combined entity. Regardless of the amount, the parent's investment account is eliminated on the worksheet so that the subsidiary's actual assets and liabilities can be consolidated. Likewise, the income figure accrued by the parent is removed each period so that the subsidiary's revenues and expenses can be included when creating an income statement for the combined business entity.

Investment Accounting by the Acquiring Company

LO2

Identify and describe the various methods available to a parent company in order to maintain its investment in subsidiary account in its internal records.

For a parent company's external financial reporting, consolidation of a subsidiary becomes necessary whenever control exists. For internal record-keeping, though, the parent has a choice for monitoring the activities of its subsidiaries. Although several variations occur in practice, three methods have emerged as the most prominent: the equity method, the initial value method,[1] and the partial equity method.

At the acquisition date, each investment accounting method (equity, initial value, and partial equity) begins with an identical value recorded in an investment account. Typically the fair value of the consideration transferred by the parent will serve as the recorded valuation basis on the parent's books.[2]

LO3

Understand that a parent's internal accounting method for its subsidiary investments has no effect on the resulting consolidated financial statements.

Subsequent to the acquisition date, the three methods produce different account balances for the parent's investment in subsidiary, income recognized from the subsidiary's activities, and retained earnings accounts. *Importantly, the selection of a particular method does not affect the totals ultimately reported for the combined companies.* However, the parent's choice of an internal accounting method does lead to distinct procedures for consolidating the financial information from the separate organizations.

Internal Investment Accounting Alternatives—The Equity Method, Initial Value Method, and Partial Equity Method

The internal reporting philosophy of the acquiring company often determines the accounting method choice for its subsidiary investment. Depending on the measures a company uses to assess the ongoing performances of its subsidiaries, parent companies may choose their own preferred internal reporting method. Regardless of this choice, however, consolidated financial statements are required for external reporting.

[1] The initial value method is sometimes referred to as the cost method.

[2] In the unusual case of a bargain purchase, the valuation basis for the investment account is the fair value of the net amount of the assets acquired and liabilities assumed.

The Equity Method

The equity method embraces full accrual accounting in maintaining the investment account and related income over time. Under the equity method, the acquiring company accrues income when the subsidiary earns it. To match the additional fair value recorded in the combination against income, amortization expense stemming from the original excess fair-value allocations is recognized through periodic adjusting entries. Unrealized gains on intra-entity transactions are deferred; subsidiary dividends serve to reduce the investment balance. As discussed in Chapter 1, the equity method creates a parallel between the parent's investment accounts and changes in the underlying equity of the acquired company.[3]

When the parent has complete ownership, equity method earnings from the subsidiary, combined with the parent's other income sources, create a total income figure reflective of the entire combined business entity. Consequently, the equity method often is referred to as a single-line consolidation. The equity method is especially popular in companies where management periodically (e.g., monthly or quarterly) measures each subsidiary's profitability using accrual-based income figures.

The Initial Value Method

Subsequent to acquisition, the initial value method (also known as the *cost method*) uses the cash basis for income recognition. Dividends received by the parent from the subsidiary are recognized as income. No recognition is given to the income earned by the subsidiary. The investment balance remains permanently on the parent's financial records at the initial fair value assigned at the acquisition date.

The initial value method might be selected because the parent does not require an accrual-based income measure of subsidiary performance. For example, the parent may wish to assess subsidiary performance on its ability to generate cash flows, on revenues generated, or some other nonincome basis. Also, some firms may find the initial value method's ease of application attractive. Because the investment account is eliminated in consolidation, and the actual subsidiary revenues and expenses are eventually combined, firms may avoid the complexity of the equity method unless they need the specific information provided by the equity income measure for internal decision making.

The Partial Equity Method

A third method available to the acquiring company is a partial application of the equity method. Under this approach, the parent recognizes the reported income accruing from the subsidiary. Dividends received reduce the investment balance. However, no other equity adjustments (amortization or deferral of unrealized gains) are recorded. Thus, in many cases, earnings figures on the parent's books approximate consolidated totals but without the effort associated with a full application of the equity method.

Exhibit 3.1 provides a summary of these three internal accounting techniques. The method adopted affects only the acquiring company's separate financial records. No changes are created in either the subsidiary's accounts or the consolidated totals.

Because specific worksheet procedures differ based on the investment method utilized by the parent, the consolidation process subsequent to the date of combination will be introduced twice. First, we review consolidations in which the acquiring company uses the equity method. Then we redevelop all procedures when the investment is recorded by one of the alternative methods.

Each acquiring company must decide for itself the appropriate approach in recording the operations of its subsidiaries. For example, Alliant Food Service, Inc., applies the equity method. According to Joe Tomczak, vice president and controller of Alliant Food

[3] In Chapter 1, the equity method was introduced in connection with the external reporting of investments in which the owner held the ability to apply significant influence over the investee (usually by possessing 20 to 50 percent of the company's voting stock). Here, the equity method is utilized for the *internal* reporting of the parent for investments in which control is maintained. Although the accounting procedures are similar, the reason for using the equity method is different.

EXHIBIT 3.1 Internal Reporting of Investment Accounts by Acquiring Company

Method	Investment Account	Income Account	Advantages
Equity	Continually adjusted to reflect ownership of acquired company.	Income accrued as earned; amortization and other adjustments are recognized.	Acquiring company totals give a true representation of consolidation figures.
Initial value	Remains at acquisition-date value assigned.	Dividends received recorded as Dividend Income.	It is easy to apply; it measures cash flows.
Partial equity	Adjusted only for accrued income and dividends received from acquired company.	Income accrued as earned; no other adjustments recognized.	It usually gives balances approximating consolidation figures, but it is easier to apply than equity method.

Service, Inc., "We maintain the parent holding company books on an equity basis. This approach provides the best method of providing information for our operational decisions."[4]

In contrast, Reynolds Metals Corporation has chosen to utilize the partial equity method approach. Allen Earehart, director of corporate accounting for Reynolds, states, "We do adjust the carrying value of our investments annually to reflect the earnings of each subsidiary. We want to be able to evaluate the parent company on a stand-alone basis and a regular equity accrual is, therefore, necessary. However, we do separate certain adjustments such as the elimination of intra-entity gains and losses and record them solely within the development of consolidated financial statements."[5]

Subsequent Consolidation—Investment Recorded by the Equity Method

Acquisition Made during the Current Year

LO4a

Prepare consolidated financial statements subsequent to acquisition when the parent has applied **the equity method** in its internal records.

As a basis for this illustration, assume that Parrot Company obtains all of the outstanding common stock of Sun Company on January 1, 2012. Parrot acquires this stock for $800,000 in cash.

The book values as well as the appraised fair values of Sun's accounts follow:

	Book Values 1/1/12	Fair Values 1/1/12	Difference
Current assets	$ 320,000	$ 320,000	–0–
Trademarks (indefinite life)	200,000	220,000	+ 20,000
Patented technology (10-year life)	320,000	450,000	+130,000
Equipment (5-year life)	180,000	150,000	(30,000)
Liabilities	(420,000)	(420,000)	–0–
Net book value	$ 600,000	$ 720,000	$120,000
Common stock—$40 par value	$(200,000)		
Additional paid-in capital	(20,000)		
Retained earnings, 1/1/12	(380,000)		

Parrot considers the economic life of Sun's trademarks as extending beyond the foreseeable future and thus having an indefinite life. Such assets are not amortized but are subject to periodic impairment testing.[6] For the definite lived assets acquired in the combination (patented technology and equipment), we assume that straight-line amortization with no salvage value is appropriate.[7]

[4] Telephone conversation with Joe Tomczak.

[5] Telephone conversation with Allen Earehart.

[6] In other cases, trademarks can have a definite life and thus would be subject to regular amortization.

[7] Unless otherwise stated, all amortization expense computations in this textbook are based on the straight-line method with no salvage value.

EXHIBIT 3.2
Excess Fair Value Allocation

PARROT COMPANY 100 Percent Acquisition of Sun Company Allocation of Acquisition-Date Subsidiary Fair Value January 1, 2012		
Sun Company fair value (consideration transferred by Parrot Company) . .		$ 800,000
Book value of Sun Company:		
Common stock	$200,000	
Additional paid-in capital	20,000	
Retained earnings, 1/1/12	380,000	(600,000)
Excess of fair value over book value		200,000
Allocation to specific accounts based on fair values:		
Trademarks	$ 20,000	
Patented technology	130,000	
Equipment (overvalued)	(30,000)	120,000
Excess fair value not identified with specific accounts—goodwill		$ 80,000

Parrot paid $800,000 cash to acquire Sun Company, clear evidence of the fair value of the consideration transferred. As shown in Exhibit 3.2, individual allocations are used to adjust Sun's accounts from their book values to their acquisition-date fair values. Because the total value of these assets and liabilities was only $720,000, goodwill of $80,000 must be recognized for consolidation purposes.

Each of these allocated amounts (other than the $20,000 attributed to trademarks and the $80,000 for goodwill) represents a valuation associated with a definite life. As discussed in Chapter 1, Parrot must amortize each allocation over its expected life. The expense recognition necessitated by this fair-value allocation is calculated in Exhibit 3.3.

One aspect of this amortization schedule warrants further explanation. The fair value of Sun's Equipment account was $30,000 *less* than book value. Therefore, instead of attributing an additional amount to this asset, the $30,000 allocation actually reflects a fair-value reduction. As such, the amortization shown in Exhibit 3.3 relating to Equipment is not an additional expense but an expense reduction.

Having determined the allocation of the acquisition-date fair value in the previous example as well as the associated amortization, the parent's separate record-keeping for its first year of Sun Company ownership can be constructed. Assume that Sun earns income of $100,000 during the year and declares and pays a $40,000 cash dividend on August 1.

In this first illustration, Parrot has adopted the equity method. Apparently, this company believes that the information derived from using the equity method is useful in its evaluation of Sun.

EXHIBIT 3.3
Annual Excess Amortization

PARROT COMPANY
100 Percent Acquisition of Sun Company
Excess Amortization Schedule—Allocation of Acquisition-Date Fair Values

Account	Allocation	Useful Life	Annual Excess Amortizations
Trademarks	$ 20,000	Indefinite	–0–
Patented technology	130,000	10 years	$13,000
Equipment	(30,000)	5 years	(6,000)
Goodwill	80,000	Indefinite	–0–
			$ 7,000*

*Total excess amortizations will be $7,000 annually for five years until the equipment allocation is fully removed. At the end of each asset's life, future amortizations will change.

Application of the Equity Method

	Parrot's Financial Records		
1/1/12	Investment in Sun Company	800,000	
	Cash		800,000
	To record the acquisition of Sun Company.		
8/1/12	Cash	40,000	
	Investment in Sun Company		40,000
	To record declaration and receipt of cash dividend from subsidiary under the equity method.		
12/31/12	Investment in Sun Company	100,000	
	Equity in Subsidiary Earnings		100,000
	To accrue income earned by 100 percent owned subsidiary.		
12/31/12	Equity in Subsidiary Earnings	7,000	
	Investment in Sun Company		7,000
	To recognize amortizations on allocations made in acquisition of subsidiary (see Exhibit 3.3).		

Parrot's application of the equity method, as shown in this series of entries, causes the Investment in Sun Company account balance to rise from $800,000 to $853,000 ($800,000 − $40,000 + $100,000 − $7,000). During the same period the parent recognizes a $93,000 equity income figure (the $100,000 earnings accrual less the $7,000 excess amortization expenses).

The consolidation procedures for Parrot and Sun one year after the date of acquisition are illustrated next. For this purpose, Exhibit 3.4 presents the separate 2012 financial statements for these two companies. Parrot recorded both investment-related accounts (the $853,000 asset balance and the $93,000 income accrual) based on applying the equity method.

Determination of Consolidated Totals

Before becoming immersed in the mechanical aspects of a consolidation, the objective of this process should be understood. As indicated in Chapter 2, in the preparation of consolidated financial reports, the subsidiary's revenue, expense, asset, and liability accounts are added to the parent company balances. Within this procedure, several important guidelines must be followed:

- Sun's assets and liabilities are adjusted to reflect the allocations originating from their acquisition-date fair values.
- Because of the passage of time, the income effects (e.g., amortizations) of these allocations must also be recognized within the consolidation process.
- Any reciprocal or intra-entity[8] accounts must be offset. If, for example, one of the companies owes money to the other, the receivable and the payable balances have no connection with an outside party. Both should be eliminated for external reporting purposes. When the companies are viewed as a single entity, the receivable and the payable are intra-entity balances to be removed.

The consolidation of the two sets of financial information in Exhibit 3.4 is a relatively uncomplicated task and can even be carried out without the use of a worksheet. Understanding the origin of each reported figure is the first step in gaining a knowledge of this process.

- *Revenues* = $1,900,000. The revenues of the parent and the subsidiary are added together.
- *Cost of goods sold* = $950,000. The cost of goods sold of the parent and subsidiary are added together.

[8] The FASB Accounting Standards Codification (ASC) uses the term *intra-entity* to describe transfers of assets across business entities affiliated though common stock ownership or other control mechanisms. The phrase indicates that although such transfers occur across separate legal entities, they are nonetheless made within a commonly controlled entity. Prior to the use of the term *intra-entity,* such amounts were routinely referred to as *intercompany* balances.

EXHIBIT 3.4
Separate Records—Equity Method Applied

PARROT COMPANY AND SUN COMPANY
Financial Statements
For Year Ending December 31, 2012

	Parrot Company	Sun Company
Income Statement		
Revenues	$(1,500,000)	$ (400,000)
Cost of goods sold	700,000	250,000
Amortization expense	120,000	20,000
Depreciation expense	80,000	30,000
Equity in subsidiary earnings	(93,000)	-0-
Net income	$ (693,000)	$ (100,000)
Statement of Retained Earnings		
Retained earnings, 1/1/12	$ (840,000)	$ (380,000)
Net income (above)	(693,000)	(100,000)
Dividends paid*	120,000	40,000
Retained earnings, 12/31/12	$(1,413,000)	$ (440,000)
Balance Sheet		
Current assets	$ 1,040,000	$ 400,000
Investment in Sun Company (at equity)	853,000	-0-
Trademarks	600,000	200,000
Patented technology	370,000	288,000
Equipment (net)	250,000	220,000
Total assets	$ 3,113,000	$ 1,108,000
Liabilities	$ (980,000)	$ (448,000)
Common stock	(600,000)	(200,000)
Additional paid-in capital	(120,000)	(20,000)
Retained earnings, 12/31/12 (above)	(1,413,000)	(440,000)
Total liabilities and equity	$(3,113,000)	$(1,108,000)

Note: Parentheses indicate a credit balance.
*Dividends declared, whether paid or not, provide the appropriate amount to include in a statement of retained earnings. To help keep the number of worksheet rows (i.e., dividends payable and receivable) at a minimum, throughout this text we assume that all dividends are paid in the same period they are declared.

- *Amortization expense* = $153,000. The balances of the parent and of the subsidiary are combined along with the additional amortization from the recognition of the excess fair value over book value attributed to the subsidiary's patented technology.
- *Depreciation expense* = $104,000. The depreciation expenses of the parent and subsidiary are added together along with the $6,000 reduction in equipment depreciation, as indicated in Exhibit 3.3.
- *Equity in subsidiary earnings* = −0−. The investment income recorded by the parent is eliminated so that the subsidiary's revenues and expenses can be included in the consolidated totals.
- *Net income* = $693,000. Consolidated revenues less consolidated expenses.
- *Retained earnings, 1/1/12* = $840,000. The parent figure only because the subsidiary was not owned prior to that date.
- *Dividends paid* = $120,000. The parent company balance only because the subsidiary's dividends were paid intra-entity to the parent, not to an outside party.
- *Retained earnings, 12/31/12* = $1,413,000. Consolidated retained earnings as of the beginning of the year plus consolidated net income less consolidated dividends paid.
- *Current assets* = $1,440,000. The parent's book value plus the subsidiary's book value.

- *Investment in Sun Company* = −0−. The asset recorded by the parent is eliminated so that the subsidiary's assets and liabilities can be included in the consolidated totals.
- *Trademarks* = $820,000. The parent's book value plus the subsidiary's book value plus the $20,000 acquisition-date fair-value allocation.
- *Patented technology* = $775,000. The parent's book value plus the subsidiary's book value plus the $130,000 acquisition-date fair-value allocation less current year amortization of $13,000.
- *Equipment* = $446,000. The parent's book value plus the subsidiary's book value less the $30,000 fair-value reduction allocation plus the current year expense reduction of $6,000.
- *Goodwill* = $80,000. The residual allocation shown in Exhibit 3.2. Note that goodwill is not amortized.
- *Total assets* = $3,561,000. A vertical summation of consolidated assets.
- *Liabilities* = $1,428,000. The parent's book value plus the subsidiary's book value.
- *Common stock* = $600,000. The parent's book value. Subsidiary shares are no longer outstanding.
- *Additional paid-in capital* = $120,000. The parent's book value. Subsidiary shares are no longer outstanding.
- *Retained earnings, 12/31/12* = $1,413,000. Computed previously.
- *Total liabilities and equities* = $3,561,000. A vertical summation of consolidated liabilities and equities.

Consolidation Worksheet

Although the consolidated figures to be reported can be computed as just shown, accountants normally prefer to use a worksheet. A worksheet provides an organized structure for this process, a benefit that becomes especially important in consolidating complex combinations.

For Parrot and Sun, only five consolidation entries are needed to arrive at the same figures previously derived for this business combination. As discussed in Chapter 2, *worksheet entries are the catalyst for developing totals to be reported by the entity but are not physically recorded in the individual account balances of either company.*

Consolidation Entry S

Common Stock (Sun Company)	200,000	
Additional Paid-In Capital (Sun Company)	20,000	
Retained Earnings, 1/1/12 (Sun Company)	380,000	
Investment in Sun Company		600,000

As shown in Exhibit 3.2, Parrot's $800,000 Investment account balance reflects two components: (1) a $600,000 amount equal to Sun's book value and (2) a $200,000 figure attributed to the difference, at January 1, 2012, between the book value and fair value of Sun's assets and liabilities (with a residual allocation made to goodwill). Entry **S** removes the $600,000 component of the Investment in Sun Company account so that the *book value* of each subsidiary asset and liability can be included in the consolidated figures. A second worksheet entry (Entry **A**) eliminates the remaining $200,000 portion of the January 1, 2012, Investment in Sun account, allowing the specific allocations to be included along with any goodwill.

Entry **S** also removes Sun's stockholders' equity accounts as of the beginning of the year. Subsidiary equity balances generated prior to the acquisition are not relevant to the business combination and should be deleted. The elimination is made through this entry because the equity accounts and the $600,000 component of the investment account represent reciprocal balances: Both provide a measure of Sun's book value as of January 1, 2012.

Before moving to the next consolidation entry, a clarification point should be made. In actual practice, worksheet entries are usually identified numerically. However, as in the previous chapter, the label "Entry **S**" used in this example refers to the elimination of Sun's beginning **S**tockholders' Equity. As a reminder of the purpose being served, all worksheet entries are identified in a similar fashion. Thus, throughout this textbook, "Entry **S**" always refers to the removal of the subsidiary's beginning stockholders' equity balances for the year against the book value portion of the investment account.

Consolidation Entry A

	Debit	Credit
Trademarks	20,000	
Patented Technology	130,000	
Goodwill	80,000	
Equipment		30,000
Investment in Sun Company		200,000

Consolidation Entry **A** adjusts the subsidiary balances from their book values to acquisition-date fair values (see Exhibit 3.2). This entry is labeled "Entry **A**" to indicate that it represents the Allocations made in connection with the excess of the subsidiary's fair values over its book values. Sun's accounts are adjusted collectively by the $200,000 excess of Sun's $800,000 acquisition-date fair value over its $600,000 book value.

Consolidation Entry I

	Debit	Credit
Equity in Subsidiary Earnings	93,000	
Investment in Sun Company		93,000

"Entry **I**" (for **I**ncome) removes the subsidiary income recognized by Parrot during the year so that Sun's underlying revenue and expense accounts (and the current amortization expense) can be brought into the consolidated totals. The $93,000 figure eliminated here represents the $100,000 income accrual recognized by Parrot, reduced by the $7,000 in excess amortizations. For consolidation purposes, the one-line amount appearing in the parent's records is not appropriate and is removed so that the individual revenues and expenses can be included. The entry originally recorded by the parent is simply reversed on the worksheet to remove its impact.

Consolidation Entry D

	Debit	Credit
Investment in Sun Company	40,000	
Dividends Paid		40,000

The dividends distributed by the subsidiary during the year also must be eliminated from the consolidated totals. The entire $40,000 payment was made to the parent so that, from the viewpoint of the consolidated entity, it is simply an intra-entity transfer of cash. The distribution did not affect any outside party. Therefore, "Entry **D**" (for **D**ividends) is designed to offset the impact of this transaction by removing the subsidiary's Dividends Paid account. Because the equity method has been applied, Parrot's receipt of this money was recorded originally as a decrease in the Investment in Sun Company account. To eliminate the impact of this reduction, the investment account is increased.

Consolidation Entry E

	Debit	Credit
Amortization Expense	13,000	
Equipment	6,000	
Patented Technology		13,000
Depreciation Expense		6,000

This final worksheet entry records the current year's excess amortization expenses relating to the adjustments of Sun's assets to acquisition-date fair values. Because the equity method amortization was eliminated within Entry **I,** "Entry **E**" (for **E**xpense) now records the current year expense attributed to each of the specific account allocations (see Exhibit 3.3). Note that we adjust depreciation expense for the tangible asset *equipment* and we adjust amortization expense for the intangible asset *patented technology*. As a matter of custom, we refer to the adjustments to all expenses resulting from excess acquisition-date fair-value allocations collectively as *excess amortization expenses*.

Thus, the worksheet entries necessary for consolidation when the parent has applied the equity method are as follows:

Entry S—Eliminates the subsidiary's stockholders' equity accounts as of the beginning of the current year along with the equivalent book value component within the parent's investment account.

Entry A—Recognizes the unamortized allocations as of the beginning of the current year associated with the original adjustments to fair value.

Entry I—Eliminates the impact of intra-entity subsidiary income accrued by the parent.

Entry D—Eliminates the impact of intra-entity subsidiary dividends.

Entry E—Recognizes excess amortization expenses for the current period on the allocations from the original adjustments to fair value.

Exhibit 3.5 provides a complete presentation of the December 31, 2012, consolidation worksheet for Parrot Company and Sun Company. The series of entries just

EXHIBIT 3.5 Consolidation Worksheet—Equity Method Applied

PARROT COMPANY AND SUN COMPANY
Consolidated Worksheet
For Year Ending December 31, 2012

Investment: Equity Method

Accounts	Parrot Company	Sun Company	Consolidation Entries Debit	Consolidation Entries Credit	Consolidated Totals
Income Statement					
Revenues	(1,500,000)	(400,000)			(1,900,000)
Cost of goods sold	700,000	250,000			950,000
Amortization expense	120,000	20,000	(E) 13,000		153,000
Depreciation expense	80,000	30,000		(E) 6,000	104,000
Equity in subsidiary earnings	(93,000)	-0-	(I) 93,000		-0-
Net income	(693,000)	(100,000)			(693,000)
Statement of Retained Earnings					
Retained earnings, 1/1/12	(840,000)	(380,000)	(S) 380,000		(840,000)
Net income (above)	(693,000)	(100,000)			(693,000)
Dividends paid	120,000	40,000		(D) 40,000	120,000
Retained earnings, 12/31/12	(1,413,000)	(440,000)			(1,413,000)
Balance Sheet					
Current assets	1,040,000	400,000			1,440,000
Investment in Sun Company	853,000	-0-	(D) 40,000	(S) 600,000 (A) 200,000 (I) 93,000	-0-
Trademarks	600,000	200,000	(A) 20,000		820,000
Patented technology	370,000	288,000	(A) 130,000	(E) 13,000	775,000
Equipment (net)	250,000	220,000	(E) 6,000	(A) 30,000	446,000
Goodwill	-0-	-0-	(A) 80,000		80,000
Total assets	3,113,000	1,108,000			3,561,000
Liabilities	(980,000)	(448,000)			(1,428,000)
Common stock	(600,000)	(200,000)	(S) 200,000		(600,000)
Additional paid-in capital	(120,000)	(20,000)	(S) 20,000		(120,000)
Retained earnings, 12/31/12 (above)	(1,413,000)	(440,000)			(1,413,000)
Total liabilities and equities	(3,113,000)	(1,108,000)	982,000	982,000	(3,561,000)

Note: Parentheses indicate a credit balance.

Consolidation entries:

(S) Elimination of Sun's stockholders' equity January 1 balances and the book value portion of the investment account.
(A) Allocation of Sun's acquisition-date excess fair values over book values.
(I) Elimination of parent's equity in subsidiary earnings accrual.
(D) Elimination of intra-entity dividend payment.
(E) Recognition of current year excess fair-value amortization and depreciation expenses.

described brings together the separate financial statements of these two organizations. Note that the consolidated totals are the same as those computed previously for this combination.

Observe that Parrot separately reports net income of $693,000 as well as ending retained earnings of $1,413,000, figures that are identical to the totals generated for the consolidated entity. However, subsidiary income earned after the date of acquisition is to be *added* to that of the parent. Thus, a question arises in this example as to why the parent company figures alone equal the consolidated balances of both operations.

In reality, Sun's income for this period is contained in both Parrot's reported balances and the consolidated totals. Through the application of the equity method, the current year earnings of the subsidiary have already been accrued by Parrot along with the appropriate amortization expense. *The parent's Equity in Subsidiary Earnings account is, therefore, an accurate representation of Sun's effect on consolidated net income.* If the equity method is employed properly, the worksheet process simply replaces this single $93,000 balance with the specific revenue and expense accounts that it represents. *Consequently, when the parent employs the equity method, its net income and retained earnings mirror consolidated totals.*

Consolidation Subsequent to Year of Acquisition—Equity Method

In many ways, every consolidation of Parrot and Sun prepared after the date of acquisition incorporates the same basic procedures outlined in the previous section. However, the continual financial evolution undergone by the companies prohibits an exact repetition of the consolidation entries demonstrated in Exhibit 3.5.

As a basis for analyzing the procedural changes necessitated by the passage of time, assume that Parrot Company continues to hold its ownership of Sun Company as of December 31, 2015. This date was selected at random; any date subsequent to 2012 would serve equally well to illustrate this process. As an additional factor, assume that Sun now has a $40,000 liability that is payable to Parrot.

For this consolidation, assume that the January 1, 2015, Sun Company's Retained Earnings balance has risen to $600,000. Because that account had a reported total of only $380,000 on January 1, 2012, Sun's book value apparently has increased by $220,000 during the 2012–2014 period. Although knowledge of individual operating figures in the past is not required, Sun's reported totals help to clarify the consolidation procedures.

Year	Sun Company Net Income	Dividends Paid	Increase in Book Value	Ending Retained Earnings
2012	$100,000	$ 40,000	$ 60,000	$440,000
2013	140,000	50,000	90,000	530,000
2014	90,000	20,000	70,000	600,000
	$330,000	$110,000	$220,000	

For 2015, the current year, we assume that Sun reports net income of $160,000 and pays cash dividends of $70,000. Because it applies the equity method, Parrot recognizes earnings of $160,000. Furthermore, as shown in Exhibit 3.3, amortization expense of $7,000 applies to 2015 and must also be recorded by the parent. Consequently, Parrot reports an Equity in Subsidiary Earnings balance for the year of $153,000 ($160,000 − $7,000).

Although this income figure can be reconstructed with little difficulty, the current balance in the Investment in Sun Company account is more complicated. Over the years, the initial $800,000 acquisition price has been subjected to adjustments for

1. The annual accrual of Sun's income.
2. The receipt of dividends from Sun.
3. The recognition of annual excess amortization expenses.

Exhibit 3.6 analyzes these changes and shows the components of the Investment in Sun Company account balance as of December 31, 2015.

EXHIBIT 3.6
Investment Account under Equity Method

PARROT COMPANY
Investment in Sun Company Account
As of December 31, 2015
Equity Method Applied

Fair value of consideration transferred at date of acquisition		$ 800,000
Entries recorded in prior years:		
Accrual of Sun Company's income		
2012	$100,000	
2013	140,000	
2014	90,000	330,000
Sun Company—Dividends paid		
2012	$ (40,000)	
2013	(50,000)	
2014	(20,000)	(110,000)
Excess amortization expenses		
2012	$ (7,000)	
2013	(7,000)	
2014	(7,000)	(21,000)
Entries recorded in current year—2015		
Accrual of Sun Company's income	$160,000	
Sun Company—Dividends paid	(70,000)	
Excess amortization expenses	(7,000)	83,000
Investment in Sun Company, 12/31/15		$1,082,000

Following the construction of the Investment in Sun Company account, the consolidation worksheet developed in Exhibit 3.7 should be easier to understand. Current figures for both companies appear in the first two columns. The parent's investment balance and equity income accrual as well as Sun's income and stockholders' equity accounts correspond to the information given previously. Worksheet entries (lettered to agree with the previous illustration) are then utilized to consolidate all balances.

Several steps are necessary to arrive at these reported totals. The subsidiary's assets, liabilities, revenues, and expenses are added to those same accounts of the parent. The unamortized portion of the original acquisition-date fair-value allocations are included along with current excess amortization expenses. The investment and equity income balances are both eliminated as are the subsidiary's stockholders' equity accounts. Intra-entity dividends are removed with the same treatment required for the debt existing between the two companies.

Consolidation Entry S

Once again, this first consolidation entry offsets reciprocal amounts representing the subsidiary's book value as of the beginning of the current year. Sun's January 1, 2015, stockholders' equity accounts are eliminated against the book value portion of the parent's investment account. Here, though, the amount eliminated is $820,000 rather than the $600,000 shown in Exhibit 3.5 for 2012. Both balances have changed during the 2012–2014 period. Sun's operations caused a $220,000 increase in retained earnings. Parrot's application of the equity method created a parallel effect on its Investment in Sun Company account (the income accrual of $330,000 less dividends collected of $110,000).

Although Sun's Retained Earnings balance is removed in this entry, the income this company earned since the acquisition date is still included in the consolidated figures. Parrot accrues these profits annually through application of the equity method. Thus, elimination of the subsidiary's entire Retained Earnings is necessary; a portion was earned prior to the acquisition and the remainder has already been recorded by the parent.

Entry **S** removes these balances as of the first day of 2015 rather than at the end of the year. The consolidation process is made a bit simpler by segregating the effect of preceding

EXHIBIT 3.7 **Consolidation Worksheet Subsequent to Year of Acquisition—Equity Method Applied**

PARROT COMPANY AND SUN COMPANY
Consolidated Worksheet
For Year Ending December 31, 2015

Investment: Equity Method

Accounts	Parrot Company	Sun Company	Consolidation Entries Debit	Consolidation Entries Credit	Consolidated Totals
Income Statement					
Revenues	(2,100,000)	(600,000)			(2,700,000)
Cost of goods sold	1,000,000	380,000			1,380,000
Amortization expense	200,000	20,000	(E) 13,000		233,000
Depreciation expense	100,000	40,000		(E) 6,000	134,000
Equity in subsidiary earnings	(153,000)	–0–	(I) 153,000		–0–
Net income	(953,000)	(160,000)			(953,000)
Statement of Retained Earnings					
Retained earnings, 1/1/15	(2,044,000)	(600,000)	(S) 600,000		(2,044,000)
Net income (above)	(953,000)	(160,000)			(953,000)
Dividends paid	420,000	70,000		(D) 70,000	420,000
Retained earnings, 12/31/15	(2,577,000)	(690,000)			(2,577,000)
Balance Sheet					
Current assets	1,705,000	500,000		(P) 40,000	2,165,000
Investment in Sun Company	1,082,000	–0–	(D) 70,000	(S) 820,000 (A) 179,000 (I) 153,000	–0–
Trademarks	600,000	240,000	(A) 20,000		860,000
Patented technology	540,000	420,000	(A) 91,000	(E) 13,000	1,038,000
Equipment (net)	420,000	210,000	(E) 6,000	(A) 12,000	624,000
Goodwill	–0–	–0–	(A) 80,000		80,000
Total assets	4,347,000	1,370,000			4,767,000
Liabilities	(1,050,000)	(460,000)	(P) 40,000		(1,470,000)
Common stock	(600,000)	(200,000)	(S) 200,000		(600,000)
Additional paid-in capital	(120,000)	(20,000)	(S) 20,000		(120,000)
Retained earnings, 12/31/15 (above)	(2,577,000)	(690,000)			(2,577,000)
Total liabilities and equities	(4,347,000)	(1,370,000)	1,293,000	1,293,000	(4,767,000)

Note: Parentheses indicate a credit balance.
Consolidation entries:
(S) Elimination of Sun's stockholders' equity January 1 balances and the book value portion of the investment account.
(A) Allocation of Sun's acquisition-date excess fair values over book values, unamortized balance as of beginning of year.
(I) Elimination of parent's equity in subsidiary earnings accrual.
(D) Elimination of intra-entity dividend payment.
(E) Recognition of current year excess fair-value amortization and depreciation expenses.
(P) Elimination of intra-entity receivable/payable.

operations from the transactions of the current year. Thus, *all worksheet entries relate specifically to either the previous years (**S** and **A**) or the current period (**I, D, E,** and **P**).*

Consolidation Entry A In the initial consolidation (2012), fair-value allocations amounting to $200,000 were entered, but these balances have now undergone three years of amortization. As computed in Exhibit 3.8, expenses for these prior years totaled $21,000, leaving a balance of $179,000. Allocation of this amount to the individual accounts is also determined in Exhibit 3.8 and reflected in worksheet Entry **A.** As with Entry **S,** these balances are calculated as of January 1, 2015, so that the current year expenses can be included separately (in Entry **E**).

Consolidation Entry I As before, this entry eliminates the equity income recorded currently by Parrot ($153,000) in connection with its ownership of Sun. The subsidiary's revenue and expense accounts are left intact so they can be included in the consolidated figures.

EXHIBIT 3.8
Excess Amortizations Relating to Individual Accounts as of January 1, 2015

Accounts	Original Allocation	Annual Excess Amortizations 2012	2013	2014	Balance 1/1/15
Trademarks	$ 20,000	–0–	–0–	–0–	$ 20,000
Patented technology	130,000	$13,000	$13,000	$13,000	91,000
Equipment	(30,000)	(6,000)	(6,000)	(6,000)	(12,000)
Goodwill	80,000	–0–	–0–	–0–	80,000
	$200,000	$ 7,000	$ 7,000	$ 7,000	$179,000
			$21,000		

Consolidation Entry D This worksheet entry offsets the $70,000 intra-entity dividend payment made by Sun to Parrot during the current period.

Consolidation Entry E Excess amortization expenses relating to acquisition-date fair-value adjustments are individually recorded for the current period.

Before progressing to the final worksheet entry, note the close similarity of these entries with the five incorporated in the 2012 consolidation (Exhibit 3.5). Except for the numerical changes created by the passage of time, the entries are identical.

Consolidation Entry P This last entry (labeled "Entry **P**" because it eliminates an intra-entity **P**ayable) introduces a new element to the consolidation process. As noted earlier, intra-entity reciprocal accounts do not relate to outside parties. Therefore, Sun's $40,000 payable and Parrot's $40,000 receivable must be removed on the worksheet because the companies are being reported as a single entity.

In reviewing Exhibit 3.7, note several aspects of the consolidation process:

- The stockholders' equity accounts of the subsidiary are removed.
- The Investment in Sun Company and the Equity in Subsidiary Earnings are both removed.
- The parent's Retained Earnings balance is not adjusted. Because the parent applies the equity method this account should be correct.
- The acquisition-date fair-value adjustments to the subsidiary's assets are recognized but only after adjustment for prior periods' annual excess amortization expenses.
- Intra-entity balances such as dividends and receivables/payables are offset.

Subsequent Consolidations—Investment Recorded Using Initial Value or Partial Equity Method

Acquisition Made during the Current Year

LO4b

Prepare consolidated financial statements subsequent to acquisition when the parent has applied **the initial value method** in its internal records.

LO4c

Prepare consolidated financial statements subsequent to acquisition when the parent has applied **the partial equity method** in its internal records.

As discussed at the beginning of this chapter, the parent company may opt to use the initial value method or the partial equity method for internal record-keeping rather than the equity method. Application of either alternative changes the balances recorded by the parent over time and, thus, the procedures followed in creating consolidations. However, *choosing one of these other approaches does not affect any of the final consolidated figures to be reported.*

When a company utilizes the equity method, it eliminates all reciprocal accounts, assigns unamortized fair-value allocations to specific accounts, and records amortization expense for the current year. Application of either the initial value method or the partial equity method has no effect on this basic process. For this reason, a number of the consolidation entries remain the same regardless of the parent's investment accounting method.

In reality, just three of the parent's accounts actually vary because of the method applied:

- The investment account.
- The income recognized from the subsidiary.
- The parent's retained earnings (in periods after the initial year of the combination).

EXHIBIT 3.9 Consolidation Worksheet—Initial Value Method Applied

PARROT COMPANY AND SUN COMPANY
Consolidated Worksheet
For Year Ending December 31, 2012

Investment: Initial Value Method

Accounts	Parrot Company	Sun Company	Consolidation Entries Debit	Consolidation Entries Credit	Consolidated Totals
Income Statement					
Revenues	(1,500,000)	(400,000)			(1,900,000)
Cost of goods sold	700,000	250,000			950,000
Amortization expense	120,000	20,000	(E) 13,000		153,000
Depreciation expense	80,000	30,000		(E) 6,000	104,000
Dividend income	(40,000) *	–0–	(I) 40,000 *		–0–
Net income	(640,000)	(100,000)			(693,000)
Statement of Retained Earnings					
Retained earnings, 1/1/12	(840,000)	(380,000)	(S) 380,000		(840,000)
Net income (above)	(640,000)	(100,000)			(693,000)
Dividends paid	120,000	40,000		(I) 40,000 *	120,000
Retained earnings, 12/31/12	(1,360,000)	(440,000)			(1,413,000)
Balance Sheet					
Current assets	1,040,000	400,000			1,440,000
Investment in Sun Company	800,000 *	–0–		(S) 600,000 (A) 200,000	–0–
Trademarks	600,000	200,000	(A) 20,000		820,000
Patented technology	370,000	288,000	(A) 130,000	(E) 13,000	775,000
Equipment (net)	250,000	220,000	(E) 6,000	(A) 30,000	446,000
Goodwill	–0–	–0–	(A) 80,000		80,000
Total assets	3,060,000	1,108,000			3,561,000
Liabilities	(980,000)	(448,000)			(1,428,000)
Common stock	(600,000)	(200,000)	(S) 200,000		(600,000)
Additional paid-in capital	(120,000)	(20,000)	(S) 20,000		(120,000)
Retained earnings, 12/31/12 (above)	(1,360,000)	(440,000)			(1,413,000)
Total liabilities and equities	(3,060,000)	(1,108,000)	889,000	889,000	(3,561,000)

Note: Parentheses indicate a credit balance.
*Boxed items highlight differences with consolidation in Exhibit 3.5.
Consolidation entries:
(S) Elimination of Sun's stockholders' equity January 1 balances and the book value portion of the investment account.
(A) Allocation of Sun's acquisition-date excess fair values over book values.
(I) Elimination of intra-entity dividend income and dividend paid by Sun.
(E) Recognition of current year excess fair-value amortization and depreciation expenses.
Note: Consolidation entry (D) is not needed when the parent applies the initial value method because entry (I) eliminates the intra-entity dividend effects.

Only the differences found in these balances affect the consolidation process when another method is applied. Thus, any time after the acquisition date, accounting for these three balances is of special importance.

To illustrate the modifications required by the adoption of an alternative accounting method, the consolidation of Parrot and Sun as of December 31, 2012, is reconstructed. Only one differing factor is introduced: the method by which Parrot accounts for its investment. Exhibit 3.9 presents the 2012 consolidation based on Parrot's use of the initial value method. Exhibit 3.10 demonstrates this same process assuming that the parent applied the partial equity method. Each entry on these worksheets is labeled to correspond with the 2012 consolidation in which the parent used the equity method (Exhibit 3.5). Furthermore, differences with the equity method (both on the parent company records and with the consolidation entries) are highlighted on each of the worksheets.

EXHIBIT 3.10 Consolidation Worksheet—Partial Equity Method Applied

PARROT COMPANY AND SUN COMPANY
Consolidated Worksheet
For Year Ending December 31, 2012

Investment: Partial Equity Method

Accounts	Parrot Company	Sun Company	Consolidation Entries Debit	Consolidation Entries Credit	Consolidated Totals
Income Statement					
Revenues	(1,500,000)	(400,000)			(1,900,000)
Cost of goods sold	700,000	250,000			950,000
Amortization expense	120,000	20,000	(E) 13,000		153,000
Depreciation expense	80,000	30,000		(E) 6,000	104,000
Equity in subsidiary earnings	(100,000) *	-0-	(I) 100,000 *		-0-
Net income	(700,000)	(100,000)			(693,000)
Statement of Retained Earnings					
Retained earnings, 1/1/12	(840,000)	(380,000)	(S) 380,000		(840,000)
Net income (above)	(700,000)	(100,000)			(693,000)
Dividends paid	120,000	40,000		(D) 40,000	120,000
Retained earnings, 12/31/12	(1,420,000)	(440,000)			(1,413,000)
Balance Sheet					
Current assets	1,040,000	400,000			1,440,000
Investment in Sun Company	860,000 *	-0-	(D) 40,000	(S) 600,000 (A) 200,000 (I) 100,000 *	-0-
Trademarks	600,000	200,000	(A) 20,000		820,000
Patented technology	370,000	288,000	(A) 130,000	(E) 13,000	775,000
Equipment (net)	250,000	220,000	(E) 6,000	(A) 30,000	446,000
Goodwill	-0-	-0-	(A) 80,000		80,000
Total assets	3,120,000	1,108,000			3,561,000
Liabilities	(980,000)	(448,000)			(1,428,000)
Common stock	(600,000)	(200,000)	(S) 200,000		(600,000)
Additional paid-in capital	(120,000)	(20,000)	(S) 20,000		(120,000)
Retained earnings, 12/31/12 (above)	(1,420,000)	(440,000)			(1,413,000)
Total liabilities and equities	(3,120,000)	(1,108,000)	989,000	989,000	(3,561,000)

Note: Parentheses indicate a credit balance.
*Boxed items highlight differences with consolidation in Exhibit 3.5.
Consolidation entries:
(S) Elimination of Sun's stockholders' equity January 1 balances and the book value portion of the investment account.
(A) Allocation of Sun's acquisition-date excess fair values over book values.
(I) Elimination of parent's equity in subsidiary earnings accrual.
(D) Elimination of intra-entity dividend payment.
(E) Recognition of current year excess fair-value amortization and depreciation expenses.

Initial Value Method Applied—2012 Consolidation

Although the initial value method theoretically stands in marked contrast to the equity method, few reporting differences actually exist. In the year of acquisition, Parrot's income and investment accounts relating to the subsidiary are the only accounts affected.

Under the initial value method, income recognition in 2012 is limited to the $40,000 dividend received by the parent; no equity income accrual is made. At the same time, the investment account retains its $800,000 initial value. Unlike the equity method, no adjustments are recorded in the parent's investment account in connection with the current year operations, subsidiary dividends, or amortization of any fair-value allocations.

After the composition of these two accounts has been established, worksheet entries can be used to produce the consolidated figures found in Exhibit 3.9 as of December 31, 2012.

Consolidation Entry S As with the previous Entry **S** in Exhibit 3.5, the $600,000 component of the investment account is eliminated against the beginning stockholders' equity account of the subsidiary. Both are equivalent to Sun's net assets at January 1, 2012, and are, therefore, reciprocal balances that must be offset. This entry is not affected by the accounting method in use.

Consolidation Entry A Sun's $200,000 excess acquisition-date fair value over book value is allocated to Sun's assets and liabilities based on their fair values at the date of acquisition. The $80,000 residual is attributed to goodwill. This procedure is identical to the corresponding entry in Exhibit 3.5 in which the equity method was applied.

Consolidation Entry I Under the initial value method, the parent records dividend collections as income. Entry **I** removes this Dividend Income account along with Sun's Dividends Paid. From a consolidated perspective, these two $40,000 balances represent an intra-entity transfer of cash that had no financial impact outside of the entity. In contrast to the equity method, Parrot has not accrued subsidiary income, nor has amortization been recorded; thus, no further income elimination is needed.

Dividend Income	40,000	
Dividends Paid		40,000
To eliminate intra-entity income.		

Consolidation Entry D When the initial value method is applied, the parent records intra-entity dividends as income. Because these distributions were already removed from the consolidated totals by Entry **I,** no separate Entry **D** is required.

Consolidation Entry E Regardless of the parent's method of accounting, the reporting entity must recognize excess amortizations for the current year in connection with the original fair-value allocations. Thus, Entry **E** serves to bring the current year expenses into the consolidated financial statements.

Consequently, using the initial value method rather than the equity method changes only Entries **I** and **D** in the year of acquisition. Despite the change in methods, reported figures are still derived by (1) eliminating all reciprocals, (2) allocating the excess portion of the acquisition-date fair values, and (3) recording amortizations on these allocations. As indicated previously, the consolidated totals appearing in Exhibit 3.9 are identical to the figures produced previously in Exhibit 3.5. Although the income and the investment accounts on the parent company's separate statements vary, the consolidated balances are not affected.

One significant difference between the initial value method and equity method does exist: The parent's separate statements do not reflect consolidated income totals when the initial value method is used. Because equity adjustments (such as excess amortizations) are ignored, neither Parrot's reported net income of $640,000 nor its retained earnings of $1,360,000 provides an accurate portrayal of consolidated figures.

Partial Equity Method Applied—2012 Consolidation

Exhibit 3.10 presents a worksheet to consolidate these two companies for 2012 (the year of acquisition) based on the assumption that Parrot applied the partial equity method. Again, the only changes from previous examples are found in (1) the parent's separate records for this investment and its related income and (2) worksheet Entries **I** and **D.**

As discussed earlier, under the partial equity approach, the parent's record-keeping is limited to two periodic journal entries: the annual accrual of subsidiary income and the receipt of dividends. Hence, within the parent's records, only a few differences exist when the partial equity method is applied rather than the initial value method. The entries recorded by Parrot in connection with Sun's 2012 operations illustrate both of these approaches.

Parrot Company Initial Value Method 2012			Parrot Company Partial Equity Method 2012		
Cash	40,000		Cash	40,000	
Dividend Income. . .		40,000	Investment in Sun Company		40,000
Dividends collected from subsidiary.			Dividends collected from subsidiary.		
			Investment in Sun Company	100,000	
			Equity in Subsidiary Earnings		100,000
			Accrual of subsidiary income.		

Therefore, by applying the partial equity method, the investment account on the parent's balance sheet rises to $860,000 by the end of 2012. This total is composed of the original $800,000 acquisition-date fair value for Sun adjusted for the $100,000 income recognition and the $40,000 cash dividend payment. The same $100,000 equity income figure appears within the parent's income statement. These two balances are appropriately found in Parrot's records in Exhibit 3.10.

Because of the handling of income recognition and dividend payments, Entries **I** and **D** again differ on the worksheet. For the partial equity method, the $100,000 equity income is eliminated (Entry **I**) by reversing the parent's entry. Removing this accrual allows the individual revenue and expense accounts of the subsidiary to be reported without double-counting. The $40,000 intra-entity dividend payment must also be removed (Entry **D**). The Dividend Paid account is simply deleted. However, elimination of the dividend from the Investment in Sun Company actually causes an increase because receipt was recorded by Parrot as a reduction in that account. All other consolidation entries (Entries **S, A,** and **E**) are the same for all three methods.

Consolidation Subsequent to Year of Acquisition—Initial Value and Partial Equity Methods

By again incorporating the December 31, 2015, financial data for Parrot and Sun (presented in Exhibit 3.7), consolidation procedures for the initial value method and the partial equity method are examined for years subsequent to the date of acquisition. *In both cases, establishment of an appropriate beginning retained earnings figure becomes a significant goal of the consolidation.*

Conversion of the Parent's Retained Earnings to a Full-Accrual (Equity) Basis

Consolidated financial statements require a *full accrual-based measurement of both income and retained earnings.* The initial value method, however, employs the cash basis for income recognition. The partial equity method only partially accrues subsidiary income. Thus, neither provides a full accrual-based measure of the subsidiary activities on the parent's income. As a result, over time the parent's retained earnings account fails to show a full accrual-based amount. Therefore, new worksheet adjustments are required to convert the parent's beginning of the year retained earnings balance to a full-accrual basis. These adjustments are made to *beginning of the year retained earnings* because current year earnings are readily converted to full-accrual basis by simply combining current year revenue and expenses. The resulting current year combined income figure is then

EXHIBIT 3.11
Retained Earnings Differences

PARROT COMPANY AND SUN COMPANY
Previous Years—2012–2014

	Equity Method	Initial Value Method	Partial Equity Method
Equity accrual	$330,000	–0–	$330,000
Dividend income	–0–	$110,000	–0–
Excess amortization expenses	(21,000)	–0–	–0–
Increase in parent's retained earnings	$309,000	$110,000	$330,000

added to the adjusted beginning of the year retained earnings to arrive at a full-accrual ending retained earnings balance.

This concern was not faced previously when the equity method was adopted. Under that approach, the parent's Retained Earnings account balance already reflects a full-accrual basis so that no adjustment is necessary. In the earlier illustration, the $330,000 income accrual for the 2012–2014 period as well as the $21,000 amortization expense were recognized by the parent in applying the equity method (see Exhibit 3.6). Having been recorded in this manner, these two balances form a permanent part of Parrot's retained earnings and are included automatically in the consolidated total. Consequently, if the equity method is applied, the process is simplified; no worksheet entries are needed to adjust the parent's Retained Earnings account to record subsidiary operations or amortization for past years.

Conversely, if a method other than the equity method is used, a worksheet change must be made to the parent's beginning Retained Earnings account (in every subsequent year) to equate this balance with a full-accrual amount. To quantify this adjustment, the parent's recognized income for these past three years under each method is first determined (Exhibit 3.11). For consolidation purposes, the beginning retained earnings account must then be increased or decreased to create the same effect as the equity method.

Initial Value Method Applied—Subsequent Consolidation

As shown in Exhibit 3.11, if Parrot applied the initial value method during the 2012–2014 period, it recognizes $199,000 less income than under the equity method ($309,000 – $110,000). Two items cause this difference. First, Parrot has not accrued the $220,000 increase in the subsidiary's book value across the periods prior to the current year. Although the $110,000 in dividends was recorded as income, the parent never recognized the remainder of the $330,000 earned by the subsidiary.[9] Second, no accounting has been made of the $21,000 excess amortization expenses. Thus, the parent's beginning Retained Earnings account is $199,000 ($220,000 − $21,000) below the appropriate consolidated total and must be adjusted.[10]

To simulate the equity method so that the parent's beginning Retained Earnings account reflects a full-accrual basis, this $199,000 increase is recorded through a worksheet entry. The initial value method figures reported by the parent effectively are converted into equity method balances.

[9] Two different calculations are available for determining the $220,000 in nonrecorded income for prior years: (1) subsidiary income less dividends paid and (2) the change in the subsidiary's book value as of the first day of the current year. The second method works only if the subsidiary has had no other equity transactions such as the issuance of new stock or the purchase of treasury shares. Unless otherwise stated, the assumption is made that no such transactions have occurred.

[10] Because neither the income in excess of dividends nor excess amortization is recorded by the parent under the initial value method, its beginning Retained Earnings account is $199,000 less than the $2,044,000 reported under the equity method (Exhibit 3.7). Thus, a $1,845,000 balance is shown in Exhibit 3.12 ($2,044,000 − this $199,000). Conversely, if the partial equity method had been applied, Parrot's absence of amortization would cause the Retained Earnings account to be $21,000 higher than the figure derived by the equity method. For this reason, Exhibit 3.13 shows the parent with a beginning Retained Earnings account of $2,065,000 rather than $2,044,000.

*Consolidation Entry *C*

Investment in Sun Company	199,000	
Retained Earnings, 1/1/15 (Parrot Company)		199,000
To convert parent's beginning retained earnings from the initial value method to equity method.		

This adjustment is labeled Entry ***C.** The *C* refers to the **c**onversion being made to equity method (full-accrual) totals. The asterisk indicates that this equity simulation relates solely to transactions of prior periods. Thus, *Entry *C should be recorded before the other worksheet entries to align the beginning balances for the year.*

Exhibit 3.12 provides a complete presentation of the consolidation of Parrot and Sun as of December 31, 2015, based on the parent's application of the initial value method. After Entry ***C** has been recorded on the worksheet, the remainder of this consolidation follows the same pattern as previous examples. Sun's stockholders' equity accounts are eliminated (Entry **S**) while the allocations stemming from the $800,000 initial fair value are recorded (Entry **A**) at their unamortized balances as of January 1, 2015 (see Exhibit 3.8). Intra-entity dividend income is removed (Entry **I**) and current year excess amortization expenses are recognized (Entry **E**). To complete this process, the intra-entity debt of $40,000 is offset (Entry **P**).

In retrospect, the only new element introduced here is the adjustment of the parent's beginning Retained Earnings. For a consolidation produced after the initial year of acquisition, an Entry ***C** is required if the parent has not applied the equity method.

Partial Equity Method Applied—Subsequent Consolidation

Exhibit 3.13 demonstrates the worksheet consolidation of Parrot and Sun as of December 31, 2015, when the investment accounts have been recorded by the parent using the partial equity method. This approach accrues subsidiary income each year but records no other equity adjustments. Therefore, as of December 31, 2015, Parrot's Investment in Sun Company account has a balance of $1,110,000:

Fair value of consideration transferred for Sun Company 1/1/12 . . .		$ 800,000
Sun Company's 2012–2014 increase in book value:		
Accrual of Sun Company's income.	$330,000	
Collection of Sun Company's dividends	(110,000)	220,000
Sun Company's 2015 operations:		
Accrual of Sun Company's income.	$160,000	
Collection of Sun Company's dividends	(70,000)	90,000
Investment in Sun Company, 12/31/15 (Partial equity method)		$1,110,000

As indicated here and in Exhibit 3.11, Parrot has recognized the yearly equity income accrual but not amortization. Consequently, if the partial equity method is in use, the parent's beginning Retained Earnings Account must be adjusted to include this expense. The three-year total of $21,000 amortization is reflected through Entry ***C** to simulate the equity method and, hence, consolidated totals.

*Consolidation Entry *C*

Retained Earnings, 1/1/15 (Parrot Company)	21,000	
Investment in Sun Company		21,000
To convert parent's beginning Retained Earnings from partial equity method to equity method by including excess amortizations.		

EXHIBIT 3.12 Consolidation Worksheet Subsequent to Year of Acquisition—Initial Value Method Applied

PARROT COMPANY AND SUN COMPANY
Consolidated Worksheet
Investment: Initial Value Method **For Year Ending December 31, 2015**

Accounts	Parrot Company	Sun Company	Consolidation Entries Debit	Consolidation Entries Credit	Consolidation Totals
Income Statement					
Revenues	(2,100,000)	(600,000)			(2,700,000)
Cost of goods sold	1,000,000	380,000			1,380,000
Amortization expense	200,000	20,000	(E) 13,000		233,000
Depreciation expense	100,000	40,000		(E) 6,000	134,000
Dividend income	(70,000) *	–0–	(I) 70,000 *		–0–
Net income	(870,000)	(160,000)			(953,000)
Statement of Retained Earnings					
Retained earnings, 1/1/15					
Parrot Company	(1,845,000)† *			(*C) 199,000 *	(2,044,000)
Sun Company		(600,000)	(S) 600,000		–0–
Net income (above)	(870,000)	(160,000)			(953,000)
Dividends paid	420,000	70,000		(I) 70,000 *	420,000
Retained earnings, 12/31/15	(2,295,000)	(690,000)			(2,577,000)
Balance Sheet					
Current assets	1,705,000	500,000		(P) 40,000	2,165,000
Investment in Sun Company	800,000 *	–0–	(*C) 199,000	(S) 820,000 (A) 179,000	–0–
Trademarks	600,000	240,000	(A) 20,000		860,000
Patented technology	540,000	420,000	(A) 91,000	(E) 13,000	1,038,000
Equipment (net)	420,000	210,000	(E) 6,000	(A) 12,000	624,000
Goodwill	–0–	–0–	(A) 80,000		80,000
Total assets	4,065,000	1,370,000			4,767,000
Liabilities	(1,050,000)	(460,000)	(P) 40,000		(1,470,000)
Common stock	(600,000)	(200,000)	(S) 200,000		(600,000)
Additional paid-in capital	(120,000)	(20,000)	(S) 20,000		(120,000)
Retained earnings, 12/31/15 (above)	(2,295,000)	(690,000)			(2,577,000)
Total liabilities and equities	(4,065,000)	(1,370,000)	1,339,000	1,339,000	(4,767,000)

Note: Parentheses indicate a credit balance.
*Boxed items highlight differences with consolidation in Exhibit 3.7.
†See footnote 10.
Consolidation entries:
(*C) To convert parent's beginning retained earnings to full-accrual basis.
(S) Elimination of Sun's stockholders' equity January 1 balances and the book value portion of investment account.
(A) Allocation of Sun's excess acquisition-date fair value over book value, unamortized balance as of beginning of year.
(I) Elimination of intra-entity dividend income and dividend paid by Sun.
(E) Recognition of current year excess fair-value amortization and depreciation expenses.
(P) Elimination of intra-entity receivable/payable.
Note: Consolidation entry (D) is not needed when the parent applies the initial value method because entry (I) eliminates the intra-entity dividend effects.

By recording Entry ***C** on the worksheet, all of the subsidiary's operational results for the 2012–2014 period are included in the consolidation. As shown in Exhibit 3.13, the remainder of the worksheet entries follow the same basic pattern as that illustrated previously for the year of acquisition (Exhibit 3.10).

Summary of Investment Methods

Having three investment methods available to the parent means that three sets of entries must be understood to arrive at reported figures appropriate for a business combination. The process can initially seem to be a confusing overlap of procedures. However, at this

EXHIBIT 3.13 Consolidation Worksheet Subsequent to Year of Acquisition—Partial Equity Method Applied

PARROT COMPANY AND SUN COMPANY
Consolidated Worksheet
For Year Ending December 31, 2015

Investment: Partial Equity Method

Accounts	Parrot Company	Sun Company	Consolidation Entries Debit	Consolidation Entries Credit	Consolidation Totals
Income Statement					
Revenues	(2,100,000)	(600,000)			(2,700,000)
Cost of goods sold	1,000,000	380,000			1,380,000
Amortization expense	200,000	20,000	(E) 13,000		233,000
Depreciation expense	100,000	40,000		(E) 6,000	134,000
Equity in subsidiary earnings	(160,000) *	-0-	(I) 160,000 *		-0-
Net income	(960,000)	(160,000)			(953,000)
Statement of Retained Earnings					
Retained earnings, 1/1/15					
Parrot Company	(2,065,000)† *		(*C) 21,000 *		(2,044,000)
Sun Company		(600,000)	(S) 600,000		-0-
Net income (above)	(960,000)	(160,000)			(953,000)
Dividends paid	420,000	70,000		(D) 70,000 *	420,000
Retained earnings, 12/31/15	(2,605,000)	(690,000)			(2,577,000)
Balance Sheet					
Current assets	1,705,000	500,000		(P) 40,000	2,165,000
Investment in Sun Company	1,110,000 *	-0-	(D) 70,000	(*C) 21,000 *	-0-
				(S) 820,000	
				(A) 179,000	
				(I) 160,000 *	
Trademarks	600,000	240,000	(A) 20,000		860,000
Patented technology	540,000	420,000	(A) 91,000	(E) 13,000	1,038,000
Equipment (net)	420,000	210,000	(E) 6,000	(A) 12,000	624,000
Goodwill	-0-	-0-	(A) 80,000		80,000
Total assets	4,375,000	1,370,000			4,767,000
Liabilities	(1,050,000)	(460,000)	(P) 40,000		(1,470,000)
Common stock	(600,000)	(200,000)	(S) 200,000		(600,000)
Additional paid-in capital	(120,000)	(20,000)	(S) 20,000		(120,000)
Retained earnings, 12/31/15 (above)	(2,605,000)	(690,000)			(2,577,000)
Total liabilities and equities	(4,375,000)	(1,370,000)	1,321,000	1,321,000	(4,767,000)

Note: Parentheses indicate a credit balance.
*Boxed items highlight differences with consolidation in Exhibit 3.7.
†See footnote 10.
Consolidation entries:
(*C) To convert parent's beginning retained earnings to full accrual basis.
(S) Elimination of Sun's stockholders' equity January 1 balances and the book value portion of investment account.
(A) Allocation of Sun's excess acquisition-date fair value over book value, unamortized balance as of beginning of year.
(I) Elimination of parent's equity in subsidiary earnings accrual.
(D) Elimination of intra-entity dividend payment.
(E) Recognition of current year excess fair-value amortization and depreciation expenses.
(P) Elimination of intra-entity receivable/payable.

point in the coverage, only three worksheet entries actually are affected by the choice of either the equity method, partial equity method, or initial value method: Entries ***C, I,** and **D.** Furthermore, accountants should never get so involved with a worksheet and its entries that they lose sight of the balances that this process is designed to calculate. These figures are never affected by the parent's choice of an accounting method.

After the appropriate balance for each account is understood, worksheet entries assist the accountant in deriving these figures. To help clarify the consolidation process

Consolidated Totals Subsequent to Acquisition*	
Current revenues	Parent revenues are included. Subsidiary revenues are included but only for the period since the acquisition.
Current expenses	Parent expenses are included. Subsidiary expenses are included but only for the period since the acquisition. Amortization expenses of the excess fair-value allocations are included by recognition on the worksheet.
Investment (or dividend) income	Income recognized by parent is eliminated and effectively replaced by the subsidiary's revenues and expenses.
Retained earnings, beginning balance	Parent balance is included. The change in the subsidiary balance since acquisition is included either as a regular accrual by the parent or through a worksheet entry to increase parent balance. Past amortization expenses of the excess fair-value allocations are included either as a part of parent balance or through a worksheet entry.
Assets and liabilities	Parent balances are included. Subsidiary balances are included after adjusting for acquisition-date fair values. Intra-entity receivable/payable balances are eliminated.
Goodwill	Original fair-value allocation is included.
Investment in subsidiary	Asset account recorded by parent is eliminated on the worksheet so that the balance is not included in consoliated figures.
Capital stock and additional paid-in capital	Parent balances only are included although they will have been adjusted at acquisition date if stock was issued.

*The next few chapters discuss the necessity of altering some of these balances for consolidation purposes. Thus, this table is not definitive but is included only to provide a basic overview of the consolidation process as it has been described to this point.

required under each of the three accounting methods, Exhibit 3.14 describes the purpose of each worksheet entry: first during the year of acquisition and second for any period following the year of acquisition.

Goodwill Impairment

LO5

Discuss the rationale for the goodwill impairment testing approach.

FASB ASC Topic 350, Intangibles—Goodwill and Other, provides accounting standards for determining, measuring, and reporting goodwill impairment losses. Because goodwill is considered to have an indefinite life, an impairment approach is used rather than amortization. The FASB reasoned that although goodwill can decrease over time, it does not do so in the "rational and systematic" manner that periodic amortization suggests. Only upon recognition of an impairment loss (or partial sale of a subsidiary) will goodwill decline from one period to the next. Goodwill impairment losses are reported as operating items in the consolidated income statement.

The notion of an indefinite life allows many firms to report the original amount of goodwill recognized in a business combination. However, goodwill at some point in time may become impaired, requiring loss recognition and a reduction in the amount reported in the consolidated balance sheet. Evidence shows that goodwill impairment losses can be substantial. Exhibit 3.15 provides examples of some recent goodwill impairment losses. Unlike amortization, which periodically reduces asset values, impairment must first be revealed before a write-down is justified. Accounting standards therefore require periodic tests for goodwill impairment.

Goodwill impairment tests are performed at the reporting unit level within a combined entity. As discussed below, all assets acquired (including goodwill) and liabilities assumed in a business combination must be assigned to *reporting units* within

EXHIBIT 3.14 Consolidation Worksheet Entries

	Equity Method Applied	Initial Value Method Applied	Partial Equity Method Applied
Any Time during Year of Acquisition			
Entry **S**	Beginning stockholders' equity of subsidiary is eliminated against book value portion of investment account.	Same as equity method.	Same as equity method.
Entry **A**	Excess fair value is allocated to assets and liabilities based on difference in book values and fair values; residual is assigned to goodwill.	Same as equity method.	Same as equity method.
Entry **I**	Equity income accrual (including amortization expense) is eliminated.	Dividend income is eliminated.	Equity income accrual is eliminated.
Entry **D**	Intra-entity dividends paid by subsidiary are eliminated.	No entry—intra-entity dividends are eliminated in Entry **I**.	Same as equity method.
Entry **E**	Current year excess amortization expenses of fair-value allocations are recorded.	Same as equity method.	Same as equity method.
Entry **P**	Intra-entity payable/receivable balances are offset.	Same as equity method.	Same as equity method.
Any Time Following Year of Acquisition			
Entry ***C**	No entry—equity income for prior years has already been recognized along with amortization expenses.	Increase in subsidiary's book value during prior years as well as excess amortization expenses are recognized (conversion is made to equity method).	Excess amortization expenses for prior years are recognized (conversion is made to equity method).
Entry **S**	Same as initial year.	Same as initial year.	Same as initial year.
Entry **A**	Unamortized excess fair value at beginning of year is allocated to specific accounts and to goodwill.	Same as equity method.	Same as equity method.
Entry **I**	Same as initial year.	Same as initial year.	Same as initial year.
Entry **D**	Same as initial year.	Same as initial year.	Same as initial year.
Entry **E**	Same as initial year.	Same as initial year.	Same as initial year.
Entry **P**	Same as initial year.	Same as initial year.	Same as initial year.

a consolidated enterprise. The goodwill residing in each reporting unit is then separately subjected to periodic impairment reviews. Current financial reporting standards require, at a minimum, an annual assessment for potential goodwill impairment.

Because impairment testing procedures can be costly, the FASB provides firms the option to first conduct a *qualitative* analysis to assess whether further testing procedures are appropriate. If circumstances indicate a potential decline in the fair value of a reporting

EXHIBIT 3.15 Recent Goodwill Impairments

Company	Impairment
Sprint-Nextel	$29.7 billion
Symantec	7.4 billion
Macy's	5.4 billion
Office Depot	1.2 billion
FedEx	910 million
Applied Micro Circuits	223 million
Ford	214 million
Nike	199 million
Dick's Sporting Goods	111 million

Discussion Question

HOW DOES A COMPANY REALLY DECIDE WHICH INVESTMENT METHOD TO APPLY?

Pilgrim Products, Inc., buys a controlling interest in the common stock of Crestwood Corporation. Shortly after the acquisition, a meeting of Pilgrim's accounting department is convened to discuss the internal reporting procedures required by the ownership of this subsidiary. Each member of the staff has a definite opinion as to whether the equity method, initial value method, or partial equity method should be adopted. To resolve this issue, Pilgrim's chief financial officer outlines several of her concerns about the decision.

> I already understand how each method works. I know the general advantages and disadvantages of all three. I realize, for example, that the equity method provides more detailed information whereas the initial value method is much easier to apply. What I need to know are the factors specific to our situation that should be considered in deciding which method to adopt. I must make a recommendation to the president on this matter, and he will want firm reasons for my favoring a particular approach. I don't want us to select a method and then find out in six months that the information is not adequate for our needs or that the cost of adapting our system to monitor Crestwood outweighs the benefits derived from the data.

What are the factors that Pilgrim's officials should evaluate when making this decision?

unit below its carrying amount, then further tests are required to see if goodwill is the source of the decline. Our coverage of goodwill impairment addresses the following:

- The assignment of acquired goodwill to reporting units.
- The option to conduct an annual qualitative test for potential goodwill impairment.
- The two-step goodwill impairment testing procedures.

Assigning Goodwill to Reporting Units

Combined companies typically organize themselves into separate *units* along distinct operating lines. Each individual operating unit has responsibility for managing its assets and liabilities to earn profits for the combined entity. These operating units report information about their earnings activities to top management to support decision making. Such operating units are known as *reporting units*.

Following a business combination, the identifiable assets and liabilities acquired are assigned to the firm's reporting units based on where they will be employed. Any amount assigned to goodwill also is assigned to reporting units expected to benefit from the synergies of the combination. Thus, any individual reporting unit where goodwill resides is the appropriate level for goodwill impairment testing.

In practice, firms often assign goodwill to reporting units either at the level of a reporting segment—as described in ASC Topic 280, Segment Reporting—or at a lower level within a segment of a combined enterprise. Reporting units may thus include the following:

- A component of an operating segment at a level below that operating segment. Segment management should review and assess performance at this level. Also, the component should be a business in which discrete financial information is available and should differ economically from other components of the operating segment.
- The segments of an enterprise.
- The entire enterprise.

For example, RF Micro Devices, a wireless technology firm, observed in its recent annual report:

> We have determined that we have two reporting units as of fiscal 2011 (CPG and MPG) for purposes of allocating and testing goodwill. In evaluating our reporting units, we first consider our operating segments and related components in accordance with FASB guidance. Goodwill is allocated to our reporting units that are anticipated to benefit from the synergies of the business combinations generating the underlying goodwill.

Thus, all goodwill impairment testing is performed at the reporting unit level, rather than collectively at the combined entity level. Separate testing of goodwill within individual reporting units also prevents the masking of goodwill impairment in one reporting unit with contemporaneous increases in the value of goodwill in other reporting units.

LO6

Describe the procedures for conducting a goodwill impairment test.

Qualitative Assessment Option

Because goodwill impairment tests require firms to calculate fair values for their reporting units each year, such a comprehensive measurement exercise can be costly. To help reduce costs, a 2011 update to ASC Topic 305 allows an entity the option to first assess qualitative factors to determine whether more rigorous testing for goodwill impairment is needed. The qualitative approach assesses the *likelihood* that a reporting unit's fair value is less than its carrying amount. The more-likely-than-not threshold is defined as having a likelihood of more than 50 percent.

In assessing whether a reporting unit's fair value exceeds its carrying amount, a firm must examine all relevant facts and circumstances, including

- Macroeconomic conditions such as a deterioration in general economic conditions, limitations on accessing capital, fluctuations in foreign exchange rates, or other developments in equity and credit markets.
- Industry and market considerations such as a deterioration in the environment in which an entity operates, an increased competitive environment, a decline (both absolute and relative to its peers) in market-dependent multiples or metrics, a change in the market for an entity's products or services, or a regulatory or political development.
- Cost factors such as increases in raw materials, labor, or other costs that have a negative effect on earnings.
- Overall financial performance such as negative or declining cash flows or a decline in actual or planned revenue or earnings.
- Other relevant entity-specific events such as changes in management, key personnel, strategy, or customers; contemplation of bankruptcy; or litigation.
- Events affecting a reporting unit such as a change in the carrying amount of its net assets, a more-likely-than-not expectation of selling or disposing all, or a portion of, a reporting unit, the testing for recoverability of a significant asset group within a reporting unit, or recognition of a goodwill impairment loss in the financial statements of a subsidiary that is a component of a reporting unit.
- If applicable, a sustained decrease (both absolute and relative to its peers) in share price. (FASB ASC para. 350-20-35-3C)

The underlying rationale for comparing a reporting unit's fair value and carrying amount is as follows. If a reporting unit's fair value is deemed greater than its carrying amount, then its collective net assets are maintaining their value. It then can be argued that a decline in any particular asset (i.e., goodwill) within the reporting unit is also unlikely and no further impairment tests are necessary. On the other hand, if the relevant facts and circumstances listed above suggest that a reporting unit's fair value is likely less than its carrying amount, then more rigorous testing for goodwill impairment is appropriate. As shown in Exhibit 3.16, a qualitative assessment of a sufficient fair value for a reporting unit circumvents further goodwill impairment testing.

The FASB ASC (paragraph 350-20-35-30) requires an entity to test for goodwill impairment annually for each of its reporting units where goodwill resides. Moreover, more frequent impairment testing is required if events or circumstances change that make it more likely than not that a reporting unit's fair value has fallen below its carrying amount.

EXHIBIT 3.16 Goodwill Impairment—Qualitative Assessment and Two-Step Goodwill Impairment Test

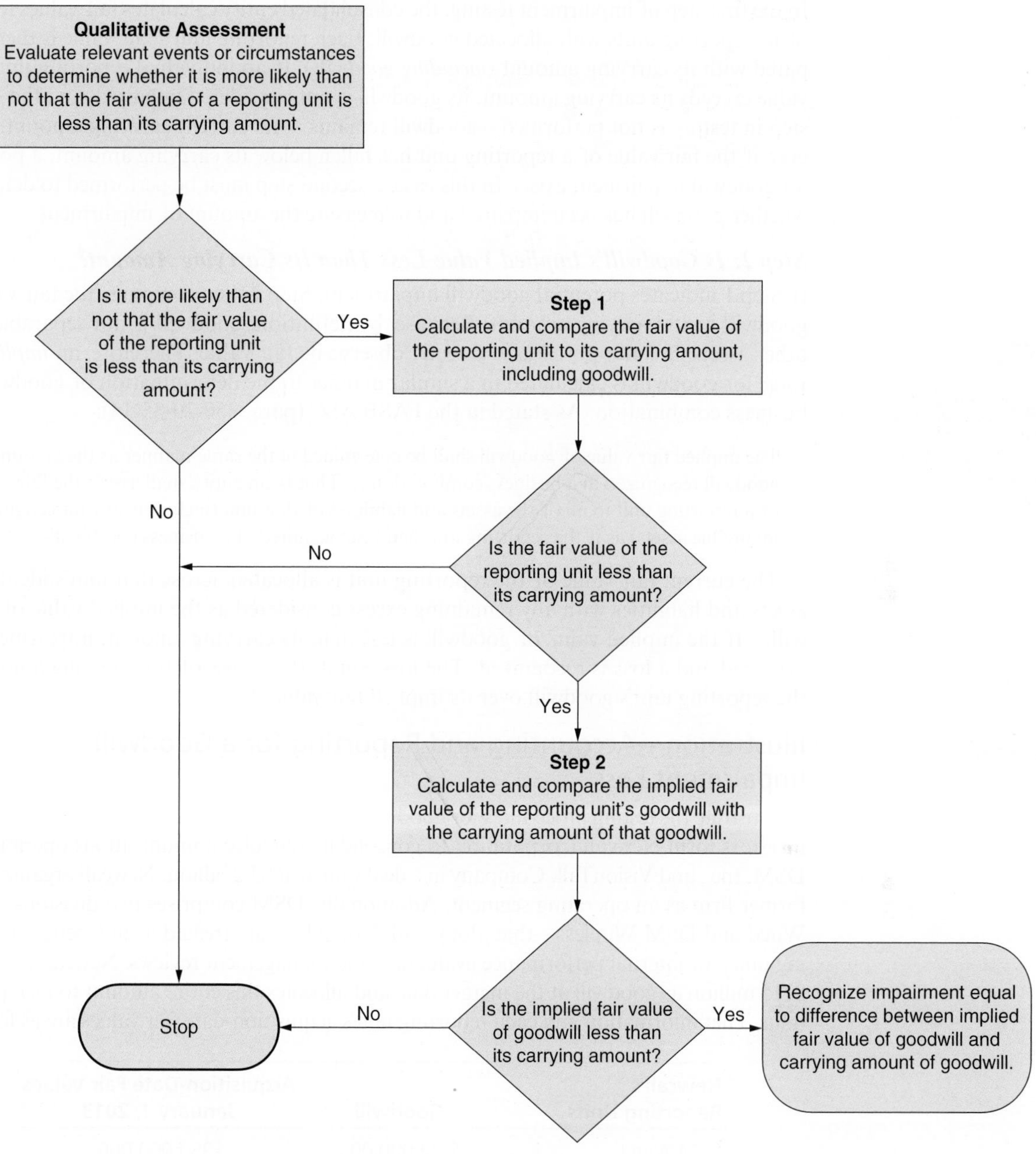

Notes:

1. An entity has the unconditional option to skip the qualitative assessment and proceed directly to performing Step 1, except in the circumstance where a reporting unit has a carrying amount that is zero or negative.
2. An entity having a reporting unit with a carrying amount that is zero or negative would proceed directly to Step 2 if it determines, as a result of performing its required qualitative assessment, that it is more likely than not that a goodwill impairment exists. To perform Step 2, an entity must calculate the fair value of a reporting unit.

From FASB Accounting Standards Update September 2011, Intangibles—Goodwill and Other (Topic 350), "Testing Goodwill for Impairment."

Testing Goodwill for Impairment—Steps 1 and 2

Exhibit 3.16 shows the two steps for goodwill impairment testing and measurement. In contrast to the qualitative assessment, Steps 1 and 2 rely on quantitative fair value measures for reporting units as a whole and for their underlying individual assets and liabilities. If, after performing the qualitative assessment described above, an entity concludes that it is more likely than not that the fair value of a reporting unit is less than its carrying amount, then the entity is required to proceed to the first step of the two-step impairment test.[11]

[11] An entity, on the basis of its discretion, may bypass the qualitative assessment for any reporting unit in any period and proceed directly to performing the first step of the impairment test. An entity may resume performing the qualitative assessment in any subsequent period (FASB ASC para. 350-20-35-3).

Step 1: Is the Carrying Amount of a Reporting Unit More Than Its Fair Value?

In the first step of impairment testing, the consolidated entity calculates fair values for each of its reporting units with allocated goodwill. Each reporting unit's fair value is then compared with its carrying amount (*including goodwill*). If an individual reporting unit's fair value exceeds its carrying amount, its goodwill is not considered impaired, and the second step in testing is not performed—goodwill remains at its current carrying amount. However, if the fair value of a reporting unit has fallen below its carrying amount, a potential for goodwill impairment exists. In this case, a second step must be performed to determine whether goodwill has been impaired and to measure the amount of impairment.

Step 2: Is Goodwill's Implied Value Less Than Its Carrying Amount?

If Step 1 indicates potential goodwill impairment, Step 2 then compares the fair value of goodwill to its carrying amount. Because, by definition, goodwill is not separable from other assets, it is not possible to directly observe its fair value. Therefore, an *implied fair value* for goodwill is calculated in a similar manner to the determination of goodwill in a business combination. As stated in the FASB ASC (para. 350-20-35-14):

> The implied fair value of goodwill shall be determined in the same manner as the amount of goodwill recognized in a business combination … That is, an entity shall assign the fair value of a reporting unit to all of the assets and liabilities of that unit (including any unrecognized intangible assets) as if the reporting unit had been acquired in a business combination …

The current fair value of the reporting unit is allocated across that unit's identifiable assets and liabilities with any remaining excess considered as the implied value of goodwill.[12] If the implied value of goodwill is less than its carrying amount, impairment has occurred and a loss is recognized. The loss equals the excess of the carrying amount of the reporting unit's goodwill over its implied fair value.[13]

Illustration—Accounting and Reporting for a Goodwill Impairment Loss

To illustrate the testing procedures for goodwill impairment, assume that on January 1, 2013, investors form Newcall Corporation to consolidate the telecommunications operations of DSM, Inc., and VisionTalk Company in a deal valued at $2.2 billion. Newcall organizes each former firm as an operating segment. Additionally, DSM comprises two divisions—DSM Wired and DSM Wireless—that along with VisionTalk are treated as independent reporting units for internal performance evaluation and management reviews. Newcall recognizes $215 million as goodwill at the merger date and allocates this entire amount to its reporting units. That information and each reporting unit's acquisition-date fair values are as follows:

Newcall's Reporting Units	**Goodwill**	**Acquisition-Date Fair Values January 1, 2013**
DSM Wired	$ 22,000,000	$950,000,000
DSM Wireless	155,000,000	748,000,000
VisionTalk	38,000,000	502,000,000

In December 2013, Newcall performs a qualitative analysis for each of its three reporting units to assess potential goodwill impairment. Accordingly, Newcall examines the relevant events and circumstances that may affect the fair values of its reporting units. The analysis reveals that the fair value of each reporting unit likely exceeds its carrying amount except for DSM Wireless. Step 1 of the goodwill impairment test then reveals that DSM Wireless's fair value has fallen to $600 million, well below its current carrying amount. Newcall attributes the decline in value to a failure to realize expected cost-saving synergies with VisionTalk. Then, in Step 2, Newcall compares the implied fair value of the DSM Wireless

[12] This procedure serves only to measure an implied fair value for goodwill. None of the other values allocated to assets and liabilities in the testing comparison are used to adjust their reported amounts.

[13] The loss cannot exceed the carrying amount of goodwill.

goodwill to its carrying amount. Newcall derived the implied fair value of goodwill through the following allocation of the December 31, 2013, fair value of DSM Wireless:

DSM Wireless December 31, 2013, fair value		$600,000,000
Fair values of DSM Wireless net assets at December 31, 2013:		
Current assets	$ 50,000,000	
Property	125,000,000	
Equipment	265,000,000	
Subscriber list	140,000,000	
Patented technology	185,000,000	
Current liabilities	(44,000,000)	
Long-term debt	(125,000,000)	
Value assigned to identifiable net assets		$596,000,000
Implied fair value of goodwill		$ 4,000,000
Carrying amount before impairment		155,000,000
Impairment loss		$151,000,000

Thus, Newcall reports a $151,000,000 goodwill impairment loss as a separate line item in the operating section of its consolidated income statement. Additional disclosures are required describing (1) the facts and circumstances leading to the impairment and (2) the method of determining the fair value of the associated reporting unit (e.g., market prices, comparable business, present value technique, etc.). The reported amounts for the other assets and liabilities of DSM Wireless remain the same and are not changed based on the goodwill testing procedure.

Reporting Units with Zero or Negative Carrying Amounts

One final issue regarding goodwill impairment testing deserves mentioning. When a reporting unit has a zero or negative carrying amount, the ASC requires a special application of the testing procedure. An exception is needed because a zero or negative carrying amount for a reporting unit accompanied by a positive fair value would always permit an entity to forego Step 2 of the impairment test even though its underlying goodwill might be impaired. Therefore, in such circumstances, the ASC requires an entity to perform Step 2 of the impairment test when it is more likely than not that a goodwill impairment exists. In judging the likelihood of goodwill impairment, an entity must consider the same factors as in the qualitative assessment for individual reporting units.

Comparisons with International Accounting Standards

International Financial Reporting Standards (IFRS) and U.S. GAAP both require goodwill recognition in a business combination when the fair value of the consideration transferred exceeds the net fair values of the assets acquired and liabilities assumed. Subsequent to acquisition, both IFRS and U.S. GAAP require an assessment for goodwill impairment at least annually and more frequently in the presence of potential impairment indicators. Also for both sets of standards, goodwill impairments, once recognized, are not recoverable. However, differences exist across the two sets of standards in the way goodwill impairment is tested for and recognized. In particular, goodwill allocation, impairment testing, and determination of the impairment loss differ across the two reporting regimes and are discussed below.

Goodwill Allocation

- *U.S. GAAP.* Goodwill acquired in a business combination is allocated to reporting units expected to benefit from the goodwill. Reporting units are operating segments or a business component one level below an operating segment.
- *IFRS.* International Accounting Standard *(IAS) 36* requires goodwill acquired in a business combination to be allocated to cash-generating units or groups of cash-generating units that are expected to benefit from the synergies of the business combination. Cash-generating groups represent the lowest level within the entity at which the goodwill is monitored for internal management purposes and are not to be larger than an operating segment or determined in accordance with *IFRS 8,* "Operating Segments."

Impairment Testing

- *U.S. GAAP.* Firms have the option to perform a qualitative assessment to evaluate possible goodwill impairment based on a greater than 50 percent likelihood that a reporting unit's fair value is less than its carrying amount. If such a likelihood exists, then a two-step testing procedure is performed. In step one, a reporting unit's total fair value is compared to its carrying amount. If the carrying amount exceeds fair value, then a second step comparing goodwill's implied fair value to its carrying amount is performed.
- *IFRS.* A one-step approach compares the fair and carrying amounts of each cash-generating unit with goodwill. If the carrying amount exceeds the fair value of the cash-generating unit, then goodwill (and possibly other assets of the cash-generating unit) is considered impaired.

Determination of the Impairment Loss

- *U.S. GAAP.* In step two, a reporting unit's implied fair value for goodwill is computed as the excess of the reporting unit's fair value over the fair value of its identifiable net assets. If the carrying amount of goodwill is greater than its implied fair value, an impairment loss is recognized for the difference.
- *IFRS.* Any excess carrying amount over fair value for a cash-generating unit is first assigned to reduce goodwill. If goodwill is reduced to zero, then the other assets of the cash-generating unit are reduced pro-rata based on the carrying amounts of the assets.

Finally, the FASB and IASB have agreed to include impairment recognition and reporting as one of their future convergence projects.

Amortization and Impairment of Other Intangibles

As discussed in Chapter 2, the acquisition method governs how we initially consolidate the assets acquired and liabilities assumed in a business combination. In periods subsequent to acquisition, income determination becomes a regular part of the consolidation process. The fair value bases (established at the acquisition date) for definite-lived subsidiary assets acquired and liabilities assumed will be amortized over their remaining lives for income recognition. For indefinite-lived assets (e.g., goodwill, certain other intangibles), an impairment model is used to assess whether asset write-downs are appropriate.

Current accounting standards suggest categories of intangible assets for possible recognition when one business acquires another. Examples include noncompetition agreements, customer lists, patents, subscriber lists, databases, trademarks, lease agreements, licenses, and many others. All identified intangible assets should be amortized over their economic useful life unless such life is considered *indefinite.* The term *indefinite life* is defined as a life that extends beyond the foreseeable future. A recognized intangible asset with an indefinite life should not be amortized unless and until its life is determined to be finite. Importantly, *indefinite* does not mean "infinite." Also, the useful life of an intangible asset should not be considered indefinite because a precise finite life is not known.

For intangible assets with finite lives, the amortization method should reflect the pattern of decline in the economic usefulness of the asset. If no such pattern is apparent, the straight-line method of amortization should be used. The amount to be amortized should be the value assigned to the intangible asset less any residual value. In most cases, the residual value is presumed to be zero. However, that presumption can be overcome if the acquiring enterprise has a commitment from a third party to purchase the intangible at the end of its useful life or an observable market exists for the intangible asset.

The length of the amortization period for identifiable intangibles (i.e., those not included in goodwill) depends primarily on the assumed economic life of the asset. Factors that should be considered in determining the useful life of an intangible asset include

- Legal, regulatory, or contractual provisions.
- The effects of obsolescence, demand, competition, industry stability, rate of technological change, and expected changes in distribution channels.

- The enterprise's expected use of the intangible asset.
- The level of maintenance expenditure required to obtain the asset's expected future benefits.

Any recognized intangible assets considered to possess indefinite lives are not amortized but instead are tested for impairment on an annual basis.[14] To test for impairment, the carrying amount of the intangible asset is compared to its fair value. If the fair value is less than the carrying amount, then the intangible asset is considered impaired and an impairment loss is recognized. The asset's carrying amount is reduced accordingly.

Contingent Consideration

LO7

Understand the accounting and reporting for contingent consideration subsequent to a business acquisition.

Contingency agreements frequently accompany business combinations. In many cases, the target firm asks for consideration based on projections of its future performance. The acquiring firm, however, may not share the projections and, thus, may be unwilling to pay now for uncertain future performance. To close the deal, agreements for the acquirer's future payments to the former owners of the target are common. Alternatively, when the acquirer's stock comprises the consideration transferred, the sellers of the target firm may request a guaranteed minimum market value of the stock for a period of time to ensure a fair price.

Accounting for Contingent Consideration in Business Combinations

Under the acquisition method, contingent consideration obligations are recognized as part of the initial value assigned in a business combination, consistent with the fair-value concept. Therefore, the acquiring firm must estimate the fair value of the contingent portion of the total business fair value. The contingency's fair value is recognized as part of the acquisition regardless of whether it is based on future performance of the target firm or the future stock prices of the acquirer.[15]

As an illustration, assume that Skeptical, Inc., acquires 100 percent of the voting stock of Rosy Pictures Company on January 1, 2013, for the following consideration:

- $550,000 market value of 10,000 shares of its $5-par common stock.
- A contingent payment of $80,000 cash if Rosy Pictures generates cash flows from operations of $20,000 or more in 2013.
- A payment of sufficient shares of Skeptical common stock to ensure a total value of $550,000 if the price per share is less than $55 on January 1, 2014.

Under the acquisition method, each of the three elements of consideration represents a portion of the negotiated fair value of Rosy Pictures and therefore must be included in the recorded value entered on Skeptical's accounting records. For the cash contingency, Skeptical estimates that there is a 30 percent chance that the $80,000 payment will be required. For the stock contingency, Skeptical estimates that there is a 20 percent probability that the 10,000 shares issued will have a market value of $540,000 on January 1, 2014, and an 80 percent probability that the market value of the 10,000 shares will exceed $550,000. Skeptical uses an interest rate of 4 percent to incorporate the time value of money.

[14] Impairment tests should also be conducted on an interim basis if an event or circumstance occurs between annual tests indicating that an intangible asset could be impaired.

[15] The FASB recommends that a probability weighted approach, such as the expected cash flow approach discussed in FASB *Concepts Statement No. 7,* "Using Cash Flow Information and Present Value in Accounting Measurements," may be useful in estimating the fair value of contingent consideration. This approach may include any or all of the following five elements:

1. An estimate of the future cash flow or, in more complex cases, series of future cash flows at different times.
2. Expectations about possible variations in the amount or timing of those cash flows.
3. The time value of money, represented by the risk-free rate of interest.
4. The price for bearing the uncertainty inherent in the asset or liability.
5. Other, sometimes unidentifiable, factors including illiquidity and market imperfections.

To determine the fair values of the contingent consideration, Skeptical computes the present value of the expected payments as follows:

- *Cash contingency* = \$80,000 × 30% × (1/[1 + .04]) = \$23,077
- *Stock contingency* = \$10,000 × 20% × (1/[1 + .04]) = \$1,923

Skeptical then records in its accounting records the acquisition of Rosy Pictures as follows:

Investment in Rosy Pictures	575,000	
Common Stock (5 par)		50,000
Additional Paid-in Capital (APIC)		500,000
Contingent Performance Obligation		23,077
Additional Paid-in Capital (APIC)—Contingent Equity Outstanding		1,923
To record acquisition of Rosy Pictures at fair value of consideration transferred including performance and stock contingencies.		

Skeptical will report the contingent cash payment under its liabilities and the contingent stock payment as a component of stockholders' equity. Subsequent to acquisition, obligations for contingent consideration that meet the definition of a liability will continue to be measured at fair value with adjustments recognized in income. Those obligations classified as equity are not subsequently remeasured at fair value, consistent with other equity issues (e.g., common stock).

To continue the preceding example, assume that in 2013 Rosy Pictures exceeds the cash flow from operations threshold of \$20,000, thus requiring an additional payment of \$80,000. Also, Skeptical's stock price had fallen to \$54.45 at January 1, 2014, thus requiring Skeptical to issue another 101 shares of its \$5 par common stock to the former owners of Rosy Pictures.

Contingent Performance Obligation	23,077	
Loss from Revaluation of Contingent Performance Obligation	56,923	
Cash		80,000
To record contingent cash payment required by original Rosy Pictures acquisition agreement.		
Additional Paid-in Capital (APIC)—Contingent Equity Outstanding	1,923	
Common Stock		505
Additional Paid-in Capital (APIC)		1,418
To record contingent stock issue required by original Rosy Pictures acquisition agreement.		

The loss from revaluation of the contingent performance obligation is reported in Skeptical's consolidated income statement as a component of ordinary income. Regarding the additional required stock issue, note that Skeptical's total paid-in capital remains unchanged from the total \$551,923 recorded at the acquisition date.

Push-Down Accounting

External Reporting

LO8

Understand in general the requirements of push-down accounting and when its use is appropriate.

In the analysis of business combinations to this point, discussion has focused on (1) the recording by the parent company and (2) required consolidation procedures. Unfortunately, official accounting pronouncements give virtually no guidance as to the impact of an acquisition on the separate financial statements of the subsidiary.

This issue has become especially significant in recent years because of acquisitions by private-equity firms. An organization, for example, might acquire a company and subsequently offer the shares back to the public in hopes of making a large profit. What should be reported in the subsidiary's financial statements being distributed with this offering? Such deals have reheated a long-standing debate over the merits of *push-down accounting*, the direct recording of fair-value allocations and subsequent amortization by a subsidiary.

For this reason, the FASB has explored various methods of reporting by a company that has been acquired or reorganized. To illustrate, assume that Yarrow Company owns one asset: a building with a book value of $200,000 but a fair value of $900,000. Mannen Corporation pays exactly $900,000 in cash to acquire Yarrow. Consolidation offers no real problem here: The building will be reported by the business combination at $900,000.

However, if Yarrow continues to issue separate financial statements (for example, to its creditors or potential stockholders), should the building be reported at $200,000 or $900,000? If adjusted, should the $700,000 increase be reported as a gain by the subsidiary or as an addition to contributed capital? Should depreciation be based on $200,000 or $900,000? If the subsidiary is to be viewed as a new entity with a new basis for its assets and liabilities, should Retained Earnings be returned to zero? If the parent acquires only 51 percent of Yarrow, does that change the answers to the previous questions? These questions represent just a few of the difficult issues currently being explored.

Proponents of push-down accounting argue that a change in ownership creates a new basis for subsidiary assets and liabilities. An unadjusted balance ($200,000 in the preceding illustration) is a cost figure applicable to previous stockholders. That total is no longer relevant information. Rather, according to this argument, it is the historical cost *paid by the current owner* that is important, a figure that is best reflected by the expenditure made in acquiring the subsidiary. Balance sheet accounts should be reported at the cost incurred by the present stockholders ($900,000 in the illustration) rather than the cost incurred by the company.

Currently, primary guidance concerning push-down accounting for external reporting purposes is provided by the Securities and Exchange Commission (SEC). Through *Staff Accounting Bulletin No. 54*, "Application of 'Push Down' Basis of Accounting in Financial Statements of Subsidiaries Acquired by Purchase," and *Staff Accounting Bulletin No. 73*, "'Push Down' Basis of Accounting for Parent Company Debt Related to Subsidiary Acquisitions," the SEC has indicated that

> push down accounting should be used in the separate financial statements of a "substantially wholly owned" subsidiary. . . . That view is based on the notion that when the form of ownership is within the control of the parent company, the accounting basis should be the same whether the entity continues to exist or is merged into the parent's operations. If a purchase of a "substantially wholly owned" subsidiary is financed by debt of the parent, that debt generally must be pushed down to the subsidiary. . . . As a general rule, the SEC requires push down accounting when the ownership change is greater than 95 percent and objects to push down accounting when the ownership change is less than 80 percent. However, if the acquired subsidiary has outstanding public debt or preferred stock, push down accounting is encouraged by the SEC but not required.

Thus, the SEC requires the use of push-down accounting for the separate financial statements of any subsidiary when no substantial outside ownership of the company's common stock, preferred stock, and publicly held debt exists. Apparently, the SEC believes that a change in ownership of that degree justifies a new basis of reporting for the subsidiary's assets and liabilities. Until the FASB takes action, though, application is required only when the subsidiary desires to issue securities (stock or debt) to the public as regulated by the SEC.

Internal Reporting

Push-down accounting has several advantages for internal reporting. For example, it simplifies the consolidation process. Because the allocations and amortization have already been entered into the records of the subsidiary, worksheet Entries **A** (to recognize the allocations originating from the fair-value adjustments) and **E** (amortization expense) are not needed. Therefore, except for eliminating the effects of intra-entity transactions, the assets, liabilities, revenues, and expenses of the subsidiary can be added directly to those of the parent to derive consolidated totals.

More important, push-down accounting provides better information for internal evaluation. Because the subsidiary's separate figures include amortization expense, the net income reported by the company reflects the impact that the acquisition has on the earnings of the business combination. As an example, assume that Ace Corporation owns 100 percent of Waxworth, Inc. Waxworth uses push-down accounting and reports net income of $500,000: $600,000 from operations less $100,000 in amortization expense resulting from fair-value allocations. Thus, Ace Corporation's officials know that this acquisition has added $500,000 to the consolidated net income of the business combination. They can then evaluate whether these earnings provide a sufficient return for the parent's investment.

Summary

1. The procedures used to consolidate financial information generated by the separate companies in a business combination are affected by both the passage of time and the method applied by the parent in accounting for the subsidiary. Thus, no single consolidation process that is applicable to all business combinations can be described.
2. The parent might elect to utilize the equity method to account for a subsidiary. As discussed in Chapter 1, the parent accrues income when earned by the subsidiary and dividend receipts are recorded as reductions in the investment account. The effects of excess fair-value amortizations or any intra-entity transactions also are reflected within the parent's financial records. The equity method provides the parent with accurate information concerning the subsidiary's impact on consolidated totals; however, it is usually somewhat complicated to apply.
3. The initial value method and the partial equity method are two alternatives to the equity method. The initial value method recognizes only the subsidiary's dividends as income while the asset balance remains at the acquisition-date fair value. This approach is simple and provides a measure of cash flows between the two companies. Under the partial equity method, the parent accrues the subsidiary's income as earned but does not record adjustments that might be required by excess fair-value amortizations or intra-entity transfers. The partial equity method is easier to apply than the equity method, and, in many cases, the parent's income is a reasonable approximation of the consolidated total.
4. For a consolidation in any subsequent period, all reciprocal balances must be eliminated. Thus, the subsidiary's equity accounts, the parent's investment balance, intra-entity income, dividends, and liabilities are removed. In addition, the remaining unamortized portions of the fair-value allocations are recognized along with excess amortization expenses for the period. If the equity method has not been applied, the parent's beginning Retained Earnings account also must be adjusted for any previous income or excess amortizations that have not yet been recorded.
5. For each subsidiary acquisition, the parent must assign the acquired assets and liabilities (including goodwill) to individual reporting units of its combined operations. The reporting units should be at the level of operating segment or lower and must provide the basis for future assessments of fair value. Any value assigned to goodwill is not amortized but instead is tested annually for impairment. Firms have the option to perform a qualitative assessment to evaluate whether a reporting unit's fair value more likely than not exceeds its carrying amount. If the assessment shows excess fair value over carrying amount for the reporting unit, a firm can forgo further testing. Otherwise, a two-step test is performed. First, if the fair value of any of the consolidated entity's reporting units falls below the carrying amount, then the implied value of the associated goodwill must be recomputed. Second, the recomputed implied value of goodwill is compared to its carrying amount. An impairment loss must then be recognized if the carrying amount of goodwill exceeds its implied value.
6. The acquisition-date fair value assigned to a subsidiary can be based, at least in part, on the fair value of any contingent consideration. For contingent obligations that meet the definition of a liability, the obligation is adjusted for changes in fair value over time with corresponding recognition of gains or losses from the revaluation. For contingent obligations classified as equity, no remeasurement to fair value takes place. In either case the initial value recognized in the combination does not change regardless of whether the contingency is eventually paid or not.
7. Push-down accounting is the adjustment of the subsidiary's account balances to recognize allocations and goodwill stemming from the parent's acquisition. Subsequent amortization of these figures also is recorded by the subsidiary as an expense. At this time, push-down accounting is required by the SEC for the separate statements of the subsidiary only when no substantial outside ownership exists.

Comprehensive Illustration

Problem

(*Estimated Time: 40 to 65 Minutes*) On January 1, 2011, Top Company acquired all of Bottom Company's outstanding common stock for $842,000 in cash. As of that date, one of Bottom's buildings with a 12-year remaining life was undervalued on its financial records by $72,000. Equipment with a 10-year life was undervalued, but only by $10,000. The book values of all of Bottom's other assets and liabilities were equal to their fair values at that time except for an unrecorded licensing agreement with an assessed value of $40,000 and a 20-year remaining useful life. Bottom's book value at the acquisition date was $720,000.

During 2011, Bottom reported net income of $100,000 and paid $30,000 in dividends. Earnings were $120,000 in 2012 with $20,000 in dividends distributed by the subsidiary. As of December 31, 2013, the companies reported the following selected balances, which include all revenues and expenses for the year:

	Top Company December 31, 2013		Bottom Company December 31, 2013	
	Debit	Credit	Debit	Credit
Buildings	$1,540,000		$460,000	
Cash and receivables	50,000		90,000	
Common stock		$ 900,000		$400,000
Dividends paid	70,000		10,000	
Equipment	280,000		200,000	
Cost of goods sold	500,000		120,000	
Depreciation expense	100,000		60,000	
Inventory	280,000		260,000	
Land	330,000		250,000	
Liabilities		480,000		260,000
Retained earnings, 1/1/13		1,360,000		490,000
Revenues		900,000		300,000

Required

a. If Top applies the equity method, what is its investment account balance as of December 31, 2013?

b. If Top applies the initial value method, what is its investment account balance as of December 31, 2013?

c. Regardless of the accounting method in use by Top, what are the consolidated totals as of December 31, 2013, for each of the following accounts?

Buildings	Revenues
Equipment	Net Income
Land	Investment in Bottom
Depreciation Expense	Dividends Paid
Amortization Expense	Cost of Goods Sold

d. Prepare the worksheet entries required on December 31, 2013, to consolidate the financial records of these two companies. Assume that Top applied the equity method to its investment account.

e. How would the worksheet entries in requirement *(d)* be altered if Top has used the initial value method?

Solution

a. To determine the investment balances under the equity method, four items must be determined: the initial value assigned, the income accrual, dividend payments, and amortization of excess acquisition-date fair value over book value. Although the first three are indicated in the problem, amortizations must be calculated separately.

An allocation of Bottom's acquisition-date fair values as well as the related amortization expense follows.

Fair value of consideration transferred by Top Company	$ 842,000
Book value of Bottom Company, 1/1/11	(720,000)
Excess fair value over book value	$ 122,000

Adjustments to specific accounts based on fair values:

		Life (years)	Annual Amortization
Buildings	$ 72,000	12	$6,000
Equipment	10,000	10	1,000
Licensing agreement	40,000	20	2,000
Totals	$122,000		$9,000

Thus, if Top adopts the equity method to account for this subsidiary, the Investment in Bottom account shows a December 31, 2013, balance of $1,095,000, computed as follows:

Initial value (fair value of consideration transferred by Top)		$ 842,000
Bottom Company's 2011–2012 increase in book value (income less dividends)		170,000
Excess amortizations for 2011–2012 ($9,000 per year for two years)		(18,000)
Current year recognition (2013):		
Equity income accrual (Bottom's revenues less its expenses)	$120,000	
Excess amortization expenses	(9,000)	
Dividend from Bottom	(10,000)	101,000
Investment in Bottom Company, 12/31/13		$1,095,000

The $120,000 income accrual and the $9,000 excess amortization expenses indicate that an Equity in Subsidiary Earnings balance of $111,000 appears in Top's income statement for the current period.

b. If Top Company applies the initial value method, the Investment in Bottom Company account permanently retains its original $842,000 balance, and the parent recognizes only the intra-entity dividend of $10,000 as income in 2013.

c.
- The consolidated Buildings account as of December 31, 2013, has a balance of $2,054,000. Although the two book value figures total only $2 million, a $72,000 allocation was made to this account based on fair value at the date of acquisition. Because this amount is being depreciated at the rate of $6,000 per year, the original allocation will have been reduced by $18,000 by the end of 2013, leaving only a $54,000 increase.
- On December 31, 2013, the consolidated Equipment account amounts to $487,000. The book values found in the financial records of Top and Bottom provide a total of $480,000. Once again, the allocation ($10,000) established by the acquisition-date fair value must be included in the consolidated balance after being adjusted for three years of depreciation ($1,000 × 3 years, or $3,000).
- Land has a consolidated total of $580,000. Because the book value and fair value of Bottom's land were in agreement at the date of acquisition, no additional allocation was made to this account. Thus, the book values are simply added together to derive a consolidated figure.
- *Cost of goods sold* = $620,000. The cost of goods sold of the parent and subsidiary are added together.
- *Depreciation expense* = $167,000. The depreciation expenses of the parent and subsidiary are added together along with the $6,000 additional building depreciation and the $1,000 additional equipment depreciation as presented in the fair-value allocation schedule.
- *Amortization expense* = $2,000. An additional expense of $2,000 is recognized from the amortization of the licensing agreement acquired in the business combination.
- The Revenues account appears as $1.2 million in the consolidated income statement. None of the worksheet entries in this example affects the individual balances of either company. Consolidation results merely from the addition of the two book values.
- Net income for this business combination is $411,000: consolidated expenses of $789,000 subtracted from revenues of $1.2 million.

- The parent's Investment in Bottom account is removed entirely on the worksheet so that no balance is reported. For consolidation purposes, this account is always eliminated so that the individual assets and liabilities of the subsidiary can be included.
- Dividends paid by the combination should be reported as $70,000, the amount Top distributed. Because Bottom's dividend payments are entirely intra-entity, they are deleted in arriving at consolidated figures.

d. Consolidation Entries Assuming Equity Method Used by Parent

Entry S

Common Stock (Bottom Company)	400,000	
Retained Earnings, 1/1/13 (Bottom Company)	490,000	
Investment in Bottom Company		890,000

Elimination of subsidiary's beginning stockholders' equity accounts against book value portion of investment account.

Entry A

Buildings	60,000	
Equipment	8,000	
Licensing Agreement	36,000	
Investment in Bottom Company		104,000

To recognize fair-value allocations to the subsidiary's assets in excess of book value. Balances represent original allocations less two years of amortization for the 2011–2013 period.

Entry I

Equity in Subsidiary Earnings	111,000	
Investment in Bottom Company		111,000

To eliminate parent's equity income accrual, balance is computed in requirement (*a*).

Entry D

Investment in Bottom	10,000	
Dividends Paid		10,000

To eliminate intra-entity dividend payment made by the subsidiary to the parent (and recorded as a reduction in the investment account because the equity method is in use).

Entry E

Depreciation Expense	7,000	
Amortization Expense	2,000	
Equipment		1,000
Buildings		6,000
Licensing Agreement		2,000

To recognize excess fair-value depreciation and amortization for 2013.

e. If Top utilizes the initial value method rather than the equity method, three changes are required in the development of consolidation entries:

(1) An Entry ***C** is required to update the parent's beginning Retained Earnings account as if the equity method had been applied. Both an income accrual as well as excess amortizations for the prior two years must be recognized because these balances were not recorded by the parent.

Entry *C

Investment in Bottom Company	152,000	
Retained Earnings, 1/1/13 (Top Company)		152,000
To convert to the equity method by accruing the net effect of the subsidiary's operations (income less dividends) for the prior two years ($170,000) along with excess amortization expenses ($18,000) for this same period.		

(2) An alteration is needed in Entry **I** because, under the initial value method, only dividend payments are recorded by the parent as income.

Entry I

Dividend Income	10,000	
Dividends Paid.		10,000
To eliminate intra-entity dividend payments recorded by parent as income.		

(3) Finally, because the intra-entity dividends have been eliminated in Entry **I**, no separate Entry **D** is needed.

Questions

1. CCES Corporation acquires a controlling interest in Schmaling, Inc. CCES may utilize any one of three methods to internally account for this investment. Describe each of these methods, and indicate their advantages and disadvantages.
2. Maguire Company obtains 100 percent control over Williams Company. Several years after the takeover, consolidated financial statements are being produced. For each of the following accounts, briefly describe the values that should be included in consolidated totals.
   a. Equipment.
   b. Investment in Williams Company.
   c. Dividends Paid.
   d. Goodwill.
   e. Revenues.
   f. Expenses.
   g. Common Stock.
   h. Net Income.
3. When a parent company uses the equity method to account for an investment in a subsidiary, why do both the parent's Net Income and Retained Earnings account balances agree with the consolidated totals?
4. When a parent company uses the equity method to account for investment in a subsidiary, the amortization expense entry recorded during the year is eliminated on a consolidation worksheet as a component of Entry **I**. What is the necessity of removing this amortization?
5. When a parent company applies the initial value method or the partial equity method to an investment, a worksheet adjustment must be made to the parent's beginning Retained Earnings account (Entry ***C**) in every period after the year of acquisition. What is the necessity for this entry? Why is no similar entry found when the parent utilizes the equity method?
6. Several years ago, Jenkins Company acquired a controlling interest in Lambert Company. Lambert recently borrowed $100,000 from Jenkins. In consolidating the financial records of these two companies, how will this debt be handled?
7. Benns adopts the equity method for its 100 percent investment in Waters. At the end of six years, Benns reports an investment in Waters of $920,000. What figures constitute this balance?
8. One company acquired another in a transaction in which $100,000 of the acquisition price is assigned to goodwill. Several years later, a worksheet is being produced to consolidate these two companies. How is the reported value of the goodwill determined at this date?
9. When should a parent consider recognizing an impairment loss for goodwill associated with a subsidiary? How should the loss be reported in the financial statements?
10. Reimers Company acquires Rollins Corporation on January 1, 2012. As part of the agreement, the parent states that an additional $100,000 payment to the former owners of Rollins will be made in 2014, if Rollins achieves certain income thresholds during the first two years following

the acquisition. How should Reimers account for this contingency in its 2012 consolidated financial statements?

11. When is the use of push-down accounting required, and what is the rationale for its application?
12. How are the individual financial records of both the parent and the subsidiary affected when push-down accounting is being applied?

Problems

LO2

1. A company acquires a subsidiary and will prepare consolidated financial statements for external reporting purposes. For internal reporting purposes, the company has decided to apply the initial value method. Why might the company have made this decision?
   a. It is a relatively easy method to apply.
   b. Operating results appearing on the parent's financial records reflect consolidated totals.
   c. GAAP now requires the use of this particular method for internal reporting purposes.
   d. Consolidation is not required when the parent uses the initial value method.

LO2

2. A company acquires a subsidiary and will prepare consolidated financial statements for external reporting purposes. For internal reporting purposes, the company has decided to apply the equity method. Why might the company have made this decision?
   a. It is a relatively easy method to apply.
   b. Operating results appearing on the parent's financial records reflect consolidated totals.
   c. GAAP now requires the use of this particular method for internal reporting purposes.
   d. Consolidation is not required when the parent uses the equity method.

LO5

3. When should a consolidated entity recognize a goodwill impairment loss?
   a. If both the fair value of a reporting unit and its associated implied goodwill fall below their respective carrying amounts.
   b. Whenever the entity's fair value declines significantly.
   c. If a reporting unit's fair value falls below its original acquisition price.
   d. Annually on a systematic and rational basis.

LO1

4. Willkom Corporation bought 100 percent of Szabo, Inc., on January 1, 2011. On that date, Willkom's equipment (10-year life) has a book value of $300,000 but a fair value of $400,000. Szabo has equipment (10-year life) with a book value of $200,000 but a fair value of $300,000. Willkom uses the equity method to record its investment in Szabo. On December 31, 2013, Willkom has equipment with a book value of $210,000 but a fair value of $330,000. Szabo has equipment with a book value of $140,000 but a fair value of $270,000. What is the consolidated balance for the Equipment account as of December 31, 2013?
   a. $600,000.
   b. $490,000.
   c. $480,000.
   d. $420,000.

LO3

5. How would the answer to problem (4) have been affected if the parent had applied the initial value method rather than the equity method?
   a. No effect: The method the parent uses is for internal reporting purposes only and has no impact on consolidated totals.
   b. The consolidated Equipment account would have a higher reported balance.
   c. The consolidated Equipment account would have a lower reported balance.
   d. The balance in the consolidated Equipment account cannot be determined for the initial value method using the information given.

LO5

6. Goodwill recognized in a business combination must be allocated among a firm's identified reporting units. If the fair value of a particular reporting unit with recognized goodwill falls below its carrying amount, which of the following is true?
   a. No goodwill impairment loss is recognized unless the implied value for goodwill exceeds its carrying amount.
   b. A goodwill impairment loss is recognized if the carrying amount for goodwill exceeds its implied value.
   c. A goodwill impairment loss is recognized for the difference between the reporting unit's fair value and carrying amount.

d. The reporting unit reduces the values assigned to its long-term assets (including any unrecognized intangibles) to reflect its fair value.

LO5

7. If no legal, regulatory, contractual, competitive, economic, or other factors limit the life of an intangible asset, the asset's assigned value is allocated to expense over which of the following?
   a. 20 years.
   b. 20 years with an annual impairment review.
   c. Infinitely.
   d. Indefinitely (no amortization) with an annual impairment review until its life becomes finite.

LO7

8. Dosmann, Inc., bought all outstanding shares of Lizzi Corporation on January 1, 2011, for $700,000 in cash. This portion of the consideration transferred results in a fair-value allocation of $35,000 to equipment and goodwill of $88,000. At the acquisition date, Dosmann also agrees to pay Lizzi's previous owners an additional $110,000 on January 1, 2013, if Lizzi earns a 10 percent return on the fair value of its assets in 2011 and 2012. Lizzi's profits exceed this threshold in both years. Which of the following is true?
   a. The additional $110,000 payment is a reduction in consolidated retained earnings.
   b. The fair value of the expected contingent payment increases goodwill at the acquisition date.
   c. Consolidated goodwill as of January 1, 2013, increases by $110,000.
   d. The $110,000 is recorded as an expense in 2013.

LO4a

Problems 9, 10, and 11 relate to the following:

On January 1, 2011, Phoenix Co. acquired 100 percent of the outstanding voting shares of Sedona Inc. for $600,000 cash. At January 1, 2011, Sedona's net assets had a total carrying amount of $420,000. Equipment (eight-year remaining life) was undervalued on Sedona's financial records by $80,000. Any remaining excess fair over book value was attributed to a customer list developed by Sedona (four-year remaining life), but not recorded on its books. Phoenix applies the equity method to account for its investment in Sedona. Each year since the acquisition, Sedona has paid a $20,000 dividend. Sedona recorded income of $70,000 in 2011 and $80,000 in 2012.

Selected account balances from the two companies' individual records were as follows:

	Phoenix	Sedona
2013 Revenues	$498,000	$285,000
2013 Expenses	350,000	195,000
2013 Income from Sedona	55,000	
Retained earnings 12/31/13	250,000	175,000

9. What is consolidated net income for Phoenix and Sedona for 2013?
   a. $148,000
   b. $203,000
   c. $228,000
   d. $238,000
10. What is Phoenix's consolidated retained earnings balance at December 31, 2013?
   a. $250,000
   b. $290,000
   c. $330,000
   d. $360,000
11. On its December 31, 2013, consolidated balance sheet, what amount should Phoenix report for Sedona's customer list?
   a. $10,000
   b. $20,000
   c. $25,000
   d. $50,000

LO7

12. Kaplan Corporation acquired Star, Inc., on January 1, 2012, by issuing 13,000 shares of common stock with a $10 per share par value and a $23 market value. This transaction resulted in recognizing $62,000 of goodwill. Kaplan also agreed to compensate Star's former owners for

any difference if Kaplan's stock is worth less than $23 on January 1, 2013. On January 1, 2013, Kaplan issues an additional 3,000 shares to Star's former owners to honor the contingent consideration agreement. Which of the following is true?

a. The fair value of the number of shares issued for the contingency increases the Goodwill account at January 1, 2013.

b. The parent's additional paid-in capital from the contingent equity recorded at the acquisition date is reclassified as a regular common stock issue on January 1, 2013.

c. All of the subsidiary's asset and liability accounts must be revalued for consolidation purposes based on their fair values as of January 1, 2013.

d. The additional shares are assumed to have been issued on January 1, 2012, so that a retrospective adjustment is required.

LO8

13. What is push-down accounting?

a. A requirement that a subsidiary must use the same accounting principles as a parent company.

b. Inventory transfers made from a parent company to a subsidiary.

c. A subsidiary's recording of the fair-value allocations as well as subsequent amortization.

d. The adjustments required for consolidation when a parent has applied the equity method of accounting for internal reporting purposes.

LO8

14. Treadway Corporation acquires Hooker, Inc. The parent pays more for it than the fair value of the subsidiary's net assets. On the acquisition date, Treadway has equipment with a book value of $420,000 and a fair value of $530,000. Hooker has equipment with a book value of $330,000 and a fair value of $390,000. Hooker is going to use push-down accounting. Immediately after the acquisition, what amounts in the Equipment account appear on Hooker's separate balance sheet and on the consolidated balance sheet?

a. $330,000 and $750,000.

b. $330,000 and $860,000.

c. $390,000 and $810,000.

d. $390,000 and $920,000.

LO4

15. Herbert, Inc., acquired all of Rambis Company's outstanding stock on January 1, 2012, for $574,000 in cash. Annual excess amortization of $12,000 results from this transaction. On the date of the takeover, Herbert reported retained earnings of $400,000, and Rambis reported a $200,000 balance. Herbert reported internal income of $40,000 in 2012 and $50,000 in 2013 and paid $10,000 in dividends each year. Rambis reported net income of $20,000 in 2012 and $30,000 in 2013 and paid $5,000 in dividends each year.

a. Assume that Herbert's internal income figures above do not include any income from the subsidiary.

- If the parent uses the equity method, what is the amount reported as consolidated retained earnings on December 31, 2013?
- Would the amount of consolidated retained earnings change if the parent had applied either the initial value or partial equity method for internal accounting purposes?

b. Under each of the following situations, what is the Investment in Rambis account balance on Herbert's books on January 1, 2013?

- The parent uses the equity method.
- The parent uses the partial equity method.
- The parent uses the initial value method.

c. Under each of the following situations, what is Entry ***C** on a 2013 consolidation worksheet?

- The parent uses the equity method.
- The parent uses the partial equity method.
- The parent uses the initial value method.

LO3, LO4

16. Haynes, Inc., obtained 100 percent of Turner Company's common stock on January 1, 2012, by issuing 9,000 shares of $10 par value common stock. Haynes's shares had a $15 per share fair value. On that date, Turner reported a net book value of $100,000. However, its equipment (with a five-year remaining life) was undervalued by $5,000 in the company's accounting records. Also, Turner had developed a customer list with an assessed value of $30,000, although

no value had been recorded on Turner's books. The customer list had an estimated remaining useful life of 10 years.

The following figures come from the individual accounting records of these two companies as of December 31, 2012:

	Haynes	Turner
Revenues	$(600,000)	$(230,000)
Expenses	440,000	120,000
Investment income	Not given	–0–
Dividends paid	80,000	50,000

The following figures come from the individual accounting records of these two companies as of December 31, 2013:

	Haynes	Turner
Revenues	$(700,000)	$(280,000)
Expenses	460,000	150,000
Investment income	Not given	–0–
Dividends paid	90,000	40,000
Equipment	500,000	300,000

a. What balance does Haynes's Investment in Turner account show on December 31, 2013, when the equity method is applied?

b. What is the consolidated net income for the year ending December 31, 2013?

c. What is the consolidated equipment balance as of December 31, 2013? How would this answer be affected by the investment method applied by the parent?

d. If Haynes has applied the initial value method to account for its investment, what adjustment is needed to the beginning of the Retained Earnings on a December 31, 2013, consolidation worksheet? How would this answer change if the partial equity method had been in use? How would this answer change if the equity method had been in use?

LO6

17. Francisco Inc. acquired 100 percent of the voting shares of Beltran Company on January 1, 2012. In exchange, Francisco paid $450,000 in cash and issued 104,000 shares of its own $1 par value common stock. On this date, Francisco's stock had a fair value of $12 per share. The combination is a statutory merger with Beltran subsequently dissolved as a legal corporation. Beltran's assets and liabilities are assigned to a new reporting unit.

The following reports the fair values for the Beltran reporting unit for January 1, 2012, and December 31, 2013, along with their respective book values on December 31, 2013.

Beltran Reporting Unit	Fair Values 1/1/12	Fair Values 12/31/13	Book Values 12/31/13
Cash	$ 75,000	$ 50,000	$ 50,000
Receivables	193,000	225,000	225,000
Inventory	281,000	305,000	300,000
Patents	525,000	600,000	500,000
Customer relationships	500,000	480,000	450,000
Equipment (net)	295,000	240,000	235,000
Goodwill	?	?	400,000
Accounts payable	(121,000)	(175,000)	(175,000)
Long-term liabilities	(450,000)	(400,000)	(400,000)

a. Prepare Francisco's journal entry to record the assets acquired and the liabilities assumed in the Beltran merger on January 1, 2012.

b. On December 31, 2013, Francisco opts to forego any goodwill impairment qualitative assessment and estimates that the total fair value of the entire Beltran reporting unit is $1,425,000. What amount of goodwill impairment, if any, should Francisco recognize on its 2013 income statement?

LO6

18. Acme Co., a consolidated enterprise, conducted an impairment review for each of its reporting units. In its qualitative assessment, one particular reporting unit, Martel, emerged as a candidate for possible goodwill impairment. Martel has recognized net assets of $780, including goodwill of $500. Martel's fair value is assessed at $650 and includes two internally developed unrecognized intangible assets (a patent and a customer list with fair values of $150 and $50, respectively). The following table summarizes current financial information for the Martel reporting unit:

	Carrying Amounts	Fair Values
Tangible assets, net	$ 80	$110
Recognized intangible assets, net	200	230
Goodwill	500	?
Unrecognized intangible assets	–0–	200
Total	$780	$650

a. Show the two quantitative steps to determine the amount of any goodwill impairment for Acme's Martel reporting unit.

b. After recognition of any goodwill impairment loss, what are the reported book values for the following assets of Acme's reporting unit Martel?
- Tangible assets, net.
- Goodwill.
- Customer list.
- Patent.

LO6

19. Destin Company recently acquired several businesses and recognized goodwill in each acquisition. Destin has allocated the resulting goodwill to its three reporting units: Sand Dollar, Salty Dog, and Baytowne. Destin performs a quantitative goodwill impairment review annually.

In its current year assessment of goodwill, Destin provides the following individual asset and liability values for each reporting unit:

	Carrying Values	Fair Values
Sand Dollar		
Tangible assets	$180,000	$190,000
Trademark	170,000	150,000
Customer list	90,000	100,000
Goodwill	120,000	?
Liabilities	(30,000)	(30,000)
Salty Dog		
Tangible assets	$200,000	$200,000
Unpatented technology	170,000	125,000
Licenses	90,000	100,000
Goodwill	150,000	?
Baytowne		
Tangible assets	140,000	150,000
Unpatented technology	–0–	100,000
Copyrights	50,000	80,000
Goodwill	90,000	?

The fair values for each reporting unit (including goodwill) are $510,000 for Sand Dollar, $580,000 for Salty Dog, and $560,000 for Baytowne. To date, Destin has reported no goodwill impairments.

a. Which of Destin's reporting units require both steps to test for goodwill impairment?

b. How much goodwill impairment should Destin report this year?

c. What changes to the valuations of Destin's tangible assets and identified intangible assets should be reported based on the goodwill impairment tests?

Problems 20 through 22 should be viewed as independent situations. They are based on the following data:

Chapman Company obtains 100 percent of Abernethy Company's stock on January 1, 2012. As of that date, Abernethy has the following trial balance:

	Debit	Credit
Accounts payable		$ 50,000
Accounts receivable	$ 40,000	
Additional paid-in capital		50,000
Buildings (net) (4-year life)	120,000	
Cash and short-term investments	60,000	
Common stock		250,000
Equipment (net) (5-year life)	200,000	
Inventory	90,000	
Land	80,000	
Long-term liabilities (mature 12/31/15)		150,000
Retained earnings, 1/1/12		100,000
Supplies	10,000	
Totals	$600,000	$600,000

During 2012, Abernethy reported income of $80,000 while paying dividends of $10,000. During 2013, Abernethy reported income of $110,000 while paying dividends of $30,000.

LO4a

20. Assume that Chapman Company acquired Abernethy's common stock for $490,000 in cash. As of January 1, 2012, Abernethy's land had a fair value of $90,000, its buildings were valued at $160,000, and its equipment was appraised at $180,000. Chapman uses the equity method for this investment. Prepare consolidation worksheet entries for December 31, 2012, and December 31, 2013.

LO4b

21. Assume that Chapman Company acquired Abernethy's common stock for $500,000 in cash. Assume that the equipment and long-term liabilities had fair values of $220,000 and $120,000, respectively, on the acquisition date. Chapman uses the initial value method to account for its investment. Prepare consolidation worksheet entries for December 31, 2012, and December 31, 2013.

LO4c

22. Assume that Chapman Company acquired Abernethy's common stock by paying $520,000 in cash. All of Abernethy's accounts are estimated to have a fair value approximately equal to present book values. Chapman uses the partial equity method to account for its investment. Prepare the consolidation worksheet entries for December 31, 2012, and December 31, 2013.

LO4a, LO4b

23. Adams, Inc., acquires Clay Corporation on January 1, 2012, in exchange for $510,000 cash. Immediately after the acquisition, the two companies have the following account balances. Clay's equipment (with a five-year life) is actually worth $440,000. Credit balances are indicated by parentheses.

	Adams	Clay
Current assets	$ 300,000	$ 220,000
Investment in Clay	510,000	–0–
Equipment	600,000	390,000
Liabilities	(200,000)	(160,000)
Common stock	(350,000)	(150,000)
Retained earnings, 1/1/12	(860,000)	(300,000)

In 2012, Clay earns a net income of $55,000 and pays a $5,000 cash dividend. In 2012, Adams reports income from its own operations (exclusive of any income from Clay) of $125,000 and declares no dividends. At the end of 2013, selected account balances for the two companies are as follows:

	Adams	Clay
Revenues	$(400,000)	$(240,000)
Expenses	290,000	180,000
Investment income	Not given	–0–
Retained earnings, 1/1/13	Not given	(350,000)

(continued)

	Adams	Clay
Dividends declared.	–0–	8,000
Common stock.	(350,000)	(150,000)
Current assets	580,000	262,000
Investment in Clay	Not given	–0–
Equipment	520,000	420,000
Liabilities	(152,000)	(130,000)

a. What are the December 31, 2013, Investment Income and Investment in Clay account balances assuming Adams uses the:

1. Equity method.
2. Initial value method.

b. How does the parent's internal investment accounting method choice affect the amount reported for expenses in its December 31, 2013, consolidated income statement?

c. How does the parent's internal investment accounting method choice affect the amount reported for equipment in its December 31, 2013, consolidated balance sheet?

d. What is Adams's January 1, 2013, Retained Earnings account balance assuming Adams accounts for its investment in Clay using the:

1. Equity value method.
2. Initial value method.

e. What worksheet adjustment to Adams's January 1, 2013, Retained Earnings account balance is required if Adams accounts for its investment in Clay using the initial value method?

f. Prepare the worksheet entry to eliminate Clay's stockholders' equity.

g. What is consolidated net income for 2013?

LO1

24. Following are selected account balances from Penske Company and Stanza Corporation as of December 31, 2013:

	Penske	Stanza
Revenues.	$(700,000)	$(400,000)
Cost of goods sold	250,000	100,000
Depreciation expense	150,000	200,000
Investment income	Not given	–0–
Dividends paid.	80,000	60,000
Retained earnings, 1/1/13	(600,000)	(200,000)
Current assets	400,000	500,000
Copyrights	900,000	400,000
Royalty agreements.	600,000	1,000,000
Investment in Stanza	Not given	–0–
Liabilities	(500,000)	(1,380,000)
Common stock	(600,000) ($20 par)	(200,000) ($10 par)
Additional paid-in capital.	(150,000)	(80,000)

On January 1, 2013, Penske acquired all of Stanza's outstanding stock for $680,000 fair value in cash and common stock. Penske also paid $10,000 in stock issuance costs. At the date of acquisition copyrights (with a six-year remaining life) have a $440,000 book value but a fair value of $560,000.

a. As of December 31, 2013, what is the consolidated copyrights balance?

b. For the year ending December 31, 2013, what is consolidated net income?

c. As of December 31, 2013, what is the consolidated retained earnings balance?

d. As of December 31, 2013, what is the consolidated balance to be reported for goodwill?

LO2, LO3, LO4

25. Foxx Corporation acquired all of Greenburg Company's outstanding stock on January 1, 2011, for $600,000 cash. Greenburg's accounting records showed net assets on that date of $470,000, although equipment with a 10-year life was undervalued on the records by $90,000. Any recognized goodwill is considered to have an indefinite life.

Greenburg reports net income in 2011 of $90,000 and $100,000 in 2012. The subsidiary paid dividends of $20,000 in each of these two years.

Financial figures for the year ending December 31, 2013, follow. Credit balances are indicated by parentheses.

	Foxx	Greenburg
Revenues	$ (800,000)	$ (600,000)
Cost of goods sold	100,000	150,000
Depreciation expense	300,000	350,000
Investment income	(20,000)	–0–
Net income	$ (420,000)	$ (100,000)
Retained earnings, 1/1/13	$(1,100,000)	$ (320,000)
Net income	(420,000)	(100,000)
Dividends paid	120,000	20,000
Retained earnings, 12/31/13	$(1,400,000)	$ (400,000)
Current assets	$ 300,000	$ 100,000
Investment in subsidiary	600,000	–0–
Equipment (net)	900,000	600,000
Buildings (net)	800,000	400,000
Land	600,000	100,000
Total assets	$ 3,200,000	$ 1,200,000
Liabilities	$ (900,000)	$ (500,000)
Common stock	(900,000)	(300,000)
Retained earnings	(1,400,000)	(400,000)
Total liabilities and equity	$(3,200,000)	$(1,200,000)

a. Determine the December 31, 2013, consolidated balance for each of the following accounts:

Depreciation Expense	Buildings
Dividends Paid	Goodwill
Revenues	Common Stock
Equipment	

b. How does the parent's choice of an accounting method for its investment affect the balances computed in requirement (*a*)?

c. Which method of accounting for this subsidiary is the parent actually using for internal reporting purposes?

d. If the parent company had used a different method of accounting for this investment, how could that method have been identified?

e. What would be Foxx's balance for retained earnings as of January 1, 2013, if each of the following methods had been in use?

Initial value method

Partial equity method

Equity method

LO1, LO4a

26. Patrick Corporation acquired 100 percent of O'Brien Company's outstanding common stock on January 1, for $550,000 in cash. O'Brien reported net assets with a carrying amount of $350,000 at that time. Some of O'Brien's assets either were unrecorded (having been internally developed) or had fair values that differed from book values as follows:

	Book Values	Fair Values
Trademarks (indefinite life)	$ 60,000	$160,000
Customer relationships (5-year life)	–0–	75,000
Equipment (10-year life)	342,000	312,000

Any goodwill is considered to have an indefinite life with no impairment charges during the year.

Following are financial statements at the end of the first year for these two companies prepared from their separately maintained accounting systems. Credit balances are indicated by parentheses.

	Patrick	O'Brien
Revenues	$(1,125,000)	$(520,000)
Cost of goods sold	300,000	228,000
Depreciation expense	75,000	70,000
Amortization expense	25,000	–0–
Income from O'Brien	(210,000)	–0–
Net Income	$ (935,000)	$(222,000)
Retained earnings 1/1	(700,000)	(250,000)
Net Income	(935,000)	(222,000)
Dividends paid	142,000	80,000
Retained earnings 12/31	$(1,493,000)	$(392,000)
Cash	$ 185,000	$ 105,000
Receivables	225,000	56,000
Inventory	175,000	135,000
Investment in O'Brien	680,000	–0–
Trademarks	474,000	60,000
Customer relationships	–0–	–0–
Equipment (net)	925,000	272,000
Goodwill	–0–	–0–
Total assets	$ 2,664,000	$ 628,000
Liabilities	(771,000)	(136,000)
Common stock	(400,000)	(100,000)
Retained earnings 12/31	(1,493,000)	(392,000)
Total liabilities and equity	$(2,664,000)	$(628,000)

a. Show how Patrick computed the $210,000 Income of O'Brien balance. Discuss how you determined which accounting method Patrick uses for its investment in O'Brien.

b. Without preparing a worksheet or consolidation entries, determine and explain the totals to be reported for this business combination for the year ending December 31.

c. Verify the totals determined in part (*b*) by producing a consolidation worksheet for Patrick and O'Brien for the year ending December 31.

LO1, LO3, LO4a, LO4b

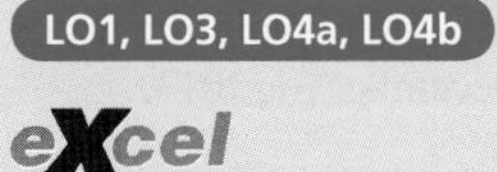

27. Following are separate financial statements of Michael Company and Aaron Company as of December 31, 2013 (credit balances indicated by parentheses). Michael acquired all of Aaron's outstanding voting stock on January 1, 2009, by issuing 20,000 shares of its own $1 par common stock. On the acquisition date, Michael Company's stock actively traded at $23.50 per share.

	Michael Company 12/31/13	Aaron Company 12/31/13
Revenues	$ (610,000)	$ (370,000)
Cost of goods sold	270,000	140,000
Amortization expense	115,000	80,000
Dividend income	(5,000)	–0–
Net income	$ (230,000)	$ (150,000)
Retained earnings, 1/1/13	$ (880,000)	$ (490,000)
Net income (above)	(230,000)	(150,000)
Dividends paid	90,000	5,000
Retained earnings, 12/31/13	$(1,020,000)	$ (635,000)
Cash	$ 110,000	$ 15,000
Receivables	380,000	220,000
Inventory	560,000	280,000
Investment in Aaron Company	470,000	–0–
Copyrights	460,000	340,000
Royalty agreements	920,000	380,000
Total assets	$ 2,900,000	$ 1,235,000

(continued)

	Michael Company 12/31/13	Aaron Company 12/31/13
Liabilities	$ (780,000)	$ (470,000)
Preferred stock	(300,000)	–0–
Common stock	(500,000)	(100,000)
Additional paid-in capital	(300,000)	(30,000)
Retained earnings, 12/31/13	(1,020,000)	(635,000)
Total liabilities and equity	$(2,900,000)	$(1,235,000)

On the date of acquisition, Aaron reported retained earnings of $230,000 and a total book value of $360,000. At that time, its royalty agreements were undervalued by $60,000. This intangible was assumed to have a six-year life with no residual value. Additionally, Aaron owned a trademark with a fair value of $50,000 and a 10-year remaining life that was not reflected on its books.

a. Using the preceding information, prepare a consolidation worksheet for these two companies as of December 31, 2013.

b. Assuming that Michael applied the equity method to this investment, what account balances would differ on the parent's individual financial statements?

c. Assuming that Michael applied the equity method to this investment, what changes would be necessary in the consolidation entries found on a December 31, 2013, worksheet?

d. Assuming that Michael applied the equity method to this investment, what changes would be created in the consolidated figures to be reported by this combination?

LO1, LO4, LO6

eXcel

28. Giant acquired all of Small's common stock on January 1, 2009. Over the next few years, Giant applied the equity method to the recording of this investment. At the date of the original acquisition, $90,000 of the fair-value price was attributed to undervalued land while $50,000 was assigned to equipment having a 10-year life. The remaining $60,000 unallocated portion of the acquisition-date excess fair value over book value was viewed as goodwill.

Following are individual financial statements for the year ending December 31, 2013. On that date, Small owes Giant $10,000. Credits are indicated by parentheses.

a. How was the $135,000 Equity in Income of Small balance computed?

b. Without preparing a worksheet or consolidation entries, determine and explain the totals to be reported by this business combination for the year ending December 31, 2013.

	Giant	Small
Revenues	$(1,175,000)	$ (360,000)
Cost of goods sold	550,000	90,000
Depreciation expense	172,000	130,000
Equity in income of Small	(135,000)	–0–
Net income	$ (588,000)	$ (140,000)
Retained earnings, 1/1/13	$(1,417,000)	$ (620,000)
Net income (above)	(588,000)	(140,000)
Dividends paid	310,000	110,000
Retained earnings, 12/31/13	$(1,695,000)	$ (650,000)
Current assets	$ 398,000	$ 318,000
Investment in Small	995,000	–0–
Land	440,000	165,000
Buildings (net)	304,000	419,000
Equipment (net)	648,000	286,000
Goodwill	–0–	–0–
Total assets	$ 2,785,000	$ 1,188,000
Liabilities	$ (840,000)	$ (368,000)
Common stock	(250,000)	(170,000)
Retained earnings (above)	(1,695,000)	(650,000)
Total liabilities and equity	$(2,785,000)	$(1,188,000)

c. Verify the figures determined in part (*b*) by producing a consolidation worksheet for Giant and Small for the year ending December 31, 2013.

d. If Giant determined that the entire amount of goodwill from its investment in Small was impaired in 2013, how would the parent's accounts reflect the impairment loss? How would the worksheet process change? What impact does an impairment loss have on consolidated financial statements?

LO1, LO3, LO4a, LO4b

29. On January 1, 2012, Pinnacle Corporation exchanged $3,200,000 cash for 100 percent of the outstanding voting stock of Strata Corporation. On the acquisition date, Strata had the following balance sheet:

Cash	$ 122,000	Accounts payable	$ 375,000
Accounts receivable	283,000	Long-term debt	2,655,000
Inventory	350,000	Common stock	1,500,000
Buildings (net)	1,875,000	Retained earnings	1,100,000
Licensing agreements	3,000,000		$5,630,000
	$5,630,000		

Pinnacle prepared the following fair-value allocation:

Fair value of Strata (consideration transferred)		$3,200,000
Carrying amount acquired		2,600,000
Excess fair value		600,000
to buildings (undervalued)	300,000	
to licensing agreements (overvalued)	(100,000)	200,000
to goodwill (indefinite life)		$ 400,000

At the acquisition date, Strata's buildings had a 10-year remaining life and its licensing agreements were due to expire in 5 years. At December 31, 2013, Strata's accounts payable included an $85,000 current liability owed to Pinnacle. Strata Corporation continues its separate legal existence as a wholly owned subsidiary of Pinnacle with independent accounting records. Pinnacle employs the initial value method in its internal accounting for its investment in Strata.

The separate financial statements for the two companies for the year ending December 31, 2013, follow. Credit balances are indicated by parentheses.

	Pinnacle	Strata
Sales	$ (7,000,000)	$(3,000,000)
Cost of goods sold	4,650,000	1,700,000
Interest expense	255,000	160,000
Depreciation expense	585,000	350,000
Amortization expense		600,000
Dividend income	(50,000)	
Net income	$ (1,560,000)	$ (190,000)
Retained earnings 1/1/13	$ (5,000,000)	$(1,350,000)
Net income	(1,560,000)	(190,000)
Dividends paid	560,000	50,000
Retained earnings 12/31/13	$ (6,000,000)	$(1,490,000)
Cash	$ 433,000	$ 165,000
Accounts receivable	1,210,000	200,000
Inventory	1,235,000	1,500,000
Investment in Strata	3,200,000	
Buildings (net)	5,572,000	2,040,000
Licensing agreements		1,800,000
Goodwill	350,000	
Total assets	$12,000,000	$ 5,705,000

(*continued*)

	Pinnacle	Strata
Accounts payable	$ (300,000)	$ (715,000)
Long-term debt	(2,700,000)	(2,000,000)
Common stock	(3,000,000)	(1,500,000)
Retained earnings 12/31/13	(6,000,000)	(1,490,000)
Total liabilities and OE	$(12,000,000)	$(5,705,000)

a. Prepare a worksheet to consolidate the financial information for these two companies.

b. Compute the following amounts that would appear on Pinnacle's 2013 separate (nonconsolidated) financial records if Pinnacle's investment accounting was based on the equity method.

1. Subsidiary income
2. Retained earnings 1/1/13
3. Investment in Strata

c. What effect does the parent's internal investment accounting method have on its consolidated financial statements?

LO1, LO3, LO4

eXcel

30. Following are selected accounts for Mergaronite Company and Hill, Inc., as of December 31, 2013. Several of Mergaronite's accounts have been omitted. Credit balances are indicated by parentheses.

	Mergaronite	Hill
Revenues	$(600,000)	$(250,000)
Cost of goods sold	280,000	100,000
Depreciation expense	120,000	50,000
Investment income	Not given	NA
Retained earnings, 1/1/13	(900,000)	(600,000)
Dividends paid	130,000	40,000
Current assets	200,000	690,000
Land	300,000	90,000
Buildings (net)	500,000	140,000
Equipment (net)	200,000	250,000
Liabilities	(400,000)	(310,000)
Common stock	(300,000)	(40,000)
Additional paid-in capital	(50,000)	(160,000)

Assume that Mergaronite took over Hill on January 1, 2009, by issuing 7,000 shares of common stock having a par value of $10 per share but a fair value of $100 each. On January 1, 2009, Hill's land was undervalued by $20,000, its buildings were overvalued by $30,000, and equipment was undervalued by $60,000. The buildings had a 10-year life; the equipment had a 5-year life. A customer list with an appraised value of $100,000 was developed internally by Hill and was to be written off over a 20-year period.

a. Determine and explain the December 31, 2013, consolidated totals for the following accounts:

Revenues	Amortization Expense	Customer List
Cost of Goods Sold	Buildings	Common Stock
Depreciation Expense	Equipment	Additional Paid-In Capital

b. In requirement (*a*), why can the consolidated totals be determined without knowing which method the parent used to account for the subsidiary?

c. If the parent uses the equity method, what consolidation entries would be used on a 2013 worksheet?

LO3, LO4, LO6

31. On January 1, 2013, Peterson Corporation exchanged $1,090,000 fair-value consideration for all of the outstanding voting stock of Santiago, Inc. At the acquisition date, Santiago had a book value equal to $950,000. Santiago's individual assets and liabilities had fair values equal to their respective book values except for the patented technology account, which was undervalued by $240,000 with an estimated remaining life of six years. The Santiago acquisition was Peterson's only business combination for the year.

In case expected synergies did not materialize, Peterson Corporation wished to prepare for a potential future spin-off of Santiago, Inc. Therefore, Peterson had Santiago maintain its separate incorporation and independent accounting information system as elements of continuing value.

On December 31, 2013, each company submitted the following financial statements for consolidation.

	Peterson Corp.	Santiago, Inc.
Income Statement		
Revenues	$ (535,000)	$ (495,000)
Cost of goods sold	170,000	155,000
Gain on bargain purchase	(100,000)	–0–
Depreciation and amortization	125,000	140,000
Equity earnings from Santiago	(160,000)	–0–
Net income	$ (500,000)	$ (200,000)
Statement of Retained Earnings		
Retained earnings, 1/1	$(1,500,000)	$ (650,000)
Net income (above)	(500,000)	(200,000)
Dividends paid	200,000	50,000
Retained earnings, 12/31	$(1,800,000)	$ (800,000)
Balance Sheet		
Current assets	$ 190,000	$ 300,000
Investment in Santiago	1,300,000	–0–
Trademarks	100,000	200,000
Patented technology	300,000	400,000
Equipment	610,000	300,000
Total assets	$ 2,500,000	$ 1,200,000
Liabilities	$ (165,000)	$ (100,000)
Common stock	(535,000)	(300,000)
Retained earnings, 12/31	(1,800,000)	(800,000)
Total liabilities and equity	$(2,500,000)	$(1,200,000)

a. Show how Peterson determined the following account balances
- Gain on bargain purchase
- Earnings from Santiago
- Investment in Santiago

b. Prepare a December 31, 2013, consolidated worksheet for Peterson and Santiago.

LO4a, LO4b

32. Branson paid $465,000 cash for all of the outstanding common stock of Wolfpack, Inc., on January 1, 2012. On that date, the subsidiary had a book value of $340,000 (common stock of $200,000 and retained earnings of $140,000), although various unrecorded royalty agreements (10-year remaining life) were assessed at a $100,000 fair value. Any remaining excess fair value was considered goodwill.

In negotiating the acquisition price, Branson also promised to pay Wolfpack's former owners an additional $50,000 if Wolfpack's income exceeded $120,000 total over the first two years after the acquisition. At the acquisition date, Branson estimated the probability adjusted present value of this contingent consideration at $35,000. On December 31, 2012, based on Wolfpack's earnings to date, Branson increased the value of the contingency to $40,000.

During the subsequent two years, Wolfpack reported the following amounts for income and dividends:

	Net Income	Dividends Paid
2012	$65,000	$25,000
2013	75,000	35,000

In keeping with the original acquisition agreement, on December 31, 2013, Branson paid the additional $50,000 performance fee to Wolfpack's previous owners.

Prepare each of the following:

a. Branson's entry to record the acquisition of the shares of its Wolfpack subsidiary.

b. Branson's entries at the end of 2012 and 2013 to adjust its contingent performance obligation for changes in fair value and the December 31, 2013, payment.

c. Consolidation worksheet entries as of December 31, 2013, assuming that Branson has applied the equity method.

d. Consolidation worksheet entries as of December 31, 2013, assuming that Branson has applied the initial value method.

LO4, LO8

33. Palm Company acquired 100 percent of Storm Company's voting stock on January 1, 2009, by issuing 10,000 shares of its $10 par value common stock (having a fair value of $14 per share). As of that date, Storm had stockholders' equity totaling $105,000. Land shown on Storm's accounting records was undervalued by $10,000. Equipment (with a five-year life) was undervalued by $5,000. A secret formula developed by Storm was appraised at $20,000 with an estimated life of 20 years.

Following are the separate financial statements for the two companies for the year ending December 31, 2013. Credit balances are indicated by parentheses.

	Palm Company	Storm Company
Revenues	$ (485,000)	$(190,000)
Cost of goods sold	160,000	70,000
Depreciation expense	130,000	52,000
Subsidiary earnings	(66,000)	–0–
Net income	$ (261,000)	$ (68,000)
Retained earnings, 1/1/13	$ (659,000)	$ (98,000)
Net income (above)	(261,000)	(68,000)
Dividends paid	175,500	40,000
Retained earnings, 12/31/13	$ (744,500)	$(126,000)
Current assets	$ 268,000	$ 75,000
Investment in Storm Company	216,000	–0–
Land	427,500	58,000
Buildings and equipment (net)	713,000	161,000
Total assets	$ 1,624,500	$ 294,000
Current liabilities	$ (110,000)	$ (19,000)
Long-term liabilities	(80,000)	(84,000)
Common stock	(600,000)	(60,000)
Additional paid-in capital	(90,000)	(5,000)
Retained earnings, 12/31/13	(744,500)	(126,000)
Total liabilities and equity	$(1,624,500)	$(294,000)

a. Explain how Palm derived the $66,000 balance in the Subsidiary Earnings account.

b. Prepare a worksheet to consolidate the financial information for these two companies.

c. Explain how Storm's individual financial records would differ if the push-down method of accounting had been applied.

LO4a

excel

34. Tyler Company acquired all of Jasmine Company's outstanding stock on January 1, 2011, for $206,000 in cash. Jasmine had a book value of only $140,000 on that date. However, equipment (having an eight-year life) was undervalued by $54,400 on Jasmine's financial records. A building with a 20-year life was overvalued by $10,000. Subsequent to the acquisition, Jasmine reported the following:

	Net Income	Dividends Paid
2011	$50,000	$10,000
2012	60,000	40,000
2013	30,000	20,000

In accounting for this investment, Tyler has used the equity method. Selected accounts taken from the financial records of these two companies as of December 31, 2013, follow:

	Tyler Company	Jasmine Company
Revenues—operating	$(310,000)	$(104,000)
Expenses	198,000	74,000
Equipment (net)	320,000	50,000
Buildings (net)	220,000	68,000
Common stock	(290,000)	(50,000)
Retained earnings, 12/31/13 balance	(410,000)	(160,000)

Determine and explain the following account balances as of December 31, 2013:

a. Investment in Jasmine Company (on Tyler's individual financial records).
b. Equity in Subsidiary Earnings (on Tyler's individual financial records).
c. Consolidated Net Income.
d. Consolidated Equipment (net).
e. Consolidated Buildings (net).
f. Consolidated Goodwill (net).
g. Consolidated Common Stock.
h. Consolidated Retained Earnings, 12/31/13.

LO4

35. On January 1, 2012, Picante Corporation acquired 100 percent of the outstanding voting stock of Salsa Corporation for $1,765,000 cash. On the acquisition date, Salsa had the following balance sheet:

Cash	$ 14,000	Accounts payable	$ 120,000
Accounts receivable	100,000	Long-term debt	930,000
Land	700,000	Common stock	1,000,000
Equipment (net)	1,886,000	Retained earnings	650,000
	$2,700,000		$2,700,000

At the acquisition date, the following allocation was prepared:

Fair value of consideration transferred		$1,765,000
Book value acquired		1,650,000
Excess fair value over book value		115,000
To in-process research and development	$44,000	
To equipment (8-year remaining life)	56,000	100,000
To goodwill (indefinite life)		$ 15,000

Although at acquisition date Picante had expected $44,000 in future benefits from Salsa's in-process research and development project, by the end of 2012, it was apparent that the research project was a failure with no future economic benefits.

On December 31, 2013, Picante and Salsa submitted the following trial balances for consolidation:

	Picante	Salsa
Sales	$ (3,500,000)	$(1,000,000)
Cost of goods sold	1,600,000	630,000
Depreciation expense	540,000	160,000
Subsidiary income	(203,000)	–0–
Net income	$ (1,563,000)	$ (210,000)
Retained earnings 1/1/13	$ (3,000,000)	$ (800,000)
Net income	(1,563,000)	(210,000)
Dividends paid	200,000	25,000
Retained earnings 12/31/13	$ (4,363,000)	$ (985,000)
Cash	$ 228,000	$ 50,000
Accounts receivable	840,000	155,000
Inventory	900,000	580,000
Investment in Salsa	2,042,000	–0–
Land	3,500,000	700,000
Equipment (net)	5,000,000	1,700,000
Goodwill	290,000	–0–
Total assets	$ 12,800,000	$ 3,185,000
Accounts payable	$ (193,000)	$ (400,000)
Long-term debt	(3,094,000)	(800,000)
Common stock	(5,150,000)	(1,000,000)
Retained earnings 12/31/13	(4,363,000)	(985,000)
Total liabilities and equities	$(12,800,000)	$(3,185,000)

a. Show how Picante derived its December 31, 2013, Investment in Salsa account balance.

b. Prepare a consolidated worksheet for Picante and Salsa as of December 31, 2013.

LO4a, LO6

36. On January 1, Prine, Inc., acquired 100 percent of Lydia Company's common stock for a fair value of $120,000,000 in cash and stock. Lydia's assets and liabilities equaled their fair values except for its equipment, which was undervalued by $500,000 and had a 10-year remaining life.

Prine specializes in media distribution and viewed its acquisition of Lydia as a strategic move into content ownership and creation. Prine expected both cost and revenue synergies from controlling Lydia's artistic content (a large library of classic movies) and its sports programming specialty video operation. Accordingly, Prine allocated Lydia's assets and liabilities (including $50,000,000 of goodwill) to a newly formed operating segment appropriately designated as a reporting unit.

The fair values of the reporting unit's identifiable assets and liabilities through the first year of operations were as follows.

	Fair Values	
Account	**1/1**	**12/31**
Cash	$ 215,000	$ 109,000
Receivables (net)	525,000	897,000
Movie library (25-year life)	40,000,000	60,000,000
Broadcast licenses (indefinite life)	15,000,000	20,000,000
Equipment (10-year life)	20,750,000	19,000,000
Current liabilities	(490,000)	(650,000)
Long-term debt	(6,000,000)	(6,250,000)

However, Lydia's assets have taken longer than anticipated to produce the expected synergies with Prine's operations. Accordingly, Prine reviewed events and circumstances and concluded that Lydia's fair value was likely less than its carrying amount. At year-end, Prine reduced its assessment of the Lydia reporting unit's fair value to $110,000,000.

At December 31, Prine and Lydia submitted the following balances for consolidation:

	Prine, Inc.	Lydia Co.
Revenues	$ (18,000,000)	$(12,000,000)
Operating expenses	10,350,000	11,800,000
Equity in Lydia earnings	(150,000)	NA
Dividends paid	300,000	80,000
Retained earnings, 1/1	(52,000,000)	(2,000,000)
Cash	260,000	109,000
Receivables (net)	210,000	897,000
Investment in Lydia	120,070,000	NA
Broadcast licenses	350,000	14,014,000
Movie library	365,000	45,000,000
Equipment (net)	136,000,000	17,500,000
Current liabilities	(755,000)	(650,000)
Long-term debt	(22,000,000)	(7,250,000)
Common stock	(175,000,000)	(67,500,000)

a. What is the relevant initial test to determine whether goodwill could be impaired?

b. At what amount should Prine record an impairment loss for its Lydia reporting unit for the year?

c. What is consolidated net income for the year?

d. What is the December 31 consolidated balance for goodwill?

e. What is the December 31 consolidated balance for broadcast licenses?

f. Prepare a consolidated worksheet for Prine and Lydia (Prine's trial balance should first be adjusted for any appropriate impairment loss).

Develop Your Skills

RESEARCH CASE

Jonas Tech Corporation recently acquired Innovation Plus Company. The combined firm consists of three related businesses that will serve as reporting units. In connection with the acquisition, Jonas requests your help with the following asset valuation and allocation issues. Support your answers with references to FASB ASC as appropriate.

Jonas recognizes several identifiable intangibles from its acquisition of Innovation Plus. It expresses the desire to have these intangible assets written down to zero in the acquisition period.

The price Jonas paid for Innovation Plus indicates that it paid a large amount for goodwill. However, Jonas worries that any future goodwill impairment may send the wrong signal to its investors about the wisdom of the Innovation Plus acquisition. Jonas thus wishes to allocate the combined goodwill of all of its reporting units to one account called *Enterprise Goodwill.* In this way, Jonas hopes to minimize the possibility of goodwill impairment because a decline in goodwill in one business unit could be offset by an increase in the value of goodwill in another business unit.

Required

1. Advise Jonas on the acceptability of its suggested immediate write-off of its identifiable intangibles.
2. Indicate the relevant factors to consider in allocating the value assigned to identifiable intangibles acquired in a business combination to expense over time.
3. Advise Jonas on the acceptability of its suggested treatment of goodwill.
4. Indicate the relevant factors to consider in allocating goodwill across an enterprise's business units.

NIKE IMPAIRMENT ANALYSIS CASE

In 2009 Nike Corporation reported a large goodwill impairment loss. Referring to Nike's 2009 financial statements and applicable financial reporting standards, answer the following questions:

1. How much goodwill impairment charge did Nike report in 2009?
2. Why did Nike write down its goodwill in 2009? What are some other indicators for goodwill impairment in general?
3. How did Nike reflect this impairment in financial statements?
4. How often does Nike test its goodwill for impairment and what are the testing steps?
5. Certain other indefinite-lived intangibles and other long-lived assets (including intangible assets with a finite life) are also subject to impairment assessment. Did Nike incur any of these impairment charges in 2009? Explain briefly when and how Nike tests these assets for impairment.

FASB ASC AND IASB RESEARCH CASE

A vice president for operations at Poncho Platforms asks for your help on a financial reporting issue concerning goodwill. Two years ago, the company suffered a goodwill impairment loss for its Chip Integration reporting unit. Since that time, however, the Chip Integration unit has recovered nicely and its current cash flows (and projected cash flows) are at an all-time high. The vice president now asks whether the goodwill loss can be reversed given the reversal of fortunes for the Chip Integration reporting unit.

1. Is impairment of goodwill reversible under U.S. GAAP? How about under IFRS? (Refer to FASB Topic 350, "Intangibles—Goodwill and Other," and *IAS 36,* "Impairment of Assets.")
2. Are goodwill impairment testing procedures the same under IFRS and U.S. GAAP? If not, how is goodwill tested for impairment under IFRS? (Refer to *IAS 36*, "Impairment of Assets.")

EXCEL CASE 1

On January 1, 2012, Innovus, Inc., acquired 100 percent of the common stock of ChipTech Company for $670,000 in cash and other fair-value consideration. ChipTech's fair value was allocated among its net assets as follows:

Fair value of consideration transferred for ChipTech		$670,000
Book value of ChipTech:		
Common stock and Additional Paid-in Capital (APIC)	$130,000	
Retained earnings	370,000	500,000
Excess fair value over book value to		170,000
Trademark (10-year remaining life)	40,000	
Existing technology (5-year remaining life)	80,000	120,000
Goodwill		$ 50,000

The December 31, 2013, trial balances for the parent and subsidiary follow:

	Innovus	ChipTech
Revenues	$ (990,000)	$(210,000)
Cost of goods sold	500,000	90,000
Depreciation expense	100,000	5,000
Amortization expense	55,000	18,000
Dividend income	(40,000)	–0–
Net income	$ (375,000)	$ (97,000)
Retained earnings 1/1/13	$(1,555,000)	$(450,000)
Net income	(375,000)	(97,000)
Dividends paid	250,000	40,000
Retained earnings 12/31/13	$(1,680,000)	$(507,000)
Current assets	$ 960,000	$ 355,000
Investment in ChipTech	670,000	
Equipment (net)	765,000	225,000
Trademark	235,000	100,000
Existing technology	–0–	45,000
Goodwill	450,000	–0–
Total assets	$ 3,080,000	$ 725,000
Liabilities	$ (780,000)	(88,000)
Common stock	(500,000)	(100,000)
Additional paid-in capital	(120,000)	(30,000)
Retained earnings 12/31/13	(1,680,000)	(507,000)
Total liabilities and equity	$(3,080,000)	$(725,000)

Required

a. Using Excel, compute consolidated balances for Innovus and ChipTech. Either use a worksheet approach or compute the balances directly.

b. Prepare a second spreadsheet that shows a 2013 impairment loss for the entire amount of goodwill from the ChipTech acquisition.

EXCEL CASE 2

On January 1, 2012, Hi-Speed.com acquired 100 percent of the common stock of Wi-Free Co. for cash of $730,000. The consideration transferred was allocated among Wi-Free's net assets as follows:

Wi-Free fair value (cash paid by Hi-Speed)		$730,000
Book value of Wi-Free:		
Common stock and Additional Paid-in Capital (APIC)	$130,000	
Retained earnings	370,000	500,000

(continued)

Excess fair value over book value to		$230,000
In-process R&D	75,000	
Computer software (overvalued)	(30,000)	
Internet domain name	120,000	165,000
Goodwill		$ 65,000

At the acquisition date, the computer software had a 4-year remaining life, and the Internet domain name was estimated to have a 10-year life. By the end of 2012, it became clear that the acquired in-process research and development would yield no economic benefits and Hi-Speed.com recognized an impairment loss. At December 31, 2013, Wi-Free's accounts payable include a $30,000 amount owed to Hi-Speed.

The December 31, 2013, trial balances for the parent and subsidiary follow:

	Hi-Speed.com	Wi-Free Co.
Revenues	$(1,100,000)	$(325,000)
Cost of goods sold	625,000	122,000
Depreciation expense	140,000	12,000
Amortization expense	50,000	11,000
Equity in subsidiary earnings	(175,500)	–0–
Net income	$ (460,500)	$(180,000)
Retained earnings 1/1/13	$(1,552,500)	$(450,000)
Net income	(460,500)	(180,000)
Dividends paid	250,000	50,000
Retained earnings 12/31/13	$(1,763,000)	$(580,000)
Current assets	$ 1,034,000	$ 345,000
Investment in Wi-Free	856,000	–0–
Equipment (net)	713,000	305,000
Computer software	650,000	130,000
Internet domain name	–0–	100,000
Goodwill	–0–	–0–
Total assets	$ 3,253,000	$ 880,000
Liabilities	$ (870,000)	$(170,000)
Common stock	(500,000)	(110,000)
Additional paid-in capital	(120,000)	(20,000)
Retained earnings 12/31/13	(1,763,000)	(580,000)
Total liabilities and equity	$(3,253,000)	$(880,000)

Required

a. Using Excel, prepare calculations showing how Hi-Speed derived the $856,000 amount for its investment in Wi-Free.

b. Using Excel, compute consolidated balances for Hi-Speed and Wi-Free. Either use a worksheet approach or compute the balances directly.

Computer Project

Alternative Investment Methods, Goodwill Impairment, and Consolidated Financial Statements

In this project, you are to provide an analysis of alternative accounting methods for controlling interest investments and subsequent effects on consolidated reporting. The project requires the use of a computer and a spreadsheet software package (e.g., Microsoft Excel, etc.). The use of these tools allows you to assess the sensitivity of alternative accounting methods on consolidated financial reporting without preparing several similar worksheets by hand. Also, by modeling a worksheet process, you can develop a better understanding of accounting for combined reporting entities.

Consolidated Worksheet Preparation

You will be creating and entering formulas to complete four worksheets. The first objective is to demonstrate the effect of different methods of accounting for the investments (equity, initial value, and partial equity) on the parent company's trial balance and on the consolidated worksheet subsequent to acquisition. The second objective is to show the effect on consolidated balances and key financial ratios of recognizing a goodwill impairment loss.

The project requires preparation of the following four separate worksheets:

a. Consolidated information worksheet (follows).
b. Equity method consolidation worksheet.
c. Initial value method consolidation worksheet.
d. Partial equity method consolidation worksheet.

If your spreadsheet package has multiple worksheet capabilities (e.g., Excel), you can use separate worksheets; otherwise, each of the four worksheets can reside in a separate area of a single spreadsheet.

In formulating your solution, each worksheet should link directly to the first worksheet. Also, feel free to create supplemental schedules to enhance the capabilities of your worksheet.

Project Scenario

Pecos Company acquired 100 percent of Suaro's outstanding stock for $1,450,000 cash on January 1, 2012, when Suaro had the following balance sheet:

Assets		Liabilities and Equity	
Cash	$ 37,000	Liabilities	$(422,000)
Receivables	82,000		
Inventory	149,000	Common stock	(350,000)
Land	90,000	Retained earnings	(126,000)
Equipment (net)	225,000		
Software	315,000		
Total assets	$898,000	Total liabilities and equity	$(898,000)

At the acquisition date, the fair values of each identifiable asset and liability that differed from book value were as follows:

Land	$ 80,000	
Brand name	60,000	(indefinite life—unrecognized on Suaro's books)
Software	415,000	(2-year estimated useful life)
In-process R&D	300,000	

Additional Information

- Although at acquisition date Pecos expected future benefits from Suaro's in-process research and development (R&D), by the end of 2012, it became clear that the research project was a failure with no future economic benefits.
- During 2012, Suaro earns $75,000 and pays no dividends.
- Selected amounts from Pecos and Suaro's separate financial statements at December 31, 2013, are presented in the consolidated information worksheet. All consolidated worksheets are to be prepared as of December 31, 2013, two years subsequent to acquisition.
- Pecos's January 1, 2013, Retained Earnings balance—before any effect from Suaro's 2012 income—is $(930,000) (credit balance).
- Pecos has 500,000 common shares outstanding for EPS calculations and reported $2,943,100 for consolidated assets at the beginning of the period.

Following is the consolidated information worksheet.

	A	B	C	D
1	**December 31, 2013, trial balances**			
2				
3		**Pecos**	**Suaro**	
4	Revenues	($1,052,000)	($427,000)	
5	Operating expenses	$ 821,000	$262,000	
6	Goodwill impairment loss	?		
7	Income of Suaro	?		
8	Net income	?	($165,000)	
9				
10	Retained earnings—Pecos 1/1/13	?		
11	Retained earnings—Suaro 1/1/13		($201,000)	
12	Net income (above)	?	($165,000)	
13	Dividends paid	$ 200,000	$ 35,000	
14	Retained earnings 12/31/13	?	($331,000)	
15				
16	Cash	$ 195,000	$ 95,000	
17	Receivables	$ 247,000	$143,000	
18	Inventory	$ 415,000	$197,000	
19	Investment in Suaro	?		
20				
21				
22				
23	Land	$ 341,000	$ 85,000	
24	Equipment (net)	$ 240,100	$100,000	
25	Software		$312,000	
26	Other intangibles	$ 145,000		
27	Goodwill			
28	Total assets	?	$932,000	
29				
30	Liabilities	($1,537,100)	($251,000)	
31	Common stock	($ 500,000)	($350,000)	
32	Retained earnings (above)	?	($331,000)	
33	Total liabilities and equity	?	($932,000)	
34				
35	Fair value allocation schedule			
36	Price paid	$1,450,000		
37	Book value	$ 476,000		
38	Excess initial value	$ 974,000	Amortizations	
39	to land	($ 10,000)	2012	2013
40	to brand name	$ 60,000	?	?
41	to software	$ 100,000	?	?
42	to IPR&D	$ 300,000	?	?
43	to goodwill	$ 524,000	?	?
44				
45	Suaro's RE changes	Income	Dividends	
46	2012	$ 75,000	$ 0	
47	2013	$ 165,000	$ 35,000	

Project Requirements

Complete the four worksheets as follows:

1. Input the **consolidated information worksheet** provided and complete the fair-value allocation schedule by computing the excess amortizations for 2012 and 2013.
2. Using separate worksheets, prepare Pecos's trial balances for each of the indicated accounting methods (equity, initial value, and partial equity). **Use only formulas for the Investment in Suaro, the Income of Suaro, and Retained Earnings accounts.**
3. **Using references to other cells only (either from the consolidated information worksheet or from the separate method sheets), prepare for each of the three consolidation worksheets:**
   - Adjustments and eliminations.
   - Consolidated balances.
4. Calculate and present the effects of a 2013 total goodwill impairment loss on the following ratios for the consolidated entity:
   - Earnings per share (EPS).
   - Return on assets.
   - Return on equity.
   - Debt to equity.

   Your worksheets should have the capability to adjust immediately for the possibility that all acquisition goodwill can be considered impaired in 2013.
5. **Prepare a word-processed report that describes and discusses the following worksheet results:**
   a. The effects of alternative investment accounting methods on the parent's trial balances and the final consolidation figures.
   b. The relation between consolidated retained earnings and the parent's retained earnings under each of the three (equity, initial value, partial equity) investment accounting methods.
   c. The effect on EPS, return on assets, return on equity, and debt-to-equity ratios of the recognition that all acquisition-related goodwill is considered impaired in 2013.

chapter 4

Consolidated Financial Statements and Outside Ownership

Wal-Mart Stores, Inc. (Walmart), in its 2011 consolidated financial statements, includes the accounts of the company and all of its subsidiaries in which a controlling interest is maintained. For those consolidated subsidiaries where Walmart's ownership is less than 100 percent, the outside stockholders' interests are shown as *noncontrolling interests* in the stockholders' equity section of its consolidated balance sheet. On its consolidated income statement, Walmart also allocates a share of the consolidated net income to the noncontrolling interest.

Walmart includes *all of the financial figures* generated by both its wholly and majority-owned subsidiaries within consolidated financial statements. How does Walmart account for the partial ownership interest of the noncontrolling owners of its subsidiaries?

A number of reasons exist for one company to hold less than 100 percent ownership of a subsidiary. The parent might not have had sufficient resources available to obtain all of the outstanding stock. As a second possibility, a few stockholders of the subsidiary could have elected to retain their ownership, perhaps in hope of getting a better price at a later date.

Lack of total ownership is frequently encountered with foreign subsidiaries. The laws of some countries prohibit outsiders from maintaining complete control of domestic business enterprises. In other areas of the world, a parent can seek to establish better relations with a subsidiary's employees, customers, and local government by maintaining some percentage of native ownership.

Regardless of the reason for owning less than 100 percent, the parent consolidates the financial data of every subsidiary when control is present. As discussed in Chapter 2, *complete ownership is not a prerequisite for consolidation.* A single economic entity is formed whenever one company is able to control the decision-making process of another.

Although most parent companies do possess 100 percent ownership of their subsidiaries, a significant number, such as Walmart, establish control with a lesser amount of stock. The remaining outside owners are collectively referred to as *a noncontrolling interest,* which replaces the traditional term *minority interest.*[1] The presence of these

[1] The term *minority interest* had been used almost universally to identify the presence of other outside owners. However, current GAAP refers to these outside owners as the *noncontrolling interest*. Because this term is more descriptive, it is used throughout this textbook.

Learning Objectives

After studying this chapter, you should be able to:

- LO1 Understand that complete ownership is not a prerequisite for the formation of a business combination.
- LO2 Describe the valuation principles underlying the acquisition method of accounting for the noncontrolling interest.
- LO3 Allocate goodwill acquired in a business combination across the controlling and noncontrolling interests.
- LO4 Understand the computation and allocation of consolidated net income in the presence of a noncontrolling interest.
- LO5 Identify and calculate the four noncontrolling interest figures that must be included within the consolidation process and prepare a consolidation worksheet in the presence of a noncontrolling interest.
- LO6 Identify appropriate placements for the components of the noncontrolling interest in consolidated financial statements.
- LO7 Determine the effect on consolidated financial statements of a control premium paid by the parent.
- LO8 Understand the impact on consolidated financial statements of a midyear acquisition.
- LO9 Understand the impact on consolidated financial statements when a step acquisition has taken place.
- LO10 Record the sale of a subsidiary (or a portion of its shares).

LO1

Understand that complete ownership is not a prerequisite for the formation of a business combination.

other stockholders poses a number of reporting questions for the accountant. Whenever less than 100 percent of a subsidiary's voting stock is held, how should the subsidiary's accounts be valued within consolidated financial statements? How should the presence of these additional owners be acknowledged?

Consolidated Financial Reporting in the Presence of a Noncontrolling Interest

Noncontrolling Interest Defined

The authoritative accounting literature defines a noncontrolling interest as follows:

> The ownership interests in the subsidiary that are held by owners other than the parent is a noncontrolling interest. The noncontrolling interest in a subsidiary is part of the equity of the consolidated group. [FASB ASC (para. 810-10-45-15)]

When a parent company acquires a controlling ownership interest with less than 100 percent of a subsidiary's voting shares, it must account for the noncontrolling shareholders' interest in its consolidated financial statements. The noncontrolling interest represents an additional set of owners who have legal claim to the subsidiary's net assets.

Exhibit 4.1 provides a framework for introducing two fundamental valuation challenges in accounting and reporting for a noncontrolling interest. The issues focus on how the parent, in its consolidated financial statements, should

- Assign values to the noncontrolling interest's share of the subsidiary's assets and liabilities.
- Value and disclose the presence of the other owners.

The solution to both of these challenges involves fair value. The acquisition method captures the subsidiary's fair value as the relevant attribute for reporting the financial effects of a business combination. Fair values also provide for managerial accountability to investors and creditors for assessing the success or failure of the combination.

Control and Accountability

In acquiring a controlling interest, a parent company becomes responsible for managing all the subsidiary's assets and liabilities even though it may own only a partial interest. If a parent can control the business activities of its subsidiary, it directly follows that the parent is accountable to its investors and creditors for all of the subsidiary's assets, liabilities, and profits. To provide a complete picture of the acquired subsidiary requires fair-value measurements for both the subsidiary and the individual assets and liabilities.

EXHIBIT 4.1
Noncontrolling Interest—Date of Acquisition

PARENT AND 70% OWNED SUBSIDIARY COMPANIES
Consolidated Balance Sheet
Date of Acquisition

Parent's assets	Parent's liabilities
Subsidiary's assets	**Subsidiary's liabilities**
	Parent company owners' equity
	• 100% of parent's net assets
	• **70% of subsidiary's net assets**
	Noncontrolling owners' interest
	• **30% of subsidiary net assets**

Thus, for business combinations involving less-than-100 percent ownership, the acquirer recognizes and measures at the acquisition date the

- Identifiable assets acquired and liabilities assumed at their full fair values.[2]
- Noncontrolling interest at fair value.
- Goodwill or a gain from a bargain purchase.

In concluding that consolidated statements involving a noncontrolling interest should initially show all of the subsidiary's assets and liabilities at their full fair values, the 2005 FASB exposure draft Business Combinations (para. B23.a.) observed

> The acquirer obtains control of the acquiree at the acquisition date and, therefore, becomes responsible and accountable for all of the acquiree's assets, liabilities, and activities, regardless of the percentage of its ownership in the investee.
>
> . . . an important purpose of financial statements is to provide users with relevant and reliable information about the performance of the entity and the resources under its control. That applies regardless of the extent of the ownership interest a parent holds in a particular subsidiary. The Boards concluded that measurement at fair value enables users to better assess the cash generating abilities of the identifiable net assets acquired in the business combination and the accountability of management for the resources entrusted to it.

Thus, even though a company acquires less than 100 percent of another firm, the acquisition method requires that the acquiring company include in its acquisition-date consolidated statements 100 percent of each of the assets acquired and each of the liabilities assumed at their full fair values. This requirement stands in marked contrast to the former purchase method that focused on cost accumulation and allocation. Under the former purchase method, the parent allocated the purchase cost only to the percentage acquired of each subsidiary asset and liability. Thus, prior to the acquisition method, subsidiary assets and liabilities were measured partially at fair value and partially at the subsidiary's carryover (book) value. The current requirements help ensure that managements are accountable for the entire fair value of their acquisitions. However, as discussed below, compared to situations where 100 percent of a firm is acquired, measuring subsidiary fair value when accompanied by a noncontrolling interest presents some special challenges.

LO2

Describe the valuation principles underlying the acquisition method of accounting for the noncontrolling interest.

Subsidiary Acquisition-Date Fair Value in the Presence of a Noncontrolling Interest

When a parent company acquires a less-than-100 percent controlling interest in another firm, the acquisition method requires a determination of the acquisition-date fair value of the acquired firm for consolidated financial reporting. The total acquired firm fair value in the presence of a partial acquisition is the sum of the following two components at the acquisition date:

- The fair value of the controlling interest.
- The fair value of the noncontrolling interest.

The sum of these two components then serves as the starting point for the parent in valuing and recording the subsidiary acquisition. If the sum exceeds the collective fair values of the net identifiable assets acquired and liabilities assumed, then goodwill is recognized. Conversely, if the collective fair values of the net identifiable assets acquired and liabilities assumed exceed the total fair value, the acquirer recognizes a gain on bargain purchase.

Measurement of the controlling interest fair value remains straightforward in the vast majority of cases—the consideration transferred by the parent typically provides the best evidence of fair value of the acquirer's interest. However, there is no parallel consideration transferred available to value the noncontrolling interest. Therefore, the parent must employ other valuation techniques to estimate the fair value of the noncontrolling interest at the acquisition date.

[2] As noted in Chapter 2, exceptions to the fair-value measurement principle include deferred taxes, certain employee benefits, indemnification assets, reacquired rights, share-based awards, and assets held for sale.

Usually, a parent can rely on readily available market trading activity to provide a fair valuation for its subsidiary's noncontrolling interest. Market trading prices for the noncontrolling interest shares in the weeks before and after the acquisition provide an objective measure of their fair value. The fair value of these shares then becomes the initial basis for reporting the noncontrolling interest in consolidated financial statements.

Acquirers frequently must pay a premium price per share to garner sufficient shares to ensure a controlling interest. A control premium, however, typically is needed only to acquire sufficient shares to obtain a controlling interest. The remaining (noncontrolling interest) shares no longer provide the added benefit of transferring control to the new owner, and, therefore, may sell at a price less than the shares that yielded control. Such control premiums are properly included in the fair value of the controlling interest, but usually do not affect the fair values of the remaining subsidiary shares. Therefore, separate independent valuations for the controlling and noncontrolling interests are typically best for measuring the total fair value of the subsidiary.

In the absence of fair value evidence based on market trades, firms must turn to less objective measures of noncontrolling interest fair value. For example, comparable investments may be available to estimate fair value. Alternatively, valuation models based on subsidiary discounted cash flows or residual income projections can be employed to estimate the acquisition-date fair value of the noncontrolling interest. Finally, if a control premium is unlikely, the consideration paid by the parent can be used to imply a fair value for the entire subsidiary. The noncontrolling interest fair value is then simply measured as its percentage of this implied subsidiary fair value.

Noncontrolling Interest Fair Value as Evidenced by Market Trades

In the majority of cases, direct evidence based on market activity in the outstanding subsidiary shares (not owned by the parent) will provide the best measure of acquisition-date fair value for the noncontrolling interest. For example, assume that Parker Corporation wished to acquire 9,000 of the 10,000 outstanding equity shares of Strong Company and projected substantial synergies from the proposed acquisition. Parker estimated that a 100 percent acquisition was not needed to extract these synergies. Also, Parker projected that financing more than a 90 percent acquisition would be too costly.

Parker then offered all of Strong's shareholders a premium price for up to 90 percent of the outstanding shares. To induce a sufficient number of shareholders to sell, Parker needed to offer \$70 per share, even though the shares had been trading in the \$59 to \$61 range. During the weeks following the acquisition, the 10 percent noncontrolling interest in Strong Company continues to trade in the \$59 to \$61 range.

In this case, the \$70 per share price paid by Parker does not appear representative of the fair value of all the shares of Strong Company. The fact that the noncontrolling interest shares continue to trade around \$60 per share indicates a \$60,000 fair value for the 1,000 shares not owned by Parker. Therefore, the valuation of the noncontrolling interest is best evidenced by the traded fair value of Strong's shares, not the price paid by Parker.

The \$70 share price paid by Parker nonetheless represents a negotiated value for the 9,000 shares. In the absence of any evidence to the contrary, Parker's shares have a fair value of \$630,000 incorporating the additional value Parker expects to extract from synergies with Strong. Thus the fair value of Strong is measured as the sum of the respective fair values of the controlling and noncontrolling interests as follows:

Fair value of controlling interest (\$70 × 9,000 shares)	\$630,000
Fair value of noncontrolling interest (\$60 × 1,000 shares)	60,000
Total acquisition-date fair value of Strong Company	\$690,000

At the acquisition date, Parker assessed the total fair value of Strong's net identifiable assets at \$600,000. Therefore, we compute goodwill as the excess of the total fair value of the firm over the sum of the fair values of the identifiable net assets as follows:

Total acquisition-date fair value of Strong Company.	$690,000
Fair value of net identifiable net assets acquired	600,000
Goodwill	$ 90,000

LO3

Allocate goodwill acquired in a business combination across the controlling and noncontrolling interests.

Allocating Acquired Goodwill to the Controlling and Noncontrolling Interests To provide a basis for potential future allocations of goodwill impairment charges, acquisition-date goodwill should be apportioned across the controlling and noncontrolling interests. The parent first allocates goodwill to its controlling interest for the excess of the fair value of the parent's equity interest over its share of the fair value of the net identifiable assets. Any remaining goodwill is then attributed to the noncontrolling interest. As a result, goodwill allocated to the controlling and noncontrolling interests will not always be proportional to the percentages owned. Continuing the Parker and Strong example, all of the acquisition goodwill is allocated to the controlling interest as follows:

	Controlling Interest	Noncontrolling Interest
Fair value at acquisition date.	$630,000	$60,000
Relative fair value of identifiable net assets acquired (90% and 10% of $600,000)	540,000	60,000
Goodwill.	$ 90,000	–0–

In the unlikely event that the noncontrolling interest's proportionate share of the subsidiary's net asset fair values exceeds its total fair value, such an excess would serve to reduce the goodwill recognized by the parent. For example, if Strong's 10 percent noncontrolling interest had a fair value of $55,000, Strong's total fair value would equal $685,000, and goodwill (all allocated to the controlling interest) would decrease to $85,000. Alternatively, if Strong's 10 percent noncontrolling interest had a fair value of $70,000, Strong's total fair value would equal $700,000. In this case, goodwill would equal $100,000 with $90,000 allocated to the controlling interest and $10,000 allocated to the noncontrolling interest. Finally, if the total fair value of the acquired firm is less than the collective sum of its net identifiable assets, a bargain purchase occurs. In such rare combinations, the parent recognizes the entire gain on bargain purchase in current income. In no case is any amount of the gain allocated to the noncontrolling interest.

Noncontrolling Interest Fair Value Implied by Parent's Consideration Transferred

In other cases, especially when a large percentage of the acquiree's voting stock is purchased, the consideration paid by the parent may be reflective of the acquiree's total fair value. For example, again assume Parker pays $70 per share for 9,000 shares of Strong Company representing a 90 percent equity interest. Also assume that the remaining 1,000 noncontrolling interest shares are not actively traded. If there was no compelling evidence that the $70 acquisition price was not representative of all of Strong's 10,000 shares, then it appears reasonable to estimate the fair value of the 10 percent noncontrolling interest using the price paid by Parker. The total fair value of Strong Company is then estimated at $700,000 and allocated as follows:

Fair value of controlling interest ($70 × 9,000 shares)	$630,000
Fair value of noncontrolling interest ($70 × 1,000 shares)	70,000
Total fair value of Strong Company	$700,000

Note that in this case, because the price per share paid by the parent equals the noncontrolling interest per share fair value, goodwill is recognized proportionately across the two ownership groups. Assuming again that the collective fair value of Strong's net identifiable assets equals $600,000, goodwill is recognized and allocated as follows:

	Controlling Interest	Noncontrolling Interest
Fair value at acquisition date	$630,000	$70,000
Relative fair value of net assets acquired (90% and 10%)	540,000	60,000
Goodwill	$ 90,000	$10,000

Allocating the Subsidiary's Net Income to the Parent and Noncontrolling Interests

LO4

Understand the computation and allocation of consolidated net income in the presence of a noncontrolling interest.

Subsequent to acquisition, the subsidiary's net income must be allocated to its owners—the parent company and the noncontrolling interest—to properly measure their respective equity in the consolidated entity. Although current accounting standards require that net income and comprehensive income be attributed to the parent and the noncontrolling interest, they do not provide detailed guidance for making that attribution. Thus it is possible that certain acquired subsidiary assets may not benefit the parent and noncontrolling interest in a manner proportional to their interests. Nonetheless, we expect that such nonproportional benefits will be the exception rather than the rule.

In this text we will assume in all cases that the relative ownership percentages of the parent and noncontrolling interest represent an appropriate basis for attributing all elements (including excess acquisition-date fair-value amortizations for identifiable assets and liabilities) of a subsidiary's income across the ownership groups. Including the excess fair-value amortizations is based on the assumption that the noncontrolling interest represents equity in the subsidiary's net assets as remeasured on the acquisition date.

To illustrate, again assume that Parker acquires 90 percent of Strong Company. Further assume that $30,000 of annual excess fair-value amortization results from increasing Strong's acquisition-date book values to fair values. If Strong reports revenues of $280,000 and expenses of $200,000 based on its internal book values, then the noncontrolling interest share of Strong's income can be computed as follows:

Noncontrolling Interest in Strong Company Net Income

Revenues	$280,000
Expenses	200,000
Subsidiary Strong net income	$ 80,000
Excess acquisition-date fair-value amortization	30,000
Net income adjusted for excess amortizations	$ 50,000
Noncontrolling interest percentage	10%
Noncontrolling interest share of subsidiary net income	$ 5,000

As a procedural matter, the $5,000 noncontrolling interest in the subsidiary net income is then simply subtracted from the combined entity's consolidated net income to derive the parent's interest in consolidated net income. Note that the noncontrolling shareholders have a 10 percent interest in the subsidiary company, but no interest in the parent firm.

Partial Ownership Consolidations (Acquisition Method)

LO5

Identify and calculate the four noncontrolling interest figures that must be included within the consolidation process and prepare a consolidation worksheet in the presence of a noncontrolling interest.

Having reviewed the basic concepts underlying the acquisition method of accounting for a noncontrolling interest, we now concentrate on the mechanical aspects of the consolidation process when an outside ownership is present. More specifically, we examine

Discussion Question

In considering its proposed statement of financial accounting standards on business combinations, the FASB received numerous comment letters. Many of these letters addressed the FASB's proposed adoption of the economic unit concept as a valuation basis for less-than-100-percent acquisitions. A sampling of these letters includes the following observations:

Bob Laux, Microsoft: Microsoft agrees with the Board that the principles underlying standards should strive to reflect the underlying economics of transactions and events. However, we do not believe the Board's conclusion that recognizing the entire economic value of the acquiree, regardless of the ownership interest in the acquiree at the acquisition date, reflects the underlying economics.

Patricia A. Little, Ford Motor Company: We agree that recognizing 100 percent of the fair value of the acquiree is appropriate. We believe that this is crucial in erasing anomalies which were created when only the incremental ownership acquired was fair valued and the minority interest was reflected at its carryover basis.

Sharilyn Gasaway, Alltell Corporation: One of the underlying principles . . . is that the acquirer should measure and recognize the fair value of the acquiree as a whole. If 100 percent of the ownership interests are acquired, measuring and recognizing 100 percent of the fair value is both appropriate and informative. However, if less than 100 percent of the ownership interests are acquired, recognizing the fair value of 100 percent of the business acquired is not representative of the value actually acquired. In the instance in which certain minority owners retain their ownership interest, recognizing the fair value of the minority interest does not provide sufficient benefit to financial statement users to justify the additional cost incurred to calculate that fair value.

PricewaterhouseCoopers: We agree that the noncontrolling interest should be recorded at its fair value when it is initially recorded in the consolidated financial statements. As such, when control is obtained in a single step, the acquirer would record 100 percent of the fair value of the assets acquired (including goodwill) and liabilities assumed.

Loretta Cangialosi, Pfizer: While we understand the motivation of the FASB to account for all elements of the acquisition transaction at fair value, we are deeply concerned about the practice issues that will result. The heavy reliance on expected value techniques, use of the hypothetical market participants, the lack of observable markets, and the obligation to affix values to "possible" and even "remote" scenarios, among other requirements, will all conspire to create a standard that will likely prove to be nonoperational, unauditable, representationally unfaithful, abuse-prone, costly, and of limited (and perhaps negative) shareholder value.

Do you think the FASB made the correct decision in requiring consolidated financial statements to recognize all subsidiary's assets and liabilities at fair value regardless of the percentage ownership acquired by the parent?

consolidations for time periods subsequent to the date of acquisition to analyze the full range of accounting complexities created by a noncontrolling interest. As indicated previously, this discussion centers on the acquisition method as required under generally accepted accounting principles.

The acquisition method focuses on incorporating in the consolidated financial statements 100 percent of the subsidiary's assets and liabilities at their acquisition-date fair values. Note that subsequent to acquisition, changes in fair values for assets and

EXHIBIT 4.2
Subsidiary Accounts—Date of Acquisition

PAWN COMPANY
Account Balances
January 1, 2012

	Book Value	Fair Value	Difference
Current assets	$ 440,000	$ 440,000	-0-
Trademarks (indefinite life)	260,000	320,000	$ 60,000
Patented technology (20-year life)	480,000	600,000	120,000
Equipment (10-year life)	110,000	100,000	(10,000)
Long-term liabilities (8 years to maturity)	(550,000)	(510,000)	40,000
Net assets	$ 740,000	$ 950,000	$210,000
Common stock	$(230,000)		
Retained earnings, 1/1/12	(510,000)		

Note: Parentheses indicate a credit balance.

liabilities are not recognized.[3] Instead, the subsidiary assets acquired and liabilities assumed are reflected in future consolidated financial statements using their acquisition-date fair values net of subsequent amortizations (or possibly reduced for impairment).

The presence of a noncontrolling interest does not dramatically alter the consolidation procedures presented in Chapter 3. The unamortized balance of the acquisition-date fair-value allocation must still be computed and included within the consolidated totals. Excess fair-value amortization expenses of these allocations are recognized each year as appropriate. Reciprocal balances are eliminated. Beyond these basic steps, the measurement and recognition of four noncontrolling interest balances add a new dimension to the process of consolidating financial information. The parent company must determine and then enter each of these figures when constructing a worksheet:

- Noncontrolling interest in the subsidiary as of the beginning of the current year.
- Noncontrolling interest in the subsidiary's current year income.
- Noncontrolling interest in the subsidiary's dividend payments.
- Noncontrolling interest as of the end of the year (found by combining the three balances above).

To illustrate, assume that King Company acquires 80 percent of Pawn Company's 100,000 outstanding voting shares on January 1, 2012, for $9.75 per share or a total of $780,000 cash consideration. Further assume that the 20 percent noncontrolling interest shares traded both before and after the acquisition date at an average of $9.75 per share. The total fair value of Pawn to be used initially in consolidation is thus as follows:

Consideration transferred by King ($9.75 × 80,000 shares)	$780,000
Noncontrolling interest fair value ($9.75 × 20,000 shares)	195,000
Pawn's total fair value at January 1, 2012	$975,000

Exhibit 4.2 presents the book value of Pawn's accounts as well as the fair value of each asset and liability on the acquisition date. Pawn's total fair value is attributed to Pawn's assets and liabilities as shown in Exhibit 4.3. Annual amortization relating to these allocations also is included in this schedule. Although expense figures are computed for only the initial years, some amount of amortization is recognized in each of the 20 years following the acquisition (the life assumed for the patented technology).

Exhibit 4.3 shows first that all identifiable assets acquired and liabilities assumed are adjusted to their full individual fair values at the acquisition date. The noncontrolling interest will share proportionately in these fair-value adjustments. Exhibit 4.3 also shows that any excess fair value not attributable to Pawn's identifiable net assets is assigned to

[3] Exceptions common to all firms (whether subject to consolidation or not) include recognizing changing fair values for marketable equity securities and other financial instruments.

EXHIBIT 4.3
Excess Fair Value Allocations

KING COMPANY AND 80% OWNED SUBSIDIARY PAWN COMPANY
Fair-Value Allocation and Amortization
January 1, 2012

	Allocation	Estimated Life (years)	Annual Excess Amortizations
Pawn's acquisition-date fair value (100%) . . .	$975,000		
Pawn's acquisition-date book value (100%) . .	(740,000)		
Fair value in excess of book value	$235,000		
Adjustments (100%) to			
Trademarks (indefinite life)	$ 60,000	indefinite	–0–
Patented technology (20-year life).	120,000	20	6,000
Equipment (10-year life)	(10,000)	10	(1,000)
Long-term liabilities (8 years to maturity). .	40,000	8	5,000
Goodwill (indefinite life).	$ 25,000	indefinite	–0–
Annual amortizations of excess fair value over book value (initial years)			$ 10,000

Goodwill Allocation to the Controlling and Noncontrolling Interests

	Controlling Interest	Noncontrolling Interest	Total
Fair value at acquisition date	$780,000	$195,000	$975,000
Relative fair value of Pawn's identifiable net assets (80% and 20%).	760,000	190,000	950,000
Goodwill	$ 20,000	$ 5,000	$ 25,000

goodwill. Because the controlling and noncontrolling interests' acquisition-date fair values are identical at $9.75 per share, the resulting goodwill is allocated proportionately across these ownership interests.

Consolidated financial statements will be produced for the year ending December 31, 2013. This date is arbitrary. Any time period subsequent to 2012 could serve to demonstrate the applicable consolidation procedures. Having already calculated the acquisition-date fair-value allocations and related amortization, the accountant can construct a consolidation of these two companies along the lines demonstrated in Chapter 3. Only the presence of the 20 percent noncontrolling interest alters this process.

To complete the information needed for this combination, assume that Pawn Company reports the following changes in retained earnings since King's acquisition:

Current year (2013)	
Net income	$ 90,000
Less: Dividends paid.	(50,000)
Increase in retained earnings	$ 40,000
Prior years (only 2012 in this illustration):	
Increase in retained earnings	$ 70,000

Assuming that King Company applies the equity method, the Investment in Pawn Company account as of December 31, 2013, can be constructed as shown in Exhibit 4.4. Note that the $852,000 balance is computed based on applying King's 80 percent ownership to Pawn's income (less amortization) and dividends. Although 100 percent of the subsidiary's assets and liabilities will be combined in consolidation, the internal accounting for King's investment in Pawn is based on its 80 percent ownership. This technique facilitates worksheet adjustments that allocate various amounts to the noncontrolling interest.

EXHIBIT 4.4
Equity Method Investment Balance

KING COMPANY
Investment in Pawn Company
Equity Method
December 31, 2013

Acquisition price for 80% interest		$780,000
Prior year (2012):		
Increase in retained earnings (80% × $70,000)	$56,000	
Excess amortization expenses (80% × $10,000) (Exhibit 4.3)	(8,000)	48,000
Current year (2013):		
Income accrual (80% × $90,000)	72,000	
Excess amortization expense (80% × $10,000) (Exhibit 4.3)	(8,000)	
Equity in subsidiary earnings	64,000*	
Dividends received (80% × $50,000)	(40,000)	24,000
Balance, 12/31/13		$852,000

*This figure appears in King's 2013 income statement. See Exhibit 4.5.

Exhibit 4.5 presents the separate financial statements for these two companies as of December 31, 2013, and the year then ended, based on the information provided.

Consolidated Totals

Although the inclusion of a 20 percent outside ownership complicates the consolidation process, the 2013 totals to be reported by this business combination can nonetheless be determined without the use of a worksheet:

- *Revenues* = $1,340,000. The revenues of the parent and the subsidiary are added together. The acquisition method includes the subsidiary's revenues in total although King owns only 80 percent of the stock.
- *Cost of Goods Sold* = $544,000. The parent and subsidiary balances are added together.
- *Depreciation Expense* = $79,000. The parent and subsidiary balances are added together along with the $1,000 reduction in equipment depreciation as indicated in Exhibit 4.3.
- *Amortization Expense* = $181,000. The parent and subsidiary balances are added together along with the $6,000 additional patented technology amortization expense as indicated in Exhibit 4.3.
- *Interest Expense* = $120,000. The parent and subsidiary balances are added along with an additional $5,000. Exhibit 4.3 shows Pawn's long-term debt reduced by $40,000 to fair value. Because the maturity value remains constant, the $40,000 represents a discount amortized to interest expense over the remaining eight-year life of the debt.
- *Equity in Subsidiary Earnings* = −0−. The parent's investment income is eliminated so that the subsidiary's revenues and expenses can be included in the consolidated totals.
- *Consolidated Net Income* = $416,000. The consolidated entity's total earnings before allocation to the controlling and noncontrolling ownership interests.
- *Noncontrolling Interest in Subsidiary's Income* = $16,000. The outside owners are assigned 20 percent of Pawn's reported income of $90,000 less $10,000 total excess fair-value amortization. The acquisition method shows this amount as an allocation of consolidated net income.
- *Net Income to Controlling Interest* = $400,000. The acquisition method shows this amount as an allocation of consolidated net income.

EXHIBIT 4.5
Separate Financial Records

KING COMPANY AND PAWN COMPANY Separate Financial Statements For December 31, 2013, and the Year Then Ended	King	Pawn
Revenues	$ (910,000)	$ (430,000)
Cost of goods sold	344,000	200,000
Depreciation expense	60,000	20,000
Amortization expense	100,000	75,000
Interest expense	70,000	45,000
Equity in subsidiary earnings (see Exhibit 4.4)	(64,000)	–0–
Net income	$ (400,000)	$ (90,000)
Retained earnings, 1/1/13	$ (860,000)	$ (580,000)
Net income (above)	(400,000)	(90,000)
Dividends paid	60,000	50,000
Retained earnings, 12/31/13	$(1,200,000)	$ (620,000)
Current assets	$ 726,000	$ 445,000
Trademarks	304,000	295,000
Patented technology	880,000	540,000
Equipment (net)	390,000	160,000
Investment in Pawn Company (see Exhibit 4.4)	852,000	–0–
Total assets	$ 3,152,000	$ 1,440,000
Long-term liabilities	$(1,082,000)	$ (590,000)
Common stock	(870,000)	(230,000)
Retained earnings, 12/31/13	(1,200,000)	(620,000)
Total liabilities and equities	$(3,152,000)	$(1,440,000)

- *Retained Earnings, 1/1* = $860,000. The parent company figure equals the consolidated total because the equity method was applied. If the initial value method or the partial equity method had been used, the parent's balance would require adjustment to include any unrecorded figures.
- *Dividends Paid* = $60,000. Only the parent company balance is reported. Eighty percent of the subsidiary's payments were made to the parent and are eliminated. The remaining distribution was made to the outside owners and serves to reduce the noncontrolling interest balance.
- *Retained Earnings, 12/31* = $1,200,000. The balance is found by adding the controlling interest's share of consolidated net income to the beginning Retained Earnings balance and then subtracting the dividends paid to the controlling interest. Because the equity method is utilized, the parent company figure reflects the total for the business combination.
- *Current Assets* = $1,171,000. The parent's and subsidiary's book values are added.
- *Trademarks* = $659,000. The parent's book value is added to the subsidiary's book value plus the $60,000 allocation of the acquisition-date fair value (see Exhibit 4.3).
- *Patented Technology* = $1,528,000. The parent's book value is added to the subsidiary's book value plus the $120,000 excess fair-value allocation less two years' excess amortizations of $6,000 per year (see Exhibit 4.3).
- *Equipment* = $542,000. The parent's book value is added to the subsidiary's book value less the $10,000 acquisition-date fair-value reduction plus two years' expense reductions of $1,000 per year (see Exhibit 4.3).

- *Investment in Pawn Company* = −0−. The balance reported by the parent is eliminated so that the subsidiary's assets and liabilities can be included in the consolidated totals.
- *Goodwill* = $25,000. The original allocation shown in Exhibit 4.3 is reported.
- *Total Assets* = $3,925,000. This balance is a summation of the consolidated assets.
- *Long-Term Liabilities* = $1,642,000. The parent's book value is added to the subsidiary's book value less the $40,000 acquisition-date fair-value allocation net of two years' amortizations of $5,000 per year (see Exhibit 4.3).
- *Noncontrolling Interest in Subsidiary* = $213,000. The outside ownership is 20 percent of the subsidiary's year-end book value adjusted for any unamortized excess fair value attributed to the noncontrolling interest:

Noncontrolling interest at 1/1/13	
20% of $810,000 beginning book value—common stock plus 1/1/13 retained earnings	$162,000
20% of unamortized excess fair-value allocations as of 1/1	45,000
Noncontrolling interest in subsidiary's income (see page 154)	16,000
Dividends paid to noncontrolling interest (20% of $50,000 total)	(10,000)
Noncontrolling interest at 12/31/13	$213,000

- *Common Stock* = $870,000. Only the parent's balance is reported.
- *Retained Earnings, 12/31* = $1,200,000. Computed on page 155.
- *Total Liabilities and Equities* = $3,925,000. This total is a summation of consolidated liabilities, noncontrolling interest, and equities.

Alternative Calculation of Noncontrolling Interest at December 31, 2013

The acquisition method requires that the noncontrolling interest be measured at fair value at the date of acquisition. Subsequent to acquisition, however, the noncontrolling interest value is adjusted for its share of subsidiary income, excess fair-value amortizations, and dividends. The following schedule demonstrates how the noncontrolling interest's acquisition-date fair value is adjusted to show the ending consolidated balance sheet amount.

Fair value of 20% noncontrolling interest at acquisition date		$195,000
20% of $70,000 change in Pawn's 2012 retained earnings	14,000	
20% of excess fair-value amortizations	(2,000)	12,000
2013 income allocation (20% × [90,000 − 10,000])		16,000
2013 dividends (20% × $50,000)		(10,000)
Noncontrolling interest at December 31, 2013		$213,000

As can be seen in the above schedule, the fair-value principle applies only to the initial noncontrolling interest valuation.

Worksheet Process—Acquisition Method

The consolidated totals for King and Pawn also can be determined by means of a worksheet as shown in Exhibit 4.6. Comparing this example with Exhibit 3.7 in Chapter 3 indicates that the presence of a noncontrolling interest does not create a significant number of changes in the consolidation procedures.

The worksheet still includes elimination of the subsidiary's stockholders' equity accounts (Entry **S**) although, as explained next, this entry is expanded to record the beginning noncontrolling interest for the year. The second worksheet entry (Entry **A**) recognizes the excess acquisition-date fair-value allocations at January 1 after one year of amortization with an additional adjustment to the beginning noncontrolling interest. Intra-entity income as well as dividend payments are removed also (Entries **I** and **D**)

EXHIBIT 4.6 Noncontrolling Interest Illustrated—Acquisition Method

KING COMPANY AND PAWN COMPANY
Consolidation Worksheet
For Year Ending December 31, 2013

Consolidation: Acquisition Method
Investment: Equity Method
Ownership: 80%

Accounts	King Company*	Pawn Company*	Consolidation Entries Debit	Consolidation Entries Credit	Noncontrolling Interest	Consolidated Totals
Revenues	(910,000)	(430,000)				(1,340,000)
Cost of goods sold	344,000	200,000				544,000
Depreciation expense	60,000	20,000		(E) 1,000		79,000
Amortization expense	100,000	75,000	(E) 6,000			181,000
Interest expense	70,000	45,000	(E) 5,000			120,000
Equity in Pawn's earnings (see Exhibit 4.4)	(64,000)	-0-	(I) 64,000			-0-
Separate company net income	(400,000)	(90,000)				
Consolidated net income						(416,000)
Noncontrolling interest in Pawn income					(16,000)	16,000
Net income to controlling interest						(400,000)
Retained earnings, 1/1	(860,000)	(580,000)	(S) 580,000			(860,000)
Net income (above)	(400,000)	(90,000)				(400,000)
Dividends paid	60,000	50,000		(D) 40,000	10,000	60,000
Retained earnings, 12/31	(1,200,000)	(620,000)				(1,200,000)
Current assets	726,000	445,000				1,171,000
Trademarks	304,000	295,000	(A) 60,000			659,000
Patented technology	880,000	540,000	(A) 114,000	(E) 6,000		1,528,000
Equipment (net)	390,000	160,000	(E) 1,000	(A) 9,000		542,000
Investment in Pawn Company	852,000	-0-	(D) 40,000	(S) 648,000		-0-
(see Exhibit 4.4)				(A) 180,000		
				(I) 64,000		
Goodwill	-0-	-0-	(A) 25,000			25,000
Total assets	3,152,000	1,440,000				3,925,000
Long-term liabilities	(1,082,000)	(590,000)	(A) 35,000	(E) 5,000		(1,642,000)
Common stock	(870,000)	(230,000)	(S) 230,000			(870,000)
				(S) 162,000		
Noncontrolling interest in Pawn 1/1				(A) 45,000	(207,000)	
Noncontrolling interest in Pawn 12/31					213,000	(213,000)
Retained earnings, 12/31	(1,200,000)	(620,000)				(1,200,000)
Total liabilities and equities	(3,152,000)	(1,440,000)	1,160,000	1,160,000		(3,925,000)

*See Exhibit 4.5.
Note: parentheses indicate credit balances.
Consolidation entries:
(S) Elimination of subsidiary's stockholders' equity along with recognition of January 1 noncontrolling interest.
(A) Allocation of subsidiary total fair value in excess of book value, unamortized balances as of January 1.
(I) Elimination of intra-entity income (equity accrual less amortization expenses).
(D) Elimination of intra-entity dividend payments.
(E) Recognition of amortization expenses of fair-value allocations.

while current-year excess amortization expenses are recognized (Entry **E**). The differences with the Chapter 3 illustrations relate exclusively to the recognition of the three components of the noncontrolling interest. In addition, *a separate Noncontrolling Interest column is added to the worksheet to accumulate these components to form the year-end figure to be reported on the consolidated balance sheet.*

Noncontrolling Interest—Beginning of Year Under the acquisition method, the noncontrolling interest shares proportionately in the fair values of the subsidiary's net identifiable assets as adjusted for excess fair-value amortizations. On the consolidated worksheet, this total net fair value is represented by two components:

1. Pawn's stockholders' equity accounts (common stock and beginning Retained Earnings) indicate a January 1, 2013, book value of $810,000.
2. The January 1, 2013, acquisition-date fair-value net of previous year's amortizations (in this case 2012 only).

Therefore, the January 1, 2013, balance of the 20 percent outside ownership is computed as follows:

20% × $810,000 subsidiary book value at 1/1/13	162,000
20% × $225,000 unamortized excess fair-value allocation at 1/1/13	45,000
1/1/13 Noncontrolling interest in Pawn.	$207,000

This balance is recognized on the worksheet through Entry **S** and Entry **A:**

Consolidation Entry S

Common Stock (Pawn).	230,000	
Retained Earnings, 1/1/13 (Pawn).	580,000	
Investment in Pawn Company (80%)		648,000
Noncontrolling Interest in Pawn Company, 1/1/13 (20%)		162,000
To eliminate beginning stockholders' equity accounts of subsidiary along with book value portion of investment (equal to 80 percent ownership). Noncontrolling interest of 20 percent is also recognized.		

Consolidation Entry A

Trademarks	60,000	
Patented Technology	114,000	
Liabilities	35,000	
Goodwill	25,000	
Equipment		9,000
Investment in Pawn Company (80%)		180,000
Noncontrolling Interest in Subsidiary, 1/1/13 (20%).		45,000
To recognize unamortized excess fair value as of January 1, 2013, to Pawn's assets acquired and liabilities assumed in the combination. Also to allocate the unamortized fair value to the noncontrolling interest. Goodwill is attributable proportionately to controlling and noncontrolling interests.		

The total $207,000 balance assigned here to the outside owners at the beginning of the year is extended to the Noncontrolling Interest worksheet column (see Exhibit 4.6).

To complete the required worksheet adjustments, Entries **I, D,** and **E** are prepared as follows:

Consolidation Entry I

Equity in Pawn's Earnings	64,000	
Investment in Pawn Company.		64,000
To eliminate intra-entity income accrual comprising subsidiary income less excess acquisition-date fair-value amortizations.		

Consolidation Entry D

Investment in Pawn Company	40,000	
Dividends Paid		40,000
To eliminate intra-entity dividend payments.		

Consolidation Entry E

Amortization Expense	6,000	
Interest Expense	5,000	
Equipment (net)	1,000	
Depreciation Expense		1,000
Patented Technology		6,000
Long-Term Liabilities		5,000
To recognize the current-income effects from excess acquisition-date fair-value allocations over their expected remaining lives.		

Noncontrolling Interest—Current Year Income Exhibit 4.6 shows the noncontrolling interest's share of current year earnings is $16,000. The amount is based on the subsidiary's $90,000 income (Pawn Company column) less excess acquisition-date fair-value amortizations. Thus, King assigns $16,000 to the outside owners computed as follows:

Noncontrolling Interest in Pawn Company Net Income

Pawn Company net income	$90,000
Excess acquisition-date fair-value amortization	10,000
Net income adjusted for excess amortizations	$80,000
Noncontrolling interest percentage	20%
Noncontrolling interest share of subsidiary net income	$16,000

In effect, 100 percent of each subsidiary revenue and expense account (including excess acquisition-date fair-value amortizations) is consolidated with an accompanying 20 percent allocation to the noncontrolling interest. The 80 percent net effect corresponds to King's ownership.

Because $16,000 of consolidated income accrues to the noncontrolling interest, this amount is added to the $207,000 beginning balance assigned (in Entries **S** and **A**) to these outside owners. The noncontrolling interest increases because the subsidiary generated a profit during the period.

Although we could record this allocation through an additional worksheet entry, the $16,000 is usually shown, as in Exhibit 4.6, by means of a columnar adjustment. The current year accrual is simultaneously entered in the Income Statement section of the consolidated column as an allocation of consolidated net income and in the Noncontrolling Interest column as an increase. This procedure assigns a portion of the combined earnings to the outside owners rather than to the parent company owners.

Noncontrolling Interest—Dividend Payments The $40,000 dividend paid to the parent company is eliminated routinely through Entry **D,** but the remainder of Pawn's dividend was paid to the noncontrolling interest. The impact of the dividend (20 percent of the subsidiary's total payment) distributed to the other owners must be acknowledged. As shown in Exhibit 4.6, this remaining $10,000 is extended directly into the Noncontrolling Interest column on the worksheet as a reduction. It represents the decrease in the underlying claim of the outside ownership that resulted from the subsidiary's asset distribution.

Noncontrolling Interest—End of Year The ending assignment for these other owners is calculated by a summation of

The beginning balance for the year	$207,000
Plus the appropriate share of the subsidiary's current income	16,000
Less the dividends paid to the outside owners	(10,000)
Noncontrolling interest end of year—credit balance	$213,000

The Noncontrolling Interest column on the worksheet in Exhibit 4.6 accumulates these figures. The $213,000 total is then transferred to the balance sheet, where it appears in the consolidated statements.

Consolidated Financial Statements

Having successfully consolidated the information for King and Pawn, the resulting financial statements for these two companies are produced in Exhibit 4.7. These figures are taken from the consolidation worksheet.

LO6

Identify appropriate placements for the components of the noncontrolling interest in consolidated financial statements.

Consolidated Financial Statement Presentations of Noncontrolling Interest

Prior to current reporting requirements, the placement of the noncontrolling interest on the consolidated balance sheet varied across reporting entities. Some firms reported their noncontrolling interests as "mezzanine" items between liabilities and equity. Others reported noncontrolling interest as liabilities or as stockholders' equity.

Noncontrolling interests in the equity of subsidiaries are now reported in the owners' equity section of the consolidated statement of financial position. The amount should be clearly identified, labeled, and distinguished from the parent's controlling interest in its subsidiaries. Also consolidated net income (or loss) and each component of other comprehensive income must be allocated to the controlling and noncontrolling interests.

Exhibit 4.7 shows first the consolidated statement of income. Consolidated net income is computed at the combined entity level as $416,000 and then allocated to the noncontrolling and controlling interests. The statement of changes in owners' equity provides details of the ownership changes for the year for both the controlling and noncontrolling interest shareholders.[4] Finally, note the placement of the noncontrolling interest in the subsidiary's equity squarely in the consolidated owners' equity section.

Alternative Fair-Value Specification—Evidence of a Control Premium

LO7

Determine the effect on consolidated financial statements of a control premium paid by the parent.

To illustrate the valuation implications for an acquisition involving a control premium, again assume that King Company acquires 80 percent of Pawn Company's 100,000 outstanding voting shares on January 1, 2012. We also again assume that Pawn's shares traded before the acquisition date at an average of $9.75 per share. In this scenario, however, we assume that to acquire sufficient shares to gain control King pays $11.00 per share or a total of $880,000 cash consideration for its 80 percent interest. King thus pays a control premium of $1.25 ($11.00 − $9.75) per share to acquire Pawn. King anticipates that synergies with Pawn will create additional value for King's shareholders. Finally, following the acquisition, the remaining 20 percent noncontrolling interest shares continue to trade at $9.75.

The total fair value of Pawn to be used initially in consolidation is thus recomputed as follows:

Consideration transferred by King ($11.00 × 80,000 shares)	$ 880,000
Noncontrolling interest fair value ($9.75 × 20,000 shares)	195,000
Pawn's total fair value at January 1, 2012	$1,075,000

[4] If appropriate, this statement of changes in owners' equity would also provide an allocation of accumulated other comprehensive income elements across the controlling and noncontrolling interests.

EXHIBIT 4.7
Consolidated Statements with Noncontrolling Interest—Acquisition Method

KING COMPANY AND PAWN COMPANY
Consolidated Financial Statements

Income Statement
Year Ended December 31, 2013

Revenues	$1,340,000
Cost of goods sold	(544,000)
Depreciation expense	(79,000)
Amortization expense	(181,000)
Interest expense	(120,000)
Consolidated net income	$ 416,000
To noncontrolling interest	16,000
To controlling interest	$ 400,000

Statement of Changes in Owners' Equity
Year Ended December 31, 2013

	King Company Owners		
	Retained Earnings	Common Stock	Noncontrolling Interest
Balance, January 1	$ 860,000	$870,000	$ 207,000
Net income	400,000		16,000
Less: Dividends	(60,000)		(10,000)
Balance, December 31	$1,200,000	$870,000	$ 213,000

Statement of Financial Position
At December 31, 2013

Assets

Current assets	$1,171,000
Trademarks	659,000
Patented technology	1,528,000
Equipment (net)	542,000
Goodwill	25,000
Total assets	$3,925,000

Liabilities

Long-term liabilities	$1,642,000

Owners' Equity

Common stock—King Company	870,000
Noncontrolling interest in subsidiary	213,000
Retained earnings	1,200,000
Total liabilities and owners' equity	$3,925,000

In keeping with the acquisition method's requirement that identifiable assets acquired and liabilities assumed be adjusted to fair value, King allocates Pawn's total fair value as follows:

Fair value of Pawn at January 1, 2012		$1,075,000
Book value of Pawn at January 1, 2012		(740,000)
Fair value in excess of book value		$ 335,000
Adjustments to		
Trademarks	$ 60,000	
Patented technology	120,000	
Equipment	(10,000)	
Long-term liabilities	40,000	210,000
Goodwill		$ 125,000

Note that the *identifiable* assets acquired and liabilities assumed are again adjusted to their full individual fair values at the acquisition date. Only the amount designated as goodwill is changed to $125,000 from $25,000 in the original fair-value allocation example as shown in Exhibit 4.3. In this case, King allocates $120,000 of the $125,000 total goodwill amount to its own interest as follows:

	Controlling Interest	Noncontrolling Interest	Total
Fair value at acquisition date	$880,000	$195,000	$1,075,000
Relative fair value of Pawn's net identifiable assets (80% and 20%)	760,000	190,000	950,000
Goodwill	$120,000	$ 5,000	$ 125,000

The initial acquisition-date fair value of $195,000 for the noncontrolling interest includes only a $5,000 goodwill allocation from the combination. Because the parent paid an extra $1.25 per share more than the fair value of the noncontrolling interest shares, more goodwill is allocated to the parent.

Next we separate the familiar consolidated worksheet entry **A** into two components labeled **A1** and **A2.** The **A1** worksheet entry allocates the excess acquisition-date fair value to the *identifiable* assets acquired and liabilities assumed (trademarks, patented technology, equipment, and liabilities). Note that the relative ownership percentages of the parent and noncontrolling interest (80 percent and 20 percent) provide the basis for allocating the net $200,000 adjustment to the parent's Investment account and the 1/1/13 balance of the noncontrolling interest.

Next, consolidated worksheet entry **A2** provides the recognition and allocation of the goodwill balance taking into account the differing per share prices of the parent's consideration transferred and the noncontrolling interest fair value. Note that the presence of a control premium affects primarily the parents' shares, and thus goodwill is disproportionately (relative to the ownership percentages) allocated to the controlling and noncontrolling interests. Exhibit 4.8 shows the consolidated worksheet for this extension to the King and Pawn example.

Consolidation Entry A1

Trademarks	60,000	
Patented Technology	114,000	
Liabilities	35,000	
Equipment		9,000
Investment in Pawn Company (80%)		160,000
Noncontrolling Interest in Subsidiary 1/1/13 (20%)		40,000

Consolidation Entry A2

Goodwill	125,000	
Investment in Pawn Company		120,000
Noncontrolling Interest in Subsidiary 1/1/13		5,000

The worksheet calculates the December 31, 2013, noncontrolling balance as follows:

EXHIBIT 4.8 Consolidated Statements with Noncontrolling Interest—Acquisition Method, Parent Pays a Control Premium

KING COMPANY AND PAWN COMPANY
Consolidation Worksheet
For Year Ending December 31, 2013

Accounts	King Company	Pawn Company	Consolidation Entries Debit	Consolidation Entries Credit	Noncontrolling Interest	Consolidated Totals
Revenues	(910,000)	(430,000)				(1,340,000)
Cost of goods sold	344,000	200,000				544,000
Depreciation expense	60,000	20,000		(E) 1,000		79,000
Amortization expense	100,000	75,000	(E) 6,000			181,000
Interest expense	70,000	45,000	(E) 5,000			120,000
Equity in Pawn's earnings	(64,000)	-0-	(I) 64,000			-0-
Separate company net income	(400,000)	(90,000)				
Consolidated net income						(416,000)
Noncontrolling interest in Pawn income					(16,000)	16,000
Net income to controlling interest						(400,000)
Retained earnings, 1/1	(860,000)	(580,000)	(S) 580,000			(860,000)
Net income (above)	(400,000)	(90,000)				(400,000)
Dividends paid	60,000	50,000		(D) 40,000	10,000	60,000
Retained earnings, 12/31	(1,200,000)	(620,000)				(1,200,000)
Current assets	626,000	445,000				1,071,000
Trademarks	304,000	295,000	(A1) 60,000			659,000
Patented technology	880,000	540,000	(A1) 114,000	(E) 6,000		1,528,000
Equipment (net)	390,000	160,000	(E) 1,000	(A1) 9,000		542,000
Investment in Pawn Company	952,000	-0-	(D) 40,000	(S) 648,000		-0-
				(A1) 160,000		
				(A2) 120,000		
				(I) 64,000		
Goodwill	-0-	-0-	(A2) 125,000			125,000
Total assets	3,152,000	1,440,000				3,925,000
Long-term liabilities	(1,082,000)	(590,000)	(A1) 35,000	(E) 5,000		(1,642,000)
Common stock	(870,000)	(230,000)	(S) 230,000			(870,000)
Noncontrolling interest in Pawn 1/1				(S) 162,000		
				(A1) 40,000		
				(A2) 5,000	(207,000)	
Noncontrolling interest in Pawn 12/31					213,000	(213,000)
Retained earnings, 12/31	(1,200,000)	(620,000)				(1,200,000)
Total liabilities and equities	(3,152,000)	(1,440,000)	1,260,000	1,260,000		(3,925,000)

Consolidation entries:

(S) Elimination of subsidiary's stockholders' equity along with recognition of January 1 noncontrolling interest.
(A1) Allocation of subsidiary identifiable net asset fair value in excess of book value, unamortized balances as of January 1.
(A2) Allocation of goodwill to parent and noncontrolling interest.
(I) Elimination of intra-entity income (equity accrual less amortization expenses).
(D) Elimination of intra-entity dividend payments.
(E) Recognition of amortization expenses of fair-value allocations.

Pawn January 1, 2013: 20% book value	$162,000
January 1, 2013: 20% excess fair-value allocation for Pawn's net identifiable assets ($200,000 × 20%) + $5,000 goodwill allocation	45,000
Noncontrolling interest at January 1, 2013	$207,000
2013 Pawn income allocation	16,000
Noncontrolling interest share of Pawn dividends	(10,000)
December 31, 2013, balance	$213,000

Note that the $45,000 January 1 excess fair-value allocation to the noncontrolling interest includes the noncontrolling interest's full share of the *identifiable* assets acquired and liabilities assumed in the combination but only $5,000 for goodwill. Because King Company paid a $100,000 control premium (80,000 shares × $1.25), the additional $100,000 is allocated entirely to the controlling interest.

By comparing Exhibits 4.6 and 4.8 we can assess the effect of the separate acquisition-date valuations for the controlling and noncontrolling interests. As seen below, the presence of King's control premium affects the goodwill component in the consolidated financial statements and little else.

	Exhibit 4.6	Exhibit 4.8	Difference
On King's Separate Financial Statements			
Current assets.	$ 726,000	$ 626,000	− $100,000
Investment in Pawn.	$ 852,000	$ 952,000	+ $100,000
On the Consolidated Balances			
Current assets.	$1,171,000	$1,071,000	− $100,000
Goodwill.	$ 25,000	$ 125,000	+ $100,000

Because King paid an additional $100,000 for its 80 percent interest in Pawn, the initial value assigned to the Investment account increases and current assets (i.e., additional cash paid for the acquisition) decreases by $100,000. The extra $100,000 then simply increases goodwill on the consolidated balance sheet. Note that the noncontrolling interest amount remains unchanged at $213,000 across Exhibits 4.6 and 4.8, consistent with underlying measurement principles for the noncontrolling interest.

Effects Created by Alternative Investment Methods

In the King and Pawn illustrations, the parent uses the equity method and bases all worksheet entries on that approach. As discussed in Chapter 3, had King incorporated the initial value method or the partial equity method, a few specific changes in the consolidation process would be required although the reported figures would be identical.

Initial Value Method

Because it employs a cash basis for income recognition, the initial value method ignores two accrual-based adjustments. First, the parent recognizes dividend income rather than an equity income accrual. Thus, the parent does not accrue the percentage of the subsidiary's income earned in past years in excess of dividends (the increase in subsidiary retained earnings). Second, the parent does not record amortization expense under the initial value method and therefore must include it in the consolidation process if proper totals are to be achieved. Because neither of these figures is recognized in applying the initial value method, an Entry ***C** is added to the worksheet to convert the previously recorded balances to the equity method. The parent's beginning Retained Earnings is affected by this adjustment as well as the Investment in Subsidiary account. The exact amount is computed as follows.

*Conversion to Equity Method from Initial Value Method (Entry *C)*

Combine:

1. The increase (since acquisition) in the subsidiary's retained earnings during past years (income less dividends) times the parent's ownership percentage, and
2. The parent's percentage of total amortization expense for these same past years.

The parent's use of the initial value method requires an additional procedural change. Under this method, the parent recognizes income from its subsidiary only when it receives a dividend. Entry (**I**) removes both intra-entity dividend income and subsidiary dividends paid to the parent. Thus, when the initial value method is used, Entry **D** is unnecessary.

Partial Equity Method

Again, an Entry ***C** is needed to convert the parent's retained earnings as of January 1 to the equity method. In this case, however, only the amortization expense for the prior years must be included. Under the partial equity method, the income accrual is appropriately recognized each period by the parent company so that no further adjustment is necessary.

Revenue and Expense Reporting for Midyear Acquisitions

LO8

Understand the impact on consolidated financial statements of a midyear acquisition.

In virtually all of our previous examples, the parent gains control of the subsidiary on the first day of the fiscal year. How is the consolidation process affected if an acquisition occurs on a midyear (any other than the first day of the fiscal year) date?

When a company gains control at a midyear date, a few obvious changes are needed. The new parent must compute the subsidiary's book value as of that date to determine excess total fair value over book value allocations (e.g., intangibles). Excess amortization expenses as well as any equity accrual and dividend collections are recognized for a period of less than a year. Finally, because only income earned by the subsidiary after the acquisition date accrues to the new owners, it is appropriate to include only postacquisition revenues and expenses in consolidated totals.

Consolidating Postacquisition Subsidiary Revenue and Expenses

Following a midyear acquisition, a parent company excludes current year subsidiary revenue and expense amounts that have accrued prior to the acquisition date from its consolidated totals. For example, when Comcast acquired AT&T Broadband, its December 31 year-end income statement included AT&T Broadband revenues and expenses only subsequent to the acquisition date. Comcast reported $8.1 billion in revenues that year. However, in a pro forma schedule, Comcast noted that had it included AT&T Broadband's revenues from January 1, total revenue for the year would have been $16.8 billion. However, because the $8.7 billion additional revenue ($16.8 billion − $8.1 billion) was not earned by Comcast owners, Comcast excluded this preacquisition revenue from its consolidated total.

To further illustrate the complexities of accounting for a midyear acquisition, assume that Tyler Company acquires 90 percent of Steven Company on July 1, 2013, for $900,000 and prepares the following fair-value allocation schedule:

Steven Company fair value, 7/1/13		$1,000,000
Steven Company book value 7/1/13		
Common stock	$600,000	
Retained earnings, 7/1/13	200,000	800,000
Excess fair value over book value		$ 200,000
Adjust trademark to fair value (4-year life)		200,000
Goodwill		–0–

The affiliates report the following 2013 income statement amounts from their own separate operations:

	Tyler	Steven
Revenues	$450,000	$300,000
Expenses	325,000	150,000
Dividends (paid quarterly)	100,000	20,000

Assuming that all revenues and expenses occurred evenly throughout the year, the December 31, 2013, consolidated income statement appears as follows:

TYLER COMPANY
Consolidated Income Statement
For the Year Ended December 31, 2013

Revenues	$600,000
Expenses	425,000
Consolidated net income	$175,000
To noncontrolling interest	5,000
To controlling interest	$170,000

The consolidated income components are computed below:

- *Revenues* = \$600,000. Combined balances of \$750,000 less \$150,000 (½ of Steven's revenues).
- *Expenses* = \$425,000. Combined balances of \$475,000 less \$75,000 (½ of Steven's expenses) plus \$25,000 excess amortization (\$200,000 ÷ 4 years × ½ year).
- *Noncontrolling interest in Steven's income* = \$5,000. 10% × (\$150,000 Steven's income − \$50,000 excess amortization) × ½ year.

In this example, preacquisition subsidiary revenue and expense accounts are eliminated from the consolidated totals. Note also that by excluding 100 percent of the preacquisition income accounts from consolidation, the noncontrolling interest is viewed as coming into being as of the parent's acquisition date.[5]

A midyear acquisition requires additional adjustments when preparing consolidating worksheets. The balances the subsidiary submits for consolidation typically include results for its entire fiscal period. Thus, in the December 31 financial statements, the book value of the firm acquired on a midyear date is reflected by a January 1 retained earnings balance plus revenues, expenses, and dividends paid from the beginning of the year to the acquisition date. To effectively eliminate subsidiary book value as of the acquisition date, Consolidation Entry **S** includes these items in addition to the other usual elements of book value (i.e., stock accounts). To illustrate, assuming that both affiliates submit fiscal year financial statements for consolidation, Tyler would make the following 2013 consolidation worksheet entry:

Consolidation Worksheet Entry S

Common Stock—Steven	600,000	
Retained Earnings—Steven (1/1/13)*	135,000	
Revenues	150,000	
Dividends Paid—Steven		10,000
Expenses		75,000
Noncontrolling Interest (7/1/13)		80,000
Investment in Steven		720,000

* July 1 balance of \$200,000 less income from first six months of \$75,000 (1/2 of \$150,000 annual Steven income) plus \$10,000 dividends paid.

[5] Current practice provides comparability across fiscal years through pro forma disclosures of various categories of revenue and expense as if the combination had occurred at the beginning of the reporting period. With the advent of modern information systems, separate cutoffs for revenues and expenses are readily available.

Through Entry **S,** preacquisition subsidiary revenues, expenses, and dividends are effectively

- Included as part of the subsidiary book value elimination in the year of acquisition.
- Included as components of the beginning value of the noncontrolling interest.
- Excluded from the consolidated income statement and statement of retained earnings.

Acquisition Following an Equity Method Investment

In many cases, a parent company owns a noncontrolling equity interest in a firm prior to obtaining control. In such cases, as the preceding example demonstrates, the parent consolidates the postacquisition revenues and expenses of its new subsidiary. Because the parent owned an equity investment in the subsidiary prior to the control date, however, the parent reports on its income statement the "equity in earnings of the investee" that accrued up to the date control was obtained. In this case, in the year of acquisition, the consolidated income statement reports both combined revenues and expenses (postacquisition) of the subsidiary and equity method income (preacquisition).

In subsequent years, the need to separate pre- and postacquisition amounts is limited to ensuring that excess amortizations correctly reflect the midyear acquisition date. Finally, if the parent employs the initial value method of accounting for the investment in subsidiary on its books, the conversion to the equity method must also reflect only postacquisition amounts.

Step Acquisitions

LO9

Understand the impact on consolidated financial statements when a step acquisition has taken place.

When Ticketmaster Entertainment Corporation increased its percentage ownership in Front Line Company from 39.4 percent to 82.3 percent, it began consolidating its investment in Front Line. Prior to the acquisition of control through majority ownership, the investment in Front Line was accounted for using the equity method of accounting.

In all previous consolidation illustrations, control over a subsidiary was assumed to have been achieved through a single transaction. Obviously, Ticketmaster's takeover of Front Line shows that a combination also can be the result of a series of stock purchases. These step acquisitions further complicate the consolidation process. The financial information of the separate companies must still be brought together, but varying amounts of consideration have been transferred to former owners at several different dates. How do the initial acquisitions affect this process?

One area where the acquisition method provides a distinct departure from past reporting practices for business combinations is when control is achieved in a series of equity acquisitions, as opposed to a single transaction. Such acquisitions are frequently referred to as *step acquisitions* or *control achieved in stages*.

Past practice under the *purchase method* emphasized cost accumulation and allocation at each date that a parent acquired a block of subsidiary shares. The purchase method treated each acquisition of a firm's shares as a separate measurement event for reporting each acquisition's percentage of subsidiary assets and liabilities in consolidated financial statements. Thus, when a parent obtained control through, for example, three separate purchases of subsidiary shares, the resulting consolidated balance sheet might combine three different valuations for individual subsidiary assets acquired and/or liabilities assumed. Moreover, if a noncontrolling interest remained, a portion of each subsidiary asset and liability would remain at its original book value, further compromising the relevance and representational faithfulness of the consolidated financial statements.

Control Achieved in Steps—Acquisition Method

Attempting to increase both the relevance and representational faithfulness of consolidated reports, the FASB requires the acquisition method when a parent achieves control over another firm in stages. At the date control is first obtained, the acquisition method measures the acquired firm at fair value, including the noncontrolling interest. The acquisition of a controlling interest is considered an important economic, and therefore measurement, event. Consequently, the parent utilizes a single uniform valuation basis for all subsidiary assets acquired and liabilities assumed—fair value at the date control is obtained.

If the parent previously held a noncontrolling interest in the acquired firm, the parent remeasures that interest to fair value and recognizes a gain or loss. If after obtaining control, the parent increases its ownership interest in the subsidiary, no further remeasurement takes place. The parent simply accounts for the additional subsidiary shares acquired as an equity transaction—consistent with any transactions with other owners, as opposed to outsiders. Below we present first an example of consolidated reporting when the parent obtains a controlling interest in a series of steps. Then, we present an example of a parent's post-control acquisition of its subsidiary's shares.

Example: Step Acquisition Resulting in Control—Acquisition Method

To illustrate, assume that Arch Company obtains control of Zion Company through two cash acquisitions. The details of each acquisition are provided in Exhibit 4.9. Assuming that Arch has gained the ability to significantly influence Zion's decision-making process, the first investment, for external reporting purposes, is accounted for by means of the equity method as discussed in Chapter 1. Thus, Arch must determine any allocations and amortization associated with its purchase price (see Exhibit 4.10). A customer base with a 22-year life represented the initial excess payment.

Application of the equity method requires the accrual of investee income by the parent while any dividends received are recorded as a decrease in the Investment account. Arch must also reduce both the income and asset balances in recognition of the annual $2,000 amortization indicated in Exhibit 4.10. Following the information provided in Exhibits 4.9 and 4.10, over the next two years, Arch Company's Investment in Zion account grows to $190,000:

Price paid for 30% investment in Zion—1/1/11	$164,000
Accrual of 2011 equity income ($60,000 × 30 percent)	18,000
Dividends received 2011 ($20,000 × 30%)	(6,000)
Amortization	(2,000)
Accrual of 2012 equity income ($80,000 × 30 percent)	24,000
Dividends received 2012 ($20,000 × 30%)	(6,000)
Amortization	(2,000)
Investment in Zion—1/1/13	$190,000

On January 1, 2013, Arch's ownership is increased to 80 percent by the purchase of another 50 percent of Zion Company's outstanding common stock for $350,000. Although the equity method can still be utilized for internal reporting, this second acquisition necessitates the preparation of consolidated financial statements beginning in 2013. Arch now controls Zion; the two companies are viewed as a single economic entity for external reporting purposes.

Once Arch gains control over Zion on January 1, 2013, the acquisition method focuses exclusively on control-date fair values and considers any previous amounts recorded by

EXHIBIT 4.9
Consolidation Information for a Step Acquisition

ARCH COMPANY'S ACQUISITIONS OF ZION COMPANY SHARES

	Consideration Transferred	Percentage Acquired	Zion Company (100%) Book Value	Zion Company (100%) Fair Value
January 1, 2011	$164,000	30%	$400,000	$546,667
January 1, 2013	350,000	50	500,000	700,000

Zion Company's Income and Dividends for 2011–2013

	Income	Dividends
2011	$ 60,000	$20,000
2012	80,000	20,000
2013	100,000	20,000

EXHIBIT 4.10
Allocation of First Noncontrolling Acquisition

ARCH COMPANY AND ZION COMPANY
Fair Value Allocation and Amortization
January 1, 2011

Fair value of consideration transferred	$ 164,000
Book value equivalent of Arch's ownership ($400,000 × 30%)	(120,000)
Customer base	$ 44,000
Assumed life	22 years
Annual amortization expense	$ 2,000

the acquirer as irrelevant for future valuations. Thus, in a step acquisition all previous values for the investment, prior to the date control is obtained, are remeasured to fair value on the date control is obtained.

We add the assumption that the $350,000 consideration transferred by Arch in its second acquisition of Zion represents the best available evidence for measuring the fair value of Zion Company at January 1, 2013. Therefore, an estimated fair value of $700,000 ($350,000 ÷ 50%) is assigned to Zion Company as of January 1, 2013, and provides the valuation basis for the assets acquired, the liabilities assumed, and the 20 percent noncontrolling interest. Exhibit 4.11 shows Arch's allocation of Zion's $700,000 acquisition-date fair value.

Note that the acquisition method views a multiple-step acquisition as essentially the same as a single-step acquisition. In the Arch Company and Zion Company example, once control is evident, the only relevant values in consolidating the accounts of Zion are fair values at January 1, 2013. A new basis of accountability arises for Zion Company on that single date because obtaining control of another firm is considered a significant remeasurement event. Previously owned noncontrolling blocks of stock are consequently revalued to fair value on the date control is obtained.

In revaluing a previous stock ownership in the acquired firm, the acquirer recognizes any resulting gain or loss in income. Therefore, on January 1, 2013, Arch increases the Investment in Zion account to $210,000 (30% × $700,000 fair value) and records the revaluation gain as follows:

Investment in Zion	20,000	
Gain on Revaluation of Zion		20,000

Fair value of Arch's 30% investment in Zion at 1/1/13 (30% × $700,000)	$210,000
Book value of Arch's 30% investment in Zion at 1/1/13	190,000
Gain on revaluation of Zion to fair value	$ 20,000

EXHIBIT 4.11
Allocation of Acquisition-Date Fair Value

ARCH COMPANY AND ZION COMPANY
Fair Value Allocation and Amortization
January 1, 2013

Zion Company fair value	$ 700,000
Zion Company book value	(500,000)
Customer base	$ 200,000
Assumed life	20 years
Annual amortization expense	$ 10,000

Worksheet Consolidation for a Step Acquisition (Acquisition Method)

To continue the example, the amount in Arch Company's 80 percent Investment in Zion account is updated for 2013:

Investment in Zion (after revaluation on 1/1/13)	$210,000
January 1, 2013—Second acquisition price paid	350,000
Equity income accrual—2013 (80% × $100,000)	80,000
Amortization of customer base (80% × $10,000)	(8,000)
Dividends received—2013 (80% × $20,000)	(16,000)
Investment in Zion—12/31/13	$616,000

The worksheet for consolidating Arch Company and Zion Company is shown in Exhibit 4.12. Observe that

- The consolidation worksheet entries are essentially the same as if Arch had acquired its entire 80 percent ownership on January 1, 2013.
- The noncontrolling interest is allocated 20 percent of the excess fair-value allocation from the customer base.
- The noncontrolling interest is allocated 20 percent of Zion's 2013 income less its share of the excess amortization attributable to the customer base.
- The gain on revaluation of Arch's initial investment in Zion is recognized as income of the current period.

Example: Step Acquisition Resulting After Control Is Obtained

The previous example demonstrates a step acquisition with control achieved with the most recent purchase. Post-control acquisitions by a parent of a subsidiary's stock, however, often continue as well. Recall that the acquisition method measures an acquired firm at its fair value on the date control is obtained. A parent's subsequent subsidiary stock acquisitions do not affect these initially recognized fair values. Once the valuation basis for the acquired firm has been established, as long as control is maintained, this valuation basis remains the same. Any further purchases (or sales) of the subsidiary's stock are treated as equity transactions.

To illustrate a post-control step acquisition, assume that on January 1, 2012, Amanda Co. obtains 70 percent of Zoe, Inc., for $350,000 cash. We also assume that the $350,000 consideration paid by Amanda represents the best available evidence for measuring the fair value of the noncontrolling interest in Zoe Company. Therefore, Zoe Company's total fair value is assessed at $500,000 ($350,000 ÷ 70%). Because Zoe's net assets' book values equal their collective fair values of $400,000, Amanda recognizes goodwill of $100,000. Then, on January 1, 2013, when Zoe's book value has increased to $420,000, Amanda buys another 20 percent of Zoe for $95,000, bringing its total ownership to 90 percent. Under the acquisition method, the valuation basis for Zoe's net assets was established on January 1, 2012, the date Amanda obtained control. Subsequent transactions in the subsidiary's stock (purchases or sales) are now viewed as transactions in the combined entity's own stock. Therefore, when Amanda acquires Zoe's shares post-control, it recognizes the difference between the fair value of the consideration transferred and the underlying subsidiary valuation as an adjustment to Additional Paid-In Capital.

The difference between the $95,000 price and the underlying consolidated subsidiary value is computed as follows:

1/1/13 price paid for 20 percent interest		$ 95,000
Noncontrolling interest (NCI) acquired:		
Book value (20% of $420,000)	$84,000	
Goodwill (20% of $100,000)	20,000	
Noncontrolling interest book value (20%) 1/1/13		104,000
Additional paid-in capital from 20 percent NCI acquisition		$ 9,000

EXHIBIT 4.12 Step Acquisition Illustrated—Acquisition Method

ARCH COMPANY AND ZION COMPANY
Consolidated Worksheet
For Year Ending December 31, 2013

Consolidation: Acquisition Method
Investment: Equity Method

Accounts	Arch Company	Zion Company	Consolidation Entries Debit	Consolidation Entries Credit	Noncontrolling Interest	Consolidated Totals
Income Statement						
Revenues	(600,000)	(260,000)				(860,000)
Expenses	425,000	160,000	(E) 10,000			595,000
Equity in subsidiary earnings	(72,000)	–0–	(I) 72,000			–0–
Gain on revaluation of Zion	(20,000)					(20,000)
Separate company net income	(267,000)	(100,000)				
Consolidated net income						(285,000)
Noncontrolling interest in Zion Company's income					(18,000)	18,000
Controlling interest in consolidated net income						(267,000)
Statement of Retained Earnings						
Retained earnings, 1/1						
Arch Company	(758,000)					(758,000)
Zion Company		(230,000)	(S) 230,000			
Net income (above)	(267,000)	(100,000)				(267,000)
Dividends paid	125,000	20,000		(D) 16,000	4,000	125,000
Retained earnings, 12/31	(900,000)	(310,000)				(900,000)
Balance Sheet						
Current assets	509,000	280,000				789,000
Land	205,000	90,000				295,000
Buildings (net)	646,000	310,000				956,000
Investment in Zion Company	616,000	–0–	(D) 16,000	(A) 160,000		–0–
				(S) 400,000		
				(I) 72,000		
Customer base	–0–	–0–	(A) 200,000	(E) 10,000		190,000
Total assets	1,976,000	680,000				2,230,000
Liabilities	(461,000)	(100,000)				(561,000)
Noncontrolling interest in Zion Company, 1/1	–0–	–0–		(S) 100,000		
				(A) 40,000	(140,000)	
Noncontrolling interest in Zion Company, 12/31	–0–	–0–			154,000	(154,000)
Common stock	(355,000)	(200,000)	(S) 200,000			(355,000)
Additional paid-in capital	(260,000)	(70,000)	(S) 70,000			(260,000)
Retained earnings, 12/31 (above)	(900,000)	(310,000)				(900,000)
Total liabilities and equities	(1,976,000)	(680,000)	798,000	798,000		(2,230,000)

Consolidation entries:
(S) Elimination of subsidiary's stockholders' equity along with recognition of 1/1 noncontrolling interest.
(A) Allocation of subsidiary total fair value in excess of book value, unamortized balances as of 1/1.
(I) Elimination of intra-entity income (equity accrual less amortization expenses).
(D) Elimination of intra-entity dividend payments.
(E) Recognition of amortization expenses on fair-value allocations.

Amanda then prepares the following journal entry to record the acquisition of the 20 percent noncontrolling interest:

Investment in Zoe	104,000	
Cash		95,000
Additional Paid-in Capital		9,000

By purchasing 20 percent of Zoe for $95,000, the consolidated entity's owners have acquired a portion of their own firm at a price $9,000 less than consolidated book value. From a worksheet perspective, the $104,000 increase in the investment account simply replaces the 20 percent allocation to the noncontrolling interest. Importantly, the $95,000 exchanged for the 20 percent interest in Zoe's net assets does not affect consolidated asset valuation. The basis for the reported values in the consolidated financial statements was established on the date control was obtained.

LO10

Record the sale of a subsidiary (or a portion of its shares).

Parent Company Sales of Subsidiary Stock—Acquisition Method

Frequently, a parent company will sell a portion or all of the shares it owns of a subsidiary. For example, General Electric Company reported the sale of its NBC Universal business in its financial statements:

> On January 28, 2011, we transferred the assets of the NBCU business and Comcast transferred certain of its assets to a newly formed entity, NBC Universal LLC (NBCU LLC). In connection with the transaction, we received $6,197 million in cash from Comcast and a 49% interest in NBCU LLC. Comcast holds the remaining 51% interest in NBCU LLC. We will account for our investment in NBCU LLC under the equity method. As a result of the transaction, we expect to recognize a small after-tax gain in the first quarter of 2011.

The accounting effect of the sale of subsidiary shares depends on whether the parent continues to maintain control after the sale. If the sale of the parent's ownership interest results in the loss of control of a subsidiary as in the GE example above, it recognizes any resulting gain or loss in consolidated net income.

If the parent sells some subsidiary shares but retains control, it recognizes no gains or losses on the sale. Under the acquisition method, as long as control remains with the parent, transactions in the stock of the subsidiary are considered to be transactions in the equity of the consolidated entity. Because such transactions are considered to occur with owners, the parent records any difference between proceeds of the sale and carrying amount as additional paid-in capital.

Sale of Subsidiary Shares with Control Maintained

To illustrate, assume Adams Company owns 100 percent of Smith Company's 25,000 voting shares and appropriately carries the investment on its books at January 1, 2013, at $750,000 using the equity method. Assuming Adams sells 5,000 shares to outside interests for $165,000 on January 1, 2013, the transaction is recorded as follows:

Cash	165,000	
Investment in Smith		150,000
Additional Paid-in Capital from Noncontrolling Interest Transaction		15,000
To record sale of 5,000 Smith shares to noncontrolling interest with excess of sale proceeds over carrying amount attributed to additional paid-in capital.		

The $15,000 "gain" on sale of the subsidiary shares is not recognized in income, but is reported as an increase in owners' equity. This equity treatment for the "gain" is consistent with the economic unit notion that as long as control is maintained, payments received from owners of the firm are considered contributions of capital. The ownership group of the consolidated entity specifically includes the noncontrolling interest. Therefore, the above treatment of sales to an ownership group is consistent with accounting for other stock transactions with owners (e.g., treasury stock transactions).

Sale of Subsidiary Shares with Control Lost

The loss of control of a subsidiary is a remeasurement event that can result in gain or loss recognition. The gain or loss is computed as the difference between the sale proceeds and the carrying amount of the shares sold. Using the Adams and Smith example above, assume now that instead of selling 5,000 shares, Adams sells 20,000 of its shares in Smith to outside interests on January 1, 2013, and keeps the remaining 5,000 shares. Assuming sale proceeds of $675,000, we record the transaction as follows:

Cash	675,000	
Investment in Smith		600,000
Gain on Sale of Smith Investment		75,000
To record sale of 20,000 Smith shares, resulting in the loss of control over Smith Company.		

If the former parent retains any of its former subsidiary's shares, the retained investment should be remeasured to fair value on the date control is lost. Any resulting gain or loss from this remeasurement should be recognized in the parent's net income.

In our Adams and Smith example, Adams still retains 5,000 shares of Smith Company (25,000 original investment less 20,000 shares sold). Assuming further that the $675,000 sale price for the 20,000 shares sold represents a reasonable value for the remaining shares of $33.75, Adams's shares now have a fair value of $168,750 ($33.75 × 5,000 shares). Adams would thus record the revaluation of its retained 5,000 shares of Smith as follows:

Investment in Smith	18,750	
Gain on Revaluation of Retained Smith Shares to Fair Value		18,750
To record the revaluation of Smith shares to a $33.75 per share fair value from their previous equity method January 1, 2013, carrying amount of $30.00 per share.		

The above revaluation of retained shares reflects the view that the loss of control of a subsidiary is a significant economic event that changes the fundamental relationship between the former parent and subsidiary. Also, the fair value of the retained investment provides the users of the parent's financial statements with more relevant information about the investment.

Cost-Flow Assumptions

If it sells less than an entire investment, the parent must select an appropriate cost-flow assumption when it has made more than one purchase. In the sale of securities, the use of specific identification based on serial numbers is acceptable, although averaging or FIFO assumptions often are applied. Use of the averaging method is especially appealing because all shares are truly identical, creating little justification for identifying different cost figures with individual shares.

Accounting for Shares That Remain

If Adams sells only a portion of the investment, it also must determine the proper method of accounting for the shares that remain. Three possible scenarios can be envisioned:

1. Adams could have so drastically reduced its interest that the parent no longer controls the subsidiary or even has the ability to significantly influence its decision making. For example, assume that Adams's ownership drops from 80 to 5 percent. In the current period prior to the sale, the 80 percent investment is reported by means of the equity method with the market-value method used for the 5 percent that remains thereafter. Consolidated financial statements are no longer applicable.
2. Adams could still apply significant influence over Smith's operations although it no longer maintains control. A drop in the level of ownership from 80 to 30 percent normally meets this condition. In this case, the parent utilizes the equity method for the entire year. Application is based on 80 percent until the time of sale and then on 30 percent for the remainder of the year. Again, consolidated statements cease to be appropriate because control has been lost.
3. The decrease in ownership could be relatively small so that the parent continues to maintain control over the subsidiary even after the sale. Adams's reduction of its

ownership in Smith from 80 to 60 percent is an example of this situation. After the disposal, consolidated financial statements are still required, but the process is based on the *end-of-year ownership percentage.* Because only the retained shares (60 percent in this case) are consolidated, the parent must separately recognize any current year income accruing to it from its terminated interest. Thus, Adams shows earnings on this portion of the investment (a 20 percent interest in Smith for the time during the year that it is held) in the consolidated income statement as a single-line item computed by means of the equity method.

Comparisons with International Accounting Standards

As observed in previous chapters of this text, the accounting and reporting for business combinations between U.S. and international standards has largely converged with FASB ASC Topic 805 and *IFRS 3R,* each of which carries the title *Business Combinations* and ASC Topic 810, Consolidation. Each set of standards requires the acquisition method and embraces a fair-value model for the assets acquired and liabilities assumed in a business combination. Both sets of standards treat exchanges between the parent and the noncontrolling interest as equity transactions, unless control is lost. However, as seen below, the accounting for the noncontrolling interest can diverge across the two reporting regimes.

- *U.S. GAAP.* In reporting the noncontrolling interest in consolidated financial statements, U.S. GAAP requires a fair-value measurement attribute, consistent with the overall valuation principles for business combinations. Thus, acquisition-date fair value provides a basis for reporting the noncontrolling interest, which is adjusted for its share of subsidiary income and dividends subsequent to acquisition.
- *IFRS.* In contrast, *IFRS 3R* allows an option for reporting the noncontrolling interest for each business combination. Under IFRS, the noncontrolling interest may be measured either at its acquisition-date fair value, which can include goodwill, or at a proportionate share of the acquiree's identifiable net asset fair value, which excludes goodwill. The IFRS proportionate-share option effectively assumes that any goodwill created through the business combination applies solely to the controlling interest.

Summary

1. A parent company need not acquire 100 percent of a subsidiary's stock to form a business combination. Only control over the decision-making process is necessary, a level that has historically been achieved by obtaining a majority of the voting shares. Ownership of any subsidiary stock that is retained by outside, unrelated parties is collectively referred to as a noncontrolling interest.
2. A consolidation takes on an added degree of complexity when a noncontrolling interest is present. The noncontrolling interest represents a group of subsidiary owners and their equity is recognized by the parent in its consolidated financial statements.
3. The valuation principle for the noncontrolling interest is acquisition-date fair value. The fair value of the noncontrolling interest is added to the consideration transferred by the parent to determine the acquisition-date fair value of the subsidiary. This fair value is then allocated to the subsidiary's assets acquired and liabilities assumed based on their individual fair values. At the acquisition date, each of the subsidiary's assets and liabilities is included in consolidation at its individual fair value regardless of the degree of parent ownership. Any remaining excess fair value beyond the total assigned to the net assets is recognized as goodwill.
4. The fair value of the noncontrolling interest is adjusted over time for subsidiary income (less excess fair-value amortization) and subsidiary dividends.
5. Consolidated goodwill is allocated across the controlling and noncontrolling interests based on the excess of their respective acquisition-date fair values less their percentage share of the identifiable subsidiary net asset fair value. The goodwill allocation, therefore, does not necessarily correspond proportionately to the ownership interest of the parent and the noncontrolling interest.
6. Four noncontrolling interest figures appear in the annual consolidation process. First, a beginning-of-the-year balance is recognized on the worksheet (through Entry **S**) followed by

the noncontrolling interest's share of the unamortized excess acquisition-date fair values of the subsidiary's assets and liabilities (including a separate amount for goodwill if appropriate). Next, the noncontrolling interest share of the subsidiary's income for the period (recorded by a columnar entry) is recognized. Subsidiary dividends paid to these unrelated owners are entered as a reduction of the noncontrolling interest. The final balance for the year is found as a summation of the Noncontrolling Interest column and is presented on the consolidated balance sheet, within the Stockholders' Equity section.

7. When a midyear business acquisition occurs, consolidated revenues and expenses should not include the subsidiary's current year preacquisition revenues and expenses. Only postacquisition subsidiary revenues and expenses are consolidated.
8. A parent can obtain control of a subsidiary by means of several separate purchases occurring over time, a process often referred to as a step acquisition. Once control is achieved, the acquisition method requires that the parent adjust to fair value all prior investments in the acquired firm and recognize any gain or loss. The fair values of these prior investments, along with the consideration transferred in the current investment that gave the parent control, and the noncontrolling interest fair value all comprise the total fair value of the acquired company.
9. When a parent sells some of its ownership shares of a subsidiary, it must establish an appropriate investment account balance to ensure an accurate accounting. If the equity method has not been used, the parent's investment balance is adjusted to recognize any income or amortization previously omitted. The resulting balance is then compared to the amount received for the stock to arrive at either an adjustment to additional paid-in capital (control maintained) or a gain or loss (control lost). Any shares still held will subsequently be reported through either consolidation, the equity method, or the fair-value method, depending on the influence retained by the parent.

Comprehensive Illustration

Problem

(*Estimated Time: 60 to 75 Minutes*) On January 1, 2009, Father Company acquired an 80 percent interest in Sun Company for $425,000. The acquisition-date fair value of the 20 percent noncontrolling interest's ownership shares was $102,500. Also as of that date, Sun reported total stockholders' equity of $400,000: $100,000 in common stock and $300,000 in retained earnings. In setting the acquisition price, Father appraised four accounts at values different from the balances reported within Sun's financial records.

Buildings (8-year life)	Undervalued by $20,000
Land	Undervalued by $50,000
Equipment (5-year life)	Undervalued by $12,500
Royalty agreement (20-year life)	Not recorded, valued at $30,000

As of December 31, 2013, the trial balances of these two companies are as follows:

	Father Company	Sun Company
Debits		
Current assets	$ 605,000	$ 280,000
Investment in Sun Company	425,000	–0–
Land	200,000	300,000
Buildings (net)	640,000	290,000
Equipment (net)	380,000	160,000
Expenses	550,000	190,000
Dividends	90,000	20,000
Total debits	$2,890,000	$1,240,000
Credits		
Liabilities	$ 910,000	$ 300,000
Common stock	480,000	100,000
Retained earnings, 1/1/13	704,000	480,000
Revenues	780,000	360,000
Dividend income	16,000	–0–
Total credits	$2,890,000	$1,240,000

Included in these figures is a $20,000 debt that Sun owes to the parent company. No goodwill impairments have occurred since the Sun Company acquisition.

Required

a. Determine consolidated totals for Father Company and Sun Company for the year 2013.

b. Prepare worksheet entries to consolidate the trial balances of Father Company and Sun Company for the year 2013.

c. Assume instead that the acquisition-date fair value of the noncontrolling interest was $104,500. What balances in the December 31, 2013, consolidated statements would change?

Solution

a. The consolidation of Father Company and Sun Company begins with the allocation of the subsidiary's acquisition-date fair value as shown in Exhibit 4.13. Because this consolidation is taking place after several years, the unamortized balances for the various allocations at the start of the current year also should be determined (see Exhibit 4.14).

Next, the parent's method of accounting for its subsidiary should be ascertained. The continuing presence of the original $425,000 acquisition price in the investment account indicates that Father is applying the initial value method. This same determination can be made from the Dividend Income account, which equals 80 percent of the subsidiary's dividends. Thus, Father's accounting records have ignored the increase in Sun's book value as well as the excess amortization expenses for the prior periods of ownership. These amounts have to be added to the parent's January 1, 2013, Retained Earnings account to arrive at a properly consolidated balance.

During the 2009–2012 period of ownership, Sun's Retained Earnings account increased by $180,000 ($480,000 − $300,000). Father's 80 percent interest necessitates an accrual of $144,000 ($180,000 × 80%) for these years. In addition, the acquisition-date fair-value allocations require

EXHIBIT 4.13
Excess Fair-Value Allocations

FATHER COMPANY AND SUN COMPANY
Acquisition-Date Fair-Value Allocation and Amortization
2009–2012

	Allocation	Estimated Life (years)	Annual Excess Amortization
Acquisition-date fair value	$527,500		
Sun book value (100%)	400,000		
Excess fair value	127,500		
Allocation to specific subsidiary accounts based on fair value:			
Buildings	$ 20,000	8	$ 2,500
Land	50,000		
Equipment	12,500	5	2,500
Royalty agreement	30,000	20	1,500
Goodwill	$ 15,000		
Annual excess amortization expenses			$ 6,500

Goodwill Allocation to the Controlling and Noncontrolling Interests

	Controlling Interest	Noncontrolling Interest	Total
Fair value at acquisition date	$425,000	$102,500	$527,500
Relative fair value of Sun's net identifiable assets (80% and 20%)	410,000	102,500	512,500
Goodwill	$ 15,000	$ -0-	$ 15,000

EXHIBIT 4.14
Excess Fair-Value Allocation Balances

FATHER COMPANY AND SUN COMPANY
Unamortized Excess Fair- over Book-Value Allocation
January 1, 2013, Balances

Account	Excess Original Allocation	Excess Amortization 2009–2012	Balance 1/1/13
Buildings	$ 20,000	$10,000	$ 10,000
Land	50,000	–0–	50,000
Equipment	12,500	10,000	2,500
Royalty agreement	30,000	6,000	24,000
Goodwill	15,000	–0–	15,000
Total	$127,500	$26,000	$101,500

the recognition of $20,800 in excess amortization expenses for this same period ($6,500 × 80% × 4 years). Thus, a net increase of $123,200 ($144,000 − $20,800) is needed to correct the parent's beginning Retained Earnings balance for the year.

Once the adjustment from the initial value method to the equity method is determined, the consolidated figures for 2013 can be calculated:

Current Assets = $865,000. The parent's book value is added to the subsidiary's book value. The $20,000 intra-entity balance is eliminated.

Investment in Sun Company = −0−. The intra-entity ownership is eliminated so that the subsidiary's specific assets and liabilities can be consolidated.

Land = $550,000. The parent's book value is added to the subsidiary's book value plus the $50,000 excess fair-value allocation (see Exhibit 4.13).

Buildings (net) = $937,500. The parent's book value is added to the subsidiary's book value plus the $20,000 fair-value allocation (see Exhibit 4.14) and less five years of amortization (2009 through 2013).

Equipment (net) = $540,000. The parent's book value is added to the subsidiary's book value. The $12,500 fair-value allocation has been completely amortized after five years.

Goodwill = $15,000. Original acquisition-date value assigned.

Expenses = $746,500. The parent's book value is added to the subsidiary's book value plus amortization expenses on the fair-value allocations for the year (see Exhibit 4.13).

Dividends Paid = $90,000. Only parent company dividends are consolidated. Subsidiary dividends paid to the parent are eliminated; the remainder reduce the Noncontrolling Interest balance.

Royalty Agreement = $22,500. The original residual allocation from the acquisition-date fair value is recognized after taking into account five years of amortization (see Exhibit 4.13).

Consolidated Net Income = $393,500. The combined total of consolidated revenues and expenses.

Noncontrolling Interest in Subsidiary's Income = $32,700. The outside owners are assigned a 20 percent share of the subsidiary's income less excess fair-value amortizations: 20% × ($170,000 − $6,500).

Controlling Interest in Consolidated Net Income = $360,800. Consolidated net income less the amount allocated to the noncontrolling interest.

Liabilities = $1,190,000. The parent's book value is added to the subsidiary's book value. The $20,000 intra-entity balance is eliminated.

Common Stock = $480,000. Only the parent company's balance is reported.

Retained Earnings, 1/1/13 = $827,200. Only the parent company's balance after a $123,200 increase to convert from the initial value method to the equity method.

Retained Earnings 12/31/13 = $1,098,000. The parent's adjusted beginning balance of $827,200, plus $360,800 net income to the controlling interest, less $90,000 dividends paid by Father Company.

Revenues = $1,140,000. The parent's book value is added to the subsidiary's book value.

Dividend Income = –0–. The intra-entity dividend receipts are eliminated.

Noncontrolling Interest in Subsidiary, 12/31/13 = $162,000.

NCI in Sun's 1/1/13 book value (20% × $580,000)	$116,000
NCI in unamortized excess fair-value allocations (20% × $86,500)	17,300
January 1, 2013, NCI in Sun's fair value	133,300
NCI in Sun's net income [20% × ($360,000 − 196,500)]	32,700
NCI dividend share (20% × $20,000)	(4,000)
Total noncontrolling interest December 31, 2013	$162,000

b. Six worksheet entries are necessary to produce a consolidation worksheet for Father Company and Sun Company.

Entry *C

Investment in Sun Company	123,200	
Retained Earnings, 1/1/13 (parent)		123,200

This increment is required to adjust the parent's Retained Earnings from the initial value method to the equity method. The amount is $144,000 (80 percent of the $180,000 increase in the subsidiary's book value during previous years) less $20,800 in excess amortization over this same four-year period ($6,500 × 80% × 4 years).

Entry S

Common Stock (subsidiary)	100,000	
Retained Earnings, 1/1/13 (subsidiary)	480,000	
Investment in Sun Company (80 percent)		464,000
Noncontrolling Interest in Sun Company (20 percent)		116,000

To eliminate beginning stockholders' equity accounts of the subsidiary and recognize the beginning balance book value attributed to the outside owners (20 percent).

Entry A1 and A2 Combined

Buildings	10,000	
Land	50,000	
Equipment	2,500	
Royalty Agreement	24,000	
Goodwill	15,000	
Investment in Sun Company		84,200
Noncontrolling Interest in Sun Company		17,300

To recognize unamortized excess fair- over book-value allocations as of the first day of the current year (see Exhibit 4.14). All goodwill is attributable to the controlling interest.

Entry I

Dividend Income	16,000	
Dividends Paid		16,000

To eliminate intra-entity dividend payments recorded by parent (using the initial value method) as income.

Entry E

Depreciation Expense	5,000	
Amortization Expense	1,500	
Buildings		2,500
Equipment		2,500
Royalty Agreement		1,500

To recognize excess amortization expenses for the current year (see Exhibit 4.13).

Entry P

Liabilities	20,000	
Current Assets		20,000
To eliminate the intra-entity debt.		

c. If the acquisition-date fair value of the noncontrolling interest were $104,500, then Sun's fair value would increase by $2,000 to $529,500 and goodwill would increase by the same $2,000 to $17,000. The entire $2,000 increase in goodwill would be allocated to the noncontrolling interest as follows:

	Controlling Interest	Noncontrolling Interest	Total
Fair value at acquisition date	$425,000	$104,500	$529,500
Relative fair value of Sun's net identifiable assets (80% and 20%)	410,000	102,500	512,500
Goodwill	$ 15,000	$ 2,000	$ 17,000

Therefore, the consolidated balance sheet would show goodwill at $17,000 (instead of $15,000) and the noncontrolling interest balance would show $164,000 (instead of $162,000).

Questions

1. What does the term *noncontrolling interest* mean?
2. Atwater Company acquires 80 percent of the outstanding voting stock of Belwood Company. On that date, Belwood possesses a building with a $160,000 book value but a $220,000 fair value. At what value would this building be consolidated?
3. What is a control premium and how does it affect consolidated financial statements?
4. Where should the noncontrolling interest's claims be reported in a set of consolidated financial statements?
5. How is the noncontrolling interest in a subsidiary company calculated as of the end of a reporting period?
6. December 31 consolidated financial statements are being prepared for Allsports Company and its new subsidiary acquired on July 1 of the current year. Should Allsports adjust its consolidated balances for the preacquisition subsidiary revenues and expenses?
7. Tree, Inc., has held a 10 percent interest in the stock of Limb Company for several years. Because of the level of ownership, this investment has been accounted for using the fair-value method. At the beginning of the current year, Tree acquires an additional 70 percent interest, which provides the company with control over Limb. In preparing consolidated financial statements for this business combination, how does Tree account for the previous 10 percent ownership interest?
8. Duke Corporation owns a 70 percent equity interest in UNCCH, a subsidiary corporation. During the current year, a portion of this stock is sold to an outside party. Before recording this transaction, Duke adjusts the book value of its investment account. What is the purpose of this adjustment?
9. In question (8), how would the parent record the sales transaction?
10. In question (8), how would Duke account for the remainder of its investment subsequent to the sale of this partial interest?

Problems

LO1

1. What is a basic premise of the acquisition method regarding accounting for a noncontrolling interest?
   a. Consolidated financial statements should be primarily for the benefit of the parent company's stockholders.
   b. Consolidated financial statements should be produced only if both the parent and the subsidiary are in the same basic industry.
   c. A subsidiary is an indivisible part of a business combination and should be included in its entirety regardless of the degree of ownership.
   d. Consolidated financial statements should not report a noncontrolling interest balance because these outside owners do not hold stock in the parent company.

LO2

2. Bailey, Inc., buys 60 percent of the outstanding stock of Luebs, Inc. Luebs owns a piece of land that cost $200,000 but was worth $500,000 at the acquisition date. What value should be attributed to this land in a consolidated balance sheet at the date of takeover?
   a. $120,000.
   b. $300,000.
   c. $380,000.
   d. $500,000.

LO2

3. Jordan, Inc., holds 75 percent of the outstanding stock of Paxson Corporation. Paxson currently owes Jordan $400,000 for inventory acquired over the past few months. In preparing consolidated financial statements, what amount of this debt should be eliminated?
   a. −0−.
   b. $100,000.
   c. $300,000.
   d. $400,000.

LO2

4. On January 1, 2012, Brendan, Inc., reports net assets of $760,000 although equipment (with a four-year life) having a book value of $440,000 is worth $500,000 and an unrecorded patent is valued at $45,000. Hope Corporation pays $692,000 on that date for an 80 percent ownership in Brendan. If the patent is to be written off over a 10-year period, at what amount should it be reported on consolidated statements at December 31, 2013?
   a. $28,800.
   b. $32,400.
   c. $36,000.
   d. $40,500.

LO6

5. The noncontrolling interest represents an outside ownership in a subsidiary that is not attributable to the parent company. Where in the consolidated balance sheet is this outside ownership interest recognized?
   a. In the liability section.
   b. In a mezzanine section between liabilities and owners' equity.
   c. In the owners' equity section.
   d. The noncontrolling interest is not recognized in the consolidated balance sheet.

LO4

6. On January 1, 2012, Chamberlain Corporation pays $388,000 for a 60 percent ownership in Neville. Annual excess fair-value amortization of $15,000 results from the acquisition. On December 31, 2013, Neville reports revenues of $400,000 and expenses of $300,000 and Chamberlain reports revenues of $700,000 and expenses of $400,000. The parent figures contain no income from the subsidiary. What is consolidated net income attributable to the controlling interest?
   a. $231,000.
   b. $351,000.
   c. $366,000.
   d. $400,000.

LO4

Questions 7 and 8 relate to the following:

On January 1, 2011, Pride Co. purchased 90 percent of the outstanding voting shares of Star Inc. for $540,000 cash. The acquisition-date fair value of the noncontrolling interest was $60,000. At January 1, 2011, Star's net assets had a total carrying amount of $420,000. Equipment (8-year remaining life) was undervalued on Star's financial records by $80,000. Any remaining excess fair value over book value was attributed to a customer list developed by Star (4-year remaining life), but not recorded on its books. Star recorded income of $70,000 in 2011 and $80,000 in 2012. Each year since the acquisition, Star has paid a $20,000 dividend. At January 1, 2013, Pride's retained earnings show a $250,000 balance.

Selected account balances for the two companies from their separate operations were as follows:

	Pride	Star
2013 Revenues	$498,000	$285,000
2013 Expenses	350,000	195,000

7. What is consolidated net income for Pride and Star for 2013?
   a. $194,000.
   b. $197,500.
   c. $203,000.
   d. $238,000.
8. Assuming that Pride, in its internal records, accounts for its investment in Star using the equity method, what is Pride's share of consolidated retained earnings at January 1, 2013?
   a. $250,000.
   b. $286,000.
   c. $315,000.
   d. $360,000.

LO8

9. James Company acquired 85 percent of Mark-Right Company on April 1. On its December 31 consolidated income statement, how should James account for Mark-Right's revenues and expenses that occurred before April 1?
   a. Include 100 percent of Mark-Right's revenues and expenses and deduct the preacquisition portion as noncontrolling interest in net income.
   b. Exclude 100 percent of the preacquisition revenues and 100 percent of the preacquisition expenses from their respective consolidated totals.
   c. Exclude 15 percent of the preacquisition revenues and 15 percent of the preacquisition expenses from consolidated expenses.
   d. Deduct 15 percent of the net combined revenues and expenses relating to the preacquisition period from consolidated net income.

LO9

10. Amie, Inc., has 100,000 shares of $2 par value stock outstanding. Prairie Corporation acquired 30,000 of Amie's shares on January 1, 2010, for $120,000 when Amie's net assets had a total fair value of $350,000. On July 1, 2013, Prairie agreed to buy an additional 60,000 shares of Amie from a single stockholder for $6 per share. Although Amie's shares were selling in the $5 range around July 1, 2013, Prairie forecasted that obtaining control of Amie would produce significant revenue synergies to justify the premium price paid. If Amie's net identifiable assets had a fair value of $500,000 at July 1, 2013, how much goodwill should Prairie report in its postcombination consolidated balance sheet?
    a. $60,000.
    b. $90,000.
    c. $100,000.
    d. $-0-.

LO9

11. A parent buys 32 percent of a subsidiary in one year and then buys an additional 40 percent in the next year. In a step acquisition of this type, the original 32 percent acquisition should be
    a. Maintained at its initial value.
    b. Adjusted to its equity method balance at the date of the second acquisition.
    c. Adjusted to fair value at the date of the second acquisition with a resulting gain or loss recorded.
    d. Adjusted to fair value at the date of the second acquisition with a resulting adjustment to additional paid-in capital.

LO4, LO8

12. On April 1, Pujols, Inc., exchanges $430,000 fair-value consideration for 70 percent of the outstanding stock of Ramirez Corporation. The remaining 30 percent of the outstanding shares continued to trade at a collective fair value of $165,000. Ramirez's identifiable assets and liabilities each had book values that equaled their fair values on April 1 for a net total of $500,000. During the remainder of the year, Ramirez generates revenues of $600,000 and expenses of $360,000 and paid no dividends. On a December 31 consolidated balance sheet, what amount should be reported as noncontrolling interest?
    a. $219,000.
    b. $237,000.
    c. $234,000.
    d. $250,500.

LO10

13. McKinley, Inc., owns 100 percent of Jackson Company's 45,000 voting shares. On June 30, McKinley's internal accounting records show a $192,000 equity method adjusted balance for

its investment in Jackson. McKinley sells 15,000 of its Jackson shares on the open market for $80,000 on June 30. How should McKinley record the excess of the sale proceeds over its carrying amount for the shares?

a. Reduce goodwill by $64,000.

b. Recognize a gain on sale for $16,000.

c. Increase its additional paid-in capital by $16,000.

d. Recognize a revaluation gain on its remaining shares of $48,000.

Use the following information for Problems 14 through 16:

West Company acquired 60 percent of Solar Company for $300,000 when Solar's book value was $400,000. The newly comprised 40 percent noncontrolling interest had an assessed fair value of $200,000. Also at the acquisition date, Solar had a trademark (with a 10-year life) that was undervalued in the financial records by $60,000. Also, patented technology (with a 5-year life) was undervalued by $40,000. Two years later, the following figures are reported by these two companies (stockholders' equity accounts have been omitted):

	West Company Book Value	Solar Company Book Value	Solar Company Fair Value
Current assets	$620,000	$300,000	$320,000
Trademarks	260,000	200,000	280,000
Patented technology	410,000	150,000	150,000
Liabilities	(390,000)	(120,000)	(120,000)
Revenues	(900,000)	(400,000)	
Expenses	500,000	300,000	
Investment income	Not given		

LO2

14. What is the consolidated net income before allocation to the controlling and noncontrolling interests?

a. $400,000.

b. $486,000.

c. $491,600.

d. $500,000.

LO4, LO5

15. Assuming Solar Company has paid no dividends, what are the noncontrolling interest's share of the subsidiary's income and the ending balance of the noncontrolling interest in the subsidiary?

a. $26,000 and $230,000.

b. $28,800 and $252,000.

c. $34,400 and $280,800.

d. $40,000 and $252,000.

LO2

16. What is the consolidated trademarks balance?

a. $508,000.

b. $514,000.

c. $520,000.

d. $540,000.

LO2

Use the following information for Problems 17 through 21:

On January 1, Park Corporation and Strand Corporation had condensed balance sheets as follows:

	Park	Strand
Current assets	$ 70,000	$20,000
Noncurrent assets	90,000	40,000
Total assets	$160,000	$60,000
Current liabilities	$ 30,000	$10,000
Long-term debt	50,000	—
Stockholders' equity	80,000	50,000
Total liabilities and equities	$160,000	$60,000

On January 2, Park borrowed $60,000 and used the proceeds to obtain 80 percent of the outstanding common shares of Strand. The acquisition price was considered proportionate to Strand's total fair value. The $60,000 debt is payable in 10 equal annual principal payments, plus interest, beginning December 31. The excess fair value of the investment over the underlying book value of the acquired net assets is allocated to inventory (60 percent) and to goodwill (40 percent). On a consolidated balance sheet as of January 2, what should be the amount for each of the following?

17. Current assets:
    a. $105,000.
    b. $102,000.
    c. $100,000.
    d. $90,000.
18. Noncurrent assets:
    a. $130,000.
    b. $134,000.
    c. $138,000.
    d. $140,000.
19. Current liabilities:
    a. $50,000.
    b. $46,000.
    c. $40,000.
    d. $30,000.
20. Noncurrent liabilities:
    a. $110,000.
    b. $104,000.
    c. $90,000.
    d. $50,000.
21. Stockholders' equity:
    a. $80,000.
    b. $90,000.
    c. $95,000.
    d. $130,000.

    (AICPA adapted)

LO4, LO5

22. On January 1, 2012, Harrison, Inc., acquired 90 percent of Starr Company in exchange for $1,125,000 fair-value consideration. The total fair value of Starr Company was assessed at $1,200,000. Harrison computed annual excess fair-value amortization of $8,000 based on the difference between Starr's total fair value and its underlying net asset fair value. The subsidiary reported earnings of $70,000 in 2012 and $90,000 in 2013 with dividend payments of $30,000 each year. Apart from its investment in Starr, Harrison had income of $220,000 in 2012 and $260,000 in 2013.
    a. What is the consolidated net income in each of these two years?
    b. What is the ending noncontrolling interest balance as of December 31, 2013?

LO2, LO4, LO5

23. On January 1, 2013, Pepper Enterprises acquired 80 percent of Harlan Company's outstanding common shares in exchange for $3,000,000 cash. The price paid for the 80 percent ownership interest was proportionately representative of the fair value of all of Harlan's shares.

    At acquisition date, Harlan's books showed assets of $4,200,000 and liabilities of $1,600,000. The recorded assets and liabilities had fair values equal to their individual book values except that a building (10-year remaining life) with book value of $195,000 had an appraised fair value of $345,000.

    Also, at acquisition date Harlan possessed unrecorded technology processes (zero book value) with an estimated fair value of $1,000,000 and a 20-year life. For 2013 Pepper reported net income of $700,000 (before recognition of Harlan's income), and Harlan separately reported earnings of $350,000. During 2013, Pepper paid dividends of $85,000 and Harlan paid $50,000 in dividends.

Compute the amounts that Pepper Enterprises should report in its December 31, 2013, consolidated financial statement for the following items:

a. Harlan's technology processes.

b. Harlan's building.

c. Controlling interest in consolidated net income.

d. Noncontrolling interest in consolidated net income.

e. Noncontrolling interest.

LO4, LO5, LO7

24. On January 1, Patterson Corporation acquired 80 percent of the 100,000 outstanding voting shares of Soriano, Inc., in exchange for $31.25 per share cash. The remaining 20 percent of Soriano's shares continued to trade for $30.00 both before and after Patterson's acquisition.

At January 1, Soriano's book and fair values were as follows:

	Book Values	Fair Values	Remaining Life
Current assets	80,000	80,000	
Buildings and equipment	1,250,000	1,000,000	5 years
Trademarks	700,000	900,000	10 years
Patented technology	940,000	2,000,000	4 years
	2,970,000		
Current liabilities	180,000	180,000	
Long-term notes payable	1,500,000	1,500,000	
Common stock	50,000		
Additional paid-in capital	500,000		
Retained earnings	740,000		
	2,970,000		

In addition, Patterson assigned a $600,000 value to certain unpatented technologies recently developed by Soriano. These technologies were estimated to have a 3-year remaining life.

During the year, Soriano paid a $30,000 dividend to its shareholders. The companies reported the following revenues and expenses from their separate operations for the year ending December 31.

	Patterson	Soriano
Revenues	3,000,000	1,400,000
Expenses	1,750,000	600,000

a. What total value should Patterson assign to its Soriano acquisition in its January 1 consolidated balance sheet?

b. What valuation principle should Patterson use to report each of Soriano's identifiable assets and liabilities in its January 1 consolidated balance sheet?

c. For years subsequent to acquisition, how will Soriano's identifiable assets and liabilities be valued in Patterson's consolidated reports?

d. How much goodwill resulted from Patterson's acquisition of Soriano?

e. What is the consolidated net income for the year and what amounts are allocated to the controlling and noncontrolling interests?

f. What is the noncontrolling interest amount reported in the December 31 consolidated balance sheet?

g. Assume instead that, based on its share prices, Soriano's January 1 total fair value was assessed at $2,250,000. How would the reported amounts for Soriano's net assets change on Patterson's acquisition-date consolidated balance sheet?

LO9

25. On January 1, 2012, Palka, Inc., acquired 70 percent of the outstanding shares of Sellinger Company for $1,141,000 in cash. The price paid was proportionate to Sellinger's total fair value, although at the acquisition date, Sellinger had a total book value of $1,380,000. All assets acquired and liabilities assumed had fair values equal to book values except for a patent (six-year remaining life) that was undervalued on Sellinger's accounting records by $240,000. On January 1, 2013, Palka acquired an additional 25 percent common stock equity interest in

Sellinger Company for $415,000 in cash. On its internal records, Palka uses the equity method to account for its shares of Sellinger.

During the two years following the acquisition, Sellinger reported the following net income and dividends:

	2012	2013
Net income	$340,000	$440,000
Dividends	150,000	180,000

a. Show Palka's journal entry to record its January 1, 2013, acquisition of an additional 25 percent ownership of Sellinger Company shares.

b. Prepare a schedule showing Palka's December 31, 2013, equity method balance for its Investment in Sellinger account.

LO2, LO7, LO8

26. Parker, Inc., acquires 70 percent of Sawyer Company for $420,000. The remaining 30 percent of Sawyer's outstanding shares continue to trade at a collective value of $174,000. On the acquisition date, Sawyer has the following accounts:

	Book Value	Fair Value
Current assets	$ 210,000	$ 210,000
Land	170,000	180,000
Buildings	300,000	330,000
Liabilities	(280,000)	(280,000)

The buildings have a 10-year life. In addition, Sawyer holds a patent worth $140,000 that has a five-year life but is not recorded on its financial records. At the end of the year, the two companies report the following balances:

	Parker	Sawyer
Revenues	$(900,000)	$(600,000)
Expenses	600,000	400,000

a. Assume that the acquisition took place on January 1. What figures would appear in a consolidated income statement for this year?

b. Assume that the acquisition took place on April 1. Sawyer's revenues and expenses occurred uniformly throughout the year. What amounts would appear in a consolidated income statement for this year?

LO2, LO4, LO5

27. On January 1, Beckman, Inc., acquires 60 percent of the outstanding stock of Calvin for $36,000. Calvin Co. has one recorded asset, a specialized production machine with a book value of $10,000 and no liabilities. The fair value of the machine is $50,000, and the remaining useful life is estimated to be 10 years. Any remaining excess fair value is attributable to an unrecorded process trade secret with an estimated future life of 4 years. Calvin's total acquisition-date fair value is $60,000.

At the end of the year, Calvin reports the following in its financial statements:

Revenues	$50,000	Machine	$ 9,000	Common stock	$10,000
Expenses	20,000	Other assets	26,000	Retained earnings	25,000
Net income	$30,000	Total assets	$35,000	Total equity	$35,000
Dividends paid	$ 5,000				

Determine the amounts that Beckman should report in its year-end consolidated financial statements for noncontrolling interest in subsidiary income, total noncontrolling interest, Calvin's machine (net of accumulated depreciation), and the process trade secret.

LO3, LO5, LO7

28. On January 1, 2011, Parflex Corporation exchanged $344,000 cash for 90% of Eagle Corporation's outstanding voting stock. Eagle's acquisition date balance sheet follows:

Cash and receivables	$ 15,000	Liabilities	$ 76,000
Inventory	35,000	Common stock	150,000
Property and equipment (net)	350,000	Retained earnings	174,000
	$400,000		$400,000

On January 1, 2011, Parflex prepared the following fair-value allocation schedule:

Consideration transferred by Parflex	$344,000
10% noncontrolling interest fair value	36,000
Fair value of Eagle	380,000
Book value of Eagle	324,000
Excess fair over book value	56,000
to equipment (undervalued, remaining life of 9 years)	18,000
to goodwill (indefinite life)	$38,000

The companies' financial statements for the year ending December 31, 2013, follow:

	Parflex	Eagle
Sales	$ (862,000)	$(366,000)
Cost of goods sold	515,000	209,000
Depreciation expense	191,200	67,000
Equity in Eagle's earnings	(79,200)	–0–
Separate company net income	$ (235,000)	$ (90,000)
Retained earnings 1/1	$ (500,000)	$(278,000)
Net income	(235,000)	(90,000)
Dividends paid	130,000	27,000
Retained earnings 12/31	$ (605,000)	$(341,000)
Cash and receivables	$ 135,000	$ 82,000
Inventory	255,000	136,000
Investment in Eagle	488,900	–0–
Property and equipment (net)	964,000	328,000
Total assets	$ 1,842,900	$ 546,000
Liabilities	$ (722,900)	(55,000)
Common stock—Parflex	(515,000)	–0–
Common stock—Eagle	–0–	(150,000)
Retained earnings 12/31	(605,000)	(341,000)
Total liabilities and owners' equity	$(1,842,900)	$(546,000)

a. Compute the goodwill allocation to the controlling and noncontrolling interest.

b. Show how Parflex determined its "Investment in Eagle" account balance.

c. Determine the amounts that should appear on Parflex's December 31, 2013, consolidated statement of financial position and its 2013 consolidated income statement.

LO8, LO9

29. On January 1, 2013, Morey, Inc., exchanged $178,000 for 25 percent of Amsterdam Corporation. Morey appropriately applied the equity method to this investment. At January 1, the book values of Amsterdam's assets and liabilities approximated their fair values.

On June 30, 2013, Morey paid $560,000 for an additional 70 percent of Amsterdam, thus increasing its overall ownership to 95 percent. The price paid for the 70 percent acquisition was proportionate to Amsterdam's total fair value. At June 30, the carrying amounts of Amsterdam's assets and liabilities approximated their fair values. Any remaining excess fair value was attributed to goodwill.

Amsterdam reports the following amounts at December 31, 2013 (credit balances shown in parentheses):

Revenues	$(210,000)
Expenses	140,000
Retained earnings, January 1	(200,000)
Dividends, October 1	20,000
Common stock	(500,000)

Amsterdam's revenue and expenses were distributed evenly throughout the year and no changes in Amsterdam's stock have occurred.

Using the acquisition method, compute the following:

a. The acquisition-date fair value of Amsterdam to be included in Morey's consolidated financial statements.

b. The revaluation gain (or loss) reported by Morey for its 25 percent investment in Amsterdam on June 30.

c. The amount of goodwill recognized by Morey on its December 31 balance sheet (assume no impairments have been recognized).

d. The noncontrolling interest amount reported by Morey on its

- June 30 consolidated balance sheet.
- December 31 consolidated balance sheet.

LO10

30. Posada Company acquired 7,000 of the 10,000 outstanding shares of Sabathia Company on January 1, 2011, for $840,000. The subsidiary's total fair value was assessed at $1,200,000 although its book value on that date was $1,130,000. The $70,000 fair value in excess of Sabathia's book value was assigned to a patent with a 5-year remaining life.

On January 1, 2013, Posada reported a $1,085,000 equity method balance in the Investment in Sabathia Company account. On October 1, 2013, Posada sells 1,000 shares of the investment for $191,000. During 2013, Sabathia reported net income of $120,000 and paid dividends of $40,000. These amounts are assumed to have occurred evenly throughout the year.

a. How should Posada report the 2013 income that accrued to the 1,000 shares prior to their sale?

b. What is the effect on Posada's financial statements from this sale of 1,000 shares?

c. How should Posada report in its financial statements the 6,000 shares of Sabathia it continues to hold?

LO5

31. On January 1, 2011, Telconnect acquires 70 percent of Bandmor for $490,000 cash. The remaining 30 percent of Bandmor's shares continued to trade at a total value of $210,000. The new subsidiary reported common stock of $300,000 on that date, with retained earnings of $180,000. A patent was undervalued in the company's financial records by $30,000. This patent had a 5-year remaining life. Goodwill of $190,000 was recognized and allocated proportionately to the controlling and noncontrolling interests. Bandmor earns income and pays cash dividends as follows:

Year	Net Income	Dividends Paid
2011	$ 75,000	$39,000
2012	96,000	44,000
2013	110,000	60,000

On December 31, 2013, Telconnect owes $22,000 to Bandmor.

a. If Telconnect has applied the equity method, what consolidation entries are needed as of December 31, 2013?

b. If Telconnect has applied the initial value method, what Entry *C is needed for a 2013 consolidation?

c. If Telconnect has applied the partial equity method, what Entry *C is needed for a 2013 consolidation?

d. What noncontrolling interest balances will appear in consolidated financial statements for 2013?

LO2, LO3, LO5

32. Miller Company acquired an 80 percent interest in Taylor Company on January 1, 2011. Miller paid $664,000 in cash to the owners of Taylor to acquire these shares. In addition, the remaining 20 percent of Taylor shares continued to trade at a total value of $166,000 both before and after Miller's acquisition.

On January 1, 2011, Taylor reported a book value of $600,000 (Common Stock = $300,000; Additional Paid-In Capital = $90,000; Retained Earnings = $210,000). Several of Taylor's buildings that had a remaining life of 20 years were undervalued by a total of $80,000.

During the next three years, Taylor reported the following figures:

Year	Net Income	Dividends Paid
2011	$ 70,000	$10,000
2012	90,000	15,000
2013	100,000	20,000

Determine the appropriate answers for each of the following questions:

a. What amount of excess depreciation expense should be recognized in the consolidated financial statements for the initial years following this acquisition?

b. If a consolidated balance sheet is prepared as of January 1, 2011, what amount of goodwill should be recognized?

c. If a consolidation worksheet is prepared as of January 1, 2011, what Entry S and Entry A should be included?

d. On the separate financial records of the parent company, what amount of investment income would be reported for 2011 under each of the following accounting methods?

(1) The equity method.

(2) The partial equity method.

(3) The initial value method.

e. On the parent company's separate financial records, what would be the December 31, 2013, balance for the Investment in Taylor Company account under each of the following accounting methods?

(1) The equity method.

(2) The partial equity method.

(3) The initial value method.

f. As of December 31, 2012, Miller's Buildings account on its separate records has a balance of $800,000 and Taylor has a similar account with a $300,000 balance. What is the consolidated balance for the Buildings account?

g. What is the balance of consolidated goodwill as of December 31, 2013?

h. Assume that the parent company has been applying the equity method to this investment. On December 31, 2013, the separate financial statements for the two companies present the following information:

	Miller Company	Taylor Company
Common stock	$500,000	$300,000
Additional paid-in capital	280,000	90,000
Retained earnings, 12/31/13	620,000	425,000

What will be the consolidated balance of each of these accounts?

LO1, LO8

33. Following are several account balances taken from the records of Karson and Reilly as of December 31, 2013. A few asset accounts have been omitted here. All revenues, expenses, and dividends occurred evenly throughout the year. Annual tests have indicated no goodwill impairment.

	Karson	Reilly
Sales	$ (800,000)	$(500,000)
Cost of goods sold	400,000	280,000
Operating expenses	200,000	100,000
Investment income	not given	–0–
Retained earnings, 1/1	(1,400,000)	(700,000)
Dividends	80,000	20,000
Trademarks	600,000	200,000
Royalty agreements	700,000	300,000
Licensing agreements	400,000	400,000
Liabilities	(500,000)	(200,000)
Common stock ($10 par value)	(400,000)	(100,000)
Additional paid-in capital	(500,000)	(600,000)

On July 1, 2013, Karson acquired 80 percent of Reilly for $1,330,000 cash consideration. In addition, Karson agreed to pay additional cash to the former owners of Reilly if certain performance measures are achieved after three years. Karson assessed a $30,000 fair value for the contingent performance obligation as of the acquisition date and as of December 31, 2013.

On July 1, 2013, Reilly's assets and liabilities had book values equal to their fair value except for some trademarks (with 5-year remaining lives) that were undervalued by $150,000. Karson estimated Reilly's total fair value at $1,700,000 on July 1, 2013.

For a consolidation prepared at December 31, 2013, what balances would be reported for the following?

Sales	Consolidated Net Income
Expenses	Retained Earnings, 1/1
Noncontrolling Interest in Subsidiary's Net Income	Trademarks
	Goodwill

LO5

34. Nascent, Inc., acquires 60 percent of Sea-Breeze Corporation for $414,000 cash on January 1, 2010. The remaining 40 percent of the Sea-Breeze shares traded near a total value of $276,000 both before and after the acquisition date. On January 1, 2010, Sea-Breeze had the following assets and liabilities:

	Book Value	Fair Value
Current assets	$150,000	$150,000
Land	200,000	200,000
Buildings (net) (6-year life)	300,000	360,000
Equipment (net) (4-year life)	300,000	280,000
Patent (10-year life)	–0–	100,000
Liabilities	(400,000)	(400,000)

The companies' financial statements for the year ending December 31, 2013, follow:

	Nascent	Sea-Breeze
Revenues	$ (600,000)	$ (300,000)
Operating expenses	410,000	210,000
Investment income	(42,000)	–0–
Net income	$ (232,000)	$ (90,000)
Retained earnings, 1/1/13	$ (700,000)	$ (300,000)
Net income	(232,000)	(90,000)
Dividends paid	92,000	70,000
Retained earnings, 12/31/13	$ (840,000)	$ (320,000)
Current assets	$ 330,000	$ 100,000
Land	220,000	200,000
Buildings (net)	700,000	200,000
Equipment (net)	400,000	500,000
Investment in Sea-Breeze	414,000	–0–
Total assets	$ 2,064,000	$ 1,000,000
Liabilities	$ (500,000)	$ (200,000)
Common stock	(724,000)	(480,000)
Retained earnings, 12/31/13	(840,000)	(320,000)
Total liabilities and equities	$(2,064,000)	$(1,000,000)

Answer the following questions:

a. How can the accountant determine that the parent has applied the initial value method?

b. What is the annual excess amortization initially recognized in connection with this acquisition?

c. If the parent had applied the equity method, what investment income would the parent have recorded in 2013?

d. What is the parent's portion of consolidated retained earnings as of January 1, 2013?

e. What is consolidated net income for 2013 and what amounts are attributable to the controlling and noncontrolling interests?

f. Within consolidated statements at January 1, 2010, what balance is included for the subsidiary's Buildings account?

g. What is the consolidated Buildings reported balance as of December 31, 2013?

LO1, LO5, LO7

35. On January 1, 2012, Pierson Corporation exchanged $1,710,000 cash for 90 percent of the outstanding voting stock of Steele Company. The consideration transferred by Pierson

provided a reasonable basis for assessing the total January 1, 2012, fair value of Steele Company. At the acquisition date, Steele reported the following owners' equity amounts in its balance sheet:

Common stock	$400,000
Additional paid-in capital	60,000
Retained earnings	265,000

In determining its acquisition offer, Pierson noted that the values for Steele's recorded assets and liabilities approximated their fair values. Pierson also observed that Steele had developed internally a customer base with an assessed fair value of $800,000 that was not reflected on Steele's books. Pierson expected both cost and revenue synergies from the combination.

At the acquisition date, Pierson prepared the following fair-value allocation schedule:

Fair value of Steele Company	$1,900,000
Book value of Steele Company	725,000
Excess fair value	1,175,000
to customer base (10-year remaining life)	800,000
to goodwill	$ 375,000

At December 31, 2013, the two companies report the following balances:

	Pierson	Steele
Revenues	$(1,843,000)	$ (675,000)
Cost of goods sold	1,100,000	322,000
Depreciation expense	125,000	120,000
Amortization expense	275,000	11,000
Interest expense	27,500	7,000
Equity in income of Steele	(121,500)	
Net income	$ (437,000)	$ (215,000)
Retained earnings, 1/1	$(2,625,000)	$ (395,000)
Net income	(437,000)	(215,000)
Dividends paid	350,000	25,000
Retained earnings, 12/31	$(2,712,000)	$ (585,000)
Current assets	$ 1,204,000	$ 430,000
Investment in Steele	1,854,000	
Buildings and equipment	931,000	863,000
Copyrights	950,000	107,000
Total assets	$ 4,939,000	$ 1,400,000
Accounts payable	$ (485,000)	$ (200,000)
Notes payable	(542,000)	(155,000)
Common stock	(900,000)	(400,000)
Additional paid-in capital	(300,000)	(60,000)
Retained earnings, 12/31	(2,712,000)	(585,000)
Total liabilities and equities	$(4,939,000)	$(1,400,000)

a. Determine the consolidated balances for this business combination as of December 31, 2013.

b. If instead the noncontrolling interest's acquisition-date fair value is assessed at $152,500, what changes would be evident in the consolidated statements?

LO5, LO6, LO7

36. The Krause Corporation acquired 80 percent of the 100,000 outstanding voting shares of Leahy, Inc., for $6.30 per share on January 1, 2012. The remaining 20 percent of Leahy's shares also traded actively at $6.30 per share before and after Krause's acquisition. An appraisal made on that date determined that all book values appropriately reflected the fair values of Leahy's underlying accounts except that a building with a 5-year life was undervalued by $45,000 and a fully amortized trademark with an estimated 10-year remaining life had a $60,000 fair value. At the acquisition date, Leahy reported common stock of $100,000 and a retained earnings balance of $280,000.

Following are the separate financial statements for the year ending December 31, 2013:

	Krause Corporation	Leahy, Inc.
Sales	$ (584,000)	$(250,000)
Cost of goods sold	194,000	95,000
Operating expenses	246,000	65,000
Dividend income	(16,000)	–0–
Net income	$ (160,000)	$ (90,000)
Retained earnings, 1/1/13	$ (700,000)	$(350,000)
Net income (above)	(160,000)	(90,000)
Dividends paid	70,000	20,000
Retained earnings, 12/31/13	$ (790,000)	$(420,000)
Current assets	$ 296,000	$ 191,000
Investment in Leahy, Inc.	504,000	–0–
Buildings and equipment (net)	680,000	390,000
Trademarks	100,000	144,000
Total assets	$ 1,580,000	$ 725,000
Liabilities	$ (470,000)	$(205,000)
Common stock	(320,000)	(100,000)
Retained earnings, 12/31/13 (above)	(790,000)	(420,000)
Total liabilities and equities	$(1,580,000)	$(725,000)

a. Prepare a worksheet to consolidate these two companies as of December 31, 2013.

b. Prepare a 2013 consolidated income statement for Krause and Leahy.

c. If instead the noncontrolling interest shares of Leahy had traded for $4.85 surrounding Krause's acquisition date, how would the consolidated statements change?

LO1, LO5, LO6

37. Father, Inc., buys 80 percent of the outstanding common stock of Sam Corporation on January 1, 2013, for $680,000 cash. At the acquisition date, Sam's total fair value, including the noncontrolling interest, was assessed at $850,000 although Sam's book value was only $600,000. Also, several individual items on Sam's financial records had fair values that differed from their book values as follows:

	Book Value	Fair Value
Land	$ 60,000	$ 225,000
Buildings and equipment (10-year remaining life)	275,000	250,000
Copyright (20-year life)	100,000	200,000
Notes payable (due in 8 years)	(130,000)	(120,000)

For internal reporting purposes, Father, Inc., employs the equity method to account for this investment.

The following account balances are for the year ending December 31, 2013, for both companies. Using the acquisition method, determine consolidated balances for this business combination (through either individual computations or the use of a worksheet).

	Father	Sam
Revenues	$(1,360,000)	$(540,000)
Cost of goods sold	700,000	385,000
Depreciation expense	260,000	10,000
Amortization expense	–0–	5,000
Interest expense	44,000	5,000
Equity in income of Sam	(105,000)	–0–
Net income	$ (461,000)	$(135,000)

(continued)

	Father	Sam
Retained earnings, 1/1/13	$(1,265,000)	$(440,000)
Net income (above)	(461,000)	(135,000)
Dividends paid	260,000	65,000
Retained earnings, 12/31/13	$(1,466,000)	$(510,000)
Current assets	$ 965,000	$ 528,000
Investment in Sam	733,000	–0–
Land	292,000	60,000
Buildings and equipment (net)	877,000	265,000
Copyright	–0–	95,000
Total assets	$ 2,867,000	$ 948,000
Accounts payable	$ (191,000)	$(148,000)
Notes payable	(460,000)	(130,000)
Common stock	(300,000)	(100,000)
Additional paid-in capital	(450,000)	(60,000)
Retained earnings (above)	(1,466,000)	(510,000)
Total liabilities and equities	$(2,867,000)	$(948,000)

Note: Credits are indicated by parentheses.

LO1, LO5

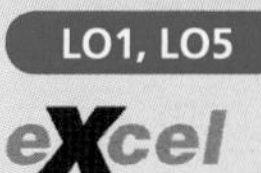

38. Adams Corporation acquired 90 percent of the outstanding voting shares of Barstow, Inc., on December 31, 2011. Adams paid a total of $603,000 in cash for these shares. The 10 percent noncontrolling interest shares traded on a daily basis at fair value of $67,000 both before and after Adams's acquisition. On December 31, 2011, Barstow had the following account balances:

	Book Value	Fair Value
Current assets	$ 160,000	$ 160,000
Land	120,000	150,000
Buildings (10-year life)	220,000	200,000
Equipment (5-year life)	160,000	200,000
Patents (10-year life)	–0–	50,000
Notes payable (5-year life)	(200,000)	(180,000)
Common stock	(180,000)	—
Retained earnings, 12/31/11	(280,000)	—

December 31, 2013, adjusted trial balances for the two companies follow:

	Adams Corporation	Barstow, Inc.
Debits		
Current assets	$ 610,000	$ 250,000
Land	380,000	150,000
Buildings	490,000	250,000
Equipment	873,000	150,000
Investment in Barstow, Inc.	702,000	–0–
Cost of goods sold	480,000	90,000
Depreciation expense	100,000	55,000
Interest expense	40,000	15,000
Dividends paid	110,000	70,000
Total debits	$3,785,000	$1,030,000
Credits		
Notes payable	$ 860,000	$ 230,000
Common stock	510,000	180,000
Retained earnings, 1/1/13	1,367,000	340,000
Revenues	940,000	280,000
Investment income	108,000	–0–
Total credits	$3,785,000	$1,030,000

a. Prepare schedules for acquisition-date fair-value allocations and amortizations for Adams's investment in Barstow.

b. Determine Adams's method of accounting for its investment in Barstow. Support your answer with a numerical explanation.

c. Without using a worksheet or consolidation entries, determine the balances to be reported as of December 31, 2013, for this business combination.

d. To verify the figures determined in requirement (*c*), prepare a consolidation worksheet for Adams Corporation and Barstow, Inc., as of December 31, 2013.

LO1, LO4, LO8

39. Following are the individual financial statements for Gibson and Davis for the year ending December 31, 2013:

	Gibson	Davis
Sales	$ (600,000)	$ (300,000)
Cost of goods sold	300,000	140,000
Operating expenses	174,000	60,000
Dividend income	(24,000)	–0–
Net income	$ (150,000)	$ (100,000)
Retained earnings, 1/1/13	$ (700,000)	$ (400,000)
Net income	(150,000)	(100,000)
Dividends paid	80,000	40,000
Retained earnings, 12/31/13	$ (770,000)	$ (460,000)
Cash and receivables	$ 248,000	$ 100,000
Inventory	500,000	190,000
Investment in Davis	528,000	–0–
Buildings (net)	524,000	600,000
Equipment (net)	400,000	400,000
Total assets	$ 2,200,000	$ 1,290,000
Liabilities	(800,000)	(490,000)
Common stock	(630,000)	(340,000)
Retained earnings, 12/31/13	(770,000)	(460,000)
Total liabilities and stockholders' equity	$(2,200,000)	$(1,290,000)

Gibson acquired 60 percent of Davis on April 1, 2013, for $528,000. On that date, equipment owned by Davis (with a five-year remaining life) was overvalued by $30,000. Also on that date, the fair value of the 40 percent noncontrolling interest was $352,000. Davis earned income evenly during the year but paid the entire dividend on November 1, 2013.

a. Prepare a consolidated income statement for the year ending December 31, 2013.

b. Determine the consolidated balance for each of the following accounts as of December 31, 2013:

Goodwill	Buildings (net)
Equipment (net)	Dividends Paid
Common Stock	

LO2, LO3, LO6, LO7, LO8

40. On July 1, 2013, Truman Company acquired a 70 percent interest in Atlanta Company in exchange for consideration of $720,000 in cash and equity securities. The remaining 30 percent of Atlanta's shares traded closely near an average price that totaled $290,000 both before and after Truman's acquisition.

In reviewing its acquisition, Truman assigned a $100,000 fair value to a patent recently developed by Atlanta, even though it was not recorded within the financial records of the subsidiary. This patent is anticipated to have a remaining life of five years.

The following financial information is available for these two companies for 2013. In addition, the subsidiary's income was earned uniformly throughout the year. Subsidiary dividend payments were made quarterly.

	Truman	Atlanta
Revenues	$ (670,000)	$ (400,000)
Operating expenses	402,000	280,000
Income of subsidiary	(35,000)	
Net income	$ (303,000)	$ (120,000)
Retained earnings, 1/1/13	$ (823,000)	$ (500,000)
Net income (above)	(303,000)	(120,000)
Dividends paid	145,000	80,000
Retained earnings, 12/31/13	$ (981,000)	$ (540,000)
Current assets	$ 481,000	$ 390,000
Investment in Atlanta	727,000	
Land	388,000	200,000
Buildings	701,000	630,000
Total assets	$ 2,297,000	$ 1,220,000
Liabilities	$ (816,000)	$ (360,000)
Common stock	(95,000)	(300,000)
Additional paid-in capital	(405,000)	(20,000)
Retained earnings, 12/31/13	(981,000)	(540,000)
Total liabilities and stockholders' equity	$(2,297,000)	$(1,220,000)

Answer each of the following:

a. How did Truman allocate Atlanta's acquisition-date fair value to the various assets acquired and liabilities assumed in the combination?

b. How did Truman allocate the goodwill from the acquisition across the controlling and noncontrolling interests?

c. How did Truman derive the Investment in Atlanta account balance at the end of 2013?

d. Prepare a worksheet to consolidate the financial statements of these two companies as of December 31, 2013.

LO9

41. On January 1, 2012, Allan Company bought a 15 percent interest in Sysinger Company. The acquisition price of $184,500 reflected an assessment that all of Sysinger's accounts were fairly valued within the company's accounting records. During 2012, Sysinger reported net income of $100,000 and paid cash dividends of $30,000. Allan possessed the ability to influence significantly Sysinger's operations and, therefore, accounted for this investment using the equity method.

On January 1, 2013, Allan acquired an additional 80 percent interest in Sysinger and provided the following fair-value assessments of Sysinger's ownership components:

Consideration transferred by Allan for 80% interest	$1,400,000
Fair value of Allan's 15% previous ownership	262,500
Noncontrolling interest's 5% fair value	87,500
Total acquisition-date fair value for Sysinger Company	$1,750,000

Also, as of January 1, 2013, Allan assessed a $400,000 value to an unrecorded customer contract recently negotiated by Sysinger. The customer contract is anticipated to have a remaining life of 4 years. Sysinger's other assets and liabilities were judged to have fair values equal to their book values. Allan elects to continue applying the equity method to this investment for internal reporting purposes.

At December 31, 2013, the following financial information is available for consolidation:

	Allan Company	Sysinger Company
Revenues	$ (931,000)	$ (380,000)
Operating expenses	615,000	230,000
Equity earnings of Sysinger	(47,500)	–0–
Gain on revaluation of Investment in Sysinger to fair value	(67,500)	–0–
Net income	$ 431,000	$ 150,000

(continued)

	Allan Company	Sysinger Company
Retained earnings, January 1	$ (965,000)	$ (600,000)
Net income (above)	(431,000)	(150,000)
Cash dividends paid to stockholders	140,000	40,000
Retained earnings, December 31	$ (1,256,000)	$ (710,000)
Current assets	$ 288,000	$ 540,000
Investment in Sysinger (equity method)	1,672,000	–0–
Property, plant, and equipment	826,000	590,000
Patented technology	850,000	370,000
Customer contract	–0–	–0–
Total assets	$ 3,636,000	$ 1,500,000
Liabilities	$ (1,300,000)	$ (90,000)
Common stock	(900,000)	(500,000)
Additional paid-in capital	(180,000)	(200,000)
Retained earnings, December 31	(1,256,000)	(710,000)
Total liabilities and equities	$ (3,636,000)	$(1,500,000)

a. How should Allan allocate Sysinger's total acquisition-date fair value (January 1, 2013) to the assets acquired and liabilities assumed for consolidation purposes?

b. Show how the following amounts on Allan's preconsolidation 2013 statements were derived:

- Equity in earnings of Sysinger.
- Gain on revaluation of Investment in Sysinger to fair value.
- Investment in Sysinger.

c. Prepare a worksheet to consolidate the financial statements of these two companies as of December 31, 2013.

LO9

42. On January 1, 2012, Bretz, Inc., acquired 60 percent of the outstanding shares of Keane Company for $573,000 in cash. The price paid was proportionate to Keane's total fair value although at the date of acquisition, Keane had a total book value of $810,000. All assets acquired and liabilities assumed had fair values equal to book values except for a copyright (six-year remaining life) that was undervalued in Keane's accounting records by $120,000. During 2012, Keane reported net income of $150,000 and paid cash dividends of $80,000. On January 1, 2013, Bretz bought an additional 30 percent interest in Keane for $300,000.

The following financial information is for these two companies for 2013. Keane issued no additional capital stock during either 2012 or 2013.

	Bretz, Inc.	Keane Company
Revenues	$ (402,000)	$ (300,000)
Operating expenses	200,000	120,000
Equity in Keane earnings	(144,000)	–0–
Net income	$ (346,000)	$ (180,000)
Retained earnings 1/1	$ (797,000)	$ (500,000)
Net income (above)	(346,000)	(180,000)
Dividends paid	143,000	60,000
Retained earnings 12/31	$(1,000,000)	$ (620,000)
Current assets	$ 224,000	$ 190,000
Investment in Keane Company	994,500	–0–
Trademarks	106,000	600,000
Copyrights	210,000	300,000
Equipment (net)	380,000	110,000
Total assets	$ 1,914,500	$ 1,200,000
Liabilities	$ (453,000)	$ (200,000)
Common stock	(400,000)	(300,000)
Additional paid-in capital	(60,000)	(80,000)
Additional paid-in capital—step acquisition	(1,500)	–0–
Retained earnings 12/31	(1,000,000)	(620,000)
Total liabilities and equities	$(1,914,500)	$(1,200,000)

a. Show the journal entry Bretz made to record its January 1, 2013, acquisition of an additional 30 percent of Keane Company shares.

b. Prepare a schedule showing how Bretz determined the Investment in Keane Company balance as of December 31, 2013.

c. Prepare a consolidated worksheet for Bretz, Inc., and Keane Company for December 31, 2013.

Develop Your Skills

ACCOUNTING THEORY RESEARCH CASE

The FASB ASC paragraph 810-10-45-16 states: "The noncontrolling interest shall be reported in the consolidated statement of financial position within equity, separately from the parent's equity. That amount shall be clearly identified and labeled, for example, as noncontrolling interest in subsidiaries."

However, prior to issuing this current reporting requirement, the FASB considered several alternative display formats for the noncontrolling interest. Access the precodification standard, *SFAS 160,* "Noncontrolling Interest in Consolidated Financial Statements," at www.fasb.org to answer the following:

- What alternative financial statement display formats did the FASB consider for the noncontrolling interest?
- What criteria did the FASB use to evaluate the desirability of each alternative?
- In what specific ways did FASB Concept Statement 6 affect the FASB's evaluation of these alternatives?

RESEARCH CASE: COCA-COLA'S ACQUISITION OF COCA-COLA ENTERPRISES (CCE)

On October 2, 2010, The Coca-Cola Company acquired the 67 percent of CCE's North American business that was not already owned by the company for consideration of $6.84 billion that included:

- The company's 33 percent indirect ownership interest in CCE's European operations.
- Cash consideration.
- Replacement awards issued to certain current and former employees of CCE's North American and corporate operations.

Access Coca-Cola's 2010 10-K annual report and answer the following.

1. How did Coca-Cola allocate the acquisition-date fair value of CCE among the assets acquired and liabilities assumed?
2. What are employee replacement awards? How did Coca-Cola account for the replacement award value provided to the former employees of CCE?
3. How did Coca-Cola account for its 33 percent interest in CCE prior to the acquisition of the 67 percent not already owned by Coca-Cola?
4. Upon acquisition of the additional 67 percent interest, how did Coca-Cola account for the change in fair value of its original 33 percent ownership interest?

CHARGING AHEAD: FASB ASC AND IFRS RESEARCH CASE

On March 1, 2013, Nu-Auto Corporation announced its plan to acquire 90 percent of the outstanding 1,000,000 shares of Battery Tech Corporation's common stock in a business combination later in the year following regulatory approval. Nu-Auto will account for the transaction in accordance with ASC 805, Business Combinations.

On October 1, 2013, Nu-Auto acquired the 90 percent controlling interest in Battery Tech. On this date, Nu-Auto paid $60 million in cash and issued 1 million shares of Nu-Auto common stock to the selling shareholders of Battery Tech. Nu-Auto's share price was $20 on the announcement date and $27 on the acquisition date. Battery Tech's remaining 100,000 shares of common stock traded in the $108 to $112 per share range in the weeks before and after October 1, 2013.

The parties agreed that Nu-Auto would issue to the selling shareholders an additional 1 million shares contingent upon the achievement of certain performance goals during the first 18 months following the acquisition. The acquisition-date fair value of the contingent stock issue was estimated at $10 million.

Battery Tech has a research and development (R&D) project underway to develop a proprietary fast-charging battery technology. The technology has a fair value of $14 million. Nu-Auto considers this R&D as in-process because it has not yet reached technological feasibility and additional R&D is needed to bring the project to completion. No assets have been recorded in Battery Tech's financial records for the research and development costs related to its fast-charging battery technology.

Battery Tech's other assets and liabilities include the following:

	Fair Value	Book Value
Cash	$ 270,000	$ 270,000
Accounts receivable	800,000	840,000
Land	2,930,000	1,500,000
Building	19,000,000	13,000,000
Machinery	46,000,000	29,000,000
Trademark	8,000,000	–0–
Accounts payable	(1,000,000)	(1,000,000)

Neither the receivables nor payables involve Nu-Auto.

Answer the following questions citing relevant support from the ASC and IFRS.

1. What is the total consideration transferred by Nu-Auto to acquire its 90 percent controlling interest in Battery Tech?
2. What values should Nu-Auto assign to identifiable assets and liabilities as part of the acquisition accounting?
3. What is the acquisition-date value assigned to the 10 percent noncontrolling interest? What are the potential noncontrolling interest valuation alternatives available under IFRS?
4. Under U.S. GAAP, what amount should Nu-Auto recognize as goodwill from the Battery Tech acquisition? What alternative valuations are available for goodwill under IFRS?

chapter

5

Consolidated Financial Statements—Intra-Entity Asset Transactions

Learning Objectives

After studying this chapter, you should be able to:

LO1 Understand why intra-entity asset transfers create accounting effects within the financial records of affiliated companies that must be eliminated or adjusted in preparing consolidated financial statements.

LO2 Understand that when companies affiliated through common control engage in intra-entity inventory transfers, consolidation procedures are required to eliminate sales and purchases balances.

LO3 Understand why consolidated entities defer intra-entity gross profit in ending inventory and the consolidation procedures required to recognize profits when actually earned.

LO4 Understand that the consolidation process for inventory transfers is designed to defer the unrealized portion of an intra-entity gross profit from the year of transfer into the year of disposal or consumption.

LO5 Understand the difference between upstream and downstream intra-entity transfers and how each affects the computation of noncontrolling interest balances.

LO6 Prepare the consolidation entry to remove any unrealized gain created by the intra-entity transfer of land from the accounting records of the year of transfer and subsequent years.

LO7 Prepare the consolidation entries to remove the effects of upstream and downstream intra-entity fixed asset transfers across affiliated entities.

Chapter 1 analyzes the deferral and subsequent recognition of gross profits created by inventory transfers between two affiliated companies in connection with equity method accounting. The central theme of that discussion is that intra-entity[1] profits are not realized until the earning process culminates in a sale to an unrelated party. This same accounting logic applies to transactions between companies within a business combination. Such sales within a single economic entity create neither profits nor losses. In reference to this issue, FASB ASC paragraph 810-10-45-1 states,

> . . . As consolidated financial statements are based on the assumption that they represent the financial position and operating results of a single economic entity, such statements shall not include gain or loss on transactions among the entities in the consolidated group. Accordingly, any intra-entity profit or loss on assets remaining within the consolidated group shall be eliminated; the concept usually applied for this purpose is gross profit or loss.

The elimination of the accounting effects created by intra-entity transactions is one of the most significant problems encountered in the consolidation process. The volume of transfers within many enterprises can be large. A recent annual report for the Ford Motor Company, for example, shows the elimination of intersegment revenues amounting to $1.898 billion.

Such transactions are especially common in companies organized as a vertically integrated chain of organizations. These entities reduce their costs by developing affiliations in which one operation furnishes products to another. As *Mergers & Acquisitions* observed,

> Downstream acquisitions . . . are aimed at securing critical sources of materials and components, streamlining manufacturing and materials planning,

[1] The FASB Accounting Standards Codification (ASC) uses the term *intra-entity* to describe transfers of assets across business entities affiliated through common stock ownership or other control mechanisms. The phrase indicates that although such transfers occur across separate legal entities, they are nonetheless made within a consolidated entity. Prior to the use of the term *intra-entity,* such transfers were routinely referred to as *intercompany* transactions.

gaining economies of scale, entering new markets, and enhancing overall competitiveness. Manufacturers that combine with suppliers are often able to assert total control over such critical areas as product quality and resource planning.[2]

Intra-entity asset transactions take several forms. In particular, inventory transfers are especially prevalent. However, the sale of land and depreciable assets also can occur between the parties within a combination. This chapter examines the consolidation procedures for each of these different types of intra-entity asset transfers.

Intra-Entity Inventory Transactions

LO1

Understand why intra-entity asset transfers create accounting effects within the financial records of affiliated companies that must be eliminated or adjusted in preparing consolidated financial statements.

As previous chapters discussed, companies that make up a business combination frequently retain their legal identities as separate operating centers and maintain their own recordkeeping. Thus, inventory sales between these companies trigger the independent accounting systems of both parties. The seller duly records revenue, and the buyer simultaneously enters the purchase into its accounts. For internal reporting purposes, recording an inventory transfer as a sale/purchase provides vital data to help measure the operational efficiency of each enterprise.[3]

Despite the internal information benefits of accounting for the transaction in this manner, from a consolidated perspective neither a sale nor a purchase has occurred. *An intra-entity transfer is merely the internal movement of inventory, an event that creates no net change in the financial position of the business combination taken as a whole.* Thus, in producing consolidated financial statements, the recorded effects of these transfers are eliminated so that consolidated statements reflect only transactions with outside parties. Worksheet entries serve this purpose; they adapt the financial information reported by the separate companies to the perspective of the consolidated enterprise. The entire impact of the intra-entity transactions must be identified and then removed. Deleting the effects of the actual transfer is described here first.

The Sales and Purchases Accounts

LO2

Understand that when companies affiliated through common control engage in intra-entity inventory transfers, consolidation procedures are required to eliminate sales and purchases balances.

To account for related companies as a single economic entity requires eliminating all intra-entity sales/purchases balances. For example, if Arlington Company makes an $80,000 inventory sale to Zirkin Company, an affiliated party within a business combination, both parties record the transfer in their internal records as a normal sale/purchase. The following consolidation worksheet entry is then necessary to remove the resulting balances from the externally reported figures. Cost of Goods Sold is reduced here under the assumption that the Purchases account usually is closed out prior to the consolidation process.

Consolidation Entry TI		
Sales	80,000	
Cost of Goods Sold (purchases component)		80,000
To eliminate effects of intra-entity transfer of inventory. (Labeled **"TI"** in reference to the transferred inventory.)		

In the preparation of consolidated financial statements, the preceding elimination must be made for all intra-entity inventory transfers. The total recorded (intra-entity) sales figure is deleted regardless of whether the transaction was downstream (from

[2] "Acquiring along the Value Chain," *Mergers & Acquisitions,* June–July 1996, p. 8.

[3] For all intra-entity transactions, the two parties involved view the events from different perspectives. Thus, the transfer is both a sale and a purchase, often creating both a receivable and a payable. To indicate the dual nature of such transactions, these accounts are indicated within this text as sales/purchases, receivables/payables, and so on.

parent to subsidiary) or upstream (from subsidiary to parent). Furthermore, any gross profit included in the transfer price does not affect the elimination. Because the entire amount of the transfer occurred between related parties, the total effect must be removed in preparing the consolidated statements.

Unrealized Gross Profit—Year of Transfer (Year 1)

Removal of the sale/purchase is often just the first in a series of consolidation entries necessitated by inventory transfers. Despite the previous elimination, unrealized gross profits created by such sales can still exist in the accounting records at year-end. These profits initially result when the merchandise is priced at more than historical cost. Actual transfer prices are established in several ways, including the normal sales price of the inventory, sales price less a specified discount, or at a predetermined markup above cost. In a footnote to recent financial statements, Ford Motor Company explains that

> Intercompany sales among geographic areas consist primarily of vehicles, parts, and components manufactured by the company and various subsidiaries and sold to different entities within the consolidated group; transfer prices for these transactions are established by agreement between the affected entities.

Regardless of the method used for this pricing decision, intra-entity profits that remain unrealized at year-end must be removed in arriving at consolidated figures.

LO3

Understand why consolidated entities defer intra-entity gross profit in ending inventory and the consolidation procedures required to recognize profits when actually earned.

All Inventory Remains at Year-End

In the preceding illustration, assume that Arlington acquired or produced this inventory at a cost of $50,000 and then sold it to Zirkin, an affiliated party, at the indicated $80,000 price. From a consolidated perspective, the inventory still has a historical cost of only $50,000. However, Zirkin's records now report it as an asset at the $80,000 transfer price. In addition, because of the markup, Arlington has recorded a $30,000 gross profit as a result of this intra-entity sale. Because the transaction did not occur with an outside party, recognition of this profit is not appropriate for the combination as a whole.

Thus, although the consolidation entry **TI** shown earlier eliminated the sale/purchase figures, the $30,000 inflation created by the transfer price still exists in two areas of the individual statements:

- Ending inventory remains overstated by $30,000.
- Gross profit is artificially overstated by this same amount.

Correcting the ending inventory requires only reducing the asset. However, before decreasing gross profit, the accounts affected by the incomplete earnings process should be identified. The ending inventory total serves as a negative component within the Cost of Goods Sold computation; it represents the portion of acquired inventory that was not sold. Thus, the $30,000 overstatement of the inventory that is still held incorrectly decreases this expense (the inventory that was sold). *Despite Entry* ***TI****, the inflated ending inventory figure causes cost of goods sold to be too low and, thus, profits to be too high by $30,000.* For consolidation purposes, the expense is increased by this amount through a worksheet adjustment that properly removes the unrealized gross profit from consolidated net income.

Consequently, if all of the transferred inventory is retained by the business combination at the end of the year, the following worksheet entry also must be included to eliminate the effects of the seller's gross profit that remains unrealized within the buyer's ending inventory:

Consolidation Entry G—Year of Transfer (Year 1) **All Inventory Remains**		
Cost of Goods Sold (ending inventory component)	30,000	
Inventory (balance sheet account)		30,000
To remove unrealized gross profit created by intra-entity sale.		

Discussion Question

EARNINGS MANAGEMENT

Enron Corporation's 2001 third-quarter 10-Q report disclosed the following transaction with LJM2, a nonconsolidated special purpose entity (SPE) that was formed by Enron:

> In June 2000, LJM2 purchased dark fiber optic cable from Enron for a purchase price of $100 million. LJM2 paid Enron $30 million in cash and the balance in an interest-bearing note for $70 million. Enron recognized $67 million in pretax earnings in 2000 related to the asset sale. Pursuant to a marketing agreement with LJM2, Enron was compensated for marketing the fiber to others and providing operation and maintenance services to LJM2 with respect to the fiber. LJM2 sold a portion of the fiber to industry participants for $40 million, which resulted in Enron recognizing agency fee revenue of $20.3 million.

As investigations later discovered, Enron controlled LJM2 in many ways.

The FASB ASC now requires the consolidation of SPEs (as variable interest entities) that are essentially controlled by their primary beneficiary.

By selling goods to SPEs that it controlled but did not consolidate, did Enron overstate its earnings? What effect does consolidation have on the financial reporting for transactions between a firm and its controlled entities?

This entry (labeled **G** for gross profit) reduces the consolidated Inventory account to its original $50,000 historical cost. Furthermore, increasing Cost of Goods Sold by $30,000 effectively removes the unrealized amount from recognized gross profit. Thus, this worksheet entry resolves both reporting problems created by the transfer price markup.

Only a Portion of Inventory Remains

Obviously, a company does not buy inventory to hold it for an indefinite time. It either uses the acquired items within the company's operations or resells them to unrelated, outside parties. Intra-entity profits ultimately are realized by subsequently consuming or reselling these goods. Therefore, only the transferred inventory still held at year-end continues to be recorded in the separate statements at a value more than the historical cost. For this reason, *the elimination of unrealized gross profit (Entry* **G***) is based not on total intra-entity sales but only on the amount of transferred merchandise retained within the business at the end of the year.*

To illustrate, assume that Arlington transferred inventory costing $50,000 to Zirkin, a related company, for $80,000, thus recording a gross profit of $30,000. Assume further that by year-end Zirkin has resold $60,000 of these goods to unrelated parties but retains the other $20,000 (for resale in the following year). From the viewpoint of the consolidated company, it has now earned the profit on the $60,000 portion of the intra-entity sale and need not make an adjustment for consolidation purposes.

Conversely, any gross profit recorded in connection with the $20,000 in merchandise that remains is still a component within Zirkin's Inventory account. Because the gross profit rate was 37½ percent ($30,000 gross profit/$80,000 transfer price), this retained inventory is stated at a value $7,500 more than its original cost ($20,000 × 37½%). The required reduction (Entry **G**) is not the entire $30,000 shown previously but only the $7,500 unrealized gross profit that remains in ending inventory.

Consolidation Entry G—Year of Transfer (Year 1)
25% of Inventory Remains (replaces previous entry)

Cost of Goods Sold (ending inventory component)	7,500	
Inventory		7,500
To remove portion of intra-entity gross profit that is unrealized in year of transfer.		

LO4

Understand that the consolidation process for inventory transfers is designed to defer the unrealized portion of an intra-entity gross profit from the year of transfer into the year of disposal or consumption.

Unrealized Gross Profit—Year Following Transfer (Year 2)

Whenever an unrealized intra-entity profit is present in ending inventory, one further consolidation entry is eventually required. Although Entry **G** removes the gross profit from the *consolidated* inventory balances in the year of transfer, the $7,500 overstatement remains within the separate financial records of the buyer and seller. The effects of this deferred gross profit are carried into their beginning balances in the subsequent year. Hence, a worksheet adjustment is necessary in the period following the transfer. For consolidation purposes, the unrealized portion of the intra-entity gross profit must be adjusted in two successive years (from ending inventory in the year of transfer and from beginning inventory of the next period).

Referring again to Arlington's sale of inventory to Zirkin, the $7,500 unrealized gross profit is still in Zirkin's Inventory account at the start of the subsequent year. Once again, the overstatement is removed within the consolidation process but this time from the beginning inventory balance (which appears in the financial statements only as a positive component of cost of goods sold). This elimination is termed *Entry *G*. The asterisk indicates that a previous year transfer created the intra-entity gross profits.

Consolidation Entry *G—Year Following Transfer (Year 2)

Retained Earnings (beginning balance of seller)	7,500	
Cost of Goods Sold (beginning inventory component)		7,500
To remove unrealized gross profit from beginning figures so that it is recognized currently in the period in which the earning process is completed.		

Reducing Cost of Goods Sold (beginning inventory) through this worksheet entry increases the gross profit reported for this second year. For consolidation purposes, the gross profit on the transfer is recognized in the period in which the items are actually sold to outside parties. As shown in the following diagram, Entry **G** initially deferred the $7,500 gross profit because this amount was unrealized in the year of transfer. Entry ***G** now increases consolidated net income (by decreasing cost of goods sold) to reflect the earning process in the current year.

In Entry ***G,** removal of the $7,500 from beginning inventory (within Cost of Goods Sold) appropriately increases current income and should not pose a significant conceptual problem. However, the rationale for decreasing the seller's beginning Retained Earnings deserves further explanation. This reduction removes the unrealized gross profit

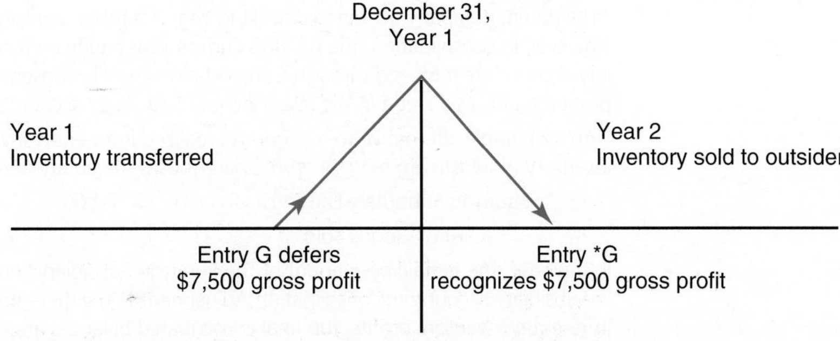

(recognized by the seller in the year of transfer) so that the profit is reported in the period when it is earned. Despite the consolidation entries in Year 1, the $7,500 gain remained on this company's separate books and was closed to Retained Earnings at the end of the period. Recall that consolidation entries are never posted to the individual affiliate's books. Therefore, from a consolidated view, the buyer's Cost of Goods Sold (through the beginning inventory component) and the seller's Retained Earnings accounts as of the beginning of Year 2 contain the unrealized profit, and must both be reduced in Entry ***G.**[4]

Intra-Entity Beginning Inventory Profit Adjustment—Downstream Sales When Parent Uses Equity Method

The worksheet elimination for the sales/purchases balances (Entry **TI**) and the entry to remove the unrealized gross profit from ending inventory in Year 1 (Entry **G**) are both standard, regardless of the circumstances of the consolidation. In contrast, for one specific situation, the procedure to eliminate the intra-entity gross profit from Year 2's beginning account balances differs from the Entry ***G** just presented. If (1) the original transfer is downstream (made by the parent) and (2) the parent applies the equity method for internal accounting purposes, then the Investment in Subsidiary account replaces beginning Retained Earnings-P in Entry ***G**.

When using the equity method in its internal records, the parent maintains income balances that appropriately reflect consolidated income. Thus, the parent defers any unrealized gross profit at the end of Year 1 through an equity method adjustment to its Equity in Subsidiary Earnings account. With the profit deferred, the retained earnings of the parent/seller at the beginning of the following year are correctly stated. The parent's beginning retained earnings do not contain the unrealized gross profit and need no adjusting.

However, prior to its elimination, the Investment in Subsidiary account must reflect the same events as the subsidiary's overall consolidated value as of the beginning of the period. In the current example, because the sales are downstream, the parent's Investment in Subsidiary account as of the beginning of the year contains a $7,500 credit reflecting the Year 1 intra-entity profit deferral.[5] This $7,500 credit creates an imbalance between the parent's Investment account and the subsidiary's overall consolidated value as of the beginning of Year 2. Worksheet Entry ***G** corrects this imbalance by transferring the original $7,500 Year 1 Investment account credit to a Year 2 earnings credit (through Cost of Goods Sold) as follows:

Consolidation Entry *G—Year Following Transfer (Year 2) (replaces previous Entry *G when transfers are downstream and the equity method is used)[6]

Investment in Subsidiary	7,500	
Cost of Goods Sold (beginning inventory component)		7,500

To recognize the previously deferred unrealized downstream inventory gross profit as part of current year income. The Investment in Subsidiary account replaces the Retained Earnings account (used for upstream profit adjustments) when adjusting for downstream sales. The parent's Retained Earnings account has already been corrected by application of the equity method.

[4] For upstream intra-entity profit in beginning inventory, the subsidiary's retained earnings remain overstated and must be adjusted through Entry ***G.**

[5] The parent company offsets this credit in Year 2 through applying the equity method in its internal records. However, in consolidation, the parent's current year equity method adjustments to its Investment in Subsidiary account are removed through Consolidation Entry **I**. Consequently, the beginning intra-entity inventory profit remains as a credit in the Investment in Subsidiary account's beginning of the year balance.

[6] An acceptable alternative to recognizing realized intra-entity inventory profits in the subsidiary's beginning inventory (downstream sale) when the parent uses the equity method (***G**) is as follows:

Equity in Subsidiary Earnings	7,500	
Cost of Goods Sold		7,500

In this case, the *remaining* amount of the Equity in Subsidiary Earnings is eliminated against the Investment in Subsidiary account in Consolidation Adjustment **I**. In either alternative adjustment for recognizing realized intra-entity inventory profits, the final consolidated balances are exactly the same: Equity in Subsidiary Earnings = 0, Investment in Subsidiary = 0, and Cost of Goods Sold is reduced by $7,500.

EXHIBIT 5.1
Relationship between Gross Profit Rate and Markup on Cost

In determining appropriate amounts of intra-entity profits for deferral and subsequent recognition in consolidated financial reports, two alternative—but mathematically related—profit percentages are often seen. Recalling that Gross Profit = Sales − Cost of Goods Sold, then

$$\textbf{Gross profit rate } (GPR) = \frac{\text{Gross profit}}{\text{Sales}} = \frac{MC}{1 + MC}$$

$$\textbf{Markup on cost } (MC) = \frac{\text{Gross profit}}{\text{Cost of goods sold}} = \frac{GPR}{1 - GPR}$$

Example:		
	Sales (transfer price)	$1,000
	Cost of goods sold	800
	Gross profit	$ 200

Here the GPR = (200/1,000) = 20% and the MC = (200/800) = 25%. In most intra-entity purchases and sales, the sales (transfer) price is known and therefore the GPR is the simplest percentage to use to determine the amount of intra-entity profit.

$$\text{Intra-entity profit} = \text{Transfer price} \times GPR$$

Instead, if the markup on cost is available, it readily converts to a GPR by the preceding formula. In this case (0.25/1.25) = 20%.

To summarize, for **intra-entity beginning inventory profits resulting from downstream transfers when the parent applies the equity method:**

a. The parent's retained earnings are appropriately stated due to intra-entity profit deferrals and subsequent recognition from its use of the equity method.
b. The subsidiary retained earnings reflect none of the intra-entity profit and therefore require no adjustment.
c. The parent's Investment in Subsidiary account as of the beginning of Year 2 contains a credit from the deferral of Year 1 intra-entity downstream profits.
d. Worksheet Entry *G transfers the Year 1 Investment account credit to a Year 2 earnings credit via Cost of Goods Sold, effectively recognizing the profit in the year of sale to outsiders.

Finally, various markup percentages determine the dollar values for intra-entity profit deferrals. Exhibit 5.1 shows formulas for both the gross profit rate and markup on cost and the relationship between the two.

LO5

Understand the difference between upstream and downstream intra-entity transfers and how each affects the computation of noncontrolling interest balances.

Unrealized Gross Profit—Effect on Noncontrolling Interest

The worksheet entries just described appropriately account for the effects of intra-entity inventory transfers on business combinations. However, one question remains: What impact do these procedures have on the measurement of a noncontrolling interest? In regard to this issue, paragraph 810-10-45-18 of the FASB ASC states,

> The amount of intra-entity profit or loss to be eliminated in accordance with paragraph 810-10-45-1 is not affected by the existence of a noncontrolling interest. The complete elimination of the intra-entity income or loss is consistent with the underlying assumption that consolidated financial statements represent the financial position and operating results of a single economic entity. The elimination of the intra-entity income or loss may be allocated between the parent and noncontrolling interests.

The last sentence indicates that alternative approaches are available in computing the noncontrolling interest's share of a subsidiary's net income. According to this pronouncement, unrealized gross profits resulting from intra-entity transfers *may or may not* affect recognition of outside ownership. Because the amount attributed to a noncontrolling interest reduces consolidated net income, the handling of this issue can affect the reported profitability of a business combination.

To illustrate, assume that Large Company owns 70 percent of the voting stock of Small Company. To avoid extraneous complications, assume that no amortization expense resulted from this acquisition. Assume further that Large reports current net income (from separate operations) of $500,000 while Small earns $100,000. During the current period, intra-entity transfers of $200,000 occur with a total markup of $90,000. At the end of the year, an unrealized intra-entity gross profit of $40,000 remains within the inventory accounts.

Clearly, the consolidated net income prior to the reduction for the 30 percent noncontrolling interest is $560,000, the two income balances less the unrealized gross profit. The problem facing the accountant is the computation of the noncontrolling interest's share of Small's income. Because of the flexibility allowed by the FASB ASC, this figure may be reported as either $30,000 (30% of the $100,000 earnings of the subsidiary) or $18,000 (30% of reported income after that figure is reduced by the $40,000 unrealized gross profit).

To appropriately measure this noncontrolling interest allocation, the relationship between an intra-entity transaction and the outside owners must be analyzed. If a transfer is downstream (the parent sells inventory to the subsidiary), a logical view would seem to be that the unrealized gross profit is that of the parent company. The parent made the original sale; therefore, the gross profit is included in its financial records. Because the subsidiary's income is unaffected, little justification exists for adjusting the noncontrolling interest to reflect the deferral of the unrealized gross profit. Consequently, in the example of Large and Small, if the transfers were downstream, the 30 percent noncontrolling interest would be $30,000 based on Small's reported income of $100,000.

In contrast, if the subsidiary sells inventory to the parent (an upstream transfer), the subsidiary's financial records would recognize the gross profit even though part of this income remains unrealized from a consolidation perspective. Because the outside owners possess their interest in the subsidiary, a reasonable conclusion would be that the noncontrolling interest measure is calculated on the income this company actually earned.

In this textbook, the noncontrolling interest's share of consolidated net income is computed based on *the reported income of the subsidiary after adjustment for any unrealized upstream gross profits.* Returning to Large Company and Small Company, if the $40,000 unrealized gross profit results from an upstream sale from subsidiary to parent, only $60,000 of Small's $100,000 reported income actually has been earned by the end of the year. The allocation to the noncontrolling interest is, therefore, reported as $18,000, or 30 percent of this realized income figure.

Although the noncontrolling interest figure is based here on the subsidiary's reported income adjusted for the effects of upstream intra-entity transfers, GAAP, as quoted earlier, does not require this treatment. Giving effect to upstream transfers in this calculation but not to downstream transfers is no more than an attempt to select the most logical approach from among acceptable alternatives.[7]

Intra-Entity Inventory Transfers Summarized

To assist in overcoming the complications created by intra-entity transfers, we demonstrate the consolidation process in three different ways:

- Before proceeding to a numerical example, review the impact of intra-entity transfers on consolidated figures. Ultimately, the accountant must understand how the balances reported by a business combination are derived when unrealized gross profits result from either upstream or downstream sales.
- Next, two different consolidation worksheets are produced: one for downstream transfers and the other for upstream. The various consolidation procedures used in these worksheets are explained and analyzed.

[7] The 100 percent allocation of downstream profits to the parent affects its application of the equity method. As seen later in this chapter, in applying the equity method, the parent removes 100 percent of intra-entity profits resulting from downstream sales from its investment and equity earnings accounts rather than its percentage ownership in the subsidiary.

- Finally, several of the consolidation worksheet entries are shown side by side to illustrate the differences created by the direction of the transfers.

The Development of Consolidated Totals

The following summarizes the effects of intra-entity inventory transfers on consolidated totals.

Revenues. Parent and subsidiary balances are combined, but all intra-entity transfers are then removed.

Cost of Goods Sold. Parent and subsidiary balances are combined, but all intra-entity transfers are removed. The resulting total is decreased by any beginning unrealized gross profit (thus raising net income) and increased by any ending unrealized gross profit (reducing net income).

Noncontrolling Interest in Subsidiary's Net Income. The subsidiary's reported net income is adjusted for any excess acquisition-date fair-value amortizations and the effects of unrealized gross profits on upstream transfers (but not downstream transfers) and then multiplied by the percentage of outside ownership.

Retained Earnings at the Beginning of the Year. As discussed in previous chapters, if the equity method is applied, the parent's balance mirrors the consolidated total. When any other method is used, the parent's beginning Retained Earnings must be converted to the equity method by Entry ***C**. Accruals for this purpose are based on the income actually earned by the subsidiary in previous years (reported income adjusted for any unrealized upstream gross profits).

Inventory. Parent and subsidiary balances are combined. Any unrealized gross profit remaining at the end of the current year is removed to adjust the reported balance to historical cost.

Noncontrolling Interest in Subsidiary at End of Year. The final total begins with the noncontrolling interest at the beginning of the year. This figure is based on the subsidiary's book value on that date plus its share of any unamortized acquisition-date excess fair value less any unrealized gross profits on upstream sales. The beginning balance is updated by adding the portion of the subsidiary's income assigned to these outside owners (as described above) and subtracting the noncontrolling interest's share of subsidiary dividends.

Intra-Entity Inventory Transfers Illustrated: Parent Uses Equity Method

To examine the various consolidation procedures required by intra-entity inventory transfers, assume that Top Company acquires 80 percent of the voting stock of Bottom Company on January 1, 2012. The parent pays $400,000 and the acquisition-date fair value of the noncontrolling interest is $100,000. Top allocates the entire $50,000 excess fair value over book value to adjust a database owned by Bottom to fair value. The database has an estimated remaining life of 20 years. Top Company applies the equity method to its investment in Bottom.[8]

The subsidiary reports net income of $30,000 in 2012 and $70,000 in 2013, the current year. Dividend payments are $20,000 in the first year and $50,000 in the second. After the takeover, intra-entity inventory transfers between the two companies occurred as shown in Exhibit 5.2. A $10,000 intra-entity receivable and payable also exists as of December 31, 2013.

The 2013 consolidation of Top and Bottom is presented twice. First, we assume the intra-entity transfers are downstream from parent to subsidiary. Second, consolidated figures are recomputed with the transfers being viewed as upstream. This distinction

[8] Later in this chapter, we extend the example to when the parent applies the initial value method.

EXHIBIT 5.2
Intra-Entity Transfers

	2012	2013
Transfer prices	$80,000	$100,000
Historical cost	60,000	70,000
Gross profit	$20,000	$ 30,000
Inventory remaining at year-end (at transfer price)	$16,000	$ 20,000
Gross profit percentage	25%	30%
Gross profit remaining in year-end inventory	$ 4,000	$ 6,000

between upstream and downstream transfer becomes significant when the parent uses the equity method and in the presence of a noncontrolling interest.

Downstream Inventory Transfers: Parent Uses the Equity Method

To understand the consolidation procedures for intra-entity inventory transfers, it's useful first to analyze the parent's internal accounting for the investment. Under the equity method, the parent's investment-related accounts are subjected to (1) income accrual, (2) excess fair over book value amortization, (3) adjustments required by unrealized intra-entity gross profits, and (4) dividends. Exhibit 5.3 shows the changes to the Investment in Bottom Company from the acquisition date until the end of the current year (2013).

Note in particular the computations of Top's equity in earnings of Bottom Company in Exhibit 5.3. First, the calculations for equity method income are identical to those presented in Chapter 4, with the addition of an adjustment for intra-entity profits. Also observe that the $4,000 intra-entity profit deferred in 2012 is subsequently recognized in 2013. Thus, the $4,000 intra-entity profit is not eliminated, but simply reallocated across time to the period when it is earned by the consolidated entity. Next observe that, because the inventory transfers are downstream from parent to subsidiary, 100 percent of the profit deferral and subsequent recognition is allocated to the parent's equity earnings and investment account. As a result, the intra-entity profit reallocation across time affects neither Bottom's income nor the noncontrolling interest.

Exhibit 5.4 presents the worksheet to consolidate these two companies for the year ending December 31, 2013. Most of the worksheet entries found in Exhibit 5.4 are described and analyzed in previous chapters of this textbook. Thus, we examine only three of these entries in detail along with the computation of the noncontrolling interest in the subsidiary's net income.

First, Consolidation Entry *G adjusts for the unrealized gross profit carried over in the beginning inventory from the 2012 intra-entity downstream transfers.

Consolidation Entry *G		
Investment in Bottom	4,000	
Cost of Goods Sold		4,000
To recognize intra-entity gross profit in beginning inventory as earned in 2013. Top uses the equity method and intra-entity sales were downstream.		

The gross profit rate (Exhibit 5.2) on these items was 25 percent ($20,000 gross profit/$80,000 transfer price), indicating an unrealized profit of $4,000 (25% of the remaining $16,000 in inventory). To recognize this gross profit in 2013, Entry *G reduces Cost of Goods Sold (or the beginning inventory component of that expense) by that amount. The reduction in Cost of Goods Sold creates an increase in current year net income. From a consolidation perspective, the gross profit is correctly recognized in 2013 when the inventory is sold to an outside party. The debit to the Investment in Bottom

EXHIBIT 5.3
Investment Balances—Equity Method—Downstream Sales

Investment in Bottom Company Analysis 1/1/12 to 12/31/13		
Consideration paid (fair value) 1/1/12		$400,000
Bottom Co. reported income for 2012	$30,000	
Database amortization	(2,500)	
Bottom Co. adjusted 2012 net income	$27,500	
Top's ownership percentage	80%	
Top's share of Bottom income	$22,000	
Deferred profit from Top's 2012 downstream sales	(4,000)	
Equity in earnings of Bottom Company, 2012		$ 18,000
Top's share of Bottom Co. dividends, 2012 (80%)		(16,000)
Balance 12/31/12		$402,000
Bottom Co. reported income for 2013	$70,000	
Database amortization	(2,500)	
Bottom Co. adjusted 2013 net income	$67,500	
Top's ownership percentage	80%	
Top's share of Bottom income	$54,000	
Recognized profit from Top's 2012 downstream sales	4,000	
Deferred profit from Top's 2013 downstream sales	(6,000)	
Equity in earnings of Bottom Company, 2013		$ 52,000
Top's share of Bottom Company dividends, 2013 (80%)		(40,000)
Balance 12/31/13		$414,000

account becomes part of the sequence of adjustments to bring that account to a zero balance in consolidation.

Consolidation Entry TI		
Sales	100,000	
Cost of Goods Sold		100,000
To eliminate current year intra-entity sales/purchases.		

Entry TI eliminates the intra-entity sales/purchases for 2013. The entire $100,000 transfer recorded by the two parties during the current period is removed to arrive at consolidated figures for the business combination.

Consolidation Entry G		
Cost of Goods Sold	6,000	
Inventory		6,000
To defer intra-entity gross profits in ending inventory.		

Entry **G** defers the unrealized gross profit remaining at the end of 2013. The $20,000 in transferred merchandise (Exhibit 5.2) that Bottom has not yet sold has a gross profit rate of 30 percent ($30,000 gross profit/$100,000 transfer price); thus, the unrealized gross profit amounts to $6,000. On the worksheet, Entry **G** eliminates this overstatement in the Inventory asset balance as well as the ending inventory (credit) component of Cost of Goods Sold. Because the gross profit remains unrealized, the increase in this expense appropriately decreases consolidated net income.

EXHIBIT 5.4 Downstream Inventory Transfers

TOP COMPANY AND BOTTOM COMPANY
Consolidation Worksheet
For Year Ending December 31, 2013

Consolidation: Acquisition Method
Investment: Equity Method
Ownership: 80%

Accounts	Top Company	Bottom Company	Consolidation Entries Debit	Consolidation Entries Credit	Noncontrolling Interest	Consolidated Totals
Income Statement						
Sales	(600,000)	(300,000)	(TI)100,000			(800,000)
Cost of goods sold	320,000	180,000	(G) 6,000	(*G) 4,000		402,000
				(TI) 100,000		
Operating expenses	170,000	50,000	(E) 2,500			222,500
Equity in earnings of Bottom	(52,000)					
			(I) 52,000‡			–0–
Separate company net income	(162,000)	(70,000)				
Consolidated net income						(175,500)
Noncontrolling interest in Bottom Company's income					(13,500)†	13,500
Top's interest in consolidated income						(162,000)
Statement of Retained Earnings						
Retained earnings 1/1/13						
Top Company	(652,000)					(652,000)
Bottom Company		(310,000)	(S)310,000			
Net income (above)	(162,000)	(70,000)				(162,000)
Dividends paid	70,000	50,000		(D) 40,000	10,000	70,000
Retained earnings 12/31/13	(744,000)	(330,000)				(744,000)
Balance Sheet						
Cash and receivables	280,000	120,000		(P) 10,000		390,000
Inventory	220,000	160,000		(G) 6,000		374,000
Investment in Bottom	414,000		(D) 40,000	(I) 52,000		
			(*G) 4,000	(S) 368,000		–0–
				(A) 38,000		
Land	410,000	200,000				610,000
Plant assets (net)	190,000	170,000				360,000
Database			(A) 47,500	(E) 2,500		45,000
Total assets	1,514,000	650,000				1,779,000
Liabilities	(340,000)	(170,000)	(P) 10,000			(500,000)
Noncontrolling interest in Bottom Company, 1/1/13				(S) 92,000		
				(A) 9,500	(101,500)	
Noncontrolling interest in Bottom Company, 12/31/13					105,000	(105,000)
Common stock	(430,000)	(150,000)	(S)150,000			(430,000)
Retained earnings 12/31/13 (above)	(744,000)	(330,000)				(744,000)
Total liabilities and equities	(1,514,000)	(650,000)	718,000	718,000		(1,779,000)

Note: Parentheses indicate a credit balance.

†Because intra-entity sales are made downstream (by the parent), the subsidiary's earned income is the $70,000 reported less $2,500 excess amortization figure with a 20% allocation to the noncontrolling interest ($13,500).

‡Boxed items highlight differences with upstream transfers examined in Exhibit 5.6.

Consolidation entries:

- (*G) Removal of unrealized gross profit from beginning figures so that it can be recognized in current period. Downstream sales attributed to parent.
- (S) Elimination of subsidiary's stockholders' equity accounts along with recognition of the noncontrolling interest as of January 1.
- (A) Allocation of excess fair value over subsidiary's book value, unamortized balance as of January 1.
- (I) Elimination of intra-entity income remaining after *G elimination.
- (D) Elimination of intra-entity dividend.
- (E) Recognition of amortization expense for current year on excess fair value allocated to database.
- (P) Elimination of intra-entity receivable/payable balances.
- (TI) Elimination of intra-entity sales/purchases balances.
- (G) Removal of unrealized gross profit from ending figures so that it can be recognized in subsequent period.

Noncontrolling Interest's Share of the Subsidiary's Income

In this first illustration, the intra-entity transfers are downstream. Thus, the unrealized gross profits are considered to relate solely to the parent company, creating no effect on the subsidiary or the outside ownership. For this reason, the noncontrolling interest's share of the subsidiary's income is unaffected by the downstream intra-entity profit deferral and subsequent recognition. Therefore, Top allocates $13,500 of Bottom's income to the noncontrolling interest computed as 20 percent of $67,500 ($70,000 reported income less $2,500 current year database excess fair-value amortization).

By including these entries along with the other routine worksheet eliminations and adjustments, the accounting information generated by Top and Bottom is brought together into a single set of consolidated financial statements. However, this process does more than simply delete intra-entity transactions; it also affects reported income. A $4,000 gross profit is removed on the worksheet from 2012 figures and subsequently recognized in 2013 (Entry *G). A $6,000 gross profit is deferred in a similar fashion from 2013 (Entry **G**) and subsequently recognized in 2014. However, these changes do not affect the noncontrolling interest because the transfers were downstream.

Special Equity Method Procedures for Unrealized Intra-Entity Profits from Downstream Transfers

Exhibit 5.3 presents the parent's equity method investment accounting procedures in the presence of unrealized intra-entity gross profits resulting from downstream inventory transfers. This application of the equity method differs from that presented in Chapter 1 for a significant influence (typically 20 to 50% ownership) investment. For significant influence investments, an investor company defers unrealized intra-entity gross profits only to the extent of its percentage ownership, regardless of whether the profits resulted from upstream or downstream transfers. In contrast, Exhibit 5.3 shows a 100 percent deferral in 2012, with a subsequent 100 percent recognition in 2013, for intra-entity gross profits resulting from Top's inventory transfers to Bottom, its 80 percent-owned subsidiary.

Why the distinction? When control (rather than just significant influence) exists, 100 percent of all intra-entity gross profits are removed from consolidated net income regardless of the direction of the underlying sale.[9] The 100 percent intra-entity profit deferral on Top's books for downstream sales ensures that none of the deferral will be allocated to the noncontrolling interest. As discussed previously, when the parent is the seller in an intra-entity transfer, little justification exists to allocate a portion of the gross profit deferral to the noncontrolling interest. In contrast, for an upstream sale, the subsidiary recognizes the gross profit on its books. Because the noncontrolling interest owns a portion of the subsidiary (but not of the parent), partial allocation of intra-entity gross profit deferrals and subsequent recognitions to the noncontrolling interest is appropriate when resulting from upstream sales.

Upstream Inventory Transfers: Parent Uses the Equity Method

A different set of consolidation procedures is necessary if the intra-entity transfers are upstream from Bottom to Top. As previously discussed, upstream gross profits are attributed to the subsidiary rather than to the parent company. Therefore, had these transfers been upstream, both the $4,000 beginning inventory gross profit recognition (Entry ***G**) and the $6,000 unrealized gross profit deferral (Entry **G**) would be considered adjustments to Bottom's reported totals.

In contrast to the downstream example in Exhibit 5.3, Exhibit 5.5 includes the intra-entity profit deferrals and subsequent recognitions in the adjustments to Bottom's

[9] When only significant influence is present, purchasing-related decisions are typically made in conjunction with the interests of other outside owners of the investee. Profits are partially deferred because sales are considered to be partially made to the other outside owners. When control is present, decision making usually rests exclusively with the majority owner, providing little basis for objective profit measurement in the presence of intra-entity sales.

EXHIBIT 5.5
Investment Balances—Equity Method—Upstream Sales

Investment in Bottom Company Analysis 1/1/12 to 12/31/13		
Consideration paid (fair value) 1/1/12		$400,000
Bottom Co. reported income for 2012	$30,000	
Database amortization	(2,500)	
Deferred profit from Bottom's 2012 upstream sales	(4,000)	
Bottom Co. adjusted 2012 net income	$23,500	
Top's ownership percentage	80%	
Equity in earnings of Bottom Company, 2012		$ 18,800
Top's share of Bottom Company dividends, 2012 (80%)		(16,000)
Balance 12/31/12		$402,800
Bottom Co. reported income for 2013	$70,000	
Database amortization	(2,500)	
Recognized profit from Bottom's 2012 upstream sales	4,000	
Deferred profit from Bottom's 2013 upstream sales	(6,000)	
Bottom Co. adjusted 2013 net income	$65,500	
Top's ownership percentage	80%	
Equity in earnings of Bottom Company, 2013		$ 52,400
Top's share of Bottom Company dividends, 2013 (80%)		(40,000)
Balance 12/31/13		$415,200

income. Because the inventory transfers are upstream from subsidiary to parent, only 80 percent of the profit deferral and subsequent recognition is allocated to the parent's equity earnings and investment account. As a result, the intra-entity profit reallocation across time affects both the subsidiary's reported income and the noncontrolling interest. Similar to the previous example, the $4,000 intra-entity profit is not eliminated, but simply reallocated across time to the period when it is earned by the consolidated entity.

To illustrate the effects of upstream inventory transfers, in Exhibit 5.6, we consolidate the financial statements of Top and Bottom again. *The individual records of the two companies are changed from Exhibit 5.4 to reflect the parent's application of the equity method for upstream sales.* This change creates several important differences between Exhibits 5.4 and 5.6.

Because the intra-entity sales are upstream, the $4,000 beginning unrealized gross profit (Entry ***G**) adjustment no longer involves a debit to the parent's Investment in Bottom account. Recall that Top and Bottom, as separate legal entities, maintain independent accounting information systems. Thus, when it transferred inventory to Top in 2012, Bottom recorded the transfer as a regular sale even though the counterparty (Top) is a member of the consolidated group. Because $16,000 of these transfers remain in Top's inventory, $4,000 of gross profit (25%) is considered unearned from a consolidated perspective as of January 1, 2013. Also from a consolidated standpoint, Bottom's January 1, 2013, Retained Earnings are overstated by the $4,000 gross profit from the 2012 intra-entity transfers. Thus, Exhibit 5.6 shows a worksheet adjustment that reduces Bottom's January 1, 2013, Retained Earnings balance. Similar to Exhibit 5.4, the credit to Cost of Goods Sold increases consolidated net income to recognize that the profit has been earned in 2013 by sales to outsiders as follows:

Consolidation Entry *G		
Retained earnings - Bottom	4,000	
Cost of Goods Sold		4,000
To recognize intra-entity gross profit in beginning inventory as earned in 2013. Top uses the equity method and intra-entity sales were upstream.		

Following this adjustment, Bottom's beginning Retained Earnings on the worksheet becomes $306,000. Reassigning the $4,000 gross profit from 2012 into 2013 dictates the

EXHIBIT 5.6 Upstream Inventory Transfers

TOP COMPANY AND BOTTOM COMPANY
Consolidation Worksheet
For Year Ending December 31, 2013

Consolidation: Acquisition Method
Investment: Equity Method
Ownership: 80%

Accounts	Top Company	Bottom Company	Consolidation Entries Debit	Consolidation Entries Credit	Noncontrolling Interest	Consolidated Totals
Income Statement						
Sales	(600,000)	(300,000)	(TI)100,000			(800,000)
Cost of goods sold	320,000	180,000	(G) 6,000	(*G) 4,000 (TI)100,000		402,000
Operating expenses	170,000	50,000	(E) 2,500			222,500
Equity in earnings of Bottom	(52,400)		(I) 52,400‡			
Separate company net income	(162,400)	(70,000)				
Consolidated net income						(175,500)
Noncontrolling interest in Bottom Company's income					(13,100)†	13,100
Top's interest in consolidated net income						(162,400)
Statement of Retained Earnings						
Retained earnings 1/1/13						
Top Company	(652,800)					(652,800)
Bottom Company		(310,000)	(*G) 4,000 (S)306,000			
Net income (above)	(162,400)	(70,000)				(162,400)
Dividends paid	70,000	50,000		(D) 40,000	10,000	70,000
Retained earnings 12/31/13	(745,200)	(330,000)				(745,200)
Balance Sheet						
Cash and receivables	280,000	120,000		(P) 10,000		390,000
Inventory	220,000	160,000		(G) 6,000		374,000
Investment in Bottom	415,200		(D) 40,000	(I) 52,400 (S)364,800 (A) 38,000		–0–
Land	410,000	200,000				610,000
Plant assets (net)	190,000	170,000				360,000
Database			(A) 47,500	(E) 2,500		45,000
Total assets	1,515,200	650,000				1,779,000
Liabilities	(340,000)	(170,000)	(P) 10,000			(500,000)
Noncontrolling interest in Bottom Company, 1/1/13				(S) 91,200 (A) 9,500	(100,700)	
Noncontrolling interest in Bottom Company, 12/31/13					103,800	(103,800)
Common stock	(430,000)	(150,000)	(S)150,000			(430,000)
Retained earnings 12/31/13 (above)	(745,200)	(330,000)				(745,200)
Total liabilities and equities	(1,515,200)	(650,000)	718,400	718,400		(1,779,000)

Note: Parentheses indicate a credit balance.
†Because intra-entity sales were upstream, the subsidiary's $70,000 income is decreased for the $6,000 gross profit deferred into next year and increased for $4,000 gross profit deferred from the previous year. After further reduction for $2,500 excess amortization, the resulting $65,500 provides the noncontrolling interest with a $13,100 allocation (20%).
‡Boxed items highlight differences with downstream transfers examined in Exhibit 5.4.
Consolidation entries:

- (*G) Removal of unrealized gross profit from beginning figures so that it can be recognized in current period. Upstream sales attributed to subsidiary.
- (S) Elimination of adjusted stockholders' equity accounts along with recognition of the noncontrolling interest as of January 1.
- (A) Allocation of excess fair value over subsidiary's book value, unamortized balance as of January 1.
- (I) Elimination of intra-entity income.
- (D) Elimination of intra-entity dividends.
- (E) Recognition of amortization expense for current year on database.
- (P) Elimination of intra-entity receivable/payable balances.
- (TI) Elimination of intra-entity sales/purchases balances.
- (G) Removal of unrealized gross profit from ending figures so that it can be recognized in subsequent period.

adjustment of the subsidiary's beginning Retained Earnings balance (as the seller of the goods) to $306,000 from the $310,000 found in the company's separate records on the worksheet.

Consolidation Entry **S** eliminates a portion of the parent's investment account and provides the initial noncontrolling interest balance. This worksheet entry also removes the stockholders' equity accounts of the subsidiary as of the beginning of the current year. Thus, the above $4,000 reduction in Bottom's January 1, 2013, Retained Earnings to defer the unrealized gross profit affects Entry **S**. After posting Entry ***G**, only $306,000 remains as the subsidiary's January 1, 2013, Retained Earnings, which along with Bottom's common stock is eliminated as follows:

Consolidation Entry S		
Common Stock—Bottom	150,000	
Retained earnings—Bottom	306,000	
Investment in Bottom		364,800
Noncontrolling Interest		91,200

This combined equity elimination figure ($456,000) above forms the basis for the 20 percent noncontrolling interest ($91,200) and the elimination of the 80 percent parent company investment ($364,800).

In comparing the consolidated totals across Exhibits 5.4 and 5.6, note that consolidated income, inventory, total assets, and total liabilities and equities are all identical. The sole effect of the direction of the intra-entity inventory transfers (upstream or downstream) resides in the allocation of the temporary income effects of profit deferral and subsequent recognition to the controlling and noncontrolling interests.

Finally, to complete the consolidation, the noncontrolling interest's share of the subsidiary's net income is recorded on the worksheet as $13,100 computed as follows:

Bottom reported net income for 2013	$70,000
Excess fair-value database amortization ($50,000/20 years)	(2,500)
2012 intra-entity gross profit recognized	4,000
2013 intra-entity gross profit deferred	(6,000)
Bottom 2013 net income adjusted	$65,500
Noncontrolling interest percentage	20%
Noncontrolling interest in Bottom's 2013 net income	$13,100

Upstream transfers affect this computation although the downstream sales in the previous example did not. Thus, the noncontrolling interest balance reported previously in the income statement in Exhibit 5.4 differs from the allocation in Exhibit 5.6.

Consolidations—Downstream versus Upstream Transfers

To help clarify the effect of downstream and upstream transfers when the parent uses the equity method, we compare two of the worksheet entries in more detail.

Downstream Transfers			**Upstream Transfers**		
(Exhibit 5.4)			(Exhibit 5.6)		
Entry *G			**Entry *G**		
Investment in Bottom	4,000		Retained Earnings, 1/1/13—Bottom	4,000	
Cost of Goods Sold		4,000	Cost of Goods Sold		4,000
To remove 2012 unrealized gross profit from beginning balances of the seller.			To remove 2012 unrealized gross profit from beginning balances of the seller.		

Downstream Transfers			**Upstream Transfers**		
Entry S			**Entry S**		
Common stock—Bottom	150,000		Common stock—Bottom	150,000	
Retained Earnings, 1/1/13—Bottom	310,000		Retaining Earnings, 1/1/13—Bottom (as adjusted)	306,000	
Investment in Bottom (80%)		368,000	Investment in Bottom (80%)		364,800
Noncontrolling interest—1/1/13 . . . . (20%)		92,000	Noncontrolling interest—1/1/13 (20%)		91,200
To remove subsidiary's stockholders' equity accounts and portion of investment balance. Book value at beginning of year is appropriate.			To remove subsidiary's stockholders' equity accounts (as adjusted in Entry ***G**) and portion of investment balance. Adjusted book value at beginning of year is appropriate.		

Noncontrolling Interest in Subsidiary's Net Income = $13,500. 20% of Bottom's reported income less excess database amortization.

Noncontrolling Interest in Subsidiary's Net Income = $13,100. 20% of Bottom's earned income (reported income after adjustment for unrealized gross profits and excess database amortization).

Effects of Alternative Investment Methods on Consolidation

In Exhibits 5.3 through 5.6 the parent company utilized the equity method. When the parent uses either the initial value or the partial equity method, consolidation procedures normally continue to follow the same patterns analyzed in the previous chapters of this textbook. However, these alternative methods lack the full accrual properties of the equity method. Therefore, an additional worksheet adjustment (***C**) is needed to ensure the consolidated financial statements reflect a full accrual GAAP basis. As was the case previously, the worksheet adjustments depend on whether the intra-entity inventories result from downstream or upstream sales.

Using the same example, we now assume the parent applies **the initial value method.** Given that the subsidiary declares and pays dividends of $20,000 in 2012 and $50,000 in 2013, Top records dividend income of $16,000 ($20,000 × 80%) and $40,000 ($50,000 × 80%) during these two years.

Exhibits 5.7 and 5.8 present the worksheets to consolidate these two companies for the year ending December 31, 2013. As in the previous examples, most of the worksheet entries found in Exhibits 5.7 and 5.8 are described and analyzed in previous chapters of this textbook. Additionally, many of the worksheet entries required by intra-entity sales are identical to those used when the parent applies the equity method. Thus, only Consolidation Entries ***C** and ***G** are examined in detail separately for downstream intra-entity sales (Exhibit 5.7) and upstream intra-entity sales (Exhibit 5.8).

*Downstream Transfers—Consolidation Entries *C and *G: Parent Uses Initial Value Method*

Consolidation Entry ***C** is required in periods subsequent to acquisition whenever the parent does not apply the equity method. This adjustment converts the parent's beginning Retained Earnings to a full-accrual consolidated total. In the current illustration, Top did not accrue its portion of the 2012 increase in Bottom's book value [($30,000 income less $20,000 paid in dividends) × 80%, or $8,000] or record the $2,000 amortization expense for this same period. Because the parent recognized neither number in its

EXHIBIT 5.7 Downstream Inventory Transfers

TOP COMPANY AND BOTTOM COMPANY
Consolidation Worksheet
For Year Ending December 31, 2013

Consolidation: Acquisition Method
Investment: Initial Value Method
Ownership: 80%

Accounts	Top Company	Bottom Company	Consolidation Entries Debit	Consolidation Entries Credit	Noncontrolling Interest	Consolidated Totals
Income Statement						
Sales	(600,000)	(300,000)	(TI)100,000			(800,000)
Cost of goods sold	320,000	180,000	(G) 6,000	(*G) 4,000 (TI)100,000		402,000
Operating expenses	170,000	50,000	(E) 2,500			222,500
Dividend income	(40,000)		(I) 40,000			
Separate company net income	(150,000)	(70,000)				
Consolidated net income						(175,500)
Noncontrolling interest in Bottom Company's income					(13,500)†	13,500
Top's interest in consolidated net income						(162,000)
Statement of Retained Earnings						
Retained Earnings 1/1/13						
Top Company	(650,000)		(*G) 4,000	(*C) 6,000		(652,000)
Bottom Company		(310,000)	(S)310,000‡			
Net income (above)	(150,000)	(70,000)				(162,000)
Dividends paid	70,000	50,000		(I) 40,000	10,000	70,000
Retained earnings 12/31/13	(730,000)	(330,000)				(744,000)
Balance Sheet						
Cash and receivables	280,000	120,000		(P) 10,000		390,000
Inventory	220,000	160,000		(G) 6,000		374,000
Investment in Bottom	400,000		(*C) 6,000	(S)368,000 (A) 38,000		-0-
Land	410,000	200,000				610,000
Plant assets (net)	190,000	170,000				360,000
Database	-0-	-0-	(A) 47,500	(E) 2,500		45,000
Total assets	1,500,000	650,000				1,779,000
Liabilities	(340,000)	(170,000)	(P) 10,000			(500,000)
Noncontrolling interest in Bottom Company, 1/1/13				(S) 92,000 (A) 9,500	(101,500)	
Noncontrolling interest in Bottom Company, 12/31/13					105,000	(105,000)
Common stock	(430,000)	(150,000)	(S)150,000			(430,000)
Retained earnings 12/31/13 (above)	(730,000)	(330,000)				(744,000)
Total liabilities and equities	(1,500,000)	(650,000)	676,000	676,000		(1,779,000)

Note: Parentheses indicate a credit balance.
†Because intra-entity sales are made downstream (by the parent), the subsidiary's earned income is the $70,000 reported figure less $2,500 excess amortization with a 20% allocation to the noncontrolling interest ($13,500).
‡Boxed items highlight differences with upstream transfers examined in Exhibit 5.8.
Consolidation entries:
(*G) Removal of unrealized gross profit from beginning figures so that it can be recognized in current period. Downstream sales attributed to parent.
(*C) Recognition of increase in book value and amortization relating to ownership of subsidiary for year prior to the current year.
(S) Elimination of subsidiary's stockholders' equity accounts along with recognition of the noncontrolling interest as of January 1.
(A) Allocation of subsidiary's fair value in excess of book value, unamortized balance as of January 1.
(I) Elimination of intra-entity dividends recorded by parent as income.
(E) Recognition of amortization expense for current year on database.
(P) Elimination of intra-entity receivable/payable balances.
(TI) Elimination of intra-entity sales/purchases balances.
(G) Removal of unrealized gross profit from ending figures so that it can be recognized in subsequent period.

EXHIBIT 5.8 Upstream Inventory Transfers

TOP COMPANY AND BOTTOM COMPANY
Consolidation Worksheet
For Year Ending December 31, 2013

Consolidation: Acquisition Method
Investment: Initial Value Method
Ownership: 80%

Accounts	Top Company	Bottom Company	Consolidation Entries Debit	Consolidation Entries Credit	Noncontrolling Interest	Consolidated Totals
Income Statement						
Sales	(600,000)	(300,000)	(TI)100,000			(800,000)
Cost of goods sold	320,000	180,000	(G) 6,000	(*G) 4,000		402,000
				(TI)100,000		
Operating expenses	170,000	50,000	(E) 2,500			222,500
Dividend income	(40,000)		(I) 40,000			
Separate company net income	(150,000)	(70,000)				
Consolidated net income						(175,500)
Noncontrolling interest in Bottom Company's income					(13,100)†	13,100
Top's interest in consolidated net income						(162,400)
Statement of Retained Earnings						
Retained earnings 1/1/13						
Top Company	(650,000)			(*C) 2,800		(652,800)
Bottom Company		(310,000)	(*G) 4,000			
			(S)306,000‡			
Net income (above)	(150,000)	(70,000)				(162,400)
Dividends paid	70,000	50,000		(I) 40,000	10,000	70,000
Retained earnings 12/31/13	(730,000)	(330,000)				(745,200)
Balance Sheet						
Cash and receivables	280,000	120,000		(P) 10,000		390,000
Inventory	220,000	160,000		(G) 6,000		374,000
Investment in Bottom	400,000		(*C) 2,800			–0–
				(S)364,800		
				(A) 38,000		
Land	410,000	200,000				610,000
Plant assets (net)	190,000	170,000				360,000
Database	–0–	–0–	(A) 47,500	(E) 2,500		45,000
Total assets	1,500,000	650,000				1,779,000
Liabilities	(340,000)	(170,000)	(P) 10,000			(500,000)
Noncontrolling interest in Bottom Company, 1/1/13				(S) 91,200		
				(A) 9,500	(100,700)	
Noncontrolling interest in Bottom Company, 12/31/13					103,800	(103,800)
Common stock	(430,000)	(150,000)	(S)150,000			(430,000)
Retained earnings 12/31/13 (above)	(730,000)	(330,000)				(745,200)
Total liabilities and equities	(1,500,000)	(650,000)	668,800	668,800		(1,779,000)

Note: Parentheses indicate a credit balance.
†Because intra-entity sales were upstream, the subsidiary's $70,000 income is decreased for the $6,000 gross profit deferred into next year and increased for $4,000 gross profit deferred from the previous year. After further reduction for $2,500 excess amortization, the resulting $65,500 provides the noncontrolling interest with a $13,100 allocation (20%).
‡Boxed items highlight differences with downstream transfers examined in Exhibit 5.7.
Consolidation entries:
(*G) Removal of unrealized gross profit from beginning figures so that it can be recognized in current period. Upstream sales attributed to subsidiary.
(*C) Recognition of earned increase in book value and amortization relating to ownership of subsidiary for year prior to the current year.
(S) Elimination of adjusted stockholders' equity accounts along with recognition of the noncontrolling interest as of January 1.
(A) Allocation of subsidiary's fair value in excess of book value, unamortized balance as of January 1.
(I) Elimination of intra-entity dividends recorded by parent as income.
(E) Recognition of amortization expense for current year on fair value allocated to value of database.
(P) Elimination of intra-entity receivable/payable balances.
(TI) Elimination of intra-entity sales/purchases balances.
(G) Removal of unrealized gross profit from ending figures so that it can be recognized in subsequent period.

Discussion Question

WHAT PRICE SHOULD WE CHARGE OURSELVES?

Slagle Corporation is a large manufacturing organization. Over the past several years, it has obtained an important component used in its production process exclusively from Harrison, Inc., a relatively small company in Topeka, Kansas. Harrison charges $90 per unit for this part:

Variable cost per unit	$40
Fixed cost assigned per unit	30
Markup	20
Total price	$90

In hope of reducing manufacturing costs, Slagle purchases all of Harrison's outstanding common stock. This new subsidiary continues to sell merchandise to a number of outside customers as well as to Slagle. Thus, for internal reporting purposes, Slagle views Harrison as a separate profit center.

A controversy has now arisen among company officials about the amount that Harrison should charge Slagle for each component. The administrator in charge of the subsidiary wants to continue the $90 price. He believes this figure best reflects the division's profitability: "If we are to be judged by our profits, why should we be punished for selling to our own parent company? If that occurs, my figures will look better if I forget Slagle as a customer and try to market my goods solely to outsiders."

In contrast, the vice president in charge of Slagle's production wants the price set at variable cost, total cost, or some derivative of these numbers. "We bought Harrison to bring our costs down. It only makes sense to reduce the transfer price; otherwise the benefits of acquiring this subsidiary are not apparent. I pushed the company to buy Harrison; if our operating results are not improved, I will get the blame."

Will the decision about the transfer price affect consolidated net income? Which method would be easiest for the company's accountant to administer? As the company's accountant, what advice would you give to these officials?

financial records, the worksheet process adjusts the parent's beginning retained earnings by $6,000 as follows:

Consolidation Entry *C		
Investment in Bottom	6,000	
Retained Earnings—Top		6,000
To convert Top's retained earnings to the accrual basis. Intra-entity sales were downstream and therefore do not affect the adjustment.		

The intra-entity inventory transfers do not affect this entry because they were downstream; the gross profits had no impact on the income recognized by the subsidiary.

Under the initial value method, the parent makes no entries in its internal financial records to adjust for the intra-entity sales. Because in this case the sales are downstream, the parent's January 1, 2013, Retained Earnings will be overstated from a consolidated view by the unrealized $4,000 gross profit recognized from its 2012 intra-entity sales.

Consolidation entry *G corrects this overstatement and appropriately recognizes (through the credit to Cost of Goods Sold) that the profit is earned in the current year as follows:

Consolidation Entry *G		
Retained Earnings—Top	4,000	
Cost of Goods Sold		4,000
To recognize intra-entity gross profit in beginning inventory as earned in 2013. Top uses the initial value method and intra-entity sales were downstream.		

Note that the above entry *G simply reassigns the intra-entity beginning inventory gross profit from downstream transfers to 2013 from 2012.

*Upstream Transfers—Consolidation Entries *C and *G: Parent Uses Initial Value Method*

We now change the example by assuming the intra-entity transfers are upstream from Bottom to Top. In this case, the $4,000 intra-entity gross profit remaining in Top's 2012 ending inventory has been recorded by Bottom as part of its 2012 net income and retained earnings. Because $4,000 of Bottom's 2012 income is deferred until 2013, the increase in the subsidiary's book value in the previous year is only $6,000 rather than $10,000 ($30,000 income less $20,000 paid in dividends) as reported. Consequently, conversion to the equity method (Entry *C) requires an increase of just $2,800:

$6,000 net increase (after intra-entity profit deferral) in subsidiary's book value during 2012 × 80%	$4,800
2012 amortization expense (80% × $2,500)	(2,000)
Increase in parent's beginning retained earnings (Entry *C)	$2,800

In applying the initial value method in its financial records, the parent did not recognize the increase in subsidiary book value, excess fair value amortization, or any effects from intra-entity transfers remaining in inventory. The worksheet process thus adjusts the parent's beginning retained earnings by $2,800 shown as follows.

Consolidation Entry *C		
Investment in Bottom	2,800	
Retained Earnings—Top		2,800
To convert Top's retained earning to the accrual basis. Intra-entity sales were upstream.		

In this case the intra-entity inventory transfers affect Consolidation Entry *C because they were downstream; the gross profits directly affected the income recognized by the subsidiary.

Using the initial value method, the parent makes no entries in its internal financial records to adjust for the intra-entity sales. Because in this case the sales are upstream, the subsidiary's January 1, 2013, Retained Earnings will be overstated from a consolidated view by the unrealized gross profit. Consolidation entry *G corrects this overstatement and appropriately recognizes that the profit is earned in the current year as follows:

Consolidation Entry *G		
Retained Earnings—Bottom	4,000	
Cost of Goods Sold		4,000
To recognize intra-entity gross profit in beginning inventory as earned in 2013. Top uses the initial value method and intra-entity sales were upstream.		

Note again how the above entry *G simply reassigns the intra-entity beginning inventory gross profit to 2013 from 2012.

Finally, if the parent had applied the partial equity method in its internal records, little would change in the consolidation processes previously described for the equity method. The primary change would involve inclusion of a Consolidation Entry *C. Because the parent would have recorded changes in reported subsidiary book value, the *C adjustment would be computed only for (1) previous years' excess fair over book value amortizations and (2) the immediate past year's intra-entity profit deferral.

Intra-Entity Land Transfers

LO6

Prepare the consolidation entry to remove any unrealized gain created by the intra-entity transfer of land from the accounting records of the year of transfer and subsequent years.

Although not as prevalent as inventory transactions, intra-entity sales of other assets occur occasionally. The final two sections of this chapter examine the worksheet procedures that noninventory transfers necessitate. We first analyze land transactions and then discuss the effects created by the intra-entity sale of depreciable assets such as buildings and equipment.

Accounting for Land Transactions

The consolidation procedures necessitated by intra-entity land transfers partially parallel those for intra-entity inventory. As with inventory, the sale of land creates a series of effects on the individual records of the two companies. The worksheet process must then adjust the account balances to reflect the perspective of a single economic entity.

By reviewing the sequence of events occurring in an intra-entity land sale, the similarities to inventory transfers can be ascertained as well as the unique features of this transaction.

1. The original seller of the land reports a gain (losses are rare in intra-entity asset transfers), even though the transaction occurred between related parties. At the same time, the acquiring company capitalizes the inflated transfer price rather than the land's historical cost to the business combination.
2. The gain the seller recorded is closed into Retained Earnings at the end of the year. From a consolidated perspective, this account has been artificially increased by a related party. Thus, both the buyer's Land account and the seller's Retained Earnings account continue to contain the unrealized profit.
3. The gain on the original transfer is actually earned only when the land is subsequently disposed of to an outside party. Therefore, appropriate consolidation techniques must be designed to eliminate the intra-entity gain each period until the time of resale.

Clearly, two characteristics encountered in inventory transfers also exist in intra-entity land transactions: inflated book values and unrealized gains subsequently culminated through sales to outside parties. Despite these similarities, significant differences exist. Because of the nature of the transaction, the individual companies do not use sales/purchases accounts when land is transferred. Instead, the seller establishes a separate gain account when it removes the land from its books. Because this gain is unearned, the balance has to be eliminated when preparing consolidated statements.

In addition, the subsequent resale of land to an outside party does not always occur in the year immediately following the transfer. Although inventory is normally disposed of within a relatively short time, the buyer often holds land for years if not permanently. Thus, the overvalued Land account can remain on the acquiring company's books indefinitely. As long as the land is retained, the effects of the unrealized gain (the equivalent of Entry ***G** in inventory transfers) must be eliminated for each subsequent consolidation. By repeating this worksheet entry every year, the consolidated financial statements properly state both the Land and the Retained Earnings accounts.

Eliminating Unrealized Gains—Land Transfers

To illustrate these worksheet procedures, assume that Hastings Company and Patrick Company are related parties. On July 1, 2013, Hastings sold land that originally cost $60,000 to Patrick at a $100,000 transfer price. The seller reports a $40,000 gain; the buyer records the land at the $100,000 acquisition price. At the end of this fiscal period, the intra-entity effect of this transaction must be eliminated for consolidation purposes:

Consolidation Entry TL (year of transfer)

Gain on Sale of Land	40,000	
Land		40,000
To eliminate effects of intra-entity transfer of land. (Labeled **"TL"** in reference to the transferred land.)		

This worksheet entry eliminates the unrealized gain from the 2013 consolidated statements and returns the land to its recorded value at date of transfer, for consolidated purposes. However, as with the transfer of inventory, the effects created by the original transaction remain in the financial records of the individual companies for as long as the property is held. The gain recorded by Hastings carries through to Retained Earnings while Patrick's Land account retains the inflated transfer price. *Therefore, for every subsequent consolidation until the land is eventually sold, the elimination process must be repeated.* Including the following entry on each subsequent worksheet removes the unrealized gain from the asset and from the earnings reported by the combination:

Consolidation Entry *GL (every year following transfer)

Retained Earnings (beginning balance of seller)	40,000	
Land		40,000
To eliminate effects of intra-entity transfer of land made in a previous year. (Labeled "***GL**" in reference to the gain on a land transfer occurring in a prior year.)		

Note that the reduction in Retained Earnings is changed to an increase in the Investment in Subsidiary account when the original sale is downstream and the parent has applied the equity method. In that specific situation, equity method adjustments have already corrected the timing of the parent's unrealized gain. Removing the gain has created a reduction in the Investment account that is appropriately allocated to the subsidiary's Land account on the worksheet. Conversely, if sales were upstream, the Retained Earnings of the seller (the subsidiary) continue to be overstated even if the parent applies the equity method.

One final consolidation concern exists in accounting for intra-entity transfers of land. If the property is ever sold to an outside party, the company making the sale records a gain or loss based on its recorded book value. However, this cost figure is actually the internal transfer price. The gain or loss being recognized is incorrect for consolidation purposes; it has not been computed by comparison to the land's historical cost. Again, the separate financial records fail to reflect the transaction from the perspective of the single economic entity.

Therefore, if the company eventually sells the land, it must recognize the gain deferred at the time of the original transfer. It has finally earned this profit by selling the property to outsiders. On the worksheet, the gain is removed one last time from beginning Retained Earnings (or the investment account, if applicable). In this instance, though, the worksheet entry reclassifies the amount as a realized gain. Thus, the gain recognition is reallocated from the year of transfer into the fiscal period in which the land is sold to the unrelated party.

Returning to the previous illustration, Hastings acquired land for $60,000 and sold it to Patrick, a related party, for $100,000. Consequently, the $40,000 unrealized gain was eliminated on the consolidation worksheet in the year of transfer as well as in each succeeding period. However, if this land is subsequently sold to an outside party for $115,000, Patrick recognizes only a $15,000 gain. From the viewpoint of the business combination, the land (having been bought for $60,000) was actually sold at a $55,000 gain. To correct the reporting, the following consolidation entry must be made in the year that the property is sold to the unrelated party. This adjustment increases the $15,000 gain recorded by Patrick to the consolidated balance of $55,000:

Consolidation Entry *GL (year of sale to outside party)		
Retained Earnings (Hastings)	40,000	
Gain on Sale of Land		40,000
To remove intra-entity gain from year of transfer so that total profit can be recognized in the current period when land is sold to an outside party.		

As in the accounting for inventory transfers, the entire consolidation process demonstrated here accomplishes two major objectives:

1. It reports historical cost for the transferred land for as long as it remains within the business combination.
2. It defers income recognition until the land is sold to outside parties.

Recognizing the Effect on Noncontrolling Interest—Land Transfers

The preceding discussion of intra-entity land transfers ignores the possible presence of a noncontrolling interest. In constructing financial statements for an economic entity that includes outside ownership, the guidelines already established for inventory transfers remain applicable.

If the original sale was a *downstream* transaction, neither the annual deferral nor the eventual recognition of the unrealized gain has any effect on the noncontrolling interest. The rationale for this treatment, as previously indicated, is that profits from downstream transfers relate solely to the parent company.

Conversely, if the transfer is made *upstream,* deferral and recognition of gains are attributed to the subsidiary and, hence, to the noncontrolling interest. As with inventory, all noncontrolling interest balances are computed on the reported earnings of the subsidiary after adjustment for any upstream transfers.

To reiterate, the accounting consequences stemming from land transfers are these:

1. In the year of transfer, any unrealized gain is deferred and the Land account is reduced to historical cost. When an upstream sale creates the gain, the amount also is excluded in calculating the noncontrolling interest's share of the subsidiary's net income for that year.
2. Each year thereafter, the unrealized gain will be removed from the seller's beginning Retained Earnings. If the transfer was upstream, eliminating this earlier gain directly affects the balances recorded within both Entry ***C** (if conversion to the equity method is required) and Entry **S.** The additional equity accrual (Entry ***C,** if needed) as well as the elimination of beginning Stockholders' Equity (Entry **S**) must be based on the newly adjusted balance in the subsidiary's Retained Earnings. This deferral process also has an impact on the noncontrolling interest's share of the subsidiary's income, but only in the year of transfer and the eventual year of sale.
3. If the land is ever sold to an outside party, the original gain is earned and must be reported by the consolidated entity.

Intra-Entity Transfer of Depreciable Assets

LO7

Prepare the consolidation entries to remove the effects of upstream and downstream intra-entity fixed asset transfers across affiliated entities.

Just as related parties can transfer land, the intra-entity sale of a host of other assets is possible. Equipment, patents, franchises, buildings, and other long-lived assets can be involved. Accounting for these transactions resembles that demonstrated for land sales. However, the subsequent calculation of depreciation or amortization provides an added challenge in the development of consolidated statements.[10]

[10] To avoid redundancy within this analysis, all further references are made to depreciation expense alone, although this discussion is equally applicable to the amortization of intangible assets and the depletion of wasting assets.

Deferral of Unrealized Gains

When faced with intra-entity sales of depreciable assets, the accountant's basic objective remains unchanged: *to defer unrealized gains to establish both historical cost balances and recognize appropriate income within the consolidated statements.* More specifically, accountants defer gains created by these transfers until such time as the subsequent use or resale of the asset consummates the original transaction. For inventory sales, the culminating disposal normally occurs currently or in the year following the transfer. In contrast, transferred land is quite often never resold, thus permanently deferring the recognition of the intra-entity profit.

For depreciable asset transfers, the ultimate realization of the gain normally occurs in a different manner; the property's use within the buyer's operations is reflected through depreciation. Recognition of this expense reduces the asset's book value every year and, hence, the overstatement within that balance.

The depreciation systematically eliminates the unrealized gain not only from the asset account but also from Retained Earnings. For the buyer, excess expense results each year because the computation is based on the inflated transfer cost. This depreciation is then closed annually into Retained Earnings. *From a consolidated perspective, the extra expense gradually offsets the unrealized gain within this equity account. In fact, over the life of the asset, the depreciation process eliminates all effects of the transfer from both the asset balance and the Retained Earnings account.*

Depreciable Asset Transfers Illustrated

To examine the consolidation procedures required by the intra-entity transfer of a depreciable asset, assume that Able Company sells equipment to Baker Company at the current market value of $90,000. Able originally acquired the equipment for $100,000 several years ago; since that time, it has recorded $40,000 in accumulated depreciation. The transfer is made on January 1, 2012, when the equipment has a 10-year remaining life.

Year of Transfer

The 2012 effects on the separate financial accounts of the two companies can be quickly enumerated:

1. Baker, as the buyer, enters the equipment into its records at the $90,000 transfer price. However, from a consolidated view, the $60,000 book value ($100,000 cost less $40,000 accumulated depreciation) is still appropriate.
2. Able, as the seller, reports a $30,000 profit, although the combination has not yet earned anything. Able then closes this gain into its Retained Earnings account at the end of 2012.
3. Assuming application of the straight-line depreciation method with no salvage value, Baker records expense of $9,000 at the end of 2012 ($90,000 transfer price/10 years). The buyer recognizes this amount rather than the $6,000 depreciation figure applicable to the consolidated entity ($60,000 book value/10 years).

To report these events as seen by the business combination, both the $30,000 unrealized gain and the $3,000 overstatement in depreciation expense must be eliminated on the worksheet. For clarification purposes, two separate consolidation entries for 2012 follow. However, they can be combined into a single adjustment:

Consolidation Entry TA (year of transfer)		
Gain on Sale of Equipment	30,000	
Equipment	10,000	
Accumulated Depreciation		40,000
To remove unrealized gain and return equipment accounts to balances based on original historical cost. (Labeled **"TA"** in reference to transferred asset.)		

Consolidation Entry ED (year of transfer)		
Accumulated Depreciation	3,000	
Depreciation Expense.		3,000
To eliminate overstatement of depreciation expense caused by inflated transfer price. (Labeled **"ED"** in reference to excess depreciation.) *Entry must be repeated for all 10 years of the equipment's life.*		

From the viewpoint of a single entity, these entries accomplish several objectives:[11]

- Reinstate the asset's historical cost of $100,000.
- Return the January 1, 2012, book value to the appropriate $60,000 figure by recognizing accumulated depreciation of $40,000.
- Eliminate the $30,000 unrealized gain recorded by Able so that this intra-entity profit does not appear in the consolidated income statement.
- Reduce depreciation for the year from $9,000 to $6,000, the appropriate expense based on historical cost.

In the year of the intra-entity depreciable asset transfer, the preceding consolidation entries **TA** and **ED** are applicable regardless of whether the transfer was upstream or downstream. They are likewise applicable regardless of whether the parent applies the equity method, initial value method, or partial equity method of accounting for its investment. As discussed subsequently, however, in the years following the intra-entity transfer, a slight modification must be made to the consolidation entry ***TA** when the equity method is applied and the transfer is downstream.

Years Following Transfer

Again, the preceding worksheet entries do not actually remove the effects of the intra-entity transfer from the individual records of these two organizations. Both the unrealized gain and the excess depreciation expense remain on the separate books and are closed into Retained Earnings of the respective companies at year-end. Similarly, the Equipment account with the related accumulated depreciation continues to hold balances based on the transfer price, not historical cost. *Thus, for every subsequent period, the separately reported figures must be adjusted on the worksheet to present the consolidated totals from a single entity's perspective.*

To derive worksheet entries at any future point, the balances in the accounts of the individual companies must be ascertained and compared to the figures appropriate for the business combination. As an illustration, the separate records of Able and Baker two years after the transfer (December 31, 2013) follow. Consolidated totals are calculated based on the original historical cost of $100,000 and accumulated depreciation of $40,000.

Account	Individual Records	Consolidated Perspective	Worksheet Adjustments
Equipment 12/31/13	$90,000	$100,000	$10,000
Accumulated Depreciation 12/31/13	(18,000)	(52,000)*	(34,000)
Depreciation Expense 12/31/13	9,000	6,000	(3,000)
1/1/13 Retained Earnings effect	(21,000)†	6,000	27,000

Note: Parentheses indicate a credit.
*Accumulated depreciation before transfer $(40,000) plus 2 years × $(6,000).
†Intra-entity transfer gain $(30,000) less one year's depreciation of $9,000.

[11] If the worksheet uses only one account for a net depreciated asset, this entry would have been

Gain on sale	30,000	
Equipment (net)		30,000
To reduce the $90,000 to original $60,000 book value at date of transfer rather than reinstating original balances.		

Because the transfer's effects remain in the separate financial records, the various accounts must be corrected in subsequent consolidations. However, the amounts involved must be updated every period because of the continual impact that depreciation has on these balances. As an example, to adjust the individual figures to the consolidated totals derived earlier, the 2013 worksheet must include the following entries:

Consolidation Entry *TA (year following transfer)		
Equipment	10,000	
Retained Earnings, 1/1/13 (Able)	27,000	
Accumulated Depreciation		37,000
To return the Equipment account to original historical cost and correct the 1/1/13 balances of Retained Earnings and Accumulated Depreciation.		

Consolidation Entry ED (year following transfer)		
Accumulated Depreciation	3,000	
Depreciation Expense		3,000
To remove excess depreciation expense on the intra-entity transfer price and adjust Accumulated Depreciation to its correct 12/31/13 balance.		
Note that the $34,000 increase in 12/31/13 consolidated Accumulated Depreciation is accomplished by a $37,000 credit in Entry ***TA** and a $3,000 debit in Entry **ED.**		

Although adjustments of the asset and depreciation expense remain constant, the change in beginning Retained Earnings and Accumulated Depreciation varies with each succeeding consolidation. At December 31, 2012, the individual companies closed out both the unrealized gain of $30,000 and the initial $3,000 overstatement of depreciation expense. Therefore, as reflected in Entry ***TA,** the beginning Retained Earnings account for 2013 is overvalued by a net amount of only $27,000 rather than $30,000. *Over the life of the asset, the unrealized gain in retained earnings will be systematically reduced to zero as excess depreciation expense ($3,000) is closed out each year.* Hence, on subsequent consolidation worksheets, the beginning Retained Earnings account decreases by this amount: $27,000 in 2013, $24,000 in 2014, and $21,000 in the following period. This reduction continues until the effect of the unrealized gain no longer exists at the end of 10 years.

If this equipment is ever resold to an outside party, the remaining portion of the gain is considered earned. As in the previous discussion of land, the intra-entity profit that exists at that date must be recognized on the consolidated income statement to arrive at the appropriate amount of gain or loss on the sale.

Depreciable Intra-Entity Asset Transfers—Downstream Transfers When the Parent Uses the Equity Method

A slight modification to consolidation entry ***TA** is required when the intra-entity depreciable asset transfer is downstream and the parent uses the equity method. In applying the equity method, the parent adjusts its book income for both the original transfer gain and periodic depreciation expense adjustments. Thus, in downstream intra-entity transfers when the equity method is used, from a consolidated view, the parent's Retained Earnings balance has been already reduced for the gain. Therefore, continuing with the previous example, the following worksheet consolidation entries would be made for a downstream sale assuming that (1) Able is the parent and (2) Able has applied the equity method to account for its investment in Baker.

Consolidation Entry *TA (year following transfer)		
Equipment	10,000	
Investment in Baker	27,000	
Accumulated Depreciation		37,000

Consolidation Entry ED (year following transfer)		
Accumulated Depreciation	3,000	
Depreciation Expense		3,000

In Entry ***TA,** note that the Investment in Baker account replaces the parent's Retained Earnings. The debit to the Investment account effectively allocates the write-down necessitated by the intra-entity transfer to the appropriate subsidiary Equipment and Accumulated Depreciation accounts.

Effect on Noncontrolling Interest—Depreciable Asset Transfers

Because of the lack of official guidance, no easy answer exists as to the assignment of any income effects created within the consolidation process. Consistent with the previous sections of this chapter, all income is assigned here to the original seller. In Entry ***TA,** for example, the beginning Retained Earnings account of Able (the seller) is reduced. Both the unrealized gain on the transfer and the excess depreciation expense subsequently recognized are assigned to that party.

Thus, again, downstream sales are assumed to have no effect on any noncontrolling interest values. The parent rather than the subsidiary made the sale. Conversely, the impact on income created by upstream sales must be considered in computing the balances attributed to these outside owners. Currently, this approach is one of many acceptable alternatives. However, in its future deliberations on consolidation policies and procedures, the FASB could mandate a specific allocation pattern.

Summary

1. The transfer of assets, especially inventory, between the members of a business combination is a common practice. In producing consolidated financial statements, any effects on the separate accounting records created by such transfers must be removed because the transactions did not occur with an outside, unrelated party.
2. Inventory transfers are the most prevalent form of intra-entity asset transaction. Despite being only a transfer, one company records a sale while the other reports a purchase. These balances are reciprocals that must be offset on the worksheet in the process of producing consolidated figures.
3. Additional accounting problems result if inventory is transferred at a markup. Any portion of the merchandise still held at year-end is valued at more than historical cost because of the inflation in price. Furthermore, the gross profit that the seller reports on these goods is unrealized from a consolidation perspective. Thus, this gross profit must be removed from the ending Inventory account, a figure that appears as an asset on the balance sheet and as a negative component within cost of goods sold.
4. Unrealized inventory gross profits also create a consolidation problem in the year following the transfer. Within the separate accounting systems, the seller closes the gross profit to Retained Earnings. The buyer's ending Inventory balance becomes the next period's beginning balance (within Cost of Goods Sold). Therefore, the inflation must be removed again but this time in the subsequent year. The seller's beginning Retained Earnings is decreased to eliminate the unrealized gross profit while Cost of Goods Sold is reduced to remove the overstatement from the beginning inventory component. However, when the parent applies the equity method and sales are downstream, the parent's Retained Earnings are correctly stated from a consolidated view. Therefore, in this case, the Investment in Subsidiary account is used in the beginning intra-entity inventory profit adjustment, instead of the parent's Retained Earnings. Through

this process, the intra-entity profit is deferred from the year of transfer so that recognition can be made at the point of disposal or consumption.

5. The deferral and subsequent realization of intra-entity gross profits raise a question concerning the measurement of noncontrolling interest balances: Does the change in the period of recognition alter these calculations? Although the issue is currently under debate, no formal answer to this question is yet found in official accounting pronouncements. In this textbook, the deferral of profits from upstream transfers (from subsidiary to parent) is assumed to affect the noncontrolling interest whereas downstream transactions (from parent to subsidiary) do not. When upstream transfers are involved, noncontrolling interest values are based on the earned figures remaining after adjustment for any unrealized profits.
6. Inventory is not the only asset that can be sold between the members of a business combination. For example, transfers of land sometimes occur. Again, if the price exceeds original cost, the buyer's records state the asset at an inflated value while the seller recognizes an unrealized gain. As with inventory, the consolidation process must return the asset's recorded balance to cost while deferring the gain. Repetition of this procedure is necessary in every consolidation for as long as the land remains within the business combination.
7. The consolidation process required by the intra-entity transfer of depreciable assets differs somewhat from that demonstrated for inventory and land. Unrealized gain created by the transaction must still be eliminated along with the asset's overstatement. However, because of subsequent depreciation, these adjustments systematically change from period to period. Following the transfer, the buyer computes depreciation based on the new inflated transfer price. Thus, an expense that reduces the carrying amount of the asset at a rate in excess of appropriate depreciation is recorded; the book value moves closer to the historical cost figure each time that depreciation is recorded. Additionally, because the excess depreciation is closed annually to Retained Earnings, the overstatement of the equity account resulting from the unrealized gain is constantly reduced. To produce consolidated figures at any point in time, the remaining inflation in these figures (as well as in the current depreciation expense) must be determined and removed.

Comprehensive Illustration

Problem

(Estimated Time: 45 to 65 Minutes) On January 1, 2011, Daisy Company acquired 80 percent of Rose Company for $594,000 in cash. Rose's total book value on that date was $610,000 and the fair value of the noncontrolling interest was $148,500. The newly acquired subsidiary possessed a trademark (10-year remaining life) that, although unrecorded on Rose's accounting records, had a fair value of $75,000. Any remaining excess acquisition-date fair value was attributed to goodwill.

Daisy decided to acquire Rose so that the subsidiary could furnish component parts for the parent's production process. During the ensuing years, Rose sold inventory to Daisy as follows:

Year	Cost to Rose Company	Transfer Price	Gross Profit Rate	Transferred Inventory Still Held at End of Year (at transfer price)
2011	$100,000	$140,000	28.6%	$20,000
2012	100,000	150,000	33.3	30,000
2013	120,000	160,000	25.0	68,000

Any transferred merchandise that Daisy retained at a year-end was always put into production during the following period.

On January 1, 2012, Daisy sold Rose several pieces of equipment that had a 10-year remaining life and were being depreciated on the straight-line method with no salvage value. This equipment was transferred at an $80,000 price, although it had an original $100,000 cost to Daisy and a $44,000 book value at the date of exchange.

On January 1, 2013, Daisy sold land to Rose for $50,000, its fair value at that date. The original cost had been only $22,000. By the end of 2013, Rose had made no payment for the land.

The following separate financial statements are for Daisy and Rose as of December 31, 2013. Daisy has applied the equity method to account for this investment.

	Daisy Company	Rose Company
Sales	$ (900,000)	$ (500,000)
Cost of goods sold	598,000	300,000
Operating expenses	210,000	80,000
Gain on sale of land	(28,000)	–0–
Income of Rose Company	(60,000)	–0–
Net income	$ (180,000)	$ (120,000)
Retained earnings, 1/1/13	$ (620,000)	$ (430,000)
Net income	(180,000)	(120,000)
Dividends paid	55,000	50,000
Retained earnings, 12/31/13	$ (745,000)	$ (500,000)
Cash and accounts receivable	$ 348,000	$ 410,000
Inventory	430,400	190,000
Investment in Rose Company	737,600	–0–
Land	454,000	280,000
Equipment	270,000	190,000
Accumulated depreciation	(180,000)	(50,000)
Total assets	$ 2,060,000	$ 1,020,000
Liabilities	(715,000)	(120,000)
Common stock	(600,000)	(400,000)
Retained earnings, 12/31/13	(745,000)	(500,000)
Total liabilities and equities	$(2,060,000)	$(1,020,000)

Required

Answer the following questions:

a. By how much did Rose's book value increase during the period from January 1, 2011, through December 31, 2012?

b. During the initial years after the takeover, what annual amortization expense was recognized in connection with the acquisition-date excess of fair value over book value?

c. What amount of unrealized gross profit exists within the parent's inventory figures at the beginning and at the end of 2013?

d. Equipment has been transferred between the companies. What amount of additional depreciation is recognized in 2013 because of this transfer?

e. The parent reports Income of Rose Company of $60,000 for 2013. How was this figure calculated?

f. Without using a worksheet, determine consolidated totals.

g. Prepare the worksheet entries required at December 31, 2013, by the transfers of inventory, land, and equipment.

Solution

a. The subsidiary's book value on the date of purchase was given as $610,000. At the beginning of 2013, the company's common stock and retained earnings total is $830,000 ($400,000 and $430,000, respectively). In the previous years, Rose's book value has apparently increased by $220,000 ($830,000 – $610,000).

b. To determine amortization, an allocation of Daisy's acquisition-date fair value must first be made. The $75,000 allocation needed to show Daisy's equipment at fair value leads to additional annual expense of $7,500 for the initial years of the combination. The $57,500 assigned to goodwill is not subject to amortization.

Acquisition-Date Fair-Value Allocation and Excess Amortization Schedule

Consideration paid by Daisy for 80% of Rose	$ 594,000
Noncontrolling interest (20%) fair value	148,500
Rose's fair value at acquisition date	$ 742,500
Book value of Rose Company	(610,000)
Excess fair value over book value	$ 132,500

		Life (Years)	Annual Excess Amortizations	Excess Amortizations 2011–2013	Unamortized Balance, 12/31/13
Trademark	$ 75,000	10	$7,500	$22,500	$52,500
Goodwill	57,500		–0–	–0–	57,500
Totals	$132,500		$7,500	$22,500	

c. Of the inventory transferred to Daisy during 2012, $30,000 is still held at the beginning of 2013. This merchandise contains an unrealized gross profit of $10,000 ($30,000 × 33.3% gross profit rate for that year). At year-end, $17,000 ($68,000 remaining inventory × 25% gross profit rate) is viewed as an unrealized gross profit.

d. Additional depreciation for the net addition of 2013 is $3,600. Equipment with a book value of $44,000 was transferred at a price of $80,000. The net of $36,000 to this asset's account balances would be written off over 10 years for an extra $3,600 per year during the consolidation process.

e. According to the separate statements given, the subsidiary reports net income of $120,000. However, in determining the income allocation between the parent and the noncontrolling interest, this reported figure must be adjusted for the effects of *any upstream transfers.* Because Rose sold the inventory upstream to Daisy, the $10,000 net profit deferred in requirement (*c*) from 2012 into the current period is attributed to the subsidiary (as the seller). Likewise, the $17,000 unrealized net profit at year-end is viewed as a reduction in Rose's net income.

All other transfers are downstream and not considered to have an effect on the subsidiary. Therefore, the Equity Income of Rose Company balance can be verified as follows:

Company's reported income—2013	$120,000
Recognition of 2012 unrealized gross profit	10,000
Deferral of 2013 unrealized gross profit	(17,000)
Excess amortization expense—2013 (see requirement [*b*])	(7,500)
Earned income of subsidiary from consolidated perspective	105,500
Parent's ownership percentage	80%
Equity income accrual	$ 84,400
Adjustments attributed to parent's ownership	
Deferral of unrealized gain—land	(28,000)
Removal of excess depreciation (see requirement [*d*])	3,600
Equity income of Rose Company—2013	$ 60,000

f. Each of the 2013 consolidated totals for this business combination can be determined as follows:

Sales = $1,240,000. The parent's balance is added to the subsidiary's balance less the $160,000 in intra-entity transfers for the period.

Cost of Goods Sold = $745,000. The computation begins by adding the parent's balance to the subsidiary's balance less the $160,000 in intra-entity transfers for the period. The $10,000 unrealized gross profit from the previous year is deducted to recognize this income currently. Next, the $17,000 ending unrealized gross profit is added to cost of goods sold to defer the income until a later year when the goods are sold to an outside party.

Operating Expenses = $293,900. The parent's balance is added to the subsidiary's balance. Annual excess fair-value amortization of $7,500 (see requirement [*b*]) is also included. Excess depreciation of $3,600 resulting from the transfer of equipment (see requirement [*e*]) is removed.

Gain on Sale of Land = –0–. This amount is eliminated for consolidation purposes because the transaction was intra-entity.

Income of Rose Company = –0–. The equity income figure is removed so that the subsidiary's actual revenues and expenses can be included in the financial statements without double-counting.

Noncontrolling Interest in Subsidiary's Income = $21,100. Requirement (*e*) shows the subsidiary's earned income from a consolidated perspective as $105,500 after adjustments for unrealized upstream gains and excess fair-value amortization. Because outsiders hold 20 percent of the subsidiary, a $21,100 allocation ($105,500 × 20%) is made.

Consolidated Net Income = $201,100 computed as Sales less Cost of Goods Sold and Operating Expenses. The consolidated net income is then distributed: $21,100 to the noncontrolling interest and $180,000 to the parent company owners.

Retained Earnings, 1/1/13 = $620,000. The equity method has been applied; therefore, the parent's balance equals the consolidated total.

Dividends Paid = $55,000. Only the amount the parent paid is shown in the consolidated statements. Distributions from the subsidiary to the parent are eliminated as intra-entity transfers. Any payment to the noncontrolling interest reduces the ending balance attributed to these outside owners.

Cash and Accounts Receivable = $708,000. The two balances are added after removal of the $50,000 intra-entity receivable created by the transfer of land.

Inventory = $603,400. The two balances are added after removal of the $17,000 ending unrealized gross profit (see requirement [*c*]).

Investment in Rose Company = –0–. The investment balance is eliminated so that the actual assets and liabilities of the subsidiary can be included.

Land = $706,000. The two balances are added. The $28,000 unrealized gain created by the transfer is removed.

Equipment = $480,000. The two balances are added. Because of the intra-entity transfer, $20,000 must also be included to adjust the $80,000 transfer price to the original $100,000 cost of the asset.

Accumulated Depreciation = $278,800. The balances are combined and adjusted for $52,400 to reinstate the historical balance for the equipment transferred across affiliates ($56,000 written off at date of transfer less $3,600 for the previous year's depreciation on the intra-entity gain). Then, an additional $3,600 is removed for the current year's depreciation on the intra-entity gain.

Trademark = $52,500. The amount from the original $75,000 acquisition-date excess fair-value allocation less 3 years' amortization at $7,500 per year.

Goodwill = $57,500. The amount from the original allocation of Rose's acquisition-date fair value.

Total Assets = $2,328,600. This figure is a summation of the preceding consolidated assets.

Liabilities = $785,000. The two balances are added after removal of the $50,000 intra-entity payable created by the transfer of land.

Noncontrolling Interest in Subsidiary, 12/31/13 = $198,600. This figure is composed of several different balances:

Rose 20% book value (adjusted for upstream intra-entity profits) at 1/1/13. . . .	$164,000
20% of 1/1/13 unamortized excess fair-value allocation for Rose's net identifiable assets and goodwill ($117,500 × 20%).	23,500
Noncontrolling interest at 1/1/13.	$187,500
2013 Rose income allocation.	21,100
Noncontrolling interest share of Rose dividends.	(10,000)
December 31, 2013, balance	$198,600

Common Stock = $600,000. Only the parent company balance is reported within the consolidated statements.

Retained Earnings, 12/31/13 = $745,000. The retained earnings amount is found by adding consolidated net income to the beginning Retained Earnings balance and then subtracting the dividends paid. All of these figures have been computed previously.

Total Liabilities and Equities = $2,328,600. This figure is the summation of all consolidated liabilities and equities.

g.

Consolidation Worksheet Entries
Intra-Entity Transactions
December 31, 2013

Inventory

Entry *G

	Debit	Credit
Retained Earnings, 1/1/13—Subsidiary	10,000	
Cost of Goods Sold		10,000

To remove 2012 unrealized gross profit from beginning balances of the current year. Because transfers were upstream, retained earnings of the subsidiary (as the original seller) are reduced. Balance is computed in requirement (c).

Entry TI

Sales	160,000	
Cost of Goods Sold		160,000
To eliminate current year intra-entity transfer of inventory.		

Entry G

Cost of Goods Sold	17,000	
Inventory		17,000
To remove 2013 unrealized gross profit from ending accounts of the current year. Balance is computed in requirement (c).		

Land

Entry TL

Gain on Sale of Land	28,000	
Land		28,000
To eliminate gross profit created on first day of current year by an intra-entity transfer of land.		

Equipment

Entry *TA

Equipment	20,000	
Investment in Rose Company	32,400	
Accumulated Depreciation		52,400
To remove unrealized gross profit (as of January 1, 2013) created by intra-entity transfer of equipment and to adjust equipment and accumulated depreciation to historical cost figures.		

Equipment is increased from the $80,000 transfer price to $100,000 cost.

Accumulated depreciation of $56,000 was eliminated at time of transfer. Excess depreciation of $3,600 per year has been recorded for the prior year ($3,600); thus, the accumulated depreciation is now only $52,400 less than the cost-based figure.

The unrealized gain on the transfer was $36,000 ($80,000 less $44,000). That figure has now been reduced by one year of excess depreciation ($3,600). Because the parent used the equity method and this transfer was downstream, the adjustment here is to the investment account rather than the parent's beginning Retained Earnings.

Entry ED

Accumulated Depreciation	3,600	
Operating Expenses (depreciation)		3,600
To eliminate the current year overstatement of depreciation created by inflated transfer price.		

Questions

1. Intra-entity transfers between the component companies of a business combination are quite common. Why do these intra-entity transactions occur so frequently?
2. Barker Company owns 80 percent of the outstanding voting stock of Walden Company. During the current year, intra-entity sales amount to $100,000. These transactions were made with a gross profit rate of 40 percent of the transfer price. In consolidating the two companies, what amount of these sales would be eliminated?
3. Padlock Corp. owns 90 percent of Safeco, Inc. During the year, Padlock sold 3,000 locking mechanisms to Safeco for $900,000. By the end of the year, Safeco had sold all but 500 of the locking mechanisms to outside parties. Padlock marks up the cost of its locking mechanisms by 60 percent in computing its sales price to affiliated and nonaffiliated customers. How much intra-entity profit remains in Safeco's inventory at year-end?

4. How are unrealized inventory gross profits created, and what consolidation entries does the presence of these gains necessitate?
5. James, Inc., sells inventory to Matthews Company, a related party, at James's standard markup. At the current fiscal year-end, Matthews still holds some portion of this inventory. If consolidated financial statements are prepared, why are worksheet entries required in two different fiscal periods?
6. How do intra-entity profits present in any year affect the noncontrolling interest calculations?
7. A worksheet is being developed to consolidate Allegan, Incorporated, and Stark Company. These two organizations have made considerable intra-entity transactions. How would the consolidation process be affected if these transfers were downstream? How would consolidated financial statements be affected if these transfers were upstream?
8. King Company owns a 90 percent interest in the outstanding voting shares of Pawn Company. No excess fair-value amortization resulted from the acquisition. Pawn reports a net income of $110,000 for the current year. Intra-entity sales occur at regular intervals between the two companies. Unrealized gross profits of $30,000 were present in the beginning inventory balances, whereas $60,000 in similar gross profits were recorded at year-end. What is the noncontrolling interest's share of the subsidiary's net income?
9. When a subsidiary sells inventory to a parent, the intra-entity profit is removed from the subsidiary's net income for consolidation and reduces the income allocation to the noncontrolling interest. Is the profit permanently eliminated from the noncontrolling interest, or is it merely shifted from one period to the next? Explain.
10. The consolidation process applicable when intra-entity land transfers have occurred differs somewhat from that used for intra-entity inventory sales. What differences should be noted?
11. A subsidiary sells land to the parent company at a significant gain. The parent holds the land for two years and then sells it to an outside party, also for a gain. How does the business combination account for these events?
12. Why does an intra-entity sale of a depreciable asset (such as equipment or a building) require subsequent adjustments to depreciation expense within the consolidation process?
13. If a seller makes an intra-entity sale of a depreciable asset at a price above book value, the seller's beginning Retained Earnings is reduced when preparing each subsequent consolidation. Why does the amount of the adjustment change from year to year?

Problems

LO1

1. What is the primary reason we defer financial statement recognition of gross profits on intra-entity sales for goods that remain within the consolidated entity at year-end?
   a. Revenues and COGS must be recognized for all intra-entity sales regardless of whether the sales are upstream or downstream.
   b. Intra-entity sales result in gross profit overstatements regardless of amounts remaining in ending inventory.
   c. Gross profits must be deferred indefinitely because sales among affiliates always remain in the consolidated group.
   d. When intra-entity sales remain in ending inventory, ownership of the goods has not changed.

LO3

2. King Corporation owns 80 percent of Lee Corporation's common stock. During October, Lee sold merchandise to King for $100,000. At December 31, 50 percent of this merchandise remains in King's inventory. Gross profit percentages were 30 percent for King and 40 percent for Lee. The amount of unrealized intra-entity profit in ending inventory at December 31 that should be eliminated in the consolidation process is
   a. $40,000.
   b. $20,000.
   c. $16,000.
   d. $15,000.
   (AICPA adapted)

LO5

3. In computing the noncontrolling interest's share of consolidated net income, how should the subsidiary's net income be adjusted for intra-entity transfers?
   a. The subsidiary's reported net income is adjusted for the impact of upstream transfers prior to computing the noncontrolling interest's allocation.

b. The subsidiary's reported income is adjusted for the impact of all transfers prior to computing the noncontrolling interest's allocation.

c. The subsidiary's reported income is not adjusted for the impact of transfers prior to computing the noncontrolling interest's allocation.

d. The subsidiary's reported income is adjusted for the impact of downstream transfers prior to computing the noncontrolling interest's allocation.

LO2, LO3

4. Bellgrade, Inc., acquired a 60 percent interest in Hansen Company several years ago. During 2012, Hansen sold inventory costing $75,000 to Bellgrade for $100,000. A total of 16 percent of this inventory was not sold to outsiders until 2013. During 2013, Hansen sold inventory costing $96,000 to Bellgrade for $120,000. A total of 35 percent of this inventory was not sold to outsiders until 2014. In 2013, Bellgrade reported cost of goods sold of $380,000 while Hansen reported $210,000. What is the consolidated cost of goods sold in 2013?

a. $465,600.
b. $473,440.
c. $474,400.
d. $522,400.

LO2, LO3

5. Top Company holds 90 percent of Bottom Company's common stock. In the current year, Top reports sales of $800,000 and cost of goods sold of $600,000. For this same period, Bottom has sales of $300,000 and cost of goods sold of $180,000. During the current year, Top sold merchandise to Bottom for $100,000. The subsidiary still possesses 40 percent of this inventory at the current year-end. Top had established the transfer price based on its normal markup. What are the consolidated sales and cost of goods sold?

a. $1,000,000 and $690,000.
b. $1,000,000 and $705,000.
c. $1,000,000 and $740,000.
d. $970,000 and $696,000.

LO2, LO3, LO5

6. Use the same information as in problem (5) except assume that the transfers were from Bottom Company to Top Company. What are the consolidated sales and cost of goods sold?

a. $1,000,000 and $720,000.
b. $1,000,000 and $755,000.
c. $1,000,000 and $696,000.
d. $970,000 and $712,000.

LO3, LO4, LO5

7. Angela, Inc., holds a 90 percent interest in Corby Company. During 2012, Corby sold inventory costing $77,000 to Angela for $110,000. Of this inventory, $40,000 worth was not sold to outsiders until 2013. During 2013, Corby sold inventory costing $72,000 to Angela for $120,000. A total of $50,000 of this inventory was not sold to outsiders until 2014. In 2013, Angela reported net income of $150,000 while Corby earned $90,000 after excess amortizations. What is the noncontrolling interest in the 2013 income of the subsidiary?

a. $8,000.
b. $8,200.
c. $9,000.
d. $9,800.

LO7

8. Dunn Corporation owns 100 percent of Grey Corporation's common stock. On January 2, 2012, Dunn sold to Grey $40,000 of machinery with a carrying amount of $30,000. Grey is depreciating the acquired machinery over a five-year life by the straight-line method. The net adjustments to compute 2012 and 2013 consolidated net income would be an increase (decrease) of

2012	2013
a. $(8,000)	$2,000
b. $(8,000)	–0–
c. $(10,000)	$2,000
d. $(10,000)	–0–

(AICPA adapted)

LO7

9. Wallton Corporation owns 70 percent of the outstanding stock of Hastings, Incorporated. On January 1, 2011, Wallton acquired a building with a 10-year life for $300,000. Wallton anticipated no salvage value, and the building was to be depreciated on the straight-line basis. On January 1, 2013, Wallton sold this building to Hastings for $280,000. At that time, the building had a remaining life of eight years but still no expected salvage value. In preparing financial statements for 2013, how does this transfer affect the computation of consolidated net income?
   a. Income must be reduced by $32,000.
   b. Income must be reduced by $35,000.
   c. Income must be reduced by $36,000.
   d. Income must be reduced by $40,000.

Use the following data for problems 10–15:

On January 1, Jarel acquired 80 percent of the outstanding voting stock of Suarez for $260,000 cash consideration. The remaining 20 percent of Suarez had an acquisition-date fair value of $65,000. On January 1, Suarez possessed equipment (5-year life) that was undervalued on its books by $25,000. Suarez also had developed several secret formulas that Jarel assessed at $50,000. These formulas, although not recorded on Suarez's financial records, were estimated to have a 20-year future life.

As of December 31, the financial statements appeared as follows:

	Jarel	Suarez
Revenues	$ (300,000)	$(200,000)
Cost of goods sold	140,000	80,000
Expenses	20,000	10,000
Net income	$ (140,000)	$(110,000)
Retained earnings, 1/1	$ (300,000)	$(150,000)
Net income	(140,000)	(110,000)
Dividends paid	–0–	–0–
Retained earnings, 12/31	$ (440,000)	$(260,000)
Cash and receivables	$ 210,000	$ 90,000
Inventory	150,000	110,000
Investment in Suarez	260,000	–0–
Equipment (net)	440,000	300,000
Total assets	$ 1,060,000	$ 500,000
Liabilities	$ (420,000)	$(140,000)
Common stock	(200,000)	(100,000)
Retained earnings, 12/31	(440,000)	(260,000)
Total liabilities and equities	$(1,060,000)	$(500,000)

During the year, Jarel bought inventory for $80,000 and sold it to Suarez for $100,000. Of these goods, Suarez still owns 60 percent on December 31.

LO2

10. What is the total of consolidated revenues?
   a. $500,000.
   b. $460,000.
   c. $420,000.
   d. $400,000.

LO2, LO3

11. What is the total of consolidated cost of goods sold?
   a. $140,000.
   b. $152,000.
   c. $132,000.
   d. $145,000.

LO1 (Chapter 3)

12. What is the total of consolidated expenses?
   a. $30,000.
   b. $36,000.
   c. $37,500.
   d. $39,000.

LO5

13. What is the consolidated total of noncontrolling interest appearing on the balance sheet?
    a. $85,500.
    b. $83,100.
    c. $87,000.
    d. $70,500.

LO7

14. What is the consolidated total for equipment (net) at December 31?
    a. $740,000.
    b. $756,000.
    c. $760,000.
    d. $765,000.

LO3

15. What is the consolidated total for inventory at December 31?
    a. $240,000.
    b. $248,000.
    c. $250,000.
    d. $260,000.

LO2, LO3, LO5

16. Following are several figures reported for Preston and Sanchez as of December 31, 2013:

	Preston	Sanchez
Inventory	$400,000	$200,000
Sales	800,000	600,000
Investment income	not given	
Cost of goods sold	400,000	300,000
Operating expenses	180,000	250,000

Preston acquired 70 percent of Sanchez in January 2012. In allocating the newly acquired subsidiary's fair value at the acquisition date, Preston noted that Sanchez had developed a customer list worth $65,000 that was unrecorded on its accounting records and had a five-year remaining life. Any remaining excess fair value over Sanchez's book value was attributed to goodwill. During 2013, Sanchez sells inventory costing $120,000 to Preston for $160,000. Of this amount, 20 percent remains unsold in Preston's warehouse at year-end. For Preston's consolidated reports, determine the following amounts to be reported for the current year.

Inventory
Sales
Cost of Goods Sold
Operating Expenses
Noncontrolling Interest in the Subsidiary's Net Income

LO3, LO4, LO5

17. On January 1, 2012, Corgan Company acquired 80 percent of the outstanding voting stock of Smashing, Inc., for a total of $980,000 in cash and other consideration. At the acquisition date, Smashing had common stock of $700,000, retained earnings of $250,000, and a noncontrolling interest fair value of $245,000. Corgan attributed the excess of fair value over Smashing's book value to various covenants with a 20-year life. Corgan uses the equity method to account for its investment in Smashing.

    During the next two years, Smashing reported the following:

	Net Income	Dividends	Inventory Purchases from Corgan
2012	$150,000	$35,000	$100,000
2013	130,000	45,000	120,000

Corgan sells inventory to Smashing using a 60 percent markup on cost. At the end of 2012 and 2013, 40 percent of the current year purchases remain in Smashing's inventory.

a. Compute the equity method balance in Corgan's Investment in Smashing, Inc., account as of December 31, 2013.

b. Prepare the worksheet adjustments for the December 31, 2013, consolidation of Corgan and Smashing.

LO1, LO3, LO4
LO5, LO6, LO7

18. Placid Lake Corporation acquired 80 percent of the outstanding voting stock of Scenic, Inc., on January 1, 2012, when Scenic had a net book value of $400,000. Any excess fair value was assigned to intangible assets and amortized at a rate of $5,000 per year.

Placid Lake's 2013 net income before consideration of its relationship with Scenic (and before adjustments for intra-entity sales) was $300,000. Scenic reported net income of $110,000. Placid Lake distributed $100,000 in dividends during this period; Scenic paid $40,000. At the end of 2013, selected figures from the two companies' balance sheets were as follows:

	Placid Lake	Scenic
Inventory	$140,000	$ 90,000
Land.	600,000	200,000
Equipment (net)	400,000	300,000

During 2012, intra-entity sales of $90,000 (original cost of $54,000) were made. Only 20 percent of this inventory was still held within the consolidated entity at the end of 2012. In 2013, $120,000 in intra-entity sales were made with an original cost of $66,000. Of this merchandise, 30 percent had not been resold to outside parties by the end of the year.

Each of the following questions should be considered as an independent situation for the year 2013.

a. What is consolidated net income for Placid Lake and its subsidiary?

b. If the intra-entity sales were upstream, how would consolidated net income be allocated to the controlling and noncontrolling interest?

c. If the intra-entity sales were downstream, how would consolidated net income be allocated to the controlling and noncontrolling interest?

d. What is the consolidated balance in the ending Inventory account?

e. Assume that no intra-entity inventory sales occurred between Placid Lake and Scenic. Instead, in 2012, Scenic sold land costing $30,000 to Placid Lake for $50,000. On the 2013 consolidated balance sheet, what value should be reported for land?

f. Assume that no intra-entity inventory or land sales occurred between Placid Lake and Scenic. Instead, on January 1, 2012, Scenic sold equipment (that originally cost $100,000 but had a $60,000 book value on that date) to Placid Lake for $80,000. At the time of sale, the equipment had a remaining useful life of five years. What worksheet entries are made for a December 31, 2013, consolidation of these two companies to eliminate the impact of the intra-entity transfer? For 2013, what is the noncontrolling interest's share of Scenic's net income?

LO2, LO3, LO4, LO5

19. On January 1, 2012, Doone Corporation acquired 60 percent of the outstanding voting stock of Rockne Company for $300,000 consideration. At the acquisition date, the fair value of the 40 percent noncontrolling interest was $200,000 and Rockne's assets and liabilities had a collective net fair value of $500,000. Doone uses the equity method in its internal records to account for its investment in Rockne. Rockne reports net income of $160,000 in 2013. Since being acquired, Rockne has regularly supplied inventory to Doone at 25 percent more than cost. Sales to Doone amounted to $250,000 in 2012 and $300,000 in 2013. Approximately 30 percent of the inventory purchased during any one year is not used until the following year.

    a. What is the noncontrolling interest's share of Rockne's 2013 income?

    b. Prepare Doone's 2013 consolidation entries required by the intra-entity inventory transfers.

LO3, LO4, LO5, LO7

20. Penguin Corporation acquired 80 percent of the outstanding voting stock of Snow Company on January 1, 2012, for $420,000 in cash and other consideration. At the acquisition date, Penguin assessed Snow's identifiable assets and liabilities at a collective net fair value of $525,000 and the fair value of the 20 percent noncontrolling interest was $105,000. No excess fair value over book value amortization accompanied the acquisition.

    The following selected account balances are from the individual financial records of these two companies as of December 31, 2013:

	Penguin	Snow
Sales.	$640,000	$360,000
Cost of goods sold	290,000	197,000
Operating expenses	150,000	105,000
Retained earnings, 1/1/13.	740,000	180,000
Inventory	346,000	110,000
Buildings (net).	358,000	157,000
Investment income	Not given	–0–

Each of the following problems is an independent situation:

a. Assume that Penguin sells Snow inventory at a markup equal to 40 percent of cost. Intra-entity transfers were $90,000 in 2012 and $110,000 in 2013. Of this inventory, Snow retained and then sold $28,000 of the 2012 transfers in 2013 and held $42,000 of the 2013 transfers until 2014.

On consolidated financial statements for 2013, determine the balances that would appear for the following accounts:

Cost of Goods Sold
Inventory
Noncontrolling Interest in Subsidiary's Net Income

b. Assume that Snow sells inventory to Penguin at a markup equal to 40 percent of cost. Intra-entity transfers were $50,000 in 2012 and $80,000 in 2013. Of this inventory, $21,000 of the 2012 transfers were retained and then sold by Penguin in 2013, whereas $35,000 of the 2013 transfers were held until 2014.

On consolidated financial statements for 2013, determine the balances that would appear for the following accounts:

Cost of Goods Sold
Inventory
Noncontrolling Interest in Subsidiary's Net Income

c. Penguin sells Snow a building on January 1, 2012, for $80,000, although its book value was only $50,000 on this date. The building had a five-year remaining life and was to be depreciated using the straight-line method with no salvage value.

Determine the balances that would appear on consolidated financial statements for 2013 for the following accounts:

Buildings (net)
Operating Expenses
Noncontrolling Interest in Subsidiary's Net Income

LO3, LO4, LO5

21. Akron, Inc., owns all outstanding stock of Toledo Corporation. Amortization expense of $15,000 per year for patented technology resulted from the original acquisition. For 2013, the companies had the following account balances:

	Akron	Toledo
Sales	$1,100,000	$600,000
Cost of goods sold	500,000	400,000
Operating expenses	400,000	220,000
Investment income	Not given	–0–
Dividends paid	80,000	30,000

Intra-entity sales of $320,000 occurred during 2012 and again in 2013. This merchandise cost $240,000 each year. Of the total transfers, $70,000 was still held on December 31, 2012, with $50,000 unsold on December 31, 2013.

a. For consolidation purposes, does the direction of the transfers (upstream or downstream) affect the balances to be reported here?

b. Prepare a consolidated income statement for the year ending December 31, 2013.

LO7

22. On January 1, 2012, QuickPort Company acquired 90 percent of the outstanding voting stock of NetSpeed, Inc., for $810,000 in cash and stock options. At the acquisition date, NetSpeed had common stock of $800,000 and Retained Earnings of $40,000. The acquisition-date fair value of the 10 percent noncontrolling interest was $90,000. QuickPort attributed the $60,000 excess of NetSpeed's fair value over book value to a database with a 5-year remaining life.

During the next two years, NetSpeed reported the following:

	Income	Dividends
2012	$ 80,000	$8,000
2013	115,000	8,000

On July 1, 2012, QuickPort sold communication equipment to NetSpeed for $42,000. The equipment originally cost $48,000 and had accumulated depreciation of $9,000 and an estimated remaining life of three years at the date of the intra-entity transfer.

a. Compute the equity method balance in QuickPort's Investment in NetSpeed, Inc., account as of December 31, 2013.

b. Prepare the worksheet adjustments for the December 31, 2013, consolidation of QuickPort and NetSpeed.

LO7

23. Padre holds 100 percent of the outstanding shares of Sonora. On January 1, 2011, Padre transferred equipment to Sonora for $95,000. The equipment had cost $130,000 originally but had a $50,000 book value and five-year remaining life at the date of transfer. Depreciation expense is computed according to the straight-line method with no salvage value.

Consolidated financial statements for 2013 currently are being prepared. What worksheet entries are needed in connection with the consolidation of this asset? Assume that the parent applies the partial equity method.

LO7

24. On January 1, 2013, Slaughter sold equipment to Bennett (a wholly owned subsidiary) for $120,000 in cash. The equipment had originally cost $100,000 but had a book value of only $70,000 when transferred. On that date, the equipment had a five-year remaining life. Depreciation expense is computed using the straight-line method.

Slaughter earned $220,000 in net income in 2013 (not including any investment income) while Bennett reported $90,000. Slaughter attributed any excess acquisition-date fair value to Bennett's unpatented technology, which was amortized at a rate of $8,000 per year.

a. What is the consolidated net income for 2013?

b. What is the parent's share of consolidated net income for 2013 if Slaughter owns only 90 percent of Bennett?

c. What is the parent's share of consolidated net income for 2013 if Slaughter owns only 90 percent of Bennett and the equipment transfer was upstream?

d. What is the consolidated net income for 2014 if Slaughter reports $240,000 (does not include investment income) and Bennett $100,000 in income? Assume that Bennett is a wholly owned subsidiary and the equipment transfer was downstream.

LO2, LO3, LO4, LO7

25. Anchovy acquired 90 percent of Yelton on January 1, 2011. Of Yelton's total acquisition-date fair value, $60,000 was allocated to undervalued equipment (with a 10-year life) and $80,000 was attributed to franchises (to be written off over a 20-year period).

Since the takeover, Yelton has transferred inventory to its parent as follows:

Year	Cost	Transfer Price	Remaining at Year-End
2011	$20,000	$ 50,000	$20,000 (at transfer price)
2012	49,000	70,000	30,000 (at transfer price)
2013	50,000	100,000	40,000 (at transfer price)

On January 1, 2012, Anchovy sold Yelton a building for $50,000 that had originally cost $70,000 but had only a $30,000 book value at the date of transfer. The building is estimated to have a five-year remaining life (straight-line depreciation is used with no salvage value).

Selected figures from the December 31, 2013, trial balances of these two companies are as follows:

	Anchovy	Yelton
Sales	$600,000	$500,000
Cost of goods sold	400,000	260,000
Operating expenses	120,000	80,000
Investment income	Not given	–0–
Inventory	220,000	80,000
Equipment (net)	140,000	110,000
Buildings (net)	350,000	190,000

Determine consolidated totals for each of these account balances.

LO3, LO4, LO5, LO7

26. On January 1, 2013, Sledge had common stock of $120,000 and retained earnings of $260,000. During that year, Sledge reported sales of $130,000, cost of goods sold of $70,000, and operating expenses of $40,000.

On January 1, 2011, Percy, Inc., acquired 80 percent of Sledge's outstanding voting stock. At that date, $60,000 of the acquisition-date fair value was assigned to unrecorded contracts (with a 20-year life) and $20,000 to an undervalued building (with a 10-year life).

In 2012, Sledge sold inventory costing $9,000 to Percy for $15,000. Of this merchandise, Percy continued to hold $5,000 at year-end. During 2013, Sledge transferred inventory costing $11,000 to Percy for $20,000. Percy still held half of these items at year-end.

On January 1, 2012, Percy sold equipment to Sledge for $12,000. This asset originally cost $16,000 but had a January 1, 2012, book value of $9,000. At the time of transfer, the equipment's remaining life was estimated to be five years.

Percy has properly applied the equity method to the investment in Sledge.

a. Prepare worksheet entries to consolidate these two companies as of December 31, 2013.

b. Compute the noncontrolling interest in the subsidiary's net income for 2013.

LO1, LO2, LO3, LO4, LO5

27. Pitino acquired 90 percent of Brey's outstanding shares on January 1, 2011, in exchange for $342,000 in cash. The subsidiary's stockholders' equity accounts totaled $326,000 and the noncontrolling interest had a fair value of $38,000 on that day. However, a building (with a nine-year remaining life) in Brey's accounting records was undervalued by $18,000. Pitino assigned the rest of the excess fair value over book value to Brey's patented technology (six-year remaining life).

Brey reported net income from its own operations of $64,000 in 2011 and $80,000 in 2012. Brey paid dividends of $19,000 in 2011 and $23,000 in 2012.

Brey sells inventory to Pitino as follows:

Year	Cost to Brey	Transfer Price to Pitino	Inventory Remaining at Year-End (at transfer price)
2011	$69,000	$115,000	$25,000
2012	81,000	135,000	37,500
2013	92,800	160,000	50,000

At December 31, 2013, Pitino owes Brey $16,000 for inventory acquired during the period.

The following separate account balances are for these two companies for December 31, 2013, and the year then ended. Credits are indicated by parentheses.

	Pitino	Brey
Sales revenues	$ (862,000)	$(366,000)
Cost of goods sold	515,000	209,000
Expenses	185,400	67,000
Investment income—Brey	(68,400)	–0–
Net income	$ (230,000)	$ (90,000)
Retained earnings, 1/1/13	$ (488,000)	$(278,000)
Net income (above)	(230,000)	(90,000)
Dividends paid	136,000	27,000
Retained earnings, 12/31/13	$ (582,000)	$(341,000)
Cash and receivables	$ 146,000	$ 98,000
Inventory	255,000	136,000
Investment in Brey	450,000	–0–
Land, buildings, and equipment (net)	964,000	328,000
Total assets	$ 1,815,000	$ 562,000
Liabilities	$ (718,000)	$ (71,000)
Common stock	(515,000)	(150,000)
Retained earnings, 12/31/13	(582,000)	(341,000)
Total liabilities and equities	$(1,815,000)	$(562,000)

Answer each of the following questions:

a. What was the annual amortization resulting from the acquisition-date fair-value allocations?

b. Were the intra-entity transfers upstream or downstream?

c. What unrealized gross profit existed as of January 1, 2013?

d. What unrealized gross profit existed as of December 31, 2013?

e. What amounts make up the $68,400 Investment Income—Brey account balance for 2013?

f. What was the noncontrolling interest's share of the subsidiary's net income for 2013?

g. What amounts make up the $450,000 Investment in Brey account balance as of December 31, 2013?

h. Prepare the 2013 worksheet entry to eliminate the subsidiary's beginning owners' equity balances.

i. Without preparing a worksheet or consolidation entries, determine the consolidation balances for these two companies.

LO2, LO3, LO4

28. Bennett acquired 70 percent of Zeigler on June 30, 2012, for $910,000 in cash. Based on Zeigler's acquisition-date fair value, only one unrecorded intangible of $400,000 was recognized and is being amortized at the rate of $10,000 per year. The noncontrolling interest fair value was assessed at $390,000 at the acquisition date. The 2013 financial statements are as follows:

	Bennett	Zeigler
Sales	$ (800,000)	$ (600,000)
Cost of goods sold	535,000	400,000
Operating expenses	100,000	100,000
Dividend income	(35,000)	–0–
Net income	$ (200,000)	$ (100,000)
Retained earnings, 1/1/13	$(1,300,000)	$ (850,000)
Net income	(200,000)	(100,000)
Dividends paid	100,000	50,000
Retained earnings, 12/31/13	$(1,400,000)	$ (900,000)
Cash and receivables	$ 400,000	$ 300,000
Inventory	290,000	700,000
Investment in Zeigler	910,000	–0–
Fixed assets	1,000,000	600,000
Accumulated depreciation	(300,000)	(200,000)
Totals	$ 2,300,000	$ 1,400,000
Liabilities	$ (600,000)	$ (400,000)
Common stock	(300,000)	(100,000)
Retained earnings	(1,400,000)	(900,000)
Totals	$(2,300,000)	$(1,400,000)

Bennett sold Zeigler inventory costing $72,000 during the last six months of 2012 for $120,000. At year-end, 30 percent remained. Bennett sells Zeigler inventory costing $200,000 during 2013 for $250,000. At year-end, 20 percent is left. With these facts, determine the consolidated balances for the accounts:

Sales
Cost of Goods Sold
Operating Expenses
Dividend Income
Noncontrolling Interest in Consolidated Income
Inventory
Noncontrolling Interest in Subsidiary, 12/31/13

LO2, LO3, LO4, LO5

29. Compute the balances in problem (28) again, assuming that all intra-entity transfers were made from Zeigler to Bennett.

LO1, LO2, LO3, LO4, LO5, LO7

30. Following are financial statements for Moore Company and Kirby Company for 2013:

	Moore	Kirby
Sales	$ (800,000)	$ (600,000)
Cost of goods sold	500,000	400,000
Operating and interest expenses	100,000	160,000
Net income	$ (200,000)	$ (40,000)

(continued)

	Moore	Kirby
Retained earnings, 1/1/13	$ (990,000)	$ (550,000)
Net income	(200,000)	(40,000)
Dividends paid	130,000	–0–
Retained earnings, 12/31/13	$(1,060,000)	$ (590,000)
Cash and receivables	$ 217,000	$ 180,000
Inventory	224,000	160,000
Investment in Kirby	657,000	–0–
Equipment (net)	600,000	420,000
Buildings	1,000,000	650,000
Accumulated depreciation—buildings	(100,000)	(200,000)
Other assets	200,000	100,000
Total assets	$ 2,798,000	$ 1,310,000
Liabilities	$(1,138,000)	$ (570,000)
Common stock	(600,000)	(150,000)
Retained earnings, 12/31/13	(1,060,000)	(590,000)
Total liabilities and equity	$(2,798,000)	$(1,310,000)

- Moore purchased 90 percent of Kirby on January 1, 2012, for $657,000 in cash. On that date, the 10 percent noncontrolling interest was assessed to have a $73,000 fair value. Also at the acquisition date, Kirby held equipment (4-year remaining life) undervalued on the financial records by $20,000 and interest-bearing liabilities (5-year remaining life) overvalued by $40,000. The rest of the excess fair value over book value was assigned to previously unrecognized brand names and amortized over a 10-year life.
- During 2012 Kirby earned a net income of $80,000 and paid no dividends.
- Each year Kirby sells Moore inventory at a 20 percent gross profit rate. Intra-entity sales were $145,000 in 2012 and $160,000 in 2013. On January 1, 2013, 30 percent of the 2012 transfers were still on hand and, on December 31, 2013, 40 percent of the 2013 transfers remained.
- Moore sold Kirby a building on January 2, 2012. It had cost Moore $100,000 but had $90,000 in accumulated depreciation at the time of this transfer. The price was $25,000 in cash. At that time, the building had a five-year remaining life.

Determine all consolidated balances either computationally or by using a worksheet.

LO2, LO3, LO4, LO5

eXcel

31. On January 1, 2012, McIlroy, Inc., acquired a 60 percent interest in the common stock of Stinson, Inc., for $372,000. Stinson's book value on that date consisted of common stock of $100,000 and retained earnings of $220,000. Also, the acquisition-date fair value of the 40 percent noncontrolling interest was $248,000. The subsidiary held patents (with a 10-year remaining life) that were undervalued within the company's accounting records by $70,000 and an unrecorded customer list (15-year remaining life) assessed at a $45,000 fair value. Any remaining excess acquisition-date fair value was assigned to goodwill. Since acquisition, McIlroy has applied the equity method to its Investment in Stinson account and no goodwill impairment has occurred.

    Intra-entity inventory sales between the two companies have been made as follows:

Year	Cost to McIlroy	Transfer Price to Stinson	Ending Balance (at transfer price)
2012	120,000	150,000	50,000
2013	112,000	160,000	40,000

The individual financial statements for these two companies as of December 31, 2013, and the year then ended follow:

	McIlroy, Inc.	Stinson, Inc.
Sales	$ (700,000)	$(335,000)
Cost of goods sold	460,000	205,000
Operating expenses	188,000	70,000
Equity earnings in Stinson	(28,000)	–0–
Net income	$ (80,000)	$ (60,000)

(continued)

	McIlroy, Inc.	Stinson, Inc.
Retained earnings, 1/1/13	$ (695,000)	$(280,000)
Net income (above)	(80,000)	(60,000)
Dividends paid	45,000	15,000
Retained earnings, 12/31/13	$ (730,000)	$(325,000)
Cash and receivables	$ 248,000	$ 148,000
Inventory	233,000	129,000
Investment in Stinson	411,000	–0–
Buildings (net)	308,000	202,000
Equipment (net)	220,000	86,000
Patents (net)	–0–	20,000
Total assets	$ 1,420,000	$ 585,000
Liabilities	$ (390,000)	$(160,000)
Common stock	(300,000)	(100,000)
Retained earnings, 12/31/13	(730,000)	(325,000)
Total liabilities and equities	$(1,420,000)	$(585,000)

a. Show how McIlroy determined the $411,000 Investment in Stinson account balance. Assume that McIlroy defers 100 percent of downstream intra-entity profits against its share of Stinson's income.

b. Prepare a consolidated worksheet to determine appropriate balances for external financial reporting as of December 31, 2013.

LO2, LO3, LO4, LO5

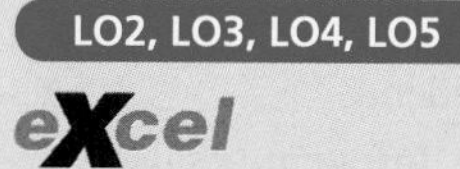

32. On January 1, 2011, Plymouth Corporation acquired 80 percent of the outstanding voting stock of Sander Company in exchange for $1,200,000 cash. At that time, although Sander's book value was $925,000, Plymouth assessed Sander's total business fair value at $1,500,000. Since that time, Sander has neither issued nor reacquired any shares of its own stock.

The book values of Sander's individual assets and liabilities approximated their acquisition-date fair values except for the patent account, which was undervalued by $350,000. The undervalued patents had a 5-year remaining life at the acquisition date. Any remaining excess fair value was attributed to goodwill. No goodwill impairments have occurred.

Sander regularly sells inventory to Plymouth. Below are details of the intra-entity inventory sales for the past three years:

Year	Intra-Entity Sales	Intra-Entity Ending Inventory at Transfer Price	Gross Profit Rate on Intra-Entity Inventory Transfers
2011	$125,000	$ 80,000	25%
2012	220,000	125,000	28%
2013	300,000	160,000	25%

Separate financial statements for these two companies as of December 31, 2013, follow:

	Plymouth	Sander
Revenues	$(1,740,000)	$ (950,000)
Cost of goods sold	820,000	500,000
Depreciation expense	104,000	85,000
Amortization expense	220,000	120,000
Interest expense	20,000	15,000
Equity in earnings of Sander	(124,000)	–0–
Net income	$ (700,000)	$ (230,000)
Retained earnings 1/1/13	$(2,800,000)	$ (345,000)
Net income	(700,000)	(230,000)
Dividends paid	200,000	25,000
Retained earnings 12/31/13	$(3,300,000)	$ (550,000)

(continued)

	Plymouth	Sander
Cash	$ 535,000	$ 115,000
Accounts receivable	575,000	215,000
Inventory	990,000	800,000
Investment in Sander	1,420,000	-0-
Buildings and equipment	1,025,000	863,000
Patents	950,000	107,000
Total assets	$ 5,495,000	$ 2,100,000
Accounts payable	$ (450,000)	$ (200,000)
Notes payable	(545,000)	(450,000)
Common stock	(900,000)	(800,000)
Additional paid-in capital	(300,000)	(100,000)
Retained earnings 12/31/13	(3,300,000)	(550,000)
Total liabilities and stockholders' equity	$(5,495,000)	$(2,100,000)

a. Prepare a schedule that calculates the Equity in Earnings of Sander account balance.

b. Prepare a worksheet to arrive at consolidated figures for external reporting purposes.

LO2, LO3, LO4, LO5, LO7

33. On January 1, 2011, Monica Company acquired 70 percent of Young Company's outstanding common stock for $665,000. The fair value of the noncontrolling interest at the acquisition date was $285,000. Young reported stockholders' equity accounts on that date as follows:

Common stock—$10 par value	$300,000
Additional paid-in capital	90,000
Retained earnings	410,000

In establishing the acquisition value, Monica appraised Young's assets and ascertained that the accounting records undervalued a building (with a five-year life) by $50,000. Any remaining excess acquisition-date fair value was allocated to a franchise agreement to be amortized over 10 years.

During the subsequent years, Young sold Monica inventory at a 30 percent gross profit rate. Monica consistently resold this merchandise in the year of acquisition or in the period immediately following. Transfers for the three years after this business combination was created amounted to the following:

Year	Transfer Price	Inventory Remaining at Year-End (at transfer price)
2011	$60,000	$10,000
2012	80,000	12,000
2013	90,000	18,000

In addition, Monica sold Young several pieces of fully depreciated equipment on January 1, 2012, for $36,000. The equipment had originally cost Monica $50,000. Young plans to depreciate these assets over a six-year period.

In 2013, Young earns a net income of $160,000 and distributes $50,000 in cash dividends. These figures increase the subsidiary's Retained Earnings to a $740,000 balance at the end of 2013. During this same year, Monica reported dividend income of $35,000 and an investment account containing the initial value balance of $665,000. No changes in Young's common stock accounts have occurred since Monica's acquisition.

Prepare the 2013 consolidation worksheet entries for Monica and Young. In addition, compute the noncontrolling interest's share of the subsidiary's net income for 2013.

LO2, LO3, LO4, LO5, LO7

34. Assume the same basic information as presented in problem (33) except that Monica employs the equity method of accounting. Hence, it reports $102,740 investment income for 2013 with an Investment account balance of $826,220. Under these circumstances, prepare the worksheet entries required for the consolidation of Monica Company and Young Company.

LO2, LO3, LO4, LO5, LO6, LO7

35. The individual financial statements for Gibson Company and Keller Company for the year ending December 31, 2013, follow. Gibson acquired a 60 percent interest in Keller on January 1, 2012, in exchange for various considerations totaling $570,000. At the acquisition date, the fair value

of the noncontrolling interest was $380,000 and Keller's book value was $850,000. Keller had developed internally a customer list that was not recorded on its books but had an acquisition-date fair value of $100,000. This intangible asset is being amortized over 20 years.

Gibson sold Keller land with a book value of $60,000 on January 2, 2012, for $100,000. Keller still holds this land at the end of the current year.

Keller regularly transfers inventory to Gibson. In 2012, it shipped inventory costing $100,000 to Gibson at a price of $150,000. During 2013, intra-entity shipments totaled $200,000, although the original cost to Keller was only $140,000. In each of these years, 20 percent of the merchandise was not resold to outside parties until the period following the transfer. Gibson owes Keller $40,000 at the end of 2013.

	Gibson Company	Keller Company
Sales	$ (800,000)	$ (500,000)
Cost of goods sold	500,000	300,000
Operating expenses	100,000	60,000
Income of Keller Company	(84,000)	–0–
Net income	$ (284,000)	$ (140,000)
Retained earnings, 1/1/13	$(1,116,000)	$ (620,000)
Net income (above)	(284,000)	(140,000)
Dividends paid	115,000	60,000
Retained earnings, 12/31/13	$(1,285,000)	$ (700,000)
Cash	$ 177,000	$ 90,000
Accounts receivable	356,000	410,000
Inventory	440,000	320,000
Investment in Keller Company	726,000	–0–
Land	180,000	390,000
Buildings and equipment (net)	496,000	300,000
Total assets	$ 2,375,000	$ 1,510,000
Liabilities	$ (480,000)	$ (400,000)
Common stock	(610,000)	(320,000)
Additional paid-in capital	–0–	(90,000)
Retained earnings, 12/31/13	(1,285,000)	(700,000)
Total liabilities and equities	$(2,375,000)	$(1,510,000)

a. Prepare a worksheet to consolidate the separate 2013 financial statements for Gibson and Keller.

b. How would the consolidation entries in requirement (*a*) have differed if Gibson had sold a building with a $60,000 book value (cost of $140,000) to Keller for $100,000 instead of land, as the problem reports? Assume that the building had a 10-year remaining life at the date of transfer.

LO2, LO3, LO4, LO6

36. On January 1, 2012, Parkway, Inc., issued securities with a total fair value of $450,000 for 100 percent of Skyline Corporation's outstanding ownership shares. Skyline has long supplied inventory to Parkway, which hopes to achieve synergies with production scheduling and product development with this combination.

Although Skyline's book value at the acquisition date was $300,000, the fair value of its trademarks was assessed to be $30,000 more than their carrying amounts. Additionally, Skyline's patented technology was undervalued in its accounting records by $120,000. The trademarks were considered to have indefinite lives, and the estimated remaining life of the patented technology was eight years.

In 2012, Skyline sold Parkway inventory costing $30,000 for $50,000. As of December 31, 2012, Parkway had resold only 28 percent of this inventory. In 2013, Parkway bought from Skyline $80,000 of inventory that had an original cost of $40,000. At the end of 2013, Parkway held $28,000 of inventory acquired from Skyline, all from its 2013 purchases.

During 2013, Parkway sold Skyline a parcel of land for $95,000 and recorded a gain of $18,000 on the sale. Skyline still owes Parkway $65,000 related to the land sale.

At the end of 2013, Parkway and Skyline prepared the following statements in preparation for consolidation.

	Parkway, Inc.	Skyline Corporation
Revenues	$ (627,000)	$(358,000)
Cost of goods sold	289,000	195,000
Other operating expenses	170,000	75,000
Gain on sale of land	(18,000)	–0–
Equity in Skyline's earnings	(55,400)	–0–
Net income	$ (241,400)	$ (88,000)
Retained earnings 1/1/13	$ (314,600)	$(292,000)
Net income	(241,400)	(88,000)
Dividends distributed	70,000	20,000
Retained earnings 12/31/13	$ (486,000)	$(360,000)
Cash and receivables	$ 134,000	$ 150,000
Inventory	281,000	112,000
Investment in Skyline	598,000	–0–
Trademarks	–0–	50,000
Land, buildings, and equip. (net)	637,000	283,000
Patented technology	–0–	130,000
Total assets	$ 1,650,000	$ 725,000
Liabilities	$ (463,000)	$(215,000)
Common stock	(410,000)	(120,000)
Additional paid-in capital	(291,000)	(30,000)
Retained earnings 12/31/13	(486,000)	(360,000)
Total liabilities and equity	$(1,650,000)	$(725,000)

a. Show how Parkway computed its $55,400 equity in Skyline's earnings balance.

b. Prepare a 2013 consolidated worksheet for Parkway and Skyline.

Develop Your Skills

EXCEL CASE

On January 1, 2012, Patrick Company purchased 100 percent of the outstanding voting stock of Shawn, Inc., for $1,000,000 in cash and other consideration. At the purchase date, Shawn had common stock of $500,000 and retained earnings of $185,000. Patrick attributed the excess of acquisition-date fair value over Shawn's book value to a trade name with a 25-year life. Patrick uses the equity method to account for its investment in Shawn.

During the next two years, Shawn reported the following:

	Income	Dividends	Inventory Transfers to Patrick at Transfer Price
2012	$78,000	$25,000	$190,000
2013	85,000	27,000	210,000

Shawn sells inventory to Patrick after a markup based on a gross profit rate. At the end of 2012 and 2013, 30 percent of the current year purchases remain in Patrick's inventory.

Required

Create an Excel spreadsheet that computes the following:

1. Equity method balance in Patrick's Investment in Shawn, Inc., account as of December 31, 2013.
2. Worksheet adjustments for the December 31, 2013, consolidation of Patrick and Shawn.

Formulate your solution so that Shawn's gross profit rate on sales to Patrick is treated as a variable.

ANALYSIS AND RESEARCH CASE: ACCOUNTING INFORMATION AND SALARY NEGOTIATIONS

Granger Eagles Players' Association and Mr. Doublecount, the CEO of Granger Eagles Baseball Company, ask your help in resolving a salary dispute. Mr. Doublecount presents the following income statement to the player representatives.

GRANGER EAGLES BASEBALL COMPANY
INCOME STATEMENT

Ticket revenues		$2,000,000
Stadium rent expense	$1,400,000	
Ticket expense	25,000	
Promotion	35,000	
Player salaries	400,000	
Staff salaries and miscellaneous	200,000	2,060,000
Net income (loss)		$ (60,000)

Mr. Doublecount argues that the Granger Eagles really lose money and, until things turn around, a salary increase is out of the question.

As a result of your inquiry, you discover that Granger Eagles Baseball Company owns 91 percent of the voting stock in Eagle Stadium, Inc. This venue is specifically designed for baseball and is where the Eagles play their entire home game schedule. However, Mr. Doublecount does not wish to consider the profits of Eagle Stadium in the negotiations with the players. He claims that "the stadium is really a separate business entity that was purchased separately from the team" and therefore does not concern the players. The Eagles Stadium income statement appears as follows:

EAGLES STADIUM, INC.
INCOME STATEMENT

Stadium rent revenue	$1,400,000	
Concession revenue	800,000	
Parking revenue	100,000	$2,300,000
Cost of goods sold	250,000	
Depreciation	80,000	
Staff salaries and miscellaneous	150,000	480,000
Net income (loss)		$1,820,000

Required

1. What advice would you provide the negotiating parties regarding the issue of considering the Eagles Stadium income statement in their discussions? What authoritative literature could you cite in supporting your advice?
2. What other pertinent information would you need to provide a specific recommendation regarding players' salaries?

chapter

6

Variable Interest Entities, Intra-Entity Debt, Consolidated Cash Flows, and Other Issues

The consolidation of financial information can be a highly complex process often encompassing a number of practical challenges. This chapter examines the procedures required by several additional issues:

- Variable interest entities.
- Intra-entity debt.
- Subsidiary preferred stock.
- The consolidated statement of cash flows.
- Computation of consolidated earnings per share.
- Subsidiary stock transactions.

Variable interest entities emerged over the past two decades as a new type of business structure that provided effective control of one firm by another without overt ownership. In response to the evolving nature of control relationships among firms, the FASB expanded its definition of control beyond the long-standing criterion of a majority voting interest to include control exercised through variable interests. This topic and some of the more traditional advanced business combination subjects listed above provide for further exploration of the complexities faced by the financial reporting community in providing relevant and reliable information to users of consolidated financial reports.

Consolidation of Variable Interest Entities

Starting in the late 1970s, many firms began establishing separate business structures to help finance their operations at favorable rates. These structures became commonly known as *special purpose entities* (SPEs), *special purpose vehicles,* or *off-balance sheet structures.* In this text, we refer to all such entities collectively as *variable interest entities,* or VIEs. Many firms have routinely included their VIEs in their consolidated financial reports. However, others sought to avoid consolidation.

VIEs can help accomplish legitimate business purposes. Nonetheless, their use was widely criticized in the aftermath of Enron Corporation's 2001 collapse. Because many firms avoided consolidation and used VIEs for off-balance sheet financing, such entities were often characterized

Learning Objectives

After studying this chapter, you should be able to:

LO1 Describe a variable interest entity, a primary beneficiary, and the factors used to decide when a variable interest entity is subject to consolidation.

LO2 Understand the consolidation procedures to eliminate all intra-entity debt accounts and recognize any associated gain or loss created whenever one company acquires an affiliate's debt instrument from an outside party.

LO3 Understand that subsidiary preferred stocks not owned by the parent are a component of the noncontrolling interest and are initially valued at acquisition-date fair value.

LO4 Prepare a consolidated statement of cash flows.

LO5 Compute basic and diluted earnings per share for a business combination.

LO6 Understand the accounting for subsidiary stock transactions that impact the underlying value recorded within the parent's Investment account and the consolidated financial statements.

LO1

Describe a variable interest entity, a primary beneficiary, and the factors used to decide when a variable interest entity is subject to consolidation.

as vehicles to hide debt and mislead investors. Other critics observed that firms with variable interests recorded questionable profits on sales to their VIEs that were not arm's-length transactions.[1] The FASB ASC Variable Interest Entities sections within the Consolidations Topic were issued in response to such financial reporting abuses.

Accounting standards for consolidating VIEs continue to evolve over time. In 2009, the FASB expanded consolidation requirements for entities previously known as qualifying special purpose entities (QSPEs). Such QSPEs are often established to transform financial assets such as trade receivables, loans, or mortgages into securities that are offered in equity markets. Additionally in 2009 the FASB adopted a new qualitative assessment for deciding whether a firm must consolidate a VIE. Consolidation criteria now focus on the power to direct the activities of the entity as well as the obligation to absorb losses and the right to receive benefits from the VIE.

What Is a VIE?

A VIE can take the form of a trust, partnership, joint venture, or corporation although sometimes it has neither independent management nor employees. Most are established for valid business purposes, and transactions involving VIEs have become widespread. Common examples of VIE activities include transfers of financial assets, leasing, hedging financial instruments, research and development, and other transactions. An enterprise often sponsors a VIE to accomplish a well-defined and limited business activity and to provide low-cost financing.

Low-cost financing of asset purchases is frequently a main benefit available through VIEs. Rather than engaging in the transaction directly, the business may sponsor a VIE to purchase and finance an asset acquisition. The VIE then leases the asset to the sponsor. This strategy saves the business money because the VIE is often eligible for a lower interest rate. This advantage is achieved for several reasons. First, the VIE typically operates with a very limited set of assets—in many cases just one asset. By isolating an asset in a VIE, the asset's risk is isolated from the sponsoring firm's overall risk. Thus the VIE creditors remain protected by the specific collateral in the asset. Second, the governing documents can strictly limit the business activities of a VIE. These limits further protect lenders by preventing the VIE from engaging in any activities not specified in its agreements. As a major public accounting firm noted,

> [t]he borrower/transferor gains access to a source of funds less expensive than would otherwise be available. This advantage derives from isolating the assets in an entity prohibited from undertaking any other business activity or taking on any additional debt, thereby creating a better security interest in the assets for the lender/investor.[2]

Because governing agreements limit activities and decision making in most VIEs, there is often little need for voting stock. In fact, a sponsoring enterprise may own very little, if any, of its VIE's voting stock. Prior to current consolidation requirements for VIEs, many businesses left such entities unconsolidated in their financial reports because technically they did not own a majority of the entity's voting stock. In utilizing the VIE as a conduit to provide financing, the related assets and debt were effectively removed from the enterprise's balance sheet.

Characteristics of Variable Interest Entities

Similar to most business entities, VIEs generally have assets, liabilities, and investors with equity interests. Unlike most businesses, because a VIE's activities can be strictly limited, the role of the equity investors can be fairly minor. The VIE may have been created specifically to benefit its sponsoring firm with low-cost financing. Thus, the equity investors may serve simply as a technical requirement to allow the VIE to function as a legal entity.

[1] In its 2001 fourth quarter 10-Q, Enron recorded earnings restatements of more than $400 million related to its failure to properly consolidate several of its SPEs (e.g., Chewco and LJM2). Enron also admitted an improper omission of $700 million of its SPE's debt. Within a month of the restatements, Enron filed for bankruptcy.

[2] KPMG, "Defining Issues: New Accounting for SPEs," March 1, 2002.

EXHIBIT 6.1
Examples of Variable Interests

Variable interests in a variable interest entity are contractual, ownership, or other pecuniary interests in an entity that change with changes in the entity's net asset value. Variable interests absorb portions of a variable interest entity's expected losses if they occur or receive portions of the entity's expected residual returns if they occur.

The following are some examples of variable interests and the related potential losses or returns:

Variable interests	Potential losses or returns
• Participation rights	• Entitles holder to residual profits
• Asset purchase options	• Entitles holder to benefit from increases in asset fair values
• Guarantees of debt	• If a VIE cannot repay liabilities, honoring a debt guarantee will produce a loss
• Subordinated debt instruments	• If a VIE's cash flow is insufficient to repay all senior debt, subordinated debt may be required to absorb the loss
• Lease residual value guarantees	• If leased asset declines below the residual value, honoring the guarantee will produce a loss

Because they bear relatively low economic risk, equity investors may be provided only a small rate of return.

The small equity investments normally are insufficient to induce lenders to provide financing for the VIE. As a result, another party (often the sponsoring firm that benefits from the VIE's activities) must contribute substantial resources—often loans and/or guarantees—to enable the VIE to secure additional financing needed to accomplish its purpose. For example, the sponsoring firm may guarantee the VIE's debt, thus assuming the risk of default. Other contractual arrangements may limit returns to equity holders while participation rights provide increased profit potential and risks to the sponsoring firm. Risks and rewards such as these cause the sponsor's economic interest to vary depending on the created entity's success—hence the term *variable interest entity*. In contrast to a traditional entity, a VIE's risks and rewards often are distributed not according to stock ownership but according to other variable interests. Exhibit 6.1 describes variable interests further and provides several examples.

Variable interests increase a firm's risk as the resources it provides (or guarantees) to the VIE increase. With increased risks come incentives to restrict the VIE's decision making. In fact, a firm with variable interests will regularly limit the equity investors' power through the VIE's governance documents. As noted by GAAP literature,

> [i]f the total equity investment at risk is not sufficient to permit the legal entity to finance its activities, the parties providing the necessary additional subordinated financial support most likely will not permit an equity investor to make decisions that may be counter to their interests. [FASB ASC (para. 810-10-05-13)]

Although the equity investors are technically the owners of the VIE, in reality they may retain little of the traditional responsibilities, risks, and benefits of ownership. In fact, the equity investors often cede financial control of the VIE to those with variable interest in exchange for a guaranteed rate of return.

Consolidation of Variable Interest Entities

Prior to current financial reporting standards, assets, liabilities, and results of operations for VIEs and other entities frequently were not consolidated with those of the firm that controlled the entity. These firms invoked a reliance on voting interests, as opposed to variable interests, to indicate a lack of a controlling financial interest. As legacy FASB standard *FIN 46R*[3]observed,

> . . . an enterprise's consolidated financial statements include subsidiaries in which the enterprise has a controlling financial interest. That requirement usually has been applied

[3] FASB *Interpretation No. 46R (FIN 46R),* "Consolidation of Variable Interest Entities," December 2003.

> to subsidiaries in which an enterprise has a majority voting interest, but in many circumstances, the enterprise's consolidated financial statements do not include variable interest entities with which it has similar relationships. The voting interest approach is not effective in identifying controlling financial interests in entities that are not controllable through voting interests or in which the equity investors do not bear residual economic risk. (Summary, page 2)

Companies must first identify a VIE that is not subject to control through voting ownership interests but is nonetheless subject to their control and therefore subject to consolidation. Each enterprise involved with a VIE must then determine whether the financial support it provides makes it the primary beneficiary of the VIE's activities. The VIE's primary beneficiary is then required to include the assets, liabilities, and results of the activities of the VIE in its consolidated financial statements.

As noted by General Electric Company in its 2010 annual report:

> Our financial statements consolidate all of our affiliates—entities in which we have a controlling financial interest, most often because we hold a majority voting interest. To determine if we hold a controlling financial interest in an entity, we first evaluate if we are required to apply the variable interest entity (VIE) model to the entity, otherwise the entity is evaluated under the voting interest model. Where we hold current or potential rights that give us the power to direct the activities of a VIE that most significantly impact the VIE's economic performance combined with a variable interest that gives us the right to receive potentially significant benefits or the obligation to absorb potentially significant losses, we have a controlling financial interest in that VIE.

Identification of a Variable Interest Entity

An entity qualifies as a VIE if either of the following conditions exists:

- The total equity at risk is not sufficient to permit the entity to finance its activities without additional subordinated financial support provided by any parties, including equity holders. In most cases, if equity at risk is less than 10 percent of total assets, the risk is deemed insufficient.[4]
- The equity investors in the VIE, as a group, lack any one of the following three characteristics of a controlling financial interest:
  1. The power, through voting rights or similar rights, to direct the activities of an entity that most significantly impact the entity's economic performance.
  2. The obligation to absorb the expected losses of the entity (e.g., the primary beneficiary may guarantee a return to the equity investors).
  3. The right to receive the expected residual returns of the entity (e.g., the investors' return may be capped by the entity's governing documents or other arrangements with variable interest holders).

Identification of the Primary Beneficiary of the VIE

Once it is established that a firm has a relationship with a VIE, the firm must determine whether it qualifies as the VIE's primary beneficiary. The primary beneficiary then must consolidate the VIE's assets, liabilities, revenues, expenses, and noncontrolling interest. An enterprise with a variable interest that provides it with a controlling financial interest in a variable interest entity will have both of the following characteristics:

- The power to direct the activities of a variable interest entity that most significantly impact the entity's economic performance.
- The obligation to absorb losses of the entity that could potentially be significant to the variable interest entity or the right to receive benefits from the entity that could potentially be significant to the variable interest entity.

[4] Alternatively, a 10 percent or higher equity interest may also be insufficient. According to GAAP, "Some entities may require an equity investment greater than 10 percent of their assets to finance their activities, especially if they engage in high-risk activities, hold high-risk assets, or have exposure to risks that are not reflected in the reported amounts of the entities' assets or liabilities." [FASB ASC (para. 810-10-25-46)]

Note that these characteristics mirror those that the equity investors often lack in a VIE. Instead, the primary beneficiary will absorb a significant share of the VIE's losses or receive a significant share of the VIE's residual returns or both. The fact that the primary beneficiary may own no voting shares whatsoever becomes inconsequential because such shares do not effectively give the equity investors power to exercise control. Thus, a careful examination of the VIE's governing documents, contractual arrangements among parties involved, and who bears the risk is necessary to determine whether a reporting entity possesses control over a VIE.

The magnitude of the effect of consolidating an enterprise's VIEs can be large. For example, Walt Disney Company now consolidates two of its international theme parks as variable interest entities. Previously, Disney accounted for these investments under the equity method. In its 2010 annual report, Disney states the following:

> The Company has a 51% effective ownership interest in the operations of Euro Disney and a 47% ownership interest in the operations of Hong Kong Disneyland, both of which are consolidated in the Company's financial statements.

As a result of the 2010 consolidation of these two VIEs, Disney's total assets increased by $4.1 billion while its total debt increased by $2.4 billion.

Example of a Primary Beneficiary and Consolidated Variable Interest Entity

Assume that Twin Peaks Electric Company seeks to acquire a generating plant for a negotiated price of $400 million from Ace Electric Company. Twin Peaks wishes to expand its market share and expects to be able to sell the electricity generated by the plant acquisition at a profit to its owners.

In reviewing financing alternatives, Twin Peaks observed that its general credit rating allowed for a 4 percent annual interest rate on a debt issue. Twin Peaks also explored the establishment of a separate legal entity whose sole purpose would be to own the electric generating plant and lease it back to Twin Peaks. Because the separate entity would isolate the electric generating plant from Twin Peaks's other risky assets and liabilities and provide specific collateral, an interest rate of 3 percent on the debt is available, producing before-tax savings of $4 million per year. To obtain the lower interest rate, however, Twin Peaks must guarantee the separate entity's debt. Twin Peaks must also maintain certain of its own predefined financial ratios and restrict the amount of additional debt it can assume.

To take advantage of the lower interest rate, on January 1, 2013, Twin Peaks establishes Power Finance Co., an entity designed solely to own, finance, and lease the electric generating plant to Twin Peaks.[5] The documents governing the new entity specify the following:

- The sole purpose of Power Finance is to purchase the Ace electric generating plant, provide equity and debt financing, and lease the plant to Twin Peaks.
- An outside investor will provide $16 million in exchange for a 100 percent nonvoting equity interest in Power Finance.
- Power Finance will issue debt in exchange for $384 million. Because the $16 million equity investment by itself is insufficient to attract low-interest debt financing, Twin Peaks will guarantee the debt.
- Twin Peaks will lease the electric generating plant from Power Finance in exchange for payments of $12 million per year based on a 3 percent fixed interest rate for both the debt and equity investors for an initial lease term of five years.
- At the end of the five-year lease term (or any extension), Twin Peaks must do one of the following:
    - Renew the lease for five years subject to the approval of the equity investor.
    - Purchase the electric generating plant for $400 million.

[5] This arrangement is similar to a "synthetic lease" commonly used in utility companies. Synthetic leases also can have tax advantages because the sponsoring firm accounts for them as capital leases for tax purposes.

- Sell the electric generating plant to an independent third party. If the proceeds of the sale are insufficient to repay the equity investor, Twin Peaks must make a payment of $16 million to the equity investor.

Once the purchase of the electric generating plant is complete and the equity and debt are issued, Power Finance Company reports the following balance sheet:

POWER FINANCE COMPANY
Balance Sheet
January 1, 2013

Electric Generating Plant	$400M	Long-Term Debt	$384M
		Owners' Equity	16M
Total Assets	$400M	Total Liabilities and OE	$400M

Exhibit 6.2 shows the relationships between Twin Peaks, Power Finance, the electric generating plant, and the parties financing the asset purchase.

In evaluating whether Twin Peaks Electric Company must consolidate Power Finance Company, two conditions must be met. First, Power Finance must qualify as a VIE by either (1) an inability to secure financing without additional subordinated support or (2) a lack of either the risk of losses or entitlement to residual returns (or both). Second, Twin Peaks must qualify as the primary beneficiary of Power Finance.

In assessing the first condition, several factors point to VIE status for Power Finance. Its owners' equity comprises only 4 percent of total assets, far short of the 10 percent benchmark. Moreover, Twin Peaks guarantees Power Finance's debt, suggesting insufficient equity to finance its operations without additional support. Finally, the equity investor appears to bear almost no risk with respect to the operations of the Ace electric plant. These characteristics indicate that Power Finance qualifies as a VIE.

In evaluating the second condition for consolidation, an assessment is made to determine whether Twin Peaks qualifies as Power Finance's primary beneficiary. Clearly, Twin

EXHIBIT 6.2
Variable Interest Entity to Facilitate Financing

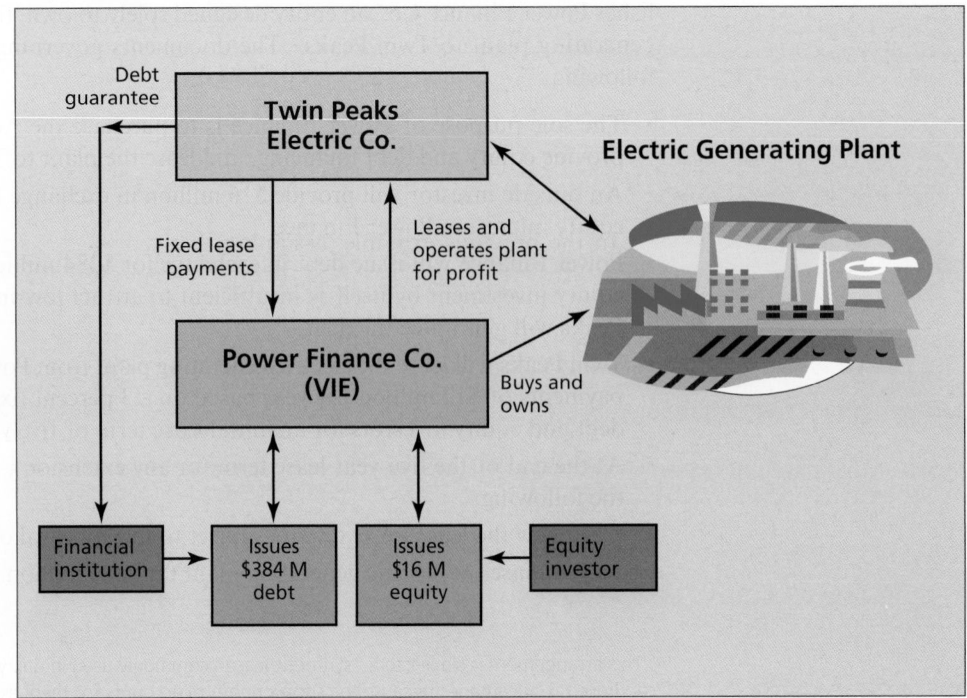

Peaks has the power to direct Power Finance's activities. But to qualify for consolidation, Twin Peaks must also have the obligation to absorb losses or the right to receive returns from Power Finance—either of which could potentially be significant to Power Finance. But what possible losses or returns would accrue to Twin Peaks? What are Twin Peaks's variable interests that rise and fall with the fortunes of Power Finance?

As stated in the VIE agreement, Twin Peaks will pay a fixed fee to lease the electric generating plant. It will then operate the plant and sell the electric power in its markets. If the business plan is successful, Twin Peaks will enjoy residual profits from operating while Power Finance's equity investors receive the fixed fee. On the other hand, if prices for electricity fall, Twin Peaks may generate revenues insufficient to cover its lease payments while Power Finance's equity investors are protected from this risk. Moreover, if the plant's fair value increases significantly, Twin Peaks can exercise its option to purchase the plant at a fixed price and either resell it or keep it for its own future use. Alternatively, if Twin Peaks were to sell the plant at a loss, it must pay the equity investors all of their initial investment, furthering the loss to Twin Peaks. Each of these elements points to Twin Peaks as the primary beneficiary of its VIE through variable interests. As the primary beneficiary, Twin Peaks must consolidate the assets, liabilities, and results of operations of Power Finance with its own.

Procedures to Consolidate Variable Interest Entities

As Power Finance's balance sheet exemplifies, VIEs typically possess only a few assets and liabilities. Also, their business activities usually are strictly limited. Thus, the actual procedures to consolidate VIEs are relatively uncomplicated.

Initial Measurement Issues

Just as in business combinations accomplished through voting interests, the financial reporting principles for consolidating variable interest entities require asset, liability, and noncontrolling interest valuations. These valuations initially, and with few exceptions, are based on fair values.

Recall that the acquisition method requires an allocation of the acquired business fair value based on the underlying fair values of its assets and liabilities. In determining the total amount to consolidate for a variable interest entity, the total business fair value of the entity is the sum of:

- Consideration transferred by the primary beneficiary.
- The fair value of the noncontrolling interest.

The fair value principle applies to consolidating VIEs in the same manner as business combinations accomplished through voting interests. If the total business fair value of the VIE exceeds the collective fair values of its net assets, goodwill is recognized.[6] Conversely, if the collective fair values of the net assets exceed the total business fair value, then the primary beneficiary recognizes a gain on bargain purchase.

In the previous example, assuming that the debt and noncontrolling interests are stated at fair values, Twin Peaks simply includes in its consolidated balance sheet the Electric Generating Plant at $400 million, the Long-Term Debt at $384 million, and a noncontrolling interest of $16 million.

Consolidation of a VIE Illustrated

To illustrate the initial measurement issues that a primary beneficiary faces, assume that Vax Company invests $5 million in TLH Property, a variable interest business entity.

[6] The FASB ASC Glossary defines a business as an integrated set of activities and assets that is capable of being conducted and managed for the purpose of providing a return in the form of dividends, lower costs, or other economic benefits directly to investors or other owners, members, or participants. Alternatively, if the activities of the VIE are so restricted that it does not qualify as a business, the excess fair value is recognized as an acquisition loss, as opposed to goodwill.

In agreements completed July 1, 2013, Vax establishes itself as the primary beneficiary of TLH Property. Previously, Vax had no interest in TLH. After Vax's investment, TLH presents the following financial information at assessed fair values:

Cash	$ 5 million
Land	20 million
Production facility	60 million
Long-term debt	(65 million)
Vax equity investment	(5 million)
Noncontrolling interest	(see following for alternative valuations)

Vax will initially include each of TLH Property's assets and liabilities at their individual fair values in its acquisition-date consolidated financial reports. Any excess of TLH Property's acquisition-date business fair value over the collective fair values assigned to the acquired net assets must be recognized as goodwill. Conversely, if the collective fair values of the acquired net assets exceed the VIE's business fair value, a "gain on bargain purchase" is credited for the difference. To demonstrate these measurement principles, we use three brief examples, each with a different business fair value depending on alternative assessed fair values of the noncontrolling interest.

Total Business Fair Value of VIE Equals Assessed Net Asset Value

In this case, assume that the noncontrolling interest fair value equals $15 million. The VIE's total fair value is then computed as follows:

Consideration transferred	$ 5,000,000
Fair value of noncontrolling interest	15,000,000
Acquisition-date VIE fair value	$20,000,000
Fair value of VIE's separately identifiable net assets	20,000,000
	–0–

Because the total fair value is identical to the $20 million collective amount of the individually assessed fair values for the net assets ($85 million total assets − $65 million long-term debt), neither goodwill nor a gain on bargain purchase is recognized. Vax simply consolidates all assets and liabilities at their respective fair values along with recognizing the noncontrolling interest.

Total Business Fair Value of VIE Is Less Than Assessed Net Asset Value

Next, assume that the value of the noncontrolling interest was assessed at $11 million. The VIE's total fair value is then computed and allocated to the identifiable assets and liabilities as follows:

Consideration transferred	$ 5,000,000
Fair value of noncontrolling interest	11,000,000
Acquisition-date VIE business fair value	$16,000,000
Fair value of VIE's separately identifiable net assets	20,000,000
Gain on bargain purchase	$ 4,000,000

The $16 million total fair value compared to the $20 million assessed fair value of TLH Property's net assets produces an excess of $4 million. In essence, the business combination receives a collective $20 million net identifiable asset fair value in exchange for $16 million. In this case, Vax recognizes a gain on bargain purchase of $4 million in its current year consolidated income statement.

Total Business Fair Value of VIE Is Greater Than Assessed Net Asset Value

Finally, assume that the value of the noncontrolling interest is assessed at $20 million. The VIE's total fair value is then computed and allocated to the identifiable assets and liabilities as follows:

Consideration transferred	$ 5,000,000
Fair value of noncontrolling interest	20,000,000
Acquisition-date VIE fair value	$25,000,000
Fair value of VIE's separately identifiable net assets	20,000,000
Goodwill	$ 5,000,000

In this case, the $25 million total fair value compared to the $20 million assessed fair value of TLH Property's net assets produces an excess total fair value of $5 million. Because TLH is a business entity, Vax Company reports the excess $5 million as goodwill in its consolidated statement of financial position.

Consolidation of VIEs Subsequent to Initial Measurement

After the initial measurement, consolidations of VIEs with their primary beneficiaries should follow the same process as if the entity were consolidated based on voting interests. Importantly, all intra-entity transactions between the primary beneficiary and the VIE (including fees, expenses, other sources of income or loss, and intra-entity inventory purchases) must be eliminated in consolidation. Finally, the VIE's income must be allocated among the parties involved (i.e., equity holders and the primary beneficiary). For a VIE, contractual arrangements, as opposed to ownership percentages, typically specify the distribution of its income. Therefore, a close examination of these contractual arrangements is needed to determine the appropriate allocation of VIE income to its equity owners and those holding variable interests.

Other Variable Interest Entity Disclosure Requirements

VIE disclosure requirements are designed to provide users of financial statements with more transparent information about an enterprise's involvement in a VIE. The enhanced disclosures are required for any enterprise that holds a variable interest in a VIE.

Included among the enhanced disclosures are requirements to show:

- The VIE's nature, purpose, size, and activities.
- The significant judgments and assumptions made by an enterprise in determining whether it must consolidate a VIE and/or disclose information about its involvement in a VIE.
- The nature of restrictions on a consolidated VIE's assets and on the settlement of its liabilities reported by an enterprise in its statement of financial position, including the carrying amounts of such assets and liabilities.
- The nature of, and changes in, the risks associated with an enterprise's involvement with the VIE.
- How an enterprise's involvement with the VIE affects the enterprise's financial position, financial performance, and cash flows.

Proposed Accounting Standards Update on Variable Interest Entities

In November 2011, the FASB issued a proposed change to ASC Topic 810 on Consolidations entitled *Principal versus Agent Analysis.* The proposal would amend the definition of a VIE by adding a principal versus agent component and also would affect determination of the primary beneficiary. The proposal defines an agent as a party that acts on behalf of and for the benefit of another party or parties (the principal(s)) and, therefore, does not control the entity when it exercises its decision-making authority.

Similar to current requirements for a primary beneficiary, a reporting entity must determine if it has the power to direct the activities that most significantly impact the VIE's economic performance. In assessing this power, however, the proposal would require that the reporting entity have the ability to use its decision-making power in a principal capacity (rather than as an agent). Moreover, assuming other primary beneficiary requirements are met, if the party exercising decision-making power is an agent for the principal, under the proposed guidance, the principal consolidates the VIE, not the agent.

Several qualitative criteria would determine whether a decision maker acts as a principal or an agent. The criteria include evaluations of the rights held by other parties, the decision maker's compensation, and the decision maker's exposure to variability of returns from other interests held in the entity. This latest FASB proposal once again demonstrates that the assessment of control continues to challenge standard setters and to evolve over time.

Comparisons with International Accounting Standards

Under both U.S. GAAP and IFRS, a controlling financial interest is the critical concept in assessing whether an entity should be consolidated by a reporting enterprise. Nonetheless, the FASB and IASB so far have employed different criteria to determine the existence of control. IFRS employs a single consolidation model for all entities regardless of whether control is evidenced by voting interests or variable interests. In contrast, U.S. GAAP employs separate models for assessing control for variable interest entities and voting interest entities. As a result, current reporting standards differ across jurisdictions for enterprises seeking to determine whether to consolidate another entity. While the FASB continues its deliberations on consolidation policies and procedures, the IASB has issued two updated standards in this area.

In May 2011, the International Accounting Standards Board issued *IFRS 10,* "Consolidated Financial Statements" and *IFRS 12,* "Disclosure of Interests in Other Entities." Included in these standards is a new definition of control that is designed to encompass all possible ways (voting power, contractual power, decision making rights, etc.) in which one entity can exercise power over another. In particular, the criteria for assessing control are:

- Power over an investee—does the reporting entity have the current ability to direct activities that significantly affect another entity's returns?
- Exposure to, or rights to, variable returns from involvement with another entity
- Linkage between power and returns—does the investor have the ability to affect its returns through its power?

These criteria recognize one entity can control another through its power to direct its operating and financing activities. For example, even with less than majority ownership, voting interests can provide an enterprise control if the non-owned shares are diffusely held and lack arrangements to act in a coordinated manner. Control can also be achieved through obtaining decision-making rights that relate to the relevant activities of an investee. Importantly, such decision-making rights can extend beyond merely voting rights. By establishing a broad concept of control as opposed to a bright line rule (e.g., consolidate if an entity has majority voting rights or the majority of risks and rewards) the IASB seeks to avoid standards that create structuring opportunities to achieve a particular accounting outcome.[7]

IFRS 12 provides for enhanced disclosures about the relationship between a parent and the entities it controls. These disclosures focus on helping investors understand first why a parent controls (or does not control) another entity and the claims of the noncontrolling interest. Second, the disclosures are designed to help investors evaluate the risks assumed by the parent.[8]

Intra-Entity Debt Transactions

LO2

Understand the consolidation procedures to eliminate all intra-entity debt accounts and recognize any associated gain or loss created whenever one company acquires an affiliate's debt instrument from an outside party.

The previous chapter explored the consolidation procedures required by the intra-entity transfer of inventory, land, and depreciable assets. In consolidating these transactions, all resulting gains were deferred until earned through either the use of the asset or its resale

[7] Patrick Finnegan, Board Member of the IASB. "At long-last—a single model for consolidation," IFRS Foundation, May 2011 perspectives.

[8] Ibid.

to outside parties. Deferral was necessary because these gains, although legitimately recognized by the individual companies, were unearned from the perspective of the consolidated entity. The separate financial information of each company was adjusted on the worksheet to be consistent with the view that the related companies actually composed a single economic concern.

This same objective applies in consolidating all other intra-entity transactions: The financial statements must represent the business combination as one enterprise rather than as a group of independent organizations. Consequently, in designing consolidation procedures for intra-entity transactions, the effects recorded by the individual companies first must be isolated. After the impact of each action is analyzed, worksheet entries recast these events from the vantage point of the business combination. Although this process involves a number of nuances and complexities, the desire for reporting financial information solely from the perspective of the consolidated entity remains constant.

We introduced the intra-entity sales of inventory, land, and depreciable assets together (in Chapter 5) because these transfers result in similar consolidation procedures. In each case, one of the affiliated companies recognizes a gain prior to the time the consolidated entity actually earned it. The worksheet entries required by these transactions simply realign the separate financial information to agree with the viewpoint of the business combination. The gain is removed and the inflated asset value is reduced to historical cost.

The next section of this chapter examines the intra-entity acquisition of bonds and notes. Although accounting for the related companies as a single economic entity continues to be the central goal, the consolidation procedures applied to intra-entity debt transactions are in diametric contrast to the process utilized in Chapter 5 for asset transfers.

Before delving into this topic, note that *direct* loans used to transfer funds between affiliated companies create no unique consolidation problems. Regardless of whether bonds or notes generate such amounts, the resulting receivable/payable balances are necessarily identical. Because no money is owed to or from an outside party, these reciprocal accounts must be eliminated in each subsequent consolidation. A worksheet entry simply offsets the two corresponding balances. Furthermore, the interest revenue/expense accounts associated with direct loans also agree and are removed in the same fashion.

Acquisition of Affiliate's Debt from an Outside Party

The difficulties encountered in consolidating intra-entity liabilities relate to a specific type of transaction: the purchase from an outside third party of an affiliate's debt instrument. A parent company, for example, could acquire a bond previously issued by a subsidiary on the open market. Despite the intra-entity nature of this transaction, the debt remains an outstanding obligation of the original issuer but is recorded as an investment by the acquiring company. Thereafter, even though related parties are involved, interest payments pass periodically between the two organizations.

Although the individual companies continue to report both the debt and the investment, from a consolidation viewpoint this liability is retired as of the acquisition date. From that time forward, the debt is no longer owed to a party outside the business combination. Subsequent interest payments are simply intra-entity cash transfers. To create consolidated statements, worksheet entries must be developed to adjust the various balances to report the debt's effective retirement.

Acquiring an affiliate's bond or note from an unrelated party poses no significant consolidation problems if the purchase price equals the corresponding book value of the liability. Reciprocal balances within the individual records would always be identical in value and easily offset in each subsequent consolidation.

Realistically, though, such reciprocity is rare when a debt is purchased from a third party. A variety of economic factors typically produce a difference between the price paid for the investment and the carrying amount of the obligation. The debt is originally sold under market conditions at a particular time. Any premium or discount associated with this issuance is then amortized over the life of the bond, creating a continuous adjustment to book value. The acquisition of this instrument at a later date is made at a price influenced by current economic conditions, prevailing interest rates, and myriad other financial and market factors.

Therefore, the cost paid to purchase the debt could be either more or less than the book value of the liability currently found within the issuing company's financial records. *To the business combination, this difference is a gain or loss because the acquisition effectively retires the bond; the debt is no longer owed to an outside party.* For external reporting purposes, this gain or loss must be recognized immediately by the consolidated entity.

Accounting for Intra-Entity Debt Transactions—Individual Financial Records

The following accounting problems emerge in consolidating intra-entity debt transactions:

1. Intra-entity investments in debt securities and related debt accounts must be eliminated in consolidation despite their differing balances.
2. Intra-entity interest revenue/expense (as well as any interest receivable/payable accounts) must be removed although these balances also fail to agree in amount.
3. The amortization process for discounts and premiums causes continual changes in each of the preceding accounts.
4. The business combination must recognize the gain or loss on the effective retirement of the debt, even though it is not recognized within the financial records of either company.

To illustrate, assume that Alpha Company possesses an 80 percent interest in the outstanding voting stock of Omega Company. On January 1, 2011, Omega issued $1 million in 10-year bonds paying cash interest of 9 percent annually. Because of market conditions prevailing on that date, Omega sold the debt for $938,555 to yield an effective interest rate of 10 percent per year. Shortly thereafter, the interest rate began to fall, and by January 1, 2013, Omega made the decision to retire this debt prematurely and refinance it at a currently lower rate. To carry out this plan, Alpha purchased all of these bonds in the open market on January 1, 2013, for $1,057,466. This price was based on an effective yield of 8 percent, which is assumed to be in line with the interest rates at the time.

Many reasons could exist for having Alpha, rather than Omega, reacquire this debt. For example, company cash levels at that date could necessitate Alpha's role as the purchasing agent. Also, contractual limitations could prohibit Omega from repurchasing its own bonds.

In accounting for this business combination, Omega Company's bonds have been effectively retired. Thus, the difference between the $1,057,466 payment and the January 1, 2013, book value of the liability must be recognized in the consolidated statements as a gain or loss. The book value for the debt on that date depends on the amortization process. Exhibit 6.3 shows the bond amortization schedule for January 1, 2011, through December 31, 2014.[9]

As seen in Exhibit 6.3, the book value of Omega Company's bonds has increased to $946,651 as of December 31, 2012, the date immediately before the day that Alpha Company acquired the bonds.

Because Alpha paid $110,815 in excess of the recorded liability ($1,057,466 − $946,651), the consolidated entity must recognize a loss of this amount. After the loss has been

EXHIBIT 6.3
Omega Company Bond Issue Amortization Schedule

Date	Face Value	Unamortized Discount	Book Value	Effective Interest	Cash Interest	Discount Amortized
1/1/11	$1,000,000	$61,445	$938,555			
12/31/11	1,000,000	57,590	942,410	93,855	90,000	3,855
12/31/12	1,000,000	53,349	946,651	94,241	90,000	4,241
12/31/13	1,000,000	48,684	951,316	94,665	90,000	4,665
12/31/14	1,000,000	43,552	956,448	95,132	90,000	5,132

[9] The effective rate method of amortization is demonstrated here because this approach is theoretically preferable. However, the straight-line method can be applied if the resulting balances are not materially different than the figures computed using the effective rate method.

acknowledged, the bond is considered to be retired and no further reporting is necessary by the *business combination* after January 1, 2013.

Despite the simplicity of this approach, neither company accounts for the event in this manner. Omega retains the $1 million debt balance within its separate financial records and amortizes the remaining discount each year. Annual cash interest payments of $90,000 (9 percent) continue to be made. At the same time, Alpha records the investment at the historical cost of $1,057,466, an amount that also requires periodic amortization. Furthermore, as the owner of these bonds, Alpha receives the $90,000 interest payments made by Omega.

To organize the accountant's approach to this consolidation, the subsequent financial recording made by each company is analyzed. Omega records only two journal entries during 2013 assuming that interest is paid each December 31:

	Omega Company's Financial Records		
12/31/13	Interest Expense	90,000	
	Cash		90,000
	To record payment of annual cash interest on $1 million, 9 percent bonds payable.		
12/31/13	Interest Expense	4,665	
	Discount on Bonds Payable		4,665
	To adjust interest expense to effective rate based on original yield rate of 10 percent ($946,651 book value for 2013 × 10% = $94,665). Book value increases to $951,316.		

Concurrently, Alpha journalizes entries to record its ownership of this investment:

	Alpha Company's Financial Records		
1/1/13	Investment in Omega Company Bonds	1,057,466	
	Cash		1,057,466
	To record acquisition of $1,000,000 in Omega Company bonds paying 9 percent cash interest, acquired to yield an effective rate of 8 percent.		
12/31/13	Cash	90,000	
	Interest Income		90,000
	To record receipt of cash interest from Omega Company bonds ($1,000,000 × 9%).		
12/31/13	Interest Income	5,403	
	Investment in Omega Company Bonds		5,403
	To reduce $90,000 interest income to effective rate based on original yield rate of 8 percent ($1,057,466 book value for 2013 × 8% = $84,597). Book value decreases to $1,052,063.		

Even a brief review of these entries indicates that the reciprocal accounts to be eliminated within the consolidation process do not agree in amount. You can see the dollar amounts appearing in each set of financial records in Exhibit 6.4. Despite the presence of these recorded balances, none of the four intra-entity accounts (the liability, investment, interest expense, and interest revenue) appears in the consolidated financial statements. *The only figure that the business combination reports is the $110,815 loss created by the extinguishment of this debt.*

Effects on Consolidation Process

As previous discussions indicated, consolidation procedures convert information generated by the individual accounting systems to the perspective of a single economic entity. A worksheet entry is therefore required on December 31, 2013, to eliminate the

EXHIBIT 6.4

ALPHA COMPANY AND OMEGA COMPANY
Effects of Intra-Entity Debt Transaction
2013

	Omega Company Reported Debt	Alpha Company Investment
2013 interest expense*	$ 94,665	$ -0-
2013 interest income†	-0-	(84,597)
Bonds payable	(1,000,000)	-0-
Discount on bonds payable*	48,684	-0-
Investment in bonds, 12/31/13†	-0-	1,052,063
Loss on retirement	-0-	-0-

Note: Parentheses indicate credit balances.
*Company total is adjusted for 2013 amortization of $4,665 (see journal entry).
†Adjusted for 2013 amortization of $5,403 (see journal entry).

intra-entity balances shown in Exhibit 6.4 and to recognize the loss resulting from the repurchase. Mechanically, the differences in the liability and investment balances as well as the interest expense and interest income accounts stem from the $110,815 difference between the purchase price of the investment and the book value of the liability. Recognition of this loss, in effect, bridges the gap between the divergent figures.

Consolidation Entry B (December 31, 2013)		
Bonds Payable	1,000,000	
Interest Income	84,597	
Loss on Retirement of Bonds	110,815	
Discount on Bond Payable		48,684
Investment in Omega Company Bonds		1,052,063
Interest Expense		94,665
To eliminate intra-entity bonds and related interest accounts and to recognize loss on effective retirement. (Labeled "**B**" in reference to bonds.)		

The preceding entry successfully transforms the separate financial reporting of Alpha and Omega to that appropriate for the business combination. The objective of the consolidation process has been met: The statements present the bonds as having been retired on January 1, 2013. The debt and the corresponding investment are eliminated along with both interest accounts. Only the loss now appears on the worksheet to be reported within the consolidated financial statements.

Assignment of Retirement Gain or Loss

An issue in accounting for intra-entity debt repurchases concerns the assignment of any retirement gains or losses. Should the $110,815 loss just reported be attributed to Alpha or to Omega? From a practical perspective, this assignment affects only the consolidated net income allocation to the controlling and noncontrolling interests. In the absence of FASB guidance on the assignment of retirement gain or loss, all income effects in this textbook relating to intra-entity debt transactions are assigned solely to the parent company. Such treatment is consistent with the perspective that the parent company ultimately controls the repurchase decision.

Intra-Entity Debt Transactions—Subsequent to Year of Acquisition

Even though the preceding Entry **B** correctly eliminates Omega's bonds in the year of retirement, the debt remains within the financial accounts of both companies until maturity. Therefore, in each succeeding time period, all balances must again be consolidated so that the liability is always reported as having been extinguished on January 1, 2013.

Discussion Question

WHO LOST THIS $300,000?

Several years ago, Penston Company purchased 90 percent of the outstanding shares of Swansan Corporation. Penston made the acquisition because Swansan produced a vital component used in Penston's manufacturing process. Penston wanted to ensure an adequate supply of this item at a reasonable price. The former owner, James Swansan, retained the remaining 10 percent of Swansan's stock and agreed to continue managing this organization. He was given responsibility for the subsidiary's daily manufacturing operations but not for any financial decisions.

Swansan's takeover has proven to be a successful undertaking for Penston. The subsidiary has managed to supply all of the parent's inventory needs and distribute a variety of items to outside customers.

At a recent meeting, Penston's president and the company's chief financial officer began discussing Swansan's debt position. The subsidiary had a debt-to-equity ratio that seemed unreasonably high considering the significant amount of cash flows being generated by both companies. Payment of the interest expense, especially on the subsidiary's outstanding bonds, was a major cost, one that the corporate officials hoped to reduce. However, the bond indenture specified that Swansan could retire this debt prior to maturity only by paying 107 percent of face value.

This premium was considered prohibitive. Thus, to avoid contractual problems, Penston acquired a large portion of Swansan's liability on the open market for 101 percent of face value. Penston's purchase created an effective loss of $300,000 on the debt, the excess of the price over the book value of the debt, as reported on Swansan's books.

Company accountants currently are computing the noncontrolling interest's share of consolidated net income to be reported for the current year. They are unsure about the impact of this $300,000 loss. The subsidiary's debt was retired, but officials of the parent company made the decision. Who lost this $300,000?

Unfortunately, a simple repetition of Entry **B** is not possible. Developing the appropriate worksheet entry is complicated by the amortization process that produces continual change in the various account balances. Thus, as a preliminary step in each subsequent consolidation, current book values, as reported by the two parties, must be identified.

To illustrate, the 2014 journal entries for Alpha and Omega follow. Exhibit 6.5 (on the following page) shows the resulting account balances as of the end of that year.

Omega Company's Financial Records—December 31, 2014		
Interest Expense	90,000	
Cash		90,000
To record payment of annual cash interest on $1 million, 9 percent bonds payable.		
Interest Expense	5,132	
Discount on Bonds Payable		5,132
To adjust interest expense to effective rate based on an original yield rate of 10 percent ($951,316 book value for 2014 × 10% = $95,132). Book value increases to $956,448.		

EXHIBIT 6.5

ALPHA COMPANY AND OMEGA COMPANY
Effects of Intra-Entity Debt Transactions
2014

	Omega Company Reported Debt	Alpha Company Investment
2014 interest expense*	$ 95,132	-0-
2014 interest income†	-0-	$ (84,165)
Bonds payable	(1,000,000)	-0-
Discount on bonds payable*	43,552	-0-
Investment in bonds, 12/31/14†	-0-	1,046,228
Income effect within retained earnings, 1/1/14‡	94,665	(84,597)

Note: Parentheses indicate credit balances.
*Company total is adjusted for 2014 amortization of $5,132 (see journal entry).
†Adjusted for 2014 amortization of $5,835 (see journal entry).
‡The balance shown for the Retained Earnings account of each company represents the 2013 reported interest figures.

Alpha Company's Financial Records—December 31, 2014		
Cash	90,000	
Interest Income		90,000
To record receipt of cash interest from Omega Company bonds.		
Interest Income	5,835	
Investment in Omega Company Bonds		5,835
To reduce $90,000 interest income to effective rate based on an original yield rate of 8 percent ($1,052,063 book value for 2014 × 8% = $84,165). Book value decreases to $1,046,228.		

After assembling the information in Exhibit 6.5, the necessary December 31, 2014, consolidation entry is prepared. We first assume that the parent applies either the initial value or the partial equity method to its Investment in Omega account. We then show this final consolidation entry assuming the parent applies the equity method.

Parent Applies the Initial Value or Partial Equity Method

To recognize the January 1, 2013, effective retirement on the December 31, 2014, consolidated financial statements, the individual affiliate's balances for the intra-entity bonds and interest income and expense must be removed. Because neither the initial value nor the partial equity method recognizes the retirement loss, the parent's retained earnings will fail to reflect the prior year effective retirement loss. However, retained earnings will reflect past interest income and expense to the extent of any discount or premium amortization.[10] A worksheet adjustment therefore reduces Alpha's January 1, 2014, retained earnings by $110,815 to reflect the original loss net of the prior year's discount and premium amortizations.

Consolidation Entry *B, when Parent Uses the Initial Value or Partial Equity Method (December 31, 2014)		
Bonds Payable	1,000,000	
Interest Income	84,165	
Retained Earnings—Alpha	100,747	
Discount on Bond Payable		43,552
Investment in Omega Company Bonds		1,046,228
Interest Expense		95,132
To eliminate intra-entity bond and related interest accounts and to adjust Alpha's Retained Earnings from $10,068 (currently recorded net debit balance) to $110,815. (Labeled "*B" in reference to prior year bond transaction.)		

[10] If there is no discount or premium amortization, interest revenue will simply offset interest expense, leaving no net effect on retained earnings.

Analysis of this latest consolidation entry should emphasize several important factors:

1. The individual account balances change during the present fiscal period so that the current consolidation entry differs from Entry **B.** These alterations are a result of the amortization process. To ensure the accuracy of the worksheet entry, the adjusted balances are isolated in Exhibit 6.5.
2. As indicated previously, all income effects arising from intra-entity debt transactions are assigned to the parent company. For this reason, the adjustment to beginning Retained Earnings in Entry ***B** is attributed to Alpha as is the $10,967 increase in current income ($95,132 interest expense elimination less the $84,165 interest revenue elimination).[11] Consequently, the noncontrolling interest balances are not altered by Entry ***B.**
3. The 2014 reduction to beginning Retained Earnings in Entry ***B** ($100,747) does not agree with the original $110,815 retirement loss. The individual companies have recorded a net deficit balance of $10,068 (the amount by which previous interest expense exceeds interest revenue) at the start of 2014. To achieve the proper consolidated total, an adjustment of only $100,747 is required ($110,815 − $10,068).

Retained earnings balance—consolidation perspective (loss on retirement of debt)		$110,815
Individual retained earnings balances, 1/1/14:		
Omega Company (interest expense—2013)	$ 94,665	
Alpha Company (interest income—2013)	(84,597)	10,068
Adjustment to consolidated retained earnings, 1/1/14		$100,747

Parentheses indicate a credit balance.

The periodic amortization of both the bond payable discount and the premium on the investment impacts the interest expense and revenue recorded by the two companies. As this schedule shows, these two interest accounts do not offset exactly; a $10,068 net residual amount remains in Retained Earnings after the first year. Because this balance continues to increase each year, the subsequent consolidation adjustments to record the loss decrease to $100,747 in 2014 and constantly lesser thereafter. *Over the life of the bond, the amortization process gradually brings the totals in the individual Retained Earnings accounts into agreement with the consolidated balance.*

Parent Applies the Equity Method

Entry ***B** as shown is appropriate for consolidations in which the parent has applied either the initial value or the partial equity method. However, a deviation is required if the parent uses the equity method for internal reporting purposes. Properly applying the equity method ensures that the parent's income and, hence, its retained earnings are correctly stated prior to consolidation. Alpha would have already recognized the loss in accounting for this investment. Consequently, when the parent applies the equity method, no adjustment to Retained Earnings is needed. In this one case, the $100,747 debit in Entry ***B** is made to the Investment in Omega Company (instead of Retained Earnings) because the loss has become a component of that account.

Consolidation Entry *B, when Parent Uses the Equity Method (December 31, 2014)

Bonds Payable	1,000,000	
Interest Income	84,165	
Investment in Omega	100,747	
Discount on Bond Payable		43,552
Investment in Omega Company Bonds		1,046,228
Interest Expense		95,132
To eliminate intra-entity bond and related interest accounts and to adjust the Investment in Omega from $10,068 (currently recorded net debit balance) to $110,815. (Labeled "***B**" in reference to prior year bond transaction.)		

[11] Had the effects of the retirement been attributed solely to the original issuer of the bonds, the $10,967 addition to current income would have been assigned to Omega (the subsidiary), thus creating a change in the noncontrolling interest computations.

The Entry *B debit to the Investment in Omega account then serves as part of the investment account elimination sequence.

Subsidiary Preferred Stock

LO3

Understand that subsidiary preferred stocks not owned by the parent are a component of the noncontrolling interest and are initially valued at acquisition-date fair value.

Although both small and large corporations routinely issue preferred shares, their presence within a subsidiary's equity structure adds a new dimension to the consolidation process. What accounting should be made of a subsidiary's preferred stock and the parent's payments that are made to acquire these shares?

Recall that preferred shares, although typically nonvoting, possess other "preferences" over common shares such as a cumulative dividend preference or participation rights. Preferred shares may even offer limited voting rights. Nonetheless, preferred shares are considered as a part of the subsidiary's stockholders' equity and their treatment in the parent's consolidated financial reports closely follows that for common shares.

The existence of subsidiary preferred shares does little to complicate the consolidation process. The acquisition method values all business acquisitions (whether 100 percent or less than 100 percent acquired) at their full fair values. In accounting for the acquisition of a subsidiary with preferred stock, the essential process of determining the acquisition-date business fair value of the subsidiary remains intact. Any preferred shares not owned by the parent simply become a component of the noncontrolling interest and are included in the subsidiary business fair-value calculation. The acquisition-date fair value for any subsidiary common and/or preferred shares owned by outsiders becomes the basis for the noncontrolling interest valuation in the parent's consolidated financial reports.

To illustrate, assume that on January 1, 2013, High Company acquires control over Low Company by purchasing 80 percent of its outstanding common stock and 60 percent of its nonvoting, cumulative, preferred stock. Low owns land undervalued in its records by $100,000, but all other assets and liabilities have fair values equal to their book values. High paid a purchase price of $1 million for the common shares and $62,400 for the preferred. On the acquisition date, the 20 percent noncontrolling interest in the common shares had a fair value of $250,000 and the 40 percent preferred stock noncontrolling interest had a fair value of $41,600.

Low's capital structure immediately prior to the acquisition is shown below:

Common stock, $20 par value (20,000 shares outstanding)	$ 400,000
Preferred stock, 6% cumulative with a par value of $100	
(1,000 shares outstanding)	100,000
Additional paid-in capital	200,000
Retained earnings	516,000
Total stockholders' equity (book value)	$1,216,000

Exhibit 6.6 shows High's calculation of the acquisition-date fair value of Low and the allocation of the difference between the fair and book values to land and goodwill.

As seen in Exhibit 6.6, the subsidiary's ownership structure (i.e., comprising both preferred and common shares) does not affect the fair-value principle for determining the basis for consolidating the subsidiary. Moreover, the acquisition method follows the same procedure for calculating business fair value regardless of the various preferences the preferred shares may possess. Any cumulative or participating preferences (or any additional rights) attributed to the preferred shares are assumed to be captured by the acquisition-date fair value of the shares and thus automatically incorporated into the subsidiary's valuation basis for consolidation.

By utilizing the information above, we next construct a basic worksheet entry as of January 1, 2013 (the acquisition date). In the presence of both common and preferred subsidiary shares, combining the customary consolidation entries S and A avoids an unnecessary allocation of the subsidiary's retained earnings across these equity shares. The combined consolidation entry also recognizes the allocations made to the undervalued land and goodwill. No other consolidation entries are needed because no time has passed since the acquisition took place.

EXHIBIT 6.6

LOW COMPANY
Acquisition-Date Fair Value
January 1, 2013

Consideration transferred for 80% interest in Low's common stock...	$1,000,000
Consideration transferred for 60% interest in Low's preferred stock ..	62,400
Noncontrolling interest in Low's common stock (20%)	250,000
Noncontrolling interest in Low's preferred stock (40%)	41,600
Total fair value of Low on 1/1/13	$1,354,000

HIGH'S ACQUISITION OF LOW
Excess Fair Value Over Book Value Allocation
January 1, 2013

Low Company business fair value		$1,354,000
Low Company book value		1,216,000
Excess acquisition-date fair value over book value		$ 138,000
Assigned to land	$100,000	
Assigned to goodwill	38,000	138,000
		–0–

Consolidation Entries S and A (combined)		
Common Stock (Low)	400,000	
Preferred Stock (Low)	100,000	
Additional Paid-In Capital (Low)	200,000	
Retained Earnings (Low)	516,000	
Land	100,000	
Goodwill	38,000	
Investment in Low's Common Stock		1,000,000
Investment in Low's Preferred Stock		62,400
Noncontrolling Interest		291,600
To eliminate the subsidiary's common and preferred shares, recognize the fair values of the subsidiary's assets, and recognize the outside ownership.		

The above combined consolidation entry recognizes the noncontrolling interest as the total of acquisition-date fair values of $250,000 for the common stock and $41,600 for the preferred shares. Consistent with previous consolidation illustrations throughout the text, the entire subsidiary's stockholders' equity section is eliminated along with the parent's investment accounts—in this case for both the common and preferred shares.

Allocation of Subsidiary Income

The final factor influencing a consolidation that includes subsidiary preferred shares is the allocation of the company's income between the two types of stock. A division must be made for every period subsequent to the takeover (1) to compute the noncontrolling interest's share and (2) for the parent's own recognition purposes. For a cumulative, non-participating preferred stock such as the one presently being examined, only the specified annual dividend is attributed to the preferred stock with all remaining income assigned to common stock. Consequently, if we assume that Low reports earnings of $100,000 in 2013 while paying the annual $6,000 dividend on its preferred stock, we allocate income for consolidation purposes as follows:

	Income
Subsidiary total	$100,000
Preferred stock (6% dividend × $100,000 par value of the stock)	$ 6,000
Common stock (residual amount)	94,000

During 2013, High Company, as the parent, is entitled to $3,600 in dividends ($6,000 × 60%) from Low's preferred stock because of its 60 percent ownership. In addition, High holds 80 percent of Low's common stock so that another $75,200 of the income ($94,000 × 80%) is attributed to the parent. The noncontrolling interest in the subsidiary's income can be calculated in a similar fashion:

		Percentage Outside Ownership	Noncontrolling Interest
Preferred stock dividend	$ 6,000	40%	$ 2,400
Income attributed to common stock	94,000	20	18,800
Noncontrolling interest in subsidiary's income			$21,200

Consolidated Statement of Cash Flows

LO4

Prepare a consolidated statement of cash flows.

Current accounting standards require that companies include a statement of cash flows among their consolidated financial reports. The main purpose of the statement of cash flows is to provide information about the entity's cash receipts and cash payments during a period. The statement is also designed to show why an entity's net income is different from its operating cash flows. For a consolidated entity, the cash flows relate to the entire business combination including the parent and all of its subsidiaries.

The statement of cash flows allocates the consolidated entity's overall change in cash during a period to three separate categories:

- Cash flows from operating activities.
- Cash flows from investing activities.
- Cash flows from financing activities.

The cash flows from operating activities can be shown using either the indirect method or the direct method. The indirect method begins with consolidated net income and then adds and subtracts various items to adjust the accrual number to a cash flow amount. The direct method examines cash flows directly from distinct sources that typically include revenues, purchases of inventory, and cash payments of other expenses. However, firms using the direct method must also supplement the statement with the calculation of cash flows from operating activities using the indirect method.

The consolidated statement of cash flows is not prepared from the individual cash flow statements of the separate companies. Instead, the consolidated income statements and balance sheets are first brought together on the worksheet. The cash flows statement is then based on the resulting consolidated figures. Thus, this statement is not actually produced by consolidation but is created from numbers generated by the process. Because special accounting procedures are needed in the period when the parent acquires a subsidiary, we first discuss preparation of the consolidated statement of cash flows for periods in which an acquisition takes place, followed by statement preparation in periods subsequent to acquisition.

Acquisition Period Statement of Cash Flows

If a business combination occurs during a particular reporting period, the consolidated cash flow statement must properly reflect several considerations. For many business combinations, the following issues frequently are present:

Business Acquisitions in Exchange for Cash

Cash purchases of businesses are an investing activity. The *net cash outflow* (cash paid less subsidiary cash acquired) is reported as the amount paid in a business acquisition.[12]

[12] For acquisitions that do not involve cash, or only partially involve cash, the details of the acquisitions should be provided in a supplemental disclosure to the statement of cash flows for "significant noncash investing and financing activities."

Operating Cash Flow Adjustments

Keeping in mind that the focus is on the consolidated entity's cash flows (not just the parent's), consolidated net income is the starting point for the indirect calculation of consolidated operating cash flows. Recall that consolidated net income includes only postacquisition subsidiary revenues and expenses. Therefore the adjustment to the accrual-based income number must also reflect only postacquisition amounts for the subsidiary. One important category of adjustments to consolidated net income to arrive at cash flows from operations involves changes in current operating accounts. Intraperiod acquisitions require special consideration in calculating changes in these current operating accounts.

For example, an increase in an accounts receivable balance typically indicates that a firm's accrual-based sales exceed the actual cash collections for sales during a period. Therefore, in computing operating cash flows, the increase in accounts receivable are deducted from the sales amount (direct method) or the net income (indirect method). However, when an acquisition takes place, the change in accounts receivable will often include amounts from the newly acquired subsidiary. Because the consolidated entity recognizes only postacquisition subsidiary revenues, such acquired receivables do not reflect sales that have been made by the consolidated entity. Therefore any subsidiary acquisition-date current operating account balances must be removed from the change in accounts receivable calculation.

In fact, any changes in operating balance sheet accounts (accounts receivable, inventory, accounts payable, etc.) must be computed net of the amounts acquired in the combination. Use of the direct method of presenting operating cash flows also reports the separate computations of cash collected from customers and cash paid for inventory net of effects of any acquired businesses.

Excess Fair Value Amortizations

Any adjustments arising from the subsidiary's revenues or expenses (e.g., depreciation, amortization) must reflect only postacquisition amounts. Closing the subsidiary's books at the date of acquisition facilitates the determination of the appropriate current year postacquisition subsidiary effects on the consolidated entity's cash flows.

Subsidiary Dividends Paid

The cash outflow from dividends paid by a subsidiary only leaves the consolidated entity when paid to the noncontrolling interest. Thus dividends paid by a subsidiary to its parent do not appear as financing outflows. However, subsidiary dividends paid to the noncontrolling interest are a component of cash outflows from financing activities.

Intra-Entity Transfers

A significant volume of transfers between affiliated companies comprising a business combination often occurs. The resulting effects of intra-entity activities are eliminated in the preparation of consolidated statements. Likewise, the consolidated statement of cash flows does not include the impact of these transfers. Intra-entity sales and purchases do not change the amount of cash held by the business combination when viewed as a whole. Because the statement of cash flows is derived from the consolidated balance sheet and income statement, the impact of all transfers is already removed. Therefore, the proper presentation of cash flows requires no special adjustments for intra-entity transfers. The worksheet entries produce correct balances for the consolidated statement of cash flows.

Statement of Cash Flows in Periods Subsequent to Acquisition

The preparation of the consolidated statement of cash flows during periods of no acquisition is relatively uncomplicated. As before, consolidated net income is the starting point for the indirect calculation of consolidated operating cash flows. If the operating accounts are free from any effects of previous years' acquisitions, no further special adjustments are required. Because the consolidation process eliminates intra-entity balances, preparation of the operating activity section of the statement of cash flows typically proceeds in a straightforward manner using the already-available consolidated income statement and balance sheet amounts. Finally, subsidiary dividends paid to the noncontrolling interest are shown as a component of cash outflows from financing activities.

Consolidated Statement of Cash Flows Illustration

Assume that on July 1, 2013, Pinto Company acquires 90 percent of Salida Company's outstanding stock for $774,000 in cash. At the acquisition date, the 10 percent noncontrolling interest has a fair value of $86,000. Exhibit 6.7 shows book and fair values of Salida's assets and liabilities and Pinto's acquisition-date fair-value allocation schedule.

At the end of 2013, the following comparative balance sheets and consolidated income statement are available:

PINTO COMPANY AND SUBSIDIARY SALIDA COMPANY
Comparative Balance Sheets

	Pinto Co. January 1, 2013	Consolidated December 31, 2013
Cash	$ 170,000	$ 431,000
Accounts receivable (net)	118,000	319,000
Inventory	310,000	395,000
Land	250,000	370,000
Buildings (net)	350,000	426,000
Equipment (net)	1,145,000	1,380,000
Database	–0–	49,000
Total assets	$2,343,000	$3,370,000
Accounts payable	$ 50,000	$ 45,000
Long-term liabilities	18,000	522,000
Common stock	1,500,000	1,500,000
Noncontrolling interest	–0–	98,250
Retained earnings	775,000	1,204,750
Total liabilities and equities	$2,343,000	$3,370,000

EXHIBIT 6.7

SALIDA COMPANY
Book and Fair Values
July 1, 2013

Account	Book Value	Fair Value
Cash	$ 35,000	$ 35,000
Accounts receivable	145,000	145,000
Inventory	90,000	90,000
Land	100,000	120,000
Buildings	136,000	136,000
Equipment	259,000	299,000
Database	–0–	50,000
Accounts payable	(15,000)	(15,000)
Net book value	$750,000	$ 860,000

PINTO'S ACQUISITION OF SALIDA
Excess Fair Value over Book Value Allocation
July 1, 2013

Consideration transferred by Pinto		$ 774,000
Noncontrolling interest fair value		86,000
Salida's total fair value		$ 860,000
Salida's book value		750,000
Excess fair over book value		$ 110,000
To land	$ 20,000	
To equipment (five-year life)	40,000	
To database (25-year life)	50,000	110,000
		–0–

PINTO COMPANY AND SUBSIDIARY SALIDA COMPANY
Consolidated Income Statement
For the Year Ended December 31, 2013

Revenues		$1,255,000
Cost of goods sold	$600,000	
Depreciation	124,000	
Database amortization	1,000	
Interest and other expenses	35,500	760,500
Consolidated net income		$ 494,500

Additional Information for 2013

- The consolidated income statement totals include Salida's postacquisition revenues and expenses.
- During the year, Pinto paid $50,000 in dividends. On August 1, Salida paid a $25,000 dividend.
- During the year, Pinto issued $504,000 in long-term debt at par value.
- No asset purchases or dispositions occurred during the year other than Pinto's acquisition of Salida.

In preparing the consolidated statement of cash flows, note that each adjustment derives from the consolidated income statement or changes from Pinto's January 1, 2013, balance sheet to the consolidated balance sheet at December 31, 2013.

Depreciation and Amortization These expenses do not represent current operating cash outflows and thus are added back to convert accrual basis income to cash provided by operating activities.

Increases in Accounts Receivable, Inventory, and Accounts Payable (net of acquisition) Changes in balance sheet accounts affecting operating cash flows must take into account amounts acquired in business acquisitions. In this case, note that the changes in Accounts Receivable, Inventory, and Accounts Payable are computed as follows:

	Accounts Receivable	Inventory	Accounts Payable
Pinto's balance 1/1/13	$118,000	$310,000	$50,000
Increase from Salida acquisition	145,000	90,000	15,000
Adjusted beginning balance	263,000	400,000	65,000
Consolidated balance 12/31/13	319,000	395,000	45,000
Operating cash flow adjustment	$ 56,000	$ 5,000	$20,000

Acquisition of Salida Company The Investing Activities section of the cash flow statement shows increases and decreases in assets purchased or sold involving cash. The cash outflow from the acquisition of Salida Company is determined as follows:

Cash paid for 90 percent interest in Salida	$774,000
Cash acquired	(35,000)
Net cash paid for Salida investment	$739,000

Note here that although Pinto acquires only 90 percent of Salida, 100 percent of Salida's cash is offset against the cash consideration paid in the acquisition in determining the investing cash outflow. Ownership divisions between the noncontrolling and controlling interests do not affect reporting for the entity's investing cash flows.

Issue of Long-Term Debt Pinto Company's issuance of long-term debt represents a cash inflow from financing activities.

Dividends The dividends paid to Pinto Company owners ($50,000) combined with the dividends paid to the noncontrolling interest ($2,500) represent cash outflows from financing activities.

Based on the consolidated totals from the comparative balance sheets and the consolidated income statement, the following consolidated statement of cash flows is then prepared. Pinto chooses to use the indirect method of reporting cash flows from operating activities.

PINTO COMPANY AND SUBSIDIARY SALIDA COMPANY
Consolidated Statement of Cash Flows
For the Year Ended December 31, 2013

Consolidated net income		$ 494,500
Depreciation expense	$ 124,000	
Amortization expense	1,000	
Increase in accounts receivable (net of acquisition effects)	(56,000)	
Decrease in inventory (net of acquisition effects)	5,000	
Decrease in accounts payable (net of acquisition effects)	(20,000)	54,000
Net cash provided by operations		$ 548,500
Purchase of Salida Company (net of cash acquired)		
Net cash used in investing activities	$(739,000)	(739,000)
Issue long-term debt	$ 504,000	
Dividends	(52,500)	
Net cash provided by financing activities		451,500
Increase in Cash 1/1/13 to 12/31/13		**$ 261,000**

Consolidated Earnings per Share

LO5

Compute basic and diluted earnings per share for a business combination.

The consolidation process affects one other intermediate accounting topic, the computation of earnings per share (EPS). Publicly held companies must disclose EPS each period. The following steps calculate such figures:

- Determine basic EPS by dividing the parent's share of consolidated net income (after reduction for preferred stock dividends) by the weighted average number of common stock shares outstanding for the period. If the reporting entity has no dilutive options, warrants, or other convertible items, only basic EPS is presented on the face of the income statement. However, diluted EPS also must be presented if any dilutive convertibles are present.
- Compute diluted EPS by combining the effects of *any dilutive securities* with basic earnings per share. Stock options, stock warrants, convertible debt, and convertible preferred stock often qualify as dilutive securities.[13]

In most instances, the computation of EPS for a business combination follows the same general pattern. Consolidated net income attributable to the parent company owners along with the number of outstanding parent shares provides the basis for calculating basic EPS. Any convertibles, warrants, or options for the parent's stock that can possibly dilute the reported figure must be included as described earlier in determining diluted EPS.

However, a problem arises if warrants, options, or convertibles that can dilute the subsidiary's earnings are outstanding. Although the parent company is not directly affected, the potential impact of these items on its share of consolidated net income must be given weight in computing diluted EPS for the consolidated income statement. Because of possible

[13] Complete coverage of the EPS computation can be found in virtually any intermediate accounting textbook. To adequately understand this process, a number of complex procedures must be mastered, including these:

- Calculation of the weighted average number of common shares outstanding.
- Understanding the method of including stock rights, convertible debt, and convertible preferred stock within the computation of diluted EPS.

conversion, the subsidiary earnings figure included in consolidated net income is not necessarily applicable to the diluted EPS computation. *Thus, the accountant must separately determine the parent's share of subsidiary income that should be used in deriving diluted EPS.*

Finally, the focus is on earnings per share for the parent company stockholders, even in the presence of a noncontrolling interest. As stated in FASB ASC (para. 260-10-45-11A):

> For purposes of computing EPS in consolidated financial statements (both basic and diluted), if one or more less-than-wholly-owned subsidiaries are included in the consolidated group, income from continuing operations and net income shall exclude the income attributable to the noncontrolling interest in subsidiaries.

Thus, consolidated income attributable to the parent's interest forms the basis for the numerator in all EPS calculations for consolidated financial reporting.

Earnings per Share Illustration

Assume that Big Corporation has 100,000 shares of its common stock outstanding during the current year. The company also has issued 20,000 shares of nonvoting preferred stock, paying an annual cumulative preferred dividend of $5 per share ($100,000 total). Each of these preferred shares is convertible into two shares of Big's common stock.

Assume also that Big owns 90 percent of Little's common stock and 60 percent of its preferred stock (which pays $12,000 in preferred dividends per year). Annual amortization is $26,000 attributable to various intangibles. EPS computations currently are being made for 2013. During the year, Big reported separate income of $600,000 and Little earned $100,000. A simplified consolidation of the figures for the year indicates consolidated net income attributable to Big of $663,000:

Big's separate income for 2013		$600,000
Little's separate income for 2013	$100,000	
Amortization expense resulting from original fair-value allocation	(26,000)	
Little's income after excess fair-value amortization		74,000
Consolidated net income		$674,000
Noncontrolling interest in Little—common stock (10% × $62,000 [$74,000 income less $12,000 preferred stock dividends])	$ (6,200)	
Noncontrolling interest in Little—preferred stock (40% of dividends)	(4,800)	
Total noncontrolling interest in consolidated net income		(11,000)
Consolidated net income attributable to Big (parent)		$663,000

Little has 20,000 shares of common stock and 4,000 shares of preferred stock outstanding. The preferred shares pay a $3 per year dividend, and each can be converted into two shares of common stock (or 8,000 shares in total). Because Big owns only 60 percent of Little's preferred stock, a $4,800 dividend is distributed each year to the outside owners (40 percent of the $12,000 total payment).

Assume finally that the subsidiary also has $200,000 in convertible bonds outstanding that were originally issued at face value. This debt has both a cash and an effective interest rate of 10 percent ($20,000 per year) and can be converted by the owners into 9,000 shares of Little's common stock. Big owns none of these bonds. Little's tax rate is 30 percent.

To better visualize these factors, the convertible items are scheduled as follows:

Company	Item	Interest or Dividend	Conversion	Big Owns
Big	Preferred stock	$100,000/year	40,000 shares	Not applicable
Little	Preferred stock	12,000/year	8,000 shares	60%
Little	Bonds	14,000/year*	9,000 shares	–0–

*Interest on the bonds is shown net of the 30 percent tax effect ($20,000 interest less $6,000 tax savings). No tax is computed for the preferred shares because distributed dividends do not create a tax impact.

EXHIBIT 6.8
Subsidiary's Diluted Earnings per Share

LITTLE COMPANY Basic and Diluted Earnings per Common Share For Year Ending December 31, 2013			
	Earnings	**Shares**	
Little's income after amortization	$74,000	20,000	
Preferred stock dividends	(12,000)		
Basic EPS	$62,000	20,000	$3.10 ($62,000/20,000)
Effect of possible preferred stock conversion:			
Dividends saved	$12,000	New shares 8,000	$1.50 impact (12,000/8,000)
Effect of possible bond conversion:			
Interest saved (net of taxes)	$14,000	9,000	$ 1.56 impact (14,000/9,000)
Diluted EPS.	$88,000	37,000	$ 2.38 (rounded)

Because the subsidiary has convertible items that can affect the company's outstanding shares and net income, Little's diluted earnings per share must be derived *before* Big's diluted EPS can be determined. As shown in Exhibit 6.8, Little's diluted EPS are $2.38. Two aspects of this schedule should be noted:

- The individual impact of the convertibles ($1.50 for the preferred stock and $1.56 for the bonds) did not raise the EPS figures above the $3.10 basic EPS. Thus, neither the preferred stock nor the bonds are antidilutive, and both are properly included in these computations.
- Absent the presence of the subsidiary's convertible bonds and preferred stock, the parent's share of consolidated net income would form the basis for computing EPS.

According to Exhibit 6.8, Little's income is $88,000 for diluted EPS. The issue for the accountant is how much of this amount should be included in computing the parent's diluted EPS. This allocation is based on the percentage of shares controlled by the parent. Note that if the subsidiary's preferred stock and bonds are converted into common shares, Big's ownership falls from 90 to 62 percent. For diluted EPS, 37,000 shares are appropriate. Big's 62 percent ownership (22,800/37,000) is the basis for allocating the subsidiary's $88,000 income to the parent.

Supporting Calculations for Diluted Earnings per Share

	Little Company Shares	Big's Percentage	Big's Ownership
Common stock	20,000	90%	18,000
Possible new shares—preferred stock	8,000	60	4,800
Possible new shares—bonds	9,000	-0-	-0-
Total	37,000		22,800

Big's ownership (diluted): 22,800/37,000 = 62% (rounded)
Income assigned to Big (diluted earnings per share computation):
$88,000 × 62% = $54,560

We can now determine Big Company's EPS. Only $54,560 of subsidiary income is appropriate for the diluted EPS computation. Because two different income figures are utilized, basic and diluted calculations are made separately as in Exhibit 6.9. Consequently, these schedules determine that Big Company should report basic EPS of $5.63, with diluted earnings per share of $4.68.

EXHIBIT 6.9

BIG COMPANY AND CONSOLIDATED SUBSIDIARY
Basic Earnings per Common Share
For Year Ending December 31, 2013

	Earnings	Shares	
Consolidated net income (to Big)	$663,000		
Big's shares outstanding		100,000	
Preferred stock dividends (Big)	(100,000)		
Basic EPS	$563,000	100,000	$5.63

Diluted Earnings per Common Share
For Year Ending December 31, 2013

	Earnings	Shares	
Computed below	$654,560*		
Big's shares outstanding		100,000	
Preferred stock dividends (Big)	(100,000)		
Effect of possible preferred stock (Big) conversion:			
Dividends saved	100,000	New shares 40,000	$2.50 impact (100,000/40,000)
Diluted EPS	$654,560	140,000	$4.68 (rounded)

*Net income computation:

Big's separate income	$600,000
Portion of Little's income assigned to diluted earnings per share calculation	54,560 (computed in supporting calculations)
Earnings of the business combination applicable to diluted earnings per share	$654,560

Subsidiary Stock Transactions

LO6

Understand the accounting for subsidiary stock transactions that impact the underlying value recorded within the parent's Investment account and the consolidated financial statements.

A note to the financial statements of Gerber Products Company disclosed a transaction carried out by one of the organization's subsidiaries: "The Company's wholly owned Mexican subsidiary sold previously unissued shares of common stock to Grupo Coral, S.A., a Mexican food company, at a price in excess of the shares' net book value." The footnote added that Gerber had increased consolidated Additional Paid-In Capital by $432,000 as a result of this stock sale.

As this illustration shows, subsidiary stock transactions can alter the level of parent ownership. A subsidiary, for example, can decide to sell previously unissued stock to raise needed capital. Although the parent company can acquire a portion or even all of these new shares, such issues frequently are marketed entirely to outsiders. A subsidiary could also be legally forced to sell additional shares of its stock. As an example, companies holding control over foreign subsidiaries occasionally encounter this problem because of laws in the individual localities. Regulations requiring a certain percentage of local ownership as a prerequisite for operating within a country can mandate issuance of new shares. Of course, changes in the level of parent ownership do not result solely from stock sales: A subsidiary also can repurchase its own stock. The acquisition, as well as the possible retirement, of such treasury shares serves as a means of reducing the percentage of outside ownership.

Changes in Subsidiary Value—Stock Transactions

When a subsidiary subsequently buys or sells its own stock, a nonoperational increase or decrease occurs in the company's fair and book value. Because the transaction need not involve the parent, the parent's investment account does not automatically reflect the effect of this change. *Thus, a separate adjustment must be recorded to maintain reciprocity between the subsidiary's stockholders' equity accounts and the parent's investment balance.*

The accountant measures the impact the stock transaction has on the parent to ensure that this effect is appropriately recorded within the consolidation process.

An overall perspective of accounting for subsidiary stock transactions follows from the fundamental notion that the parent establishes the subsidiary's valuation basis at fair value as of the acquisition date. Over time, the parent adjusts this initial fair value for subsidiary income less excess amortization and subsidiary dividends. If the subsidiary issues (or buys) any of its own stock subsequent to acquisition, the effect on the parent will depend on whether the price received (or paid) is greater or less than the per share subsidiary adjusted fair value at that point in time.

An example demonstrates the mechanics of this issue. Assume that on January 1, 2012, Giant Company acquires in the open market 60,000 of Small Company's outstanding 80,000 shares and prepares the following fair-value allocation schedule:

Consideration transferred by Giant	$480,000	
Noncontrolling interest fair value	160,000	
Small Company acquisition-date fair value		$640,000
Small Company acquisition-date book value		
Common stock (80,000 shares outstanding)	$ 80,000	
Additional paid-in capital	200,000	
Retained earnings, 1/1/12	260,000	540,000
Excess fair value assigned to trademark (10-year life)		$100,000

Assuming Small reports earnings of $50,000 in 2012 and pays no dividends, Giant prepares the following routine consolidation entries for the December 31, 2012, worksheet. Giant uses the equity method to account for its 75 percent interest in Small.

December 31, 2012, Consolidation Worksheet Entries

Consolidation Entry S		
Common Stock (Small Company)	80,000	
Additional Paid-In Capital (Small Company)	200,000	
Retained Earnings, 1/1/12 (Small Company)	260,000	
Investment in Small Company (75%)		405,000
Noncontrolling Interest in Small Company (25%)		135,000
To eliminate subsidiary's stockholders' equity accounts and recognize noncontrolling interest book value beginning balance.		

Consolidation Entry A		
Trademark	100,000	
Investment in Small Company (75%)		75,000
Noncontrolling Interest in Small Company (25%)		25,000
To recognize the excess acquisition-date fair value assigned to Small's trademark with allocations to the controlling and noncontrolling interest.		

Consolidation Entry I		
Equity in Small's Earnings	30,000	
Investment in Small Company		30,000
To eliminate Giant's equity in Small's earnings (75% × [$50,000 less $10,000 trademark excess amortization]).		

Consolidation Entry E		
Amortization Expense	10,000	
Trademark		10,000
To recognize the excess trademark amortization ($100,000 ÷ 10 years).		

We now introduce a subsidiary stock transaction to demonstrate the effect created on the consolidation process. Assume that on January 1, 2013, Giant announces plans for expansion of Small's operations. To help finance the expansion, Small sells 20,000 previously unissued shares of its common stock to outside parties for $10 per share. After the stock issue, Small's book value is as follows:

Common stock ($1.00 par value with 100,000 shares issued and outstanding) . .	$100,000
Additional paid-in capital	380,000
Retained earnings, 1/1/13	310,000
Total stockholders' equity, 1/1/13	$790,000

Note that the common stock and additional paid-in capital balances reflect increases from the new stock issue. Retained earnings have also increased from Small's $50,000 income in 2012 (no dividends). Although Small's book value is now $790,000, its valuation for the consolidated entity is derived from its acquisition-date fair value as adjusted through time as follows:

Consideration transferred	$480,000
Noncontrolling interest acquisition-date fair value	160,000
2012 Small income less excess amortization	40,000
Adjusted subsidiary value, 1/1/13	$680,000
Stock issue proceeds ($10 × 20,000 shares)	200,000
Subsidiary valuation basis, 1/1/13	$880,000

Because of Small's stock issue, Giant no longer possesses a 75 percent interest. Instead, the parent now holds 60 percent (60,000 shares of a total of 100,000 shares) of Small Company. The effect on the parent's ownership can be computed as follows:

Small's valuation basis 1/1/13 (above)	$880,000
Giant's post-issue ownership (60,000 shares ÷ 100,000 shares)	60%
Giant's post-stock issue ownership balance	$528,000
Giant's equity-adjusted investment account ($480,000 + [75% × $40,000]) . . .	510,000
Required adjustment—increase in Giant's additional paid-in capital	$ 18,000

Independent of any action by the parent company, the assigned fair-value equivalency of this investment has risen from $510,000 to $528,000. Small's ability to sell shares of stock at more than the per share consolidated subsidiary value ($680,000 ÷ 80,000 shares = $8.50 per share) created an increased value for the parent. Therefore, Giant records the $18,000 increment as an adjustment to both its investment account (because the underlying value of the subsidiary has increased) and additional paid-in capital:

Giant Company's Financial Records—January 1, 2013		
Investment in Small Company	18,000	
Additional Paid-In Capital (Giant Company)		18,000
To recognize change in equity of business combination created by Small Company issuing 20,000 additional shares of common stock at above the previously assigned fair value.		

Note that the parent reports a change in stockholders' equity (i.e., Additional Paid-In Capital) for effects from subsidiary stock transactions. GAAP literature states that:

> [c]hanges in a parent's ownership interest while the parent retains its controlling financial interest in its subsidiary shall be accounted for as equity transactions (investments by owners and distributions to owners acting in their capacity as owners). Therefore, no gain or loss shall be recognized in consolidated net income or comprehensive income. The carrying amount of the noncontrolling interest shall be adjusted to reflect the change in its ownership interest in the subsidiary. Any difference between the fair value of the consideration received or paid and the amount by which the noncontrolling interest is adjusted shall be recognized in equity attributable to the parent. [FASB ASC (para. 810-10-45-23)]

Consistent with this view, this textbook treats the effects from subsidiary stock transactions on the consolidated entity as adjustments to Additional Paid-In Capital.

After the change in the parent's records has been made, the consolidation process can proceed in a normal fashion. Assuming Small reports earnings of $85,000 in 2013 and pays no dividends, Giant prepares the following routine consolidation entries for the December 31, 2013, worksheet. *Although the investment and subsidiary equity accounts are removed here, the change recorded earlier in Giant's Additional Paid-In Capital remains within the consolidated figures.*

December 31, 2013, Consolidation Worksheet Entries

Consolidation Entry S		
Common Stock (Small Company)	100,000	
Additional Paid-In Capital (Small Company)	380,000	
Retained Earnings (Small Company)	310,000	
Investment in Small Company (60%)		474,000
Noncontrolling Interest in Small Company (40%)		316,000
To eliminate subsidiary's stockholders' equity accounts and recognize noncontrolling interest book value beginning balance. Small's capital accounts have been updated to reflect the issuance of 20,000 shares of $1 par value common stock at $10 per share.		

Consolidation Entry A		
Trademark	90,000	
Investment in Small Company (60%)		54,000
Noncontrolling Interest in Small Company (40%)		36,000
To recognize the unamortized excess acquisition-date fair value assigned to Small's trademark as of the beginning of the period with allocations to the controlling and noncontrolling interests' adjusted ownership percentages.		

Consolidation Entry I		
Equity in Small's Earnings	45,000	
Investment in Small Company		45,000
To eliminate Giant's equity in Small's earnings (60% × [$85,000 − $10,000 trademark excess amortization]).		

Consolidation Entry E		
Amortization Expense	10,000	
Trademark		10,000
To recognize the excess trademark amortization ($100,000 ÷ 10 years).		

The noncontrolling interest now stands at 40 percent ownership. Because these 40 percent owners will share in the profits generated by the subsidiary's trademark, they are allocated a 40 percent share to their overall equity balance in the consolidated financial statements. The noncontrolling interest is also assigned 40 percent of the excess fair-value trademark amortization.

Subsidiary Stock Transactions—Illustrated

No single example can demonstrate the many possible variations that different types of subsidiary stock transactions could create. To provide a working knowledge of this process, we analyze four additional cases briefly, each based on the following scenario:

Assume that Antioch Company acquires 90 percent of the common stock of Westminster Company on January 1, 2012, in exchange for $1,350,000 cash. The acquisition-date fair value of the 10 percent noncontrolling interest is $150,000. At that date, Westminster has the following stockholders' equity accounts:

Common stock—100,000 shares outstanding	$ 200,000
Additional paid-in capital	450,000
Retained earnings, 1/1/12	750,000
Total stockholders' equity	$1,400,000

The $100,000 excess acquisition-date fair over book value was allocated to a customer list with a five-year remaining life. In 2012, Westminster reports $190,000 in earnings and pays a $30,000 dividend. Antioch accrues its share of Westminster's income (less excess fair-value amortization related to the customer list) through application of the equity method. Antioch's equity method balance for its investment in Westminster is computed as follows:

Consideration transferred for 90% of Westminster	$1,350,000
Equity earnings of Westminster (90% × [$190,000 − $20,000 excess amortization])	153,000
Dividends received (90% × $30,000)	(27,000)
Equity method balance, 12/31/12	$1,476,000

View each of the following cases as an independent situation.

Case 1

Assume that on January 1, 2013, Westminster Company sells 25,000 shares of previously unissued common stock to outside parties for $14.40 per share. This stock issue changes both the parent's percentage interest in the subsidiary and the subsidiary's consolidated valuation basis. The parent's percentage ownership declines to 72 percent (90,000 shares ÷ 125,000 total shares). The subsidiary's valuation basis for consolidation becomes:

Consideration transferred	$1,350,000
Noncontrolling interest acquisition-date fair value	150,000
2012 Westminster income less excess amortization	170,000
Westminster dividends	(30,000)
Stock issue proceeds ($14.40 × 25,000 shares)	360,000
Subsidiary valuation basis 1/1/13	$2,000,000

Next, the effect on the parent's ownership can be computed as follows:

Westminster's valuation basis 1/1/13 (above)	$2,000,000
Antioch's post–stock issue ownership (90,000 shares ÷ 125,000 shares)	72%
Antioch's post–stock issue ownership balance	$1,440,000
Antioch's pre–stock issue equity-adjusted investment account (above)	1,476,000
Required adjustment—decrease in Antioch's additional paid-in capital	$ 36,000

To reflect this effect of the stock issue change on its valuation of the subsidiary, the parent makes the following journal entry on its financial records.

Antioch Company's Financial Records		
Additional Paid-In Capital (Antioch Company)	36,000	
Investment in Westminster Company		36,000
To recognize change in equity of business combination created by issuance of 25,000 additional shares of Westminster's common stock.		

Case 2

Assume that on January 1, 2013, Westminster issues 20,000 new shares of common stock for $16 per share. Of this total, Antioch acquires 18,000 shares to maintain its 90 percent level of ownership. Antioch pays a total of $288,000 (18,000 shares × $16) for this additional stock. Outside parties buy the remaining shares.

Under these circumstances, the stock transaction alters the consolidated valuation basis of the subsidiary but not the percentage owned by the parent. Thus, only the subsidiary value must be updated prior to determining the necessity of an equity revaluation:

Consideration transferred	$1,350,000
Noncontrolling interest acquisition-date fair value	150,000
2012 Westminster income less excess amortization	170,000
Westminster dividends	(30,000)
Stock issue proceeds ($16 × 20,000 shares)	320,000
Subsidiary valuation basis 1/1/13	$1,960,000

The effect on the parent's ownership is computed as follows:

Westminster's valuation basis 1/1/13 (above)		$1,960,000
Antioch's post–stock issue ownership (108,000 shares ÷ 120,000 shares)		90%
Antioch's post–stock issue ownership balance		$1,764,000
Antioch's equity-adjusted investment account before stock purchase	$1,476,000	
Additional payment for 18,000 shares of Westminster	288,000	1,764,000
Required adjustment		$ -0-

This case requires no adjustment because Antioch's underlying interest remains aligned with the subsidiary's consolidated valuation basis. Any purchase of new stock by the parent in the same ratio as previous ownership does not affect consolidated Additional Paid-In Capital. The transaction creates no proportionate increase or decrease.

Case 3

Assume that instead of issuing new stock, on January 1, 2013, Westminster reacquires all 10,000 shares owned by the noncontrolling interest. It pays $16 per share for this treasury stock.

This illustration presents another type of subsidiary stock transaction: the acquisition of treasury stock. In this case the effect on the parent can be computed by reference to the amount of noncontrolling interest that must be reduced to zero in the consolidated financial statements.

Noncontrolling interest (NCI) acquisition-date fair value	$ 150,000
NCI share of 2012 Westminster income less excess amortization ($170,000 × 10%)	17,000
NCI share of Westminster dividends ($30,000 × 10%)	(3,000)
Noncontrolling interest valuation basis at 1/1/13	$ 164,000
Treasury stock purchase ($16 × 10,000 shares)	(160,000)
Required adjustment—increase in Antioch's additional paid-in capital	$ 4,000

The consolidated entity paid $160,000 to reduce a $164,000 owners' equity interest (the noncontrolling interest) to zero, thus increasing its own equity by $4,000. As usual, the increase in equity is attributed to additional paid-in capital and is recorded on the parent's records.

Antioch Company's Financial Records

Investment in Westminster Company	4,000	
Additional Paid-In Capital (Antioch Company)		4,000
To recognize change in equity of business combination created by acquisition of 10,000 treasury shares by Westminster.		

This third illustration represents a newly introduced subsidiary stock transaction, the purchase of treasury stock. Therefore, display of consolidation Entries **S** and **A** are also presented. These entries demonstrate the worksheet eliminations required when the subsidiary holds treasury shares:

Consolidation Entry S		
Common Stock (Westminster Company)	200,000	
Additional Paid-In Capital (Westminster Company)	450,000	
Retained Earnings, 1/1/13 (Westminster Company)	910,000	
Treasury Stock		160,000
Investment in Westminster Company		1,400,000
To eliminate equity accounts of Westminster Company		

Consolidation Entry A		
Customer List	80,000	
Investment in Westminster Company		80,000
To recognize the beginning-of-year unamortized excess acquisition-date fair value allocated to the customer list.		

Note first the absence of a noncontrolling interest entry. Also note that the sum of the credits to the Investment in Westminster account is $1,480,000, which is the pretreasury stock purchase equity method balance of $1,476,000 plus the $4,000 addition from the acquisition of the noncontrolling interest.

Case 4

Assume that on January 1, 2013, Westminster issues a 10 percent stock dividend (10,000 new shares) to its owners when the stock's fair value is $15 per share.

This final case illustrates another example of a subsidiary stock transaction producing no effect on the parent's records. Stock dividends, whether large or small, capitalize a portion of the issuing company's retained earnings without altering total book value. Shareholders recognize the receipt of a stock dividend as a change in the per share value rather than as an adjustment to the investment balance. Because neither party perceives a net effect, the consolidation process proceeds in a routine fashion. Therefore, a subsidiary stock dividend requires no special treatment prior to development of a worksheet.

Consideration transferred	$1,350,000
Noncontrolling interest acquisition-date fair value	150,000
2012 Westminster income less excess amortization	170,000
Westminster dividends	(30,000)
Subsidiary valuation basis 1/1/13	$1,640,000
Antioch's ownership (adjusted for 10% stock dividend 99,000 ÷ 110,000 shares)	90%
Antioch's post–stock dividend ownership interest	$1,476,000
Antioch's equity-adjusted investment account	1,476,000
Adjustment required by stock dividend	$ –0–

The consolidation Entries **S** and **A** made just after the stock dividend follow. The $1,404,000 component of the investment account is offset against the stockholders' equity of the subsidiary. Although the stock dividend did not affect the parent's investment, the equity accounts of the subsidiary have been realigned in recognition of the $150,000 stock dividend (10,000 shares of $2 par value stock valued at $15 per share):

Consolidation Entry S		
Common Stock (Westminster Company)	220,000	
Additional Paid-In Capital (Westminster Company)	580,000	
Retained Earnings, 1/1/13 (Westminster Company)	760,000	
Investment in Westminster Company (90%)		1,404,000
Noncontrolling Interest (10%)		156,000
To eliminate the equity accounts of Westminster Company.		

Consolidation Entry A		
Customer List	80,000	
Investment in Westminster Company		72,000
Noncontrolling Interest		8,000
To recognize the beginning-of-year unamortized excess fair value attributable to the customer list.		

Note here that the sum of the credits to the Investment in Westminster account is \$1,476,000, which equals the pre–stock dividend equity method balance.

Summary

1. Variable interest entities (VIEs) typically take the form of a trust, partnership, joint venture, or corporation. In most cases, a sponsoring firm creates these entities to engage in a limited and well-defined set of business activities. Control of VIEs, by design, often does not rest with their equity holders. Instead, control is exercised through contractual arrangements with the sponsoring firm that becomes the entity's "primary beneficiary." These contracts can take the form of leases, participation rights, guarantees, or other residual interests. Through contracting, the primary beneficiary bears a significant portion of the risks and receives a significant portion of the rewards of the entity, often without owning any voting shares. Current accounting standards require a business that has a controlling financial interest in a VIE to consolidate the financial statements of the VIE with its own.
2. If one member of a business combination acquires an affiliate's debt instrument (e.g., a bond or note) from an outside party, the purchase price usually differs from the book value of the liability. Thus, a gain or loss has been incurred from the perspective of the business combination. However, both the debt and investment remain in the individual financial accounts of the two companies, but the gain or loss goes unrecorded. The consolidation process must adjust all balances to reflect the effective retirement of the debt.
3. Following a related party's acquisition of a company's debt, Interest Income and Expense are recognized. Because these accounts result from intra-entity transactions, they also must be removed in every subsequent consolidation along with the debt and investment figures. Retained Earnings also requires adjustment in each year after the purchase to record the impact of the gain or loss.
4. Amortization of intra-entity debt/investment balances often is necessary because of discounts and/or premiums. Consequently, the Interest Income and Interest Expense figures reported by the two parties will not agree. The closing of these two accounts into Retained Earnings each year gradually reduces the consolidation adjustment that must be made to this equity account.
5. When acquired, many subsidiaries have preferred stock outstanding as well as common stock. The existence of subsidiary preferred shares does little to complicate the consolidation process. The acquisition method values all business acquisitions at their full fair values. If a subsidiary has preferred stock, the essential process of determining its acquisition-date business fair value remains intact. Any preferred shares not owned by the parent simply become a component of the noncontrolling interest and are included in the acquisition-date measure of subsidiary fair value.
6. Every business combination must prepare a statement of cash flows. This statement is not created by consolidating the individual cash flows of the separate companies. Instead, both a consolidated income statement and balance sheet are produced, and the cash flows statement is developed from these figures. Dividends paid to the noncontrolling interest must be listed as a financing activity.
7. For most business combinations, the determination of earnings per share (EPS) follows the normal pattern presented in intermediate accounting textbooks. However, if the subsidiary has potentially dilutive items outstanding (stock warrants, convertible preferred stock, convertible bonds, etc.), a different process must be followed. The subsidiary's own diluted EPS are computed as a preliminary procedure. The parent and the outside owners then allocate the earnings used in each of these calculations based on the ownership levels of the subsidiary's shares and the dilutive items. The determination of the EPS figures to be reported for the business combination is based on the portion of consolidated net income assigned to the parent.
8. After the combination is created, a subsidiary may enter into stock transactions such as issuing additional shares or acquiring treasury stock. Such actions normally create a

proportional increase or decrease in the subsidiary's equity when compared with the parent's investment. The change is measured and then reflected in the consolidated statements through the Additional Paid-In Capital account. To achieve the appropriate accounting, the parent adjusts the Investment in Subsidiary account as well as its own Additional Paid-In Capital. Because the worksheet does not eliminate this equity balance, the required increase or decrease carries over to the consolidated figures.

Comprehensive Illustration

Problem: Consolidated Statement of Cash Flows and Earnings per Share

(*Estimated Time: 35 to 45 Minutes*) Pop, Inc., acquires 90 percent of the 20,000 shares of Son Company's outstanding common stock on December 31, 2011. Of the acquisition-date fair value, it allocates $80,000 to covenants, a figure amortized at the rate of $2,000 per year. Comparative consolidated balance sheets for 2013 and 2012 are as follows:

	2013	2012
Cash	$ 210,000	$ 130,000
Accounts receivable	350,000	220,000
Inventory	320,000	278,000
Land, buildings, and equipment (net)	1,090,000	1,120,000
Covenants	78,000	80,000
Total assets	$2,048,000	$1,828,000
Accounts payable	$ 290,000	$ 296,000
Long-term liabilities	650,000	550,000
Noncontrolling interest	37,800	34,000
Preferred stock (10% cumulative)	100,000	100,000
Common stock (26,000 shares outstanding)	520,000	520,000
Retained earnings, 12/31	450,200	328,000
Total liabilities and stockholders' equity	$2,048,000	$1,828,000

Additional Information for 2013

- Consolidated net income (after adjustments for all intra-entity items) was $178,000.
- Consolidated depreciation and amortization equaled $52,000.
- On April 10, Son sold a building with a $40,000 book value, receiving cash of $50,000. Later that month, Pop borrowed $100,000 from a local bank and purchased equipment for $60,000. These transactions were all with outside parties.
- During the year, Pop paid $40,000 dividends on its common stock and $10,000 on its preferred stock, and Son paid a $20,000 dividend on its common stock.
- Son has long-term convertible debt of $180,000 outstanding included in consolidated liabilities. It recognized interest expense of $16,000 (net of taxes) on this debt during the year. This debt can be exchanged for 10,000 shares of the subsidiary's common stock. Pop owns none of this debt.
- Son recorded $60,000 net income from its own operations. Noncontrolling interest in Son's income was $5,800.
- Pop recorded $4,000 in profits on sales of goods to Son. These goods remain in Son's warehouse at December 31.
- Pop applies the equity method to account for its investment in Son. On its own books, Pop recognized $48,200 equity in earnings from Son (90% × [$60,000 less $2,000 amortization] and $4,000 unrealized intra-entity profit on its sales to Son).

Required

a. Prepare a consolidated statement of cash flows for Pop, Inc., and Son Company for the year ending December 31, 2013. Use the indirect method for determining the amount of cash generated by normal operations.[14]

b. Compute basic earnings per share and diluted earnings per share for Pop. Inc.

Solution

a. Consolidated Statement of Cash Flows

The problem specifies that the indirect method should be used in preparing the consolidated statement of cash flows. Therefore, all items that do not represent cash flows from operations must be removed from the $178,000 consolidated net income. For example, both the depreciation and amortization are eliminated (noncash items) as well as the gain on the sale of the building (a nonoperational item). As the chapter discussed, the noncontrolling interest's share of Son's net income is another noncash reduction that also is removed. In addition, each of the changes in consolidated Accounts Receivable, Inventory, and Accounts Payable produces a noncash impact on net income. The increase in Accounts Receivable, for example, indicates that the sales figure for the period was larger than the amount of cash collected so that adjustment is required in producing this statement.

From the information given, several nonoperational changes in cash can be determined: the bank loan, the acquisition of equipment, the sale of a building, the dividend paid by Son to the noncontrolling interest, and the dividend paid by the parent. Each of these transactions is included in the consolidated statement of cash flows shown in Exhibit 6.10, which explains the $80,000 increase in cash experienced by the entity during 2013.

b. Earnings per Share

The subsidiary's convertible debt has a potentially dilutive effect on earnings per share. Therefore, diluted EPS cannot be determined for the business combination directly from consolidated

EXHIBIT 6.10

POP, INC., AND SON COMPANY
Consolidated Statement of Cash Flows
Year Ending December 31, 2013

Cash flows from operating activities		
Consolidated net income		$ 178,000
Adjustments to reconcile consolidated net income to net cash provided by operating activities:		
Depreciation and amortization	$ 52,000	
Gain on sale of building	(10,000)	
Increase in accounts receivable	(130,000)	
Increase in inventory	(42,000)	
Decrease in accounts payable	(6,000)	(136,000)
Net cash provided by operations		$ 42,000
Cash flows from investing activities		
Purchase of equipment	$ (60,000)	
Sale of building	50,000	
Net cash used in investing activities		(10,000)
Cash flows from financing activities		
Payment of cash dividends—Pop	$ (50,000)	
Payment of cash dividend to noncontrolling owners of Son	(2,000)	
Borrowed from bank	100,000	
Net cash provided by financing activities		48,000
Net increase in cash		$ 80,000
Cash, January 1, 2013		130,000
Cash, December 31, 2013		$ 210,000

[14] Prior to attempting this problem, a review of an intermediate accounting textbook might be useful to obtain a complete overview of the production of a statement of cash flows.

EXHIBIT 6.11

POP, INC., AND SON COMPANY
Earnings per Share
Year Ending December 31, 2013

	Earnings	Shares	
	Basic Earnings per Share		
Pop's share of consolidated net income	$172,200		
Preferred dividend paid by Pop	(10,000)		
Basic EPS	162,200	26,000	$6.24 (rounded)
	Diluted Earnings per Share		
Pop's share of consolidated net income	$172,200		
Remove equity income	(48,200)		
Remove unrealized gain	(4,000)		
Preferred stock dividend	(10,000)		
Common shares outstanding (Pop, Inc.)		26,000	
Common stock income—Pop (for EPS computations)	$110,000		
Income of Son (for diluted EPS)	44,400		
Diluted EPS	$154,400	26,000	$5.94 (rounded)

net income. First, the diluted EPS figure must be calculated for the subsidiary. This information then is used in the computations made by the consolidated entity.

Diluted EPS of $2.47 for the subsidiary is determined as follows:

Son Company—Diluted Earnings per Share

	Earnings		Shares	
As reported less excess amortization	$58,000		20,000	$2.90
Effect of possible debt conversion:				
Interest saved (net of taxes)	16,000	New shares	10,000	$1.60 impact (16,000/10,000)
Diluted EPS	$74,000		30,000	$2.47 (rounded)

The parent owns none of the convertible debt included in computing diluted EPS. Pop holds only 18,000 (90 percent of the outstanding common stock) of the 30,000 shares used in this EPS calculation. Consequently, in determining diluted EPS for the parent company, only $44,400 of the subsidiary's income is applicable:

$$\$74{,}000 \times 18{,}000/30{,}000 = \$44{,}400$$

Exhibit 6.11 reveals basic EPS of $6.24 and diluted EPS of $5.94. Because the subsidiary's earnings figure is included separately in the computation of diluted EPS, the parent's individual income must be identified in the same manner. Thus, the effect of the equity income and intra-entity (downstream) transactions are taken into account in arriving at the parent's separate earnings.

Questions

1. What is a variable interest entity (VIE)?
2. What are variable interests in an entity and how might they provide financial control over an entity?
3. When is a sponsoring firm required to consolidate the financial statements of a VIE with its own financial statements?
4. A parent company acquires from a third party bonds that had been issued originally by one of its subsidiaries. What accounting problems are created by this purchase?

5. In question (4), why is the consolidation process simpler if the bonds had been acquired directly from the subsidiary than from a third party?
6. When a company acquires an affiliated company's debt instruments from a third party, how is the gain or loss on extinguishment of the debt calculated? When should this balance be recognized?
7. Several years ago, Bennett, Inc., bought a portion of the outstanding bonds of Smith Corporation, a subsidiary organization. The acquisition was made from an outside party. In the current year, how should these intra-entity bonds be accounted for within the consolidation process?
8. One company purchases the outstanding debt instruments of an affiliated company on the open market. This transaction creates a gain that is appropriately recognized in the consolidated financial statements of that year. Thereafter, a worksheet adjustment is required to correct the beginning balance of the consolidated Retained Earnings. Why is the amount of this adjustment reduced from year to year?
9. A parent acquires the outstanding bonds of a subsidiary company directly from an outside third party. For consolidation purposes, this transaction creates a gain of $45,000. Should this gain be allocated to the parent or the subsidiary? Why?
10. Perkins Company acquires 90 percent of the outstanding common stock of the Butterfly Corporation as well as 55 percent of its preferred stock. How should these preferred shares be accounted for within the consolidation process?
11. The income statement and the balance sheet are produced using a worksheet, but a consolidated statement of cash flows is not. What process is followed in preparing a consolidated statement of cash flows?
12. How do noncontrolling interest balances affect the consolidated statement of cash flows?
13. In many cases, EPS is computed based on the parent's portion of consolidated net income and parent company shares and convertibles. However, a different process must be used for some business combinations. When is this alternative approach required?
14. A subsidiary has (1) a convertible preferred stock and (2) a convertible bond. How are these items factored into the computation of earnings per share for the parent company?
15. Why might a subsidiary decide to issue new shares of common stock to parties outside the business combination?
16. Washburn Company owns 75 percent of Metcalf Company's outstanding common stock. During the current year, Metcalf issues additional shares to outside parties at a price more than its per share consolidated value. How does this transaction affect the business combination? How is this impact recorded within the consolidated statements?
17. Assume the same information as in question (16) except that Metcalf issues a 10 percent stock dividend instead of selling new shares of stock. How does this transaction affect the business combination?

Problems

LO1

1. An enterprise that holds a variable interest in a variable interest entity (VIE) is required to consolidate the assets, liabilities, revenues, expenses, and noncontrolling interest of that entity if:
   a. The VIE has issued no voting stock.
   b. The variable interest held by the enterprise involves a lease.
   c. The enterprise has a controlling financial interest in the VIE.
   d. Other equity interests in the VIE have the obligation to absorb the expected losses of the VIE.

LO2

2. A subsidiary has a debt outstanding that was originally issued at a discount. At the beginning of the current year, the parent company acquired the debt at a slight premium from outside parties. Which of the following statements is true?
   a. Whether the balances agree or not, both the subsequent interest income and interest expense should be reported in a consolidated income statement.
   b. The interest income and interest expense will agree in amount and should be offset for consolidation purposes.
   c. In computing any noncontrolling interest allocation, the interest income should be included but not the interest expense.
   d. Although subsequent interest income and interest expense will not agree in amount, both balances should be eliminated for consolidation purposes.

LO3

3. The parent company acquires all of a subsidiary's common stock but only 70 percent of its preferred shares. This preferred stock pays a 7 percent annual cumulative dividend. No dividends are in arrears at the current time. How is the noncontrolling interest's share of the subsidiary's income computed?
   a. As 30 percent of the subsidiary's preferred dividend.
   b. No allocation is made because the dividends have been paid.
   c. As 30 percent of the subsidiary's income after all dividends have been subtracted.
   d. Income is assigned to the preferred stock based on total par value and 30 percent of that amount is allocated to the noncontrolling interest.

LO4

4. Aceton Corporation owns 80 percent of the outstanding stock of Voctax, Inc. During the current year, Voctax made $140,000 in sales to Aceton. How does this transfer affect the consolidated statement of cash flows?
   a. The transaction should be included if payment has been made.
   b. Only 80 percent of the transfers should be included because the subsidiary made the sales.
   c. Because the transfers were from a subsidiary organization, the cash flows are reported as investing activities.
   d. Because of the intra-entity nature of the transfers, the amount is not reported in the consolidated cash flow statement.

LO4

5. Warrenton, Inc., owns 80 percent of Aminable Corporation. On a consolidated income statement, the Noncontrolling Interest in the Subsidiary's Income is reported as $37,000. Aminable paid a total cash dividend of $100,000 for the year. How does this impact the consolidated statement of cash flows?
   a. The dividends paid to the outside owners are reported as a financing activity, but the noncontrolling interest figure is not viewed as a cash flow.
   b. The noncontrolling interest figure is reported as an investing activity, but the dividends amount paid to the outside owners is omitted entirely.
   c. Neither figure is reported on the statement of cash flows.
   d. Both dividends paid and the noncontrolling interest are viewed as financing activities.

Problems 6 and 7 are based on the following information.
Comparative consolidated balance sheet data for Iverson, Inc., and its 80 percent–owned subsidiary Oakley Co. follow:

	2013	2012
Cash	$ 7,000	$ 20,000
Accounts receivable (net)	55,000	38,000
Merchandise inventory	85,000	45,000
Buildings and equipment (net)	95,000	105,000
Trademark	85,000	100,000
Totals	$327,000	$308,000
Accounts payable	$ 75,000	$ 63,000
Notes payable, long-term	–0–	25,000
Noncontrolling interest	39,000	35,000
Common stock, $10 par	200,000	200,000
Retained earnings (deficit)	13,000	(15,000)
Totals	$327,000	$308,000

Additional Information for Fiscal Year 2013

- Iverson and Oakley's consolidated net income was $45,000.
- Oakley paid $5,000 in dividends during the year. Iverson paid $12,000 in dividends.
- Oakley sold $11,000 worth of merchandise to Iverson during the year.
- There were no purchases or sales of long-term assets during the year.

In the 2013 consolidated statement of cash flows for Iverson Company:

LO4

6. Net cash flows from operating activities were
   a. $12,000.
   b. $20,000.
   c. $24,000.
   d. $25,000.

LO4

7. Net cash flows from financing activities were
   a. $(25,000).
   b. $(37,000).
   c. $(38,000).
   d. $(42,000).

LO5

8. Bensman Corporation is computing EPS. One of its subsidiaries has stock warrants outstanding. How do these convertible items affect Bensman's EPS computation?
   a. No effect is created because the stock warrants were for the subsidiary company's shares.
   b. The stock warrants are not included in the computation unless they are antidilutive.
   c. The effect of the stock warrants must be computed in deriving the amount of subsidiary income to be included in making the diluted EPS calculation.
   d. The stock warrants are included only in basic EPS but never in diluted EPS.

LO6

9. Arcola, Inc., acquires all 40,000 shares of Tuscola Company for $725,000. A year later, when Arcola's equity adjusted balance in its investment in Tuscola equals $800,000, Tuscola issues an additional 10,000 shares to outside investors for $25 per share. Which of the following best describes the effect of Tuscola's stock issue on Arcola's investment account?
   a. No effect because the shares were all sold to outside parties.
   b. The investment account is reduced because Arcola now owns a smaller percentage of Tuscola.
   c. The investment account is increased because Arcola's share of Tuscola's value has increased.
   d. No effect because Arcola maintains control over Tuscola despite the new stock issue.

LO2

10. Jordan, Inc., owns Fey Corporation. For the current year, Jordan reports net income (without consideration of its investment in Fey) of $200,000 and the subsidiary reports $80,000. The parent had a bond payable outstanding on January 1, with a book value of $212,000. The subsidiary acquired the bond on that date for $199,000. During the current year, Jordan reported interest expense of $22,000 while Fey reported interest income of $21,000. What is consolidated net income?
    a. $266,000.
    b. $268,000.
    c. $292,000.
    d. $294,000.

LO5

11. Mattoon, Inc., owns 80 percent of Effingham Company. For the current year, this combined entity reported consolidated net income of $500,000. Of this amount $465,000 was attributable to Mattoon's controlling interest while the remaining $35,000 was attributable to the noncontrolling interest. Mattoon has 100,000 shares of common stock outstanding and Effingham has 25,000 shares outstanding. Neither company has issued preferred shares or has any convertible securities outstanding. On the face of the consolidated income statement, how much should be reported as Mattoon's earnings per share?
    a. $5.00
    b. $4.65
    c. $4.00
    d. $3.88

LO2

12. Ace Company reports current earnings of $400,000 while paying $40,000 in cash dividends. Byrd Company earns $100,000 in net income and distributes $10,000 in dividends. Ace has held a 70 percent interest in Byrd for several years, an investment with an acquisition-date fair value equal to the book value of its underlying net assets. Ace uses the initial value method to account for these shares.

    On January 1 of the current year, Byrd acquired in the open market $50,000 of Ace's 8 percent bonds. The bonds had originally been issued several years ago for 92, reflecting a 10 percent effective interest rate. On the date of purchase, the book value of the bonds payable was $48,300. Byrd paid $46,600 based on a 12 percent effective interest rate over the remaining life of the bonds.

    What is consolidated net income for this year?
    a. $492,160.
    b. $493,938.
    c. $499,160.
    d. $500,258.

LO2

13. Using the same information presented in problem (12), what is the noncontrolling interest's share of the subsidiary's net income?
    a. $27,000.
    b. $28,290.
    c. $28,620.
    d. $30,000.

LO2

14. Pesto Company possesses 80 percent of Salerno Company's outstanding voting stock. Pesto uses the initial value method to account for this investment. On January 1, 2009, Pesto sold 9 percent bonds payable with a $10 million face value (maturing in 20 years) on the open market at a premium of $600,000. On January 1, 2012, Salerno acquired 40 percent of these same bonds from an outside party at 96.6 of face value. Both companies use the straight-line method of amortization. For a 2013 consolidation, what adjustment should be made to Pesto's beginning Retained Earnings as a result of this bond acquisition?
    a. $320,000 increase.
    b. $326,000 increase.
    c. $331,000 increase.
    d. $340,000 increase.

LO3

15. On January 1, Tesco Company spent a total of $4,384,000 to acquire control over Blondel Company. This price was based on paying $424,000 for 20 percent of Blondel's preferred stock and $3,960,000 for 90 percent of its outstanding common stock. At the acquisition date, the fair value of the 10 percent noncontrolling interest in Blondel's common stock was $440,000. The fair value of the 80 percent of Blondel's preferred shares not owned by Tesco was $1,696,000. Blondel's stockholders' equity accounts at January 1 were as follows:

Preferred stock—9%, $100 par value, cumulative and participating; 10,000 shares outstanding	$1,000,000
Common stock—$50 par value; 40,000 shares outstanding	2,000,000
Retained earnings	3,000,000
Total stockholders' equity	$6,000,000

    Tesco believes that all of Blondel's accounts approximate their fair values within the company's financial statements. What amount of consolidated goodwill should be recognized?
    a. $300,000.
    b. $316,000.
    c. $364,000.
    d. $520,000.

LO3

16. On January 1, Morgan Company has a net book value of $1,460,000 as follows:

1,000 shares of preferred stock; par value $100 per share; cumulative, nonparticipating, nonvoting; call value $108 per share	$ 100,000
20,000 shares of common stock; par value $40 per share	800,000
Retained earnings	560,000
Total	$1,460,000

    Leinen Company acquires all outstanding preferred shares for $106,000 and 60 percent of the common stock for $870,000. The acquisition-date fair value of the noncontrolling interest in Morgan's common stock was $580,000. Leinen believed that one of Morgan's buildings, with a 12-year life, was undervalued by $50,000 on the company's financial records.
    What amount of consolidated goodwill would be recognized from this acquisition?
    a. $40,000.
    b. $41,200.
    c. $42,400.
    d. $46,000.

LO4

17. Aedion Company owns control over Breedlove, Inc. Aedion reports sales of $300,000 during 2013 and Breedlove reports $200,000. Inventory costing $20,000 was transferred from

Breedlove to Aedion (upstream) during the year for $40,000. Of this amount, 25 percent is still in ending inventory at year-end. Total receivables on the consolidated balance sheet were $80,000 at the first of the year and $110,000 at year-end. No intra-entity debt existed at the beginning or ending of the year. Using the direct method, what is the consolidated amount of cash collected by the business combination from its customers?

a. $430,000.

b. $460,000.

c. $490,000.

d. $510,000.

LO6

18. Aaron owns 100 percent of the 12,000 shares of Veritable, Inc. The Investment in Veritable account has a balance of $588,000, corresponding to the subsidiary's unamortized acquisition-date fair value of $49 per share. Veritable issues 3,000 new shares to the public for $50 per share. How does this transaction affect the Investment in Veritable account?

a. It is not affected because the shares were sold to outside parties.

b. It should be increased by $2,400.

c. It should be increased by $3,000.

d. It should be decreased by $117,600.

Problems 19 through 21 are based on the following information.

Neill Company purchases 80 percent of the common stock of Stamford Company on January 1, 2012, when Stamford has the following stockholders' equity accounts:

Common stock—40,000 shares outstanding	$100,000
Additional paid-in capital	75,000
Retained earnings, 1/1/12	540,000
Total stockholders' equity	$715,000

To acquire this interest in Stamford, Neill pays a total of $592,000. The acquisition-date fair value of the 20 percent noncontrolling interest was $148,000. Any excess fair value was allocated to goodwill, which has not experienced any impairment.

On January 1, 2013, Stamford reports retained earnings of $620,000. Neill has accrued the increase in Stamford's retained earnings through application of the equity method.

View the following problems as independent situations:

LO6

19. On January 1, 2013, Stamford issues 10,000 additional shares of common stock for $25 per share. Neill acquires 8,000 of these shares. How will this transaction affect the parent company's Additional Paid-In Capital account?

a. Has no effect on it.

b. Increases it by $20,500.

c. Increases it by $36,400.

d. Increases it by $82,300.

LO6

20. On January 1, 2013, Stamford issues 10,000 additional shares of common stock for $15 per share. Neill does not acquire any of this newly issued stock. How does this transaction affect the parent company's Additional Paid-In Capital account?

a. Has no effect on it.

b. Increases it by $44,000.

c. Decreases it by $35,200.

d. Decreases it by $55,000.

LO6

21. On January 1, 2013, Stamford reacquires 8,000 of the outstanding shares of its own common stock for $24 per share. None of these shares belonged to Neill. How does this transaction affect the parent company's Additional Paid-In Capital account?

a. Has no effect on it.

b. Decreases it by $55,000.

c. Decreases it by $35,000.

d. Decreases it by $28,000.

LO1

22. Hillsborough Country Outfitters, Inc., entered into an agreement for HCO Media LLC to exclusively conduct Hillsborough's e-commerce initiatives through a jointly owned (50 percent each) Internet site known as HCO.com. HCO Media receives 2 percent of all sales revenue generated through the site up to a maximum of $500,000 per year. Both Hillsborough and HCO Media pay 50 percent of the costs to maintain the Internet site. However, if HCO Media's fees are insufficient to cover its 50 percent share of the costs, Hillsborough absorbs the loss.

    Assuming that HCO Media qualifies as a VIE, should Hillsborough consolidate HCO Media LLC?

LO1

23. The following describes a set of arrangements between TecPC Company and a variable interest entity (VIE) as of December 31, 2013. TecPC agrees to design and construct a new research and development (R&D) facility. The VIE's sole purpose is to finance and own the R&D facility and lease it to TecPC Company after construction is completed. Payments under the operating lease are expected to begin in the first quarter of 2015.

    The VIE has financing commitments sufficient for the construction project from equity and debt participants (investors) of $4 million and $42 million, respectively. TecPC, in its role as the VIE's construction agent, is responsible for completing construction by December 31, 2014. TecPC has guaranteed a portion of the VIE's obligations during the construction and postconstruction periods.

    TecPC agrees to lease the R&D facility for five years with multiple extension options. The lease is a variable rate obligation indexed to a three-month market rate. As market interest rates increase or decrease, the payments under this operating lease also increase or decrease, sufficient to provide a return to the investors. If all extension options are exercised, the total lease term is 35 years.

    At the end of the first five-year lease term or any extension, TecPC may choose one of the following:

    - Renew the lease at fair value subject to investor approval.
    - Purchase the facility at its original construction cost.
    - Sell the facility on the VIE's behalf, to an independent third party. If TecPC sells the project and the proceeds from the sale are insufficient to repay the investors their original cost, TecPC may be required to pay the VIE up to 85 percent of the project's cost.

    a. What is the purpose of reporting consolidated statements for a company and the entities that it controls?

    b. When should a VIE's financial statements be consolidated with those of another company?

    c. Identify the risks of ownership of the R&D facility that (1) TecPC has effectively shifted to the VIE's owners and (2) remain with TecPC.

    d. What characteristics of a primary beneficiary does TecPC possess?

LO1

24. On December 31, 2013, PanTech Company invests $20,000 in SoftPlus, a variable interest entity. In contractual agreements completed on that date, PanTech established itself as the primary beneficiary of SoftPlus. Previously, PanTech had no equity interest in SoftPlus. Immediately after PanTech's investment, SoftPlus presents the following balance sheet:

Cash	$ 20,000	Long-term debt	$120,000
Marketing software	140,000	Noncontrolling interest	60,000
Computer equipment	40,000	PanTech equity interest	20,000
Total assets	$200,000	Total liabilities and equity	$200,000

    Each of the above amounts represents an assessed fair value at December 31, 2013, except for the marketing software.

    a. If the marketing software was undervalued by $20,000, what amounts for SoftPlus would appear in PanTech's December 31, 2013, consolidated financial statements?

    b. If the marketing software was overvalued by $20,000, what amounts for SoftPlus would appear in PanTech's December 31, 2013, consolidated financial statements?

LO1

25. On January 1, 2013, Anywhere Tech Company exchanged $840,000 for 40 percent of the outstanding voting stock of Cloud Computing. Especially attractive to Anywhere Tech was a research project underway at Cloud Computing that would enhance both the speed and quantity of client accessible data. Although not recorded in Cloud Computing's financial records, the fair value of the research project was considered to be $1,800,000.

In contractual agreements with the sole owner of the remaining 60 percent of Cloud Computing, Anywhere Tech was granted (1) various decision-making rights over Cloud Computing's operating decisions and (2) special service purchase provisions at below market rates. As a result of these contractual agreements, Anywhere Tech established itself as the primary beneficiary of Cloud Computing. Immediately after the purchase, Anywhere Tech and Cloud Computing presented the following balance sheets:

	Anywhere Tech	Cloud Computing
Cash	$ 45,000	$ 25,000
Investment in Cloud Computing	840,000	
Capitalized software	965,000	140,000
Computer equipment	1,050,000	40,000
Communications equipment	900,000	320,000
Patent		175,000
Total assets	$ 3,800,000	$ 700,000
Long-term debt	(925,000)	(600,000)
Common stock-Anywhere Tech	(2,500,000)	
Common stock-Cloud Computing		(25,000)
Retained earnings	(375,000)	(75,000)
Total liabilities and equity	$(3,800,000)	$(700,000)

Each of the above amounts represents a fair value at January 1, 2013. The fair value of the 60 percent of Cloud Computing shares not owned by Anywhere Tech was $1,260,000.

Prepare an acquisition-date consolidated worksheet for Anywhere Tech and its variable interest entity.

LO2

26. Cairns owns 75 percent of the voting stock of Hamilton, Inc. The parent's interest was acquired several years ago on the date that the subsidiary was formed. Consequently, no goodwill or other allocation was recorded in connection with the acquisition. Cairns uses the equity method in its internal records to account for its investment in Hamilton.

On January 1, 2010, Hamilton sold $1,000,000 in 10-year bonds to the public at 105. The bonds had a cash interest rate of 9 percent payable every December 31. Cairns acquired 40 percent of these bonds at 96 percent of face value on January 1, 2012. Both companies utilize the straight-line method of amortization. Prepare the consolidation worksheet entries to recognize the effects of the intra-entity bonds at each of the following dates.

a. December 31, 2012.

b. December 31, 2013.

c. December 31, 2014.

LO2

27. Highlight, Inc., owns all outstanding stock of Kiort Corporation. The two companies report the following balances for the year ending December 31, 2013:

	Highlight	Kiort
Revenues and interest income	$(670,000)	$(390,000)
Operating and interest expense	540,000	221,000
Other gains and losses	(120,000)	(32,000)
Net income	$(250,000)	$(201,000)

On January 1, 2013, Highlight acquired on the open market bonds for $108,000 originally issued by Kiort. This investment had an effective rate of 8 percent. The bonds had a face value of $100,000 and a cash interest rate of 9 percent. At the date of acquisition, these bonds were shown as liabilities by Kiort with a book value of $84,000 (based on an effective rate of 11 percent). Determine the balances that should appear on a consolidated income statement for 2013.

LO2

28. Several years ago Abrams, Inc., sold $800,000 in bonds to the public. Annual cash interest of 8 percent ($64,000) was to be paid on this debt. The bonds were issued at a discount to yield 10 percent. At the beginning of 2012, Bierman Corporation (a wholly owned subsidiary of Abrams) purchased $100,000 of these bonds on the open market for $121,655, a price based

on an effective interest rate of 6 percent. The bond liability had a book value on that date of $668,778. Assume Abrams uses the equity method to account internally for its investment in Bierman. What consolidation entry would be required for these bonds on

a. December 31, 2012?

b. December 31, 2014?

LO2

29. Opus, Incorporated, owns 90 percent of Bloom Company. On December 31, 2012, Opus acquires half of Bloom's $500,000 outstanding bonds. These bonds had been sold on the open market on January 1, 2010, at a 12 percent effective rate. The bonds pay a cash interest rate of 10 percent every December 31 and are scheduled to come due on December 31, 2020. Bloom issued this debt originally for $435,763. Opus paid $283,550 for this investment, indicating an 8 percent effective yield.

    a. Assuming that both parties use the effective rate method, what gain or loss from the retirement of this debt should be reported on the consolidated income statement for 2012?

    b. Assuming that both parties use the effective rate method, what balances should appear in the Investment in Bloom Bonds account on Opus's records and the Bonds Payable account of Bloom as of December 31, 2013?

    c. Assuming that both parties use the straight-line method, what consolidation entry would be required on December 31, 2013, because of these bonds? Assume that the parent is not applying the equity method.

LO3

30. Hepner Corporation has the following stockholders' equity accounts:

Preferred stock (6% cumulative dividend)	$500,000
Common stock	750,000
Additional paid-in capital	300,000
Retained earnings	950,000

The preferred stock is participating. Wasatch Corporation buys 80 percent of this common stock for $1,600,000 and 70 percent of the preferred stock for $630,000. The acquisition-date fair value of the noncontrolling interest in the common shares was $400,000 and was $270,000 for the preferred shares. All of the subsidiary's assets and liabilities are viewed as having fair values equal to their book values. What amount is attributed to goodwill on the date of acquisition?

LO3

31. Smith, Inc., has the following stockholders' equity accounts as of January 1, 2013:

Preferred stock—$100 par, nonvoting and nonparticipating, 8 percent cumulative dividend	$ 2,000,000
Common stock—$20 par value	4,000,000
Retained earnings	10,000,000

Haried Company purchases all of Smith's common stock on January 1, 2013, for $14,040,000. The preferred stock remains in the hands of outside parties. Any excess acquisition-date fair value will be assigned to franchise contracts with a 40-year life.

During 2013, Smith reports earning $450,000 in net income and pays $360,000 in cash dividends. Haried applies the equity method to this investment.

a. What is the noncontrolling interest's share of consolidated net income for this period?

b. What is the balance in the Investment in Smith account as of December 31, 2013?

c. What consolidation entries are needed for 2013?

LO3

32. Through the payment of $10,468,000 in cash, Drexel Company acquires voting control over Young Company. This price is paid for 60 percent of the subsidiary's 100,000 outstanding common shares ($40 par value) as well as all 10,000 shares of 8 percent, cumulative, $100 par value preferred stock. Of the total payment, $3.1 million is attributed to the fully participating preferred stock with the remainder paid for the common. This acquisition is carried out on January 1, 2013, when Young reports retained earnings of $10 million and a total book value of $15 million. The acquisition-date fair value of the noncontrolling interest in Young's common stock was $4,912,000. On this same date, a building owned by Young (with a 5-year remaining life) is undervalued in the financial records by $200,000, while equipment with a 10-year life is overvalued by $100,000. Any further excess acquisition-date fair value is assigned to a brand name with a 20-year life.

During 2013, Young reports net income of $900,000 while paying $400,000 in cash dividends. Drexel uses the initial value method to account for both of these investments.

Prepare appropriate consolidation entries for 2013.

LO4

33. The following information has been taken from the consolidation worksheet of Peak and its 90 percent–owned subsidiary, Valley:
    - Peak reports a $12,000 gain on the sale of a building. The building had a book value of $32,000 but was sold for $44,000 cash.
    - Intra-entity inventory transfers of $129,000 occurred during the current period.
    - Valley paid a $30,000 dividend during the year with $27,000 of this amount going to Peak.
    - Amortization of an intangible asset recognized by Peak's worksheet was $16,000 for the current period.
    - Consolidated accounts payable decreased by $11,000 during the year.

    Indicate how to reflect each of these events on a consolidated statement of cash flows.

LO4

34. Alford Company and its 80 percent–owned subsidiary, Knight, have the following income statements for 2013:

	Alford	Knight
Revenues	$(500,000)	$(230,000)
Cost of goods sold	300,000	140,000
Depreciation and amortization	40,000	10,000
Other expenses	20,000	20,000
Gain on sale of equipment	(30,000)	–0–
Equity in earnings of Knight	(36,200)	–0–
Net income	$(206,200)	$ (60,000)

Additional Information for 2013

- Intra-entity inventory transfers during the year amounted to $90,000. All intra-entity transfers were downstream from Alford to Knight.
- Unrealized inventory profits at January 1 were $6,000, but at December 31, they are $9,000.
- Annual excess amortization expense resulting from the acquisition is $11,000.
- Knight paid dividends totaling $20,000.
- The noncontrolling interest's share of the subsidiary's income is $9,800.
- During the year, consolidated inventory rose by $11,000 while accounts receivable and accounts payable declined by $8,000 and $6,000, respectively.

Using either the direct or indirect method, compute net cash flows from operating activities during the period for the business combination.

LO5

35. Porter Corporation owns all 30,000 shares of the common stock of Street, Inc. Porter has 60,000 shares of its own common stock outstanding. During the current year, Porter earns income (without any consideration of its investment in Street) of $150,000 while Street reports $130,000. Annual amortization of $10,000 is recognized each year on the consolidation worksheet based on acquisition-date fair-value allocations. Both companies have convertible bonds outstanding. During the current year, bond-related interest expense (net of taxes) is $32,000 for Porter and $24,000 for Street. Porter's bonds can be converted into 8,000 shares of common stock; Street's bonds can be converted into 10,000 shares. Porter owns none of these bonds. What are the earnings per share amounts that Porter should report in its current year consolidated income statement?

LO5

36. Primus, Inc., owns all outstanding stock of Sonston, Inc. For the current year, Primus reports income (exclusive of any investment income) of $600,000. Primus has 100,000 shares of common stock outstanding. Sonston reports net income of $200,000 for the period with 40,000 shares of common stock outstanding. Sonston also has 10,000 stock warrants outstanding that allow the holder to acquire shares at $10 per share. The value of this stock was $20 per share throughout the year. Primus owns 2,000 of these warrants. What amount should Primus report for diluted earnings per share?

LO5

37. Garfun, Inc., owns all of the stock of Simon, Inc. For 2013, Garfun reports income (exclusive of any investment income) of $480,000. Garfun has 80,000 shares of common stock outstanding. It also has 5,000 shares of preferred stock outstanding that pay a dividend of $15,000

per year. Simon reports net income of $290,000 for the period with 80,000 shares of common stock outstanding. Simon also has a liability for 10,000 of $100 bonds that pay annual interest of $8 per bond. Each of these bonds can be converted into three shares of common stock. Garfun owns none of these bonds. Assume a tax rate of 30 percent. What amount should Garfun report as diluted earnings per share?

LO5

38. The following separate income statements are for Mason and its 80 percent–owned subsidiary, Dixon:

	Mason	Dixon
Revenues	$(400,000)	$(300,000)
Expenses	290,000	225,000
Gain on sale of equipment	–0–	(15,000)
Equity earnings of subsidiary	(52,000)	–0–
Net income	$(162,000)	$ (90,000)
Outstanding common shares	50,000	30,000

Additional Information

- Amortization expense resulting from Dixon's excess acquisition-date fair value is $25,000 per year.
- Mason has convertible preferred stock outstanding. Each of these 5,000 shares is paid a dividend of $4 per year. Each share can be converted into four shares of common stock.
- Stock warrants to buy 10,000 shares of Dixon are also outstanding. For $20, each warrant can be converted into a share of Dixon's common stock. The fair value of this stock is $25 throughout the year. Mason owns none of these warrants.
- Dixon has convertible bonds payable that paid interest of $30,000 (after taxes) during the year. These bonds can be exchanged for 20,000 shares of common stock. Mason holds 15 percent of these bonds, which it bought at book value directly from Dixon.

Compute Mason's basic and diluted EPS.

LO6

39. DeMilo, Inc., owns 100 percent of the 40,000 outstanding shares of Ricardo, Inc. DeMilo currently carries the Investment in Ricardo account at $490,000 using the equity method.

Ricardo issues 10,000 new shares to the public for $15.75 per share. How does this transaction affect the Investment in Ricardo account that appears on DeMilo's financial records?

LO6

40. Albuquerque, Inc., acquired 16,000 shares of Marmon Company several years ago for $600,000. At the acquisition date, Marmon reported a book value of $710,000, and Albuquerque assessed the fair value of the noncontrolling interest at $150,000. Any excess of acquisition-date fair value over book value was assigned to broadcast licenses with indefinite lives. Since the acquisition date and until this point, Marmon has issued no additional shares. No impairment has been recognized for the broadcast licenses.

At the present time, Marmon reports $800,000 as total stockholders' equity, which is broken down as follows:

Common stock ($10 par value)	$200,000
Additional paid-in capital	230,000
Retained earnings	370,000
Total	$800,000

View the following as independent situations:

a. Marmon sells 5,000 shares of previously unissued common stock to the public for $47 per share. Albuquerque purchased none of this stock. What journal entry should Albuquerque make to recognize the impact of this stock transaction?

b. Marmon sells 4,000 shares of previously unissued common stock to the public for $33 per share. Albuquerque purchased none of this stock. What journal entry should Albuquerque make to recognize the impact of this stock transaction?

LO6

41. On January 1, 2011, Aronsen Company acquired 90 percent of Siedel Company's outstanding shares. Siedel had a net book value on that date of $480,000: common stock ($10 par value) of $200,000 and retained earnings of $280,000.

Aronsen paid $584,100 for this investment. The acquisition-date fair value of the 10 percent noncontrolling interest was $64,900. The excess fair value over book value associated with the acquisition was used to increase land by $89,000 and to recognize copyrights (16-year remaining life) at $80,000. Subsequent to the acquisition, Aronsen applied the initial value method to its investment account.

In the 2011–2012 period, the subsidiary's retained earnings increased by $100,000. During 2013, Siedel earned income of $80,000 while paying $20,000 in dividends. Also, at the beginning of 2013, Siedel issued 4,000 new shares of common stock for $38 per share to finance the expansion of its corporate facilities. Aronsen purchased none of these additional shares and therefore recorded no entry. Prepare the appropriate 2013 consolidation entries for these two companies.

LO2

42. Pavin acquires all of Stabler's outstanding shares on January 1, 2011, for $460,000 in cash. Of this amount, $30,000 was attributed to equipment with a 10-year remaining life and $40,000 was assigned to trademarks expensed over a 20-year period. Pavin applies the partial equity method so that income is accrued each period based solely on the earnings reported by the subsidiary.

On January 1, 2014, Pavin reports $300,000 in bonds outstanding with a book value of $282,000. Stabler purchases half of these bonds on the open market for $145,500.

During 2014, Pavin begins to sell merchandise to Stabler. During that year, inventory costing $80,000 was transferred at a price of $100,000. All but $10,000 (at sales price) of these goods were resold to outside parties by year-end. Stabler still owes $33,000 for inventory shipped from Pavin during December.

The following financial figures are for the two companies for the year ending December 31, 2014. Prepare a worksheet to produce consolidated balances. (Credits are indicated by parentheses.)

	Pavin	Stabler
Revenues	$ (740,000)	$(505,000)
Cost of goods sold	455,000	240,000
Expenses	125,000	158,500
Interest expense—bonds	36,000	-0-
Interest income—bond investment	-0-	(16,500)
Loss on extinguishment of bonds	-0-	-0-
Equity in Stabler's income	(123,000)	-0-
Net income	$ (247,000)	$(123,000)
Retained earnings, 1/1/14	$ (345,000)	$(361,000)
Net income (above)	(247,000)	(123,000)
Dividends paid	155,000	61,000
Retained earnings, 12/31/14	$ (437,000)	$(423,000)
Cash and receivables	$ 217,000	$ 35,000
Inventory	175,000	87,000
Investment in Stabler	613,000	-0-
Investment in Pavin bonds	-0-	147,000
Land, buildings, and equipment (net)	245,000	541,000
Trademarks	-0-	-0-
Total assets	$ 1,250,000	$ 810,000
Accounts payable	$ (225,000)	$(167,000)
Bonds payable	(300,000)	(100,000)
Discount on bonds	12,000	-0-
Common stock	(300,000)	(120,000)
Retained earnings (above)	(437,000)	(423,000)
Total liabilities and stockholders' equity	$(1,250,000)	$(810,000)

LO2

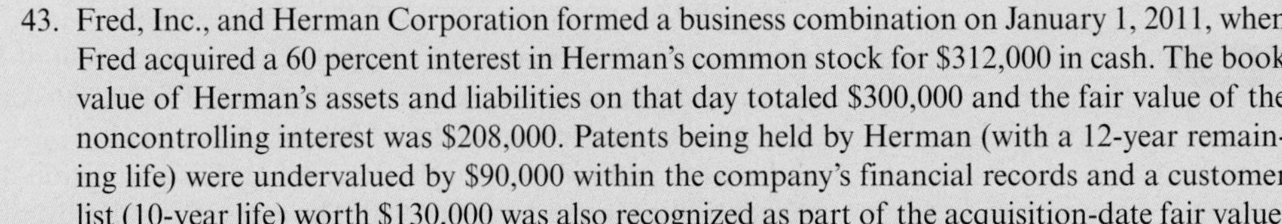

43. Fred, Inc., and Herman Corporation formed a business combination on January 1, 2011, when Fred acquired a 60 percent interest in Herman's common stock for $312,000 in cash. The book value of Herman's assets and liabilities on that day totaled $300,000 and the fair value of the noncontrolling interest was $208,000. Patents being held by Herman (with a 12-year remaining life) were undervalued by $90,000 within the company's financial records and a customer list (10-year life) worth $130,000 was also recognized as part of the acquisition-date fair value.

Intra-entity inventory transfers occur regularly between the two companies. Merchandise carried over from one year to the next is always sold in the subsequent period.

Year	Original Cost to Herman	Transfer Price to Fred	Ending Balance at Transfer Price
2011	80,000	100,000	20,000
2012	100,000	125,000	40,000
2013	90,000	120,000	30,000

Fred had not paid for half of the 2013 inventory transfers by year-end.

On January 1, 2012, Fred sold $15,000 in land to Herman for $22,000. Herman is still holding this land.

On January 1, 2013, Herman acquired $20,000 (face value) of Fred's bonds on the open market. These bonds had an 8 percent cash interest rate. On the date of repurchase, the liability was shown within Fred's records at $21,386, indicating an effective yield of 6 percent. Herman's acquisition price was $18,732 based on an effective interest rate of 10 percent.

Herman indicated earning a net income of $25,000 within its 2013 financial statements. The subsidiary also reported a beginning Retained Earnings balance of $300,000, dividends paid of $4,000, and common stock of $100,000. Herman has not issued any additional common stock since its takeover. The parent company has applied the equity method to record its investment in Herman.

a. Prepare consolidation worksheet adjustments for 2013.

b. Calculate the 2013 balance for the noncontrolling interest's share of consolidated net income. In addition, determine the ending 2013 balance for noncontrolling interest in the consolidated balance sheet.

c. Determine the consolidation worksheet adjustments needed in 2014 in connection with the intra-entity bonds.

LO2, LO3

44. On January 1, 2012, Mona, Inc., acquired 80 percent of Lisa Company's common stock as well as 60 percent of its preferred shares. Mona paid $65,000 in cash for the preferred stock, with a call value of 110 percent of the $50 per share par value. The remaining 40 percent of the preferred shares traded at a $34,000 fair value. Mona paid $552,800 for the common stock. At the acquisition date, the noncontrolling interest in the common stock had a fair value of $138,200. The excess fair value over Lisa's book value was attributed to franchise contracts of $40,000. This intangible asset is being amortized over a 40-year period. Lisa pays all preferred stock dividends (a total of $8,000 per year) on an annual basis. During 2012, Lisa's book value increased by $50,000.

On January 2, 2012, Mona acquired one-half of Lisa's outstanding bonds payable to reduce the business combination's debt position. Lisa's bonds had a face value of $100,000 and paid cash interest of 10 percent per year. These bonds had been issued to the public to yield 14 percent. Interest is paid each December 31. On January 2, 2012, these bonds had a total $88,350 book value. Mona paid $53,310, indicating an effective interest rate of 8 percent.

On January 3, 2012, Mona sold Lisa fixed assets that had originally cost $100,000 but had accumulated depreciation of $60,000 when transferred. The transfer was made at a price of $120,000. These assets were estimated to have a remaining useful life of 10 years.

The individual financial statements for these two companies for the year ending December 31, 2013, are as follows:

	Mona, Inc.	Lisa Company
Sales and other revenues	$ (500,000)	$ (200,000)
Expenses	220,000	120,000
Dividend income—Lisa common stock	(8,000)	–0–
Dividend income—Lisa preferred stock	(4,800)	–0–
Net income	$ (292,800)	$ (80,000)
Retained earnings, 1/1/13	$ (700,000)	$ (500,000)
Net income (above)	(292,800)	(80,000)
Dividends paid—common stock	92,800	10,000
Dividends paid—preferred stock	–0–	8,000
Retained earnings, 12/31/13	$ (900,000)	$ (562,000)

(continued)

	Mona, Inc.	Lisa Company
Current assets	$ 130,419	$ 500,000
Investment in Lisa—common stock	552,800	-0-
Investment in Lisa—preferred stock	65,000	-0-
Investment in Lisa—bonds	51,781	-0-
Fixed assets	1,100,000	800,000
Accumulated depreciation	(300,000)	(200,000)
Total assets	$ 1,600,000	$ 1,100,000
Accounts payable	$ (400,000)	$ (144,580)
Bonds payable	-0-	(100,000)
Discount on bonds payable	-0-	6,580
Common stock	(300,000)	(200,000)
Preferred stock	-0-	(100,000)
Retained earnings, 12/31/13	(900,000)	(562,000)
Total liabilities and equities	$(1,600,000)	$(1,100,000)

a. What consolidation worksheet adjustments would have been required as of January 1, 2012, to eliminate the subsidiary's common and preferred stocks?

b. What consolidation worksheet adjustments would have been required as of December 31, 2012, to account for Mona's purchase of Lisa's bonds?

c. What consolidation worksheet adjustments would have been required as of December 31, 2012, to account for the intra-entity sale of fixed assets?

d. Assume that consolidated financial statements are being prepared for the year ending December 31, 2013. Calculate the consolidated balance for each of the following accounts:

Franchises
Fixed Assets
Accumulated Depreciation
Expenses

LO4

45. Rodriguez Company holds 80 percent of the common stock of Molina, Inc., and 30 percent of this subsidiary's convertible bonds. The following consolidated financial statements are for 2012 and 2013:

Rodriguez Company and Consolidated Subsidiary Molina

	2012	2013
Revenues	$ (850,000)	$ (980,000)
Cost of goods sold	600,000	640,000
Depreciation and amortization	90,000	100,000
Gain on sale of building	-0-	(20,000)
Interest expense	30,000	30,000
Consolidated net income	(130,000)	(230,000)
to noncontrolling interest	9,000	11,000
to parent company	$ (121,000)	$ (219,000)
Retained earnings, 1/1	$ (300,000)	$ (371,000)
Net income	(121,000)	(219,000)
Dividends paid	50,000	100,000
Retained earnings, 12/31	$ (371,000)	$ (490,000)
Cash	$ 80,000	$ 150,000
Accounts receivable	150,000	140,000
Inventory	200,000	340,000
Buildings and equipment (net)	640,000	690,000
Databases	150,000	145,000
Total assets	$ 1,220,000	$ 1,465,000

(continued)

Rodriguez Company and Consolidated Subsidiary Molina

Accounts payable	$ (140,000)	$ (100,000)
Bonds payable	(400,000)	(500,000)
Noncontrolling interest in Molina	(32,000)	(41,000)
Common stock	(100,000)	(130,000)
Additional paid-in capital	(177,000)	(204,000)
Retained earnings	(371,000)	(490,000)
Total liabilities and equities	$(1,220,000)	$(1,465,000)

Additional Information for 2013

- The parent issued bonds during the year for cash.
- Amortization of databases amounts to $5,000 per year.
- The parent sold a building with a cost of $60,000 but a $30,000 book value for cash on May 11.
- The subsidiary purchased equipment on July 23 using cash.
- Late in November, the parent issued stock for cash.
- During the year, the subsidiary paid dividends of $10,000.

Prepare a consolidated statement of cash flows for this business combination for the year ending December 31, 2013. Either the direct or the indirect method may be used.

LO5

46. Following are separate income statements for Austin, Inc., and its 80 percent owned subsidiary, Rio Grande Corporation as well as a consolidated statement for the business combination as a whole.

	Austin	Rio Grande	Consolidated
Revenues	$(700,000)	$(500,000)	$(1,200,000)
Cost of goods sold	400,000	300,000	700,000
Operating expenses	100,000	70,000	195,000
Equity in earnings of Rio Grande	(84,000)		
Individual company net income	$(284,000)	$(130,000)	
Consolidated net income			$ (305,000)
Noncontrolling interest in Rio Grande's income			(21,000)
Consolidated net income attributable to Austin			$ (284,000)

Additional Information

- Annual excess fair over book value amortization of $25,000 resulted from the acquisition.
- The parent applies the equity method to this investment.
- Austin has 50,000 shares of common stock and 10,000 shares of preferred stock outstanding. Owners of the preferred stock are paid an annual dividend of $40,000, and each share can be exchanged for two shares of common stock.
- Rio Grande has 30,000 shares of common stock outstanding. The company also has 5,000 stock warrants outstanding. For $10, each warrant can be converted into a share of Rio Grande's common stock. Austin holds half of these warrants. The price of Rio Grande's common stock was $20 per share throughout the year.
- Rio Grande also has convertible bonds, none of which Austin owned. During the current year, total interest expense (net of taxes) was $22,000. These bonds can be exchanged for 10,000 shares of the subsidiary's common stock.

Determine Austin's basic and diluted EPS.

LO3

47. On January 1, Paisley, Inc., paid $560,000 for all of Skyler Corporation's outstanding stock. This cash payment was based on a price of $180 per share for Skyler's $100 par value preferred stock and $38 per share for its $20 par value common stock. The preferred shares are voting, cumulative, and fully participating. At the acquisition date, the book values of Skyler's accounts equaled their fair values. Any excess fair value is assigned to an intangible asset and will be amortized over a 10-year period.

During the year, Skyler sold inventory costing $60,000 to Paisley for $90,000. All but $18,000 (measured at transfer price) of this merchandise has been resold to outsiders by the end of the year. At the end of the year, Paisley continues to owe Skyler for the last shipment of inventory priced at $28,000.

Also, on January 2, Paisley sold Skyler equipment for $20,000 although it had a book value of only $12,000 (original cost of $30,000). Both companies depreciate such property according to the straight-line method with no salvage value. The remaining life at this date was four years.

The following financial statements are for each company for the year ending December 31. Determine consolidated financial totals for this business combination.

	Paisley, Inc.	Skyler Corporation
Sales	$ (800,000)	$(400,000)
Cost of goods sold	528,000	260,000
Expenses	180,000	130,000
Gain on sale of equipment	(8,000)	–0–
Net income	$ (100,000)	$ (10,000)
Retained earnings, 1/1	$ (400,000)	$(150,000)
Net income	(100,000)	(10,000)
Dividends paid	60,000	–0–
Retained earnings, 12/31	$ (440,000)	$(160,000)
Cash	$ 30,000	$ 40,000
Accounts receivable	300,000	100,000
Inventory	260,000	180,000
Investment in Skyler Corporation	560,000	–0–
Land, buildings, and equipment	680,000	500,000
Accumulated depreciation	(180,000)	(90,000)
Total assets	$ 1,650,000	$ 730,000
Accounts payable	$ (140,000)	$ (90,000)
Long-term liabilities	(240,000)	(180,000)
Preferred stock	–0–	(100,000)
Common stock	(620,000)	(200,000)
Additional paid-in capital	(210,000)	–0–
Retained earnings, 12/31	(440,000)	(160,000)
Total liabilities and equity	$(1,650,000)	$(730,000)

Note: Parentheses indicate a credit balance.

LO4

48. On June 30, 2013, Plaster, Inc., paid $916,000 for 80 percent of Stucco Company's outstanding stock. Plaster assessed the acquisition-date fair value of the 20 percent noncontrolling interest at $229,000. At acquisition date, Stucco reported the following book values for its assets and liabilities:

Cash	$ 60,000
Accounts receivable	127,000
Inventory	203,000
Land	65,000
Buildings	175,000
Equipment	300,000
Accounts payable	(35,000)

On June 30, Plaster allocated the excess acquisition-date fair value over book value to Stucco's assets as follows:

Equipment (3-year life)	$ 75,000
Database (10-year life)	175,000

At the end of 2013, the following comparative (2012 and 2013) balance sheets and consolidated income statement were available:

	Plaster, Inc. December 31, 2012	Consolidated December 31, 2013
Cash	$ 43,000	$ 242,850
Accounts receivable (net)	362,000	485,400
Inventory	415,000	720,000
Land	300,000	365,000
Buildings (net)	245,000	370,000
Equipment (net)	1,800,000	2,037,500
Database	–0–	166,250
Total assets	$3,165,000	$4,387,000
Accounts payable	$ 80,000	$ 107,000
Long-term liabilities	400,000	1,200,000
Common stock	1,800,000	1,800,000
Noncontrolling interest	–0–	255,500
Retained earnings	885,000	1,024,500
Total liabilities and equities	$3,165,000	$4,387,000

PLASTER, INC., AND SUBSIDIARY STUCCO COMPANY
Consolidated Income Statement
For the Year Ended December 31, 2013

Revenues		$1,217,500
Cost of goods sold	$737,500	
Depreciation	187,500	
Database amortization	8,750	
Interest and other expenses	9,750	943,500
Consolidated net income		$ 274,000

Additional Information for 2013

- On December 1, Stucco paid a $40,000 dividend. During the year, Plaster paid $100,000 in dividends.
- During the year, Plaster issued $800,000 in long-term debt at par.
- Plaster reported no asset purchases or dispositions other than the acquisition of Stucco.

Prepare a 2013 consolidated statement of cash flows for Plaster and Stucco. Use the indirect method of reporting cash flows from operating activities.

Develop Your Skills

EXCEL CASE: INTRA-ENTITY BONDS

Place Company owns a majority voting interest in Sassano, Inc. On January 1, 2011, Place issued $1,000,000 of 11 percent 10-year bonds at $943,497.77 to yield 12 percent. On January 1, 2013, Sassano purchased all of these bonds in the open market at a price of $904,024.59 with an effective yield of 13 percent.

Required

Using an Excel spreadsheet, do the following:

1. Prepare amortization schedules for the Place Company bonds payable and the Investment in Place Bonds for Sassano, Inc.
2. Using the values from the amortization schedules, compute the worksheet adjustment for a December 31, 2013, consolidation of Place and Sassano to reflect the effective retirement of the Place bonds. Formulate your solution to be able to accommodate various yield rates (and therefore prices) on the repurchase of the bonds.

Hints

Present value of 1 = $1/(1 + r)^n$
Present value of an annuity of 1 = $(1 - 1/[1 + r]^n)/r$
Where r = effective yield and n = years remaining to maturity

RESEARCH CASE

Find a recent annual report for a firm with business acquisitions (e.g., Compaq, GE). Locate the firm's consolidated statement of cash flows and answer the following:

- Does the firm employ the direct or indirect method of accounting for operating cash flows?
- How does the firm account for the balances in balance sheet operating accounts (e.g., accounts receivable, inventory, accounts payable) in determining operating cash flows?
- Describe the accounting for cash paid for business acquisitions in the statement of cash flows.
- Describe the accounting for any noncontrolling subsidiary interest, acquired in-process research and development costs, and any other business combination–related items in the consolidated statement of cash flows.

FINANCIAL REPORTING RESEARCH AND ANALYSIS CASE

The FASB ASC Subtopic Variable Interest Entities affects thousands of business enterprises that now, as primary beneficiaries, consolidate entities that qualify as controlled VIEs. Retrieve the annual reports of one or more of the following companies (or any others you may find) that consolidate VIEs:

- The Walt Disney Company.
- General Electric.
- ConAgra Foods.
- Time Warner.
- Allegheny Energy.

Required

Write a brief report that describes

1. The reasons for consolidation of the company's VIE(s).
2. The effect of the consolidation of the VIE(s) on the company's financial statements.

chapter

7

Consolidated Financial Statements—Ownership Patterns and Income Taxes

Learning Objectives

After studying this chapter, you should be able to:

- LO1 Understand the implications for the consolidation process when indirect control is present in a grandfather-father-son ownership configuration.
- LO2 Understand the implications for the consolidation process when a corporate ownership structure is characterized by a connecting affiliation.
- LO3 Understand the implications for the consolidation process when a corporate ownership structure is characterized by mutual ownership.
- LO4 List the criteria for being a member of an affiliated group for income tax filing purposes.
- LO5 Compute taxable income and deferred tax amounts for an affiliated group based on information presented in a consolidated set of financial statements.
- LO6 Compute taxable income and deferred tax amounts to be recognized when separate tax returns are filed by any of the affiliates of a business combination.
- LO7 Determine the deferred tax consequences for temporary differences generated when a business combination is created.
- LO8 Explain the impact that a net operating loss of an acquired affiliate has on consolidated figures.

Chapter 7 concludes coverage of the accounting for business combinations by analyzing two additional aspects of consolidated financial statements. First, we present the various ownership patterns that can exist within a combination. We examine indirect control of a subsidiary, connecting affiliations, and mutual ownership as well as the consolidation procedures applicable to each organizational structure. The chapter then provides an overview of the income tax considerations relevant to the members of a business combination. We discuss income tax accounting for both consolidated and separate corporate returns in light of current laws.

Indirect Subsidiary Control

Previous chapters presented primarily one type of business combination. Specifically, a parent typically holds a direct financial interest in a single subsidiary. This ownership pattern expedites the explanation of consolidation theories and techniques. In practice, though, more elaborate corporate structures commonly exist. General Electric Company (GE), for example, controls literally scores of subsidiaries. However, GE directly owns voting stock in relatively few of these companies. It maintains control through indirect ownership because GE's subsidiaries hold the stock of many of the companies within the business combination. For example, GE, the parent company, owns GE Capital, which in turn has controlling interests in other companies. This type of corporate configuration is referred to as a *father-son-grandson relationship* because of the pattern the descending tiers create.

Forming a business combination as a series of indirect ownerships is not an unusual practice. Many businesses organize their operations in this manner to group individual companies along product lines, geographic districts, or other logical criteria. The philosophy behind this structuring is that placing direct control in proximity to each subsidiary can develop clearer lines of communication and responsibility reporting. However, other indirect ownership patterns are simply the result of

LO1

Understand the implications for the consolidation process when indirect control is present in a grandfather-father-son ownership configuration.

years of acquisition and growth. As an example, when Procter & Gamble acquired the Gillette Company in 2005, it gained control over Gillette's subsidiaries including Oral-B Laboratories, Braun AG, and others. Procter & Gamble did not achieve this control directly, but indirectly through the acquisition of the parent company.

The Consolidation Process When Indirect Control Is Present

Regardless of a company's reason for establishing indirect control over a subsidiary, a new accounting problem emerges: The parent must consolidate financial information from each of the connecting corporations into a single set of financial statements. Fortunately, indirect ownership does not introduce any new conceptual issues but affects only the mechanical elements of this process. For example, in preparing consolidated statements, the parent company must allocate acquisition-date fair values and recognize any related excess amortizations for each affiliate regardless of whether control is direct or indirect. In addition, all worksheet entries previously demonstrated continue to apply. For business combinations involving indirect control, the entire consolidation process is basically repeated for each separate affiliate.

Calculation of Subsidiary Income

Although the presence of an indirect ownership does not change most consolidation procedures, a calculation of each subsidiary's accrual-based income does pose some difficulty. Appropriate income determination is essential for calculating (1) equity income accruals and (2) the noncontrolling interest's share of consolidated net income.

In combinations with indirect control, at least one company (and possibly many) holds both a parent and a subsidiary position. A company in that position must first recognize the equity income accruing from its subsidiaries before computing its own income total. The process begins with the grandson, then moves to the son, and finishes with the father. Only by following this systematic approach is the correct amount of accrual-based income determined for each individual company.

In computing consolidated net income, we adjust the subsidiary's reported earnings for excess fair-value amortizations and any upstream intra-entity transfers. In combinations with indirect control, these same adjustments are made for each company's separate operating income, beginning at the lowest level. The respective accrual-based income figures for each affiliate in the consolidated entity therefore must take into account

- Excess acquisition-date fair over book value amortizations.
- Deferrals and subsequent income recognition from intra-entity transfers. The income effects can include gains from long-term asset transfers or gross profits from inventory transfers. In subsequent illustrations, we refer to both types as "gains."

Income Computation Illustrated

For example, assume that three companies form a business combination: Top Company owns 70 percent of Midway Company, which, in turn, possesses 60 percent of Bottom Company. As the following display indicates, Top controls both subsidiaries, although the parent's relationship with Bottom is only of an indirect nature.

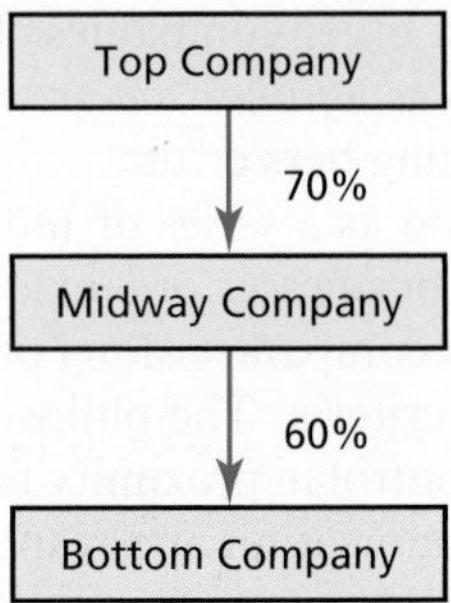

Assume next that the following information comes from the 2013 individual financial records of the three companies making up this combination:

	Top Company	Midway Company	Bottom Company
Internally calculated operating income	$600,000	$300,000	$100,000
Dividend income from investment in subsidiary (based on initial value method) . . .	80,000	50,000	
Internally calculated net income	$680,000	$350,000	$100,000
Additional information:			
Net deferred intra-entity gains within current year income	$110,000	$ 80,000	$ 20,000
Amortization expense relating to excess fair value over book value of investment . .	30,000	25,000	–0–

As specified, we begin with the grandson of the organization and calculate each company's 2013 accrual-based income. From the perspective of the business combination, Bottom's income for the period is only $55,000 after deferring the $20,000 in net intra-entity gains and recognizing the $25,000 excess amortization associated with the acquisition by Midway. Thus, $55,000 is the basis for the equity accrual by its parent and noncontrolling interest recognition. Once the grandson's income has been derived, this figure then is used to compute the accrual-based earnings of the son, Midway:

Internally calculated operating income—Midway Company		$300,000
Equity income accruing from Bottom Company—		
Bottom's income from internal records	$100,000	
Excess amortization related to Midway acquisition.	(25,000)	
Intra-entity gain deferral	(20,000)	
Bottom's accrual-based income	$ 55,000	
Midway's percentage ownership	60%	
Midway's share of Bottom's income		33,000
Excess amortization from Top's acquisition of Midway.		(30,000)
Deferral of Midway's intra-entity gain (above)		(80,000)
Accrual-based income of Midway Company		$223,000

Midway's $223,000 accrual-based income figure varies significantly from the company's internally calculated profit of $350,000. This difference is not unusual and merely reflects an appropriate consolidated perspective in viewing the position of the company within the affiliated ownership structure and the consequent effects of excess amortization and intra-entity transfers. Continuing with the successive derivation of each company's earnings, we now can determine Top's income. After computing the son's earnings, the father's earnings are derived as follows:

Internally calculated operating income —Top Company	$600,000
Equity income accruing from Midway Company—70% of $223,000	156,100
Deferral of Top's intra-entity gain (above)	(110,000)
Accrual-based income of Top.	$646,100

We should note several aspects of the accrual-based income data:

1. The 2013 income statement for Top Company and its consolidated subsidiaries discloses an $88,900 balance as the "noncontrolling interests' share of subsidiary

income." The total accrual-based income figures of the two subsidiaries provide the basis for the calculation as follows:

	Accrual-Based Income	Outside Ownership	Noncontrolling Interest in Income
Bottom Company.	$ 55,000	40%	$22,000
Midway Company	223,000	30	66,900
Total			$88,900

2. Although this illustration applies the initial value method to both investments, the parent's individual accounting does not affect accrual-based income totals. The initial value figures are simply replaced with equity accruals in preparation for consolidation. The selection of a particular method is relevant only for internal reporting purposes; earnings, as shown here, are based entirely on the equity income accruing from each subsidiary.
3. As demonstrated previously, if appropriate equity accruals are recognized, the sum of the parent's accrual-based income and the noncontrolling interest income share serves as a "proof figure" for the consolidated total. Thus, if the consolidation process is performed correctly, the earnings this entire organization reports should equal $735,000 ($646,100 + $88,900). Observe that consolidated net income can also be computed as follows:

Sum of Top, Midway, and Bottom operating incomes	$1,000,000
Less: Combined excess fair-value amortizations	(55,000)
Less: Combined intra-entity gain deferrals	(210,000)
Consolidated net income	$ 735,000

4. When indirect control is established, a difference exists between the percentage of stock held and the income contributed to the business combination by a subsidiary. In this illustration, Midway possesses 60 percent of Bottom's voting stock, but, mathematically, only 42 percent of Bottom's income is attributed to Top's controlling interest (70% direct ownership of Midway × 60% indirect ownership of Bottom). The remaining income earned by this subsidiary is assigned to the owners outside the combination.

   The validity of this 42 percent accrual is not readily apparent. Therefore, we construct an elementary example to demonstrate the mathematical accuracy of this percentage. Assume that neither Top nor Midway reports any earnings during the year but that Bottom has $100 in accrual-based income. If Bottom declares a $100 cash dividend, $60 goes to Midway and the remaining $40 goes to Bottom's noncontrolling interest. Assuming then that Midway uses this $60 to pay its own dividend, $42 (70 percent) is transferred to Top and $18 goes to Midway's outside owners.

   Thus, 58 percent of Bottom's income should be attributed to parties outside the business combination. An initial 40 percent belongs to Bottom's own noncontrolling interest and an additional 18 percent accrues eventually to Midway's other shareholders. Consequently, only 42 percent of Bottom's original income is considered earned by the combination. Consolidated financial statements reflect this allocation by including 100 percent of the subsidiary's revenues and expenses and simultaneously recognizing a reduction for the 58 percent of the subsidiary's net income attributable to the noncontrolling interest.

Consolidation Process—Indirect Control

After analyzing the income calculations within a father-son-grandson configuration, a full-scale consolidation can be produced. As demonstrated, this type of ownership pattern does not alter significantly the worksheet process. Most worksheet entries are simply made twice: first for the son's investment in the grandson and then for the father's ownership of the son. Although this sudden doubling of entries may seem overwhelming, close examination reveals that the individual procedures remain unaffected.

To illustrate, assume that on January 1, 2011, Big acquires 80 percent of Middle's outstanding common stock for $640,000. On that date, Middle has a book value (total stockholders' equity) of $700,000 and the 20 percent noncontrolling interest has a fair value of $160,000. The resulting excess of subsidiary fair value over book value is assigned to franchises and amortized at the rate of $10,000 per year.

Following the acquisition, Middle's book value rises to $1,080,000 by the end of 2013, denoting a $380,000 increment during this three-year period ($1,080,000 − $700,000). Big applies the partial equity method; therefore, the parent accrues a $304,000 ($380,000 × 80%) increase in the investment account (to $944,000) over this same time span.

On January 1, 2012, Middle acquires 70 percent of Little for $462,000. Little's stockholders' equity accounts total $630,000 and the fair value of the 30 percent noncontrolling interest is $198,000. Middle allocates this entire $30,000 excess fair value to franchises so that, over a 6-year assumed life, the business combination amortization recognizes an expense of $5,000 each year. During 2012–2013, Little's book value increases by $150,000, to a $780,000 total. Because Middle also applies the partial equity method, it adds $105,000 ($150,000 × 70%) to the investment account to arrive at a $567,000 balance ($462,000 + $105,000).

To complete the introductory information for this illustration, assume that a number of intra-entity upstream transfers occurred over the past two years. The following table shows the dollar volume of these transactions and the unrealized gross profit in each year's ending inventory:

	Little Company Transfers to Middle Company		Middle Company Transfers to Big Company	
Year	Transfer Price	Year-End Deferred Gross Profit	Transfer Price	Year-End Deferred Gross Profit
2012	$ 75,000	$17,500	$200,000	$30,000
2013	120,000	25,000	250,000	40,000

Exhibit 7.1, on pages 306–307, presents the worksheet to consolidate these three companies for the year ending December 31, 2013. The first three columns represent the individual statements for each organization. The entries required to consolidate the various balances follow this information. To identify the separate procedures, entries concerning the relationship between Big (father) and Middle (son) are marked with a "B," whereas an "L" denotes Middle's ownership of Little (grandson). Duplicating entries in this exhibit are designed to facilitate a clearer understanding of this consolidation. A number of these dual entries can be combined later.

To arrive at consolidated figures, Exhibit 7.1 incorporates the worksheet entries described next. Analyzing each of these adjustments and eliminations can identify the consolidation procedures necessitated by a father-son-grandson ownership pattern. Despite the presence of indirect control over Little, financial statements are created for the business combination as a whole utilizing the process described in previous chapters.

*Consolidation Entry *G*

Entry ***G** defers the intra-entity gross profits contained in the beginning financial figures. Within their separate accounting systems, two of the companies prematurely recorded income ($17,500 by Little and $30,000 by Middle) in 2012 at the transfer. For consolidation purposes, a 2013 worksheet entry eliminates these gross profits from both beginning Retained Earnings as well as Cost of Goods Sold (the present location of the beginning inventory). Consequently, the consolidated income statement recognizes the appropriate gross profit for the current period.

EXHIBIT 7.1

BIG COMPANY AND CONSOLIDATED SUBSIDIARIES
Consolidation Worksheet
For Year Ending December 31, 2013

Indirect Control: Father-Son-Grandson
Investment: Partial Equity Method

Accounts	Big Company	Middle Company	Little Company	Consolidation Entries Debit	Consolidation Entries Credit	Noncontrolling Interest	Consolidated Totals
Income Statement							
Sales	(800,000)	(500,000)	(300,000)	(LTI) 120,000			(1,230,000)
				(BTI) 250,000			
Cost of goods sold	300,000	220,000	140,000	(LG) 25,000	(L*G) 17,500		307,500
					(LTI) 120,000		
				(BG) 40,000	(B*G) 30,000		
					(BTI) 250,000		
Expenses	200,000	80,000	60,000	(LE) 5,000			355,000
				(BE) 10,000			
Income of Little Company	–0–	(70,000)	–0–	(LI) 70,000			–0–
Income of Middle Company	(216,000)	–0–	–0–	(BI) 216,000			–0–
Separate company income	(516,000)	(270,000)	100,000				
Consolidated net income							(567,500)
Noncontrolling interest in Little Company's net income						(26,250)	26,250
Noncontrolling interest in Middle Company's net income						(48,250)	48,250
Consolidated net income to parent							(493,000)
Statement of Retained Earnings							
Retained earnings, 1/1/13:							
Big Company	(900,000)	–0–	–0–	(B*C) 52,600			(847,400)
Middle Company	–0–	(800,000)	–0–	(B*G) 30,000			–0–
				(L*C) 15,750			
				(BS) 754,250			
Little Company	–0–	–0–	(600,000)	(L*G) 17,500			–0–
				(LS) 582,500			
Net income (from above)	(516,000)	(270,000)	(100,000)				(493,000)
Dividends paid:							
Big Company	120,000	–0–	–0–				120,000
Middle Company	–0–	90,000	–0–		(BD) 72,000	18,000	–0–
Little Company	–0–	–0–	50,000		(LD) 35,000	15,000	–0–
Retained earnings, 12/31/13	(1,296,000)	(980,000)	(650,000)				(1,220,400)

Accounts	Big Company	Middle Company	Little Company	Consolidation Entries Debit	Consolidation Entries Credit	Noncontrolling Interest	Consolidated Totals
Balance Sheet							
Cash and receivables	600,000	300,000	280,000				1,180,000
Inventory	300,000	260,000	290,000		(LG) 25,000		785,000
					(BG) 40,000		
Investment in Middle Company	944,000	–0–	–0–	(BD) 72,000	(B*C) 52,600		–0–
					(BS) 683,400		
					(BI) 216,000		
					(BA) 64,000		
Investment in Little Company	–0–	567,000	–0–	(LD) 35,000	(L*C) 15,750		–0–
					(LS) 498,750		
					(LI) 70,000		
					(LA) 17,500		
Land, buildings, equipment	192,000	153,000	510,000				855,000
Franchises	–0–	–0–	–0–	(LA) 25,000	(LE) 5,000		90,000
				(BA) 80,000	(BE) 10,000		
Total assets	2,036,000	1,280,000	1,080,000				2,910,000
Liabilities	(340,000)	(200,000)	(300,000)				(840,000)
Noncontrolling interest in Little Company, 1/1/13	–0–	–0–	–0–		(LS) 213,750 (LA) 7,500	(221,250)	
Noncontrolling interest in Middle Company, 1/1/13	–0–	–0–	–0–		(BS) 170,850 (BA) 16,000	(186,850)	
Total noncontrolling interest, 12/31/13	–0–	–0–	–0–			449,600	(449,600)
Common stock:							
Big Company	(400,000)	–0–	–0–				(400,000)
Middle Company	–0–	(100,000)	–0–	(BS) 100,000			–0–
Little Company	–0–	–0–	(130,000)	(LS) 130,000			–0–
Retained earnings (above)	(1,296,000)	(980,000)	(650,000)				(1,220,400)
Total liabilities and equities	(2,036,000)	(1,280,000)	(1,080,000)	2,630,600	2,630,600		(2,910,000)

Note: Parentheses indicate a credit balance.
Consolidation entries: Entries labeled with a "B" refer to the investment relationship between Big and Middle. Entries with an "L" refer to Middle's ownership of Little.

(*G) Removal of unrealized gross profit from beginning inventory figures so that it can be recognized in current period.
(*C) Conversion of partial equity method to equity method. Amortization for prior years is recognized along with effects of beginning unrealized upstream gross profits.
(S) Elimination of subsidiaries' stockholders' equity accounts along with recognition of January 1, noncontrolling interests.
(A) Allocation to franchises, unamortized balance being recognized as of January 1.
(I) Elimination of intra-entity income accrued during the period.
(D) Elimination of intra-entity dividends.
(E) Recognition of amortization expense for the current period.
(TI) Elimination of intra-entity sales/purchases balances created by the transfer of inventory.
(G) Removal of unrealized inventory gross profit from ending figures so that it can be recognized in subsequent period.

*Consolidation Entry *C*

Neither Big nor Middle applies the full equity method to its investments; therefore, the figures recognized during the years prior to the current period (2013) must now be updated on the worksheet. This process begins with the son's ownership of the grandson. Hence, Middle must reduce its 2012 income (now closed into Retained Earnings) by $3,500 to reflect the amortization applicable to that year. Middle did not record this expense in applying the partial equity method.

In addition, because $17,500 of Little's previously reported earnings have just been deferred (in preceding Entry ***G**), the effect of this reduction on Middle's ownership must also be recognized. The parent's original equity accrual for 2012 is based on reported rather than accrual-based profit, thus recording too much income. Little's deferral necessitates Middle's parallel $12,250 decrease ($17,500 × 70%). Consequently, the worksheet reduces Middle's Retained Earnings balance as of January 1, 2013, and the Investment in Little account by a total of $15,750:

Reduction in Middle's Beginning Retained Earnings

2012 amortization expense ($5,000 × 70%)	$ 3,500
Income effect created by Little's deferral of 2012 unrealized gross profit (reduction of previous accrual) ($17,500 × 70%)	12,250
Required reduction to Middle's beginning retained earnings (Entry **L*C**)	$15,750

A similar equity adjustment is required in connection with Big's ownership of Middle. The calculation of the specific amount to be recorded follows the same procedure identified earlier for Middle's investment in Little. Again, amortization expense for all prior years (2011 and 2012, in this case) is brought into the consolidation as well as the income reduction created by the deferral of Middle's $30,000 unrealized gross profit (Entry ***G**). *However, recognition also must be given to the effects associated with the $15,750 decrease in Middle's pre-2013 earnings described in the previous paragraph.* Although recorded only on the worksheet, this adjustment is a change in Middle's originally reported income. To reflect Big's ownership of Middle, the effect of this reduction must be included in determining the income balances actually accruing to the parent company. Thus, a $52,600 decrease is needed in Big's beginning Retained Earnings to establish the proper accounting for its subsidiaries:

Reduction in Big's Beginning Retained Earnings

Amortization expense relating to Middle Company acquisition—2011–2012 ($10,000 per year × 80%).	$16,000
Income effect created by Middle Company's deferral of intra-entity gross profit ($30,000 × 80%).	24,000
Income effect created by Middle Company's adjustment to its prior year's investment income ($15,750 × 80%) (above).	12,600
Required reduction to Big's beginning retained earnings (Entry **B*C**)	$52,600

Consolidation Entry S

The beginning stockholders' equity accounts of each subsidiary are eliminated here and noncontrolling interest balances as of the beginning of the year are recognized. As in previous chapters, the preliminary adjustments described earlier directly affect the amounts involved in this entry. Because Entry ***G** removed a $17,500 beginning inventory profit, Little's January 1, 2013, book value on the worksheet is $712,500, not $730,000. This total is the basis for the $213,750 beginning noncontrolling interest (30%) and the $498,750 elimination (70%) from the parent's investment account.

Similarly, Entries ***G** ($30,000) and ***C** ($15,750) have already decreased Middle's book value by $45,750. Thus, this company's beginning stockholders' equity accounts are now adjusted to a total of $854,250 ($900,000 − $45,750). This balance leads to a $170,850 initial noncontrolling interest valuation (20%) and a $683,400 (80%) offset against Big's Investment in Middle account.

Consolidation Entry A

The unamortized franchise balances remaining as of January 1, 2013, are removed from the two investment accounts so that this intangible asset can be identified separately on the consolidated balance sheet. Because Entry *C already recognizes amortization expense for the previous periods, only beginning totals for the year of $25,000 ($30,000 − $5,000) and $80,000 ($100,000 − $20,000) still remain from the original amounts paid. These totals are allocated across the controlling and noncontrolling interests.

Consolidation Entry I

This entry eliminates the current intra-entity income figures accrued by each parent through its application of the partial equity method.

Consolidation Entry D

Intra-entity dividends distributed during the year are removed here from the consolidated financial totals.

Consolidation Entry E

The annual amortization expense relating to each of the franchise balances is recorded.

Consolidation Entry TI

The intra-entity sales/purchases figures created by the transfer of inventory during 2013 are eliminated on the worksheet.

Consolidation Entry G

This final consolidation entry defers the intra-entity inventory gross profits that remain unearned as of December 31, 2013. The profit on these transfers is removed until the merchandise is subsequently sold to unrelated parties.

Noncontrolling Interests' Share of Consolidated Income

To complete the steps that constitute this consolidation worksheet, the 2013 income accruing to owners outside the business combination must be recognized. This allocation is based on the accrual-based earnings of the two subsidiaries, which, as previously discussed, are calculated beginning with the grandson (Little) followed by the son (Middle):

Little Company's Accrual-Based Income and Noncontrolling Interest

Internally calculated operating income (from Exhibit 7.1)	$100,000
Excess fair-value franchise amortization from acquisition by Middle	(5,000)
Recognition of previously deferred gross profits from 2012 (Entry **L*G**)	17,500
Deferral of intra-entity gross profits as of 12/31/13 (Entry **LG**)	(25,000)
Little Company's accrual-based income, 2013	$ 87,500
Outside ownership	30%
Noncontrolling interest in Little Company's income	$ 26,250

Middle Company's Accrual-Based Income and Noncontrolling Interest

Internally calculated operating income (from Exhibit 7.1 after removing income of Little Company)	$200,000
Excess fair-value franchise amortization from acquisition by Big	(10,000)
Recognition of gross profits previously deferred from 2012 (Entry **B*G**)	30,000
Deferral of intra-entity gross profits as of 12/31/13 (Entry **BG**)	(40,000)
Equity income accruing from Little Company (70% of $87,500 accrual-based income [above])	61,250
Middle Company's accrual-based income, 2013	$241,250
Outside ownership	20%
Noncontrolling interest in Middle Company's income	$ 48,250

Although computation of Big's earnings is not required here, this figure, along with the consolidated income allocations to the noncontrolling interests, verifies the accuracy of the worksheet process:

Big Company's Accrual-Based Income

Internally calculated operating income (from Exhibit 7.1, not including income of Middle Company)	$300,000
Equity income accruing from Middle Company (80% of $241,250 accrual-based income [prior schedule])	193,000
Big Company's accrual-based income, 2013	$493,000

This $493,000 figure represents the income derived by the parent from its own operations plus the earnings accrued from the company's two subsidiaries (one directly owned and the other indirectly controlled). This balance equals Big Company's share of the consolidated income of the business combination. As Exhibit 7.1 shows, the income reported by Big Company does, indeed, net to this same total: $493,000.

Indirect Subsidiary Control—Connecting Affiliation

LO2

Understand the implications for the consolidation process when a corporate ownership structure is characterized by a connecting affiliation.

The father-son-grandson organization is only one of many corporate ownership patterns. The number of possible configurations found in today's business world is almost limitless. To illustrate the consolidation procedures that accompany these alternative patterns, we briefly discuss a second basic ownership structure referred to as a *connecting affiliation*.

It exists when two or more companies within a business combination own an interest in another member of that organization. The simplest form of this configuration is frequently drawn as a triangle:

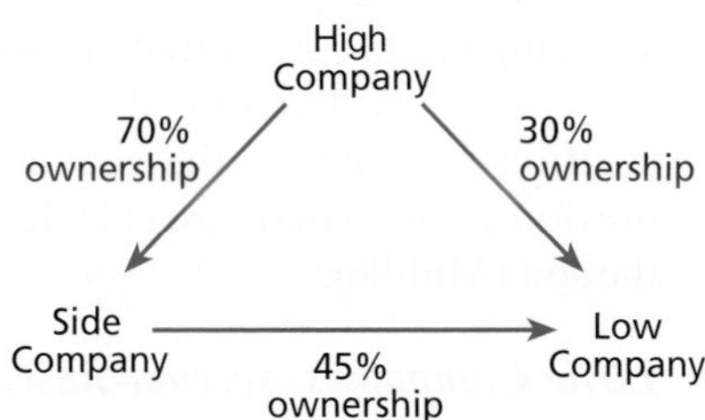

In this example, both High Company and Side Company maintain an ownership interest in Low Company, thus creating a connecting affiliation. Although neither of these individual companies possesses enough voting stock to establish direct control over Low's operations, the combination's members hold a total of 75 percent of the outstanding shares. Consequently, control lies within the single economic entity's boundaries and requires inclusion of Low's financial information as a part of consolidated statements.

On the date the parent obtains control, the valuation basis for the subsidiary in the parent's consolidated statements is established. For Low, we assume that Side Company's ownership preceded that of High's. Subsequently, High obtained control upon acquiring its 30 percent interest in Low and the valuation basis for inclusion of Low's assets and liabilities (and related excess fair value over book value amortization) was established at that date.

The process for consolidating a connecting affiliation is essentially the same as for a father-son-grandson organization. Perhaps the most noticeable difference is that more than two investments are always present. In this triangular business combination, High owns an interest in both Side and Low while Side also maintains an investment in Low. Thus, unless combined in some manner, three separate sets of consolidation entries appear on the worksheet. Although the added number of entries certainly provides a degree of mechanical complication, the basic concepts involved in the consolidation process remain the same regardless of the number of investments.

As with the father-son-grandson structure, one key aspect of the consolidation process warrants additional illustration: the determination of accrual-based income figures for each individual company. Therefore, assume that High, Side, and Low have separate internally calculated operating incomes (without inclusion of any earnings from their subsidiaries) of $300,000, $200,000, and $100,000, respectively. Each company also retains a $30,000 net intra-entity gain in its current year income figures. Assume that annual amortization expense of $10,000 has been identified within the acquisition-date excess fair value over book value for each of the two subsidiaries.

In the same manner as a father-son-grandson organization, determining accrual-based earnings begins with any companies solely in a subsidiary position (Low, in this case). Next companies that are both parents and subsidiaries (Side) compute their accrual-based income. Finally, this same calculation is made for the one company (High) that has ultimate control over the entire combination. Accrual-based income figures for the three companies in this combination are derived as follows:

Low Company's Accrual-Based Income and Noncontrolling Interest

Internally computed operating income	$100,000
Amortization expense from High and Side Companies' acquisition	(10,000)
Deferral of Low Company's net intra-entity gain	(30,000)
Low Company's accrual-based income	$ 60,000
Outside ownership	25%
Noncontrolling interest in Low Company's income	$ 15,000

Side Company's Accrual-Based Income and Noncontrolling Interest

Internally computed operating income	$200,000
Amortization expense relating to High Company's acquisition	(10,000)
Deferral of Side Company's net intra-entity gain	(30,000)
Equity income accruing from Low Company (45% × $60,000)	27,000
Side Company's accrual-based income	$187,000
Outside ownership	30%
Noncontrolling interest in Side Company's income	$ 56,100

High Company's Accrual-Based Income

Internally computed operating income	$300,000
Deferral of High Company's net intra-entity gain	(30,000)
Equity income accruing from Side Company (70% × $187,000)	130,900
Equity income accruing from Low Company—direct ownership (30% × $60,000)	18,000
High Company's income	$418,900

Although in this illustration a connecting affiliation exists, the basic tenets of the consolidation process remain the same:

- Remove all effects from intra-entity transfers.
- Adjust the parents' beginning Retained Earnings to recognize the equity income resulting from ownership of the subsidiaries in prior years. Determining accrual-based earnings for this period properly aligns the balances with the perspective of a single economic entity.
- Eliminate the beginning stockholders' equity accounts of each subsidiary and recognize the noncontrolling interests' figures as of the first day of the year.
- Enter all unamortized balances created by the original acquisition-date excess of fair value over book value onto the worksheet and allocated to controlling and noncontrolling interests.

- Recognize amortization expense for the current year.
- Remove intra-entity income and dividends.
- Compute the noncontrolling interests' share of the subsidiaries' net income (as just shown) and include it in the business combination's financial statements.

Mutual Ownership

LO3

Understand the implications for the consolidation process when a corporate ownership structure is characterized by mutual ownership.

One specific corporate structure that requires further analysis is a mutual ownership. This type of configuration exists when two companies within a business combination hold an equity interest in each other. This ownership pattern is sometimes created as a result of financial battles that occur during takeover attempts. A defensive strategy (often called the *Pac-Man Defense*) is occasionally adopted whereby the target company attempts to avoid takeover by reversing roles and acquiring shares of its investor. Consequently, the two parties hold shares of each other, and one usually gains control.

Two typical mutual ownership patterns follow. In situation A, the parent and the subsidiary possess a percentage of each other's voting shares; in situation B, the mutual ownership exists between two subsidiary companies:

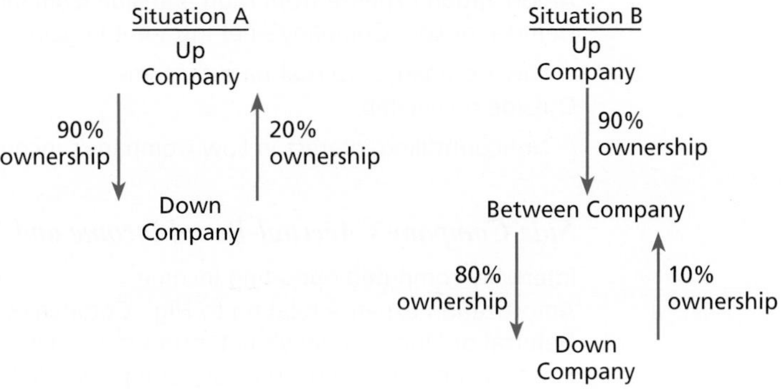

Accounting for mutual ownership raises unique conceptual issues. These concerns center on handling any parent company stock owned by a subsidiary. According to the FASB ASC (para. 810-10-45-5):

> Shares of the parent held by a subsidiary shall not be treated as outstanding shares in the consolidated statement of financial position and, therefore, shall be eliminated in the consolidated financial statements and reflected as treasury shares.

This approach has theoretical merit because ownership of parent shares by its subsidiary does not involve parties outside of the affiliated group. For consolidation purposes, no accounting distinction is drawn between the parent reacquiring its own shares and the same transaction made by its subsidiary. The acquisition of treasury shares by either a parent or its controlled subsidiary represents an identical economic event that should have identical financial reporting implications.

Treasury Stock Approach

The treasury stock approach to mutual ownership focuses on the parent's control over the subsidiary. Although the affiliated companies maintain separate legal incorporation, only a single economic entity exists, and the parent dominates it. Hence, either company can purchase stock or other items, but all reporting for the business combination must be from the parent's perspective. The focus on the parent's perspective is underscored by the fundamental purpose of consolidated financial statements as observed in the FASB ASC (para. 810-10-10-1):

> The purpose of consolidated financial statements is to present, primarily for the benefit of the owners and creditors of the parent, the results of operations and the financial position of a parent and all its subsidiaries as if the consolidated group were a single economic entity.

Therefore, as a single economic entity, the purchase of the parent's shares by any of the affiliated members is reported as treasury stock in the consolidated financial statements.

The treasury stock approach has always been common in practice, although its popularity was undoubtedly based as much on the ease of application as on theoretical merit. *The cost of parent shares held by the subsidiary is simply reclassified on the worksheet into a treasury stock account.* Any dividend payments on this stock are considered intra-entity cash transfers that must be eliminated. This reporting technique is straightforward, and the shares are indeed no longer accounted for as if they were outstanding.

Mutual Ownership Illustrated

To illustrate the treasury stock approach, assume that on January 1, 2011, Sun Company purchased 10 percent of Pop Company. Sun paid $120,000 for these shares, an amount that exactly equaled Pop's proportionate book value. Many possible reasons exist for this transaction. The acquisition could be simply an investment or an attempt to forestall a takeover move by Pop. To simplify the illustration, it is assumed that Pop's shares are not traded actively and therefore continuous market values are unavailable. Under these circumstances, Sun's books appropriately carry the investment in Pop at the $120,000 initial value.

On January 1, 2012, Pop manages to gain control over Sun by acquiring a 70 percent ownership interest, thus creating a business combination. Details of the acquisition are as follows:

Consideration transferred for 70% interest	$504,000
30% noncontrolling interest acquisition-date fair value	216,000
Sun Company total fair value	$720,000
Sun Company's reported book value	600,000
Excess fair value over book value—assigned to franchise contracts (40-year life)	$120,000
Annual additional amortization ($120,000 over 40 years)	$ 3,000
Investment is accounted for internally by the initial value method.	

During the ensuing years, the two companies report these balances and transactions:

	Sun Company			Pop Company		
Year	Reported Operating Income	Dividend Income (10% ownership)	Dividends Paid	Reported Operating Income	Dividend Income (70% ownership)	Dividends Paid
2011	$20,000	$3,000	$ 8,000	$ 90,000	–0–	$30,000
2012	30,000	5,000	10,000	130,000	$ 7,000	50,000
2013	40,000	8,000	15,000	160,500	10,500	80,000

Treasury Stock Approach Illustrated

Exhibit 7.2 presents the consolidation of Pop and Sun for 2013. This worksheet has been developed under the treasury stock approach to mutual ownership so that Pop's investment in Sun is consolidated along routine lines.

Following the calculation of the franchise value and amortization, regular worksheet entries are developed for Pop's investment. Because the initial value method is applied, the $7,000 dividend income recognized in the prior years of ownership (only 2012, in this case) is converted to an equity accrual in Entry ***C.** The parent should recognize 70 percent of the subsidiary's $35,000 income for 2012, or $24,500.[1] However, inclusion

[1] Although an intra-entity transfer, the $5,000 dividend received from Pop is included here in measuring the subsidiary's previous income. This cash distribution increased Sun's book value; thus, some accounting must be made within the consolidation process. In addition, at the time of payment, the parent reduced its Retained Earnings. Hence, the intra-entity portion of this dividend must be reinstated or consolidated Retained Earnings will be too low.

EXHIBIT 7.2

Investment: Initial Value Method
Mutual Ownership:
Treasury Stock Approach

POP AND CONSOLIDATED SUBSIDIARY
Consolidation Worksheet
For Year Ending December 31, 2013

Accounts	Pop Company	Sun Company	Consolidation Entries Debit	Consolidation Entries Credit	Noncontrolling Interest	Consolidated Totals
Income Statement						
Revenues	(900,000)	(400,000)				(1,300,000)
Expenses	739,500	360,000	(E) 3,000			1,102,500
Dividend income	(10,500)	(8,000)	(I) 18,500			–0–
Separate company net income	(171,000)	(48,000)				
Consolidated net income						(197,500)
Noncontrolling interest in Sun Company's income [($48,000 − 3,000) × 30%)]					(13,500)	13,500
to controlling interest						(184,000)
Statement of Retained Earnings						
Retained earnings, 1/1/13:						
Pop Company	(747,000)	–0–		(*C) 15,400		(762,400)
Sun Company	–0–	(425,000)	(S) 425,000			–0–
Net income (above)	(171,000)	(48,000)				(184,000)
Dividends paid:						
Pop Company	80,000	–0–		(I) 8,000		72,000
Sun Company	–0–	15,000		(I) 10,500	4,500	–0–
Retained earnings, 12/31/13	(838,000)	(458,000)				(874,400)
Balance Sheet						
Current assets	842,000	332,000				1,174,000
Investment in Sun Company	504,000	–0–	(*C) 15,400	(S) 437,500 (A) 81,900		–0–
Investment in Pop Company	–0–	120,000		(TS) 120,000		–0–
Land, buildings, equipment (net)	642,000	516,000				1,158,000
Franchises	–0–	–0–	(A) 117,000	(E) 3,000		114,000
Total assets	1,988,000	968,000				2,446,000
Liabilities	(550,000)	(310,000)				(860,000)
Noncontrolling interest in Sun Company, 1/1/13	–0–	–0–		(S) 187,500 (A) 35,100	(222,600)	
Noncontrolling interest in Sun Company, 12/31/13	–0–	–0–			231,600	(231,600)
Common stock	(600,000)	(200,000)	(S) 200,000			(600,000)
Retained earnings, 12/31/13 (above)	(838,000)	(458,000)				(874,400)
Treasury stock	–0–	–0–	(TS) 120,000			120,000
Total liabilities and equities	(1,988,000)	(968,000)	898,900	898,900		(2,446,000)

Note: Parentheses indicate a credit balance.
Consolidation entries:
(*C) Conversion of initial value method to equity method. This entry recognizes 70 percent of the increase in Sun Company's book value less amortization expense applicable to the previous year [70% ($25,000 − $3,000)].
(S) Elimination of subsidiary's stockholders' equity accounts along with recognition of January 1, noncontrolling interest.
(TS) Reclassification of Sun Company's ownership in Pop Company into a treasury stock account.
(A) Allocation to franchises, unamortized balance being recorded as of January 1.
(I) Elimination of intra-entity dividend income for the period.
(E) Recognition of amortization expense for the current year.

of the $2,100 amortization expense (the parent's 70 percent share) dictates that $22,400 is the appropriate equity accrual. Because the parent has already recognized $7,000 in dividend income, Entry ***C** records the necessary increase as $15,400 ($22,400 − $7,000).[2]

The remaining entries relating to Pop's investment are standard: The subsidiary's stockholders' equity accounts are eliminated (Entry **S**), the franchises' allocation is recognized (Entry **A**), and so on. The existence of the mutual ownership actually affects only two facets of Exhibit 7.2. First, Sun's $120,000 payment made for the parent's shares is reclassified into a treasury stock account (through Entry **TS**). Second, the $8,000 intra-entity dividend flowing from Pop to Sun during the current year of 2013 is eliminated within Entry **I** (used because the collection was recorded as income). The simplicity of applying the treasury stock approach should be apparent from this one example.

Before leaving the treasury stock approach, a final comment is needed regarding the computation of the noncontrolling interest's share of Sun's income. In Exhibit 7.2, this balance is recorded as $13,500, or 30 percent of the subsidiary's $45,000 adjusted net income ($48,000 reported net income less $3,000 excess fair-value amortization). A question can be raised as to the validity of including the $8,000 dividend within this income total because that payment is eliminated within the consolidation.

These dividends, although intra-entity in nature, increase the subsidiary company's book value (see footnote 1). Therefore, the increment must be reflected in some manner to indicate the change in the amount attributed to the outside owners. For example, the increase could be recognized as a direct adjustment of $2,400 (30 percent of $8,000) in the noncontrolling interest balance. More often, as shown here, such cash transfers are considered to be income *when viewed from the perspective of these other unrelated parties.*

Income Tax Accounting for a Business Combination

To this point, this textbook has not attempted to analyze the income tax implications involved in corporate mergers and acquisitions. Only a comprehensive tax course can provide complete coverage of the numerous complexities inherent in the tax laws in this area. Furthermore, essential accounting issues can be overshadowed by intermingling an explanation of the financial reporting process with an in-depth study of related tax consequences.

Despite the desire to focus attention on basic accounting issues, income taxes can never be ignored. Certain elements of the tax laws have a direct impact on the financial reporting of any business combination. At a minimum, a fair presentation of the consolidated entity's financial statements requires recognition of current income tax expense figures and deferred income taxes. Therefore, a complete understanding of the financial reporting process requires an introduction to the income taxation of a business combination.

Affiliated Groups

LO4

List the criteria for being a member of an affiliated group for income tax filing purposes.

A central issue in accounting for the income taxes of a business combination involves the entity filing its tax returns. Many combinations require only a single consolidated return; in other cases, some, or even all, of the component corporations prepare separate returns. According to current tax laws, a business combination may elect to file a consolidated return encompassing all companies that compose an *affiliated group* as defined

[2] The necessary adjustment to beginning retained earnings also can be computed as follows:

Income of subsidiary—2012	$ 35,000
Dividends paid	(10,000)
Increase in book value	$ 25,000
Ownership percentage	70%
Income accrual	$ 17,500
Amortization—2012 (70% × $3,000)	(2,100)
Increase in beginning retained earnings	$ 15,400

by the Internal Revenue Code. The Code automatically requires all other corporations to submit separate income tax returns. Consequently, a first step in the taxation process is to delineate the boundaries of an affiliated group. Because of specific requirements outlined in the tax laws, this designation does not necessarily cover the same constituents as a business combination.

According to the Internal Revenue Code, the essential criterion for including a subsidiary within an affiliated group is the parent's ownership of at least 80 percent of the voting stock and at least 80 percent of each class of nonvoting stock. This ownership may be direct or indirect, although the parent must meet these requirements in connection with at least one directly owned subsidiary. As another condition, each company in the affiliated group must be a domestic (rather than a foreign) corporation. A company's options can be described as follows:

- *Domestic subsidiary, 80 percent to 100 percent owned:* May file as part of consolidated return or may file separately.
- *Domestic subsidiary, less than 80 percent owned:* Must file separately.
- *Foreign subsidiary:* Must file separately.

Clearly, a distinction exists between business combinations (identified for financial reporting) and affiliated groups as defined for tax purposes. Chapter 2 described a business combination as comprising all subsidiaries controlled by a parent company unless control is only temporary. The possession (either directly or indirectly) of a mere majority of voting stock normally supports control. Conversely, the Internal Revenue Code's 80 percent rule creates a smaller circle of companies qualifying for inclusion in an affiliated group.

For the companies of an affiliated group, filing a consolidated tax return provides several distinct benefits:

- Intra-entity profits are not taxed until realized (through use or sale to an outside party); similarly, intra-entity losses (which are rare) are not deducted until realized.
- Intra-entity dividends are nontaxable (this exclusion applies to all dividends between members of an affiliated group regardless of whether a consolidated return is filed).
- Losses incurred by one affiliated company can be used to reduce taxable income earned by other group members.

LO5

Compute taxable income and deferred tax amounts for an affiliated group based on information presented in a consolidated set of financial statements.

Deferred Income Taxes

Some deviations between generally accepted accounting principles and income tax laws create *temporary differences* whereby (1) a variation between an asset or liability's recorded book value and its tax basis exists and (2) this difference results in taxable or deductible amounts in future years. When a temporary difference is present, financial reporting principles require recognizing a deferred tax asset or liability. The specific amount of this income tax deferral depends somewhat on whether consolidated or separate returns are being filed. Thus, we analyze here the tax consequences of several common transactions to demonstrate a business combination's income tax expense reporting.

Intra-Entity Dividends

For financial reporting, dividends between the members of a business combination always are eliminated; they represent intra-entity cash transfers. In tax accounting, dividends also are removed from income but only if at least 80 percent of the subsidiary's stock is held. Consequently, at this ownership level, no difference between financial and tax reporting exists; both eliminate all intra-entity dividends. Income tax expense is not recorded. Deferred tax recognition is also ignored because no temporary difference has been created.

However, if less than 80 percent of a subsidiary's stock is held, tax recognition becomes necessary. Intra-entity dividends are taxed partially because, at that ownership level, 20 percent is taxable. The dividends-received deduction on the tax return (the nontaxable portion) is only 80 percent.[3] Thus, an income tax liability is immediately created for the recipient. *In addition, deferred income taxes are required for any of the subsidiary's income not paid currently as a dividend.* A temporary difference is created because tax payments will occur in future years when the subsidiary's earnings eventually are distributed to the parent. Hence, a current tax liability is recorded based on the dividends collected, and a deferred tax liability is recorded for the taxable portion of any income not paid to the parent during the year.

The Impact of Goodwill

Current law allows, in some cases, the amortization of goodwill and other purchased intangibles (referred to as *Section 197 property*) over a 15-year period. For financial reporting, goodwill is written off if it is impaired or if the related business is disposed of in some manner. Because of the difference in the periods in which taxable income and financial income are reduced, the presence of tax-deductible goodwill creates a temporary difference that necessitates recognizing deferred income taxes. The same is true for other purchased intangibles if a life other than 15 years is used for financial reporting.

Unrealized Intra-Entity Gains

Taxes on unrealized gains that result from transfers between related companies within a business combination create a special accounting problem. On consolidated financial statements, the impact of all such transactions is deferred. The same is true for a consolidated tax return; the gains are removed until realized. No temporary difference is created.

If separate returns are filed, though, tax laws require the profits to be reported in the period of transfer even though unearned by the business combination. Thus, the income is taxed immediately, prior to being earned from a financial reporting perspective. This "prepayment" of the tax creates a deferred income tax asset.[4]

Consolidated Tax Returns—Illustration

To illustrate accounting effects created by filing a consolidated tax return, assume that Great Company possesses 90 percent of Small Company's voting and nonvoting stocks. Subsequent to the acquisition, the two companies continue normal operations, which includes significant intra-entity transactions. Each company's operating and dividend incomes for the current time period are presented below, along with the effects of unrealized gains. No income tax accruals have been recognized within these totals:

	Great Company	Small Company (90% owned)
Operating income (excludes equity or dividend income from subsidiary)	$160,000	$40,000
Net unrealized gains in current year income (included in operating income above)	30,000	8,000
Dividend income (from Small)	9,000	–0–
Dividends paid	20,000	10,000

From the perspective of the single economic entity, Great's individual income for the period amounts to $130,000: $160,000 in internal operating incomes less $30,000 in

[3] If less than 20 percent of a company's stock is owned, the dividends-received deduction is only 70 percent. However, this level of ownership is not applicable to a subsidiary within a business combination.

[4] Deferral is required for the amount of taxes paid on the unrealized gain by the seller. This approach was taken rather than computing the deferral based on the future tax effect caused by the difference between the buyer's book value and tax basis, a procedure typically followed. This deferral treatment helps eliminate the need for complex cross-currency deferred tax computations when the parties are in separate tax jurisdictions.

unrealized gains. Using this same approach, Small's income is \$32,000 after removing the effects of the intra-entity transfers (\$40,000 operating income less \$8,000 in unrealized gains). Thus, the income to report in consolidated financial statements before the reduction for noncontrolling interest is \$162,000 (\$130,000 + \$32,000). For financial reporting, both intra-entity dividends and unrealized gains are omitted in arriving at this total. Income prior to the noncontrolling interest is computed here because any allocation to these other owners is not deductible for tax purposes.

Because the parent owns more than 80 percent of Small's stock, dividends collected from the subsidiary are tax-free. Likewise, intra-entity gains are not taxable presently because a consolidated return is filed. Hence, *financial and tax accounting are the same for both items;* neither of these figures produces a temporary difference and deferred income taxes are not needed.

The affiliated group pays taxes on \$162,000 and, assuming an effective rate of 30 percent, must convey \$48,600 (\$162,000 × 30%) to the government this year. Because no temporary differences exist, deferred income tax recognition is not applicable. Consequently, \$48,600 is the only tax expense reported. This amount is recorded for the consolidated entity by means of a worksheet entry or through an individual accrual by each company.

Income Tax Expense Assignment—Consolidated Return

Whenever a firm files a consolidated tax return, it allocates the total expense between the two parties. This figure is especially important to the subsidiary if it must produce separate financial statements for a loan or a future issuance of equity. The subsidiary's expense also serves as a basis for calculating the noncontrolling interest's share of consolidated net income.

Several techniques can accomplish this proration. For example, the expense charged to the subsidiary often is based on the percentage of the total taxable income from each company (the percentage allocation method) or on the appropriate taxable income figures if separate returns were filed (the separate return method).

To illustrate, we again use the figures from Great and Small in the previous example. Great owned 90 percent of Small's outstanding stock. Based on filing a consolidated return, total income tax expense of \$48,600 was recognized. How should these two companies allocate this figure?

Percentage Allocation Method

Total taxable income on this consolidated return was \$162,000. Of this amount, \$130,000 was applied to the parent (operating income after deferral of unrealized gain), and \$32,000 came from the subsidiary (computed in the same manner). Thus, 19.753 percent (\$32,000/\$162,000) of total expense should be assigned to the subsidiary, an amount that equals \$9,600 (19.753% of \$48,600).

Separate Return Method

On separate returns, intra-entity gains are taxable. Therefore, the separate returns of these two companies appear as follows:

	Great	Small	Total
Operating income	\$160,000	\$40,000	
Assumed tax rate	30%	30%	
Income tax expense—separate returns	\$ 48,000	\$12,000	\$60,000

By filing a consolidated return, an expense of only \$48,600 is recorded for the business combination. Because 20 percent of income tax expense on the separate returns (\$12,000/\$60,000) came from the subsidiary, \$9,720 of the expense (\$48,600 × 20%) is assigned to Small.

Under this second approach, the noncontrolling interest's share of this subsidiary's income is computed as follows:

Small Company—reported income	$40,000
Less: Unrealized intra-entity gains	(8,000)
Less: Assigned income tax expense	(9,720)
Small Company—realized income	$22,280
Outside ownership	10%
Noncontrolling interest in Small Company's income	$ 2,228

LO6

Compute taxable income and deferred tax amounts to be recognized when separate tax returns are filed by any of the affiliates of a business combination.

Filing of Separate Tax Returns

Despite the advantages of filing as an affiliated group, a single consolidated return cannot always encompass every member of a business combination. Separate returns are mandatory for foreign subsidiaries and for domestic corporations not meeting the 80 percent ownership rule. Also, a company may still elect to file separately even if it meets the conditions for inclusion within an affiliated group. If all companies in an affiliated group are profitable and few intra-entity transactions occur, they may prefer separate returns. Filing in this manner gives the various companies more flexibility in their choice of accounting methods and fiscal tax years.[5] Tax laws, though, do not allow a company to switch back and forth between consolidated and separate returns. Once a company elects to file a consolidated tax return as part of an affiliated group, obtaining Internal Revenue Service permission to file separately can be difficult.

When members of a business combination do file separate tax returns, temporary differences often emerge across income recognized for consolidated financial reporting and for income tax reporting. The sources of such differences include (1) the immediate taxation of unrealized intra-entity gains (and losses) and (2) possible future tax effects of subsidiary income in excess of dividend payments. Differences in the timing of income recognition across consolidated reporting and income tax purposes create deferred tax assets and/or liabilities. For example, intra-entity gains and losses must be included on a separate tax return at the time of transfer rather than when the earnings process is culminated. Because the tax is paid in the current year, but the profit is not recognized until a subsequent year, a deferred tax asset is created—similar to a prepaid item. On the other hand when a parent recognizes subsidiary profits for financial reporting purposes, both current income and net assets increase. But if the parent delays paying tax on the profits until the subsidiary pays a dividend, the parent also needs to account for the delayed tax effect. Accordingly the parent recognizes and reports a deferred tax liability.

However, not all subsidiary dividend distributions result in deferred taxes. For dividend payments, deferred taxes are not required when ownership equals or exceeds 80 percent. Because the tax law provides a 100 percent dividends-received deduction, the transfer is nontaxable even on a separate return; no expense recognition is required.

If the amount distributed by a subsidiary that is less than 80 percent owned equals current earnings, 20 percent of the collection is taxed immediately to the recipient, but no temporary difference is created because no future tax effect is produced. Hence, again, deferred income tax recognition is not appropriate.

Conceptually, questions about the recognition of deferred taxes arise when a less than 80 percent owned subsidiary pays less in dividends than its current income. If a subsidiary earns $100,000, for example, but pays dividends of only $60,000, will the parent's share of the $40,000 remainder ever become taxable income? Do these undistributed earnings represent temporary differences? If so, immediate recognition of the associated tax effect is required even though payment of this $40,000 is not anticipated for the foreseeable future.

[5] At one time, the filing of separate returns was especially popular to take advantage of reduced tax rates on lower income levels. However, Congress eliminated the availability of this tax savings.

The FASB ASC (para. 740-30-25-4) addresses this issue as follows, "A deferred tax liability shall be recognized for . . . an excess of the amount for financial reporting over the tax basis of an investment in a domestic subsidiary." Therefore, other than one exception noted later in this chapter, any portion of the subsidiary's income not distributed in the form of dividends creates a temporary difference but is not taxed until a later date; thus, a deferred tax liability is created. Because many companies retain a substantial portion of their income to finance growth, an expense recognized here may never be paid.

Deferred Tax on Undistributed Earnings—Illustrated

Assume that Parent Company owns 70 percent of Child Company. Because ownership is less than 80 percent, filing separate tax returns for the two companies is mandatory. In the current year, Parent's operating earnings (excluding taxes and any income from this investment) amount to $200,000, and Child reports a pretax net income of $100,000. During the period, the subsidiary paid a total of $20,000 in cash dividends, $14,000 (70%) to Parent and the remainder to the other owners. To avoid complications in this initial example, we assume that no unrealized intra-entity gains and losses are present.

The reporting of Child's income taxes does not provide a significant difficulty because it involves no temporary differences. Using an assumed tax rate of 30 percent, the subsidiary accrues income tax expense of $30,000 ($100,000 × 30%), leaving an after-tax profit of $70,000. *Because it paid only $20,000 in dividends, undistributed earnings for the period amount to $50,000.*

For Parent, Child's undistributed earnings represent a temporary tax difference. The following schedules have been developed to calculate Parent's current tax liability and deferred tax liability.

Income Tax Currently Payable—Parent Company

Reported operating income—Parent Company		$200,000
Dividends received	$ 14,000	
Less: Dividends-received deduction (80%)	(11,200)	2,800
Taxable income—current year		$202,800
Tax rate		30%
Income tax payable—current period (Parent)		$ 60,840

Deferred Income Tax Payable—Parent Company

Undistributed earnings of Child Company	$ 50,000
Parent Company's ownership	70%
Undistributed earnings accruing to Parent	$ 35,000
Dividends-received deduction upon eventual distribution (80%)	(28,000)
Income to be taxed—subsequent dividend payments	$ 7,000
Tax rate	30%
Deferred income tax payable	$ 2,100

These computations show a total income tax expense of $62,940: a current liability of $60,840 and a deferred liability of $2,100. The deferred balance results entirely from Child's undistributed earnings. Although the subsidiary has a $70,000 after-tax income, it distributes only $20,000 in the form of dividends. The $50,000 that Child retains represents a temporary tax difference to the stockholders. Thus, it recognizes the deferred income tax associated with these undistributed earnings. The income is earned now; therefore, the liability is recorded in the current period.

The FASB ASC Topic 740, Income Taxes, provides one important exception to the recognition of deferred income taxes on a subsidiary's undistributed income. FASB ASC 740-30-25-18 states that a deferred tax liability is not recognized for the excess amount for financial reporting over the tax basis of an investment in a *foreign* subsidiary that is essentially permanent in duration. Thus, in the previous example, if the subsidiary is foreign and the retention of these excess earnings seems to be permanent, the $2,100 deferred tax liability is omitted, reducing the total reported expense to $60,840.

Separate Tax Returns Illustrated

A complete example best demonstrates the full accounting impact created by filing separate tax returns. As a basis for this illustration, assume that Lion Corporation reported the following data with its 60 percent owned subsidiary, Cub Company (a domestic corporation), for the current year:

	Lion Corporation	Cub Company (60% owned by Lion)
Operating income	$500,000	$200,000
Unrealized intra-entity inventory gross profits (included in operating income)	40,000	30,000
Dividend income from Cub Company	24,000	Not applicable
Dividends paid	Not applicable	40,000
Applicable tax rate	30%	30%

Subsidiary's Income Tax Expense Because the companies must file separate tax returns, they do not defer the unrealized gross profits but leave them in both companies' operating incomes. Thus, Cub's taxable income is $200,000, an amount that creates a current payable of $60,000 ($200,000 × 30%). The unrealized gross profit is a temporary difference for financial reporting purposes, creating a deferred income tax asset (payment of the tax comes before the income actually is earned) of $9,000 ($30,000 × 30%). Therefore, the subsidiary recognizes only $51,000 as the period's appropriate expense.

Income Tax Expense—Cub

Income currently taxable	$200,000	
Tax rate	30%	$60,000
Temporary difference (unrealized gross profit is taxed before being earned)	$ (30,000)	
Tax rate	30%	(9,000)
Income tax expense—Cub		$51,000

Consequently, Cub reports after-tax income of $119,000 ($200,000 operating income less $30,000 unrealized gross profit less $51,000 in income tax expense). This profit figure is the basis for recognizing $47,600 ($119,000 × 40% outside ownership) as the noncontrolling interest's share of consolidated income.

Parent's Income Tax Expense On Lion's separate return, its own unrealized gross profits remain within income. The taxable portion of the dividends received from Cub also must be included. Hence, the parent's taxable earnings total $504,800, a balance that creates a $151,440 current tax liability for the company.

Income Tax Currently Payable—Lion

Operating income—Lion Corporation (includes $40,000 unrealized gains)		$500,000
Dividends received from Cub Company (60%)	$24,000	
Less: 80% dividends-received deduction	(19,200)	4,800
Taxable income		$504,800
Tax rate		30%
Income tax payable—current (Lion)		$151,440

Although we present Lion's tax return information here, Lion determines its total tax expense for the period only by accounting for the impact of the two temporary differences: the parent's $40,000 in unrealized gross profits and the undistributed earnings of the subsidiary. The undistributed earnings amount to $47,400, computed as follows:

After-tax income of Cub (above)	$119,000
Dividends paid	(40,000)
Undistributed earnings	$ 79,000
Lion's ownership	60%
Lion's portion of undistributed earnings	$ 47,400

Now the parent can derive its deferred income tax effects for financial reporting.

Deferred Income Taxes—Lion Company

Unrealized Gross Profits

Amount taxable now prior to being earned	$40,000
Tax rate	30%
Deferred income tax asset	$12,000

Undistributed Earnings of Subsidiary

Undistributed earnings of Cub—to be taxed later (computed above)	$ 47,400
Dividends-received deduction upon eventual distribution (80%)	(37,920)
Income eventually taxable	$ 9,480
Tax rate	30%
Deferred income tax liability	$ 2,844

The two temporary differences exert opposite effects on Lion's reported income taxes. Because the firms file separate returns, the unrealized gross profits are taxable in the current period despite not actually having been earned. From an accounting perspective, paying the tax on these gross profits now creates a deferred income tax asset of $12,000 ($40,000 × 30%). In contrast, the parent currently recognizes the undistributed earnings (through consolidation of the investment). However, this portion of the subsidiary's income is not yet taxable to the parent. Because the tax payment is not due until the parent receives the dividends, a $2,844 deferred income tax liability ($9,480 × 30%) occurs.

The parent reports the deferred tax asset as a current asset because it relates to inventory whereas the deferred tax liability is long term because ownership of the investment created it. Lion's reported income tax expense results from the creation of these three accounts:

Lion's Financial Records		
Deferred Income Tax Asset—Current	12,000	
Income Tax Expense	142,284	
Deferred Income Tax Liability—Long-Term		2,844
Income Tax Currently Payable		151,440
To record current and deferred taxes of parent company.		

Temporary Differences Generated by Business Combinations

LO7

Determine the deferred tax consequences for temporary differences generated when a business combination is created.

Based on the transaction's nature, the tax laws deem some acquisitions to be tax-free (to the seller) but others to be taxable. In most tax-free acquisitions and in a few taxable acquisitions, the resulting book values of the acquired company's assets and liabilities differ from their tax bases. Such differences result because the subsidiary's cost is retained for tax purposes (in tax-free exchanges) or because the allocations for tax purposes vary from those used for financial reporting (a situation found in some taxable transactions).

Thus, formation of a business combination can create temporary differences. Any deferred income tax assets and liabilities the subsidiary previously recorded are not at issue; the parent consolidates these accounts in the same manner as other subsidiary assets and liabilities. The question here concerns differences in book value and tax basis that stem from the takeover.

As an illustration, assume that Son Company owns a single asset, a building that has a $150,000 tax basis (cost less accumulated depreciation) but presently has a $210,000 fair value. Pop Corporation conveys a total value of $300,000 to acquire this company. The exchange is structured to be tax-free. After this transaction, the building continues to have a tax basis of only $150,000. However, its consolidated book value is $210,000, an amount $60,000 more than the figure applicable for tax purposes. How does this $60,000 difference affect the consolidated statements?

GAAP provides extensive guidance on reporting deferred tax assets and deferred tax liabilities created in a business combination. According to the FASB ASC (para. 805-740-25-2):

> An acquirer shall recognize a deferred tax asset or deferred tax liability arising from the assets acquired and liabilities assumed in a business combination and shall account for the potential tax effects of temporary differences, carryforwards, and any income tax uncertainties of an acquiree that exist at the acquisition date . . .

Thus, any temporary difference that is found in Pop's acquisition of Son creates a deferred tax asset or liability. Because the asset's tax basis is $150,000 but its recorded value within consolidated statements is $210,000, a temporary difference of $60,000 exists. Assuming that a 30 percent tax rate is appropriate, the newly formed business combination must recognize a deferred income tax liability of $18,000 ($60,000 × 30%).

Consequently, in a consolidated balance sheet prepared immediately after Pop obtains control over Son, the building is recorded at $210,000 fair value. In addition, Pop reports the new deferred tax liability of $18,000. Because the net value of these two accounts is $192,000, goodwill of $108,000 emerges as the figure remaining from the $300,000 acquisition value.

This $18,000 liability systematically declines to zero over the building's life. The consolidated entity must compute depreciation for tax purposes based on the $150,000 basis and is, therefore, less each year than the expense shown for financial reporting purposes (based on $210,000). With less expense, taxable income is more than book income for the remaining years of the asset's life. However, the extra payment that results is not charged to expense but reduces the deferred tax liability (initially established at the acquisition date) the additional amount. To illustrate, assume that this building generates revenues of $40,000 per year. Assume also that it has a 10-year life and that the company uses the straight-line method of depreciation.

	Financial Reporting	Income Tax Reporting
Revenues	$40,000	$40,000
Depreciation expense:		
10% of $210,000	21,000	
10% of $150,000		15,000
Income	$19,000	$25,000
Tax rate	30%	30%
Tax effect	$ 5,700	$ 7,500

Although the combination must pay $7,500 to the government, currently reported income caused only $5,700 of that amount. The other $1,800 ($6,000 reversal of temporary difference × 30%) resulted because of the use of the previous basis for tax purposes. Therefore, the following entry is made:

Income Tax Expense	5,700	
Deferred Income Tax Liability (to remove part of balance created at acquisition date)	1,800	
Income Tax Currently Payable		7,500
To accrue current income taxes as well as impact of temporary difference in asset of subsidiary.		

LO8

Explain the impact that a net operating loss of an acquired affiliate has on consolidated figures.

Business Combinations and Operating Loss Carryforwards

Tax laws in the United States provide a measure of relief for companies incurring net operating losses (NOLs) when they file current tax returns. They may carry such losses back for two years and apply them as a reduction to taxable income figures previously reported. This procedure generates a cash refund of income taxes the company paid during these earlier periods.

If a loss still exists after the carryback (or if the taxpayer elects not to carry the loss back), a carryforward for the subsequent 20 years also is allowed.[6] Carrying the loss forward reduces subsequent taxable income levels until the NOL is entirely eliminated or the time period expires. *Thus, NOL carryforwards can benefit the company only if taxable income can be generated in the future*. The immediate recognition of NOL carryforwards has always been controversial because it requires the company to anticipate making profits.

In the past, some companies created business combinations, at least in part, to take advantage of tax carryforwards. If an acquired company had an unused NOL while the parent projected significant profitability, the combination used the carryforward on a consolidated return to reduce income taxes after the acquisition. U.S. laws have now been changed so that only the company that reported the loss can use virtually all of an NOL carryforward. Hence, acquiring companies with an NOL carryforward has ceased to be a popular business strategy. However, because the practice has not disappeared, reporting rules for a subsidiary's NOL carryforward are still needed.

FASB ASC Topic 740, Income Taxes, requires an acquiring firm to recognize a deferred income tax asset for any NOL carryforward. However, a valuation allowance also must be recognized

> if, based on the weight of available evidence, it is *more likely than not* (a likelihood of more than 50 percent) that some portion or all of the deferred tax assets will not be realized. The valuation allowance should be sufficient to reduce the deferred tax asset to the amount that is more likely than not to be realized. [FASB ASC (para. 740-10-30-5)]

As an example, assume that a company has one asset (a building) worth $500,000. Because of recent losses, this company has a $200,000 NOL carryforward. The assumed tax rate is 30 percent so that the company will derive a $60,000 benefit ($200,000 × 30%) if it earns future taxable profits.

Assume that the parent acquired this company for $640,000. In accounting for the acquisition, the parent must anticipate the likelihood that the new subsidiary will utilize some or all of the NOL carryforward. If it is more likely than not that the benefit will be realized, goodwill of $80,000 results:

Consideration paid		$640,000
Subsidiary assets:		
Building.	$500,000	
Deferred income tax asset	60,000	560,000
Goodwill.		$ 80,000

[6] If a taxpayer believes that future tax rates will increase, choosing not to carry a loss back in favor of only a carryforward could be financially preferable.

Conversely, if the chances that this subsidiary will use the NOL carryforward are 50 percent or less, the parent must recognize a valuation allowance and $140,000 of consolidated goodwill.

Consideration paid			$640,000
Subsidiary assets:			
Building		$500,000	
Deferred income tax asset	$ 60,000		
Valuation allowance	(60,000)	–0–	500,000
Goodwill			$140,000

In this second case, a question arises if this carryforward successfully reduces future taxes: How should the company remove the valuation allowance? Any changes in a valuation allowance for an acquired entity's deferred tax asset must be reported as a reduction or increase to income tax expense.[7] However, changes within the measurement period that result from new information about facts and circumstances that existed at the acquisition date are recognized through a corresponding adjustment to goodwill.[8]

Income Taxes and Business Combinations—Comparisons with International Accounting Standards

U.S. GAAP on accounting for income taxes and *International Accounting Standard (IAS) 12* each require business combinations to recognize both current tax effects and anticipated future tax consequences using deferred tax assets and liabilities. For many financial reporting tax issues that arise from business combinations, the standards are the same.

One area, however, where a difference remains concerns taxes on intra-entity asset transfers that remain within the consolidated group. U.S. GAAP prohibits the recognition of unrealized intra-entity profits and therefore the selling firm defers any related current tax effects until the profit is realized when the asset is sold to a third party. In contrast, IFRS requires the taxes paid by the selling firm on intra-entity profits to be recognized as incurred. Further, although prohibited by U.S. GAAP, IFRS allows tax deferral on differences between the tax bases of assets transferred across entities (and tax jurisdictions) that remain within the consolidated group.[9]

Summary

1. For consolidation purposes, a parent need not possess majority ownership of each of the component companies constituting a business combination. Often control is indirect: One subsidiary owns a majority of an affiliated subsidiary's shares. Although the parent might own stock in only one of these companies, control has been established over both. Such an arrangement often is referred to as a *father-son-grandson configuration*.
2. The consolidation of financial information for a father-son-grandson business combination does not differ conceptually from a consolidation involving only direct ownership. All intra-entity, reciprocal balances are eliminated. Goodwill, other allocations, and amortization usually must be recognized if an acquisition has taken place. Because more than one investment is involved, the number of worksheet entries increases, but that is more of a mechanical inconvenience than a conceptual concern.

[7] Alternatively, a postacquisition change in the valuation allowance may result in a direct adjustment to contributed capital if the original transaction was accounted for directly through other comprehensive income or other elements of stockholders' equity.

[8] However, once goodwill is reduced to zero, an acquirer recognizes any additional decrease in the valuation allowance as a bargain purchase.

[9] Ernst & Young LLP, *US GAAP vs. IFRS: The Basics,* March 2010.

3. One aspect of a father-son-grandson consolidation that warrants attention is determining accrual-based income figures for each subsidiary. Any company within a business combination that holds both a parent and subsidiary position must determine the income accruing from ownership of its subsidiary before computing its own earnings. This procedure is important because income is the basis for each parent's equity accruals and noncontrolling interest allocations.
4. If a subsidiary possesses shares of its parent, a mutual affiliation exists. This investment is intra-entity in nature and must be eliminated for consolidation purposes. The treasury stock approach simply reclassifies the cost of these shares as treasury stock with no equity accrual recorded.
5. Under present tax laws, an affiliated group of only domestic corporations can file a single consolidated income tax return. The parent must control 80 percent of the voting stock as well as 80 percent of the nonvoting stock (either directly or indirectly). A consolidated return allows the companies to defer recognition of intra-entity gains and gross profits until realized. Furthermore, losses incurred by one member of the group reduce taxable income earned by the others. Intra-entity dividends are also nontaxable on a consolidated return, although such distributions are never taxable when paid between companies within an affiliated group.
6. Separate tax returns apply to some members of a business combination. Foreign corporations and any company not meeting the 80 percent ownership rule, as examples, must report in this manner. In addition, a company might simply elect to file in this manner if a consolidated return provides no advantages. For financial reporting purposes, a separate return often necessitates recognition of deferred income taxes because temporary differences can result from unrealized transfer gains as well as intra-entity dividends (if 80 percent ownership is not held).
7. When a business combination is created, the subsidiary's assets and liabilities sometimes have a tax basis that differs from their assigned values. In such cases, the company must recognize a deferred tax asset or liability at the time of acquisition to reflect the tax impact of these differences.

Comprehensive Illustration

Problem

(*Estimated Time: 60 to 75 Minutes*) On January 1, 2011, Gold Company acquired 90 percent of Silver Company. Details of the acquisition are as follows:

Consideration transferred by Gold	$576,000
Noncontrolling interest acquisition-date fair value	64,000
Silver total fair value	$640,000
Silver book value	600,000
Excess fair value over book value assigned to brand name (20-year life)	$ 40,000

Subsequently, on January 1, 2012, Silver purchased 10 percent of Gold for $150,000. This price equaled the book value of Gold's underlying net assets and no allocation was made to either goodwill or any specific accounts.

On January 1, 2013, Gold and Silver each acquired 30 percent of the outstanding shares of Bronze for $105,000 apiece, which resulted in Gold obtaining control over Bronze. Details of this acquisition are as follows:

Consideration transferred by Gold and Silver ($105,000 each)	$210,000
Noncontrolling interest acquisition-date fair value	140,000
Bronze total fair value	$350,000
Bronze book value	300,000
Excess fair value over book value assigned to copyright (10-year life)	$ 50,000

After the formation of this business combination Silver made significant intra-entity inventory sales to Gold. The volume of these transfers follows:

Year	Transfer Price to Gold Company	Markup on Transfer Price	Inventory Retained at Year-End (at transfer price)
2011	$100,000	30%	$ 60,000
2012	160,000	25	90,000
2013	200,000	28	120,000

EXHIBIT 7.3
Individual Financial Statements—2013

	Gold Company	Silver Company	Bronze Company
Sales	$ (800,000)	$ (600,000)	$(300,000)
Cost of goods sold	380,000	300,000	120,000
Operating expenses	193,000	100,000	90,000
Gain on sale of land	(13,000)	–0–	–0–
Dividend income from Gold Company	–0–	(10,000)	–0–
Dividend income from Silver Company	(36,000)	–0–	–0–
Dividend income from Bronze Company	(6,000)	(6,000)	–0–
Net income	$ (282,000)	$ (216,000)	$ (90,000)
Retained earnings, 1/1/13	$ (923,200)	$ (609,000)	$(200,000)
Net income (above)	(282,000)	(216,000)	(90,000)
Dividends paid	100,000	40,000	20,000
Retained earnings, 12/31/13	$(1,105,200)	$ (785,000)	$(270,000)
Cash and receivables	$ 295,000	$ 190,000	$ 130,000
Inventory	459,000	410,000	110,000
Investment in Silver Company	570,000	–0–	–0–
Investment in Gold Company	–0–	150,000	–0–
Investment in Bronze Company	105,000	105,000	–0–
Land, buildings, and equipment (net)	980,000	670,000	380,000
Total assets	$ 2,409,000	$ 1,525,000	$ 620,000
Liabilities	$ (603,800)	$ (540,000)	$(250,000)
Common stock	(700,000)	(200,000)	(100,000)
Retained earnings, 12/31/13	(1,105,200)	(785,000)	(270,000)
Total liabilities and equities	$(2,409,000)	$(1,525,000)	$(620,000)

In addition, on July 1, 2013, Gold sold Bronze a tract of land for $25,000. This property cost $12,000 when the parent acquired it several years ago.

The initial value method is used to account for all investments. The individual firms recognize income from the investments when dividends are received. Because consolidated statements are prepared for the business combination, accounting for the investments affects internal reporting only. During 2011 and 2012, Gold and Silver individually reported the following information:

	Gold Company	Silver Company
2011:		
Operating income	$180,000	$120,000
Dividend income—Silver Company (90%)	36,000	–0–
Dividends paid	80,000	40,000
2012:		
Operating income	240,000	150,000
Dividend income—Gold Company (10%)	–0–	9,000
Dividend income—Silver Company (90%)	27,000	–0–
Dividends paid	90,000	30,000

The 2013 financial statements for each of the three companies comprising this business combination are presented in Exhibit 7.3. These figures ignore income tax effects.

Required

a. Prepare worksheet entries to consolidate the 2013 financial statements for this combination. Assume that the mutual ownership between Gold and Silver is accounted for by means of the treasury stock approach. Compute the noncontrolling interests in Bronze's income and in Silver's income.

b. Assume that consolidated net income (before deducting any balance for the noncontrolling interests) amounts to $498,900. Assume also that the effective tax rate is 40 percent and that Gold and Silver file a consolidated tax return but Bronze files separately. Calculate the income tax expense recognized within the consolidated income statement for 2013.

Solution

a. The 2013 consolidation entries for Gold, Silver, and Bronze follow.

Entry *G

The consolidation process begins with Entry ***G,** which recognizes the intra-entity gross profit (on transfers from Silver to Gold) created in the previous period. The unrealized gross profit within ending inventory is deferred from the previous period into the current period.

Consolidation Entry *G

Retained earnings, 1/1/13 (Silver Company)	22,500	
Cost of goods sold		22,500

To recognize gross profits on intra-entity sales made from Silver to Gold during the preceding year (25% markup × $90,000).

Consolidation Entry *C (Gold)

Investment in Silver Company	164,250	
Retained Earnings, 1/1/13 (Gold Company)		164,250

To convert Gold's investment income figures for the two preceding years to equity income accruals computed as follows:

Increase in Silver's book value from 1/1/11 to 1/1/13 ($809,000 − 600,000)	$209,000
Excess fair-value amortization ($2,000 × 2 years)	(4,000)
Deferral of 12/31/12 intra-entity profit (25% × $90,000)	(22,500)
Silver's increase in book value adjusted for accruals recognized in combination	$182,500
Gold's ownership percentage	90%
Conversion from initial value method to equity method	$164,250

Consolidation Entry S1

Common Stock (Silver Company)	200,000	
Retained Earnings, 1/1/13 (Silver Company)	586,500	
Investment in Silver Company (90%)		707,850
Noncontrolling Interest in Silver Company, 1/1/13 (10%)		78,650

To eliminate the beginning stockholders' equity accounts of Silver and to recognize a 10 percent noncontrolling interest in the subsidiary. Retained Earnings has been adjusted for Entry ***G**.

Consolidation Entry S2

Common Stock (Bronze Company)	100,000	
Retained Earnings, 1/1/13 (Bronze Company)	200,000	
Investment in Bronze Company (60%)		180,000
Noncontrolling Interest in Bronze Company, 1/1/13 (40%)		120,000

To eliminate Bronze's beginning stockholders' equity accounts and to recognize outside ownership of the company's remaining shares. The investments of both Gold and Silver are accounted for concurrently through this one entry.

Consolidation Entry TS

Treasury Stock	150,000	
Investment in Gold		150,000

To reclassify Silver's investment in Gold as treasury stock.

Consolidation Entry A

Brand Name	36,000	
Copyright	50,000	
Investment in Silver		32,400
Noncontrolling Interest in Silver		3,600
Investment in Bronze		30,000
Noncontrolling Interest in Bronze		20,000

To recognize unamortized beginning-of-the-year balances from the excess fair value over book value acquisition-date allocations.

Consolidation Entry I

Dividend Income from Gold Company	10,000	
Dividend Income from Silver Company	36,000	
Dividend Income from Bronze Company	12,000	
Dividends Paid (Gold Company)		10,000
Dividends Paid (Silver Company)		36,000
Dividends Paid (Bronze Company)		12,000

To eliminate dividend payments made between the companies and recorded as income based on application of the initial value method.

Consolidation Entry E

Amortization Expense	7,000	
Brand Name		2,000
Copyright		5,000

To recognize current year amortizations of the acquisition-date excess fair-value allocations.

Consolidation Entry TI

Sales	200,000	
Cost of Goods Sold		200,000

To eliminate the intra-entity transfer of inventory made in the current year by Silver.

Consolidation Entry G

Cost of Goods Sold	33,600	
Inventory		33,600

To eliminate intra-entity gross profits remaining in Gold's December 31 current year inventory (28% gross profit rate × the parent's $120,000 ending inventory balance).

Consolidation Entry GL

Gain on Sale of Land	13,000	
Land		13,000

To eliminate gross profit on intra-entity transfer of land from Gold to Bronze during the year.

Noncontrolling Interest in Bronze Company's Income

As in all previous examples, the noncontrolling interest calculates its claim to a portion of consolidated income based on the subsidiary's income after amortizations and intra-entity profit deferrals and recognitions. Because this subsidiary has no unrealized intra-entity profits, the $90,000 income figure reported in Exhibit 7.3 is applicable and is adjusted only for the $5,000 excess fair-value amortization. Thus, the noncontrolling interest in Bronze's income is $34,000 [40% × ($90,000 − $5,000)].

Noncontrolling Interest in Silver Company's Income

Again, the noncontrolling interest calculates its claim to a portion of consolidated income based on the subsidiary's income after amortizations and intra-entity profit deferrals and recognitions. For Silver Company the adjustments are as follows:

Silver's internally computed net income	$210,000
Excess fair-value amortization	(2,000)
Equity in earnings of Bronze (30%)	27,000
Beginning inventory intra-entity profit recognized	22,500
Ending inventory intra-entity profit deferral	(33,600)
Silver's income adjusted for combination accruals	$223,900
Noncontrolling interest percentage	10%
Noncontrolling interest in Silver's net income	$ 22,390

b. No differences exist between Bronze's book values and tax basis. No computation of deferred income taxes is required; thus, this company's separate tax return is relatively straightforward. The $90,000 income figure creates a current tax liability of $36,000 (using the 40% tax rate).

In contrast, the consolidated tax return filed for Gold and Silver must include the following financial information. When applicable, figures reported in Exhibit 7.3 have been combined for the two companies.

Tax Return Information—Consolidated Return

Sales	$1,400,000	
Less: Intra-entity sales (2013)	(200,000)	$1,200,000
Cost of goods sold	$ 680,000	
Less: 2013 intra-entity purchases	(200,000)	
Less: 2012 intra-entity gross profits recognized in 2013 ($90,000 × 25%)	(22,500)	
Add: 2013 unrealized intra-entity gross profits ($120,000 × 28%)	33,600	491,100
Gross profit		$ 708,900
Operating expenses (including amortization)		300,000
Operating income		$ 408,900
Other income (since Bronze is not part of affiliated group):		
Gain on sale of land		13,000
Dividend income—Bronze Company	$ 12,000	
Less: 80% dividends-received deduction	(9,600)	2,400
Taxable income		$ 424,300
Tax rate		40%
Income tax payable by Gold Company and Silver Company for 2013		$ 169,720

Members of this business combination must pay a total of $205,720 to the government in 2013 ($36,000 for Bronze and $169,720 in connection with the consolidated return of Gold and Silver). Any temporary differences that originate or reverse during the year necessitate accounting for deferred income tax assets and/or liabilities. *In this illustration, only the dividend payments from Bronze and the unrealized gain on the sale of land to Bronze actually create such differences.* For example, amortization of the intangible assets is the same for book and tax purposes. Other items encountered do not lead to deferred income taxes:

- Because Gold and Silver file a consolidated return, they defer the unrealized inventory profits for both tax purposes and financial reporting so that no difference is created.
- The dividends that Silver paid to Gold are not subject to taxation because these distributions were made between members of an affiliated group.

However, recognition of a deferred tax liability is required because Bronze's realized income ($54,000 after income tax expense of $36,000) is higher than its $20,000 dividend distribution. Gold and Silver own 60 percent of Bronze, indicating that the consolidated income statement includes $32,400 ($54,000 × 60%) of its income. Because this figure is $20,400 more than the amount of dividends it paid Gold and Silver ($12,000, or 60% of $20,000), a deferred tax liability is required. The temporary difference is actually $4,080 (20% of $20,400) because of the 80 percent dividends-received deduction. The future tax effect on this difference is $1,632 based on the 40 percent tax rate applied.

A deferred tax asset also is needed in connection with Gold's intra-entity sale of land to Bronze. These companies file separate returns. Thus, the gain is taxed immediately, although this $13,000 is not realized for reporting purposes until a future resale occurs. From an accounting perspective, the tax of $5,200 ($13,000 × 40%) is being prepaid in 2013.

Recognition of the current payable as well as the two deferrals leads to an income tax expense of $202,152:

Income Tax Expense	202,152	
Deferred Income Tax—Asset.	5,200	
Income Taxes Payable—Current.		205,720
Deferred Income Tax—Liability		1,632

Questions

1. What is a *father-son-grandson relationship?*
2. When an indirect ownership is present, why is a specific ordering necessary for determining the incomes of the component corporations?
3. Able Company owns 70 percent of the outstanding voting stock of Baker Company, which, in turn, holds 80 percent of Carter Company. Carter possesses 60 percent of Dexter Company's capital stock. How much income actually accrues to the consolidated entity from each of these companies after considering the various noncontrolling interests?
4. How does the presence of an indirect ownership (such as a father-son-grandson relationship) affect the mechanical aspects of the consolidation process?
5. What is the difference between a connecting affiliation and a mutual ownership?
6. In accounting for mutual ownerships, what is the treasury stock approach?
7. For income tax purposes, how is *affiliated group* defined?
8. What are the advantages to a business combination filing a consolidated tax return? Considering these advantages, why do some members of a business combination file separate tax returns?
9. Why is the allocation of the income tax expense figure between the members of a business combination important? By what methods can this allocation be made?
10. If a parent and its subsidiary file separate income tax returns, why will the parent frequently have to recognize deferred income taxes? Why might the subsidiary have to recognize deferred income taxes?
11. In a recent acquisition, the consolidated value of a subsidiary's assets exceeded the basis appropriate for tax purposes. How does this difference affect the consolidated balance sheet?
12. Jones acquires Wilson, in part because the new subsidiary has an unused net operating loss carryforward for tax purposes. How does this carryforward affect the consolidated figures at the acquisition date?
13. A subsidiary that has a net operating loss carryforward is acquired. The related deferred income tax asset is $230,000. Because the parent believes that a portion of this carryforward likely will never be used, it also recognizes a valuation allowance of $150,000. At the end of the first year of ownership, the parent reassesses the situation and determines that the valuation allowance should be reduced to $110,000. What effect does this change have on the business combination's reporting?

Problems

LO1

1. In a father-son-grandson business combination, which of the following is true?
   a. The father company always must have its realized income computed first.
   b. The computation of a company's realized income has no effect on the realized income of other companies within a business combination.
   c. A father-son-grandson configuration does not require consolidation unless one company owns shares in all of the other companies.
   d. All companies solely in subsidiary positions must have their realized income computed first within the consolidation process.

LO3

2. A subsidiary owns shares of its parent company. Which of the following is true concerning the treasury stock approach?

a. It is one of several options to account for mutual holdings available under current accounting standards.

b. The original cost of the subsidiary's investment is a reduction in consolidated stockholders' equity.

c. The subsidiary accrues income on its investment by using the equity method.

d. The treasury stock approach eliminates these shares entirely within the consolidation process.

LO3

3. On January 1, Stanton Company buys 10 percent of the outstanding shares of its parent, ProMart, Inc. Although the total book and fair values of ProMart's net assets equaled $4 million, the price paid for these shares was $420,000. During the year, ProMart reported $510,000 of operating income (no subsidiary income was included) and paid dividends of $140,000. How are the shares of the parent owned by the subsidiary reported at December 31?

   a. An investment balance of $457,000 is eliminated for consolidation purposes.

   b. Consolidated stockholders' equity is reduced by $457,000.

   c. An investment balance of $437,000 is eliminated for consolidation purposes.

   d. Consolidated stockholders' equity is reduced by $420,000.

LO4

4. Which of the following is correct for two companies that want to file a consolidated tax return as an affiliated group?

   a. One company must hold at least 51 percent of the other company's voting stock.

   b. One company must hold at least 65 percent of the other company's voting stock.

   c. One company must hold at least 80 percent of the other company's voting stock.

   d. They cannot file one unless one company owns 100 percent of the other's voting stock.

LO5

5. How does the amortization of tax-deductible goodwill affect the computation of a parent company's income taxes?

   a. It is a deductible expense only if the parent owns at least 80 percent of subsidiary's voting stock.

   b. It is deductible only as impairments are recognized.

   c. It is a deductible item over a 15-year period.

   d. It is deductible only if a consolidated tax return is filed.

LO4

6. Which of the following is *not* a reason for two companies to file separate tax returns?

   a. The parent owns 68 percent of the subsidiary.

   b. They have no intra-entity transactions.

   c. Intra-entity dividends are tax-free only on separate returns.

   d. Neither company historically has had an operating tax loss.

LO1

7. Bassett Company owns 80 percent of Crimson and Crimson owns 90 percent of Damson, Inc. Operating income totals for the current year follow; they contain no investment income. None of these acquisitions required amortization expense. Included in Damson's income is a $40,000 unrealized gain on intra-entity transfers to Crimson.

	Bassett	Crimson	Damson
Operating income	$300,000	$200,000	$200,000

   What is Bassett's accrual-based income for the year?

   a. $575,200.

   b. $588,000.

   c. $596,400.

   d. $604,000.

LO1

8. Alder Corporation holds 80 percent of Beech, which, in turn, owns 80 percent of Cherry. Operating income figures (excluding investment income) and unrealized upstream gains included in the income for the current year follow:

	Alder	Beech	Cherry
Operating income	$525,000	$315,000	$280,000
Unrealized gains	–0–	19,000	50,000

What is the noncontrolling interest's share of consolidated net income?

a. $105,200.
b. $119,000.
c. $142,000.
d. $163,800.

LO3

9. Phelps, Inc. owns 85 percent of Satellite Corporation's voting stock. The acquisition price exceeded book and fair value by $80,000 and was appropriately attributed to goodwill. Satellite holds 20 percent of Phelps's voting stock. The price paid for the shares by Satellite equaled 20 percent of the parent's book value and net fair values of its assets and liabilities.

   During the current year, Phelps reported operating income of $160,000 and dividend income from Satellite of $27,000. At the same time, Satellite reported operating income of $50,000 and dividend income from Phelps of $14,000.

   What is the noncontrolling interest in Satellite's net income under the treasury stock approach?

   a. $31,500.
   b. $29,400.
   c. $9,600.
   d. $7,500.

LO7

10. Pike, Inc., owns 60 percent of Stark Company. During the current year, Stark reported net income of $200,000 but paid a total cash dividend of only $40,000. What deferred income tax liability must be recognized in the consolidated balance sheet? Assume the tax rate is 30 percent.

    a. $5,760.
    b. $9,600.
    c. $12,840.
    d. $28,800.

LO7

11. Plumas, Inc., owns 85 percent of Santa Cruz Corporation. Both companies have been profitable for many years. During the current year, the parent sold for $100,000 merchandise costing $70,000 to the subsidiary, which still held 20 percent of this merchandise at the end of the year. Assume that the tax rate is 25 percent and that separate tax returns are filed. What deferred income tax asset is created?

    a. –0–.
    b. $300.
    c. $1,500.
    d. $7,500.

LO5

12. What would be the answer to problem (11) if a consolidated tax return were filed?

    a. –0–.
    b. $300.
    c. $1,500.
    d. $7,500.

LO7

13. Hastoon Company purchases all of Zedner Company for $420,000 in cash. On that date, the subsidiary has net assets with a $400,000 fair value but a $300,000 book value and tax basis. The tax rate is 30 percent. Neither company has reported any deferred income tax assets or liabilities. What amount of goodwill should be recognized on the date of the acquisition?

    a. $20,000.
    b. $36,000.
    c. $50,000.
    d. $120,000.

LO1

14. On January 1, 2011, Aspen Company acquired 80 percent of Birch Company's outstanding voting stock for $288,000. Birch reported a $300,000 book value and the fair value of the noncontrolling interest was $72,000 on that date. Also, on January 1, 2012, Birch acquired 80 percent of Cedar Company for $104,000 when Cedar had a $100,000 book value and the 20 percent noncontrolling interest was valued at $26,000. In each acquisition, the subsidiary's excess acquisition-date fair over book value was assigned to a trade name with a 30-year life.

    These companies report the following financial information. Investment income figures are not included.

	2011	2012	2013
Sales:			
Aspen Company	$415,000	$545,000	$688,000
Birch Company	200,000	280,000	400,000
Cedar Company	Not available	160,000	210,000
Expenses:			
Aspen Company	$310,000	$420,000	$510,000
Birch Company	160,000	220,000	335,000
Cedar Company	Not available	150,000	180,000
Dividends paid:			
Aspen Company	$ 20,000	$ 40,000	$ 50,000
Birch Company	10,000	20,000	20,000
Cedar Company	Not available	2,000	10,000

Assume that each of the following questions is independent:

a. If all companies use the equity method for internal reporting purposes, what is the December 31, 2012, balance in Aspen's Investment in Birch Company account?

b. What is the consolidated net income for this business combination for 2013?

c. What is the noncontrolling interests' share of the consolidated net income in 2013?

d. Assume that Birch made intra-entity inventory transfers to Aspen that have resulted in the following unrealized gross profits at the end of each year:

Date	Amount
12/31/11	$10,000
12/31/12	16,000
12/31/13	25,000

What is the realized income of Birch in 2012 and 2013, respectively?

LO3

15. On January 1, 2011, Uncle Company purchased 80 percent of Nephew Company's capital stock for $500,000 in cash and other assets. Nephew had a book value of $600,000 and the 20 percent noncontrolling interest fair value was $125,000 on that date. On January 1, 2010, Nephew had acquired 30 percent of Uncle for $280,000. Uncle's appropriately adjusted book value as of that date was $900,000.

Operating income figures (not including investment income) for these two companies follow. In addition, Uncle pays $20,000 in dividends to shareholders each year and Nephew distributes $5,000 annually. Any excess fair-value allocations are amortized over a 10-year period.

Year	Uncle Company	Nephew Company
2011	$ 90,000	$30,000
2012	120,000	40,000
2013	140,000	50,000

a. Assume that Uncle applies the equity method to account for this investment in Nephew. What is the subsidiary's income recognized by Uncle in 2013?

b. What is the noncontrolling interest's share of the subsidiary's 2013 income?

LO1

16. Mesa, Inc., obtained 80 percent of Butte Corporation on January 1, 2011. Annual amortization of $22,500 is to be recorded on the allocations of Butte's acquisition-date business fair value. On January 1, 2012, Butte acquired 55 percent of Valley Company's voting stock. Excess business fair-value amortization on this second acquisition amounted to $8,000 per year. For 2013, each of the three companies reported the following information accumulated by its separate accounting system. Operating income figures do not include any investment or dividend income.

	Operating Income	Dividends Paid
Mesa	$250,000	$150,000
Butte	98,000	25,000
Valley	140,000	30,000

a. What is consolidated net income for 2013?

b. How is consolidated net income distributed to the controlling and noncontrolling interests?

LO2

17. Baxter, Inc., owns 90 percent of Wisconsin, Inc., and 20 percent of Cleveland Company. Wisconsin, in turn, holds 60 percent of Cleveland's outstanding stock. No excess amortization resulted from these acquisitions. During the current year, Cleveland sold a variety of inventory items to Wisconsin for $40,000 although the original cost was $30,000. Of this total, Wisconsin still held $12,000 in inventory (at transfer price) at year-end.

    During this same period, Wisconsin sold merchandise to Baxter for $100,000 although the original cost was only $70,000. At year-end, $40,000 of these goods (at the transfer price) was still on hand.

    The initial value method was used to record each of these investments. None of the companies holds any other investments.

    Using the following separate income statements, determine the figures that would appear on a consolidated income statement:

	Baxter	Wisconsin	Cleveland
Sales	$(1,000,000)	$(450,000)	$(280,000)
Cost of goods sold	670,000	280,000	190,000
Expenses	110,000	60,000	30,000
Dividend income:			
Wisconsin	(36,000)	–0–	–0–
Cleveland	(4,000)	(12,000)	–0–
Net income	$ (260,000)	$(122,000)	$ (60,000)

LO8

18. Fontana Company developed a specialized banking application software program that it licenses to various financial institutions through multiple-year agreements. On January 1, 2013, these licensing agreements have a fair value of $750,000 and represent Fontana's sole asset. Although Fontana currently has no liabilities, because of recent operating losses, the company has a $120,000 net operating loss (NOL) carryforward.

    On January 1, 2013, Catalan, Inc., acquired all of Fontana's voting stock for $900,000. Catalan expects to extract operating synergies by integrating Fontana's software into its own products. Catalan also hopes that Fontana will be able to receive a future tax reduction from its NOL. Assume an applicable federal income tax rate of 35 percent.

    a. If there is a greater than 50 percent chance that the subsidiary will be able to utilize the NOL carryforward, how much goodwill should Catalan recognize from the acquisition?

    b. If there is a less than 50 percent chance that the subsidiary will be able to utilize the NOL carryforward, how much goodwill should Catalan recognize from the acquisition?

LO6

19. Up and its 80 percent owned subsidiary (Down) reported the following figures for the year ending December 31, 2013. Down paid dividends of $30,000 during this period.

	Up	Down
Sales	$(600,000)	$(300,000)
Cost of goods sold	300,000	140,000
Operating expenses	174,000	60,000
Dividend income	(24,000)	–0–
Net income	$(150,000)	$(100,000)

    In 2012, unrealized gross profits of $30,000 on upstream transfers of $90,000 were deferred into 2013. In 2013, unrealized gross profits of $40,000 on upstream transfers of $110,000 were deferred into 2014.

    a. What amounts appear for each line in a consolidated income statement? Explain your computations.

    b. What income tax expense should appear on the consolidated income statement if each company files a separate return? Assume that the tax rate is 30 percent.

LO5, LO6

20. Clarke has a controlling interest in Rogers's outstanding stock. At the current year-end, the following information has been accumulated for these two companies:

	Operating Income	Dividends Paid
Clarke	$500,000 (includes a $90,000 net unrealized gross profit on intra-entity inventory transfers)	$90,000
Rogers	240,000	80,000

Clarke uses the initial value method to account for the investment in Rogers. The operating income figures just presented include neither dividend nor other investment income. The effective tax rate for both companies is 40 percent.

a. Assume that Clarke owns 100 percent of Rogers's voting stock and is filing a consolidated tax return. What income tax amount does this affiliated group pay for the current period?

b. Assume that Clarke owns 92 percent of Rogers's voting stock and is filing a consolidated tax return. What amount of income taxes does this affiliated group pay for the current period?

c. Assume that Clarke owns 80 percent of Rogers's voting stock, but the companies elect to file separate tax returns. What is the total amount of income taxes that these two companies pay for the current period?

d. Assume that Clarke owns 70 percent of Rogers's voting stock, requiring separate tax returns. What is the total amount of income tax expense to be recognized in the consolidated income statement for the current period?

e. Assume that Clarke owns 70 percent of Rogers's voting stock so that separate tax returns are required. What amount of income taxes does Clarke have to pay for the current year?

LO5, LO6

21. On January 1, 2012, Piranto acquires 90 percent of Slinton's outstanding shares. Financial information for these two companies for the years of 2012 and 2013 follows:

	2012	**2013**
Piranto Company:		
Sales	$(600,000)	$(800,000)
Operating expenses	400,000	500,000
Unrealized gross profits as of end of year (included in above figures)	(120,000)	(150,000)
Dividend income—Slinton Company	(18,000)	(36,000)
Slinton Company:		
Sales	(200,000)	(250,000)
Operating expenses	120,000	150,000
Dividends paid	(20,000)	(40,000)

Assume that a tax rate of 40 percent is applicable to both companies.

a. On consolidated financial statements for 2013, what are the income tax expense and the income tax currently payable if Piranto and Slinton file a consolidated tax return as an affiliated group?

b. On consolidated financial statements for 2013, what are the income tax expense and income tax currently payable if they choose to file separate returns?

LO6

22. Lake acquired a controlling interest in Boxwood several years ago. During the current fiscal period, the two companies individually reported the following income (exclusive of any investment income):

Lake	$300,000
Boxwood	100,000

Lake paid a $90,000 cash dividend during the current year and Boxwood distributed $10,000.

Boxwood sells inventory to Lake each period. Unrealized intra-entity gross profits of $18,000 were present in Lake's beginning inventory for the current year, and its ending inventory carried $32,000 in unrealized profits.

View each of the following questions as an independent situation. The effective tax rate for both companies is 40 percent.

a. If Lake owns a 60 percent interest in Boxwood, what total income tax expense must be reported on a consolidated income statement for this period?

b. If Lake owns a 60 percent interest in Boxwood, what total amount of income taxes must be paid by these two companies for the current year?

c. If Lake owns a 90 percent interest in Boxwood and a consolidated tax return is filed, what amount of income tax expense would be reported on a consolidated income statement for the year?

LO5, LO6

23. Garrison holds a controlling interest in Robertson's outstanding stock. For the current year, the following information has been gathered about these two companies:

	Garrison	Robertson
Operating income	$300,000 (includes a $50,000 net unrealized gain on an intra-entity transfer)	$200,000
Dividends paid	32,000	50,000
Tax rate	40%	40%

Garrison uses the initial value method to account for the investment in Robertson. Garrison's operating income figure does not include dividend income for the current year.

a. Assume that Garrison owns 80 percent of Robertson's voting stock. On a consolidated tax return, what amount of income tax is paid?

b. Assume that Garrison owns 80 percent of Robertson's voting stock. On separate tax returns, what total amount of income tax is paid?

c. Assume that Garrison owns 70 percent of Robertson's voting stock. What total amount of income tax expense does a consolidated income statement recognize?

d. Assume that Garrison holds 60 percent of Robertson's voting stock. On a separate income tax return, what amount of income tax does Garrison have to pay?

LO7

24. Leftwich recently acquired all of Kew Corporation's stock and is now consolidating the financial data of this new subsidiary. Leftwich paid a total of $650,000 for the company, which has the following accounts:

	Fair Value	Tax Basis
Accounts receivable	$110,000	$110,000
Inventory	130,000	130,000
Land	100,000	100,000
Buildings	180,000	140,000
Equipment	200,000	150,000
Liabilities	(220,000)	(220,000)

Assume that the effective tax rate is 30 percent. On a consolidated balance sheet prepared immediately after this takeover, what impact does the acquisition of Kew have on the individual asset and liability accounts reported by the business combination?

LO2

25. House Corporation has been operating profitably since its creation in 1959. At the beginning of 2011, House acquired a 70 percent ownership in Wilson Company. At the acquisition date, House prepared the following fair-value allocation schedule:

Consideration transferred for 70 percent interest in Wilson		$ 707,000
Fair value of the 30% noncontrolling interest		303,000
Wilson business fair value		$1,010,000
Wilson book value		790,000
Excess fair value over book value		$ 220,000
Assignments to adjust Wilson's assets to fair value:		
To buildings (20-year life)	$ 60,000	
To equipment (4-year life)	(20,000)	
To franchises (10-year life)	40,000	80,000
To goodwill (indefinite life)		$ 140,000

House regularly buys inventory from Wilson at a markup of 25 percent more than cost. House's purchases during 2011 and 2012 and related ending inventory balances follow:

Year	Intra-Entity Purchases	Remaining Intra-Entity Inventory—End of Year (at transfer price)
2011	$120,000	$40,000
2012	150,000	60,000

On January 1, 2013, House and Wilson acted together as co-acquirers of 80 percent of Cuddy Company's outstanding common stock. The total price of these shares was $240,000, indicating neither goodwill nor other specific fair-value allocations. Each company put up one-half of the consideration transferred. During 2013, House acquired additional inventory from Wilson at a price of $200,000. Of this merchandise, 45 percent is still held at year-end.

Using the three companies' following financial records for 2013, prepare a consolidation worksheet. The partial equity method based on *operating income* has been applied to each investment.

	House Corporation	Wilson Company	Cuddy Company
Sales and other revenues	$ (900,000)	$ (700,000)	$(300,000)
Cost of goods sold	551,000	300,000	140,000
Operating expenses	219,000	270,000	90,000
Income of Wilson Company	(91,000)	–0–	–0–
Income of Cuddy Company	(28,000)	(28,000)	–0–
Net income	$ (249,000)	$ (158,000)	$ (70,000)
Retained earnings, 1/1/13	$ (820,000)	$ (590,000)	$(150,000)
Net income (above)	(249,000)	(158,000)	(70,000)
Dividends paid	100,000	96,000	50,000
Retained earnings, 12/31/13	$ (969,000)	$ (652,000)	$(170,000)
Cash and receivables	$ 220,000	$ 334,000	$ 67,000
Inventory	390,200	320,000	103,000
Investment in Wilson Company	807,800	–0–	–0–
Investment in Cuddy Company	128,000	128,000	–0–
Buildings	385,000	320,000	144,000
Equipment	310,000	130,000	88,000
Land	180,000	300,000	16,000
Total assets	$ 2,421,000	$ 1,532,000	$ 418,000
Liabilities	$ (632,000)	$ (570,000)	$ (98,000)
Common stock	(820,000)	(310,000)	(150,000)
Retained earnings, 12/31/13	(969,000)	(652,000)	(170,000)
Total liabilities and equities	$(2,421,000)	$(1,532,000)	$(418,000)

LO3

26. Mighty Company purchased a 60 percent interest in Lowly Company on January 1, 2012, for $420,000 in cash. Lowly's book value at that date was reported as $600,000 and the fair value of the noncontrolling interest was assessed at $280,000. Any excess acquisition-date fair value over Lowly's book value is assigned to trademarks to be amortized over 20 years. Subsequently, on January 1, 2013, Lowly acquired a 20 percent interest in Mighty. The price of $240,000 was equivalent to 20 percent of Mighty's book and fair value.

    Neither company has paid dividends since these acquisitions occurred. On January 1, 2013, Lowly's book value was $800,000, a figure that rises to $840,000 (Common Stock of $300,000 and Retained Earnings of $540,000) by year-end. Mighty's book value was $1.7 million at the beginning of 2013 and $1.8 million (Common Stock of $1 million and Retained Earnings of $800,000) at December 31, 2013. No intra-entity transactions have occurred and no additional stock has been sold. Each company applies the initial value method in accounting for the individual investments. What worksheet entries are required to consolidate these two companies for 2013? What is the noncontrolling interest in the subsidiary's net income for this year?

LO1, LO5, LO6

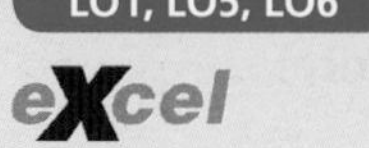

27. On January 1, 2012, Travers Company acquired 90 percent of Yarrow Company's outstanding stock for $720,000. The 10 percent noncontrolling interest had an assessed fair value of $80,000 on that date. Any acquisition-date excess fair value over book value was

attributed to an unrecorded customer list developed by Yarrow with a remaining life of 15 years.

On the same date, Yarrow acquired an 80 percent interest in Stookey Company for $344,000. At the acquisition date, the 20 percent noncontrolling interest fair value was $86,000. Any excess fair value was attributed to a fully amortized copyright that had a remaining life of 10 years. Although both investments are accounted for using the initial value method, neither Yarrow nor Stookey have distributed dividends since the acquisition date. Travers has a policy to pay cash dividends each year equal to 40 percent of operating earnings. Reported income totals for 2012 follow:

Travers Company	$300,000
Yarrow Company.	160,000
Stookey Company	120,000

Following are the 2013 financial statements for these three companies. Stookey has transferred numerous amounts of inventory to Yarrow since the takeover amounting to $80,000 (2012) and $100,000 (2013). These transactions include the same markup applicable to Stookey's outside sales. In each year, Yarrow carried 20 percent of this inventory into the succeeding year before disposing of it. An effective tax rate of 45 percent is applicable to all companies.

	Travers Company	Yarrow Company	Stookey Company
Sales.	$ (900,000)	$ (600,000)	$(500,000)
Cost of goods sold	480,000	320,000	260,000
Operating expenses	100,000	80,000	140,000
Net income	$ (320,000)	$ (200,000)	$(100,000)
Retained earnings, 1/1/13.	$ (700,000)	$ (600,000)	$(300,000)
Net income (above).	(320,000)	(200,000)	(100,000)
Dividends paid	128,000	–0–	–0–
Retained earnings, 12/31/13	$ (892,000)	$ (800,000)	$(400,000)
Current assets.	$ 444,000	$ 380,000	$ 280,000
Investment in Yarrow Company	720,000	–0–	–0–
Investment in Stookey Company.	–0–	344,000	–0–
Land, buildings, and equipment (net) .	949,000	836,000	520,000
Total assets	$ 2,113,000	$ 1,560,000	$ 800,000
Liabilities.	$ (721,000)	$ (460,000)	$(200,000)
Common stock.	(500,000)	(300,000)	(200,000)
Retained earnings, 12/31/13.	(892,000)	(800,000)	(400,000)
Total liabilities and equities	$(2,113,000)	$(1,560,000)	$(800,000)

a. Prepare the business combination's 2013 consolidation worksheet; ignore income tax effects.

b. Determine the amount of income tax for Travers and Yarrow on a consolidated tax return for 2013.

c. Determine the amount of Stookey's income tax on a separate tax return for 2013.

d. Based on the answers to requirements (*b*) and (*c*), what journal entry does this combination make to record 2013 income tax?

LO5, LO6

28. Politan Company acquired an 80 percent interest in Soludan Company on January 1, 2012. Any portion of Soludan's business fair value in excess of its corresponding book value was assigned to trademarks. This intangible asset has subsequently undergone annual amortization based on a 15-year life. Over the past two years, regular intra-entity inventory sales transpired between the two companies. No payment has yet been made on the latest transfer.

Following are the individual financial statements for the two companies as well as consolidated totals for 2013:

	Politan Company	Soludan Company	Consolidated Totals
Sales	$ (800,000)	$(600,000)	$(1,280,000)
Cost of goods sold	500,000	400,000	784,000
Operating expenses	100,000	100,000	202,500
Income of Soludan	(80,000)	–0–	–0–
Separate company net income	$ (280,000)	$(100,000)	
Consolidated net income			$ (293,500)
Noncontrolling interest in Soludan Company's income			18,700
Controlling interest in consolidated net income			$ (274,800)
Retained earnings, 1/1/13	$ (620,000)	$(290,000)	$ (611,600)
Net income (above)	(280,000)	(100,000)	(274,800)
Dividends paid	70,000	20,000	70,000
Retained earnings, 12/31/13	$ (830,000)	$(370,000)	$ (816,400)
Cash and receivables	$ 290,000	$ 90,000	$ 360,000
Inventory	190,000	160,000	338,000
Investment in Soludan Company	390,000	–0–	–0–
Land, buildings, and equipment	380,000	260,000	640,000
Trademarks	–0–	–0–	32,500
Total assets	$ 1,250,000	$ 510,000	$ 1,370,500
Liabilities	$ (270,000)	$ (60,000)	$ (310,000)
Noncontrolling interest in Soludan Company	–0–	–0–	(94,100)
Common stock	(120,000)	(80,000)	(120,000)
Additional paid-in capital	(30,000)	–0–	(30,000)
Retained earnings (above)	(830,000)	(370,000)	(816,400)
Total liabilities and equities	$(1,250,000)	$(510,000)	$(1,370,500)

a. What method does Politan use to account for its investment in Soludan?

b. What is the balance of the unrealized inventory gross profit deferred at the end of the current period?

c. What amount was originally allocated to the trademarks?

d. What is the amount of the current year intra-entity inventory sales?

e. Were the intra-entity inventory sales made upstream or downstream?

f. What is the balance of the intra-entity liability at the end of the current year?

g. What unrealized gross profit was deferred into the current year from the preceding period?

h. The beginning consolidated Retained Earnings account shows a balance of $611,600 rather than the $620,000 reported by the parent. What creates this difference?

i. How was the ending Noncontrolling Interest in Soludan Company computed?

j. With a tax rate of 40 percent, what income tax journal entry is recorded if the companies prepare a consolidated tax return?

k. With a tax rate of 40 percent, what income tax journal entry is recorded if these two companies prepare separate tax returns?

LO1

29. On January 1, 2011, Alpha acquired 80 percent of Delta. Of Delta's total business fair value, $125,000 was allocated to copyrights with a 20-year remaining life. Subsequently, on January 1, 2012, Delta obtained 70 percent of Omega's outstanding voting shares. In this second acquisition, $120,000 of Omega's total business fair value was assigned to copyrights that had a remaining life of 12 years. Delta's book value was $490,000 on January 1, 2011, and Omega reported a book value of $140,000 on January 1, 2012.

Delta has made numerous inventory transfers to Alpha since the business combination was formed. Unrealized gross profits of $15,000 were present in Alpha's inventory as of January 1, 2013. During the year, $200,000 in additional intra-entity sales were made with $22,000 in gross profits remaining unrealized at the end of the period.

Both Alpha and Delta utilized the partial equity method to account for their investment balances.

Following are the individual financial statements for the companies for 2013 with consolidated totals. Develop the worksheet entries necessary to derive these reported balances:

	Alpha Company	Delta Company	Omega Company	Consolidated Totals
Sales	$ (900,000)	$ (500,000)	$(200,000)	$(1,400,000)
Cost of goods sold	500,000	240,000	80,000	627,000
Operating expenses	294,000	129,000	50,000	489,250
Income of subsidiary	(144,000)	(49,000)	–0–	–0–
Separate company net income	$ (250,000)	$ (180,000)	$ (70,000)	
Consolidated net income				$ (283,750)
Noncontrolling interest in income of Delta Company				31,950
Noncontrolling interest in income of Omega Company				18,000
Controlling interest in consolidated net income				$ (233,800)
Retained earnings, 1/1/13	$ (600,000)	$ (400,000)	$(100,000)	$ (572,400)
Net income (above)	(250,000)	(180,000)	(70,000)	(233,800)
Dividends paid	50,000	40,000	50,000	50,000
Retained earnings, 12/31/13	$ (800,000)	$ (540,000)	$(120,000)	$ (756,200)
Cash and receivables	$ 262,000	$ 206,000	$ 70,000	$ 538,000
Inventory	290,000	310,000	160,000	738,000
Investment in Delta Company	628,000	–0–	–0–	–0–
Investment in Omega Company	–0–	238,000	–0–	–0–
Property, plant, and equipment	420,000	316,000	270,000	1,006,000
Copyrights	–0–	–0–	–0–	206,250
Total assets	$ 1,600,000	$ 1,070,000	$ 500,000	$ 2,488,250
Liabilities	$ (600,000)	$ (410,000)	$(280,000)	$(1,290,000)
Common stock	(200,000)	(120,000)	(100,000)	(200,000)
Retained earnings, 12/31/13	(800,000)	(540,000)	(120,000)	(756,200)
Noncontrolling interest in Delta Company, 12/31/13	–0–	–0–	–0–	(146,050)
Noncontrolling interest in Omega Company, 12/31/13	–0–	–0–	–0–	(96,000)
Total liabilities and equities	$(1,600,000)	$(1,070,000)	$(500,000)	$(2,488,250)

Develop Your Skills

EXCEL CASE: INDIRECT SUBSIDIARY CONTROL

Summit owns a 90 percent majority voting interest in Treeline. In turn, Treeline owns a 70 percent majority voting interest in Basecamp. In the current year, each firm reports the following income and dividends. Operating income figures do not include any investment or dividend income.

	Operating Income	Dividends Paid
Summit	$345,000	$150,000
Treeline	280,000	100,000
Basecamp	175,000	40,000

In addition, in computing its income on a full accrual basis, Treeline's acquisition of Basecamp necessitates excess acquisition-date fair value over book value amortizations of $25,000 per year. Similarly, Summit's acquisition of Treeline requires $20,000 of excess fair-value amortizations.

Required

Prepare an Excel spreadsheet that computes the following:

1. Treeline's income including its equity in Basecamp earnings.
2. Summit's income including its equity in Treeline's total earnings.
3. Total entity net income for the three companies.
4. Total noncontrolling interest in the total entity's net income.
5. Difference between these elements:
   - Summit's net income.
   - Total entity net income for the three companies less noncontrolling interest in the total entity's net income.

   (*Hint:* The difference between these two amounts should be zero.)

RESEARCH CASE: CONSOLIDATED TAX EXPENSE

Using the web, access The Coca-Cola Company's 2010 financial statements (www.thecoca-colacompany.com). Identify and discuss the following aspects of consolidated tax expense disclosed in the financial statements:

1. Loss carryforwards and carrybacks.
2. Components of deferred tax assets and liabilities.
3. Deferred tax impacts of stock sales by equity investees.
4. Deferred tax impacts of sales of interests in investees.
5. Valuation allowances on deferred taxes.
6. The impact of Coca-Cola's acquisition of Coca-Cola Enterprises (CCE) on the company's deferred taxes.

chapter 8

Segment and Interim Reporting

As one of the largest companies in the United States, The Walt Disney Company reported consolidated revenues of $38.1 billion in 2010. The Walt Disney Company is well known as a filmmaker and operator of theme parks, but it is perhaps less well known as the owner of the ESPN and ABC television networks. How much of the company's consolidated revenues did these different lines of business generate? Knowing this could be very useful to potential investors as opportunities for future growth and profitability in these different industries could differ significantly.

To comply with U.S. GAAP, Disney disaggregated its 2010 consolidated operating revenues and reported that the company's revenues were generated from these different ventures: approximately $17.2 billion came from Media Networks, $10.8 billion from Parks and Resorts, $6.7 billion from Studio Entertainment, $2.7 billion from Consumer Products, and $0.8 billion from Interactive Media. Additional information disclosed by Disney indicated that $28.3 billion of the 2010 consolidated revenues were generated in the United States and Canada, $6.6 billion in Europe, $2.3 billion in Asia Pacific, and $0.9 billion in Latin America and other parts of the world. Such information, describing the various components of Disney's operations (both by line of business and by geographic area), can often be more useful to an analyst than the single sales figure reported in the consolidated income statement. "All investors like segment reporting—separate financials for each division—because it enables them to analyze how well each part of a corporation is doing."[1]

In its 2010 Annual Report, the Boeing Company reported earnings of $3,307 million for the year ended December 31, 2010. This information was not made available to the public until early in 2011 after the company had closed the books on 2010. To provide more timely information on which investors could base their decisions about the company, Boeing published separate interim reports for each of the first three quarters of 2010. Earnings were $519 million in the first quarter, $787 million in the second quarter, and $837 million in the third quarter, and then earnings climbed in the fourth quarter to $1,164 million. Information about the results of operations for time intervals of less than one year can be very useful to an analyst.

The first part of this chapter examines the specific requirements for disaggregating financial statement information as required by

Learning Objectives

After studying this chapter, you should be able to:

- LO1 Understand how an enterprise determines its operating segments and the factors that influence this determination.
- LO2 Apply the three tests that are used to determine which operating segments are of significant size to warrant separate disclosure.
- LO3 List the basic disclosure requirements for operating segments.
- LO4 Determine when and what types of information must be disclosed for geographic areas.
- LO5 Apply the criterion for determining when disclosure of a major customer is required.
- LO6 Recognize differences between U.S. GAAP and IFRS in segment reporting.
- LO7 Understand and apply procedures used in interim reports to treat an interim period as an integral part of the annual period.
- LO8 List the minimum disclosure requirements for interim financial reports.
- LO9 Recognize differences between U.S. GAAP and IFRS in interim reporting.

[1] Robert A. Parker, "How Do You Play the New Annual Report Game?" *Communication World*, September 1990, p. 26.

authoritative accounting literature. Companies must disclose specific items of information for each reportable operating segment and provide additional enterprisewide disclosures. The second part of the chapter concentrates on the special rules required to be applied in preparing interim reports. All publicly traded companies in the United States are required to prepare interim reports on a quarterly basis.

Segment Reporting

To facilitate the analysis and evaluation of financial data, in the 1960s several groups began to push the accounting profession to require disclosure of segment information. Not surprisingly, the timing of this movement corresponded to a period of significant corporate merger and acquisition activity. As business organizations expanded through ever-widening diversification, financial statement analysis became increasingly difficult. The broadening of an enterprise's activities into different products, industries, or geographic areas complicates the analysis of conditions, trends, and ratios. The various industry segments or geographic areas of an enterprise's operations can have different rates of profitability, degrees and types of risk, and opportunities for growth.

Because of the increasingly diverse activities of many organizations, disclosure of additional information was sought to help financial statement readers. The identity of the significant elements of an entity's operations was viewed as an important complement to consolidated totals. Thus, organizations such as the Financial Analysts Federation, the Financial Executives Institute, and the New York Stock Exchange supported the inclusion of data describing the major components (or segments) of an enterprise as a way to enhance the informational content of corporate financial statements.

The move toward dissemination of disaggregated information culminated in December 1976 with the FASB's release of *SFAS 14,* "Financial Reporting for Segments of a Business Enterprise." This pronouncement established guidelines for the presentation within corporate financial statements of information to describe the various segments that constitute each reporting entity. It also prescribed disclosures related to foreign operations, major customers, and export sales.

Over time, however, financial analysts deemed *SFAS 14* to be inadequate and organizations such as the Association for Investment Management and Research (AIMR) and the AICPA recommended an overhaul of segment reporting rules. In response, the FASB approved FASB *Statement 131,* "Disclosures about Segments of an Enterprise and Related Information," in 1997. Effective for fiscal years beginning after December 15, 1997, this statement made substantial changes to the segment disclosures required to be provided by U.S. companies. *How reportable segments are determined,* and *amount and types of information* to be provided significantly changed. *SFAS 131* was incorporated into the FASB Accounting Standards Codification (ASC) in 2009 under Topic 280, Segment Reporting.

Operating Segments

LO1

Understand how an enterprise determines its operating segments and the factors that influence this determination.

The objective of segment reporting is to provide information about the different business activities in which an enterprise engages and the different economic environments in which it operates to help users of financial statements:

- Better understand the enterprise's performance.
- Better assess its prospects for future net cash flows.
- Make more informed judgments about the enterprise as a whole.

The Management Approach

To achieve this objective, U.S. GAAP follows a so-called management approach for determining segments. The management approach is based on the way that management disaggregates the enterprise for making operating decisions. These disaggregated components are *operating segments,* which will be evident from the enterprise's organization structure. More specifically, an operating segment is a component of an enterprise if:

- It engages in business activities from which it earns revenues and incurs expenses.
- The chief operating decision maker regularly reviews its operating results to assess performance and make resource allocation decisions.
- Its discrete financial information is available.

An organizational unit can be an operating segment even if all of its revenues or expenses result from transactions with other segments as might be the case in a vertically integrated company. However, not all parts of a company are necessarily included in an operating segment. For example, a research and development unit that incurs expenses but does not earn revenues would not be an operating segment. Similarly, corporate headquarters might not earn revenues or might earn revenues that are only incidental to the enterprise's activities and therefore would not be considered an operating segment.

For many companies, only one set of organizational units qualifies as operating segments. In some companies, however, business activities are disaggregated in more than one way and the chief operating decision maker uses multiple sets of reports. For example, a company might generate reports by geographic region *and* by product line. In those cases, two additional criteria must be considered to identify operating segments:

1. An operating segment has a segment manager who is directly accountable to the chief operating decision maker for its financial performance. If more than one set of organizational units exist but segment managers are held responsible for only one set, that set constitutes the operating segments.
2. If segment managers exist for two or more overlapping sets of organizational units (as in a matrix form of organization), the nature of the business activities must be considered, and the organizational units based on products and services constitute the operating segments. For example, if certain managers are responsible for different product lines and other managers are responsible for different geographic areas, the enterprise components based on products would constitute the operating segments.

Determination of Reportable Operating Segments

LO2

Apply the three tests that are used to determine which operating segments are of significant size to warrant separate disclosure.

After a company has identified its operating segments based on its internal reporting system, management must decide which segments to report separately. Generally, information must be reported separately for each operating segment that meets one or more quantitative thresholds. *However, if two or more operating segments have essentially the same business activities in essentially the same economic environments, information for those individual segments may be combined.* For example, a retail chain may have five stores, each of which meets the definition of an operating segment, but each store is essentially the same as the others. In that case, the benefit to be derived from separately reporting each operating segment would not justify the cost of disclosure. In determining whether business activities and environments are similar, management must consider these aggregation criteria:

1. The nature of the products and services provided by each operating segment.
2. The nature of the production process.
3. The type or class of customer.
4. The distribution methods.
5. If applicable, the nature of the regulatory environment.

Segments must be similar in each and every one of these areas to be combined. However, aggregation of similar segments is not required.

Quantitative Thresholds

After determining whether any segments are to be combined, management next must decide which of its operating segments are significant enough to justify separate disclosure. The

FASB established three tests for identifying operating segments for which separate disclosure is required:

- A revenue test.
- A profit or loss test.
- An asset test.

An operating segment needs to satisfy only one of these tests to be considered of significant size to necessitate separate disclosure.

To apply these three tests, a segment's revenues, profit or loss, and assets must be determined. Authoritative literature does not stipulate a specific measure of profit or loss, such as operating profit or income before taxes, to be used in applying these tests. Instead, the profit measure used by the chief operating decision maker in evaluating operating segments is to be used. An operating segment is considered to be significant if it meets any one of the following tests:

1. *Revenue test.* Segment revenues, both external and intersegment, are 10 percent or more of the combined revenue, internal and external, of all reported operating segments.
2. *Profit or loss test.* Segment profit or loss is 10 percent or more of the larger (in absolute terms) of the combined reported profit of all profitable segments or the combined reported loss of all segments incurring a loss.
3. *Asset test.* Segment assets are 10 percent or more of the combined assets of all operating segments.

Application of the revenue and asset tests appears to pose few problems. In contrast, the profit or loss test is more complicated and warrants illustration. For this purpose, assume that Durham Company has five separate operating segments with the following profits or losses:

Durham Company Segments—Profits and Losses

Soft drinks	$1,700,000
Wine	(600,000)
Food products	240,000
Paper packaging	880,000
Recreation parks	(130,000)
Net operating profit	$2,090,000

Three of these industry segments (soft drinks, food products, and paper packaging) report profits that total $2,820,000. The two remaining segments have losses of $730,000 for the year.

Profits		Losses	
Soft drinks	$1,700,000	Wine	$600,000
Food products	240,000	Recreation parks	130,000
Paper packaging	880,000		
Total	$2,820,000	Total	$730,000

Consequently, $2,820,000 serves as the basis for the profit or loss test because that figure is larger in absolute terms than $730,000. Based on the 10 percent threshold, any operating segment with either a profit *or loss* of more than $282,000 (10% × $2,820,000) is considered material and, thus, must be disclosed separately. According to this one test, the soft drink and paper packaging segments (with operating profits of $1.7 million and $880,000, respectively) are both judged to be reportable, as is the wine segment, despite having a loss of $600,000.

Operating segments that do not meet any of the quantitative thresholds may be combined to produce a reportable segment if they share *a majority* of the aggregation criteria listed earlier. Durham Company's food products and recreation parks operating segments do not meet any of the aggregation criteria. Operating segments that are not individually significant and that cannot be aggregated with other segments are combined and disclosed in an *All Other* category. The sources of the revenues included in the All Other category must be disclosed.

Testing Procedures—Complete Illustration

To provide a comprehensive example of all three of these testing procedures, assume that Atkinson Company is a large business combination comprising six operating segments: automotive, furniture, textbook, motion picture, appliance, and finance. Complete information about each of these segments, as reported internally to the chief operating decision maker, appears in Exhibit 8.1.

The Revenue Test

In applying the revenue test to Atkinson Company's operating segments, the combined revenue of all segments must be determined:

Operating Segment	Total Revenues
Automotive	$41.6*
Furniture	9.0
Textbook	6.8
Motion picture	22.8
Appliance	5.3
Finance	12.3
Combined total	$97.8

*All figures are in millions.

EXHIBIT 8.1 Reportable Segment Testing

ATKINSON COMPANY

	Automotive	Furniture	Textbook	Motion Picture	Appliance	Finance
Revenues:						
Sales to outsiders	$32.6*	$6.9	$ 6.6	$22.2	$3.1	-0-
Intersegment transfers	6.6	1.2	-0-	-0-	1.9	-0-
Interest revenue—outsiders	2.4	0.9	0.2	0.6	0.3	$ 8.7
Interest revenue—intersegment loans	-0-	-0-	-0-	-0-	-0-	$ 3.6
Total revenues	$41.6	$9.0	$ 6.8	$22.8	$5.3	$12.3
Expenses:						
Operating expenses—outsiders	$17.1	$3.6	$ 7.3	$24.0	$3.6	$ 2.3
Operating expenses—intersegment transfers	4.8	1.0	-0-	-0-	0.8	0.8
Interest expense	2.1	1.0	2.2	4.6	-0-	6.1
Income taxes	6.6	1.4	(1.5)	(3.1)	0.4	0.1
Total expenses	$30.6	$7.0	$ 8.0	$25.5	$4.8	$ 9.3
Assets:						
Tangible	$ 9.6	$1.1	$ 0.8	$10.9	$0.9	$ 9.2
Intangible	1.8	0.2	0.7	3.6	0.1	-0-
Intersegment loans	-0-	-0-	-0-	-0-	-0-	5.4
Total assets	$11.4	$1.3	$ 1.5	$14.5	$1.0	$14.6

*All figures in millions.

Because these six segments have total revenues of $97.8 million, that figure is used in applying the revenue test. Based on the 10 percent significance level, any segment with revenues of more than $9.78 million qualifies for required disclosure. Accordingly, the automotive, motion picture, and finance segments have satisfied this particular criterion. Atkinson must present appropriate disaggregated information for each of these three operating segments within its financial statements.

The Profit or Loss Test

Subtracting segment expenses from total segment revenues determines the profit or loss of each operating segment. Common costs are not required to be allocated to individual segments to determine segment profit or loss if this is not normally done for internal purposes. For example, an enterprise that accounts for pension expense only on a consolidated basis is not required to allocate pension expense to each operating segment. Any allocations that are made must be done on a reasonable basis. Moreover, segment profit or loss does not have to be calculated in accordance with generally accepted accounting principles if the measure reported internally is calculated on another basis. To assist the readers of financial statements in understanding segment disclosures, any differences in the basis of measurement between segment and consolidated amounts must be disclosed.

Each operating segment's profit or loss is calculated as follows:

Operating Segment	Total Revenues	Total Expenses	Profit	Loss
Automotive	$41.6*	$30.6	$11.0	–0–
Furniture	9.0	7.0	2.0	–0–
Textbook	6.8	8.0	–0–	$ 1.2
Motion picture	22.8	25.5	–0–	2.7
Appliance	5.3	4.8	0.5	–0–
Finance	12.3	9.3	3.0	–0–
Totals	$97.8	$85.2	$16.5	$ 3.9

*All figures are in millions.

The $16.5 million total (the four profit figures) is larger in an absolute sense than the $3.9 million in losses. Therefore, this larger balance is the basis for the second quantitative test. As a result of the 10 percent criterion, either a profit or loss of $1.65 million or more qualifies a segment for disaggregation. According to the income totals just calculated, Atkinson Company's automotive, furniture, motion picture, and finance segments are large enough to warrant separate disclosure.

The Asset Test

The final test is based on the operating segments' combined total assets:

Operating Segment	Assets
Automotive	$11.4*
Furniture	1.3
Textbook	1.5
Motion picture	14.5
Appliance	1.0
Finance	14.6
Combined total	$44.3

*All figures are in millions.

Because 10 percent of the combined total equals $4.43 million, any segment holding at least that amount of assets is viewed as a reportable segment. Consequently, according to this final significance test, the automotive, motion picture, and finance segments are all considered of sufficient size to require disaggregation. The three remaining segments do not have sufficient assets to pass this particular test.

Analysis of Test Results

A summary of all three significance tests as applied to Atkinson Company follows:

Operating Segments	Revenue Test	Profit or Loss Test	Asset Test
Automotive	✔	✔	✔
Furniture		✔	
Textbook			
Motion picture	✔	✔	✔
Appliance			
Finance	✔	✔	✔

Four of this company's operating segments meet at least one of the quantitative thresholds (automotive, furniture, motion picture, and finance) and therefore are separately reportable. Because neither the appliance nor the textbook segment has met any of these three tests, disaggregated information describing their *individual* operations is not required. However, the financial data accumulated from these two nonsignificant segments still have to be presented. The figures can be combined and disclosed as aggregate amounts in an All Other category with appropriate disclosure of the source of revenues.

Other Guidelines

Additional guidelines apply to the disclosure of operating segment information. These rules are designed to ensure that the disaggregated data are consistent from year to year and relevant to the needs of financial statement users. For example, any operating segment that has been reportable in the past and is judged by management to be of continuing significance should be disclosed separately in the current statements regardless of the outcome of the testing process. This degree of flexibility is included within the rules to ensure the ongoing usefulness of the disaggregated information, especially for comparison purposes.

In a similar manner, if an operating segment newly qualifies for disclosure in the current year, prior period segment data presented for comparative purposes must be restated to reflect the newly reportable segment as a separate segment. Again, the comparability of information has high priority in setting the standards for disclosure.

Another issue concerns the number of operating segments that should be disclosed. To enhance the value of the disaggregated information, a substantial portion of a company's operations should be presented individually. A sufficient number of segments are presumed to be included only if their combined sales to unaffiliated customers are at least 75 percent of total company sales made to outsiders. If this lower limit is not achieved, additional segments must be disclosed separately despite their failure to satisfy even one of the three quantitative thresholds.

As an illustration, assume that Brendan Corporation identified seven operating segments that generated revenues as follows (in millions):

Operating Segments	Sales to Unaffiliated Customers	Intersegment Transfers	Segment Revenues (and percentage of total)	
Housewares	$ 5.5	$ 1.6	$ 7.1	9.3%
Toys	6.2	–0–	6.2	8.1
Pottery	3.4	7.9	11.3	14.8 ✔
Lumber	6.6	10.4	17.0	22.3 ✔
Lawn mowers	7.2	–0–	7.2	9.4
Appliances	2.1	6.2	8.3	10.9 ✔
Construction	19.2	–0–	19.2	25.2 ✔
Totals	$50.2	$26.1	$76.3	100%

Based on the 10 percent revenue test, four of these segments are reportable (because each has total revenues of more than $7.63 million): pottery, lumber, appliances, and construction. Assuming that none of the other segments qualifies as significant in either of the two remaining tests, disclosure of disaggregated data is required for only these four segments. However, the 75 percent rule has not been met; the reportable segments generate just 62.4 percent of the company's total sales to unrelated parties (in millions):

Reportable Segments	**Sales to Unaffiliated Customers**
Pottery	$ 3.4
Lumber	6.6
Appliances	2.1
Construction	19.2
Total	$31.3
Information being disaggregated: $31.3 million/$50.2 million = 62.4%	

To satisfy the 75 percent requirement, Brendan Corporation must also include the lawn mower segment within the disaggregated data. With the addition of this nonsignificant segment, sales of $38.5 million ($31.3 + $7.2) to outside parties now are disclosed. This figure amounts to 76.7 percent of the company total ($38.5 million/$50.2 million). The two remaining segments—housewares and toys—could still be included separately within the disaggregated data; disclosure is not prohibited. However, information for these two segments probably would be combined and reported as aggregate amounts in an All Other category.

One final aspect of these reporting requirements should be mentioned. Some companies might be organized in such a fashion that a relatively large number of operating segments exist. The authoritative guidance suggests that there could be a practical limit to the number of operating segments that should be reported separately. Beyond that limit, the information becomes too detailed to be useful. Although a maximum number is not prescribed, authoritative literature suggests that 10 separately reported segments might be the practical limit. Exhibit 8.2 provides a flowchart summarizing the procedures for determining separately reportable operating segments.

Information to Be Disclosed by Reportable Operating Segment

List the basic disclosure requirements for operating segments.

Consistent with requests from the financial analyst community, a significant amount of information is required to be disclosed for each operating segment:

1. *General information* about the operating segment:
   - Factors used to identify reportable operating segments.
   - Types of products and services from which each operating segment reported derives its revenues.
2. *Segment profit or loss* and the following revenues and expenses included in segment profit or loss:
   - Revenues from external customers.
   - Revenues from transactions with other operating segments.
   - Interest revenue and interest expense (reported separately); net interest revenue may be reported for finance segments if this measure is used internally for evaluation.
   - Depreciation, depletion, and amortization expenses.
   - Other significant noncash items included in segment profit or loss.
   - Unusual items and extraordinary items.
   - Income tax expense or benefit.

EXHIBIT 8.2 Flowchart for Determining Reportable Operating Segments

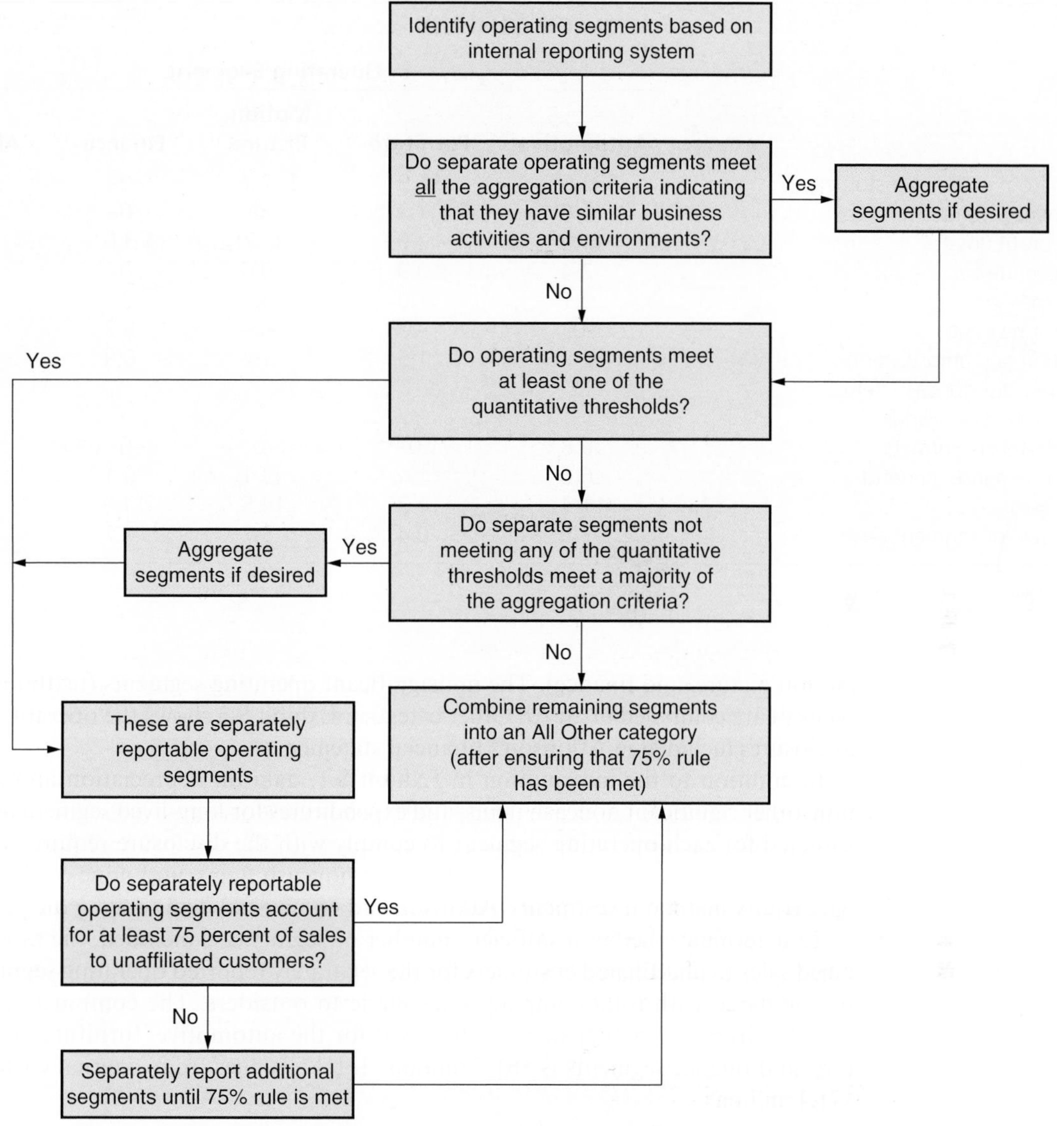

3. *Total segment assets* and the following related items:
    - Investment in equity method affiliates.
    - Expenditures for additions to long-lived assets.

Authoritative guidance does not specifically require cash flow information to be reported for each operating segment because this information often is not generated by segment for internal reporting purposes. The requirement to disclose significant noncash items other than depreciation is an attempt to provide information that might enhance users' ability to estimate cash flow from operations.

Immaterial items need not be disclosed. For example, some segments do not have material amounts of interest revenue and expense, and therefore disclosure of these items of information is not necessary. In addition, if the internal financial reporting system does not generate information for an item on a segment basis, that item need not be disclosed. This is consistent with the rationale that segment reporting should create as little additional cost to an enterprise as possible.

To demonstrate how the operating segment information might be disclosed, we return to the Atkinson Company example earlier in this chapter. Application of the quantitative threshold tests resulted in four separately reportable segments (automotive, furniture,

EXHIBIT 8.3 Operating Segment Disclosures

ATKINSON COMPANY

	Operating Segment				
	Automotive	Furniture	Motion Picture	Finance	All Other
Revenues from external customers	$32.6*	$6.9	$22.2	–0–	$ 9.7
Intersegment revenues	6.6	1.2	–0–	–0–	1.9
Segment profit (loss)	11.0	2.0	(2.7)	$ 3.0	(0.7)
Interest revenue	2.4	0.9	0.6	–0–	0.5
Interest expense	2.1	1.0	4.6	–0–	2.2
Net interest revenue	–0–	–0–	–0–	6.2	–0–
Depreciation and amortization	2.7	1.5	2.4	0.9	0.4
Other significant noncash items:					
Cost in excess of billings on long-term contracts	0.8	–0–	–0–	–0–	–0–
Income tax expense (benefit)	6.6	1.4	(3.1)	0.1	(1.1)
Segment assets	11.4	1.3	14.5	14.6	2.5
Expenditures for segment assets	3.5	0.4	3.7	1.7	1.3

*All figures in millions.

motion picture, and finance). The nonsignificant operating segments (textbook and appliance) are combined in an All Other category. Exhibit 8.3 shows the operating segment disclosures included in Atkinson's financial statements.

In addition to the information in Exhibit 8.1, data on depreciation and amortization, other significant noncash items, and expenditures for long-lived segment assets were gathered for each operating segment to comply with the disclosure requirements. Only the automotive segment has other significant noncash items, and none of the segments have equity method investments. Atkinson had no unusual items during the year.

To determine whether a sufficient number of segments is included, the ratio of combined sales to unaffiliated customers for the separately reported operating segments must be compared with total company sales made to outsiders. The combined amount of revenues from external customers disclosed for the automotive, furniture, motion picture, and finance segments is $61.7 million. Total revenues from external customers are $71.4 million:

$$\$61.7 \text{ million}/\$71.4 \text{ million} = 86.4\%$$

Because 86.4 percent exceeds the FASB's lower limit of 75 percent, Atkinson's level of disaggregation is adequate.

Reconciliations to Consolidated Totals

As noted earlier, information is to be provided as the company's internal reporting system prepares it even if not based on GAAP. Preparing segment information in accordance with authoritative accounting literature used at the consolidated level would be difficult because some GAAP is not intended to apply at the segment level. Examples are accounting for (1) inventory on a LIFO basis when inventory pools include items in more than one segment, (2) companywide pension plans, and (3) acquired goodwill. Accordingly, allocation of these items to individual operating segments is not required.

However, the total of the reportable segments' revenues must be reconciled to consolidated revenues, and the total of reportable segments' profit or loss must be reconciled to income before tax for the company as a whole. Adjustments and eliminations that have been made to develop enterprise financial statements in compliance with generally accepted accounting principles must be identified. Examples are the elimination of intersegment revenues and an adjustment for companywide pension expense. The same is true for reconciliation of total segments' assets to the enterprise's total assets.

EXHIBIT 8.4
Reconciliation of Segment Results to Consolidated Totals

ATKINSON COMPANY

Revenues:	
Total segment revenues	$ 97.8*
Elimination of intersegment revenues	(13.3)
Total consolidated revenues	$ 84.5
Profit or loss:	
Total segment profit or loss	$ 12.6
Total segment income taxes	3.9
Total segment profit before income taxes	$ 16.5
Elimination of intersegment profits	(5.9)
Unallocated amounts:	
Litigation settlement received	3.6
Other corporate expenses	(2.7)
Adjustment to pension expense in consolidation	(0.8)
Consolidated income before income taxes	$ 10.7
Assets:	
Total for reported segments	$ 44.3
Elimination of intersegment loans	(5.4)
Goodwill not allocated to segments	3.2
Other unallocated amounts	2.6
Total consolidated assets	$ 44.7

*All figures in millions.

In addition, in reconciling the total of segments' revenues, profit or loss, and assets to the enterprise totals, the aggregate amount of revenues, profit or loss, and assets from immaterial operating segments must be disclosed. The company also must disclose assets, revenues, expenses, gains, losses, interest expense, and depreciation, depletion, and amortization expense for components of the enterprise that are not operating segments. This includes, for example, assets and expenses associated with corporate headquarters. See Exhibit 8.4 for an example of how Atkinson might present these reconciliations.

Atkinson Company must make three adjustments in reconciling segment results with consolidated totals. The first adjustment is to eliminate intra-entity revenues, profit or loss, and assets that are not included in consolidated totals. The elimination of intersegment revenues includes intersegment transfers amounting to $9.7 million plus $3.6 million of intersegment interest revenue generated by the finance segment (total $13.3 million). The second adjustment relates to corporate items that have not been allocated to the operating segments, including acquired goodwill, a litigation settlement received by the company, and corporate headquarters expenses and assets. The third adjustment reconciles differences in segment accounting practices from accounting practices used in the consolidated financial statements. The only adjustment of this nature that Atkinson made relates to the accounting for pension expense. Individual operating segments measure pension expense based on cash payments made to the pension plan. Because GAAP requires measuring pension expense on an accrual basis, an adjustment for the amount of pension expense to be recognized in the consolidated statements is necessary.

Explanation of Measurement

In addition to the operating segment disclosures and reconciliation of segment results to consolidated totals, companies also must explain the measurement of segment profit or loss and segment assets, including a description of any differences in measuring (1) segment profit or loss and consolidated income before tax, (2) segment assets and consolidated assets, and (3) segment profit or loss and segment assets. An example of this last item is the allocation of depreciation expense to segments but not of the related depreciable assets. The basis of accounting for intersegment transactions also must be described.

Examples of Operating Segment Disclosures

A majority of companies are organized along product and/or service lines. Exhibit 8.5 shows operating segment disclosures for Pfizer Inc. Pfizer does not disclose interest revenue and interest expense by operating segment because these relate only to the corporate/other

EXHIBIT 8.5 Operating Segment Disclosures in Pfizer's 2010 Annual Report

20. Segment, Geographic and Revenue Information

Business Segments

Effective with the acquisition of Wyeth, we operate in the following two distinct commercial organizations, which constitute our two business segments:

- **Biopharmaceutical**
  consists of the Primary Care, Specialty Care, Oncology, Established Products and Emerging Markets units and includes products that prevent and treat cardiovascular and metabolic diseases, central nervous system disorders, arthritis and pain, infectious and respiratory diseases, urogenital conditions, cancer, eye diseases and endocrine disorders, among others. Biopharmaceutical's segment profit includes costs related to research and development, manufacturing, and sales and marketing activities that are associated with the products in our Biopharmaceutical segment.
- **Diversified**
  includes Animal Health products and services that prevent and treat diseases in livestock and companion animals, including vaccines, parasiticides and anti-infectives; Consumer Healthcare products that include over-the-counter healthcare products such as pain management therapies (analgesics and heat wraps), cough/cold/allergy remedies, dietary supplements, hemorrhoidal care and personal care items; Nutrition products that consist mainly of infant and toddler nutritional products; and Capsugel, which represents our capsule products and services business. Diversified's segment profit includes costs related to research and development, manufacturing, and sales and marketing activities that are associated with the products in our Diversified segment.

Segment profit/(loss) is measured based on income from continuing operations before provision for taxes on income and income attributable to noncontrolling interests. Certain costs, such as significant impacts of purchase accounting for acquisitions, restructuring and acquisition-related costs, costs related to our cost-reduction initiatives and certain asset impairment charges are included in *Corporate/Other* only. This methodology is utilized by management to evaluate our businesses. We regularly review our segments and the approach used by management to evaluate performance and allocate resources.

Segment ($ in millions)	Year Ended December 31,		
	2010	2009	2008
Revenues			
Biopharmaceutical	**$ 58,523**	$ 45,448	$ 44,174
Diversified	**8,966**	4,189	3,592
Corporate/Other	**320**	372	530
Total revenues	**$ 67,809**	$ 50,009	$ 48,296
Segment Profit/(Loss)			
Biopharmaceutical	**$ 28,981**	$ 21,939	$ 21,786
Diversified	**2,042**	935	972
Corporate/Other	**(21,601)**	(12,047)	(13,064)
Total profit/(loss)	**$ 9,422**	$ 10,827	$ 9,694
Identifiable Assets			
Biopharmaceutical	**$123,560**	$140,008	$ 60,591
Diversified	**18,255**	19,470	2,808
Discontinued operations/Held for sale	**561**	496	148
Corporate/Other	**52,638**	52,975	47,601
Total identifiable assets	**$195,014**	$212,949	$111,148
Property, Plant, and Equipment Additions			
Biopharmaceutical	**$ 1,263**	$ 985	$ 1,351
Diversified	**160**	147	265
Corporate/Other	**90**	73	85
Total property, plant and equipment additions	**$ 1,513**	$ 1,205	$ 1,701
Depreciation and Amortization			
Biopharmaceutical	**$ 2,731**	$ 1,672	$ 2,223
Diversified	**183**	113	108
Corporate/Other	**5,573**	2,972	2,759
Total depreciation and amortization	**$ 8,487**	$ 4,757	$ 5,090

category. Nor does it report income tax expense or benefit by segment because the company evaluates the performance of its operating segments based on income before taxes.

Some companies, such as McDonald's, Coca-Cola, and Nike, are organized geographically and define operating segments as regions of the world. McDonald's has four operating segments: United States; Europe; Asia, Pacific, Middle East, Africa (APMEA); and Other Countries and Corporate. Some companies report a combination of products or services and international segments. Walmart has four operating segments: Walmart U.S., Walmart International, Sam's Club, and Other. PepsiCo has six reportable segments: Frito-Lay North America (FLNA); Quaker Foods North America (QFNA); Latin America Foods (LAF); PepsiCo Americas Beverages (PAB); Europe; and Asia, Middle East, and Africa (AMEA). The nature of these companies' segmentation provides considerable insight into the way upper management views and evaluates the various parts of the consolidated enterprise.

Entity-Wide Information

Information about Products and Services

The authoritative literature recognizes that some enterprises are not organized along product or service lines. For example, some enterprises organize by geographic areas. Moreover, some enterprises may have only one operating segment yet provide a range of different products and services. To provide some comparability between enterprises, the authoritative literature requires *disclosure of revenues derived from transactions with external customers from each product or service* if operating segments have not been determined based on differences in products or services. An enterprise with only one operating segment also must disclose revenues from external customers on the basis of product or service. However, providing this information is not required if impracticable; that is, the information is not available and the cost to develop it would be excessive.

Lowe's Companies, Inc., operates in only one segment; nevertheless, it reported "sales by product category," as required in its 2010 annual report. See Exhibit 8.6 for that information.

EXHIBIT 8.6 **Sales by Product Category in Lowe's Companies, Inc., 2010 Annual Report**

	Sales by Product Category ($ in millions)					
	2010		2009		2008	
Product Category	**Total Sales**	**%**	**Total Sales**	**%**	**Total Sales**	**%**
Appliances	$ 5,365	11%	$ 4,904	10%	$ 4,752	10%
Lumber	3,402	7	3,242	7	3,506	7
Paint	3,003	6	2,913	6	2,791	6
Millwork	2,884	6	2,786	6	2,965	6
Building materials	2,879	6	2,924	6	2,966	6
Lawn & landscape products	2,812	6	2,690	6	2,585	5
Flooring	2,779	6	2,765	6	2,879	6
Rough plumbing	2,709	6	2,659	6	2,618	6
Seasonal living	2,654	5	2,413	5	2,449	5
Tools	2,604	5	2,439	5	2,563	5
Hardware	2,526	5	2,497	5	2,516	5
Fashion plumbing	2,433	5	2,475	5	2,573	5
Lighting	2,396	5	2,407	5	2,508	5
Nursery	1,962	4	1,942	4	1,850	4
Outdoor power equipment	1,932	4	1,834	4	1,963	4
Cabinets & countertops	1,700	3	1,715	4	1,935	4
Home organization	1,695	3	1,662	3	1,662	4
Rough electrical	1,409	3	1,316	3	1,446	3
Home fashion	1,337	3	1,309	3	1,408	3
Other	334	1	328	1	295	1
Totals	**$48,815**	**100%**	**$47,220**	**100%**	**$48,230**	**100%**

LO4

Determine when and what types of information must be disclosed for geographic areas.

Information about Geographic Areas

Two items of information—revenues from external customers and long-lived assets—must be reported (1) for the *domestic country* and (2) for *all foreign countries in total* in which the enterprise derives revenues or holds assets. In addition, if revenues from external customers attributed to an *individual foreign country* are material, the specific country and amount of revenues must be disclosed separately as must a material amount of long-lived assets located in an individual foreign country. Even if the company has only one operating segment and therefore does not otherwise provide segment information, it must report geographic area information.

Thus, U.S.-based companies are required to disclose the amount of revenues generated and long-lived assets held in (1) the United States, (2) all other countries in total, and (3) each material foreign country. Requiring disclosure at the individual country level is a significant change from previous accounting standards, which required disclosures according to groups of countries in the same geographic area. Current U.S. GAAP does not preclude companies from continuing to provide this information and for consistency purposes, many companies continue to do so even if they determine no single foreign country to be material. The reporting requirement was changed from geographic regions to individual countries because reporting information about individual countries has two benefits. First, it reduces the burden on financial statement preparers because most companies likely have material operations in only a few countries, perhaps only their country of domicile. Second, and more important, country-specific information is easier to interpret and therefore more useful. Individual countries within a geographic area often experience very different rates of economic growth and economic conditions. Disclosures by individual country rather than broad geographic area provide investors and other financial statement readers better information for assessing the risk level associated with a company's foreign operations.

Although a 10 percent threshold was considered for determining when a country is material, ultimately it was decided to leave this to management's judgment. In determining materiality, management should apply the concept that an item is material if its omission could change a user's decision about the enterprise as a whole. U.S. GAAP does not provide more specific guidance on this issue.

Considerable variation exists with respect to how companies apply the materiality rule for determining separately reportable countries. For example, International Business Machines Corporation (IBM) provides disclosures only for those countries with 10 percent or more of revenues or net plant, property, and equipment. Exhibit 8.7

EXHIBIT 8.7
IBM's Geographic Area Disclosures

INTERNATIONAL BUSINESS MACHINES CORPORATION

GEOGRAPHIC INFORMATION

The following provides information for those countries that are 10 percent or more of the specific category.

Revenue* ($ in millions) *For the year ended December 31:*	**2010**	**2009**	**2008**
United States	**$35,581**	$34,150	$ 36,686
Japan	**10,701**	10,222	10,403
Other countries	**53,589**	51,386	56,541
Total IBM consolidated revenue	**$99,870**	$95,758	$103,630

Net Plant, Property, and Equipment ($ in millions) *At December 31:*	**2010**	**2009**	**2008**
United States	**$ 6,134**	$ 6,313	$ 6,469
Japan	**1,163**	1,050	1,055
Other countries	**5,135**	5,092	4,797
Total	**$12,432**	$12,455	$12,321

*Revenues are attributed to countries based on the location of the client.

EXHIBIT 8.8 **DuPont's Geographic Area Disclosures**

E. I. DU PONT DE NEMOURS AND COMPANY

Geographic Information

	2010		2009		2008	
	Net Sales[1]	**Net Property[2]**	**Net Sales[1]**	**Net Property[2]**	**Net Sales[1]**	**Net Property[2]**
United States	**$11,451**	**$ 7,835**	$ 9,814	$ 7,641	$11,091	$ 7,784
EMEA[3]						
Belgium	**$ 298**	**$ 139**	$ 240	$ 146	$ 350	$ 157
France.	**777**	**102**	837	100	1,072	115
Germany.	**1,939**	**289**	1,645	294	2,220	309
Italy.	**767**	**36**	684	39	912	28
Luxembourg	**67**	**244**	50	243	88	247
Russia	**306**	**7**	253	7	359	7
Spain	**427**	**259**	389	291	521	297
The Netherlands	**264**	**216**	215	220	240	229
United Kingdom	**503**	**116**	452	126	605	138
Other	**2,769**	**327**	2,400	329	3,119	325
Total EMEA	**$ 8,117**	**$ 1,735**	$ 7,165	$ 1,795	$ 9,486	$ 1,852
Asia Pacific						
Australia	**$ 236**	**$ 9**	$ 178	$ 8	$ 255	$ 9
China/Hong Kong	**2,759**	**494**	1,827	427	1,656	309
India	**695**	**81**	492	65	485	60
Japan	**1,464**	**102**	1,096	97	1,302	102
Korea	**614**	**65**	482	74	534	78
Singapore	**179**	**31**	135	32	153	42
Taiwan	**534**	**129**	362	129	420	132
Thailand	**266**	**3**	190	3	236	4
Other	**562**	**69**	427	47	442	26
Total Asia Pacific	**$ 7,309**	**$ 983**	$ 5,189	$ 882	$ 5,483	$ 762
Latin America						
Argentina	**$ 321**	**$ 26**	$ 282	$ 27	$ 335	$ 28
Brazil.	**1,892**	**317**	1,584	316	1,775	300
Mexico	**915**	**215**	757	215	843	225
Other	**592**	**58**	559	53	609	46
Total Latin America	**$ 3,720**	**$ 616**	$ 3,182	$ 611	$ 3,562	$ 599
Canada	**$ 908**	**$ 170**	$ 759	$ 165	$ 907	$ 157
Total	**$31,505**	**$11,339**	$26,109	$11,094	$30,529	$ 11,154

[1] Net sales are attributed to countries based on the location of the customer.
[2] Includes property, plant, and equipment less accumulated depreciation.
[3] Europe, Middle East, and Africa (EMEA).

contains the geographic area information included in IBM's 2010 Annual Report. Only the United States and Japan meet the company's materiality threshold of 10 percent. As a result, the location of more than 50 percent of IBM's revenues is not disclosed. In contrast, Exhibit 8.8 provides the geographic area disclosures made by E.I. du Pont de Nemours and Company in its 2010 Annual Report. DuPont defines materiality at a very low amount. For example, Singapore generated only one-half of one percent (0.5%) of net sales. DuPont provides disclosures for 22 individual countries (including the United States) that comprise 88 percent of the company's total net sales.

LO5

Apply the criterion for determining when disclosure of a major customer is required.

Information about Major Customers

Authoritative accounting literature requires one final but important disclosure. A reporting entity must indicate its reliance on any major external customer. *Presentation of this*

Discussion Question

HOW DOES A COMPANY DETERMINE WHETHER A FOREIGN COUNTRY IS MATERIAL?

Segment reporting can provide useful information for investors and competitors. Segment disclosures could result in competitive harm for the company making the disclosures. By analyzing segment information, potential competitors can identify and concentrate on the more successful areas of a disclosing company's business. Indeed, the FASB recognized competitive harm as an issue of concern for companies disclosing segment information. In developing the current segment reporting guidelines, the FASB considered but ultimately decided not to provide companies an exemption from providing segment information if they believed that doing so would result in competitive harm. The FASB believed that such an exemption would be inappropriate because it would provide a means for broad noncompliance with the new standard.

The previous segment reporting standard required geographic segments with 10 percent or more of total firm revenues, operating profit, or identifiable assets to be reported separately. In contrast, the current guidelines require disclosures to be provided by country when revenues or long-lived assets in an individual country are material. However, U.S. GAAP does not specify what is material for this purpose but leaves this to management judgment. Some commentators have expressed a concern that firms might use high materiality thresholds to avoid making individual country disclosures, perhaps to avoid potential competitive harm. Anecdotally, the very different levels of disclosure provided in 2010 by IBM and DuPont shown in Exhibits 8.7 and 8.8, respectively, suggest that companies define materiality differently.

What factors might a company consider in determining whether an individual foreign country is material to its operations? Should U.S. GAAP require a percentage test to determine when an individual country is material?

information is required whenever 10 percent or more of a company's consolidated revenues is derived from a single external customer. The existence of all major customers must be disclosed along with the related amount of revenues and the identity of the operating segment generating the revenues. Interestingly enough, the company need not reveal the customer's identity.

The 2010 Annual Report of toy manufacturer Hasbro, Inc., provides an example of how this information is disclosed. In Note 18, Segment Reporting, Hasbro discloses: "Sales to the Company's three largest customers, Wal-Mart Stores, Inc., Target Corporation, and Toys 'R' Us, Inc., amounted to 23 percent, 12 percent and 11 percent, respectively, of consolidated revenues during 2010, 25 percent, 13 percent and 11 percent during 2009, and 25 percent, 12 percent and 10 percent during 2008. These net revenues were primarily related to the U.S. and Canada Segment." Of 500 companies surveyed in *Accounting Trends & Techniques,* 117 indicated the existence of a major customer in their 2008 annual reports.[2]

The authoritative literature requires major customer disclosures even if a company operates in only one segment and therefore does not provide segment information. Also, to avoid any confusion, a group of entities under common control is considered to be a

[2] AICPA, *Accounting Trends & Techniques,* 2009, p. 36.

single customer, and federal, state, local, and foreign governments are each considered to be a single customer.

In addition to requiring information about major customers, previous accounting standards also required information about export sales. Providing information on export sales, however, is no longer necessary. *Accounting Trends & Techniques* indicates that the number of companies reporting export sales dropped from 168 in 1997 to only 19 in 2008.[3]

IFRS—Segment Reporting

LO6

Recognize differences between U.S. GAAP and IFRS in segment reporting.

IFRS 8, "Operating Segments," became effective for annual periods beginning on or after January 1, 2009, and substantially converges IFRS with U.S. GAAP. *IFRS 8* requires disclosures to be provided for separately reportable operating segments as well as certain enterprisewide disclosures. Paragraph 1 establishes the "core principle" of *IFRS 8* to be:

> An entity shall disclose information to enable users of its financial statements to evaluate the nature and financial effects of the business activities in which it engages and the economic environments in which it operates.

The major differences between *IFRS 8* and U.S. GAAP are:

1. *IFRS 8* requires disclosure of total assets and total liabilities by operating segment, but only if such information is provided to the chief operating decision maker. U.S. GAAP requires disclosure of segment assets in general, and is silent with respect to the disclosure of liabilities, even if this information is provided to the chief operating decision maker.
2. *IFRS 8* indicates that intangible assets are to be included in providing disclosure of long-lived assets attributable to geographic segments. In contrast, U.S. GAAP does not define what is intended to be included in long-lived assets. However, FASB ASC (para. 280-10-55-23) indicates long-lived assets "implies hard assets that cannot be readily removed, which would exclude intangibles." Many U.S. companies define long-lived assets as property, plant, and equipment only, which is inconsistent with *IFRS 8.*
3. When a company has a matrix form of organization, *IFRS 8* indicates operating segments are to be determined based on the core principle of the Standard. As a result, operating segments can be based on either products and services or geographic areas. U.S. GAAP stipulates that in a matrix form of organization, segments must be based on products and services, not geographic areas.

Interim Reporting

LO7

Understand and apply procedures used in interim reports to treat an interim period as an integral part of the annual period.

To give investors and creditors more timely information than an annual report provides, companies show financial information for periods of less than one year. The SEC requires publicly traded companies in the United States to provide financial statements on a quarterly basis. Unlike annual financial statements, financial statements included in quarterly reports filed with the SEC need not be audited. This allows companies to disseminate the information to investors and creditors as quickly as possible.

APB Opinion No. 28 issued in 1973 provides guidance to companies as to how to prepare interim statements. That opinion has stood the test of time with only two subsequent authoritative pronouncements related to interim reporting. The FASB's *SFAS 3* amended *APB Opinion No. 28* with regard to reporting accounting changes in interim statements, and FASB *Interpretation No. 18* clarifies the application of *APB Opinion No. 28* with regard to income taxes. Each of these pronouncements was incorporated into the FASB ASC in 2009 under Topic 270, Interim Reporting.

Some inherent problems are associated with determining the results of operations for time periods of less than one year, especially with regard to expenses that do not

[3] Ibid., p. 28.

occur evenly throughout the year. Two approaches can be followed in preparing interim reports: (1) treat the interim period as a **discrete** accounting period, standing on its own, or (2) treat it as an **integral** portion of a longer period. Considering the annual bonus a company pays to key employees in December of each year illustrates the distinction between these two approaches. Under the *discrete* period approach, the company reports the entire bonus as an expense in December, reducing fourth quarter income only. Under the *integral* part of an annual period approach, a company accrues a portion of the bonus to be paid in December as an expense in each of the first three quarters of the year. Obviously, application of the integral approach requires estimating the annual bonus early in the year and developing a method for allocating the bonus to the four quarters of the year. The advantage of this approach is that there is less volatility in quarterly earnings as irregularly occurring costs are spread over the entire year.

Current accounting guidelines require companies to treat interim periods as integral parts of an annual period rather than as discrete accounting periods in their own right. Generally speaking, companies should prepare interim financial statements following the same accounting principles and practices they use in preparing annual statements. However, deviation from this general rule is necessary for several items so that the interim statements better reflect the expected annual amounts. Special rules related to revenues, inventory and cost of goods sold, other costs and expenses, extraordinary items, income taxes, accounting changes, and seasonal items are discussed in turn in the following sections.

Revenues

Companies should recognize revenues in interim periods in the same way they recognize revenues on an annual basis. For example, a company that accounts for revenue from long-term construction projects under the percentage of completion method for annual purposes should also recognize revenue in interim statements on a percentage of completion basis. Moreover, a company should recognize projected losses on long-term contracts to their full extent in the interim period in which it becomes apparent that a loss will arise.

Inventory and Cost of Goods Sold

Interim period accounting for inventory and cost of goods sold requires several modifications to procedures used on an annual basis. The modifications relate to (1) a LIFO liquidation, (2) application of the lower-of-cost-or-market rule, and (3) standard costing.

1. *LIFO liquidation:* Companies using the last-in, first-out (LIFO) cost-flow assumption to value inventory experience a LIFO liquidation at the end of an interim period when the number of units of inventory sold exceeds the number of units added to inventory during the period. When prices are rising, matching beginning inventory cost (carried at low LIFO amounts) against the current period sales revenue results in an unusually high amount of gross profit. If, by year-end, the company expects to replace the units of beginning inventory sold, there is no LIFO liquidation on an annual basis. In that case, gross profit for the interim period should not reflect the temporary LIFO liquidation, and inventory reported on the interim balance sheet should include the expected cost to replace the beginning inventory sold.

To illustrate, assume that Liquid Products Company began the first quarter with 100 units of inventory that cost $10 per unit. During the first quarter, it purchased 200 units at a cost of $15 per unit, and sold 240 units at $20 per unit. During the first quarter, the company experienced a liquidation of 40 units of beginning inventory. It calculates gross profit as follows:

Sales (240 units @ $20)		$4,800
Cost of goods sold:		
200 units @ $15	$3,000	
40 units @ $10 (LIFO historical cost)	400	3,400
Gross profit		$1,400

However, during the second quarter, the company expects to replace the units of beginning inventory sold at a cost of $17 per unit and that inventory at year-end will be at least 100 units. Therefore, it calculates gross profit for the first quarter as follows:

Sales (240 units @ $20)		$4,800
Cost of goods sold:		
200 units @ $15	$3,000	
40 units @ $17 (replacement cost)	680	3,680
Gross profit		$1,120

The journal entry to record cost of goods sold in the first quarter is as follows:

Cost of Goods Sold	3,680	
Inventory		3,400
Excess of Replacement Cost over Historical Cost of LIFO Liquidation		280
To record cost of goods sold with a historical cost of $3,400 and an excess of replacement cost over historical cost for beginning inventory liquidated of $280 [($17 − $10) × 40 units].		

2. *Lower-of-cost-or-market rule:* If at the end of an interim period, the fair value of inventory is less than its cost, the company should write down inventory and recognize a loss so long as it deems the fair value decline to be permanent. However, if it expects the fair value to recover above the inventory's original cost by year-end, it should not write down inventory at the interim balance sheet date. Instead, it should continue to carry inventory at cost.

3. *Standard costing:* A company should not reflect in interim financial statements planned price, volume, or capacity variances arising from the use of a standard cost system that are expected to be absorbed by the end of the annual period. However, it should report unplanned variances at the end of the interim period in the same fashion as it would in the annual financial statements.

Other Costs and Expenses

A company should charge costs and expenses not directly matched with revenues to income in the interim period in which they occur unless they can be identified with activities or benefits of other interim periods. In that case, the cost should be allocated among interim periods on a reasonable basis through the use of accruals and deferrals. For example, assume that a company required to prepare quarterly financial statements pays annual property taxes of $100,000 on April 10. One-fourth of the estimated property tax should be accrued as expense in the first quarter of the year. When it makes the payment, it should apply one-fourth against the accrued property tax payable from the previous quarter and charge one-fourth to second-quarter income. The company should defer one-half of the payment as a prepaid expense to be allocated to the third and fourth quarters of the year. The following journal entries demonstrate the procedures for ensuring that the company recognizes one-fourth of the annual payment as expense in each quarter of the year.

March 31

Property Tax Expense	25,000	
Accrued Property Tax Payable		25,000
To accrue one-fourth of the estimated annual property tax as expense for the quarter ended March 31.		

April 10

Accrued Property Tax Payable	25,000	
Property Tax Expense	25,000	
Prepaid Property Tax (Current Asset)	50,000	
Cash		100,000
To record the payment of the annual property tax, recognize one-fourth as property tax expense for the quarter ending June 30, and defer one-half as a prepaid expense.		

September 30

Property Tax Expense.	25,000	
Prepaid Property Tax		25,000
To record property tax expense for the quarter ended September 30.		

December 31

Property Tax Expense	25,000	
Prepaid Property Tax		25,000
To record property tax expense for the quarter ended December 31.		

Other items requiring similar treatment include annual major repairs and advertising. In addition, a number of adjustments such as bad debt expense, executive bonuses, and quantity discounts based on annual sales volume that are normally made at year-end actually relate to the entire year. To the extent that the company can estimate annual amounts, it should make adjustments at the end of each interim period so that the interim periods bear a reasonable portion of the expected annual amount.

Extraordinary Items

Companies should report extraordinary gains and losses separately and in full in the interim period in which they occur. Companies should deem gains and losses extraordinary if they are (1) unusual in nature, (2) infrequent in occurrence, and (3) material in amount. The materiality of extraordinary items should be determined by comparing the amount of the gain or loss to the expected income for the full year. Companies should separately disclose unusual and infrequent gains and losses material to the interim period even if not material to the year as a whole. Likewise, they should separately disclose gains and losses on the disposal of a business segment in the interim period in which the disposal occurs.

For example, assume that Charleston Company incurred a hurricane loss of $100,000 in the first quarter that it deems to be both unusual and infrequent. First-quarter income before subtracting the hurricane loss is $800,000, and annual income is expected to be $10 million. The loss is clearly material with respect to first-quarter income (12.5%) but is not material for the year as a whole (1%). Charleston should not label this loss an extraordinary item on its first-quarter income statement but nevertheless should separately disclose the loss (either as a separate line item on the income statement or in the notes).

Companies should disclose contingencies in interim reports the same way they disclose them in annual reports. The contingency should continue to be reported in subsequent interim and annual reports until it is resolved or becomes immaterial. Materiality should be judged with respect to the year as a whole.

Income Taxes

Companies should compute income tax related to ordinary income at an estimated *annual* effective tax rate. At the end of each interim period, a company makes its best estimate of the effective tax rate for the entire year. The effective tax rate reflects anticipated tax credits, foreign tax rates, and tax planning activities for the year. It then applies this rate to the pretax ordinary income earned to date during the year, resulting in the cumulative income tax expense to recognize to date. The difference between the cumulative income tax recognized to date and income tax recognized in earlier interim periods is the amount of income tax expense recognized in the current interim period.

Assume that Viertel Company estimated its effective annual tax rate at 42 percent in the first quarter of 2013. Pretax income for the first quarter was $500,000. At the end of the second quarter of 2013, the company expects its effective annual tax rate will be only 40 percent because of the planned usage of foreign tax credits. Pretax income in the second quarter of 2013 is also $500,000. No items require net-of-tax presentation in either quarter. The income tax expense recognized in each of the first two quarters of 2013 is determined as follows:

First Quarter	
Pretax income for first quarter of 2013	$500,000
Estimated annual income tax rate	42%
Income tax expense	$210,000

Second Quarter		
Pretax income for first quarter of 2013	$500,000	
Pretax income for second quarter of 2013	500,000	
Year-to-date income statement		$1,000,000
Estimated annual income tax rate		40%
Year-to-date income tax expense		$ 400,000
Income tax expense recognized in first quarter		210,000
Income tax expense recognized in second quarter		$ 190,000

The same process is followed for the third and fourth quarters of the year.

Companies should compute income tax related to those special items reported net of tax (extraordinary items and discontinued operations) and recognize them when the item occurs. The income tax on an interim period special item is calculated at the margin as the difference between income tax on income including this item and income tax on income excluding this item.

Change in Accounting Principle

Current accounting guidelines require retrospective application of a new accounting principle to prior periods' financial statements. *Retrospective application* means that comparative financial statements will be restated as if the new accounting principle had always been used. Whether an accounting change occurs in the first or in a subsequent interim period has no bearing on the manner in which the change is reflected in the interim financial statements. Changes in accounting principle, regardless of when the accounting change is made, are handled as follows (according to FASB ASC 250-10-45-5):

a. The cumulative effect of the change to the new accounting principle on periods prior to those presented is reflected in the carrying amounts of assets and liabilities as of the beginning of the first period presented.

b. An offsetting adjustment, if any, is made to the opening balance of retained earnings (or other appropriate components of equity or net assets in the statement of financial position) for that period.

c. Financial statements for each individual prior period are adjusted to reflect the period-specific effects of applying the new accounting principle.

When the accounting change takes place in other than the first interim period, current guidelines require information for the interim periods prior to the change to be reported by retrospectively applying the new accounting principle to those prechange interim periods. If retrospective application is impracticable, the accounting change is not allowed to be made in an interim period but may be made at the beginning of the next fiscal year. Situations in which the retrospective application of a new accounting principle to prechange interim periods is not feasible should be rare.

Illustration of Accounting Change Made in Other Than First Interim Period

Modal Company began operations on January 1, 2012. The company's interim income statements as originally reported under the LIFO inventory valuation method follow:

	2012				2013
	1stQ	2ndQ	3rdQ	4thQ	1stQ
Sales	$2,000	$2,000	$2,000	$2,000	$2,200
Cost of goods sold (LIFO)	900	950	1,000	1,000	1,050
Operating expenses	500	500	500	500	600
Income before income taxes	$ 600	$ 550	$ 500	$ 500	$ 550
Income taxes (40%)	240	220	200	200	220
Net income	$ 360	$ 330	$ 300	$ 300	$ 330

Modal has 500 shares of common stock outstanding. The company's interim report for the first quarter of 2013 included the following information:

	Three Months Ended March 31	
	2012	2013
Net income	$ 360	$ 330
Net income per common share	$0.72	$0.66

In June 2013, Modal adopts the FIFO method of inventory valuation for both financial reporting and tax purposes. Retrospective application of the FIFO method to previous quarters results in the following amounts of cost of goods sold:

	2012				2013
	1stQ	2ndQ	3rdQ	4thQ	1stQ
Cost of goods sold (FIFO)	$800	$850	$1,000	$900	$950

Retrospective application of the FIFO method results in the following restatements of income:

	2012				2013
	1stQ	2ndQ	3rdQ	4thQ	1stQ
Sales	$2,000	$2,000	$2,000	$2,000	$2,200
Cost of goods sold (FIFO)	800	850	1,000	900	950
Operating expenses	500	500	500	500	600
Income before income taxes	$ 700	$ 650	$ 500	$ 600	$ 650
Income taxes (40%)	280	260	200	240	260
Net income	$ 420	$ 390	$ 300	$ 360	$ 390

Sales for the second quarter of 2013 are $2,400, cost of goods sold under the FIFO method is $1,000, and operating expenses are $600. Income before income taxes in the second quarter of 2013 is $800, income taxes are $320, and net income is $480.

To prepare interim statements for the second quarter of 2013 in accordance with U.S. GAAP, net income as originally reported in the first and second quarters of 2012, as well as in the first quarter of 2013, is restated to reflect the change to FIFO. The manner in which the accounting change is reflected in the second quarter of 2013, with year-to-date information, and comparative information for similar periods in 2012 follow:

	Three Months Ended June 30		Six Months Ended June 30	
	2012	**2013**	**2012**	**2013**
Net income	$ 390	$ 480	$ 810	$ 870
Net income per common share	$0.78	$0.96	$1.62	$1.74

Seasonal Items

The sales volume of some companies experiences significant seasonal variation. Summer sports equipment manufacturers, for example, are likely to have a significant upward spike in sales during the second quarter of the year. To avoid the risk that investors and creditors will be misled into believing that second-quarter earnings indicate earnings for the entire year, FASB ASC 270-10-45 requires companies to disclose the seasonal nature of their business operations. In addition, such companies should consider supplementing their interim reports with reports on the 12-month period ended at the interim date for both the current and preceding years.

Minimum Disclosures in Interim Reports

LO8

List the minimum disclosure requirements for interim financial reports.

Many companies provide summary financial statements and notes in their interim reports that contain less information than is included in the annual financial statements. Authoritative accounting literature requires companies to provide the following minimum information in their interim reports:

- Sales or gross revenues, provision for income taxes, extraordinary items, and net income.
- Earnings per share.
- Seasonal revenues and expenses.
- Significant changes in estimates or provisions for income taxes.
- Disposal of a segment of a business and unusual or infrequently occurring items.
- Contingent items.
- Changes in accounting principles or estimates.
- Significant changes in financial position.

Authoritative guidelines also encourage, but do not require, companies to publish balance sheet and cash flow information in interim reports. If they do not include this information, companies must disclose significant changes since the last period in cash and cash equivalents, net working capital, long-term liabilities, and stockholders' equity.

Companies that provide interim reports on a quarterly basis are not required to publish a fourth-quarter report because this coincides with the end of the annual period. When they do not provide separate fourth-quarter financial statements, they should disclose special accounting items occurring in the fourth quarter in the notes to the annual financial statements. These items include extraordinary or unusual and infrequently occurring items, disposals of a segment of the business, and the aggregate effect of year-end adjustments that are material to the results of the fourth quarter.

The SEC requires companies to include selected quarterly financial data in their annual report to shareholders. Southwest Airlines Co. provided quarterly data in its 2010 annual report as shown in Exhibit 8.9.

EXHIBIT 8.9
Quarterly Financial Data from Southwest Airlines Co.'s 2010 Annual Report

QUARTERLY FINANCIAL DATA (Unaudited) (GAAP)				
	Three Months Ended			
(in millions, except per share amounts)	March 31	June 30	September 30	December 31
2010				
Operating revenues	$2,630	$3,168	$3,192	$3,114
Operating income (loss) . .	54	363	355	216
Income (loss) before income taxes.	17	184	332	213
Net income (loss)	11	112	205	131
Net income (loss) per share, basic.	.01	.15	.27	.18
Net income (loss) per share, diluted	.01	.15	.27	.18

Segment Information in Interim Reports

The management approach to determining operating segments should result in less costly disclosure because, by definition, management already collects this information. Because the information is readily available, segment disclosures also must be included in interim reports. This was one of AIMR's major recommendations for improving segment reporting. U.S. GAAP requires that the following information be included in interim reports for each operating segment:

- Revenues from external customers.
- Intersegment revenues.
- Segment profit or loss.
- Total assets, if there has been a material change from the last annual report.

In addition, an enterprise must reconcile total segments' profit or loss to the company's total income before taxes and disclose any change from the last annual report in the basis for measuring segment profit or loss. Requiring only a few items of information in interim reports is a compromise between users' desire to have the same information as is provided in annual financial statements and preparers' cost in reporting the information. There is no requirement to provide information about geographic areas or major customers in interim reports.

IFRS—Interim Reporting

LO9

Recognize differences between U.S. GAAP and IFRS in interim reporting.

IAS 34, "Interim Financial Reporting," provides guidance with respect to the form and content of interim financial statements, and the recognition and measurement principles to be followed in preparing them.[4] *IAS 34* requires the following minimum components in an interim report:

- A condensed statement of financial position (balance sheet).
- A condensed statement of comprehensive income, presented as:
  a. A condensed single statement of net income and comprehensive income, or
  b. Separate condensed statements of net income and comprehensive income.
- A condensed statement of changes in equity.

[4] Note that the IASB has no jurisdictional authority to require the preparation of interim reports; it simply provides requirements (through *IAS 34*) for how those reports should be prepared. *IAS 34* must be followed in those jurisdictions that require the use of IFRS and require the preparation of interim reports.

- A condensed statement of cash flows.
- Selected explanatory notes.

Unlike U.S. GAAP, *IAS 34* requires each interim period to be treated as a discrete period in determining the amounts to be recognized. Thus, expenses that are incurred in one quarter are recognized in full in that quarter, even though the expenditure benefits the entire year. In addition, there is no accrual in earlier quarters for expenses expected to be incurred in a later quarter of the year. The only exception to this rule is the accrual of income tax expense at the end of each interim period.

Summary

1. The consolidation of information from many, varied companies into a set of consolidated financial statements tends to camouflage the characteristics of the individual components. Consequently, during the 1960s, several groups made a strong push to require that disaggregated information be included as an integral part of financial reporting to provide a means for analyzing the components of a business combination. The FASB responded by issuing *SFAS 14,* "Financial Reporting for Segments of a Business Enterprise" in 1976.
2. Over the years after *SFAS 14* was introduced, financial analysts consistently requested that financial statements be disaggregated to a much greater degree than was done in practice. In direct response to the financial analyst community's criticisms and suggestions, the FASB issued a new standard for segment reporting in 1997—*SFAS 131*. This standard was incorporated into the FASB's Accounting Standards Codification in 2009.
3. The management approach bases operating segments on a company's organization structure and internal reporting system. The management approach should enhance the usefulness of segment information because it highlights the risks and opportunities that management believes are important and allows the analyst to see the company through management's eyes. This approach also has the advantage of reducing the cost of providing segment information because that information already is being produced for internal use.
4. Once operating segments have been identified, a company must determine which segments are of significant magnitude to warrant separate disclosure. Three quantitative threshold tests (revenue, profit or loss, and asset) are used to identify reportable segments. A segment need satisfy only one of these tests to be considered of sufficient size to necessitate disclosure. Each test is based on identifying segments that meet a 10 percent minimum of the related combined total. The profit and loss test has a 10 percent criterion based on the higher (in an absolute sense) of the total profit from all segments with profits or the total loss from all segments with losses.
5. Companies must report several information types for each reportable operating segment, including selected revenues, profit or loss, selected expenses, assets, capital expenditures, and equity method investment and income. Companies must report revenues from external customers separately from intersegment revenues. In addition, the types of products and services from which each segment derives its revenues must be disclosed.
6. A set of parameters determines the number of segments an enterprise reports. As a minimum, the separately disclosed units must generate at least 75 percent of the total sales made to unaffiliated parties. For an upper limit, authoritative literature suggests that the disclosure of more than 10 operating segments reduces the usefulness of the information.
7. Companies must reconcile the total of all segments' revenues, profit or loss, and assets to the consolidated totals. The major reconciliation adjustments relate to intra-entity revenues, profit or loss, and assets eliminated in consolidation; revenues, profit or loss, and assets that have not been allocated to individual operating segments; and differences in accounting methods used by segments and in preparing consolidated financial statements.
8. U.S. GAAP requires several entity-wide disclosures. If an enterprise does not define operating segments internally on a product line basis or has only one operating segment, disclosure of revenues derived from each product or service is required.
9. In addition, companies must report revenues from external customers and long-lived assets for the domestic country, for each foreign country that generates a material amount of revenues or holds assets, and for all foreign countries in total. Current guidelines do not provide any threshold tests for determining when operations in a foreign country are material.

10. Authoritative accounting literature requires disclosure of one other type of information. The reporting entity must indicate the existence of major customers when 10 percent or more of consolidated revenues are derived from a single unaffiliated party.
11. To converge with U.S. GAAP, the IASB issued *IFRS 8*, "Operating Segments," which became effective in 2009. The major differences between IFRS and U.S. GAAP are that *IFRS 8* (1) requires the disclosure of liabilities by operating segment if this information is reported to the chief operating decision maker, (2) requires the inclusion of intangible assets in the disclosure of long-lived assets by geographic area, and (3) allows companies with matrix organizations to define operating segments on the basis of either products and services or geographic areas.
12. For interim reporting purposes, U.S. GAAP requires time intervals of less than one year to be treated as an integral part of the annual period.
13. Costs and expenses not directly matched with revenues should be charged to income in the interim period in which they occur unless they can be identified with activities or benefits of other interim periods. In that case, the cost should be allocated among interim periods on a reasonable basis by using accruals and deferrals. Items related to the whole year but recorded as an adjustment only at year-end should be estimated and accrued in each interim period of the year.
14. Companies must report extraordinary gains and losses separately and in full in the interim period in which they occur. The materiality of extraordinary items should be determined by comparing the amount of the gain or loss to the expected income for the full year. Unusual and infrequent gains and losses that are material to the interim period but not to the year as a whole should be disclosed separately.
15. Companies determine interim period income tax expense by applying the estimated annual effective income tax rate to year-to-date pretax ordinary income, resulting in the cumulative income tax expense to be recognized to date. The cumulative income tax to be recognized to date less income tax recognized in earlier interim periods is the amount of income tax expense recognized in the current interim period.
16. When an accounting change is made in other than the first interim period, information for the prechange interim periods should be reported based on retrospective application of the new accounting principle to those periods. An accounting change may be made only at the beginning of a fiscal year if retrospective application of the new accounting principle to prechange interim periods is not practicable.
17. The minimum information to disclose in interim reports includes sales, income taxes, extraordinary items, net income, earnings per share, seasonal revenues and expenses, and significant changes in financial position. Publication of balance sheet and cash flow information in interim reports is not required. If this information is not included, significant changes since the last period in cash and cash equivalents, net working capital, long-term liabilities, and stockholders' equity must be disclosed.
18. Certain segment information items need to be disclosed in interim reports. Specifically, companies must disclose revenues from outside customers, intersegment revenues, and segment profit or loss in interim reports for each operating segment. In addition, companies must report total assets by segment if a material change occurred since the last annual report.
19. Unlike U.S. GAAP, the IASB's *IAS 34*, "Interim Financial Reporting," requires that each interim period be treated as a discrete period in determining amounts to be recognized. The exception to this rule is the accrual of income tax expense to determine net income for each interim period.

Comprehensive Illustration

Problem

(*Estimated Time: 25 to 40 Minutes*) Battey Corporation manufactures several products: natural fibers, synthetic fibers, leather, plastics, and wood. It is organized into five operating divisions based on these different products. The company has a number of subsidiaries that perform operations throughout the world. At the end of 2013 as part of the internal reporting process, Battey reported the revenues, profits, and assets (in millions) to the chief operating decision maker:

Revenues by Operating Segment	United States	Canada	Mexico	France	Italy	Brazil
Natural fibers:						
Sales to external customers	$1,739	–0–	$342	$606	–0–	$1,171
Intersegment sales.	–0–	–0–	–0–	–0–	–0–	146
Synthetic fibers:						
Sales to external customers	290	$116	–0–	–0–	–0–	37
Intersegment sales.	12	5	–0–	–0–	–0–	–0–
Leather:						
Sales to external customers	230	–0–	57	–0–	$278	55
Intersegment sales.	22	–0–	9	–0–	34	9
Plastics:						
Sales to external customers	748	286	–0–	83	92	528
Intersegment sales.	21	12	–0–	–0–	–0–	72
Wood:						
Sales to external customers	116	22	–0–	–0–	–0–	149
Intersegment sales.	17	3	–0–	–0–	–0–	28

Operating Profit or Loss by Operating Segment	United States	Canada	Mexico	France	Italy	Brazil
Natural fibers	$526	–0–	$ 92	$146	–0–	$404
Synthetic fibers	21	$ 8	–0–	–0–	–0–	10
Leather	70	–0–	27	–0–	$ 94	24
Plastics	182	74	–0–	18	24	68
Wood	18	5	–0–	–0–	–0–	37

Assets by Operating Segment	United States	Canada	Mexico	France	Italy	Brazil
Natural fibers	$1,005	–0–	$223	$296	–0–	$817
Synthetic fibers	163	$ 50	–0–	–0–	–0–	74
Leather	146	–0–	41	–0–	$150	38
Plastics	425	173	–0–	54	58	327
Wood	66	19	–0–	–0–	–0–	143

Required

a. Determine the operating segments that should be reported separately in Battey's 2013 financial statements.

b. Determine the geographic areas for which Battey should report revenues separately in its 2013 financial statements. Assume that Battey has elected to define a material country as one in which sales to external customers are 10 percent or more of consolidated sales.

c. Determine the volume of revenues that a single customer must generate to necessitate disclosure of a major customer.

Solution

a. Battey Corporation determines its reportable operating segments by following a three-step process. First, it identifies operating segments. Second, it examines aggregation criteria to determine whether any operating segments may be combined. Third, it determines reportable operating segments by applying the three quantitative threshold tests.

Identification of Operating Segments Battey's internal reporting system provides information to the chief operating decision maker by operating division and by country. Either of these components conceivably could be identified as operating segments for segment reporting purposes. However, U.S. GAAP stipulates that, in this situation, the components based on products and services constitute the operating segments. Thus, the five operating divisions are identified as Battey's operating segments.

Aggregation Criteria Aggregation criteria are examined next to determine whether any operating segments can be combined. Management determines that the economic characteristics of the natural fibers and synthetic fibers operating divisions are very similar. In addition, they are considerably similar with regard to the nature of the product, production process, customers, and distribution methods. Because each aggregation criterion is met, Battey elects to combine these two segments into a single fibers category.

Quantitative Threshold Tests Determining Battey's reportable operating segments depends on the three materiality tests described in this chapter. The revenue test can be performed directly from the information provided. Any operating segment with total revenues (including intersegment sales) equal to 10 percent or more of combined revenue (internal and external) must be reported separately:

Revenue Test (in millions)

Operating Segments	Total Revenues (including intersegment)	
Fibers	$4,464	60.8%
Leather	694	9.5
Plastics	1,842	25.1
Wood	335	4.6
Total combined revenues	$7,335	100.0%

Reportable segments are fibers and plastics.

The profit or loss test is performed next. Battey must separately report any operating segment with profit or loss equal to 10 percent or more of the larger, in absolute amount, of combined segment profit (for those segments with a profit) or combined segment loss (for those segments with a loss). Because each of Battey's operating segments generated a profit in 2013, this test can be applied by determining the total combined profit:

Profit or Loss Test (in millions)

Operating Segments	Total Profit or Loss	
Fibers	$1,207	65.3%
Leather	215	11.6
Plastics	366	19.8
Wood	60	3.3
Total combined segment profit	$1,848	100.0%

Reportable segments are fibers, leather, and plastics.

Finally, Battey performs the asset test:

Asset Test (in millions)

Operating Segments	Total Assets	
Fibers	$2,628	61.6%
Leather	375	8.8
Plastics	1,037	24.3
Wood	228	5.3
Total combined segment assets	$4,268	100.0%

Reportable segments are fibers and plastics.

Based on these three tests, data about the fibers, leather, and plastics operating segments must be reported separately. Information on the immaterial wood segment need not be reported. However, the revenues, profit, and assets of this segment are included in reconciliations to consolidated totals.

b. Battey must report revenues from U.S. external customers, for all foreign countries, and for each foreign country in which the company generates a material amount of revenues. Authoritative accounting literature does not provide quantitative tests for determining when a foreign country is material but leaves this to management's judgment. Battey has decided to define *materiality* as sales to external customers equal to 10 percent or more of consolidated revenues.

Revenue Test (in millions)

Country	Sales to External Customers	
United States	$3,123	45.0%
Canada	424	6.1
Mexico	399	5.8
France	689	9.9
Italy	370	5.3
Brazil	1,940	27.9
Total consolidated revenues	$6,945	100.0%

Using this criterion, Battey reports results for the United States and Brazil separately and combines the remaining countries into an All Other category. Alternatively, if Battey had established a materiality threshold of 5 percent, it would report separately each of the foreign countries in which it generates revenues. Again, determination of materiality is left to management's judgment.

c. The significance test for disclosure of a major customer is 10 percent of consolidated revenues. Battey must report the existence of any major customer from which it generated $694.5 million or more in revenues during 2013.

Questions

1. How does the consolidation process tend to disguise information needed to analyze the financial operations of a diversified organization?
2. What is disaggregated financial information?
3. According to the FASB, what is the major objective of segment reporting?
4. The management approach requires a firm to define segments on the basis of its internal organization structure. What are the advantages in defining segments on this basis?
5. What is an operating segment?
6. How should a company determine operating segments when it disaggregates business activities in more than one way and the chief operating decision maker uses multiple sets of reports?
7. Describe the three tests to identify reportable operating segments.
8. What information must an enterprise report for each of its material operating segments?
9. Under what conditions must an enterprise provide information about products and services?
10. Under what conditions must an enterprise provide information about geographic areas?
11. What information must an enterprise report by geographic area?
12. To satisfy geographic area disclosure requirements, what are the minimum and maximum numbers of countries for which information should be reported separately?
13. Under what conditions should a company disclose the amount of sales from a major customer?
14. What are the major differences between U.S. GAAP and *IFRS 8* with respect to the disclosures that are required to be provided for each separately reportable operating segment?
15. Why are publicly traded companies in the United States required to prepare interim reports on a quarterly basis?
16. What approach are companies required to follow in preparing interim financial statements?
17. How should a company handle LIFO liquidation in an interim period when the liquidated inventory is expected to be replaced by year-end?
18. How does a company determine the amount of income tax expense to report in an interim period?

19. What procedures must companies follow to account for a change in accounting principle made in other than the first interim period of the year?
20. What minimum information must an enterprise provide in an interim report?
21. What type of segment information must companies provide in interim financial statements?
22. How would an annual bonus paid at year-end be treated under *IAS 34* and how does this treatment differ from what is required under U.S. GAAP?

Problems

LO1

1. Which of the following does U.S. GAAP *not* consider to be an objective of segment reporting?
   a. It helps users better understand the enterprise's performance.
   b. It helps users better assess the enterprise's prospects for future cash flows.
   c. It helps users make more informed judgments about the enterprise as a whole.
   d. It helps users make comparisons between a segment of one enterprise and a similar segment of another enterprise.

LO3

2. Under current U.S. accounting guidelines, which of the following items of information is Most Company *not* required to disclose, even if it were material in amount?
   a. Revenues generated from sales of its consumer products line of goods.
   b. Revenues generated by its Japanese subsidiary.
   c. Revenues generated from export sales.
   d. Revenues generated from sales to Walmart.

LO3

3. Which of the following operating segment disclosures is *not* required under current U.S. accounting guidelines?
   a. Liabilities.
   b. Interest expense.
   c. Intersegment sales.
   d. Unusual items and extraordinary items.

LO2

4. In determining whether a particular operating segment is of significant size to warrant disclosure, which of the following is true?
   a. Three tests are applied, and all three must be met.
   b. Four tests are applied, and only one must be met.
   c. Three tests are applied, and only one must be met.
   d. Four tests are applied, and all four must be met.

LO1, LO3, LO4

5. Which of the following statements is *not* true under U.S. GAAP?
   a. Operating segments can be determined by looking at a company's organization chart.
   b. Companies must combine individual foreign countries into geographic areas to comply with the geographic area disclosure requirements.
   c. Companies that define their operating segments by product lines must provide revenue and asset information for the domestic country, for all foreign countries in total, and for each material foreign country.
   d. Companies must disclose total assets, investment in equity method affiliates, and total expenditures for long-lived assets by operating segment.

LO1

6. Which of the following is not necessarily true for an operating segment?
   a. An operating segment earns revenues and incurs expenses.
   b. The chief operating decision maker regularly reviews an operating segment to assess performance and make resource allocation decisions.
   c. Discrete financial information generated by the internal accounting system is available for an operating segment.
   d. An operating segment regularly generates a profit from its normal, ongoing operations.

LO2

7. Which of the following is a criterion for determining whether an operating segment is separately reportable?
   a. Segment liabilities are 10 percent or more of consolidated liabilities.
   b. Segment profit or loss is 10 percent or more of consolidated net income.
   c. Segment assets are 10 percent or more of combined segment assets.

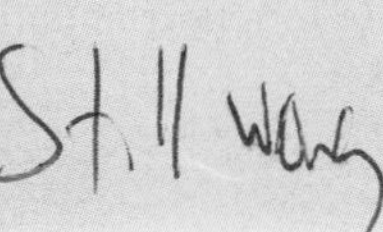

d. Segment revenues from external sales are 5 percent or more of combined segment revenues from external sales.

LO1, LO3, LO4, LO5

8. Which of the following statements concerning U.S. GAAP is true?
   a. Does not require segment information to be reported in accordance with generally accepted accounting principles.
   b. Does not require a reconciliation of segment assets to consolidated assets.
   c. Requires geographic area information to be disclosed in interim financial statements.
   d. Requires disclosure of a major customer's identity.

LO3

9. Plume Company has a paper products operating segment. Which of the following items does it *not* have to report for this segment?
   a. Interest expense.
   b. Research and development expense.
   c. Depreciation and amortization expense.
   d. Interest income.

LO4

10. Which of the following items is required to be disclosed by geographic area?
    a. Total assets.
    b. Revenues from external customers.
    c. Profit or loss.
    d. Capital expenditures.

LO4

11. According to U.S. GAAP, which of the following is an acceptable grouping of countries for providing information by geographic area?
    a. United States, Mexico, Japan, Spain, All Other Countries.
    b. United States, Canada and Mexico, Germany, Italy.
    c. Europe, Asia, Africa.
    d. Canada, Germany, France, All Other Countries.

LO4

12. What information about revenues by geographic area should a company present?
    a. Disclose separately the amount of sales to unaffiliated customers and the amount of intra-entity sales between geographic areas.
    b. Disclose as a combined amount sales to unaffiliated customers and intra-entity sales between geographic areas.
    c. Disclose separately the amount of sales to unaffiliated customers but not the amount of intra-entity sales between geographic areas.
    d. No disclosure of revenues from foreign operations need be reported.

LO5

13. Which of the following information items with regard to a major customer must be disclosed?
    a. The identity of the customer.
    b. The percentage of total sales derived from the major customer.
    c. The operating segment making the sale.
    d. The geographic area from which the sale was made.

LO8

14. Which of the following statements is true for a company that has managers responsible for product and service lines of business and managers responsible for geographic areas (matrix form of organization)?
    a. Under U.S. GAAP, the company must base operating segments on geographic areas.
    b. Under IFRS, the company must base operating segments on product and service lines of business.
    c. Under U.S. GAAP, the company may choose to define operating segments on the basis of either products and services or geographic areas.
    d. Under IFRS, the company must refer to the core principle of *IFRS 8* to determine operating segments.

LO6

15. In considering interim financial reporting, how does current U.S. GAAP require that such reporting be viewed?
    a. As a special type of reporting that need not follow generally accepted accounting principles.

    b. As useful only if activity is evenly spread throughout the year making estimates unnecessary.
    c. As reporting for a basic accounting period.
    d. As reporting for an integral part of an annual period.

LO6 16. How should material seasonal variations in revenue be reflected in interim financial statements?

a. The seasonal nature should be disclosed, and the interim report should be supplemented with a report on the 12-month period ended at the interim date for both the current and preceding years.

b. The seasonal nature should be disclosed, but no attempt should be made to reflect the effect of past seasonality on financial statements.

c. The seasonal nature should be reflected by providing pro forma financial statements for the current interim period.

d. No attempt should be made to reflect seasonality in interim financial statements.

LO6 17. For interim financial reporting, an extraordinary gain occurring in the second quarter should be

a. Recognized ratably over the last three quarters.

b. Recognized ratably over all four quarters, with the first quarter being restated.

c. Recognized in the second quarter.

d. Disclosed by footnote only in the second quarter.

LO7 18. Which of the following items must be disclosed in interim reports?

a. Total assets.

b. Total liabilities.

c. Cash flow from operating activities.

d. Gross revenues.

LO7 19. Which of the following items is *not* required to be reported in interim financial statements for each material operating segment?

a. Revenues from external customers.

b. Intersegment revenues.

c. Segment assets.

d. Segment profit or loss.

LO8 20. Niceville Company pays property taxes of $100,000 in the second quarter of the year. Which of the following statements is true with respect to the recognition of property tax expense in interim financial statements?

a. Under U.S. GAAP, the company would report property tax expense of $100,000 in the second quarter of the year.

b. Under IFRS, the company would report property tax expense of $100,000 in the second quarter of the year.

c. Under U.S. GAAP, the company would report property tax expense of $33,333 in each of the second, third, and fourth quarters of the year.

d. Under IFRS, the company would report property tax expense of $25,000 in the first quarter of the year.

LO2 21. Estilo Company has three operating segments with the following information:

	Paper	Pencils	Hats
Sales to outsiders	$8,000	$4,000	$6,000
Intersegment transfers	600	1,000	1,400

In addition, corporate headquarters generates revenues of $1,000.

What is the minimum amount of revenue that each of these segments must generate to be considered separately reportable?

a. $1,800.

b. $1,900.

c. $2,000.

d. $2,100.

LO5 22. Carson Company has four separate operating segments:

	Apples	Oranges	Pears	Peaches
Sales to outsiders.	$123,000	$81,000	$95,000	$77,000
Intersegment transfers.	31,000	26,000	13,000	18,000

What revenue amount must one customer generate before it must be identified as a major customer?

a. $37,600.

b. $41,200.

c. $46,400.

d. $56,400.

LO2

23. Jarvis Corporation has six different operating segments reporting the following operating profit and loss figures:

K	$ 80,000 loss	N	$440,000 profit
L	140,000 profit	O	90,000 profit
M	940,000 loss	P	100,000 profit

With respect to the profit or loss test, which of the following statements is *not* true?

a. K is not a reportable segment based on this one test.

b. L is a reportable segment based on this one test.

c. O is not a reportable segment based on this one test.

d. P is a reportable segment based on this one test.

LO2

24. Quatro Corp. engages solely in manufacturing operations. The following data pertain to the operating segments for the current year:

Operating Segment	Total Revenues	Profit	Assets at 12/31
A	$10,000,000	$1,750,000	$20,000,000
B	8,000,000	1,400,000	17,500,000
C	6,000,000	1,200,000	12,500,000
D	3,000,000	550,000	7,500,000
E	4,250,000	675,000	7,000,000
F	1,500,000	225,000	3,000,000
Total	$32,750,000	$5,800,000	$67,500,000

In its segment information for the current year, how many reportable segments does Quatro have?

a. Three.

b. Four.

c. Five.

d. Six.

LO2

25. What is the minimum number of operating segments that must be separately reported?

a. Ten.

b. Segments with at least 75 percent of revenues as measured by the revenue test.

c. At least 75 percent of the segments must be separately reported.

d. Segments with at least 75 percent of the revenues generated from outside parties.

LO2

26. Medford Company has seven operating segments but only four (G, H, I, and J) are of significant size to warrant separate disclosure. As a whole, the segments generated revenues of $710,000 ($520,000 + $190,000) from outside parties. In addition, the segments had $260,000 in intersegment transfers ($220,000 + $40,000).

	Outside Sales	Intersegment Sales
G	$120,000	$ 80,000
H	150,000	50,000
I	160,000	20,000
J	90,000	70,000
Totals	$520,000	$220,000
K	$ 60,000	–0–
L	70,000	$ 20,000
M	60,000	20,000
Totals	$190,000	$ 40,000

Which of the following statements is true?

a. A sufficient number of segments are being reported because those segments have $740,000 in revenues of a total of $970,000 for the company as a whole.

b. Not enough segments are being reported because those segments have $520,000 in outside sales of a total of $710,000 for the company as a whole.

c. Not enough segments are being reported because those segments have $740,000 in revenues of a total of $970,000 for the company as a whole.

d. A sufficient number of segments are being reported because those segments have $520,000 in outside sales of a total of $710,000 for the company as a whole.

LO6

27. Philo Company estimates that the amounts for total depreciation expense for the year ending December 31 will be $60,000 and for year-end bonuses to employees will be $120,000. What total amount of expense relating to these two items should Philo report in its quarterly income statement for the three months ended June 30?

a. $15,000.

b. $30,000.

c. $45,000.

d. $90,000.

LO6

28. Ming Company's $100,000 income for the quarter ended September 30 included the following after-tax items:

- $20,000 of a $40,000 extraordinary loss, realized on August 15; the other $20,000 was allocated to the fourth quarter of the year.
- A $16,000 cumulative effect loss resulting from a change in inventory valuation method made on September 1.
- $12,000 of the $48,000 annual property taxes paid on February 1.

For the quarter ended September 30, the amount of net income that Ming should report is

a. $80,000.

b. $88,000.

c. $96,000.

d. $116,000.

LO6

29. In March 2013, Archibald Company estimated its year-end executive bonuses to be $1,000,000. The executive bonus paid in 2012 was $950,000. What amount of bonus expense, if any, should Archibald recognize in determining net income for the first quarter of 2013?

a. –0–.

b. $237,500.

c. $250,000.

d. $1,000,000.

Use the following information for problems 30 and 31.

On March 15, Calloway, Inc., paid property taxes of $480,000 for the calendar year.

LO6

30. How much of this expense should Calloway's income statement reflect for the quarter ending March 31?

a. –0–.

b. $40,000.

c. $120,000.

d. $480,000.

LO6

31. The journal entry at March 15 to record the payment of property taxes would include which of the following?

a. A debit to Property Tax Expense of $480,000.

b. A credit to Cash of $120,000.

c. A debit to Prepaid Property Taxes of $360,000.

d. A credit to Prepaid Property Taxes of $40,000.

Use the following information for problems 32 and 33.

Lifetime Sports, Inc., uses the LIFO cost-flow assumption to value inventory. It began the current year with 1,000 units of inventory carried at LIFO cost of $50 per unit. During the first quarter, it purchased 5,000 units at an average cost of $80 per unit and sold 5,300 units at $100 per unit.

LO6

32. The company does not expect to replace the units of beginning inventory sold; it plans to reduce inventory by year-end to 500 units. What amount of cost of goods sold is to be recorded for the quarter ended March 31?
    a. $415,000.
    b. $424,000.
    c. $424,600.
    d. $434,600.

LO6

33. The company expects to replace the units of beginning inventory sold in April at a cost of $82 per unit and expects inventory at year-end to be between 1,500 and 2,000 units. What amount of cost of goods sold is to be recorded for the quarter ended March 31?
    a. $415,000.
    b. $424,000.
    c. $424,600.
    d. $434,600.

LO2

34. Fireside Corporation is organized into four operating segments. The internal reporting system generated the following segment information:

	Revenues from Outsiders	Intersegment Transfers	Operating Expenses
Cards	$1,200,000	$100,000	$ 900,000
Calendars	900,000	200,000	1,350,000
Clothing	1,000,000	–0–	700,000
Books	800,000	50,000	770,000

The company incurred additional operating expenses (of a general nature) of $700,000.

What is the profit or loss of each of these segments? Perform the profit or loss test to determine which of these segments is separately reportable.

LO2

35. Ecru Company has identified five industry segments: plastics, metals, lumber, paper, and finance. It appropriately consolidated each of these segments in producing its annual financial statements. Information describing each segment (in thousands) follows:

	Plastics	Metals	Lumber	Paper	Finance
Sales to outside parties	$6,319	$2,144	$636	$347	–0–
Intersegment transfers	106	131	96	108	–0–
Interest income from outside parties	–0–	19	6	–0–	$ 27
Interest income from intersegment loans	–0–	–0–	–0–	–0–	159
Operating expenses	3,914	1,612	916	579	16
Interest expense	61	16	51	31	87
Tangible assets	1,291	2,986	314	561	104
Intangible assets	72	361	–0–	48	–0–
Intersegment loans	–0–	–0–	–0–	–0–	664

Ecru does not allocate its $1,250,000 in common expenses to the various segments.

Perform testing procedures to determine Ecru's reportable operating segments.

LO2, LO5

36. Following is financial information describing the six operating segments that make up Fairfield, Inc. (in thousands):

	Segments					
	Red	Blue	Green	Pink	Black	White
Sales to outside parties	$1,811	$812	$514	$309	$121	$ 99
Intersegment revenues	16	91	109	–0–	16	302
Salary expense	614	379	402	312	317	62
Rent expense	139	166	81	92	42	31
Interest expense	65	59	82	49	14	5
Income tax expense (savings) .	141	87	61	(86)	(64)	–0–

Consider the following questions independently. None of the six segments has a primarily financial nature.

a. What minimum revenue amount must any one segment generate to be of significant size to require disaggregated disclosure?

b. If only Red, Blue, and Green necessitate separate disclosure, is Fairfield disclosing disaggregated data for enough segments?

c. What volume of revenues must a single client generate to necessitate disclosing the existence of a major customer?

d. If each of these six segments has a profit or loss (in thousands) as follows, which warrants separate disclosure?

Red	$1,074	Pink	$ (94)
Blue	449	Black	(222)
Green	140	White	308

LO2

37. Mason Company has prepared consolidated financial statements for the current year and is now gathering information in connection with the following five operating segments it has identified.

Determine the reportable segments by performing each applicable test. Also describe the procedure utilized to ensure that a sufficient number of segments are being separately disclosed. (Figures are in thousands.)

	Company Total	Books	Computers	Maps	Travel	Finance
Sales to outside parties	$1,547	$121	$ 696	$416	$314	–0–
Intersegment sales	421	24	240	39	118	–0–
Interest income—external	97	60	–0–	–0–	–0–	$ 37
Interest income—intersegment loans	147	–0–	–0–	–0–	–0–	147
Assets	3,398	206	1,378	248	326	1,240
Operating expenses	1,460	115	818	304	190	33
Expenses—intersegment sales	198	70	51	31	46	–0–
Interest expense—external	107	–0–	–0–	–0–	–0–	107
Interest expense—intersegment loans	177	21	71	38	47	–0–
Income tax expense (savings)	21	12	(41)	27	31	(8)
General corporate expenses	55					
Unallocated operating costs	80					

LO4

38. Slatter Corporation operates primarily in the United States. However, a few years ago, it opened a plant in Spain to produce merchandise to sell there. This foreign operation has been so successful that during the past 24 months the company started a manufacturing plant in Italy and another in Greece. Financial information for each of these facilities follows:

	Spain	Italy	Greece
Sales	$395,000	$272,000	$463,000
Intersegment transfers	–0–	–0–	62,000
Operating expenses	172,000	206,000	190,000
Interest expense	16,000	29,000	19,000
Income taxes	67,000	19,000	34,000
Long-lived assets	191,000	106,000	72,000

The company's domestic (U.S.) operations reported the following information for the current year:

Sales to unaffiliated customers	$4,610,000
Intersegment transfers	427,000
Operating expenses	2,410,000
Interest expense	136,000
Income taxes	819,000
Long-lived assets	1,894,000

Slatter has adopted the following criteria for determining the materiality of an individual foreign country: (1) sales to unaffiliated customers within a country are 10 percent or more of consolidated sales or (2) long-lived assets within a country are 10 percent or more of consolidated long-lived assets.

Apply Slatter's materiality tests to identify the countries to report separately.

LO6

39. Noventis Corporation prepared the following estimates for the four quarters of the current year:

	First Quarter	Second Quarter	Third Quarter	Fourth Quarter
Sales	$1,000,000	$1,200,000	$1,400,000	$1,600,000
Cost of goods sold	400,000	480,000	550,000	600,000
Administrative costs	250,000	155,000	160,000	170,000
Advertising costs	–0–	100,000	–0–	–0–
Executive bonuses	–0–	–0–	–0–	80,000
Provision for bad debts	–0–	–0–	–0–	52,000
Annual maintenance costs	60,000	–0–	–0–	–0–

Additional Information

- First-quarter administrative costs include the $100,000 annual insurance premium.
- Advertising costs paid in the second quarter relate to television advertisements that will be broadcast throughout the entire year.
- No special items affect income during the year.
- Noventis estimates an effective income tax rate for the year of 40 percent.

a. Assuming that actual results do *not* vary from the estimates provided, determine the amount of income to be reported each quarter of the current year.

b. Assume that actual results do *not* vary from the estimates provided except for that in the third quarter, the estimated annual effective income tax rate is revised downward to 38 percent. Determine the amount of income to be reported each quarter of the current year.

LO6

40. Cambi Company began operations on January 1, 2012. In the second quarter of 2013, it adopted the FIFO method of inventory valuation. In the past, it used the LIFO method. The company's interim income statements as originally reported under the LIFO method follow:

	2012				2013
	1stQ	2ndQ	3rdQ	4thQ	1stQ
Sales	$10,000	$12,000	$14,000	$16,000	$18,000
Cost of goods sold (LIFO)	4,000	5,000	5,800	7,000	8,500
Operating expenses	2,000	2,200	2,600	3,000	3,200
Income before income taxes	$ 4,000	$ 4,800	$ 5,600	$ 6,000	$ 6,300
Income taxes (40%)	1,600	1,920	2,240	2,400	2,520
Net income	$ 2,400	$ 2,880	$ 3,360	$ 3,600	$ 3,780

If the FIFO method had been used since the company began operations, cost of goods sold in each of the previous quarters would have been as follows:

	2012				2013
	1stQ	2ndQ	3rdQ	4thQ	1stQ
Cost of goods sold (FIFO)	$3,800	$4,600	$5,200	$6,000	$7,400

Sales for the second quarter of 2013 are $20,000, cost of goods sold under the FIFO method is $9,000, and operating expenses are $3,400. The effective tax rate remains 40 percent. Cambi Company has 1,000 shares of common stock outstanding.

Prepare a schedule showing the calculation of net income and earnings per share that Cambi reports for the three-month period and the six-month period ended June 30, 2013.

LO6

41. The following information for Quadrado Corporation relates to the three-month period ending September 30, 2013.

	Units	Price per Unit
Sales	110,000	$20
Beginning inventory.	20,000	12
Purchases.	100,000	14
Ending inventory	10,000	–0–

Quadrado expects to purchase 150,000 units of inventory in the fourth quarter of 2013 at a cost of $15 per unit, and to have on hand 30,000 units of inventory at year-end. Quadrado uses the last-in, first-out (LIFO) method to account for inventory costs.

Determine the cost of goods sold and gross profit amounts to record for the three months ending September 30, 2013. Prepare journal entries to reflect these amounts.

Develop Your Skills

RESEARCH CASE 1—SEGMENT REPORTING

Many companies make annual reports available on their corporate Internet home page. Annual reports also can be accessed through the SEC's EDGAR system at www.sec.gov (under Filing Type, search for 10-K). Access the most recent annual report for a company with which you are familiar to complete the following requirements.

Required

Prepare a one-page report describing your findings for the following:

1. The company's reported operating segments and whether they are based on product lines, geographic areas, or some other basis.
2. The importance of each operating segment for the company as a whole in terms of revenues, income, and assets.
3. Whether the company provides any enterprisewide disclosures in addition to disclosures related to its operating segments.
4. Whether the company provides disclosures about major customers.

RESEARCH CASE 2—INTERIM REPORTING

Many companies make quarterly reports available on their corporate Internet home page. Quarterly reports also can be accessed through the SEC's EDGAR system at www.sec.gov (under Filing Type, search for 10-Q). Access the most recent quarterly report for a company with which you are familiar to complete the following requirements.

Required

Prepare a one-page report describing your findings for the following:

1. Whether the company provides the minimum disclosures required for interim reports.
2. Any disclosures the company provides that exceed the minimum disclosures required.
3. The various year-to-year comparisons that can be made using the disclosures provided in the quarterly report.

RESEARCH CASE 3—OPERATING SEGMENTS

Many companies make annual reports available on their corporate Internet home page. Annual reports also can be accessed through the SEC's EDGAR system at www.sec.gov (under Filing Type, search for 10-K). Access the most recent annual report for each of the following companies:

Abbott Laboratories
Eaton
General Electric
United Technologies

Required

Prepare a one-page report summarizing your findings for the following:

1. The two most important operating segments in terms of percentage of total revenues.
2. The two operating segments with the largest growth in revenues.
3. The two most profitable operating segments in terms of profit margin.

RESEARCH CASE 4—COMPARABILITY OF GEOGRAPHIC AREA INFORMATION

CPA skills

Many companies make annual reports available on their corporate Internet home page. Annual reports also can be accessed through the SEC's EDGAR system at www.sec.gov (under Filing Type, search for 10-K). Access the most recent annual report for each of the following companies:

Bristol Myers Squibb
Eli Lilly
Merck
Pfizer

Required

Prepare a one-page report describing the comparability of the geographic area information provided by these companies.

RESEARCH CASE 5—WITHIN INDUSTRY COMPARISON OF SEGMENT INFORMATION

CPA skills

Many companies make annual reports available on their corporate Internet home page. Annual reports also can be accessed through the SEC's EDGAR system at www.sec.gov (under Filing Type, search for 10-K). Access the most recent annual report for two companies generally considered to be competitors. Possible companies include these:

Beverages: Coca-Cola, PepsiCo
Chemical: Dow Chemical, DuPont, Monsanto, Union Carbide
Computer: Apple Computer, Dell, Hewlett-Packard, IBM
Food products: Campbell Soup, Heinz, Sara Lee
Petroleum: Chevron, ExxonMobil
Pharmaceutical: Eli Lilly, Merck, Pfizer
Toys: Hasbro, Mattel

Required

Based solely on the segment information provided, prepare a one-page report describing and comparing the two companies.

ACCOUNTING STANDARDS CASE 1—SEGMENT REPORTING

Nuland International Corporation recently acquired 40 percent of Scott Trading Company and appropriately accounts for this investment under the equity method. Nuland's corporate controller is in the process of determining the company's operating segments for purposes of preparing financial statements for the current year. He has determined that the investment in Scott meets the definition of an operating segment (i.e., Scott earns revenues and incurs expenses, Nuland's chief operating officer regularly reviews Scott's operating results, and Scott provides Nuland with a complete set of financial statements). However, because Nuland does not control Scott, the controller is not sure whether the investment in Scott can be considered a separate operating segment.

Required

Search current U.S. authoritative accounting literature to determine whether an equity method investment can be treated as an operating segment for financial reporting purposes. If so, explain the conditions under which this would be possible. Identify the source of guidance for answering this question.

ACCOUNTING STANDARDS CASE 2—INTERIM REPORTING

Caplan Pharma, Inc., recently was sued by a competitor for possible infringement of the competitor's patent on a top-selling flu vaccine. The plaintiff is suing for damages of $15 million. Caplan's CFO has discussed the case with legal counsel, who believes it is possible that Caplan will not be able to successfully defend the lawsuit. The CFO knows that current U.S. accounting guidelines require that contingencies (such as lawsuits) must be disclosed in the annual report when a loss is possible. However, she is unsure whether this rule must be applied in the preparation of interim financial statements. She also knows that disclosure is necessary only if the amount is material, but she is unsure whether materiality should be assessed in relation to results for the interim period or for the entire year.

Required

Search current U.S. accounting standards to determine whether contingencies are required to be disclosed in interim reports, and, if so, how materiality is to be determined. Identify the source of guidance for answering these questions.

ANALYSIS CASE—WALMART INTERIM AND SEGMENT REPORTING

The following information was extracted from quarterly reports for Wal-Mart Stores, Inc. (amounts in millions):

	Three Months Ended April 30		Three Months Ended July 31		Three Months Ended October 31	
Operating Income	**2010**	**2009**	**2010**	**2009**	**2010**	**2009**
Walmart U.S.	$4,638	$4,391	$4,879	$4,890	$4,399	$4,318
Walmart International	1,095	857	1,299	1,112	1,223	1,078
Sam's Club.	429	393	428	418	367	395

The following information was extracted from the notes to the financial statements in the Wal-Mart Stores, Inc., Annual Report (for the fiscal year ended January 31, 2011, amounts in millions):

16 Segments
Fiscal Year Ended January 31, 2011

	Walmart U.S.	Walmart International	Sam's Club	Other	Consolidated
Net sales	$260,261	$109,232	$49,459	—	$418,952
Operating income (loss)	19,914	5,606	1,711	(1,689)	25,542
Total assets of continuing operations	89,725	72,021	12,531	6,255	180,532

18 Quarterly Financial Data (Unaudited)
(amounts in millions except per share data)

	Fiscal Year Ended January 31, 2011			
	Q1	**Q2**	**Q3**	**Q4**
Net sales	$99,097	$103,016	$101,239	$115,600
Cost of sales	74,700	77,523	75,906	87,158
Income from continuing operations . . .	$ 3,444	$ 3,747	$ 3,590	$ 5,178

Required

1. Assess the seasonal nature of Walmart's sales and income for the company as a whole and by operating segment.
2. Assess Walmart's profitability by quarter and by operating segment.

EXCEL CASE—COCA-COLA GEOGRAPHIC SEGMENT INFORMATION

The Coca-Cola Company is organized geographically and defines reportable operating segments as regions of the world. The following information was extracted from Note 19 Operating Segments in the Coca-Cola Company 2010 Annual Report:

Information about our Company's operations by operating segment for the years ended December 31, 2010, 2009, and 2008, is as follows (in millions):

	Eurasia & Africa	Europe	Latin America	North America	Pacific	Bottling Investments	Corporate	Eliminations	Consolidated
2010									
Net operating revenues:									
Third party	**$2,426**	**$4,424**	**$3,880**	**$11,140**	**$4,941**	**$8,216**	**$ 92**	**$ —**	**$35,119**
Intersegment	**130**	**825**	**241**	**65**	**330**	**97**	**—**	**(1,688)**	**—**
Total net revenues	**2,556**	**5,249**	**4,121**	**11,205**	**5,271**	**8,313**	**92**	**(1,688)**	**35,119**
Operating income (loss)	**980**	**2,976**	**2,405**	**1,520**	**2,048**	**227**	**(1,707)**	**—**	**8,449**
Interest income	**—**	**—**	**—**	**—**	**—**	**—**	**317**	**—**	**317**
Interest expense	**—**	**—**	**—**	**—**	**—**	**—**	**733**	**—**	**733**
Depreciation and amortization	**31**	**106**	**54**	**575**	**101**	**430**	**146**	**—**	**1,433**
Equity income (loss)—net	**18**	**33**	**24**	**(4)**	**1**	**971**	**(18)**	**—**	**1,025**
Income (loss) before income taxes	**1,000**	**3,020**	**2,426**	**1,523**	**2,049**	**1,205**	**3,020**	**—**	**14,243**
Identifiable operating assets	**1,278**	**2,724**	**2,298**	**32,793**	**1,827**	**8,398**	**16,018**	**—**	**65,336**
Investments	**291**	**243**	**379**	**57**	**123**	**6,426**	**66**	**—**	**7,585**
Capital expenditures	**59**	**33**	**94**	**711**	**101**	**942**	**275**	**—**	**2,215**
2009									
Net operating revenues:									
Third party	$1,977	$4,308	$3,700	$ 8,191	$4,533	$8,193	$ 88	$ —	$30,990
Intersegment	220	895	182	80	342	127	—	(1,846)	—
Total net revenues	2,197	5,203	3,882	8,271	4,875	8,320	88	(1,846)	30,990
Operating income (loss)	810	2,946	2,042	1,699	1,887	179	(1,332)	—	8,231
Interest income	—	—	—	—	—	—	249	—	249
Interest expense	—	—	—	—	—	—	355	—	355
Depreciation and amortization	27	132	52	365	95	424	141	—	1,236
Equity income (loss)—net	(1)	20	(4)	(1)	(23)	785	5	—	781
Income (loss) before income taxes	810	2,976	2,039	1,701	1,866	980	(1,426)	—	8,946
Identifiable operating assets	1,155	3,047	2,480	10,941	1,929	9,140	13,224	—	41,916
Investments	331	214	248	8	82	5,809	63	—	6,755
Capital expenditures	70	68	123	458	91	826	357	—	1,993
2008									
Net operating revenues:									
Third party	$2,135	$4,785	$3,623	$ 8,205	$4,358	$8,731	$ 107	$ —	$31,944
Intersegment	192	1,016	212	75	337	200	—	(2,032)	—
Total net revenues	2,327	5,801	3,835	8,280	4,695	8,931	107	(2,032)	31,944
Operating income (loss)	834	3,175	2,099	1,584	1,858	264	(1,368)	—	8,446
Interest income	—	—	—	—	—	—	333	—	333
Interest expense	—	—	—	—	—	—	438	—	438
Depreciation and amortization	26	169	42	376	78	409	128	—	1,228
Equity income (loss)—net	(14)	(4)	6	(2)	(19)	(844)	3	—	(874)
Income (loss) before income taxes	823	3,182	2,098	1,579	1,841	(582)	(1,435)	—	7,506
Identifiable operating assets	956	3,012	1,849	10,845	1,444	7,935	8,699	—	34,740
Investments	395	179	199	4	72	4,873	57	—	5,779
Capital expenditures	67	76	58	493	177	818	279	—	1,968

Required

1. Use an electronic spreadsheet to calculate the following measures for each of Coca-Cola's operating segments (excluding Bottling Investments and Corporate):
   Percentage of total net revenues, 2009 and 2010.
   Percentage change in total net revenues, 2008 to 2009 and 2009 to 2010.
   Operating income as a percentage of total net revenues (profit margin), 2009 and 2010.
2. Determine whether you believe Coca-Cola should attempt to expand its operations in a particular region of the world to increase operating revenues and operating income.
3. List any additional information you would like to have to conduct your analysis.

chapter 9

Foreign Currency Transactions and Hedging Foreign Exchange Risk

Learning Objectives

After studying this chapter, you should be able to:

- LO1 Understand concepts related to foreign currency, exchange rates, and foreign exchange risk.
- LO2 Account for foreign currency transactions using the two-transaction perspective, accrual approach.
- LO3 Understand how foreign currency forward contracts and foreign currency options can be used to hedge foreign exchange risk.
- LO4 Account for forward contracts and options used as hedges of foreign currency denominated assets and liabilities.
- LO5 Account for forward contracts and options used as hedges of foreign currency firm commitments.
- LO6 Account for forward contracts and options used as hedges of forecasted foreign currency transactions.
- LO7 Prepare journal entries to account for foreign currency borrowings.

Today, international business transactions are a regular occurrence. In its 2010 annual report, Lockheed Martin Corporation reported export sales of $7.1 billion, representing 15 percent of total sales. Even small businesses are significantly involved in transactions occurring throughout the world as evidenced by this excerpt from Cirrus Logic, Inc.'s 2010 Annual Report: "Export sales, principally to Asia, include sales to U.S.–based customers with manufacturing plants overseas and represented 79 percent, 68 percent, and 62 percent of our net sales in fiscal years 2010, 2009, and 2008, respectively." Collections from export sales or payments for imported items might be made not in U.S. dollars but in pesos, pounds, yen, and the like depending on the negotiated terms of the transaction. As the foreign currency exchange rates fluctuate, so does the U.S. dollar value of these export sales and import purchases. Companies often find it necessary to engage in some form of hedging activity to reduce losses arising from fluctuating exchange rates. At the end of fiscal year 2010 as part of its foreign currency hedging activities, Google, Inc., reported having outstanding foreign currency forward contracts and options with a notional value of $7.5 billion.

This chapter covers accounting issues related to foreign currency transactions and foreign currency hedging activities. To provide background for subsequent discussions of the accounting issues, the chapter begins by describing foreign exchange markets. The chapter then discusses accounting for import and export transactions, followed by coverage of various hedging techniques. Because they are most popular, the discussion concentrates on forward contracts and options. Understanding how to account for these items is important for any company engaged in international transactions.

Foreign Exchange Markets

Each country uses its own currency as the unit of value for the purchase and sale of goods and services. The currency used in the United States is the U.S. dollar, the currency used in Mexico is the Mexican peso, and so on. If a U.S. citizen travels to Mexico and wishes to purchase local

LO1

Understand concepts related to foreign currency, exchange rates, and foreign exchange risk.

goods, Mexican merchants require payment to be made in Mexican pesos. To make a purchase, a U.S. citizen has to acquire pesos using U.S. dollars. The *foreign exchange rate* is the price at which the foreign currency can be acquired. A variety of factors determine the exchange rate between two currencies; unfortunately for those engaged in international business, the exchange rate can fluctuate over time.[1]

Exchange Rate Mechanisms

Exchange rates have not always fluctuated. During the period 1945–1973, countries fixed the par value of their currency in terms of the U.S. dollar, and the value of the U.S. dollar was fixed in terms of gold. Countries agreed to maintain the value of their currency within 1 percent of the par value. If the exchange rate for a particular currency began to move outside this 1 percent range, the country's central bank was required to intervene by buying or selling its currency in the foreign exchange market. Because of the law of supply and demand, a central bank's purchase of currency would cause the price of the currency to stop falling, and its sale of currency would cause the price to stop rising.

The integrity of the system hinged on the U.S. dollar maintaining its value in gold and the ability of foreign countries to convert their U.S. dollar holdings into gold at the fixed rate of $35 per ounce. As the United States began to incur balance of payment deficits in the 1960s, a glut of U.S. dollars arose worldwide, and foreign countries began converting their U.S. dollars into gold. This resulted in a decline in the U.S. government's gold reserve from a high of $24.6 billion in 1949 to a low of $10.2 billion in 1971. In that year, the United States suspended the convertibility of the U.S. dollar into gold, signaling the beginning of the end for the fixed exchange rate system. In March 1973, most currencies were allowed to float in value.

Today, several different currency arrangements exist. Some of the more important ones and the countries affected follow:

1. *Independent float:* The value of the currency is allowed to fluctuate freely according to market forces with little or no intervention from the central bank (Canada, Japan, Sweden, Switzerland, United States).
2. *Pegged to another currency:* The value of the currency is fixed (pegged) in terms of a particular foreign currency and the central bank intervenes as necessary to maintain the fixed value. For example, the Bahamas, Panama, and Saudi Arabia peg their currency to the U.S. dollar.
3. *European Monetary System (euro):* In 1998, the countries comprising the European Monetary System adopted a common currency called the *euro* and established a European Central Bank.[2] Until 2002, local currencies such as the German mark and French franc continued to exist but were fixed in value in terms of the euro. On January 1, 2002, local currencies disappeared, and the euro became the currency in 12 European countries. Today, 17 countries are part of the euro area. The value of the euro floats against other currencies such as the U.S. dollar.

Foreign Exchange Rates

Exchange rates between the U.S. dollar and many foreign currencies are published on a daily basis in *The Wall Street Journal* and major U.S. newspapers. Exchange rates also are available on the Internet at www.oanda.com and www.x-rates.com. To better illustrate exchange rates and the foreign currency market, next we examine the exchange rates reported by *The Wall Street Journal* for Monday, February 28, 2011, as shown in Exhibit 9.1.

These exchange rates were quoted in New York at 4:00 P.M. Eastern time (ET). The U.S. dollar price for one Argentinian peso on Monday, February 28, 2011, at 4:00 P.M.

[1] Several theories attempt to explain exchange rate fluctuations but with little success, at least in the short term. An understanding of the causes of exchange rate changes is not necessary to comprehend the concepts underlying the accounting for changes in exchange rates.

[2] Most longtime members of the European Union (EU) are "euro zone" countries. The major exception is the United Kingdom, which elected not to participate. Switzerland is another important European country not part of the euro zone because it is not a member of the EU.

EXHIBIT 9.1 The Wall Street Journal Foreign Exchange Quotes, Monday, February 28, 2011

Country/currency	Mon in US$	Mon per US$	US$ vs. YTD chg (%)	Country/currency	Mon in US$	Mon per US$	US$ vs. YTD chg (%)
Americas				**Europe**			
Argentina peso*	0.2484	4.0258	**1.4**	**Czech Rep.** koruna**	0.0567	17.637	**−5.8**
Brazil real	0.6011	1.6636	**0.2**	**Denmark** krone	0.1851	5.4025	**−3.1**
Canada dollar	1.0294	0.9714	**−2.6**	**Euro area** euro	1.3799	0.7247	**−3.1**
1-mos forward	1.0287	0.9721	**−2.6**	**Hungary** forint	0.005089	196.5	**−5.6**
3-mos forward	1.0273	0.9734	**−2.6**	**Norway** krone	0.1786	5.5991	**−3.9**
6-mos forward	1.0245	0.9761	**−2.6**	**Poland** zloty	0.3486	2.8686	**−3.2**
Chile peso	0.002105	475.06	**1.5**	**Romania** leu	0.3283	3.0459	**−3.9**
Colombia peso	0.0005244	1906.94	**−0.7**	**Russia** ruble‡	0.03464	28.868	**−5.6**
Ecuador US dollar	1	1	**unch**	**Sweden** krona	0.1579	6.3331	**−5.8**
Mexico peso*	0.0826	12.1021	**−1.9**	**Switzerland** franc	1.0764	0.929	**−0.6**
Peru new sol	0.3605	2.7739	**−1.2**	1-mos forward	1.0767	0.9288	**−0.6**
Uruguay peso†	0.0514	19.46	**−2.1**	3-mos forward	1.0773	0.9282	**−0.5**
Venezuela b. fuerte	0.23285	4.2946	**unch**	6-mos forward	1.0781	0.9276	**−0.5**
Asia-Pacific				**Turkey** lira**	0.6255	1.5987	**3.7**
				UK pound	1.6256	0.6152	**−4**
Australian dollar	1.0181	0.9822	**0.4**	1-mos forward	1.6252	0.6153	**−4**
China yuan	0.1522	6.5716	**−0.3**	3-mos forward	1.624	0.6158	**−4**
Hong Kong dollar	0.1284	7.788	**0.2**	6-mos forward	1.6213	0.6168	**−4**
India rupee	0.02209	45.2694	**1.3**				
Indonesia rupiah	0.0001134	8818	**−2.1**	**Middle East/Africa**			
Japan yen	0.012224	81.81	**0.7**	**Bahrain** dinar	2.6522	0.377	**unch**
1-mos forward	0.012227	81.79	**0.7**	**Egypt** pound*	0.1698	5.891	**1.5**
3-mos forward	0.012233	81.75	**0.8**	**Israel** shekel	0.2759	3.6245	**2.8**
6-mos forward	0.012245	81.67	**0.8**	**Jordan** dinar	1.4109	0.7088	**unch**
Malaysia ringgit§	0.3278	3.0506	**−1.1**	**Kenya** shilling	0.01211	82.57	**2.3**
New Zealand dollar	0.7524	1.3291	**3.5**	**Kuwait** dinar	3.5907	0.2785	**−1.1**
Pakistan rupee	0.01166	85.763	**0.1**	**Lebanon** pound	0.000666	1501.5	**0.1**
Philippines peso	0.023	43.554	**−0.2**	**Saudi Arabia** riyal	0.2666	3.7509	**unch**
Singapore dollar	0.7862	1.2719	**−0.9**	**South Africa** rand	0.1436	6.9638	**5.1**
South Korea won	0.0008886	1125.37	**0.4**	**UAE** dirham	0.2723	3.6724	**unch**
Taiwan dollar	0.03361	29.753	**2**				
Thailand baht	0.03269	30.59	**1.7**	**SDR**††	1.5731	0.6357	**−2.1**
Vietnam dong	0.00005	20878	**7.1**				

*Floating rate.
†Financial.
§Government rate.
‡Russian Central Bank rate.
**Commercial rate
††Special Drawing Rights (SDR); from the International Monetary Fund; based on exchange rates for U.S., British, and Japanese currencies.
Note: Based on trading among banks of $1 million and more, as quoted at 4 P.M. ET by Thomson Reuters.
Source: The Wall Street Journal Online, http://online.wsj.com/mdc/public/page/2_3021-forex-20110228.html?mod=mdc_pastcalendarm, accessed May 30, 2011.

in New York was $0.2484. The U.S. dollar price for a peso at 4:01 P.M. Eastern time in New York was probably something different, as was the U.S. dollar price for a peso in Buenos Aires at 4:00 P.M. ET. These exchange rates are for trades between banks in amounts of $1 million or more; that is, these are interbank or wholesale prices. Prices charged to retail customers, such as companies engaged in international business, are higher. These are selling rates at which banks in New York will sell currency to one another. The prices that banks are willing to pay to buy foreign currency (buying rates) are somewhat less than the selling rates. The difference between the buying and selling rates is the spread through which the banks earn a profit on foreign exchange trades.

Two columns of information are published for each day's exchange rates. The first column, in US$, indicates the number of U.S. dollars needed to purchase one unit of foreign currency. These are known as *direct quotes*. The direct quote for the Swedish krona on

February 28 was $0.1579; in other words, 1.0 krona could be purchased with $0.1579. The second column, per US$, indicates the number of foreign currency units that could be purchased with one U.S. dollar. These are called *indirect quotes,* which are simply the inverse of direct quotes. If one krona can be purchased with $0.1579, then 6.3331 kroner can be purchased with $1.00. To avoid confusion, *direct quotes are used exclusively in this chapter.*

The third column indicates the year-to-date change in the value of each foreign currency. In the two months following January 1, 2011, the U.S. dollar decreased in value against the Canadian dollar by 2.6 percent, whereas during the same time period it increased in value against the Chilean peso by 1.5 percent. Several currencies, such as the Bahraini dinar and the Venezuelan bolivar fuerte, did not change in value because they were pegged to the U.S. dollar.

Spot and Forward Rates

Foreign currency trades can be executed on a spot or forward basis. The *spot rate* is the price at which a foreign currency can be purchased or sold today. In contrast, the *forward rate* is the price today at which foreign currency can be purchased or sold sometime in the future. Because many international business transactions take some time to be completed, the ability to lock in a price today at which foreign currency can be purchased or sold at some future date has definite advantages.

Most of the quotes published in *The Wall Street Journal* are *spot rates*. In addition, it publishes forward rates quoted by New York banks for several major currencies (British pound, Canadian dollar, Japanese yen, and Swiss franc) on a daily basis. This is only a partial listing of possible forward contracts. A firm and its bank can tailor forward contracts in other currencies and for other time periods to meet the firm's needs. Entering into a forward contract has no up-front cost.

The forward rate can exceed the spot rate on a given date, in which case the foreign currency is said to be selling at a *premium* in the forward market, or the forward rate can be less than the spot rate, in which case it is selling at a *discount*. Currencies sell at a premium or a discount because of differences in interest rates between two countries. When the interest rate in the foreign country exceeds the domestic interest rate, the foreign currency sells at a discount in the forward market. Conversely, if the foreign interest rate is less than the domestic rate, the foreign currency sells at a premium.[3] Forward rates are said to be unbiased predictors of the future spot rate.

The spot rate for British pounds on February 28, 2011, indicates that 1 pound could have been purchased on that date for $1.6256. On the same day, the three-month forward rate was $1.624. By entering into a forward contract on February 28, it was possible to guarantee that pounds could be purchased on May 28 at a price of $1.624, regardless of what the spot rate turned out to be on May 28. Entering into the forward contract to purchase pounds would have been beneficial if the spot rate on May 28 was more than $1.624. On the other hand, such a forward contract would have been detrimental if the spot rate was less than $1.624. In either case, the forward contract must be honored and pounds must be purchased on May 28 at $1.624.

As it turned out, the spot rate for pounds on May 28, 2011, was $1.6481, so entering into a three-month forward contract on February 28, 2011, to purchase pounds at $1.624 would have resulted in a gain.

Option Contracts

To provide companies more flexibility than exists with a forward contract, a market for *foreign currency options* has developed. A foreign currency option gives the holder of the option *the right but not the obligation* to trade foreign currency in the future. A *put* option is for the sale of foreign currency by the holder of the option; a *call* is for the purchase of foreign currency by the holder of the option. The *strike price* is the exchange rate at which the option will be executed if the option holder decides to exercise the option. The

[3] This relationship is based on the theory of interest rate parity that indicates the difference in national interest rates should be equal to, but opposite in sign to, the forward rate discount or premium. This topic is covered in detail in international finance textbooks.

strike price is similar to a forward rate. There are generally several strike prices to choose from at any particular time. Foreign currency options can be purchased on the Philadelphia Stock Exchange, on the Chicago Mercantile Exchange, or directly from a bank in the so-called over-the-counter market.

Unlike a forward contract, for which banks earn their profit through the spread between buying and selling rates, options must actually be purchased by paying an *option premium,* which is a function of two components: intrinsic value and time value. An option's *intrinsic value* is equal to the gain that could be realized by exercising the option immediately. For example, if a spot rate for a foreign currency is $1.00, a *call* option (to purchase foreign currency) with a strike price of $0.97 has an intrinsic value of $0.03, whereas a *put* option (to sell foreign currency) with a strike price of $0.97 has an intrinsic value of zero. An option with a positive intrinsic value is said to be "in the money." The *time value* of an option relates to the fact that the spot rate can change over time and cause the option to become in the money. Even though a 90-day call option with a strike price of $1.00 has zero intrinsic value when the spot rate is $1.00, it will still have a positive time value because there is a chance that the spot rate could increase over the next 90 days and bring the option into the money.

The value of a foreign currency option can be determined by applying an adaptation of the Black-Scholes option pricing formula. This formula is discussed in detail in international finance books. In very general terms, the value of an option is a function of the difference between the current spot rate and strike price, the difference between domestic and foreign interest rates, the length of time to expiration, and the potential volatility of changes in the spot rate. For purposes of this book, the premium originally paid for a foreign currency option and its subsequent fair value up to the date of expiration derived from applying the pricing formula will be given.

On May 30, 2011, the Chicago Mercantile Exchange indicated that a June 2011 call option in euros with a strike price of $1.425 could have been purchased by paying a premium of $0.0079 per euro. Thus, the right to purchase a standard contract of 62,500 euros in June 2011 at a price of $1.425 per euro could have been acquired by paying $493.75 ($0.0079 × 62,500 euros). If the spot rate for euros in June 2011 turned out to be more than $1.425, the option would be exercised and euros purchased at the strike price of $1.425. If, on the other hand, the June spot rate is less than $1.425, the option would not be exercised; instead, euros would be purchased at the lower spot rate. The call option establishes the maximum amount that would have to be paid for euros but does not lock in a disadvantageous price should the spot rate fall below the option strike price.

Foreign Currency Transactions

LO2

Account for foreign currency transactions using the two-transaction perspective, accrual approach.

Export sales and import purchases are international transactions; they are components of what is called *trade*. When two parties from different countries enter into a transaction, they must decide which of the two countries' currencies to use to settle the transaction. For example, if a U.S. computer manufacturer sells to a customer in Japan, the parties must decide whether the transaction will be denominated (payment will be made) in U.S. dollars or Japanese yen.

Assume that a U.S. exporter (Amerco) sells goods to a German importer that will pay in euros (€). In this situation, Amerco has entered into a foreign currency transaction. It must restate the euro amount that it actually will receive into U.S. dollars to account for this transaction. This happens because Amerco keeps its books and prepares financial statements in U.S. dollars. Although the German importer has entered into an international transaction, it does not have a foreign currency transaction (payment will be made in its currency) and no restatement is necessary.

Assume that, as is customary in its industry, Amerco does not require immediate payment and allows its German customer 30 days to pay for its purchases. By doing this, Amerco runs the risk that the euro might depreciate against the U.S. dollar between the sale date and the date of payment. If so, the sale would generate fewer U.S. dollars than it would have had the euro not decreased in value, and the sale is less profitable because it was made on a credit basis. In this situation Amerco is said to have an *exposure to foreign exchange risk*. Specifically, Amerco has a transaction exposure that can be summarized as follows:

- *Export sale:* A transaction exposure exists when the exporter allows the buyer to pay in a foreign currency and allows the buyer to pay sometime after the sale has been made. The exporter is exposed to the risk that the foreign currency might depreciate (decrease in value) between the date of sale and the date payment is received, thereby decreasing the U.S. dollars ultimately collected.
- *Import purchase:* A transaction exposure exists when the importer is required to pay in foreign currency and is allowed to pay sometime after the purchase has been made. The importer is exposed to the risk that the foreign currency might appreciate (increase in price) between the date of purchase and the date of payment, thereby increasing the U.S. dollars that have to be paid for the imported goods.

Accounting Issue

The major issue in accounting for foreign currency transactions is how to deal with the change in U.S. dollar value of the sales revenue and account receivable resulting from the export when the foreign currency changes in value. (The corollary issue is how to deal with the change in the U.S. dollar value of the account payable and goods being acquired in an import purchase.) For example, assume that Amerco, a U.S. company, sells goods to a German customer at the price of 1 million euros when the spot exchange rate is $1.32 per euro. If payment were received at the sale date, Amerco could have converted 1 million euros into $1,320,000; this amount clearly would be the amount at which the sales revenue would be recognized. Instead, Amerco allows the German customer 30 days to pay for its purchase. At the end of 30 days, the euro has depreciated to $1.30 and Amerco is able to convert the 1 million euros received on that date into only $1,300,000. How should Amerco account for this $20,000 decrease in value?

Accounting Alternatives

Conceptually, the two methods of accounting for changes in the value of a foreign currency transaction are the one-transaction perspective and the two-transaction perspective. The *one-transaction perspective* assumes that an export sale is not complete until the foreign currency receivable has been collected and converted into U.S. dollars. Any change in the U.S. dollar value of the foreign currency is accounted for as an adjustment to Accounts Receivable and to Sales. Under this perspective, Amerco would ultimately report Sales at $1,300,000 and an increase in the Cash account of the same amount. This approach can be criticized because it hides the fact that the company could have received $1,320,000 if the German customer had been required to pay at the date of sale. Amerco incurs a $20,000 loss because of the depreciation in the euro, but that loss is buried in an adjustment to Sales. This approach is not acceptable under U.S. GAAP.

Instead, U.S. GAAP requires companies to use a *two-transaction perspective* in accounting for foreign currency transactions.[4] This perspective treats the export sale and the subsequent collection of cash as two separate transactions. Because management has made two decisions—(1) to make the export sale and (2) to extend credit in foreign currency to the customer—the company should report the income effect from each of these decisions separately. The U.S. dollar value of the sale is recorded at the date the sale occurs. At that point, the sale has been completed; there are no subsequent adjustments to the Sales account. Any difference between the number of U.S. dollars that could have been received at the date of sale and the number of U.S. dollars actually received at the date of collection due to fluctuations in the exchange rate is a result of the decision to extend foreign currency credit to the customer. This difference is treated as a foreign exchange gain or loss that is reported separately from Sales in the income statement. Using the two-transaction perspective to account for its export sale to the German customer, Amerco would make the following journal entries:

[4] Accounting for foreign currency transactions is covered in Topic 830, Foreign Currency Matters, in the FASB Accounting Standards Codification (ASC).

Date of Sale:	Accounts Receivable (€).	1,320,000	
	Sales.		1,320,000
	To record the sale and euro receivable at the spot rate of $1.32.		
Date of Collection:	Foreign Exchange Loss	20,000	
	Accounts Receivable (€)		20,000
	To adjust the value of the euro receivable to the new spot rate of $1.30 and record a foreign exchange loss resulting from the depreciation in the euro.		
	Cash	1,300,000	
	Accounts Receivable (€)		1,300,000
	To record the receipt of 1 million euros and conversion at the spot rate of $1.30.		

Sales are reported in income at the amount that would have been received if the customer had not been given 30 days to pay the 1 million euros—that is, $1,320,000. A separate Foreign Exchange Loss of $20,000 is reported in income to indicate that because of the decision to extend foreign currency credit to the German customer and because the euro decreased in value, Amerco actually received fewer U.S. dollars.[5]

Note that Amerco keeps its Account Receivable (€) account separate from its U.S. dollar receivables. Companies engaged in international trade need to keep separate receivable and payable accounts in each of the currencies in which they have transactions. Each foreign currency receivable and payable should have a separate account number in the company's chart of accounts.

We can summarize the relationship between fluctuations in exchange rates and foreign exchange gains and losses as follows:

		Foreign Currency (FC)	
Transaction	**Type of Exposure**	**Appreciates**	**Depreciates**
Export sale	Asset	Gain	Loss
Import purchase	Liability	Loss	Gain

A foreign currency receivable arising from an export sale creates an *asset exposure* to foreign exchange risk. If the foreign currency appreciates, the foreign currency asset increases in U.S. dollar value and a foreign exchange gain arises; depreciation of the foreign currency causes a foreign exchange loss. A foreign currency payable arising from an import purchase creates a *liability exposure* to foreign exchange risk. If the foreign currency appreciates, the foreign currency liability increases in U.S. dollar value and a foreign exchange loss results; depreciation of the currency results in a foreign exchange gain.

Balance Sheet Date before Date of Payment

The question arises as to what adjustments should be made if a balance sheet date falls between the date of sale and the date of payment. For example, assume that Amerco shipped goods to its German customer on December 1, 2013, with payment to be received on March 1, 2014. Assume that at December 1, the spot rate for the euro was $1.32, but by December 31, the euro has appreciated to $1.33. Is any adjustment needed at December 31, 2013, when the books are closed to account for the fact that the foreign currency receivable has changed in U.S. dollar value since December 1?

The general consensus worldwide is that a foreign currency receivable or foreign currency payable should be revalued at the balance sheet date to account for the change in exchange rates. Under the two-transaction perspective, this means that a foreign

[5] Note that the foreign exchange loss results because the customer is allowed to pay in euros and is given 30 days to pay. If the transaction were denominated in U.S. dollars, no loss would result, nor would there be a loss if the euros had been received at the date the sale was made.

exchange gain or loss arises at the balance sheet date. The next question then is what should be done with these foreign exchange gains and losses that have not yet been realized in cash. Should they be included in net income?

The two approaches to accounting for unrealized foreign exchange gains and losses are the deferral approach and the accrual approach. Under the *deferral approach,* unrealized foreign exchange gains and losses are deferred on the balance sheet until cash is actually paid or received. When cash is paid or received, a *realized* foreign exchange gain or loss is included in income. This approach is not acceptable under U.S. GAAP.

U.S. GAAP requires U.S. companies to use the *accrual approach* to account for unrealized foreign exchange gains and losses. Under this approach, a firm reports unrealized foreign exchange gains and losses in net income in the period in which the exchange rate changes. This is consistent with accrual accounting as it results in reporting the effect of a rate change that will have an impact on cash flow in the period when the event causing the impact takes place. Thus, any change in the exchange rate from the date of sale to the balance sheet date results in a foreign exchange gain or loss to be reported in income in that period. Any change in the exchange rate from the balance sheet date to the date of payment results in a second foreign exchange gain or loss that is reported in the second accounting period. Amerco makes the following journal entries under the accrual approach:

12/1/13	Accounts Receivable (€)	1,320,000	
	Sales		1,320,000
	To record the sale and euro receivable at the spot rate of $1.32.		
12/31/13	Accounts Receivable (€)	10,000	
	Foreign Exchange Gain		10,000
	To adjust the value of the euro receivable to the new spot rate of $1.33 and record a foreign exchange gain resulting from the appreciation in the euro since December 1.		
3/1/14	Foreign Exchange Loss	30,000	
	Accounts Receivable (€).		30,000
	To adjust the value of the euro receivable to the new spot rate of $1.30 and record a foreign exchange loss resulting from the depreciation in the euro since December 31.		
	Cash	1,300,000	
	Accounts Receivable (€).		1,300,000
	To record the receipt of 1 million euros and conversion at the spot rate of $1.30.		

The net impact on income in 2013 is a sale of $1,320,000 and a foreign exchange gain of $10,000; in 2014, Amerco records a foreign exchange loss of $30,000. This results in a net increase of $1,300,000 in Retained Earnings that is balanced by an equal increase in Cash over the two-year period. Over the two-year period Amerco recognizes a net foreign exchange loss of $20,000.

One criticism of the accrual approach is that it leads to a violation of conservatism when an unrealized foreign exchange gain arises at the balance sheet date. In fact, this is one of only two situations in U.S. GAAP in which it is acceptable to recognize an unrealized gain in income. (The other situation relates to trading marketable securities reported at fair value.)

Restatement at the balance sheet date is required for all foreign currency assets and liabilities carried on a company's books. In addition to foreign currency payables and receivables arising from import and export transactions, companies might have dividends receivable from foreign subsidiaries, loans payable to foreign lenders, or lease payments receivable from foreign customers that are denominated in a foreign currency and therefore must be restated at the balance sheet date. Each of these foreign currency denominated assets and liabilities is exposed to foreign exchange risk; therefore, fluctuation in the exchange rate results in foreign exchange gains and losses.

Many U.S. companies report foreign exchange gains and losses on the income statement in a line item often titled Other Income (Expense). Companies include other incidental gains and losses such as gains and losses on sales of assets in this line item as well. Companies are required to disclose the magnitude of foreign exchange gains and losses if material. For example, in the Notes to Financial Statements in its 2010 annual report, Merck indicated that the income statement item Other (Income) Expense, Net included exchange losses of $214 million in 2010 and $147 million in 2008, and an exchange gain of $12 million in 2009.

Hedges of Foreign Exchange Risk

LO3

Understand how foreign currency forward contracts and foreign currency options can be used to hedge foreign exchange risk.

In the preceding example, Amerco has an asset exposure in euros when it sells goods to the German customer and allows the customer three months to pay for its purchase. If the euro depreciates over the next three months, Amerco will incur a net foreign exchange loss. For many companies, the uncertainty of not knowing exactly how many U.S. dollars an export sale will generate is of great concern. To avoid this uncertainty, companies often use foreign currency derivatives to hedge against the effect of unfavorable changes in the value of foreign currencies. The two most common derivatives used to hedge foreign exchange risk are *foreign currency forward contracts* and *foreign currency options*. Through a forward contract, Amerco can lock in the price at which it will sell the euros it receives in three months. An option establishes a price at which Amerco will be able, but is not required, to sell the euros it receives in three months. If Amerco enters into a forward contract or purchases a put option on the date the sale is made, the derivative is being used as a *hedge of a recognized foreign currency denominated asset* (the euro account receivable).

Companies engaged in foreign currency activities often enter into hedging arrangements as soon as they receive a noncancelable sales order or place a noncancelable purchase order. A noncancelable order that specifies the foreign currency price and date of delivery is known as a *foreign currency firm commitment*. Assume that on June 1, Amerco accepts an order to sell parts to a customer in South Korea at a price of 5 million Korean won. The parts will be delivered and payment will be received on August 15. On June 1, before the sale has been made, Amerco enters into a forward contract to sell 5 million Korean won on August 15. In this case, Amerco is using a foreign currency derivative as a *hedge of an unrecognized foreign currency firm commitment*.

Some companies have foreign currency transactions that occur on a regular basis and can be reliably forecasted. For example, Amerco regularly purchases materials from a supplier in Hong Kong for which it pays in Hong Kong dollars. Even if Amerco has no contract to make future purchases, it has an exposure to foreign currency risk if it plans to continue making purchases from the Hong Kong supplier. Assume that on October 1, Amerco forecasts that it will make a purchase from the Hong Kong supplier in one month. To hedge against a possible increase in the price of the Hong Kong dollar, Amerco acquires a call option on October 1 to purchase Hong Kong dollars in one month. The foreign currency option represents a *hedge of a forecasted foreign currency denominated transaction*.

Derivatives Accounting

Topic 815, Derivatives and Hedging, of the FASB Accounting Standards Codification governs the accounting for derivatives, including those used to hedge foreign exchange risk. This authoritative literature provides guidance for hedges of the following sources of foreign exchange risk:

1. Recognized foreign currency denominated assets and liabilities.
2. Unrecognized foreign currency firm commitments.
3. Forecasted foreign currency denominated transactions.
4. Net investments in foreign operations.

Different accounting applies to each type of foreign currency hedge. This chapter demonstrates the accounting for the first three types of hedges. The next chapter covers hedges of net investments in foreign operations.

Fundamental Requirement of Derivatives Accounting

The fundamental requirement is that companies carry all derivatives on the balance sheet at their fair value. Derivatives are reported on the balance sheet as assets when they have a positive fair value and as liabilities when they have a negative fair value. The first issue in accounting for derivatives is the determination of fair value.

The fair value of derivatives can change over time, causing adjustments to be made to the carrying values of the assets and liabilities. The second issue in accounting for derivatives is the treatment of the gains and losses that arise from these adjustments.

Determination of Fair Value of Derivatives

The *fair value of a foreign currency forward contract* is determined by reference to changes in the forward rate over the life of the contract, discounted to the present value. Three pieces of information are needed to determine the fair value of a forward contract at any point in time:

1. The forward rate when the forward contract was entered into.
2. The current forward rate for a contract that matures on the same date as the forward contract entered into.
3. A discount rate—typically, the company's incremental borrowing rate.

Assume that Exim Company enters into a forward contract on December 1 to sell 1 million Mexican pesos on March 1 at a forward rate of $0.085 per peso, or a total of $85,000. Exim incurs no cost to enter into the forward contract, which has no value on December 1. On December 31, when Exim closes its books to prepare financial statements, the forward rate to sell Mexican pesos on March 1 has changed to $0.082. On that date, a forward contract for the delivery of 1 million pesos could be negotiated, resulting in a cash inflow of only $82,000 on March 1. This represents a favorable change in the value of Exim's forward contract of $3,000 ($85,000 − $82,000). The undiscounted fair value of the forward contract on December 31 is $3,000. Assuming that the company's incremental borrowing rate is 12 percent per annum, the undiscounted fair value of the forward contract must be discounted at the rate of 1 percent per month for two months (from the current date of December 31 to the settlement date of March 1). The fair value of the forward contract at December 31 is $2,940.90 ($3,000 × 0.9803).[6]

The manner in which the *fair value of a foreign currency option* is determined depends on whether the option is traded on an exchange or has been acquired in the over-the-counter market. The fair value of an exchange-traded foreign currency option is its current market price quoted on the exchange. For over-the-counter options, fair value can be determined by obtaining a price quote from an option dealer (such as a bank). If dealer price quotes are unavailable, the company can estimate the value of an option using the modified Black-Scholes option pricing model (briefly mentioned earlier). Regardless of who does the calculation, principles similar to those of the Black-Scholes pricing model can be used to determine the fair value of the option.

Accounting for Changes in the Fair Value of Derivatives

Changes in the fair value of derivatives must be included in *comprehensive income,* which is defined as all changes in equity from nonowner sources. It consists of two components: *net income* and *other comprehensive income*. Other comprehensive income consists of income items that current authoritative accounting literature require to be deferred in stockholders' equity such as gains and losses on available-for-sale marketable securities. Other comprehensive income is accumulated and reported as a separate line in the

[6] The present value factor for two months at 1 percent per month is calculated as $1/1.01^2$, or 0.9803.

stockholders' equity section of the balance sheet. This book uses the account title *Accumulated Other Comprehensive Income* to describe this stockholders' equity line item.

In accordance with U.S. GAAP, gains and losses arising from changes in the fair value of derivatives are recognized initially either (1) on the income statement as a part of net income or (2) on the balance sheet in accumulated other comprehensive income. Recognition treatment depends partly on whether the company uses derivatives for hedging purposes or for speculation.[7] For speculative derivatives, the company recognizes the change in the fair value of the derivative (the gain or loss) immediately in net income. The accounting for changes in the fair value of derivatives used for hedging depends on the nature of the foreign exchange risk being hedged and on whether the derivative qualifies for *hedge accounting*.

Hedge Accounting

Companies enter into hedging relationships to minimize the adverse effect that changes in exchange rates have on cash flows and net income. As such, companies would like to account for hedges in a way that recognizes the gain or loss from the hedge in net income in the same period as the loss or gain on the risk being hedged. This approach is known as *hedge accounting.* U.S. GAAP allows hedge accounting for foreign currency derivatives only if three conditions are satisfied:

1. The derivative is used to hedge either a cash flow exposure or fair-value exposure to foreign exchange risk.
2. The derivative is highly effective in offsetting changes in the cash flows or fair value related to the hedged item.
3. The derivative is properly documented as a hedge.

Each of these conditions is discussed in turn.

Nature of the Hedged Risk

Derivatives for which companies wish to use hedge accounting must be designated as either a *cash flow hedge* or a *fair value hedge*. For hedges of recognized foreign currency assets and liabilities and hedges of foreign currency firm commitments, companies must choose between the two types of designation. Hedges of forecasted foreign currency transactions can qualify only as cash flow hedges. Accounting procedures differ for the two types of hedges. In general, gains and losses on cash flow hedges are included in other comprehensive income, and gains and losses on fair value hedges are recognized immediately in net income.

A *fair-value exposure* exists if changes in exchange rates can affect the fair value of an asset or liability reported on the balance sheet. To qualify for hedge accounting, the fair-value risk must have the potential to affect net income if it is not hedged. For example, a fair-value risk is associated with a foreign currency account receivable. If the foreign currency depreciates, the receivable must be written down with an offsetting loss recognized in net income. The authoritative literature has determined that a fair-value exposure also exists for foreign currency firm commitments.

A *cash flow exposure* exists if changes in exchange rates can affect the amount of cash flow to be realized from a transaction with changes in cash flow reflected in net income. A foreign currency account receivable, for example, has both a fair-value exposure and a cash flow exposure. A cash flow exposure exists for (1) recognized foreign currency

[7] Companies can acquire derivative financial instruments as investments for speculative purposes. For example, assume that the three-month forward rate for British pounds is $2.00, and a speculator believes the British pound spot rate in three months will be $1.97. In that case, the speculator would enter into a three-month forward contract to sell British pounds. At the future date, the speculator purchases pounds at the spot rate of $1.97 and sells them at the contracted forward rate of $2.00, reaping a gain of $0.03 per pound. Of course, such an investment might as easily generate a loss if the spot rate does not move as expected.

assets and liabilities, (2) foreign currency firm commitments, and (3) forecasted foreign currency transactions.

Hedge Effectiveness

For hedge accounting to be used initially, the hedge must be expected to be highly effective in generating gains and losses that offset losses and gains on the item being hedged. The hedge actually must be effective in generating offsetting gains and losses for hedge accounting to continue to be applied.

At inception, a foreign currency derivative can be considered an effective hedge if the critical terms of the hedging instrument match those of the hedged item. Critical terms include the currency type, currency amount, and settlement date. For example, a forward contract to purchase 100,000 Canadian dollars in 30 days would be an effective hedge of a 100,000 Canadian dollar liability that is payable in 30 days. Assessing hedge effectiveness on an ongoing basis can be accomplished using a cumulative dollar offset method.

Hedge Documentation

For hedge accounting to be applied, U.S. GAAP requires formal documentation of the hedging relationship at the inception of the hedge (i.e., on the date a foreign currency forward contract is entered into or a foreign currency option is acquired). The hedging company must prepare a document that identifies the hedged item, the hedging instrument, the nature of the risk being hedged, how the hedging instrument's effectiveness will be assessed, and the risk management objective and strategy for undertaking the hedge.

Hedging Combinations

The specific accounting procedures followed and journal entries needed to account for a foreign currency hedging relationship are determined by a combination of the following factors:

1. The type of foreign currency item being hedged:
    a. Foreign currency denominated asset or liability.
    b. Foreign currency firm commitment.
    c. Forecasted foreign currency transaction.
2. The type of hedging instrument used:
    a. Forward contract.
    b. Option.
3. The nature of the hedged risk:
    a. Cash flow exposure.
    b. Fair-value exposure.
4. The nature of the underlying foreign currency item being hedged:
    a. Asset (existing or future).
    b. Liability (existing or future).

In the next three sections in this chapter we discuss the accounting for hedges of (1) foreign currency denominated assets/liabilities, (2) foreign currency firm commitments, and (3) forecasted foreign currency transactions. We demonstrate through examples the use of both forward contracts and options to hedge these items, and we selectively demonstrate the accounting for both cash flow and fair value hedges. We focus on hedges entered into by an exporter that has a current or future foreign currency asset that is exposed to foreign exchange risk. The comprehensive example at the end of this chapter demonstrates the accounting for hedges entered into by an importer that has an existing or future foreign currency liability. Exhibit 9.2 provides an overall summary of the procedures followed in accounting for hedges of foreign exchange risk for those combinations presented in this chapter. By examining this exhibit, the similarities and differences in the procedures followed and accounting entries prepared to account for each hedge combination can be discerned.

EXHIBIT 9.2 **Summary of Accounting for Hedges of Foreign Exchange Risk**

Date	Hedge of a Foreign Currency Denominated Asset or Liability				Hedge of a Foreign Currency Firm Commitment		Hedge of a Forecasted Foreign Currency Transaction	
	Cash Flow Hedge		Fair Value Hedge		Fair Value Hedge		Cash Flow Hedge	
	Forward Contract	Option	Forward Contract	Option	Forward Contract	Option	Forward Contract	Option
A. Initiation Date	1. Recognize the transaction (sale or purchase) and foreign currency denominated asset or liability	1. Recognize the transaction (sale or purchase) and foreign currency denominated asset or liability	1. Recognize the transaction (sale or purchase) and foreign currency denominated asset or liability	1. Recognize the transaction (sale or purchase) and foreign currency denominated asset or liability	1. No entry related to the firm commitment (zero value)	1. No entry related to the firm commitment	1. No entry related to the forecasted transaction	1. No entry related to the forecasted transaction
	2. No entry related to forward contract (zero fair value)	2. Recognize option as an asset (purchase price is fair value)	2. No entry related to forward contract (zero fair value)	2. Recognize option as an asset (purchase price is fair value)	2. No entry related to forward contract (zero fair value)	2. Recognize option as an asset (purchase price is fair value)	2. No entry related to forward contract (zero fair value)	2. Recognize option as an asset (purchase price is fair value)
B. Balance Sheet Date	1. Adjust hedged asset or liability to fair value, with counterpart (change in fair value) reported as foreign exchange gain or loss in net income	1. Adjust hedged asset or liability to fair value, with counterpart (change in fair value) reported as foreign exchange gain or loss in net income	1. Adjust hedged asset or liability to fair value, with counterpart (change in fair value) reported as foreign exchange gain or loss in net income	1. Adjust hedged asset or liability to fair value, with counterpart (change in fair value) reported as foreign exchange gain or loss in net income	1. Adjust forward contract to fair value (either an asset or a liability), with counterpart (change in fair value) reported as gain or loss in net income	1. Adjust option to fair value (either an asset or zero value), with counterpart (change in fair value) reported as gain or loss in net income	1. N/A	1. N/A
	2. Adjust forward contract to fair value (either an asset or a liability), with counterpart (change in fair value) reported in AOCI	2. Adjust option to fair value (either an asset or zero value), with counterpart (change in fair value) reported in AOCI	2. Adjust forward contract to fair value (either an asset or a liability), with counterpart (change in fair value) reported as gain or loss in net income	2. Adjust option to fair value (either an asset or zero value), with counterpart (change in fair value) reported as gain or loss in net income	2. Adjust firm commitment to fair value (based on change in forward rate), with counterpart (change in fair value) reported as gain or loss in net income	2. Adjust firm commitment to fair value (based on change in spot rate), with counterpart (change in fair value) reported as gain or loss in net income	2. Adjust forward contract to fair value (either an asset or a liability), with counterpart (change in fair value) reported in AOCI	2. Adjust option to fair value (either an asset or zero value), with counterpart (change in fair value) reported in AOCI

(continued)

EXHIBIT 9.2 **(Continued)**

Date	Hedge of a Foreign Currency Denominated Asset or Liability				Hedge of a Foreign Currency Firm Commitment		Hedge of a Forecasted Foreign Currency Transaction	
	Cash Flow Hedge		Fair Value Hedge		Fair Value Hedge		Cash Flow Hedge	
	Forward Contract	Option	Forward Contract	Option	Forward Contract	Option	Forward Contract	Option
	3. Transfer an amount from AOCI to net income to offset the foreign exchange gain or loss on the hedged asset or liability recognized in B.1	3. Transfer an amount from AOCI to net income to offset the foreign exchange gain or loss on the hedged asset or liability recognized in B.1	3. N/A	3. N/A	3. N/A	3. N/A	3. N/A	3. N/A
	4. Transfer from AOCI to net income (as discount expense or premium revenue) the current period's amortization of discount or premium	4. Transfer from AOCI to net income (as expense) the change in time value on the option	4. N/A	4. N/A	4. N/A	4. N/A	4. Transfer from AOCI to net income (as discount expense or premium revenue) the current period's amortization of discount or premium	4. Transfer from AOCI to net income (as option expense) the change in time value on the option
C. Settlement Date	1.–4. Repeat steps B.1.–B.4	1.–4. Repeat steps B.1.–B.4	1.–2. Repeat steps B.1. and B.2	1.–2. Repeat steps B.1. and B.2	1.–2. Repeat steps B.1. and B.2	1.–2. Repeat steps B.1. and B.2	1.–2. Repeat steps B.2. and B.4	1.–2. Repeat steps B.2. and B.4
	5. Recognize settlement of the foreign currency denominated asset or liability	5. Recognize settlement of the foreign currency denominated asset or liability	3. Recognize settlement of the foreign currency denominated asset or liability	3. Recognize settlement of the foreign currency denominated asset or liability	3. Recognize the transaction (sale or purchase)	3. Recognize the transaction (sale or purchase)	3. Recognize the transaction (sale or purchase)	3. Recognize the transaction (sale or purchase)
	6. Recognize settlement of the forward contract*	6. Recognize exercise (or expiration) of the option*	4. Recognize settlement of the forward contract&	4. Recognize exercise (or expiration) of the option&	4. Recognize settlement of the forward contract#	4. Recognize exercise (or expiration) of the option#	4. Recognize settlement of the forward contract#	4. Recognize exercise (or expiration) of the option#
					5. Close the balance in the firm commitment account as an adjustment to net income	5. Close the balance in the firm commitment account as an adjustment to net income	5. Close the balance in AOCI related to the forward contract as an adjustment to net income	5. Close the balance in AOCI related to the option as an adjustment to net income

*Step 6 precedes step 5 in the case of a foreign currency denominated liability
&Step 4 precedes step 3 in the case of a foreign currency denominated liability
#Step 4 precedes step 3 in the case of a foreign currency purchase transaction

Hedges of Foreign Currency Denominated Assets and Liabilities

LO4

Account for forward contracts and options used as hedges of foreign currency denominated assets and liabilities.

Hedges of foreign currency denominated assets and liabilities, such as accounts receivable and accounts payable, can qualify as either *cash flow hedges* or *fair value hedges*. To qualify as a cash flow hedge, the hedging instrument must completely offset the variability in the cash flows associated with the foreign currency receivable or payable. If the hedging instrument does not qualify as a cash flow hedge or if the company elects not to designate the hedging instrument as a cash flow hedge, the hedge is designated as a fair value hedge. The following summarizes the basic accounting for the two types of hedges of foreign currency denominated assets and liabilities.

Cash Flow Hedge

At each balance sheet date, the following procedures are required:

1. The hedged asset or liability is adjusted to fair value based on changes in the spot exchange rate, and a foreign exchange gain or loss is recognized in net income (Cash Flow Hedge Step B.1. in Exhibit 9.2).
2. The derivative hedging instrument is adjusted to fair value (resulting in an asset or liability reported on the balance sheet) with the counterpart recognized as a change in Accumulated Other Comprehensive Income (AOCI) (Cash Flow Hedge Step B.2. in Exhibit 9.2).
3. An amount equal to the foreign exchange gain or loss on the hedged asset or liability is then transferred from AOCI to net income; the net effect is to offset any gain or loss on the hedged asset or liability (Cash Flow Hedge Step B.3. in Exhibit 9.2).
4. An additional amount is removed from AOCI and recognized in net income to reflect (a) the current period's amortization of the original discount or premium on the forward contract (if a forward contract is the hedging instrument) or (b) the change in the *time value* of the option (if an option is the hedging instrument) (Cash Flow Hedge Step B.4. in Exhibit 9.2).

Fair Value Hedge

At each balance sheet date, the following procedures are required:

1. Adjust the hedged asset or liability to fair value based on changes in the spot exchange rate and recognize a foreign exchange gain or loss in net income (Fair Value Hedge Step B.1. in Exhibit 9.2).
2. Adjust the derivative hedging instrument to fair value (resulting in an asset or liability reported on the balance sheet) and recognize the counterpart as a gain or loss in net income (Fair Value Hedge Step B.2. in Exhibit 9.2).

Forward Contract Used to Hedge a Foreign Currency Denominated Asset

We now return to the Amerco example in which the company has a foreign currency account receivable to demonstrate the accounting for a hedge of a recognized foreign currency denominated asset.[8] In the preceding example, Amerco has an asset exposure in euros when it sells goods to the German customer and allows the customer three months to pay for its purchase. To hedge its exposure to a possible decline in the U.S. dollar value of the euro, Amerco enters into a forward contract.

[8] The comprehensive illustration at the end of this chapter demonstrates the accounting for the hedge of a foreign currency denominated liability.

Assume that on December 1, 2013, the three-month forward rate for euros is $1.305 and Amerco signs a contract with New Manhattan Bank to deliver 1 million euros in three months in exchange for $1,305,000. No cash changes hands on December 1, 2013. Because the spot rate on December 1 is $1.32, the euro (€) is selling at a discount in the three-month forward market (the forward rate is less than the spot rate). Because the euro is selling at a discount of $0.015 per euro, Amerco receives $15,000 less than it would had payment been received at the date the goods are delivered ($1,305,000 versus $1,320,000). This $15,000 reduction in cash flow can be considered as an expense; it is the cost of extending foreign currency credit to the foreign customer.[9] Conceptually, this expense is similar to the transaction loss that arises on the export sale. It exists only because the transaction is denominated in a foreign currency. The major difference is that Amerco knows the exact amount of the discount expense at the date of sale, whereas when it is left unhedged, Amerco does not know the size of the transaction loss until three months pass. (In fact, it is possible that the unhedged receivable could result in a transaction gain rather than a transaction loss.)

Because the future spot rate turns out to be only $1.30, selling euros at a forward rate of $1.305 is obviously better than leaving the euro receivable unhedged: Amerco will receive $5,000 more as a result of the hedge. This can be viewed as a gain resulting from the use of the forward contract. Unlike the discount expense, the exact size of this gain is not known until three months pass. (In fact, it is possible that use of the forward contract could result in an additional loss. This would occur if the spot rate on March 1, 2014, is more than the forward rate of $1.305.)

Amerco must account for its foreign currency transaction and the related forward contract simultaneously but separately. The process can be better understood by referring to the steps involving the three parties—Amerco, the German customer, and New Manhattan Bank—shown in Exhibit 9.3.

Because the settlement date, currency type, and currency amount of the forward contract match the corresponding terms of the account receivable, the hedge is expected to be highly effective. If Amerco properly designates the forward contract as a hedge of its euro account receivable position, it may apply hedge accounting. Because it completely offsets the variability in the cash flows related to the account receivable, Amerco may designate the forward contract as a cash flow hedge. Alternatively, because changes in the spot rate affect not only the cash flows but also the fair value of the foreign currency receivable, Amerco may elect to account for this forward contract as a fair value hedge.

In either case, Amerco determines the fair value of the forward contract by referring to the change in the forward rate for a contract maturing on March 1, 2014. The relevant exchange rates, U.S. dollar value of the euro receivable, and fair value of the forward contract are determined as follows:

		Account Receivable (€)		Forward	Forward Contract	
Date	Spot Rate	U.S. Dollar Value	Change in U.S. Dollar Value	Rate to 3/1/14	Fair Value	Change in Fair Value
12/1/13	$1.32	$1,320,000	—	$1.305	–0–	—
12/31/13	1.33	1,330,000	+$10,000	1.316	$(10,783)*	−$10,783
3/1/14	1.30	1,300,000	−$30,000	1.30	5,000†	+ 15,783

*$1,305,000 − $1,316,000 = $(11,000) × 0.9803 = $(10,783), where 0.9803 is the present value factor for two months at an annual interest rate of 12 percent (1 percent per month) calculated as $1/1.01^2$.
†$1,305,000 − $1,300,000 = $5,000.

Amerco pays nothing to enter into the forward contract at December 1, 2013, and the forward contract has a fair value of zero on that date. At December 31, 2013, the forward

[9] This should not be confused with the cost associated with normal credit risk—that is, the risk that the customer will not pay for its purchase. That is a separate issue unrelated to the currency in which the transaction is denominated.

EXHIBIT 9.3
Hedge of a Foreign Currency Account Receivable with a Forward Contract

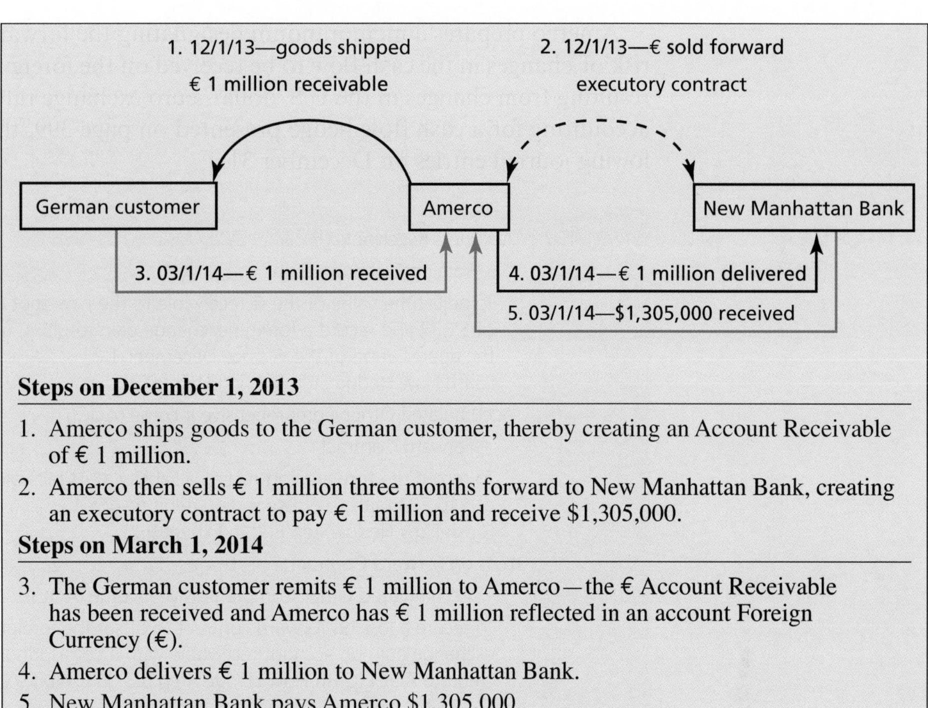

Steps on December 1, 2013

1. Amerco ships goods to the German customer, thereby creating an Account Receivable of € 1 million.
2. Amerco then sells € 1 million three months forward to New Manhattan Bank, creating an executory contract to pay € 1 million and receive $1,305,000.

Steps on March 1, 2014

3. The German customer remits € 1 million to Amerco—the € Account Receivable has been received and Amerco has € 1 million reflected in an account Foreign Currency (€).
4. Amerco delivers € 1 million to New Manhattan Bank.
5. New Manhattan Bank pays Amerco $1,305,000.

rate for a contract to deliver euros on March 1, 2014, is $1.316. Amerco could enter into a forward contract on December 31, 2013, to sell 1 million euros for $1,316,000 on March 1, 2014. Because Amerco is committed to sell 1 million euros for $1,305,000, the nominal value of the forward contract is $(11,000). The fair value of the forward contract is the present value of this amount. Assuming that Amerco has an incremental borrowing rate of 12 percent per year (1% per month) and discounting for two months (from December 31, 2013, to March 1, 2014), the fair value of the forward contract at December 31, 2013, is $(10,783), a liability. On March 1, 2014, the forward rate to sell euros on that date is, by definition, the spot rate, $1.30. At that rate, Amerco could sell 1 million euros for $1,300,000. Because Amerco has a contract to sell euros for $1,305,000, the fair value of the forward contract on March 1, 2014, is $5,000. This represents an increase of $15,783 in fair value from December 31, 2013. The original discount on the forward contract is determined by the difference in the euro spot rate and three-month forward rate on December 1, 2013: ($1.305 − $1.32) × € 1 million = $15,000.

Forward Contract Designated as Cash Flow Hedge

Assume that Amerco designates the forward contract as a *cash flow hedge* of a foreign currency denominated asset. In this case, it allocates the original forward discount or premium to net income over the life of the forward contract using an effective interest method. The company prepares the following journal entries to account for the foreign currency transaction and the related forward contract:

2013 Journal Entries—Forward Contract Designated as a Cash Flow Hedge

Date	Account	Debit	Credit
12/1/13	Accounts Receivable (€)	1,320,000	
	Sales		1,320,000
	To record the sale and € 1 million account receivable at the spot rate of $1.32 (Cash Flow Hedge Step A.1. in Exhibit 9.2).		
	Amerco makes no formal entry for the forward contract because it is an executory contract (no cash changes hands) and has a fair value of zero (Cash Flow Hedge Step A.2. in Exhibit 9.2).		

Amerco prepares a memorandum designating the forward contract as a hedge of the risk of changes in the cash flow to be received on the foreign currency account receivable resulting from changes in the U.S. dollar–euro exchange rate. Following the four steps in accounting for a cash flow hedge presented on page 399, the company prepares the following journal entries on December 31:

12/31/13	Accounts Receivable (€).	10,000	
	Foreign Exchange Gain		10,000
	To adjust the value of the € receivable to the new spot rate of $1.33 and record a foreign exchange gain resulting from the appreciation of the € since December 1 (Cash Flow Hedge Step B.1. in Exhibit 9.2).		
	Accumulated Other Comprehensive Income (AOCI)	10,783	
	Forward Contract		10,783
	To record the forward contract as a liability at its fair value of $10,783 with a corresponding debit to AOCI (Cash Flow Hedge Step B.2. in Exhibit 9.2).		
	Loss on Forward Contract	10,000	
	Accumulated Other Comprehensive Income (AOCI)		10,000
	To record a loss on forward contract to offset the foreign exchange gain on account receivable with a corresponding credit to AOCI (Cash Flow Hedge Step B.3. in Exhibit 9.2).		
	Discount Expense.	5,019	
	Accumulated Other Comprehensive Income (AOCI)		5,019
	To allocate the forward contract discount to net income over the life of the contract using the effective interest method with a corresponding credit to AOCI (Cash Flow Hedge Step B.4. in Exhibit 9.2).		

The first entry at December 31, 2013, serves to revalue the foreign currency account receivable and recognize a foreign exchange gain of $10,000 in net income. The second entry recognizes the forward contract as a liability of $10,783 on the balance sheet. Because the forward contract has been designated as a cash flow hedge, the debit of $10,783 in the second entry is made to AOCI, which decreases stockholders' equity. The third entry achieves the objective of hedge accounting by transferring $10,000 from AOCI to a loss on forward contract. As a result of this entry, the loss on forward contract of $10,000 and the foreign exchange gain on the account receivable of $10,000 exactly offset one another, and the net impact on income is zero. As a result of the second and third entries, the forward contract is reported on the balance sheet as a liability at fair value of $(10,783); a loss on forward contract is recognized in the amount of $10,000 to offset the foreign exchange gain; and AOCI has a negative (debit) balance of $783. The second and third entries could be combined into one entry as follows:

Loss on Forward Contract	10,000	
Accumulated Other Comprehensive Income (AOCI).	783	
Forward Contract.		10,783

The negative balance in AOCI of $783 can be viewed as that portion of the loss on the forward contract (decrease in fair value of the forward contract) that is not recognized in net income but instead is deferred in stockholders' equity. Under cash flow hedge accounting, a loss on the hedging instrument (forward contract) is recognized only to the extent that it offsets a gain on the item being hedged (account receivable).

The last entry uses the effective interest method to allocate a portion of the $15,000 forward contract discount as an expense to net income. The company calculates the implicit interest rate associated with the forward contract by considering the fact that the forward contract will generate cash flow of $1,305,000 from a foreign currency asset with an initial value of \$1,320,000. Because the discount of \$15,000 accrues over a three-month period, the effective interest rate is calculated as $[1 - \sqrt[3]{\$1,305,000/\$1,320,000}] = .0038023$. The amount of discount to be allocated to net income for the month of December 2013 is \$1,320,000 × .0038023 = \$5,019.

The impact on net income for the year 2013 follows:

Sales		\$1,320,000
Foreign exchange gain	\$ 10,000	
Loss on forward contract	(10,000)	
Net gain (loss)		–0–
Discount expense		(5,019)
Impact on net income		\$1,314,981

The effect on the December 31, 2013, balance sheet is as follows:

Assets		Liabilities and Stockholders' Equity	
Accounts receivable (€)	\$1,330,000	Forward contract	\$ 10,783
		Retained earnings	1,314,981
		AOCI	4,236
			\$1,330,000

2014 Journal Entries—Forward Contract Designated as Cash Flow Hedge

From December 31, 2013, to March 1, 2014, the euro account receivable decreases in value by \$30,000 and the forward contract increases in value by \$15,873. In addition, on March 1, 2014, the remaining discount on forward contract must be amortized to expense. The company prepares the following journal entries on March 1 to reflect these changes:

Date	Account	Debit	Credit
3/1/14	Foreign Exchange Loss	30,000	
	Accounts Receivable (€)		30,000
	To adjust the value of the € receivable to the new spot rate of \$1.30 and record a foreign exchange loss resulting from the depreciation of the € since December 31 (Cash Flow Hedge Step C.1. in Exhibit 9.2).		
	Forward Contract	15,783	
	Accumulated Other Comprehensive Income (AOCI)		15,783
	To adjust the carrying value of the forward contract to its current fair value of \$5,000 with a corresponding credit to AOCI (Cash Flow Hedge Step C.2. in Exhibit 9.2).		
	Accumulated Other Comprehensive Income (AOCI)	30,000	
	Gain on Forward Contract		30,000
	To record a gain on forward contract to offset the foreign exchange loss on account receivable with a corresponding debit to AOCI (Cash Flow Hedge Step C.3. in Exhibit 9.2).		
	Discount Expense	9,981	
	Accumulated Other Comprehensive Income (AOCI)		9,981
	To allocate the remaining forward contract discount to net income (\$15,000 − 5,019 = \$9,981) with a corresponding credit to AOCI (Cash Flow Hedge Step C.4. in Exhibit 9.2).		

As a result of these entries, the balance in AOCI is zero: \$4,236 + \$15,783 − \$30,000 + \$9,981 = \$0.

The next two journal entries recognize the receipt of euros from the customer, close out the euro account receivable, and record the settlement of the forward contract.

3/1/14	Foreign Currency (€)	1,300,000	
	Accounts Receivable (€)		1,300,000
	To record receipt of € 1 million from the German customer as an asset (Foreign Currency) at the spot rate of $1.30 (Cash Flow Hedge Step C.5. in Exhibit 9.2).		
	Cash	1,305,000	
	Foreign Currency (€)		1,300,000
	Forward Contract		5,000
	To record settlement of the forward contract (i.e., record receipt of $1,305,000 in exchange for delivery of € 1 million) and remove the forward contract from the accounts (Cash Flow Hedge Step C.6. in Exhibit 9.2).		

The impact on net income for the year 2014 follows:

Foreign exchange loss	$(30,000)	
Gain on forward contract	30,000	
Net gain (loss)		–0–
Discount expense		$(9,981)
Impact on net income		$(9,981)

The net effect on the balance sheet over the two years is a $1,305,000 increase in Cash with a corresponding increase in Retained Earnings of $1,305,000 ($1,314,981 – $9,981). The cumulative amount recognized as Discount Expense of $15,000 reflects the cost of extending credit to the German customer.

The net benefit from entering into the forward contract is $5,000. This "gain" is not directly reflected in net income. However, it can be calculated as the difference between the net gain on the forward contract and the cumulative amount of discount expense ($20,000 – $15,000 = $5,000) recognized over the two periods.

Effective Interest versus Straight-Line Methods

Use of the effective interest method results in allocating the forward contract discount $5,019 at the end of the first month and $9,981 at the end of the next two months. Straight-line allocation of the $15,000 discount on a monthly basis results in a reasonable approximation of these amounts:

12/31/13	$15,000 × 1/3 = $5,000
3/1/14	$15,000 × 2/3 = $10,000

Determining the effective interest rate is complex and provides no conceptual insights. For the remainder of this chapter, we use straight-line allocation of forward contract discounts and premiums. The important thing to keep in mind in this example is that with a cash flow hedge, an expense equal to the original forward contract discount is recognized in net income over the life of the contract.

What if the forward rate on December 1, 2013, had been $1.326 (i.e., the euro was selling at a premium in the forward market)? In that case, Amerco would receive $6,000 more through the forward sale of euros ($1,326,000) than had it received the euros at the date of sale ($1,320,000). Amerco would allocate the forward contract premium as an increase in net income at the rate of $2,000 per month: $2,000 at December 31, 2013, and $4,000 at March 1, 2014.

Forward Contract Designated as Fair Value Hedge

Assume that Amerco decides to designate the forward contract not as a cash flow hedge but as a fair value hedge. In that case, it takes the gain or loss on the forward contract directly to net income and does not separately amortize the original discount on the forward contract.

2013 Journal Entries—Forward Contract Designated as a Fair Value Hedge

12/1/13	Accounts Receivable (€)	1,320,000	
	Sales		1,320,000
	To record the sale and € 1 million account receivable at the spot rate of $1.32 (Fair Value Hedge Step A.1. in Exhibit 9.2).		

The forward contract requires no formal entry (Fair Value Hedge Step A.2. in Exhibit 9.2). A memorandum designates the forward contract as a hedge of the risk of changes in the fair value of the foreign currency account receivable resulting from changes in the U.S. dollar–euro exchange rate.

Following the two steps in accounting for a fair value hedge presented in Exhibit 9.2, the company prepares the following entries on December 31:

12/31/13	Accounts Receivable (€)	10,000	
	Foreign Exchange Gain		10,000
	To adjust the value of the € receivable to the new spot rate of $1.33 and record a foreign exchange gain resulting from the appreciation of the € since December 1 (Fair Value Hedge Step B.1. in Exhibit 9.2).		
	Loss on Forward Contract	10,783	
	Forward Contract		10,783
	To record the forward contract as a liability at its fair value of $10,783 and record a forward contract loss for the change in the fair value of the forward contract since December 1 (Fair Value Hedge Step B.2. in Exhibit 9.2).		

The first entry at December 31, 2013, serves to revalue the foreign currency account receivable and recognize a foreign exchange gain of $10,000. The second entry recognizes the forward contract as a liability of $10,783 on the balance sheet. Because the forward contract has been designated as a fair value hedge, the debit in the second entry recognizes the entire change in fair value of the forward contract as a loss in net income; there is no deferral of loss in stockholders' equity. A net loss of $783 is reported in net income as a result of these two entries.

The impact on net income for the year 2013 is as follows:

Sales		$1,320,000
Foreign exchange gain	$10,000	
Loss on forward contract	(10,783)	
Net gain (loss)		(783)
Impact on net income		$1,319,217

The effect on the December 31, 2013, balance sheet follows:

Assets		Liabilities and Stockholders' Equity	
Accounts receivable (€)	$1,330,000	Forward contract	$ 10,783
		Retained earnings	1,319,217
			$1,330,000

Discussion Question

DO WE HAVE A GAIN OR WHAT?

Ahnuld Corporation, a health juice producer, recently expanded its sales through exports to foreign markets. Earlier this year, the company negotiated the sale of several thousand cases of turnip juice to a retailer in the country of Tcheckia. The customer is unwilling to assume the risk of having to pay in U.S. dollars. Desperate to enter the Tcheckian market, the vice president for international sales agrees to denominate the sale in tchecks, the national currency of Tcheckia. The current exchange rate for 1 tcheck is $2.00. In addition, the customer indicates that it cannot pay until it sells all of the juice. Payment is scheduled for six months from the date of sale.

Fearful that the tcheck might depreciate in value over the next six months, the head of the risk management department at Ahnuld Corporation enters into a forward contract to sell tchecks in six months at a forward rate of $1.80. The forward contract is designated as a fair value hedge of the tcheck receivable. Six months later, when Ahnuld receives payment from the Tcheckian customer, the exchange rate for the tcheck is $1.70. The corporate treasurer calls the head of the risk management department into her office.

Treasurer: I see that your decision to hedge our foreign currency position on that sale to Tcheckia was a bad one.

Department head: What do you mean? We have a gain on that forward contract. We're $10,000 better off from having entered into that hedge.

Treasurer: That's not what the books say. The accountants have recorded a net loss of $20,000 on that particular deal. I'm afraid I'm not going to be able to pay you a bonus this year. Another bad deal like this one and I'm going to have to demote you back to the interest rate swap department.

Department head: Those bean counters have messed up again. I told those guys in international sales that selling to customers in Tcheckia was risky, but at least by hedging our exposure, we managed to receive a reasonable amount of cash on that deal. In fact, we ended up with a gain of $10,000 on the hedge. Tell the accountants to check their debits and credits again. I'm sure they just put a debit in the wrong place or some accounting thing like that.

Have the accountants made a mistake? Does the company have a loss, a gain, or both from this forward contract?

2014 Journal Entries—Forward Contract Designated as a Fair Value Hedge

The company prepares the following entries on March 1:

3/1/14	Foreign Exchange Loss	30,000	
	Accounts Receivable (€).		30,000
	To adjust the value of the € receivable to the new spot rate of $1.30 and record a foreign exchange loss resulting from the depreciation of the € since December 31 (Fair Value Hedge Step C.1. in Exhibit 9.2).		
	Forward Contract	15,783	
	Gain on Forward Contract		15,783
	To adjust the carrying value of the forward contract to its current fair value of $5,000 and record a forward contract gain for the change in the fair value since December 31 (Fair Value Hedge Step C.2. in Exhibit 9.2).		

3/1/14	Foreign Currency (€)	1,300,000	
	Accounts Receivable (€)		1,300,000
	To record receipt of € 1 million from the German customer as an asset at the spot rate of $1.30 (Fair Value Hedge Step C.3. in Exhibit 9.2).		
	Cash	1,305,000	
	Foreign Currency (€)		1,300,000
	Forward Contract		5,000
	To record settlement of the forward contract (i.e., record receipt of $1,305,000 in exchange for delivery of € 1 million) and remove the forward contract from the accounts (Fair Value Hedge Step C.4. in Exhibit 9.2).		

The impact on net income for the year 2014 follows:

Foreign exchange loss	$(30,000)
Gain on forward contract	15,783
Impact on net income	$(14,217)

The net effect on the balance sheet for the two periods is an increase of $1,305,000 in Cash with a corresponding increase in Retained Earnings of $1,305,000 ($1,319,217 − $14,217).

Under fair value hedge accounting, the company does not amortize the original forward contract discount systematically over the life of the contract. Instead, it recognizes the discount in income as the difference between the foreign exchange Gain (Loss) on the account receivable and the Gain (Loss) on the forward contract—that is, $(783) in 2013 and $(14,217) in 2014. The net impact on net income over the two years is $(15,000), which reflects the cost of extending credit to the German customer. The net gain on the forward contract of $5,000 ($10,783 loss in 2013 and $15,783 gain in 2014) reflects the net benefit (i.e., increase in cash inflow) from Amerco's decision to hedge the euro receivable.

Companies often cannot or do not bother to designate as hedges the forward contracts they use to hedge foreign currency denominated assets and liabilities. In those cases, the company accounts for the forward contract in exactly the same way it would if it had designated it as a fair value hedge. The company reports an undesignated forward contract on the balance sheet at fair value as an asset or liability and immediately recognizes changes in the fair value of the forward contract in income. The only difference between a forward contract designated as a fair value hedge of a foreign currency denominated asset or liability and an undesignated forward contract is the manner in which the company discloses it in the notes to the financial statements. E.I. du Pont de Nemours and Company provided the following disclosure related to this in its 2010 Form 10-K (page F-45):

Derivatives Not Designated in Hedging Relationships

The company uses forward exchange contracts to reduce its net exposure, by currency, related to foreign currency-denominated monetary assets and liabilities. The netting of such exposures precludes the use of hedge accounting. However, the required revaluation of the forward contract and the associated foreign currency-denominated monetary assets and liabilities results in a minimal earnings impact, after taxes.

Cash Flow Hedge versus Fair Value Hedge

A forward contract used to hedge a foreign currency denominated asset or liability can be designated as either a cash flow hedge or a fair value hedge when it completely offsets the variability in cash flows associated with the hedged item. The total impact on income is the same regardless of whether the forward contract is designated as a fair value hedge or as a cash flow hedge. In our example, Amerco recognized an expense (or loss) of $15,000 in both cases, and the company knew what the total expense was going to be as soon as the contract was signed.

A benefit to designating a forward contract as a cash flow hedge is that the company knows the forward contract's effect on net income *each year* as soon as the contract is signed.

The net impact on income is the periodic amortization of the forward contract discount or premium. In our example, Amerco knew on December 1, 2013, that it would recognize a discount expense of $5,000 in 2013 and $10,000 in 2014. The impact on each year's income is not as systematic when the forward contract is designated as a fair value hedge—loss of $783 in 2013 and $14,217 in 2014. Moreover, the company does not know what the net impact on 2013 income will be until December 31, 2013, when the euro account receivable and the forward contract are revalued. Because of the potential for greater volatility in periodic net income that results from a fair value hedge, companies may prefer to designate forward contracts used to hedge a foreign currency denominated asset or liability as cash flow hedges.

Foreign Currency Option Used to Hedge a Foreign Currency Denominated Asset

As an alternative to a forward contract, Amerco could hedge its exposure to foreign exchange risk arising from the euro account receivable by purchasing a foreign currency put option. A put option would give Amerco the right but not the obligation to sell 1 million euros on March 1, 2014, at a predetermined strike price. Assume that on December 1, 2013, Amerco purchases an over-the-counter option from its bank with a strike price of $1.32 when the spot rate is $1.32 and pays a premium of $0.009 per euro.[10] Thus, the purchase price for the option is $9,000 (€1 million × $0.009).

Because the strike price and spot rate are the same, no intrinsic value is associated with this option. The premium is based solely on time value; that is, it is possible that the euro will depreciate and the spot rate on March 1, 2014, will be less than $1.32, in which case the option will be "in the money." If the spot rate for euros on March 1, 2014, is less than the strike price of $1.32, Amerco will exercise its option and sell its 1 million euros at the strike price of $1.32. If the spot rate for euros in three months is more than the strike price of $1.32, Amerco will not exercise its option but will sell euros at the higher spot rate. By purchasing this option, Amerco is guaranteed a minimum cash flow from the export sale of $1,311,000 ($1,320,000 from exercising the option less the $9,000 cost of the option). There is no limit to the maximum number of U.S. dollars that Amerco could receive.

As is true for other derivative financial instruments, authoritative accounting literature requires foreign currency options to be reported on the balance sheet at fair value. The fair value of a foreign currency option at the balance sheet date is determined by reference to the premium quoted by banks on that date for an option with a similar expiration date. Banks (and other sellers of options) determine the current premium by incorporating relevant variables at the balance sheet date into the modified Black-Scholes option pricing model. Changes in value for the euro account receivable and the foreign currency option are summarized as follows:

		Account Receivable (€)		Option	Foreign Currency Option	
Date	**Spot Rate**	**U.S. Dollar Value**	**Change in U.S. Dollar Value**	**Premium for 3/1/14**	**Fair Value**	**Change in Fair Value**
12/1/13	$1.32	$1,320,000	–0–	$0.009	$ 9,000	–0–
12/31/13	1.33	1,330,000	+$10,000	0.006	6,000	–$ 3,000
3/1/14	1.30	1,300,000	– 30,000	0.020	20,000	+ 14,000

The fair value of the foreign currency put option at December 1 is its cost of $9,000. The spot rate for the euro increases during December, which causes a decrease in the fair value of the put option; the right to sell euros at $1.32 is of even less value when the spot rate is $1.33 (on December 31) than when the spot rate was $1.32 (on December 1).

[10] The seller of the option determined the price of the option (the premium) by using a variation of the Black-Scholes option pricing formula.

The bank determines the fair value of the option at December 31 to be $6,000. By March 1, the euro spot rate has decreased to $1.30. By exercising its option on March 1 at the strike price of $1.32, Amerco will receive $1,320,000 from its export sale, rather than only $1,300,000 if it were required to sell euros in the spot market on March 1. Thus, the option has a fair value of $20,000 on March 1.

We can decompose the fair value of the foreign currency option into its intrinsic value and time value components as follows:

Date	Fair Value	Intrinsic Value	Time Value	Change in Time Value
12/1/13	$ 9,000	-0-	$9,000	-0-
12/31/13	6,000	-0-	6,000	−$3,000
3/1/14	20,000	$20,000	-0-	− 6,000

Because the option strike price is less than or equal to the spot rate at both December 1 and December 31, the option has no intrinsic value at those dates. The entire fair value is attributable to time value only. On March 1, the date of expiration, no time value remains, and the entire amount of fair value is attributable to intrinsic value.

Option Designated as Cash Flow Hedge

Assume that Amerco designates the foreign currency option as a *cash flow hedge* of a foreign currency denominated asset. In this case, Amerco recognizes the change in the option's time value immediately in net income. The company prepares the following journal entries to account for the foreign currency transaction and the related foreign currency option:

2013 Journal Entries—Option Designated as a Cash Flow Hedge

Date	Account	Debit	Credit
12/1/13	Accounts Receivable (€)	1,320,000	
	Sales		1,320,000
	To record the sale and € 1 million account receivable at the spot rate of $1.32 (Cash Flow Hedge Step A.1. in Exhibit 9.2).		
	Foreign Currency Option	9,000	
	Cash		9,000
	To record the purchase of the foreign currency option as an asset at its fair value of $9,000 (Cash Flow Hedge Step A.2. in Exhibit 9.2).		

From December 1 to December 31, the euro account receivable increases in value by $10,000 and the option decreases in value by $3,000. The company prepares the following journal entries on December 31 to reflect these changes:

Date	Account	Debit	Credit
12/31/13	Accounts Receivable (€)	10,000	
	Foreign Exchange Gain		10,000
	To adjust the value of the € receivable to the new spot rate of $1.33 and record a foreign exchange gain resulting from the appreciation of the € since December 1 (Cash Flow Hedge Step B.1. in Exhibit 9.2).		
	Accumulated Other Comprehensive Income (AOCI).	3,000	
	Foreign Currency Option		3,000
	To adjust the fair value of the option from $9,000 to $6,000 with a corresponding debit to AOCI (Cash Flow Hedge Step B.2. in Exhibit 9.2).		
	Loss on Foreign Currency Option.	10,000	
	Accumulated Other Comprehensive Income (AOCI)		10,000
	To record a loss on foreign currency option to offset the foreign exchange gain on the account receivable with a corresponding credit to AOCI (Cash Flow Hedge Step B.3. in Exhibit 9.2).		

	Option Expense.	3,000	
	Accumulated Other Comprehensive Income (AOCI)		3,000
	To recognize the change in the time value of the option as a decrease in net income with a corresponding credit to AOCI (Cash Flow Hedge Step B.4. in Exhibit 9.2).		

The first three journal entries prepared on December 31 result in the euro account receivable and the foreign currency option being reported on the balance sheet at fair value with a net gain (loss) of zero reflected in net income, which is consistent with the concept of hedge accounting. The final entry serves to amortize a portion of the option cost to expense in net income. On March 1, the remaining $6,000 of option cost will be expensed.

The impact on net income for the year 2013 follows:

Sales		$1,320,000
Foreign exchange gain	$ 10,000	
Loss on foreign currency option.	(10,000)	
Net gain (loss)		–0–
Option expense.		(3,000)
Impact on net income		$1,317,000

The effect on the December 31, 2013, balance sheet is as follows:

Assets		Liabilities and Stockholders' Equity	
Cash.	$ (9,000)	Retained earnings	$1,317,000
Accounts receivable (€).	1,330,000	AOCI	10,000
Foreign currency option	6,000		$1,327,000
	$1,327,000		

At March 1, 2014, the option has increased in fair value by $14,000—time value decreases by $6,000 and intrinsic value increases by $20,000. The accounting entries made in 2014 are presented next:

2014 Journal Entries—Option Designated as a Cash Flow Hedge

3/1/14	Foreign Exchange Loss	30,000	
	Accounts Receivable (€).		30,000
	To adjust the value of the € receivable to the new spot rate of $1.30 and record a foreign exchange loss resulting from the depreciation of the € since December 31 (Cash Flow Hedge Step C.1. in Exhibit 9.2).		
	Foreign Currency Option.	14,000	
	Accumulated Other Comprehensive Income (AOCI)		14,000
	To adjust the fair value of the option from $6,000 to $20,000 with a corresponding credit to AOCI (Cash Flow Hedge Step C.2. in Exhibit 9.2).		
	Accumulated Other Comprehensive Income (AOCI).	30,000	
	Gain on Foreign Currency Option.		30,000
	To record a gain on foreign currency option to offset the foreign exchange gain on account receivable with a corresponding debit to AOCI (Cash Flow Hedge Step C.3. in Exhibit 9.2).		
	Option Expense.	6,000	
	Accumulated Other Comprehensive Income (AOCI)		6,000
	To recognize the change in the time value of the option as a decrease in net income with a corresponding credit to AOCI (Cash Flow Hedge Step C.4. in Exhibit 9.2).		

The first three entries above result in the euro account receivable and the foreign currency option being reported at their fair values, with a net gain (loss) of zero. The fourth entry amortizes the remaining cost of the option to expense. As a result of these entries, the balance in AOCI is zero: $10,000 + $14,000 − $30,000 + $6,000 = $0.

The next two journal entries recognize the receipt of euros from the customer, close out the euro account receivable, and record the exercise of the foreign currency option.

3/1/14	Foreign Currency (€)	1,300,000	
	Accounts Receivable (€)		1,300,000
	To record receipt of € 1 million from the German customer as an asset at the spot rate of $1.30 (Cash Flow Hedge Step C.5. in Exhibit 9.2).		
	Cash	1,320,000	
	Foreign Currency (€)		1,300,000
	Foreign Currency Option		20,000
	To record exercise of the option (i.e., record receipt of $1,320,000 in exchange for delivery of € 1 million) and remove the foreign currency option from the accounts (Cash Flow Hedge Step C.6. in Exhibit 9.2).		

The impact on net income for the year 2014 follows:

Foreign exchange loss	$(30,000)	
Gain on foreign currency option	30,000	
Net gain (loss)		–0–
Option expense		(6,000)
Impact on net income		$(6,000)

Over the two accounting periods, Amerco reports Sales of $1,320,000 and a cumulative Option Expense of $9,000. The net effect on the balance sheet is an increase in the Cash account of $1,311,000 ($1,320,000 − $9,000) with a corresponding increase in the Retained Earnings account of $1,311,000 ($1,317,000 − $6,000).

The net benefit from having acquired the option is $11,000. Amerco reflects this "gain" in net income as the net Gain on Foreign Currency Option less the cumulative Option Expense ($20,000 − $9,000 = $11,000) recognized over the two accounting periods.

Option Designated as Fair Value Hedge

Assume that Amerco decides not to designate the foreign currency option as a cash flow hedge but to treat it as a fair value hedge. In that case, it takes the gain or loss on the option directly to net income and does not separately recognize the change in the time value of the option.

2013 Journal Entries—Option Designated as a Fair Value Hedge

12/1/13	Accounts Receivable (€)	1,320,000	
	Sales		1,320,000
	To record the sale and € 1 million account receivable at the spot rate of $1.32 (Fair Value Hedge Step A.1. in Exhibit 9.2).		
	Foreign Currency Option	9,000	
	Cash		9,000
	To record the purchase of the foreign currency option as an asset at its fair value of $9,000 (Fair Value Hedge Step A.2. in Exhibit 9.2).		
12/31/13	Accounts Receivable (€)	10,000	
	Foreign Exchange Gain		10,000
	To adjust the value of the € receivable to the new spot rate of $1.33 and record a foreign exchange gain resulting from the appreciation of the € since December 1 (Fair Value Hedge Step B.1. in Exhibit 9.2).		

Date	Account	Debit	Credit
	Loss on Foreign Currency Option.	3,000	
	Foreign Currency Option		3,000
	To adjust the fair value of the option from $9,000 to $6,000 and record a loss on foreign currency option for the change in the fair value of the option since December 1 (Fair Value Hedge Step B.2. in Exhibit 9.2).		

The impact on net income for the year 2013 follows:

Sales.		$1,320,000
Foreign exchange gain	$10,000	
Loss on foreign currency option	(3,000)	
Net gain (loss).		7,000
Impact on net income		$1,327,000

2014 Journal Entries—Option Designated as a Fair Value Hedge

Date	Account	Debit	Credit
3/1/14	Foreign Exchange Loss	30,000	
	Accounts Receivable (€).		30,000
	To adjust the value of the € receivable to the new spot rate of $1.30 and record a foreign exchange loss resulting from the depreciation of the € since December 31 (Fair Value Hedge Step C.1. in Exhibit 9.2).		
	Foreign Currency Option.	14,000	
	Gain on Foreign Currency Option.		14,000
	To adjust the fair value of the option from $6,000 to $20,000 and record a gain on foreign currency option for the change in fair value since December 31 (Fair Value Hedge Step C.2. in Exhibit 9.2).		
	Foreign Currency (€).	1,300,000	
	Accounts Receivable (€).		1,300,000
	To record receipt of € 1 million from the German customer as an asset at the spot rate of $1.30 (Fair Value Hedge Step C.3. in Exhibit 9.2).		
	Cash.	1,320,000	
	Foreign Currency (€)		1,300,000
	Foreign Currency Option		20,000
	To record exercise of the option (i.e., record receipt of $1,320,000 in exchange for delivery of € 1 million) and remove the foreign currency option from the accounts (Fair Value Hedge Step C.4. in Exhibit 9.2).		

The impact on net income for the year 2014 follows:

Foreign exchange loss.	$(30,000)
Gain on foreign currency option	14,000
Impact on net income	$(16,000)

Over the two accounting periods, Amerco reports Sales of $1,320,000 and a cumulative net loss of $9,000 ($7,000 net gain in 2013 and $16,000 net loss in 2014). The net effect on the balance sheet is an increase in Cash of $1,311,000 ($1,320,000 − $9,000) with a corresponding increase in Retained Earnings of $1,311,000 ($1,327,000 − $16,000). The net benefit from having acquired the option is $11,000. Amerco reflects this in net income through the net Gain on Foreign Currency Option ($3,000 loss in 2013 and $14,000 gain in 2014) recognized over the two accounting periods.

The accounting for an option used as a fair value hedge of a foreign currency denominated asset or liability is the same as if the option had been considered a speculative derivative. The only advantage to designating the option as a fair value hedge relates to the disclosures made in the notes to the financial statements.

Spot Rate Exceeds Strike Price

If the spot rate at March 1, 2014, had been more than the strike price of $1.32, Amerco would allow its option to expire unexercised. Instead it would sell its foreign currency (€) at the spot rate. The fair value of the foreign currency option on March 1, 2014, would be zero. The journal entries for 2013 to reflect this scenario would be the same as the preceding ones. The option would be reported as an asset on the December 31, 2013, balance sheet at $6,000 and the € receivable would have a carrying value of $1,330,000. The entries on March 1, 2014, assuming a spot rate on that date of $1.325 (rather than $1.30), would be as follows:

Date	Account	Debit	Credit
3/1/14	Foreign Exchange Loss	5,000	
	Accounts Receivable (€)		5,000
	To adjust the value of the € receivable to the new spot rate of $1.325 and record a foreign exchange loss resulting from the depreciation of the € since December 31 (Fair Value Hedge Step C.1. in Exhibit 9.2).		
	Loss on Foreign Currency Option	6,000	
	Foreign Currency Option		6,000
	To adjust the fair value of the option from $6,000 to $0 and record a loss on foreign currency option for the change in fair value since December 31 (Fair Value Hedge Step C.2. in Exhibit 9.2).		
	Foreign Currency (€)	1,325,000	
	Accounts Receivable (€)		1,325,000
	To record receipt of € 1 million from the German customer as an asset at the spot rate of $1.325 (Fair Value Hedge Step C.3. in Exhibit 9.2).		
	Cash	1,325,000	
	Foreign Currency (€)		1,325,000
	To record the sale of € 1 million at the spot rate of $1.325 (Fair Value Hedge Step C.4. in Exhibit 9.2).		

The overall impact on net income for the year 2014 is as follows:

Foreign exchange loss	$ (5,000)
Loss on foreign currency option	(6,000)
Impact on net income	$(11,000)

Hedges of Unrecognized Foreign Currency Firm Commitments

LO5

Account for forward contracts and options used as hedges of foreign currency firm commitments.

In the examples thus far, Amerco does not enter into a hedge of its export sale until it actually makes the sale. Assume now that on December 1, 2013, Amerco receives and accepts an order from a German customer to deliver goods on March 1, 2014, at a price of 1 million euros. Assume further that under the terms of the sales agreement, Amerco will ship the goods to the German customer on March 1, 2014, and will receive immediate payment on delivery. In other words, Amerco will not allow the German customer time to pay. Although Amerco will not make the sale until March 1, 2014, it has a firm commitment to make the sale and receive 1 million euros in three months. This creates a euro asset exposure to foreign exchange risk as of December 1, 2013. On that date, Amerco wants to hedge against an adverse change in the value of the euro over the next three months. This is known as a *hedge of a foreign currency firm commitment*. U.S. GAAP allows hedges of firm commitments to be designated either as cash flow or fair value hedges. However, because the results of fair value hedge accounting are intuitively more appealing, we do not cover cash flow hedge accounting for firm commitments.

A firm commitment is an executory contract; the company has not delivered goods nor has the customer paid for them. Normally, executory contracts are not recognized in financial statements. However, when a firm commitment is hedged using a derivative financial instrument, hedge accounting requires explicit recognition on the balance sheet at fair value of both the derivative financial instrument (forward contract or option) and the firm commitment. The change in fair value of the firm commitment results in a gain or loss that offsets the loss or gain on the hedging instrument (forward contract or option), thus achieving the goal of hedge accounting. This raises the conceptual question of how to measure the fair value of the firm commitment. When a forward contract is used as the hedging instrument, the fair value of the firm commitment is determined through reference to changes in the forward exchange rate. Changes in the spot exchange rate are used to determine the fair value of the firm commitment when a foreign currency option is the hedging instrument.

Forward Contract Used as Fair Value Hedge of a Firm Commitment

To hedge its firm commitment exposure to a decline in the U.S. dollar value of the euro, Amerco decides to enter into a forward contract on December 1, 2013. Assume that on that date, the three-month forward rate for euros is $1.305 and Amerco signs a contract with New Manhattan Bank to deliver 1 million euros in three months in exchange for $1,305,000. No cash changes hands on December 1, 2013. Amerco measures the fair value of the firm commitment through changes in the forward rate. Because the fair value of the forward contract is also measured using changes in the forward rate, the gains and losses on the firm commitment and forward contract exactly offset. The fair value of the forward contract and firm commitment are determined as follows:

		Forward Contract		Firm Commitment	
Date	Forward Rate to 3/1/14	Fair Value	Change in Fair Value	Fair Value	Change in Fair Value
12/1/13	$1.305	–0–	–0–	–0–	–0–
12/31/13	1.316	$(10,783)*	−$10,783	$10,783*	+$10,783
3/1/14	1.30 (spot)	5,000†	+ 15,783	(5,000)†	− 15,783

*($1,305,000 − $1,316,000) = $(11,000) × 0.9803 = $(10,783), where 0.9803 is the present value factor for two months at an annual interest rate of 12 percent (1 percent per month) calculated as $1/1.01^2$.
†($1,305,000 − $1,300,000) = $5,000.

Amerco pays nothing to enter into the forward contract at December 1, 2013. Both the forward contract and the firm commitment have a fair value of zero on that date. As a result, there are no journal entries needed on December 1, 2013. At December 31, 2013, the forward rate for a contract to deliver euros on March 1, 2014, is $1.316. A forward contract could be entered into on December 31, 2013, to sell 1 million euros for $1,316,000 on March 1, 2014. Because Amerco is committed to sell 1 million euros for $1,305,000, the value of the forward contract is $(11,000); present value is $(10,783), a liability. The fair value of the firm commitment is also measured through reference to changes in the forward rate. As a result, the fair value of the firm commitment is equal in amount but of opposite sign to the fair value of the forward contract. At December 31, 2013, the firm commitment is an asset of $10,783. To apply the two steps in accounting for a fair value hedge of a firm commitment at the balance sheet date, on December 31, 2013, Amerco will:

1. Adjust the forward contract to fair value, which results in the recognition of a liability of $10,783, and recognize the counterpart as a loss in net income (Fair Value Hedge Step B.1. in Exhibit 9.2).
2. Adjust the firm commitment to fair value, which results in the recognition of an asset of $10,783, and recognize the counterpart as a gain on firm commitment in net income (Fair Value Hedge Step B.2. in Exhibit 9.2).

The journal entries in 2013 to account for the forward contract fair value hedge of a foreign currency firm commitment are as follows:

2013 Journal Entries—Forward Contract Fair Value Hedge of Firm Commitment

12/1/13	There is no entry to record either the sales agreement or the forward contract because both are executory contracts. A memorandum designates the forward contract as a hedge of the risk of changes in the fair value of the firm commitment resulting from changes in the U.S. dollar–euro forward exchange rate (Fair Value Hedge Steps A.1. and A.2. in Exhibit 9.2).		
12/31/13	Loss on Forward Contract	10,783	
	Forward Contract.		10,783
	To record the forward contract as a liability at its fair value of $(10,783) and record a forward contract loss for the change in the fair value of the forward contract since December 1 (Fair Value Hedge Step B.1. in Exhibit 9.2).		
	Firm Commitment.	10,783	
	Gain on Firm Commitment		10,783
	To record the firm commitment as an asset at its fair value of $10,783 and record a firm commitment gain for the change in the fair value of the firm commitment since December 1 (Fair Value Hedge Step B.2. in Exhibit 9.2).		

Consistent with the objective of hedge accounting, the gain on the firm commitment offsets the loss on the forward contract, and the impact on 2013 net income is zero. Amerco reports the forward contract as a liability and reports the firm commitment as an asset on the December 31, 2013, balance sheet. This achieves the objective of making sure that derivatives are reported on the balance sheet and ensures that there is no impact on net income.

On March 1, 2014, the forward rate to sell euros on that date, by definition, is the spot rate, $1.30. At that rate, Amerco could sell 1 million euros for $1,300,000. Because Amerco has a contract to sell euros for $1,305,000, the fair value of the forward contract on March 1, 2014, is $5,000 (an asset). The firm commitment has a value of $(5,000), a liability.

On March 1, 2014, Amerco first recognizes changes in the fair value of the forward contract and firm commitment since December 31. The company then records the sale and the settlement of the forward contract. Finally, the $5,000 balance in the firm commitment account is closed as an adjustment to net income. The required journal entries are as follows:

2014 Journal Entries—Forward Contract Fair Value Hedge of Firm Commitment

3/1/14	Forward Contract	15,783	
	Gain on Forward Contract		15,783
	To adjust the fair value of the forward contract from $(10,783) to $5,000 and record a forward contract gain for the change in fair value since December 31 (Fair Value Hedge Step C.1. in Exhibit 9.2).		
	Loss on Firm Commitment	15,783	
	Firm Commitment		15,783
	To adjust the fair value of the firm commitment from $10,783 to $(5,000) and record a firm commitment loss for the change in fair value since December 31 (Fair Value Hedge Step C.2. in Exhibit 9.2).		
	Foreign Currency (€).	1,300,000	
	Sales		1,300,000
	To record the sale and the receipt of € 1 million as an asset at the spot rate of $1.30 (Fair Value Hedge Step C.3. in Exhibit 9.2).		
	Cash	1,305,000	
	Foreign Currency (€)		1,300,000
	Forward Contract.		5,000
	To record settlement of the forward contract (receipt of $1,305,000 in exchange for delivery of € 1 million) and remove the forward contract from the accounts (Fair Value Hedge Step C.4. in Exhibit 9.2).		

	Firm Commitment.	5,000	
	Adjustment to Net Income—Firm Commitment		5,000
	To close the firm commitment as an adjustment to net income (Fair Value Hedge Step C.5. in Exhibit 9.2).		

Once again, the gain on forward contract and the loss on firm commitment offset. As a result of the last entry, the export sale increases 2014 net income by $1,305,000 ($1,300,000 in sales plus a $5,000 adjustment to net income). This exactly equals the amount of cash received. In practice, companies use a variety of account titles for the adjustment to net income that results from closing the firm commitment account.

The net gain on forward contract of $5,000 ($10,783 loss in 2013 plus $15,783 gain in 2014) measures the net benefit to the company from hedging its firm commitment. Without the forward contract, Amerco would have sold the 1 million euros received on March 1, 2014, at the spot rate of $1.30 generating cash flow of $1,300,000. Through the forward contract, Amerco is able to sell the euros for $1,305,000, a net gain of $5,000.

Option Used as Fair Value Hedge of Firm Commitment

Now assume that to hedge its exposure to a decline in the U.S. dollar value of the euro, Amerco purchases a put option to sell 1 million euros on March 1, 2014, at a strike price of $1.32. The premium for such an option on December 1, 2013, is $0.009 per euro. With this option, Amerco is guaranteed a minimum cash flow from the export sale of $1,311,000 ($1,320,000 from option exercise less $9,000 cost of the option).

Amerco measures the fair value of the firm commitment by referring to changes in the U.S. dollar–euro spot rate. In this case, Amerco must discount the fair value of the firm commitment to its present value. The fair value and changes in fair value for the firm commitment and foreign currency option are summarized here:

	Foreign Currency Option				Firm Commitment	
Date	Option Premium for 3/1/14	Fair Value	Change in Fair Value	Spot Rate	Fair Value	Change in Fair Value
12/1/13	$0.009	$ 9,000	–0–	$1.32	–0–	–0–
12/31/13	0.006	6,000	−$ 3,000	1.33	$ 9,803*	+$ 9,803
3/1/14	0.020	20,000	+ 14,000	1.30	(20,000)†	− 29,803

*$1,330,000 − $1,320,000 = $10,000 × 0.9803 = $9,803, where 0.9803 is the present value factor for two months at an annual interest rate of 12 percent (1 percent per month) calculated as $1/1.01^2$.
†$1,300,000 − $1,320,000 = $(20,000).

At December 1, 2013, given the spot rate of $1.32, the firm commitment to receive 1 million euros in three months would generate a cash flow of $1,320,000. At December 31, 2013, the cash flow that the firm commitment could generate increases by $10,000 to $1,330,000. The fair value of the firm commitment at December 31, 2013, is the present value of $10,000 discounted at 1 percent per month for two months. Amerco determines the fair value of the firm commitment on March 1, 2014, by referring to the change in the spot rate from December 1, 2013, to March 1, 2014. Because the spot rate declines by $0.02 over that period, the firm commitment to receive 1 million euros has a fair value of $(20,000) on March 1, 2014. The journal entries to account for the foreign currency option and related foreign currency firm commitment are discussed next:

2013 Journal Entries—Option Fair Value Hedge of Firm Commitment

12/1/13	Foreign Currency Option.	9,000	
	Cash		9,000
	To record the purchase of the foreign currency option as an asset (Fair Value Hedge Step A.2. in Exhibit 9.2).		

There is no entry to record the sales agreement because it is an executory contract (Fair Value Hedge Step A.1. in Exhibit 9.2). Amerco prepares a memorandum to designate the option as a hedge of the risk of changes in the fair value of the firm commitment resulting from changes in the spot exchange rate.

12/31/13	Loss on Foreign Currency Option	3,000	
	Foreign Currency Option		3,000
	To adjust the fair value of the option from $9,000 to $6,000 and record the change in the value of the option as a loss (Fair Value Hedge Step B.1. in Exhibit 9.2).		
	Firm Commitment	9,803	
	Gain on Firm Commitment		9,803
	To record the firm commitment as an asset at its fair value of $9,803 and record a firm commitment gain for the change in the fair value of the firm commitment since December 1 (Fair Value Hedge Step B.2. in Exhibit 9.2).		

Because the fair value of the firm commitment is based on changes in the spot rate whereas the fair value of the option is based on a variety of factors, the gain on the firm commitment and loss on the option do not exactly offset.

The impact on net income for the year 2013 is as follows:

Gain on firm commitment.	$ 9,803
Loss on foreign currency option	(3,000)
Impact on net income.	$ 6,803

The effect on the December 31, 2013, balance sheet follows:

Assets		Liabilities and Stockholders' Equity	
Cash.	$(9,000)	Retained earnings	$6,803
Foreign currency option	6,000		
Firm commitment	9,803		
	$ 6,803		

On March 1, 2014, following fair value hedge accounting procedures, Amerco first recognizes changes in the fair value of the option and of the firm commitment since December 31. The company then records the sale and the exercise of the option. Finally, the $20,000 balance in the firm commitment account is closed as an adjustment to net income. The required journal entries are as follows:

2014 Journal Entries—Option Fair Value Hedge of Firm Commitment

3/1/14	Foreign Currency Option.	14,000	
	Gain on Foreign Currency Option.		14,000
	To adjust the fair value of the foreign currency option from $6,000 to $20,000 and record a gain on foreign currency option for the change in fair value since December 31 (Fair Value Hedge Step C.1. in Exhibit 9.2).		
	Loss on Firm Commitment	29,803	
	Firm Commitment		29,803
	To adjust the fair value of the firm commitment from $9,803 to $(20,000) and record a firm commitment loss for the change in fair value since December 31 (Fair Value Hedge Step C.2. in Exhibit 9.2).		
	Foreign Currency (€).	1,300,000	
	Sales		1,300,000
	To record the sale and the receipt of € 1 million as an asset at the spot rate of $1.30 (Fair Value Hedge Step C.3. in Exhibit 9.2).		

Cash	1,320,000	
Foreign Currency (€)		1,300,000
Foreign Currency Option		20,000
To record exercise of the foreign currency option (receipt of $1,320,000 in exchange for delivery of € 1 million) and remove the foreign currency option from the accounts (Fair Value Hedge Step C.4. in Exhibit 9.2).		
Firm Commitment	20,000	
Adjustment to Net Income—Firm Commitment		20,000
To close the firm commitment as an adjustment to net income (Fair Value Hedge Step C.5. in Exhibit 9.2).		

The following is the impact on net income for the year 2014:

Sales	$1,300,000
Loss on firm commitment	(29,803)
Gain on foreign currency option	14,000
Adjustment to net income–firm commitment	20,000
Impact on net income	$1,304,197

The net increase in net income over the two accounting periods is $1,311,000 ($6,803 in 2013 plus $1,304,197 in 2014), which exactly equals the net cash flow realized on the export sale ($1,320,000 from exercising the option less $9,000 to purchase the option). The net gain on the option of $11,000 (loss of $3,000 in 2013 plus gain of $14,000 in 2014) reflects the net benefit from having entered into the hedge. Without the option, Amerco would have sold the 1 million euros received on March 1, 2014, at the spot rate of $1.30 for $1,300,000.

Hedge of Forecasted Foreign Currency Denominated Transaction

LO6

Account for forward contracts and options used as hedges of forecasted foreign currency transactions.

Cash flow hedge accounting also is used for foreign currency derivatives used to hedge the cash flow risk associated with a forecasted foreign currency transaction. For hedge accounting to apply, the forecasted transaction must be probable (likely to occur), the hedge must be highly effective in offsetting fluctuations in the cash flow associated with the foreign currency risk, and the hedging relationship must be properly documented.

Accounting for a hedge of a forecasted transaction differs from accounting for a hedge of a foreign currency firm commitment in two ways:

1. Unlike the accounting for a firm commitment, there is no recognition of the forecasted transaction or gains and losses on the forecasted transaction.
2. The company reports the hedging instrument (forward contract or option) at fair value, but because no gain or loss occurs on the forecasted transaction to offset against, the company does not report changes in the fair value of the hedging instrument as gains and losses in net income. Instead, it reports them in other comprehensive income. On the projected date of the forecasted transaction, the company transfers the cumulative change in the fair value of the hedging instrument from accumulated other comprehensive income (balance sheet) to net income (income statement).

Forward Contract Cash Flow Hedge of a Forecasted Transaction

To demonstrate the accounting for a hedge of a forecasted foreign currency transaction, assume that Amerco has a long-term relationship with its German customer and can reliably forecast that the customer will require delivery of goods costing 1 million euros in March 2014. Confident that it will receive 1 million euros on March 1, 2014, Amerco enters into a forward contract on December 1, 2013, to sell 1 million euros on March 1, 2014, at a rate of $1.30. The facts are essentially the same as those for the hedge of a firm commitment except that Amerco does not receive a sales order from the German customer until late February 2014. Relevant exchange rates and the fair value of the forward contract are as follows:

		Forward Contract	
Date	Forward Rate to 3/1/14	Fair Value	Change in Fair Value
12/1/13	$1.305	–0–	–0–
12/31/13	1.316	$(10,783)*	−$10,783
3/1/14	1.30 (spot)	5,000	+ 15,783

*($1,305,000 − $1,316,000) = $(11,000) × 0.9803 = $(10,783), where 0.9803 is the present value factor for two months at an annual interest rate of 12 percent (1 percent per month) calculated as $1/1.01^2$. The original discount on the forward contract is determined by the difference in the € spot rate and the three-month forward rate on December 1, 2013: ($1.305 − $1.32) × € 1 million = $15,000.

2013 Journal Entries—Forward Contract Hedge of a Forecasted Transaction

12/1/13	There is no entry to record either the forecasted sale or the forward contract. A memorandum designates the forward contract as a hedge of the risk of changes in the cash flows related to the forecasted sale resulting from changes in the spot rate (Cash Flow Hedge Steps A.1. and A.2. in Exhibit 9.2).		

On December 31, the forward contract is recognized as a liability at its fair value, with the counterpart reflected in AOCI, and discount expense is recognized due to the passage of time, with the counterpart also reflected in AOCI. The necessary journal entries are:

12/31/13	Accumulated Other Comprehensive Income (AOCI)	10,783	
	Forward Contract		10,783
	To record the forward contract as a liability at its fair value of $10,783 with a corresponding debit to AOCI (Cash Flow Hedge Step B.2. in Exhibit 9.2).		
	Discount Expense	5,000	
	Accumulated Other Comprehensive Income (AOCI)		5,000
	To record straight-line allocation of the forward contract discount: $15,000 × ⅓ = $5,000 (Cash Flow Hedge Step B.4. in Exhibit 9.2).		

Discount expense reduces 2013 net income by $5,000. The impact on the December 31, 2013, balance sheet is as follows:

Assets	Liabilities and Stockholders' Equity	
No effect	Forward contract	$10,783
	Retained earnings	(5,000)
	AOCI	(5,783)
		$ 0

On March 1, 2014, the carrying value of the forward contract is adjusted to fair value and the discount is amortized to expense. Then, the sale and the settlement of the forward contract are recorded. Finally, the balance in AOCI related to the hedge of the forecasted transaction is closed as an adjustment to net income. The following entries are required:

2014 Journal Entries—Forward Contract Hedge of a Forecasted Transaction

3/1/14	Forward Contract	15,783	
	Accumulated Other Comprehensive Income (AOCI)		15,783
	To adjust the carrying value of the forward contract to its current fair value of $5,000 with a corresponding credit to AOCI (Cash Flow Hedge Step C.1. in Exhibit 9.2).		

3/1/14	Discount Expense	10,000	
	Accumulated Other Comprehensive Income (AOCI)		10,000
	To record straight-line allocation of the forward contract discount: \$15,000 × ⅔ = \$10,000 (Cash Flow Hedge Step C.2. in Exhibit 9.2).		
	Foreign Currency (€).	1,300,000	
	Sales		1,300,000
	To record the sale and the receipt of € 1 million as an asset at the spot rate of \$1.30 (Cash Flow Hedge Step C.3. in Exhibit 9.2).		
	Cash	1,305,000	
	Foreign Currency (€)		1,300,000
	Forward Contract.		5,000
	To record settlement of the forward contract (receipt of \$1,305,000 in exchange for delivery of € 1 million) and remove the forward contract from the accounts (Cash Flow Hedge Step C.4. in Exhibit 9.2).		
	Accumulated Other Comprehensive Income (AOCI).	20,000	
	Adjustment to Net Income–Forecasted Transaction.		20,000
	To close AOCI as an adjustment to net income (Cash Flow Hedge Step C.5. in Exhibit 9.2).		

The impact on net income for the year 2014 follows:

Sales.	\$1,300,000
Discount expense	(10,000)
Adjustment to net income–forecasted transaction . .	20,000
Impact on net income	\$1,310,000

Over the two accounting periods, the net impact on net income is \$1,305,000, which equals the amount of net cash inflow realized from the sale.

Option Designated as a Cash Flow Hedge of a Forecasted Transaction

Now assume that Amerco hedges its forecasted foreign currency transaction by purchasing a 1 million euro put option on December 1, 2013. The option, which expires on March 1, 2014, has a strike price of \$1.32 and a premium of \$0.009 per euro. The fair value of the option at relevant dates is as follows (same as in previous examples):

		Foreign Currency Option				
Date	**Option Premium for 3/1/14**	**Fair Value**	**Change in Fair Value**	**Intrinsic Value**	**Time Value**	**Change in Time Value**
12/1/13	\$0.009	\$ 9,000	–0–	–0–	\$9,000	–0–
12/31/13	0.006	6,000	−\$ 3,000	–0–	6,000	−\$3,000
3/1/14	0.020	20,000	+ 14,000	\$20,000	–0–	− 6,000

2013 Journal Entries—Option Hedge of a Forecasted Transaction

12/1/13	Foreign Currency Option.	9,000	
	Cash		9,000
	To record the purchase of the foreign currency option as an asset (Cash Flow Hedge Step A.2. in Exhibit 9.2).		
	There is no entry to record the forecasted sale. A memorandum designates the foreign currency option as a hedge of the risk of changes in the cash flows related to the forecasted sale (Cash Flow Hedge Step A.1. in Exhibit 9.2).		

At December 31, the carrying value of the option is decreased for the change in fair value since December 1, and the change in the time value of the option is recognized as option expense. The required journal entries are as follows:

Date	Account	Debit	Credit
12/31/13	Accumulated Other Comprehensive Income (AOCI).	3,000	
	Foreign Currency Option		3,000
	To adjust the carrying value of the option to its fair value with a corresponding debit to AOCI (Cash Flow Hedge Step B.2. in Exhibit 9.2).		
	Option Expense.	3,000	
	Accumulated Other Comprehensive Income (AOCI)		3,000
	To recognize the change in the time value of the option as a decrease in net income with a corresponding credit to AOCI (Cash Flow Hedge Step B.4. in Exhibit 9.2).		

The impact on net income for the year 2013 follows:

Option expense.	$(3,000)
Impact on net income	$(3,000)

A foreign currency option of $6,000 is reported as an asset on the December 31, 2013, balance sheet. Cash is decreased by $9,000, and Retained Earnings is decreased by $3,000.

On March 1, 2014, first the carrying value of the option is adjusted to fair value and the change in the time value of the option is recognized as option expense. Then, the sale and the exercise of the foreign currency option are recorded. Finally, the balance in AOCI related to the hedge of the forecasted transaction is closed as an adjustment to net income. The following entries are required:

2014 Journal Entries—Option Hedge of a Forecasted Transaction

Date	Account	Debit	Credit
3/1/14	Foreign Currency Option	14,000	
	Accumulated Other Comprehensive Income (AOCI)		14,000
	To adjust the carrying value of the option to its fair value with a corresponding credit to AOCI (Cash Flow Hedge Step C.1. in Exhibit 9.2).		
	Option Expense.	6,000	
	Accumulated Other Comprehensive Income (AOCI)		6,000
	To recognize the change in the time value of the option as a decrease in net income with a corresponding credit to AOCI (Cash Flow Hedge Step C.2. in Exhibit 9.2).		
	Foreign Currency (€).	1,300,000	
	Sales		1,300,000
	To record the sale and the receipt of € 1 million as an asset at the spot rate of $1.30 (Cash Flow Hedge Step C.3. in Exhibit 9.2).		
	Cash	1,320,000	
	Foreign Currency (€)		1,300,000
	Foreign Currency Option		20,000
	To record the exercise of the foreign currency option (receipt of $1,320,000 in exchange for delivery of € 1 million) and remove the foreign currency option from the accounts (Cash Flow Hedge Step C.4. in Exhibit 9.2).		
	Accumulated Other Comprehensive Income (AOCI).	20,000	
	Adjustment to Net Income–Forecasted Transaction.		20,000
	To close AOCI as an adjustment to net income (Cash Flow Hedge Step C.5. in Exhibit 9.2).		

The following is the impact on net income for the year 2014:

Sales.	$1,300,000
Option expense.	(6,000)
Adjustment to net income–forecasted transaction . .	20,000
Impact on net income	$1,314,000

Over the two periods, a total of $1,311,000 is recognized as net income, which is equal to the net cash inflow realized from the export sale ($1,320,000 from the sale less $9,000 for the option).

Use of Hedging Instruments

There are probably as many different corporate strategies regarding hedging foreign exchange risk as there are companies exposed to that risk. Some companies require hedges of all foreign currency transactions. Others require the use of a forward contract hedge when the forward rate results in a larger cash inflow or smaller cash outflow than with the spot rate. Still other companies have proportional hedging policies that require hedging on some predetermined percentage (e.g., 50 percent, 60 percent, or 70 percent) of transaction exposure.

Companies are required to provide information on the use of derivative financial instruments to hedge foreign exchange risk in the notes to financial statements. Exhibit 9.4 presents disclosures made by Abbott Laboratories in its 2010 annual report. Abbott Labs uses forward contracts to hedge foreign exchange risk associated with anticipated foreign currency transactions, foreign currency denominated payables and receivables, and foreign currency borrowings. Much of its hedging activity relates to intercompany transactions involving foreign subsidiaries. The table in Exhibit 9.4 discloses that (1) Abbott's forward contracts primarily are to sell foreign currencies to receive U.S. dollars,

EXHIBIT 9.4 Disclosures Related to Hedging Foreign Exchange Risk in Abbott Laboratories' 2010 Annual Report

Foreign Currency Sensitive Financial Instruments

Abbott enters into foreign currency forward exchange contracts to manage its exposure to foreign currency denominated intercompany loans and trade payables and third-party trade payables and receivables. The contracts are marked-to-market, and resulting gains or losses are reflected in income and are generally offset by losses or gains on the foreign currency exposure being managed. At December 31, 2010 and 2009, Abbott held $10.8 billion and $7.5 billion, respectively, of such contracts, which all mature in the next twelve months.

In addition, certain Abbott foreign subsidiaries enter into foreign currency forward exchange contracts to manage exposures to changes in foreign exchange rates for anticipated intercompany purchases by those subsidiaries whose functional currencies are not the U.S. dollar. These contracts are designated as cash flow hedges of the variability of the cash flows due to changes in foreign exchange rates and are marked-to-market with the resulting gains or losses reflected in Accumulated other comprehensive income (loss). Gains or losses will be included in Cost of Products Sold at the time the products are sold, generally within the next 12 months. At December 31, 2010 and 2009, Abbott held $1.3 billion and $2.0 billion, respectively, of such contracts, which all mature in the following calendar year.

The following table reflects the total foreign currency forward contracts outstanding at December 31, 2010.

(dollars in millions)	**Contract Amount**	**Weighted Average Exchange Rate**	**Fair and Carrying Value Receivable/ (Payable)**
Receive primarily U.S. Dollars in exchange for the following currencies:			
Euro	$ 5,803	1.347	$ 16
British pound	1,422	1.581	2
Japanese yen	2,256	82.7	(2)
Canadian dollar	538	1.021	4
All other currencies	2,090	N/A	(25)
Total	$12,109		$ (5)

(2) 48 percent of Abbott's $12.109 billion in forward contracts at December 31, 2010, was in euros, and (3) the net fair value of all the company's forward contracts was negative and reported on the balance sheet as a liability (payable).

Abbott Labs uses forward contracts exclusively to manage its foreign exchange risk. Dell Inc. uses foreign currency forward contracts as well as options to hedge exposures on firm commitments and forecasted transactions in more than 20 currencies in which the company conducts business. In contrast, The Coca-Cola Company employs a combination of forward contracts, currency options, and collars[11] in its foreign exchange risk-hedging strategy.

The Euro

The introduction of the euro as a common currency throughout much of Europe in 2002 reduced the need for hedging in that region of the world. For example, a German company purchasing goods from a Spanish supplier no longer has an exposure to foreign exchange risk because both countries use a common currency. This is also true for German subsidiaries of U.S. parent companies. However, any euro-denominated transactions between the U.S. parent and its German (or other euro zone) subsidiary continue to be exposed to foreign exchange risk.

One advantage of the euro for U.S. companies is that a euro account receivable from sales to a customer in, say, the Netherlands acts as a natural hedge of a euro account payable on purchases from, say, a supplier in Italy. Assuming that similar amounts and time periods are involved, any foreign exchange loss (gain) arising from the euro payable is offset by a foreign exchange gain (loss) on the euro receivable. A company does not need to hedge the euro account payable with a hedging instrument such as a foreign currency option.

Foreign Currency Borrowing

LO7

Prepare journal entries to account for foreign currency borrowings.

In addition to the receivables and payables that arise from import and export activities, companies often must account for foreign currency borrowings, another type of foreign currency transaction. Companies borrow foreign currency from foreign lenders either to finance foreign operations or perhaps to take advantage of more favorable interest rates. The facts that both the principal and interest are denominated in foreign currency and both create an exposure to foreign exchange risk complicate accounting for a foreign currency borrowing.

To demonstrate the accounting for foreign currency debt, assume that on July 1, 2013, Multicorp International borrowed 1 billion Japanese yen (¥) on a one-year note at a per annum interest rate of 5 percent. Interest is payable and the note comes due on July 1, 2014. The following exchange rates apply:

Date	U.S. Dollars per Japanese Yen Spot Rate
July 1, 2013	$0.00921
December 31, 2013	0.00932
July 1, 2014	0.00937

On July 1, 2013, Multicorp borrows ¥ 1 billion and converts it into $9,210,000 in the spot market. On December 31, 2013, Multicorp must revalue the Japanese yen note payable with an offsetting foreign exchange gain or loss reported in income and must accrue interest expense and interest payable. Interest is calculated by multiplying the loan principal in yen by the relevant interest rate. The amount of interest payable in yen is then translated to U.S. dollars at the spot rate to record the accrual journal entry. On July 1, 2014, any difference between the amount of interest accrued at year-end and the actual U.S. dollar amount that must be spent to pay the accrued interest is recognized as a foreign exchange gain or loss. These journal entries account for this foreign currency borrowing:

[11] A foreign currency collar is created by simultaneously purchasing a call option and selling a put option in a foreign currency to fix a range of prices at which the foreign currency can be purchased at a predetermined future date.

7/1/13	Cash	9,210,000	
	Note Payable (¥)		9,210,000
	To record the ¥ note payable at the spot rate of $0.00921 and the conversion of ¥ 1 billion into U.S. dollars.		
12/31/13	Interest Expense	233,000	
	Accrued Interest Payable (¥)		233,000
	To accrue interest for the period July 1–December 31, 2013: ¥ 1 billion × 5% × ½ year = ¥ 25 million × $0.00932 = $233,000.		
	Foreign Exchange Loss	110,000	
	Note Payable (¥)		110,000
	To revalue the ¥ note payable at the spot rate of $0.00932 and record a foreign exchange loss of $110,000 [¥ 1 billion × ($0.00932 − $0.00921)].		
7/1/14	Interest Expense	234,250	
	Accrued Interest Payable (¥)	233,000	
	Foreign Exchange Loss	1,250	
	Cash		468,500
	To record the interest payment of ¥ 50 million acquired at the spot rate of $0.00937 for $468,500; interest expense for the period of January 1–July 1, 2014: ¥ 25 million × $0.00937; and a foreign exchange loss on the ¥ accrued interest payable: ¥ 25 million × ($0.00937 − $0.00932).		
	Foreign Exchange Loss	50,000	
	Note Payable (¥)		50,000
	To revalue the ¥ note payable at the spot rate of $0.00937 and record a foreign exchange loss of $50,000 [¥ 1 billion × ($0.00937 − $0.00932)].		
	Note Payable (¥)	9,370,000	
	Cash		9,370,000
	To record repayment of the ¥ 1 billion note through purchase of ¥ at the spot rate of $0.00937.		

Foreign Currency Loan

At times companies lend foreign currency to related parties, creating the opposite situation from a foreign currency borrowing. The accounting involves keeping track of a note receivable and interest receivable, both of which are denominated in foreign currency. Fluctuations in the U.S. dollar value of the principal and interest generally give rise to foreign exchange gains and losses that would be included in income. An exception arises when the foreign currency loan is made on a long-term basis to a foreign branch, subsidiary, or equity method affiliate. Foreign exchange gains and losses on "intra-entity foreign currency transactions that are of a long-term investment nature (that is, settlement is not planned or anticipated in the foreseeable future)" are deferred in accumulated other comprehensive income until the loan is repaid.[12] Only the foreign exchange gains and losses related to the interest receivable are recorded currently in net income.

IFRS—Foreign Currency Transactions and Hedges

Similar to U.S. GAAP, *IAS 21*, "The Effects of Changes in Foreign Exchange Rates," also requires the use of a two-transaction perspective in accounting for foreign currency transactions with unrealized foreign exchange gains and losses accrued in net income in the period of exchange rate change. There are no substantive differences between IFRS and U.S. GAAP in the accounting for foreign currency transactions.

[12] FASB ASC (para. 830-20-35-3b).

IAS 39, "Financial Instruments: Recognition and Measurement," governs the accounting for hedging instruments including those used to hedge foreign exchange risk. Rules and procedures in *IAS 39* related to foreign currency hedge accounting generally are consistent with U.S. GAAP. Similar to current U.S. standards, *IAS 39* allows hedge accounting for recognized assets and liabilities, firm commitments, and forecasted transactions when documentation requirements and effectiveness tests are met, and requires hedges to be designated as cash flow or fair value hedges. One difference between the two sets of standards relates to the type of financial instrument that can be designated as a foreign currency cash flow hedge. Under U.S. GAAP, only derivative financial instruments can be used as a cash flow hedge, whereas IFRS also allows nonderivative financial instruments, such as foreign currency loans, to be designated as hedging instruments in a foreign currency cash flow hedge.

In 2010, the IASB issued an Exposure Draft (ED) on hedge accounting as a possible amendment to *IFRS 9*, "Financial Instruments," that would result in significant differences between IFRS and U.S. GAAP if it becomes a standard. The proposal would replace the rules-based hedge accounting requirements in *IAS 39* and more closely align accounting with a company's risk management activities. The ED proposes that changes in fair value related to fair value hedges be reflected in AOCI (similar to cash flow hedges). The IASB believes this will improve transparency by including all information about hedging in AOCI. In addition, the ED proposes that changes in the time value of options be reflected in AOCI rather than in net income.

The ED also proposes extensive disclosures that focus on the risks that are being managed, how those risks are managed, and the outcomes of risk management, including the effect on the financial statements. The objective is to help users of financial statements better understand the extent and effect of a company's hedging activities and to assist them in forecasting future cash flows.

Summary

1. Several exchange rate mechanisms are used around the world. Most national currencies fluctuate in value against other currencies over time.
2. Exposure to foreign exchange risk exists when a payment to be made or to be received is denominated (stated) in terms of a foreign currency. Appreciation in a foreign currency results in a foreign exchange gain when the foreign currency is to be received and a foreign exchange loss when the foreign currency is to be paid. Conversely, a decrease in the value of a foreign currency results in a foreign exchange loss when the foreign currency is to be received and a foreign exchange gain when the foreign currency is to be paid.
3. Companies must revalue foreign currency assets and liabilities to their current U.S. dollar value using current exchange rates when financial statements are prepared. The change in U.S. dollar value of foreign currency balances is recognized as a foreign exchange gain or loss in income in the period in which the exchange rate change occurs. This is known as the two-transaction perspective, accrual approach.
4. Exposure to foreign exchange risk can be eliminated through hedging. Hedging involves establishing a price today at which a foreign currency to be received in the future can be sold in the future or at which a foreign currency to be paid in the future can be purchased in the future.
5. The two most popular instruments for hedging foreign exchange risk are foreign currency forward contracts and foreign currency options. A *forward contract* is a binding agreement to exchange currencies at a predetermined rate. An *option* gives the buyer the right, but not the obligation, to exchange currencies at a predetermined rate.
6. Hedge accounting is appropriate if the derivative is used to hedge either a fair value exposure or cash flow exposure to foreign exchange risk, the derivative is highly effective in offsetting changes in the fair value or cash flows related to the hedged item, and the derivative is properly documented as a hedge. Hedge accounting requires reporting gains and losses on the hedging instrument in net income in the same period as gains and losses on the item being hedged.
7. Companies must report all derivatives, including forward contracts and options, on the balance sheet at their fair value. Changes in fair value are included in accumulated other comprehensive income if the derivative is designated as a cash flow hedge and in net income if it is designated as a fair value hedge.

8. Authoritative accounting literature provides guidance for hedges of (a) recognized foreign currency denominated assets and liabilities, (b) unrecognized foreign currency firm commitments, and (c) forecasted foreign currency denominated transactions. Cash flow hedge accounting can be used for all three types of hedges; fair value hedge accounting can be used only for (a) and (b).
9. If a company hedges a foreign currency firm commitment (fair value hedge), it should recognize gains and losses on the hedging instrument as well as on the underlying firm commitment in net income. The firm commitment account created to offset the gain or loss on firm commitment is treated as an adjustment to the underlying transaction when it takes place.
10. If a company hedges a forecasted transaction (cash flow hedge), it reports changes in the fair value of the hedging instrument in accumulated other comprehensive income. The cumulative change in fair value reported in other comprehensive income is included in net income in the period in which the forecasted transaction was originally anticipated to take place.
11. Borrowing foreign currency creates two exposures to foreign exchange risk. Foreign exchange gains and losses related to both the foreign currency note payable and accrued foreign currency interest payable are recognized in income over the life of the loan.
12. IFRS rules related to the accounting for foreign currency transactions and foreign currency hedges generally are consistent with U.S. GAAP. *IAS 21* requires a two-transaction, accrual approach in accounting for foreign currency transactions. *IAS 39* requires foreign currency hedging instruments to be designated either as a cash flow or fair value hedge; in either case the hedging instrument must be reported at fair value. Hedge accounting is allowed for hedges of foreign currency assets and liabilities, firm commitments, and forecasted transactions, provided that the hedge is properly documented and is effective.

Comprehensive Illustration

Problem

(*Estimated Time: 60 to 75 minutes*) Zelm Company is a U.S. company that produces electronic switches for the telecommunications industry. Zelm regularly imports component parts from a supplier located in Guadalajara, Mexico, and makes payments in Mexican pesos. The following spot exchange rates, forward exchange rates, and call option premium for Mexican pesos exist during the period August to October.

	U.S. Dollar per Mexican Peso		
Date	Spot Rate	Forward Rate to October 31	Call Option Premium for October 31 (strike price $0.080)
August 1	$0.080	$0.085	$0.0052
September 30	0.086	0.088	0.0095
October 31	0.091	0.091	0.0110

Part A

On August 1, Zelm imports parts from its Mexican supplier at a price of 1 million Mexican pesos. It receives the parts on August 1 but does not pay for them until October 31. In addition, on August 1, Zelm enters into a forward contract to purchase 1 million pesos on October 31. It appropriately designates the forward contract as a *cash flow hedge* of the Mexican peso liability exposure. Zelm's incremental borrowing rate is 12 percent per annum (1 percent per month), and the company uses a straight-line method on a monthly basis for allocating forward discounts and premiums.

Part B

The facts are the same as in Part A with the exception that Zelm designates the forward contract as a *fair value hedge* of the Mexican peso liability exposure.

Part C

On August 1, Zelm imports parts from its Mexican supplier at a price of 1 million Mexican pesos. It receives the parts on August 1 but does not pay for them until October 31. In addition, on August 1, Zelm purchases a three-month call option on 1 million Mexican pesos with a strike price of $0.080. The option is appropriately designated as a *cash flow hedge* of the Mexican peso liability exposure.

Part D

On August 1, Zelm orders parts from its Mexican supplier at a price of 1 million Mexican pesos. It receives the parts and pays for them on October 31. On August 1, Zelm enters into a forward contract to purchase 1 million Mexican pesos on October 31. It designates the forward contract as a *fair value hedge* of the Mexican peso firm commitment. Zelm determines the fair value of the firm commitment by referring to changes in the forward exchange rate.

Part E

On August 1, Zelm orders parts from its Mexican supplier at a price of 1 million Mexican pesos. It receives the parts and pays for them on October 31. On August 1, Zelm purchases a three-month call option on 1 million Mexican pesos with a strike price of $0.080. The option is appropriately designated as a *fair value hedge* of the Mexican peso firm commitment. The fair value of the firm commitment is by reference to changes in the spot exchange rate.

Part F

Zelm anticipates that it will import component parts from its Mexican supplier in the near future. On August 1, Zelm purchases a three-month call option on 1 million Mexican pesos with a strike price of $0.080. It appropriately designates the option as a *cash flow hedge* of a forecasted Mexican peso transaction. Zelm receives and pays for parts costing 1 million Mexican pesos on October 31.

Required

Prepare journal entries for each of these independent situations in accordance with U.S. GAAP and determine the impact each situation has on the September 30 and October 31 trial balances.

Solution

Part A. Forward Contract Cash Flow Hedge of a Recognized Foreign Currency Liability

8/1	Parts Inventory	80,000	
	Accounts Payable (Mexican pesos)		80,000
	To record the purchase of parts and a Mexican peso account payable at the spot rate of $0.080.		

The forward contract requires no formal entry. Zelm prepares a memorandum to designate the forward contract as a hedge of the risk of changes in the cash flow to be paid on the foreign currency payable resulting from changes in the U.S. dollar–Mexican peso exchange rate.

9/30	Foreign Exchange Loss	6,000	
	Accounts Payable (Mexican pesos)		6,000
	To adjust the value of the Mexican peso payable to the new spot rate of $0.086 and record a foreign exchange loss resulting from the appreciation of the peso since August 1.		
	Forward Contract	2,970	
	Accumulated Other Comprehensive Income (AOCI)		2,970
	To record the forward contract as an asset at its fair value of $2,970 with a corresponding credit to AOCI.		

Zelm determines the fair value of the forward contract by referring to the change in the forward rate for a contract that settles on October 31: ([$0.088 − $0.085] × 1 million pesos = $3,000. The present value of $3,000 discounted for one month [from October 31 to September 30] at an interest rate of 12 percent per year [1 percent per month] is calculated as follows: $3,000 × 0.9901 = $2,970.)

	Accumulated Other Comprehensive Income (AOCI)	6,000	
	Gain on Forward Contract		6,000
	To record a gain on forward contract to offset the foreign exchange loss on account payable with a corresponding debit to AOCI.		

		Debit	Credit
	Premium Expense	3,333	
	Accumulated Other Comprehensive Income (AOCI)		3,333
	To allocate the forward contract premium to income over the life of the contract using a straight-line method on a monthly basis ($5,000 × 2/3 = $3,333).		

The original premium on the forward contract is determined by the difference in the peso spot rate and three-month forward rate on August 1: ($0.085 − $0.080) × 1 million pesos = $5,000.

Trial Balance—September 30	Debit	Credit
Parts Inventory	$80,000	–0–
Accounts Payable (Mexican pesos)		$86,000
Forward Contract (asset)	2,970	
AOCI		303
Foreign Exchange Loss	6,000	
Gain on Forward Contract		6,000
Premium Expense	3,333	–0–
	$92,303	$92,303

		Debit	Credit
10/31	Foreign Exchange Loss	5,000	
	Accounts Payable (Mexican pesos)		5,000
	To adjust the value of the Mexican peso payable to the new spot rate of $0.091 and record a foreign exchange loss resulting from the appreciation of the peso since September 30.		
	Forward Contract	3,030	
	Accumulated Other Comprehensive Income (AOCI)		3,030
	To adjust the carrying value of the forward contract to its current fair value of $6,000 with a corresponding credit to AOCI.		

The current fair value of the forward contract is determined by referring to the difference in the spot rate on October 31 and the original forward rate: ($0.091 − $0.085) × 1 million pesos = $6,000. The forward contract adjustment on October 31 is calculated as the difference in the current fair value and the carrying value at September 30: $6,000 − $2,970 = $3,030.

	Debit	Credit
Accumulated Other Comprehensive Income (AOCI)	5,000	
Gain on Forward Contract		5,000
To record a gain on forward contract to offset the foreign exchange loss on account payable with a corresponding debit to AOCI.		
Premium Expense	1,667	
Accumulated Other Comprehensive Income (AOCI)		1,667
To allocate the forward contract premium to income over the life of the contract using a straight-line method on a monthly basis ($5,000 × 1/3 = $1,667).		
Foreign Currency (Mexican pesos)	91,000	
Cash		85,000
Forward Contract		6,000
To record settlement of the forward contract: Record payment of $85,000 in exchange for 1 million pesos, record the receipt of 1 million pesos as an asset at the spot rate of $0.091, and remove the forward contract from the accounts.		
Accounts Payable (pesos)	91,000	
Foreign Currency (pesos)		91,000
To record remittance of 1 million pesos to the Mexican supplier.		

Trial Balance—October 31	Debit	Credit
Cash		$85,000
Parts Inventory	$80,000	–0–
Retained Earnings, 9/30	3,333	–0–
Foreign Exchange Loss	5,000	–0–
Gain on Forward Contract	–0–	5,000
Premium Expense	1,667	–0–
	$90,000	$90,000

Part B. Forward Contract Fair Value Hedge of a Recognized Foreign Currency Liability

8/1	Parts Inventory	80,000	
	Accounts Payable (Mexican pesos)		80,000
	To record the purchase of parts and a peso account payable at the spot rate of $0.080.		

The forward contract requires no formal entry. A memorandum designates the forward contract as a hedge of the risk of changes in the cash flow to be paid on the foreign currency payable resulting from changes in the U.S. dollar–peso exchange rate.

9/30	Foreign Exchange Loss	6,000	
	Accounts Payable (Mexican pesos)		6,000
	To adjust the value of the peso payable to the new spot rate of $0.086 and record a foreign exchange loss resulting from the appreciation of the peso since August 1.		
	Forward Contract	2,970	
	Gain on Forward Contract		2,970
	To record the forward contract as an asset at its fair value of $2,970 and record a forward contract gain for the change in the fair value of the forward contract since August 1.		

Trial Balance—September 30	Debit	Credit
Parts Inventory	$80,000	–0–
Accounts Payable (Mexican pesos)		$86,000
Forward Contract (asset)	2,970	–0–
Foreign Exchange Loss	6,000	–0–
Gain on Forward Contract	–0–	2,970
	$88,970	$88,970

10/31	Foreign Exchange Loss	5,000	
	Accounts Payable (Mexican pesos)		5,000
	To adjust the value of the peso payable to the new spot rate of $0.091 and record a foreign exchange loss resulting from the appreciation of the peso since September 30.		
	Forward Contract	3,030	
	Gain on Forward Contract		3,030
	To adjust the carrying value of the forward contract to its current fair value of $6,000 and record a forward contract gain for the change in fair value since September 30.		
	Foreign Currency (Mexican pesos)	91,000	
	Cash		85,000
	Forward Contract		6,000

To record settlement of the forward contract: Record payment of $85,000 in exchange for 1 million pesos, record the receipt of 1 million pesos as an asset at the spot rate of $0.091, and remove the forward contract from the accounts.

	Debit	Credit
Accounts Payable (pesos)	91,000	
Foreign Currency (pesos)		91,000

To record remittance of 1 million pesos to the Mexican supplier.

Trial Balance—October 31	Debit	Credit
Cash	–0–	$85,000
Parts Inventory	$80,000	–0–
Retained Earnings, 9/30.	3,030	–0–
Foreign Exchange Loss.	5,000	–0–
Gain on Forward Contract.	–0–	3,030
	$88,030	$88,030

Part C. Option Cash Flow Hedge of a Recognized Foreign Currency Liability

The following schedule summarizes the changes in the components of the fair value of the peso call option with a strike price of $0.080:

Date	Spot Rate	Option Premium	Fair Value	Change in Fair Value	Intrinsic Value	Time Value	Change in Time Value
8/1	$0.080	$0.0052	$ 5,200	–0–	–0–	$5,200*	–0–
9/30	0.086	0.0095	9,500	+$4,300	$ 6,000†	3,500†	−$1,700
10/31	0.091	0.0110	11,000	+ 1,500	11,000	–0–‡	− 3,500

*Because the strike price and spot rate are the same, the option has no intrinsic value. Fair value is attributable solely to the time value of the option.

†With a spot rate of $0.086 and a strike price of $0.08, the option has an intrinsic value of $6,000. The remaining $3,500 of fair value is attributable to time value.

‡The time value of the option at maturity is zero.

Date		Debit	Credit
8/1	Parts Inventory	80,000	
	Accounts Payable (Mexican pesos)		80,000
	To record the purchase of parts and a peso account payable at the spot rate of $0.080.		
	Foreign Currency Option	5,200	
	Cash		5,200
	To record the purchase of a foreign currency option as an asset.		
9/30	Foreign Exchange Loss	6,000	
	Accounts Payable (pesos)		6,000
	To adjust the value of the peso payable to the new spot rate of $0.086 and record a foreign exchange loss resulting from the appreciation of the peso since August 1.		
	Foreign Currency Option	4,300	
	Accumulated Other Comprehensive Income (AOCI)		4,300
	To adjust the fair value of the option from $5,200 to $9,500 with a corresponding credit to AOCI.		
	Accumulated Other Comprehensive Income (AOCI)	6,000	
	Gain on Foreign Currency Option		6,000
	To record a gain on forward currency option to offset the foreign exchange loss on account payable with a corresponding debit to AOCI.		
	Option Expense	1,700	
	Accumulated Other Comprehensive Income (AOCI)		1,700
	To recognize the change in the time value of the foreign currency option as an expense with a corresponding credit to AOCI.		

Trial Balance—September 30	Debit	Credit
Cash.		$ 5,200
Parts Inventory	$80,000	–0–
Foreign Currency Option (asset)	9,500	–0–
Accounts Payable (Mexican pesos)	–0–	86,000
Foreign Exchange Loss	6,000	–0–
Gain on Foreign Currency Option	–0–	6,000
Option Expense	1,700	–0–
	$97,200	$97,200

Date	Account	Debit	Credit
10/31	Foreign Exchange Loss.	5,000	
	Accounts Payable (Mexican pesos)		5,000
	To adjust the value of the peso payable to the new spot rate of $0.091 and record a foreign exchange loss resulting from the appreciation of the peso since September 30.		
	Foreign Currency Option	1,500	
	Accumulated Other Comprehensive Income (AOCI)		1,500
	To adjust the carrying value of the foreign currency option to its current fair value of $11,000 with a corresponding credit to AOCI.		
	Accumulated Other Comprehensive Income (AOCI).	5,000	
	Gain on Foreign Currency Option		5,000
	To record a gain on foreign currency option to offset the foreign exchange loss on account payable with a corresponding debit to AOCI.		
	Option Expense	3,500	
	Accumulated Other Comprehensive Income (AOCI)		3,500
	To recognize the change in the time value of the foreign currency option as an expense with a corresponding credit to AOCI.		
	Foreign Currency (Mexican pesos)	91,000	
	Cash		80,000
	Foreign Currency Option		11,000
	To record exercise of the foreign currency option: Record payment of $80,000 in exchange for 1 million pesos, record the receipt of 1 million pesos as an asset at the spot rate of $0.091, and remove the option from the accounts.		
	Accounts Payable (pesos).	91,000	
	Foreign Currency (pesos)		91,000
	To record remittance of 1 million pesos to the Mexican supplier.		

Trial Balance—October 31	Debit	Credit
Cash ($5,200 credit balance + $80,000 credit) . . .	–0–	$85,200
Parts Inventory	$80,000	–0–
Retained Earnings, 9/30	1,700	–0–
Foreign Exchange Loss	5,000	–0–
Gain on Foreign Currency Option	–0–	5,000
Option Expense	3,500	–0–
	$90,200	$90,200

Part D. Forward Contract Fair Value Hedge of a Foreign Currency Firm Commitment

Date	Account	Debit	Credit
8/1	The forward contract or the purchase order requires no formal entry. A memorandum would be prepared designating the forward contract as a fair value hedge of the foreign currency firm commitment.		
9/30	Forward Contract	2,970	
	Gain on Forward Contract		2,970

Date	Accounts	Debit	Credit
	To record the forward contract as an asset at its fair value of $2,970 and record a forward contract gain for the change in the fair value of the forward contract since August 1.		
	Loss on Firm Commitment	2,970	
	Firm Commitment		2,970
	To record the firm commitment as a liability at its fair value of $2,970 based on changes in the forward rate and record a firm commitment loss for the change in fair value since August 1.		

Trial Balance—September 30	Debit	Credit
Forward Contract (asset)	$2,970	–0–
Firm Commitment (liability)	–0–	$2,970
Gain on Forward Contract	–0–	2,970
Loss on Firm Commitment	2,970	–0–
	$5,940	$5,940

Date	Accounts	Debit	Credit
10/31	Forward Contract	3,030	
	Gain on Forward Contract		3,030
	To adjust the carrying value of the forward contract to its current fair value of $6,000 and record a forward contract gain for the change in fair value since September 30.		
	Loss on Firm Commitment	3,030	
	Firm Commitment		3,030
	To adjust the value of the firm commitment to $6,000 based on changes in the forward rate and record a firm commitment loss for the change in fair value since September 30.		
	Foreign Currency (Mexican pesos)	91,000	
	Cash		85,000
	Forward Contract		6,000
	To record settlement of the forward contract: Record payment of $85,000 in exchange for 1 million pesos, record the receipt of 1 million pesos as an asset at the spot rate of $0.091, and remove the forward contract from the accounts.		
	Parts Inventory	91,000	
	Foreign Currency (Mexican pesos)		91,000
	To record the purchase of parts through the payment of 1 million pesos to the Mexican supplier.		
	Firm Commitment	6,000	
	Adjustment to Net Income–Firm Commitment		6,000
	To close the firm commitment account as an adjustment to net income.		

(*Note:* The final entry to close the Firm Commitment account to Adjustment to Net Income must be made *only* in the period in which Parts Inventory affects net income through Cost of Goods Sold. The Firm Commitment account remains on the books as a liability until that point in time.)

Trial Balance—October 31	Debit	Credit
Cash	–0–	$85,000
Parts Inventory (Cost of Goods Sold)	$91,000	–0–
Gain on Forward Contract	–0–	3,030
Loss on Firm Commitment	3,030	–0–
Adjustment to Net Income–Firm Commitment	–0–	6,000
	$94,030	$94,030

Part E. Option Fair Value Hedge of a Foreign Currency Firm Commitment

		Debit	Credit
8/1	Foreign Currency Option	5,200	
	Cash		5,200
	To record the purchase of a foreign currency option as an asset.		
9/30	Foreign Currency Option	4,300	
	Gain on Foreign Currency Option		4,300
	To adjust the fair value of the option from $5,200 to $9,500 and record an option gain for the change in fair value since August 1.		
	Loss on Firm Commitment	5,940	
	Firm Commitment		5,940
	To record the firm commitment as a liability at its fair value of $5,940 based on changes in the spot rate and record a firm commitment loss for the change in fair value since August 1.		

The fair value of the firm commitment is determined by referring to changes in the spot rate from August 1 to September 30: ($0.080 − $0.086) × 1 million pesos = $(6,000). This amount must be discounted for one month at 12 percent per annum (1 percent per month): $(6,000) × 0.9901 = $(5,940).

Trial Balance—September 30	Debit	Credit
Cash	–0–	$ 5,200
Foreign Currency Option (asset)	$ 9,500	–0–
Firm Commitment (liability)	–0–	5,940
Gain on Foreign Currency Option	–0–	4,300
Loss on Firm Commitment	5,940	–0–
	$15,440	$15,440

		Debit	Credit
10/31	Foreign Currency Option	1,500	
	Gain on Foreign Currency Option		1,500
	To adjust fair value of the option from $9,500 to $11,000 and record an option gain for the change in fair value since September 30.		
	Loss on Firm Commitment.	5,060	
	Firm Commitment		5,060
	To adjust the fair value of the firm commitment from $5,940 to $11,000 and record a firm commitment loss for the change in fair value since September 30.		

The fair value of the firm commitment is determined by referring to changes in the spot rate from August 1 to October 31: ($0.080 − $0.091) × 1 million pesos = $(11,000).

		Debit	Credit
	Foreign Currency (Mexican pesos)	91,000	
	Cash		80,000
	Foreign Currency Option		11,000
	To record exercise of the foreign currency option: Record payment of $80,000 in exchange for 1 million pesos, record the receipt of 1 million pesos as an asset at the spot rate of $0.091, and remove the option from the accounts.		
	Parts Inventory.	91,000	
	Foreign Currency (pesos)		91,000
	To record the purchase of parts through the payment of 1 million pesos to the Mexican supplier.		
	Firm Commitment	11,000	
	Adjustment to Net Income–Firm Commitment		11,000
	To close Firm Commitment account to Adjustment to Net Income.		

(*Note:* The final entry to close the Firm Commitment to Adjustment to Net Income is made *only* in the period in which Parts Inventory affects net income through Cost of Goods Sold. The Firm Commitment account remains on the books as a liability until that point in time.)

Trial Balance—October 31	Debit	Credit
Cash ($5,200 credit balance + $80,000 credit). . .	–0–	$85,200
Parts Inventory (Cost of Goods Sold).	$91,000	–0–
Retained Earnings, 9/30	1,640	–0–
Gain on Foreign Currency Option	–0–	1,500
Loss on Firm Commitment	5,060	–0–
Adjustment to Net Income–Firm Commitment . . .	–0–	11,000
	$97,700	$97,700

Part F. Option Cash Flow Hedge of a Forecasted Foreign Currency Transaction

Date	Account	Debit	Credit
8/1	Foreign Currency Option	5,200	
	Cash		5,200
	To record the purchase of a foreign currency option as an asset.		
9/30	Foreign Currency Option	4,300	
	Accumulated Other Comprehensive Income (AOCI)		4,300
	To adjust the fair value of the option from $5,200 to $9,500 with a corresponding adjustment to AOCI.		
	Option Expense	1,700	
	Accumulated Other Comprehensive Income (AOCI)		1,700
	To recognize the change in the time value of the foreign currency option as an expense with a corresponding credit to AOCI.		

Trial Balance—September 30	Debit	Credit
Cash.	–0–	$ 5,200
Foreign Currency Option (asset)	$ 9,500	–0–
Accumulated Other Comprehensive Income . . .	–0–	6,000
Option Expense	1,700	–0–
	$11,200	$11,200

Date	Account	Debit	Credit
10/31	Foreign Currency Option	1,500	
	Accumulated Other Comprehensive Income (AOCI)		1,500
	To adjust the fair value of the option from $9,500 to $11,000 with a corresponding adjustment to AOCI.		
	Option Expense	3,500	
	Accumulated Other Comprehensive Income (AOCI)		3,500
	To recognize the change in the time value of the foreign currency option as an expense with a corresponding credit to AOCI.		
	Foreign Currency (Mexican pesos)	91,000	
	Cash		80,000
	Foreign Currency Option		11,000
	To record exercise of the foreign currency option: Record payment of $80,000 in exchange for 1 million pesos, record the receipt of 1 million pesos as an asset at the spot rate of $0.091, and remove the option from the accounts.		
	Parts Inventory.	91,000	
	Foreign Currency (Mexican pesos).		91,000

To record the purchase of parts through the payment of 1 million pesos to the Mexican supplier.		
Accumulated Other Comprehensive Income (AOCI)	11,000	
Adjustment to Net Income–Forecasted Transaction		11,000
To close AOCI as an adjustment to net income.		

(*Note:* The final entry to close AOCI to Adjustment to Net Income is made at the date that the forecasted transaction was expected to occur, regardless of when the parts inventory affects net income.)

Trial Balance—October 31	Debit	Credit
Cash ($5,200 credit balance + $80,000 credit). . .	–0–	$85,200
Parts Inventory (Cost of Goods Sold).	$91,000	–0–
Retained Earnings, 9/30	1,700	–0–
Foreign Currency Option expense	3,500	–0–
Adjustment to Net Income–Forecasted Transaction.	–0–	11,000
	$96,200	$96,200

Questions

1. What concept underlies the two-transaction perspective in accounting for foreign currency transactions?
2. A company makes an export sale denominated in a foreign currency and allows the customer one month to pay. Under the two-transaction perspective, accrual approach, how does the company account for fluctuations in the exchange rate for the foreign currency?
3. What factors create a foreign exchange gain on a foreign currency transaction? What factors create a foreign exchange loss?
4. What does the term *hedging* mean? Why do companies elect to follow this strategy?
5. How does a foreign currency option differ from a foreign currency forward contract?
6. How does the timing of hedges of (*a*) foreign currency denominated assets and liabilities, (*b*) foreign currency firm commitments, and (*c*) forecasted foreign currency transactions differ?
7. Why would a company prefer a foreign currency option over a forward contract in hedging a foreign currency firm commitment? Why would a company prefer a forward contract over an option in hedging a foreign currency asset or liability?
8. How do companies report foreign currency derivatives, such as forward contracts and options, on the balance sheet?
9. How does a company determine the fair value of a foreign currency forward contract? How does it determine the fair value of an option?
10. What is hedge accounting?
11. Under what conditions can companies use hedge accounting to account for a foreign currency option used to hedge a forecasted foreign currency transaction?
12. What are the differences in accounting for a forward contract used as (*a*) a cash flow hedge and (*b*) a fair value hedge of a foreign currency denominated asset or liability?
13. What are the differences in accounting for a forward contract used as a fair value hedge of (*a*) a foreign currency denominated asset or liability and (*b*) a foreign currency firm commitment?
14. What are the differences in accounting for a forward contract used as a cash flow hedge of (*a*) a foreign currency denominated asset or liability and (*b*) a forecasted foreign currency transaction?
15. How are changes in the fair value of an option accounted for in a cash flow hedge? In a fair value hedge?
16. In what way is the accounting for a foreign currency borrowing more complicated than the accounting for a foreign currency account payable?

Problems

LO1

1. Which of the following combinations correctly describes the relationship between foreign currency transactions, exchange rate changes, and foreign exchange gains and losses?

	Type of Transaction	Foreign Currency	Foreign Exchange Gain or Loss
a.	Export sale	Appreciates	Loss
b.	Import purchase	Appreciates	Gain
c.	Import purchase	Depreciates	Gain
d.	Export sale	Depreciates	Gain

LO2

2. In accounting for foreign currency transactions, which of the following approaches is used in the United States?
   a. One-transaction perspective; accrue foreign exchange gains and losses.
   b. One-transaction perspective; defer foreign exchange gains and losses.
   c. Two-transaction perspective; defer foreign exchange gains and losses.
   d. Two-transaction perspective; accrue foreign exchange gains and losses.

LO2

3. On October 1, 2013, Mud Co., a U.S. company, purchased parts from Terra, a Portuguese company, with payment due on December 1, 2013. If Mud's 2013 operating income included no foreign exchange gain or loss, the transaction could have
   a. Resulted in an extraordinary gain.
   b. Been denominated in U.S. dollars.
   c. Generated a foreign exchange gain to be reported as a deferred charge on the balance sheet.
   d. Generated a foreign exchange loss to be reported as a separate component of stockholders' equity.

LO2

4. Post, Inc., had a receivable from a foreign customer that is payable in the customer's local currency. On December 31, 2013, Post correctly included this receivable for 200,000 local currency units (LCU) in its balance sheet at $110,000. When Post collected the receivable on February 15, 2014, the U.S. dollar equivalent was $95,000. In Post's 2014 consolidated income statement, how much should it report as a foreign exchange loss?
   a. $–0–.
   b. $10,000.
   c. $15,000.
   d. $25,000.

LO2, LO7

5. On July 1, 2013, Houghton Company borrowed 200,000 euros from a foreign lender evidenced by an interest-bearing note due on July 1, 2014. The note is denominated in euros. The U.S. dollar equivalent of the note principal is as follows:

Date	Amount
July 1, 2013 (date borrowed)	$195,000
December 31, 2013 (Houghton's year-end)	220,000
July 1, 2014 (date repaid)	230,000

   In its 2014 income statement, what amount should Houghton include as a foreign exchange gain or loss on the note?
   a. $35,000 gain.
   b. $35,000 loss.
   c. $10,000 gain.
   d. $10,000 loss.

LO1, LO2

6. Slick Co. had a Swiss franc receivable resulting from exports to Switzerland and a Mexican peso payable resulting from imports from Mexico. Slick recorded foreign exchange gains related to both its franc receivable and peso payable. Did the foreign currencies increase or decrease in dollar value from the date of the transaction to the settlement date?

	Franc	Peso
a.	Increase	Increase
b.	Decrease	Decrease
c.	Decrease	Increase
d.	Increase	Decrease

LO2 7. Grete Corp. had the following foreign currency transactions during 2013:

- Purchased merchandise from a foreign supplier on January 20, 2013, for the U.S. dollar equivalent of $60,000 and paid the invoice on April 20, 2013, at the U.S. dollar equivalent of $68,000.
- On September 1, 2013, borrowed the U.S. dollar equivalent of $300,000 evidenced by a note that is payable in the lender's local currency on September 1, 2014. On December 31, 2013, the U.S. dollar equivalent of the principal amount was $320,000.

In Grete's 2013 income statement, what amount should be included as a foreign exchange loss?

a. $4,000.
b. $20,000.
c. $22,000.
d. $28,000.

LO4 8. A U.S. exporter has a Thai baht account receivable resulting from an export sale on April 1 to a customer in Thailand. The exporter signed a forward contract on April 1 to sell Thai baht and designated it as a cash flow hedge of a recognized Thai baht receivable. The spot rate was $0.022 on that date, and the forward rate was $0.023. Which of the following did the U.S. exporter report in net income?

a. Discount expense.
b. Discount revenue.
c. Premium expense.
d. Premium revenue.

LO5 9. Lawrence Company ordered parts costing FC100,000 from a foreign supplier on May 12 when the spot rate was $0.20 per FC. A one-month forward contract was signed on that date to purchase FC100,000 at a forward rate of $0.21. The forward contract is properly designated as a fair value hedge of the FC100,000 firm commitment. On June 12, when the company receives the parts, the spot rate is $0.23. At what amount should Lawrence Company carry the parts inventory on its books?

a. $20,000.
b. $21,000.
c. $22,000.
d. $23,000.

LO3 10. On December 1, 2013, Barnum Company (a U.S.–based company) entered into a three-month forward contract to purchase 1,000,000 ringgits on March 1, 2014. The following U.S. dollar per ringgit exchange rates apply:

Date	Spot Rate	Forward Rate (to March 1, 2012)
December 1, 2013	$0.044	$0.042
December 31, 2013	0.040	0.037
March 1, 2014	0.038	N/A

Barnum's incremental borrowing rate is 12 percent. The present value factor for two months at an annual interest rate of 12 percent (1 percent per month) is 0.9803.

Which of the following correctly describes the manner in which Barnum Company will report the forward contract on its December 31, 2013, balance sheet?

a. As an asset in the amount of $1,960.60.
b. As an asset in the amount of $3,921.20.
c. As a liability in the amount of $6,862.10.
d. As a liability in the amount of $4,901.50.

Use the following information for Problems 11 and 12.

MNC Corp. (a U.S.–based company) sold parts to a South Korean customer on December 1, 2013, with payment of 10 million South Korean won to be received on March 31, 2014. The following exchange rates apply:

Date	Spot Rate	Forward Rate (to March 31, 2014)
December 1, 2013	$0.0035	$0.0034
December 31, 2013	0.0033	0.0032
March 31, 2014	0.0038	N/A

MNC's incremental borrowing rate is 12 percent. The present value factor for three months at an annual interest rate of 12 percent (1 percent per month) is 0.9706.

LO2

11. Assuming that MNC did not enter into a forward contract, how much foreign exchange gain or loss should it report on its 2013 income statement with regard to this transaction?
   a. $5,000 gain.
   b. $3,000 gain.
   c. $2,000 loss.
   d. $1,000 loss.

LO4

12. Assuming that MNC entered into a forward contract to sell 10 million South Korean won on December 1, 2013, as a fair value hedge of a foreign currency receivable, what is the net impact on its net income in 2013 resulting from a fluctuation in the value of the won?
   a. No impact on net income.
   b. $58.80 decrease in net income.
   c. $2,000 decrease in net income.
   d. $1,941.20 increase in net income.

LO6

13. On March 1, Pimlico Corporation (a U.S.–based company) expects to order merchandise from a supplier in Sweden in three months. On March 1, when the spot rate is $0.10 per Swedish krona, Pimlico enters into a forward contract to purchase 500,000 Swedish kroner at a three-month forward rate of $0.12. At the end of three months, when the spot rate is $0.115 per Swedish krona, Pimlico orders and receives the merchandise, paying 500,000 kroner. What amount does Pimlico report in net income as a result of this cash flow hedge of a forecasted transaction?
   a. $10,000 Premium Expense plus a $7,500 positive Adjustment to Net Income when the merchandise is purchased.
   b. $10,000 Discount Expense plus a $5,000 positive Adjustment to Net Income when the merchandise is purchased.
   c. $2,500 Premium Expense plus a $5,000 negative Adjustment to Net Income when the merchandise is purchased.
   d. $2,500 Premium Expense plus a $2,500 positive Adjustment to Net Income when the merchandise is purchased.

LO6

14. Palmer Corporation, operating as a U.S. corporation, expects to order goods from a foreign supplier at a price of 200,000 pounds, with delivery and payment to be made on April 15. On January 15, Palmer purchased a three-month call option on 200,000 pounds and designated this option as a cash flow hedge of a forecasted foreign currency transaction. The option has a strike price of $0.25 per pound and costs $2,000. The spot rate for pounds is $0.25 on January 15 and $0.22 on April 15. What amount will Palmer Corporation report as an option expense in net income during the period January 15 to April 15?
   a. $600.
   b. $1,000.
   c. $2,000.
   d. $4,400.

Use the following information for Problems 15 through 17.

On September 1, 2013, Jensen Company received an order to sell a machine to a customer in Canada at a price of 100,000 Canadian dollars. Jensen shipped the machine and received payment on March 1, 2014. On September 1, 2013, Jensen purchased a put option giving it the right to sell 100,000 Canadian dollars on March 1, 2014, at a price of $80,000. Jensen properly designated the option as a fair value hedge of the Canadian dollar firm commitment. The option cost $2,000 and had a fair value of $2,300 on December 31, 2013. The fair value of the firm commitment was measured by referring to changes in the spot rate. The following spot exchange rates apply:

Date	U.S. Dollar per Canadian Dollar
September 1, 2013	$0.80
December 31, 2013	0.79
March 1, 2014	0.77

Jensen Company's incremental borrowing rate is 12 percent. The present value factor for two months at an annual interest rate of 12 percent (1 percent per month) is 0.9803.

LO5

15. What was the net impact on Jensen Company's 2013 income as a result of this fair value hedge of a firm commitment?
    a. $-0-.
    b. $680.30 decrease in income.
    c. $300 increase in income.
    d. $980.30 increase in income.

LO5

16. What was the net impact on Jensen Company's 2014 income as a result of this fair value hedge of a firm commitment?
    a. $-0-.
    b. $1,319.70 decrease in income.
    c. $77,980.30 increase in income.
    d. $78,680.30 increase in income.

LO5

17. What was the net increase or decrease in cash flow from having purchased the foreign currency option to hedge this exposure to foreign exchange risk?
    a. $-0-.
    b. $1,000 increase in cash flow.
    c. $1,500 decrease in cash flow.
    d. $3,000 increase in cash flow.

Use the following information for Problems 18 through 20.
On March 1, 2013, Werner Corp. received an order for parts from a Mexican customer at a price of 500,000 Mexican pesos with a delivery date of April 30, 2013. On March 1, when the U.S. dollar–Mexican peso spot rate is $0.115, Werner Corp. entered into a two-month forward contract to sell 500,000 pesos at a forward rate of $0.12 per peso. It designates the forward contract as a fair value hedge of the firm commitment to receive pesos, and the fair value of the firm commitment is measured by referring to changes in the peso forward rate. Werner delivers the parts and receives payment on April 30, 2013, when the peso spot rate is $0.118. On March 31, 2013, the Mexican peso spot rate is $0.123, and the forward contract has a fair value of $1,250.

LO5

18. What is the net impact on Werner's net income for the quarter ended March 31, 2013, as a result of this forward contract hedge of a firm commitment?
    a. $-0-.
    b. $1,250 increase in net income.
    c. $1,500 decrease in net income.
    d. $1,500 increase in net income.

LO5

19. What is the net impact on Werner's net income for the quarter ended June 30, 2013, as a result of this forward contract hedge of a firm commitment?
    a. $-0-.
    b. $59,000 increase in net income.
    c. $60,000 increase in net income.
    d. $61,500 increase in net income.

LO5 20. What is the net increase or decrease in cash flow from having entered into this forward contract hedge?

a. $–0–.

b. $1,000 increase in cash flow.

c. $1,500 decrease in cash flow.

d. $2,500 increase in cash flow.

Use the following information for Problems 21 and 22.

On November 1, 2013, Dos Santos Company forecasts the purchase of raw materials from a Brazilian supplier on February 1, 2014, at a price of 200,000 Brazilian reals. On November 1, 2013, Dos Santos pays $1,500 for a three-month call option on 200,000 reals with a strike price of $0.40 per real. Dos Santos properly designates the option as a cash flow hedge of a forecasted foreign currency transaction. On December 31, 2013, the option has a fair value of $1,100. The following spot exchange rates apply:

Date	U.S. Dollar per Brazilian Real
November 1, 2013	$0.40
December 31, 2013	0.38
February 1, 2014	0.41

LO6 21. What is the net impact on Dos Santos Company's 2013 net income as a result of this hedge of a forecasted foreign currency transaction?

a. $–0–.

b. $400 decrease in net income.

c. $1,000 decrease in net income.

d. $1,400 decrease in net income.

LO6 22. What is the net impact on Dos Santos Company's 2014 net income as a result of this hedge of a forecasted foreign currency transaction? Assume that the raw materials are consumed and become a part of the cost of goods sold in 2014.

a. $80,000 decrease in net income.

b. $80,600 decrease in net income.

c. $81,100 decrease in net income.

d. $83,100 decrease in net income.

LO2 23. Rabato Corporation acquired merchandise on account from a foreign supplier on November 1, 2013, for 60,000 LCU (local currency units). It paid the foreign currency account payable on January 15, 2014. The following exchange rates for 1 LCU are known:

November 1, 2013	$0.345
December 31, 2013	0.333
January 15, 2014	0.359

a. How does the fluctuation in exchange rates affect Rabato's 2013 income statement?

b. How does the fluctuation in exchange rates affect Rabato's 2014 income statement?

LO2 24. On December 20, 2013, Butanta Company (a U.S. company headquartered in Miami, Florida) sold parts to a foreign customer at a price of 50,000 ostras. Payment is received on January 10, 2014. Currency exchange rates for 1 ostra are as follows:

December 20, 2013	$1.05
December 31, 2013	1.02
January 10, 2014	0.98

a. How does the fluctuation in exchange rates affect Butanta's 2013 income statement?

b. How does the fluctuation in exchange rates affect Butanta's 2014 income statement?

LO2 25. New Colony Corporation (a U.S. company) made a sale to a foreign customer on September 15, 2013, for 100,000 foreign currency units (FCU). It received payment on October 15, 2013. The following exchange rates for 1 FCU apply:

September 15, 2013	$0.40
September 30, 2013	0.42
October 15, 2013	0.37

Prepare all journal entries for New Colony in connection with this sale, assuming that the company closes its books on September 30 to prepare interim financial statements.

LO2

26. On December 1, 2013, Dresden Company (a U.S. company located in Albany, New York) purchases inventory from a foreign supplier for 60,000 local currency units (LCU). Dresden will pay in 90 days after it sells this merchandise. It makes sales rather quickly and pays this entire obligation on January 28, 2014. Currency exchange rates for 1 LCU are as follows:

December 1, 2013	$0.88
December 31, 2013	0.82
January 28, 2014	0.90

Prepare all journal entries for Dresden Company in connection with the purchase and payment.

LO2

27. Acme Corporation (a U.S. company located in Sarasota, Florida) has the following import/export transactions in 2013:

March 1	Bought inventory costing 50,000 pesos on credit.
May 1	Sold 60 percent of the inventory for 45,000 pesos on credit.
August 1	Collected 40,000 pesos from customers.
September 1	Paid 30,000 pesos to creditors.

Currency exchange rates for 1 peso for 2013 are as follows:

March 1	$0.17
May 1	0.18
August 1	0.19
September 1	0.20
December 31	0.21

For each of the following accounts, how much will Acme report on its 2013 financial statements?

a. Inventory.
b. Cost of Goods Sold.
c. Sales.
d. Accounts Receivable.
e. Accounts Payable.
f. Cash.

LO2

28. Bartlett Company, headquartered in Cincinnati, Ohio, has occasional transactions with companies in a foreign country whose currency is the lira. Prepare journal entries for the following transactions in U.S. dollars. Also prepare any necessary adjusting entries at December 31 caused by fluctuations in the value of the lira. Assume that the company uses a perpetual inventory system.

Transactions in 2013

February 1	Bought equipment for 40,000 lira on credit.
April 1	Paid for the equipment purchased February 1.
June 1	Bought inventory for 30,000 lira on credit.
August 1	Sold 70 percent of inventory purchased June 1 for 40,000 lira on credit.
October 1	Collected 30,000 lira from the sales made on August 1, 2013.
November 1	Paid 20,000 lira on the debts incurred on June 1, 2013.

Transactions in 2014

February 1	Collected remaining 10,000 lira from August 1, 2013, sales.
March 1	Paid remaining 10,000 lira on the debts incurred on June 1, 2013.

Currency exchange rates for 1 lira for 2013

February 1	$0.44
April 1	0.45
June 1	0.47
August 1	0.48
October 1	0.49
November 1	0.50
December 31	0.52

Currency exchange rates for 1 lira for 2014

February 1	$0.54
March 1	0.55

LO2

29. Benjamin, Inc., operates an export/import business. The company has considerable dealings with companies in the country of Camerrand. The denomination of all transactions with these companies is alaries (AL), the Camerrand currency. During 2013, Benjamin acquires 20,000 widgets at a price of 8 alaries per widget. It will pay for them when it sells them. Currency exchange rates for 1 AL are as follows:

September 1, 2013	$0.46
December 1, 2013	0.44
December 31, 2013	0.48
March 1, 2014	0.45

a. Assume that Benjamin acquired the widgets on December 1, 2013, and made payment on March 1, 2014. What is the effect of the exchange rate fluctuations on reported income in 2013 and in 2014?

b. Assume that Benjamin acquired the widgets on September 1, 2013, and made payment on December 1, 2013. What is the effect of the exchange rate fluctuations on reported income in 2013?

c. Assume that Benjamin acquired the widgets on September 1, 2013, and made payment on March 1, 2014. What is the effect of the exchange rate fluctuations on reported income in 2013 and in 2014?

LO7

30. On September 30, 2013, Ericson Company negotiated a two-year, 1,000,000 dudek loan from a foreign bank at an interest rate of 2 percent per year. It makes interest payments annually on September 30 and will repay the principal on September 30, 2015. Ericson prepares U.S.-dollar financial statements and has a December 31 year-end.

a. Prepare all journal entries related to this foreign currency borrowing assuming the following exchange rates for 1 dudek:

September 30, 2013	$0.100
December 31, 2013	0.105
September 30, 2014	0.120
December 31, 2014	0.125
September 30, 2015	0.150

b. Determine the effective cost of borrowing in dollars in each of the three years 2013, 2014, and 2015.

LO4

31. Brandlin Company of Anaheim, California, sells parts to a foreign customer on December 1, 2013, with payment of 20,000 korunas to be received on March 1, 2014. Brandlin enters into a forward contract on December 1, 2013, to sell 20,000 korunas on March 1, 2014. Relevant exchange rates for the koruna on various dates are as follows:

Date	Spot Rate	Forward Rate (to March 1, 2014)
December 1, 2013	$2.00	$2.075
December 31, 2013	2.10	2.200
March 1, 2014	2.25	N/A

Brandlin's incremental borrowing rate is 12 percent. The present value factor for two months at an annual interest rate of 12 percent (1 percent per month) is 0.9803. Brandlin must close its books and prepare financial statements at December 31.

a. Assuming that Brandlin designates the forward contract as a cash flow hedge of a foreign currency receivable and recognizes any premium or discount using the straight-line method, prepare journal entries for these transactions in U.S. dollars. What is the impact on 2013 net income? What is the impact on 2014 net income? What is the impact on net income over the two accounting periods?

b. Assuming that Brandlin designates the forward contract as a fair value hedge of a foreign currency receivable, prepare journal entries for these transactions in U.S. dollars. What is the impact on 2013 net income? What is the impact on 2014 net income? What is the impact on net income over the two accounting periods?

LO4

32. Use the same facts as in Problem (31) except that Brandlin Company purchases parts from a foreign supplier on December 1, 2013, with payment of 20,000 korunas to be made on March 1, 2014. On December 1, 2013, Brandlin enters into a forward contract to purchase 20,000 korunas on March 1, 2014.

    a. Assuming that Brandlin designates the forward contract as a cash flow hedge of a foreign currency payable and recognizes any premium or discount using the straight-line method, prepare journal entries for these transactions in U.S. dollars. What is the impact on 2013 net income? What is the impact on 2014 net income? What is the impact on net income over the two accounting periods?

    b. Assuming that Brandlin designates the forward contract as a fair value hedge of a foreign currency payable, prepare journal entries for these transactions in U.S. dollars. What is the impact on net income in 2013 and in 2014? What is the impact on net income over the two accounting periods?

LO4

33. On June 1, Alexander Corporation sold goods to a foreign customer at a price of 1,000,000 pesos. It will receive payment in three months on September 1. On June 1, Alexander acquired an option to sell 1,000,000 pesos in three months at a strike price of $0.045. Relevant exchange rates and option premiums for the peso are as follows:

Date	Spot Rate	Put Option Premium for September 1 (strike price $0.045)
June 1	$0.045	$0.0020
June 30	0.048	0.0018
September 1	0.044	N/A

Alexander must close its books and prepare its second-quarter financial statements on June 30.

a. Assuming that Alexander designates the foreign currency option as a cash flow hedge of a foreign currency receivable, prepare journal entries for these transactions in U.S. dollars. What is the impact on net income over the two accounting periods?

b. Assuming that Alexander designates the foreign currency option as a fair value hedge of a foreign currency receivable, prepare journal entries for these transactions in U.S. dollars. What is the impact on net income over the two accounting periods?

LO4

34. On June 1, Hamilton Corporation purchased goods from a foreign supplier at a price of 1,000,000 markkas. It will make payment in three months on September 1. On June 1, Hamilton acquired an option to purchase 1,000,000 markkas in three months at a strike price of $0.085. Relevant exchange rates and option premiums for the markka are as follows:

Date	Spot Rate	Call Option Premium for September 1 (strike price $0.085)
June 1	$0.085	$0.002
June 30	0.088	0.004
September 1	0.090	N/A

Hamilton must close its books and prepare its second-quarter financial statements on June 30.

a. Assuming that Hamilton designates the foreign currency option as a cash flow hedge of a foreign currency payable, prepare journal entries for these transactions in U.S. dollars. What is the impact on net income over the two accounting periods?

b. Assuming that Hamilton designates the foreign currency option as a fair value hedge of a foreign currency payable, prepare journal entries for these transactions in U.S. dollars. What is the impact on net income over the two accounting periods?

LO4

35. On November 1, 2013, Ambrose Company sold merchandise to a foreign customer for 100,000 FCUs with payment to be received on April 30, 2014. At the date of sale, Ambrose entered into a six-month forward contract to sell 100,000 LCUs. It properly designates the forward contract as a cash flow hedge of a foreign currency receivable. The following exchange rates apply:

Date	Spot Rate	Forward Rate (to April 30, 2014)
November 1, 2013	$0.53	$0.52
December 31, 2013	0.50	0.48
April 30, 2014	0.49	N/A

Ambrose's incremental borrowing rate is 12 percent. The present value factor for four months at an annual interest rate of 12 percent (1 percent per month) is 0.9610.

a. Prepare all journal entries, including December 31 adjusting entries, to record the sale and forward contract.

b. What is the impact on net income in 2013?

c. What is the impact on net income in 2014?

LO4

36. Eximco Corporation (based in Champaign, Illinois) has a number of transactions with companies in the country of Mongagua, where the currency is the mong. On November 30, 2013, Eximco sold equipment at a price of 500,000 mongs to a Mongaguan customer that will make payment on January 31, 2014. In addition, on November 30, 2013, Eximco purchased raw materials from a Mongaguan supplier at a price of 300,000 mongs; it will make payment on January 31, 2014. To hedge its net exposure in mongs, Eximco entered into a two-month forward contract on November 30, 2013, to deliver 200,000 mongs to the foreign currency broker in exchange for $104,000. Eximco properly designates its forward contract as a fair value hedge of a foreign currency receivable. The following rates for the mong apply:

Date	Spot Rate	Forward Rate (to January 31, 2014)
November 30, 2013	$0.53	$0.52
December 31, 2013	0.50	0.48
January 31, 2014	0.49	N/A

Eximco's incremental borrowing rate is 12 percent. The present value factor for one month at an annual interest rate of 12 percent (1 percent per month) is 0.9901.

a. Prepare all journal entries, including December 31 adjusting entries, to record these transactions and the forward contract.

b. What is the impact on net income in 2013?

c. What is the impact on net income in 2014?

LO4, LO5

37. On October 1, 2013, Hanks Company entered into a forward contract to sell 100,000 LCUs in four months (on January 31, 2014) and receive $65,000 in U.S. dollars. Exchange rates for the LCU follow:

Date	Spot Rate	Forward Rate (to January 31, 2014)
October 1, 2013	$0.69	$0.65
December 31, 2013	0.71	0.74
January 31, 2014	0.72	N/A

Hanks's incremental borrowing rate is 12 percent. The present value factor for one month at an annual interest rate of 12 percent (1 percent per month) is 0.9901. Hanks must close its books and prepare financial statements on December 31.

a. Prepare journal entries, assuming that Hanks entered into the forward contract as a fair value hedge of a 100,000 LCU receivable arising from a sale made on October 1, 2013. Include entries for both the sale and the forward contract.

b. Prepare journal entries, assuming that Hanks entered into the forward contract as a fair value hedge of a firm commitment related to a 100,000 LCU sale that will be made on January 31, 2014. Include entries for both the firm commitment and the forward contract. The fair value of the firm commitment is measured referring to changes in the forward rate.

LO5

38. On August 1, Jackson Corporation (a U.S.–based importer) placed an order to purchase merchandise from a foreign supplier at a price of 200,000 rupees. Jackson will receive and make payment for the merchandise in three months on October 31. On August 1, Jackson entered into a forward contract to purchase 200,000 rupees in three months at a forward rate of $0.30. It properly designates the forward contract as a fair value hedge of a foreign currency firm commitment. The fair value of the firm commitment is measured by referring to changes in the forward rate. Relevant exchange rates for the rupee are as follows:

Date	Spot Rate	Forward Rate (to October 31)
August 1	$0.300	$0.300
September 30	0.305	0.325
October 31	0.320	N/A

Jackson's incremental borrowing rate is 12 percent. The present value factor for one month at an annual interest rate of 12 percent (1 percent per month) is 0.9901. Jackson must close its books and prepare its third-quarter financial statements on September 30.

a. Prepare journal entries for the forward contract and firm commitment through October 31.

b. Assuming the inventory is sold in the fourth quarter, what is the impact on net income over the two accounting periods?

c. What net cash outflow results from the purchase of merchandise from the foreign supplier?

LO5

39. On June 1, Vandervelde Corporation (a U.S.–based manufacturing firm) received an order to sell goods to a foreign customer at a price of 500,000 leks. Vandervelde will ship the goods and receive payment in three months on September 1. On June 1, Vandervelde purchased an option to sell 500,000 leks in three months at a strike price of $1.00. It properly designated the option as a fair value hedge of a foreign currency firm commitment. The fair value of the firm commitment is measured by referring to changes in the spot rate. Relevant exchange rates and option premiums for the lek are as follows:

Date	Spot Rate	Put Option Premium for September 1 (strike price $1.00)
June 1	$1.00	$0.010
June 30	0.99	0.016
September 1	0.97	N/A

Vandervelde's incremental borrowing rate is 12 percent. The present value factor for two months at an annual interest rate of 12 percent (1 percent per month) is 0.9803. Vandervelde Corporation must close its books and prepare its second-quarter financial statements on June 30.

a. Prepare journal entries for the foreign currency option and firm commitment.

b. What is the impact on net income over the two accounting periods?

c. What is the net cash inflow resulting from the sale of goods to the foreign customer?

LO5

40. Big Arber Company ordered parts from a foreign supplier on November 20 at a price of 50,000 pijios when the spot rate was $0.20 per pijio. Delivery and payment were scheduled for December 20. On November 20, Big Arber acquired a call option on 50,000 pijios at a strike price of $0.20, paying a premium of $0.008 per pijio. It designates the option as a fair value hedge of a foreign currency firm commitment. The fair value of the firm commitment is measured by referring to changes in the spot rate. The parts arrive and Big Arber makes payment according to schedule. Big Arber does not close its books until December 31.

a. Assuming a spot rate of $0.21 per pijio on December 20, prepare all journal entries to account for the option and firm commitment.

b. Assuming a spot rate of $0.18 per pijio on December 20, prepare all journal entries to account for the option and firm commitment.

LO6

41. Based on past experience, Leickner Company expects to purchase raw materials from a foreign supplier at a cost of 1,000,000 marks on March 15, 2014. To hedge this forecasted transaction, the company acquires a three-month call option to purchase 1,000,000 marks on December 15, 2013. Leickner selects a strike price of $0.58 per mark, paying a premium of $0.005 per unit, when the spot rate is $0.58. The spot rate increases to $0.584 at December 31, 2013, causing the fair value of the option to increase to $8,000. By March 15, 2014, when the raw materials are purchased, the spot rate has climbed to $0.59, resulting in a fair value for the option of $10,000.

a. Prepare all journal entries for the option hedge of a forecasted transaction and for the purchase of raw materials, assuming that December 31 is Leickner's year-end and that the raw materials are included in the cost of goods sold in 2014.

b. What is the overall impact on net income over the two accounting periods?

c. What is the net cash outflow to acquire the raw materials?

LO2, LO4, LO5

42. Vino Veritas Company, a U.S.–based importer of wines and spirits, placed an order with a French supplier for 1,000 cases of wine at a price of 200 euros per case. The total purchase price is 200,000 euros. Relevant exchange rates for the euro are as follows:

Date	Spot Rate	Forward Rate to October 31, 2013	Call Option Premium for October 31, 2013 (strike price $1.00)
September 15, 2013	$1.00	$1.06	$0.035
September 30, 2013	1.05	1.09	0.070
October 31, 2013	1.10	1.10	0.100

Vino Veritas Company has an incremental borrowing rate of 12 percent (1 percent per month) and closes the books and prepares financial statements at September 30.

a. Assume that the wine arrived on September 15, 2013, and the company made payment on October 31, 2013. There was no attempt to hedge the exposure to foreign exchange risk. Prepare journal entries to account for this import purchase.

b. Assume that the wine arrived on September 15, 2013, and the company made payment on October 31, 2013. On September 15, Vino Veritas entered into a 45-day forward contract to purchase 200,000 euros. It properly designated the forward contract as a fair value hedge of a foreign currency payable. Prepare journal entries to account for the import purchase and foreign currency forward contract.

c. Vino Veritas ordered the wine on September 15, 2013. The wine arrived and the company paid for it on October 31, 2013. On September 15, Vino Veritas entered into a 45-day forward contract to purchase 200,000 euros. The company properly designated the forward contract as a fair value hedge of a foreign currency firm commitment. The fair value of the firm commitment is measured by referring to changes in the forward rate. Prepare journal entries to account for the foreign currency forward contract, firm commitment, and import purchase.

d. The wine arrived on September 15, 2013, and the company made payment on October 31, 2013. On September 15, Vino Veritas purchased a 45-day call option for 200,000 euros. It properly designated the option as a cash flow hedge of a foreign currency payable. Prepare journal entries to account for the import purchase and foreign currency option.

e. The company ordered the wine on September 15, 2013. It arrived on October 31, 2013, and the company made payment on that date. On September 15, Vino Veritas purchased a 45-day call option for 200,000 euros. It properly designated the option as a fair value hedge of a foreign currency firm commitment. The fair value of the firm commitment is measured by referring to changes in the spot rate. Prepare journal entries to account for the foreign currency option, firm commitment, and import purchase.

Develop Your Skills

RESEARCH CASE—INTERNATIONAL FLAVORS AND FRAGRANCES

Many companies make annual reports available on their corporate Internet home page. Annual reports also can be accessed through the SEC's EDGAR system at www.sec.gov (under Filing Type, search for 10-K). Access the most recent annual report for International Flavors and Fragrances (IFF).

Required

1. Identify the location(s) in the annual report where IFF provides disclosures related to its management of foreign exchange risk.
2. Determine the types of hedging instruments the company uses and the types of hedges in which it engages.
3. Determine the manner in which the company discloses the fact that its foreign exchange hedges are effective in offsetting gains and losses on the underlying items being hedged.

ACCOUNTING STANDARDS CASE—FORECASTED TRANSACTIONS

Fergusson Corporation, a U.S. company, manufactures components for the automobile industry. In the past, Fergusson purchased actuators used in its products from a supplier in the United States. The company plans to shift its purchases to a supplier in Portugal. Fergusson's CFO expects to place an order with the Portuguese supplier in the amount of 200,000 euros in three months. In contemplation of this future import, the CFO purchased a euro call option to hedge the cash flow risk that the euro might appreciate against the U.S. dollar over the next three months. The CFO is aware that a foreign currency option used to hedge the cash flow risk associated with a forecasted foreign currency transaction may be designated as a hedge for accounting purposes only if the forecasted transaction is probable. However, he is unsure how he should demonstrate that the anticipated import purchase from Portugal is likely to occur. He wonders whether management's intention to make the purchase is sufficient.

Required

Search current U.S. authoritative accounting literature to determine whether management's intent is sufficient to assess that a forecasted foreign currency transaction is likely to occur. If not, what additional evidence must be considered? Identify the FASB ASC guidance for answering these questions.

EXCEL CASE—DETERMINE FOREIGN EXCHANGE GAINS AND LOSSES

CPA skills

Import/Export Company, a U.S. company, made a number of import purchases and export sales denominated in foreign currency in 2010. Information related to these transactions is summarized in the following table. The company made each purchase or sale on the date in the Transaction Date column and made payment in foreign currency or received payment on the date in the Settlement Date column.

Foreign Currency	Type of Transaction	Amount in Foreign Currency	Transaction Date	Settlement Date
Brazilian real (BRL)	Import purchase	(87,000)	1/4/2010	5/4/2010
Swiss franc (CHF)	Export sale	51,700	1/4/2010	5/4/2010
Swiss franc (CHF)	Import purchase	(55,000)	5/4/2010	10/4/2010
Euro	Export sale	37,200	4/1/2010	9/1/2010
Euro	Export sale	37,200	4/1/2010	10/1/2010
Chinese yuan (CNY)	Import purchase	(342,000)	1/4/2010	10/4/2010
South Korean won (KRW)	Import purchase	(55,600,000)	1/4/2010	10/4/2010

Required

1. Create an electronic spreadsheet with the information from the preceding table. Label columns as follows:

   Foreign Currency
   Type of Transaction
   Amount in Foreign Currency
   Transaction Date
   Exchange Rate at Transaction Date
   $ Value at Transaction Date
   Settlement Date
   Exchange Rate at Settlement Date
   $ Value at Settlement Date
   Foreign Exchange Gain (Loss)
2. Use historical exchange rate information available on the Internet at www.x-rates.com, Historic Lookup, to find the 2010 exchange rates between the U.S. dollar and each foreign currency on the relevant transaction and settlement dates.
3. Complete the electronic spreadsheet to determine the foreign exchange gain (loss) on each transaction. Determine the total net foreign exchange gain (loss) reported in Import/Export Company's 2010 income statement.

ANALYSIS CASE—CASH FLOW HEDGE

CPA skills

On February 1, 2013, Linber Company forecasted the purchase of component parts on May 1, 2013, at a price of 100,000 euros. On that date, Linber entered into a forward contract to purchase 100,000 euros on May 1, 2013. It designated the forward contract as a cash flow hedge of the forecasted transaction. The spot rate for euros on February 1, 2013, was $1 per euro. On May 1, 2013, the forward contract was settled, and the component parts were received and paid for. The parts were consumed in the second quarter of 2013.

Linber's financial statements reported the following amounts related to this cash flow hedge (credit balances in parentheses):

Income Statement	First Quarter 2013	Second Quarter 2013
Premium expense	$4,000	$ 2,000
Cost of goods sold	–0–	103,000
Adjustment to net income	–0–	3,000

Balance Sheet	3/31/13	5/1/13
Forward contract (liability)	$(1,980)*	–0–
AOCI (credit)	(2,020)	–0–
Change in cash	–0–	$(106,000)

*$2,000 × 0.9901 = $1,980, where 0.9901 is the present value factor for one month at an annual interest rate of 12 percent calculated as 1/1.01.

Required

1. On February 1, 2013, what was the U.S. dollar per euro forward rate to May 1, 2013?
2. On March 31, 2013, what was the U.S. dollar per euro forward rate to May 1, 2013?
3. Was Linber better off or worse off as a result of having entered into this cash flow hedge of a forecasted transaction? By what amount?
4. What does the total premium expense of $6,000 reflect?

INTERNET CASE—HISTORICAL EXCHANGE RATES

The Pier Ten Company, a U.S. company, made credit sales to four customers in Asia on December 15, 2010, and received payment on January 15, 2011. Information related to these sales is as follows:

Customer	Location	Invoice Price
Rama Properties Ltd.	New Delhi	898,000 Indian rupees (INR)
Luzon Island Group	Manila	874,000 Philippine pesos (PHP)
Mishima Industries Inc.	Tokyo	1,662,500 Japanese yen (JPY)
Melayu Trading Company	Kuala Lumpur	62,550 Malaysian ringgit (MYR)

The Pier Ten Company's fiscal year ends December 31.

Required

1. Use historical exchange rate information available on the Internet at www.x-rates.com, Historical Lookup, to find exchange rates between the U.S. dollar and each foreign currency for December 14, 2010, December 31, 2010, and January 14, 2011.
2. Determine the foreign exchange gains and losses that Pier Ten would have recognized in net income in 2010 and 2011, and the overall foreign exchange gain or loss for each transaction. Determine for which transaction it would have been most important for Pier Ten to hedge its foreign exchange risk.
3. Pier Ten could have acquired a one-month put option on December 15, 2010, to hedge the foreign exchange risk associated with each of the four export sales. In each case, the put option would have cost $100 with the strike price equal to the December 15, 2010, spot rate. Determine for which hedges, if any, Pier Ten would have recognized a net gain on the foreign currency option.

COMMUNICATION CASE—FORWARD CONTRACTS AND OPTIONS

Palmetto Bug Extermination Corporation (PBEC), a U.S. company, regularly purchases chemicals from a supplier in Switzerland with the invoice price denominated in Swiss francs. PBEC has experienced several foreign exchange losses in the past year due to increases in the U.S. dollar price of the Swiss currency. As a result, Dewey Nukem, PBEC's CEO, has asked you to investigate the possibility of using derivative financial instruments, specifically foreign currency forward contracts and foreign currency options, to hedge the company's exposure to foreign exchange risk.

Required

Draft a memo to CEO Nukem comparing the advantages and disadvantages of using forward contracts and options to hedge foreign exchange risk. Recommend the type of hedging instrument you believe the company should employ and justify this recommendation.

chapter 10

Translation of Foreign Currency Financial Statements

- After months of negotiations, Kraft (KFT) announced last month that it would acquire U.K. confection giant Cadbury (CBY) with a revised bid of $19.5 billion. The acquisition of Cadbury by Kraft will generate a joint portfolio of more than 40 confectionary brands, each with annual sales in excess of $100 million, essentially creating the world's biggest confectionary company.[1]
- Sanofi-Aventis (SNY), France's biggest drugmaker, agreed to buy Genzyme (GENZ) for at least $20.1 billion, ending its nine-month pursuit of the U.S. biotech company.[2]
- International Paper (IP) made its first investment in India, buying a 53.5 percent stake in Andhra Pradesh Paper Mills, for $257 million.[3]

Recent announcements such as these have become more the norm than the exception in today's global economy. Companies establish operations in foreign countries for a variety of reasons including to develop new markets for their products, take advantage of lower production costs, or gain access to raw materials. Some multinational companies have reached a stage in their development in which domestic operations are no longer considered to be of higher priority than international operations. For example, in 2010, U.S.-based International Flavors and Fragrances, Inc., had operations in 40 countries and 75 percent of its net sales outside North America; Merck & Co., Inc., generated 57 percent of its sales and had 35 percent of its property, plant, and equipment outside of the United States.

Foreign operations create numerous managerial problems for the parent company that do not exist for domestic operations. Some of these problems arise from cultural differences between the home and foreign countries. Other problems exist because foreign operations generally are required to comply with the laws and regulations of the

Learning Objectives

After studying this chapter, you should be able to:

LO1 Explain the theoretical underpinnings and the limitations of the current rate and temporal methods.

LO2 Describe guidelines as to when foreign currency financial statements are to be translated using the current rate method and when they are to be translated using the temporal method.

LO3 Translate a foreign subsidiary's financial statements into its parent's reporting currency using the current rate method and calculate the related translation adjustment.

LO4 Remeasure a foreign subsidiary's financial statements using the temporal method and calculate the associated remeasurement gain or loss.

LO5 Understand the rationale for hedging a net investment in a foreign operation and describe the treatment of gains and losses on hedges used for this purpose.

LO6 Prepare a consolidation worksheet for a parent and its foreign subsidiary.

[1] "Kraft-Cadbury: Making Acquisitions Work," *Bloomberg Businessweek* online edition, February 9, 2010, www.businessweek.com.

[2] "Bid & Ask," *Bloomberg Businessweek* online edition, February 17, 2011, www.businessweek.com.

[3] "Bid & Ask," *Bloomberg Businessweek* online edition, March 31, 2011, www.businessweek.com.

foreign country. For example, most countries require companies to prepare financial statements in the local currency using local accounting rules.

To prepare worldwide consolidated financial statements, a U.S. parent company must (1) convert the foreign GAAP financial statements of its foreign operations into U.S. GAAP and (2) translate the financial statements from the foreign currency into U.S. dollars. This conversion and translation process must be carried out regardless of whether the foreign operation is a branch, joint venture, majority-owned subsidiary, or affiliate accounted for under the equity method. This chapter deals with the issue of translating foreign currency financial statements into the parent's reporting currency.

Two major theoretical issues are related to the translation process: (1) which *translation method* should be used and (2) where the resulting *translation adjustment* should be reported in the consolidated financial statements. In this chapter, these two issues are examined first from a conceptual perspective and second by the manner in which the FASB in the United States has resolved these issues. The chapter concludes with a discussion of IFRS on this topic.

Exchange Rates Used in Translation

Two types of exchange rates are used in translating financial statements:

1. *Historical exchange rate:* the exchange rate that exists when a transaction occurs.
2. *Current exchange rate:* the exchange rate that exists at the balance sheet date.

Translation methods differ as to which balance sheet and income statement accounts to translate at historical exchange rates and which to translate at current exchange rates.

Assume that the company described in the discussion question on the next page began operations in Gualos on December 31, 2012, when the exchange rate was $0.20 per vilsek. When Southwestern Corporation prepared its consolidated balance sheet at December 31, 2012, it had no choice about the exchange rate used to translate the Land account into U.S. dollars. It translated the Land account carried on the foreign subsidiary's books at 150,000 vilseks at an exchange rate of $0.20; $0.20 was both the *historical* and *current* exchange rate for the Land account at December 31, 2012.

Consolidated Balance Sheet: 12/31/12	
Land (150,000 vilseks × $0.20).	$30,000

During the first quarter of 2013, the vilsek appreciates relative to the U.S. dollar by 15 percent; the exchange rate at March 31, 2013, is $0.23 per vilsek. In preparing its balance sheet at the end of the first quarter of 2013, Southwestern must decide whether the Land account carried on the subsidiary's balance sheet at 150,000 vilseks should be translated into dollars using the *historical exchange rate* of $0.20 or the *current exchange rate* of $0.23.

If the historical exchange rate is used at March 31, 2013, Land continues to be carried on the consolidated balance sheet at $30,000 with no change from December 31, 2012.

Historical Rate—Consolidated Balance Sheet: 3/31/13	
Land (150,000 vilseks × $0.20).	$30,000

If the current exchange rate is used, Land is carried on the consolidated balance sheet at $34,500, an increase of $4,500 from December 31, 2012.

Current Rate—Consolidated Balance Sheet: 3/31/13	
Land (150,000 vilseks × $0.23).	$34,500

Discussion Question

HOW DO WE REPORT THIS?

Southwestern Corporation operates throughout Texas buying and selling widgets. To expand into more profitable markets, the company recently decided to open a small subsidiary in the nearby country of Gualos. The currency in Gualos is the vilsek. For some time, the government of that country held the exchange rate constant: 1 vilsek equaled \$0.20 (or 5 vilseks equaled \$1.00). Initially, Southwestern invested cash in this new operation; its \$90,000 was converted into 450,000 vilseks (\$90,000 × 5). Southwestern used one-third of this money (150,000 vilseks, or \$30,000) to purchase land to hold for the possible construction of a plant, invested one-third in short-term marketable securities, and spent one-third in acquiring inventory for future resale.

Shortly thereafter, the Gualos government officially revalued the currency so that 1 vilsek was worth \$0.23. Because of the strength of the local economy, the vilsek gained buying power in relation to the U.S. dollar. The vilsek then was considered more valuable than in the past. Southwestern's accountants realized that a change had occurred; each of the assets was now worth more in U.S. dollars than the original \$30,000 investment: 150,000 vilseks × \$0.23 = \$34,500. Two of the company's top officers met to determine the appropriate method for reporting this change in currency values.

Controller: Nothing has changed. Our cost is still \$30,000 for each item. That's what we spent. Accounting uses historical cost wherever possible. Thus, we should do nothing.

Finance director: Yes, but the old rates are meaningless now. We would be foolish to report figures based on a rate that no longer exists. The cost is still 150,000 vilseks for each item. You are right, the cost has not changed. However, the vilsek is now worth \$0.23, so our reported value must change.

Controller: The new rate affects us only if we take money out of the country. We don't plan to do that for many years. The rate will probably change 20 more times before we remove money from Gualos. We've got to stick to our \$30,000 historical cost. That's our cost and that's good, basic accounting.

Finance director: You mean that for the next 20 years we will be translating balances for external reporting purposes using an exchange rate that has not existed for years? That doesn't make sense. I have a real problem using an antiquated rate for the investments and inventory. They will be sold for cash when the new rate is in effect. These balances have no remaining relation to the original exchange rate.

Controller: You misunderstand the impact of an exchange rate fluctuation. Within Gualos, no impact occurs. One vilsek is still one vilsek. The effect is realized only when an actual conversion takes place into U.S. dollars at a new rate. At that point, we will properly measure and report the gain or loss. That is when realization takes place. Until then our cost has not changed.

Finance director: I simply see no value at all in producing financial information based entirely on an exchange rate that does not exist. I don't care when realization takes place.

Controller: You've got to stick with historical cost, believe me. The exchange rate today isn't important unless we actually convert vilseks to dollars.

How should Southwestern report each of these three assets on its current balance sheet? Does the company have a gain because the value of the vilsek has increased relative to the U.S. dollar?

Translation Adjustments

To keep the accounting equation (A = L + OE) in balance, the increase of $4,500 on the asset (A) side of the consolidated balance sheet when the current exchange rate is used must be offset by an equal $4,500 *increase* in owners' equity (OE) on the other side of the balance sheet. The increase in owners' equity is called a *positive translation adjustment.* It has a *credit* balance.

The increase in dollar value of the Land due to the vilsek's appreciation creates a positive translation adjustment. This is true for any asset on the Gualos subsidiary's balance sheet that is translated at the *current* exchange rate. *Assets translated at the current exchange rate when the foreign currency has appreciated generate a positive (credit) translation adjustment.*

Liabilities on the Gualos subsidiary's balance sheet that are translated at the current exchange rate also increase in dollar value when the vilsek appreciates. For example, Southwestern would report Notes Payable of 10,000 vilseks at $2,000 on the December 31, 2012, balance sheet and at $2,300 on the March 31, 2013, balance sheet. To keep the accounting equation in balance, the increase in liabilities (L) must be offset by a *decrease* in owners' equity (OE), giving rise to a *negative translation adjustment.* This has a *debit* balance. *Liabilities translated at the current exchange rate when the foreign currency has appreciated generate a negative (debit) translation adjustment.*

Balance Sheet Exposure

Balance sheet items (assets and liabilities) translated at the *current* exchange rate change in dollar value from balance sheet to balance sheet as a result of the change in exchange rate. These items are *exposed* to translation adjustment. Balance sheet items translated at *historical* exchange rates do not change in dollar value from one balance sheet to the next. These items are *not* exposed to translation adjustment. Exposure to translation adjustment is referred to as *balance sheet, translation,* or *accounting exposure. Balance sheet exposure* can be contrasted with the *transaction exposure* discussed in Chapter 9 that arises when a company has foreign currency receivables and payables in the following way: *Transaction exposure gives rise to foreign exchange gains and losses that are ultimately realized in cash; translation adjustments arising from balance sheet exposure do not directly result in cash inflows or outflows.*

Each item translated at the current exchange rate is exposed to translation adjustment. In effect, a separate translation adjustment exists for each of these exposed items. However, negative translation adjustments on liabilities offset positive translation adjustments on assets when the foreign currency appreciates. If total exposed assets equal total exposed liabilities throughout the year, the translation adjustments (although perhaps significant on an individual basis) net to a zero balance. The *net* translation adjustment needed to keep the consolidated balance sheet in balance is based solely on the *net asset* or *net liability* exposure.

A foreign operation has a *net asset balance sheet exposure* when assets translated at the current exchange rate are higher in amount than liabilities translated at the current exchange rate. A *net liability balance sheet exposure* exists when liabilities translated at the current exchange rate are higher than assets translated at the current exchange rate. The following summarizes the relationship between exchange rate fluctuations, balance sheet exposure, and translation adjustments:

Balance Sheet	Foreign Currency (FC)	
Exposure	**Appreciates**	**Depreciates**
Net asset	Positive translation adjustment	Negative translation adjustment
Net liability	Negative translation adjustment	Positive translation adjustment

Exactly how to handle the translation adjustment in the consolidated financial statements is a matter of some debate. The major issue is whether the translation adjustment should be treated as a *translation gain or loss reported in net income* or whether the translation adjustment should be treated as a *direct adjustment to owners' equity without affecting net income*. We consider this issue in more detail later after examining methods of translation.

Translation Methods

LO1

Explain the theoretical underpinnings and the limitations of the current rate and temporal methods.

Two major translation methods are currently used: (1) the current rate (or closing rate) method and (2) the temporal method. We discuss each method from the perspective of a U.S.–based multinational company translating foreign currency financial statements into U.S. dollars.

Current Rate Method

The basic assumption underlying the *current rate method* is that a company's *net investment* in a foreign operation is *exposed* to foreign exchange risk. In other words, a foreign operation represents a foreign currency net asset and if the foreign currency *decreases* in value against the U.S. dollar, a *decrease in the U.S. dollar value of the foreign currency net asset* occurs. This decrease in U.S. dollar value of the net investment will be reflected by reporting a *negative* (debit balance) translation adjustment in the consolidated financial statements. If the foreign currency *increases* in value, an *increase in the U.S. dollar value of the net asset* occurs and will be reflected through a *positive* (credit balance) translation adjustment.

To measure the net investment's exposure to foreign exchange risk, *all assets and all liabilities* of the foreign operation are translated at the *current* exchange rate. Stockholders' equity items are translated at historical rates. *The balance sheet exposure under the current rate method is equal to the foreign operation's net asset (total assets minus total liabilities) position.*[4]

Total assets > Total liabilities → Net asset exposure

A positive translation adjustment arises when the foreign currency appreciates, and a negative translation adjustment arises when the foreign currency depreciates.

As mentioned, the major difference between the translation adjustment and a foreign exchange gain or loss is that the translation adjustment is not necessarily realized through inflows and outflows of cash. The translation adjustment that arises when using the current rate method is unrealized. It can become a realized gain or loss only if the foreign operation is sold (for its book value) and the foreign currency proceeds from the sale are converted into U.S. dollars.

The current rate method requires translation of all income statement items at the exchange rate in effect at the date of accounting recognition. In most cases, an assumption can be made that the revenue or expense is incurred evenly throughout the accounting period and a weighted average-for-the-period exchange rate can be used for translation. However, when an income account, such as a gain or loss, occurs at a specific point in time, the exchange rate at that date should be used for translation.[5]

Temporal Method

The basic objective underlying the *temporal method* of translation is to produce a set of U.S. dollar–translated financial statements as if the foreign subsidiary had actually used U.S. dollars in conducting its operations. Continuing with the Gualos subsidiary example, Southwestern, the U.S. parent, should report the Land account on the consolidated

[4] In rare cases, a foreign subsidiary could have liabilities higher than assets (negative stockholders' equity). In those cases, a net liability exposure exists under the current rate method.

[5] Alternatively, all income statement items may be translated at the current exchange rate. Later we demonstrate that translation at the current rate has a slight advantage over translation at the average-for-the-period rate.

balance sheet at the amount of U.S. dollars that it would have spent if it had sent dollars to the subsidiary to purchase land. Because the land cost 150,000 vilseks at a time when one vilsek could be acquired with $0.20, the parent would have sent $30,000 to the subsidiary to acquire the land; this is the land's historical cost *in U.S. dollar terms*. The following rule is consistent with the temporal method's underlying objective:

1. Assets and liabilities carried on the foreign operation's balance sheet at *historical cost* are translated at *historical* exchange rates to yield an equivalent historical cost in U.S. dollars.
2. Conversely, assets and liabilities carried at a *current or future value* are translated at the *current* exchange rate to yield an equivalent current value in U.S. dollars.

Application of this rule maintains the underlying valuation method (current value or historical cost) that the foreign subsidiary uses in accounting for its assets and liabilities. In addition, stockholders' equity accounts are translated at historical exchange rates.

Cash, marketable securities, receivables, and most liabilities are carried at current or future value and translated at the *current* exchange rate under the temporal method.[6] The temporal method generates either a net asset or a net liability balance sheet exposure, depending on whether cash plus marketable securities plus receivables are more than or less than liabilities.

Cash + Marketable securities + Receivables $>$ Liabilities $\rightarrow$ Net asset exposure

Cash + Marketable securities + Receivables $<$ Liabilities $\rightarrow$ Net liability exposure

Because liabilities (current plus long term) usually are more than assets translated at the current exchange rate, *a net liability exposure generally exists when the temporal method is used.*

One way to understand the concept of exposure underlying the temporal method is to pretend that the parent actually carries on its balance sheet the foreign operation's cash, marketable securities, receivables, and payables. For example, consider the Japanese subsidiary of a U.S. parent company. The Japanese subsidiary's yen receivables that result from sales in Japan may be thought of as Japanese yen receivables of the U.S. parent that result from export sales to Japan. If the U.S. parent had yen receivables on its balance sheet, a decrease in the yen's value would result in a *foreign exchange loss*. A foreign exchange loss also occurs on the Japanese yen held in cash by the U.S. parent and on the Japanese yen denominated marketable securities. A foreign exchange gain on the parent's Japanese yen payables resulting from foreign purchases would offset these foreign exchange losses. Whether a net gain or a net loss exists depends on the relative amount of yen cash, marketable securities, and receivables versus yen payables. Under the temporal method, the translation adjustment measures the "net foreign exchange gain or loss" on the foreign operation's cash, marketable securities, receivables, and payables, *as if those items were actually carried on the parent's books.*

Again, the major difference between the translation adjustment resulting from the use of the temporal method and a foreign exchange gain or loss is that the translation adjustment is not necessarily realized through inflows or outflows of cash. The U.S. dollar translation adjustment in this case *is realized* only if (1) the parent sends U.S. dollars to the Japanese subsidiary to pay all of its yen liabilities and (2) the subsidiary converts its yen receivables and marketable securities into yen cash and then sends this amount plus the amount in its yen cash account to the U.S. parent, which converts it into U.S. dollars.

The temporal method translates income statement items at exchange rates that exist when the revenue is generated or the expense is incurred. For most items, an assumption

[6] Under current authoritative literature, all marketable equity securities and marketable debt securities that are classified as "trading" or "available for sale" are carried at current market value. Marketable debt securities classified as "held to maturity" are carried at amortized cost. Throughout the remainder of this chapter, we will assume that all marketable securities are reported at current value.

EXHIBIT 10.1
Exchange Rates for Selected Financial Statement Items

	Temporal Method Exchange Rate	Current Rate Method Exchange Rate
	Balance Sheet	
Assets		
Cash and receivables	Current	Current
Marketable securities	Current*	Current
Inventory at market	Current	Current
Inventory at cost	Historical	Current
Prepaid expenses	Historical	Current
Property, plant, and equipment	Historical	Current
Intangible assets	Historical	Current
Liabilities		
Current liabilities	Current	Current
Deferred income	Historical	Current
Long-term debt	Current	Current
Stockholders' equity		
Capital stock	Historical	Historical
Additional paid-in capital	Historical	Historical
Retained earnings	Composite	Composite
Dividends	Historical	Historical
	Income Statement	
Revenues	Average	Average
Most expenses	Average	Average
Cost of goods sold	Historical	Average
Depreciation of property, plant, and equipment	Historical	Average
Amortization of intangibles	Historical	Average

*Marketable debt securities classified as held to maturity are carried at amortized cost and translated at the historical exchange rate under the temporal method.

can be made that the revenue or expense is incurred evenly throughout the accounting period and an average-for-the-period exchange rate can be used for translation. However, some expenses are related to assets carried at historical cost—for example, cost of goods sold, depreciation of fixed assets, and amortization of intangibles. Because the related assets are translated at historical exchange rates, these expenses must be translated at historical rates as well.

The current rate method and temporal method are the two methods currently used in the United States. They are also the predominant methods used worldwide. A summary of the appropriate exchange rate for selected financial statement items under these two methods is presented in Exhibit 10.1.

Translation of Retained Earnings

Stockholders' equity items are translated at historical exchange rates under both the temporal and current rate methods. This creates somewhat of a problem in translating retained earnings. This figure is actually a composite of many previous transactions: all revenues, expenses, gains, losses, and declared dividends occurring over the company's life. At the end of the first year of operations, foreign currency (FC) retained earnings (R/E) is translated as follows:

Net income in FC	[translated per method used to translate income statement items]	=	Net income in $
− Dividends in FC	× historical exchange rate when declared	=	− Dividends in $
Ending R/E in FC			Ending R/E in $

The ending dollar amount of retained earnings in Year 1 becomes the beginning dollar retained earnings for Year 2, and the translated retained earnings in Year 2 (and subsequent years) are then determined as follows:

Beginning R/E in FC	(from last year's translation)	=	Beginning R/E in $
+ Net income in FC	[translated per method used to translate income statement items]	=	+ Net income in $
− Dividends in FC	× historical exchange rate when declared	=	− Dividends in $
Ending R/E in FC			Ending R/E in $

The same approach translates retained earnings under both the current rate and the temporal methods. The only difference is that translation of the current period net income is calculated differently under the two methods.

Complicating Aspects of the Temporal Method

Under the temporal method, keeping a record of the exchange rates is necessary when acquiring inventory, prepaid expenses, fixed assets, and intangible assets because these assets, carried at historical cost, are translated at historical exchange rates. Keeping track of the historical rates for these assets is not necessary under the current rate method. Translating these assets at historical rates makes the application of the temporal method more complicated than the current rate method.

Calculation of Cost of Goods Sold

Under the *current rate method,* the account Cost of Goods Sold (COGS) in foreign currency (FC) is simply translated using the average-for-the-period exchange rate (ER):

COGS in FC × Average ER = COGS in $

Under the *temporal method,* COGS must be decomposed into beginning inventory, purchases, and ending inventory, and each component of COGS must then be translated at its appropriate historical rate. For example, if a company acquires beginning inventory (FIFO basis) in the year 2013 evenly throughout the fourth quarter of 2012, then it uses the average exchange rate in the fourth quarter of 2012 to translate beginning inventory. Likewise, it uses the fourth quarter (4thQ) 2013 exchange rate to translate ending inventory. When purchases can be assumed to have been made evenly throughout 2013, the average 2013 exchange rate is used to translate purchases:

Beginning inventory in FC	×	Historical ER (4thQ 2012)	=	Beginning inventory in $
+ Purchases in FC	×	Average ER (2013)	=	+ Purchases in $
− Ending inventory in FC	×	Historical ER (4thQ 2013)	=	− Ending inventory in $
COGS in FC				COGS in $

No single exchange rate can be used to directly translate COGS in FC into COGS in dollars.

Application of the Lower-of-Cost-or-Market Rule

Under the *current rate method,* the ending inventory reported on the foreign currency balance sheet is translated at the current exchange rate regardless of whether it is carried at cost or a lower market value. Application of the *temporal method* requires the inventory's foreign currency cost and foreign currency market value to be translated into U.S. dollars at appropriate exchange rates, and the *lower of the dollar cost and dollar market value* is reported on the consolidated balance sheet. As a result, inventory can be carried at cost on the foreign currency balance sheet and at market value on the U.S. dollar consolidated balance sheet, and vice versa.

Fixed Assets, Depreciation, and Accumulated Depreciation

The *temporal method* requires translating fixed assets acquired at different times at different (historical) exchange rates. The same is true for depreciation of fixed assets and accumulated depreciation related to fixed assets.

For example, assume that a company purchases a piece of equipment on January 1, 2012, for FC 1,000 when the exchange rate is $1.00 per FC. It purchases another item of equipment on January 1, 2013, for FC 5,000 when the exchange rate is $1.20 per FC. Both pieces of equipment have a five-year useful life. The temporal method reports the amount of the equipment on the consolidated balance sheet on December 31, 2014, when the exchange rate is $1.50 per FC, as follows:

FC 1,000	× $1.00 =	$1,000
5,000	× 1.20 =	6,000
FC 6,000		$7,000

Depreciation expense for 2014 under the temporal method is calculated as shown here:

FC 200	× $1.00 =	$ 200
1,000	× 1.20 =	1,200
FC 1,200		$1,400

Accumulated depreciation under the temporal method is calculated as shown:

FC 600	× $1.00 =	$ 600
2,000	× 1.20 =	2,400
FC 2,600		$3,000

Similar procedures apply for intangible assets as well.

The *current rate method* reports equipment on the December 31, 2014, balance sheet at FC 6,000 × $1.50 = $9,000. Depreciation expense is translated at the average exchange rate of $1.40, FC 1,200 × $1.40 = $1,680, and accumulated depreciation is FC 2,600 × $1.50 = $3,900.

In this example, the foreign subsidiary has only two fixed assets requiring translation. In comparison with the current rate method, the temporal method can require substantial additional work for subsidiaries that own hundreds and thousands of fixed assets.

Gain or Loss on the Sale of an Asset

Assume that a foreign subsidiary sells land that cost FC 1,000 at a selling price of FC 1,200. The subsidiary reports an FC 200 gain on the sale of land on its income statement. It acquired the land when the exchange rate was $1.00 per FC; it made the sale when the exchange rate was $1.20 per FC; and the exchange rate at the balance sheet date is $1.50 per FC.

The *current rate method* translates the gain on sale of land at the exchange rate in effect at the date of sale:

FC 200 × $1.20 = $240

The *temporal method* cannot translate the gain on the sale of land directly. Instead, it requires translating the cash received and the cost of the land sold into U.S. dollars separately, with the difference being the U.S. dollar value of the gain. In accordance with the rules of the temporal method, the Cash account is translated at the exchange rate on the date of sale, and the Land account is translated at the historical rate:

Cash	FC 1,200	× $1.20 =	$1,440
Land	1,000	× 1.00 =	1,000
Gain	FC 200		$ 440

Treatment of Translation Adjustment

The *first issue* related to the translation of foreign currency financial statements is selecting the appropriate method. The *second issue* in financial statement translation relates to deciding *where to report the resulting translation adjustment in the consolidated financial statements.* There are two prevailing schools of thought with regard to this issue:

1. *Translation gain or loss:* This treatment considers the translation adjustment to be a gain or loss analogous to the gains and losses arising from foreign currency transactions and reports it in net income in the period in which the fluctuation in the exchange rate occurs.

The first of two conceptual problems with treating translation adjustments as gains or losses in income is that the gain or loss is unrealized; that is, no cash inflow or outflow accompanies it. The second problem is that the gain or loss could be inconsistent with economic reality. For example, the depreciation of a foreign currency can have a *positive* impact on the foreign operation's export sales and income, but the particular translation method used gives rise to a translation *loss.*

2. *Cumulative translation adjustment in other comprehensive income:* The alternative to reporting the translation adjustment as a gain or loss in net income is to include it in Other Comprehensive Income. In effect, this treatment defers the gain or loss in stockholders' equity until it is realized in some way. As a balance sheet account, the cumulative translation adjustment is not closed at the end of an accounting period and fluctuates in amount over time.

The two major translation methods and the two possible treatments for the translation adjustment give rise to these four possible combinations:

Combination	Translation Method	Treatment of Translation Adjustment
A	Temporal	Gain or loss in Net Income
B	Temporal	Deferred in Other Comprehensive Income
C	Current rate	Gain or loss in Net Income
D	Current rate	Deferred in Other Comprehensive Income

U.S. Rules

Prior to 1975, the United States had no authoritative rules about which translation method to use or where to report the translation adjustment in the consolidated financial statements. Different companies used different combinations. As an indication of the importance of this particular accounting issue, the first official pronouncement issued by the newly created FASB in 1974 was *SFAS 1,* "Disclosure of Foreign Currency Translation Information." It did not express a preference for any particular combination but simply required disclosure of the method used and the treatment of the translation adjustment.

The use of different combinations by different companies created a lack of comparability across companies. To eliminate this noncomparability, in 1975 the FASB issued *SFAS 8,* "Accounting for the Translation of Foreign Currency Transactions and Foreign Currency Financial Statements." It mandated use of the *temporal method* with all companies reporting *translation gains or losses* in net income for all foreign operations (Combination A in the preceding table).

U.S. multinational companies (MNCs) strongly opposed *SFAS 8.* Specifically, they considered reporting translation gains and losses in income to be inappropriate because they are unrealized. Moreover, because currency fluctuations often reversed themselves in subsequent quarters, artificial volatility in quarterly earnings resulted.

After releasing two exposure drafts proposing new translation rules, the FASB finally issued *SFAS 52,* "Foreign Currency Translation," in 1981. This resulted in a complete overhaul of U.S. GAAP with regard to foreign currency translation. A narrow four-to-three vote of the board approving *SFAS 52* indicates how contentious the issue of foreign currency translation has been. Despite the narrow vote, *SFAS 52* has stood the test of time and was incorporated into the FASB Accounting Standards Codification (ASC) in 2009 as part of Topic 830 Foreign Currency Matters.

LO2

Describe guidelines as to when foreign currency financial statements are to be translated using the current rate method and when they are to be translated using the temporal method.

Two Translation Combinations

Implicit in the *temporal method* is the assumption that foreign subsidiaries of U.S. MNCs have very close ties to their parent companies and that they would actually carry out their day-to-day operations and keep their books in the U.S. dollar if they could. To reflect the integrated nature of the foreign subsidiary with its U.S. parent, the translation process should create a set of U.S. dollar–translated financial statements as if the foreign subsidiary had actually used the dollar in carrying out its activities. This is the *U.S. dollar perspective* to translation.

In developing the current rules, the FASB recognized two types of foreign entities. First, some foreign entities are so closely integrated with their parents that they conduct much of their business in U.S. dollars. *Second, other foreign entities are relatively self-contained and integrated with the local economy; primarily, they use a foreign currency in their daily operations.* For the first type of entity, the FASB determined that the U.S. dollar perspective still applies and, therefore, Combination A is still relevant.

For the second relatively independent type of entity, a *local currency perspective* to translation is applicable. For this type of entity, the FASB determined that a different translation methodology, namely the *current rate method,* should be used for translation and that translation adjustments should be reported as a *separate component in other comprehensive income* (Combination D on the previous page). In addition, the FASB requires using the *average-for-the-period* exchange rate to translate income when the current rate method is used.

In rationalizing the placement of the translation adjustment in stockholders' equity rather than net income, the FASB offered two contrasting positions on the conceptual nature of the translation adjustment. One view is that the "change in the dollar equivalent of the net investment is an unrealized enhancement or reduction, having no effect on the functional currency net cash flow generated by the foreign entity which may be currently reinvested or distributed to the parent." Philosophically, this position holds that even though changes in the exchange rate create gains and losses, they are unrealized in nature and should, therefore, not be included within net income.

The alternative perspective put forth by the FASB "regards the translation adjustment as merely a mechanical by-product of the translation process." This second contention argues that exchange rate fluctuation creates no meaningful effect; the resulting translation adjustment merely serves to keep the balance sheet in equilibrium.

Interestingly enough, the FASB chose not to express preference for either of these theoretical views. The board felt no need to offer a hint of guidance as to the essential nature of the translation adjustment because both explanations point to its exclusion from net income. Thus, a balance sheet figure that can amount to millions of dollars is basically undefined by the FASB.

Functional Currency

To determine whether a specific foreign operation is integrated with its parent or self-contained and integrated with the local economy, the FASB created the concept of the *functional currency.* The functional currency is the primary currency of the foreign entity's operating environment. It can be either the parent's currency (U.S.$) or a foreign currency (generally the local currency). The functional currency orientation results in the following rule:

Functional Currency	Translation Method	Translation Adjustment
U.S. dollar	Temporal method	Gain (loss) in Net Income
Foreign currency	Current rate method	Separate component of Other Comprehensive Income (Stockholders' Equity)

EXHIBIT 10.2
Indicators for Determining the Functional Currency

	Indication That Functional Currency Is the	
Indicator	**Foreign Currency**	**Parent's Currency**
Cash flow	Primarily in FC and does not affect parent's cash flows	Directly impacts parent's cash flows on a current basis
Sales price	Not affected on short-term basis by changes in exchange rate	Affected on short-term basis by changes in exchange rate
Sales market	Active local sales market	Sales market mostly in parent's country or sales denominated in parent's currency
Expenses	Primarily local costs	Primarily costs for components obtained from parent's country
Financing	Primarily denominated in foreign currency and FC cash flows adequate to service obligations	Primarily from parent or denominated in parent currency or FC cash flows not adequate to service obligations
Intra-entity transactions	Low volume of intra-entity transactions, not extensive interrelationship with parent's operations	High volume of intra-entity transactions and extensive interrelationship with parent's operations

In addition to introducing the concept of the *functional currency,* the FASB introduced some new terminology. The *reporting currency* is the currency in which the entity prepares its financial statements. For U.S.–based corporations, this is the U.S. dollar. If a foreign operation's functional currency is the U.S. dollar, foreign currency balances must be *remeasured* into U.S. dollars using the temporal method with translation adjustments reported as *remeasurement gains and losses* in income. When a foreign currency is the functional currency, foreign currency balances are *translated* using the current rate method and a *translation adjustment* is reported on the balance sheet.

The functional currency is essentially a matter of fact. However, in some cases the facts will not clearly indicate a single functional currency. Management's judgment is essential in assessing the facts to determine the functional currency. Indicators to guide parent company management in its determination of a foreign entity's functional currency are presented in Exhibit 10.2. Current authoritative literature provides no guidance as to how to weight these indicators in determining the functional currency. Leaving the decision about identifying the functional currency up to management allows some leeway in this process.

Research has shown that the weighting schemes used by U.S. multinationals to determine the functional currency might be biased toward selection of the *foreign currency* as the functional currency.[7] This would be rational behavior for multinationals because, when the foreign currency is the functional currency, the translation adjustment is reported in stockholders' equity and does not affect net income.

Highly Inflationary Economies

Multinationals do not need to determine the functional currency of those foreign entities located in a *highly inflationary economy.* In those cases, entities must use the *temporal method with remeasurement gains or losses reported in income.*

A country is defined as having a *highly inflationary economy* when its cumulative three-year inflation exceeds 100 percent. With compounding, this equates to an average of approximately 26 percent per year for three years in a row. Countries that have met this definition at some time include Argentina, Brazil, Israel, Mexico, and Turkey. In any given year, a country may or may not be classified as highly inflationary, depending on its most recent three-year experience with inflation.

[7] Timothy S. Doupnik and Thomas G. Evans, "Functional Currency as a Strategy to Smooth Income," *Advances in International Accounting*, 1988.

One reason for this rule is to avoid a "disappearing plant problem" caused by using the current rate method in a country with high inflation. Remember that under the current rate method, all assets (including fixed assets) are translated at the current exchange rate. To see the problem this creates in a highly inflationary economy, consider the following hypothetical example.

The Brazilian subsidiary of a U.S. parent purchased land at the end of 1984 for 10,000,000 cruzeiros (Cr$) when the exchange rate was $0.001 per Cr$. Under the *current rate method,* the land is reported in the parent's consolidated balance sheet (B.S.) at $10,000:

	Historical Cost		Current ER		Consolidated B.S.
1984	Cr$ 10,000,000	×	$0.001	=	$10,000

In 1985, Brazil experienced roughly 200 percent inflation. Accordingly, with the forces of purchasing power parity at work, the cruzeiro plummeted against the U.S. dollar to a value of $0.00025 at the end of 1985. Under the current rate method, the parent's consolidated balance sheet reports land at $2,500, and a negative translation adjustment of $7,500 results:

1985 Cr$ 10,000,000 × $0.00025 = $2,500

Using the current rate method, the land has lost 75 percent of its U.S. dollar value in one year—and land is not even a depreciable asset!

In the exposure draft leading to the current authoritative guidance on translation, the FASB proposed requiring companies with operations in highly inflationary countries to first *restate* the historical costs for inflation and then *translate* using the current rate method. For example, with 200 percent inflation in 1985, the Land account would have been written up to Cr$ 40,000,000 and then translated at the current exchange rate of $0.00025, producing a translated amount of $10,000, the same as in 1984.

Companies objected to making inflation adjustments, however, because of a lack of reliable inflation indices in many countries. The FASB backed off from requiring the *restate/translate* approach; instead it requires using the temporal method in highly inflationary countries. In the previous example, under the *temporal method,* a firm uses the historical rate of $0.001 to translate the land value year after year. The firm carries land on the consolidated balance sheet at $10,000 each year, thereby avoiding the disappearing plant problem.

Once a country is classified as highly inflationary, a decrease in the cumulative three-year inflation rate below 100 percent is not necessarily sufficient to remove it from this classification. FASB ASC 830-10-55-25 and the SEC staff suggest that if there is no evidence to suggest that the drop below 100 percent is "other than temporary," the country should continue to be viewed as highly inflationary. The magnitude of the decrease below 100 percent, the length of time the rate is under 100 percent, and the country's current economic conditions should be taken into account in the "other than temporary" analysis.

Currently, there are few countries in the world that meet the FASB's definition of highly inflationary. Arguably the most significant country exceeding this threshold is Venezuela, which was deemed to be highly inflationary in January 2010.[8] Many U.S. companies, especially those in the energy industry, have subsidiaries in Venezuela. In 2010, those U.S. parent companies that previously designated their Venezuelan operation as having the local currency as functional currency, and therefore used the current rate method for translation, were compelled to change their translation method to the temporal method.

[8] The International Practices Task Force (IPTF) of the Center for Audit Quality (CAQ) SEC Regulations Committee monitors the inflationary status of certain countries and identifies those that meet the FASB's definition of highly inflationary.

Appropriate Exchange Rate

In some countries, such as Venezuela, there is more than one rate at which the local currency can be converted into foreign currency. Often there is an "official rate" that is available from the Central Bank, and a "parallel rate" that is available in the open (sometimes illegal) market. Or in some countries there is one rate for certain types of products and another rate for other products. For example, in January 2010, in conjunction with an official devaluation of the local currency, the Venezuelan government established an exchange rate of 2.6 bolivar fuertes (BsF) per one U.S. dollar for essential imports (such as food and medicine), and an exchange rate of BsF 4.3 per U.S.$ for the import of nonessential goods. The existence of multiple exchange rates raises the question of which exchange rate to use in the financial statement translation process.

When the temporal method is used, ASC 830-20-30-3 indicates that the appropriate rate to use is the applicable rate at which a transaction could be settled, which is a matter for management judgment. In the case of Venezuela, for example, the Center for Audit Quality's International Practices Task Force (IPTF) determined that while Venezuelan law generally requires foreign currency transactions to be settled at the official exchange rate, because some transactions denominated in U.S. dollars may be settled using the parallel rate of exchange, either exchange rate might be appropriate for the translation of US$-denominated assets and liabilities.

In contrast, when the current rate method is used, ASC 830-30-45-6 states that the exchange rate applicable for converting dividend remittances into U.S. dollars should be used to translate financial statements. Generally, this will be the official rate established by the Central Bank or other governmental authority.

The Process Illustrated

To provide a basis for demonstrating the translation and remeasurement procedures prescribed by current authoritative literature, assume that USCO (a U.S.–based company) forms a wholly owned subsidiary in Switzerland (SWISSCO) on December 31, 2012. On that date, USCO invested $300,000 in exchange for all of the subsidiary's common stock. Given the exchange rate of $0.60 per Swiss franc (CHF), the initial capital investment was CHF 500,000, of which CHF 150,000 was immediately invested in inventory and the remainder held in cash. Thus, SWISSCO began operations on January 1, 2013, with stockholders' equity (net assets) of CHF 500,000 and net monetary assets of CHF 350,000.

SWISSCO
Opening Balance Sheet
January 1, 2013

Assets	CHF	Liabilities and Equity	CHF
Cash	CHF 350,000	Common stock	CHF 100,000
Inventory	150,000	Additional paid-in capital	400,000
	CHF 500,000		CHF 500,000

During 2013, SWISSCO purchased property and equipment, acquired a patent, and purchased additional inventory, primarily on account. It negotiated a five-year loan to help finance the purchase of equipment. It sold goods, primarily on account, and incurred expenses. It generated income after taxes of CHF 470,000 and declared dividends of CHF 150,000 on October 1, 2013.

As a company incorporated in Switzerland, SWISSCO must account for its activities using Swiss accounting rules, which differ from U.S. GAAP in many respects. As noted in the introduction to this chapter, to prepare consolidated financial statements, USCO must first convert SWISSCO's financial statements to a U.S. GAAP basis.[9] SWISSCO's U.S. GAAP financial statements for the year 2013 in Swiss francs appear in Exhibit 10.3.

[9] Differences in accounting rules across countries are discussed in more detail in Chapter 11.

EXHIBIT 10.3
Foreign Currency Financial Statements

SWISSCO
Income Statement
For Year Ending December 31, 2013

	CHF
Sales	4,000,000
Cost of goods sold	(3,000,000)
Gross profit	1,000,000
Depreciation expense	(100,000)
Amortization expense	(10,000)
Other expenses	(220,000)
Income before income taxes	670,000
Income taxes	(200,000)
Net income	470,000

Statement of Retained Earnings
For Year Ending December 31, 2013

	CHF
Retained earnings, 1/1/13	–0–
Net income, 2013	470,000
Less: Dividends, 10/1/13	(150,000)
Retained earnings, 12/31/13	320,000

Balance Sheet
December 31, 2013

Assets	CHF	Liabilities and Equity	CHF
Cash	130,000	Accounts payable	600,000
Accounts receivable	200,000	Total current liabilities	600,000
Inventory*	400,000	Long-term debt	250,000
Total current assets	730,000	Total liabilities	850,000
Property and equipment	1,000,000	Common stock	100,000
Accumulated depreciation	(100,000)	Additional paid-in capital	400,000
Patents, net	40,000	Retained earnings	320,000
Total assets	1,670,000	Total equity	820,000
		Total liabilities and equity	1,670,000

*Inventory is valued at FIFO cost under the lower-of-cost-or-market-value rule; ending inventory was acquired evenly throughout the fourth quarter.

Statement of Cash Flows
For Year Ending December 31, 2013

	CHF
Operating activities:	
Net income	470,000
Add: Depreciation expense	100,000
Amortization expense	10,000
Increase in accounts receivable	(200,000)
Increase in inventory	(250,000)
Increase in accounts payable	600,000
Net cash from operations	730,000
Investing activities:	
Purchase of property and equipment	(1,000,000)
Acquisition of patent	(50,000)
Net cash from investing activities	(1,050,000)
Financing activities:	
Proceeds from long-term debt	250,000
Payment of dividends	(150,000)
Net cash from financing activities	100,000
Decrease in cash	(220,000)
Cash at 12/31/12	350,000
Cash at 12/31/13	130,000

To properly translate the Swiss franc financial statements into U.S. dollars, USCO must gather exchange rates between the Swiss franc and U.S. dollar at various points in time. Relevant exchange rates (in U.S. dollars) are as follows:

January 1, 2013	$0.60
Rate when property and equipment were acquired and long-term debt was incurred, March 15, 2013	0.61
Rate when patent was acquired, April 10, 2013	0.62
Average 2013	0.65
Rate when dividends were declared, October 1, 2013	0.67
Average fourth quarter 2013	0.68
December 31, 2013	0.70

As you can see, the Swiss franc steadily appreciated against the dollar during the year.

Translation of Financial Statements—Current Rate Method

LO3

Translate a foreign subsidiary's financial statements into its parent's reporting currency using the current rate method and calculate the related translation adjustment.

The first step in translating foreign currency financial statements is to determine the functional currency. Assuming that the Swiss franc is the functional currency, the income statement and statement of retained earnings are translated into U.S. dollars using the current rate method as shown in Exhibit 10.4.

All revenues and expenses are translated at the exchange rate in effect at the date of accounting recognition. We utilize the weighted average exchange rate for 2013 here because each revenue and expense in this illustration would have been recognized evenly throughout the year. However, when an income account, such as a gain or loss, occurs at a specific point in time, the exchange rate as of that date is applied. Depreciation and amortization expenses also are translated at the average rate for the year. These expenses accrue evenly throughout the year even though the journal entry could have been delayed until year-end for convenience.

EXHIBIT 10.4
Translation of Income Statement and Statement of Retained Earnings—Current Rate Method

SWISSCO
Income Statement
For Year Ending December 31, 2013

	CHF	Translation Rate*	US$
Sales	CHF 4,000,000	0.65 A	$ 2,600,000
Cost of goods sold	(3,000,000)	0.65 A	(1,950,000)
Gross profit	1,000,000		650,000
Depreciation expense	(100,000)	0.65 A	(65,000)
Amortization expense	(10,000)	0.65 A	(6,500)
Other expenses	(220,000)	0.65 A	(143,000)
Income before income taxes	670,000		435,500
Income taxes	(200,000)	0.65 A	(130,000)
Net income	CHF 470,000		$ 305,500

Statement of Retained Earnings
For Year Ending December 31, 2013

	CHF	Translation Rate*	US$
Retained earnings, 1/1/13	CHF -0-		$ -0-
Net income, 2013	470,000	Above	305,500
Dividends, 10/1/13	(150,000)	0.67 H	(100,500)
Retained earnings, 12/31/13	CHF 320,000		$ 205,000

*Indicates the exchange rate used and whether the rate is the current (C), average (A), or a historical (H) rate.

EXHIBIT 10.5
Translation of Balance Sheet—Current Rate Method

SWISSCO
Balance Sheet
December 31, 2013

	CHF	Translation Rate	US$
Assets			
Cash	CHF 130,000	0.70 C	$ 91,000
Accounts receivable	200,000	0.70 C	140,000
Inventory	400,000	0.70 C	280,000
Total current assets	730,000		511,000
Property and equipment	1,000,000	0.70 C	700,000
Less: Accumulated depreciation	(100,000)	0.70 C	(70,000)
Patents, net	40,000	0.70 C	28,000
Total assets	CHF 1,670,000		$1,169,000
Liabilities and Equities			
Accounts payable	CHF 600,000	0.70 C	$ 420,000
Total current liabilities	600,000		420,000
Long-term debt	250,000	0.70 C	175,000
Total liabilities	850,000		595,000
Common stock	100,000	0.60 H	60,000
Additional paid-in capital	400,000	0.60 H	240,000
Retained earnings	320,000	Above	205,000
Cumulative translation adjustment		To balance	69,000
Total equity	820,000		574,000
Total liabilities and equity	CHF 1,670,000		$1,169,000

The translated amount of net income for 2013 is brought down from the income statement into the statement of retained earnings. Dividends are translated at the exchange rate on the date of declaration.

Translation of the Balance Sheet

Looking at SWISSCO's translated balance sheet in Exhibit 10.5, note that all assets and liabilities are translated at the current exchange rate. Common stock and additional paid-in capital are translated at the exchange rate on the day the common stock was originally sold. Retained earnings at December 31, 2013, is brought down from the statement of retained earnings. Application of these procedures results in total assets of $1,169,000 and total liabilities and equities of $1,100,000. The balance sheet is brought into balance by creating a positive translation adjustment of $69,000 that is treated as an increase in Stockholders' Equity.

Note that the translation adjustment for 2013 is a *positive* $69,000 (credit balance). The sign of the translation adjustment (positive or negative) is a function of two factors: (1) the nature of the balance sheet exposure (asset or liability) and (2) the change in the exchange rate (appreciation or depreciation). In this illustration, SWISSCO has a *net asset exposure* (total assets translated at the current exchange rate are more than total liabilities translated at the current exchange rate), and the Swiss franc has *appreciated,* creating a *positive translation adjustment.*

The translation adjustment can be derived as the amount needed to bring the balance sheet back into balance. The translation adjustment also can be calculated by considering the impact of exchange rate changes on the beginning balance and subsequent changes in the net asset position summarized as follows:

1. Translate the net asset balance of the subsidiary at the beginning of the year at the exchange rate in effect on that date (*a*).
2. Translate individual increases and decreases in the net asset balance during the year at the rates in effect when those increases and decreases occurred (*b*). Only a few events,

such as net income, dividends, stock issuance, and the acquisition of treasury stock, actually change net assets. Transactions such as the acquisition of equipment or the payment of a liability have no effect on total net assets.

3. Combine the translated beginning net asset balance (*a*) and the translated value of the individual changes (*b*) to arrive at the relative value of the net assets being held prior to the impact of any exchange rate fluctuations during the year (*c*).
4. Translate the ending net asset balance at the current exchange rate to determine the reported value after all exchange rate changes have occurred (*d*).
5. Compare the translated value of the net assets prior to any rate changes (*c*) with the ending translated value (*d*). The difference is the result of exchange rate changes during the period. If (*c*) is higher than (*d*), a negative (debit) translation adjustment arises. If (*d*) is higher than (*c*), a positive (credit) translation adjustment results.

Computation of Translation Adjustment

Based on the process just described, the translation adjustment for SWISSCO in this example is calculated as follows:

Net asset balance, 1/1/13	CHF 500,000	×	0.60	=	$ 300,000	(*a*)
Change in net assets:						
Net income, 2013	470,000	×	0.65	=	305,500	(*b*)
Dividends declared, 10/1/13	(150,000)	×	0.67	=	(100,500)	(*b*)
Net asset balance, 12/31/13	CHF 820,000				$ 505,000	(*c*)
Net asset balance, 12/31/13 at current exchange rate	CHF 820,000	×	0.70	=	574,000	(*d*)
Translation adjustment, 2013 (positive)					$ (69,000)	

The process described and demonstrated above is used to calculate the current period's translation adjustment. Because SWISSCO began operations at the beginning of the current year, the $69,000 translation adjustment is the only amount that will be needed to keep the U.S. dollar consolidated balance sheet in balance. In subsequent years, a cumulative translation adjustment comprised of the current year's translation adjustment plus translation adjustments from prior years will be included in stockholders' equity on the U.S. dollar consolidated balance sheet. Most companies report the cumulative translation adjustment in Accumulated Other Comprehensive Income, along with unrealized foreign exchange gains and losses, gains and losses on cash flow hedges, unrealized gains and losses on available-for-sale marketable securities, and adjustments for pension accounting.

The cumulative translation adjustment is carried in accumulated other comprehensive income only until the foreign operation is sold or liquidated. In the period in which sale or liquidation occurs, the cumulative translation adjustment related to the particular entity is removed from accumulated other comprehensive income and included as part of the gain or loss on the sale of the investment. In effect, the accumulated unrealized foreign exchange gain or loss that has been deferred in accumulated other comprehensive income becomes realized when the entity is disposed of.

Translation of the Statement of Cash Flows

The current rate method requires translating all operating items in the statement of cash flows at the average-for-the-period exchange rate (see Exhibit 10.6). This is the same rate used for translating income statement items. Although the ending balances in Accounts Receivable, Inventory, and Accounts Payable on the balance sheet are translated at the current exchange rate, the average rate is used for the *changes* in these accounts because those changes are caused by operating activities (such as sales and purchases) that are translated at the average rate.

Investing and financing activities are translated at the exchange rate on the day the activity took place. Although long-term debt is translated in the balance sheet at the current rate, in the statement of cash flows, it is translated at the historical rate when the debt was incurred.

EXHIBIT 10.6
Translated Statement of Cash Flows—Current Rate Method

SWISSCO
Statement of Cash Flows
For Year Ending December 31, 2013

	CHF	Translation Rate	US$
Operating activities:			
Net income.	CHF 470,000	0.65 A	$ 305,500
Add: Depreciation.	100,000	0.65 A	65,000
Amortization	10,000	0.65 A	6,500
Increase in accounts receivable	(200,000)	0.65 A	(130,000)
Increase in inventory.	(250,000)	0.65 A	(162,500)
Increase in accounts payable.	600,000	0.65 A	390,000
Net cash from operations	730,000		474,500
Investing activities:			
Purchase of property and equipment . . .	(1,000,000)	0.61 H	(610,000)
Acquisition of patent	(50,000)	0.62 H	(31,000)
Net cash from investing activities.	(1,050,000)		(641,000)
Financing activities:			
Proceeds from long-term debt	250,000	0.61 H	152,500
Payment of dividends	(150,000)	0.67 H	(100,500)
Net cash from financing activities	100,000		52,000
Decrease in cash.	(220,000)		(114,500)
Effect of exchange rate change on cash.		To balance	(4,500)
Cash at December 31, 2012.	CHF 350,000	0.60 H	210,000
Cash at December 31, 2013.	CHF 130,000	0.70 C	$ 91,000

The $(4,500) "effect of exchange rate change on cash" is a part of the overall translation adjustment of $69,000. It represents that part of the translation adjustment attributable to a decrease in Cash and is derived as a balancing amount.

Remeasurement of Financial Statements—Temporal Method

LO4

Remeasure a foreign subsidiary's financial statements using the temporal method and calculate the associated remeasurement gain or loss.

Now assume that a careful examination of the functional currency indicators in Exhibit 10.2 leads USCO's management to conclude that SWISSCO's functional currency is the U.S. dollar. In that case, the Swiss franc financial statements must be remeasured into U.S. dollars using the temporal method and the remeasurement gain or loss reported in income. To ensure that the remeasurement gain or loss is reported in income, it is easiest to remeasure the balance sheet first (as shown in Exhibit 10.7).

According to the procedures outlined in Exhibit 10.1, the temporal method remeasures cash, receivables, and liabilities into U.S. dollars using the current exchange rate of $0.70. Inventory (carried at FIFO cost), property and equipment, patents, and the contributed capital accounts (Common Stock and Additional Paid-In Capital) are remeasured at historical rates. These procedures result in total assets of $1,076,800 and liabilities and contributed capital of $895,000. To balance the balance sheet, Retained Earnings must total $181,800. We verify the accuracy of this amount later.

Remeasurement of the Income Statement

Exhibit 10.8 shows the remeasurement of SWISSCO's income statement and statement of retained earnings. Revenues and expenses incurred evenly throughout the year (sales, other expenses, and income taxes) are remeasured at the average exchange rate of $0.65. Expenses related to assets remeasured at historical exchange rates (depreciation expense and amortization expense) are remeasured at relevant historical rates.

EXHIBIT 10.7
Remeasurement of Balance Sheet—Temporal Method

SWISSCO
Balance Sheet
December 31, 2013

	CHF	Remeasurement Rate	US$
Assets			
Cash	CHF 130,000	0.70 C	$ 91,000
Accounts receivable	200,000	0.70 C	140,000
Inventory	400,000	0.68 H	272,000
Total current assets	730,000		503,000
Property and equipment	1,000,000	0.61 H	610,000
Less: Accumulated depreciation	(100,000)	0.61 H	(61,000)
Patents, net	40,000	0.62 H	24,800
Total assets	CHF 1,670,000		$1,076,800
Liabilities and Equities			
Accounts payable	CHF 600,000	0.70 C	$ 420,000
Total current liabilities	600,000		420,000
Long-term debt	250,000	0.70 C	175,000
Total liabilities	850,000		595,000
Common stock	100,000	0.60 H	60,000
Additional paid-in capital	400,000	0.60 H	240,000
Retained earnings	320,000	To balance	181,800
Total equity	820,000		481,800
Total liabilities and equity	CHF 1,670,000		$1,076,800

The following procedure remeasures cost of goods sold at historical exchange rates. Beginning inventory acquired on January 1 is remeasured at the exchange rate on that date ($0.60). Purchases made evenly throughout the year are remeasured at the average rate for the year ($0.65). Ending inventory (at FIFO cost) is purchased evenly throughout the fourth quarter of 2013 and the average exchange rate for the quarter ($0.68) is used

EXHIBIT 10.8
Remeasurement of Income Statement and Statement of Retained Earnings—Temporal Method

SWISSCO
Income Statement
For Year Ending December 31, 2013

	CHF	Remeasurement Rate	US$
Sales	CHF 4,000,000	0.65 A	$ 2,600,000
Cost of goods sold	(3,000,000)	Calculation	(1,930,500)
Gross profit	1,000,000		669,500
Depreciation expense	(100,000)	0.61 H	(61,000)
Amortization expense	(10,000)	0.62 H	(6,200)
Other expenses	(220,000)	0.65 A	(143,000)
Income before income taxes	670,000		459,300
Income taxes	(200,000)	0.65 A	(130,000)
Remeasurement Loss		To balance	(47,000)
Net income	CHF 470,000	Below	$ 282,300

Statement of Retained Earnings
For Year Ending December 31, 2013

	CHF	Remeasurement Rate	US$
Retained earnings, 1/1/13	CHF -0-		$ -0-
Net income, 2013	470,000	To balance	282,300
Dividends	(150,000)	0.67 H	(100,500)
Retained earnings, 12/31/13	CHF 320,000	Above	$ 181,800

to remeasure that component of cost of goods sold. These procedures result in Cost of Goods Sold of $1,930,500, calculated as follows:

Beginning inventory, 1/1/13	CHF 150,000	×	0.60	=	$ 90,000
Plus: Purchases, 2013	3,250,000	×	0.65	=	2,112,500
Less: Ending inventory, 12/31/13	(400,000)	×	0.68	=	(272,000)
Cost of goods sold, 2013	CHF 3,000,000				$1,930,500

The ending balances in Retained Earnings on the balance sheet and on the statement of retained earnings must reconcile with one another. Because dividends are remeasured into a U.S. dollar equivalent of $100,500 and the ending balance in Retained Earnings on the balance sheet is $181,800, net income must be $282,300.

Reconciling the amount of income reported in the statement of retained earnings and in the income statement requires a remeasurement loss of $47,000 in calculating net income. Without this remeasurement loss, the income statement, statement of retained earnings, and balance sheet are not consistent with one another.

The remeasurement loss can be calculated by considering the impact of exchange rate changes on the subsidiary's balance sheet exposure. Under the temporal method, SWISSCO's balance sheet exposure is defined by its net monetary asset or net monetary liability position. SWISSCO began 2013 with net monetary assets (cash) of CHF 350,000. During the year, however, expenditures of cash and the incurrence of liabilities caused monetary liabilities (accounts payable + long-term debt = CHF 850,000) to exceed monetary assets (cash + accounts receivable = CHF 330,000). A net monetary liability position of CHF 520,000 exists at December 31, 2013. The remeasurement loss is computed by translating the beginning net monetary asset position and subsequent changes in monetary items at appropriate exchange rates and then comparing this with the dollar value of net monetary liabilities at year-end based on the current exchange rate:

Computation of Remeasurement Loss

Net monetary assets, 1/1/13	CHF 350,000	×	0.60	=	$ 210,000
Increase in monetary assets:					
Sales, 2013	4,000,000	×	0.65	=	2,600,000
Decreases in monetary assets and increases in monetary liabilities:					
Purchases, 2013	(3,250,000)	×	0.65	=	(2,112,500)
Other expenses, 2013	(220,000)	×	0.65	=	(143,000)
Income taxes, 2013	(200,000)	×	0.65	=	(130,000)
Purchase of property and equipment, 3/15/13	(1,000,000)	×	0.61	=	(610,000)
Acquisition of patent, 4/10/13	(50,000)	×	0.62	=	(31,000)
Dividends, 10/1/13	(150,000)	×	0.67	=	(100,500)
Net monetary liabilities, 12/31/13	CHF (520,000)				$ (317,000)
Net monetary liabilities, 12/31/11 at the current exchange rate	CHF (520,000)	×	0.70	=	(364,000)
Remeasurement loss					$ 47,000

Had SWISSCO maintained its net monetary asset position of CHF 350,000 for the entire year, a $35,000 remeasurement gain would have resulted. The CHF held in cash was worth $210,000 (CHF 350,000 × $0.60) at the beginning of the year and $245,000 (CHF 350,000 × $0.70) at year-end. However, the net monetary asset position is not maintained because of changes during the year in monetary items other than the original cash balance. Indeed, a net monetary liability position arises. The foreign currency *appreciation* coupled with an increase in *net monetary liabilities* generates a *remeasurement loss* for the year.

Remeasurement of the Statement of Cash Flows

In remeasuring the statement of cash flows (shown in Exhibit 10.9), the U.S. dollar value for net income comes directly from the remeasured income statement. Depreciation and

EXHIBIT 10.9
Remeasurement of Statement of Cash Flows—Temporal Method

SWISSCO
Statement of Cash Flows
For Year Ending December 31, 2013

	CHF	Remeasurement Rate	US$
Operating activities:			
Net income	CHF 470,000	From I/S	$ 282,300
Add: Depreciation expense	100,000	0.61 H	61,000
Amortization expense	10,000	0.62 H	6,200
Remeasurement loss		From I/S	47,000
Increase in accounts receivable	(200,000)	0.65 A	(130,000)
Increase in inventory	(250,000)	*	(182,000)
Increase in accounts payable	600,000	0.65 A	390,000
Net cash from operations	730,000		474,500
Investing activities:			
Purchase of property and equipment	(1,000,000)	0.61 H	(610,000)
Acquisition of patent	(50,000)	0.62 H	(31,000)
Net cash from investing activities	(1,050,000)		(641,000)
Financing activities:			
Proceeds from long-term debt	250,000	0.61 H	152,500
Payment of dividends	(150,000)	0.67 H	(100,500)
Net cash from financing activities	100,000		52,000
Decrease in cash	(220,000)		(114,500)
Effect of exchange rate changes on cash		To balance	(4,500)
Cash at December 31, 2012	CHF 350,000	0.60 H	$ 210,000
Cash at December 31, 2013	CHF 130,000	0.70 C	$ 91,000

*In remeasuring cost of goods sold earlier, beginning inventory was remeasured as $90,000 and ending inventory was remeasured as $272,000: an increase of $182,000.

amortization are remeasured at the rates used in the income statement, and the remeasurement loss is added back to net income because it is a noncash item. The increases in accounts receivable and accounts payable relate to sales and purchases and therefore are remeasured at the average rate. The U.S. dollar value for the increase in inventory is determined by referring to the remeasurement of the cost of goods sold.

The resulting U.S. dollar amount of "net cash from operations" ($474,500) is exactly the same as when the current rate method was used in translation. In addition, the investing and financing activities are translated in the same manner under both methods. This makes sense; the amount of cash inflows and outflows is a matter of fact and is not affected by the particular translation methodology employed.

Nonlocal Currency Balances

One additional issue related to the translation of foreign currency financial statements needs to be considered. How should a company deal with nonlocal currency balances in the foreign currency financial statements of their foreign operations? For example, if any of the accounts of the Swiss subsidiary are denominated in a currency other than the Swiss franc, those balances would first have to be restated into francs in accordance with the rules discussed in Chapter 9. Both the foreign currency balance and any related foreign exchange gain or loss would then be translated (or remeasured) into U.S. dollars.

For example, assume that SWISSCO borrows 100,000 euros on January 1, 2013. Exchange rates in 2013 between the Swiss franc (CHF) and euro (€) and between the CHF and U.S. dollar ($) are as follows:

	CHF per €	$ per CHF
January 1, 2013	CHF 1.20	$0.60
Average, 2013	CHF 1.22	$0.65
December 31, 2013	CHF 1.25	$0.70

On December 31, 2013, SWISSCO remeasures the €100,000 note payable into CHF using the current rate as follows: €100,000 × CHF 1.25 = CHF 125,000. SWISSCO also recognizes a CHF 5,000 [€100,000 × (CHF 1.25 − CHF 1.20)] foreign exchange loss. To consolidate SWISSCO's CHF financial statements with those of its parent, the note payable remeasured in CHF is then translated into $ using the current exchange rate and the related foreign exchange loss in CHF is translated into $ using the average exchange rate as follows:

Note payable	CHF 125,000 × $0.70 C = $87,500
Foreign exchange loss	CHF 5,000 × $0.65 A = $3,250

A note payable of $87,500 will be reported on the consolidated balance sheet and a loss of $3,250 will be reflected in the measurement of consolidated net income.

Comparison of the Results from Applying the Two Different Methods

LO1

Explain the theoretical underpinnings and the limitations of the current rate and temporal methods.

The determination of the foreign subsidiary's functional currency (and the use of different translation methods) can have a significant impact on consolidated financial statements. The following chart shows differences for SWISSCO in several key items under the two different translation methods:

	Translation Method		
Item	**Current Rate**	**Temporal**	**Difference**
Net income	$ 305,500	$ 282,300	+ 8.2%
Total assets	1,169,000	1,076,800	+ 8.6
Total equity	574,000	481,800	+19.1
Return on equity	53.2%	58.6%	− 9.2

In this illustration, if the Swiss franc is determined to be SWISSCO's functional currency (and the current rate method is applied), net income reported in the consolidated income statement would be 8.2 percent more than if the U.S. dollar is the functional currency (and the temporal method is applied). In addition, total assets would be 8.6 percent more and total equity would be 19.1 percent more using the current rate method. Because of the larger amount of equity, return on equity using the current rate method is 9.2 percent less.

Note that the current rate method does not always result in higher net income and a higher amount of equity than the temporal method. For example, had SWISSCO maintained its net monetary asset position, it would have computed a remeasurement gain under the temporal method leading to higher income than under the current rate method. Moreover, if the Swiss franc had depreciated during 2013, the temporal method would have resulted in higher net income.

The important point is that determining the functional currency and resulting translation method can have a significant impact on the amounts a parent company reports in its consolidated financial statements. The appropriate determination of the functional currency is an important issue.

> "Within rather broad parameters," says Peat, Marwick, Mitchell partner James Weir, choosing the functional currency is basically a management call. So much so, in fact, that Texaco, Occidental, and Unocal settled on the dollar as the functional currency for most of their foreign operations, whereas competitors Exxon, Mobil, and Amoco chose primarily the local currencies as the functional currencies for their foreign businesses.[10]

Different functional currencies selected by different companies in the same industry could have a significant impact on the comparability of financial statements within that industry. Indeed, one concern that those FASB members dissenting on the current

[10] John Heins, "Plenty of Opportunity to Fool Around," *Forbes*, June 2, 1986, p. 139.

standard raised was that the functional currency rules might not result in similar accounting for similar situations.

In addition to differences in amounts reported in the consolidated financial statements, the results of the SWISSCO illustration demonstrate several conceptual differences between the two translation methods.

Underlying Valuation Method

Using the temporal method, SWISSCO remeasured its property and equipment as follows:

Property and equipment CHF 1,000,000 × $0.61 H = $610,000

By multiplying the historical cost in Swiss francs by the historical exchange rate, $610,000 represents the U.S. dollar–equivalent historical cost of this asset. It is the amount of U.S. dollars that the parent company would have had to pay to acquire assets having a cost of CHF 1,000,000 when the exchange rate was $0.61 per Swiss franc.

Property and equipment were translated under the current rate method as follows:

Property and equipment CHF 1,000,000 × $0.70 C = $700,000

The $700,000 amount is not readily interpretable. It does not represent the U.S. dollar equivalent historical cost of the asset; that amount is $610,000. Nor does it represent the U.S. dollar equivalent current cost of the asset because CHF 1,000,000 is not the current cost of the asset in Switzerland. The $700,000 amount is simply the product of multiplying two numbers together!

Underlying Relationships

The following table reports the values for selected financial ratios calculated from the original foreign currency financial statements and from the U.S. dollar–translated statements using the two different translation methods:

Ratio	CHF	US$ Temporal	US$ Current Rate
Current ratio (current assets/current liabilities)	1.22	1.20	1.22
Debt/equity ratio (total liabilities/total equities). . . .	1.04	1.23	1.04
Gross profit ratio (gross profit/sales)	25%	25.8%	25%
Return on equity (net income/total equity)	57.3%	58.6%	53.2%

The temporal method distorts all of the ratios measured in the foreign currency. The subsidiary appears to be less liquid, more highly leveraged, and more profitable than it does in Swiss franc terms.

The current rate method maintains the first three ratios but distorts return on equity. The distortion occurs because income was translated at the average-for-the-period exchange rate whereas total equity was translated at the current exchange rate. In fact, the use of the average rate for income and the current rate for assets and liabilities distorts any ratio combining balance sheet and income statement figures, such as turnover ratios.

Conceptually, when the current rate method is employed, income statement items can be translated at either the average or the current exchange rate. U.S. GAAP requires using the average exchange rate. In this illustration, if revenues and expenses had been translated at the current exchange rate, net income would have been $329,000 (CHF 470,000 × $0.70), and the return on equity would have been 57.3 percent ($329,000/$574,000), exactly the amount reflected in the Swiss franc financial statements.

LO5

Understand the rationale for hedging a net investment in a foreign operation and describe the treatment of gains and losses on hedges used for this purpose.

Hedging Balance Sheet Exposure

When the U.S. dollar is the functional currency or when a foreign operation is located in a highly inflationary economy, remeasurement gains and losses are reported in the consolidated income statement. Management of U.S. multinational companies could wish to avoid reporting remeasurement losses in net income because of the perceived negative impact this has on the company's stock price. Likewise, when the foreign currency is the functional currency, management could wish to avoid negative translation adjustments because of the adverse impact on the debt-to-equity ratio.

> More and more corporations are hedging their translation exposure—the recorded value of international assets such as plant, equipment and inventory—to prevent gyrations in their quarterly accounts. Though technically only paper gains or losses, translation adjustments can play havoc with balance-sheet ratios and can spook analysts and creditors alike.[11]

Translation adjustments and remeasurement gains or losses are functions of two factors: (1) changes in the exchange rate and (2) balance sheet exposure. Although a company can do little if anything to influence exchange rates, parent companies can use several techniques to hedge the balance sheet exposures of their foreign operations.

Parent companies can hedge balance sheet exposure by using a derivative financial instrument, such as a forward contract or foreign currency option, or a nonderivative hedging instrument, such as a foreign currency borrowing. To illustrate, assume that SWISSCO's functional currency is the Swiss franc; this creates a net asset balance sheet exposure. USCO believes that the Swiss franc will depreciate, thereby generating a negative translation adjustment that will reduce consolidated stockholders' equity. USCO could hedge this balance sheet exposure by borrowing Swiss francs for a period of time, thus creating an offsetting Swiss franc liability exposure. As the Swiss franc depreciates, the U.S. dollar value of the Swiss franc borrowing decreases and USCO will be able to repay the Swiss franc borrowing using fewer U.S. dollars. This generates a foreign exchange gain, which offsets the negative translation adjustment arising from the translation of SWISSCO's financial statements. As an alternative to the Swiss franc borrowing, USCO might have acquired a Swiss franc put option to hedge its balance sheet exposure. A put option gives the company the right to sell Swiss francs at a predetermined strike price. As the Swiss franc depreciates, the fair value of the put option should increase, resulting in a gain. Current standards provide that the gain or loss on a hedging instrument designated and effective as a *hedge of the net investment in a foreign operation* should be reported in the same manner as the translation adjustment being hedged. Thus, the foreign exchange gain on the Swiss franc borrowing or the gain on the foreign currency option would be included in Accumulated Other Comprehensive Income along with the negative translation adjustment arising from the translation of SWISSCO's financial statements. In the event that the gain on the hedging instrument is larger than the translation adjustment being hedged, the excess is taken to net income.

The paradox of hedging a balance sheet exposure is that in the process of avoiding an unrealized translation adjustment, realized foreign exchange gains and losses can result. Consider USCO's foreign currency borrowing to hedge a Swiss franc balance sheet exposure. At the initiation of the loan, USCO converts the borrowed Swiss francs into U.S. dollars at the spot exchange rate. When the liability matures, USCO purchases Swiss francs at the spot rate prevailing at that date to repay the loan. The change in exchange rate over the life of the loan generates a *realized* gain or loss. If the Swiss franc depreciates as expected, a realized foreign exchange gain that offsets the negative translation adjustment in Accumulated Other Comprehensive Income results. Although the net effect on Accumulated Other Comprehensive Income is zero, a net increase in cash occurs as a result of the hedge. If the Swiss franc unexpectedly appreciates, a realized foreign exchange loss occurs. This is offset by a positive translation adjustment in Accumulated Other Comprehensive Income, but a net decrease in cash exists. While a hedge of a net investment in a foreign operation eliminates the possibility of reporting a negative translation adjustment in Accumulated Other Comprehensive Income, gains and losses realized in cash can result.

[11] Ida Picker, "Indecent Exposure," *Institutional Investor*, September 1991, p. 82.

EXHIBIT 10.10
Sonoco Products Company, 2010 Annual Report

18 Accumulated Other Comprehensive Loss

The following table summarizes the components of accumulated other comprehensive loss and the changes in accumulated comprehensive loss, net of tax as applicable, for the years ended December 31, 2010, and 2009:

	Foreign Currency Translation Adjustments	Defined Benefit Plans	Derivative Financial Instruments	Accumulated Other Comprehensive Loss
Balance at December 31, 2008	$(68,737)	$(372,807)	$(13,135)	$(454,679)
Change during 2009	79,535	56,149	8,526	144,210
Balance at December 31, 2009	$(10,798)	$(316,658)	$ (4,609)	(310,469)
Change during 2010	6,887	13,621	2,906	17,602
Balance at December 31, 2010	$ 17,685	$(303,037)	$ (7,515)	$(292,867)

Disclosures Related to Translation

Current standards require firms to present an analysis of the change in the cumulative translation adjustment account in the financial statements or notes thereto. Many companies comply with this requirement directly in their statement of comprehensive income. Other companies provide separate disclosure in the notes; see Exhibit 10.10 for an example of this disclosure for Sonoco Products Company.

An analysis of the Foreign Currency Translation Adjustments column indicates a positive translation adjustment of $79,535 in 2009 and a positive translation adjustment of $6,887 in 2010. From the signs of these adjustments, one can infer that, in aggregate, the foreign currencies in which Sonoco has operations appreciated against the U.S. dollar in both 2009 and 2010.

Although not specifically required to do so, many companies describe their translation procedures in their "summary of significant accounting policies" in the notes to the financial statements. The following excerpt from International Business Machines Corporation's 2010 annual report illustrates this type of disclosure:

> **Translation of Non-U.S. Currency Amounts**—Assets and liabilities of non-U.S. subsidiaries that have a local functional currency are translated to United States (U.S.) dollars at year-end exchange rates. Translation adjustments are recorded in accumulated other comprehensive income/(loss) in the Consolidated Statement of Stockholders' Equity. Income and expense items are translated at weighted-average rates of exchange prevailing during the year.
>
> Inventories, plant, rental machines and other properties—net, and other non-monetary assets and liabilities of non-U.S. subsidiaries and branches that operate in U.S. dollars are translated at the approximate exchange rates prevailing when the company acquired the assets or liabilities. All other assets and liabilities denominated in a currency other than U.S. dollars are translated at year-end exchange rates with the transaction gain or loss recognized in other (income) and expense. Cost of sales and depreciation are translated at historical exchange rates. All other income and expense items are translated at the weighted-average rates of exchange prevailing during the year. These translation gains and losses are included in net income for the period in which exchange rates change.

Consolidation of a Foreign Subsidiary

LO6

Prepare a consolidation worksheet for a parent and its foreign subsidiary.

This section of the chapter demonstrates the procedures used to consolidate a foreign subsidiary's financial statements with those of its parent. The treatment of the excess of fair value over book value requires special attention. As an item denominated in foreign currency, translation of the excess gives rise to a translation adjustment recorded on the consolidation worksheet.

On January 1, 2012, Altman, Inc., a U.S.–based manufacturing firm, acquired 100 percent of Bradford Ltd. in Great Britain. Altman paid £25,000,000, which was equal to Bradford's fair value. Bradford's balance sheet on January 1, 2012, was as follows:

Cash	£ 925,000	Accounts payable	£ 675,000
Accounts receivable	1,400,000	Long-term debt	4,000,000
Inventory	6,050,000	Common stock	20,000,000
Plant and equipment (net)	19,000,000	Retained earnings	2,700,000
Total	£27,375,000	Total	£27,375,000

The £2,300,000 excess of fair value over book value resulted from undervalued land (part of plant and equipment) and therefore is not subject to amortization. Altman uses the equity method to account for its investment in Bradford.

On December 31, 2013, two years after the acquisition date, Bradford submitted the following trial balance for consolidation (credit balances are in parentheses):

Cash	£ 600,000
Accounts Receivable	2,700,000
Inventory	9,000,000
Plant and Equipment (net)	17,200,000
Accounts Payable	(500,000)
Long-Term Debt	(2,000,000)
Common Stock	(20,000,000)
Retained Earnings, 1/1/13	(3,800,000)
Sales	(13,900,000)
Cost of Goods Sold	8,100,000
Depreciation Expense	900,000
Other Expenses	950,000
Dividends Declared, 6/30/13	750,000
	£ –0–

Although Bradford generated net income of £1,100,000 in 2012, it declared or paid no dividends that year. Other than the payment of dividends in 2013, no intra-entity transactions occurred between the two affiliates. Altman has determined the British pound to be Bradford's functional currency.

Relevant exchange rates for the British pound were as follows:

	January 1	June 30	December 31	Average
2012	$1.51	–0–	$1.56	$1.54
2013	1.56	$1.58	1.53	1.55

Translation of Foreign Subsidiary Trial Balance

The initial step in consolidating the foreign subsidiary is to translate its trial balance from British pounds into U.S. dollars. Because the British pound has been determined to be the functional currency, this translation uses the current rate method. The historical exchange rate for translating Bradford's common stock and January 1, 2012, retained earnings is the exchange rate that existed at the acquisition date—$1.51.

	British Pounds	Rate	U.S. Dollars
Cash	£ 600,000	1.53 C	$ 918,000
Accounts Receivable	2,700,000	1.53 C	4,131,000
Inventory	9,000,000	1.53 C	13,770,000
Plant and Equipment (net)	17,200,000	1.53 C	26,316,000
Accounts Payable	(500,000)	1.53 C	(765,000)
Long-Term Debt	(2,000,000)	1.53 C	(3,060,000)
Common Stock	(20,000,000)	1.51 H	(30,200,000)

(continued)

	British Pounds	Rate	U.S. Dollars
Retained Earnings, 1/1/13	(3,800,000)	*	(5,771,000)
Sales	(13,900,000)	1.55 A	(21,545,000)
Cost of Goods Sold	8,100,000	1.55 A	12,555,000
Depreciation Expense	900,000	1.55 A	1,395,000
Other Expenses	950,000	1.55 A	1,472,500
Dividends Declared, 6/30/13	750,000	1.58 H	1,185,000
Cumulative translation adjustment			(401,500)
	£ -0-		$ -0-
*Retained Earnings, 1/1/12	£2,700,000	1.51 H	$4,077,000
Net Income, 2012	1,100,000	1.54 A	1,694,000
Retained Earnings, 12/31/12	£3,800,000		$5,771,000

A positive (credit balance) cumulative translation adjustment is required to make the trial balance actually balance. The cumulative translation adjustment is calculated as follows:

Net assets, 1/1/12	£22,700,000	1.51 H	$34,277,000	
Change in net assets, 2012				
Net income, 2012	1,100,000	1.54 A	1,694,000	
Net assets, 12/31/12	£23,800,000		$35,971,000	
Net assets, 12/31/12, at current exchange rate	£23,800,000	1.56 C	37,128,000	
Translation adjustment, 2012 (positive)				$(1,157,000)
Net assets, 1/1/13	£23,800,000	1.56 H	$37,128,000	
Change in net assets, 2013				
Net income, 2013	3,950,000	1.55 A	6,122,500	
Dividends 6/30/13	(750,000)	1.58 H	(1,185,000)	
Net assets, 12/31/13	£27,000,000		$42,065,500	
Net assets, 12/31/13, at current exchange rate	£27,000,000	1.53 C	41,310,000	
Translation adjustment, 2013 (negative)				755,500
Cumulative translation adjustment, 12/31/13 (positive)				$ (401,500)

The translation adjustment in 2012 is positive because the British pound appreciated against the U.S. dollar that year; the translation adjustment in 2013 is negative because the British pound depreciated.

Determination of Balance in Investment Account—Equity Method

The original value of the investment in Bradford, the net income earned by Bradford, and the dividends paid by Bradford are all denominated in British pounds. Relevant amounts must be translated from pounds into U.S. dollars so Altman can account for its investment in Bradford under the equity method. In addition, the translation adjustment calculated each year is included in the Investment in Bradford account to update the foreign currency investment to its U.S. dollar equivalent. The counterpart is recorded as a translation adjustment on Altman's books:

12/31/12	Investment in Bradford	$1,157,000	
	Cumulative Translation Adjustment		$1,157,000
	To record the positive translation adjustment related to the investment in a British subsidiary when the British pound appreciated.		
12/31/13	Cumulative Translation Adjustment	$ 755,500	
	Investment in Bradford		$ 755,500
	To record the negative translation adjustment related to the investment in a British subsidiary when the British pound depreciated.		

As a result of these two journal entries, Altman has a Cumulative Translation Adjustment of $401,500 on its separate balance sheet.

The carrying value of the investment account in U.S. dollar terms at December 31, 2013, is determined as follows:

Investment in Bradford	British Pounds	Exchange Rate	U.S. Dollars
Original value.	£25,000,000	1.51 H	$37,750,000
Bradford net income, 2012	1,100,000	1.54 A	1,694,000
Translation adjustment, 2012.			1,157,000
Balance, 12/31/12	£26,100,000		$40,601,000
Bradford net income, 2013	3,950,000	1.55 A	6,122,500
Bradford dividends, 6/30/13.	(750,000)	1.58 H	(1,185,000)
Translation adjustment, 2013.			(755,500)
Balance, 12/31/13	£29,300,000		$44,783,000

In addition to Altman's $44,783,000 investment in Bradford, it has equity income on its December 31, 2013, trial balance in the amount of $6,122,500.

Consolidation Worksheet

Once the subsidiary's trial balance has been translated into dollars and the carrying value of the investment is known, the consolidation worksheet at December 31, 2013, can be prepared. As is true in the consolidation of domestic subsidiaries, the investment account, the subsidiary's equity accounts, and the effects of intra-entity transactions must be eliminated. The excess of fair value over book value at the date of acquisition also must be allocated to the appropriate accounts (in this example, plant and equipment).

Unique to the consolidation of foreign subsidiaries is the fact that the excess of fair value over book value, denominated in foreign currency, also must be translated into the parent's reporting currency. When the foreign currency is the functional currency, the excess is translated at the current exchange rate with a resulting translation adjustment. The excess is not carried on either the parent's or the subsidiary's books but is recorded only in the consolidation worksheet. *Neither the parent nor the subsidiary has recognized the translation adjustment related to the excess, and it must be recorded in the consolidation worksheet.* Exhibit 10.11 presents the consolidation worksheet of Altman and Bradford at December 31, 2013.

Explanation of Consolidation Entries

S—Eliminates the subsidiary's stockholders' equity accounts as of the beginning of the current year along with the equivalent book value component within the original value of the Investment in Bradford account.

A—Allocates the excess of fair value over book value at the date of acquisition to land (plant and equipment) and eliminates that amount within the original value of the Investment in Bradford account.

I—Eliminates the amount of equity income recognized by the parent in the current year and included in the Investment in Bradford account under the equity method.

D—Eliminates the subsidiary's dividend payment that was a reduction in the Investment in Bradford account under the equity method.

T—Eliminates the cumulative translation adjustment included in the Investment in Bradford account under the equity method and eliminates the cumulative translation adjustment carried on the parent's books.

E—Revalues the excess of fair value over book value for the change in exchange rate since the date of acquisition with the counterpart recognized as an increase in

EXHIBIT 10.11 Consolidation Worksheet—Parent and Foreign Subsidiary

ALTMAN, INC., AND BRADFORD LTD.
Consolidation Worksheet
For Year Ending December 31, 2013

Accounts	Altman	Bradford	Consolidated Entries Debits	Consolidated Entries Credits	Consolidated Totals
Income Statement					
Sales	$ (32,489,000)	$(21,545,000)			$ (54,034,000)
Cost of goods sold	16,000,000	12,555,000			28,555,000
Depreciation expense	9,700,000	1,395,000			11,095,000
Other expenses	2,900,000	1,472,500			4,372,500
Equity income	(6,122,500)		(I) 6,122,500		-0-
Net income	$ (10,011,500)	$ (6,122,500)			$ (10,011,500)
Statement of Retained Earnings					
Retained earnings, 1/1/13	$ (25,194,000)	$ (5,771,000)	(S) 5,771,000		$ (25,194,000)
Net income (above)	(10,011,500)	(6,122,500)			(10,011,500)
Dividends paid	1,500,000	1,185,000		(D) 1,185,000	1,500,000
Retained earnings, 12/31/13	$ (33,705,500)	$(10,708,500)			$ (33,705,500)
Balance Sheet					
Cash	$ 3,649,800	$ 918,000			$ 4,567,800
Accounts receivable	3,100,000	4,131,000			7,231,000
Inventory	11,410,000	13,770,000			25,180,000
Investment in Bradford	44,783,000			(S) 35,971,000	-0-
				(A) 3,473,000	
			(D) 1,185,000	(I) 6,122,500	
				(T) 401,500	
Plant and equipment (net)	39,500,000	26,316,000	(A) 3,473,000		
			(E) 46,000		69,335,000
Total assets	$ 102,442,800	$ 45,135,000			$ 106,313,800
Accounts payable	$ (2,500,000)	$ (765,000)			$ (3,265,000)
Long-term debt	(22,728,800)	(3,060,000)			(25,788,800)
Common stock	(43,107,000)	(30,200,000)	(S) 30,200,000		(43,107,000)
Retained earnings, 12/31/13 (above)	(33,705,500)	(10,708,500)			(33,705,500)
Cumulative translation adjustment	(401,500)	(401,500)	(T) 401,500	(E) 46,000	(447,500)
Total liabilities and equities	$(102,422,800)	$(45,135,000)	$47,199,000	$47,199,000	$(106,313,800)

the consolidated cumulative translation adjustment. The revaluation is calculated as follows:

Excess of Fair Value over Book Value

U.S. dollar equivalent at 12/31/13	£2,300,000 × $1.53	=	$3,519,000
U.S. dollar equivalent at 1/1/12	2,300,000 × $1.51	=	3,473,000
Cumulative translation adjustment related to excess, 12/31/13			$ 46,000

IFRS—Translation of Foreign Currency Financial Statements

IAS 21, "The Effects of Changes in Foreign Exchange Rates," provides guidance in IFRS with respect to the translation of foreign currency financial statements. *IAS 21* generally follows the functional currency approach introduced by the FASB. Under

IAS 21, as is true under U.S. GAAP, a foreign subsidiary's financial statements are translated using the current rate method when a foreign currency is the functional currency and using the temporal method when the parent company's currency is the functional currency. Significant differences between IFRS and U.S. GAAP relate to (*a*) the hierarchy of factors used to determine the functional currency and (*b*) the method used to translate the foreign currency statements of a subsidiary located in a hyperinflationary country.

Although stated differently, the factors to be considered in determining the functional currency of a foreign subsidiary in *IAS 21* generally are consistent with U.S. GAAP functional currency indicators. Specifically, *IAS 21* indicates that the *primary* factors to be considered are:

1. The currency that mainly influences sales price.
2. The currency of the country whose competitive forces and regulations mainly determine sales price.
3. The currency that mainly influences labor, material, and other costs of providing goods and services.

Other factors to be considered are:

1. The currency in which funds from financing activities are generated.
2. The currency in which receipts from operating activities are retained.
3. Whether the foreign operation carries out its activities as an extension of the parent or with a significant degree of autonomy.
4. The volume of transactions with the parent.
5. Whether cash flows generated by the foreign operation directly affect the cash flows of the parent.
6. Whether cash flows generated by the foreign operation are sufficient to service its debt.

IAS 21 states that when the above indicators are mixed and the functional currency is not obvious, the parent must give priority to the primary indicators in determining the foreign entity's functional currency.

As noted earlier, U.S. GAAP is silent with respect to weights to be assigned to various indicators to determine the functional currency and there is no hierarchy provided. Because of this difference in the functional currency determination process, it is possible that a foreign subsidiary could be determined to have a functional currency under IFRS that would be different from the functional currency determined under U.S. GAAP.

Under *IAS 21,* the financial statements of a foreign subsidiary located in a hyperinflationary economy are translated into the parent's currency using a two-step process. First, the financial statements are restated for local inflation in accordance with *IAS 29*, "Financial Reporting in Hyperinflationary Economies." Second, each financial statement line item, which has now been restated for local inflation, is translated using the current exchange rate. In effect, neither the temporal method nor the current rate method is used when the subsidiary is located in a country experiencing hyperinflation. Because all balance sheet accounts, including stockholders' equity, are translated at the current exchange rate, a translation adjustment does not exist. Unlike U.S. GAAP, IFRS does not provide a bright-line threshold to identify a hyperinflationary economy. Instead, *IAS 29* provides a list of characteristics that indicate hyperinflation, including (*a*) the general population prefers to keep its wealth in a relatively stable foreign currency; (*b*) interest rates, wages, and other prices are linked to a price index; and (*c*) the cumulative rate of inflation over three years is approaching, or exceeds, 100 percent. As noted earlier in this chapter, under current U.S. GAAP, the financial statements of a foreign subsidiary located in a highly inflationary economy must be translated using the temporal method, and high inflation is defined as a cumulative three-year inflation of 100 percent or more.

As noted in Chapter 9, there is considerable similarity between IFRS and U.S. GAAP with respect to the accounting for derivative financial instruments used to hedge foreign exchange risk. Similar to U.S. GAAP, *IAS 39* also allows hedge accounting for hedges of net investments in a foreign operation. The gain or loss on the hedging instrument is recognized in Accumulated Other Comprehensive Income (AOCI) along with the translation adjustment that is being hedged. Under both IFRS and U.S. GAAP, the cumulative translation adjustment and cumulative net gain or loss on the net investment hedge are transferred from AOCI to net income when the foreign subsidiary is sold or otherwise disposed of.

Summary

1. Because many companies have significant financial involvement in foreign countries, the process by which foreign currency financial statements are translated into U.S. dollars has special accounting importance. The two major issues related to the translation process are (1) which method to use and (2) where to report the resulting translation adjustment in the consolidated financial statements.
2. Translation methods differ on the basis of which accounts are translated at the current exchange rate and which are translated at historical rates. Accounts translated at the current exchange rate are exposed to translation adjustment. Different translation methods give rise to different concepts of balance sheet exposure and translation adjustments of differing signs and magnitude.
3. The temporal method translates assets carried at current value (cash, marketable securities, receivables) and liabilities at the current exchange rate. This method translates assets carried at historical cost and stockholders' equity at historical exchange rates. When liabilities are more than the sum of cash, marketable securities, and receivables, a net liability balance sheet exposure exists. Foreign currency appreciation results in a negative translation adjustment (remeasurement loss). Foreign currency depreciation results in a positive translation adjustment (remeasurement gain). By translating assets carried at historical cost at historical exchange rates, the temporal method maintains the underlying valuation method used by the foreign operation but distorts relationships in the foreign currency financial statements.
4. The current rate method translates all assets and liabilities at the current exchange rate, giving rise to a net asset balance sheet exposure. Foreign currency appreciation results in a positive translation adjustment. Foreign currency depreciation results in a negative translation adjustment. By translating assets carried at historical cost at the current exchange rate, the current rate method maintains relationships in the foreign currency financial statements but distorts the underlying valuation method used by the foreign operation.
5. Current U.S. accounting procedures require two separate procedures for translating foreign currency financial statements into the parent's reporting currency. *Translation* through use of the current rate method is appropriate when the foreign operation's functional currency is a foreign currency. In this case, the translation adjustment is reported in Accumulated Other Comprehensive Income and reflected on the balance sheet as a separate component of stockholders' equity. *Remeasurement* by using the temporal method is appropriate when the operation's functional currency is the U.S. dollar. Remeasurement also is applied when the operation is in a country with a highly inflationary economy. In these situations, the translation adjustment is treated as a remeasurement gain or loss in net income.
6. Some companies hedge their balance sheet exposures to avoid reporting remeasurement losses in net income and/or negative translation adjustments in Accumulated Other Comprehensive Income. Gains and losses on derivative or nonderivative instruments used to hedge net investments in foreign operations are reported in the same manner as the translation adjustment being hedged.
7. IFRS and U.S. GAAP have broadly similar rules with regard to the translation of foreign currency financial statements. Differences exist with respect to the determination of functional currency, with *IAS 21* establishing a hierarchy of functional currency indicators, and in translating financial statements of foreign entities located in high inflation countries. For these entities, *IAS 21* requires financial statements to first be restated for local inflation and then translated into the parent's currency using the current exchange rate for all financial statement items.

Comprehensive Illustration

Problem

(*Estimated Time: 55 to 65 Minutes*) Arlington Company is a U.S.–based organization with numerous foreign subsidiaries. As a preliminary step in preparing consolidated financial statements for 2013, it must translate the financial information from each foreign operation into its reporting currency, the U.S. dollar.

Arlington owns a Swedish subsidiary that has been in business for several years. On December 31, 2012, this entity's balance sheet was translated from Swedish kroner (SEK) (its functional currency) into U.S. dollars as prescribed by U.S. GAAP. Equity accounts at that date follow (all credit balances):

Common stock	SEK 110,000	=	$21,000
Retained earnings	194,800	=	36,100
Cumulative translation adjustment			3,860

At the end of 2013, the Swedish subsidiary produced the following trial balance. These figures include all of the entity's transactions for the year except for the results of several transactions related to sales made to a Chinese customer. A separate ledger has been maintained for these transactions denominated in Chinese renminbi (RMB). This ledger follows the company's trial balance.

Trial Balance—Swedish Subsidiary
December 31, 2013

	Debit	Credit
Cash	SEK 41,000	
Accounts Receivable	126,000	
Inventory	128,000	
Land	160,000	
Fixed Assets	228,000	
Accumulated Depreciation		SEK 98,100
Accounts Payable		39,000
Notes Payable		56,000
Bonds Payable		125,000
Common Stock		110,000
Retained Earnings, 1/1/13		194,800
Sales		350,000
Cost of Goods Sold	165,000	
Depreciation Expense	10,900	
Salary Expense	36,000	
Rent Expense	12,000	
Other Expenses	41,000	
Dividends Paid, 7/1/13	25,000	
Totals	SEK 972,900	SEK 972,900

Ledger—Transactions in Chinese Renminbi
December 31, 2013

	Debit	Credit
Cash	RMB 10,000	
Accounts Receivable	28,000	
Fixed Assets	20,000	
Accumulated Depreciation		RMB 4,000
Notes Payable		15,000
Sales		44,000
Depreciation Expense	4,000	
Interest Expense	1,000	
Totals	RMB 63,000	RMB 63,000

Additional Information

- The Swedish subsidiary began selling to the Chinese customer at the beginning of the current year. At that time, it borrowed 20,000 RMB to acquire a truck for delivery purposes. It paid one-fourth of that debt before the end of the year. The subsidiary made sales to China evenly during the period.
- The U.S. dollar exchange rates for 1 SEK are as follows:

January 1, 2013	$0.200 = 1.00 SEK
Weighted average rate for 2013	0.192 = 1.00
July 1, 2013	0.190 = 1.00
December 31, 2013	0.182 = 1.00

- The exchange rates applicable for the remeasurement of 1 RMB into Swedish kroner are as follows:

January 1, 2013	1.25 SEK = 1.00 RMB
Weighted average rate for 2013	1.16 = 1.00
December 1, 2013	1.10 = 1.00
December 31, 2013	1.04 = 1.00

- The Swedish subsidiary expended SEK 10,000 during the year on development activities. In accordance with IFRS, this cost has been capitalized within the Fixed Assets account. This expenditure had no effect on the depreciation recognized for the year.

Required

Prepare financial statements for the year ending December 31, 2013, for the Swedish subsidiary. Translate these statements into U.S. dollars in accordance with U.S. accounting standards to facilitate the preparation of consolidated statements. The Swedish krona is the subsidiary's functional currency.

Solution

Remeasurement of Foreign Currency Balances

A portion of the Swedish subsidiary's operating results are presently stated in Chinese renminbi. These balances must be remeasured into the functional currency, the Swedish krona, before the translation process can begin. In remeasuring these accounts using the temporal method, the krona value of the monetary assets and liabilities is determined by using the current (C) exchange rate (1.04 SEK per RMB) whereas all other accounts are remeasured at historical (H) or average (A) rates.

Remeasurement of Foreign Currency Balances

	Renminbi		Rate		Kroner
Sales	RMB 44,000	×	1.16 A	=	SEK 51,040
Interest Expense	(1,000)	×	1.16 A	=	(1,160)
Depreciation Expense	(4,000)	×	1.25 H	=	(5,000)
Income from renminbi transactions	39,000				44,880
Cash	10,000	×	1.04 C	=	10,400
Accounts Receivable	28,000	×	1.04 C	=	29,120
Fixed Assets	20,000	×	1.25 H	=	25,000
Accumulated Depreciation	(4,000)	×	1.25 H	=	(5,000)
Total assets	54,000				59,520
Notes Payable	15,000	×	1.04 C	=	15,600
Income from renminbi transactions	39,000		From above		44,880
	54,000				60,480
Remeasurement Loss					(960)
Total					59,520

(continued)

Remeasurement of Foreign Currency Balances (Continued)

	Renminbi		Rate		Kroner
Remeasurement Loss for 2013					
Net monetary asset balance, 1/1/13	–0–				–0–
Increases in net monetary items:					
Operations (sales less interest expense)	RMB 43,000	×	1.16	=	SEK 49,880
Decreases in net monetary items:					
Purchased truck, 1/1/13	(20,000)	×	1.25	=	(25,000)
Net monetary assets, 12/31/13	RMB 23,000				SEK 24,880
Net monetary assets, 12/31/13, at current exchange rate	RMB 23,000	×	1.04	=	SEK 23,920
Remeasurement loss (gain)					SEK 960

The net monetary asset exposure (cash and accounts receivable > notes payable) and depreciation of the Chinese renminbi create a remeasurement loss of SEK 960.

The remeasured figures from the Chinese operation must be combined in some manner with the subsidiary's trial balance denominated in Swedish kroner. For example, the accounts can simply be added together on a worksheet. As an alternative, a year-end adjustment can be recorded in the Swedish subsidiary's accounting system to add the remeasured balances for financial reporting purposes, as follows:

12/31/13 Adjustment	Debit	Credit
Cash	10,400	
Accounts receivable	29,120	
Fixed assets	25,000	
Depreciation expense	5,000	
Interest expense	1,160	
Remeasurement loss	960	
Accumulated depreciation		5,000
Notes payable		15,600
Sales		51,040
To record in Swedish kroner the foreign currency transactions originally denominated in renminbi.		

One more adjustment is necessary before translating the subsidiary's Swedish krona financial statements into the parent's reporting currency. The development costs incurred by the Swedish entity should be reclassified as an expense as required by U.S. authoritative literature. After this adjustment, the Swedish subsidiary's statements conform with U.S. GAAP.

12/31/13 Adjustment	Debit	Credit
Other expenses	10,000	
Fixed assets		10,000
To adjust fixed assets and expenses in Swedish kroner to be in compliance with U.S. GAAP.		

Combining all remeasured and adjusted balances with the Swedish subsidiary's trial balance allows totals to be derived. For example, total sales for the subsidiary are SEK 401,040 (350,000 + 51,040), cash is SEK 51,400 (41,000 + 10,400), and so on. Having established all account balances in the functional currency (Swedish kroner), the subsidiary's statements now can be translated into U.S. dollars. Under the current rate method, the dollar values to be reported for income statement items are based on the average exchange rate for the current year. All assets and liabilities are translated at the current exchange rate at the balance sheet date, and equity accounts are translated at historical rates in effect at the date of accounting recognition.

Swedish Subsidiary
Income Statement for Year Ending December 31, 2013

Sales	SEK 401,040	×	0.192 A =	$ 76,999.68
Cost of goods sold	(165,000)	×	0.192 A =	(31,680.00)
Gross profit	236,040			45,319.68
Depreciation expense	(15,900)	×	0.192 A =	(3,052.80)
Salary expense	(36,000)	×	0.192 A =	(6,912.00)
Rent expense	(12,000)	×	0.192 A =	(2,304.00)
Other expenses	(51,000)	×	0.192 A =	(9,792.00)
Interest expense	(1,160)	×	0.192 A =	(222.72)
Remeasurement loss	(960)	×	0.192 A =	(184.32)
Net income	SEK 119,020			$ 22,851.84

Statement of Retained Earnings for Year Ending December 31, 2013

Retained earnings, 1/1/13	SEK 194,800	Given above	$ 36,100.00
Net income, 2013	119,020		22,851.84
Dividends paid, 7/1/13	(25,000)	× 0.190 H =	(4,750.00)
Retained earnings, 12/31/13	SEK 288,820		$ 54,201.84

Balance Sheet
December 31, 2013

Cash	SEK 51,400	×	0.182 C=	$ 9,354.80
Accounts receivable	155,120	×	0.182 C=	28,231.84
Inventory	128,000	×	0.182 C=	23,296.00
Land	160,000	×	0.182 C=	29,120.00
Fixed assets	243,000	×	0.182 C=	44,226.00
Accumulated depreciation	(103,100)	×	0.182 C=	(18,764.20)
Total	SEK 634,420			$115,464.44
Accounts payable	SEK 39,000	×	0.182 C=	$ 7,098.00
Notes payable	71,600	×	0.182 C=	13,031.20
Bonds payable	125,000	×	0.182 C=	22,750.00
Common stock	110,000		Given above	21,000.00
Retained earnings	288,820			54,201.84
Cumulative translation adjustment				(2,616.60)
Total	SEK 634,420			$115,464.44

The cumulative translation adjustment at 12/31/13 comprises the beginning balance (given) plus the translation adjustment for the current year:

Cumulative Translation Adjustment

Balance, 1/1/13	$ 3,860.00
Translation adjustment for 2013	(6,476.60)
Balance, 12/31/13	$(2,616.60)

The negative translation adjustment for 2013 of $6,476.60 is calculated by considering the effect of exchange rate changes on net assets:

Translation Adjustment for 2013

Net assets, 1/1/13	SEK 304,800*	×	0.200	=	$60,960.00
Increase in net assets:					
Net income, 2013	119,020	×	0.192	=	22,851.84
Decrease in net assets:					
Dividends, 7/1/13	(25,000)	×	0.190	=	(4,750.00)
Net assets, 12/31/13	SEK 398,820†				$79,061.84

(continued)

Translation Adjustment for 2013 (Continued)

Net assets, 12/31/13, at current exchange rate	SEK 398,820	×	0.182	=	72,585.24
Translation adjustment, 2013—negative					$ 6,476.60

*Indicated by January 1, 2013, stockholders' equity balances—Common Stock, SEK 110,000; Retained Earnings, SEK 194,800.
†Indicated by December 31, 2013, stockholders' equity balances—Common Stock, SEK 110,000; Retained Earnings, SEK 288,820.

Questions

1. What are the two major issues related to the translation of foreign currency financial statements?
2. What causes balance sheet (or translation) exposure to foreign exchange risk? How does balance sheet exposure compare with transaction exposure?
3. Why might a company want to hedge its balance sheet exposure? What is the paradox associated with hedging balance sheet exposure?
4. How are gains and losses on financial instruments used to hedge the net investment in a foreign operation reported in the consolidated financial statements?
5. What concept underlies the temporal method of translation? What concept underlies the current rate method of translation? How does balance sheet exposure differ under these two methods?
6. In translating the financial statements of a foreign subsidiary, why is the value assigned to retained earnings especially difficult to determine? How is this problem normally resolved?
7. What are the major procedural differences in applying the current rate and temporal methods of translation?
8. Clarke Company has a subsidiary operating in a foreign country. In relation to this subsidiary, what does the term *functional currency* mean? How is the functional currency determined?
9. A translation adjustment must be calculated and disclosed when financial statements of a foreign subsidiary are translated into the parent's reporting currency. How is this figure computed, and where is the amount reported in the financial statements?
10. The FASB put forth two theories about the underlying nature of a translation adjustment. What are these theories, and which one did the FASB consider correct?
11. When is remeasurement rather than translation appropriate? How does remeasurement differ from translation?
12. Which translation method does U.S. GAAP require for operations in highly inflationary countries? What is the rationale for mandating use of this method?
13. In what ways does IFRS differ from U.S. GAAP with respect to the translation of foreign currency financial statements?

Problems

LO2

1. What is a subsidiary's functional currency?
   a. The parent's reporting currency.
   b. The currency in which transactions are denominated.
   c. The currency in which the entity primarily generates and expends cash.
   d. Always the currency of the country in which the company has its headquarters.

LO3, LO4

2. In comparing the translation and the remeasurement process, which of the following is true?
   a. The reported balance of inventory is normally the same under both methods.
   b. The reported balance of equipment is normally the same under both methods.
   c. The reported balance of sales is normally the same under both methods.
   d. The reported balance of depreciation expense is normally the same under both methods.

LO3

3. Which of the following statements is true for the translation process (as opposed to remeasurement)?
   a. A translation adjustment can affect consolidated net income.
   b. Equipment is translated at the historical exchange rate in effect at the date of its purchase.
   c. A translation adjustment is created by the change in the relative value of a subsidiary's net assets caused by exchange rate fluctuations.
   d. A translation adjustment is created by the change in the relative value of a subsidiary's monetary assets and monetary liabilities caused by exchange rate fluctuations.

LO2, LO3

4. A subsidiary of Byner Corporation has one asset (inventory) and no liabilities. The functional currency for this subsidiary is the peso. The inventory was acquired for 100,000 pesos when the exchange rate was \$0.16 = 1 peso. Consolidated statements are to be produced, and the current exchange rate is \$0.19 = 1 peso. Which of the following statements is true for the consolidated financial statements?
   a. A remeasurement gain must be reported.
   b. A positive translation adjustment must be reported.
   c. A negative translation adjustment must be reported.
   d. A remeasurement loss must be reported.

LO3

5. At what rates should the following balance sheet accounts in foreign statements be translated (rather than remeasured) into U.S. dollars?

	Accumulated Depreciation—Equipment	Equipment
a.	Current	Current
b.	Current	Average for year
c.	Historical	Current
d.	Historical	Historical

Problems 6 and 7 are based on the following information.
Certain balance sheet accounts of a foreign subsidiary of Rose Company have been stated in U.S. dollars as follows:

	Stated at	
	Current Rates	Historical Rates
Accounts receivable, current	\$200,000	\$220,000
Accounts receivable, long term	100,000	110,000
Prepaid insurance	50,000	55,000
Goodwill	80,000	85,000
	\$430,000	\$470,000

LO2, LO3

6. This subsidiary's functional currency is a foreign currency. What total should Rose's balance sheet include for the preceding items?
   a. \$430,000.
   b. \$435,000.
   c. \$440,000.
   d. \$450,000.

LO2, LO4

7. This subsidiary's functional currency is the U.S. dollar. What total should Rose's balance sheet include for the preceding items?
   a. \$430,000.
   b. \$435,000.
   c. \$440,000.
   d. \$450,000.

Problems 8 and 9 are based on the following information.
A subsidiary of Salisbury, Inc., is located in a foreign country whose functional currency is the schweikart (SWK). The subsidiary acquires inventory on credit on November 1, 2012, for SWK 100,000 that is sold on January 17, 2013, for SWK 130,000. The subsidiary pays for the inventory on January 31, 2013. Currency exchange rates for 1 SWK are as follows:

November 1, 2012	\$0.16 = 1 SWK
December 31, 2012	0.17 = 1
January 17, 2013	0.18 = 1
January 31, 2013	0.19 = 1
Average for 2013	0.20 = 1

LO2, LO3

8. What amount does Salisbury's consolidated balance sheet report for this inventory at December 31, 2012?
   a. $16,000.
   b. $17,000.
   c. $18,000.
   d. $19,000.

LO2, LO3

9. What amount does Salisbury's consolidated income statement report for cost of goods sold for the year ending December 31, 2013?
   a. $16,000.
   b. $17,000.
   c. $18,000.
   d. $19,000.

Problems 10 and 11 are based on the following information.
A Clarke Corporation subsidiary buys marketable equity securities and inventory on April 1, 2013, for 100,000 pesos each. It pays for both items on June 1, 2013, and they are still on hand at year-end. Inventory is carried at cost under the lower-of-cost-or-market rule. Currency exchange rates for 1 peso follow:

January 1, 2013	$0.15 = 1 peso
April 1, 2013	0.16 = 1
June 1, 2013	0.17 = 1
December 31, 2013	0.19 = 1

LO2, LO4

10. Assume that the peso is the subsidiary's functional currency. What balances does a consolidated balance sheet report as of December 31, 2013?
    a. Marketable equity securities = $16,000 and Inventory = $16,000.
    b. Marketable equity securities = $17,000 and Inventory = $17,000.
    c. Marketable equity securities = $19,000 and Inventory = $16,000.
    d. Marketable equity securities = $19,000 and Inventory = $19,000.

LO2, LO4

11. Assume that the U.S. dollar is the subsidiary's functional currency. What balances does a consolidated balance sheet report as of December 31, 2013?
    a. Marketable equity securities = $16,000 and Inventory = $16,000.
    b. Marketable equity securities = $17,000 and Inventory = $17,000.
    c. Marketable equity securities = $19,000 and Inventory = $16,000.
    d. Marketable equity securities = $19,000 and Inventory = $19,000.

LO2, LO4

12. A U.S. company's foreign subsidiary had these amounts in foreign currency units (FCU) in 2013:

Cost of goods sold	FCU 10,000,000
Ending inventory	500,000
Beginning inventory	200,000

    The average exchange rate during 2013 was $0.80 = FCU 1. The beginning inventory was acquired when the exchange rate was $1.00 = FCU 1. Ending inventory was acquired when the exchange rate was $0.75 = FCU 1. The exchange rate at December 31, 2013, was $0.70 = FCU 1. Assuming that the foreign country is highly inflationary, at what amount should the foreign subsidiary's cost of goods sold be reflected in the U.S. dollar income statement?
    a. $7,815,000.
    b. $8,040,000.
    c. $8,065,000.
    d. $8,090,000.

LO3

13. Ace Corporation starts a subsidiary in a foreign country; the subsidiary has the peso as its functional currency. On January 1, Ace buys all of the subsidiary's common stock for 20,000 pesos. On April 1, the subsidiary purchases inventory for 20,000 pesos with payment made on May 1,

and sells this inventory on August 1 for 30,000 pesos, which it collects on October 1. Currency exchange rates for 1 peso are as follows:

January 1	$0.15 = 1 peso
April 1	0.17 = 1
May 1	0.18 = 1
August 1	0.19 = 1
October 1	0.20 = 1
December 31	0.21 = 1

In preparing consolidated financial statements, what translation adjustment will Ace report at the end of the current year?

a. $400 positive (credit).
b. $600 positive (credit).
c. $1,400 positive (credit).
d. $1,800 positive (credit).

LO1

14. In the translated financial statements, which method of translation maintains the underlying valuation methods used in the foreign currency financial statements?

a. Current rate method; income statement translated at average exchange rate for the year.
b. Current rate method; income statement translated at exchange rate at the balance sheet date.
c. Temporal method.
d. Monetary/nonmonetary method.

LO4

15. Houston Corporation operates a branch operation in a foreign country. Although this branch deals in pesos, the U.S. dollar is viewed as its functional currency. Thus, a remeasurement is necessary to produce financial information for external reporting purposes. The branch began the year with 100,000 pesos in cash and no other assets or liabilities. However, the branch immediately used 60,000 pesos to acquire equipment. On May 1, it purchased inventory costing 30,000 pesos for cash that it sold on July 1 for 50,000 pesos cash. The branch transferred 10,000 pesos to the parent on October 1 and recorded depreciation on the equipment of 6,000 pesos for the year. Currency exchange rates for 1 peso follow:

January 1	$0.16 = 1 peso
May 1	0.18 = 1
July 1	0.20 = 1
October 1	0.21 = 1
December 31	0.22 = 1
Average for the year	0.19 = 1

What is the remeasurement gain to be recognized in the consolidated income statement?

a. $2,100.
b. $2,400.
c. $2,700.
d. $3,000.

LO4

16. Which of the following items is *not* remeasured using historical exchange rates under the temporal method?

a. Accumulated depreciation on equipment.
b. Cost of goods sold.
c. Marketable equity securities.
d. Retained earnings.

LO2

17. In accordance with U.S. generally accepted accounting principles, which translation combination is appropriate for a foreign operation whose functional currency is the U.S. dollar?

Method	Treatment of Translation Adjustment
a. Temporal	Other comprehensive income
b. Temporal	Gain or loss in net income
c. Current rate	Other comprehensive income
d. Current rate	Gain or loss in net income

LO3

18. A foreign subsidiary's functional currency is its local currency, which has not experienced significant inflation. The weighted average exchange rate for the current year is the appropriate exchange rate for translating

	Wages Expense	Wages Payable
a.	Yes	Yes
b.	Yes	No
c.	No	Yes
d.	No	No

LO5

19. The functional currency of DeZoort, Inc.'s British subsidiary is the British pound. DeZoort borrowed pounds as a partial hedge of its investment in the subsidiary. In preparing consolidated financial statements, DeZoort's negative translation adjustment on its investment in the subsidiary exceeded its foreign exchange gain on its borrowing. How should DeZoort report the effects of the negative translation adjustment and foreign exchange gain in its consolidated financial statements?
    a. Report the translation adjustment in Other Comprehensive Income on the balance sheet and the foreign exchange gain in the income statement.
    b. Report the translation adjustment in the income statement and defer the foreign exchange gain in Other Comprehensive Income on the balance sheet.
    c. Report the translation adjustment less the foreign exchange gain in Other Comprehensive Income on the balance sheet.
    d. Report the translation adjustment less the foreign exchange gain in the income statement.

LO4

20. Gains from remeasuring a foreign subsidiary's financial statements from the local currency, which is not the functional currency, into the parent's currency should be reported as a(n)
    a. Deferred foreign exchange gain.
    b. Translation adjustment in Other Comprehensive Income.
    c. Extraordinary item, net of income taxes.
    d. Part of continuing operations.

LO3

21. The foreign currency is the functional currency for a foreign subsidiary. At what exchange rate should each of the following accounts be translated?
    a. Rent Expense.
    b. Dividends Paid.
    c. Equipment.
    d. Notes Payable.
    e. Sales.
    f. Depreciation Expense.
    g. Cash.
    h. Accumulated Depreciation.
    i. Common Stock.

LO3

22. On January 1, Dandu Corporation started a subsidiary in a foreign country. On April 1, the subsidiary purchased inventory at a cost of 120,000 local currency units (LCU). One-fourth of this inventory remained unsold at the end of the year while 40 percent of the liability from the purchase had not yet been paid. The exchange rates for $1 were as follows:

January 1	$1 = 2.5 LCU
April 1	1 = 2.8
Average for the current year	1 = 2.7
December 31	1 = 3.0

What should be the December 31 Inventory and Accounts Payable balances for this foreign subsidiary as translated into U.S. dollars using the current rate method?

LO3, LO4

23. The following accounts are denominated in pesos as of December 31, 2013. For reporting purposes, these amounts need to be stated in U.S. dollars. For each balance, indicate the exchange rate that would be used if a translation is made under the current rate method. Then, again for each account, provide the exchange rate that would be necessary if a remeasurement is being made using the temporal method. The company was started in 2000. The buildings were acquired in 2002 and the patents in 2003.

	Translation	Remeasurement
Accounts payable		
Accounts receivable		
Accumulated depreciation		
Advertising expense		
Amortization expense (patents)		
Buildings		
Cash		
Common stock		
Depreciation expense		
Dividends paid (10/1/13)		
Notes payable—due in 2016		
Patents (net)		
Salary expense		
Sales		

Exchange rates for 1 peso are as follows:

2000	1 peso = $0.28
2002	1 = 0.26
2003	1 = 0.25
January 1, 2013	1 = 0.24
April 1, 2013	1 = 0.23
July 1, 2013	1 = 0.22
October 1, 2013	1 = 0.20
December 31, 2013	1 = 0.16
Average for 2013	1 = 0.19

LO1, LO3, LO4

24. On December 18, 2013, Stephanie Corporation acquired 100 percent of a Swiss company for 3.7 million Swiss francs (CHF), which is indicative of fair value. At the acquisition date, the exchange rate was $0.70 = CHF 1. On December 18, 2013, the fair values of the subsidiary's assets and liabilities were:

Cash	CHF 500,000
Inventory	1,000,000
Fixed assets	3,000,000
Notes payable	(800,000)

Stephanie prepares consolidated financial statements on December 31, 2013. By that date, the Swiss franc has appreciated to $0.75 = CHF 1. Because of the year-end holidays, no transactions took place prior to consolidation.

a. Determine the translation adjustment to be reported on Stephanie's December 31, 2013, consolidated balance sheet, assuming that the Swiss franc is the Swiss subsidiary's functional currency. What is the economic relevance of this translation adjustment?

b. Determine the remeasurement gain or loss to be reported in Stephanie's 2013 consolidated net income, assuming that the U.S. dollar is the functional currency. What is the economic relevance of this remeasurement gain or loss?

LO3

25. Fenwicke Company began operating a subsidiary in a foreign country on January 1, 2013, by acquiring all of its common stock for LCU 40,000, which was equal to fair value. This subsidiary immediately borrowed LCU 100,000 on a five-year note with 10 percent interest payable annually beginning on January 1, 2014. The subsidiary then purchased for LCU 140,000 a building that had a 10-year anticipated life and no salvage value and is to be depreciated using the straight-line method. The subsidiary rents the building for three years to a group of local doctors for LCU 5,000 per month. By year-end, payments totaling LCU 50,000 had been received. On October 1, LCU 4,000 was paid for a repair made on that date. The subsidiary transferred a cash dividend of LCU 5,000 back to Fenwicke on December 31, 2013. The functional currency for the subsidiary is the LCU. Currency exchange rates for 1 LCU follow:

January 1, 2013	$2.00 = 1 LCU
October 1, 2013	1.85 = 1
Average for 2013.	1.90 = 1
December 31, 2013.	1.80 = 1

Prepare an income statement, statement of retained earnings, and balance sheet for this subsidiary in LCU and then translate these amounts into U.S. dollars.

LO3

26. Refer to the information in problem (25). Prepare a statement of cash flows in LCU for Fenwicke's foreign subsidiary and then translate these amounts into U.S. dollars.

LO3, LO4

27. Watson Company has a subsidiary in the country of Alonza where the local currency unit is the kamel (KM). On December 31, 2012, the subsidiary has the following balance sheet:

Cash	KM 16,000	Notes payable (due 2012) . . .	KM 19,000
Inventory.	10,000	Common stock	20,000
Land	4,000	Retained earnings	10,000
Building.	40,000		
Accumulated depreciation . . .	(21,000)		
	KM 49,000		KM 49,000

The subsidiary acquired the inventory on August 1, 2012, and the land and buildings in 2000. It issued the common stock in 1998. During 2013, the following transactions took place:

2013	
Feb. 1	Paid 5,000 KM on the note payable.
May 1	Sold entire inventory for 15,000 KM on account.
June 1	Sold land for 5,000 KM cash.
Aug. 1	Collected all accounts receivable.
Sept. 1	Signed long-term note to receive 6,000 KM cash.
Oct. 1	Bought inventory for 12,000 KM cash.
Nov. 1	Bought land for 4,000 KM on account.
Dec. 1	Paid 3,000 KM cash dividend to parent.
Dec. 31	Recorded depreciation for the entire year of 2,000 KM.

The exchange rates for 1 KM are as follows:

1998	KM 1 = $0.24
2000	1 = 0.21
August 1, 2012	1 = 0.31
December 31, 2012.	1 = 0.32
February 1, 2013	1 = 0.33
May 1, 2013	1 = 0.34
June 1, 2013	1 = 0.35
August 1, 2013	1 = 0.37
September 1, 2013	1 = 0.38
October 1, 2013	1 = 0.39
November 1, 2013.	1 = 0.40
December 1, 2013.	1 = 0.41
December 31, 2013.	1 = 0.42
Average for 2013.	1 = 0.37

a. If this is a translation, what is the translation adjustment determined solely for 2013?

b. If this is a remeasurement, what is the remeasurement gain or loss determined solely for 2013?

LO3, LO4

28. Aerkion Company starts 2013 with two assets: cash of 22,000 LCU (local currency units) and land that originally cost 60,000 LCU when acquired on April 4, 2005. On May 1, 2013, Aerkion rendered services to a customer for 30,000 LCU, an amount immediately paid in cash. On October 1, 2013, the company incurred an 18,000 LCU operating expense that was

immediately paid. No other transactions occurred during the year. Currency exchange rates for 1 LCU follow:

April 4, 2005	LCU 1 = $0.23
January 1, 2013	1 = 0.24
May 1, 2013	1 = 0.25
October 1, 2013	1 = 0.26
Average for 2013	1 = 0.27
December 31, 2013	1 = 0.29

a. Assume that Aerkion is a foreign subsidiary of a U.S. multinational company that uses the U.S. dollar as its reporting currency. Assume also that the LCU is the subsidiary's functional currency. What is the translation adjustment for this subsidiary for the year 2013?

b. Assume that Aerkion is a foreign subsidiary of a U.S. multinational company that uses the U.S. dollar as its reporting currency. Assume also that the U.S. dollar is the subsidiary's functional currency. What is the remeasurement gain or loss for 2013?

c. Assume that Aerkion is a foreign subsidiary of a U.S. multinational company. On the December 31, 2013, balance sheet, what is the translated value of the Land account? On the December 31, 2013, balance sheet, what is the remeasured value of the Land account?

LO3, LO4

29. Lancer, Inc., starts a subsidiary in a foreign country on January 1, 2012. The following account balances for the year ending December 31, 2013, are stated in kanquo (KQ), the local currency:

Sales	KQ 200,000
Inventory (bought on 3/1/13)	100,000
Equipment (bought on 1/1/12)	80,000
Rent expense	10,000
Dividends (paid on 10/1/13)	20,000
Notes receivable (to be collected in 2016)	30,000
Accumulated depreciation—equipment	24,000
Salary payable	5,000
Depreciation expense	8,000

The following exchange rates for $1 are applicable:

January 1, 2012	13 KQ
January 1, 2013	18
March 1, 2013	19
October 1, 2013	21
December 31, 2013	22
Average for 2012	14
Average for 2013	20

Lancer is preparing account balances to produce consolidated financial statements.

a. Assuming that the kanquo is the functional currency, what exchange rate would be used to report each of these accounts in U.S. dollar consolidated financial statements?

b. Assuming that the U.S. dollar is the functional currency, what exchange rate would be used to report each of these accounts in U.S. dollar consolidated financial statements?

LO3, LO5

30. Board Company has a foreign subsidiary that began operations at the start of 2013 with assets of 132,000 kites (the local currency unit) and liabilities of 54,000 kites. During this initial year of operation, the subsidiary reported a profit of 26,000 kites. It distributed two dividends, each for 5,000 kites with one dividend paid on March 1 and the other on October 1. Applicable exchange rates for 1 kite follow:

January 1, 2013 (start of business)	$0.80
March 1, 2013	0.78
Weighted average rate for 2013	0.77
October 1, 2013	0.76
December 31, 2013	0.75

a. Assume that the kite is this subsidiary's functional currency. What translation adjustment would Board report for the year 2013?

b. Assume that on October 1, 2013, Board entered into a forward exchange contract to hedge the net investment in this subsidiary. On that date, Board agreed to sell 200,000 kites in three months at a forward exchange rate of $0.76/1 kite. Prepare the journal entries required by this forward contract.

c. Compute the net translation adjustment for Board to report in Accumulated Other Comprehensive Income for the year 2013 under this second set of circumstances.

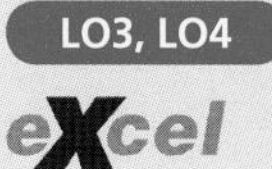

31. Kingsfield starts a subsidiary operation in a foreign country on January 1, 2013. The country's currency is the kumquat (KQ). To start this business, Kingsfield invests 10,000 kumquats. Of this amount, it spends 3,000 kumquats immediately to acquire equipment. Later, on April 1, 2013, it also purchases land. All subsidiary operational activities occur at an even rate throughout the year. The currency exchange rates for the kumquat for this year follow:

January 1, 2013	$1.71
April 1, 2013	1.59
June 1, 2013	1.66
Weighted average—2013	1.64
December 31, 2013	1.62

As of December 31, 2013, the subsidiary reports the following trial balance:

	Debits	Credits
Cash	KQ 8,000	
Accounts Receivable	9,000	
Equipment	3,000	
Accumulated Depreciation		KQ 600
Land	5,000	
Accounts Payable		3,000
Notes Payable (due 2016)		5,000
Common Stock		10,000
Dividends Paid (6/1/13)	4,000	
Sales		25,000
Salary Expense	5,000	
Depreciation Expense	600	
Miscellaneous Expenses	9,000	
Totals	KQ 43,600	KQ 43,600

A corporation based in East Lansing, Michigan, Kingsfield uses the U.S. dollar as its reporting currency.

a. Assume that the subsidiary's functional currency is the kumquat. Prepare a trial balance for it in U.S. dollars so that consolidated financial statements can be prepared.

b. Assume that the subsidiary's functional currency is the U.S. dollar. Prepare a trial balance for it in U.S. dollars so that consolidated financial statements can be prepared.

32. Livingston Company is a wholly owned subsidiary of Rose Corporation. Livingston operates in a foreign country with financial statements recorded in goghs (GH), the company's functional currency. Financial statements for the year of 2013 are as follows:

Income Statement
For Year Ending December 31, 2013

Sales	GH 270,000
Cost of goods sold	(155,000)
Gross profit	115,000
Less: Operating expenses	(54,000)
Gain on sale of equipment	10,000
Net income	GH 71,000

(continued)

Statement of Retained Earnings
For Year Ending December 31, 2013

Retained earnings, 1/1/13	GH 216,000
Net income	71,000
Less: Dividends paid	(26,000)
Retained earnings, 12/31/13	GH 261,000

Balance Sheet
December 31, 2013

Assets	
Cash	GH 44,000
Receivables	116,000
Inventory	58,000
Fixed assets (net)	339,000
Total assets	GH 557,000
Liabilities and Equities	
Liabilities	GH 176,000
Common stock	120,000
Retained earnings, 12/31/13	261,000
Total liabilities and equities	GH 557,000

Additional Information

- The common stock was issued in 2004 when the exchange rate was $1.00 = 0.48 GH; fixed assets were acquired in 2005 when the rate was $1.00 = 0.50 GH.
- As of January 1, 2013, the Retained Earnings balance was translated as $395,000.
- The currency exchange rates for $1 for the current year follow:

January 1, 2013	0.60 GH
April 1, 2013	0.62
September 1, 2013	0.58
December 31, 2013	0.65
Weighted average rate for 2013	0.63

- Inventory was acquired evenly throughout the year.
- The December 31, 2012, balance sheet reported a translation adjustment with a $85,000 debit balance.
- Dividends were paid on April 1, 2013, and a piece of equipment was sold on September 1, 2013.

Translate the foreign currency statements into the parent's reporting currency, the U.S. dollar.

LO3, LO4

33. The following account balances are for the Agee Company as of January 1, 2013, and December 31, 2013. All figures are denominated in kroner (Kr).

	January 1, 2013	December 31, 2013
Accounts payable	(18,000)	(24,000)
Accounts receivable	35,000	79,000
Accumulated depreciation—buildings	(20,000)	(25,000)
Accumulated depreciation—equipment	–0–	(5,000)
Bonds payable—due 2016	(50,000)	(50,000)
Buildings	118,000	97,000
Cash	35,000	8,000
Common stock	(70,000)	(80,000)
Depreciation expense	–0–	15,000
Dividends (10/1/13)	–0–	32,000
Equipment	–0–	30,000
Gain on sale of building	–0–	(6,000)
Rent expense	–0–	14,000
Retained earnings	(30,000)	(30,000)
Salary expense	–0–	20,000
Sales	–0–	(80,000)
Utilities expense	–0–	5,000

Additional Information

- Agee issued additional shares of common stock during the year on April 1, 2013. Common stock at January 1, 2013, was sold at the start of operations in 2004.
- It purchased buildings in 2005 and sold one building with a book value of Kr 16,000 on July 1 of the current year.
- Equipment was acquired on April 1, 2013.

Relevant exchange rates for 1 Kr were as follows:

2004	$2.40
2005	2.20
January 1, 2013	2.50
April 1, 2013	2.60
July 1, 2013	2.80
October 1, 2013	2.90
December 31, 2013	3.00
Average for 2013	2.70

a. Assuming the U.S. dollar is the functional currency and retained earnings at January 1, 2013, total $52,600, what is the remeasurement gain or loss for 2013?

b. Assuming the foreign currency is the functional currency and retained earnings at January 1, 2013, total $62,319, what is the translation adjustment for 2013?

LO3, LO4

excel

34. Sendelbach Corporation is a U.S.–based organization with operations throughout the world. One of its subsidiaries is headquartered in Toronto. Although this wholly owned company operates primarily in Canada, it engages in some transactions through a branch in Mexico. Therefore, the subsidiary maintains a ledger denominated in Mexican pesos (Ps) and a general ledger in Canadian dollars (C$). As of December 31, 2013, the subsidiary is preparing financial statements in anticipation of consolidation with the U.S. parent corporation. Both ledgers for the subsidiary are as follows:

Main Operation—Canada

	Debit	Credit
Accounts payable		C$ 35,000
Accumulated depreciation		27,000
Buildings and equipment	C$167,000	
Cash	26,000	
Common stock		50,000
Cost of goods sold	203,000	
Depreciation expense	8,000	
Dividends paid, 4/1/13	28,000	
Gain on sale of equipment, 6/1/13		5,000
Inventory	98,000	
Notes payable—due in 2016		76,000
Receivables	68,000	
Retained earnings, 1/1/13		135,530
Salary expense	26,000	
Sales		312,000
Utility expense	9,000	
Branch operation	7,530	
Totals	C$640,530	C$640,530

Branch Operation—Mexico

	Debit	Credit
Accounts payable		Ps 49,000
Accumulated depreciation		19,000
Building and equipment	Ps 40,000	
Cash	59,000	
Depreciation expense	2,000	

(continued)

Branch Operation—Mexico (Continued)

	Debit	Credit
Inventory (beginning—income statement)	23,000	
Inventory (ending—income statement)		28,000
Inventory (ending—balance sheet)	28,000	
Purchases	68,000	
Receivables	21,000	
Salary expense	9,000	
Sales		124,000
Main office		30,000
Totals	Ps 250,000	Ps 250,000

Additional Information

- The Canadian subsidiary's functional currency is the Canadian dollar, and Sendelbach's reporting currency is the U.S. dollar. The Canadian and Mexican operations are not viewed as separate accounting entities.
- The building and equipment used in the Mexican operation were acquired in 2005 when the currency exchange rate was C$0.25 = Ps 1.
- Purchases should be assumed as having been made evenly throughout the fiscal year.
- Beginning inventory was acquired evenly throughout 2012; ending inventory was acquired evenly throughout 2013.
- The Main Office account on the Mexican records should be considered an equity account. This balance was remeasured into C$7,530 on December 31, 2013.
- Currency exchange rates for 1 Ps applicable to the Mexican operation follow:

Weighted average, 2012	C$0.30
January 1, 2013	0.32
Weighted average rate for 2013	0.34
December 31, 2013	0.35

- The December 31, 2012, consolidated balance sheet reported a cumulative translation adjustment with a $36,950 credit (positive) balance.
- The subsidiary's common stock was issued in 2004 when the exchange rate was $0.45 = C$1.
- The subsidiary's December 31, 2012, Retained Earnings balance was C$135,530, a figure that has been translated into US$70,421.
- The applicable currency exchange rates for 1 C$ for translation purposes are as follows:

January 1, 2013	US$0.70
April 1, 2013	0.69
June 1, 2013	0.68
Weighted average rate for 2013	0.67
December 31, 2013	0.65

a. Remeasure the Mexican operation's figures into Canadian dollars. (*Hint:* Back into the beginning net monetary asset or liability position.)

b. Prepare financial statements (income statement, statement of retained earnings, and balance sheet) for the Canadian subsidiary in its functional currency.

c. Translate the Canadian dollar functional currency financial statements into U.S. dollars so that Sendelbach can prepare consolidated financial statements.

LO3, LO6

35. On January 1, 2012, Cayce Corporation acquired 100 percent of Simbel Company for consideration paid of $126,000, which was equal to fair value. Cayce is a U.S.–based company headquartered in Buffalo, New York, and Simbel is in Cairo, Egypt. Cayce accounts for its investment in Simbel under the cost method. Any excess of fair value over book value is attributable to undervalued land on Simbel's books. Simbel had no retained earnings at the date of acquisition. Following are the 2013 financial statements for the two operations. Information for Cayce and for Simbel is in U.S. dollars ($) and Egyptian pounds (£E), respectively.

	Cayce Corporation	Simbel Company
Sales	$200,000	£E 800,000
Cost of goods sold	(93,800)	(420,000)
Salary expense	(19,000)	(74,000)
Rent expense	(7,000)	(46,000)
Other expenses	(21,000)	(59,000)
Dividend income—from Simbel	13,750	–0–
Gain on sale of fixed asset, 10/1/13	–0–	30,000
Net income	$ 72,950	£E 231,000
Retained earnings, 1/1/13	$318,000	£E 133,000
Net income	72,950	231,000
Dividends paid	(24,000)	(50,000)
Retained earnings, 12/31/13	$366,950	£E 314,000
Cash and receivables	$110,750	£E 146,000
Inventory	98,000	297,000
Prepaid expenses	30,000	–0–
Investment in Simbel (cost)	126,000	–0–
Fixed assets (net)	398,000	455,000
Total assets	$762,750	£E 898,000
Accounts payable	$ 60,800	£E 54,000
Notes payable—due in 2015	132,000	140,000
Common stock	120,000	240,000
Additional paid-in capital	83,000	150,000
Retained earnings, 12/31/13	366,950	314,000
Total liabilities and equities	$762,750	£E 898,000

Additional Information

- During 2012, the first year of joint operation, Simbel reported income of £E 163,000 earned evenly throughout the year. Simbel paid a dividend of £E 30,000 to Cayce on June 1 of that year. Simbel also paid the 2013 dividend on June 1.
- On December 9, 2013, Simbel classified a £E 10,000 expenditure as a rent expense, although this payment related to prepayment of rent for the first few months of 2014.
- The exchange rates for 1 £E are as follows:

January 1, 2012	$0.300
June 1, 2012	0.290
Weighted average rate for 2012	0.288
December 31, 2012	0.280
June 1, 2013	0.275
October 1, 2013	0.273
Weighted average rate for 2013	0.274
December 31, 2013	0.270

Translate Simbel's 2013 financial statements into U.S. dollars and prepare a consolidation worksheet for Cayce and its Egyptian subsidiary. Assume that the Egyptian pound is the subsidiary's functional currency.

LO1, LO3, LO4

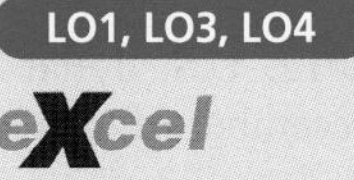

36. Diekmann Company, a U.S.–based company, acquired a 100 percent interest in Rakona A.S. in the Czech Republic on January 1, 2012, when the exchange rate for the Czech koruna (Kčs) was $0.05. Rakona's financial statements as of December 31, 2013, two years later, follow:

Balance Sheet
December 31, 2013

Assets	
Cash	Kčs 2,000,000
Accounts receivable (net)	3,300,000
Inventory	8,500,000

(continued)

Balance Sheet (Continued)
December 31, 2013

Assets	
Equipment	25,000,000
Less: Accumulated depreciation	(8,500,000)
Building	72,000,000
Less: Accumulated depreciation	(30,300,000)
Land	6,000,000
Total assets	Kčs 78,000,000
Liabilities and Stockholders' Equity	
Accounts payable	Kčs 2,500,000
Long-term debt	50,000,000
Common stock	5,000,000
Additional paid-in capital	15,000,000
Retained earnings	5,500,000
Total liabilities and stockholders' equity	Kčs 78,000,000

Income Statement
For Year Ending December 31, 2013

Sales	Kčs 25,000,000
Cost of goods sold	(12,000,000)
Depreciation expense—equipment	(2,500,000)
Depreciation expense—building	(1,800,000)
Research and development expense	(1,200,000)
Other expenses (including taxes)	(1,000,000)
Net income	Kčs 6,500,000
Plus: Retained earnings, 1/1/13	500,000
Less: Dividends, 2013	(1,500,000)
Retained earnings, 12/31/13	Kčs 5,500,000

Additional Information

- The January 1, 2013, beginning inventory of Kčs 6,000,000 was acquired on December 18, 2012, when the exchange rate was $0.043. Purchases of inventory were acquired uniformly during 2013. The December 31, 2013, ending inventory of Kčs 8,500,000 was acquired in the latter part of 2013 when the exchange rate was $0.032. All fixed assets were on the books when the subsidiary was acquired except for Kčs 5,000,000 of equipment acquired on January 3, 2013, when the exchange rate was $0.036, and Kčs 12,000,000 in buildings acquired on March 5, 2013, when the exchange rate was $0.034. Straight-line depreciation is 10 years for equipment and 40 years for buildings. A full year's depreciation is taken in the year of acquisition.
- Dividends were declared and paid on December 15, 2013, when the exchange rate was $0.031.
- Other exchange rates for 1 Kčs follow:

January 1, 2013	$0.040
Average 2013	0.035
December 31, 2013	0.030

Part I. Translate the Czech koruna financial statements at December 31, 2013, in the following three situations:

a. The Czech koruna is the functional currency. The December 31, 2012, U.S. dollar–translated balance sheet reported retained earnings of $22,500. The December 31, 2012, cumulative translation adjustment was negative $202,500 (debit balance).

b. The U.S. dollar is the functional currency. The December 31, 2012, Retained Earnings account in U.S. dollars (including a 2012 remeasurement gain) that appeared in Rakona's remeasured financial statements was $353,000.

c. The U.S. dollar is the functional currency. Rakona has no long-term debt. Instead, it has common stock of Kčs 20,000,000 and additional paid-in capital of Kčs 50,000,000. The December 31, 2012, U.S. dollar–translated balance sheet reported a negative balance in retained earnings of $147,000 (including a 2012 remeasurement loss).

Part II. Explain the positive or negative sign of the translation adjustment in Part I(*a*) and explain why a remeasurement gain or loss exists in Parts I(*b*) and I(*c*).

Develop Your Skills

RESEARCH CASE 1—FOREIGN CURRENCY TRANSLATION AND HEDGING ACTIVITIES

CPA skills

Many companies make annual reports available on their corporate Internet home page. Annual reports also can be accessed through the SEC's EDGAR system at www.sec.gov (under Filing Type, search for 10-K).

Access the most recent annual report for a U.S.–based multinational company with which you are familiar.

Required

a. Identify the location(s) in the annual report that provides disclosures related to the translation of foreign currency financial statements and foreign currency hedging.

b. Determine whether the company's foreign operations have a predominant functional currency.

c. Determine the amount of remeasurement gain or loss, if any, reported in net income in each of the three most recent years.

d. Determine the amount of translation adjustment, if any, reported in other comprehensive income in each of the three most recent years. Explain the sign (positive or negative) of the translation adjustment in each of the three most recent years.

e. Determine whether the company hedges net investments in foreign operations. If so, determine the type(s) of hedging instrument used.

RESEARCH CASE 2—FOREIGN CURRENCY TRANSLATION DISCLOSURES IN THE COMPUTER INDUSTRY

CPA skills

Many companies make annual reports available on their corporate Internet home page. Annual reports also can be accessed through the SEC's EDGAR system at www.sec.gov (under Filing Type, search for 10-K).

Access the most recent annual report for the following U.S.–based multinational corporations:
International Business Machines Corporation.
Dell Computer Company.

Required

a. Identify the location(s) in the annual report that provides disclosures related to foreign currency translation and foreign currency hedging.

b. Determine whether the company's foreign operations have a predominant functional currency. Discuss the implication this has for the comparability of financial statements of the two companies.

c. Determine the amount of translation adjustment, if any, reported in other comprehensive income in each of the three most recent years. Explain the sign (positive or negative) of the translation adjustment in each of the three most recent years. Compare the relative magnitude of these translation adjustments for the two companies.

d. Determine whether each company hedges the net investment in foreign operations. If so, determine the type(s) of hedging instrument used.

e. Prepare a brief report comparing and contrasting the foreign currency translation and foreign currency hedging policies of these two companies.

ACCOUNTING STANDARDS CASE 1—MORE THAN ONE FUNCTIONAL CURRENCY

CPA skills

Lynch Corporation has a wholly owned subsidiary in Mexico (Lynmex) with two distinct and unrelated lines of business. Lynmex's Small Appliance Division manufactures small household appliances such as toasters and coffeemakers at a factory in Monterrey, Nuevo Leon, and sells them directly to retailers such as Gigantes throughout Mexico. Lynmex's Electronics Division imports finished products produced by Lynch Corporation in the United States and sells them to a network of distributors operating throughout Mexico.

Lynch's CFO believes that the two divisions have different functional currencies. The functional currency of the Small Appliance Division is the Mexican peso, whereas the functional currency of the Electronics Division is the U.S. dollar. The CFO is unsure whether to designate the Mexican peso or the U.S. dollar as Lynmex's functional currency, or whether the subsidiary can be treated as two separate foreign operations with different functional currencies.

Required

Search current U.S. authoritative accounting literature to determine how the functional currency should be determined for a foreign entity that has more than one distinct and separable operation. Identify the source of guidance for answering this question.

ACCOUNTING STANDARDS CASE 2—CHANGE IN FUNCTIONAL CURRENCY

Hughes Inc. has a wholly owned subsidiary in Canada that previously had been determined as having the Canadian dollar as its functional currency. Due to a recent restructuring, Hughes Inc.'s CFO believes that the functional currency of the Canadian company has changed to the U.S. dollar. A large cumulative translation adjustment related to the Canadian subsidiary is included in Accumulated Other Comprehensive Income on Hughes Inc.'s balance sheet. The CFO is unsure whether the cumulative translation adjustment should be removed from equity, and if so, to what other account it should be transferred. He also questions whether the change in functional currency qualifies as a change in accounting principle, which would require retrospective application of the temporal method in translating the Canadian subsidiary's financial statements. He wonders, for example, whether the Canadian subsidiary's nonmonetary assets need to be restated as if the temporal method had been applied in previous years.

Required

Search current U.S. authoritative accounting literature for guidance on how to handle a change in functional currency from a foreign currency to the U.S. dollar. Summarize that guidance to answer the CFO's questions. Identify the source of guidance for answering these questions.

EXCEL CASE—TRANSLATING FOREIGN CURRENCY FINANCIAL STATEMENTS

Charles Edward Company established a subsidiary in a foreign country on January 1, 2013, by investing FC 3,200,000 when the exchange rate was $0.50/FC. Charles Edward negotiated a bank loan of FC 3,000,000 on January 5, 2013, and purchased plant and equipment in the amount of FC 6,000,000 on January 8, 2013. It depreciated plant and equipment on a straight-line basis over a 10-year useful life. It purchased its beginning inventory of FC 1,000,000 on January 10, 2013, and acquired additional inventory of FC 4,000,000 at three points in time during the year at an average exchange rate of $0.43/FC. It uses the first-in, first-out (FIFO) method to determine cost of goods sold. Additional exchange rates per FC 1 during the year 2013 follow:

January 1–31, 2013	$0.50
Average 2013	0.45
December 31, 2013	0.38

The foreign subsidiary's income statement for 2013 and balance sheet at December 31, 2013, follow:

INCOME STATEMENT
For the Year Ended December 31, 2013
FC (in thousands)

Sales	FC 5,000
Cost of goods sold	3,000
Gross profit	2,000
Selling expense	400
Depreciation expense	600

(continued)

Income before tax	1,000
Income taxes	300
Net income	700
Retained earnings, 1/1/13	–0–
Retained earnings, 12/31/13	FC 700

BALANCE SHEET
At December 31, 2013
FC (in thousands)

Cash	FC 1,000
Inventory	2,000
Fixed assets	6,000
Less: Accumulated depreciation	(600)
Total assets	FC 8,400
Current liabilities	FC 1,500
Long-term debt	3,000
Contributed capital	3,200
Retained earnings	700
Total liabilities and stockholders' equity	FC 8,400

As the controller for Charles Edward Company, you have evaluated the characteristics of the foreign subsidiary to determine that the FC is the subsidiary's functional currency.

Required

a. Use an electronic spreadsheet to translate the foreign subsidiary's FC financial statements into U.S. dollars at December 31, 2013, in accordance with U.S. GAAP. Insert a row in the spreadsheet after retained earnings and before total liabilities and stockholders' equity for the cumulative translation adjustment. Calculate the translation adjustment separately to verify the amount obtained as a balancing figure in the translation worksheet.

b. Use an electronic spreadsheet to remeasure the foreign subsidiary's FC financial statements in U.S. dollars at December 31, 2013, assuming that the U.S. dollar is the subsidiary's functional currency. Insert a row in the spreadsheet after depreciation expense and before income before taxes for the remeasurement gain (loss).

c. Prepare a report for James Edward, CEO of Charles Edward, summarizing the differences that will be reported in the company's 2013 consolidated financial statements because the FC, rather than the U.S. dollar, is the foreign subsidiary's functional currency. In your report, discuss the relationship between the current ratio, the debt-to-equity ratio, and profit margin calculated from the FC financial statements and from the translated U.S. dollar financial statements. Also discuss the meaning of the translated U.S. dollar amounts for inventory and for fixed assets.

EXCEL AND ANALYSIS CASE—PARKER, INC., AND SUFFOLK PLC

On January 1, 2012, Parker, Inc., a U.S.–based firm, acquired 100 percent of Suffolk PLC located in Great Britain for consideration paid of 52,000,000 British pounds (£), which was equal to fair value. The excess of fair value over book value is attributable to land (part of property, plant, and equipment) and is not subject to depreciation. Parker accounts for its investment in Suffolk at cost. On January 1, 2012, Suffolk reported the following balance sheet:

Cash	£ 2,000,000	Accounts payable	£ 1,000,000
Accounts receivable	3,000,000	Long-term debt	8,000,000
Inventory	14,000,000	Common stock	44,000,000
Property, plant, and equipment (net)	40,000,000	Retained earnings	6,000,000
	£ 59,000,000		£59,000,000

Suffolk's 2012 income was recorded at £2,000,000. It declared and paid no dividends in 2012.

On December 31, 2013, two years after the date of acquisition, Suffolk submitted the following trial balance to Parker for consolidation:

Cash	£ 1,500,000
Accounts Receivable	5,200,000
Inventory	18,000,000
Property, Plant, and Equipment (net)	36,000,000
Accounts Payable	(1,450,000)
Long-Term Debt	(5,000,000)
Common Stock	(44,000,000)
Retained Earnings (1/1/13)	(8,000,000)
Sales	(28,000,000)
Cost of Goods Sold	16,000,000
Depreciation	2,000,000
Other Expenses	6,000,000
Dividends Paid (1/30/13)	1,750,000
	–0–

Other than paying dividends, no intra-entity transactions occurred between the two companies. Relevant exchange rates for the British pound follow:

	January 1	January 30	Average	December 31
2012	$1.60	$1.61	$1.62	$1.64
2013	1.64	1.65	1.66	1.68

The December 31, 2013, financial statements (before consolidation with Suffolk) follow. Dividend income is the U.S. dollar amount of dividends received from Suffolk translated at the $1.65/£ exchange rate at January 30, 2013. The amounts listed for dividend income and all affected accounts (i.e., net income, December 31 retained earnings, and cash) reflect the $1.65/£ exchange rate at January 30, 2013. Credit balances are in parentheses.

	Parker
Sales	$ (70,000,000)
Cost of goods sold	34,000,000
Depreciation	20,000,000
Other expenses	6,000,000
Dividend income	(2,887,500)
Net income	$ (12,887,500)
Retained earnings, 1/1/13	$ (48,000,000)
Net income, 2013	(12,887,500)
Dividends, 1/30/13	4,500,000
Retained earnings, 12/31/13	$ (56,387,500)
Cash	$ 3,687,500
Accounts receivable	10,000,000
Inventory	30,000,000
Investment in Suffolk	83,200,000
Plant and equipment (net)	105,000,000
Accounts payable	(25,500,000)
Long-term debt	(50,000,000)
Common stock	(100,000,000)
Retained earnings, 12/31/13	(56,387,500)
	–0–

Parker's chief financial officer (CFO) wishes to determine the effect that a change in the value of the British pound would have on consolidated net income and consolidated stockholders' equity. To help assess the foreign currency exposure associated with the investment in Suffolk, the CFO requests assistance in comparing consolidated results under actual exchange rate fluctuations with results that would have occurred had the dollar value of the pound remained constant or declined during the first two years of Parker's ownership.

Required

Use an electronic spreadsheet to complete the following four parts:

Part I. Given the relevant exchange rates presented,

a. Translate Suffolk's December 31, 2013, trial balance from British pounds to U.S. dollars. The British pound is Suffolk's functional currency.

b. Prepare a schedule that details the change in Suffolk's cumulative translation adjustment (beginning net assets, income, dividends, etc.) for 2012 and 2013.

c. Prepare the December 31, 2013, consolidation worksheet for Parker and Suffolk.

d. Prepare the 2013 consolidated income statement and the December 31, 2013, consolidated balance sheet.

Note: Worksheets should possess the following qualities:

- Each spreadsheet should be programmed so that all relevant amounts adjust appropriately when different values of exchange rates (subsequent to January 1, 2012) are entered into it.
- Be sure to program Parker's dividend income, cash, and retained earnings to reflect the dollar value of alternative January 30, 2013, exchange rates.

Part II. Repeat tasks (*a*), (*b*), (*c*), and (*d*) from Part I to determine consolidated net income and consolidated stockholders' equity if the exchange rate had remained at $1.60/£ over the period 2012 to 2013.

Part III. Repeat tasks (*a*), (*b*), (*c*), and (*d*) from Part I to determine consolidated net income and consolidated stockholders' equity if the following exchange rates had existed:

	January 1	January 30	Average	December 31
2012	$1.60	$1.59	$1.58	$1.56
2013	1.56	1.55	1.54	1.52

Part IV. Prepare a report that provides Parker's CFO the risk assessments requested. Focus on profitability, cash flow, and the debt-to-equity ratio.

CPA REVIEW

Please visit the text website for the online Kaplan CPA simulation:

Montana Company

Situation: The Montana Company, based in Billings, transacts business in the United States and Mexico. Its wholly owned subsidiary (Cabo, Inc.) is located in Mexico. Both companies assume the United States dollar as its functional currency.

Consolidated financial statements are being prepared for Year 1. Montana Co. and Cabo, Inc., have a December 31 year-end. The currency exchange rates are as follows for the current year (Year 1):

- January 1, Year 1: 1 peso equals $.088
- Average for Year 1: 1 peso equals $.090
- November 1, Year 1: 1 peso equals $.092
- December 1, Year 1: 1 peso equals $.094
- December 31, Year 1: 1 peso equals $.095
- January 31, Year 2: 1 peso equals $.098

Topics to be covered:

- Foreign currency translation
- Foreign currency remeasurement

chapter 11

Worldwide Accounting Diversity and International Standards

Learning Objectives

After studying this chapter, you should be able to:

LO1 Explain the major factors influencing the international development of accounting systems.

LO2 Understand the problems created by differences in accounting standards across countries and the reasons to develop a set of internationally accepted accounting standards.

LO3 List the authoritative pronouncements that constitute International Financial Reporting Standards (IFRS).

LO4 Describe the ways and the extent to which IFRS are used around the world.

LO5 Describe the FASB–IASB convergence process and the SEC's IFRS Roadmap.

LO6 Recognize acceptable accounting treatments under IFRS and identify key differences between IFRS and U.S. GAAP.

LO7 Determine the impact that specific differences between IFRS and U.S. GAAP have on the measurement of income and stockholders' equity.

Considerable differences exist across countries with respect to how financial statements are prepared and presented. For example, companies in the United States are not allowed to report property, plant, and equipment at amounts greater than historical cost. In contrast, companies in Germany are allowed to report their assets on the balance sheet at revalued amounts. Research and development costs must be expensed as incurred in Japan, but development costs may be capitalized as an asset in Canada and France. Chinese companies use the direct method in preparing the statement of cash flows, whereas most companies in the United States and Europe use the indirect method. Numerous other differences exist across countries, and all of these differences can result in significantly different amounts being reported on the balance sheet and income statement.

In its 2009 annual report, the Brazilian chemical company, Braskem SA, described 13 significant differences between Brazilian and U.S. accounting rules. Under Brazilian accounting rules, Braskem reported 2009 net income of 767.8 million Brazilian reais (BRL). If Braskem had used U.S. GAAP in 2009, its net income would have been only BRL 232.7 million, a difference of 70 percent. The largest difference related to income taxes, specifically the valuation allowance on deferred tax assets. Similarly, stockholders' equity of BRL 4,592.5 million on a Brazilian GAAP basis would have been only BRL 4,379.4 million under U.S. GAAP. Russian telecommunications company Rostelecom reported its 2009 net income under Russian accounting rules to be 5.1 billion Russian rubles (RUR); under International Financial Reporting Standards, the company reported net profit of RUR 3.5 billion for the same period, a reduction of 31 percent. These examples show that diversity in accounting principles across countries can have a significant impact on the amounts reported in financial statements. The first part of this chapter presents additional evidence of accounting diversity, explores the reasons for that diversity, and describes problems caused by accounting diversity.

Efforts have been underway for over three decades to reduce the diversity that exists in financial reporting across countries. The most important of these efforts has been the work that was begun by the International Accounting Standards Committee (IASC) and continues with the International Accounting Standards Board (IASB) to develop International Financial Reporting Standards (IFRS). Today, publicly traded companies in more than 100 countries around the world are using IFRS to prepare consolidated financial statements. The second part of this chapter describes the process of international convergence of financial reporting, focusing on the work of the IASB and current efforts to converge U.S. GAAP with IFRS.

Evidence of Accounting Diversity

Exhibit 11.1 presents the 2010 consolidated balance sheet for Jardine Matheson, a diversified company incorporated in Bermuda with significant holdings in Asia. Jardine Matheson is one of the thousands of companies around the world that prepares its

EXHIBIT 11.1
Jardine Matheson 2010 Balance Sheet

Consolidated Balance Sheet at 31st December 2010

	Note	**2010 US$m**	**2009 US$m (restated)**
Assets			
Intangible assets	*14*	**1,958**	1,759
Tangible assets	*15*	**4,816**	4,116
Investment properties	*16*	**18,426**	15,201
Plantations	*17*	**954**	425
Associates and joint ventures	*18*	**6,385**	4,811
Other Investments	*19*	**1,044**	841
Noncurrent debtors	*20*	**1,898**	1,375
Deferred tax assets	*21*	**133**	126
Pension assets	*22*	**102**	92
Noncurrent assets		**35,716**	28,746
Properties for sale	*23*	**1,184**	787
Stocks and work in progress	*24*	**2,680**	1,960
Current debtors	*20*	**4,085**	3,055
Current investments	*19*	**6**	3
Current tax assets		**130**	84
Bank balances and other liquid funds	*25*		
– nonfinancial services companies		**4,099**	3,937
– financial services companies		**176**	156
		4,275	4,093
		12,360	9,982
Noncurrent assets classified as held for sale	*26*	**—**	107
Current assets		**12,360**	10,089
Total assets		**48,076**	38,835
Equity			
Share capital	*27*	**162**	159
Share premium and capital reserves	*29*	**69**	48
Revenue and other reserves		**14,980**	11,717
Own shares held	*31*	**(1,501)**	(1,230)
Shareholders' funds		**13,710**	10,694
Minority Interests	*32*	**18,250**	14,446
Total equity		**31,960**	25,140

(*continued*)

EXHIBIT 11.1 (Continued)

Consolidated Balance Sheet at 31st December 2010

	Note	2010 US$m	2009 US$m (restated)
Liabilities			
Long-term borrowings	33		
– nonfinancial services companies		4,294	5,228
– financial services companies		1,128	718
		5,422	5,946
Deferred tax liabilities	21	572	444
Pension liabilities	22	176	179
Noncurrent creditors	34	216	158
Noncurrent provisions	35	94	72
Noncurrent liabilities		6,480	6,799
Current creditors	34	5,848	4,683
Current borrowings	33		
– nonfinancial services companies		2,057	909
– financial services companies		1,403	918
		3,460	1,827
Current tax liabilities		273	333
Current provisions	35	55	53
Current liabilities		9,636	6,896
Total liabilities		16,116	13,695
Total equity and liabilities		48,076	38,835

financial statements in accordance with IFRS. A quick examination of this statement reveals several format and terminology differences compared with what is usually found in the balance sheets of U.S.–based companies. The company classifies assets as current and noncurrent but lists them in reverse order of liquidity starting with intangibles. Likewise, it lists long-term liabilities before current liabilities, both of which are reported below shareholders' equity.

Fixed assets are referred to as *tangible assets*, receivables are called *debtors*, and inventories are reported as *stocks and work in progress*. Cash and cash equivalents are called *bank balances and other liquid funds*. Accounts payable are referred to as *creditors*, and *provisions*, found in both noncurrent and current liabilities, are estimated obligations related to things such as warranties and restructuring plans. *Share capital* reflects the par value of common stock and *share premium* shows the paid-in capital in excess of par value. Retained earnings are not reported separately but are included in *revenue and other reserves*. One of the *other reserves* is related to the revaluation of assets, which is an unacceptable practice in the United States. Treasury stock is aptly called *own shares held*.

Exhibit 11.2 presents the 2010 consolidated income statement for the Dutch company Heineken N.V., the producer of one of the most popular brands of beer in the world. Heineken also uses IFRS in preparing its consolidated financial statements. Inspection of this statement reveals a significant difference in format compared with the format normally found in the United States. U.S. companies typically report operating expenses on the income statement according to their function, as follows:

Sales
Less: Cost of goods sold
Equals: Gross profit
Less: Selling costs
Less: Administrative costs
Equals: Operating profit

EXHIBIT 11.2
Heineken N.V. 2010 Income Statement

Consolidated Income Statement
For the Year Ended 31 December 2010

(In millions of EUR)	Note	2010	2009
Revenue	5	**16,133**	**14,701**
Other income	8	**239**	**41**
Raw materials, consumables and services	9	(10,291)	(9,650)
Personnel expenses	10	(2,680)	(2,379)
Amortisation, depreciation and impairments	11	(1,118)	(1,083)
Total expenses		**(14,089)**	**(13,112)**
Results from operating activities		**2,283**	**1,630**
Interest income	12	100	90
Interest expenses	12	(590)	(633)
Other net finance expenses	12	(19)	214
Net finance expenses		**(509)**	**(329)**
Share of profit of associates and joint ventures and impairments thereof (net of income tax)	16	193	127
Profit before income tax		**1,967**	**1,428**
Income tax expenses	13	(399)	(286)
Profit		**1,568**	**1,142**
Attributable to:			
Equity holders of the Company (net profit)		1,436	1,018
Noncontrolling interest		132	124
Profit		**1,568**	**1,142**
Weighted average number of shares—basic	23	562,234,726	488,666,607
Weighted average number of shares—diluted	23	563,387,135	489,974,594
Basic earnings per share (€)	23	2.55	2.08
Diluted earnings per share (€)	23	2.55	2.08

This format combines manufacturing costs (materials and supplies, labor costs, and overhead) and reports them as cost of goods sold. Selling costs and administrative costs (which also consist of supplies, labor costs, and overhead) are reported separately from cost of goods sold. Gross profit is reported as the difference between sales and cost of goods sold.

Heineken does not report operating expenses on the basis of their function but on the basis of their nature. Materials costs are reported as *raw material, consumables and services*, labor costs are reported as *personnel expenses*, and overhead is reported in these line items as well as in *amortisation, depreciation, and impairments*. Each of these line items includes amounts that cut across functional areas. *Personnel expenses*, for example, includes the wages, salaries, and benefits paid to employees involved in manufacturing, selling, and administration. As a result, cost of goods sold is not reported as a separate amount and therefore gross profit cannot be calculated. The nature of expenses format used by Heineken in preparing its income statement is the format traditionally used in continental European countries. Today, however, it is common to find companies in the Netherlands, Germany, and other European countries using the function of expenses (or cost of sales) format familiar in the United States.

The examples of accounting diversity demonstrated thus far relate to differences in terminology and presentation in the financial statements. However, as alluded to in the first paragraph of this chapter, differences also exist across countries with regard to the recognition and measurement principles followed in determining the amounts reported on financial statements.

Foreign companies whose stock is listed on a U.S. stock exchange are required to be registered and file financial statements with the U.S. Securities and Exchange Commission (SEC). Foreign registrants must file their annual report with the SEC on Form 20-F.

EXHIBIT 11.3 SK Telecom Co., Ltd., 2009 Reconciliation of Net Income to U.S. GAAP

	Note Reference	Year Ended December 31, 2007	2008	2009
Net income based on Korean GAAP		₩ 1,562,265	₩ 972,338	₩ 1,055,606
Adjustments:				
Loss on impairment of investment securities	34.a	(2,427)	172,597	2,896
Reversal of amortization of goodwill	34.b	151,589	185,483	168,590
Goodwill impairment	34.b	—	(106,046)	—
Intangible assets	34.b	(4,836)	(10,932)	(3,032)
Capitalization of foreign exchange losses and interest expenses related to tangible assets	34.c	954	4,356	7,616
Capitalization of interest expenses related to purchases of intangible assets	34.c	5,272	5,272	5,272
Nonrefundable activation fees for wireless service only	34.d	(50,325)	(21,991)	40,659
Convertible bonds payable	34.e	(19,340)	(30,407)	103,657
Currency and interest rate swap	34.f	8,295	(478,874)	543,802
Sales of stock by the equity method investee	34.g	(6,392)	—	—
Consolidation of variable interest entity	34.h	(20,651)	(34,303)	(36,260)
Convertible notes receivable	34.i	(412,383)	—	—
Scope of consolidation	34.j	48,009	187,833	(3,920)
Reclassification of SK C&C investment	34.k	83,785	47,645	(94,327)
Retroactive application of equity method of accounting on SKBB investment	34.l	(797)	(21,025)	—
Business combination	34.m	—	—	(340,979)
Asset Securitization Transactions	34.n	—	—	15,489
FIN 48 effect	34.o	(1,320)	2,778	2,711
Effect of changes in tax law	34.o	—	30,066	—
Tax effect of the reconciling items	34.p	109,368	46,947	(111,098)
Net income based on U.S. GAAP		₩ 1,451,066	₩ 951,737	₩ 1,356,682
Less net loss attributable to noncontrolling interest		54,281	121,129	123,044
Net income attributable to the Company		₩ 1,505,347	₩ 1,072,866	₩ 1,479,726
Weighted average number of common shares outstanding		72,650,909	72,765,557	72,346,763
Earnings per share based on U.S.GAAP:				
Continuing operation—Basic earnings per share		₩ 19,528	₩ 11,399	₩ 17,805
—Diluted earnings per share		₩ 19,213	₩ 11,321	₩ 17,569
Discontinued operation—Basic earnings per share		₩ 1,192	₩ 3,345	₩ 2,648
—Diluted earnings per share		₩ 1,166	₩ 3,285	₩ 2,576

The financial statements included in Form 20-F may be prepared in accordance with a foreign GAAP, but the SEC requires income and stockholders' equity under foreign GAAP to be reconciled to U.S. GAAP.[1] Examination of these reconciliations provides considerable insight into the significant differences that exist in recognition and measurement principles between U.S. GAAP and accounting principles in other countries.

As an example, Exhibit 11.3 presents the reconciliation of net income provided by South Korean wireless phone services provider SK Telecom Co, Ltd., in its 2009 Form 20-F. Adjustments are made for 20 differences between Korean and U.S. GAAP. Some of the accounting differences requiring the largest adjustments relate to the accounting for noncontrolling interests, amortization of goodwill, convertible notes receivable, impairment of investment securities, and currency and interest rate swaps. Note that net income

[1] As noted later in this chapter, this requirement was removed in 2007 for those foreign registrants using IFRS to prepare the financial statements included in Form 20-F.

under U.S. GAAP is less than net income under Korean GAAP in 2007 and 2008, but the opposite is true in 2009. The difference in net income in 2009 is highly material; SK Telecom's net income under U.S. GAAP that year was 28.5 percent higher than its net income based on Korean GAAP.

In addition to providing the reconciliation schedule as shown in Exhibit 11.3, SK Telecom also provides notes that explain the accounting differences that underlie each adjustment. For example, the company provided the following disclosure related to the adjustment for currency and interest rate swap:

> Under Korean GAAP, when all critical terms of the hedging instrument and the hedged item are the same, a hedging relationship is considered to be highly effective without a formal assessment of hedge effectiveness. Under Korean GAAP, the Company qualified for certain cash flow hedge accounting. Under U.S. GAAP, at inception of the hedge, a formal hedge effectiveness assessment is required to qualify for hedge accounting or a company can be exempted if it meets the shortcut method requirements. Under U.S. GAAP, the Company did not qualify for any hedge accounting. As a result, the has [sic] Company's currency and interest rate swap, which qualified as a cash flow hedge under Korean GAAP, but did not qualify under U.S. GAAP.[2]

Thus, a difference in the rules related to hedge accounting between U.S. and Korean GAAP resulted in SK Telecom's single largest adjustments in 2008 and 2009.

Reasons for Accounting Diversity

LO1

Explain the major factors influencing the international development of accounting systems.

Why do differences in financial reporting practices across countries exist? Accounting scholars have hypothesized numerous influences on a country's accounting system, including factors as varied as the nature of the political system, the stage of economic development, and the state of accounting education and research. A survey of the relevant literature identified the following five items as commonly accepted factors influencing a country's financial reporting practices: (1) legal system, (2) taxation, (3) financing system, (4) inflation, and (5) political and economic ties.[3] In addition, many believe that national culture has played an important role in shaping the nature of a country's accounting system.

Legal System

The two major types of legal systems used around the world are common law and codified Roman law. Common law began in England and is found primarily in the English-speaking countries of the world. Common law countries rely on a limited amount of statute law interpreted by the courts. Court decisions establish precedents, thereby developing case law that supplements the statutes. A system of code law, followed in most non-English-speaking countries, originated in the Roman *jus civile* and was developed further in European universities during the Middle Ages. Code law countries tend to have relatively more statute or codified law governing a wider range of human activity.

What does a country's legal system have to do with accounting? Code law countries generally have a corporation law (sometimes called a *commercial code* or *companies act*) that establishes the basic legal parameters governing business enterprises. Corporation law often stipulates which financial statements must be published in accordance with a prescribed format. Additional accounting measurement and disclosure rules are included in an accounting law that has been debated and passed by the national legislature. The accounting profession tends to have little influence on the development of accounting standards. In countries with a tradition of common law, although a corporation law laying the basic framework for accounting might exist (such as in the United Kingdom), the profession or an independent, nongovernmental body representing a variety of

[2] SK Telecom Co., Ltd. and Subsidiaries, 2009 Form 20-F, p. F-80.

[3] Gary K. Meek and Sharokh M. Saudagaran, "A Survey of Research on Financial Reporting in a Transnational Context," *Journal of Accounting Literature,* 1990, pp. 145–82.

constituencies establishes specific accounting rules. Thus, the type of legal system in a country determines whether the primary source of accounting rules is the government or the accounting profession.

In code law countries, the accounting law is rather general; it does not provide much detail regarding specific accounting practices and may provide no guidance at all in certain areas. Germany is a good example of a code law country. Its accounting law passed in 1985 is only 47 pages long and is silent with regard to issues such as leases, foreign currency translation, and a cash flows statement.[4] In those situations for which the law provides no guidance, German companies must refer to other sources, including tax law and opinions of the German auditing profession, to decide how to do their accounting. Common law countries, where a nongovernment organization is likely to develop accounting standards, have much more detailed rules. The extreme case might be the FASB in the United States. It provides very specific detail in its authoritative pronouncements about how to apply the rules and has been accused of producing a standards overload.

Taxation

In some countries, published financial statements form the basis for taxation; in other countries, financial statements are adjusted for tax purposes and submitted to the government separately from the reports sent to stockholders. Continuing to focus on Germany, its so-called conformity principle (*Massgeblichkeitsprinzip*) requires that, in most cases, an expense also must be used in calculating financial statement income to be deductible for tax purposes. Well-managed German companies attempt to minimize income for tax purposes, for example, by using accelerated depreciation to reduce their tax liability. As a result of the conformity principle, accelerated depreciation also must be taken in calculating accounting income.

In the United States, on the other hand, conformity between the tax statement and financial statements is required only for the use of the LIFO inventory cost-flow assumption. U.S. companies are allowed to use accelerated depreciation for tax purposes and straight-line depreciation in the financial statements. All else being equal, a U.S. company is likely to report higher income than its German counterpart.

Financing System

The major providers of financing for business enterprises are family members, banks, governments, and shareholders. Those countries in which families, banks, or the state dominate company financing have less pressure for public accountability and information disclosure. Banks and the state often are represented on the board of directors and therefore are able to obtain information necessary for decision making from inside the company. As companies depend more on financing from the general populace through the public offerings of shares of stock, the demand for more information made available outside the company increases. It simply is not feasible for the company to allow the hundreds, thousands, or hundreds of thousands of shareholders access to internal accounting records. The information needs of those financial statement users can be satisfied only by extensive disclosures in accounting reports.

There also can be a difference in orientation, with stockholders more interested in profit (emphasis on the income statement) and banks more interested in solvency and liquidity (emphasis on the balance sheet). Bankers prefer companies to practice rather conservative accounting with regard to assets and liabilities.

Inflation

Countries with chronically high rates of inflation have been forced to adopt accounting rules that require the inflation adjustment of historical cost amounts. This has been especially true in Latin America, which as a region has had more inflation than any other part of the world. For example, prior to economic reform in the mid-1990s, Brazil

[4] Jermyn Paul Brooks and Dietz Mertin, *Neues Deutsches Bilanzrecht* (Düsseldorf: IDW-Verlag GmbH, 1986).

EXHIBIT 11.4
Framework for the Development of Accounting Systems Internationally

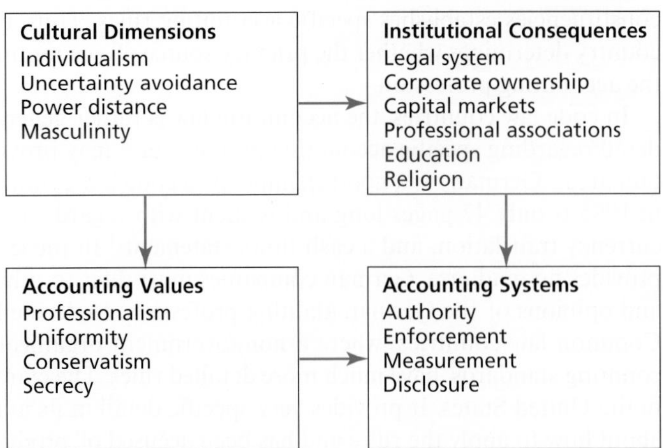

Source: Adapted from S. J. Gray, "Towards a Theory of Cultural Influence on the Development of Accounting Systems Internationally," *Abacus*, March 1988, p. 7.

regularly experienced annual inflation rates exceeding 100 percent. The high point was reached in 1993 when annual inflation was nearly 1,800 percent. Double- and triple-digit inflation rates render historical costs meaningless. This factor primarily distinguishes accounting in Latin America from the rest of the world.

Political and Economic Ties

Accounting is a technology that can be borrowed relatively easily from or imposed on another country. Through political and economic linkages, accounting rules have been conveyed from one country to another. For example, through previous colonialism, both England and France have transferred their accounting frameworks to a variety of countries around the world. British accounting systems can be found in countries as far-flung as Australia and Zimbabwe. French accounting is prevalent in the former French colonies of western Africa. More recently, economic ties with the United States have had an impact on accounting in Canada, Mexico, and Israel.

Culture

From a worldwide survey of IBM Corporation employees, Hofstede identified four societal values that can be used to describe similarities and differences in national cultures: (1) individualism, (2) uncertainty avoidance, (3) power distance, and (4) masculinity.[5] Gray developed a model of the development of accounting systems internationally, an adaptation of which is depicted in Exhibit 11.4.[6] In this model, Gray suggested that societal values influence a country's accounting system in two ways. First, they help shape a country's institutions, such as its legal system and capital market (financing system), which in turn affect the development of the accounting system. Second, societal values influence the accounting values shared by members of the accounting subculture, which in turn influences the nature of the accounting system. Focusing on the links between culture, accounting values, and accounting systems, Gray developed a number of specific hypotheses. For example, he hypothesized that in a society with a low tolerance for uncertainty (high uncertainty avoidance), accountants prefer more conservative measures of profits and assets (high conservatism). This manifests itself in the accounting system through accounting measurement rules that emphasize the accounting value of conservatism. As another example, Gray hypothesized that in countries in which hierarchy and unequal distribution of power in organizations is readily accepted (high power distance), the preference is for secrecy (high secrecy) to preserve power inequalities. This results in

[5] Geert Hofstede, *Culture's Consequences: International Differences in Work-Related Values* (Beverly Hills, CA: Sage Publications, 1980).

[6] Sidney J. Gray, "Towards a Theory of Cultural Influence on the Development of Accounting Systems Internationally," *Abacus,* March 1988, pp. 1–15.

an accounting system in which financial statements disclose a minimal amount of information. Several research studies have found support for a number of Gray's hypotheses.[7]

A General Model of the Reasons for International Differences in Financial Reporting

In 1998, Nobes developed a simplified model of the reasons for international accounting diversity that has only two explanatory factors: (1) national culture, including institutional structures, and (2) the nature of a country's financing system.[8] Nobes argued that differences in the purpose for financial reporting across countries is the major reason for international differences in financial reporting and that the most relevant factor in determining the purpose of financial reporting is the nature of a country's financing system. Specifically, whether or not a country has a strong equity financing system with large numbers of outside shareholders determines the type of financial reporting system a country uses.

Nobes divided financial reporting systems into two classes, A and B. Countries with a strong equity-outsider financing system use a Class A accounting system and countries with a weak equity-outsider financing system have a Class B system. Class A accounting is less conservative, provides more disclosure, and does not follow tax rules. Class B accounting is more conservative and disclosure is not as extensive and more closely follows tax rules. U.S. GAAP is a Class A accounting system.

Nobes stated that a country's culture determines the nature of its financing system. He assumed (without explaining how) that some cultures lead to strong equity-outsider financing systems and other cultures lead to weak equity-outsider financing systems. His model of reasons for international accounting differences is summarized as follows:

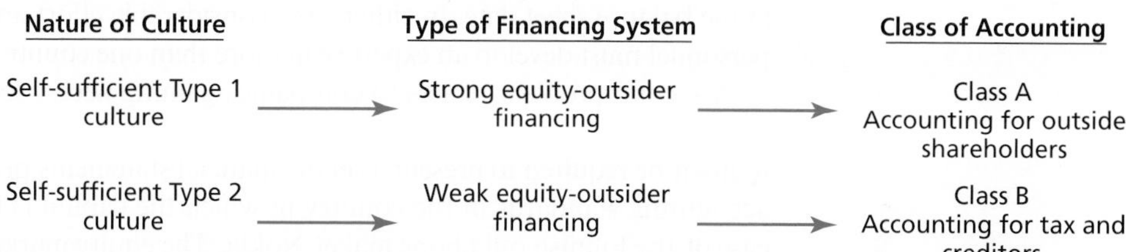

Many countries in the developing world are culturally dominated by another country, often as a result of European colonialism. Nobes argued that culturally dominated countries use the accounting system of their dominating country regardless of the nature of the equity financing system. This explains, for example, why the African nation of Malawi, a former British colony, uses a Class A accounting system even though it has a weak equity-outsider financing system.

As the financing system in a country evolves from weak equity to strong equity, Nobes suggests that the accounting system also evolves in the direction of Class A accounting. He cites China as an example of a country in which this is already taking place. Nobes also argues that individual companies with strong equity-outsider financing attempt to use Class A accounting even if they are located in a Class B accounting system country; some evidence suggests that this also has occurred. To enhance companies' ability to compete in attracting international equity investment, several European countries (with weak equity-outsider financing and Class B accounting systems) developed a two-tiered financial reporting system in the late 1990s. Austria, France, Germany, Italy, and Switzerland gave stock exchange–listed companies the option to use International Financial Reporting Standards (IFRS) (a Class A accounting system) in preparing their

[7] For a review of this literature, see Timothy S. Doupnik and George T. Tsakumis, "A Critical Review of Tests of Gray's Theory of Cultural Relevance and Suggestions for Future Research," *Journal of Accounting Literature,* 2004, pp. 1–48.

[8] Christopher W. Nobes, "Towards a General Model of the Reasons for International Differences in Financial Reporting," *Abacus,* September 1998, pp. 162–87.

consolidated financial statements. Large numbers of German and Swiss multinational companies (including Deutsche Bank, Bayer, and Nestlé), in particular, took advantage of this option. Other companies continued to use local GAAP.

The desire for companies to be competitive in the international capital market led the European Union in 2005 to require all publicly traded companies to use IFRS in preparing their consolidated financial statements. As time passes, it will be interesting to see whether adoption of a Class A accounting system results in a stronger equity-outsider financing system within the countries comprising the European Union.

Problems Caused by Diverse Accounting Practices

LO2

Understand the problems created by differences in accounting standards across countries and the reasons to develop a set of internationally accepted accounting standards.

The diversity in accounting practices across countries causes problems that can be quite serious for some parties. One problem relates to the preparation of consolidated financial statements by companies with foreign operations. Consider The Coca-Cola Company, which has subsidiaries in more than 40 countries around the world. Each subsidiary incorporated in the country in which it is located is required to prepare financial statements in accordance with local regulations. These regulations usually require companies to keep books in the local currency and follow local accounting principles. Thus, Coca-Cola Italia S.r.L. prepares financial statements in euros using Italian accounting rules, and Coca-Cola de Chile, S.A., prepares financial statements in Chilean pesos using Chilean accounting standards. To prepare consolidated financial statements in the United States, in addition to translating the foreign currency financial statements into U.S. dollars, the parent company also must convert the financial statements of its foreign subsidiaries into U.S. GAAP. Each foreign subsidiary must either maintain two sets of books prepared in accordance with both local and U.S. GAAP or, as is more common, make reconciliations from local GAAP to U.S. GAAP at the balance sheet date. In either case, considerable effort and cost are involved; company personnel must develop an expertise in more than one country's accounting standards.

A second problem relates to companies gaining access to foreign capital markets. If a company desires to obtain capital by selling stock or borrowing money in a foreign country, it might be required to present a set of financial statements prepared in accordance with the accounting standards in the country in which the capital is being obtained. Consider the case of the Finnish cell phone maker Nokia. The equity market in Finland is so small (there are fewer than 6 million Finns) and Nokia's capital needs are so great that the company found it necessary to have its common shares listed on foreign stock exchanges in Germany and the United States. To have their stock traded in the United States, foreign companies must reconcile financial statements to U.S. accounting standards. This can be quite costly. To prepare for a New York Stock Exchange (NYSE) listing in 1993, the German automaker Daimler-Benz estimated it spent $60 million to initially prepare U.S. GAAP financial statements; it planned to spend $15 million to $20 million each year thereafter.[9]

A third problem relates to the lack of comparability of financial statements between companies from different countries. This can significantly affect the analysis of foreign financial statements for making investment and lending decisions. In 2005 alone, U.S. investors bought nearly $180 billion in debt and equity of foreign entities while foreign investors pumped approximately $474 billion into U.S. entities through similar acquisitions.[10] In the 1990s, there was an explosion in mutual funds that invest in the stock of foreign companies—from 123 in 1989[11] to 1,621 at the end of 1999.[12] T. Rowe Price's New Asia Fund, for example, invests exclusively in stocks and bonds of companies located in Asian countries other than Japan. The job of deciding which foreign company to invest

[9] Allan B. Afterman, *International Accounting, Financial Reporting, and Analysis* (New York: Warren, Gorham & Lamont, 1995), pp. C1-17 and C1-22.

[10] U.S. Department of Commerce, *Survey of Current Business,* December 2006, p. D-64.

[11] James L. Cochrane, James E. Shapiro, and Jean E. Tobin, "Foreign Equities and U.S. Investors: Breaking Down the Barriers Separating Supply and Demand," NYSE Working Paper 95-04, 1995.

[12] Paula A. Tkac, "The Performance of Open-End International Mutual Funds," *Economic Review,* Third Quarter 2001, pp. 1–17.

in is complicated by the fact that foreign companies use accounting rules that differ from those used in the United States, and those rules differ from country to country. It is very difficult, if not impossible, for a potential investor to directly compare the financial position and performance of, for example, chemical companies in Germany (BASF), China (Sinopec), and the U.S. (DuPont) because these three countries have different financial accounting and reporting standards.

International Harmonization of Financial Reporting

Because of the problems associated with worldwide accounting diversity, attempts to reduce accounting differences across countries known as *harmonization* have been ongoing for more than three decades. The ultimate goal of harmonization is to have all companies around the world following similar accounting standards.

While numerous organizations have been involved in the international harmonization of financial reporting the two most important players in this effort have been the European Union on a regional basis and the International Accounting Standards Board on a global basis.

European Union

The major objective embodied in the Treaty of Rome that created the European Economic Community in 1957 (now called the *European Union*) was the establishment of free movement of persons, goods and services, and capital across member countries. To achieve a common capital market, the European Union (EU) attempted to harmonize financial reporting practices within the community. To do this, the EU issued directives that had to be incorporated into the laws of member nations. Two directives helped harmonize accounting. The Fourth Directive, issued in 1978, dealt with valuation rules, disclosure requirements, and the format of financial statements. The Seventh Directive, issued in 1983, related to the preparation of consolidated financial statements.

The Seventh Directive required companies to prepare consolidated financial statements and outlined the procedures for their preparation. This directive significantly impacted European accounting because consolidations were previously uncommon on the Continent.

The Fourth Directive provided considerable flexibility with dozens of provisions beginning with the expression "member states may require or permit companies to"; these allowed countries to choose from among acceptable alternatives. One manifestation of this flexibility resulted in Dutch and British law allowing companies to write up assets to higher market values, but in Germany this was strictly forbidden. Notwithstanding this flexibility, implementation of the directives into local law caused extensive change in accounting practice in several countries.

The Fourth and Seventh Directives did not create complete harmonization within the European Union. As an illustration of the effects of differing principles within the EU, the profits of one case study company were measured in European currency units (ECUs) using the accounting principles of various member states. The results are almost startling:

Most Likely Profit—Case Study Company

Country	ECUs (millions)
Spain	131
Germany	133
Belgium	135
Netherlands	140
France	149
Italy	174
United Kingdom	192

Source: Anthony Carey, "Harmonization: Europe Moves Forward," *Accountancy,* March 1990, pp. 92–93.

Part of the difference in the measurement of profit across EU countries resulted from several important topics not being covered in the directives including lease accounting, foreign currency translation, accounting changes, contingencies, income taxes, and long-term construction contracts. In 1990, the EU Commission indicated that there would be no further accounting directives. Instead, the Commission indicated in 1995 that it would associate the EU with efforts undertaken by the International Accounting Standards Committee toward a broader international harmonization of accounting standards.

International Accounting Standards Committee

In hopes of eliminating the diversity of principles used throughout the world, the International Accounting Standards Committee (IASC) was formed in June 1973 by accountancy bodies in Australia, Canada, France, Germany, Japan, Mexico, the Netherlands, the United Kingdom and Ireland, and the United States. The IASC operated until April 1, 2001, when it was succeeded by the International Accounting Standards Board (IASB).

Based in London, the IASC's primary objective was to develop international accounting standards (IASs). The IASC had no power to require the use of its standards, but member accountancy bodies pledged to work toward adoption of IASs in their countries. IASs were approved by a board consisting of representatives from 14 countries. The part-time board members normally met only three times a year for three or four days. The publication of a final IAS required approval of at least 11 of the 14 board members.

Early IASs tended to follow a lowest common denominator approach and often allowed at least two methods for dealing with a particular accounting issue. For example, *IAS 2,* originally issued in 1975, allowed the use of specific identification, FIFO, LIFO, average cost, and the base stock method for valuing inventories, effectively sanctioning most of the alternative methods in worldwide use. For the same reason, the IASC initially allowed both the traditional U.S. treatment of expensing goodwill over a period of up to 40 years and the U.K. approach of writing off goodwill directly to stockholders' equity. Although perhaps necessary from a political perspective, such compromise brought the IASC under heavy criticism.

The IOSCO Agreement

In 1987, the International Organization of Securities Commissions (IOSCO) became a member of the IASC's Consultative Group. IOSCO is composed of the stock exchange regulators in more than 100 countries, including the U.S. SEC. As one of its objectives, IOSCO works to facilitate cross-border securities offerings and listings by multinational issuers. To this end, IOSCO supported the IASC's efforts at developing IASs that foreign issuers could use in lieu of local accounting standards when entering capital markets outside of their home country. "This could mean, for example, that if a French company had a simultaneous stock offering in the United States, Canada, and Japan, financial statements prepared in accordance with international standards could be used in all three nations."[13]

IOSCO supported the IASC's Comparability Project (begun in 1987) "to eliminate most of the choices of accounting treatment currently permitted under International Accounting Standards."[14] As a result of the Comparability Project, 10 revised IASs were approved in 1993 to become effective in 1995. In 1993, IOSCO and the IASC agreed upon a list of "core" standards to use in financial statements of companies involved in cross-border securities offerings and listings. Upon their completion, IOSCO agreed to evaluate the core standards for possible endorsement for cross-border listing purposes.

The IASC accelerated its pace of standards development, issuing or revising 16 standards in the period 1997–1998. With the publication of *IAS 39* in December 1998, the IASC completed its work program to develop the core set of standards. In 2000, IOSCO's Technical Committee recommended that securities regulators permit foreign issuers to

[13] Stephen H. Collins, "The SEC on Full and Fair Disclosure," *Journal of Accountancy,* January 1989, p. 84.

[14] International Accounting Standards Committee, *International Accounting Standards 1990* (London: IASC, 1990), p. 13.

use IASC standards to gain access to a country's capital market as an alternative to using local standards.

International Accounting Standards Board

On completion of its core set of standards, the IASC proposed a new structure that would allow it and national standard setters to better work together toward global harmonization. The restructuring created the International Accounting Standards Board (IASB). In April 2001, the IASB assumed accounting standard-setting responsibilities from its predecessor body, the IASC.

The IASB consists of 16 full-time members. To ensure the IASB's independence all members are required to sever their employment relationships with former employers and are not allowed to hold any position giving rise to perceived economic incentives that might call their independence into question. Seven of the full-time IASB members have a formal liaison responsibility with one or more national standard setters. A minimum of five IASB members must have a background as practicing auditors, three must have a background as preparers of financial statements, and three as users of financial statements, and at least one member must come from academia. The most important criterion for selection as an IASB member is technical competence. The initial IASB members came from nine countries: Australia, Canada, France, Germany, Japan, South Africa, Switzerland, the United Kingdom (4), and the United States (3).

LO3

List the authoritative pronouncements that constitute International Financial Reporting Standards (IFRS).

International Financial Reporting Standards (IFRS)

In April 2001, the IASB adopted all international accounting standards issued by the IASC and announced that its accounting standards would be called *international financial reporting standards* (IFRS). *IAS 1*, "Presentation of Financial Statements," was amended in 2003 and defines IFRS as standards and interpretations adopted by the IASB. The authoritative pronouncements that make up IFRS consist of these:

- International Financial Reporting Standards (IFRSs) issued by the IASB.
- International Accounting Standards (IASs) issued by the IASC (and adopted by the IASB).
- Interpretations originated by the Standing Interpretations Committee (SIC) (until 2001) and the International Financial Reporting Interpretations Committee (IFRIC).

Under the new structure, the IASB has sole responsibility for establishing IFRS.

The IASC issued 41 IASs from 1975 to 2001, and the IASB had issued 13 IFRSs as of July 1, 2011. Several IASs have been withdrawn or superseded by subsequent standards. For example, later standards dealing with property, plant, and equipment and intangible assets have superseded *IAS 4,* "Depreciation Accounting," originally issued in 1976. Other IASs have been revised one or more times since their original issuance. For example, *IAS 2*, "Inventories," was originally issued in 1975 but was then revised as part of the Comparability Project in 1993. As part of an improvements project undertaken by the IASB, *IAS 2* was again updated in 2003. Of 41 IASs issued by the IASC, only 28 were still in force as of July 1, 2011. The IASB issued the first IFRS in 2003; it deals with the important question of how a company should restate its financial statements when it adopts IFRS for the first time.

Exhibit 11.5 provides a complete list of the 41 IASs and IFRSs as of July 1, 2011. Together these two sets of standards (along with several interpretations) create what the IASB refers to as IFRS and what can be thought of as IASB GAAP. IFRS constitute a comprehensive set of financial reporting standards that cover the major accounting issues. In addition, the IASB's Framework for the Preparation and Presentation of Financial Statements, which is very similar in scope to the FASB's Conceptual Framework, provides a basis for determining the appropriate accounting treatment for items not covered by a specific standard or interpretation. As was true for its predecessor, the IASB does not have the ability to enforce its standards. It develops IFRS for the public good and makes them available to any organization or nation that wishes to use them.

EXHIBIT 11.5
International Financial Reporting Standards as of July 2011

	Title	Originally Issued
IAS 1	Presentation of Financial Statements	1975
IAS 2	Inventories	1975
IAS 7	Statement of Cash Flows	1977
IAS 8	Accounting Policies, Changes in Accounting Estimates and Errors	1978
IAS 10	Events after the Reporting Period	1978
IAS 11	Construction Contracts	1979
IAS 12	Income Taxes	1979
IAS 16	Property, Plant, and Equipment	1982
IAS 17	Leases	1982
IAS 18	Revenue	1982
IAS 19	Employee Benefits	1983
IAS 20	Accounting for Government Grants and Disclosure of Government Assistance	1983
IAS 21	The Effects of Changes in Foreign Exchange Rates	1983
IAS 23	Borrowing Costs	1984
IAS 24	Related Party Disclosures	1984
IAS 26	Accounting and Reporting by Retirement Benefit Plans	1987
IAS 27	Separate Financial Statements	1989
IAS 28	Investments in Associates and Joint Ventures	1989
IAS 29	Financial Reporting in Hyperinflationary Economies	1989
IAS 32	Financial Instruments: Presentation	1995
IAS 33	Earnings per Share	1997
IAS 34	Interim Financial Reporting	1998
IAS 36	Impairment of Assets	1998
IAS 37	Provisions, Contingent Liabilities and Contingent Assets	1998
IAS 38	Intangible Assets	1998
IAS 39	Financial Instruments: Recognition and Measurement	1998
IAS 40	Investment Property	2000
IAS 41	Agriculture	2001
IFRS 1	First-Time Adoption of IFRS	2003
IFRS 2	Share-Based Payment	2004
IFRS 3	Business Combinations	2004
IFRS 4	Insurance Contracts	2004
IFRS 5	Noncurrent Assets Held for Sale and Discontinued Operations	2004
IFRS 6	Exploration for and Evaluation of Mineral Resources	2004
IFRS 7	Financial Instruments: Disclosures	2005
IFRS 8	Operating Segments	2006
IFRS 9	Financial Instruments	2009
IFRS 10	Consolidated Financial Statements	2011
IFRS 11	Joint Arrangements	2011
IFRS 12	Disclosure of Interests in Other Entities	2011
IFRS 13	Fair Value Measurement	2011

The IASB Framework states that the "objective of financial statements is to provide information about the financial position, performance and changes in financial position of an entity that is useful to a wide range of users in making economic decisions."[15] The Framework lists the range of users of financial statements to include investors, lenders, employees, customers, suppliers, government agencies, and the public. However, the objective of financial statements can be achieved by focusing on the information needs of investors because the "provision of financial statements that meet their needs also will meet most of the needs of other users that financial statements can satisfy."[16] With its emphasis on providing relevant information to investors, IFRS clearly fall into the category of being a Class A accounting system as defined by Nobes.

[15] IASB, *Framework for the Preparation and Presentation of Financial Statements,* para. 12.

[16] Ibid., para. 10.

Describe the ways and the extent to which IFRS are used around the world.

Use of IFRS

A country can use IFRS in a number of different ways. For example, a country could (1) adopt IFRS as its national GAAP, (2) *require* domestic listed companies to use IFRS in preparing their *consolidated* financial statements, (3) *allow* domestic listed companies to use IFRS, and/or (4) require or allow *foreign* companies listed on a domestic stock exchange to use IFRS. See Exhibit 11.6 for a summary of the extent to which IFRS are

EXHIBIT 11.6
Use of IFRS in Preparing Consolidated Financial Statements July 2011

IFRS Required for all Domestic Listed Companies			
Anguilla	Estonia*	Kuwait	Papua New Guinea
Antigua and Barbuda	Fiji	Kyrgyzstan	Peru
Argentina (2012)	Finland	Latvia*	Poland*
Armenia	France*	Lebanon	Portugal*
Australia[#]	Georgia	Libya	Qatar
Austria*	Germany*	Liechtenstein	Romania*
Bahamas	Ghana	Lithuania*	Serbia
Bahrain	Greece*	Luxembourg*	Slovak Republic*
Barbados	Grenada	Macedonia	Slovenia*
Belgium*	Guatemala	Malawi	South Africa
Bosnia & Herzegovina	Guyana	Malta*	South Korea
Botswana	Haiti	Mauritius	Spain*
Brazil	Honduras	Mexico (2012)	St. Kitts and Nevis
Bulgaria*	Hong Kong[†]	Mongolia	Sweden*
Canada	Hungary*	Montenegro	Tajikistan
Chile	Iceland	Namibia	Tanzania
Costa Rica	India (2012–2014)	Nepal	Trinidad & Tobago
Croatia	Iraq	Netherlands*	United Arab Emirates
Cyprus*	Ireland*	New Zealand[#]	United Kingdom*
Czech Republic*	Italy*	Nicaragua	West Bank Gaza
Denmark*	Jamaica	Nigeria (2012)	Zambia
Dominican Republic	Jordan	Norway	
Ecuador	Kazakhstan	Oman	
Egypt	Kenya	Panama	

IFRS Required for Some Domestic Listed Companies			
Azerbaijan	Israel	Morocco	Saudi Arabia
Belarus			

IFRS Permitted for Domestic Listed Companies			
Aruba	Gibraltar	Mozambique	Swaziland
Bermuda	Haiti	Myanmar	Switzerland[§]
Bolivia	Japan	Netherlands Antilles	Turkey
Cayman Islands	Laos	Paraguay	Uganda
Dominica	Lesotho	Sri Lanka	Virgin Is. (British)
El Salvador	Maldives	Suriname	Zimbabwe

IFRS Not Permitted for Domestic Listed Companies			
Bangladesh	Indonesia	Russia	Turkmenistan
Benin	Iran	Senegal	Ukraine
Bhutan	Malaysia	Singapore[‡]	United States
Burkina Faso	Mali	Syria	Uruguay
China	Moldova	Taiwan	Uzbekistan
Cote d'Ivoire	Niger	Thailand	Venezuela
Colombia	Pakistan	Togo	Vietnam
Cuba	Philippines	Tunisia	

[#]Australia and New Zealand have national standards described as IFRS equivalents.
*Denotes EU membership. The EU has not adopted portions of *IAS 39*.
[†]Hong Kong has adopted standards that are identical to IFRS.
[‡]Singapore has adopted many IFRSs word for word but has changed several IFRSs when adopting them as national standards.
[§]Switzerland requires Swiss-based multinational companies to use either IFRS or U.S. GAAP.
Source: Deloitte Touche Tohmatsu, "Use of IFRSs by Jurisdiction," www.iasplus.com (accessed July 1, 2011).

required or permitted to be used by domestic listed companies in preparing consolidated financial statements in countries around the world.

Of the 153 countries included in Exhibit 11.6, as of July 2011, 93 required all domestic listed companies to use IFRS. In addition, Argentina, India, Mexico, and Nigeria were scheduled to adopt IFRS in 2012. Most significant among this group of IFRS users are the 27 countries of the European Union. All publicly traded companies in the EU have been required to use IFRS to prepare their consolidated financial statements since January 1, 2005. The only exceptions were those companies that were using U.S. GAAP, which several jurisdictions allowed, or that had publicly traded debt securities only. These companies began using IFRS in 2007. In most cases, EU companies continue to use domestic GAAP to prepare parent company financial statements, which often serve as the basis for taxation. With the EU's adoption of IFRS, the IASB gained a substantial amount of legitimacy as the global accounting standard setter.

Most countries of economic importance require or permit domestic listed companies to use IFRS in preparing their consolidated financial statements. The most important exceptions are China and the United States, the two largest economies in the world. In 2006, China adopted a completely new set of Chinese Accounting Standards that is based on IFRS. In addition, Chinese companies listed on the Hong Kong stock exchange are permitted to use either Hong Kong GAAP or IFRS.

There are two primary methods used by countries to incorporate IFRS into their financial reporting requirements for listed companies: (1) full adoption of IFRS as issued by the IASB, without any intervening review or approval by a local body and (2) adoption of IFRS after some form of national or multinational review and approval process. The EU follows the second method with individual IFRSs going through a multistep process of review and formal endorsement by the European Commission (EC). The EC has adopted all IFRSs as issued by the IASB without modification, with one exception. Certain provisions on hedge accounting in *IAS 39,* "Financial Instruments: Recognition and Measurement," have been carved out from the standard endorsed by the EC. Typically, auditor reports of EU–based companies are careful to state that the company's consolidated financial statements comply with IFRS *as adopted by the European Union.*

FASB–IASB Convergence

LO5

Describe the FASB–IASB convergence process and the SEC's IFRS Roadmap.

At a joint meeting in Norwalk, Connecticut, in September 2002, the FASB and IASB agreed to "use their best efforts to (a) make their existing financial reporting standards fully compatible as soon as is practicable and (b) to coordinate their work program to ensure that once achieved, compatibility is maintained."[17] This so-called Norwalk Agreement set the FASB and IASB along the path of convergence of accounting standards. Convergence can occur by the FASB adopting an existing IASB standard, the IASB adopting an existing FASB standard, or the two boards working together to develop a new standard. In a Memorandum of Understanding (MoU) developed in 2006, the FASB and IASB agreed that trying to eliminate differences between two standards that are in need of significant improvement is not a good use of resources. Instead, standards in need of improvement should be replaced with new jointly developed standards. The idea behind convergence is to have similar, but not necessarily identical standards. Indeed, the boards acknowledge that the development of identical standards, even if jointly developed, is not realistic. One impetus for the FASB–IASB convergence project can be found in the Sarbanes-Oxley Act of 2002, which requires the U.S. accounting standard setters to consider "the extent to which international convergence on high quality accounting standards is necessary or appropriate in the public interest and for the protection of investors."[18] Note that the process of convergence as is being pursued by the FASB is different from the outright adoption of IFRS as national accounting standards, which is the approach that has been taken by many countries including those in the European Union.

[17] FASB–IASB, Memorandum of Understanding, "The Norwalk Agreement," available at www.iasplus.com.

[18] Sarbanes-Oxley Act of 2002, Section 108(b).

The six key FASB initiatives to further convergence[19] between IFRS and U.S. GAAP are:

1. *Short-term convergence project:* The objective of the short-term convergence project is to eliminate those differences between U.S. GAAP and IFRS in which convergence is likely to be achievable in the short term. Convergence is expected to occur by selecting either existing U.S. GAAP or IASB requirements as the high-quality solution.
2. *Joint projects:* Joint projects involve sharing FASB and IASB staff resources and working on a similar time schedule.
3. *The convergence research project:* The FASB staff embarked on a project to identify all substantive differences between U.S. GAAP and IFRS and catalog differences based on the FASB's strategy for resolving them.
4. *Liaison IASB member on-site at the FASB offices:* To facilitate information exchange and foster cooperation, a full-time IASB member is in residence at the FASB offices. Former FASB Vice-Chair James Leisenring was the first IASB member to serve in this capacity.
5. *Monitoring IASB projects:* The FASB monitors IASB projects based on the level of interest in the topic being addressed.
6. *Explicit consideration of convergence potential in board agenda decisions:* As part of the process for considering topics to add to its agenda, the FASB explicitly considers the potential for cooperation with the IASB.

SEC Acceptance of IFRS

As a result of the IOSCO agreement discussed earlier, the SEC's early focus on international standards related to whether it should allow foreign companies to use IFRS without reconciliation to U.S. GAAP. The SEC began formal consideration of this question in 2000 by issuing a Concept Release to solicit comments on whether it should modify its GAAP reconciliation requirement. Pressure put on the SEC to make this change intensified with the adoption of IFRS in the European Union in 2005. Finally, in November 2007, the SEC issued a final rule aptly titled "Acceptance from Foreign Private Issuers of Financial Statements Prepared in Accordance with International Financial Reporting Standards without Reconciliation to U.S. GAAP." Beginning with financial statements filed for fiscal years ended after November 15, 2007, foreign companies using IFRS no longer provide U.S. GAAP information in their annual reports filed with the SEC. Approximately 180 companies were able to file their 2007 annual reports with the SEC without providing a reconciliation to U.S. GAAP. Among these companies was Rostelecom, introduced at the beginning of this chapter. However, foreign companies using foreign GAAP other than IFRS must continue to provide a U.S. GAAP reconciliation in their Form 20-F.

Elimination of the U.S. GAAP reconciliation requirement for foreign filers using IFRS results in an asymmetric situation for U.S. domestic companies that are required to use U.S. GAAP. To level the playing field, the SEC issued a Concept Release in July 2007 to solicit public comment on the idea of allowing U.S. companies to choose between U.S. GAAP and IFRS. A majority of comment letters were not in favor of allowing a *choice* between IFRS or U.S. GAAP, but instead recommended that the SEC *require* the use of IFRS by U.S. companies. Even the chairmen of the FASB and the Financial Accounting Foundation (FAF), which oversees the FASB, expressed approval for a move toward the use of IFRS in the United States. They concluded that: "Investors would be better served if all U.S. public companies used accounting standards promulgated by a single global standard setter as the basis for preparing their financial reports. This would be best accomplished by *moving U.S. public companies to an improved version of International Financial Reporting Standards (IFRS)*" (emphasis added).[20] However, they also noted that

[19] Extensive information on the FASB's international convergence project can be found on the organization's website at www.fasb.org.

[20] Letter to Ms. Nancy M. Morris, Securities and Exchange Commission, signed by Robert E. Denham, Chairman, Financial Accounting Foundation, and Robert H. Herz, Chairman, Financial Accounting Standards Board, dated November 7, 2007 (accessed December 6, 2007, at www.fasb.org/FASB_FAF_Response_SEC_Release_msw.pdf).

the switch to IFRS would be a complex, multiyear process that would involve significant changes to the U.S. financial reporting system, including changes in auditing standards, licensing requirements, and how accountants are educated.

IFRS Roadmap

In reaction to the support expressed for IFRS, the SEC issued a proposed rule for the potential use of IFRS by U.S. public companies in November 2008.[21] This so-called IFRS Roadmap sets forth several milestones that, if achieved, could lead to the *required* use of IFRS by U.S. issuers. The SEC indicated that it would monitor these milestones until 2011, and if significant progress had been made at that time the SEC would then require the mandatory adoption of IFRS by U.S. public companies over a three-year phase-in period. Large companies with market capitalization greater than $700 million (so-called large accelerated filers) would be the first required to use IFRS. Accelerated filers would adopt IFRS in the second year, and nonaccelerated filers in year three. The roadmap indicated 2014 as the first year of IFRS adoption, but a subsequent SEC Release in February 2010 pushed that date back to "approximately 2015 or 2016."[22]

The milestones the SEC indicated it would monitor are:

1. *Improvements in IFRS.* The SEC is interested in seeing improvements made to IFRS prior to 2011, especially from the IASB–FASB convergence process, and it urges the two boards to continue their efforts in this regard. The roadmap specifically mentions completion of joint projects such as those on revenue recognition and financial statement presentation as being important.
2. *Accountability and funding for the IASB.* The Commission will carefully consider the degree to which the IASC Foundation, which oversees the IASB, is able to develop a secure, stable funding mechanism that permits the IASB to function in an independent manner. The roadmap indicates that compulsory financial contributions from a broad-based constituency would help to ensure the independent functioning of the IASB in its standard-setting process.
3. *Improvement in the ability to use interactive data for IFRS reporting.* The SEC will evaluate progress made by the IASB in completing a detailed XBRL taxonomy that will allow firms to file IFRS financial statements in an interactive data format at a greater level of detail than is currently possible.
4. *Education and training.* The SEC also will evaluate the overall level of education and training in the United States on IFRS before requiring their mandatory adoption. Investor education is especially important because the benefits to be derived from a single set of high-quality globally accepted accounting standards can be realized only if investors understand the basis for the reported results.

The SEC received more than 170 comment letters on the IFRS Roadmap with a wide range of views expressed, from no support to complete support for IFRS. Some of the negative comments expressed by constituents related to:

- IFRS are an incomplete set of standards (e.g., lacking industry-specific guidance).
- IFRS are not compatible with the U.S. litigation environment.
- The U.S. economy has more important issues to deal with (i.e., the financial crisis).
- Congress might not allow the SEC to designate the IASB as the U.S. standard setter.

Several letters written by audit firms recommended that the SEC go ahead and make the decision to adopt IFRS and establish a certain date for IFRS adoption to avoid the uncertainty associated with measurement against milestones in 2011. On the other

[21] The SEC's "Roadmap for the Potential Use of Financial Statements Prepared in Accordance with International Financial Reporting Standards by U.S. Issuers" is available at www.sec.gov/rules/proposed/2008/33-8982.pdf.

[22] SEC Release Nos. 33-9109; 34-61578, "Commission Statement in Support of Convergence and Global Accounting Standards," February 2010, p. 15, available at www.sec.gov.

hand, a significant number of letters written by financial statement preparers expressed a preference for convergence of IFRS and U.S. GAAP rather than conversion to IFRS. In their comment letter, the chairs of the FASB and FAF expressed concerns with the IFRS Roadmap and reiterated their commitment to continue the convergence process as follows:

> . . . we remain committed to continuing to work closely with the IASB to improve both U.S. GAAP and IFRS and to eliminate differences between them. We believe these joint efforts will improve the quality of the standards and the comparability of financial information globally and will advance the efforts toward a single set of high-quality global accounting standards."[23]

In the meantime, they call upon the SEC to conduct additional study to "better identify, understand, and evaluate the strengths, weaknesses, costs, and benefits of possible approaches the U.S. should take in moving toward that goal."

A Possible Framework for Incorporating IFRS into U.S. Financial Reporting

The SEC has jurisdiction over the financial reporting of U.S. publicly listed companies only. The possible adoption of IFRS by the SEC would not necessarily affect the financial reporting done by the millions of nonpublic companies that currently use U.S. GAAP. Two important questions associated with the possible SEC adoption of IFRS are: (1) will U.S. GAAP continue to exist, and (2) what role, if any, will the FASB play in financial reporting.

As the self-imposed deadline for monitoring roadmap milestones approached, the SEC staff published a discussion paper in May 2011 that suggests a possible framework for incorporating IFRS into the U.S. financial reporting system.[24] This framework combines the existing FASB–IASB convergence project with the endorsement process followed in many countries and the EU. Some refer to this method as "condorsement." The framework would retain both U.S. GAAP and the FASB as the U.S. accounting standard setter. At the end of a transition period, a U.S. company following U.S. GAAP also would be able to represent that its financial statements are in compliance with IFRS.

The two components of the framework are:

1. The FASB continues to participate in the process of developing *new* IFRSs and incorporates those standards into U.S. GAAP by means of an endorsement process.
2. The FASB would incorporate *existing* IFRSs into U.S. GAAP over a defined period of time, for example, five to seven years, with a focus on minimizing transition costs for U.S. companies.

This approach would maintain U.S. GAAP, which could continue to be used by both public and nonpublic companies. It would achieve the objective of having a single set of high-quality, globally accepted accounting standards. At the same time, it would retain the FASB's authority for establishing financial reporting standards in the United States, and provide the flexibility to modify the requirements of IFRS. These modifications could include:

- Requiring additional disclosures beyond what is required by an IFRS.
- Prescribing which of two or more alternative accounting treatments allowed by IFRS should be followed by U.S. issuers.
- Promulgating standards on issues not specifically addressed in IFRS.

[23] Letter to Ms. Florence E. Harmon, Securities and Exchange Commission, signed by John J. Brennan, Chairman, Financial Accounting Foundation, and Robert H. Herz, Chairman, Financial Accounting Standards Board, dated March 11, 2009 (accessed July 23, 2009, at http://www.fasb.org/).

[24] SEC, "Work Plan for the Consideration of Incorporating International Financial Reporting Standards into the Financial Reporting System for U.S. Issuers: Exploring a Possible Method of Incorporation," SEC Staff Paper, May 26, 2011, available at http://www.sec.gov/spotlight/globalaccountingstandards/ifrs-work-plan-paper-052611.pdf).

The suggested "condorsement" framework for incorporating IFRS into U.S. GAAP is very different from the adoption process proposed in the IFRS Roadmap. At the time this book went to press, it was very unclear whether, when, or how IFRS might be incorporated into the U.S. financial reporting system.

First-Time Adoption of IFRS

Under the SEC's IFRS Roadmap, large U.S. companies could be required to adopt IFRS in preparing their fiscal year financial statements. The process of converting from one set of GAAP to another is quite complex and there are many questions to be answered. To provide guidance on this issue, the first standard developed by the IASB was *IFRS 1,* "First-Time Adoption of IFRS." *IFRS 1* establishes the procedures to be followed in converting from previously used accounting standards to IFRS for the first time, and introduces the concept of the "opening balance sheet."

IFRS 1 requires companies transitioning to IFRS to prepare an opening balance sheet at the "date of transition." The transition date is the beginning of the earliest period for which an entity presents full comparative information under IFRS. The following timeline shows how the transition date is determined:

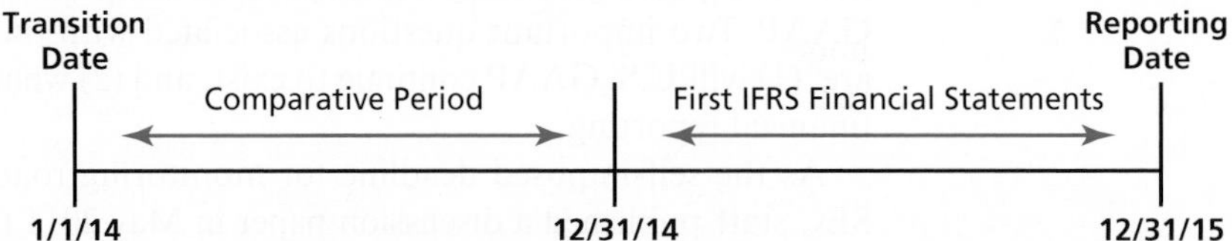

If a company is preparing financial statements for the year ended December 31, 2015, under *IFRS 1* it also must provide comparative financial statements for the year ended December 31, 2014. January 1, 2014, is the beginning of the earliest period for which the comparative information must be provided, and therefore is the transition date. This means that a company must begin using IFRS on January 1, 2014, to be able to prepare IFRS financial statements for 2015.

An entity must complete the following steps to prepare the opening IFRS balance sheet:

Step 1—Determine Applicable IFRS Accounting Policies Based on Standards in Force on the Reporting Date.

This requirement implies that companies must know two years in advance what the applicable standards will be on the reporting date. European Union companies were required to present IFRS financial statements for the first time on December 31, 2005. To assist EU companies in their transition to IFRS, the IASB adopted a "stable platform" policy in which new IASB standards issued after March 1, 2004, did not go into effect until after January 1, 2006. Thus, EU companies knew what the standards in force on December 31, 2005, were going to be as early as March 2004.

Step 2—Recognize Assets and Liabilities Required to Be Recognized under IFRS That Were Not Recognized under Previous GAAP and Derecognize Assets and Liabilities Previously Recognized That Are Not Allowed to Be Recognized under IFRS.

Deferred development costs are an example of an asset recognized under IFRS that is not allowed under U.S. GAAP. A U.S. company transitioning to IFRS on January 1, 2014, would be required to assess whether development costs incurred in prior years met the criteria for capitalization in *IAS 38,* "Intangible Assets." If so, then the costs previously expensed would be reversed and recognized on the opening balance sheet as an asset. The counterpart would be an adjustment to stockholders' equity. Restructuring is an area in which a U.S. company might need to derecognize a liability. A restructuring charge and related liability can be recognized at an earlier date under U.S. GAAP than under IFRS.

Going forward, new IFRS adopters will need to amend their asset and liability recognition policies to make sure that they are in compliance with IFRS. For example, development costs incurred after January 1, 2014, will have to be evaluated for possible capitalization.

Step 3—Measure Assets and Liabilities Recognized on the Opening Balance Sheet in Accordance with IFRS.

An entity must retroactively apply applicable IASB standards to each asset and liability reported on the opening balance sheet. As an example, a company previously using LIFO to measure inventory will have to select a method acceptable under IFRS (FIFO or weighted average cost) and retroactively apply that method to the inventory carried on the opening balance sheet. This represents a change in accounting principle. *IFRS 1* indicates that the effect of the change should be recognized in stockholders' equity on the opening balance sheet, and not in net income.

Step 4—Reclassify Items Previously Classified in a Different Manner from What Is Acceptable under IFRS.

There are several situations in which accounting elements are classified differently under IFRS and U.S. GAAP. For example, U.S. companies classify deferred tax assets and liabilities as current or noncurrent depending on the classification of the underlying asset or liability giving rise to the deferred tax. Deferred taxes are classified as noncurrent only under IFRS. To comply with *IAS 12,* "Income Taxes," deferred taxes classified as current under U.S. GAAP would have to be reclassified as noncurrent on the IFRS opening balance sheet. As another example, in some cases, convertible debt that is classified as a liability under U.S. GAAP would have to be reclassified as equity under IFRS.

Step 5—Comply with All Disclosure and Presentation Requirements.

First time adopters of IFRS will have to be careful to comply with all disclosure and presentation requirements, especially those contained in *IAS 1,* "Presentation of Financial Statements." Several public accounting firms provide IFRS disclosure checklists that can be used for this purpose.[25]

In preparing the opening balance sheet, *IFRS 1* provides several optional exemptions from complying with IFRS where retrospective application would be extremely difficult and the benefit to users is unlikely to exceed the cost. First-time adopters of IFRS have an option *not* to (*a*) adjust the carrying amount of goodwill recognized under previous GAAP, (*b*) restate a business combination originally accounted for under the pooling method, (*c*) retrospectively apply *IFRS 2* to stock options, or (*d*) recognize any cumulative translation adjustment for foreign subsidiaries.

Once the opening IFRS balance sheet has been prepared, the company continues to use IFRS for the next two years so that comparative information can be included in the first set of annual financial statements prepared under IFRS. *IFRS 1* also requires a company to provide the following reconciliations in its first set of IFRS financial statements:

1. Reconciliation of total equity measured under previous GAAP to total equity measured under IFRS at:
   (*a*) the date of transition to IFRS (e.g., January 1, 2014).
   (*b*) the end of the comparative period (e.g., December 31, 2014).
2. Reconciliation of net income measured under previous GAAP to net income measured under IFRS for the comparative period (e.g., for the year ended December 31, 2014).

IFRS 1 also requires disclosures explaining the company's adoption of IFRS, including notes to accompany the IFRS reconciliations.

Exhibit 11.7 presents Note 4 from the 2005 Annual Report of the Spanish airline company Iberia, Líneas Aéreas de España, S.A. In accordance with European Union regulations, Iberia adopted IFRS in 2005, with January 1, 2004, as the transition date.

[25] For example, the KPMG International Financial Reporting Group (IFRG) prepared an IFRS Disclosure Checklist dated June 2010, which is available for download at www.kpmg.com/.

EXHIBIT 11.7
Iberia Group
2005 Annual Report

4. Reconciliation of the Beginning and Ending Balances for 2004 per Spanish GAAP and IFRS

Reconciliation of equity at 1 January 2004 and at 31 December 2004

Concept	Equity at 1 January 2004	Equity at 31 December 2004
	(Thousands of Euros)	
Balance per Spanish GAAP in force at that date[a]	1,432,760	1,645,765
Impacts due to transition to IFRS[b]		
Derecognition of amortisation of goodwill	(98,098)	(91,485)
Reversal of provisions and other contingent liabilities	116,682	124,507
Derecognition of deferred income	19,090	1,981
Reversal of provision for major repairs	5,114	—
Conversion to IFRSs of financial statements of companies accounted for using the equity method	4,618	2,262
Derecognition of negative consolidation differences	1,494	998
Derecognition of deferred charges and start-up expenses	(1,905)	(5,189)
Other	—	6
Total impact on equity	46,995	33,080
Minority interests	9,204	5,324
Balance per IFRSs	1,488,959	1,684,169

[a]Obtained from the consolidated financial statements at the date shown, as approved by the shareholders at the related Annual General Meetings.
[b]Taking into consideration tax effects.

Reconciliation of profit for 2004

Concept	Increase/ (Reduction) 2004 Profit
	(Thousands of Euros)
Balance per Spanish GAAP in force at that date*	218,402
Impacts due to transition to IFRS:	
Amortisation of goodwill	6,613
Provisions and other contingent liabilities	7,825
Derecognition of deferred income	(17,109)
Reversal of provision for major repairs	(3,521)
Conversion to IFRSs of financial statements of companies accounted for using the equity method	(2,356)
Share options	(4,969)
Derecognition of negative consolidation differences	(496)
Derecognition of deferred charges and start-up expenses	(3,284)
Other	6
Total impact on equity/profit	(17,291)
Balance per IFRSs	201,111

*Obtained from the consolidated financial statements at the date shown, as approved by the shareholders at the related Annual General Meeting.

The main changes arose in the following items:

Goodwill

Goodwill was calculated as the positive difference between the amount paid by Iberia, Líneas Aéreas de España, S.A. for the acquisition of 67% of Aviación y Comercio, S.A. and the related underlying carrying amount at 31 December 1997. This goodwill was attributed basically to the value of the market presence, size and image of Aviación y Comercio, S.A. at that date. Since it

(continued)

EXHIBIT 11.7
(Continued)

was not possible to reasonably allocate these items to a single cash-generating unit on the basis of which to evaluate possible changes in value in the future, the Company opted to write this goodwill off against the reserves for first-time application of IFRSs. Also, the Group reversed EUR 6,613 thousand relating to the amortisation recognised in 2004 in accordance with Spanish GAAP.

Provisions and Other Contingent Liabilities

The Group reversed, with a credit to reserves, certain provisions recorded to cover potential contingencies which do not meet all the requirements under *IAS 37* to be recognised in the financial statements.

Deferred Income

In accordance with *IAS 17*, the gains recognised as a result of a sale and operating leaseback transaction, which until 2004 were recognised over the subsequent lease term, must be recognised in the income statement at the moment when the transaction is arranged. The Group therefore eliminated the deferred gains with a charge to reserves on first-time application of IFRSs. Also, the deferred income credited to the income statement in this connection in 2004 was reversed.

Note 4 provides the reconciliation of equity and net income from Spanish GAAP to IFRS for the comparative period 2004, and explains the major adjustments made. The notes indicate that Iberia opted not to restate goodwill and instead wrote existing goodwill off against equity on the opening balance sheet. In addition, the notes explain that the company retroactively applied IFRS to remeasure the amounts reported on the opening balance sheet for provisions and other contingent liabilities, and deferred income.

IFRS Accounting Policy Hierarchy

With respect to the issue of determining appropriate accounting policies to use in preparing IFRS financial statements, *IAS 8,* "Accounting Policies, Changes in Accounting Estimates and Errors," establishes the following hierarchy that firms must follow:

1. Apply specifically relevant standards (IASs, IFRSs, or Interpretations) dealing with an accounting issue.
2. Refer to other IASB standards dealing with similar or related issues.
3. Refer to the definitions, recognition criteria, and measurement concepts in the IASB Framework.
4. Consider the most recent pronouncements of other standard-setting bodies that use a similar conceptual framework, other accounting literature, and accepted industry practice to the extent that these do not conflict with sources in items 2 and 3 above.

Two aspects of this hierarchy are noteworthy. First, the Framework is specifically listed as part of the hierarchy and must be consulted before considering sources of guidance listed in item 4. Second, because the FASB and IASB conceptual frameworks are similar, step 4 provides an opportunity for entities to adopt FASB standards in dealing with accounting issues where steps 1 through 3 are not helpful.

In establishing accounting policies to be followed under IFRS, the two extreme approaches that companies can follow are:

1. *Minimize change.* Under this approach a company would adopt accounting policies consistent with IFRS that are most consistent with current accounting policies.
2. *Fresh start.* Under this approach a company would ignore current accounting policies and adopt accounting policies consistent with the IFRS that best reflect economic reality.

The first approach is likely to be less costly than the second approach. However, many commentators encourage companies to take advantage of the opportunity to start from a clean slate and adopt a fresh start approach. For example, in an IFRS newsletter for U.S. companies, Deloitte states: "While IFRS conversion can involve a significant amount of work, there may be a unique opportunity to make needed improvements in your financial reporting and accounting operations, systems, tax accounting, and processes."[26]

Differences between IFRS and U.S. GAAP

LO6

Recognize acceptable accounting treatments under IFRS and identify key differences between IFRS and U.S. GAAP.

In a comparison of IFRS and U.S. GAAP published in July 2008, Deloitte Touche Tohmatsu identified more than 200 differences in the two sets of standards. Exhibit 11.8 summarizes some of these differences. Note that a number of these differences are within the scope of the FASB–IASB convergence projects and therefore are likely to be eliminated over time.

The types of differences that exist between IFRS and U.S. GAAP can be generally classified as follows:

1. Recognition differences.
2. Measurement differences.
3. Presentation and disclosure differences.

Examples of each type of difference are described next.

Recognition Differences

Several differences between IFRS and U.S. GAAP relate to (1) whether an item is recognized or not, (2) how it is recognized, or (3) when it is recognized. A good example of this type of difference relates to the accounting for research and development (R&D) costs. Under U.S. GAAP, R&D costs must be expensed immediately. The only exception relates to costs incurred in developing computer software, which must be capitalized when several restrictive criteria are met. *IAS 38,* "Intangible Assets," also requires immediate expensing of all research costs. Development costs, on the other hand, must be recognized as an internally generated intangible asset when certain criteria are met. Deferred development costs are amortized over their useful life but not to exceed 20 years. Development costs include all costs directly attributable to or that can be reasonably allocated to development activities including personnel costs, materials and services costs, depreciation on fixed assets, amortization of patents and licenses, and overhead costs other than general administration. The types of development costs that might qualify as an internally generated intangible asset under *IAS 38* include computer software costs, patents and copyrights, customer or supplier relationships, market share, fishing licenses, and franchises. Brands, advertising costs, training costs, and customer lists are specifically excluded from recognition as an intangible asset.

Other recognition differences relate to (1) gains on sale and leaseback transactions, (2) past service costs related to vested pension benefits, and (3) deferred tax assets (refer to Exhibit 11.8).

Measurement Differences

Measurement differences result in the recognition of different amounts in the financial statements under IFRS and U.S. GAAP. In some cases, these differences result from different measurement methods required under the two sets of standards. For example, although both IFRS and U.S. GAAP require the use of a lower-of-cost-or-market rule in valuing inventory, the two sets of standards measure "market" differently. Under U.S. GAAP, market value is measured as *replacement cost* (with net realizable value as a ceiling and net realizable value minus a normal profit as a floor). *IAS 2,* "Inventory," requires inventory to be carried on the balance sheet at the lower of cost or *net realizable value*.

In other cases, measurement differences can exist because of alternatives allowed by one set of standards but not the other. Permitting the use of LIFO under U.S. GAAP but not allowing its use under IFRS is an example of this type of difference.

[26] Deloitte Development LLC, "IFRS Conversion: Some Important Lessons Learned," *IFRS Insights,* March 2009, p. 2, available at http://www.iasplus.com/usa/ifrsinsights/0903ifrsinsights.pdf.

EXHIBIT 11.8
Some Key Differences between IFRS and U.S. GAAP at July 2008

Accounting Item	IFRS	U.S. GAAP
Inventory		
Cost-flow assumption	LIFO not allowed	LIFO allowed
"Market" in lower-of-cost-or-market rule	Net realizable value	Replacement cost (with ceiling and floor)
Reversal of inventory writedown	Required if certain criteria are met	Not allowed
Property, plant, and equipment		
Measurement subsequent to acquisition	Based on historical cost or a revalued amount	Based on historical cost
Major inspection or overhaul costs	Generally capitalized	Either capitalized or expensed
Asset impairment		
Indication of impairment	Asset's carrying value exceeds the higher of its (1) value in use (discounted expected future cash flows) or (2) fair value less costs to sell	Asset's carrying value exceeds the undiscounted expected future cash flows from the asset
Subsequent reversal of an impairment loss	Required if certain criteria are met	Not allowed
Construction contracts		
Method used when percentage of completion not appropriate	Cost recovery method	Completed contract method
Research and development costs		
Development costs	Capitalized if certain criteria are met	Expensed immediately (except computer software development)
Leases		
Recognition of gain on sale and leaseback on an operating lease	Recognized immediately	Amortized over the lease term
Pensions		
Recognition of past (prior) service costs related to benefits that have vested*	Recognized immediately	Amortized over the remaining service period or life expectancy
Income taxes		
Recognition of deferred tax assets	Recognized only if realization of tax benefit is probable	Always recognized but a valuation allowance is provided
Classification of deferred taxes	Always noncurrent	Split between current and noncurrent
Consolidated financial statements		
Different accounting policies of parent and subsidiaries	Must conform policies	No requirement to conform policies
Presentation of "extraordinary" items	Not allowed	Required when certain criteria are met
Definition of a "discontinued operation"	A reportable business or geographic segment	A reportable segment, operating segment, reporting unit, subsidiary, or asset group
Interim reporting	Interim period treated as discrete accounting period	Interim period treated as integral part of full year
Statement of cash flows		
Classification of:		
• Interest paid	Operating or financing	Operating
• Interest received	Operating or investing	Operating

*IFRS uses the term *past* service costs, whereas U.S. GAAP calls these *prior* service costs.

Source: Deloitte Touche Tohmatsu, *IFRSs and U.S. GAAP—A Pocket Comparison,* July 2008.

Discussion Question

WHICH ACCOUNTING METHOD REALLY IS APPROPRIATE?

In this era of rapidly changing technology, research and development (R&D) expenditures represent one of the most important factors in the future success of many companies. Organizations that spend too little on R&D risk being left behind by the competition. Conversely, companies that spend too much may waste money or not be able to make efficient use of the results.

In the United States, all R&D expenditures are expensed as incurred. However, expensing all R&D costs is not an approach used in much of the world. Firms using IFRS must capitalize development costs as an intangible asset when they can demonstrate (1) the technical feasibility of completing the project, (2) the intention to complete the project, (3) the ability to use or sell the intangible asset, (4) how the intangible asset will generate future benefits, (5) the availability of adequate resources to complete the asset, and (6) the ability to measure development costs associated with the intangible asset.

Should any portion of R&D costs be capitalized? Is expensing all R&D expenditures the best method of reporting these costs? Is the U.S. approach better than the international standard? Which approach provides the best representation of the company's activities?

One of the greatest potential differences between the application of IFRS and U.S. GAAP is found in *IAS 16,* "Property, Plant, and Equipment." In measuring fixed assets subsequent to acquisition, *IAS 16* allows companies to choose between two approaches: (1) the cost model and (2) the revaluation model. Under the cost model, property, plant, and equipment is measured and carried on the balance sheet at cost less accumulated depreciation and any impairment losses. This is consistent with U.S. GAAP. Under the revaluation model, fixed assets are carried on the balance sheet subsequent to acquisition at a revalued amount, which is measured as fair value at the date of revaluation less any subsequent accumulated depreciation and impairment losses. If a company adopts the revaluation model, it must make revaluations regularly enough that the carrying value reported on the balance sheet does not differ materially from fair value. Companies following the revaluation model need not adopt this treatment for all classes of property, plant, and equipment. However, they must apply it to all items within a class of assets. A company could choose to revalue land but not buildings, for example, but it would need to revalue each and every parcel of land it owns at the same time.

Presentation and Disclosure Differences

Presentation and disclosure differences relate to the manner in which items are presented on the financial statements or disclosed in the notes to the financial statements. Presentation of certain gains and losses as *extraordinary items* under U.S. GAAP, which is not allowed under IFRS, is one example. Another is the difference between the two sets of standards in what is considered a discontinued operation and therefore presented separately on the income statement. The U.S. GAAP definition of a discontinued operation is less restrictive.

Perhaps the greatest difference between IFRS and U.S. GAAP with respect to presentation is the fact that IFRS contain a single standard—*IAS 1,* "Presentation of Financial Statements"—that governs the presentation of financial statements. U.S. GAAP has no equivalent to *IAS 1.*

IAS 1, "Presentation of Financial Statements"

IAS 1, "Presentation of Financial Statements," provides guidance with respect to the following issues:

1. *Purpose of financial statements:* Financial statements provide information about the financial position, financial performance, and cash flows useful to a wide range of users in making economic decisions.
2. *Overriding principle of fair presentation:* Financial statements should present fairly an entity's financial position, financial performance, and cash flows. Compliance with IFRS generally ensures fair presentation. In extremely rare circumstances, an entity might need to depart from IFRS to ensure fair presentation.
3. *Basic principles and assumptions: IAS 1* emphasizes the going concern assumption, the accrual basis of accounting, the consistency principle, the principle of comparative information, and the separate presentation of material items. The standard also precludes the offsetting of assets and liabilities and of revenues and expenses unless specifically permitted by another standard.
4. *Components of financial statements: IAS 1* requires a complete set of financial statements to include:
   a. A statement of financial position (balance sheet).
   b. A statement of comprehensive income (or a separate income statement and statement of comprehensive income).
   c. A statement of changes in equity.
   d. A statement of cash flows.
   e. Accompanying notes, including a summary of significant accounting policies.
5. *Structure and content of financial statements: IAS 1* also provides guidance with respect to the structure of each financial statement and prescribes items that must be presented (a) on the face of financial statements and (b) either on the face of financial statements or disclosed in the notes.

IAS 1 requires an entity to classify assets and liabilities as current and noncurrent unless presentation according to liquidity provides more reliable information. The income statement can be presented using either a *function of expenses* (cost of sales) format or a *nature of expenses* format. See Exhibit 11.9 for illustrations of the alternative formats for classifying expenses on the income statement. Note that the amount reported as *Operating income (loss)* is the same under both formats. Additional required disclosures must be made either on the face of the income statement or in the notes. For example, a company using the function of expenses format must disclose additional information on the nature of expenses, including depreciation and amortization expense and employee benefits expense. For both formats, the total amount distributed as dividends as well as dividends per share must be disclosed. In addition, *IAS 33*, "Earnings per Share," requires basic and diluted earnings per share to be reported on the face of the income statement.

LO7

Determine the impact that specific differences between IFRS and U.S. GAAP have on the measurement of income and stockholders' equity.

U.S. GAAP Reconciliations

Prior to the SEC removing the U.S. GAAP reconciliation requirement for foreign companies using IFRS, a good source of information for understanding the differences between IFRS and U.S. GAAP and their impact on financial statements was the U.S. GAAP reconciliations prepared by foreign companies listed on U.S. stock exchanges in compliance with SEC regulations. Studying these reconciliations was instrumental in determining which were the most important issues to address in the FASB–IASB convergence project.[27] See Exhibit 11.10 for an excerpt from the U.S. GAAP reconciliation included in the 2005 Form 20-F of China Southern Airlines Company Limited (CSA). CSA is one

[27] International Accounting Standards Committee Foundation (IASCF), Annual Report 2003, p. 5. The IASCF oversees, funds, and selects the members of the IASB.

EXHIBIT 11.9
Illustrative IFRS Income Statement

IFRS COMPANY
Income Statement for the Year Ended December 31, Year 1 (in thousands of currency units)

Nature of Expenses Format	*Function of Expenses Format*
Revenue	**Revenue**
Other income	Cost of sales
Changes in inventories of finished goods and work in progress	**Gross profit**
Raw materials and consumables used	Other income
Employee benefits expense	Distribution costs
Depreciation and amortization expense	Administrative expenses
Other expenses	Other expenses
Operating income (loss)	**Operating income (loss)**
Finance costs	Finance costs
Equity method income (loss)	Equity method income (loss)
Profit (or loss) before tax	**Profit (or loss) before tax**
Income tax expense	Income tax expense
Profit (loss) for the period	**Profit (loss) for the period**
Attributable to:	Attributable to:
Parent company shareholders	Parent company shareholders
Noncontrolling interest (Minority interest)	Noncontrolling interest (Minority interest)

Source: *IAS 1*, "Presentation of Financial Statements," paras. 102, 103.

of several Chinese companies listed on the New York Stock Exchange that prepare their consolidated financial statements in accordance with IFRS.

Note 51, Significant Differences between IFRS and U.S. GAAP, indicates that CSA made six adjustments to net income (loss) under IFRS in 2005 to reconcile to U.S. GAAP. The last of these adjustments relates to deferred tax effects arising from differences in the amount of income (loss) reported under IFRS and U.S. GAAP.

Adjustment (a) relates to the acquisition of two airlines, China Northern Airlines (CNA) and Xinjiang Airlines (XJA), in 2004. Under IFRS, these business combinations were accounted for using the purchase method. When the acquisitions took place, U.S. GAAP required that they be accounted for as poolings of interests. Under the purchase method, acquired assets are consolidated at their fair value, and subsequent expenses

EXHIBIT 11.10 China Southern Airlines Company Limited—2005 Form 20-F Excerpt from Note 51

51. SIGNIFICANT DIFFERENCES BETWEEN IFRS AND U.S. GAAP

Effect on net income/(loss) of significant differences between IFRS and U.S. GAAP is as follows:

	Reference in Note above	2004 RMB	2005 RMB
Loss to equity shareholders of the Company under IFRSs		(48)	(1,848)
U.S. GAAP adjustments:			
Net (loss)/income before tax attributable to airline operations of CNA and XJA	(a)	354	159
Sale and leaseback accounting	(b)	115	115
Lease arrangements	(c)	7	7
Capitalized interest	(d)	(13)	(9)
Reversal of additional depreciation arising from revaluation of property, plant and equipment	(e)	13	—
Investments in affiliated company and jointly controlled entity	(f)	7	7
Deferred tax effects		(196)	39
Net (loss)/income under U.S. GAAP		239	(1,530)
Basic (loss)/earnings per share under U.S. GAAP		0.055	(0.350)

related to those assets, such as depreciation, are based on fair value at the date of purchase. Under the pooling of interests method, acquired assets are consolidated at their book value, which remains the basis for determining future expenses. Adjustment (a) adds back the additional expense recognized by CSA under the purchase method on the difference between the acquired assets' fair value and book value. Adjustment (f) is similar in nature. In that case, CSA invested in an affiliated company and a jointly controlled entity that were accounted for as purchases under IFRS. These investments would have been treated as poolings of interests under U.S. GAAP.

Adjustment (b) arises from the difference between IFRS and U.S. GAAP in accounting for gains on sale and leaseback transactions. U.S. GAAP requires such gains to be amortized over the life of the lease, whereas IFRS require immediate recognition in net income. The addition of RMB 115 million in 2005 to determine net income under U.S. GAAP is the current year portion of a gain that originated several years earlier and was fully recognized under IFRS at that time. Adjustment (c) is made for a similar reason.

CSA adopted the allowed alternative in *IAS 23,* "Borrowing Costs," to capitalize interest associated with self-constructed assets. However, the amount of interest to be capitalized (rather than expensed) differs between IFRS and U.S. GAAP and adjustment (d) reflects this difference. Under IFRS, interest costs are capitalized to the extent the related borrowings are directly attributable to an asset's construction. Under U.S. GAAP, if the average accumulated costs for the asset exceed the amount of specific new borrowings, additional interest cost is capitalized based on the average interest rate applicable to other borrowings. The additional amount capitalized as part of the cost of an asset under U.S. GAAP gives rise to a higher amount of annual depreciation expense. The additional depreciation related to capitalized interest is subtracted from IFRS-based income to calculate income under U.S. GAAP.

Adjustment (e) relates to the company's use of the revaluation model in *IAS 16,* "Property, Plant, and Equipment," to revalue fixed assets subsequent to initial recognition. CSA revalued fixed assets in 1996 as part of the transformation from a state-owned enterprise to a publicly traded company. This resulted in an increase in the carrying value of fixed assets accompanied by an increase in stockholders' equity. The revaluation of fixed assets also resulted in an increase in the amount of annual depreciation expense. Adjustment (e) reverses the additional depreciation taken under IFRS on the revaluation amount that would not be allowed under U.S. GAAP. Because this reversal of additional depreciation was made in 2004, not in 2005, one can assume that the revalued assets were fully depreciated in 2004.

Exhibit 11.11 presents the U.S. GAAP reconciliation provided by the German company Bayer AG in its 2005 Form 20-F. Bayer made nine adjustments to convert net income under IFRS to a U.S. GAAP basis, including an adjustment for the deferred tax effect of reconciling net income to U.S. GAAP. The adjustment pertaining to business combinations in 2003 and 2004 relates to the systematically amortized goodwill under IFRS until 2004. That practice was eliminated in U.S. GAAP in 2002. As a result, goodwill amortization expense taken by Bayer under IFRS was added back to calculate net income under U.S. GAAP in 2003 and 2004. With the adoption of *IFRS 3,* "Business Combinations," in 2004, IFRS no longer allow goodwill amortization but require annual impairment testing.

Prior to 1995, IFRS allowed purchased goodwill to be reported as a negative amount in stockholders' equity, in effect, as a *goodwill reserve,* rather than as an asset. Bayer's positive adjustments to stockholders' equity for business combinations primarily relate to the reinstatement of goodwill as an asset and removal of the goodwill reserve under U.S. GAAP.

Bayer makes a small positive adjustment to net income and a larger negative adjustment to stockholders' equity with respect to in-process research and development (IPRD). Prior to 2007, U.S. GAAP required IPRD to be expensed at the time of business combination, whereas IFRS require development costs to be capitalized as an asset when certain criteria have been met. The capitalized development costs then are amortized to expense over their useful life. Bayer must have capitalized in-process development costs acquired in a business combination at some point prior to 2003. The net income adjustment adds back the current year's amortization expense recognized under

EXHIBIT 11.11 Bayer AG—2005 Form 20-F Excerpt from Note 44

[44] U.S. GAAP Information

The Group's consolidated financial statements have been prepared in accordance with IFRS, which as applied by the Group, differs in certain significant respects from U.S. GAAP. The effects of the application of U.S. GAAP to net income and stockholders' equity are set out in the tables below:

	Notes	2003 (€ million)	2004 (€ million)	2005 (€ million)
Net income (loss) reported under IFRS		(1,291)	682	1,595
Business combinations	a	28	192	(4)
Pensions and other postemployment benefits	b	(121)	(325)	(450)
In-process research and development	c	12	38	8
Asset impairment	d	(360)	(7)	23
Early retirement program	e	178	(58)	(20)
Revaluation surplus	f	—	—	4
Minority interest	g	(12)	3	2
Other	h	(13)	(14)	(12)
Deferred tax effect on U.S. GAAP adjustments		134	142	181
Net income (loss) reported under U.S. GAAP		(1,445)	653	1,327
Basic and diluted earnings (loss) per share under U.S. GAAP		(1.98)	0.89	1.82

	Notes	2004 (€ million)	2005 (€ million)
Stockholders' equity reported under IFRS		10,943	11,157
Business combinations	a	1,003	1,013
Pensions and other postemployment benefits	b	2,317	691
In-process research and development	c	(93)	(87)
Asset impairment	d	(162)	(138)
Early retirement program	e	151	101
Revaluation surplus	f	(66)	(62)
Minority interest	g	(111)	(80)
Other	h	28	19
Deferred tax effect on U.S. GAAP adjustments		(964)	(267)
Stockholders' equity reported under U.S. GAAP		13,046	12,347

IFRS. That amortization expense would not exist under U.S. GAAP because all IPRD already would have been expensed at the time of business combination. The adjustment to stockholders' equity reflects the amount of capitalized development costs that has not yet been amortized under IFRS but would have been fully expensed under U.S. GAAP. The adjustment reflects the appropriate amount of retained earnings under U.S. GAAP.

Although both IFRS and U.S. GAAP require long-lived assets to be tested for impairment, they differ as to the method for determining whether an impairment loss has occurred and the way in which an impairment loss is measured. Under IFRS, impairments on long-lived assets are recognized when an asset's recoverable amount is less than its book value. An asset's recoverable amount is the higher of its net selling price, which is the sales price less the cost to dispose, and its value in use, which is the present value of future cash flows expected from the use and disposal of the asset. The amount recognized as impairment loss is the difference between the asset's recoverable amount and its book value. Under U.S. GAAP, an impairment exists when the sum of undiscounted future cash flows expected from the use and disposal of the asset is less than the asset's book value. In that case, the impairment loss is measured as the difference between the asset's carrying value and its fair value. Bayer made adjustments to both net income and stockholders' equity to account for differences in the recognition of impairment losses. An impairment loss recognized under IFRS but not under U.S. GAAP causes IFRS income to be smaller than U.S. GAAP income in the year in which the impairment occurs. In future years, however, U.S. GAAP income will be smaller because depreciation expense is based on a higher book value. Over the life of the impaired asset, the total amount of depreciation and impairment loss will be the same under both sets of rules. The reconciliations prepared by Bayer and China Southern Airlines reflect only a few of the many differences that exist between IFRS and U.S. GAAP.

A Principles-Based Approach to Standard Setting

The IASB has taken a principles-based approach to establishing accounting standards rather than the so-called rules-based approach followed by the FASB in the United States. Principles-based standards focus on providing general principles for the recognition and measurement of a specific item with a limited amount of guidance; they avoid the use of "bright-line" tests. Application of principles-based standards requires a greater degree of professional judgment than does application of rules-based standards. IASB Chair Sir David Tweedie explains the approach taken by the IASB:

> The IASB concluded that a body of detailed guidance (sometimes referred to as *bright lines*) encourages a rule-based mentality of "where does it say I can't do this?" We take the view that this is counter-productive and helps those who are intent on finding ways around standards more than it helps those seeking to apply standards in a way that gives useful information.[28]

Classification of leases is an accounting issue that demonstrates the difference in the standard-setting approach taken by the IASB and the FASB. U.S. GAAP requires leases to be classified as either capital or operating. Capital leases are reported on the balance sheet as both an asset and a liability whereas operating leases are not. Criteria for classifying leases are set out in FASB ASC Topic 840, which clearly states: "If at its inception a lease meets any one of the four lease classification criteria . . . , the lease shall be classified by the lessee as a capital lease" [ASC 840-10-25-29]. Otherwise a lease shall be classified as an operating lease. The four criteria follow [ASC 840-10-25-1]:

1. The lease transfers property ownership to the lessee by the end of the lease term.
2. The lease contains a bargain purchase option.
3. The lease term equals 75 percent or more of the economic life of the leased property.
4. The present value of minimum lease payments is 90 percent or more of the lease property's fair value.

Accounting for leases under U.S. GAAP is very prescriptive. A lease *shall be* classified as a capital lease if at least one of four criteria is met, and two of the criteria are based on bright-line thresholds—*75 percent or more* of the economic life and *90 percent or more* of the fair value. The bright-line tests have come under considerable criticism because they give companies the opportunity to engineer lease agreements so as to avoid meeting the tests and thereby to keep leases off the balance sheet. In a Financial Reporting Issues Conference sponsored by the FASB in 1996, the FASB standard on lease accounting was deemed to be the worst standard in U.S. GAAP.[29]

IAS 17, "Accounting for Leases," is similar to U.S. GAAP in many respects. It also distinguishes between capital (finance) leases and operating leases, but IFRS guidance for classifying leases is much less prescriptive than the U.S. guidance. Paragraph 8 of *IAS 17* provides the following general principle for lease classification:

> A lease is classified as a finance lease if it transfers substantially all risks and rewards incidental to ownership. A lease is classified as an operating lease if it does not transfer substantially all risks and rewards incidental to ownership.

[28] Excerpt from a speech delivered to the Committee on Banking, Housing and Urban Affairs of the United States Senate, Washington, D.C., February 14, 2002.

[29] Cheri L. Reither, "What Are the Best and the Worst Accounting Standards?" *Accounting Horizons,* September 1998, pp. 283–92.

Clearly, *IAS 17*'s general principle for classifying leases does not provide sufficient guidance to ensure consistent application across companies. Paragraphs 10 and 11 provide additional guidance that is suggestive rather than prescriptive. These paragraphs describe examples of situations that individually or in combination *would normally lead to* or *could lead to* the classification of a lease as a finance lease. Note that the standard does not indicate that in these situations a lease *must be* capitalized.

Four of the examples provided in paragraph 10 are similar to the four U.S. GAAP criteria for lease classification. However, the IASB standard is careful not to establish bright-line tests. Rather than the 75 percent of economic life rule in U.S. GAAP, *IAS 17* indicates that if the lease term is for the *major part* of the asset's economic life, it normally would be classified as a capital lease. In the example relating the present value of minimum lease payments to the fair value of the lease property, a less specific test of *at least substantially all* is used instead of the FASB's bright line of 90 percent or more. Presumably, writing a lease contract whose lease term is only 74 percent of the asset's economic life and the present value of lease payments is only 89 percent of the asset's fair value would not in and of itself preclude the lease from being classified as a finance lease under *IAS 17,* whereas it clearly would not meet the test for capitalization under U.S. GAAP. *IAS 17* reiterates in paragraph 10 that "whether a lease is a finance lease or an operating lease depends on the substance of the transaction rather than the form of the contract."

Concerned that the rules-based standards in U.S. GAAP could have contributed to the spate of accounting scandals at U.S. companies, the Sarbanes-Oxley Act of 2002 required the SEC to study the adoption of a principles-based accounting system in the United States. In conducting its study, the SEC evaluated IFRS but concluded that they did not represent a cohesive set of principles-based standards that could act as a model for the United States. The SEC report to Congress issued in 2003 stated that "a careful examination of the IFRS shows that many of those standards are more properly described as rules based. Other IFRS could fairly be characterized as principles only because they are overly general."[30] Principles-only standards do not contain sufficient guidance to ensure relatively consistent application across companies.

Some observers have expressed concern that the FASB–IASB convergence project might result in IASB standards becoming more rules based. In 2003, the IASB issued exposure draft ED 4, "Disposal of Non-current Assets and Presentation of Discontinued Operations," intended to converge IFRS with U.S. standards. Consistent with U.S. GAAP, the IASB's exposure draft included a list of criteria for determining when assets are being "held for sale" and therefore must be classified as such on the balance sheet. In a letter commenting on ED 4, representatives from the National Association of German Banks *(Bundesverband deutscher Banken)* took issue with the fact that the proposed standard included a list of criteria for identifying assets held for sale. According to the authors, such a "list of criteria is at odds with the IAS objective of producing standards based on principles."[31] Moreover, they argue that "in our view, setting out detailed sets of individual circumstances will result in more, not less, discretionary leeway."

Obstacles to Worldwide Comparability of Financial Statements

IFRS and U.S. GAAP are the dominant accounting standards worldwide. In January 2007, a study conducted by the *Financial Times* determined that U.S. GAAP was used by companies comprising 35 percent of global market capitalization; companies

[30] U.S. Securities and Exchange Commission, "Study Pursuant to Section 108(d) of the Sarbanes-Oxley Act of 2002 on the Adoption by the United States Financial Reporting System of a Principles-Based Accounting System," www.sec.gov/news/studies/principlesbasedstand.htm (accessed January 28, 2007).

[31] Katrin Burkhardt and Silvia Schütte, representing the Bundesverband deutscher Banken, in a letter written to Sir David Tweedie, chairman of the IASB, dated October 21, 2003, and cataloged by the IASB as CL59 Bundesverband deutscher Banken.

making up 55 percent of global market capitalization were using or planning to use IFRS; and only 10 percent were using some other set of rules for financial reporting purposes.[32] If the FASB–IASB convergence project progresses to the point where most substantive differences between the two sets of standards have been eliminated, or the SEC requires adoption of IFRS by U.S. companies, some day most major companies worldwide could use similar accounting rules. When that day arrives, will the objective of accounting harmonization have been achieved? Will financial statements truly be comparable across countries? The use of a common set of accounting standards is a necessary but perhaps not a sufficient condition for ensuring worldwide comparability. Several obstacles stand in the way of a common set of standards being interpreted and applied in a consistent manner across all countries.[33]

Translation of IFRS into Other Languages

IFRS are written in English and therefore must be translated into other languages for use by non-English-speaking accountants. The IASB created an official translation process in 1997, and by 2011, IFRS had been translated into more than 40 other languages. Most translations are into European languages because of the European Union's required usage of IFRS. However, IFRS also have been translated into Chinese, Japanese, and Arabic. Despite the care the IASB took in the translation process, several research studies suggest that certain English-language expressions used in IFRS are difficult to translate without some distortion of meaning. In one study, Canadian researchers examined English-speaking and French-speaking students' interpretations of probability expressions such as *probable, not likely,* and *reasonable assurance* used to establish recognition and disclosure thresholds in IASs.[34] English-speaking students' interpretations of these expressions differed significantly from the interpretations made by French-speaking students of the French-language translation. In another study, German accountants fluent in English assigned values to both the English original and the German translation of probability expressions used in IFRS.[35] For several expressions, the original and translation were interpreted differently, suggesting that the German translation distorted the original meaning.

As an example, IFRS (and U.S. GAAP) use the term *remote* that appears particularly difficult to translate in a consistent fashion. *IAS 37,* "Provisions, Contingent Liabilities and Contingent Assets," indicates that a contingent liability is disclosed "unless the possibility of an outflow of resources embodying economic benefits is *remote*" (para. 28), and *IAS 31,* "Interests in Joint Ventures," requires separate disclosure of specific types of contingent liabilities "unless the probability of loss is *remote*" (para. 54). It would appear that *remote* is intended to establish a similar threshold for disclosure in both standards.

French translations of *remote* in both *IAS 31* and *IAS 37* use the word *faible (weak)*. However, the adjective *trés (very)* is added to form the expression *trés faible* in *IAS 31*. Thus, *remote* is literally translated as "weak" *(faible)* in *IAS 37* and "very weak" *(trés faible)* in *IAS 31*. Preparers of financial statements using the French translation of IFRS might interpret *IAS 31* as establishing a stronger test than *IAS 37* for avoiding disclosure.

Translating *remote* into German presents even greater difficulty. *IAS 31* uses the German word *unwahrscheinlich (improbable)*, and *IAS 37* uses the phrase *äußerst gering (extremely remote)*. The German translation of *IAS 31* appears to establish a more stringent threshold for nondisclosure of contingent liabilities than does the German translation of *IAS 37,* and it is questionable whether either threshold is the same as the original in English. The SEC implicitly acknowledged the potential problem in translating IFRS

[32] *Financial Times,* "IFRS vs US GAAP," January 9, 2007, www.ft.com.

[33] The following discussion is based on George T. Tsakumis, David R. Campbell Sr., and Timothy S. Doupnik, "IFRS: Beyond the Standards," *Journal of Accountancy,* February 2009, pp. 34–39.

[34] Ronald A. Davidson and Heidi Hadlich Chrisman, "Interlinguistic Comparison of International Accounting Standards: The Case of Uncertainty Expressions," *The International Journal of Accounting* 28 (1993), pp. 1–16.

[35] Timothy S. Doupnik and Martin Richter, "Interpretation of Uncertainty Expressions: A Cross-National Study," *Accounting, Organizations and Society* 28 (2003), pp. 15–35.

to other languages in its rule eliminating the U.S. GAAP reconciliation requirement for foreign registrants. That rule applies only to those foreign companies that prepare financial statements in accordance with the *English language version* of IFRS.

The Impact of Culture on Financial Reporting

Even if translating IFRS into languages other than English was not difficult, differences in national culture values could lead to differences in the interpretation and application of IFRS. As described earlier in this chapter, Gray proposed a model that hypothesizes a relationship between cultural values, accounting values, and the financial reporting rules developed in a country. More recently, Gray's model was extended to hypothesize that accounting values not only affect a country's accounting rules but also the manner in which those rules are applied.[36] This hypothesis has important implications for a world in which countries with different national cultures use the same accounting standards. It implies that for accounting issues in which accountants must use their judgment in applying an accounting principle, culturally based biases could cause accountants in one country to apply the standard differently from accountants in another country.

Several research studies support this hypothesis.[37] For example, one study found that, given the same set of facts, accountants in France and Germany estimated higher amounts of warranty expense than did accountants in the United Kingdom.[38] This result was consistent with differences in the level of the accounting value of conservatism across these countries resulting from differences in their cultural values. Financial statement users need to be aware that the use of a common set of accounting standards will not lead to complete financial statement comparability across countries. However, a greater degree of comparability will exist than if each country were to continue to use a different set of standards.

Summary

1. Historically, considerable diversity existed with respect to financial reporting across countries. Differences include the format and presentation of financial statements, the measurement and recognition rules followed in preparing financial statements, disclosures provided in the notes to financial statements, and even the terminology used to describe items reported on financial statements.
2. Accounting systems differ across countries partially because of differences in environmental factors such as the type of legal system followed in the country, the importance of equity as a source of financing, and the extent to which accounting statements serve as the basis for taxation. Culture also plays a role in the development of accounting systems and can influence the manner in which accountants interpret and apply accounting standards.
3. Nobes argues that the primary cause for differences in accounting systems involves differences in the extent to which countries use an equity-outsider financing system. Countries with a strong equity-outsider financing system have a Class A accounting system geared toward providing information that is useful in making investment decisions. Weak equity-outsider financing system countries have a Class B accounting system oriented more toward creditors and provides a basis for taxation. Empirical research supports Nobes's notion of two dominant classes of accounting system.
4. The worldwide diversity in accounting practices causes problems that can be quite serious for some parties. Parent companies with foreign subsidiaries must convert from foreign GAAP to parent company GAAP to prepare worldwide consolidated financial statements. To gain access to a foreign capital market, companies often find it necessary to prepare information based on foreign GAAP. This is especially true for foreign companies wishing to gain access to the U.S. capital market. Accounting diversity makes it difficult for potential investors to

[36] Doupnik and Tsakumis, "A Critical Review of Tests of Gray's Theory."

[37] See Joseph J. Schultz and Thomas J. Lopez, "The Impact of National Influence on Accounting Estimates: Implications for International Accounting Standard-Setters," *The International Journal of Accounting* 36 (2001), pp. 271–90; Timothy S. Doupnik and Martin Richter, "The Impact of Culture on the Interpretation of 'In Context' Verbal Probability Expressions," *Journal of International Accounting Research* 3(1), 2004, pp. 1–20; and George T. Tsakumis, "The Influence of Culture on Accountants' Application of Financial Reporting Rules," *Abacus,* March 2007, pp. 27–48.

[38] Schultz and Lopez, "The Impact of National Influence on Accounting Estimates."

compare financial statements between companies from different countries in making international investment decisions.

5. *Harmonization* is the process of reducing differences in financial reporting across countries, thereby increasing the comparability of financial statements. The ultimate form of harmonization would be the use of similar financial reporting standards by all companies in the world.
6. The European Union attempted to harmonize accounting standards across its member nations through the issuance of the Fourth and Seventh Directives. Although these directives significantly reduced the differences that had existed previously, they did not result in complete comparability of financial statements across the European Union.
7. The International Accounting Standards Committee (IASC) was formed in 1973 to develop international accounting standards (IASs) universally acceptable in all countries. The so-called IOSCO agreement significantly enhanced the IASC's legitimacy as the international accounting standard setter.
8. In 2001, the International Accounting Standards Board (IASB) replaced the IASC and adopted the IASs developed by its predecessor. The IASB creates its own international financial reporting standards (IFRSs). Together, IASs, IFRSs, and Interpretations make up IASB GAAP and are referred to collectively as IFRS.
9. The IASB does not have the ability to require the use of its standards. However, a relatively large number of countries either require or allow domestic companies to use IFRS. Since 2005, all publicly traded companies in the European Union have been required to use IFRS in preparing their consolidated financial statements.
10. In 2002, the FASB and the IASB announced the Norwalk Agreement to converge their financial reporting standards as soon as is practicable. The FASB's initiatives to further convergence include a short-term project to eliminate differences in which convergence is likely to be achievable in the short term by selecting either existing U.S. GAAP or IASB requirements. The FASB and IASB also are jointly working on several projects that deal with broader issues, including a project to create a common conceptual framework. In addition, a full-time member of the IASB serves as a liaison with the FASB.
11. In 2007, the U.S. SEC eliminated the U.S. GAAP reconciliation requirement for foreign companies that use IFRS, and in 2008, it issued an IFRS Roadmap that proposes the use of IFRS by U.S. companies. The SEC indicated it would monitor several milestones until 2011 and then make a decision whether to require U.S. publicly traded companies to use IFRS beginning as early as 2015.
12. In 2011, the SEC staff suggested a "condorsement" approach to incorporating IFRS into U.S. financial reporting. Under this approach, U.S. GAAP would continue with the FASB as national standard setter. The FASB would continue to participate in the development of new IFRSs and would incorporate existing IFRSs into U.S. GAAP over a specified transition period, for example, five to seven years.
13. *IFRS 1* establishes procedures to be followed in the first-time adoption of IFRS. *IFRS 1* requires the preparation of an opening IFRS balance sheet two years prior to when a company publishes its first set of IFRS financial statements. In preparing the opening IFRS balance sheet a company would need to (a) recognize assets and liabilities required by IFRS but not by previous GAAP and derecognize items previously recognized that are not allowed under IFRS, (b) measure assets and liabilities in accordance with IFRS, (c) reclassify items previously classified in a different manner from what it required by IFRS, and (d) comply with all disclosure and presentation requirements.
14. Numerous differences between IFRS and U.S. GAAP exist. These differences can be categorized as relating to (a) recognition, (b) measurement, (c) presentation, and (d) disclosure. Recognizing development costs as an asset when certain criteria are met under IFRS while requiring they be expensed under U.S. GAAP is an example of a recognition difference. Carrying fixed assets on the balance sheet at revalued amounts under IFRS versus depreciated historical cost under U.S. GAAP is a measurement difference. Presenting certain gains and losses on the income statement as extraordinary items under U.S. GAAP, which is not acceptable under IFRS, is an example of a presentation difference.
15. The IASB has taken a principles-based approach to standard setting rather than the rules-based approach of the FASB. IASB standards provide a general principle with some guidance but try to avoid overly detailed guidance and bright-line tests. The classification of leases is an area that highlights the difference in standard-setting approach. Some have expressed concern that the FASB–IASB convergence process may result in IASB standards becoming more rules based.

16. The use of the same set of accounting standards by all companies is a necessary but possibly insufficient condition for achieving the goal of worldwide comparability of financial statements. Translation and culture are two obstacles in achieving this goal. It might not be possible to translate IFRS into non-English languages without some distortion of meaning. Differences in societal values across countries might lead to culturally determined biases in interpreting and applying a common set of standards. However, although these obstacles exist, worldwide adoption of a single set of standards results in a greater degree of comparability than would exist with a different set of standards used by each country.

Comprehensive Illustration

Problem

(*Estimated Time: 60 minutes*) Bastion Company is a U.S.-based company that prepares its consolidated financial statements in accordance with U.S. GAAP. The company reported income in 2013 of $2,000,000 and stockholders' equity at December 31, 2013, of $15,000,000.

Bastion is aware that the U.S. Securities and Exchange Commission might require U.S. companies to use IFRS in preparing consolidated financial statements. The company wishes to determine the impact that a switch to IFRS would have on its financial statements and has engaged you to prepare a reconciliation of income and stockholders' equity from U.S. GAAP to IFRS. You have identified the following six areas in which Bastion's accounting principles based on U.S. GAAP differ from IFRS.

1. Inventory—lower of cost or market.
2. Property, plant, and equipment—measurement subsequent to initial recognition.
3. Intangible assets—research and development costs.
4. Sale and leaseback—gain on sale.
5. Pension plan—prior service costs.
6. Property, plant, and equipment—impairment.

Bastion provides the following information with respect to each of these accounting differences.

Inventory

At year-end 2013, inventory had a historical cost of $400,000, a replacement cost of $360,000, and a net realizable value of $380,000; the normal profit margin was 20 percent.

Property, Plant, and Equipment

Bastion acquired a building at the beginning of 2012 at a cost of $5,000,000. The building has an estimated useful life of 25 years, has an estimated residual value of $1,000,000, and is being depreciated on a straight-line basis. At the beginning of 2013, the building was appraised and determined to have a fair value of $5,440,000. There is no change in estimated useful life or residual value. In a switch to IFRS, the company would use the revaluation model in *IAS 16* to determine the carrying value of property, plant, and equipment subsequent to acquisition.

Research and Development Costs

Bastion incurred research and development costs of $2,000,000 in 2013. Of this amount, 40 percent related to development activities subsequent to the point at which criteria indicating the creation of an intangible asset had been met. As of the end of the year, development of the new product had not been completed.

Sale and Leaseback

In January 2011, Bastion realized a gain on the sale and leaseback of an office building in the amount of $3,000,000. The lease is accounted for as an operating lease and the term of the lease is five years.

Pension Plan

In 2012 the company amended its pension plan creating a prior service cost of $240,000. The average remaining number of years to be worked by the employees affected by the amendment is

15 years. Half of the prior service cost was attributable to already vested employees and half of the prior service cost was attributable to nonvested employees who on average had three more years until vesting. The company has no retired employees.

Property, Plant, and Equipment

Bastion owns machinery on December 31, 2013, that has a book value of $440,000, an estimated salvage value of $40,000, and an estimated remaining useful life of 10 years. On that date, the machinery is expected to generate future cash flows of $450,000 and it is estimated to have a fair value, after deducting costs to sell, of $360,000. The present value of expected future cash flows is $375,000.

Required

Prepare a schedule reconciling U.S. GAAP net income and stockholders' equity to IFRS.

Solution

Bastion Company Reconciliation from U.S. GAAP to IFRS

	2013
Income under U.S. GAAP	**$2,000,000**
Adjustments:	
1. Inventory writedown	20,000
2. Building revaluation	(25,000)
3. Deferred development costs	800,000
4. Gain on sale and leaseback	(600,000)
5. Prior (past) service cost	(24,000)
6. Impairment loss on machinery	(65,000)
Income under IFRS	**$2,106,000**

	2013
Stockholders' equity under U.S. GAAP	**$15,000,000**
Adjustments:	
1. Inventory writedown	20,000
2. Building revaluation	575,000
3. Deferred development costs	800,000
4. Gain on sale and leaseback	1,200,000
5. Prior (past) service cost	(168,000)
6. Impairment of machinery	(65,000)
Stockholders' equity under IFRS	**$17,362,000**

Explanation

1. Inventory Writedown. Under U.S. GAAP, the company reports inventory on the balance sheet at the lower of cost or market, where market is defined as replacement cost ($360,000), with net realizable value ($380,000) as a ceiling and net realizable value less a normal profit ($380,000 × 80% = $304,000) as a floor. In this case, inventory was written down to replacement cost and reported on the December 31, 2013, balance sheet at $360,000. A $40,000 loss was included in 2013 income.

In accordance with *IAS 2,* the company would report inventory on the balance sheet at the lower of cost ($400,000) and net realizable value ($380,000). The inventory would have been reported on the December 31, 2013, balance sheet at net realizable value of $380,000 and a loss on writedown of inventory of $20,000 would have been reflected in net income. As a result, IFRS income would be $20,000 larger than U.S. GAAP net income. IFRS retained earnings would be larger by the same amount.

2. Building Revaluation. Under U.S. GAAP, the company reports depreciation expense of $160,000 [($5,000,000 − $1,000,000)/25 years] in 2009 and in 2013.

Under *IAS 16*'s revaluation model, depreciation expense on the building in 2012 was $160,000, resulting in a book value at the end of 2012 of $4,840,000. The building then would have been revalued upward at the beginning of 2013 to its fair value of $5,440,000. The appropriate journal entry to recognize the revaluation would be:

Building	600,000	
Revaluation Surplus (a stockholders' equity account)		600,000

In 2013, depreciation expense would be $185,000 [($5,440,000 − $1,000,000)/24 years].

The additional depreciation under IFRS causes IFRS-based income in 2013 to be $25,000 smaller than U.S. GAAP income. IFRS-based stockholders' equity is $575,000 larger than U.S. GAAP stockholders' equity. This is equal to the amount of the revaluation surplus ($600,000) less the additional depreciation in 2013 under IFRS ($25,000), which reduced retained earnings.

3. Deferred Development Costs. Under U.S. GAAP, research and development expense in the amount of $2,000,000 would be recognized in determining 2013 income.

Under *IAS 38,* $1,200,000 (60% × $2,000,000) of research and development costs would be expensed in 2013, and $800,000 (40% × $2,000,000) of development costs would be capitalized as an intangible asset (deferred development costs). IFRS income in 2013 would be $800,000 larger than U.S. GAAP income. Because the new product has not yet been brought to market, there is no amortization of the deferred development costs under IFRS in 2013. Stockholders' equity under IFRS at the end of 2013 would be $800,000 larger than under U.S. GAAP.

4. Gain on Sale and Leaseback. Under U.S. GAAP, the gain on the sale and leaseback (operating lease) is recognized in income over the life of the lease. With a lease term of five years, $600,000 of the gain would be recognized in 2013. $600,000 also would have been recognized in 2011 and 2012, resulting in a cumulative amount of retained earnings at year-end 2013 of $1,800,000.

Under *IAS 17,* the entire gain on the sale and leaseback of $3,000,000 would have been recognized in income in 2011. This resulted in an increase in retained earnings of $3,000,000 in that year. No gain would be recognized in 2013. IFRS income in 2013 would be $600,000 smaller than U.S. GAAP income, but stockholders' equity at December 31, 2013, under IFRS would be $1,200,000 ($3,000,000 − $1,800,000) larger than under U.S. GAAP.

5. Prior Service Costs. Under U.S. GAAP, the prior service cost of $240,000 is amortized over the remaining service period (number of years to be worked) of the employees. Expense recognized in 2013 is $16,000 [$240,000/15 years]. The cumulative expense recognized since the plan was changed in 2012 is $32,000 [$16,000 × 2 years].

Under *IAS 19,* the prior (past) service cost attributable to the vested employees would have been expensed in 2012—$120,000 [50% × $240,000]. The past service cost attributable to nonvested employees would be expensed over the three remaining years until vesting. Expense recognized in 2013 would be $40,000 [$120,000/3 years]. The cumulative expense recognized since the plan was changed is $200,000 [$120,000 + ($40,000 × 2 years)]. IFRS income in 2013 would be $24,000 less than U.S. GAAP income [$40,000 − $16,000], and stockholders' equity at year-end 2013 under IFRS would be $168,000 less than under U.S. GAAP [$200,000 − $32,000].

6. Impairment of Machinery. Under U.S. GAAP, an impairment occurs when an asset's carrying value exceeds its undiscounted expected future cash flows. In this case, the expected future cash flows are $450,000, which is higher than the machinery's carrying value of $440,000, so no impairment occurred.

Under *IAS 36,* an asset is impaired when its carrying value exceeds the higher of (1) its value in use (present value of expected future cash flows) and (2) its fair value less costs to sell. The machinery has a value in use of $375,000 and its fair value less costs to sell is $360,000. An impairment loss of $65,000 [$440,000 − $375,000] would be recognized in determining 2013 net income, with a corresponding reduction in retained earnings. IFRS income in 2013 is $65,000 smaller than U.S. GAAP income, and stockholders' equity at year-end 2013 under IFRS would be $65,000 smaller than under U.S. GAAP.

Questions

1. What factors contribute to the diversity of accounting systems worldwide?
2. Nestlé S.A. is a very large company headquartered in a very small country (Switzerland). It has operations in more than 50 different countries around the world. Much of the company's international expansion has been through the acquisition of local (i.e., foreign) companies. What major problems does worldwide accounting diversity cause for a company like Nestlé?

3. According to Gray, how do societal values affect national accounting systems?
4. According to Nobes, what is the relationship between culture, type of financing system, and class of accounting?
5. Why were several original standards issued by the IASC revised in 1993?
6. In what ways does the IASB differ from the IASC?
7. Some say that IFRS are now GAAP in the European Union. How is this statement true, and how is it false?
8. What are three countries that do not allow domestic publicly traded companies to use IFRS to prepare consolidated financial statements?
9. What have the FASB and IASB agreed to do in the Norwalk Agreement?
10. What are the FASB's key initiatives in its international convergence project?
11. How is the process of convergence with IASB standards as followed by the FASB different from the adoption of IFRS as occurred in the European Union?
12. How are IFRS currently used in the United States and how might they be used in the future based upon the SEC's IFRS Roadmap?
13. What are the steps that a company must follow in preparing its initial set of IFRS financial statements upon the company's first-time adoption of IFRS?
14. What are the two extreme approaches that a company might follow in determining appropriate accounting policies for preparing its initial set of IFRS financial statements?
15. Under what circumstances might it be acceptable for a company preparing IFRS financial statements to follow an accounting treatment developed by the FASB?
16. What are three potentially significant differences between IFRS and U.S. GAAP with respect to the recognition or measurement of assets?
17. Even if all companies in the world were to use IFRS, what are two obstacles to the worldwide comparability of financial statements?

Problems

LO1

1. Which of the following could explain why accounting is more conservative in some countries than in others?
   a. Accounting is oriented toward stockholders as a major source of financing.
   b. Published financial statements are the basis for taxation.
   c. A common law legal system is used.
   d. Full disclosure in financial statements is emphasized.

LO2

2. Which of the following is *not* a problem caused by differences in financial reporting practices across countries?
   a. Consolidation of financial statements by firms with foreign operations is more difficult.
   b. Firms incur additional costs when attempting to obtain financing in foreign countries.
   c. Firms face double taxation on income earned by foreign operations.
   d. Comparisons of financial ratios across firms in different countries may not be meaningful.

LO2

3. Which of the following is *not* a reason for establishing international accounting standards?
   a. Some countries do not have the resources to develop accounting standards on their own.
   b. Comparability is needed between companies operating in different areas of the world.
   c. It would simplify the preparation of consolidated financial statements by multinational corporations.
   d. Demand in the United States is heavy for an alternative to U.S. generally accepted accounting principles.

LO3

4. According to the IASB, IFRS are composed of
   a. International financial reporting standards issued by the IASB only.
   b. International accounting standards issued by the IASC only.
   c. International financial reporting standards issued by the IASB and international accounting standards issued by the IASC.
   d. International financial reporting standards issued by the IASB and statements of financial accounting standards issued by the FASB.

LO4

5. After 2012, which of the following countries will be using IFRS?
   a. Canada.
   b. Mexico.
   c. Brazil.
   d. All of the above.

LO5

6. What is the so-called Norwalk Agreement?
   a. An agreement between the FASB and SEC to allow foreign companies to use IFRSs in their filing of financial statements with the SEC.
   b. An agreement between the U.S. FASB and the U.K. Accounting Standards Board to converge their respective accounting standards as soon as practicable.
   c. An agreement between the SEC chairman and the EU Internal Market commissioner to allow EU companies to list securities in the United States without providing a U.S. GAAP reconciliation.
   d. An agreement between the FASB and the IASB to make their existing standards compatible as soon as practicable and to work together to ensure compatibility in the future.

LO5

7. Which of the following is *not* one of the FASB's initiatives to converge with IASB standards?
   a. The FASB eliminates differences between FASB and IASB standards by adopting IASB requirements, or vice versa, in a short-term convergence project.
   b. The FASB considers the possibility of convergence with IASB standards when deciding which topics to add to its work agenda.
   c. A member of the FASB serves as a liaison with the IASB by working out of the IASB's offices in London.
   d. A joint project develops a common conceptual framework that both the FASB and IASB could use as a basis for future standards.

LO5

8. Which of the following does *not* accurately describe a requirement that a company must fulfill when adopting IFRS for the first time?
   a. The company must prepare an opening IFRS balance sheet at the beginning of the year for which the company is preparing its first set of IFRS financial statements.
   b. At the IFRS transition date, the company must select IFRS accounting policies based on those that will be in effect for the accounting period that will be covered by the first set of IFRS financial statements.
   c. At the IFRS transition date, the company must derecognize assets and liabilities that were recognized under previous GAAP that are not allowed to be recognized under IFRS.
   d. The company must provide a reconciliation of net income and stockholders' equity under previous GAAP to net income and stockholders' equity under IFRS in its first set of IFRS financial statements.

LO6

9. In which of the following areas does the IASB allow firms to choose between two acceptable treatments?
   a. Measuring property, plant, and equipment subsequent to acquisition.
   b. Presenting gains and losses as extraordinary on the face of the income statement.
   c. Recognizing development costs that meet criteria for capitalization as an asset.
   d. Recognizing prior (past) service costs related to pension benefits that have already vested.

LO5

10. Under the "condorsement" framework suggested by the SEC staff in 2011, which of the following is most likely:
    a. IFRS would replace U.S. GAAP and the IASB would become the national accounting standard setter in the United States.
    b. The FASB would continue its U.S. GAAP–IFRS convergence project until a specified future date at which point U.S. companies would be required to adopt IFRS.
    c. The FASB would participate in developing new IFRSs and then adopt them as part of U.S. GAAP.
    d. The FASB would endorse existing IFRSs and adopt them as part of U.S. GAAP immediately.

LO5

11. Which of the following statements is correct with respect to the IFRS accounting policy hierarchy in situations where a specifically relevant IASB standard dealing with an accounting issue does not exist?
    a. The IASB Framework takes precedence over other IASB standards that deal with related issues.

b. The IASB Framework takes precedence over standards developed by standard-setting bodies in other countries that deal with the specific accounting issue.

c. The most recent specifically relevant pronouncement of any other standard-setting body may be used when IASB standards and Framework provide no helpful guidance.

d. IFRSs take precedence over IASs and Interpretations in identifying appropriate guidance.

LO6

12. Which companies are required to provide a U.S. GAAP reconciliation in their annual report filed with the SEC?

a. All foreign companies listed on a U.S. securities exchange.

b. Foreign companies listed on a U.S. securities exchange that use IFRS in preparing financial statements.

c. Domestic U.S. companies listed on a U.S. securities exchange that use IFRS in preparing financial statements.

d. Foreign companies listed on a U.S. securities exchange that use something other than U.S. GAAP or IFRS in preparing financial statements.

LO6

13. Under IFRS, when an entity chooses the revaluation model as its accounting policy for measuring property, plant, and equipment, which of the following statements is correct?

a. When an asset is revalued, the entire class of property, plant, and equipment (such as Land) to which that asset belongs must be revalued.

b. When an asset is revalued, it is reported on the balance sheet at its current replacement cost.

c. Revaluations of property, plant, and equipment must be made at least every three years.

d. The revalued assets must be reported in a special section of the balance sheet separate from those assets measured using the cost model.

LO6

14. *IAS 1,* "Presentation of Financial Statements," does not provide guidance with respect to which of the following?

a. The statements that must be included in a complete set of financial statements.

b. The basic principles and assumptions to be used in preparing financial statements.

c. The importance of prudence in preparing financial statements.

d. The items that must be presented on the face of the financial statements.

Problems 15–19 are based on the Comprehensive Illustration at the end of the chapter.

LO7

15. Lisali Company gathered the following information related to inventory that it owned on December 31, 2013:

Historical cost	$100,000
Replacement cost	95,000
Net realizable value	98,000
Normal profit margin	20%

a. Determine the amount at which Lisali should carry inventory on the December 31, 2013, balance sheet and the amount, if any, that should be reported in net income related to this inventory using (1) U.S. GAAP and (2) IFRS.

b. Determine the adjustments that Lisali would make in 2013 to reconcile net income and stockholders' equity under U.S. GAAP to IFRS.

LO7

16. Bracy Company acquired a new piece of construction equipment on January 1, 2013, at a cost of $100,000. The equipment was expected to have a useful life of 10 years and a residual value of $20,000 and is being depreciated on a straight-line basis. On January 1, 2014, the equipment was appraised and determined to have a fair value of $101,000, a salvage value of $20,000, and a remaining useful life of nine years.

a. Determine the amount of depreciation expense that Bracy should recognize in determining net income in 2013, 2014, and 2015 and the amount at which equipment should be carried on the December 31, 2013, 2014, and 2015 balance sheets using (1) U.S. GAAP and (2) IFRS. In measuring property, plant, and equipment subsequent to acquisition, Bracy uses the revaluation model in *IAS 16*.

b. Determine the adjustments that Bracy would make in 2013, 2014, and 2015 to reconcile net income and stockholders' equity under U.S. GAAP to IFRS.

LO7

17. Moxie Corporation incurs research and development costs of $500,000 in 2013, 30 percent of which relates to development activities subsequent to certain criteria having been met that suggest that an intangible asset has been created. The newly developed product is brought to market in January 2014 and is expected to generate sales revenue for 10 years.
    a. Determine the amount Moxie should recognize as research and development expense in 2013 under (1) U.S. GAAP and (2) IFRS.
    b. Determine the adjustments that Moxie would make in 2013 and 2014 to reconcile net income and stockholders' equity under U.S. GAAP to IFRS.

LO7

18. Ilmanov Ltd. sold a building to a bank at the beginning of 2013 at a gain of $50,000 and immediately leased the building back for a period of five years. The lease is accounted for as an operating lease.
    a. Determine the amount of gain on the sale and leaseback that Ilmanov should recognize in 2013 under (1) U.S. GAAP and (2) IFRS.
    b. Determine the adjustments that Ilmanov would make in 2013 and 2014 to reconcile net income and stockholders' equity under U.S. GAAP to IFRS.

LO7

19. Ramshare Company acquired equipment at the beginning of 2013 at a cost of $100,000. The equipment has a five-year life with no expected salvage value and is depreciated on a straight-line basis. At December 31, 2013, Ramshare compiled the following information related to this equipment:

Expected future cash flows from use of the equipment	$85,000
Present value of expected future cash flows from use of the equipment	75,000
Fair value (net selling price), less costs to dispose	72,000

    a. Determine the amount at which Ramshare should carry this equipment on its December 31, 2013, balance sheet and the amount, if any, that it should report in net income related to this inventory using (1) U.S. GAAP and (2) IFRS.
    b. Determine the adjustments that Ramshare would make in 2013 and 2014 to reconcile net income and stockholders' equity under U.S. GAAP to IFRS. Ignore the possibility of any additional impairment at the end of 2012.

Develop Your Skills

ANALYSIS CASE 1—APPLICATION OF *IAS 16*

Abacab Company's shares are listed on the New Market Stock Exchange, which allows the use of either international financial reporting standards (IFRS) or U.S. GAAP. On January 1, Year 1, Abacab Company acquired a building at a cost of $10 million. The building has a 20-year useful life and no residual value and is depreciated on a straight-line basis. On January 1, Year 3, the company hired an appraiser who determines the fair value of the building (net of any accumulated depreciation) to be $12 million.

IAS 16, "Property, Plant, and Equipment," requires assets to be initially measured at cost. Subsequent to initial recognition, assets may be carried either at cost less accumulated depreciation and any impairment losses (the cost model) or at a revalued amount equal to fair value at the date of the revaluation less any subsequent accumulated depreciation and impairment losses (the revaluation model). If a firm chooses to use the revaluation model, the counterpart to the revaluation of the asset is recorded as an increase in Accumulated Other Comprehensive Income (stockholders' equity). Subsequent depreciation is based on the revalued amount less any residual value.

U.S. GAAP requires items of property, plant, and equipment to be initially measured at cost. U.S. GAAP does not allow property, plant, and equipment to be revalued above original cost at subsequent balance sheet dates. The cost of property, plant, and equipment must be depreciated on a systematic basis over its useful life. Subsequent to initial recognition, assets must be carried at cost less accumulated depreciation and any impairment losses.

Required

a. Determine the amount of depreciation expense recognized in Year 2, Year 3, and Year 4 under (*a*) the revaluation model in *IAS 16* and (*b*) U.S. GAAP.

b. Determine the book value of the building under the two different sets of accounting rules at January 2, Year 3; December 31, Year 3; and December 31, Year 4.

c. Summarize the difference in net income and in stockholders' equity over the 20-year life of the building using the two different sets of accounting rules.

ANALYSIS CASE 2—RECONCILIATION OF IFRS TO U.S. GAAP

Quantacc Ltd. began operations on January 1, 2011, and uses IFRS to prepare its consolidated financial statements. Although not required to do so, to facilitate comparisons with companies in the United States, Quantacc reconciles its net income and stockholders' equity to U.S. GAAP. Information relevant for preparing this reconciliation is as follows:

1. Quantacc carries fixed assets at revalued amounts. Fixed assets were revalued upward on January 1, 2013, by $35,000. At that time, fixed assets had a remaining useful life of 10 years.
2. On January 1, 2012, Quantacc realized a gain on the sale and leaseback of an office building in the amount of $200,000. The lease is classified as an operating lease and has a term of 20 years.
3. Quantacc capitalized development costs related to a new pharmaceutical product in 2012 in the amount of $80,000. Quantacc began selling the new product on January 1, 2013, and expects the product to be marketable for a total of 5 years.

Net income under IFRS in 2013 is $100,000 and stockholders' equity under IFRS at December 31, 2013, is $1,000,000.

Required

a. Prepare a schedule to reconcile Quantacc's 2013 net income and December 31, 2013, stockholders' equity under IFRS to U.S. GAAP.

b. Provide a brief title/description for each reconciling adjustment made, indicate the dollar amount of the adjustment, and calculate total amounts for net income and stockholders' equity under U.S. GAAP.

RESEARCH CASE—RECONCILIATION TO U.S. GAAP

Unless they use IFRS, foreign companies with securities listed in the United States (in the form of ADRs) are required to reconcile their net income and stockholders' equity to U.S. GAAP in the annual report (Form 20–F) they file with the Securities and Exchange Commission (SEC). Lists of foreign SEC registrants are available on the Internet at www.adrbnymellon.com; click on DR Directory & Profiles. Annual reports of foreign SEC registrants may be accessed through the SEC's EDGAR system at www.sec.gov (under Filing Type, search for 20–F). However, not all foreign registrants file their reports with the SEC electronically. Many non-U.S. companies make annual reports available on their corporate Internet home page. Access a recent annual report (Form 20–F) for a foreign company listed on the New York Stock Exchange that does not use IFRS to complete the following requirements.

Required

a. Determine the nationality of the company selected and the accounting rules and regulations it used (company GAAP) to prepare its financial statements.

b. Summarize the major differences in measuring net income between company GAAP and U.S. GAAP.

c. Compare the company's profitability using company GAAP and U.S. GAAP.

COMMUNICATION CASE—SEC "IFRS ROADMAP"

In November 2008, the SEC released its "Roadmap for the Potential Use of Financial Statements Prepared in Accordance with International Financial Reporting Standards by U.S. Issuers." The Roadmap originally proposed allowing U.S. companies that meet certain criteria to adopt IFRS on a voluntary basis several years before requiring the use of IFRS. Conglomerate Company meets the criteria for early use of IFRS. As the company's external auditor, you have been asked to provide a recommendation as to whether the company should early adopt IFRS on a voluntary basis.

Required

Draft a memo to the CEO of Conglomerate Company describing the potential benefits and the potential risks associated with the early use of IFRS.

INTERNET CASE—FOREIGN COMPANY ANNUAL REPORT

Many non-U.S. companies make annual reports available on their corporate Internet home page. Access the financial statements from the most recent annual report for a foreign company with which you are familiar to complete this assignment.

Required

a. Determine the set of accounting rules (GAAP) the company uses to prepare its financial statements.

b. Determine whether the company provides a set of financial statements comparable to the set of financial statements provided by U.S. companies (consolidated balance sheet, consolidated income statement, consolidated cash flow statement).

c. List major differences between the company's income statement and the income statement of a typical U.S. corporation.

d. List major differences between the company's balance sheet and the balance sheet of a typical U.S. corporation.

e. Determine whether the scope and content of the information provided in the notes to the financial statements are comparable to the information provided in the notes to the financial statements by a typical U.S. corporation.

f. Evaluate the overall presentation of financial statements and notes to financial statements by the company in comparison with a typical U.S. corporation.

chapter 12

Financial Reporting and the Securities and Exchange Commission

The Securities and Exchange Commission was born on June 6, 1934—a time of despair in the markets. Americans were still suffering from the 1929 market crash after a roaring 1920s when they bought about $50 billion in new securities—half of which turned out to be worthless. Their confidence also was eroded by the 1932 indictment (later acquittal) of Samuel Insull for alleged wrongs in the collapse of his utility "empire," and by the 1933–34 Senate hearings on improper market activity.[1]

The financing of U.S. industry depends on raising vast amounts of capital. During every business day in the United States, tens of billions of dollars of stocks, bonds, and other securities are sold to thousands of individuals, corporations, trust funds, pension plans, mutual funds, and other investors. Such investors cannot be expected to venture their money without forethought. They have to be able to assess the risks involved: the possibility of either a profit or loss being returned to them as well as the expected amount.

Consequently, disclosure of sufficient, accurate information is absolutely necessary to stimulate the inflow of large quantities of capital. Enough data must be available to encourage investors to consider buying and selling securities in hopes of generating profits. With inadequate or unreliable information on which to base these decisions, investing becomes little more than gambling.

Learning Objectives

After studying this chapter, you should be able to:

- LO1 Understand the origin and expansive role of the Securities and Exchange Commission.
- LO2 Describe the purpose(s) of various federal securities laws.
- LO3 Understand the Congressional rationale for enacting the Sarbanes-Oxley Act and the responsibilities of the Public Accounting Oversight Board.
- LO4 Describe the SEC's role in establishing generally accepted accounting principles (GAAP).
- LO5 Define and describe an issuer's filings with the Securities and Exchange Commission.
- LO6 Describe an issuer's registration process, various forms used by the issuers, and the exemption(s) from registration.

The Work of the Securities and Exchange Commission

In the United States, the responsibility for ensuring that complete and reliable information is available to investors lies with the Securities and Exchange Commission (SEC), an independent agency of the federal government created by the Securities Exchange Act of 1934. Although the SEC's authority applies mainly to publicly held companies, the commission's guidelines and requirements have had a major influence in the United States on the development of all generally accepted accounting principles (GAAP).

[1]"D-Day for the Securities Industry, 1934," *The Wall Street Journal,* May 9, 1989, p. B1.

LO1

Understand the origin and expansive role of the securities and Exchange Commission.

As described on the SEC's website:

> The mission of the U.S. Securities and Exchange Commission is to protect investors, maintain fair, orderly, and efficient markets, and facilitate capital formation.
>
> As more and more first-time investors turn to the markets to help secure their futures, pay for homes, and send children to college, our investor protection mission is more compelling than ever.
>
> As our nation's securities exchanges mature into global for-profit competitors, there is even greater need for sound market regulation.
>
> And the common interest of all Americans in a growing economy that produces jobs, improves our standard of living, and protects the value of our savings means that all of the SEC's actions must be taken with an eye toward promoting the capital formation that is necessary to sustain economic growth.
>
> The world of investing is fascinating and complex, and it can be very fruitful. But unlike the banking world, where deposits are guaranteed by the federal government, stocks, bonds and other securities can lose value. There are no guarantees. That's why investing is not a spectator sport. By far the best way for investors to protect the money they put into the securities markets is to do research and ask questions.
>
> The laws and rules that govern the securities industry in the United States derive from a simple and straightforward concept: all investors, whether large institutions or private individuals, should have access to certain basic facts about an investment prior to buying it, and so long as they hold it. To achieve this, the SEC requires public companies to disclose meaningful financial and other information to the public. This provides a common pool of knowledge for all investors to use to judge for themselves whether to buy, sell, or hold a particular security. Only through the steady flow of timely, comprehensive, and accurate information can people make sound investment decisions.[2]

The SEC is headed by five commissioners appointed by the president of the United States (with the consent of the Senate) to serve five-year staggered terms. To ensure the bipartisan nature of this group, no more than three of these individuals can belong to the same political party. The chairman is from the same political party as the president. The commissioners provide leadership for an agency that has grown over the years into an organization with approximately 3,700 employees in 11 regional locations. Despite its importance, the SEC is a relatively small component of the federal government. However, the SEC generates significant fees primarily from issuers, relative to 8–K, 10–K, 10–Q, and registration statement fees. In 2010, the SEC deposited $1.095 billion in the U.S. Treasury. Furthermore, the SEC collected disgorgements and penalties of $1.8 billion in fiscal year 2006, $1.9 billion in 2008, and an additional $2.8 billion in 2010.

The SEC is composed of four divisions and 18 offices including the following:

- The *Division of Corporation Finance* has responsibility to ensure that publicly held companies meet disclosure requirements. This division reviews registration statements, annual and quarterly filings, proxy materials, annual reports, and tender offers.
- The *Division of Trading and Markets* oversees the securities markets in this country and is responsible for registering and regulating brokerage firms. This division also oversees the Securities Investor Protection Corporation (SIPC), a nonprofit corporation that provides insurance for cash and securities held by customers in member brokerage firms. This insurance protects ("insures") against the failure of the member brokerage firms.
- The *Division of Enforcement* helps to ensure compliance with federal securities laws. This division investigates possible violations of securities laws and recommends appropriate remedies. The most common issues facing this division are insider trading, misrepresentation or omission of important information about securities, manipulation of the market price of a security, and issuance of securities without proper registration. According to the SEC's annual report, 681 investigations of possible violations were initiated during 2010.

[2] The U.S. Securities and Exchange Commission, SEC website, July 2011. Available at www.sec.gov/about/whatwedo.shtml.

- The *Division of Investment Management* oversees the $26 trillion investment management industry and administers the securities laws affecting investment companies including mutual funds and investment advisers. This division also interprets laws and regulations for the public and the SEC staff.
- The *Office of Information Technology* supports the SEC and its staff in all aspects of information technology. This office operates the Electronic Data Gathering Analysis and Retrieval (EDGAR) system, which electronically receives, processes, and disseminates more than half a million financial statements every year. This office also maintains a very active website that contains a tremendous amount of data about the SEC and the securities industry and free access to EDGAR.[3]
- The *Office of Compliance Inspections and Examinations* determines whether brokers, dealers, and investment companies and advisers comply with federal securities laws.
- The *Office of the Chief Accountant* is the principal adviser to the commission on accounting and auditing matters that arise in connection with the securities laws. The office also works closely with private sector bodies such as the FASB and the AICPA that set various accounting and auditing standards.

This chapter provides an overview of the workings of the Securities and Exchange Commission as well as the agency's relationship to the accounting profession. Because complete examination of the organization is beyond the scope of this textbook, we discuss only a portion of the SEC's extensive functions here. This coverage introduces the role the agency currently plays in the world of U.S. business.

LO2

Describe the purpose(s) of various federal securities laws.

Purpose of the Federal Securities Laws

Before examining the SEC and its various functions in more detail, a historical perspective should be established. The development of laws regulating companies involved in interstate commerce was discussed as early as 1885. In fact, the Industrial Commission created by Congress suggested in 1902 that all publicly held companies should be required to disclose material information including annual financial reports. However, the crisis following the stock market crash of 1929 and the widespread fraud that was subsequently discovered were necessary to prompt Congress to act in hope of reestablishing the trust and stability needed for the capital markets.

> Before the Great Crash of 1929, there was little support for federal regulation of the securities markets. This was particularly true during the post-World War I surge of securities activity. Proposals that the federal government require financial disclosure and prevent the fraudulent sale of stock were never seriously pursued. Tempted by promises of "rags to riches" transformations and easy credit, most investors gave little thought to the dangers inherent in uncontrolled market operation. During the 1920s, approximately 20 million large and small shareholders took advantage of post-war prosperity and set out to make their fortunes in the stock market. It is estimated that of the $50 billion in new securities offered during this period, half became worthless. When the stock market crashed in October 1929, the fortunes of countless investors were lost. . . . With the Crash and ensuing depression, public confidence in the markets plummeted. There was a consensus that for the economy to recover, the public's faith in the capital markets needed to be restored.[4]

As a result, Congress enacted two primary pieces of securities legislation designed to restore investor trust in the capital markets by providing more structure and government oversight:

- The Securities Act of 1933, often referred to as the *truth in securities law,* regulates the initial offering of securities by a company or underwriter.
- The Securities Exchange Act of 1934, which actually created the SEC, regulates the subsequent trading of securities through brokers and exchanges.

[3] www.sec.gov/edgar/shtml.

[4] U.S. Securities and Exchange Commission, SEC website, July 2011. Available at www.sec.gov/about/whatwedo.shtml.

These laws put an end to the legality of many abuses that had been common practices such as the manipulation of stock market prices and the misuse of corporate information by officials and directors (often referred to as *inside parties*[5]) for their own personal gain. Just as important, these two legislative actions were designed to help rebuild public confidence in the capital market system. Because of the large losses suffered during the 1929 market crash and subsequent depression, many investors had begun to avoid buying stocks, bonds, or other securities.

This reduction in the pool of available capital dramatically compounded the economic problems of the day.

The creation of federal securities laws did not end with the 1933 Act and the 1934 Act. During the decades since the first commissioners were appointed, the SEC has administered rules and regulations created by a number of different congressional actions. Despite the passage of subsequent legislation, this organization's major objectives have remained relatively constant. Over the years, the SEC has attempted to achieve several interconnected goals including:

- Ensuring that full and fair information is disclosed to all investors before the securities of a company are allowed to be bought and sold.
- Prohibiting the dissemination of materially misstated information.
- Preventing the misuse of information especially by inside parties.
- Regulating the operation of securities markets such as the New York Stock Exchange and the various over-the-counter exchanges.

In many ways, the SEC's work has been a huge success. The value of the securities that have been registered as well as the volume of these securities bought and sold each business day are staggering by any standard. Over the decades, the number of individuals and institutions (from both inside and outside the United States) willing to take the risk of making financial investments has grown to incredible numbers. In 2010 alone, more than 1.27 trillion shares were exchanged on just the New York Stock Exchange.[6] However, a cloud recently has rested over the entire U.S. capital market system. During the early 2000s, a number of highly publicized corporate scandals shook public confidence in the financial information available for decision-making purposes. Where once most investors appeared to believe in the overall integrity of the stock markets, that faith has clearly been diminished although the problem has not reached the magnitude seen in the 1930s. This lack of confidence has been a drag on the general willingness to invest and, thus, on the economy as a whole.

An unlimited number of reasons can be put forth for these scandals:

- Greed by corporate executives.
- Failure in the corporate governance process as practiced by many boards of directors.
- Failure of public accounting firms to apply appropriate quality control measures to ensure independent judgments.
- Shortcomings in promulgated standards used to self-regulate the accounting profession.
- Unreasonable market expectations brought on by years of skyrocketing stock values fueled in part by technology stocks.
- A workload that overburdened the Securities and Exchange Commission, which the relatively small agency could not handle in an adequate fashion.

As a result, on July 30, 2002, President George W. Bush signed the Sarbanes-Oxley Act of 2002. This wide-ranging legislation was designed to end many of the problems that

[5] *Inside parties* usually are identified as the officers of a company as well as its directors and any owners of more than 10 percent of any class of equity security. An individual's level of ownership is measured by a person's own holdings of equity securities as well as ownership by related parties such as a spouse, minor children, relatives living in the same house as the person in question, or a trust in which the person is the beneficiary.

[6] NYSE website, July 2011. Available at www.nyxdata.com/.

have plagued corporate reporting and the securities markets in recent years in the hope of restoring public confidence. This new law has had an enormous impact on public accounting as well as the reporting required in connection with the issuance of securities.

In light of additional financial market scandals, Congress passed and President Obama signed the Wall Street Reform and Consumer Protection Act of 2010.[7] This new legislation marks a significant expansion of the federal government's role in regulating corporate governance and provides expanded authority to the SEC to require extensive disclosures concerning corporate compensation.

Full and Fair Disclosure

No responsibility of the SEC is more vital than that of ensuring that a company has disclosed sufficient, reliable information before its stocks, bonds, or other securities are publicly traded. Problems with companies such as Enron, WorldCom, Adelphia, and Tyco have drawn increased attention to this role.

Unless specifically exempted, all publicly held companies (frequently referred to as *registrants*) must periodically file detailed reports with the SEC. The SEC requires and regulates these filings as a result of a number of laws passed by Congress over the years:

1. *Securities Act of 1933:* Requires the registration of new securities offered for public sale so that potential investors can have adequate information. The act is also intended to prevent deceit and misrepresentation in connection with the sale of securities.[8]
2. *Securities Exchange Act of 1934:* Created the SEC and empowered it to require reporting by publicly owned companies and registration of securities, security exchanges, and certain brokers and dealers. This act prohibits fraudulent and unfair behavior such as sales practice abuses and insider trading.
3. *Public Utility Holding Company Act of 1935:* Requires registration of interstate holding companies of public utilities covered by this law. This act was passed because of abuses in the 1920s in which huge, complex utility empires were created to minimize the need for equity financing.
4. *Trust Indenture Act of 1939:* Requires registration of trust indenture documents and supporting data in connection with the public sale of bonds, debentures, notes, and other debt securities.
5. *Investment Company Act of 1940:* Requires registration of investment companies, including mutual funds, that engage in investing and trading in securities. This act is designed in part to minimize conflicts of interest that arise with fund management.
6. *Investment Advisers Act of 1940 and Securities Investor Protection Act of 1970:* Require investment advisers to register and to follow certain standards created to protect investors.
7. *Foreign Corrupt Practices Act of 1977:* Affects registration indirectly through amendment to the Securities Exchange Act of 1934. This act requires the maintenance of accounting records and adequate internal accounting controls.
8. *Insider Trading Sanctions Act of 1984 and Insider Trading and Securities Fraud Enforcement Act of 1988:* Also affect registration indirectly. Increase the penalties against persons who profit from illegal use of inside information and who are associated with market manipulation and securities fraud.
9. *Sarbanes-Oxley Act of 2002:* As discussed in a later section of this chapter, designed as an answer to the numerous corporate accounting scandals that came to light in 2001 and 2002. This act mandated a number of reforms to bolster corporate responsibility, strengthen disclosure, and combat fraud. It also created the Public Company Accounting Oversight Board (PCAOB) to oversee the accounting profession.

[7] Public Law No. 111–203, 124 stat. 1376 (2010). This statute is commonly referred to as the "Dodd-Frank Act."

[8] Interestingly, one of the provisions originally suggested for this act would have created a federal corps of auditors. The defeat of this proposal (after some debate) has allowed for the rise of the independent auditing profession as it is currently structured in the United States. For more information, see Mark Moran and Gary John Previts, "The SEC and the Profession, 1934–1984: The Realities of Self-Regulation," *Journal of Accountancy*, July 1984.

SEC Requirements

As is obvious from the previous list of statutes, the SEC administers extensive filing requirements. Thus, accountants who specialize in working with the federal securities laws must develop a broad knowledge of a great many reporting rules and regulations. The SEC specifies most of these disclosure requirements in two basic documents, *Regulation S–K* and *Regulation S–X,* which are supplemented by periodic releases and staff bulletins.

Regulation S–K established requirements for all nonfinancial information contained in filings with the SEC. Descriptions of the registrant's business and its securities are just two items covered by these regulations. A partial list of other nonfinancial data to be disclosed includes specified data about the company's directors, officers, and other management; management's discussion and analysis of the current financial condition and the results of operations; and descriptions of both legal proceedings and the company's properties.

Regulation S–X prescribed the form and content of the financial statements (and the accompanying notes and related schedules) included in the various reports filed with the SEC. Thus, before being accepted, all financial information must meet a number of clearly specified requirements.

The SEC's Impact on Financial Reporting to Stockholders

The SEC's disclosure and accounting requirements are not limited to the filings made directly with that body. *Rule 14c–3* of the 1934 Act states that the annual reports of publicly held companies should include financial statements that have been audited. This information (referred to as *proxy information* because it accompanies the management's request to cast votes for absentee stockholders at the annual shareholders meeting) must present balance sheets as of the end of the two most recent fiscal years along with income statements and cash flow statements for the three most recent fiscal years. *Rule 14c–3* also states that additional information, as specified in *Regulation S–K,* should be included in this annual report. The result has been a significant demand for CPAs to provide services as independent auditors.

Over the years, the SEC has moved toward an *integrated disclosure system.* Under this approach, much of the same reported information that the SEC requires must also go to the shareholders. Thus, the overall reporting process is simplified because only a single set of information must be generated in most cases. The integrated disclosure system is also intended as a way to improve the quality of the disclosures received directly by the shareholders.

Information required in proxy statements, which the shareholders receive directly, includes the following:

1. Five-year summary of operations including sales, total assets, income from continuing operations, and cash dividends per share.
2. Description of the business activities including principal products and sources and availability of raw materials.
3. Three-year summary of industry segments, export sales, and foreign and domestic operations.
4. List of company directors and executive officers.
5. Market price of the company's common stock for each quarterly period within the two most recent fiscal years.
6. Any restrictions on the company's ability to continue paying dividends.
7. Management's discussion and analysis of financial condition, changes in financial condition, and results of operations. This discussion should include liquidity, trends and significant events, causes of material changes in the financial statements, and the impact of inflation on the company.

In addition, even prior to passage of the Sarbanes-Oxley Act, the SEC required certain disclosures in proxy statements describing the services provided by the registrant's independent external auditor. This information helped to ensure that true independence was not endangered. Apparently, mere disclosure was not adequate in all cases.

Such disclosure must include the following:

1. All nonaudit services provided by the independent audit firm.
2. A statement as to whether the board of directors (or its audit committee) approved all nonaudit services after considering the possibility that such services might impair the external auditor's independence.
3. The percentage of nonaudit fees to the total annual audit fee. This disclosure helps indicate the importance of the audit work to the firm versus the reward from any other services provided to the registrant.
4. Individual nonaudit fees that are more than 3 percent of the annual audit fee.

Corporate Accounting Scandals and the Sarbanes-Oxley Act

LO3

Understand the Congressional rationale for enacting the Sarbanes-Oxley Act and the responsibilities of the Public Accounting Oversight Board.

When William H. Donaldson entered his cavernous corner office on the sixth floor of the Securities and Exchange Commission in 2003, he headed an agency at one of its lowest points since its creation nearly 70 years ago.[9]

Enron's former chairman and chief executive, Kenneth Lay, received $152.7 million in payments and stock in the year leading up to the company's collapse amid revelations that it hid debt and inflated profit for years. Lay's take in 2001 was more than 11,000 times the maximum amount of severance paid to laid-off workers.

Former WorldCom CEO Bernard Ebbers borrowed $408 million from the telecommunications company that had improperly accounted for $9 billion and was forced into bankruptcy. Ebbers had pledged company shares as collateral, but with those shares, once valued at $286 million, worthless, he was said to be considering forgoing his $1.5 million annual pension to help settle the debt.

Adelphia Communications's founder and former CEO, John J. Rigas, allegedly conspired with four other executives to loot the company, leading prosecutors to seek the forfeiture of more than $2.5 billion.[10]

Hardly a day passed during 2002 without a new revelation of corporate wrongdoing. The list of companies whose executives virtually robbed the corporate treasury or whose accounting practices ranged from dubious to outrageous is unfortunately long. Throughout this excruciating disclosure process, many in the investing public began to raise two related questions:

Why didn't the independent auditor stop these practices?

How can the SEC allow such activities to occur?

As indicated previously, a number of theories can suggest the cause of the ethical meltdown during this period, ranging from human greed to inappropriate auditing practices. In truth, as the history of this time continues to unfold, a variety of culprits share the blame for such reprehensible behavior on both the corporate and the individual levels.

Regardless of the reasons, drastic actions had to be taken to reduce or eliminate future abuses (actual and perceived) to begin restoring public confidence in publicly traded entities and their disclosed accounting information. A capitalistic economy needs readily accepted investments, and that is possible only if investors believe they can make wise decisions to buy and sell securities based on the information available. Thus, Congress

[9] Stephen Labaton, "Can a Bloodied S.E.C. Dust Itself Off and Get Moving?" *The New York Times,* December 16, 2002, p. C-2.

[10] Brad Foss, "Unearthing of Corporate Scandals Exposed Market's Vulnerabilities," Associated Press Newswires, December 12, 2002.

passed the Sarbanes-Oxley Act in July 2002[11] by a virtually unanimous vote. The scope and potential consequences of this legislation are extremely broad; the actual impact will probably not be determined for decades. "The Sarbanes-Oxley Act of 2002 is a major reform package mandating the most far-reaching changes Congress has imposed on the business world since FDR's New Deal."[12]

The act is so wide-ranging that this text describes only a general overview of some of the more frequently discussed statutory provisions here.

Creation of the Public Company Accounting Oversight Board

The public accounting profession has long taken pride in its own self-regulation. Through its major professional body, the American Institute of Certified Public Accountants (AICPA), the profession has established and enforced its own code of conduct and, through its Auditing Standards Board (ASB), created its own auditing standards for decades. The maintenance of public trust was often heard as a litany for the creation of such professional guidelines. Unfortunately, self-regulation obviously was not always successful in the public auditing arena. One of the inherent flaws in the system was that the professional body, the AICPA, was considerably smaller than many of the international audit firms that it sought to control. Discipline and conformity are simply difficult to maintain when the students are many times bigger, richer, and more powerful than the principal.

The Sarbanes-Oxley Act created the Public Company Accounting Oversight Board (PCAOB) to oversee auditors of public companies. The creation of the Oversight Board—a governmental board under the control of the SEC—effectively minimizes self-regulation in the accounting profession. The board

- Has five members appointed by the SEC to staggered five-year terms.[13]
- Allows only two members to be accountants, past or present.[14]
- Enforces auditing, quality control, and independence standards and rules.
- Is under the oversight and enforcement authority of the SEC.
- Is funded from fees levied on all publicly traded companies.

These few provisions show that this Oversight Board rather than the accounting profession is now ultimately in charge of regulating public accounting for publicly traded companies. Although the board itself is not a government agency, the SEC has control of it and, thus, is a much more active participant in the work of the independent auditor. For example, the SEC is to pick the five members of the board (after consultation with the chair of the Board of Governors of the Federal Reserve System and the secretary of the U.S. Department of the Treasury). The act requires the board members to be prominent individuals of integrity and good reputation who must cease all other professional and business activities to help ensure independence and adequate time commitment.

One of the most interesting issues is how the Oversight Board interacts with the Auditing Standards Board to promulgate audit and attestation standards. While the AICPA authorizes the ASB to issue such pronouncements, the mandate of the Sarbanes-Oxley Act requires the Oversight Board to play a significant role in this process. Although directed to cooperate with the accounting profession, the PCAOB has the authority to amend, modify, repeal, or reject any auditing standard.[15] ASB standards, unless later modified or superseded by the PCAOB, are adopted for audits of securities issuers. The Oversight Board has since taken an active role in developing its own pronouncements and many new ASB pronouncements apply only to nonissuers.

[11] Public Law 107–204; 107th Congress, July 30, 2002.

[12] Richard I. Miller and Paul H. Pashkoff, "Regulations under the Sarbanes-Oxley Act," *Journal of Accountancy,* October 2002, p. 33.

[13] Sarbanes-Oxley Act of 2002, Sec. 101(e)(1).

[14] Ibid., at Sec. 101(e)(2).

[15] Ibid., at Sec. 103(a)(1).

The future of the Financial Accounting Standards Board (FASB) is much less in doubt at this time. From its inception, the FASB has been a free-standing organization entirely separate from the AICPA. As we discuss later, the SEC has always held the ability to significantly impact accounting standards. Furthermore, the problems that led to the recent corporate scandals have been less about accounting issues and more about audit failures. Some observers, however, contend that the rules-based orientation of U.S. generally accepted accounting principles encourages income manipulation, which also could encourage more activity by the SEC in this area.

Registration of Public Accounting Firms

Registration of public accounting firms is required only of firms that prepare, issue, or participate in preparing an audit report for an issuer—basically an entity that issues securities on a publicly traded exchange. Consequently, virtually all public accounting firms of significant size must register, but most small firms do not need to register. Even foreign firms that play a substantial role in the audit of an organization that has securities registered in the United States must register with the PCAOB and follow the rules of the Sarbanes-Oxley Act. This act has a significant impact on the activities of foreign companies that sell their securities on U.S. markets, an impact not necessarily appreciated outside the United States. "Under the law, CEOs are required to vouch for financial statements, boards must have audit committees drawn from independent directors, and companies can no longer make loans to corporate directors. All of that conflicts with some other countries' rules and customs."[16]

The application process for PCAOB registration provides the Oversight Board a significant amount of information about the audit firms. The firms must identify each of their audit clients that qualifies as an issuer and the Oversight Board then assesses an annual fee on the issuer based on the size of its market capitalization. These fees serve, in part, as the financial support for the work of the Oversight Board.[17]

Other information required of the accounting firms in this application process includes the following:

- A list of all accountants participating in the audit report of any client qualifying as an issuer.
- Annual fees received from each issuer with the amounts separated as to audit and nonaudit services.
- Information about any criminal, civil, or administrative actions pending against the firm or any person associated with the firm.
- Information regarding disagreements between the issuer and the auditing firm during the previous year.

Inspections of Registered Firms

After registration, each audit firm is subject to periodic inspections by the PCAOB. This process is to eliminate the peer reviews that one firm conducted on another. Now any firm that audits more than 100 issuers per year will be inspected annually. All other registered firms will be inspected every three years. The Oversight Board has the power to take disciplinary action as a result of the findings of these inspections. In addition, deficiencies can be made public if the firm does not address them in an appropriate fashion within 12 months.

The PCAOB's power is not limited just to reacting to the findings of annual inspections. "The new board has a full range of sanctions at its disposal, including suspension or revocation of registration, censure, and significant fines. It has authority to investigate any act or practice that may violate the act, the new board's rules, the provisions of the

[16] Louis Lavelle and Mike McNamee, "Will Overseas Boards Play by American Rules?" *BusinessWeek*, December 16, 2002, p. 36.

[17] Sarbanes-Oxley Act of 2002, Sec. 102(b)(2).

federal securities laws relating to audit reports or applicable professional standards."[18] Clearly, Congress provided the new Oversight Board extensive powers to enable it to clean up any problems discovered in public accounting.

Auditor Independence

One of the most discussed issues surrounding accounting scandals is the failure of audit firms to act independently in dealing with audit clients. Not surprisingly, a significant portion of the Sarbanes-Oxley Act ensures that public accounting firms are, indeed, independent. Certain services that could previously be provided to an audit client are now forbidden.[19] These include financial information system design and implementation as well as internal audit outsourcing. The client's audit committee must preapprove any allowed services and disclose them in reports to the SEC.

Audit committees have long been considered an important element in maintaining an appropriate distance between the external auditors and the management of the client. The committee has been composed of members of the company's board of directors and served as a liaison with the auditors. However, in actual practice, the work and the composition of the audit committee tended to vary greatly from company to company. The Sarbanes-Oxley Act formalized the liaison role by making the audit committee responsible for the appointment and compensation of the external auditor. To help ensure impartiality, the committee must be made up of individuals who are independent from management. The Act directs the auditor to report to the audit committee rather than to company management. To further ensure independence from management, the lead partner of the audit firm must be rotated off the job after five years.[20]

These provisions, as well as the many other elements of the Sarbanes-Oxley Act, have changed public accounting as it was known in the past. Drastic action was needed and was taken.[21] This Act is strengthening the independent audit to help eliminate the dubious practices that have haunted public accounting. Some of these steps may not have been necessary, but the need to reestablish public confidence in the capital market system forced the legislators to avoid any "quick-fix" solutions.

The SEC's Authority over Generally Accepted Accounting Principles

LO4

Describe the SEC's role in establishing generally accepted accounting principles (GAAP).

The primary focus of the Sarbanes-Oxley Act was on the regulation of independent auditor and auditing standards. Therefore, it had little impact on accounting standards and the registration of securities. Those regulations continue to evolve over time. Because financial reporting standards can be changed merely by amending *Regulation S–X,* the SEC holds the ultimate legal authority for establishing accounting principles for most publicly held companies in this country. In the past, the SEC has usually restricted the application of this power to disclosure issues while looking to the private sector (with the SEC's oversight) to formulate accounting principles. For this reason, the FASB rather than the SEC is generally viewed as the main standards-setting body for financial accounting in the United States. "Under federal law, the SEC has the mandate to determine accounting principles for publicly traded companies. But it has generally ceded that authority to private-sector accounting bodies such as the Financial Accounting Standards Board."[22]

[18] Miller and Pashkoff, "Regulations under the Sarbanes-Oxley Act," pp. 35 and 36.

[19] Sarbanes-Oxley Act of 2002, Sec. 201.

[20] Ibid., at Sec. 203.

[21] The Sarbanes-Oxley Act, particularly Section 404 requirements, adds a significant cost to reporting operations for public companies. However, the SEC is attempting to provide "Section 404 relief" from the "multi-million-dollar expenses," while still ensuring proper disclosure. "Getting it Right," *Journal of Accountancy,* March 2007, p. 29.

[22] Kevin G. Salwen and Robin Goldwyn Blumenthal, "Tackling Accounting, SEC Pushes Changes with Broad Impact," *The Wall Street Journal,* September 27, 1990, p. A1.

However, the SEC does retain the ability to exercise its power with regard to the continuing evolution of accounting principles. The chief accountant of the SEC is responsible for providing the commissioners and the commission staff with advice on all current accounting and auditing matters and helps to draft rules for the form and content of financial statement disclosure and other reporting requirements. Because he or she is the principal adviser to the SEC on all accounting and auditing matters,[23] the most powerful accounting position in the United States is that of Chief Accountant of the SEC. The work of the chief accountant can lead the SEC to pass amendments as needed to alter various aspects of *Regulation S–X.*

The SEC issued *Financial Reporting Releases (FRRs)* as needed to supplement *Regulation S–X* and *Regulation S–K.* They explain desired changes in the reporting requirements. By the end of 1998, 50 FRRs had been issued.[24] By 2004 this number was 72. In addition, the staff of the SEC publishes a series of *Staff Accounting Bulletins (SABs)* as a means of informing the financial community of its positions.

> Staff Accounting Bulletins reflect the SEC staff's views regarding accounting-related disclosure practices. They represent interpretations and policies followed by the Division of Corporation Finance and the Office of the Chief Accountant in administering the disclosure requirements of the federal securities laws.[25]

For example, *SAB 101* was released in 1999 to provide guidance in connection with the recognition of revenue. The bulletin first stated that any transaction that fell within the scope of specific authoritative literature (e.g., a FASB statement) should be reported based on that pronouncement. *SAB 101* then established guidelines for revenue recognition situations when authoritative standards were not available. In such cases, a reporting entity should recognize revenue when realized (or realizable) and earned. However, *SAB 101* then went further to establish four criteria for revenue recognition: evidence that an arrangement exists, delivery has occurred or services have been rendered, the price is fixed or can be determined, and collectibility is reasonably assured. To help apply these criteria in actual practice, *SAB 101* included nine examples to show how to judge revenue recognition in such cases as the receipt of money in layaway programs and annual membership fees received by discount retailers.

Additional Disclosure Requirements

Historically, the SEC has restricted the use of its authority (as in *SAB 101*) to the gray areas of accounting for which official guidance is not available. New reporting problems arise each year while no authoritive body has ever completely addressed many other accounting issues, even after years of discussion. As another response to such problems, the SEC often requires the disclosure of additional data if current rules are viewed as insufficient.

> It was in the 1970s that the SEC seemed to single out disclosure as the area in which it would take the standard-setting lead, leaving measurement issues to the FASB. This was when the SEC was expanding the coverage of Management's Discussion & Analysis (MD&A), an extensive narrative disclosure that is required to be appended to the financial statements.[26]

For example, in the early part of 1997, while the FASB worked on a project concerning the accounting for derivatives, the SEC approved rules so that more information would be available immediately. Note disclosure in financial statements had to include more information about accounting policies used. In addition, information about the

[23] www.sec.gov/about/whatwedo.shtml, July 2011.

[24] From 1937 until 1982, the SEC issued more than 300 *Accounting Series Releases* (ASRs) to (1) amend *Regulation S-X,* (2) express interpretations regarding accounting and auditing issues, and (3) report disciplinary actions against public accountants. The SEC codified the ASRs that dealt with financial reporting matters of continuing interest and issued it as *Financial Reporting Release No. 1.*

[25] See footnote 2.

[26] Stephen A. Zeff, "A Perspective on the U.S. Public/Private-Sector Approach to the Regulation of Financial Reporting," *Accounting Horizons,* March 1995, pp. 58–59.

risk of loss from market rate or price changes inherent in derivatives and other financial instruments was required. By means of these disclosures, the SEC enabled investors to have data about the potential consequences of the company's financial position.

Moratorium on Specific Accounting Practices

The commission also can exert its power by declaring a moratorium on the use of specified accounting practices. When authoritative guidance is not present, the SEC can simply prohibit a particular method from being applied. As an example, in the 1980s, companies utilized a variety of procedures to account for internal computer software costs because no official pronouncement had yet been issued. Consequently, the SEC

> imposed a moratorium that will prohibit companies that plan to go public from capitalizing the internal costs of developing computer software for sale or lease or marketed to customers in other ways. . . . The decision doesn't prevent companies currently capitalizing internal software expenses from continuing, but the companies must disclose the effect of not expensing such costs as incurred. The moratorium continues until the Financial Accounting Standards Board issues a standard on the issue.[27]

When the FASB eventually arrived at a resolution of this question in August 1985 and issued *SFAS 86,* "Accounting for the Costs of Computer Software to Be Sold, Leased, or Otherwise Marketed," the SEC dropped the moratorium. Hence, the FASB set the accounting rule, but the SEC ensured appropriate reporting until that time.

Challenging Individual Statements

As described, officially requiring additional disclosure and prohibiting the application of certain accounting practices are two methods the SEC uses to control the financial reporting process. Forcing a specific registrant to change its filed statements is another, less formal approach that can create the same effect. For example:

> Advanced Micro Devices, Inc., agreed to settle an investigation by the Securities and Exchange Commission of the semiconductor company's public disclosures. The SEC found AMD "made inaccurate and misleading statements" concerning development of its 486 microprocessor. In 1992 and 1993, AMD "led the public to believe that it was independently designing the microcode for its 486 microprocessor without access" to the code of its rival chipmaker, Intel Corp., the SEC said, "when, in fact, AMD had provided its engineers . . . with Intel's copyright 386 microcode to accelerate the company's development efforts." Without admitting or denying the commission's findings, AMD, based in Sunnyvale, California, consented to an order barring it from committing future violations of SEC rules. No fines were imposed.[28]

Following the SEC's action, any company involved in a similar event would certainly be well advised to provide the suggested disclosure. Failing to do so could result in the SEC's refusal to approve an issuer's future registrations.

The Dodd-Frank Act strengthens the SEC's role in challenging, or at least questioning, financial statements. The act added a new provision to the Securities Exchange Act, pursuant to which the SEC may require listed companies to adopt and publish policies by which they will disgorge or "claw back" executive compensation when restated financial statements are necessitated by executive misconduct. Failure to adopt such policies results in mandatory delisting.[29]

Overruling the FASB

The SEC's actions are not necessarily limited, however, to the gray areas of accounting. Although the commission generally has allowed the FASB (and previous authoritative groups) to establish accounting principles, the SEC retains the authority to override or negate any pronouncements produced in the private sector. This power was dramatically

[27] "SEC Imposes 'Software Costs' Moratorium," *Journal of Accountancy,* September 1983, p. 3.

[28] "SEC Inquiry on Disclosure to Public Is Being Settled," *The Wall Street Journal,* October 1, 1996, p. B4.

[29] Dodd–Frank §954.

demonstrated in 1977 when the FASB issued *SFAS 19,* "Financial Accounting and Reporting by Oil and Gas Producing Companies." After an extended debate over the merits of alternative methods, the FASB issued this statement requiring oil- and gas-producing companies to apply the successful-efforts method when accounting for unsuccessful exploration and drilling costs.

In response, the SEC almost immediately invoked a moratorium on the use of this practice until an alternative approach could be evaluated. Thus, companies filing with the SEC were not allowed to follow the method established by the FASB (after years of formal study and deliberation by that body). Although the commission's reaction toward the accounting profession was a unique instance, the handling of this one issue clearly demonstrates the veto power that the SEC maintains over the work of the FASB.[30]

LO5

Define and describe an issuer's filings with the Securities and Exchange Commission.

Filings with the SEC

Because of legislation and regulations, registrants may be required to make numerous different filings with the SEC. The SEC actually receives hundreds of thousands of filings per year. However, for the overview presented here, the reporting process is divided into two very broad categories:

- Registration statements.
- Periodic filings.

Registration statements ensure the disclosure of sufficient, relevant financial data before either a company or its underwriters can *initially offer* a security to the public. The Securities Act of 1933 mandates dissemination of such information. Registration is necessary except in certain situations described at a later point in this chapter. The SEC charges a registration fee based on the value of the securities offered.[31] This fee is a very small fraction of the value of the securities being issued. In 2011, it was $116.10 for each $1 million of security offering. The SEC collects fees vastly in excess of its operating costs and, in fact, has a net position at the end of most fiscal years.

For years, the existence of this surplus has caused debate. Some view it as a source of general revenue for the federal government, and others have argued that it indicated that corporations were being overcharged for the registration process. However, another possibility emerged as a result of the corporate accounting scandals in 2001 and 2002: The surplus probably meant that the resources being invested in the SEC's work were not adequate. In other words, the agency could simply not meet its responsibilities with the money allotted. Not surprisingly, the Sarbanes-Oxley Act authorized a 77 percent increase in the agency's budget as well as a substantial increase in the size of its staff. However, this authorization did not necessarily mean that the SEC would actually receive more money in the budgeting process.

> Instead of supporting the 77 percent budget hike promised by Congress, the White House wants the SEC to make do with a more modest $568 million next year. The Commission's 2002 budget was $438 million. While this might seem like a lot, Harvey Goldschmid [SEC Commissioner] said that it is not enough to pay for the effective policing of 17,000 companies, 34,000 investment portfolios, and 7,500 financial advisers, especially in a climate where so much emphasis is placed on the quality of oversight.[32]

[30] For a detailed account of the activities surrounding the SEC's rejection of *SFAS 19,* see Donald Gorton, "The SEC Decision Not to Support SFAS 19: A Case Study of the Effect of Lobbying on Standard Setting," *Accounting Horizons,* March 1991.

[31] Self-Regulatory Organizations also impose similar fees. For instance, the National Association of Security Dealers imposes a .01 percent fee (with a $75,000.00 cap) based on the proposed maximum aggregate offering price. This permits the NASD to fulfill its functions in regard to its role with the SEC. SEC Release No. 34-50984, File No. SR-NASD-2004-177.

[32] Howard Stock, "Don't Short-Change SEC, Goldschmid Tells Bush," *Investors Relations Business,* December 16, 2002.

After initial registration, a number of federal laws, the most important of which is the Securities Exchange Act of 1934, require registrants to provide periodic filings. This legislation has resulted in the *continual reporting of specified data* by all companies that have securities publicly traded on either a national securities exchange or an over-the-counter market.[33]

For registration statements as well as periodic filings, the SEC has established forms that provide the format and content to be followed in providing required information. "These forms contain no blanks to be filled in as do tax forms. Instead, they are narrative in character, giving general instructions about the items of information to be furnished. Detailed information must be assembled by the companies using the form designed for the type of security being offered as well as the type of company making the offer."[34]

Registration Statements (1933 Act)

As indicated, a registration statement must be filed with and made effective by the Securities and Exchange Commission before a company can offer a security publicly. A security is very broadly defined to include items such as a note, stock, treasury stock, bond, debenture, investment contract, evidence of indebtedness, or transferable share.

The SEC's role is not to evaluate the quality of the investment. Rather, the SEC seeks to ensure that the content and disclosure of the filing comply with all applicable regulations. The responsibility for the information always rests with corporate officials. The SEC is charged with ensuring full and fair disclosure of relevant financial information. The registrant has the responsibility to provide such data, but the decision to invest must remain with the public.

A number of different forms are available for this purpose, depending on the specific circumstances. Some of the most commonly encountered registration statement forms follow:[35]

- S–1 Used when no other form is prescribed. Usually used by new registrants or by companies that have been filing reports with the SEC for less than 36 months.
- S–3 Used by companies that are large and already have a significant following in the stock market (at least $75 million of the voting stock is held by nonaffiliates). Disclosure is reduced for these organizations because the public is assumed to already have access to a considerable amount of information. Form F–3 is used if registration is by a foreign issuer.
- S–4 Used for securities issued in connection with business combination transactions.
- S–8 Used as a registration statement for employee stock plans.
- S–11 Used for the registration of securities by certain real estate companies.

The use of several of these forms, especially Form S–3, offers a distinct advantage to established companies that are issuing securities. Rather than duplicate voluminous information already disclosed in other filings with the SEC—frequently the annual report to shareholders—the registrant can simply indicate the location of the data in these other documents, a process referred to as *incorporation by reference.*

LO6

Describe an issuer's registration process, various forms used by the issuers, and the exemption(s) from registration.

Registration Procedures

The actual registration process is composed of a series of events leading up to the SEC's permission to "go effective." Because the registrant is seeking to obtain significant financial resources through the issuance of new securities in public markets, each of these procedures is vitally important.

[33] A company that has securities traded on an over-the-counter market does not have to file under the 1934 Act unless it has at least $10 million in assets and 500 shareholders.

[34] K. Fred Skousen, *An Introduction to the SEC* (Cincinnati: South-Western Publishing, 1991), p. 47.

[35] www.sec.gov/about/forms/secforms.htm.

After selecting the appropriate form, the company accumulates information according to the requirements of *Regulation S–K* and *Regulation S–X*. If it anticipates problems or questions, the company may request a prefiling conference with the SEC staff to seek guidance prior to beginning the registration. For example, if uncertainty concerning the handling or disclosure of an unusual transaction exists, a prefiling conference can save all parties considerable time and effort.

> The Commission has a long-established policy of holding its staff available for conferences with prospective registrants or their representatives in advance of filing a registration statement. These conferences may be held for the purpose of discussing generally the problems confronting a registrant in effecting registration or to resolve specific problems of an unusual nature which are sometimes presented by involved or complicated financial transactions.[36]

When the SEC receives it, the Division of Corporation Finance[37] reviews the registration statement. An analyst determines whether all nonfinancial information complies with the SEC's disclosure requirements in *Regulation S–K*. At the same time, an accountant verifies that the financial statement data included in the filing meet the standards of *Regulation S–X* and have been prepared according to generally accepted accounting principles. *Because the SEC does not conduct a formal audit, the report of the company's independent CPA is essential to this particular evaluation.* In addition, an SEC lawyer reviews the registration statement to verify its legal aspects.

The Division of Corporation Finance regularly requests clarifications, changes, or additional information, especially for those filings involving an initial registration. A *letter of comments* (also known as a *deficiency letter*) is issued to the company to communicate these findings. In most cases, the registrant attempts to provide the necessary data or changes to expedite the process. However, in controversial areas, the issuer may begin discussions directly with the SEC staff in hope of resolving the problem without making the requested adjustments or disclosure or, at least, with limited inconvenience.

When the Division of Corporation Finance is eventually satisfied that the company has fulfilled all SEC regulations, the registration statement is made effective and the securities can be sold. *Effectiveness does not, however, indicate an endorsement of the securities by the SEC.* With most offerings, the company actually sells the stock using one or more underwriters (stock brokerage firms) that market the shares to their clients to earn commissions.

For convenience and to save time and money, large companies are allowed to use a process known as *shelf registration*. They file once with the SEC and are then allowed to offer those securities at any time over the subsequent two years without having to go back to the SEC. For example, "Enterprise Products Partners L. P. announced today that it has filed an $800 million universal shelf registration statement with the Securities and Exchange Commission for the proposed sale of debt and equity securities over the next two years."[38]

The registration statement is physically composed of two parts. Part I, referred to as a *prospectus*, contains extensive information that includes these items:

1. Financial statements for the issuing company audited by an independent CPA along with appropriate supplementary data.
2. An explanation of the intended use of the proceeds to be generated by the sale of the new securities.
3. A description of the risks associated with the securities.
4. A description of the business and the properties owned by the issuer.

[36] Stanley Weinstein, Daniel Schechtman, and Michael A. Walker, *SEC Compliance*, vol. 4 (Englewood Cliffs, NJ: Prentice Hall, 1999), para. 30,641.

[37] All registration statements filed by issuers offering securities to the public for the first time are reviewed. Subsequent registration statements and periodic filings are reviewed only on a selective basis.

[38] "Enterprise Files $800 Million Universal Shelf Registration with SEC," *Business Wire*, December 27, 1999.

The registrant must furnish every potential buyer of the securities with a copy of this prospectus, thus ensuring the adequate availability of information for their investment analysis.

Part II of the registration statement is primarily for the informational needs of the SEC staff. Additional data should be disclosed about the company and the securities being issued such as marketing arrangements, expenses of issuance, sales to special parties, and the like. The registrant is not required to provide this information to prospective buyers, although the entire registration statement is available to the public through the SEC.

Securities Exempt from Registration According to the 1933 Act, not all securities issued by companies and their underwriters require registration prior to their sale. For example, securities sold to the residents of the state in which the issuing company is chartered and principally doing business are exempted. However, these offerings may still be regulated by the securities laws of the individual states (commonly known as *blue sky laws*), which vary significantly.[39]

Other exempt offerings include but are not limited to the following:

- Securities issued by governments, banks, and savings and loan associations.
- Securities issued that are restricted to a company's own existing stockholders for which no commission is paid to solicit the exchange.
- Securities, such as bonds, issued by nonprofit organizations such as religious, educational, or charitable groups.
- Small offerings of no more than $5 million within a 12-month period. In most cases, though, a Regulation A offering circular must still be filed with the SEC and given to prospective buyers. However, an offering circular requires much less information than a registration statement.
- Offerings of no more than $1 million made to any number of investors within a 12-month period. No specific disclosure of information is required. General solicitations are allowed. The issuer must give notice of the offering to the SEC within 15 days of the first sale.
- Offerings of no more than $5 million made to 35 or fewer purchasers in a 12-month period. No general solicitation is allowed for securities issued in this manner. Accredited investors (such as banks, insurance companies, and individuals with net worth of more than $1 million) are not included in the restriction on the number of buyers. Unaccredited investors must still be furnished an audited balance sheet and other specified information. Parties making purchases have to hold the securities for at least two years or lose the filing exemption.
- The private placement of securities to no more than 35 sophisticated investors (having knowledge and experience in financial matters) who already have sufficient information available to them about the issuing company. General solicitation is not permitted. These private placement rules have become quite important in recent years. Private placements in the United States rose from $16 billion in 1980 to more than $200 billion in 1996. By 2004, private equity placements nearly approached this figure, approximating $177 billion. For example, "SYS Technologies, a leading provider of real time information technology solutions to industrial and U.S. government customers, announced today that it has completed a private placement with institutional investors raising gross proceeds of $3.35 million on June 3, 2005."[40]

Periodic Filings with the SEC

Once a company has issued securities that are publicly traded on a securities exchange or an over-the-counter market, it must continually file information with the SEC so that

[39] "These early laws became known as 'blue sky' laws after a judicial decision characterized some transactions as 'speculative schemes which have no more basis than so many feet of blue sky.'" (Skousen, *An Introduction to the SEC*, p. 3.)

[40] "SYS Technologies Completes Private Placement Transaction," www.freshnews.com/news/fresh-money/article_24429.html.

adequate disclosure is available. As with registration statements, several different forms are utilized for this purpose. However, for most companies with actively traded securities, three of these are common: Form 10–K (an annual report), Form 10–Q (a quarterly report), and Form 8–K (disclosure of significant events). Smaller businesses use Form 10–KSB for annual reports and Form 10–QSB for quarterly reports.

In addition, as mentioned previously, proxy statements must be filed with the SEC. Management or another interested party issues these statements to a company's owners in hope of securing voting rights to be used at stockholders' meetings.

Form 10–K A 10–K form is an annual report filed with the SEC to provide information and disclosures required by *Regulation S–K* and *Regulation S–X*. Fortunately, because of the integrated disclosure system, the annual report distributed by companies to their stockholders now includes most of the basic financial disclosures required by the SEC in Form 10–K. Thus, many companies simply attach the stockholders' annual report to the Form 10–K each year and use the incorporation by reference procedure to meet most of the SEC's filing requirements. This process is sometimes known as a *wraparound filing.*

Form 10–K, as with the various other SEC filings, is constantly undergoing assessment to determine whether it is meeting investor needs.[41] Thus, the SEC's reporting requirements are evolutionary and change over time.

> The Securities and Exchange Commission issued guidelines aimed at making public companies provide a more detailed look at the trends and business changes that management expects in the future. . . . In the main part of yesterday's interpretation, the commissioners said that in the 10–K reports, companies must discuss "trends, demands, commitments or events" that it knows are "reasonably likely" to occur and have a material effect on financial condition or results.[42]

As this quote indicates, the SEC is especially interested in the quality of the information provided by the MD&A section of a registrant's filings. Basically, management should describe the company's past, present, and future. This information can furnish investors with a feel for the prospects of the company; it is a candid narrative to provide statement readers with a sense of management's priorities, accomplishments, and concerns. The SEC staff carefully reviews the MD&A feature. "If the management of a company knows something that could have a material impact on earnings in the future, officials have an obligation to share that information with shareholders."[43]

Form 10–Q A 10–Q form contains condensed interim financial statements for the registrant and must be filed with the SEC shortly after the end of each quarter. However, no Form 10–Q is required following the fourth quarter of the year since a Form 10–K is forthcoming shortly thereafter. A Form 10–Q does not have to be audited by an independent CPA.

Information to be contained in each Form 10–Q includes the following:

- Income statements must be included for the most recent quarter and for the year to date as well as for the comparative periods in the previous year.
- A statement of cash flows is also necessary, but only for the year to date as well as for the corresponding period in the preceding year.
- Two balance sheets are reported: one as of the end of the most recent quarter and the second showing the company's financial position at the end of the previous fiscal year.
- Each Form 10–Q should also include any needed disclosures pertaining to the current period including the MD&A of the financial condition of the company and results of operations.

[41] The current Form 10–K instructions can be viewed at www.sec.gov/about/forms/form10-K.pdf. This version of the Form 10–K has been approved for use through May 31, 2014.

[42] Paul Duke Jr., "SEC Issues Guidelines for 10–K Filings Seeking More Details on Trends, Changes," *The Wall Street Journal,* May 19, 1989, p. A2.

[43] Kevin G. Salwen, "SEC Charges Caterpillar Failed to Warn Holders of Earnings Risk Posed by Unit," *The Wall Street Journal,* April 2, 1992, p. A3.

Form 8–K An 8–K form is used to disclose a unique or significant happening.[44] Consequently, the 8–K is not filed at regular time intervals but within 15 calendar days of the event (or within 5 business days in certain specified instances). The SEC receives thousands of 8–K reports each year. According to the SEC's guidelines, Form 8–K may be filed to report any action that company officials believe is important to security holders. However, the following events are designated for required disclosure in this manner:

- Resignation of a director.
- Changes in control of the registrant.
- Acquisition or disposition of assets.
- Changes in the registrant's certified public accountants (independent auditors).
- Bankruptcy or receivership.

Proxy Statements As previously mentioned, most of the significant actions undertaken by a company first must be approved at stockholders' meetings. For example, the members of the board of directors are elected in this meeting to oversee the company's operations. Although such votes are essential to the operations of a business, few major companies could possibly assemble enough shareholders at any one time and place for a voting quorum. The geographic distances are simply too great. Hence, before each of the periodic meetings, the management (or any other interested party) usually requests signed proxies from shareholders granting the legal authority to cast votes for the owners in connection with the various actions to be taken at such stockholders' meetings.[45]

Because of the power conveyed by a proxy, any such solicitation sent to shareholders (by any party) must include specific information as the SEC required in its *Regulation 14A.* This proxy statement has to be filed with the SEC at least 10 days before being distributed. In addition to the disclosed items previously described, other data must be reported to the owners:

- The proxy statement needs to indicate on whose behalf the solicitation is being made.
- The proxy statement must disclose fully all matters that are to be voted on at the meeting.
- In most cases, the proxy statement has to be accompanied (or preceded) by an annual report to the shareholders.

As with all areas of disclosure, the SEC's regulation of proxy statements has greatly enhanced the information available to investors. Historically, shareholders have not always been able to get adequate information.

> Thus was the president of one company able to respond cavalierly to a shareholder's request for information, "I can assure you that the company is in a good financial position. I trust that you will sign and mail your proxy at an early date." Quaint. But that was nothing. One unlisted company printed its proxy on the back of the dividend check—so when you endorsed the check you voted for management.[46]
>
> From a 1902 annual report to shareholders: "The settled plan has been to withhold all information from stockholders and others that is not called for by the stockholders in a body. So far no request for information has been made in the manner prescribed by the directors."[47]

Electronic Data Gathering, Analysis, and Retrieval System (EDGAR)

During recent years, the SEC has been almost overwhelmed by the sheer mountains of documents that it receives, reviews, and makes available to the public. Filings with the

[44] The current Form 8–K instructions can be viewed at www.sec.gov/about/forms/form8-K.pdf. The SEC estimates that an issuer can complete an 8–K filing in approximately five hours.

[45] Any person who owns at least 5 percent of the company's stock or has been an owner for six months or longer has the right to look at a list of shareholders to make a proxy solicitation.

[46] Laura Jereski, "You've Come a Long Way, Shareholder," *Forbes,* July 13, 1987, p. 282.

[47] Skousen, *An Introduction to the SEC,* p. 75.

Discussion Question

IS THE DISCLOSURE WORTH THE COST?

Filing with the SEC requires a very significant amount of time and effort on the registrant's part. Companies frequently resist attempts by the SEC to increase the levels of disclosure. Usually, they argue that additional information will not necessarily be useful to a great majority of investors. Regardless of the issue being debated, critics claim that the cost of the extra data far outweighs any benefits that might be derived from this disclosure.

Such contentions are not necessarily made just to avoid disclosing information. This cost analysis has continued for most of the past four decades. One survey from the late 1970s estimated the cost of SEC disclosures to be more than $400 million in 1975 alone.

> The table reports an estimated $213,500,000 for the fully variable costs of 10–K, 10–Q, and 8–K disclosures in 1975. To this should be added the separate estimate (not shown) of $191,900,000 for disclosure related to new issues in 1975, for a total estimate of about $400,000,000 for SEC disclosure costs in 1975. These estimates are biased downward because they do not include various fixed costs.*

Such costs are either passed along to the consumer in the form of higher prices or serve to retard the growth of the reporting company.

Additional SEC requirements continue to concern issuers, many of which conclude that "the costs of mandatory SEC disclosures outweigh the benefits" and accept delisting from the various exchanges, rather than incurring the costs of such disclosure.† SEC revenues, which constitute real out-of-pocket costs to issuers, exceeded $2 billion in 2003. This represents a 10-fold increase in the past 30 years.

The author of one survey (that has been widely discussed and debated over the years) held that federal securities laws are not actually helpful to investors.

> I found that there was little evidence of fraud related to financial statements in the period prior to the enactment of the Securities Acts. Nor was there a widespread lack of disclosure. . . . Hence, I conclude that there was little justification for the accounting disclosure required by the Acts. . . . These findings indicate that the data required by the SEC do not seem to be useful to investors.‡

The SEC was created, in part, to ensure that the public has fair and full disclosure about companies whose securities are publicly traded. However, the commission must be mindful of the cost of such disclosures. How can the SEC determine whether the cost of a proposed disclosure is more or less than the benefits to be derived by the public? After all, despite SEC investigations, Bernard Madoff avoided detection for decades.

*J. Richard Zecher, "An Economic Perspective of SEC Corporate Disclosure," *The SEC and Accounting: The First 50 Years,* ed. Robert H. Mundheim and Noyes E. Leech (Amsterdam: North-Holland, 1985), pp. 75–76.

†Brian J. Bushee and Christian Leuz, "Economic Consequences of SEC Disclosure Regulation," The Wharton School, University of Pennsylvania, February 2004, p. 3.

‡George J. Benston, "The Value of the SEC's Accounting Disclosure Requirements," *The Accounting Review,* July 1969, p. 351.

SEC contain millions of pieces of paper each year. Not surprisingly, some problems in the capital markets during the last few years have been blamed, in part, on this overload. "[The SEC's] corporation finance division cannot keep up with the deluge of company filings."[48]

[48] Labaton, "Can a Bloodied S.E.C. Dust Itself Off and Get Moving?"

In 1984, the SEC began to develop an electronic data gathering, analysis, and retrieval system nicknamed EDGAR. As originally envisioned, all filings would arrive at the SEC on disks or through some other electronic transmission. Each filing could be reviewed, analyzed, and stored by SEC personnel on a computer so they would no longer constantly have to sift through stacks of paper. Perhaps more important, investors would have the ability to access these data through the Internet. Thus, investors throughout the world could have information available for their decisions literally minutes after the documents are made effective by the SEC.

Because of the ambitious nature of the EDGAR project, approximately a decade was required to get the system effectively operational. For years, EDGAR was the object of much scorn; "one member of the House Energy and Commerce Committee suggested renaming the project Mr. Ed, 'since the SEC has a much better chance of finding a talking horse than it does of achieving an efficient computer filing system.'"[49] However, the beginning of the explosive use of the Internet in the mid-1990s corresponded with the widespread availability of information on EDGAR. Not surprisingly, EDGAR's popularity has expanded.

> If you're suspicious about a certain stock, then go to the Securities and Exchange Commission's EDGAR database—chockablock with annual reports, prospectuses and all the other paperwork demanded of public companies.[50]
>
> Since Congress went to all the trouble in the 1930s of creating the SEC and requiring these corporate disclosures, it seems like somebody should give them an occasional good read. The Edgar database at the SEC's Web site gives any individual free access to the filings of thousands of public companies. . . . It's sometimes amazing what kind of information typing someone's name, address or phone number into an Edgar search engine can generate.[51]

Today, virtually all publicly held companies are required to file their SEC reports electronically. Paper filings, when permitted, are also converted to electronic files and available to the general public.[52] The resultant EDGAR filings are typically available via the SEC's website within 24 hours of filings. These public filings, combined with the ease of access via the Internet, have resulted in the virtually immediate dissemination of vital investment-related data to accounting professionals, financial advisers, government regulators, and the investing public. EDGAR users can locate filings based on entity names, standard industrial classification (SIC) codes, central index keys (CIK), addresses, date–time frames, and a variety of other variables. This extensive database has helped move financial reporting to a significantly higher level of transparency.

Summary

1. In the United States, the Securities and Exchange Commission (SEC) has been entrusted with the responsibility for ensuring that complete and reliable information is available to investors who buy and sell securities in public capital markets. Since being created in 1934, this agency has administered numerous reporting rules and regulations created by congressional actions starting with the Securities Act of 1933 and the Securities Exchange Act of 1934.
2. The corporate accounting scandals that rocked the U.S. financial community during 2001 and 2002 led Congress to pass the Sarbanes-Oxley Act. This legislation addressed a number of problems. Its main provision was the creation of the Public Company Accounting Oversight Board to monitor and regulate the auditors of public companies. Audit firms of public companies must register with this board and are subject to periodic inspections as well as various types of possible disciplinary actions. This act also contains rules to help ensure the independence of the external auditor.

[49] Sandra Block, "SEC Gets Closer to Electronic Filing," *The Wall Street Journal,* August 30, 1991, p. C1.

[50] The address for EDGAR is www.sec.gov. A quick EDGAR tutorial is available at www.sec.gov/edgar/quickedgar.htm to familiarize users with the retrieval system. Joseph R. Garber, "Click Before You Leap," *Forbes,* February 24, 1997, p. 162.

[51] John Emshwiller, "Financial Filings Hold Key to Investigative Pieces, Big and Small," *The Wall Street Journal,* May 31, 2005.

[52] www.sec.gov/edgar/quickedgar.htm.

3. Before a company's securities (either equity or debt) can be publicly traded, appropriate filings must be made with the SEC to ensure that sufficient data are made available to potential investors. Disclosure requirements for this process are outlined in two documents: *Regulation S–K* (for nonfinancial information) and *Regulation S–X* (describing the form and content of all included financial statements).
4. The ability to require the reporting of special information gives the SEC enormous legal power over the accounting standards in the United States. Traditionally, this authority has been wielded only on rare occasions and only to increase disclosure requirements and to provide guidance where none was otherwise available. However, in a significant demonstration of its authority, the SEC overruled the FASB's decision in 1977 as to the appropriate method to account for unsuccessful exploration and drilling costs incurred by oil- and gas-producing companies.
5. Filings with the SEC are divided generally into two broad categories: registration statements and periodic filings. Registration statements are designed to provide information about a company prior to its issuance of a security to the public. Depending on the circumstances, several different registration forms are available for this purpose. After the registrant produces the statement and the SEC initially reviews it, a letter of comments describing desired explanations or changes is furnished. These concerns must be resolved before the security can be sold.
6. Not all securities issued in the United States require registration with the SEC. As an example, formal registration is not necessary for securities sold by either government units or banks. Certain issues for relatively small amounts are also exempt although some amount of disclosure is normally required. Securities sold solely within the state in which the business operates are not subject to federal securities laws but must comply with state laws frequently referred to as *blue sky laws.*
7. Companies whose stocks or bonds are publicly traded on a securities exchange must also submit periodic filings to the SEC to ensure that adequate disclosure is constantly maintained. Among the most common of these filings are Form 10–K (an annual report) and Form 10–Q (condensed interim financial information). Form 8–K also is required to report any significant events that occur. In addition, proxy statements (documents that are used to solicit votes at stockholders' meetings) also come under the filing requirements monitored by the SEC.
8. The SEC created the EDGAR database to allow companies to make electronic filings with the commission. More importantly, EDGAR allows any person with access to the Internet to review these documents in a timely fashion. Thus, access to financial and other information about filing entities has become much more widely available.

Questions

(Students may wish to visit the SEC website, www.sec.gov, for supplemental resources.)

1. Why were federal securities laws originally enacted by Congress?
2. What are some of the possible reasons for the numerous corporate accounting scandals discovered during 2001 and 2002?
3. List several provisions of the Sarbanes-Oxley Act that are designed to restore public confidence in the U.S. capital market system.
4. What is the SEC's relationship to the Public Company Accounting Oversight Board?
5. Who must register with the Public Company Accounting Oversight Board?
6. What is the impact of being registered with the PCAOB?
7. How has the Sarbanes-Oxley Act attempted to ensure that external auditors will be completely independent in the future?
8. What is the purpose of the inspection process created by the Sarbanes-Oxley Act?
9. What is covered by *Regulation S–K?*
10. What is covered by *Regulation S–X?*
11. What are some of the major divisions within the SEC?
12. What does the Securities Act of 1933 cover?
13. What does the Securities Exchange Act of 1934 cover?
14. What are the goals of the SEC?
15. What information is required in a proxy statement?
16. Why is the content of a proxy statement considered to be so important?
17. How does the SEC affect the development of generally accepted accounting principles in the United States?

18. What is the purpose of *Financial Reporting Releases* and *Staff Accounting Bulletins?*
19. What was the SEC's response to the FASB's handling of accounting for oil- and gas-producing companies, and why was this action considered so significant?
20. What is the purpose of a registration statement?
21. Under what law is a registration statement filed?
22. What are the two parts of a registration statement? What does each part contain?
23. How does the SEC generate revenues?
24. Two forms commonly used in the registration process are Form S–1 and Form S–3. Which registrants should use each form?
25. What is incorporation by reference?
26. What is a prefiling conference, and why might it be helpful to a registrant?
27. What is a letter of comments? By what other name is it often called?
28. What is a prospectus? What does a prospectus contain?
29. Under what circumstances is a company exempt from filing a registration statement with the SEC prior to the issuance of securities?
30. What is a private placement of securities?
31. What are blue sky laws?
32. What is a wraparound filing?
33. When is a Form 8–K issued by a company? What specific information does a Form 8–K convey?
34. What is the purpose of the Management's Discussion and Analysis?
35. What is the difference between a Form 10–K and a Form 10–Q?
36. What was the purpose of creating the EDGAR system?

Problems

LO1

1. Which of the following statements is true?
   a. The Securities Exchange Act of 1934 regulates intrastate stock offerings made by a company.
   b. The Securities Act of 1933 regulates the subsequent public trading of securities through brokers and markets.
   c. The Securities Exchange Act of 1934 is commonly referred to as blue sky legislation.
   d. The Securities Act of 1933 regulates the initial offering of securities by a company.

LO2

2. What is the purpose of *Regulation S–K?*
   a. Defines generally accepted accounting principles in the United States.
   b. Establishes required disclosure of nonfinancial information with the SEC.
   c. Establishes required financial disclosures with the SEC.
   d. Indicates which companies must file with the SEC on an annual basis.

LO2

3. What is the difference between *Regulation S–K* and *Regulation S–X?*
   a. *Regulation S–K* establishes reporting requirements for companies in their initial issuance of securities whereas *Regulation S–X* is directed toward the subsequent issuance of securities.
   b. *Regulation S–K* establishes reporting requirements for companies smaller than a certain size whereas *Regulation S–X* is directed toward companies larger than that size.
   c. *Regulation S–K* establishes regulations for nonfinancial information filed with the SEC whereas *Regulation S–X* prescribes the form and content of financial statements included in SEC filings.
   d. *Regulation S–K* establishes reporting requirements for publicly held companies whereas *Regulation S–X* is directed toward private companies.

LO2

4. The Securities Exchange Act of 1934
   a. Regulates the public trading of previously issued securities through brokers and exchanges.
   b. Prohibits blue sky laws.
   c. Regulates the initial offering of securities by a company.
   d. Requires the registration of investment advisers.

LO3

5. Which of the following is a requirement of the Sarbanes-Oxley Act of 2002?
   a. Registration of all auditing firms with the Public Company Accounting Oversight Board.
   b. Annual inspection of all auditing firms registered with the Public Company Accounting Oversight Board.
   c. A monetary fee assessed on organizations issuing securities.
   d. Overall assessment of the work of the SEC each year.

LO3

6. Which of the following is *not* correct with regard to the Public Company Accounting Oversight Board?
   a. The board can expel a registered auditing firm without SEC approval.
   b. All registered auditing firms must be inspected at least every three years.
   c. The board members must be appointed by Congress.
   d. The board has the authority to set auditing standards rather than utilize the work of the Auditing Standards Board.

LO3

7. Which of the following is *not* a way by which the Sarbanes-Oxley Act attempts to ensure auditor independence from an audit client?
   a. The auditing firm must be appointed by the client's audit committee.
   b. Audit fees must be approved by the Public Company Accounting Oversight Board.
   c. The audit committee must be composed of members of the client's board of directors who are independent of the management.
   d. The external auditor cannot also perform financial information system design and implementation work.

LO5

8. What is a registration statement?
   a. A statement that must be filed with the SEC before a company can begin an initial offering of securities to the public.
   b. A required filing with the SEC before a large amount of stock can be obtained by an inside party.
   c. An annual filing made with the New York Stock Exchange.
   d. A filing made by a company with the SEC to indicate that a significant change has occurred.

LO5

9. Which of the following is a registration statement used by large companies that already have a significant following in the stock market?
   a. Form 8–K.
   b. Form 10–K.
   c. Form S–1.
   d. Form S–3.

LO4

10. What was the significance of the controversy in 1977 over the appropriate accounting principles to be used by oil- and gas-producing companies?
   a. Several major lawsuits resulted.
   b. Companies refused to follow the SEC's dictates.
   c. Partners of a major accounting firm were indicted on criminal charges.
   d. The SEC overruled the FASB on its handling of this matter.

LO6

11. Which of the following must be provided to every potential buyer of a new security?
   a. A letter of comments.
   b. A deficiency letter.
   c. A prospectus.
   d. A Form S–16.

LO5

12. What does the term *incorporation by reference* mean?
   a. The legal incorporation of a company in more than one state.
   b. Filing information with the SEC by indicating that the information is already available in another document.
   c. A reference guide indicating informational requirements specified in *Regulation S–X.*
   d. Incorporating a company in a state outside of its base of operations.

LO6

13. What is a letter of comments?
    a. A letter the SEC sends to a company indicating needed changes or clarifications in a registration statement.
    b. A questionnaire supplied to the SEC by a company suggesting changes in *Regulation S–X.*
    c. A letter included in a Form 10–K to indicate the management's assessment of the company's financial position.
    d. A letter composed by a company asking for information or clarification prior to the filing of a registration statement.

LO6

14. What is a prospectus?
    a. A document attached to a Form 8–K.
    b. A potential stockholder as defined by *Regulation S–K.*
    c. A document a company files with the SEC prior to filing a registration statement.
    d. The first part of a registration statement that a company must furnish to all potential buyers of a new security.

LO6

15. Which of the following is *not* exempt from registration with the SEC under the Securities Act of 1933?
    a. Securities issued by a nonprofit religious organization.
    b. Securities issued by a government unit.
    c. A public offering of no more than $5.9 million.
    d. An offering made to only 26 sophisticated investors.

LO6

16. Which of the following is usually *not* filed with the SEC on a regular periodic basis?
    a. A Form 10–Q.
    b. A prospectus.
    c. A proxy statement.
    d. A Form 10–K.

LO6

17. What is a shelf registration?
    a. A registration statement that the SEC formally rejects.
    b. A registration statement that the SEC rejects due to the lapse of a specified period of time.
    c. A registration process for large companies that allows them to offer securities over a period of time without seeking additional approval by the SEC.
    d. A registration form that is withdrawn by the registrant without any action having been taken.

LO6

18. What is EDGAR?
    a. A system the SEC uses to reject registration statements that do not contain adequate information.
    b. The enforcement arm of the SEC.
    c. A system designed by the SEC to allow electronic filings.
    d. A branch of the government that oversees the work of the SEC.

LO1, LO3, LO5, LO6

19. Identify each of the following as they pertain to the SEC.
    a. Blue sky laws.
    b. S–8 Statement.
    c. Letter of comments.
    d. Public Company Accounting Oversight Board.
    e. Prospectus.

LO2

20. Discuss the objectives of the Securities Act of 1933 and the Securities Exchange Act of 1934. How are these objectives accomplished?

LO6

21. What are the general steps involved in filing a registration statement with the SEC?

LO4

22. Discuss the methods by which the SEC can influence the development of generally accepted accounting principles in the United States.

LO6

23. Which forms do most companies file with the SEC on a periodic basis? Explain the purpose of each form and its primary contents.

LO5

24. Which forms do most companies file with the SEC in connection with the offering of securities to the public?

LO6

25. What is the importance of a Form 8–K? What is the importance of a proxy statement?

LO3

26. Describe the provisions of the Sarbanes-Oxley Act as they relate to the creation and responsibilities of the Public Company Accounting Oversight Board.

LO1, LO2, LO4, LO5, LO6

27. Explain each of the following items:
    - *a.* *Staff Accounting Bulletins.*
    - *b.* Wraparound filing.
    - *c.* Incorporation by reference.
    - *d.* Division of Corporation Finance.
    - *e.* Integrated disclosure system.
    - *f.* Management's discussion and analysis.
    - *g.* Chief accountant of the SEC.

LO6

28. Which organizations are normally exempted from the SEC's registration requirements?

Develop Your Skills

RESEARCH CASE 1

Domer Corporation is preparing to issue a relatively small amount of securities and does not want to go to the trouble and expense of filing a registration statement with the SEC. Company officials hope to be exempt under provisions of Regulation A. These officials want to be certain that they meet these provisions precisely so that no later legal problems arise.

Required

Go to the website www.sec.gov and then select Corporate Finance under Divisions. Then select the link for Statutes, Rules, and Forms, followed by the Rules and Regulations Link. Based on the information provided for Regulation A, prepare a report for Domer Corporation officials as to the requirements for exemption and advise as to the maximum amount of capital that may be raised through such issuance. Assuming that Domer Corporation is a development stage company, revise the report. Note specifically Regulation §230.251.

RESEARCH CASE 2

Tasch Corporation, a multilevel marketing and sales organization, plans to sell approximately $10,000,000 worth of "service agreements" to many of its customers. These service agreements guarantee a set return to the customer in exchange for an up-front purchase price, with Tasch Corporation managing the various business interests of its customers. Jerry Tasch, the corporation's president, needs advice concerning the necessity of SEC filings prior to the sale of these service agreements.

Required

Assume that the only (initial) question to be addressed is whether the service agreements constitute securities under the Securities Act of 1933. Perform research utilizing an Internet search engine to determine whether the service agreements are in fact securities. Note that courts interpret statutes and regulations, so it is often useful to look at judicial determinations to reach a conclusion. To that end, consider locating and reviewing the following case: *SEC v. Calvo,* 378 F.3d 1211 (11th Cir. 2004). Students can locate this case using many web links including FINDLAW and LexisNexis. This web link will direct the student directly to the specific opinion (http://www.ca11.uscourts.gov/opinions/ops/200213445.pdf).

ANALYSIS CASE 1

Go to the website www.sec.gov and, under the Filings & Forms (EDGAR) heading, click on "Search for Company Filings" and then click on "Company or Fund Name." Enter the name of a well-known company such as Dell. A list of available documents should be shown for that company.

Required

Using these available documents, answer the following questions:

1. Has the company filed an 8–K during the most recent time period? If so, open that document and determine the reason that the form was filed with the SEC.
2. Has the company filed a 10–K during the recent time period? If so, open that document and determine the total reported net income for the latest period of time.
3. Has the company filed a 14A (a proxy statement) during the most recent time period? If so, open that document and determine what issues were to be voted on at the annual meeting.

COMMUNICATION CASE 1

The senior partner of Wojtysiak & Co., CPAs, has been approached by a small, publicly traded corporation wishing to change auditors. The Wojtysiak firm does not audit any other public companies. Because of the Sarbanes-Oxley Act of 2002, Mike Wojtysiak, the senior partner, needs to know the regulatory issues facing his firm if it accepts the new engagement.

Required

Draft a report that outlines the Sarbanes-Oxley considerations for a firm such as the Wojtysiak firm. Locate the actual act (Public Law 107-204) or perform a thorough summary and review it prior to preparing the report. The full act may be found at http://corporate.findlaw.com/industry/corporate/docs/publ107.204.html.

chapter 13

Accounting for Legal Reorganizations and Liquidations

One common thread that runs throughout a significant portion of this textbook is the accounting for an organization when viewed as a whole.[1] Several chapters, for example, examine the consolidation of financial information generated by two or more companies that have been united in a business combination. Although that coverage included the handling of specific accounts, the primary emphasis was on reporting these organizations as a single economic entity.

Likewise, the analysis of foreign currency translation demonstrated the procedures used in consolidating the assets and liabilities as well as operating results of a subsidiary doing business anywhere in the world.

The various reporting requirements for disaggregated information have also been presented as a means to help disclose complete information to describe an entity. Again, the accounting goal was to convey data about the entire operation.

Continuing with this theme, subsequent chapters present the specialized accounting that partnerships, state and local government units, not-for-profit organizations, estates, and trusts utilize.

The presentation of financial data to describe a particular type of organization is not a rigid structure. Accounting is adaptable. Numerous factors influence its development in specific circumstances: the purpose of the information, the nature of the organization, the environment in which it operates, and so on. In reporting the operations and financial position of a business combination, a foreign subsidiary, an operating segment, a partnership, a government unit, an estate, or a not-for-profit organization, accountants must develop unique reporting techniques that address particular needs and problems.

The current chapter extends this coverage by presenting accounting procedures required in bankruptcy cases. At such times, the financially troubled company and its owners and creditors face the prospect of incurring significant losses. Once again, the accountant must adapt financial reporting to meet many and varied informational needs. The large number of failed businesses during the last few years has made this accounting process especially important.

[1] Intermediate accounting textbooks, in contrast, tend to present the reporting of specific assets and liabilities such as leases, pensions, deferred income taxes, and bonds.

Learning Objectives

After studying this chapter, you should be able to:

- LO1 Describe the history and current status of bankruptcy and bankruptcy laws.
- LO2 Explain the difference between a voluntary and involuntary bankruptcy.
- LO3 Identify the various types of creditors as they are labeled during a bankruptcy.
- LO4 Describe the difference between a Chapter 7 bankruptcy and a Chapter 11 bankruptcy.
- LO5 Account for a company as it enters bankruptcy.
- LO6 Account for the liquidation of a company in bankruptcy.
- LO7 List the provisions that are often found in a bankruptcy reorganization plan.
- LO8 Account for a company as it moves through reorganization.
- LO9 Describe the financial reporting for a company that successfully exits bankruptcy as a reorganized entity.

Accounting for Legal Reorganizations and Liquidations

LO1

Describe the history and current status of bankruptcy and bankruptcy laws.

Centuries ago in Italy the bankrupt merchant would be forced into an odd form of pillory. He would have the table he did business at in the town square broken. At least one source says the word *bankruptcy* derives from the Italian words for this practice, which translate to *broken bench.*[2]

A basic assumption of accounting is that a business is considered a *going concern* unless evidence to the contrary is discovered. As a result, assets such as inventory, land, buildings, and equipment are traditionally reported based on historical cost rather than net realizable value. Unfortunately, not all organizations prove to be going concerns. The number of companies experiencing financial difficulties varies from year to year as economic and other conditions change.

> According to numbers released this week by BankruptcyData.com, the number of Chapter 7 and Chapter 11 filings by public companies in 2010 fell by more than half compared to the number of filings in 2009. The 106 filings in 2010 also had a net asset value of $89 billion, a steep drop-off from the $594 billion in combined asset value for companies entering bankruptcy the year before.[3]

The size of some of the more renowned bankruptcies has become astronomical. Notice how many of the 10 largest U. S. bankruptcies have occurred in the last few years:

- Lehman Brothers Holdings Inc., September 15, 2008, $691 billion in assets.
- Washington Mutual Inc., September 26, 2008, $328 billion.
- WorldCom Inc., July 21, 2002, $104 billion.
- General Motors Corp., June 1, 2009, $91 billion.
- CIT Group, Inc., November 1, 2009, $71 billion.
- Enron Corp., December 2, 2001, $66 billion.
- Conseco Inc., December 17, 2002, $61 billion.
- Chrysler LLC, April 30, 2009, $39 billion.
- Thornburg Mortgage Inc., May 1, 2009, $37 billion.
- Pacific Gas and Electric Co., April 6, 2001, $36 billion.[4]

What happens to these businesses after they fail? Is bankruptcy the equivalent of a death sentence? Who gets the assets? Are the creditors protected? How does the accountant reflect the economic plight of the company?

Virtually all businesses undergo financial difficulties at various times. Economic downturns, poor product performance, intense competition, rapid technological changes, and litigation losses can create cash flow difficulties for even the best-managed organizations. Most companies take remedial actions and work to return operations to normal profitability. However, as the preceding list indicates, not all companies are able to solve their monetary difficulties. If problems persist, a company can eventually become *insolvent,* unable to pay debts as the obligations come due. When creditors are not paid, they take whatever actions they can to protect their financial interests in hopes of reducing the possibility of loss. They may seek recovery from the distressed company in several ways: repossessing assets, filing lawsuits, foreclosing on loans, and so on. An insolvent company can literally become besieged by its creditors.

If left unchecked, pandemonium would be the possible outcome of a company's insolvency. As a result, some of the creditors and stockholders as well as the company itself could find themselves treated unfairly. One party might be able to collect in full while

[2] "In Pursuit of a Balanced Bankruptcy Law," *ABA Banking Journal,* May 1993, p. 50.

[3] Briana Baxter, "Corporate Bankruptcies Fell in 2010," *The Am Law Daily,* January 11, 2011.

[4] "Largest Bankruptcies in World History," posted February 11, 2011, http://sandimba.blogspot.com/2011/02/largest-bankruptcies-in-world-history.html.

another is left with a total loss. *Not surprisingly, bankruptcy laws have been established in the United States to structure this process, provide protection for all parties, and ensure fair and equitable treatment.*

Although a complete coverage of bankruptcy statutes is more appropriate for a business law textbook, significant aspects of this process directly involve accountants.

> In many small business situations, the company accountant is the sole outside financial adviser and the first to recognize that the deteriorating financial picture mandates consideration of bankruptcy in one form or another. In many such situations, the accountant's role in convincing management that a timely reorganization under the bankruptcy law is the sole means of salvaging any part of the business may be critical.[5]

In addition, the information that the accountant prepares serves as the basis for assessing whether an organization is at risk for bankruptcy.

> There are a number of broadly accepted bankruptcy models commonly used by corporate credit officers to gauge their exposure, both academic and practical, which are based on accounting factors that have been found to be predictive of bankruptcy. Measures of liquidity, leverage and profitability have formed the basis for these accounting-based bankruptcy models, the best known of which are the Altman Z-Score and the Ohlson O-Score.[6]

Bankruptcy Reform Act of 1978

> Over the ages debtors who found themselves unable to meet obligations were dealt with harshly. Not only were all their assets taken from them, but they were given little or no relief through legal forgiveness of debts. Many of them ended up in debtors' prisons with all means of rehabilitation removed. A large number of the early settlers in this country left their homelands to escape such a fate.[7]

Based on an original provision of the U.S. Constitution, Congress is responsible for creating bankruptcy laws. However, virtually no federal bankruptcy laws were actually passed until the Bankruptcy Act of 1898 (subsequently revised in 1938 by the Chandler Act). Later, following a decade of study and debate by Congress, the Bankruptcy Reform Act of 1978 replaced these laws. Congress has amended this act several times since 1978.[8]

Consequently, the Bankruptcy Reform Act of 1978 as amended continues to provide the legal structure for most bankruptcy proceedings. *It strives to achieve two goals in connection with insolvency cases: (1) the fair distribution of assets to creditors and (2) the discharge of an honest debtor from debt.*

LO2

Explain the difference between a voluntary and involuntary bankruptcy.

Voluntary and Involuntary Petitions

When insolvency occurs, any interested party has the right to seek protection under the Bankruptcy Reform Act.[9] Thus, the company itself can file a petition with the court to begin bankruptcy proceedings.[10] If the company is the initiator, the process is referred to as a

[5] John K. Pearson, "The Role of the Accountant in Business Bankruptcies," *The National Public Accountant,* November 1982, p. 22.

[6] Jack Zwingli, "Identifying Bankruptcy Risk," *Business Credit,* February 1, 2010.

[7] Homer A. Bonhiver, *The Expanded Role of the Accountant under the 1978 Bankruptcy Code* (New York: Deloitte Haskins & Sells, 1980), p. 7.

[8] An excellent overview of the bankruptcy process from a legal perspective can be downloaded at http://www.uscourts.gov/FederalCourts/Bankruptcy/BankruptcyBasics.aspx. It is titled "Bankruptcy Basics" and is produced by the Administrative Office of the United States Courts, James C. Duff, Director. Bankruptcy can be viewed in an entirely different light in the book *Comic Wars* written by Dan Raviv and published in 2002 by Broadway Books in New York. *Comic Wars* follows the battle between several financial icons as they seek to gain control over Marvel Entertainment as it struggles to avoid liquidation.

[9] As is discussed later in this chapter, insolvency (not being able to pay debts as they come due) is not necessary for filing a bankruptcy petition. During the 1980s, such companies as Manville Corporation, Texaco, and A. H. Robins filed for protection under the Bankruptcy Reform Act in hopes of settling massive litigation claims.

[10] The bankruptcy petition filed by Circuit City on November 10, 2008, can be found at http://www.creditslips.org/creditslips/CircuitCity.pdf. This document shows that the company owed Hewlett-Packard, the biggest unsecured creditor, $118,797,964. The petition was originally for a reorganization but that quickly became a liquidation in January 2009 after an unsuccessful attempt to cash in on Christmas sales.

voluntary bankruptcy. In such cases, the company's petition must be accompanied by exhibits listing all debts and assets (reported at fair value). Company officials also must respond to questions concerning various aspects of the business's affairs. Such questions include:

- When did the business commence?
- In whose possession are the books of account and records?
- When was the last inventory of property taken?

Creditors also can seek to force a debtor into bankruptcy (known as an *involuntary* bankruptcy) in hopes of reducing their potential losses. To avoid nuisance actions, bankruptcy laws regulate the filing of involuntary petitions. If a company has 12 or more unsecured creditors, at least 3 must sign the petition. In addition, under current rules, the creditors that sign must have unsecured debts of at least $14,425.[11] If fewer than 12 unsecured creditors exist, only a single signer is required, but the $14,425 minimum debt limit remains.

> Lenders owed at least $54 million by Conex International LLC are trying to push the mechanical contracting and industrial services company into involuntary bankruptcy protection. Wells Fargo Bank, Bank of Montreal, and the Prudential Insurance Co. of America on Sunday filed an involuntary Chapter 11 bankruptcy petition against Conex in the U.S. Bankruptcy Court in Wilmington, Del., court papers show. The creditors each list "credit agreement default" as the nature of their claims, which they say total $54 million. The figure excludes an as-yet undetermined amount of interest.[12]

Neither a voluntary nor an involuntary petition automatically creates a bankruptcy case. Bankruptcy courts can reject voluntary petitions if the action is considered detrimental to the creditors. Involuntary petitions also can be rejected unless evidence exists to indicate that the debtor is not actually able to meet obligations as they come due. Merely being slow to pay is not sufficient. The debtor may well fight an involuntary petition fearing that its reputation will be tainted in the business community.

If the court accepts the petition, an *order for relief* is granted. This order halts all actions against the debtor, thus providing time for the various parties involved to develop a course of action. In addition, the company comes under the authority of the bankruptcy court so that any distributions must be made in a fair manner.

> To prevent creditors from seizing whatever is handy once the bankruptcy is filed, the Bankruptcy Code provides for an automatic stay or injunction that prohibits actions by creditors to collect debts from the debtor or the debtor's property without the court's permission. The automatic stay bars any creditor (including governmental creditors such as the Internal Revenue Service) from taking any action against the debtor or the debtor's property.[13]

LO3

Identify the various types of creditors as they are labeled during a bankruptcy.

Classification of Creditors

Following the issuance of an order for relief, the possible risk of loss obviously influences each creditor's view of a bankruptcy case. However, many creditors may have already obtained some measure of security for themselves. When a debt is created, the parties can agree to attach a mortgage lien or security interest to specified assets (known as *collateral*) owned by the debtor. Such action is most likely when the amounts involved are great or the debtor is experiencing financial difficulty. In the event that the liability is not paid when due, the creditor has the right to force the sale (or, in some cases, the return) of the pledged property with the proceeds being used to satisfy all or part of the obligation. Thus, in bankruptcy proceedings, a secured creditor holds a much less vulnerable position than an unsecured creditor.

[11] Throughout the bankruptcy laws, a number of monetary standards such as this exist. Such dollar amounts were last adjusted for inflation on April 1, 2010. These balances are to be adjusted every three years based on the Consumer Price Index for All Urban Consumers.

[12] Jacqueline Palank, "Lenders Seek to Push Conex, Affiliates Into Bankruptcy," *Dow Jones News Service*, February 22, 2011.

[13] Pearson, "The Role of the Accountant," p. 24.

Because of the possible presence of liens, all loans and other liabilities are reported to the court according to their degree of protection against loss. Some debts are identified as *fully secured* to indicate that the net realizable value of the collateral exceeds the amount of the obligation. Despite the debtor's insolvency, these creditors will not suffer loss; they are completely protected by the pledged property. Any money received from the asset that is in excess of the balance of the debt is then used to pay unsecured creditors.

Conversely, a liability is *partially secured* if the value of the collateral covers only a portion of the obligation. The remainder is considered *unsecured;* the creditor risks losing some or all of this additional amount. For example, a bank might have a $90,000 loan due from an insolvent party that is protected by a lien attached to land valued at $64,000. This debt is only partially secured; the asset would not satisfy $26,000 of the balance. This residual portion is reported to the court as unsecured.

All other liabilities are unsecured; these creditors have no legal right to any of the debtor's specific assets. They are entitled to share only in any funds that remain after all secured claims have been settled. Obviously, unsecured creditors are in a precarious position. Unless a debtor's assets greatly exceed secured liabilities (which is unlikely in most insolvency cases), these creditors can expect significant losses if liquidation proves to be necessary. Hence, one of the most important aspects of the bankruptcy laws is the ranking of unsecured claims.

The Bankruptcy Reform Act identifies several types of unsecured liabilities that have priority and must be paid before other unsecured debts are settled. *These obligations are ranked with each level having to be satisfied in full before any payment is made to the next.* Only in this manner is a systematic distribution of any remaining assets possible.

Unsecured Liabilities Having Priority The following liabilities have priority:[14]

1. Claims for administrative expenses such as the costs of preserving and liquidating the estate. All trustee expenses and the costs of outside attorneys, accountants, or other consultants are included in this category. Without this high-priority ranking, insolvent companies would have difficulty convincing qualified individuals to serve in these essential positions.

    > Though big corporate bankruptcies routinely leave losers—shareholders, bondholders, employees, the plumber or electrician left with unpaid bills—they also create a class of winners. The lawyers and other professionals have lots to do. And they are ordinarily given a priority claim on whatever assets the failed business still has. For example, in the bankruptcy of the investment firm Lehman Brothers, administrative fees as of Sept. 30 totaled about $420 million.[15]

2. Obligations arising between the date that a petition is filed with the bankruptcy court and the appointment of a trustee or the issuance of an order for relief. In voluntary cases, such claims are rare because an order for relief is usually entered when the petition is filed. This provision is important, however, in helping the debtor continue operations if an involuntary petition is presented but no legal action is immediately taken. With this high ranking, the debtor can hope to continue to buy goods and stay in business while resisting an involuntary petition.
3. Employee claims for wages earned during the 180 days preceding the filing of a petition. The amount of this priority is limited, though, to $11,725 (raised from $10,950 in 2010) per individual. This priority ranking does not include officers' salaries. It is designed to prevent employees from being too heavily penalized by the company's problems and encourages them to continue working until the bankruptcy issue is settled. In addition, employees are not company creditors in the traditional sense of that

[14] Only the most significant unsecured liabilities given priority are included here. For a complete list, check a current business law textbook.

[15] David S. Hilzenrath, "Cleanup of Madoff Mess Has Its Own Mounting Cost," *The Washington Post*, April 1, 2011, A-section.

Discussion Question

WHAT DO WE DO NOW?

The Toledo Shirt Company manufactures men's shirts sold to department stores and other outlets throughout Ohio, Illinois, and Indiana. For the past 14 years, one of Toledo's major customers has been Abraham and Sons, a chain of nine stores selling men's clothing. Mr. Abraham retired 18 months ago and his two sons took complete control of the organization. Since that time, they have invested significant sums of money in an attempt to expand each store by also selling women's clothing. Success in this new market has been difficult. Abraham and Sons is not known for selling women's clothing, and no one in the company has much expertise in the area.

Approximately seven months ago, James Thurber, Toledo's chief financial officer, began to notice that it was taking longer than usual to collect payments from Abraham and Sons. Instead of the normal 30 days, the retailer was taking 45 days—and frequently longer—to pay each invoice. Because of the amount of money involved, Thurber began to monitor the balance daily. When the age of the receivable ($343,000) hit 65 days, he called Abraham and Sons. The treasurer assured him that the company was merely having seasonal cash flow issues but that payments would soon be back on a normal schedule.

Thurber was still concerned and shortly thereafter placed Abraham and Sons on a "cash and carry" basis. No new sales were to be made unless cash was collected in advance. The company's treasurer immediately called Thurber to complain bitterly. "We have been one of your best customers for well over a decade, but now that we have gotten into a bit of trouble you stab us in the back. When we straighten things out here, we will remember this. We can get our shirts from someone else. Our expansions are now complete; we have hired an expert to help us market women's clothing. We can see the light at the end of the tunnel. Abraham and Sons will soon be more profitable than ever." In hopes of appeasing the customer while still protecting his own position, Thurber agreed to sell merchandise to Abraham and Sons on a very limited credit basis.

A few days later, Thurber received a disturbing phone call from a vice president with another clothing manufacturer. "We've got to force Abraham and Sons into bankruptcy immediately to protect ourselves. Those guys are running the company straight into the ground. They owe me $230,000, and I can only hope to collect a small portion of it now. I need two other creditors to sign the petition and I want Toledo Shirt to be one of them. Abraham and Sons has already mortgaged all of its buildings and equipment so we can't get anything from those assets. Inventory stocks are dwindling and sales have disappeared since they've tried to change the image of their stores. We can still get some of our money but if we wait much longer nothing will be left but the bones."

Should the Toledo Shirt Company be loyal to a good customer or start the bankruptcy process to protect itself? What actions should Thurber take?

term. They did not enter employment to serve as lenders to the corporation. However, employees can still be financially damaged by bankruptcy.

> The $32 million claim filed on behalf of former Heller employees, represented by Garfield Granett, Carl Goodman, and Anna Scarpa, asks for at least $11,725 for each of the firm's 861 former employees. Called a priority claim, that amount is guaranteed to employees of a company in bankruptcy, after secured creditors are paid.[16]

[16] Amanda Royal, "Thelen, Heller Face Huge Wage Claims," *The Recorder*, April 2, 2009.

4. Employee claims for contributions to benefit plans earned during the 180 days preceding the filing of a petition. Again, an $11,725 limit per individual (reduced by certain specified payments) is enforced.
5. Claims for the return of deposits made by customers to acquire property or services that the debtor never delivered or provided. The priority figure, in this case, is limited to $2,600. These claimants did not intend to be creditors; they were merely trying to make a purchase.
6. Government claims for unpaid taxes.

All other obligations of an insolvent company are classified as general unsecured claims that can be repaid only after creditors with priority have been satisfied. *If the funds that remain for the general unsecured debts are not sufficient to settle all claims, the available money must be divided proportionally.* Periodic changes in this priority listing are made and can impact the amounts various types of creditors will receive. For example, in 2005, Congress reclassified prior rent still due as an administrative expense rather than as an unsecured claim as it had been previously classified. Consequently, such rental debts are now more likely to be paid in full, leaving less for the remaining unsecured creditors.

LO4

Describe the difference between a Chapter 7 bankruptcy and a Chapter 11 bankruptcy.

Liquidation versus Reorganization

The most important decision in any bankruptcy filing (either voluntary or involuntary) is the method by which the debtor will be discharged from its obligations. One obvious option is to liquidate the company's assets with the proceeds distributed to creditors based on their secured positions and the priority ranking system just outlined. However, a very important alternative to liquidation does exist. The debtor company may survive insolvency and continue operations if the parties involved accept a proposal for *reorganization*.

Not everyone agrees with the wisdom of allowing reorganization. This argument holds that keeping inefficient organizations alive and competing does not serve the industry or the economy well.

> There are many reasons why a business gets sick, but they don't necessarily mean it should be destroyed. Hundreds of thousands of businesses that at one time or another had financial difficulties survive today as the result of Chapter 11 proceedings. They continue to contribute to employment, to tax revenues, to overall growth. It's counterproductive to destroy the business value of an asset by liquidating it and paying it out in a Chapter 7 if that company shows signs of being able to recover in a reorganization.[17]

Contrast that statement with the following:

> The efficiency of Chapter 11 is undergoing scrutiny. A particular concern, in industries such as telecoms and now airlines, is that bankrupt firms will return with manageable debts and thus be better able to compete, with the result that they force hitherto healthier rivals into bankruptcy in their turn. Does Chapter 11 create zombie companies that live on, only to drag other firms into their graves?[18]

Under most reorganization plans, creditors agree to absorb a partial loss rather than force the insolvent company to liquidate. Before accepting such an arrangement, creditors (as well as the bankruptcy court) must be convinced that helping to rehabilitate the debtor will lead to a higher return. One benefit associated with reorganizations is that the creditor may be able to retain the insolvent company as a customer. In many cases, continuation of this relationship is an important concern if the debtor historically has been a good client. Furthermore, the priority ranking system often leaves the general unsecured creditors very little to gain by trying to force a liquidation.

Legal guidelines for the liquidation of a debtor are contained in Chapter 7 of Title I of the Bankruptcy Reform Act. Chapter 11 describes the reorganization process. Consequently,

[17] James A. Goodman as interviewed by Robert A. Mamis, "Why Bankruptcy Works," *Inc.*, October 1996, p. 39.
[18] "The Night of the Killer Zombies," *The Economist*, December 14, 2002.

Discussion Question

HOW MUCH IS THAT BUILDING REALLY WORTH?

Viron, Inc., was created in 2006 to recycle plastic products and manufacture a variety of new items. The actual production process was quite complex because the old plastic had to be divided into categories and then reclaimed based on the composition. Viron made new products based on the type of plastic available and the market demand.

In December 2008, the company spent $7.1 million to construct a building for manufacturing purposes. It was designed specifically to meet Viron's needs. The building was constructed near Gaffney, South Carolina, to take advantage of a large labor force available because of high unemployment in the area.

Unfortunately, because of the lingering recession, the company was not able to generate revenues quickly enough to reach a break-even point and was forced to file for bankruptcy. An accountant was hired to produce a statement of financial affairs to aid the parties in deciding whether to liquidate or reorganize.

In producing the statement of financial affairs, the accountant needed to establish a liquidation value for the building in Gaffney that was the company's largest asset. A real estate appraiser was brought in and made the following comments about the structure.

> The building is well constructed and practically new. It is clearly worth in excess of $7 million. However, I doubt that anyone is going to pay that much for it. We don't get a lot of new industry in this area, so not many companies need to buy large buildings. Even if a company did buy the building, it would have to spend a significant amount of money for conversion. Unless a company just wanted to recycle plastics, the building would have to be completely adapted to any other purpose. To tell you the truth, I am not sure it can be sold at any price. There are a lot of abandoned buildings in the area. Of course, if someone wants to recycle plastics, it just might bring $7 million.

In producing the statement of financial affairs, how should the accountant report this building?

the proceedings have come to be referred to as a *Chapter 7 bankruptcy* (liquidation) or a *Chapter 11 bankruptcy* (reorganization). Accountants face two entirely different reporting situations depending on the type of bankruptcy encountered. However, in both cases, accountants must keep all parties informed about relevant events as they occur.

LO5

Account for a company as it enters bankruptcy.

Statement of Financial Affairs

> A new bankruptcy court filing by General Growth Properties Inc. sheds light on the finances of Boston's Faneuil Hall Marketplace. The shopping and tourist mecca generated annual revenue of $24.6 million in 2007 and $24.85 million in 2008 for the Chicago real estate investment trust, which operates it through a lease with the city. The revenue figures were detailed in a statement of financial affairs filed Wednesday by General Growth.[19]

At the start of bankruptcy proceedings, the *debtor* normally prepares a statement of financial affairs. This schedule provides information about the company's current financial position and helps all parties as they consider what actions to take. This statement is

[19] Donna Goodison, "Faneuil Hall Pulls in $25 Million; Mall Co. Reveals Finances," *Boston Herald*, August 28, 2009.

especially important in assisting unsecured creditors as they decide whether to push for reorganization or liquidation. The debtor's assets and liabilities are reported according to the classifications relevant to a liquidation.

Consequently, assets are labeled as follows:

1. Pledged with fully secured creditors.
2. Pledged with partially secured creditors.
3. Available for priority liabilities and unsecured creditors (often referred to as free assets).

The company's debts are then listed in a parallel fashion:

1. Liabilities with priority.
2. Fully secured creditors.
3. Partially secured creditors.
4. Unsecured creditors.

Stockholders are included in this final group.

The statement of financial affairs is produced under the assumption that liquidation will occur. Thus, historical cost figures are not relevant. The various parties to the bankruptcy desire information that reflects (1) the net realizable value of the debtor's assets and (2) the ultimate application of these proceeds to specific liabilities. With this knowledge, both creditors and stockholders can estimate the monetary resources that will be available after all secured claims and priority liabilities have been settled. By comparing this total with the amount of unsecured liabilities, interested parties can approximate the potential loss they face.

The information found in a statement of financial affairs can affect the outcome of the bankruptcy. If, for example, the statement indicates that unsecured creditors are destined to suffer a material loss in a liquidation, this group will probably favor reorganizing the company in hopes of averting such a consequence. Conversely, if the statement shows that all creditors will be paid in full and that a distribution to the stockholders is also possible, liquidation becomes a much more viable option. Thus, all parties involved with an insolvent company should consult a statement of financial affairs before deciding the fate of the operation.

Statement of Financial Affairs Illustrated

Chaplin Company recently experienced severe financial difficulties and is currently insolvent. It will soon file a voluntary bankruptcy petition, and company officials are trying to decide whether to seek liquidation or reorganization. They have asked their accountant to produce a statement of financial affairs to assist them in formulating an appropriate strategy. A current balance sheet for Chaplin, prepared as if the company were a going concern, is presented in Exhibit 13.1.

Prior to the creation of a statement of financial affairs, additional data must be ascertained concerning the insolvent company and its assets and liabilities. In this illustration, the following information about Chaplin Company has been accumulated:

- The investment reported on the balance sheet has appreciated in value since being acquired and is now worth $20,000. Dividends of $500 are currently due from this investment, although Chaplin has not yet recognized the revenue.
- Officials estimate that $12,000 of the company's accounts receivable can still be collected despite the bankruptcy proceedings.
- By spending $5,000 for repairs and marketing, Chaplin can sell its inventory for $50,000.
- The company will receive a $1,000 refund from the various prepaid expenses, but its intangible assets have no resale value.
- The land and building are in an excellent location and can be sold for a figure 10 percent more than book value. However, the equipment was specially designed for Chaplin.

EXHIBIT 13.1
Financial Position Prior to Bankruptcy Petition

CHAPLIN COMPANY
Balance Sheet
June 30, 2012

Assets

Current assets:		
Cash	$ 2,000	
Investment (equity method)	15,000	
Accounts receivable (net)	23,000	
Inventory	41,000	
Prepaid expenses	3,000	$ 84,000
Land, building, equipment, and other assets:		
Land	100,000	
Building (net)	110,000	
Equipment (net)	80,000	
Intangible assets	15,000	305,000
Total assets		$389,000

Liabilities and Stockholders' Equity

Current liabilities:		
Notes payable (secured by inventory)	$ 75,000	
Accounts payable	60,000	
Accrued expenses	18,000	$153,000
Long term liabilities:		
Notes payable (secured by lien on land and buildings)		200,000
Stockholders' equity:		
Common stock	100,000	
Retained earnings (deficit)	(64,000)	36,000
Total liabilities and stockholders' equity		$389,000

Company officials anticipate having trouble finding a buyer unless the price is reduced considerably. Hence, they expect to receive only 40 percent of current book value for these assets.

- Administrative costs of $21,500 are projected if the company does liquidate.
- Accrued expenses include salaries of $13,000. Of this figure, one person is owed a total of $12,725 but is the only employee due an amount in excess of $11,725. Payroll taxes withheld from wages but not yet paid to the government total $3,000. Company records currently show only a $1,000 portion of this liability.
- Interest of $5,000 on the company's long-term liabilities has not been accrued for the first six months of 2012.

From this information, the statement of financial affairs presented in Exhibit 13.2 for Chaplin Company was prepared. Several aspects of this statement should be specifically noted:

1. The current and long-term distinctions usually applied to assets and liabilities are omitted. Because the company is on the verge of going out of business, such classifications are meaningless. Instead, the statement is designed to separate the secured and unsecured balances.
2. Book values are included on the left side of the schedule but only for informational purposes. These figures are not relevant in a bankruptcy. *All assets are reported at estimated net realizable value, whereas liabilities are shown at the amount required for settlement.*
3. Both the dividend receivable and the interest payable are included in Exhibit 13.2, although neither has been recorded on the balance sheet. The payroll tax liability also is reported at the amount the company presently owes. The statement of financial affairs must disclose currently updated figures.
4. Liabilities having priority are individually identified within the liability section (point A). Because these claims will be paid before other unsecured creditors, the

EXHIBIT 13.2

CHAPLIN COMPANY
Statement of Financial Affairs
June 30, 2012

Book Values			Available for Unsecured Creditors
	Assets		
	Pledged with fully secured creditors:		
$210,000	Land and building	$ 231,000	
	Less: Notes payable (long term)	(200,000)	
	Interest payable	(5,000)	$ 26,000
	Pledged with partially secured creditors:		
41,000	Inventory	$ 45,000	
	Less: Notes payable (current)	(75,000)	–0–
	Free assets:		
2,000	Cash		2,000
15,000	Investment in marketable securities		20,000
–0–	Dividends receivable		500
23,000	Accounts receivable		12,000
3,000	Prepaid expenses		1,000
80,000	Equipment		32,000
15,000	Intangible assets		–0–
	Total available to pay liabilities with priority and unsecured creditors		93,500
	Less: Liabilities with priority (see Ⓐ below in Liabilities)		(36,500) Ⓑ
	Available for unsecured creditors		57,000 Ⓓ
	Estimated deficiency		38,000 Ⓔ
$389,000			$ 95,000

Book Values			Unsecured—Nonpriority Liabilities
	Liabilities and Stockholders' Equity		
	Liabilities with priority:		
–0–	Administrative expenses (estimated)	$ 21,500	
$ 13,000	Salaries payable (accrued expenses)	12,000	$ 1,000 Ⓒ
1,000	Payroll taxes payable (accrued expenses)	3,000	
	Total	$ 36,500 Ⓐ	
	Fully secured creditors:		
200,000	Notes payable	$ 200,000	
–0–	Interest payable	5,000	
	Less: Land and building	(231,000)	–0–
	Partially secured creditors:		
75,000	Notes payable	$ 75,000	
	Less: Inventory	(45,000)	30,000
	Unsecured creditors:		
60,000	Accounts payable		60,000
4,000	Accrued expenses (other than salaries and payroll taxes)		4,000
36,000	Stockholders' equity		–0–
$389,000			$ 95,000

$36,500 total is subtracted directly from the free assets (point B). Although not yet incurred, estimated administrative costs are included in this category because such expenses will be necessary for a liquidation. Salaries are also considered priority liabilities. However, the $1,000 owed to one employee in excess of the individual $11,725 limit is separated as an unsecured claim (point C).

5. According to this statement, if liquidation occurs, Chaplin expects to have $57,000 in free assets remaining after settling all liabilities with priority (point D). Unfortunately,

the liability section shows unsecured claims of $95,000. These creditors, therefore, face a $38,000 loss ($95,000 − $57,000) if the company is liquidated (point E). This final distribution is often stated as a percentage:

$$\frac{\text{Free assets}}{\text{Unsecured claims}} = \frac{\$57,000}{\$95,000} = 60\%$$

Unsecured creditors can anticipate receiving only 60 percent of their claims. An individual, for example, to whom this company owes $400 should anticipate collecting $240 ($400 × 60%) following liquidation. However, this is merely an estimation.

6. If the statement of financial affairs had shown the company with more free assets (after subtracting liabilities with priority) than unsecured claims, all creditors could expect to be paid in full with any excess money going to Chaplin's stockholders.

Liquidation—Chapter 7 Bankruptcy

LO6

Account for the liquidation of a company in bankruptcy.

When an insolvent company is to be liquidated, the provisions established by Chapter 7 of the Bankruptcy Reform Act regulate the process. This set of laws was written to provide an orderly and equitable structure for selling assets and paying debts. To this end, several events occur after the court has entered an order for relief in either a voluntary or involuntary liquidation.

To begin, the court appoints an interim trustee to oversee the company and its liquidation. This individual is charged with preserving the assets and preventing loss of the estate. Thus, creditors are protected from any detrimental actions that management, the ownership, or any of the other creditors might undertake. The interim trustee (as well as the permanent trustee, if the creditors subsequently select one) must perform a number of tasks shortly after being appointed. These functions include (but are not limited to):

- Changing locks and moving all assets and records to locations the trustee controls.
- Posting notices that the U.S. trustee now possesses all business assets and that tampering with or removing any contents is a violation of federal law.
- Compiling all financial records and placing them in the custody of the trustee's own accountant.
- Obtaining possession of any corporate records including minute books and other official documents.[20]

The court then calls for a meeting of all creditors who have appropriately filed a proof of claim against the debtor. This group may choose to elect a permanent trustee to replace the person temporarily appointed by the court. A majority (in number as well as in dollars due from the company) of the unsecured, nonpriority creditors must agree to this new trustee. If the creditors cannot reach a decision, the interim trustee is retained.

To ensure fairness, a committee of between 3 and 11 unsecured creditors is selected to help protect the group's interests. This committee of creditors does the following:

- Consults with the trustee regarding the administration of the estate.
- Makes recommendations to the trustee regarding the performance of the trustee's duties.
- Submits to the court any questions affecting the administration of the estate.[21]

Role of the Trustee

In the liquidation of any company, the trustee is a central figure. This individual must recover all property belonging to the insolvent company, preserve the estate from any further deterioration, liquidate noncash assets, and make distributions to the proper claimants.

[20] Bonhiver, *The Expanded Role of the Accountant*, pp. 50–51.

[21] Ibid., p. 26.

Additionally, the trustee may need to continue operating the company to complete business activities that were in progress when the order for relief was entered. To accomplish such a multitude of objectives, this individual holds wide-ranging authority in bankruptcy matters, including the right to obtain professional assistance from attorneys and accountants.

The trustee can also void any transfer of property (known as a *preference*) made by the debtor within 90 days *prior* to filing the bankruptcy petition if the company was already insolvent at the time. The recipient must then return these payments so that they can be included in the debtor's estate.[22]

> The preference avoidance statute is designed to ensure that any distributions from a bankruptcy estate are made in accordance with the scheme established by Congress. The preference avoidance statute looks back for a period of 90 days to a full year before the bankruptcy filing to examine whether any creditors received more than their proportionate share of the debtor's assets during that time. If a creditor did receive more than its fair share of the debtor's assets, the bankruptcy trustee is empowered to void such transactions and to recover the value of the transfers from the recipient for the benefit of the debtor's bankruptcy estate as a whole.[23]

Return of the asset is not necessary, however, if the transfer was for no more than would have been paid to this party in a liquidation.

Not surprisingly, the trustee must properly record all activities and report them periodically to the court and other interested parties. The actual reporting rules that the Bankruptcy Reform Act created are quite general: "Each trustee, examiner, and debtor-in-possession is required to file 'such reports as are necessary or as the court orders.' . . . In the past there have been no specific guidelines or forms used in the preparation of these reports."[24] Consequently, a wide variety of statements and reports may be encountered in liquidations. However, the trustee commonly uses *a statement of realization and liquidation* to report the major events of the liquidation process. This statement is designed to convey the following information:

- Account balances reported by the company at the date on which the order for relief was filed.
- Cash receipts generated by the sale of the debtor's property.
- Cash disbursements the trustee made to wind up the affairs of the business and to pay the secured creditors.
- Any other transactions such as the write-off of assets and the recognition of unrecorded liabilities.

Any cash that remains following this series of events is paid to the unsecured creditors after the priority claims have first been settled.

Statement of Realization and Liquidation Illustrated

To demonstrate the production of a statement of realization and liquidation, the information previously presented for Chaplin Company will be used again. Assume that company officials decide to liquidate the business, a procedure regulated by Chapter 7 of the Bankruptcy Reform Act.

The dollar amounts resulting from this liquidation will not necessarily agree with the balances used in creating the statement of financial affairs in Exhibit 13.2. The previous statement was based on projected sales and other estimations, whereas a statement of realization and liquidation reports the actual transactions and other

[22] The 90-day limit is extended to one year if the transfer is made to an inside party such as an officer or a director or an affiliated company. The one-year limit also applies to any transfer made by the debtor with the intent to defraud another party. Transfers of less than $5,000 cannot be challenged as preferences.

[23] Bradley S. Schmarak and Tracy L. Treger, "Avoiding the Preference Pitfall in Workouts," *Commercial Lending Review,* October 11, 1997, p. 37.

[24] Bonhiver, *The Expanded Role of the Accountant,* p. 69.

events as they occur. Discrepancies should be expected. Assume the following transactions occur in liquidating this company:

Liquidation Transactions of Chaplin Company—2012

July 1	The accounting records in Exhibit 13.1 are adjusted to the correct balances as of June 30, 2012, the date on which the order for relief was entered. Hence, the dividends receivable, interest payable, and additional payroll tax liability are recognized.
July 23	The trustee expends $7,000 to dispose of the company's inventory at a negotiated price of $51,000. The net cash results are applied to the notes payable for which the inventory served as partial security.
July 29	Cash dividend of $500, accrued as of June 30, is collected. The related investments (reported at $15,000) are then sold for $19,600.
Aug. 17	Accounts receivable of $16,000 are collected. The remaining balances are all written off as bad debts.
Aug. 30	The trustee determines that no refund is available from any of the company's prepaid expenses. The intangible assets also are removed from the financial records because they have no cash value. The land and building are sold for $208,000. The trustee immediately uses $205,000 of this money to pay off the secured creditors.
Oct. 9	After an extended search for a buyer, the equipment is sold for $42,000 in cash.
Nov. 1	A $24,900 invoice is received for various administrative expenses incurred in liquidating the company. The trustee also reclassifies the remaining portion of the partially secured liabilities as unsecured.
Nov. 9	Noncash assets have now been converted into cash and all secured claims settled, so the trustee begins to distribute any remaining funds. The liabilities with priority are paid first. The excess is then applied to the claims of unsecured nonpriority creditors.

The physical structure used to prepare a statement of realization and liquidation can vary significantly. One popular form presents the various account groups on a horizontal plane with the liquidating transactions shown vertically. In this manner, accountants can record the events as they occur to show their effects on each account classification. Exhibit 13.3 has been constructed in this style to display the liquidation of Chaplin Company.

Probably the most significant information presented in this statement is the measurement and classification of the insolvent company's liabilities. In the same manner as the statement of financial affairs, fully and partially secured claims are reported separately from liabilities with priority and unsecured nonpriority claims.

For Chaplin Company, Exhibit 13.3 discloses that $135,900 in debts remain as of November 9 ($39,900 in priority claims and $96,000 in unsecured nonpriority liabilities). Unfortunately, after satisfying all secured liabilities, the company retains only $83,100 in cash. The trustee must first use this money to pay the three liabilities with priority according to the following ranking:

Administrative expenses	$24,900
Salaries payable (within the $11,725 per person limitation)	12,000
Payroll taxes payable	3,000
Total	$39,900

These disbursements leave the company with $43,200 ($83,100 − $39,900) in cash but $96,000 in unsecured liabilities. Consequently, the unsecured creditors can collect only 45 percent of their claims against Chaplin Company:

$$\frac{\$43{,}200}{\$96{,}000} = 45\%$$

EXHIBIT 13.3 **Final Statement**

CHAPLIN COMPANY
Statement of Realization and Liquidation
June 30, 2012, to November 9, 2012

Date		Cash	Noncash Assets	Liabilities with Priority	Fully Secured Creditors	Partially Secured Creditors	Unsecured—Nonpriority Liabilities	Stockholders' Equity (Deficit)
6/30/12	Book balances	$ 2,000	$ 387,000	$13,000*	$ 200,000	$ 75,000	$65,000†	$ 36,000
7/1/12	Adjustments for dividends, interest, and payroll taxes		500	2,000	5,000			(6,500)
7/1/12	Adjusted book balances.	2,000	387,500	15,000	205,000	75,000	65,000	29,500
7/23/12	Inventory sold—recorded net of disposal costs.	44,000	(41,000)					3,000
7/23/12	Proceeds from inventory paid to secured creditors	(44,000)				(44,000)		
7/29/12	Investments sold and dividends received	20,100	(15,500)					4,600
8/17/12	Receivables collected with remainder written off	16,000	(23,000)					(7,000)
8/30/12	Intangible assets and prepaid expenses written off.		(18,000)					(18,000)
	Land and building sold.	208,000	(210,000)					(2,000)
	Proceeds from land and building paid to secured creditors	(205,000)			(205,000)			
10/9/12	Equipment sold	42,000	(80,000)					(38,000)
11/1/12	Administrative expenses accrued			24,900				(24,900)
11/1/12	Excess of partially secured liabilities reclassified as an unsecured claim					(31,000)	31,000	
11/9/12	Final balances remaining for unsecured creditors	$ 83,100	–0–	$39,900	–0–	–0–	$96,000	$(52,800)

*Includes salaries payable of $12,000 (amount due employees but limited to $11,725 per individual) and $1,000 in payroll taxes owed to the government.
†Accounts payable plus accrued expenses other than salaries payable (within $11,725 per person limitation) and payroll tax liability.

Because all liabilities have not been paid in full, the stockholders receive nothing, a common outcome of a bankruptcy liquidation.

Interestingly, the unsecured nonpriority creditors receive a smaller percentage of their claims than the 60 percent figure projected in the statement of financial affairs (produced in Exhibit 13.2). Although this earlier statement plays an important role in bankruptcy planning and proceedings, the preparer's ability to foretell future events limits the statement's accuracy.

Reorganization—Chapter 11 Bankruptcy

LO7

List the provisions that are often found in a bankruptcy reorganization plan.

> Reorganization under the federal Bankruptcy Code is a way to salvage a company rather than liquidate it. Although the original owners of a company rescued in this way are often left without anything, others whose livelihoods depend on the company's fortunes may come out with their interests intact. The company's creditors, for example, may take over as the new owners. Its suppliers might be able to maintain the company as a customer. Its customers still may count on the company as a supplier. And perhaps most important, many of its employees may be able to keep the jobs that otherwise would have been sacrificed in a liquidation.[25]

For the 12 months ended December 31, 2010, 11,774 Chapter 11 business reorganizations were begun in the United States.[26] Reorganizations attempt to salvage the company so that operations can continue. Although this legal procedure offers the company hope of survival, reorganization is certainly not a guarantee of future prosperity. Companies that attempt to reorganize are often eventually liquidated. Whitehall Jewelers filed for Chapter 11 bankruptcy on June 23, 2008, and began liquidation on August 13, 2008. Circuit City filed for Chapter 11 on November 10, 2008, and began liquidation on January 19, 2009.

Many reorganizations may actually fail because the debtor resists for too long before filing a petition:

> Seeking bankruptcy because disaster looms—not after it has arrived—helps (gives the corporation time and provides equality of treatment). . . . Once a company files under the bankruptcy laws, suppliers are likely to demand cash on delivery. So management that moves before liquid assets are depleted has a better chance of making a go of reorganization.[27]

Obviously, the activities and events surrounding a reorganization differ significantly from a liquidation. One important distinction is that control over the company is normally retained by the ownership (referred to as a *debtor in possession*). However, if fraud or gross mismanagement can be proven, the court has the authority to appoint an independent trustee to assume control. Unless replaced, the debtor in possession continues to operate the company and has the primary responsibility for developing an acceptable plan of reorganization. Not everyone, though, agrees with the wisdom of leaving the ownership in charge of the company: "One philosophical objection raised increasingly often is the rule that puts the debtor in control of the bankruptcy process, an idea that often leaves foreigners 'stunned,' says one bankruptcy lawyer. This typically means that the managers who bankrupt a firm can have a go at restructuring it to keep it alive."[28]

While a reorganization is in process, the owners and managers are legally required to preserve the company's estate as of the date that the order for relief is entered. In this

[25] John Robbins, Al Goll, and Paul Rosenfield, "Accounting for Companies in Chapter 11 Reorganization," *Journal of Accountancy,* January 1991, p. 75.

[26] http://www.uscourts.gov/uscourts/Statistics/BankruptcyStatistics/BankruptcyFilings/2010/1210_f2.pdf. This source also indicates that 39,485 businesses began Chapter 7 bankruptcies during 2010.

[27] Daniel B. Moskowitz and Mark Ivey, "You Don't Have to Be Broke to Need Chapter 11," *BusinessWeek,* April 27, 1987, p. 108.

[28] "The Night of the Killer Zombies."

way, the bankruptcy regulations seek to reduce the losses that creditors and stockholders may have to absorb when either reorganization or liquidation eventually occurs.

The Plan for Reorganization

> The plan is the heart of every Chapter 11 reorganization. The provisions of the plan specify the treatment of all creditors and equity holders upon its approval by the Bankruptcy Court. Moreover, the plan shapes the financial structure of the entity that emerges.[29]

The most intriguing aspect of a Chapter 11 bankruptcy is the plan developed to rescue the company from insolvency. Initially, only the debtor in possession can file proposals with the court. However, if a plan for reorganization is not put forth within 120 days of the order for relief or accepted within 180 days (unless the court grants an extension although the debtor's exclusivity to propose a plan cannot be extended beyond 18 months), any interested party has the right to prepare and file a proposal.

A reorganization plan may contain an unlimited number of provisions: proposed changes in the company, additional financing arrangements, alterations in the debt structure, and the like. Regardless of the specific contents, the intent of all such plans is to provide a feasible long-term solution to the company's monetary difficulties. However, to gain acceptance by the parties involved, a plan must present convincing evidence that it will enable the business to emerge from bankruptcy as a viable going concern.

Although a definitive list of elements that could be included in a reorganization proposal is not possible, some of the most common follow:

1. *Plans proposing changes in the company's operations.* In hopes of improving liquidity, officials may decide to introduce new product lines or sell off unprofitable assets or even entire businesses. Closing failing operations is especially common. A debtor in possession bears the burden of proving that the problems that led to insolvency can be eliminated.

> Borders Group, Inc. today announced that the U.S. Bankruptcy Court for the Southern District of New York has approved its previously-disclosed strategic Store Reduction Program to facilitate its reorganization and repositioning. Borders said that it has entered into agreements with experienced liquidators to conduct an orderly wind down of the 200 underperforming stores that are part of the program. Borders expects these stores to be closed by the end of April.[30]

2. *Plans for generating additional monetary resources.* Companies facing insolvency must develop new sources of cash, often in a short time period. Loans and the sale of both common and preferred stocks are frequently negotiated during reorganization to provide funding to continue the business. "The U.S. government will take about a 61 percent stake in the new GM after lending the automaker more than $50 billion."[31]

3. *Plans for changes in company management.* Frequently, a financial crisis is blamed on poor leadership. In that situation, proposing to reorganize a company with the management team intact is probably not a practical suggestion. Therefore, many plans include hiring new individuals to implement the reorganization and run important aspects of the company. These changes may even affect the board of directors elected by the stockholders to oversee the company and its operations:

> Chicago-based Tribune Co. and its creditors are in the early stages of negotiating a plan of reorganization in U.S. Bankruptcy Court that sources say likely will transfer control of the troubled media conglomerate from Chicago billionaire Sam Zell to a group of large banks and investors that hold $8.6 billion in senior debt.[32]

[29] FASB ASC (para. 852-10-05-4).

[30] "Borders Receives Court Approval for Store Reduction Program," Press Release from Borders Group, Inc., February 17, 2011. Unfortunately, Borders's plans were not sufficient and the entire company had to be liquidated.

[31] Mike Spector, "GM Asset Sale Gets Judge's Nod," *The Wall Street Journal,* July 6, 2009, p. B-1.

[32] Michael Oneal, "Zell Could Lose Control of Tribune Co.," *McClatchy–Tribune Business News*, June 8, 2009.

4. *Plans to settle the debts of the company that existed when the order for relief was entered.* No element of a reorganization plan is more important than the proposal for satisfying the claims of the company's various creditors. In most cases, their agreement is necessary before the court will confirm any plan of reorganization. Actual proposals to settle these debts may include numerous provisions.

- Assets can be transferred to creditors who accept this payment in exchange for extinguishing a specified amount of debt. The amount of the liability being canceled is usually higher (often substantially higher) than the fair value of the assets rendered.

> Dow Corning Corp. made public a $4.4 billion bankruptcy-reorganization plan, its third attempt to forge a solution for exiting from bankruptcy court and hammering out a way to resolve thousands of claims that silicone breast implants cause diseases and injuries. The company, which for years was the leading maker of silicone implants in the United States, offered $3 billion of that total to resolve an estimated 200,000 existing silicone claims.[33]

- An equity interest (such as common stock, preferred stock, or stock rights) can be conveyed to creditors to settle an outstanding debt. For example, the announcement that Garden Ridge was moving to exit from bankruptcy indicated that the "reorganization plan will call for the distribution of preferred stock to general unsecured creditors."[34]
- The terms of the outstanding liabilities can be modified: maturity dates extended, interest rates lowered, face values reduced, accrued interest forgiven, and so on.

One recent development is the use of prepackaged or prearranged bankruptcies. In such cases, the company and its debtors agree on the terms of the reorganization plan before a bankruptcy petition is signed. Thus, the parties go into the bankruptcy with an agreement to present to the court. In this manner, extensive legal fees can be avoided. An increasing number of these bankruptcy reorganizations take only two to three months instead of years. Furthermore, the parties have more protection because the Bankruptcy Court is likely to accept the plan without requiring extensive changes or revisions.

> Prearranged bankruptcies are on the rise and for good reason. A well-executed prearranged bankruptcy—where most of the biggest creditors agree to a reorganization plan before going to court—allows a company to secure attractive financing, maintain the trust of employees, customers and suppliers, and move through the bankruptcy process much more quickly and inexpensively than a standard filing.[35]

Acceptance and Confirmation of Reorganization Plan

The creation of a plan for reorganization does not guarantee its implementation. The Bankruptcy Reform Act specifies that a plan must be voted on by both the company's creditors and stockholders before the court confirms. *To be accepted, each class of creditors must vote for the plan.* Acceptance requires the approval of two-thirds in dollar amount and more than one-half in the number of claims that cast votes. A separate vote is also required of each class of shareholders. For approval, at least two-thirds (measured by the number of shares held) of the owners who vote must agree to the proposed reorganization. In fact, convincing any of the parties to support a specific plan is not an easy task because agreement often means accepting a significant loss. Eventually, though, acceptance is necessary if progress is ever to be made.

[33] Thomas M. Burton, "Dow Corning Has $4.4 Billion Plan on Chapter 11 and Implant Claims," *The Wall Street Journal*, February 18, 1998, p. B2.

[34] "Garden Ridge Gets Bankruptcy Plans OK'd," *Home Textiles Today,* April 4, 2005, p. 8.

[35] Jim Hogan, "Keys to a Prearranged Bankruptcy; A powerful tool to move a company through Chapter 11 proceedings quickly, inexpensively and with minimal disruption to the business," *Investment Dealers Digest*, March 25, 2011.

Although the plan may gain creditor and stockholder approval, court confirmation is still required. The court reviews the proposal and can reject the reorganization plan if a claimant (who did not vote for acceptance) would receive more through liquidation. The court also has the authority to confirm a reorganization plan that was not accepted by a particular class of creditors or stockholders. This provision is referred to as a *cram down;* it occurs when the court determines that the plan is fair and equitable. As an alternative, the court may convert a Chapter 11 reorganization into a Chapter 7 liquidation at any time if the development of an acceptable plan does not appear to be possible. That threat often encourages the parties to work together to achieve a workable resolution.

LO8

Account for a company as it moves through reorganization.

Financial Reporting during Reorganization

Developing and gaining approval for a reorganization plan can take years. During that period, the company continues operating under the assumption that it will eventually emerge from the bankruptcy proceedings. While going through reorganization, the company faces several specific accounting questions:

- Should the income effects resulting from operating activities be differentiated from transactions connected solely with the reorganization process?
- How should liabilities be reported? Because some debts may not be paid for years and then might require payment of an amount considerably less than face value, how should this information be conveyed?
- Does reorganization necessitate a change in the reporting basis of the company's assets?

Answers to such questions can be found in FASB's Accounting Standards Codification, Topic 852, Reorganizations, which provides guidelines for the preparation of financial statements at two times:

1. During the period when an entity is going through reorganization.
2. At the point that the entity emerges from reorganization.

The Income Statement during Reorganization

According to U.S. GAAP, any gains, losses, revenues, and expenses resulting from the reorganization of a business should be reported separately. Such items are placed on the income statement before any income tax expense or benefits.[36]

These separately reported reorganization items include gains and losses on the sale of assets necessitated by the reorganization. In addition, as mentioned previously, enormous amounts of professional fees may be incurred. The authoritative literature requires that these costs be expensed as incurred.

U.S. GAAP also establishes the approved reporting of interest expense and interest revenue. During reorganization, interest usually does not accrue on debts owed at the date on which the order for relief is granted. The amount of liability on that date is frozen. Thus, recognition of interest expense is necessary only if payment will be made during the proceeding (for example, on debts incurred during the bankruptcy) or if the interest will probably be an allowed claim (for example, if the amount was owed but unrecorded prior to the granting of the order for relief). Any interest expense to be recognized is not really a result of the reorganization process and should not be separately reported as a reorganization item.

In contrast, interest revenue can increase to quite a substantial amount during reorganization. Because the company is not forced to pay debts incurred prior to the date of the order for relief, cash reserves often grow so that the resulting interest becomes a significant source of income. Any interest revenue that would not have been earned except for the bankruptcy is reported separately as a reorganization item.

[36] In a similar manner, the statement of cash flows should be constructed so that reorganization items are shown separately within the operating, investing, and financing categories.

For example, Delta Air Lines Inc. reported the following amounts as reorganization items within its income statement for the six months ended June 30, 2006 (in millions):

Pilot collective bargaining agreement	$2,100
Aircraft financing renegotiations, rejections and returns	1,590
Compensation expense	55
Professional fees	53
Facility leases	24
Debt issuance costs	13
Interest income	(47)
Other items	(5)
Total reorganization items net	$3,783

To illustrate, assume that Crawford Corporation files a voluntary bankruptcy petition and is granted an order for relief on January 1, 2013. Thereafter, the company's ownership and management begin to (1) work on a reorganization plan and (2) rehabilitate the company. It closes several branch operations and hires accountants, lawyers, and other professionals to assist in the reorganization. At the end of 2013, the bankruptcy is still in progress. The company should prepare an income statement that is structured so that the reader can distinguish the results of operating activities from reorganization items (see Exhibit 13.4).

The Balance Sheet during Reorganization

A new entity is not created when a company moves *into* reorganization. Therefore, traditional generally accepted accounting principles continue to apply. Assets, for example, should still be reported at their book values. However, a successful reorganization plan will likely reduce many liabilities. In addition, because of the order for relief, the current/noncurrent classification system is no longer applicable; payments may be delayed for years.

Thus, in reporting the liabilities of a company in reorganization, debts subject to compromise (possible reduction by the court through acceptance of a reorganization plan) must be disclosed separately. Unsecured and partially secured obligations existing as of the granting of the order for relief fall into this category. Fully secured liabilities and all debts incurred subsequent to that date are not subject to compromise and must be reported in a normal manner as either a current or noncurrent liability.

EXHIBIT 13.4
Income Statement during Reorganization

CRAWFORD CORPORATION
(Debtor in Possession)
Income Statement
For Year Ended December 31, 2013
(In thousands except for the loss per common share)

Revenues:		
Sales		$650,000
Cost and expenses:		
Cost of goods sold	$346,000	
General and administrative expenses	165,000	
Selling expenses	86,000	
Interest expense	4,000	601,000
Earnings before reorganization items and tax effects		49,000
Reorganization items:		
Loss on closing of branches	(86,000)	
Professional fees	(75,000)	
Interest revenue	26,000	(135,000)
Loss before income tax benefit		(86,000)
Income tax benefit		18,800
Net loss		$ (67,200)
Loss per common share		$ (0.56)

Liabilities that are subject to compromise must be shown at the expected amount of allowable claims rather than an estimated settlement amount. Thus, the company does not have to anticipate the payment required by a final plan but simply discloses the amount of these claims. For example, the March 31, 2009, balance sheet for Frontier Airlines Holdings, Inc., reported current liabilities of $293 million and noncurrent liabilities of $22 million. The company separately reported liabilities of $709 million subject to compromise.

LO9

Describe the financial reporting for a company that successfully exits bankruptcy as a reorganized entity.

Financial Reporting for Companies Emerging from Reorganization

Is a company that successfully leaves Chapter 11 status considered a new entity so that fair values should be assigned to its asset and liability accounts (referred to as *fresh start reporting*)? Or is the company simply a continuation of the organization that entered bankruptcy so that historical figures are still applicable? According to U.S. GAAP, assets and liabilities should be adjusted to fair value if two criteria are met:

- The reorganization (or fair) value of the assets of the emerging company is less than the total of the allowed claims as of the date of the order for relief plus the liabilities incurred subsequently.
- The previous owners of the voting stock are left with less than 50 percent of the voting stock of the company when it emerges from bankruptcy.

Meeting the first criterion shows that the old company could not have continued in business as a going concern. The second criterion indicates that control of the company has changed.

Many, if not most, Chapter 11 bankruptcies meet these two criteria. Consequently, the entity is reported as if it were a brand new business. For example, a note to the 2008 financial statements of Kaiser Aluminum explains: "The Company's emergence from Chapter 11 bankruptcy and adoption of fresh start accounting resulted in a new reporting entity for accounting purposes."

In applying fresh start accounting, the reorganization value of the entity that emerges from bankruptcy must first be determined. This reorganization value is an estimation of the amount a willing buyer would pay for the company's assets after restructuring. This total value is then assigned to the specific tangible and intangible assets of the company in the same way as in a business combination as described in earlier chapters of this book.

Unfortunately, determining the reorganization value for a large and complex business can be a difficult assignment. The 2010 financial statements for General Motors describe its approach to this computation.

> Based on our estimated reorganization value, we determined that on July 10, 2009, both the criteria of ASC 852 were met and, as a result, we applied fresh-start reporting.
>
> Our reorganization value was determined using the sum of:
>
> - Our discounted forecast of expected future cash flows from our business subsequent to the 363 Sale,[37] discounted at rates reflecting perceived business and financial risks;
> - The fair value of operating liabilities;
> - The fair value of our non-operating assets, primarily our investments in nonconsolidated affiliates and cost method investments; and
> - The amount of cash we maintained at July 10, 2009, that we determined to be in excess of the amount necessary to conduct our normal business activities.

In applying fresh start accounting, the assets held by a company on the day when it exits from reorganization should be reported based on individual current values, not historical book values. The entity is viewed as a newly created organization. For that

[37] A 363 Sale refers to the section of the bankruptcy code that allows the old company to sell its assets to the new company as a means of going forward with the business.

reason, Kmart Holdings indicated when it emerged from reorganization that the "fair value adjustments included the recognition of approximately $2.2 billion of intangible assets that were previously not recorded in the Predecessor Company's financial statements, such as favorable leasehold interests, Kmart brand rights, pharmacy customer relationships and other lease and license agreements." As with a consolidation, any unallocated portion of the reorganization value is reported as goodwill. For example, General Motors reported goodwill of $30.5 billion upon application of fresh start accounting.

Reporting liabilities following a reorganization also creates a concern because many of these balances will be reduced and the payment period extended. Consequently, all liabilities (except for deferred income taxes) are reported at the present value of the future cash payments.

To make the necessary asset adjustments to fresh start accounting, Additional Paid-In Capital is normally increased or decreased. However, any write-down of a liability creates a recognized gain. Finally, because the company is viewed as a new entity, it must leave reorganization with a zero balance reported for retained earnings.

Fresh Start Accounting Illustrated

Assume that a company has the following trial balance just prior to emerging from bankruptcy:

	Debit	Credit
Current assets	$ 50,000	
Land	100,000	
Buildings	400,000	
Equipment	250,000	
Accounts payable (incurred since the order for relief was granted)		$ 100,000
Liabilities when the order for relief was granted:		
Accounts payable		60,000
Accrued expenses		50,000
Notes payable (due in 3 years)		300,000
Bonds payable (due in 5 years)		600,000
Common stock (50,000 shares with a $1 par value)		50,000
Additional paid-in capital		40,000
Retained earnings (deficit)	400,000	
Totals	$1,200,000	$1,200,000

Other Information

- *Assets.* The company's land has a fair value of $120,000, whereas the building is worth $500,000. Other assets appearing above are valued at their book values. A trademark is worth $10,000 although it has not previously been recorded. The reorganization value of the company's assets is assumed to be $1,000,000 based on discounting the projected future cash flows for the new entity.
- *Liabilities.* The $100,000 of accounts payable incurred after the order for relief was granted must be paid in full as the individual balances come due. Liabilities when the order for relief was granted were $1,010,000 ($60,000 + $50,000 + $300,000 + $600,000). The accounts payable and accrued expenses that were owed at that time will be converted into one-year notes payable of $70,000, paying interest of 10 percent. The $300,000 in notes payable listed on the trial balance will be converted into a 10-year $100,000 note paying annual interest of 8 percent. These creditors also get 20,000 shares of stock that the common stockholders are to turn in to the company. Finally, the $600,000 of bonds payable will be converted into eight-year, 9 percent notes with a face value of $430,000. These interest rates are assumed to be reasonable. The bondholders also get 15,000 shares of common stock turned in by the current owners.

- *Stockholders' equity:* The common stock owners will return 70 percent of their stock (35,000 shares) to the company to be issued as specified above. The reorganization value of the assets is calculated as $1,000,000, and the debts of the company after these events total $700,000 ($100,000 + $70,000 + $100,000 + $430,000). Thus, stockholders' equity must be the $300,000 difference in the assets and liabilities. Because shares with a $50,000 par value will still be outstanding, Additional Paid-In Capital (APIC) needs to be adjusted to $250,000. Retained earnings will be zero as the company comes out of bankruptcy.

In accounting for this reorganization, the initial question to be resolved is whether fresh start accounting is appropriate. The first criterion is met because the reorganization value of the assets ($1,000,000) is less than the sum of all postpetition liabilities ($100,000 in Accounts Payable) plus allowed claims (the $1,010,000 total of liabilities remaining from the date of the order for relief before any write-down). The second criterion is also met because the previous stockholders retain less than 50 percent of the shares after the plan takes effect. At that point, they will hold only 15,000 of the 50,000 outstanding shares.

Because fresh start accounting is required, the assets must be adjusted to fair value rather than retain their historical book value. The reorganization value is $1 million, but the individual assets' fair value totals only $930,000 (current assets $50,000, trademark $10,000, land $120,000 [adjusted], buildings $500,000 [adjusted], and equipment $250,000). Therefore, goodwill is recognized for the $70,000 reorganization value of the company in excess of the value assigned to these specific assets.

The accounts are already recorded at book value; adjustment is necessary only when fair value differs from book value:

Trademark	10,000	
Land	20,000	
Buildings	100,000	
Goodwill	70,000	
Additional Paid-In Capital		200,000
To adjust asset accounts from book value to fresh start accounting and to recognize excess value as goodwill.		

Next, the 35,000 shares of common stock (with a $1 per share par value) returned to the company by the previous owners are recorded as follows:

Common Stock	35,000	
Additional Paid-In Capital		35,000
To remove shares of common stock returned to the company by owners as part of the reorganization agreement.		

Liability accounts on the records at the date of the order for relief must now be adjusted for the provisions of the bankruptcy reorganization plan. Because the new debts in the illustration bear a reasonable interest rate, present value computations are not necessary. The first entry is a straight conversion with a gain recorded for the difference between the old debt and the new:

Accounts Payable	60,000	
Accrued Expenses	50,000	
Notes Payable (1 year)		70,000
Gain on Debt Discharge		40,000
To convert liabilities to a one-year note as per reorganization plan.		

Discussion Question

IS THIS THE REAL PURPOSE OF THE BANKRUPTCY LAWS?

> Insolvency is not a necessary condition for bankruptcy. Moreover a firm may petition the court for protection under Chapter 11 even though it is not insolvent. If the business can demonstrate real financial trouble, the court will generally not dismiss the petition. In recent years, Chapter 11 has been looked upon as a safe harbor for gaining time to restructure the business and to head off more serious financial problems. *For example, when Johns Manville filed a petition under Chapter 11, it was a profitable, financially sound company.* Yet it faced numerous lawsuits for damages resulting from asbestos products it sold. Reorganization helped Johns Manville deal with its financial problems. [emphasis added]*

Over the years, the filing of a voluntary Chapter 11 bankruptcy petition has become a tool that companies sometimes use to settle significant financial problems. Just as Johns Manville reorganized to settle the claims of asbestos victims, A. H. Robins followed a similar path to resolve thousands of lawsuits stemming from injuries resulting from the Dalkon Shield intrauterine device. The Wilson Foods Corporation managed to reduce union wages by filing under Chapter 11, as did Continental Airlines Corporation.

Not surprisingly, seeking protection under Chapter 11 to force a bargained resolution of a financial difficulty is a controversial legal maneuver. Creditors and claimants often argue that this procedure is used to avoid responsibility. Companies counter that bankruptcy can become the only realistic means of achieving any settlement.

Should companies be allowed to use the provisions of Chapter 11 in this manner?

*Paul J. Corr and Donald D. Bourque, "Managing in a Reorganization," *Management Accounting,* January 1988, p. 34.

The two remaining debts (the note payable and the bond payable) will be exchanged, at least in part, for shares of common stock. Each of these entries will require a computation of the amount to be assigned to additional paid-in capital (APIC). The reported total of APIC for the company was derived previously as $250,000. Because the holders of the notes receive 20,000 shares of stock (or 40 percent of the company's 50,000 share total), this stock is assigned APIC of $100,000 (40 percent of that total). The holders of the bonds are to receive 15,000 shares (30 percent of the total). Hence, APIC of $75,000 (30 percent) is recorded. Gains are entered for the differences.

Notes Payable (3 years)	300,000	
Notes Payable (10 years)		100,000
Common Stock (par value of 20,000 shares)		20,000
Additional Paid-In Capital (40 percent of company total)		100,000
Gain on Debt Discharge		80,000
To record exchange with gain recorded for difference between book value of old note and the amount recorded for new note and shares of stock.		
Bonds Payable	600,000	
Notes Payable (8 years)		430,000
Common Stock (par value of 15,000 shares)		15,000
Additional Paid-In Capital (30 percent of company total)		75,000
Gain on Debt Discharge		80,000
To record exchange with gain recorded for difference between book value of old bonds and the amount recorded for new notes and shares of stock.		

At this point, all asset, liability, and common stock amounts are reported based on the amounts appropriate for the company as it leaves reorganization. Only additional paid-in capital and retained earnings remain to be finalized. Additional paid-in capital now has a balance of $450,000 ($40,000 beginning balance plus $200,000 for adjusting assets plus $35,000 for shares returned by owners plus $100,000 because of shares issued for notes and $75,000 because of shares issued for bonds). Therefore, this balance is $200,000 more than the amount to be reported as established through the provisions of the reorganization agreement. In addition, the Gain on Debt Discharge account has a balance of $200,000 ($40,000 + $80,000 + $80,000), a figure that must be closed out. Adjusting and closing these accounts eliminates the $400,000 deficit shown previously in retained earnings so that the emerging company has no balance in this equity account after its reorganization.

Additional Paid-In Capital	200,000	
Gain on Debt Discharge	200,000	
Retained Earnings (Deficit)		400,000
To adjust Additional Paid-In Capital balance to correct amount, close out Gain account, and eliminate deficit balance.		

After posting these entries, this company emerges from bankruptcy with the following:

1. Assets are reported at fair value except for goodwill, which is a residual figure.
2. Debts equal the present value of the future cash payments (except for any deferred income taxes).
3. The deficit in retained earnings has been removed.

	Debit	Credit
Current assets	$ 50,000	
Trademark	10,000	
Land	120,000	
Buildings	500,000	
Equipment	250,000	
Goodwill	70,000	
Accounts payable		$ 100,000
Note payable (due in 1 year)		70,000
Note payable (due in 10 years)		100,000
Notes payable (due in 8 years)		430,000
Common stock (50,000 shares with a $1 par value)		50,000
Additional paid-in capital		250,000
Retained earnings	–0–	–0–
Totals	$1,000,000	$1,000,000

Summary

1. Every year a significant number of businesses in the United States become insolvent, unable to pay debts as they come due. Because creditors and investors hold financial interests in these failed companies, bankruptcy laws have been created to provide protection for all parties. The Bankruptcy Reform Act of 1978 (as amended) currently is the primary structure for these legal proceedings. This act was designed to ensure a fair distribution of all remaining properties while discharging an honest debtor's obligations.
2. Bankruptcy proceedings can be voluntary (instigated by the insolvent debtor) or involuntary (instigated by a group of creditors). In either case, the court usually grants an order for relief to halt all actions against the debtor. Some creditors may have already gained protection for themselves by having a mortgage lien or security interest attached to specific assets. A creditor is considered fully secured if the value of any collateral exceeds the related debt balance but is only partially secured if the obligation is larger. All other liabilities are unsecured; these creditors have legal rights but not to any of the debtor's specific assets. The Bankruptcy Reform Act lists several types of unsecured liabilities (including administrative expenses and government claims for unpaid taxes) that have priority and must be paid before other unsecured debts are settled.

3. The parties involved in a bankruptcy want, and need, to be informed of the possible outcome, especially if liquidation is being considered. Thus, a statement of financial affairs can be prepared for an insolvent company. This document lists the net realizable value of all remaining assets and indicates any property pledged to specific creditors. In addition, the liabilities of the business are segregated and disclosed within four classifications: fully secured, partially secured, unsecured with priority, and unsecured. Prior to filing a bankruptcy petition, the parties can use this information to help decide whether liquidation or reorganization is the best course of action. However, this statement should be viewed as a projection because many reported values are merely estimations.
4. If the insolvent company's assets will be liquidated to satisfy obligations (a Chapter 7 bankruptcy), a trustee is appointed to oversee the process. This individual must recover all property belonging to the company, liquidate noncash assets, possibly continue running operations to complete any business in progress, and make appropriate payments. To convey information about these events and transactions, the trustee commonly prepares a statement of realization and liquidation as a current report of all remaining account balances and any transactions to date.
5. Liquidation is not the only outcome available to an insolvent business. The company may seek to survive by developing a reorganization plan (a Chapter 11 bankruptcy). Reorganization is possible only if creditors, shareholders, and the court accept the plan. While a reorganization is in process, the owners and management must preserve the company's estate as of the date on which the order of relief was entered. Although the ownership has the initial opportunity for creating a proposal for action, any interested party has the right to file a reorganization plan after a period of time.
6. Reorganization plans usually contain a number of provisions for modifying operations, generating new financing by equity or debt, and settling the liabilities existing when the order for relief was entered. To be accepted, each class of creditors and shareholders must support the agreement. Thereafter, the court must confirm the reorganization plan.
7. During reorganization, a company reports its liabilities as those subject to compromise or not subject to compromise. The first category includes all unsecured and partially secured debts that existed on the day the order for relief was granted. The balance to be reported is the amount of allowed claims rather than the estimated amount of settlement. Liabilities not subject to compromise are those debts fully secured or incurred following the granting of the order for relief.
8. An income statement prepared during the reorganization period should disclose operating activities separately from reorganization items. Professional fees associated with the reorganization such as lawyers' fees are reorganization items and expensed as incurred. Any interest revenue earned during this period because of an increase in the company's cash reserves should also be reported as a reorganization item.
9. Many companies that emerge from reorganization proceedings must apply fresh start accounting as a new entity. Such companies record assets at fair value, and recognition of intangible assets and goodwill might also be necessary. Liabilities (except for deferred income taxes) are reported at the present value of required cash flows. Retained earnings (or a deficit) must be eliminated. Additional Paid-In Capital is adjusted to keep the balance sheet in equilibrium.

Comprehensive Illustration

Problem

(*Estimated Time: 50 to 65 Minutes*) Roth Company is insolvent and in the process of filing for relief under the provisions of the Bankruptcy Reform Act of 1978. Roth has no cash, and the company's balance sheet currently shows Accounts Payable of $48,000. Roth owes an additional $8,000 in connection with various expenses but has not yet recorded these amounts. The company's assets with an indication of both book value and anticipated net realizable value follow:

	Book Value	Expected Net Realizable Value
Accounts receivable	$ 31,000	$ 9,000
Inventory	48,000	36,000
Investments	10,000	18,000
Land	80,000	75,000
Buildings	190,000	160,000
Accumulated depreciation	(38,000)	
Equipment	110,000	20,000
Accumulated depreciation	(61,000)	
Other assets	5,000	–0–
Totals	$375,000	$318,000

Roth has three notes payable, each with a different maturity date:

- Note 1 due in 5 years—$220,000, secured by a mortgage lien on Roth's land and buildings.
- Note 2 due in 8 years—$30,000, secured by Roth's investments.
- Note 3 due in 10 years—$35,000, unsecured.

Of the accounts payable that Roth owes, $10,000 represents salaries to employees. However, no individual is entitled to receive more than $4,100. An additional $3,000 due to the U.S. government in connection with taxes is included in this liability amount.

The company reported the stockholders' equity balance of $42,000 at the current date: common stock of $140,000 and a deficit of $98,000. Liquidating the company will lead to administrative expenses of approximately $20,000.

Required

a. Prepare a statement of financial affairs for Roth to indicate the expected availability of funds if the company is liquidated.

b. Assume that Roth owes Philip, Inc., $2,000. This liability is unsecured. If Roth is liquidated, what amount can Philip expect to receive?

c. What amount will be paid on note 2 if Roth is liquidated?

d. Assume that Roth is immediately reorganized. Assume that the company has a reorganization value of $330,000, based on discounted cash flows, and the net realizable value is to be the assigned balance for each asset. The accounts payable and accrued expenses are reduced by the parties to $20,000. Note 1 is decreased to a $130,000 note due in four years with a 7 percent annual interest rate. This creditor also receives half of the company's outstanding stock from the owners. Note 2 is reduced to a $12,000 note due in five years with an 8 percent annual interest rate. This creditor also receives 10 percent of the outstanding stock of the company from the owners. Note 3 is decreased to $5,000 due in three years with a 9 percent annual interest rate. All interest rates are considered reasonable.

Prepare a trial balance for this company after it emerges from bankruptcy.

Solution

a. To develop a statement of financial affairs for this company, the following preliminary actions must be taken:

- The $8,000 total for the unrecorded accounts payable is entered into the company's accounting records. Because these debts were incurred in connection with expenses, the deficit is increased by a corresponding amount.
- Unsecured liabilities that have priority are identified:

Administrative costs (estimated)	$20,000
Salaries payable	10,000
Amount due to government for taxes	3,000
Total liabilities with priority	$33,000

- Secured claims should be appropriately classified:

  Note 1 is fully secured because Roth's land and buildings can be sold for an amount in excess of the $220,000 balance.

  Note 2 is only partially secured because Roth's investments are worth less than the $30,000 balance.

With this information, the statement of financial affairs in Exhibit 13.5 can be produced.

b. Based on the information provided by the statement of financial affairs, Roth anticipates having $47,000 (Point A) in free assets remaining at the end of the liquidation. This amount must be distributed to unsecured creditors with total claims of $90,000 (Point B). Therefore, only 52.2 percent of each obligation can be paid:

$$\frac{\$47,000}{\$90,000} = 52.2\% \text{ (rounded)}$$

Philip, Inc., should receive 52.2 percent of its $2,000 unsecured claim, or $1,044.

EXHIBIT 13.5

ROTH COMPANY
Statement of Financial Affairs

Book Values	Assets		Available for Unsecured Creditors
	Pledged with fully secured creditors:		
$232,000	Land and buildings	$ 235,000	
	Less: Note payable	(220,000)	$ 15,000
	Pledged with partially secured creditors:		
10,000	Investments	18,000	
	Less: Note payable	(30,000)	–0–
	Free assets:		
31,000	Accounts receivable		9,000
48,000	Inventory		36,000
49,000	Equipment		20,000
5,000	Other assets		–0–
	Total available for liabilities with priority and unsecured creditors		80,000
	Less: Liabilities with priority (listed below)		(33,000)
	Available for unsecured creditors		47,000 Ⓐ
	Estimated deficiency		43,000
$375,000			$ 90,000

Book Values	Liabilities and Stockholders' Equity		Available for Nonpriority Liabilities
	Liabilities with priority:		
–0–	Administrative expenses (estimated)	$ 20,000	
	Accounts payable:		
$ 10,000	Salaries payable	10,000	
3,000	Taxes payable	3,000	
	Total	$ 33,000	
	Fully secured creditors:		
220,000	Note payable	220,000	
	Less: Land and buildings	(235,000)	–0–
	Partially secured creditors:		
30,000	Note payable	30,000	
	Less: investments	(18,000)	$ 12,000
	Unsecured creditors:		
35,000	Note payable		35,000
43,000	Accounts payable (other than salaries and taxes but plus $8,000 in unrecorded liabilities that have been included)		43,000
34,000	Stockholders' equity (adjusted for unrecorded liabilities)		–0–
$375,000			$ 90,000 Ⓑ

c. The $30,000 note payable is partially secured by Roth's investments, an asset having a net realizable value of only $18,000. The remaining $12,000 is an unsecured claim, which (as computed in the previous requirement) will be paid 52.2 percent of face value. Thus, the holder of this note can expect to receive $24,264:

Net realizable value of investments	$18,000
Payment on $12,000 unsecured claim (52.2 percent)	6,264
Amount to be received	$24,264

d. Fresh start accounting is appropriate. The reorganization value of $330,000 is less than the $341,000 total amount of claims (no liabilities after the issuance of the order for relief are indicated).

Accounts payable	$ 48,000
Accrued expenses	8,000
Note 1	220,000
Note 2	30,000
Note 3	35,000
Total claims	$341,000

In addition, the original owners of the stock retain only 40 percent of the shares after the company leaves the bankruptcy proceeding.

The company's assets are assigned values equal to their net realizable value based on the information provided. Because the reorganization value of $330,000 is $12,000 in excess of the $318,000 total net realizable value of company assets, goodwill is recognized for that amount.

Each liability is adjusted to the newly agreed-on amounts. Present value computations are not required because a reasonable interest rate is included in each case. These debts now total $167,000 ($20,000 + $130,000 + $12,000 + $5,000).

Because the reorganization value is $330,000 and the liabilities are $167,000, stockholders' equity must be $163,000 ($330,000 − $167,000). The number of outstanding shares of common stock has not changed, so that account retains its balance of $140,000. The other $23,000 of stockholders' equity is recorded as additional paid-in capital leaving the proper zero balance for retained earnings.

	Debit	Credit
Accounts receivable	$ 9,000	
Inventory	36,000	
Investments	18,000	
Land	75,000	
Buildings	160,000	
Equipment	20,000	
Goodwill	12,000	
Accounts payable and accrued expenses		$ 20,000
Note payable 1		130,000
Note payable 2		12,000
Note payable 3		5,000
Common stock		140,000
Additional paid-in capital		23,000
Totals	$330,000	$330,000

Questions

1. What does the term *insolvent* mean?
2. At present, what federal legislation governs most bankruptcy proceedings?
3. What are the primary objectives of a bankruptcy proceeding?
4. A bankruptcy case may begin with either a voluntary or an involuntary petition. What is the difference? What are the requirements for an involuntary petition?
5. A bankruptcy court enters an order for relief. How does this action affect an insolvent company and its creditors?
6. What is the difference between fully secured liabilities, partially secured liabilities, and unsecured liabilities?
7. In a bankruptcy proceeding, what is the significance of a liability with priority? What are the general categories of liabilities that have priority in a liquidation?
8. Why are administrative expenses incurred during a liquidation classified as liabilities having priority?
9. What is the difference between a Chapter 7 bankruptcy and a Chapter 11 bankruptcy?
10. Why might unsecured creditors favor reorganizing an insolvent company rather than forcing it into liquidation?

11. What is the purpose of a statement of financial affairs? Why might this statement be prepared before a bankruptcy petition has been filed?
12. In a bankruptcy liquidation, what actions does the trustee perform?
13. A trustee for a company that is being liquidated voids a preference transfer. What has happened, and why did the trustee take this action?
14. A statement of realization and liquidation is prepared for a company being liquidated. What information can be gained from this statement?
15. What does the term *debtor in possession* mean?
16. Who can develop reorganization plans in a Chapter 11 bankruptcy?
17. What types of proposals might a reorganization plan include?
18. Under normal conditions, how does a reorganization plan become effective?
19. In a bankruptcy proceeding, what is a *cram down?*
20. While a company goes through reorganization, how should its liabilities be reported?
21. During reorganization, how should a company's income statement be structured?
22. What accounting is made of the professional fees incurred during a reorganization?
23. What does *fresh start accounting* mean?
24. Under what conditions does a company emerging from a bankruptcy reorganization use fresh start accounting?
25. When fresh start accounting is utilized, how are a company's assets and its liabilities reported?
26. How is goodwill computed if fresh start accounting is applied to a reorganized company?

Problems

LO1

1. What are the objectives of the bankruptcy laws in the United States?
   a. Provide relief for the court system and ensure that all debtors are treated the same.
   b. Distribute assets fairly and discharge honest debtors from their obligations.
   c. Protect the economy and stimulate growth.
   d. Prevent insolvency and protect shareholders.

LO1, LO2, LO3, LO4, LO5

2. In a bankruptcy, which of the following statements is true?
   a. An order for relief results only from a voluntary petition.
   b. Creditors entering an involuntary petition must have debts totaling at least $20,000.
   c. Secured notes payable are considered liabilities with priority on a statement of affairs.
   d. A liquidation is referred to as a *Chapter 7 bankruptcy,* and a reorganization is referred to as a *Chapter 11 bankruptcy*.

LO6

3. In reporting a company that is to be liquidated, assets are shown at
   a. Present value calculated using an appropriate effective rate.
   b. Net realizable value.
   c. Historical cost.
   d. Book value.

LO2

4. An involuntary bankruptcy petition must be filed by
   a. The insolvent company's attorney.
   b. The holders of the insolvent company's debenture bonds.
   c. Unsecured creditors with total debts of at least $14,425.
   d. The company's management.

LO2

5. An order for relief
   a. Prohibits creditors from taking action to collect from an insolvent company without court approval.
   b. Calls for the immediate distribution of free assets to unsecured creditors.
   c. Can be entered only in an involuntary bankruptcy proceeding.
   d. Gives an insolvent company time to file a voluntary bankruptcy petition.

LO3

6. Which of the following is *not* a liability that has priority in a liquidation?
   a. Administrative expenses incurred in the liquidation.
   b. Salary payable of $800 per person owed to 26 employees.
   c. Payroll taxes due to the federal government.
   d. Advertising expense incurred before the company became insolvent.

LO2 7. Which of the following is the minimum limitation necessary for filing an involuntary bankruptcy petition?
   a. The signature of 12 creditors to whom the debtor owes at least $10,000 in unsecured debt.
   b. The signature of six creditors to whom the debtor owes at least $20,000 in unsecured debt.
   c. The signature of three creditors to whom the debtor owes at least $14,425 in unsecured debt.
   d. The signature of nine creditors to whom the debtor owes at least $25,000 in unsecured debt.

LO5 8. On a statement of financial affairs, how are liabilities classified?
   a. Current and noncurrent.
   b. Secured and unsecured.
   c. Monetary and nonmonetary.
   d. Historic and futuristic.

LO5 9. What is a *debtor in possession?*
   a. The holder of a note receivable issued by an insolvent company prior to the granting of an order for relief.
   b. A fully secured creditor.
   c. The ownership of an insolvent company that continues to control the organization during a bankruptcy reorganization.
   d. The stockholders in a Chapter 7 bankruptcy.

LO5 10. How are anticipated administrative expenses reported on a statement of financial affairs?
   a. As a footnote until actually incurred.
   b. As a liability with priority.
   c. As a partially secured liability.
   d. As an unsecured liability.

LO6 11. Prior to filing a voluntary Chapter 7 bankruptcy petition, Haynes Company pays a supplier $13,000 to satisfy an unsecured claim. Haynes was insolvent at the time. Subsequently, the trustee appointed to oversee this liquidation forces the return of this $13,000. Which of the following is correct?
   a. A preference transfer has been voided.
   b. All transactions just prior to a voluntary bankruptcy proceeding must be nullified.
   c. The supplier should sue for the return of this money.
   d. The $13,000 claim becomes a liability with priority.

LO6 12. Which of the following is *not* an expected function of a bankruptcy trustee?
   a. Filing a plan of reorganization.
   b. Recovering all property belonging to a company.
   c. Liquidating noncash assets.
   d. Distributing assets to the proper claimants.

LO5 13. What is an inherent limitation of the statement of financial affairs?
   a. Many of the amounts reported are only estimations that might prove to be inaccurate.
   b. The statement is applicable only to a Chapter 11 bankruptcy.
   c. The statement covers only a short time, whereas a bankruptcy may last much longer.
   d. The figures on the statement vary as to a voluntary and an involuntary bankruptcy.

LO7 14. What is a *cram down?*
   a. An agreement about the total amount of money to be reserved to pay creditors who have priority.
   b. The bankruptcy court's confirmation of a reorganization even though a class of creditors or stockholders did not accept it.
   c. The filing of an involuntary bankruptcy petition, especially by the holders of partially secured debts.
   d. The court's decision as to whether a particular creditor has priority.

LO8 15. On a balance sheet prepared for a company during its reorganization, how are liabilities reported?
   a. As current and long term.
   b. As monetary and nonmonetary.
   c. As subject to compromise and not subject to compromise.
   d. As equity related and debt related.

LO8

16. On a balance sheet prepared for a company during its reorganization, at what balance are liabilities reported?
    a. At the expected amount of the allowed claims.
    b. At the present value of the expected future cash flows.
    c. At the expected amount of the settlement.
    d. At the amount of the anticipated final payment.

LO8

17. Which of the following is *not* a reorganization item for purposes of reporting a company's income statement during a Chapter 11 bankruptcy?
    a. Professional fees.
    b. Interest income.
    c. Interest expense.
    d. Gains and losses on closing facilities.

LO8

18. What accounting is made for professional fees incurred during a bankruptcy reorganization?
    a. They must be expensed immediately.
    b. They must be capitalized and written off over 40 years or less.
    c. They must be capitalized until the company emerges from the reorganization.
    d. They are either expensed or capitalized, depending on the nature of the expenditure.

LO9

19. Which of the following is necessary for a company to use fresh start accounting?
    a. The previous owners must hold at least 50 percent of the stock of the company when it emerges from bankruptcy.
    b. The reorganization value of the company must exceed the value of all assets.
    c. The reorganization value of the company must exceed the value of all liabilities.
    d. The original owners must hold less than 50 percent of the stock of the company when it emerges from bankruptcy.

LO9

20. If the reorganization value of a company emerging from bankruptcy is larger than the fair values that can be assigned to specific assets, what accounting is made of the difference?
    a. Because of conservatism, the difference is simply ignored.
    b. The difference is expensed immediately.
    c. The difference is capitalized as an intangible asset.
    d. The difference is recorded as a professional fee.

LO9

21. For a company emerging from bankruptcy, how are its liabilities (other than deferred income taxes) reported?
    a. At their historical value.
    b. At zero because of fresh start accounting.
    c. At the present value of the future cash flows.
    d. At the negotiated value less all professional fees incurred in the reorganization.

LO3, LO5, LO6

22. A company is to be liquidated and has the following liabilities:

Income taxes	$ 8,000
Notes payable (secured by land)	120,000
Accounts payable	85,000
Salaries payable (evenly divided between two employees)	6,000
Bonds payable	70,000
Administrative expenses for liquidation	20,000

The company has the following assets:

	Book Value	Fair Value
Current assets	$ 80,000	$ 35,000
Land	100,000	90,000
Buildings and equipment	100,000	110,000

How much money will the holders of the notes payable collect following the liquidation?

LO3, LO6

23. Xavier Company is going through a Chapter 7 bankruptcy. All assets have been liquidated, and the company retains only $25,200 in free cash. The following debts, totaling $38,050, remain:

Government claims to unpaid taxes	$ 6,000
Salary during last month owed to Mr. Key (not an officer)	17,825
Administrative expenses	2,450
Salary during last month owed to Ms. Rankin (not an officer)	5,225
Unsecured accounts payable	6,550

Indicate how much money will be paid to the creditor associated with each debt.

LO3, LO5

24. Ataway Company has severe financial difficulties and is considering filing a bankruptcy petition. At this time, it has the following assets (stated at net realizable value) and liabilities:

Assets (pledged against debts of $70,000)	$116,000
Assets (pledged against debts of $130,000)	50,000
Other assets	80,000
Liabilities with priority	42,000
Unsecured creditors	200,000

In a liquidation, how much money would be paid on the partially secured debt?

LO3, LO5, LO6

25. Chesterfield Company has cash of $50,000, inventory worth $90,000, and a building worth $130,000. Unfortunately, the company also has accounts payable of $180,000, a note payable of $80,000 (secured by the inventory), liabilities with priority of $20,000, and a bond payable of $150,000 (secured by the building). In a Chapter 7 bankruptcy, how much money will the holder of the bond expect to receive?

LO3, LO6

26. Mondesto Company has the following:

Unsecured creditors	$230,000
Liabilities with priority	110,000
Secured liabilities:	
Debt 1, $210,000; value of pledged asset	180,000
Debt 2, $170,000; value of pledged asset	100,000
Debt 3, $120,000; value of pledged asset	140,000

The company also has a number of other assets that are not pledged in any way. The creditors holding Debt 2 want to receive at least $142,000. For how much do these free assets have to be sold so that the creditors associated with Debt 2 receive exactly $142,000?

LO3, LO5

27. A statement of financial affairs created for an insolvent corporation that is beginning the process of liquidation discloses the following data (assets are shown at net realizable values):

Assets pledged with fully secured creditors	$200,000
Fully secured liabilities	150,000
Assets pledged with partially secured creditors	380,000
Partially secured liabilities	490,000
Assets not pledged	300,000
Unsecured liabilities with priority	160,000
Accounts payable (unsecured)	390,000

a. This company owes $3,000 to an unsecured creditor (without priority). How much money can this creditor expect to collect?

b. This company owes $100,000 to a bank on a note payable that is secured by a security interest attached to property with an estimated net realizable value of $80,000. How much money can this bank expect to collect?

LO3, LO6

28. A company preparing for a Chapter 7 liquidation has the following liabilities:

- Note payable A of $90,000 secured by land having a book value of $50,000 and a fair value of $70,000.
- Note payable B of $120,000 secured by a building having a $60,000 book value and a $40,000 fair value.
- Note payable C of $60,000, unsecured.
- Administrative expenses payable of $20,000.

- Accounts payable of $120,000.
- Income taxes payable of $30,000.

It has these other assets:

- Cash of $10,000.
- Inventory of $100,000 but with fair value of $60,000.
- Equipment of $90,000 but with fair value of $50,000.

How much will each of the company's liabilities be paid at liquidation?

LO5

29. Olds Company declares Chapter 7 bankruptcy. The following are the asset and liability book values at that time; administrative expenses are estimated to be $12,000:

Cash	$ 24,000	
Accounts receivable	60,000	(worth $28,000)
Inventory	70,000	(worth $56,000)
Land (secures note A)	200,000	(worth $160,000)
Building (secures bonds)	400,000	(worth $320,000)
Equipment	120,000	(worth unknown)
Accounts payable	180,000	
Taxes payable to government	20,000	
Note payable A	170,000	
Note payable B	250,000	
Bonds payable	300,000	

The holders of note payable B want to collect at least $125,000. To achieve that goal, how much does the company have to receive in the liquidation of its equipment?

LO3, LO6

30. A company going through a Chapter 7 bankruptcy has the following account balances:

Cash	$ 30,000
Receivables (30% collectible)	50,000
Inventory (worth $39,000)	90,000
Land (worth $120,000) (secures note payable)	100,000
Buildings (worth $180,000) (secures bonds payable)	200,000
Salaries payable (7 workers owed equal amounts for last 2 weeks)	10,000
Accounts payable	90,000
Note payable (secured by land)	110,000
Bonds payable (secured by building)	300,000
Common stock	100,000
Retained earnings	(140,000)

How much will be paid to each of the following?

Salaries payable
Accounts payable
Note payable
Bonds payable

LO8

31. Pumpkin Company is going through bankruptcy reorganization. It has a $200,000 note payable incurred prior to the order for relief. The company believes that the note will be settled for $60,000 in cash. It is also possible that the creditor will instead take a piece of land that cost the company $50,000 but is worth $72,000. On a balance sheet during the reorganization period, how will this debt be reported?

LO9

32. A company is coming out of reorganization with the following accounts:

	Book Value	Fair Value
Receivables	$ 80,000	$ 90,000
Inventory	200,000	210,000
Buildings	300,000	400,000
Liabilities	300,000	300,000
Common stock	330,000	
Additional paid-in capital	20,000	
Retained earnings (deficit)	(70,000)	

The company's assets have a $760,000 reorganization value. As part of the reorganization, the company's owners transferred 80 percent of the outstanding stock to the creditors.

Prepare the journal entry that is necessary to adjust the company's records to fresh start accounting.

LO8

33. Addison Corporation is currently going through a Chapter 11 bankruptcy. The company has the following account balances for the current year. Prepare an income statement for this organization. The effective tax rate is 20 percent (realization of any tax benefits is anticipated).

	Debit	Credit
Advertising expense	$ 24,000	
Cost of goods sold	211,000	
Depreciation expense	22,000	
Interest expense	4,000	
Interest revenue		$ 32,000
Loss on closing of branch	109,000	
Professional fees	71,000	
Rent expense	16,000	
Revenues		467,000
Salaries expense	70,000	

LO9

34. Kansas City Corporation holds three assets when it comes out of Chapter 11 bankruptcy:

	Book Value	Fair Value
Inventory	$ 86,000	$ 50,000
Land and buildings	250,000	400,000
Equipment	123,000	110,000

The company has a reorganization value of $600,000.

a. Describe the rules to determine whether to apply fresh start accounting to Kansas City.

b. If fresh start accounting is appropriate, how will this company's assets be reported?

c. If a Goodwill account is recognized in a reorganization, where should it be reported? What happens to this balance?

LO8

35. Jaez Corporation is in the process of going through a reorganization. As of December 31, 2013, the company's accountant has determined the following information although the company is still several months away from emerging from the bankruptcy proceeding. Prepare a balance sheet in appropriate form.

	Book Value	Fair Value
Assets		
Cash	$ 23,000	$ 23,000
Inventory	45,000	47,000
Land	140,000	210,000
Buildings	220,000	260,000
Equipment	154,000	157,000

	Allowed Claims	Expected Settlement
Liabilities as of the date of the order for relief		
Accounts payable	$ 123,000	$ 20,000
Accrued expenses	30,000	4,000
Income taxes payable	22,000	18,000
Note payable (due 2016, secured by land)	100,000	100,000
Note payable (due 2018)	170,000	80,000
Liabilities since the date of the order for relief		
Accounts payable	$ 60,000	
Note payable (due 2015)	110,000	
Stockholders' equity		
Common stock	$ 200,000	
Deficit	(233,000)	

LO9

36. Ristoni Company is in the process of emerging from a Chapter 11 bankruptcy. It will apply fresh start accounting as of December 31, 2013. The company currently has 30,000 shares of common stock outstanding with a $240,000 par value. As part of the reorganization, the owners will contribute 18,000 shares of this stock back to the company. A retained earnings deficit balance of $330,000 exists at the time of this reorganization.

    The company has the following asset accounts:

	Book Value	Fair Value
Accounts receivable.	$100,000	$ 80,000
Inventory.	112,000	90,000
Land and buildings	420,000	500,000
Equipment.	78,000	65,000

The company's liabilities will be settled as follows. Assume that all notes will be issued at reasonable interest rates.

- Accounts payable of $80,000 will be settled with a note for $5,000. These creditors will also get 1,000 shares of the stock contributed by the owners.
- Accrued expenses of $35,000 will be settled with a note for $4,000.
- Note payable of $100,000 (due 2017) was fully secured and has not been renegotiated.
- Note payable of $200,000 (due 2016) will be settled with a note for $50,000 and 10,000 shares of the stock contributed by the owners.
- Note payable of $185,000 (due 2014) will be settled with a note for $71,000 and 7,000 shares of the stock contributed by the owners.
- Note payable of $200,000 (due 2015) will be settled with a note for $110,000.

The company has a reorganization value of $780,000.

    Prepare all journal entries for Ristoni so that the company can emerge from the bankruptcy proceeding.

LO9

37. Smith Corporation has gone through bankruptcy and is ready to emerge as a reorganized entity on December 31, 2013. On this date, the company has the following assets (fair value is based on discounting the anticipated future cash flows):

	Book Value	Fair Value
Accounts receivable.	$ 20,000	$ 18,000
Inventory.	143,000	111,000
Land and buildings	250,000	278,000
Machinery.	144,000	121,000
Patents	100,000	125,000

The company has a reorganization value of $800,000.

    Smith has 50,000 shares of $10 par value common stock outstanding. A deficit Retained Earnings balance of $670,000 also is reported. The owners will distribute 30,000 shares of this stock as part of the reorganization plan.

The company's liabilities will be settled as follows:

- Accounts payable of $180,000 (existing at the date on which the order for relief was granted) will be settled with an 8 percent, two-year note for $35,000.
- Accounts payable of $97,000 (incurred since the date on which the order for relief was granted) will be paid in the regular course of business.
- Note payable—First Metropolitan Bank of $200,000 will be settled with an 8 percent, five-year note for $50,000 and 15,000 shares of the stock contributed by the owners.
- Note payable—Northwestern Bank of Tulsa of $350,000 will be settled with a 7 percent, eight-year note for $100,000 and 15,000 shares of the stock contributed by the owners.

a. How does Smith Corporation's accountant know that fresh start accounting must be utilized?

b. Prepare a balance sheet for Smith Corporation upon its emergence from reorganization.

LO3, LO6

38. Ambrose Corporation reports the following information:

	Book Value	Liquidation Value
Assets pledged with fully secured creditors	$220,000	$245,000
Assets pledged with partially secured creditors	111,000	103,000
Other assets	140,000	81,000
Liabilities with priority	36,000	
Fully secured liabilities	200,000	
Partially secured liabilities	180,000	
Accounts payable (unsecured)	283,000	

In liquidation, what amount of cash should each class of liabilities expect to collect?

LO3, LO5

39. The following balance sheet has been prepared by the accountant for Limestone Company as of June 3, 2013, the date on which the company is to file a voluntary petition of bankruptcy:

LIMESTONE COMPANY
Balance Sheet
June 3, 2013

Assets	
Cash	$ 3,000
Accounts receivable (net)	65,000
Inventory	88,000
Land	100,000
Buildings (net)	300,000
Equipment (net)	180,000
Total assets	$736,000
Liabilities and Equities	
Accounts payable	$ 98,000
Notes payable—current (secured by equipment)	250,000
Notes payable—long term (secured by land and buildings)	190,000
Common stock	120,000
Retained earnings	78,000
Total liabilities and equities	$736,000

Additional Information

- If the company is liquidated, administrative expenses are estimated at $18,000.
- The Accounts Payable figure includes $10,000 in wages earned by the company's 12 employees during May. No one earned more than $2,200.
- Liabilities do not include taxes of $14,000 owed to the U.S. government.
- Company officials estimate that 40 percent of the accounts receivable will be collected in a liquidation and that the inventory disposal will bring $80,000. The land and buildings will be sold together for approximately $310,000; the equipment should bring $130,000 at auction.

Prepare a statement of financial affairs for Limestone Company as of June 3, 2013.

LO3, LO5, LO6

40. Creditors of Jones Corporation are considering petitioning the courts to force the company into Chapter 7 bankruptcy. The following information has been determined. Administrative expenses in connection with the liquidation are estimated to be $22,000. Indicate the amount of money that each class of creditors can anticipate receiving.

	Book Value	Net Realizable Value
Cash	$ 6,000	$ 6,000
Accounts receivable	32,000	18,000
Inventory	45,000	31,000
Supplies	3,000	–0–

(continued)

	Book Value	Net Realizable Value
Investments	$ 2,000	$ 8,000
Land	60,000	72,000
Buildings	90,000	68,000
Equipment	50,000	35,000
Notes payable (secured by land)	65,000	
Notes payable (secured by buildings)	78,000	
Bonds payable (secured by equipment)	115,000	
Accounts payable	70,000	
Salaries payable (two weeks' salary for three employees)	6,000	
Taxes payable	10,000	

LO5, LO6, LO9

41. Anteium Company owes $80,000 on a note payable that is currently due. The note is held by a local bank and is secured by a mortgage lien attached to three acres of land worth $48,000. The land originally cost Anteium $31,000 when acquired several years ago. The only other account balances for this company are Investments of $20,000 (but worth $25,000), Accounts Payable of $20,000, Common Stock of $40,000, and a deficit of $89,000. Anteium is insolvent and attempting to arrange a reorganization so that the business can continue to operate. The reorganization value of the company is $82,000.

    View each of the following as an independent situation:

    a. On a statement of financial affairs, how would this note be reported? How would the land be shown?

    b. Assume that Anteium develops an acceptable reorganization plan. Sixty percent of the common stock is transferred to the bank to settle that particular obligation. A 7 percent, three-year note payable for $5,000 is used to settle the accounts payable. How would Anteium record the reorganization?

    c. Assume that Anteium is liquidated. The land and investments are sold for $50,000 and $26,000, respectively. Administrative expenses amount to $11,000. How much will the various parties collect?

LO3, LO6

42. The following balance sheet has been produced for Litz Corporation as of August 8, 2013, the date on which the company is to begin selling assets as part of a corporate liquidation:

LITZ CORPORATION
Balance Sheet
August 8, 2013

Assets	
Cash	$ 16,000
Accounts receivable (net)	82,000
Investments	32,000
Inventory (net realizable value is expected to approximate cost)	69,000
Land	30,000
Buildings (net)	340,000
Equipment (net)	210,000
Total assets	$779,000
Liabilities and Equities	
Accounts payable	$150,000
Notes payable—current (secured by inventory)	132,000
Notes payable—long term (secured by land and buildings [valued at $300,000])	259,000
Common stock	135,000
Retained earnings	103,000
Total liabilities and equities	$779,000

The following events occur during the liquidation process:

- The investments are sold for $39,000.
- The inventory is sold at auction for $48,000.

- The money derived from the inventory is applied against the current notes payable.
- Administrative expenses of $15,000 are incurred in connection with the liquidation.
- The land and buildings are sold for $315,000. The long-term notes payable are paid.
- The accountant determines that $34,000 of the accounts payable are liabilities with priority.
- The company's equipment is sold for $84,000.
- Accounts receivable of $34,000 are collected. The remainder of the receivables is considered uncollectible.
- The administrative expenses are paid.

a. Prepare a statement of realization and liquidation for the period just described.

b. What percentage of their claims should the unsecured creditors receive?

LO7, LO9

43. Becket Corporation's accountant has prepared the following balance sheet as of November 10, 2013, the date on which the company is to release a plan for reorganizing operations under Chapter 11 of the Bankruptcy Reform Act:

BECKET CORPORATION
Balance Sheet
November 10, 2013

Assets	
Cash	$ 12,000
Accounts receivable (net)	61,000
Investments	26,000
Inventory (net realizable value is expected to approximate 80% of cost)	80,000
Land	57,000
Buildings (net)	248,000
Equipment (net)	117,000
Total assets	$601,000
Liabilities and Equities	
Accounts payable	$129,000
Notes payable—current (secured by equipment)	220,000
Notes payable—(due in 2016) (secured by land and buildings)	325,000
Common stock ($10 par value)	60,000
Retained earnings (deficit)	(133,000)
Total liabilities and equities	$601,000

The company presented the following proposal:

- The reorganization value of the company's assets just prior to issuing additional shares below, selling the company's investment, and conveying title to the land is set at $650,000 based on discounted future cash flows.
- Accounts receivable of $20,000 are written off as uncollectible. Investments are worth $40,000, land is worth $80,000, the buildings are worth $300,000, and the equipment is worth $86,000.
- An outside investor has been found to buy 7,000 shares of common stock at $11 per share.
- The company's investments are to be sold for $40,000 in cash with the proceeds going to the holders of the current note payable. The remainder of these short-term notes will be converted into $130,000 of notes due in 2017 and paying 10 percent annual cash interest.
- All accounts payable will be exchanged for $40,000 in notes payable due in 2014 that pay 8 percent annual interest.
- Title to land costing $20,000 but worth $50,000 will be transferred to the holders of the note payable due in 2016. In addition, these creditors will receive $180,000 in notes payable (paying 10 percent annual interest) coming due in 2020. These creditors also are issued 3,000 shares of previously unissued common stock.

Prepare journal entries for Becket to record the transactions as put forth in this reorganization plan.

LO2, LO3, LO5, LO6

44. Oregon Corporation has filed a voluntary petition to reorganize under Chapter 11 of the Bankruptcy Reform Act. Its creditors are considering an attempt to force liquidation. The company currently holds cash of $6,000 and accounts receivable of $25,000. In addition, the company owns four plots of land. The first two (labeled A and B) cost $8,000 each. Plots C and D cost the company $20,000 and $25,000, respectively. A mortgage lien is attached to each parcel of land as security for four different notes payable of $15,000 each. Presently, the land can be sold for the following:

Plot A	$16,000
Plot B	$11,000
Plot C	$14,000
Plot D	$27,000

Another $25,000 note payable is unsecured. Accounts payable at this time total $32,000. Of this amount, $12,000 is salary owed to the company's workers. No employee is due more than $3,400.

The company expects to collect $12,000 from the accounts receivable if liquidation becomes necessary. Administrative expenses required for liquidation are anticipated to be $16,000.

a. Prepare a statement of financial affairs for Oregon Corporation.

b. If the company is liquidated, how much cash would be paid on the note payable secured by plot B?

c. If the company is liquidated, how much cash would be paid on the unsecured note payable?

d. If the company is liquidated and plot D is sold for $30,000, how much cash would be paid on the note payable secured by plot B?

LO3, LO5

45. Lynch, Inc., is a hardware store operating in Boulder, Colorado. Management recently made some poor inventory acquisitions that have loaded the store with unsalable merchandise. Because of the drop in revenues, the company is now insolvent. The entire inventory can be sold for only $33,000. Following is a trial balance as of March 14, 2013, the day the company files for a Chapter 7 liquidation:

	Debit	Credit
Accounts payable		$ 33,000
Accounts receivable	$ 25,000	
Accumulated depreciation, building		50,000
Accumulated depreciation, equipment		16,000
Additional paid-in capital		8,000
Advertising payable		4,000
Building	80,000	
Cash	1,000	
Common stock		50,000
Equipment	30,000	
Inventory	100,000	
Investments	15,000	
Land	10,000	
Note Payable—Colorado Savings and Loan (secured by lien on land and building)		70,000
Note Payable—First National Bank (secured by equipment)		150,000
Payroll taxes payable		1,000
Retained earnings (deficit)	126,000	
Salaries payable (owed equally to two employees)		5,000
Totals	$387,000	$387,000

Company officials believe that 60 percent of the accounts receivable can be collected if the company is liquidated. The building and land have a fair value of $75,000, and the equipment is worth $19,000. The investments represent shares of a nationally traded company that can be sold at the current time for $21,000. Administrative expenses necessary to carry out a liquidation would approximate $16,000.

Prepare a statement of financial affairs for Lynch, Inc., as of March 14, 2013.

LO3, LO6

46. Use the trial balance presented for Lynch, Inc., in problem (45). Assume that the company will be liquidated and the following transactions will occur:

- Accounts receivable of $18,000 are collected with remainder written off.
- All of the company's inventory is sold for $40,000.
- Additional accounts payable of $10,000 incurred for various expenses such as utilities and maintenance are discovered.
- The land and building are sold for $71,000.
- The note payable due to the Colorado Savings and Loan is paid.
- The equipment is sold at auction for only $11,000 with the proceeds applied to the note owed to the First National Bank.
- The investments are sold for $21,000.
- Administrative expenses total $20,000 as of July 23, 2013, but no payment has yet been made.

a. Prepare a statement of realization and liquidation for the period from March 14, 2013, through July 23, 2013.

b. How much cash would be paid to an unsecured, nonpriority creditor that Lynch, Inc., owes a total of $1,000?

LO2, LO3, LO7, LO9

47. Holmes Corporation has filed a voluntary petition with the bankruptcy court in hopes of reorganizing. A statement of financial affairs has been prepared for the company showing these debts:

Liabilities with priority:	
Salaries payable	$ 18,000
Fully secured creditors:	
Notes payable (secured by land and buildings valued at $84,000)	70,000
Partially secured creditors:	
Notes payable (secured by inventory valued at $30,000)	140,000
Unsecured creditors:	
Notes payable	50,000
Accounts payable	10,000
Accrued expenses	4,000

Holmes has 10,000 shares of common stock outstanding with a par value of $5 per share. In addition, it is currently reporting a deficit balance of $132,000.

Company officials have proposed the following reorganization plan:

- The company's assets have a total book value of $210,000, an amount considered to be equal to fair value. The reorganization value of the assets as a whole, though, is set at $225,000.
- Employees will receive a one-year note in lieu of all salaries owed. Interest will be 10 percent, a normal rate for this type of liability.
- The fully secured note will have all future interest dropped from a 15 percent rate, which is now unrealistic, to a 10 percent rate.
- The partially secured note payable will be satisfied by signing a new six-year $30,000 note paying 10 percent annual interest. In addition, this creditor will receive 5,000 new shares of Holmes's common stock.
- An outside investor has been enlisted to buy 6,000 new shares of common stock at $6 per share.
- The unsecured creditors will be offered 20 cents on the dollar to settle the remaining liabilities.

If this plan of reorganization is accepted and becomes effective, what journal entries would Holmes Corporation record?

Develop Your Skills

RESEARCH CASE 1

Aberdeen Corporation is considering the possibility of filing a voluntary petition of bankruptcy because of its huge debt load. The company is publicly traded on a national stock exchange and, therefore, company officials are concerned about the role of the Securities and Exchange Commission in this legal action.

Required

Go to the following website: www.sec.gov/investor/pubs/bankrupt.htm. List the information that the SEC provides in connection with the bankruptcy of a publicly held company.

RESEARCH CASE 2

An investment analyst has been studying the long-term prospects of Six Flags Entertainment Corporation and has asked for your assistance. Go to www.sixflags.com and click on "Investor Relations" on the top of the page. Then, click on "Annual Reports" on the left side of the next page. Finally, click on "2010 Annual Report." Scroll down until you find the company's financial statements and look them over very carefully. Focus on Note 1, "Chapter 11 Reorganization," and especially parts (a) "Plan of Reorganization" and (g) "Fresh Start Accounting and Effects of the Plan."

Required

Write a memo to summarize the information found in this note and the impact on the financial statements of applying fresh start accounting.

ANALYSIS CASE 1

Go to the website of a company that has recently emerged from Chapter 11 bankruptcy—for example, Dex One Corporation (successor company to R.H. Donnelley Corporation) at www.dexone.com or General Motors at www.gm.com. By doing a search of the website or by looking at areas such as "Investor Relations" or "About Us," what information can you determine about the bankruptcy plan that was approved?

Then go to the Securities and Exchange Commission website (www.sec.gov) and click on "Search for Company Filings" under "Filings & Forms." Then click on "Company or Fund name" and enter the name of the same company. After you receive a list of filings, click on the most recent 10–K form. What information is available from this source about the bankruptcy reorganization plan?

Finally, if available, go to an online index of business publications or obtain a hard copy index of *The Wall Street Journal.* Again, search for available information concerning this company's bankruptcy reorganization plan.

Required

Based on these searches:

1. What were the main provisions of the bankruptcy reorganization plan that brought the company out of Chapter 11?
2. Which of these sources provided the best information?

ANALYSIS CASE 2

Go to the website of a company that is currently in bankruptcy reorganization such as Nortel Networks (www.nortel.com) or the Tribune Group (www.tribune.com). Or go to www.epiqbankruptcysolutions.com and click on one of the firm's current cases.

Required

By reviewing the site map or by looking at areas of the website such as "Investor Information," "Reorganization," or "About Us," find what information the company is making available about its current financial difficulties. List the various operations of the company that are being affected.

COMMUNICATION CASE 1

If available, go to an online business publication database such as Factiva, WilsonWeb, or ABI-Inform. Look up a recent, well-known bankruptcy case such as CIT Group, General Motors, or Tribune Group. Search for articles that discuss the issues and problems that led this company to file for bankruptcy.

Required

Write a short report on that company and the problems and mistakes that led to its insolvency and declaration of bankruptcy. If possible, indicate actions that the company could have taken to avoid its decline into bankruptcy.

COMMUNICATION CASE 2

Read the following articles as well as any other published pieces that describe the work of the accountant in bankruptcy cases:

"Restructuring for a Positive Return," *CMA Management,* December 2005/January 2006.

"Alternatives to Bankruptcy Liquidation," *Agency Sales,* February 2005.

"Management Accounting—How a Workout Specialist Operates," *Journal of Accountancy,* January 1992.

"Fresh-start Reporting: An Opportunity for Debtor Companies Emerging from Bankruptcy," *American Bankruptcy Journal*, July/August 2009.

"Statements of Financial Affairs and Schedules as a Corporate X-Ray," *American Bankruptcy Institute Journal*, March 2010.

"Fresh-Start Accounting Becomes Part of the Daily Financial Intake," *American Bankruptcy Institute Journal*, February 2010.

"Assisting Troubled Business Clients: A Midsize Dilemma for CPAs," *Journal of Accountancy,* March 2008.

"Stanford Business School Research: Financial Statements Are Still Valuable Tools for Predicting Bankruptcy," *Business Wire,* May 12, 2006.

Required

Write a report describing the services that an accountant can perform during a corporate bankruptcy. Include activities to be carried out prior to filing a petition and thereafter.

chapter 14

Partnerships: Formation and Operation

A reader of college accounting textbooks might well conclude that business activity is carried out exclusively by corporations. Because most large companies are legally incorporated, a vast majority of textbook references and illustrations concern corporate organizations. Contrary to the perception being relayed, partnerships (as well as sole proprietorships) make up a vital element of the business community. The Internal Revenue Service projects that by 2014, nearly 4.5 million partnership income tax returns will be filed (as compared to nearly 7.7 million corporation income tax returns).[1]

The partnership form serves a wide range of business activities, from small local operations to worldwide enterprises. The following examples exist in the U.S. economy:

- Individual proprietors often join together to form a partnership as a way to reduce expenses, expand services, and add increased expertise. As will be discussed, partnerships also provide important tax benefits.
- A partnership is a common means by which friends and relatives can easily create and organize a business endeavor.
- Historically doctors, lawyers, and other professionals have formed partnerships because of legal prohibitions against the incorporation of their practices. Although most states now permit alternative forms for such organizations, operating as a partnership or sole proprietorship is still necessary in many areas.

Over the years, some partnerships have grown to enormous sizes. Buckeye Partners, for example, primarily operates pipeline systems in the United States; in 2010 Buckeye had revenues of more than $3 billion. The international accounting firm of PriceWaterhouseCoopers recently reported revenues of more than $26 billion.[2] In 2010, Deloitte indicated operations in nearly 140 countries,[3] and Ernst & Young reported having more than 141,000 employees.[4]

[1] www.irs.gov/taxstats.

[2] "America's Largest Private Companies," *Forbes,* 2010.

[3] www.deloitte.com.

[4] "America's Largest Private Companies," *Forbes,* 2010.

Learning Objectives

After studying this chapter, you should be able to:

- LO1 Discuss the advantages and disadvantages of the partnership versus the corporate form of business.
- LO2 Describe the purpose of the articles of partnership and list specific items that should be included in this agreement.
- LO3 Prepare the journal entry to record the initial capital investment made by a partner.
- LO4 Use both the bonus method and the goodwill method to record a partner's capital investment.
- LO5 Understand the impact that the allocation of partnership income has on the partners' individual capital balances.
- LO6 Allocate income to partners when interest and/or salary factors are included.
- LO7 Discuss the meaning of partnership dissolution and understand that a dissolution will often have little or no effect on the operations of the partnership business.
- LO8 Prepare journal entries to record the acquisition by a new partner of either all or a portion of a current partner's interest.
- LO9 Prepare journal entries to record a new partner's admission by a contribution made directly to the partnership.
- LO10 Prepare journal entries to record the withdrawal of a current partner.

Partnerships—Advantages and Disadvantages

LO1

Discuss the advantages and disadvantages of the partnership versus the corporate form of business.

The popularity of partnerships derives from several advantages inherent to this type of organization. An analysis of these attributes explains why nearly 3.6 million enterprises in the United States are partnerships rather than corporations.

One of the most common motives is the ease of formation. Only an oral agreement is necessary to create a legally binding partnership. In contrast, depending on specific state laws, incorporation requires filing a formal application and completing various other forms and documents. Operators of small businesses may find the convenience and reduced cost involved in creating a partnership to be an especially appealing characteristic. As the American Bar Association noted:

> The principal advantage of partnerships is the ability to make virtually any arrangements defining their relationship to each other that the partners desire. There is no necessity, as there is in a corporation, to have the ownership interest in capital and profits proportionate to the investment made; and losses can be allocated on a different basis from profits. It is also generally much easier to achieve a desirable format for control of the business in a partnership than in a corporation, since the control of a corporation, which is based on ownership of voting stock, is much more difficult to alter.
>
> Partnerships are taxed on a conduit or flow-through basis under subchapter K of the Internal Revenue Code. This means that the partnership itself does not pay any taxes. Instead the net income and various deductions and tax credits from the partnership are passed through to the partners based on their respective percentage interest in the profits and losses of the partnership, and the partners include the income and deductions in their individual tax returns.[5]

Thus, partnership revenue and expense items (as defined by the tax laws) must be assigned directly each year to the individual partners who pay the income taxes. Passing income balances through to the partners in this manner avoids double taxation of the profits that are earned by a business and then distributed to its owners. A corporation's income is taxed twice: when earned and again when conveyed as a dividend. A partnership's income is taxed only at the time that the business initially earns it.

For example, assume that a business earns $100. After paying any income taxes, the remainder is immediately conveyed to its owners. An income tax rate of 30 percent is assumed for both individuals and corporations. Corporate dividends paid to owners, however, are taxed at a 15 percent rate.[6] As the following table shows, if this business is a partnership rather than a corporation, the owners have $10.50 more expendable income, which is 10.5 percent of the business income. Although significant in amount, this difference narrows as tax rates are lowered.

	Partnership	Corporation
Income before income taxes	$100.00	$100.00
Income taxes paid by business (30%)	–0–	(30.00)
Income distributed to owners	$100.00	$ 70.00
Income taxes paid by owners*	(30.00)	(10.50)
Expendable income	$ 70.00	$ 59.50

*30% assumed rate on ordinary income.
15% assumed rate on dividend income.

Historically, a second tax advantage has long been associated with partnerships. Because income is taxable to the partners as the business earns it, any operating losses can be used to reduce their personal taxable income directly. In contrast, a corporation is viewed as legally separate from its owners, so losses cannot be passed through to them.

[5] American Bar Association, *Family Legal Guide,* 3rd ed. (New York: Random House Reference, 2004).

[6] The Tax Increase Prevention and Reconciliation Act of 2005 limits the top tax rate on both dividend income and capital gains to 15 percent through 2010. The Tax Relief Act of 2010 keeps these rates in effect through 2012.

A corporation has the ability to carry back any net operating losses and reduce previously taxed income (usually for the two prior years) and carry forward remaining losses to decrease future taxable income (for up to 20 years). However, if a corporation is newly formed or has not been profitable, operating losses provide no immediate benefit to a corporation or its owners as losses do for a partnership.

The tax advantage of deducting partnership losses is limited however. For tax purposes, ownership of a partnership is labeled as a passive activity unless the partner materially participates in the actual business activities. Passive activity losses thus serve only to offset other passive activity profits. In most cases, these partnership losses cannot be used to reduce earned income such as salaries. Thus, unless a taxpayer has significant passive activity income (from rents, for example), losses reported by a partnership create little or no tax advantage unless the partner materially participates in the actual business activity.

The partnership form of business also has certain significant disadvantages. Perhaps the most severe problem is the unlimited liability that each partner automatically incurs. Partnership law specifies that any partner can be held personally liable for *all* debts of the business. The potential risk is especially significant when coupled with the concept of *mutual agency*. This legal term refers to the right that each partner has to incur liabilities in the name of the partnership. Consequently, partners acting within the normal scope of the business have the power to obligate the company for any amount. If the partnership fails to pay these debts, creditors can seek satisfactory remuneration from any partner that they choose.

Such legal concepts as unlimited liability and mutual agency describe partnership characteristics that have been defined and interpreted over a number of years. To provide consistent application across state lines in regard to these terms as well as many other legal aspects of a partnership, the Uniform Partnership Act (UPA) was created. This act, which was first proposed in 1914 (and revised in 1997), now has been adopted by all states in some form. It establishes uniform standards in such areas as the nature of a partnership, the relationship of the partners to outside parties, and the dissolution of the partnership. For example, Section 6 of the act provides the most common legal definition of a partnership: "an association of two or more persons to carry on a business as co-owners for profit."

Alternative Legal Forms

Because of the possible owner liability, partnerships often experience difficulty in attracting large amounts of capital. Potential partners frequently prefer to avoid the risk that is a basic characteristic of a partnership. However, the tax benefits of avoiding double taxation still provide a strong pull toward the partnership form. Hence, in recent years, a number of alternative types of organizations have been developed. The availability of these legal forms depends on state laws as well as applicable tax laws. In each case, however, the purpose is to limit the owners' personal liability while providing the tax benefits of a partnership.[7]

Subchapter S Corporation

A Subchapter S corporation (often referred to as an *S corporation*) is created as a corporation and, therefore, has all of the legal characteristics of that form.[8] According to the U.S. tax laws, if the corporation meets certain regulations, it will be taxed in virtually the same way as a partnership. Thus, the Subchapter S corporation pays no income taxes although any income (and losses) pass directly through to the taxable income of the individual owners. This form avoids double taxation, and the owners do not face unlimited liability. To qualify, the business can have only one class of stock and is limited to 100 stockholders. All owners must be individuals, estates, certain tax-exempt entities, or certain types of trusts. The most significant problem associated with this business form is that its growth potential is limited because of the restriction on the number and type of owners.

[7] Many factors should be considered in choosing a specific legal form for an organization. The information shown here is merely an overview. For more information, consult a tax guide or a business law textbook.

[8] Unless a corporation qualifies as a Subchapter S corporation or some other legal variation, it is referred to as a *Subchapter C corporation*. Therefore, a vast majority of all businesses are C corporations.

Limited Partnerships (LPs)

A *limited partnership* is a type of investment designed primarily for individuals who want the tax benefits of a partnership but who do not wish to work in a partnership or have unlimited liability. In such organizations, a number of limited partners invest money as owners but are not allowed to participate in the company's management. These partners can still incur a loss on their investment, but the amount is restricted to what has been contributed. To protect the creditors of a limited partnership, one or more general partners must be designated to assume responsibility for all obligations created in the name of the business.

Buckeye Partners, L.P. (with annual revenues of more than $3.0 billion), is an example of a limited partnership that trades on the New York Stock Exchange. Buckeye's December 31, 2010, balance sheet reported capital of $1.4 billion for its limited partners.

Many limited partnerships were originally formed as tax shelters to create immediate losses (to reduce the taxable income of the partners) with profits spread out into the future. As mentioned earlier, tax laws limit the deduction of passive activity losses, and this significantly reduced the formation of limited partnerships.

Limited Liability Partnerships (LLPs)

The *limited liability partnership* has most of the characteristics of a general partnership except that it significantly reduces the partners' liability. Partners may lose their investment in the business and are responsible for the contractual debts of the business. The advantage here is created in connection with any liability resulting from damages. In such cases, the partners are responsible for only their own acts or omissions plus the acts and omissions of individuals under their supervision.

As Section 306(c) of the Uniform Partnership Act notes

> An obligation of a partnership incurred while the partnership is a limited liability partnership, whether arising in contract, tort, or otherwise, is solely the obligation of the partnership. A partner is not personally liable, directly or indirectly, by way of contribution or otherwise, for such an obligation solely by reason of being or so acting as a partner.

Thus, a partner in the Houston office of a public accounting firm would probably not be held liable for a poor audit performed by that firm's San Francisco office. Not surprisingly, limited liability partnerships have become very popular with professional service organizations that have multiple offices. For example, all of the four largest accounting firms are LLPs.

Limited Liability Companies (LLCs)

The limited liability company is a new type of organization in the United States although it has long been used in Europe and other areas of the world. It is classified as a partnership for tax purposes. However, depending on state laws, the owners risk only their own investments. In contrast to a Subchapter S corporation, the number of owners is not usually restricted so that growth is easier to accomplish.

Partnership Accounting—Capital Accounts

Despite legal distinctions, questions should be raised as to the need for an entirely separate study of partnership accounting:

- Does an association of two or more persons require accounting procedures significantly different from those of a corporation?
- Does proper accounting depend on the legal form of an organization?

The answers to these questions are both yes and no. Accounting procedures are normally standardized for assets, liabilities, revenues, and expenses regardless of the legal form of a business. *Partnership accounting, though, does exhibit unique aspects that warrant study, but they lie primarily in the handling of the partners' capital accounts.*

The stockholders' equity accounts of a corporation do not correspond directly with the capital balances found in a partnership's financial records. The various equity accounts reported by an incorporated enterprise display a greater range of information. This characteristic reflects the wide variety of equity transactions that can occur in a corporation as well as the influence of state and federal laws. Government regulation has had enormous effect on the accounting for corporate equity transactions in that extensive disclosure is required to protect stockholders and other outside parties such as potential investors.

To provide adequate information and to meet legal requirements, corporate accounting must provide details about numerous equity transactions and account balances. For example, the amount of a corporation's paid-in capital is shown separately from earned capital and other comprehensive income; the par value of each class of stock is disclosed; treasury stock, stock options, stock dividends, and other capital transactions are reported based on prescribed accounting principles.

In comparison, partnerships provide only a limited amount of equity disclosure primarily in the form of individual capital accounts that are accumulated for every partner or every class of partners. These balances measure each partner or group's interest in the book value of the net assets of the business. Thus, the equity section of a partnership balance sheet is composed solely of capital accounts that can be affected by many different events: contributions from partners as well as distributions to them, earnings, and any other equity transactions.

However, partnership accounting makes no differentiation between the various sources of ownership capital. Disclosing the composition of the partners' capital balances has not been judged necessary because partnerships have historically tended to be small with equity transactions that were rarely complex. Additionally, absentee ownership is not common, a factor that minimizes both the need for government regulation and outside interest in detailed information about the capital balances.

LO2

Describe the purpose of the articles of partnership and list specific items that should be included in this agreement.

Articles of Partnership

Because the demand for information about capital balances is limited, accounting principles specific to partnerships are based primarily on traditional approaches that have evolved over the years rather than on official pronouncements. These procedures attempt to mirror the relationship between the partners and their business especially as defined by the partnership agreement. This legal covenant, which may be either oral or written, is often referred to as the *articles of partnership* and forms the central governance for a partnership's operation. The financial arrangements spelled out in this contract establish guidelines for the various capital transactions. Therefore, the articles of partnership, rather than either laws or official rules, provide much of the underlying basis for partnership accounting.

Because the articles of partnership are a negotiated agreement that the partners create, an unlimited number of variations can be encountered in practice. Partners' rights and responsibilities frequently differ from business to business. Consequently, firms often hire accountants in an advisory capacity to participate in creating this document to ensure the equitable treatment of all parties. Although the articles of partnership may contain a number of provisions, an explicit understanding should always be reached in regard to the following:

- Name and address of each partner.
- Business location.
- Description of the nature of the business.
- Rights and responsibilities of each partner.
- Initial contribution to be made by each partner and the method to be used for valuation.
- Specific method by which profits and losses are to be allocated.
- Periodic withdrawal of assets by each partner.
- Procedure for admitting new partners.
- Method for arbitrating partnership disputes.
- Life insurance provisions enabling remaining partners to acquire the interest of any deceased partner.
- Method for settling a partner's share in the business upon withdrawal, retirement, or death.

Discussion Question

WHAT KIND OF BUSINESS IS THIS?

After graduating from college, Shelley Williams held several different jobs but found that she did not enjoy working for other people. Finally, she and Yvonne Hargrove, her college roommate, decided to start a business of their own. They rented a small building and opened a florist shop selling cut flowers such as roses and chrysanthemums that they bought from a local greenhouse.

Williams and Hargrove agreed orally to share profits and losses equally, although they also decided to take no money from the operation for at least four months. No other arrangements were made, but the business did reasonably well and, after the first four months had passed, each began to draw out $500 in cash every week.

At year-end, they took their financial records to a local accountant so that they could get their income tax returns completed. He informed them that they had been operating as a partnership and that they should draw up a formal articles of partnership agreement or consider incorporation or some other legal form of organization. They confessed that they had never really considered the issue and asked for his advice on the matter.

What advice should the accountant give to these clients?

LO3

Prepare the journal entry to record the initial capital investment made by a partner.

Accounting for Capital Contributions

Several types of capital transactions occur in a partnership: allocation of profits and losses, retirement of a current partner, admission of a new partner, and so on. The initial transaction, however, is the contribution the original partners make to begin the business. In the simplest situation, the partners invest only cash amounts. For example, assume that Carter and Green form a business to be operated as a partnership. Carter contributes $50,000 in cash and Green invests $20,000. The initial journal entry to record the creation of this partnership follows:

Cash	70,000	
Carter, Capital		50,000
Green, Capital		20,000
To record cash contributed to start new partnership.		

The assumption that only cash was invested avoids complications in this first illustration. Often, though, one or more of the partners transfers noncash assets such as inventory, land, equipment, or a building to the business. Although fair value is used to record these assets, a case could be developed for initially valuing any contributed asset at the partner's current book value. According to the concept of unlimited liability (as well as present tax laws), a partnership does not exist as an entity apart from its owners. A logical extension of the idea is that the investment of an asset is not a transaction occurring between two independent parties such as would warrant revaluation. This contention holds that the semblance of an arm's-length transaction is necessary to justify a change in the book value of any account.

Although retaining the recorded value for assets contributed to a partnership may seem reasonable, this method of valuation proves to be inequitable to any partner investing appreciated property. A $50,000 capital balance always results from a cash investment of that amount, but recording other assets depends entirely on the original book value.

For example, should a partner who contributes a building having a recorded value of $18,000 but a fair value of $50,000 be credited with only an $18,000 interest in the partnership? Because $50,000 in cash and $50,000 in appreciated property are equivalent contributions, a $32,000 difference in the partners' capital balances cannot be justified. To prevent such inequities, each item transferred to a partnership is initially recorded for external reporting purposes at current value.[9]

Requiring revaluation of contributed assets can, however, be advocated for reasons other than just the fair treatment of all partners. Despite some evidence to the contrary, a partnership can be viewed legitimately as an entity standing apart from its owners. As an example, a partnership maintains legal ownership of its assets and (depending on state law) can initiate lawsuits. For this reason, accounting practice traditionally has held that the contribution of assets (and liabilities) to a partnership is an exchange between two separately identifiable parties that should be recorded based on fair values.

The determination of an appropriate valuation for each capital balance is more than just an accounting exercise. Over the life of a partnership, these figures serve in a number of important capacities:

1. The totals in the individual capital accounts often influence the assignment of profits and losses to the partners.
2. The capital account balance is usually one factor in determining the final distribution that will be received by a partner at the time of withdrawal or retirement.
3. Ending capital balances indicate the allocation to be made of any assets that remain following the liquidation of a partnership.

To demonstrate, assume that Carter invests $50,000 in cash to begin the previously discussed partnership and Green contributes the following assets:

	Book Value to Green	Fair Value
Inventory	$ 9,000	$10,000
Land	14,000	11,000
Building	32,000	46,000
Totals	$55,000	$67,000

As an added factor, Green's building is encumbered by a $23,600 mortgage that the partnership has agreed to assume.

Green's net investment is equal to $43,400 ($67,000 less $23,600). The following journal entry records the formation of the partnership created by these contributions:

Cash	50,000	
Inventory	10,000	
Land	11,000	
Building	46,000	
Mortgage Payable		23,600
Carter, Capital		50,000
Green, Capital		43,400
To record properties contributed to start partnership. Assets and liabilities are recorded at fair value.		

We should make one additional point before leaving this illustration. Although having contributed inventory, land, and a building, Green holds no further right to these

[9] For federal income tax purposes, the $18,000 book value is retained as the basis for this building, even after transfer to the partnership. Within the tax laws, no difference is seen between partners and their partnership so that no adjustment to fair value is warranted.

individual assets; they now belong to the partnership. The $43,400 capital balance represents an ownership interest in the business as a whole but does not constitute a specific claim to any asset. Having transferred title to the partnership, Green has no more right to these assets than does Carter.

LO4

Use both the bonus method and the goodwill method to record a partner's capital investment.

Intangible Contributions

In forming a partnership, the contributions made by one or more of the partners may go beyond assets and liabilities. A doctor, for example, can bring a particular line of expertise to a partnership, and a practicing dentist might have already developed an established patient list. These attributes, as well as many others, are frequently as valuable to a partnership as cash and fixed assets. *Hence, formal accounting recognition of such special contributions may be appropriately included as a provision of any partnership agreement.*

To illustrate, assume that James and Joyce plan to open an advertising agency and decide to organize the endeavor as a partnership. James contributes cash of $70,000, and Joyce invests only $10,000. Joyce, however, is an accomplished graphic artist, a skill that is considered especially valuable to this business. Therefore, in producing the articles of partnership, the partners agree to start the business with equal capital balances. Often such decisions result only after long, and sometimes heated, negotiations. Because the value assigned to an intangible contribution such as artistic talent is arbitrary at best, proper reporting depends on the partners' ability to arrive at an equitable arrangement.

In recording this agreement, James and Joyce have two options: (1) the bonus method and (2) the goodwill method. Each of these approaches achieves the desired result of establishing equal capital account balances. Recorded figures can vary significantly, however, depending on the procedure selected. Thus, the partners should reach an understanding prior to beginning business operations as to the method to be used. The accountant can help avoid conflicts by assisting the partners in evaluating the impact created by each of these alternatives.

The Bonus Method The bonus method assumes that a specialization such as Joyce's artistic abilities does *not* constitute a recordable partnership asset with a measurable cost. Hence, this approach recognizes only the assets that are physically transferred to the business (such as cash, patents, inventory). Although these contributions determine total partnership capital, the establishment of specific capital balances is viewed as an independent process based solely on the partners' agreement. Because the initial equity figures result from negotiation, they do not need to correspond directly with the individual investments.

James and Joyce have contributed a total of $80,000 in identifiable assets to their partnership and have decided on equal capital balances. According to the bonus method, this agreement is fulfilled simply by splitting the $80,000 capital evenly between the two partners. The following entry records the formation of this partnership under this assumption:

	Debit	Credit
Cash	80,000	
James, Capital		40,000
Joyce, Capital		40,000
To record cash contributions with bonus to Joyce because of artistic abilities.		

Joyce received a *capital bonus* here of $30,000 (the $40,000 recorded capital balance in excess of the $10,000 cash contribution) from James in recognition of the artistic abilities she brought into the business.

The Goodwill Method The goodwill method is based on the assumption that an implied value can be calculated mathematically and recorded for any intangible contribution made by a partner. In the present illustration, Joyce invested $60,000 less cash than James but receives an equal amount of capital according to the partnership agreement.

Proponents of the goodwill method argue that Joyce's artistic talent has an apparent value of $60,000, a figure that should be included as part of this partner's capital investment. If not recorded, Joyce's primary contribution to the business is ignored completely within the accounting records.

Cash	80,000	
Goodwill	60,000	
James, Capital		70,000
Joyce, Capital		70,000
To record cash contributions with goodwill attributed to Joyce in recognition of artistic abilities.		

Comparison of Methods Both approaches achieve the intent of the partnership agreement: to record equal capital balances despite a difference in the partners' cash contributions. The bonus method allocates the $80,000 invested capital according to the percentages designated by the partners, whereas the goodwill method capitalizes the implied value of Joyce's intangible contribution.

Although nothing prohibits the use of either technique, the recognition of goodwill poses definite theoretical problems. In previous discussions of both the equity method (Chapter 1) and business combinations (Chapter 2), goodwill was recognized but only as a result of an acquisition made by the reporting entity. Consequently, this asset had a historical cost in the traditional accounting sense. Partnership goodwill has no such cost; the business recognizes an asset even though no funds have been spent.

The partnership of James and Joyce, for example, is able to record $60,000 in goodwill without any expenditure. Furthermore, the value attributed to this asset is based solely on a negotiated agreement between the partners; the $60,000 balance has no objectively verifiable basis. Thus, although partnership goodwill is sometimes encountered in actual practice, this "asset" should be viewed with a strong degree of professional skepticism.

Additional Capital Contributions and Withdrawals

Subsequent to forming a partnership, the owners may choose to contribute additional capital amounts during the life of the business. These investments can be made to stimulate expansion or to assist the business in overcoming working capital shortages or other problems. Regardless of the reason, the contribution is again recorded as an increment in the partner's capital account based on fair value. For example, in the previous illustration, assume that James decides to invest another $5,000 cash in the partnership to help finance the purchase of new office furnishings. The partner's capital account balance is immediately increased by this amount to reflect the transfer to the partnership.

The partners also may reverse this process by withdrawing assets from the business for their own personal use. For example, one partnership, Andersons, reported recently in its financial statements partner withdrawals of $1,759,072 for the year as well as increases in invested capital of $733,675. To protect the interests of the other partners, the articles of partnership should clearly specify the amount and timing of such withdrawals.

In many instances, the articles of partnership allow withdrawals on a regular periodic basis as a reward for ownership or as compensation for work performed for the business. Often such distributions are recorded initially in a separate drawing account that is closed into the individual partner's capital account at year-end. Assume, for illustration purposes, that James and Joyce take out $1,200 and $1,500, respectively, from their business. The journal entry to record these payments is as follows:

James, Drawing	1,200	
Joyce, Drawing	1,500	
Cash		2,700
To record withdrawal of cash by partners.		

Discussion Question

HOW WILL THE PROFITS BE SPLIT?

James J. Dewars has been the sole owner of a small CPA firm for the past 20 years. Now 52 years old, Dewars is concerned about the continuation of his practice after he retires. He would like to begin taking more time off now although he wants to remain active in the firm for at least another 8 to 10 years. He has worked hard over the decades to build up the practice so that he presently makes a profit of $180,000 annually.

Lewis Huffman has been working for Dewars for the past four years. He now earns a salary of $68,000 per year. He is a very dedicated employee who generally works 44 to 60 hours per week. In the past, Dewars has been in charge of the larger, more profitable audit clients whereas Huffman, with less experience, worked with the smaller clients. Both Dewars and Huffman do some tax work although that segment of the business has never been emphasized.

Sally Scriba has been employed for the past seven years with another CPA firm as a tax specialist. She has no auditing experience but has a great reputation in tax planning and preparation. She currently earns an annual salary of $80,000.

Dewars, Huffman, and Scriba are negotiating the creation of a new CPA firm as a partnership. Dewars plans to reduce his time in this firm although he will continue to work with many of the clients that he has served for the past two decades. Huffman will begin to take over some of the major audit jobs. Scriba will start to develop an extensive tax practice for the firm.

Because of the changes in the firm, the three potential partners anticipate earning a total net income in the first year of operations of between $130,000 and $260,000. Thereafter, they hope that profits will increase at the rate of 10 to 20 percent annually for the next five years or so.

How should this new partnership allocate its future net income among these partners?

Larger amounts might also be withdrawn from a partnership on occasion. A partner may have a special need for money or just desire to reduce the basic investment that has been made in the business. Such transactions are usually sporadic occurrences and entail amounts significantly higher than the partner's periodic drawing. The articles of partnership may require prior approval by the other partners.

Allocation of Income

LO5

Understand the impact that the allocation of partnership income has on the partners' individual capital balances.

At the end of each fiscal period, partnership revenues and expenses are closed out, accompanied by an allocation of the resulting net income or loss to the partners' capital accounts. Because a separate capital balance is maintained for each partner, a method must be devised for this assignment of annual income. Because of the importance of the process, the articles of partnership should always stipulate the procedure the partners established. If no arrangement has been specified, state partnership law normally holds that all partners receive an equal allocation of any income or loss earned by the business. If the partnership agreement specifies only the division of profits, then losses must be divided in the same manner as directed for profit allocation.

An allocation pattern can be extremely important to the success of an organization because it can help emphasize and reward outstanding performance.

> The goal of a partner compensation plan is to inspire each principal's most profitable performance—and make a firm grow. When a CPA firm's success depends on partner

> contributions other than accounting expertise—such as bringing in business, developing a specialty or being a good manager—its compensation plan has to encourage those qualities, for both fairness and firm health.[10]

Actual procedures for allocating profits and losses can range from the simple to the elaborate.

> Our system is as follows: a base draw to all partners, which grows over an eight-year period from 0.63x to a maximum of x, to which is added a 7 percent return on our accrual capital and our intangible capital. (Intangible capital is defined as the goodwill of the firm valued at 75 percent of gross revenues.) A separate pool of funds (about 20 percent of our compensation) is reserved for the performance pool. Each partner assesses how his or her goals helped firm goals for the year, reviews the other partners' assessment reports and then prepares an allocation schedule. Bonus pool shares are based on a group vote.[11]

Partnerships can avoid all complications by assigning net income on an equal basis among all partners. Other organizations attempt to devise plans that reward such factors as the expertise of the individuals, number of years with the organization, or the amount of time that each works. Some agreements also consider the capital invested in the business as an element that should be recognized within the allocation process.

As an initial illustration, assume that Tinker, Evers, and Chance form a partnership by investing cash of $120,000, $90,000, and $75,000, respectively. The articles of partnership agreement specifies that Evers will be allotted 40 percent of all profits and losses because of previous business experience. Tinker and Chance are to divide the remaining 60 percent equally. This agreement also stipulates that each partner is allowed to withdraw $10,000 in cash annually from the business. The amount of this withdrawal does not directly depend on the method utilized for income allocation. *From an accounting perspective, the assignment of income and the setting of withdrawal limits are two separate decisions.*

At the end of the first year of operations, the partnership reports net income of $60,000. To reflect the changes made in the partners' capital balances, the closing process consists of the following two journal entries. The assumption is made here that each partner has taken the allowed amount of drawing during the year. In addition, for convenience, all revenues and expenses already have been closed into the Income Summary account.

	Debit	Credit
Tinker, Capital	10,000	
Evers, Capital	10,000	
Chance, Capital	10,000	
Tinker, Drawing		10,000
Evers, Drawing		10,000
Chance, Drawing		10,000
To close out drawing accounts recording payments made to the three partners.		

	Debit	Credit
Income Summary	60,000	
Tinker, Capital (30%)		18,000
Evers, Capital (40%)		24,000
Chance, Capital (30%)		18,000
To allocate net income based on provisions of partnership agreement.		

Statement of Partners' Capital

Because a partnership does not separately disclose a retained earnings balance, the statement of retained earnings usually reported by a corporation is replaced by a statement of partners' capital. The following financial statement is based on the data presented for

[10] Michael Hayes, "Pay for Performance," *Journal of Accountancy*, June 2002, p. 24.

[11] Richard Kretz, "You Want to Minimize the Pain," *Journal of Accountancy*, June 2002, p. 28.

the partnership of Tinker, Evers, and Chance. The changes made during the year in the individual capital accounts are outlined along with totals representing the partnership as a whole:

TINKER, EVERS, AND CHANCE
Statement of Partners' Capital
For Year Ending December 31, Year 1

	Tinker, Capital	Evers, Capital	Chance, Capital	Totals
Capital balances beginning of year	$120,000	$ 90,000	$ 75,000	$285,000
Allocation of net income.	18,000	24,000	18,000	60,000
Drawings	(10,000)	(10,000)	(10,000)	(30,000)
Capital balances end of year	$128,000	$104,000	$ 83,000	$315,000

LO6

Allocate income to partners when interest and/or salary factors are included.

Alternative Allocation Techniques—Example 1

Assigning net income based on a ratio may be simple, but this approach is not necessarily equitable to all partners. For example, assume that Tinker does not participate in the partnership's operations but is the contributor of the highest amount of capital. Evers and Chance both work full-time in the business, but Evers has considerably more experience in this line of work.

Under these circumstances, no single ratio is likely to reflect properly the various contributions made by each partner. Indeed, an unlimited number of alternative allocation plans could be devised in hopes of achieving fair treatment for all parties. For example, because of the different levels of capital investments, consideration should be given to including interest within the allocation process to reward the contributions. A compensation allowance is also a possibility, usually in an amount corresponding to the number of hours worked or the level of a partner's business expertise.

To demonstrate one possible option, assume that Tinker, Evers, and Chance begin their partnership based on the original facts except that they arrive at a more detailed method of allocating profits and losses. After considerable negotiation, an articles of partnership agreement credits each partner annually for interest in an amount equal to 10 percent of that partner's beginning capital balance for the year. Evers and Chance also will be allotted $15,000 each as a compensation allowance in recognition of their participation in daily operations. Any remaining profit or loss will be split 3:4:3, with the largest share going to Evers because of the work experience that this partner brings to the business. As with any appropriate allocation, this pattern attempts to provide fair treatment for all three partners.

Under this arrangement, the $60,000 net income earned by the partnership in the first year of operation would be prorated as follows. The sequential alignment of the various provisions is irrelevant except that the ratio, which is used to assign the remaining profit or loss, must be calculated last.

	Tinker	Evers	Chance	Totals
Interest (10% of beginning capital)	$12,000	$ 9,000	$ 7,500	$28,500
Compensation allowance . . .	–0–	15,000	15,000	30,000
Remaining income:				
$ 60,000				
(28,500)				
(30,000)				
$ 1,500	450 (30%)	600 (40%)	450 (30%)	1,500
Totals	$12,450	$24,600	$22,950	$60,000

For the Tinker, Evers, and Chance partnership, the allocations just calculated lead to the following year-end closing entry:

Income Summary	60,000	
Tinker, Capital.		12,450
Evers, Capital		24,600
Chance, Capital		22,950
To allocate income for the year to the individual partners' capital accounts based on partnership agreement.		

Alternative Allocation Techniques—Example 2

As the preceding illustration indicates, the assignment process is no more than a series of mechanical steps reflecting the change in each partner's capital balance resulting from the provisions of the partnership agreement. The number of different allocation procedures that could be employed is limited solely by the partners' imagination. Although interest, compensation allowances, and various ratios are the predominant factors encountered in practice, other possibilities exist. Therefore, another approach to the allocation process is presented to further illustrate some of the variations that can be utilized. A two-person partnership is used here to simplify the computations.

Assume that Webber and Rice formed a partnership in 2010 to operate a bookstore. Webber contributed the initial capital, and Rice manages the business. With the assistance of their accountant, they wrote an articles of partnership agreement that contains the following provisions:

1. Each partner is allowed to draw $1,000 in cash from the business every month. Any withdrawal in excess of that figure will be accounted for as a direct reduction to the partner's capital balance.
2. Partnership profits and losses will be allocated each year according to the following plan:

   a. Each partner will earn 15 percent interest based on the monthly average capital balance for the year (calculated without regard for normal drawings or current income).

   b. As a reward for operating the business, Rice is to receive credit for a bonus equal to 20 percent of the year's net income. However, no bonus is earned if the partnership reports a net loss.

   c. The two partners will divide any remaining profit or loss equally.

Assume that Webber and Rice subsequently begin the year 2013 with capital balances of $150,000 and $30,000, respectively. On April 1 of that year, Webber invests an additional $8,000 cash in the business, and on July 1, Rice withdraws $6,000 in excess of the specified drawing allowance. Assume further that the partnership reports income of $30,000 for 2013.

Because the interest factor established in this allocation plan is based on a monthly average figure, the specific amount to be credited to each partner is determined by means of a preliminary calculation:

Webber—Interest Allocation

Beginning balance:	$150,000 × 3 months =	$ 450,000
Balance, 4/1/13:	$158,000 × 9 months =	1,422,000
		1,872,000
		× 1/12
Monthly average capital balance.		156,000
Interest rate		× 15%
Interest credited to Webber.		$ 23,400

Rice—Interest Allocation

Beginning balance:	$30,000 × 6 months =	$180,000
Balance, 7/1/13:	$24,000 × 6 months =	144,000
		324,000
		× 1/12
Monthly average capital balance.		27,000
Interest rate		× 15%
Interest credited to Rice.		$ 4,050

Following this initial computation, the actual income assignment can proceed according to the provisions specified in the articles of partnership. The stipulations drawn by Webber and Rice must be followed exactly, even though the business's $30,000 profit in 2013 is not sufficient to cover both the interest and the bonus. Income allocation is a mechanical process that should always be carried out as stated in the articles of partnership without regard to the specific level of income or loss.

Based on the plan that was created, Webber's capital increases by $21,675 during 2013 but Rice's account increases by only $8,325:

	Webber	Rice	Totals
Interest (above).	$23,400	$4,050	$27,450
Bonus (20% × $30,000).	–0–	6,000	6,000
Remaining income (loss):			
$ 30,000			
(27,450)			
(6,000)			
$ (3,450).	(1,725) (50%)	(1,725) (50%)	(3,450)
Totals	$21,675	$8,325	$30,000

Accounting for Partnership Dissolution

LO7

Discuss the meaning of partnership dissolution and understand that a dissolution will often have little or no effect on the operations of the partnership business.

Many partnerships limit capital transactions almost exclusively to contributions, drawings, and profit and loss allocations. Normally, though, over any extended period, changes in the members who make up a partnership occur. Employees may be promoted into the partnership or new owners brought in from outside the organization to add capital or expertise to the business. Current partners eventually retire, die, or simply elect to leave the partnership. Large operations may even experience such changes on a routine basis.

Regardless of the nature or the frequency of the event, any alteration in the specific individuals composing a partnership automatically leads to legal dissolution. In many instances, the breakup is merely a prerequisite to the formation of a new partnership. For example, if Abernethy and Chapman decide to allow Miller to become a partner in their business, the legally recognized partnership of Abernethy and Chapman has to be dissolved first. The business property as well as the right to future profits can then be conveyed to the newly formed partnership of Abernethy, Chapman, and Miller. The change is a legal one. Actual operations of the business would probably continue unimpeded by this alteration in ownership.

Conversely, should the partners so choose, dissolution can be a preliminary step in the termination and liquidation of the business. The death of a partner, lack of sufficient profits, or internal management differences can lead the partners to break up the partnership business. Under this circumstance, the partnership sells properties, pays debts, and distributes any remaining assets to the individual partners. Thus, in liquidations (which are analyzed in detail in the next chapter), both the partnership and the business cease to exist.

Dissolution—Admission of a New Partner

One of the most prevalent changes in the makeup of a partnership is the addition of a new partner. An employee may have worked for years to gain this opportunity, or a prospective partner might offer the new investment capital or business experience necessary for future business success. An individual can gain admittance to a partnership in one of two ways: (1) by purchasing an ownership interest from a current partner or (2) by contributing assets directly to the business.

In recording either type of transaction, the accountant has the option, once again, to retain the book value of all partnership assets and liabilities (as exemplified by the bonus method) or revalue these accounts to their present fair values (the goodwill method). The decision as to a theoretical preference between the bonus and goodwill methods hinges on one single question: *Should the dissolved partnership and the newly formed partnership be viewed as two separate reporting entities?*

If the new partnership is merely an extension of the old, no basis exists for restatement. The transfer of ownership is a change only in a legal sense and has no direct impact on business assets and liabilities. However, if the continuation of the business represents a legitimate transfer of property from one partnership to another, revaluation of all accounts and recognition of goodwill can be justified.

Because both approaches are encountered in practice, this textbook presents each. However, the concerns previously discussed in connection with partnership goodwill still exist: Recognition is not based on historical cost and no objective verification of the capitalized amount can be made. One alternative revaluation approach that attempts to circumvent the problems involved with partnership goodwill has been devised. This hybrid method revalues all partnership assets and liabilities to fair value without making any corresponding recognition of goodwill.

LO8

Prepare journal entries to record the acquisition by a new partner of either all or a portion of a current partner's interest.

Admission through Purchase of a Current Interest

As mentioned, one method of gaining admittance to a partnership is by the purchase of a current interest. One or more partners can choose to sell their portion of the business to an outside party. This type of transaction is most common in operations that rely primarily on monetary capital rather than on the business expertise of the partners.

In making a transfer of ownership, a partner can actually convey only three rights:

1. *The right of co-ownership in the business property.* This right justifies the partner's periodic drawings from the business as well as the distribution settlement paid at liquidation or at the time of a partner's withdrawal.
2. *The right to share in profits and losses as specified in the articles of partnership.*
3. *The right to participate in the management of the business.*

Unless restricted by the articles of partnership, every partner has the power to sell or assign the first two of these rights at any time. Their transfer poses no threat of financial harm to the remaining partners. In contrast, partnership law states that the right to participate in the management of the business can be conveyed only with the consent of all partners. This particular right is considered essential to the future earning power of the enterprise as well as the maintenance of business assets. Therefore, current partners are protected from the intrusion of parties who might be considered detrimental to the management of the company.

As an illustration, assume that Scott, Thompson, and York formed a partnership several years ago. Subsequently, York decides to leave the partnership and offers to sell his interest to Morgan. Although York may transfer the right of property ownership as well as the specified share of future profits and losses, the partnership does not automatically admit Morgan. York legally remains a partner until such time as both Scott and Thompson agree to allow Morgan to participate in the management of the business.

To demonstrate the accounting procedures applicable to the transfer of a partnership interest, assume that the following information is available relating to the partnership of Scott, Thompson, and York:

Partner	Capital Balance	Profit and Loss Ratio
Scott	$ 50,000	20%
Thompson	30,000	50
York.	20,000	30
Total capital	$100,000	

As often happens, the relationship of the capital accounts to one another does not correspond with the partners' profit and loss ratio. Capital balances are historical cost figures. They result from contributions and withdrawals made throughout the life of the business as well as from the allocation of partnership income. Therefore, any correlation between a partner's recorded capital at a particular point in time and the profit and loss percentage would probably be coincidental. Scott, for example, has 50 percent of the current partnership capital ($50,000/$100,000) but is entitled to only a 20 percent allocation of income.

Instead of York selling his interest to Morgan, assume that each of these three partners elects to transfer a 20 percent interest to Morgan for a total payment of $30,000. According to the sales contract, *the money is to be paid directly to the owners.*

One approach to recording this transaction is that, because Morgan's purchase is carried out between the individual parties, the acquisition has no impact on partnership assets and liabilities. Because the business is not involved directly, the transfer of ownership requires a simple capital reclassification without any accompanying revaluation. This approach is similar to the bonus method; only a legal change in ownership is occurring so that revaluation of neither assets or liabilities nor goodwill is appropriate.

Book Value Method

Scott, Capital (20% of capital balance).	10,000	
Thompson, Capital (20%)	6,000	
York, Capital (20%)	4,000	
Morgan, Capital (20% of total).		20,000
To reclassify capital to reflect Morgan's acquisition. Money is paid directly to partners.		

An alternative for recording Morgan's acquisition relies on a different perspective of the new partner's admission. Legally, the partnership of Scott, Thompson, and York is transferring all assets and liabilities to the partnership of Scott, Thompson, York, and Morgan. Therefore, according to the logic underlying the goodwill method, a transaction is occurring between two separate reporting entities, an event that necessitates the complete revaluation of all assets and liabilities.

Because Morgan is paying $30,000 for a 20 percent interest in the partnership, the implied value of the business as a whole is $150,000 ($30,000/20%). However, the book value is only $100,000; thus, a $50,000 upward revaluation is indicated. This adjustment is reflected by restating specific partnership asset and liability accounts to fair value with any remaining balance recorded as goodwill.

Goodwill (Revaluation) Method

Goodwill (or specific accounts).	50,000	
Scott, Capital (20% of goodwill).		10,000
Thompson, Capital (50%).		25,000
York, Capital (30%)		15,000
To recognize goodwill and revaluation of assets and liabilities based on value of business implied by Morgan's purchase price.		

Note that this entry credits the $50,000 revaluation to the original partners based on the profit and loss ratio rather than on capital percentages. Recognition of goodwill (or an increase in the book value of specific accounts) indicates that unrecorded gains have accrued to the business during previous years of operation. Therefore, the equitable treatment is to allocate this increment among the partners according to their profit and loss percentages. After the implied value of the partnership is established, the reclassification of ownership can be recorded based on the new capital balances as follows:

Scott, Capital (20% × new $60,000 capital balance)	12,000	
Thompson, Capital (20% × $55,000)	11,000	
York, Capital (20% × $35,000)	7,000	
Morgan, Capital (20% × $150,000 new total)		30,000
To reclassify capital to reflect Morgan's acquisition. Money is paid directly to partners.		

LO9

Prepare journal entries to record a new partner's admission by a contribution made directly to the partnership.

Admission by a Contribution Made to the Partnership

Entrance into a partnership is not limited solely to the purchase of a current partner's interest. An outsider may be admitted to the ownership by contributing cash or other assets directly to the business rather than to the partners. For example, assume that King and Wilson maintain a partnership and presently report capital balances of $80,000 and $20,000, respectively. According to the articles of partnership, King is entitled to 60 percent of all profits and losses with the remaining 40 percent credited each year to Wilson. By agreement of the partners, Goldman is allowed to enter the partnership for a payment of $20,000 *with this money going into the business.* Based on negotiations that preceded the acquisition, all parties have agreed that Goldman receives an initial 10 percent interest in the net assets of the partnership.

Bonus Credited to Original Partners The bonus (or no revaluation) method maintains the same recorded value for all partnership assets and liabilities despite Goldman's admittance. The capital balance for this new partner is simply set at the appropriate 10 percent level based on the total net assets of the partnership after the payment is recorded. Because $20,000 is invested, total reported capital increases to $120,000. Thus, Goldman's 10 percent interest is computed as $12,000. *The $8,000 difference between the amount contributed and this allotted capital balance is viewed as a bonus.* Because Goldman is willing to accept a capital balance that is less than his investment, this bonus is attributed to the original partners (again based on their profit and loss ratio). As a result of the nature of the transaction, no need exists to recognize goodwill or revalue any of the assets or liabilities.

Cash	20,000	
Goldman, Capital (10% of total capital)		12,000
King, Capital (60% of bonus)		4,800
Wilson, Capital (40% of bonus)		3,200
To record Goldman's entrance into partnership with $8,000 extra payment recorded as a bonus to the original partners.		

Goodwill Credited to Original Partners The goodwill method views Goldman's payment as evidence that the partnership as a whole possesses an actual value of $200,000 ($20,000/10%). Because, even with the new partner's investment, only $120,000 in net assets is reported, a valuation adjustment of $80,000 is implied.[12] Over the previous years,

[12] In this example, because $20,000 is invested in the business, total capital to be used in the goodwill computation has increased to $120,000. If, as in the previous illustration, payment had been made directly to the partners, the original capital of $100,000 is retained in determining goodwill.

unrecorded gains have apparently accrued to the business. This $80,000 figure might reflect the need to revalue specific accounts such as inventory or equipment, although the entire amount, or some portion of it, may simply be recorded as goodwill.

Goodwill (or specific accounts)	80,000	
King, Capital (60% of goodwill)		48,000
Wilson, Capital (40%)		32,000
To recognize goodwill based on Goldman's purchase price.		
Cash	20,000	
Goldman, Capital		20,000
To record Goldman's admission into partnership.		

Comparison of Bonus Method and Goodwill Method Completely different capital balances as well as asset and liability figures result from these two approaches. In both cases, however, the new partner is credited with the appropriate 10 percent of total partnership capital.

	Bonus Method	Goodwill Method
Assets less liabilities (as reported)	$100,000	$100,000
Goldman's contribution	20,000	20,000
Goodwill	-0-	80,000
Total	$120,000	$200,000
Goldman's capital	$ 12,000	$ 20,000

Because Goldman contributed an amount more than 10 percent of the partnership's resulting book value, this business is perceived as being worth more than the recorded accounts indicate. Therefore, the bonus in the first instance and the goodwill in the second were both assumed as accruing to the two original partners. Such a presumption is not unusual in an established business, especially if profitable operations have developed over a number of years.

Hybrid Method of Recording Admission of New Partner One other approach to Goldman's admission can be devised. Assume that the assets and liabilities of the King and Wilson partnership have a book value of $100,000 as stated earlier. Also assume that a piece of land held by the business is actually worth $30,000 more than its currently recorded book value. Thus, the identifiable assets of the partnership are worth $130,000. Goldman pays $20,000 for a 10 percent interest.

In this approach, the identifiable assets (such as land) are revalued but no goodwill is recognized.

Land	30,000	
King, Capital (60% of revaluation)		18,000
Wilson, Capital (40%)		12,000
To record current fair value of land in preparation for admission of new partner.		

The admission of Goldman and the payment of $20,000 bring the total capital balance to $150,000. Because Goldman is acquiring a 10 percent interest, a capital balance of $15,000 is recorded. The extra $5,000 payment ($20,000 − $15,000) is attributed as a bonus to the original partners. In this way, asset revaluation and a capital bonus are both used to align the accounts.

Cash	20,000	
Goldman, Capital (10% of total capital)		15,000
King, Capital (60% of bonus)		3,000
Wilson, Capital (40% of bonus)		2,000
To record entrance of Goldman into partnership and bonus assigned to original partners.		

Bonus or Goodwill Credited to New Partner As previously discussed, Goldman also may be contributing some attribute other than tangible assets to this partnership. Therefore, the articles of partnership may be written to credit the new partner, rather than the original partners, with either a bonus or goodwill. Because of an excellent professional reputation, valuable business contacts, or myriad other possible factors, Goldman might be able to negotiate a beginning capital balance in excess of the $20,000 cash contribution. This same circumstance may also result if the business is desperate for new capital and is willing to offer favorable terms as an enticement to the potential partner.

To illustrate, assume that Goldman receives a 20 percent interest in the partnership (rather than the originally stated 10 percent) in exchange for the $20,000 cash investment. The specific rationale for the higher ownership percentage need not be identified.

The bonus method sets Goldman's initial capital at $24,000 (20 percent of the $120,000 book value). To achieve this balance, a capital bonus of $4,000 must be credited to Goldman and taken from the present partners:

Cash	20,000	
King, Capital (60% of bonus).	2,400	
Wilson, Capital (40% of bonus)	1,600	
Goldman, Capital		24,000
To record Goldman's entrance into partnership with reduced payment reported as a bonus from original partners.		

If goodwill rather than a bonus is attributed to the *entering partner,* a mathematical problem arises in determining the implicit value of the business as a whole. In the current illustration, Goldman paid $20,000 for a 20 percent interest. Therefore, the value of the company is calculated as only $100,000 ($20,000/20%), a figure that is less than the $120,000 in net assets reported after the new contribution. Negative goodwill appears to exist. One possibility is that individual partnership assets are overvalued and require reduction. As an alternative, the cash contribution might not be an accurate representation of the new partner's investment. Goldman could be bringing an intangible contribution (goodwill) to the business along with the $20,000. This additional amount must be determined algebraically:

$$\text{Goldman's capital} = 20\% \text{ of partnership capital}$$

Therefore:

$$\$20{,}000 + \text{Goodwill} = 0.20\ (\$100{,}000 + \$20{,}000 + \text{Goodwill})$$
$$\$20{,}000 + \text{Goodwill} = \$20{,}000 + \$4{,}000 + 0.20\ \text{Goodwill}$$
$$0.80\ \text{Goodwill} = \$4{,}000$$
$$\text{Goodwill} = \$5{,}000$$

If the partners determine that Goldman is, indeed, making an intangible contribution (a particular skill, for example, or a loyal clientele), Goldman should be credited with a $25,000 capital investment: $20,000 cash and $5,000 goodwill. When added to the original $100,000 in net assets reported by the partnership, this contribution raises the total capital for the business to $125,000. As the articles of partnership specified, Goldman's interest now represents a 20 percent share of the partnership ($25,000/$125,000).

Recognizing $5,000 in goodwill has established the proper relationship between the new partner and the partnership. Therefore, the following journal entry reflects this transaction:

Cash	20,000	
Goodwill	5,000	
Goldman, Capital		25,000
To record Goldman's entrance into partnership with goodwill attributed to this new partner.		

LO10

Prepare journal entries to record the withdrawal of a current partner.

Dissolution—Withdrawal of a Partner

Admission of a new partner is not the only method by which a partnership can undergo a change in composition. Over the life of the business, partners might leave the organization. Death or retirement can occur, or a partner may simply elect to withdraw from the partnership. The articles of partnership also can allow for the expulsion of a partner under certain conditions. Again, any change in membership legally dissolves the partnership, although its operations usually continue uninterrupted under the remaining partners' ownership.

Regardless of the reason for dissolution, some method of establishing an equitable settlement of the withdrawing partner's interest in the business is necessary. Often, the partner (or the partner's estate) may simply sell the interest to an outside party, with approval, or to one or more of the remaining partners. As an alternative, the business can distribute cash or other assets as a means of settling a partner's right of co-ownership. Consequently, many partnerships hold life insurance policies solely to provide adequate cash to liquidate a partner's interest upon death.

Whether death or some other reason caused the withdrawal, a final distribution will not necessarily equal the book value of the partner's capital account. A capital balance is only a recording of historical transactions and rarely represents the true value inherent in a business. Instead, payment is frequently based on the value of the partner's interest as ascertained by either negotiation or appraisal. Because a settlement determination can be derived in many ways, the articles of partnership should contain exact provisions regulating this procedure.

The withdrawal of an individual partner and the resulting distribution of partnership property can, as before, be accounted for by either the bonus (no revaluation) method or the goodwill (revaluation) method. Again, a hybrid option is also available.

As in earlier illustrations, if a bonus is recorded, the amount can be attributed to either of the parties involved: the withdrawing partner or the remaining partners. Conversely, any revaluation of partnership property (as well as the establishment of a goodwill balance) is allocated among all partners to recognize possible unrecorded gains. The hybrid approach restates assets and liabilities to fair value but does not record goodwill. This last alternative reflects the legal change in ownership but avoids the theoretical problems associated with partnership goodwill.

Accounting for the Withdrawal of a Partner—Illustration

To demonstrate the various approaches that can be taken to account for a partner's withdrawal, assume that the partnership of Duncan, Smith, and Windsor has existed for a number of years. At the present time, the partners have the following capital balances as well as the indicated profit and loss percentages:

Partner	Capital Balance	Profit and Loss Ratio
Duncan	$ 70,000	50%
Smith	20,000	30
Windsor	10,000	20
Total capital	$100,000	

Windsor decides to withdraw from the partnership, but Duncan and Smith plan to continue operating the business. As per the original partnership agreement, a final settlement distribution for any withdrawing partner is computed based on the following specified provisions:

1. An independent expert will appraise the business to determine its estimated fair value.
2. Any individual who leaves the partnership will receive cash or other assets equal to that partner's current capital balance after including an appropriate share of any adjustment indicated by the previous valuation. The allocation of unrecorded gains and losses is based on the normal profit and loss ratio.

Following Windsor's decision to withdraw from the partnership, its property is immediately appraised. Total fair value is estimated at $180,000, a figure $80,000 in excess of book value. According to this valuation, land held by the partnership is currently worth $50,000 more than its original cost. In addition, $30,000 in goodwill is attributed to the partnership based on its value as a going concern. *Therefore, Windsor receives $26,000 on leaving the partnership: the original $10,000 capital balance plus a 20 percent share of this $80,000 increment.* The amount of payment is not in dispute, but the method of recording the withdrawal is.

Bonus Method Applied

If the partnership used the bonus method to record this transaction, the extra $16,000 paid to Windsor is simply assigned as a decrease in the remaining partners' capital accounts. Historically, Duncan and Smith have been credited with 50 percent and 30 percent of all profits and losses, respectively. This same relative ratio is used now to allocate the reduction between these two remaining partners on a ⅝ and ⅜ basis:

Bonus Method		
Windsor, Capital (to remove account balance)	10,000	
Duncan, Capital (⅝ of excess distribution)	10,000	
Smith, Capital (⅜ of excess distribution)	6,000	
Cash		26,000
To record Windsor's withdrawal with $16,000 excess distribution taken from remaining partners.		

Goodwill Method Applied

This same transaction can also be accounted for by means of the goodwill (or revaluation) approach. The appraisal indicates that land is undervalued on the partnership's records by $50,000 and that goodwill of $30,000 has apparently accrued to the business over the years. The first of the following entries recognizes these valuations. This adjustment properly equates Windsor's capital balance with the $26,000 cash amount to be distributed. Windsor's equity balance is merely removed in the second entry at the time of payment.

Goodwill Method		
Land	50,000	
Goodwill	30,000	
Duncan, Capital (50%)		40,000
Smith, Capital (30%)		24,000
Windsor, Capital (20%)		16,000
To recognize land value and goodwill as a preliminary step to Windsor's withdrawal.		
Windsor, Capital (to remove account balance)	26,000	
Cash		26,000
To distribute cash to Windsor in settlement of partnership interest.		

The implied value of a partnership as a whole cannot be determined directly from the amount distributed to a withdrawing partner. For example, paying Windsor $26,000 did not indicate that total capital should be $130,000 ($26,000/20%). This computation is appropriate only when (1) a new partner is admitted or (2) the percentage of capital is the same as the profit and loss ratio. Here, an outside valuation of the business indicated that it was worth $80,000 more than book value. As a 20 percent owner, Windsor was entitled to $16,000 of that amount, raising the partner's capital account from $10,000 to $26,000, the amount of the final payment.

Hybrid Method Applied

As indicated previously, a hybrid approach also can be adopted to record a partner's withdrawal. It also recognizes asset and liability revaluations but ignores goodwill. A bonus must then be recorded to reconcile the partner's adjusted capital balance with the final distribution.

The following journal entry, for example, does not record goodwill. However, the book value of the land is increased by $50,000 in recognition of present worth. This adjustment increases Windsor's capital balance to $20,000, a figure that is still less than the $26,000 distribution. The $6,000 difference is recorded as a bonus taken from the remaining two partners according to their relative profit and loss ratio.

Hybrid Method		
Land	50,000	
Duncan, Capital (50%)		25,000
Smith, Capital (30%)		15,000
Windsor, Capital (20%)		10,000
To adjust Land account to fair value as a preliminary step in Windsor's withdrawal.		
Windsor, Capital (to remove account balance)	20,000	
Duncan, Capital (⅝ of bonus)	3,750	
Smith, Capital (⅜ of bonus)	2,250	
Cash		26,000
To record final distribution to Windsor with $6,000 bonus taken from remaining partners.		

Summary

1. A partnership is defined as "an association of two or more persons to carry on a business as co-owners for profit." This form of business organization exists throughout the U.S. economy ranging in size from small, part-time operations to international enterprises. The partnership format is popular for many reasons, including the ease of creation and the avoidance of the double taxation that is inherent in corporate ownership. However, the unlimited liability incurred by each general partner normally restricts the growth potential of most partnerships. Thus, although the number of partnerships in the United States is large, the size of each tends to be small.
2. Over the years, a number of different types of organizations have been developed to take advantage of both the single taxation of partnerships and the limited liability afforded to corporate stockholders. Such legal forms include S corporations, limited partnerships, limited liability partnerships, and limited liability companies.
3. The unique elements of partnership accounting are found primarily in the capital accounts accumulated for each partner. The basis for recording these balances is the articles of partnership, a document that should be established as a prerequisite to the formation of any partnership. One of the principal provisions of this agreement is each partner's initial investment. Noncash contributions such as inventory or land are entered into the partnership's accounting records at fair value.
4. In forming a partnership, the partners' contributions need not be limited to tangible assets. A particular line of expertise possessed by a partner and an established clientele are attributes that can have a significant value to a partnership. Two methods of recording this type

of investment are found in practice. The bonus method recognizes only identifiable assets. The capital accounts are then aligned to indicate the balances negotiated by the partners. According to the goodwill approach, all contributions (even those of a nebulous nature such as expertise) are valued and recorded, often as goodwill.

5. Another accounting issue to be resolved in forming a partnership is the allocation of annual net income. In closing out the revenue and expense accounts at the end of each period, some assignment must be made to the individual capital balances. Although an equal division can be used to allocate any profit or loss, partners frequently devise unique plans in an attempt to be equitable. Such factors as time worked, expertise, and invested capital should be considered in creating an allocation procedure.
6. Over time, changes occur in the makeup of a partnership because of death or retirement or because of the admission of new partners. Such changes dissolve the existing partnership, although the business frequently continues uninterrupted through a newly formed partnership. If, for example, a new partner is admitted by the acquisition of a present interest, the capital balances can simply be reclassified to reflect the change in ownership. As an alternative, the purchase price may be viewed as evidence of the underlying value of the organization as a whole. Based on this calculation, asset and liability balances are adjusted to fair value, and any residual goodwill is recognized.
7. Admission into an existing partnership also can be achieved by a direct capital contribution from the new partner. Because of the parties' negotiations, the amount invested will not always agree with the beginning capital balance attributed to the new partner. The bonus method resolves this conflict by simply reclassifying the various capital accounts to align the balances with specified totals and percentages. No revaluation is carried out under this approach. Conversely, according to the goodwill method, all asset and liability accounts are adjusted first to fair value. The price the new partner paid is used to compute an implied value for the partnership, and any excess over fair value is recorded as goodwill.
8. The composition of a partnership also can undergo changes because of the death or retirement of a partner. Individuals may decide to withdraw. Such changes legally dissolve the partnership, although business operations frequently continue under the remaining partners' ownership. In compensating the departing partner, the final asset distribution may differ from the ending capital balance. This disparity can, again, be accounted for by means of the bonus method, which adjusts the remaining capital accounts to absorb the bonus. The goodwill approach by which all assets and liabilities are restated to fair value with any goodwill being recognized also can be applied. Finally, a hybrid method revalues the assets and liabilities but ignores goodwill. Under this last approach, any amount paid to the departing partner in excess of the newly adjusted capital balance is accounted for by means of the bonus method.

Comprehensive Illustration

Problem

(*Estimated Time: 30 to 55 Minutes*) Heyman and Mullins begin a partnership on January 1, 2012. Heyman invests $40,000 cash and inventory costing $15,000 but with a current appraised value of only $12,000. Mullins contributes a building with a $40,000 book value and a $48,000 fair value. The partnership also accepts responsibility for a $10,000 note payable owed in connection with this building.

The partners agree to begin operations with equal capital balances. The articles of partnership also provide that at each year-end, profits and losses are allocated as follows:

1. For managing the business, Heyman is credited with a bonus of 10 percent of partnership income after subtracting the bonus. No bonus is accrued if the partnership records a loss.
2. Both partners are entitled to interest equal to 10 percent of the average monthly capital balance for the year without regard for the income or drawings of that year.
3. Any remaining profit or loss is divided 60 percent to Heyman and 40 percent to Mullins.
4. Each partner is allowed to withdraw $800 per month in cash from the business.

On October 1, 2012, Heyman invested an additional $12,000 cash in the business. For 2012, the partnership reported income of $33,000.

Lewis, an employee, is allowed to join the partnership on January 1, 2013. The new partner invests $66,000 directly into the business for a one-third interest in the partnership property. The revised partnership agreement still allows for both the bonus to Heyman and the 10 percent interest, but all remaining profits and losses are now split 40 percent each to Heyman and Lewis with the remaining 20 percent to Mullins. Lewis is also entitled to $800 per month in drawings.

Mullins chooses to withdraw from the partnership a few years later. After negotiations, all parties agree that Mullins should be paid a $90,000 settlement. The capital balances on that date were as follows:

Heyman, capital	$88,000
Mullins, capital	78,000
Lewis, capital	72,000

Required

a. Assuming that this partnership uses the bonus method exclusively, make all necessary journal entries. Entries for the monthly drawings of the partners are not required.

b. Assuming that this partnership uses the goodwill method exclusively, make all necessary journal entries. Again, entries for the monthly drawings are not required.

Solution

a. **Bonus Method**

2012

Jan. 1 All contributed property is recorded at fair value. Under the bonus method, total capital is then divided as specified between the partners.

Cash	40,000	
Inventory	12,000	
Building	48,000	
Note Payable		10,000
Heyman, Capital (50%)		45,000
Mullins, Capital (50%)		45,000

To record initial contributions to partnership along with equal capital balances.

Oct. 1

Cash	12,000	
Heyman, Capital		12,000

To record additional investment by partner.

Dec. 31 Both the bonus assigned to Heyman and the interest accrual must be computed as preliminary steps in the income allocation process. Because the bonus is based on income after subtracting the bonus, the amount must be calculated algebraically:

Bonus = 0.10 ($33,000 − Bonus)
Bonus = $3,300 − 0.10 Bonus
1.10 Bonus = $3,300
Bonus = $3,000

According to the articles of partnership, the interest allocation is based on a monthly average figure. Mullins's capital balance of $45,000 did not change during the year; therefore $4,500 (10%) is the appropriate interest accrual for that partner. However, because of the October 1, 2012, contribution, Heyman's interest must be determined as follows:

Beginning balance:	$45,000 × 9 months =	$405,000
New balance:	$57,000 × 3 months =	171,000
		576,000
		× 1/12
Monthly average—capital balance		48,000
Interest rate		× 10%
Interest credited to Heyman		$ 4,800

Following the bonus and interest computations, the $33,000 income earned by the business is allocated according to the previously specified arrangement:

	Heyman	Mullins	Totals
Bonus	$ 3,000	–0–	$ 3,000
Interest	4,800	$ 4,500	9,300
Remaining income:			
$33,000			
(3,000)			
(9,300)			
$20,700	12,420 (60%)	8,280 (40%)	20,700
Income allocation	$20,220	$12,780	$33,000

The partnership's closing entries for the year would be recorded as follows:

Heyman, Capital	9,600	
Mullins, Capital	9,600	
Heyman, Drawing		9,600
Mullins, Drawing		9,600
To close out $800 per month drawing accounts for the year.		
Income Summary	33,000	
Heyman, Capital		20,220
Mullins, Capital		12,780
To close out profit for year to capital accounts as computed above.		

At the end of this initial year of operation, the partners' capital accounts hold these balances:

	Heyman	Mullins	Totals
Beginning balance	$45,000	$45,000	$ 90,000
Additional investment.	12,000	–0–	12,000
Drawing	(9,600)	(9,600)	(19,200)
Net income (above)	20,220	12,780	33,000
Total capital	$67,620	$48,180	$115,800

2013

Jan. 1 Lewis contributed $66,000 to the business for a one-third interest in the partnership property. Combined with the $115,800 balance previously computed, the partnership now has total capital of $181,800. Because no revaluation is recorded under the bonus approach, a one-third interest in the partnership equals $60,600 ($181,800 × ⅓). Lewis has invested $5,400 in excess of this amount, a balance viewed as a bonus accruing to the original partners:

Cash.	66,000	
Lewis, Capital		60,600
Heyman, Capital (60% of bonus)		3,240
Mullins, Capital (40% of bonus)		2,160
To record Lewis's entrance into partnership with bonus to original partners.		

Several years later The final event in this illustration is Mullins's withdrawal from the partnership. Although this partner's capital balance reports only $78,000, the final distribution is set at $90,000. The extra $12,000 payment represents a bonus assigned to Mullins, an amount that decreases the capital of the remaining two partners. Because Heyman and Lewis have previously accrued equal 40 percent shares of all profits and losses, the reduction is split evenly between the two.

Mullins, Capital	78,000	
Heyman, Capital (½ of bonus payment)	6,000	
Lewis, Capital (½ of bonus payment)	6,000	
Cash		90,000
To record withdrawal of Mullins with a bonus from remaining partners.		

b. **Goodwill Method**

2012

Jan. 1 The fair value of Heyman's contribution is $52,000, whereas Mullins is investing only a net $38,000 (the value of the building less the accompanying debt). Because the capital accounts are initially to be equal, Mullins is presumed to be contributing goodwill of $14,000.

	Debit	Credit
Cash	40,000	
Inventory	12,000	
Building	48,000	
Goodwill	14,000	
Note payable		10,000
Heyman, Capital		52,000
Mullins, Capital		52,000
Creation of partnership with goodwill attributed to Mullins.		

Oct. 1

	Debit	Credit
Cash	12,000	
Heyman, Capital		12,000
To record additional contribution by partner.		

Dec. 31 Although Heyman's bonus is still $3,000 as derived in requirement (*a*), the interest accruals must be recalculated because the capital balances are different. Mullins's capital for the entire year was $52,000; thus, interest of $5,200 (10%) is appropriate. However, Heyman's balance changed during the year so that a monthly average must be determined as a basis for computing interest:

Beginning balance:	$52,000 × 9 months =	$468,000
New balance:	$64,000 × 3 months =	192,000
		660,000
		× 1/12
Monthly average—capital balance		55,000
Interest rate		× 10%
Interest credited to Heyman		$5,500

The $33,000 partnership income is allocated as follows:

	Heyman	Mullins	Totals
Bonus (above)	$ 3,000	–0–	$ 3,000
Interest (above)	5,500	$ 5,200	10,700
Remaining income:			
$33,000			
(3,000)			
(10,700)			
$19,300	11,580 (60%)	7,720 (40%)	19,300
Income allocation	$20,080	$12,920	$33,000

The closing entries made under the goodwill approach would be as follows:

	Debit	Credit
Heyman, Capital	9,600	
Mullins, Capital	9,600	
Heyman, Drawing		9,600
Mullins, Drawing		9,600
To close out drawing accounts for the year.		
Income Summary	33,000	
Heyman, Capital		20,080
Mullins, Capital		12,920
To assign profits per allocation schedule.		

After the closing process, the capital balances are composed of the following items:

	Heyman	Mullins	Totals
Beginning balance	$52,000	$52,000	$104,000
Additional investment	12,000	–0–	12,000
Drawing	(9,600)	(9,600)	(19,200)
Net income	20,080	12,920	33,000
Total capital	$74,480	$55,320	$129,800

2013

Jan. 1 Lewis's investment of $66,000 for a one-third interest in the partnership property implies that the business as a whole is worth $198,000 ($66,000 divided by ⅓). After adding Lewis's contribution to the present capital balance of $129,800, the business reports total net assets of only $195,800. Thus, a $2,200 increase in value ($198,000 − $195,800) is indicated and will be recognized at this time. Under the assumption that all partnership assets and liabilities are valued appropriately, this entire balance is attributed to goodwill.

Goodwill	2,200	
Heyman, Capital (60%).		1,320
Mullins, Capital (40%).		880
To recognize goodwill based on Lewis's acquisition price.		
Cash.	66,000	
Lewis, Capital		66,000
To admit Lewis to the partnership.		

Several years later To conclude this illustration, Mullins's withdrawal must be recorded. This partner is to receive a distribution that is $12,000 more than the corresponding capital balance of $78,000. Because Mullins is entitled to a 20 percent share of profits and losses, the additional $12,000 payment indicates that the partnership as a whole is undervalued by $60,000 ($12,000/20%). Only in that circumstance would the extra payment to Mullins be justified. Therefore, once again, goodwill is recognized and is followed by the final distribution.

Goodwill	60,000	
Heyman, Capital (40%).		24,000
Mullins, Capital (20%)		12,000
Lewis, Capital (40%).		24,000
Recognition of goodwill based on withdrawal amount paid to Mullins.		
Mullins, Capital	90,000	
Cash		90,000
To distribute money to partner.		

Questions

1. What are the advantages of operating a business as a partnership rather than as a corporation? What are the disadvantages?
2. How does partnership accounting differ from corporate accounting?
3. What information do the capital accounts found in partnership accounting convey?
4. Describe the differences between a Subchapter S corporation and a Subchapter C corporation.
5. A company is being created and the owners are trying to decide whether to form a general partnership, a limited liability partnership, or a limited liability company. What are the advantages and disadvantages of each of these legal forms?
6. What is an articles of partnership agreement, and what information should this document contain?
7. What valuation should be recorded for noncash assets transferred to a partnership by one of the partners?
8. If a partner is contributing attributes to a partnership such as an established clientele or a particular expertise, what two methods can be used to record the contribution? Describe each method.
9. What is the purpose of a drawing account in a partnership's financial records?

10. At what point in the accounting process does the allocation of partnership income become significant?
11. What provisions in a partnership agreement can be used to establish an equitable allocation of income among all partners?
12. If no agreement exists in a partnership as to the allocation of income, what method is appropriate?
13. What is a partnership dissolution? Does dissolution automatically necessitate the cessation of business and the liquidation of partnership assets?
14. By what methods can a new partner gain admittance into a partnership?
15. When a partner sells an ownership interest in a partnership, what rights are conveyed to the new owner?
16. A new partner enters a partnership and goodwill is calculated and credited to the original partners. How is the specific amount of goodwill assigned to these partners?
17. Under what circumstance might goodwill be allocated to a new partner entering a partnership?
18. When a partner withdraws from a partnership, why is the final distribution often based on the appraised value of the business rather than on the book value of the capital account balance?

Problems

LO1

1. Which of the following is *not* a reason for the popularity of partnerships as a legal form for businesses?
   a. Partnerships may be formed merely by an oral agreement.
   b. Partnerships can more easily generate significant amounts of capital.
   c. Partnerships avoid the double taxation of income that is found in corporations.
   d. In some cases, losses may be used to offset gains for tax purposes.

LO1

2. How does partnership accounting differ from corporate accounting?
   a. The matching principle is not considered appropriate for partnership accounting.
   b. Revenues are recognized at a different time by a partnership than is appropriate for a corporation.
   c. Individual capital accounts replace the contributed capital and retained earnings balances found in corporate accounting.
   d. Partnerships report all assets at fair value as of the latest balance sheet date.

LO2

3. Which of the following best describes the articles of partnership agreement?
   a. The purpose of the partnership and partners' rights and responsibilities are required elements of the articles of partnership.
   b. The articles of partnership are a legal covenant and must be expressed in writing to be valid.
   c. The articles of partnership are an agreement that limits partners' liability to partnership assets.
   d. The articles of partnership are a legal covenant that may be expressed orally or in writing, and forms the central governance for a partnership's operations.

LO9

4. Pat, Jean Lou, and Diane are partners with capital balances of $50,000, $30,000, and $20,000, respectively. These three partners share profits and losses equally. For an investment of $50,000 cash (paid to the business), MaryAnn will be admitted as a partner with a one-fourth interest in capital and profits. Based on this information, which of the following best justifies the amount of MaryAnn's investment?
   a. MaryAnn will receive a bonus from the other partners upon her admission to the partnership.
   b. Assets of the partnership were overvalued immediately prior to MaryAnn's investment.
   c. The book value of the partnership's net assets was less than the fair value immediately prior to MaryAnn's investment.
   d. MaryAnn is apparently bringing goodwill into the partnership, and her capital account will be credited for the appropriate amount.

LO9

5. A partnership has the following capital balances:

Albert (50% of gains and losses)	$ 80,000
Barrymore (20%)	60,000
Candroth (30%)	140,000

Danville is going to invest $70,000 into the business to acquire a 30 percent ownership interest. Goodwill is to be recorded. What will be Danville's beginning capital balance?

a. $70,000.

b. $90,000.

c. $105,000.

d. $120,000.

LO8

6. A partnership has the following capital balances:

Elgin (40% of gains and losses)	$100,000
Jethro (30%)	200,000
Foy (30%)	300,000

Oscar is going to pay a total of $200,000 to these three partners to acquire a 25 percent ownership interest from each. Goodwill is to be recorded. What is Jethro's capital balance after the transaction?

a. $150,000.

b. $175,000.

c. $195,000.

d. $200,000.

LO9

7. The capital balance for Bolcar is $110,000 and for Neary is $40,000. These two partners share profits and losses 70 percent (Bolcar) and 30 percent (Neary). Kansas invests $50,000 in cash into the partnership for a 30 percent ownership. The bonus method will be used. What is Neary's capital balance after Kansas's investment?

a. $35,000.

b. $37,000.

c. $40,000.

d. $43,000.

LO9

8. Bishop has a capital balance of $120,000 in a local partnership, and Cotton has a $90,000 balance. These two partners share profits and losses by a ratio of 60 percent to Bishop and 40 percent to Cotton. Lovett invests $60,000 in cash in the partnership for a 20 percent ownership. The goodwill method will be used. What is Cotton's capital balance after this new investment?

a. $99,600.

b. $102,000.

c. $112,000.

d. $126,000.

LO9

9. The capital balance for Messalina is $210,000 and for Romulus is $140,000. These two partners share profits and losses 60 percent (Messalina) and 40 percent (Romulus). Claudius invests $100,000 in cash in the partnership for a 20 percent ownership. The bonus method will be used. What are the capital balances for Messalina, Romulus, and Claudius after this investment is recorded?

a. $216,000, $144,000, $90,000.

b. $218,000, $142,000, $88,000.

c. $222,000, $148,000, $80,000.

d. $240,000, $160,000, $100,000.

LO6

10. A partnership begins its first year with the following capital balances:

Arthur, Capital	$ 60,000
Baxter, Capital	80,000
Cartwright, Capital	100,000

The articles of partnership stipulate that profits and losses be assigned in the following manner:

- Each partner is allocated interest equal to 10 percent of the beginning capital balance.
- Baxter is allocated compensation of $20,000 per year.
- Any remaining profits and losses are allocated on a 3:3:4 basis, respectively.
- Each partner is allowed to withdraw up to $5,000 cash per year.

Assuming that the net income is $50,000 and that each partner withdraws the maximum amount allowed, what is the balance in Cartwright's capital account at the end of that year?

a. $105,800.

b. $106,200.

c. $106,900.

d. $107,400.

LO4, LO5, LO6

11. A partnership begins its first year of operations with the following capital balances:

Winston, Capital	$110,000
Durham, Capital	80,000
Salem, Capital	110,000

According to the articles of partnership, all profits will be assigned as follows:

- Winston will be awarded an annual salary of $20,000 with $10,000 assigned to Salem.
- The partners will be attributed interest equal to 10 percent of the capital balance as of the first day of the year.
- The remainder will be assigned on a 5:2:3 basis, respectively.
- Each partner is allowed to withdraw up to $10,000 per year.

The net loss for the first year of operations is $20,000 and net income for the subsequent year is $40,000. Each partner withdraws the maximum amount from the business each period. What is the balance in Winston's capital account at the end of the second year?

a. $102,600.

b. $104,400.

c. $108,600.

d. $109,200.

LO10

12. A partnership has the following capital balances:

Allen, Capital	$60,000
Burns, Capital	30,000
Costello, Capital	90,000

Profits and losses are split as follows: Allen (20%), Burns (30%), and Costello (50%). Costello wants to leave the partnership and is paid $100,000 from the business based on provisions in the articles of partnership. If the partnership uses the bonus method, what is the balance of Burns's capital account after Costello withdraws?

a. $24,000.

b. $27,000.

c. $33,000.

d. $36,000.

Problems 13 and 14 are *independent* problems based on the following scenario:

At year-end, the Circle City partnership has the following capital balances:

Manning, Capital	$130,000
Gonzalez, Capital	110,000
Clark, Capital	80,000
Freeney, Capital	70,000

Profits and losses are split on a 3:3:2:2 basis, respectively. Clark decides to leave the partnership and is paid $90,000 from the business based on the original contractual agreement.

LO10

13. Using the goodwill method, what is Manning's capital balance after Clark withdraws?

a. $133,000.

b. $137,500.

c. $140,000.

d. $145,000.

LO10

14. If instead the partnership uses the bonus method, what is the balance of Manning's capital account after Clark withdraws?
    a. $100,000.
    b. $126,250.
    c. $130,000.
    d. $133,750.

Problems 15 and 16 are *independent* problems based on the following capital account balances:

William (40% of gains and losses).	$220,000
Jennings (40%).	160,000
Bryan (20%)	110,000

LO8

15. Darrow invests $270,000 in cash for a 30 percent ownership interest. The money goes to the original partners. Goodwill is to be recorded. How much goodwill should be recognized, and what is Darrow's beginning capital balance?
    a. $410,000 and $270,000.
    b. $140,000 and $270,000.
    c. $140,000 and $189,000.
    d. $410,000 and $189,000.

LO9

16. Darrow invests $250,000 in cash for a 30 percent ownership interest. The money goes to the business. No goodwill or other revaluation is to be recorded. After the transaction, what is Jennings's capital balance?
    a. $160,000.
    b. $168,000.
    c. $170,200.
    d. $171,200.

LO9

17. Lear is to become a partner in the WS partnership by paying $80,000 in cash to the business. At present, the capital balance for Hamlet is $70,000 and for MacBeth is $40,000. Hamlet and MacBeth share profits on a 7:3 basis. Lear is acquiring 40 percent of the new partnership.
    a. If the goodwill method is applied, what will the three capital balances be following the payment by Lear?
    b. If the bonus method is applied, what will the three capital balances be following the payment by Lear?

LO9

18. The Distance Plus partnership has the following capital balances at the beginning of the current year:

Tiger (50% of profits and losses).	$85,000
Phil (30%).	60,000
Ernie (20%)	55,000

Each of the following questions should be viewed independently.
    a. If Sergio invests $100,000 in cash in the business for a 25 percent interest, what journal entry is recorded? Assume that the bonus method is used.
    b. If Sergio invests $60,000 in cash in the business for a 25 percent interest, what journal entry is recorded? Assume that the bonus method is used.
    c. If Sergio invests $72,000 in cash in the business for a 25 percent interest, what journal entry is recorded? Assume that the goodwill method is used.

LO9

19. A partnership has the following account balances: Cash $50,000; Other Assets $600,000; Liabilities $240,000; Nixon, Capital (50% of profits and losses) $200,000; Hoover, Capital (20%) $120,000; and Polk, Capital (30%) $90,000. Each of the following questions should be viewed as an independent situation:
    a. Grant invests $80,000 in the partnership for an 18 percent capital interest. Goodwill is to be recognized. What are the capital accounts thereafter?
    b. Grant invests $100,000 in the partnership to get a 20 percent capital balance. Goodwill is not to be recorded. What are the capital accounts thereafter?

LO9

20. The C-P partnership has the following capital account balances on January 1, 2013:

Com, Capital	$150,000
Pack, Capital.	110,000

Com is allocated 60 percent of all profits and losses with the remaining 40 percent assigned to Pack after interest of 10 percent is given to each partner based on beginning capital balances.

On January 2, 2013, Hal invests $76,000 cash for a 20 percent interest in the partnership. This transaction is recorded by the goodwill method. After this transaction, 10 percent interest is still to go to each partner. Profits and losses will then be split as follows: Com (50%), Pack (30%), and Hal (20%). In 2013, the partnership reports a net income of $36,000.

a. Prepare the journal entry to record Hal's entrance into the partnership on January 2, 2013.

b. Determine the allocation of income at the end of 2013.

LO6

21. The partnership agreement of Jones, King, and Lane provides for the annual allocation of the business's profit or loss in the following sequence:

- Jones, the managing partner, receives a bonus equal to 20 percent of the business's profit.
- Each partner receives 15 percent interest on average capital investment.
- Any residual profit or loss is divided equally.

The average capital investments for 2013 were as follows:

Jones	$100,000
King	200,000
Lane	300,000

How much of the $90,000 partnership profit for 2013 should be assigned to each partner?

LO4, LO5, LO6

22. Purkerson, Smith, and Traynor have operated a bookstore for a number of years as a partnership. At the beginning of 2013, capital balances were as follows:

Purkerson	$60,000
Smith	40,000
Traynor	20,000

Due to a cash shortage, Purkerson invests an additional $8,000 in the business on April 1, 2013.

Each partner is allowed to withdraw $1,000 cash each month.

The partners have used the same method of allocating profits and losses since the business's inception:

- Each partner is given the following compensation allowance for work done in the business: Purkerson, $18,000; Smith, $25,000; and Traynor, $8,000.
- Each partner is credited with interest equal to 10 percent of the average monthly capital balance for the year without regard for normal drawings.
- Any remaining profit or loss is allocated 4:2:4 to Purkerson, Smith, and Traynor, respectively. The net income for 2013 is $23,600. Each partner withdraws the allotted amount each month.

What are the ending capital balances for 2013?

LO4, LO5, LO6

23. On January 1, 2012, the dental partnership of Left, Center, and Right was formed when the partners contributed $20,000, $60,000, and $50,000, respectively. Over the next three years, the business reported net income and (loss) as follows:

2012.	$(30,000)
2013.	20,000
2014.	40,000

During this period, each partner withdrew cash of $10,000 per year. Right invested an additional $12,000 in cash on February 9, 2013.

At the time that the partnership was created, the three partners agreed to allocate all profits and losses according to a specified plan written as follows:

- Each partner is entitled to interest computed at the rate of 12 percent per year based on the individual capital balances at the beginning of that year.
- Because of prior work experience, Left is entitled to an annual salary allowance of $12,000, and Center is credited with $8,000 per year.
- Any remaining profit will be split as follows: Left, 20 percent; Center, 40 percent; and Right, 40 percent. If a loss remains, the balance will be allocated: Left, 30 percent; Center, 50 percent; and Right, 20 percent.

Determine the ending capital balance for each partner as of the end of each of these three years.

LO10

24. The E.N.D. partnership has the following capital balances as of the end of the current year:

Pineda	$230,000
Adams	190,000
Fergie	160,000
Gomez	140,000
Total capital	$720,000

Answer each of the following *independent* questions:

a. Assume that the partners share profits and losses 3:3:2:2, respectively. Fergie retires and is paid $190,000 based on the terms of the original partnership agreement. If the goodwill method is used, what is the capital balance of the remaining three partners?

b. Assume that the partners share profits and losses 4:3:2:1, respectively. Pineda retires and is paid $280,000 based on the terms of the original partnership agreement. If the bonus method is used, what is the capital balance of the remaining three partners?

LO10

25. The partnership of Matteson, Richton, and O'Toole has existed for a number of years. At the present time the partners have the following capital balances and profit and loss sharing percentages:

Partner	Capital Balance	Profit and Loss Percentage
Matteson	$ 90,000	30%
Richton	150,000	50
O'Toole	100,000	20

O'Toole elects to withdraw from the partnership, leaving Matteson and Richton to operate the business. Following the original partnership agreement, when a partner withdraws, the partnership and all of its individual assets are to be reassessed to current fair values by an independent appraiser. The withdrawing partner will receive cash or other assets equal to that partner's current capital balance after including an appropriate share of any adjustment indicated by the appraisal. Gains and losses indicated by the appraisal are allocated using the regular profit and loss percentages.

An independent appraiser is hired and estimates that the partnership as a whole is worth $600,000. Regarding the individual assets, the appraiser finds a building with a book value of $180,000 has a fair value of $220,000. The book values for all other identifiable assets and liabilities are the same as their appraised fair values.

Accordingly, the partnership agrees to pay O'Toole $120,000 upon withdrawal. Matteson and Richton, however, do not wish to record any goodwill in connection with the change in ownership.

Prepare the journal entry to record O'Toole's withdrawal from the partnership.

LO2, LO4, LO6, LO9

26. In the early part of 2013, the partners of Page, Childers, and Smith sought assistance from a local accountant. They had begun a new business in 2012 but had never used an accountant's services.

Page and Childers began the partnership by contributing $80,000 and $30,000 in cash, respectively. Page was to work occasionally at the business, and Childers was to be employed full-time. They decided that year-end profits and losses should be assigned as follows:

- Each partner was to be allocated 10 percent interest computed on the beginning capital balances for the period.
- A compensation allowance of $5,000 was to go to Page with a $20,000 amount assigned to Childers.
- Any remaining income would be split on a 4:6 basis to Page and Childers, respectively.

In 2012, revenues totaled $90,000, and expenses were $64,000 (not including the compensation allowance assigned to the partners). Page withdrew cash of $8,000 during the year, and Childers took out $11,000. In addition, the business paid $5,000 for repairs made to Page's home and charged it to repair expense.

On January 1, 2013, the partnership sold a 20 percent interest to Smith for $43,000 cash. This money was contributed to the business with the bonus method used for accounting purposes.

Answer the following questions:

a. Why was the original profit and loss allocation, as just outlined, designed by the partners?

b. Why did the drawings for 2012 not agree with the compensation allowances provided for in the partnership agreement?

c. What journal entries should the partnership have recorded on December 31, 2012?

d. What journal entry should the partnership have recorded on January 1, 2013?

LO3, LO9, LO10

27. Following is the current balance sheet for a local partnership of doctors:

Cash and current assets	$ 30,000	Liabilities	$ 40,000
		A, capital	20,000
Land	180,000	B, capital	40,000
		C, capital	90,000
Building and equipment (net)	100,000	D, capital	120,000
Totals	$310,000	Totals	$310,000

The following questions represent *independent* situations:

a. E is going to invest enough money in this partnership to receive a 25 percent interest. No goodwill or bonus is to be recorded. How much should E invest?

b. E contributes $36,000 in cash to the business to receive a 10 percent interest in the partnership. Goodwill is to be recorded. Profits and losses have previously been split according to the following percentages: A, 30 percent; B, 10 percent; C, 40 percent; and D, 20 percent. After E makes this investment, what are the individual capital balances?

c. E contributes $42,000 in cash to the business to receive a 20 percent interest in the partnership. Goodwill is to be recorded. The four original partners share all profits and losses equally. After E makes this investment, what are the individual capital balances?

d. E contributes $55,000 in cash to the business to receive a 20 percent interest in the partnership. No goodwill or other asset revaluation is to be recorded. Profits and losses have previously been split according to the following percentages: A, 10 percent; B, 30 percent; C, 20 percent; and D, 40 percent. After E makes this investment, what are the individual capital balances?

e. C retires from the partnership and, as per the original partnership agreement, is to receive cash equal to 125 percent of her final capital balance. No goodwill or other asset revaluation is to be recognized. All partners share profits and losses equally. After the withdrawal, what are the individual capital balances of the remaining partners?

LO5, LO6, LO9

28. Boswell and Johnson form a partnership on May 1, 2011. Boswell contributes cash of $50,000; Johnson conveys title to the following properties to the partnership:

	Book Value	Fair Value
Land	$15,000	$28,000
Building and equipment	35,000	36,000

The partners agree to start their partnership with equal capital balances. No goodwill is to be recognized.

According to the articles of partnership written by the partners, profits and losses are allocated based on the following formula:

- Boswell receives a compensation allowance of $1,000 per month.
- All remaining profits and losses are split 60:40 to Johnson and Boswell, respectively.
- Each partner can make annual cash drawings of $5,000 beginning in 2012.

Net income of $11,000 is earned by the business during 2011.

Walpole is invited to join the partnership on January 1, 2012. Because of her business reputation and financial expertise, she is given a 40 percent interest for $54,000 cash. The bonus approach is used to record this investment, made directly to the business. The articles of partnership are amended to give Walpole a $2,000 compensation allowance per month and an annual cash drawing of $10,000. Remaining profits are now allocated:

Johnson	48%
Boswell	12
Walpole	40

All drawings are taken by the partners during 2012. At year-end, the partnership reports an earned net income of $28,000.

On January 1, 2013, Pope (previously a partnership employee) is admitted into the partnership. Each partner transfers 10 percent to Pope, who makes the following payments directly to the partners:

Johnson	$5,672
Boswell	7,880
Walpole	8,688

Once again, the articles of partnership must be amended to allow for the entrance of the new partner. This change entitles Pope to a compensation allowance of $800 per month and an annual drawing of $4,000. Profits and losses are now assigned as follows:

Johnson	40.5%
Boswell	13.5
Walpole	36.0
Pope	10.0

For the year of 2013, the partnership earned a profit of $46,000, and each partner withdrew the allowed amount of cash.

Determine the capital balances for the individual partners as of the end of each year: 2011 through 2013.

LO4, LO5, LO6, LO9

29. Gray, Stone, and Lawson open an accounting practice on January 1, 2011, in San Diego, California, to be operated as a partnership. Gray and Stone will serve as the senior partners because of their years of experience. To establish the business, Gray, Stone, and Lawson contribute cash and other properties valued at $210,000, $180,000, and $90,000, respectively. An articles of partnership agreement is drawn up. It has the following stipulations:

- Personal drawings are allowed annually up to an amount equal to 10 percent of the beginning capital balance for the year.
- Profits and losses are allocated according to the following plan:
  (1) A salary allowance is credited to each partner in an amount equal to $8 per billable hour worked by that individual during the year.
  (2) Interest is credited to the partners' capital accounts at the rate of 12 percent of the average monthly balance for the year (computed without regard for current income or drawings).
  (3) An annual bonus is to be credited to Gray and Stone. Each bonus is to be 10 percent of net income after subtracting the bonus, the salary allowance, and the interest. Also included in the agreement is the provision that the bonus cannot be a negative amount.
  (4) Any remaining partnership profit or loss is to be divided evenly among all partners.

Because of monetary problems encountered in getting the business started, Gray invests an additional $9,100 on May 1, 2011. On January 1, 2012, the partners allow Monet to buy into the partnership. Monet contributes cash directly to the business in an amount equal to a 25 percent interest in the book value of the partnership property subsequent to this contribution.

The partnership agreement as to splitting profits and losses is not altered upon Monet's entrance into the firm; the general provisions continue to be applicable.

The billable hours for the partners during the first three years of operation follow:

	2011	2012	2013
Gray.	1,710	1,800	1,880
Stone.	1,440	1,500	1,620
Lawson	1,300	1,380	1,310
Monet	–0–	1,190	1,580

The partnership reports net income for 2011 through 2013 as follows:

2011	$ 65,000
2012	(20,400)
2013	152,800

Each partner withdraws the maximum allowable amount each year.

a. Determine the allocation of income for each of these three years (to the nearest dollar).

b. Prepare in appropriate form a statement of partners' capital for the year ending December 31, 2013.

LO8, LO9, LO10

30. A partnership of attorneys in the St. Louis, Missouri, area has the following balance sheet accounts as of January 1, 2013:

Assets.	$320,000	Liabilities	$120,000
		Athos, capital	80,000
		Porthos, capital	70,000
		Aramis, capital.	50,000

According to the articles of partnership, Athos is to receive an allocation of 50 percent of all partnership profits and losses while Porthos receives 30 percent and Aramis, 20 percent. The book value of each asset and liability should be considered an accurate representation of fair value.

For each of the following *independent* situations, prepare the journal entry or entries to be recorded by the partnership. (Round to nearest dollar.)

a. Porthos, with permission of the other partners, decides to sell half of his partnership interest to D'Artagnan for $50,000 in cash. No asset revaluation or goodwill is to be recorded by the partnership.

b. All three of the present partners agree to sell 10 percent of each partnership interest to D'Artagnan for a total cash payment of $25,000. Each partner receives a negotiated portion of this amount. Goodwill is recorded as a result of the transaction.

c. D'Artagnan is allowed to become a partner with a 10 percent ownership interest by contributing $30,000 in cash directly into the business. The bonus method is used to record this admission.

d. Use the same facts as in requirement (*c*) except that the entrance into the partnership is recorded by the goodwill method.

e. D'Artagnan is allowed to become a partner with a 10 percent ownership interest by contributing $12,222 in cash directly to the business. The goodwill method is used to record this transaction.

f. Aramis decides to retire and leave the partnership. An independent appraisal of the business and its assets indicates a current fair value of $280,000. Goodwill is to be recorded. Aramis will then be given the exact amount of cash that will close out his capital account.

LO2, LO3, LO5, LO6, LO8, LO10

31. Steve Reese is a well-known interior designer in Fort Worth, Texas. He wants to start his own business and convinces Rob O'Donnell, a local merchant, to contribute the capital to form a partnership. On January 1, 2011, O'Donnell invests a building worth $52,000 and equipment valued at $16,000 as well as $12,000 in cash. Although Reese makes no tangible contribution to the partnership, he will operate the business and be an equal partner in the beginning capital balances.

To entice O'Donnell to join this partnership, Reese draws up the following profit and loss agreement:

- O'Donnell will be credited annually with interest equal to 20 percent of the beginning capital balance for the year.
- O'Donnell will also have added to his capital account 15 percent of partnership income each year (without regard for the preceding interest figure) or $4,000, whichever is larger. All remaining income is credited to Reese.
- Neither partner is allowed to withdraw funds from the partnership during 2011. Thereafter, each can draw $5,000 annually or 20 percent of the beginning capital balance for the year, whichever is larger.

The partnership reported a net loss of $10,000 during the first year of its operation. On January 1, 2012, Terri Dunn becomes a third partner in this business by contributing $15,000 cash to the partnership. Dunn receives a 20 percent share of the business's capital. The profit and loss agreement is altered as follows:

- O'Donnell is still entitled to (1) interest on his beginning capital balance as well as (2) the share of partnership income just specified.
- Any remaining profit or loss will be split on a 6:4 basis between Reese and Dunn, respectively.

Partnership income for 2012 is reported as $44,000. Each partner withdraws the full amount that is allowed.

On January 1, 2013, Dunn becomes ill and sells her interest in the partnership (with the consent of the other two partners) to Judy Postner. Postner pays $46,000 directly to Dunn. Net income for 2013 is $61,000 with the partners again taking their full drawing allowance.

On January 1, 2014, Postner withdraws from the business for personal reasons. The articles of partnership state that any partner may leave the partnership at any time and is entitled to receive cash in an amount equal to the recorded capital balance at that time plus 10 percent.

a. Prepare journal entries to record the preceding transactions on the assumption that the bonus (or no revaluation) method is used. Drawings need not be recorded, although the balances should be included in the closing entries.

b. Prepare journal entries to record the previous transactions on the assumption that the goodwill (or revaluation) method is used. Drawings need not be recorded, although the balances should be included in the closing entries.

(Round all amounts to the nearest dollar.)

Develop Your Skills

RESEARCH CASE

Go to the website www.sec.gov where forms filed with the SEC are available. Look for a section entitled "Filings & Forms (EDGAR)," and click on "Search for Company Filings" within that section. On the next screen that appears, click on "Search Companies and Filings." On the next screen, enter the following company name: Buckeye Partners. A list of SEC filings made by that company will appear; scroll down to the first 10–K (annual report) filing from Buckeye Partners. Click on that 10–K. This path will provide the latest financial information available for Buckeye Partners. Scroll through the statement information until the actual financial statements, followed by the notes, appear.

Required

Review this set of financial statements as well as the accompanying notes. List information included for this partnership that would typically not appear in financial statements produced for a corporation.

ANALYSIS CASE

Brenda Wilson, Elizabeth Higgins, and Helen Poncelet form a partnership as a first step in creating a business. Wilson invests most of the capital but does not plan to be actively involved in the day-to-day operations. Higgins has had some experience and is expected to do a majority of the daily work. Poncelet has been in this line of business for some time and has many connections. Therefore, she will devote a majority of her time to getting new clients.

Required

Write a memo to these three partners suggesting at least two different ways in which the profits of the partnership can be allocated each year in order to be fair to all parties.

COMMUNICATION CASE 1

Heidi Birmingham and James T. Roberts have decided to create a business. They have financing available and have a well-developed business plan. However, they have not yet decided which type of legal business structure would be best for them.

Required

Write a report for these two individuals outlining the types of situations in which the corporate form of legal structure would be the best choice.

COMMUNICATION CASE 2

Use the information in Communication Case 1.

Required

Write a report for these two individuals outlining the types of situations in which the partnership form of legal structure would be the best choice.

EXCEL CASE

The Red and Blue partnership has been created to operate a law firm. The partners have been attempting to devise a fair system to allocate profits and losses. Red plans to work more billable hours each year than Blue. However, Blue has more experience and can charge a higher hourly rate. Red expects to invest more money in the business than Blue.

Required

Build a spreadsheet that can be used to allocate profits and losses to these two partners each year. The spreadsheet should be constructed so that the following variables can be entered:

Net income for the year.
Number of billable hours for each partner.
Hourly rate for each partner.
Capital investment by each partner.
Interest rate on capital investment.
Profit and loss ratio.

Use this spreadsheet to determine the allocation if partnership net income for the current year is $200,000, the number of billable hours is 2,000 for Red and 1,500 for Blue, the hourly rate for Red is $20 and for Blue is $30, and investment by Red is $80,000 and by Blue is $50,000. Interest on capital will be accrued each year at 10 percent of the beginning balance. Any remaining income amount will be split 50–50.

Use the spreadsheet a second time but make these changes: Blue reports 1,700 billable hours, Red invests $100,000, and interest will be recognized at a 12 percent annual rate. How do these three changes impact the allocation of the $200,000?

chapter 15

Partnerships: Termination and Liquidation

Learning Objectives

After studying this chapter, you should be able to:

LO1 Determine amounts to be paid to partners in a liquidation.

LO2 Prepare journal entries to record the transactions incurred in the liquidation of a partnership.

LO3 Determine the distribution of available cash when one or more partners have a deficit capital balance or become personally insolvent.

LO4 Prepare a proposed schedule of liquidation from safe capital balances to determine an equitable preliminary distribution of available partnership assets.

LO5 Develop a predistribution plan to guide the distribution of assets in a partnership liquidation.

Partnerships can be rather frail organizations. Termination of business activities followed by the liquidation of partnership property can take place for a variety of reasons, both legal and personal.

> In any firm, unless there is continuous open and candid communication among equity partners, and acceptance and buy-in for the business plan chosen by the firm, sooner or later there will be a dissolution of the firm.
>
> The form of the dissolution is irrelevant, whether by withdrawal of individual partners or wholesale departure and formal liquidation. The end result will be the same: The original dream of harmonious and collegial growth of the firm will come to an end.[1]

Although a business organized as a partnership can exist indefinitely through periodic changes within the ownership, the actual cessation of operations is not an uncommon occurrence. "Sooner or later, all partnerships end, whether a partner dies, moves to Hawaii, or gets into a different line of business."[2] The partners simply may be incompatible and choose to cease operations. The same decision could be made if profits fail to reach projected levels. "In the best of times, partnerships are fragile."[3]

The death of a partner is an event that dissolves a partnership and frequently leads to the termination of business operations. Rather than continuing under a new partnership arrangement, the remaining owners could discover that liquidation is necessary to settle the claims of the deceased partner's estate. A similar action could be required if one or more partners elect to change careers or retire. Under that circumstance, liquidation is often the most convenient method for winding up the financial affairs of the business.

As a final possibility, bankruptcy can legally force a partnership into selling its noncash assets. Laventhol & Horwath, the seventh largest public accounting firm in the United States at the time, filed for bankruptcy protection after the firm came under intense financial pressure from numerous lawsuits. "Laventhol said that at least 100 lawsuits are pending in state and federal courts. Bankruptcy court protection 'is absolutely

[1] Edward Poll, "Commentary: Coach's Corner: Reuniting a Firm Divided," *Massachusetts Lawyers Weekly,* pNA. Retrieved July 11, 2007, from *InfoTrac OneFile* via Thomson Gale.

[2] Camilla Cornell, "Breaking Up (with a Business Partner) Is Hard to Do," *Profit,* November 2004, p. 69.

[3] Sue Shellenbarger, "Cutting Losses When Partners Face a Breakup," *The Wall Street Journal,* May 21, 1991, p. B1.

necessary in order to protect the debtor and its creditors from the devastating results a destructive race for assets will cause,' the firm said."[4]

The bankruptcy of Laventhol & Horwath was not an isolated incident. During the period 1998–2004, a study conducted by Hildebrandt International identified 80 U.S. law firms with more than 10 lawyers that dissolved. In investigating the reasons for failure, the researcher identified internal dysfunction, the inability to pay market compensation levels, and a weak competitive market position as major factors leading to law firms going out of business.[5]

Termination and Liquidation—Protecting the Interests of All Parties

As the chapter on bankruptcy discussed, accounting for the termination and liquidation of a business can prove to be a delicate task. Losses are commonly incurred. For example, "[f]ormer partners in Keck, Mahin and Cate have pledged to pay slightly over $3 million to general unsecured creditors to settle the bankrupt firm's debts . . . this figure represents about 36 percent of the money owed."[6] Here, both the partners and the creditors suffered heavy losses.

Other partnerships have experienced a similar fate.

> In 1990, prior to the advent of limited-liability partnerships, the accounting firm of Laventhol & Horwath filed for Chapter 11 bankruptcy-court protection, in part due to lawsuits over questionable accounting. The firm's assets were insufficient to cover the claims of creditors and litigants. Under a plan negotiated with the firm's creditors, the 360 partners and former partners who had spent time at the firm since 1984 were required to dig into their own pockets to share a $46 million liability. Under a formula hammered out by partner Jacob Brandzel, now an executive at American Express Co. in Chicago, they were obligated to contribute between about $5,000 and $450,000, depending on factors including seniority. Managers were levied a 5 percent to 10 percent surcharge on top. Everyone was given 10 years to pay.[7]

Consequently, throughout any liquidation, both creditors and partners demand continuous accounting information that enables them to monitor and assess their financial risks. In generating these data for a partnership, the accountant must record the following:

- The conversion of partnership assets into cash.
- The allocation of the resulting gains and losses.
- The payment of liabilities and expenses.
- Any remaining unpaid debts to be settled or the distribution of any remaining assets to the partners based on their final capital balances.

Beyond the goal of merely reporting these transactions, the accountant must work to ensure the equitable treatment of all parties involved in the liquidation. The accounting records, for example, are the basis for allocating available assets to creditors and to the individual partners. If assets are limited, the accountant also may have to make recommendations as to the appropriate method for distributing any remaining funds. Protecting the interests of partnership creditors is an especially significant duty because the Uniform Partnership Act specifies that they have first priority to the assets held by

[4] Peter Pae, "Laventhol Bankruptcy Filing Indicates Liabilities May Be as Much as $2 Billion," *The Wall Street Journal,* November 23, 1990, p. A4.

[5] William G. Johnston, "Anatomy of Law Firm Failures: A Look at US Law Firm Dissolutions from 1998–2004," Hildebrandt International, March 2004, p. 16. Retrieved July 11, 2007, from www.hildebrandt.com/publicdocs/doc_id_1739_492004850218.pdf.

[6] Chicago *Daily Law Bulletin,* August 13, 1999, p. 3.

[7] Mitchell Pacelle and Ianthe Jeanne Dugan, "Partners Forever? Within Andersen, Personal Liability May Bring Ruin," *The Wall Street Journal,* April 2, 2002, p. C1.

the business at dissolution. The accountant's desire for an equitable settlement is enhanced, no doubt, in that any party to a liquidation who is not treated fairly can seek legal recovery from the responsible party.

Not only the creditors but also the partners themselves have a great interest in the financial data produced during the period of liquidation. They must be concerned, as indicated, by the possibility of incurring substantial monetary losses. The potential for loss is especially significant because of the unlimited liability to which the partners are exposed. Even the new legal formats that have been developed do not necessarily provide safety.

> Because it is unclear how much protection the LLP structure will provide Andersen partners, partnership and bankruptcy lawyers are expected to be following the matter closely. "As far as I know, there has never been a litigation test of the extent of the LLP shield, and there have been very few LLP cases about liability at all," said Larry Ribstein, a law professor at George Mason University.[8]

As long as a partnership can meet all of its obligations, a partner's risk is normally no more than that of a corporate stockholder. However, should the partnership become insolvent, each partner faces the possibility of having to satisfy *all* remaining obligations personally. Although any partner suffering more than a proportionate share of these losses can seek legal retribution from the other partners, this process is not always an effective remedy. The other partners may themselves be insolvent, or anticipated legal costs might discourage the damaged party from seeking recovery. Therefore, each partner usually has a keen interest in monitoring the progress of a liquidation as it transpires.

Termination and Liquidation Procedures Illustrated

LO1

Determine amounts to be paid to partners in a liquidation.

The procedures involved in terminating and liquidating a partnership are basically mechanical. Partnership assets are converted into cash that is then used to pay business obligations as well as liquidation expenses. *Any remaining assets are distributed to the individual partners based on their final capital balances.* Once assets have been distributed, the partnership's books are permanently closed. If each partner has a capital balance large enough to absorb all liquidation losses, the accountant should experience little difficulty in recording this series of transactions.

To illustrate the typical process, assume that Morgan and Houseman have been operating an art gallery as a partnership for a number of years. Morgan and Houseman allocate all profits and losses on a 6:4 basis, respectively. On May 1, 2013, the partners decide to terminate business activities, liquidate all noncash assets, and dissolve their partnership. Although they give no specific explanation for this action, any number of reasons could exist. The partners, for example, could have come to a disagreement so that they no longer believe they can work together. Another possibility is that business profits have become inadequate to warrant the continuing investment of their time and capital.

Following is a balance sheet for the partnership of Morgan and Houseman as of the termination date. The revenue, expense, and drawing accounts have been closed as a preliminary step in terminating the business. A separate reporting of the gains and losses that occur during the final winding-down process will subsequently be made.

MORGAN AND HOUSEMAN
Balance Sheet
May 1, 2013

Assets		Liabilities and Capital	
Cash	$ 45,000	Liabilities	$ 32,000
Accounts receivable	12,000	Morgan, capital	50,000
Inventory	22,000	Houseman, capital	38,000
Land, building, and equipment (net)	41,000		
Total assets	$120,000	Total liabilities and capital	$120,000

[8] Ibid.

We assume here that the liquidation of Morgan and Houseman proceeds in an orderly fashion through the following events:

2013

June 1	The inventory is sold at auction for $15,000.
July 15	Of the total accounts receivable, the partnership collected $9,000 and wrote off the remainder as bad debts.
Aug. 20	The fixed assets are sold for a total of $29,000.
Aug. 25	All partnership liabilities are paid.
Sept. 10	A total of $3,000 in liquidation expenses is paid to cover costs such as accounting and legal fees as well as the commissions incurred in disposing of partnership property.
Oct. 15	All remaining cash is distributed to the owners based on their final capital account balances.

Accordingly, the partnership of Morgan and Houseman incurred a number of losses in liquidating its property. Such losses are almost anticipated because the need for immediate sale usually holds a high priority in a liquidation. Furthermore, a portion of the assets used by any business, such as its equipment and buildings, could have a utility that is strictly limited to a particular type of operation. If the property is not easily adaptable, disposal at any reasonable price often proves to be a problem.

LO2

Prepare journal entries to record the transactions incurred in the liquidation of a partnership.

To record the liquidation of Morgan and Houseman, the following journal entries would be made. Rather than report specific income and expense balances, gains and losses are traditionally recorded directly to the partners' capital accounts. Because operations have ceased, determination of a separate net income figure for this period would provide little informational value. *Instead, a primary concern of the parties involved in any liquidation is the continuing changes in each partner's capital balance.*

6/1/13	Cash	15,000	
	Morgan, Capital (60% of loss)	4,200	
	Houseman, Capital (40% of loss)	2,800	
	Inventory		22,000
	To record sale of partnership inventory at a $7,000 loss.		
7/15/13	Cash	9,000	
	Morgan, Capital	1,800	
	Houseman, Capital	1,200	
	Accounts Receivable		12,000
	To record collection of accounts receivable with write-off of remaining $3,000 in accounts as bad debts.		
8/20/13	Cash	29,000	
	Morgan, Capital	7,200	
	Houseman, Capital	4,800	
	Land, Building, and Equipment (net)		41,000
	To record sale of fixed assets and allocation of $12,000 loss.		
8/25/13	Liabilities	32,000	
	Cash		32,000
	To record payment made to settle the liabilities of the partnership.		
9/10/13	Morgan, Capital	1,800	
	Houseman, Capital	1,200	
	Cash		3,000
	To record payment of liquidation expenses with the amounts recorded as direct reductions to the partners' capital accounts.		

After liquidating the partnership assets and paying off all obligations, the cash that remains can be divided between Morgan and Houseman personally. The following schedule is utilized to determine the partners' ending capital account balances and, thus, the appropriate distribution for this final payment:

Cash and Capital Account Balances

	Cash	Morgan, Capital	Houseman, Capital
Beginning balances*	$ 45,000	$50,000	$38,000
Sold inventory	15,000	(4,200)	(2,800)
Collected accounts receivable	9,000	(1,800)	(1,200)
Sold fixed assets	29,000	(7,200)	(4,800)
Paid liabilities	(32,000)	–0–	–0–
Paid liquidation expenses	(3,000)	(1,800)	(1,200)
Final totals	$ 63,000	$35,000	$28,000

*Because of the presence of other assets as well as liabilities, the beginning balances in Cash and in the capital accounts are not equal.

After the ending capital balances have been calculated, the remaining cash can be distributed to the partners to close out the financial records of the partnership:

10/15/13	Morgan, Capital	35,000	
	Houseman, Capital	28,000	
	Cash		63,000
	To record distribution of cash to partners in accordance with final capital balances.		

Schedule of Liquidation

Liquidation can take a considerable length of time to complete. Because the various parties involved seek continually updated financial information, the accountant should produce frequent reports summarizing the transactions as they occur. Consequently, a statement (often referred to as the *schedule of liquidation*) can be prepared at periodic intervals to disclose

- Transactions to date.
- Property still being held by the partnership.
- Liabilities remaining to be paid.
- Current cash and capital balances.

Although the preceding Morgan and Houseman example has been condensed into a few events occurring during a relatively brief period of time, partnership liquidations usually require numerous transactions that transpire over months and, perhaps, even years. By receiving frequent schedules of liquidation, both the creditors and the partners are able to stay apprised of the results of this lengthy process.

See Exhibit 15.1 for the final schedule of liquidation for the partnership of Morgan and Houseman. The accountant should have distributed previous statements at each important juncture of this liquidation to meet the informational needs of the parties involved. The example here demonstrates the stair-step approach incorporated in preparing a schedule of liquidation. The effects of each transaction (or group of transactions) are outlined in a horizontal fashion so that current account balances and all prior transactions are evident. This structuring also facilitates the preparation of future statements: A new layer summarizing recent events can simply be added at the bottom each time a new schedule is to be produced.

EXHIBIT 15.1

MORGAN AND HOUSEMAN
Schedule of Partnership Liquidation
Final Balances

	Cash	Noncash Assets	Liabilities	Morgan, Capital (60%)	Houseman, Capital (40%)
Beginning balances, 5/1/13	$ 45,000	$ 75,000	$ 32,000	$ 50,000	$ 38,000
Sold inventory, 6/1/13	15,000	(22,000)	–0–	(4,200)	(2,800)
Updated balances	60,000	53,000	32,000	45,800	35,200
Collected receivables, 7/15/13	9,000	(12,000)	–0–	(1,800)	(1,200)
Updated balances	69,000	41,000	32,000	44,000	34,000
Sold fixed assets, 8/20/13	29,000	(41,000)	–0–	(7,200)	(4,800)
Updated balances	98,000	–0–	32,000	36,800	29,200
Paid liabilities, 8/25/13	(32,000)		(32,000)	–0–	–0–
Updated balances	66,000	–0–	–0–	36,800	29,200
Paid liquidation expenses, 9/10/13	(3,000)			(1,800)	(1,200)
Updated balances	63,000	–0–	–0–	35,000	28,000
Distributed remaining cash, 10/15/13	(63,000)			(35,000)	(28,000)
Closing balances	–0–	–0–	–0–	–0–	–0–

LO3

Determine the distribution of available cash when one or more partners have a deficit capital balance or become personally insolvent.

Deficit Capital Balance—Contribution by Partner

In Exhibit 15.1, the liquidation process ended with both partners continuing to report positive capital balances. Thus, each partner was able to share in the remaining $63,000 cash. Unfortunately, such an outcome is not always possible. At the end of a liquidation, one or more partners could have a negative capital account, or the partnership could be unable to generate even enough cash to satisfy all of its creditors' claims. Such deficits are most likely to occur when the partnership is already insolvent at the start of the liquidation or when the disposal of noncash assets results in material losses. Under these circumstances, the accounting procedures to be applied depend on legal regulations as well as the individual actions of the partners.

To illustrate, assume that the partnership of Holland, Dozier, and Ross was dissolved at the beginning of the current year. Business activities were terminated and all noncash assets were subsequently converted into cash. During the liquidation process, the partnership incurred a number of large losses that have been allocated to the partners' capital accounts on a 4:4:2 basis, respectively. A portion of the resulting cash is then used to pay all partnership liabilities and liquidation expenses.

Following these transactions, assume that only the following four account balances remain open within the partnership's records:

Cash	$20,000	Holland, Capital	$ (6,000)
		Dozier, Capital	15,000
		Ross, Capital	11,000
		Total	$20,000

Holland has a negative capital balance of $6,000; the assigned share of partnership losses has exceeded this partner's net contribution. In such cases, the Uniform Partnership Act (Section 807[b]) stipulates that the partner "shall contribute to the partnership an amount equal to any excess charges over the credits in the partner's account . . ." Therefore, Holland legally is required to convey an additional $6,000 to the partnership to eliminate the deficit balance. This contribution raises the cash balance to $26,000, which allows a complete distribution to be made to Dozier ($15,000) and Ross ($11,000) in line with their capital accounts. The journal entry for this final payment closes out the partnership records:

	Debit	Credit
Cash	6,000	
Holland, Capital		6,000
To record contribution made by Holland to extinguish negative capital balance.		
Dozier, Capital	15,000	
Ross, Capital	11,000	
Cash		26,000
To record distribution of remaining cash to partners in accordance with their ending capital balances.		

Deficit Capital Balance—Loss to Remaining Partners

Unfortunately, an alternative scenario can easily be conceived for the previous partnership liquidation. Although Holland's capital account shows a $6,000 deficit balance, this partner could resist any attempt to force an additional investment, especially because the business is in the process of being terminated. The possibility of such recalcitrance is enhanced if the individual is having personal financial difficulties. Thus, the remaining partners may eventually have to resort to formal litigation to gain Holland's contribution. Until that legal action is concluded, the partnership records remain open although inactive.

Distribution of Safe Payments

While awaiting the final resolution of this matter, no compelling reason exists for the partnership to continue holding $20,000 in cash. These funds will eventually be paid to Dozier and Ross regardless of any action that Holland takes. An immediate transfer should be made to these two partners to allow them the use of their money. However, because Dozier has a $15,000 capital account balance and Ross currently reports $11,000, a complete distribution is not possible. A method must be devised, therefore, to allow for a fair allocation of the available $20,000.

To ensure the equitable treatment of all parties, this initial distribution is based on the assumption that the $6,000 capital deficit will prove to be a total loss to the partnership. Holland may, for example, be completely insolvent so that no additional payment will ever be forthcoming. By making this conservative presumption, the accountant is able to calculate the lowest possible amounts (or *safe balances*) that Dozier and Ross must retain in their capital accounts to be able to absorb all future losses.

Should Holland's $6,000 deficit (or any portion of it) prove uncollectible, the loss will be written off against the capital accounts of Dozier and Ross. Allocation of this amount is based on the relative profit and loss ratio specified in the articles of partnership. According to the information provided, Dozier and Ross are credited with 40 percent and 20 percent of all partnership income, respectively. This 40:20 ratio equates to a 2:1 relationship (or ⅔:⅓) between the two. Thus, if no part of the $6,000 deficit balance is ever recovered from Holland, $4,000 (two-thirds) of the loss will be assigned to Dozier and $2,000 (one-third) to Ross:

Allocation of Potential $6,000 Loss

Dozier	⅔ of $(6,000) = $(4,000)
Ross	⅓ of $(6,000) = $(2,000)

These amounts represent the maximum potential reductions that the two remaining partners could still incur. Depending on Holland's actions, Dozier could be forced to absorb an additional $4,000 loss, and Ross's capital account could decrease by as much as

$2,000. These balances must therefore remain in the respective capital accounts until the issue is resolved. Hence, Dozier is entitled to receive $11,000 in cash at the present time; this distribution reduces that partner's capital account from $15,000 to the minimum $4,000 level. Likewise, a $9,000 payment to Ross decreases the $11,000 capital balance to the $2,000 limit. These $11,000 and $9,000 amounts represent safe payments that can be distributed to the partners without fear of creating new deficits in the future.

Dozier, Capital	11,000	
Ross, Capital	9,000	
Cash		20,000
To record distribution of cash to Dozier and Ross based on safe capital balances, using the assumption that Holland will not contribute further to the partnership.		

After this $20,000 cash distribution, only a few other events can occur during the remaining life of the partnership. Holland, either voluntarily or through legal persuasion, may contribute the entire $6,000 needed to eradicate the capital deficit. If so, the money should be immediately turned over to Dozier ($4,000) and Ross ($2,000) based on their remaining capital balances. This final distribution effectively closes the partnership records.

A second possibility is that Dozier and Ross could be unable to recover any part of the deficit from Holland. These two remaining partners must then absorb the $6,000 loss themselves. Because adequate safe capital balances have been maintained, recording a complete default by Holland serves to close out the partnership books.

Dozier, Capital (⅔ of loss)	4,000	
Ross, Capital (⅓ of loss)	2,000	
Holland, Capital		6,000
To record allocation of deficit capital balance of insolvent partner.		

Deficit Is Partly Collectible

One other ending to this partnership liquidation is conceivable. The partnership could recover a portion of the $6,000 from Holland, but the remainder could prove to be uncollectible. This partner could become bankrupt, or the other partners could simply give up trying to collect. The partners could also negotiate this settlement to avoid protracted legal actions.

To illustrate, assume that Holland manages to contribute $3,600 to the partnership but subsequently files for relief under the provisions of the bankruptcy laws. In a later legal arrangement, $1,000 additional cash goes to the partnership, but the final $1,400 will never be collected. This series of events creates the following effects within the liquidation process:

1. The $3,600 contribution is distributed to Dozier and Ross based on a new computation of their safe capital balances.
2. The $1,400 default is charged against the two positive capital balances in accordance with the relative profit and loss ratio.
3. The final $1,000 contribution is then paid to Dozier and Ross in amounts equal to their ending capital accounts, a transaction that closes the partnership's financial records.

The distribution of the first $3,600 depends on a recalculation of the minimum capital balances that Dozier and Ross must maintain to absorb all potential losses. Each of these computations is necessary because of a basic realization: Holland's remaining deficit balance ($2,400 at this time) could prove to be a total loss. This approach guarantees that the other two partners will continue to report sufficient capital until the liquidation is ultimately resolved.

	Current Capital	Allocation of Potential Loss	Safe Capital Payments
Dozier	$4,000	⅔ of $(2,400) = $(1,600)	$2,400
Ross	2,000	⅓ of (2,400) = (800)	1,200

Thus, the $3,600 in cash that is now available is distributed immediately to Dozier and Ross based on their safe balances:

Cash	3,600	
Holland, Capital		3,600
Dozier, Capital	2,400	
Ross, Capital	1,200	
Cash		3,600
To record capital contribution by Holland and subsequent distribution of funds to Dozier and Ross based on safe capital balances.		

After recording this $3,600 contribution from Holland and the subsequent disbursement, the partnership's capital accounts stay open, registering the following individual balances:

Holland, Capital (deficit)	$(2,400)
Dozier, Capital (safe balance)	1,600
Ross, Capital (safe balance)	800

These accounts continue to remain on the partnership books until the final resolution of Holland's obligation.

In this illustration, the $1,000 legal settlement and the remaining $1,400 loss ultimately allow the parties to close out the records:

Cash	1,000	
Dozier, Capital (⅔ of loss)	933	
Ross, Capital (⅓ of loss)	467	
Holland, Capital		2,400
To record final $1,000 cash settlement of Holland's interest and resulting $1,400 loss.		
Dozier, Capital	667	
Ross, Capital	333	
Cash		1,000
To record distribution of final cash balance based upon remaining capital account totals.		

In the previous example, one partner (Holland) became insolvent during the liquidation process. Personal bankruptcy is not uncommon and raises questions as to the legal right that damaged partners have to proceed against an insolvent partner. We now consider another example in which two partners are insolvent.

The following balance sheet is presented for the partnership of Morris, Newton, Olsen, and Prince and indicates the applicable profit and loss percentages. Both Morris and Prince are personally insolvent. Morris's creditors have brought an $8,000 claim against the partnership's assets, and Prince's creditors are seeking $15,000. These claims have forced the partnership to terminate operations so that the business property can be liquidated and the insolvent partners can settle their personal obligations. The question as to which partner is entitled to any cash balance that remains is again raised.

Cash	$ 10,000	Liabilities	$ 70,000
Noncash assets	140,000	Morris, capital (40%)	15,000
		Newton, capital (20%)	10,000
		Olsen, capital (20%)	23,000
		Prince, capital (20%)	32,000
Total assets	$150,000	Total liabilities and capital	$150,000

Assume that the partnership sells the noncash assets for a total of $80,000, creating a $60,000 loss, and pays all its liabilities. The partnership's accounting system records these two events as follows:

Cash	80,000	
Morris, Capital (40% of loss)	24,000	
Newton, Capital (20% of loss)	12,000	
Olsen, Capital (20% of loss)	12,000	
Prince, Capital (20% of loss)	12,000	
Noncash Assets (or specific accounts)		140,000
To record sale of noncash assets and allocation of resulting $60,000 loss.		
Liabilities	70,000	
Cash		70,000
To record extinguishment of partnership obligations.		

Because of these two transactions, the partnership's cash has increased from $10,000 to $20,000.

After the allocation of this loss, the capital accounts for Morris and Newton report deficit balances of $9,000 ($15,000 − $24,000) and $2,000 ($10,000 − $12,000), respectively. Although Newton is solvent and would be expected to compensate the partnership, Morris's personal financial condition does not allow for any further contribution. Therefore, Newton, Olsen, and Prince must absorb Morris's $9,000 deficit. Because these three partners have historically shared profits evenly (20:20:20), they continue to do so in recording this additional capital loss:

Newton, Capital (⅓ of loss)	3,000	
Olsen, Capital (⅓ of loss)	3,000	
Prince, Capital (⅓ of loss)	3,000	
Morris, Capital		9,000
To record write-off of deficit capital balance of insolvent partner.		

This last allocation increases Newton's deficit to a $5,000 balance ($2,000 + $3,000), an amount that the partner should now contribute in accordance with partnership law:

Cash	5,000	
Newton, Capital		5,000
To record contribution from solvent partner necessitated by negative capital balance.		

Following this series of transactions, only the cash balance (now $25,000) and Olsen's and Prince's capital accounts remain open within the partnership records:

	Cash	Morris, Capital	Newton, Capital	Olsen, Capital	Prince, Capital
Beginning balances	$10,000	$15,000	$10,000	$23,000	$32,000
Sold assets	80,000	(24,000)	(12,000)	(12,000)	(12,000)
Paid liabilities	(70,000)	–0–	–0–	–0–	–0–
Default by Morris	–0–	9,000	(3,000)	(3,000)	(3,000)
Contribution by Newton	5,000	–0–	5,000	–0–	–0–
Current balances	$25,000	–0–	–0–	$ 8,000	$17,000

Although $8,000 of the partnership's remaining cash goes directly to Olsen, the $17,000 attributed to Prince is first subjected to the claims of the partner's personal creditors. Because of their claims, $15,000 of this amount must be used to satisfy these obligations, with only the final $2,000 being paid to Prince. Because Morris receives no distribution of cash from the partnership, no assets become available to settle claims of this partner's personal creditors.

Insolvent Partnership

The two previous illustrations analyzed liquidations in which one or more of the partners is personally insolvent. Another possibility is that the partnership itself is insolvent. In an active partnership, insolvency can occur if losses, partner drawings, or litigation deplete the operation's working capital. A bankruptcy petition could follow if the partnership cannot meet its debts as they come due. Liquidation of business assets could be necessary unless the partnership can generate additional capital quickly. Even a financially sound partnership can become insolvent if it incurs material losses during a voluntary liquidation.

To serve as a basis for examining the accounting and legal ramifications of an insolvent partnership, assume that the law firm of Keller, Lewis, Monroe, and Norris is in the final stages of liquidation. The firm has sold all noncash assets and has used available cash to pay a portion of the business's liabilities. After these transactions, the following account balances remain open within the partnership's records. The four partners share profits and losses equally.

Liabilities	$ 20,000
Keller, capital	(30,000)
Lewis, capital	(5,000)
Monroe, capital	5,000
Norris, capital	10,000

Note: Parentheses indicate deficit.

This partnership is insolvent; it continues to owe creditors $20,000, even after liquidation and distribution of all assets. However, additional money should be forthcoming from two of the partners. Because of their deficit capital accounts, Keller and Lewis are legally required to contribute an additional $30,000 and $5,000, respectively, to the business. With these newly available funds, the partnership will be able to pay all $20,000 of its remaining liabilities as well as make cash distributions to Monroe ($5,000) and Norris ($10,000) in accordance with their capital account balances. This final payment would close the partnership books.

Once again, the possibility exists that one or more of the partners who are reporting a negative capital balance will not step forward to make any further investment. Assume, for example, that Keller is personally insolvent and cannot contribute, whereas Lewis simply refuses to supply additional funds in hopes of avoiding the obligation. *At this point, the remaining creditors can initiate legal recovery proceedings against any or all of the partners regardless of their capital balances.* Any action, however, against the insolvent partner could prove to be a futile effort.

Discussion Question

WHAT HAPPENS IF A PARTNER BECOMES INSOLVENT?

In 2001, three dentists—Ben Rogers, Judy Wilkinson, and Henry Walker—formed a partnership to open a practice in Toledo, Ohio. The partnership's primary purpose was to reduce expenses by sharing building and equipment costs, supplies, and the services of a clerical staff. Each contributed $70,000 in cash and, with the help of a bank loan, constructed a building and acquired furniture, fixtures, and equipment. Because the partners maintained their own separate clients, annual net income has been allocated as follows: Each partner receives the specific amount of revenues that he or she generated during the period less one-third of all expenses. From the beginning, the partners did not anticipate expansion of the practice; consequently, they could withdraw cash each year up to 90 percent of their share of income for the period.

The partnership had been profitable for a number of years. Over the years, Rogers has used much of his income to speculate in real estate in the Toledo area. By 2013 he was spending less time with the dental practice so that he could concentrate on his investments. Unfortunately, a number of these deals proved to be bad decisions and he incurred significant losses. On November 8, 2013, while Rogers was out of town, his personal creditors filed a $97,000 claim against the partnership assets. Unbeknownst to Wilkinson and Walker, Rogers had become insolvent.

Wilkinson and Walker hurriedly met to discuss the problem because Rogers could not be located. Rogers's capital account was currently at $105,000, but the partnership had only $27,000 in cash and liquid assets. The partners knew that Rogers's equipment had been used for a number of years and could be sold for relatively little. In contrast, the building had appreciated in value, and the claim could be satisfied by selling the property. However, this action would have a tremendously adverse impact on the dental practices of the remaining two partners.

What alternatives are available to Wilkinson and Walker, and what are the advantages and disadvantages of each?

Predicting the exact outcome of litigation is rarely possible. Thus, we assume here that Norris is forced to contribute $20,000 cash to settle the remaining liabilities. The following journal entries would then be required for this partnership:

Cash	20,000	
Norris, Capital		20,000
Liabilities	20,000	
Cash		20,000
To record capital contribution by Norris and payment to remaining partnership creditors.		

After all liabilities have been extinguished, the partners who still maintain positive capital accounts can demand remuneration from any partner with a negative balance. Despite this legal obligation, the chances of a significant recovery from the insolvent Keller is not likely. Thus, the partners could choose to write off this deficit as a step toward closing the partnership's financial records. Legal recovery proceedings can still continue against Keller regardless of the accounting treatment. As equal partners, Lewis, Monroe, and Norris absorb the $30,000 loss evenly.

Lewis, Capital (⅓ of loss)	10,000	
Monroe, Capital (⅓ of loss)	10,000	
Norris, Capital (⅓ of loss)	10,000	
Keller, Capital		30,000
To record write-off of deficit capital balance of insolvent partner.		

The partners' capital accounts now have the following balances:

	Keller, Capital	Lewis, Capital	Monroe, Capital	Norris, Capital
Beginning balances	$(30,000)	$ (5,000)	$ 5,000	$ 10,000
Capital contribution	–0–	–0–	–0–	20,000
Write-off of deficit balance	30,000	(10,000)	(10,000)	(10,000)
Current balances	–0–	$(15,000)	$ (5,000)	$ 20,000

Both Lewis and Monroe now have a legal obligation to reimburse the partnership to offset their deficit capital balances. Upon their payment of $15,000 and $5,000, respectively, the entire $20,000 will be distributed to Norris (the only partner with a positive balance), and the partnership's books will be closed. Should either Lewis or Monroe fail to make the appropriate contribution, the additional loss must be allocated between the two remaining partners.

Preliminary Distribution of Partnership Assets

LO4

Prepare a proposed schedule of liquidation from safe capital balances to determine an equitable preliminary distribution of available partnership assets.

In all of the illustrations analyzed in this chapter, distributions were made to the partners only after all assets were sold and all liabilities paid. As previously mentioned, a liquidation can take an extended time to complete. During this lengthy process, the partnership need not retain any assets that will eventually be disbursed to the partners. If the business is safely solvent, waiting until all affairs have been settled before transferring property to the owners is not warranted. The partners should be allowed to use their own funds at the earliest possible time.

The objective in making any type of preliminary distribution is to ensure that the partnership maintains enough capital to absorb all future losses. Any capital in excess of this maximum requirement is a safe balance, an amount that can be immediately conveyed to the partner. To determine safe capital balances at any time, the accountant assumes that all subsequent events will result in maximum losses: No cash will be received in liquidating remaining noncash assets and each partner is personally insolvent. Any positive capital balance that would remain even after the inclusion of all potential losses can be paid to the partner without delay. Although the assumption that no further funds will be generated could be unrealistic, it does ensure that negative capital balances are not created by premature payments being made to any of the partners.

Preliminary Distribution Illustrated

To demonstrate the computation of safe capital distributions, assume that a liquidating partnership reports the following balance sheet:

Cash	$ 60,000	Liabilities	$ 40,000
Noncash assets	140,000	Mason, loan	20,000
		Mason, capital (50%)	60,000
		Lee, capital (30%)	30,000
		Dixon, capital (20%)	50,000
Total assets	$200,000	Total liabilities and capital	$200,000

Assume also that the partners estimate that $6,000 will be the maximum expense incurred in carrying out this liquidation. Consequently, the partnership needs $46,000 to meet all obligations: $40,000 to satisfy partnership liabilities and $6,000 for these final expenses. Because the partnership holds $60,000 in cash, it can transfer the extra $14,000 to the partners immediately without fear of injuring any participants in the liquidation. However, the appropriate allocation of this money is not readily apparent; safe capital balances must be computed to guide the actual distribution.

Before demonstrating the allocation of this $14,000, we examine the appropriate handling of a partner's loan balance. According to the balance sheet, Mason has conveyed $20,000 to the business at some point in the past, an amount that was considered a loan rather than additional capital. Perhaps the partnership was in desperate need of funds and Mason was willing to contribute only if the contribution was structured as a loan. Regardless of the reason, the question as to the status of this account remains: Is the $20,000 to be viewed as a liability to the partner or as a capital balance? The answer becomes especially significant during the liquidation process because available funds often are limited. In this regard, the Uniform Partnership Act (UPA) (Section 807[a]) indicates that the assets of the partnership must be applied to pay obligations to creditors, including partners who are creditors; any surplus is distributed to partners based on their capital balances.

Although the UPA indicates that the debt to Mason should be repaid entirely before any distribution of capital can be made to the other partners, actual accounting practice takes a different view. "In preparing predistribution schedules, accountants typically offset partners' loans with the partners' capital accounts and then distribute funds accordingly."[9]

In other words, the loan is merged with the partner's capital account balance at the beginning of liquidation. Thus, accounting practice and the UPA seem to differ in the handling of a loan from a partner.

To illustrate the potential problem with this conflict, assume that a partnership has $20,000 in cash left after liquidation. Partner A has a positive capital balance of $20,000 whereas Partner B has a negative capital balance of $20,000. In addition, Partner B has previously loaned the partnership $20,000. If Partner B is insolvent, a distribution problem arises.[10] If the provisions of the UPA are followed literally, the $20,000 cash should be given to Partner B (probably to the creditors of Partner B) to repay the loan. Because Partner B is insolvent, no more assets can be expected from this individual. Thus, Partner A would have to absorb the entire $20,000 deficit capital balance and will get no portion of the $20,000 in cash that the business holds.

However, despite the UPA, common practice appears to be that the loan from Partner B will be used to offset that partner's negative capital balance. Using that approach, Partner B is left with a zero capital balance so that the entire $20,000 goes to Partner A; neither Partner B nor the creditors of Partner B get anything. Thus, when a loan comes from a partner who later becomes insolvent and reports a negative capital balance, the handling of the loan becomes significant. Unfortunately, further legal guidance does not exist at this time because "no reported state or federal opinion has directly ruled on the right of offset of potential capital deficits."[11]

To follow common practice, this textbook accounts for a loan from a partner in liquidation as if the balance were a component of the partner's capital. By this offset, the accountant can reduce the amount accumulated as a negative capital balance for any insolvent partner. Any such loan can be transferred into the corresponding capital account at the start of the liquidation process. Similarly, any loans due from a partner should be shown as a reduction in the appropriate capital balance.

Proposed Schedule of Liquidation

Returning to the current illustration, the accountant needs to determine an equitable distribution for the $14,000 cash presently available. To structure this computation, a proposed schedule of liquidation is developed *based on the underlying assumption that all*

[9] Robert E. Whitis and Jeffrey R. Pittman, "Inconsistencies between Accounting Practices and Statutory Law in Partnership Liquidations," *Accounting Educators' Journal,* Fall 1996, p. 99.

[10] The same problem should not exist if the partner is solvent. The partner is legally required to contribute enough funds to delete any capital deficit. Thus, in this case, Partner B would be entitled to the $20,000 loan repayment but then must contribute $20,000 because of the negative capital balance. That cash amount would go to Partner A because of that partner's positive capital balance.

[11] Whitis and Pittman, "Inconsistencies between Accounting Practices," p. 93.

EXHIBIT 15.2

MASON, LEE, AND DIXON
Proposed Schedule of Liquidation—Initial Safe Capital Balances

	Cash	Noncash Assets	Liabilities	Mason, Capital (50%)	Lee, Capital (30%)	Dixon, Capital (20%)
Beginning balances	$ 60,000	$140,000	$40,000	$80,000	$ 30,000	$ 50,000
Maximum loss on noncash assets	–0–	(140,000)	–0–	(70,000)	(42,000)	(28,000)
Maximum liquidation expenses	(6,000)	–0–	–0–	(3,000)	(1,800)	(1,200)
Payment of liabilities	(40,000)	–0–	(40,000)	–0–	–0–	–0–
Potential balances	14,000	–0–	–0–	7,000	(13,800)	20,800
Assume Lee to be insolvent	–0–	–0–	–0–	(9,857) (5/7)	13,800	(3,943) (2/7)
Potential balances	14,000	–0–	–0–	(2,857)	–0–	16,857
Assume Mason to be insolvent	–0–	–0–	–0–	2,857	–0–	(2,857)
Safe balances	$ 14,000	–0–	–0–	–0–	–0–	$ 14,000

future events will result in total losses. Exhibit 15.2 presents this statement for the Mason, Lee, and Dixon partnership. To expedite coverage, the $20,000 loan has already been transferred into Mason's capital account. Thus, regardless of whether this partner arrives at a deficit or a safe capital balance, the loan figure already has been included.

The preparation of Exhibit 15.2 forecasts complete losses ($140,000) in connection with the disposition of all noncash assets and anticipates liquidation expenses at maximum amounts ($6,000). Following the projected payment of liabilities, any partner reporting a negative capital account is assumed to be personally insolvent. These potential deficit balances are written off and the losses are assigned to the remaining solvent partners based on their relative profit and loss ratio. Lee, with a negative $13,800, is eliminated first. This allocation creates a deficit of $2,857 for Mason, an amount that Dixon alone must absorb. After this series of maximum losses is simulated, any positive capital balance that still remains is considered safe; a cash distribution of that amount can be made to the specific partners.

Exhibit 15.2 indicates that only Dixon has a large enough capital balance at the present time to absorb all possible future losses. Thus, the entire $14,000 can be distributed to this partner with no fear that the capital account will ever report a deficit. Based on current practice, Mason, despite having made a $20,000 loan to the partnership, is entitled to no part of this initial distribution. The loan is of insufficient size to prevent potential deficits from occurring in Mason's capital account.

One series of computations found in this proposed schedule of liquidation merits additional attention. The simulated losses initially create a $13,800 negative balance in Lee's capital account while the other two partners continue to report positive figures. Mason and Dixon must then absorb Lee's projected deficit according to their relative profit and loss percentages. Previously, Mason was allocated 50 percent of net income with 20 percent recorded to Dixon. These figures equate to a 50/70:20/70, or a 5/7:2/7 ratio. Based on this realigned relationship, the $13,800 potential deficit is allocated between Mason (5/7, or $9,857) and Dixon (2/7, or $3,943), reducing Mason's own capital account to a negative balance as shown in Exhibit 15.2.

Continuing with the assumption that maximum losses occur in all cases, Mason's $2,857 deficit is accounted for as if that partner were also personally insolvent. Therefore, the entire negative balance is assigned to Dixon, the only partner still in a positive capital position. Because all potential losses have been recognized at this point, the remaining $14,000 capital is a safe balance that should be paid to Dixon. Even after the money is distributed, Dixon's capital account will still be large enough to absorb all future losses.

Liquidation in Installments

In practice, complete losses are not likely to occur in the liquidation of any business. Thus, at various points during this process, additional cash amounts can become available as partnership property is sold. If the assets are disposed of in a piecemeal fashion,

EXHIBIT 15.3 Liquidation for Installments

MASON, LEE, AND DIXON
Proposed Schedule of Liquidation—Subsequent Safe Capital Balances

	Cash	Noncash Assets	Liabilities	Mason, Capital (50%)	Lee, Capital (30%)	Dixon, Capital (20%)
Beginning balances	$ 60,000	$140,000	$ 40,000	$ 80,000	$ 30,000	$ 50,000
Capital distribution—safe balances	(14,000)	-0-	-0-	-0-	-0-	(14,000)
Disposal of noncash assets	20,000	(50,000)	-0-	(15,000)	(9,000)	(6,000)
Liabilities paid	(40,000)	-0-	(40,000)	-0-	-0-	-0-
Liquidation expenses	(2,000)	-0-	-0-	(1,000)	(600)	(400)
Current balances	24,000	90,000	-0-	64,000	20,400	29,600
Maximum loss on remaining noncash assets	-0-	(90,000)	-0-	(45,000)	(27,000)	(18,000)
Maximum liquidation expenses	(3,000)	-0-	-0-	(1,500)	(900)	(600)
Potential balances	21,000	-0-	-0-	17,500	(7,500)	11,000
Assume Lee to be insolvent	-0-	-0-	-0-	(5,357) (5/7)	7,500	(2,143) (2/7)
Safe balances—current	$ 21,000	-0-	-0-	$ 12,143	-0-	$ 8,857

cash can actually flow into the company on a regular basis for an extended period of time. As needed, updated safe capital schedules must be developed to determine the recipients of newly available funds. Because numerous capital distributions could be required, this process is often referred to as a *liquidation made in installments.*

To illustrate, assume that the partnership of Mason, Lee, and Dixon actually undergoes the following events in connection with its liquidation:

- As the proposed schedule of liquidation in Exhibit 15.2 indicates, Dixon receives $14,000 in cash as a preliminary capital distribution.
- Noncash assets with a book value of $50,000 are sold for $20,000.
- All $40,000 in liabilities are settled.
- Liquidation expenses of $2,000 are paid; the partners now believe that only a maximum of $3,000 more will be expended in this manner. The original estimation of $6,000 was apparently too high.

As a result of these transactions, the partnership has an additional $21,000 in cash now available to distribute to the partners: $20,000 received from the sale of noncash assets and another $1,000 because of the reduced estimation of liquidation expenses. Once again, the accountant must assume maximum future losses as a means of determining the appropriate distribution of these funds. The accountant produces a second proposed schedule of liquidation (Exhibit 15.3), indicating that $12,143 of this amount should go to Mason with the remaining $8,857 to Dixon. To facilitate a better visual understanding, actual transactions are recorded first on this schedule, followed by the assumed losses. *A dotted line separates the real from the potential occurrences.*

LO5

Develop a predistribution plan to guide the distribution of assets in a partnership liquidation.

Predistribution Plan

The liquidation of a partnership can require numerous transactions occurring over a lengthy period of time. The continual production of proposed schedules of liquidation could become a burdensome chore. The previous illustration already has required two separate statements, and the partnership still possesses $90,000 in noncash assets awaiting conversion to cash. *Therefore, at the start of a liquidation, most accountants produce a single predistribution plan to serve as a guideline for all future payments.* Thereafter, whenever cash becomes available, this plan indicates the appropriate recipient(s) without the necessity of drawing up ever-changing proposed schedules of liquidation.

A predistribution plan is developed by simulating a series of losses, each of which is just large enough to eliminate, one at a time, all of the partners' claims to partnership property. This approach recognizes that the individual capital accounts exhibit differing degrees of sensitivity to losses. Capital accounts possess varying balances and could be charged with losses at different rates. Consequently, a predistribution plan is based on calculating the losses (the "maximum loss allowable") that would eliminate each of these capital balances in a sequential pattern. This series of absorbed losses then forms the basis for the predistribution plan.

To demonstrate the creation of a predistribution plan, assume that the following partnership is to be liquidated:

Cash	–0–	Liabilities	$100,000
Noncash assets	$221,000	Rubens, capital (50%)	30,000
		Smith, capital (20%)	40,000
		Trice, capital (30%)	51,000
Total assets	$221,000	Total liabilities and capital	$221,000

The partnership capital reported by this organization totals $121,000. However, the individual balances for the partners range from $30,000 to $51,000, and profits and losses are assigned according to three different percentages. Thus, differing losses would reduce each partner's current capital balance to zero. *As a prerequisite to developing a predistribution plan, the sensitivity to losses exhibited by each of these capital accounts must be measured:*

Partner	Capital Balance/ Loss Allocation	Maximum Loss That Can Be Absorbed
Rubens	$30,000/50%	$ 60,000 ✔
Smith	40,000/20%	200,000
Trice	51,000/30%	170,000

According to this initial computation, Rubens is the partner in the most vulnerable position at the present time. Based on a 50 percent share of income, a loss of only $60,000 would reduce this partner's capital account to a zero balance. If the partnership does incur a loss of this amount, Rubens can no longer hope to recover any funds from the liquidation process. Thus, the following schedule simulates the potential effects of this loss (referred to as a *Step 1 loss*):

	Rubens, Capital	Smith, Capital	Trice, Capital
Beginning balances	$ 30,000	$ 40,000	$ 51,000
Assumed $60,000 loss	(30,000) (50%)	(12,000) (20%)	(18,000) (30%)
Step 1 balances	–0–	$ 28,000	$ 33,000

As previously discussed, the predistribution plan is based on describing the series of losses that would eliminate each partner's capital in turn and, thus, all claims to cash. In the previous Step 1 schedule, the $60,000 loss did reduce Rubens's capital account to zero. Assuming, as a precautionary step, that Rubens is personally insolvent, all further losses would have to be allocated between Smith and Trice. Because these two partners have previously shared partnership profits and losses on a 20 percent and 30 percent basis, a 20/50:30/50 (or 40%:60%) relationship exists between them. Therefore, these realigned percentages must now be utilized in calculating a *Step 2 loss,* the amount just large enough to exclude another of the remaining partners from sharing in any future cash distributions:

Partner	Capital Balance/ Loss Allocation	Maximum Loss That Can Be Absorbed
Smith	$28,000/40%	$70,000
Trice	33,000/60%	55,000 ✔

Because Rubens's capital balance already has been eliminated, Trice is now in the most vulnerable position: Only a $55,000 Step 2 loss is required to reduce this partner's capital account to a zero balance.

	Rubens, Capital	Smith, Capital	Trice, Capital
Beginning balances	$ 30,000	$ 40,000	$ 51,000
Assumed $60,000 loss	(30,000) (50%)	(12,000) (20%)	(18,000) (30%)
Step 1 balances	–0–	$ 28,000	$ 33,000
Assumed $55,000 loss	–0–	(22,000) (40%)	(33,000) (60%)
Step 2 balances	–0–	$ 6,000	–0–

According to this second schedule, a total loss of $115,000 ($60,000 from Step 1 plus $55,000 from Step 2) leaves capital of only $6,000, a balance attributed entirely to Smith. At this final point in the simulation, an additional loss of this amount also ends Smith's right to receive any funds from the liquidation process. Having the sole positive capital account remaining, this partner would have to absorb the entire amount of the final loss.

	Rubens, Capital	Smith, Capital	Trice, Capital
Beginning balances	$ 30,000	$ 40,000	$ 51,000
Assumed $60,000 loss	(30,000) (50%)	(12,000) (20%)	(18,000) (30%)
Step 1 balances	–0–	$ 28,000	$ 33,000
Assumed $55,000 loss	–0–	(22,000) (40%)	(33,000) (60%)
Step 2 balances	–0–	6,000	–0–
Assumed $6,000 loss	–0–	(6,000) (100%)	–0–
Final balances	–0–	–0–	–0–

Once this series of simulated losses has reduced each partner's capital account to zero, a predistribution plan for the liquidation can be devised. *This procedure requires working backward through the preceding final schedule to determine the effects that will result if the assumed losses do not occur.* Without these losses, cash becomes available for the partners; therefore, a direct relationship exists between the volume of losses and the distribution pattern. For example, Smith will entirely absorb the last $6,000 loss. Should that loss fail to materialize, Smith is left with a positive safe capital balance of this amount. Thus, as cash becomes available, the first $6,000 received (in excess of partnership obligations and anticipated liquidation expenses) should be distributed solely to Smith.

Similarly, the preceding $55,000 Step 2 loss was divided between Smith and Trice on a 4:6 basis. Again, if such losses do not occur, these balances need not be retained to protect the partnership against capital deficits. Therefore, after Smith has received the initial $6,000, any additional cash that becomes available (up to $55,000) will be split between Smith (40%) and Trice (60%). For example, if the partnership holds exactly $61,000 in cash in excess of liabilities and possible liquidation expenses, this distribution should be made:

	Rubens	Smith	Trice
First $6,000	–0–	$ 6,000	–0–
Next $55,000	–0–	22,000 (40%)	$33,000 (60%)
Cash distribution	–0–	$28,000	$33,000

The predistribution plan can be completed by including the Step 1 loss, an amount that was to be absorbed by the partners on a 5:2:3 basis. Thus, all money that becomes available to the partners after the initial $61,000 is to be distributed according to the original profit and loss ratio. At this point in the liquidation, enough cash would have been generated to ensure that each partner has a safe capital balance: No possibility exists that a future deficit can occur. Any additional increases in the projected capital balances will be allocated by the

5:2:3 allocation pattern. *For this reason, once all partners begin to receive a portion of the cash disbursements, any remaining funds are divided based on the original profit and loss percentages.*

To inform all parties of the pattern by which available cash will be disbursed, the predistribution plan should be formally prepared in a schedule format prior to beginning liquidation. Following is the predistribution plan for the partnership of Rubens, Smith, and Trice. To complete this illustration, liquidation expenses of $12,000 have been estimated. Because these expenses have the same effect on the capital accounts as losses, they do not change the sequential pattern by which assets eventually will be distributed.

RUBENS, SMITH, AND TRICE
Predistribution Plan

Available Cash		Recipient
First	$112,000	Creditors ($100,000) and liquidation expenses (estimated at $12,000)
Next	6,000	Smith
Next	55,000	Smith (40%) and Trice (60%)
All further cash balances		Rubens (50%), Smith (20%), and Trice (30%)

Summary

1. Although a partnership can exist indefinitely through the periodic admission of new partners, termination of business activities and liquidation of property can take place for a number of reasons. A partner's death or retirement and the insolvency of a partner or even the partnership itself can trigger this process. Because of the risk that the partnership will incur large losses during liquidation, all parties usually seek frequent and timely information describing ongoing developments. The accountant is expected to furnish these data while also working to ensure the equitable treatment of all parties.
2. The liquidation process entails (*a*) converting partnership property into cash, (*b*) paying off liabilities and liquidation expenses, and (*c*) conveying any remaining property to the partners based on their final capital balances. As a means of reporting these transactions, a schedule of liquidation should be produced at periodic intervals. This statement discloses all recent transactions, the assets and liabilities still being held, and the current capital balances. Distribution of this schedule on a regular basis allows the various parties involved in the liquidation to monitor the progress being made.
3. During a liquidation, negative capital balances can arise for one or more of the partners, especially if the partnership incurs material losses in disposing of its property. In such cases, the specific partner or partners should contribute enough additional assets to eliminate their deficits. If payment is slow in coming, the partners who have safe capital balances can immediately divide any cash still held by the partnership. A *safe balance* is the amount of capital that would remain even if maximum future losses occur: Noncash assets are lost in total and all partners with deficits fail to fulfill their legal obligations. In making these computations, the remaining partners absorb negative capital balances based on their relative profit and loss ratio.
4. Completion of the actual liquidation of a partnership can take an extended period. Often, cash is generated during the early stages of this process in excess of the amount needed to cover liabilities and liquidation expenses. The accountant should propose a fair and immediate distribution of these available funds. A proposed schedule of liquidation can be created as a guide for such cash distributions. This statement is based on a *simulated* series of transactions: sale of all noncash assets, payment of liquidation expenses, and so on. At every point, maximum losses are assumed: Noncash assets have no resale value, liquidation expenses are set at the maximum level, and all partners are personally insolvent. Any safe capital balance remaining after incurring such losses represents a distribution that can be made at the present time. Even after this payment, the capital account will still be large enough to absorb all potential losses.
5. A partnership liquidation can require numerous transactions over a lengthy time period. Thus, the accountant could discover that the continual production of proposed schedules of liquidation becomes burdensome. For this reason, at the start of the liquidation process the accountant usually produces a single predistribution plan that serves as a definitive guideline for all payments to be made to the partners. To create this plan, the accountant simulates a series of losses with each loss, in turn, exactly eliminating a partner's capital balance. After these assumed losses have reduced all capital accounts to zero, the accountant devises the predistribution plan by working backward through the series of simulated losses. In effect, the accountant is measuring the cash that will become available if such losses do not occur.

Comprehensive Illustration

Problem

(*Estimated Time: 30 to 40 Minutes*) For the past several years, the Andrews, Caso, Quinn, and Sheridan partnership has operated a local department store. Based on the provisions of the original articles of partnership, all profits and losses have been allocated on a 4:3:2:1 ratio, respectively. Recently, both Caso and Quinn have undergone personal financial problems and, as a result, are now insolvent. Caso's creditors have filed a $20,000 claim against the partnership's assets, and $22,000 is being sought to repay Quinn's personal debts. To satisfy these legal obligations, the partnership property must liquidate. The partners estimate that they will incur $12,000 in expenses to dispose of all noncash assets.

At the time that active operations cease and the liquidation begins, the following partnership balance sheet is produced. All measurement accounts have been closed out to arrive at the current capital balances.

Cash	$ 20,000	Liabilities	$140,000
Noncash assets	280,000	Caso, loan	10,000
		Andrews, capital (40%)	76,000
		Caso, capital (30%)	14,000
		Quinn, capital (20%)	51,000
		Sheridan, capital (10%)	9,000
Total assets	$300,000	Total liabilities and capital	$300,000

During the lengthy liquidation process, the following transactions take place:

- Sale of noncash assets with a book value of $190,000 for $140,000 cash.
- Payment of $14,000 liquidation expenses. No further expenses are expected.
- Distribution of safe capital balances to the partners.
- Payment of all business liabilities.
- Sale of the remaining noncash assets for $10,000.
- Determination of deficit capital balances for any insolvent partners as uncollectible.
- Receipt of appropriate cash contributions from any solvent partner who is reporting a negative capital balance.
- Distribution of final cash.

Required

a. Using the information available prior to the start of the liquidation process, develop a predistribution plan for this partnership.

b. Prepare journal entries to record the actual liquidation transactions.

Solution

a. This partnership begins the liquidation process with capital amounting to $160,000. This total includes the $10,000 loan from Caso because the partnership must retain the liability as a possible offset against any eventual deficit capital balance. Therefore, the predistribution plan is based on the assumption that $160,000 in losses will be incurred, entirely eliminating all partnership capital. As discussed in this chapter, these simulated losses are arranged in a series so that each capital account is sequentially reduced to a zero balance.

At the start of the liquidation, Caso's capital position is the most vulnerable.

Partner	Capital Balance/ Loss Allocation	Maximum Loss That Can Be Absorbed
Andrews	$76,000/40%	$190,000
Caso	24,000/30%	80,000 ✔
Quinn	51,000/20%	255,000
Sheridan	9,000/10%	90,000

As this schedule indicates, an $80,000 loss would eradicate both Caso's $14,000 capital balance and the $10,000 loan. Therefore, to start the development of a predistribution plan, this loss is assumed to have occurred.

	Andrews, Capital	Caso, Loan and Capital	Quinn, Capital	Sheridan, Capital
Beginning balances	$ 76,000	$ 24,000	$ 51,000	$ 9,000
Assumed $80,000 loss	(32,000) (40%)	(24,000) (30%)	(16,000) (20%)	(8,000) (10%)
Step 1 balances	$ 44,000	–0–	$ 35,000	$ 1,000

With Caso's capital account eliminated, further losses are to be split among the remaining partners in the ratio of 4:2:1 (or 4/7:2/7:1/7). Because only an additional $7,000 loss (the preceding $1,000 Step 1 capital balance divided by 1/7) is now needed to reduce Sheridan's account to zero, this partner is in the second most vulnerable position.

	Andrews	Caso	Quinn	Sheridan
Step 1 balances (above)	$44,000	–0–	$35,000	$ 1,000
Assumed $7,000 loss	(4,000) (4/7)	–0–	(2,000) (2/7)	(1,000) (1/7)
Step 2 balances	$40,000	–0–	$33,000	–0–

Following these two simulated losses, only Andrews and Quinn continue to report positive capital balances. Thus, they divide any additional losses on a 4:2 basis, or 2/3:1/3. Based on these realigned percentages, Andrews's position has become the more vulnerable. An additional loss of $60,000 ($40,000/2/3) reduces this partner's remaining capital to zero whereas a $99,000 loss ($33,000/1/3) is required to eliminate Quinn's balance.

	Andrews	Caso	Quinn	Sheridan
Step 2 balances (above)	$ 40,000	–0–	$33,000	–0–
Assumed $60,000 loss	(40,000) (2/3)	–0–	(20,000) (1/3)	–0–
Step 3 balances	–0–	–0–	$13,000	–0–

The final $13,000 capital balance belongs to Quinn; an additional loss of this amount is necessary to remove the last element of partnership capital.

Based on the results of this series of simulated losses, the accountant can create a predistribution plan. However, the $140,000 in liabilities owed by the partnership still retains first priority to any available cash. Additionally, $12,000 must be held to cover the anticipated liquidation expenses.

ANDREWS, CASO, QUINN, AND SHERIDAN
Predistribution Plan

Available Cash		Recipient
First	$152,000	Creditors and anticipated liquidation expenses
Next	13,000	Quinn
Next	60,000	Andrews (2/3) and Quinn (1/3)
Next	7,000	Andrews (4/7), Quinn (2/7), and Sheridan (1/7)
All further cash		Andrews (40%), Caso (30%), Quinn (20%), and Sheridan (10%)

b. Journal entries for the liquidation:

Caso, Loan	10,000	
Caso, Capital		10,000
To record offset of loan against capital balance in anticipation of liquidation.		
Cash	140,000	
Andrews, Capital (40% of loss)	20,000	
Caso, Capital (30% of loss)	15,000	
Quinn, Capital (20% of loss)	10,000	
Sheridan, Capital (10% of loss)	5,000	
Noncash Assets		190,000
To record sale of noncash assets and allocation of $50,000 loss.		
Andrews, Capital (40%)	5,600	
Caso, Capital (30%)	4,200	
Quinn, Capital (20%)	2,800	
Sheridan, Capital (10%)	1,400	
Cash		14,000
To record payment of liquidation expenses.		

- The partnership now holds $146,000 in cash, $6,000 more than is needed to satisfy all liabilities and estimated expenses. According to the predistribution plan drawn up in requirement (*a*), this entire amount can be safely distributed to Quinn (or to Quinn's creditors).

Quinn, Capital	6,000	
Cash		6,000
To record distribution of available cash based on safe capital balance.		
Liabilities	140,000	
Cash		140,000
To record extinguishment of all partnership debts.		
Cash	10,000	
Andrews, Capital (40% of loss)	32,000	
Caso, Capital (30% of loss)	24,000	
Quinn, Capital (20% of loss)	16,000	
Sheridan, Capital (10% of loss)	8,000	
Noncash Assets		90,000
To record sale of remaining noncash assets and allocation of $80,000 loss.		

- At this point in the liquidation, only the cash and the capital accounts remain open on the partnership books.

	Cash	Andrews, Capital	Caso, Capital	Quinn, Capital	Sheridan, Capital
Beginning balances	$ 20,000	$ 76,000	$ 14,000	$ 51,000	$ 9,000
Loan offset	–0–	–0–	10,000	–0–	–0–
Sale of noncash assets	140,000	(20,000)	(15,000)	(10,000)	(5,000)
Liquidation expenses	(14,000)	(5,600)	(4,200)	(2,800)	(1,400)
Cash distribution	(6,000)	–0–	–0–	(6,000)	–0–
Payment of liabilities	(140,000)	–0–	–0–	–0–	–0–
Sale of noncash assets	10,000	(32,000)	(24,000)	(16,000)	(8,000)
Current balances	$ 10,000	$ 18,400	$(19,200)	$ 16,200	$(5,400)

Because Caso is personally insolvent, the $19,200 deficit balance will not be repaid, and the remaining three partners must absorb it on a 4:2:1 basis.

Andrews, Capital (4/7 of loss)	10,971	
Quinn, Capital (2/7 of loss)	5,486	
Sheridan, Capital (1/7 of loss)	2,743	
Caso, Capital		19,200
To record write-off of deficit capital balance of insolvent partner.		

- This last allocation decreases Sheridan's capital account to an $8,143 negative total. Because this partner is personally solvent, that amount should be contributed to the partnership in accordance with regulations of the Uniform Partnership Act.

Cash	8,143	
Sheridan, Capital		8,143
To record contribution made to eliminate deficit capital balance.		

- Sheridan's contribution brings the final cash total for the partnership to $18,143. This amount is distributed to the two partners who continue to maintain positive capital balances: Andrews and Quinn (or Quinn's creditors).

	Andrews, Capital	Quinn, Capital
Balances above	$18,400	$16,200
Caso deficit	(10,971)	(5,486)
Final balances	$ 7,429	$10,714

Andrews, Capital	7,429	
Quinn, Capital	10,714	
Cash		18,143
To record distribution of remaining cash according to final capital balances.		

Questions

1. What is the difference between the dissolution of a partnership and the liquidation of partnership property?
2. Why would the members of a partnership elect to terminate business operations and liquidate all noncash assets?
3. Why are liquidation gains and losses usually recorded as direct adjustments to the partners' capital accounts?
4. After liquidating all property and paying partnership obligations, what is the basis for allocating remaining cash among the partners?
5. What is the purpose of a schedule of liquidation? What information does it convey to its readers?
6. According to the Uniform Partnership Act, what events should occur if a partner incurs a negative capital balance during the liquidation process?
7. How are safe capital balances computed when preliminary distributions of cash are to be made during a partnership liquidation?
8. How do loans from partners affect the distribution of assets in a partnership liquidation? What alternatives can affect the handling of such loans?
9. What is the purpose of a proposed schedule of liquidation, and how is it developed?
10. How is a predistribution plan created for a partnership liquidation?

Problems

LO1

1. If a partnership is liquidated, how is the final allocation of business assets made to the partners?
   a. Equally.
   b. According to the profit and loss ratio.
   c. According to the final capital account balances.
   d. According to the initial investment made by each of the partners.

LO1

2. Which of the following statements is true concerning the accounting for a partnership going through liquidation?
   a. Gains and losses are reported directly as increases and decreases in the appropriate capital account.
   b. A separate income statement is created to measure only the profit or loss generated during liquidation.
   c. Because gains and losses rarely occur during liquidation, no special accounting treatment is warranted.
   d. Within a liquidation, all gains and losses are divided equally among the partners.

LO3

3. During a liquidation, if a partner's capital account balance drops below zero, what *should* happen?
   a. The other partners file a legal suit against the partner with the deficit balance.
   b. The partner with the highest capital balance contributes sufficient assets to eliminate the deficit.
   c. The deficit balance is removed from the accounting records with only the remaining partners sharing in future gains and losses.
   d. The partner with a deficit contributes enough assets to offset the deficit balance.

LO3

4. A local partnership is liquidating and is currently reporting the following capital balances:

Angela, capital (50% share of all profits and losses)	$ 19,000
Woodrow, capital (30%)	18,000
Cassidy, capital (20%)	(12,000)

   Cassidy has indicated that a forthcoming contribution will cover the $12,000 deficit. However, the two remaining partners have asked to receive the $25,000 in cash that is presently available. How much of this money should each of the partners be given?
   a. Angela, $13,000; Woodrow, $12,000.
   b. Angela, $11,500; Woodrow, $13,500.
   c. Angela, $12,000; Woodrow, $13,000.
   d. Angela, $12,500; Woodrow, $12,500.

LO3

5. A local partnership is considering possible liquidation because one of the partners (Bell) is insolvent. Capital balances at the current time are as follows. Profits and losses are divided on a 4:3:2:1 basis, respectively.

Bell, capital	$50,000
Hardy, capital	56,000
Dennard, capital	14,000
Suddath, capital	80,000

   Bell's creditors have filed a $21,000 claim against the partnership's assets. The partnership currently holds assets reported at $300,000 and liabilities of $100,000. If the assets can be sold for $190,000, what is the minimum amount that Bell's creditors would receive?
   a. –0–
   b. $2,000.
   c. $2,800.
   d. $6,000.

LO5

6. What is a predistribution plan?
   a. A guideline for the cash distributions to partners during a liquidation.
   b. A list of the procedures to be performed during a liquidation.

c. A determination of the final cash distribution to the partners on the settlement date.

d. A detailed list of the transactions that will transpire in the reorganization of a partnership.

LO3, LO4

7. A partnership has the following balance sheet just before final liquidation is to begin:

Cash	$ 26,000	Liabilities	$ 50,000
Inventory	31,000	Art, capital (40% of profits and losses)	18,000
Other assets	62,000	Raymond, capital (30%)	25,000
		Darby, capital (30%)	26,000
Total	$119,000	Total	$119,000

Liquidation expenses are estimated to be $12,000. The other assets are sold for $40,000. What distribution can be made to the partners?

a. –0– to Art, $1,500 to Raymond, $2,500 to Darby.

b. $1,333 to Art, $1,333 to Raymond, $1,334 to Darby.

c. –0– to Art, $1,200 to Raymond, $2,800 to Darby.

d. $600 to Art, $1,200 to Raymond, $2,200 to Darby.

LO1, LO3, LO4

8. A partnership has the following capital balances: A (20% of profits and losses) = $100,000; B (30% of profits and losses) = $120,000; C (50% of profits and losses) = $180,000. If the partnership is to be liquidated and $30,000 becomes immediately available, who gets that money?

a. $6,000 to A, $9,000 to B, $15,000 to C.

b. $22,000 to A, $3,000 to B, $5,000 to C.

c. $22,000 to A, $8,000 to B, –0– to C.

d. $24,000 to A, $6,000 to B, –0– to C.

LO5

9. A partnership is currently holding $400,000 in assets and $234,000 in liabilities. The partnership is to be liquidated, and $20,000 is the best estimation of the expenses that will be incurred during this process. The four partners share profits and losses as shown. Capital balances at the start of the liquidation follow:

Kevin, capital (40%)	$59,000
Michael, capital (30%)	39,000
Brendan, capital (10%)	34,000
Jonathan, capital (20%)	34,000

The partners realize that Brendan will be the first partner to start receiving cash. How much cash will Brendan receive before any of the other partners collect any cash?

a. $12,250.

b. $14,750.

c. $17,000.

d. $19,500.

LO5

10. Carney, Pierce, Menton, and Hoehn are partners who share profits and losses on a 4:3:2:1 basis, respectively. They are beginning to liquidate the business. At the start of this process, capital balances are as follows:

Carney, capital	$60,000
Pierce, capital	27,000
Menton, capital	43,000
Hoehn, capital	20,000

Which of the following statements is true?

a. The first available $2,000 will go to Hoehn.

b. Carney will be the last partner to receive any available cash.

c. The first available $3,000 will go to Menton.

d. Carney will collect a portion of any available cash before Hoehn receives money.

LO3, LO4

11. A partnership has gone through liquidation and now reports the following account balances:

Cash	$16,000
Loan from Jones	3,000
Wayman, capital	(2,000) (deficit)
Jones, capital	(5,000) (deficit)
Fuller, capital	13,000
Rogers, capital	7,000

Profits and losses are allocated on the following basis: Wayman, 30 percent; Jones, 20 percent; Fuller, 30 percent; and Rogers, 20 percent. Which of the following events should occur now?

a. Jones should receive $3,000 cash because of the loan balance.

b. Fuller should receive $11,800 and Rogers $4,200.

c. Fuller should receive $10,600 and Rogers $5,400.

d. Jones should receive $3,000, Fuller $8,800, and Rogers $4,200.

LO1, LO3, LO4

12. A partnership has the following account balances: Cash, $70,000; Other Assets, $540,000; Liabilities, $260,000; Nixon (50% of profits and losses), $170,000; Cleveland (30%), $110,000; Pierce (20%), $70,000. The company liquidates, and $8,000 becomes available to the partners. Who gets the $8,000?

LO1, LO3

13. A local partnership has only two assets (cash of $10,000 and land with a cost of $35,000). All liabilities have been paid and the following capital balances are currently being recorded. The partners share profits and losses as follows. All partners are insolvent.

Brown, capital (40%)	$25,000
Fish, capital (30%)	15,000
Stone, capital (30%)	5,000

a. If the land is sold for $25,000, how much cash does each partner receive in a final settlement?

b. If the land is sold for $15,000, how much cash does each partner receive in a final settlement?

c. If the land is sold for $5,000, how much cash does each partner receive in a final settlement?

LO3

14. A local dental partnership has been liquidated and the final capital balances are as follows:

Atkinson, capital (40% of all profits and losses)	$ 60,000
Kaporale, capital (30%)	20,000
Dennsmore, capital (20%)	(30,000)
Rasputin, capital (10%)	(50,000)

If Rasputin contributes additional cash of $20,000 to the partnership, what should happen to it?

LO4

15. A partnership currently holds three assets: cash, $10,000; land, $35,000; and a building, $50,000. The partners anticipate that expenses required to liquidate their partnership will amount to $5,000. Capital balances are as follows:

Ace, capital	$25,000
Ball, capital	28,000
Eaton, capital	20,000
Lake, capital	22,000

The partners share profits and losses as follows: Ace (30%), Ball (30%), Eaton (20%), and Lake (20%). If a preliminary distribution of cash is to be made, how much will each partner receive?

LO4

16. The following condensed balance sheet is for the partnership of Hardwick, Saunders, and Ferris, who share profits and losses in the ratio of 4:3:3, respectively:

Cash	$ 90,000	Accounts payable	$210,000
Other assets	820,000	Ferris, loan	40,000
Hardwick, loan	30,000	Hardwick, capital	300,000
		Saunders, capital	200,000
		Ferris, capital	190,000
Total assets	$940,000	Total liabilities and capital	$940,000

The partners decide to liquidate the partnership. Forty percent of the other assets are sold for $200,000. Prepare a proposed schedule of liquidation.

LO5

17. The following condensed balance sheet is for the partnership of Miller, Tyson, and Watson, who share profits and losses in the ratio of 6:2:2, respectively:

Cash	$ 40,000	Liabilities	$ 70,000
Other assets	140,000	Miller, capital	50,000
		Tyson, capital	50,000
		Watson, capital	10,000
Total assets	$180,000	Total liabilities and capital	$180,000

For how much money must the other assets be sold so that each partner receives some amount of cash in a liquidation?

LO4

18. A partnership's balance sheet is as follows:

Cash	$ 60,000	Liabilities	$ 50,000
Noncash assets	120,000	Babb, capital	60,000
		Whitaker, capital	20,000
		Edwards, capital	50,000
Total assets	$180,000	Total liabilities and capital	$180,000

Babb, Whitaker, and Edwards share profits and losses in the ratio of 4:2:4, respectively. This business is to be terminated, and the partners estimate that $8,000 in liquidation expenses will be incurred. How should the $2,000 in safe cash that is presently held be disbursed?

LO3

19. A partnership has liquidated all assets but still reports the following account balances:

Loan from White	$ 6,000
Black, capital	3,000
White, capital	(9,000) (deficit)
Green, capital	(3,000) (deficit)
Brown, capital	15,000
Blue, capital	(12,000) (deficit)

The partners split profits and losses as follows: Black, 30 percent; White, 30 percent; Green, 10 percent; Brown, 20 percent; and Blue, 10 percent.

Assuming that all partners are personally insolvent except for Green and Brown, how much cash must Green now contribute to this partnership?

LO4, LO5

20. The following balance sheet is for a local partnership in which the partners have become very unhappy with each other.

Cash	$ 40,000	Liabilities	$ 30,000
Land	130,000	Adams, capital	80,000
Building	120,000	Baker, capital	30,000
		Carvil, capital	60,000
		Dobbs, capital	90,000
Total assets	$290,000	Total liabilities and capital	$290,000

To avoid more conflict, the partners have decided to cease operations and sell all assets. Using this information, answer the following questions. Each question should be viewed as an *independent* situation related to the partnership's liquidation.

a. The $10,000 cash that exceeds the partnership liabilities is to be disbursed immediately. If profits and losses are allocated to Adams, Baker, Carvil, and Dobbs on a 2:3:3:2 basis, respectively, how will the $10,000 be divided?

b. The $10,000 cash that exceeds the partnership liabilities is to be disbursed immediately. If profits and losses are allocated on a 2:2:3:3 basis, respectively, how will the $10,000 be divided?

c. The building is immediately sold for $70,000 to give total cash of $110,000. The liabilities are then paid, leaving a cash balance of $80,000. This cash is to be distributed to the partners. How much of this money will each partner receive if profits and losses are allocated to Adams, Baker, Carvil, and Dobbs on a 1:3:3:3 basis, respectively?

d. Assume that profits and losses are allocated to Adams, Baker, Carvil, and Dobbs on a 1:3:4:2 basis, respectively. How much money must the firm receive from selling the land and building to ensure that Carvil receives a portion?

LO5

21. The partnership of Larson, Norris, Spencer, and Harrison has decided to terminate operations and liquidate all business property. During this process, the partners expect to incur $8,000 in liquidation expenses. All partners are currently solvent.

The balance sheet reported by this partnership at the time that the liquidation commenced follows. The percentages indicate the allocation of profits and losses to each of the four partners.

Cash	$ 28,250	Liabilities	$ 47,000
Accounts receivable	44,000	Larson, capital (20%)	15,000
Inventory	39,000	Norris, capital (30%)	60,000
Land and buildings	23,000	Spencer, capital (20%)	75,000
Equipment	104,000	Harrison, capital (30%)	41,250
Total assets	$238,250	Total liabilities and capital	$238,250

Based on the information provided, prepare a predistribution plan for liquidating this partnership.

LO5

22. The following partnership is being liquidated:

Cash	$ 36,000	Liabilities	$50,000
Noncash assets	174,000	Able, loan	10,000
		Able, capital (20%)	40,000
		Moon, capital (30%)	60,000
		Yerkl, capital (50%)	50,000

a. Liquidation expenses are estimated to be $12,000. Prepare a predistribution schedule to guide the distribution of cash.

b. Assume that assets costing $28,000 are sold for $40,000. How is the available cash to be divided?

LO5

23. A local partnership is to be liquidated. Commissions and other liquidation expenses are expected to total $19,000. The business's balance sheet prior to the commencement of liquidation is as follows:

Cash	$ 27,000	Liabilities	$ 40,000
Noncash assets	254,000	Simpson, capital (20%)	18,000
		Hart, capital (40%)	40,000
		Bobb, capital (20%)	48,000
		Reidl, capital (20%)	135,000
Total assets	$281,000	Total liabilities and capital	$281,000

Prepare a predistribution plan for this partnership.

LO3

24. The following information concerns two different partnerships. These problems should be viewed as independent situations.

Part A

The partnership of Ross, Milburn, and Thomas has the following account balances:

Cash	$ 36,000	Liabilities	$17,000
Noncash assets	100,000	Ross, capital	69,000
		Milburn, capital	(8,000) (deficit)
		Thomas, capital	58,000

This partnership is being liquidated. Ross and Milburn are each entitled to 40 percent of all profits and losses with the remaining 20 percent to Thomas.

a. What is the maximum amount that Milburn might have to contribute to this partnership because of the deficit capital balance?

b. How should the $19,000 cash that is presently available in excess of liabilities be distributed?

c. If the noncash assets are sold for a total of $41,000, what is the minimum amount of cash that Thomas could receive?

Part B

The partnership of Sampson, Klingon, Carton, and Romulan is being liquidated. It currently holds cash of $9,000 but no other assets. Liabilities amount to $24,000. The capital balances are as follows:

Sampson	$ 9,000
Klingon	(17,000)
Carton.	5,000
Romulan	(12,000)

Profits and losses are allocated on the following basis: Sampson, 40 percent, Klingon, 20 percent, Carton, 30 percent, and Romulan, 10 percent.

a. If both Klingon and Romulan are personally insolvent, how much money must Carton contribute to this partnership?

b. If only Romulan is personally insolvent, how much money must Klingon contribute? How will these funds be disbursed?

c. If only Klingon is personally insolvent, how much money should Sampson receive from the liquidation?

LO2

25. March, April, and May have been in partnership for a number of years. The partners allocate all profits and losses on a 2:3:1 basis, respectively. Recently, each partner has become personally insolvent and, thus, the partners have decided to liquidate the business in hopes of remedying their personal financial problems. As of September 1, the partnership's balance sheet is as follows:

Cash.	$ 11,000	Liabilities.	$ 61,000
Accounts receivable	84,000	March, capital.	25,000
Inventory	74,000	April, capital	75,000
Land, building, and equipment (net)	38,000	May, capital.	46,000
Total assets	$207,000	Total liabilities and capital	$207,000

Prepare journal entries for the following transactions:

a. Sold all inventory for $56,000 cash.

b. Paid $7,500 in liquidation expenses.

c. Paid $40,000 of the partnership's liabilities.

d. Collected $45,000 of the accounts receivable.

e. Distributed safe cash balances; the partners anticipate no further liquidation expenses.

f. Sold remaining accounts receivable for 30 percent of face value.

g. Sold land, building, and equipment for $17,000.

h. Paid all remaining liabilities of the partnership.

i. Distributed cash held by the business to the partners.

LO5

26. The partnership of W, X, Y, and Z has the following balance sheet:

Cash.	$ 30,000	Liabilities.	$42,000
Other assets	220,000	W, capital (50% of profits and losses)	60,000
		X, capital (30%)	78,000
		Y, capital (10%).	40,000
		Z, capital (10%)	30,000

Z is personally insolvent, and one of his creditors is considering suing the partnership for the $5,000 that is currently due. The creditor realizes that liquidation could result from this litigation and does not wish to force such an extreme action unless the creditor is reasonably sure of getting the money that is due. If the partnership sells the other assets, how much money must it receive to ensure that $5,000 would be available from Z's portion of the business? Liquidation expenses are expected to be $15,000.

LO4

27. On January 1, the partners of Van, Bakel, and Cox (who share profits and losses in the ratio of 5:3:2, respectively) decide to liquidate their partnership. The trial balance at this date follows:

	Debit	Credit
Cash	$ 18,000	
Accounts receivable	66,000	
Inventory	52,000	
Machinery and equipment, net	189,000	
Van, loan	30,000	
Accounts payable		$ 53,000
Bakel, loan		20,000
Van, capital		118,000
Bakel, capital		90,000
Cox, capital		74,000
Totals	$355,000	$355,000

The partners plan a program of piecemeal conversion of the business's assets to minimize liquidation losses. All available cash, less an amount retained to provide for future expenses, is to be distributed to the partners at the end of each month. A summary of the liquidation transactions follows:

January	Collected $51,000 of the accounts receivable; the balance is deemed uncollectible.
	Received $38,000 for the entire inventory.
	Paid $2,000 in liquidation expenses.
	Paid $50,000 to the outside creditors after offsetting a $3,000 credit memorandum received by the partnership on January 11.
	Retained $10,000 cash in the business at the end of January to cover any unrecorded liabilities and anticipated expenses. The remainder is distributed to the partners.
February	Paid $3,000 in liquidation expenses.
	Retained $6,000 cash in the business at the end of the month to cover unrecorded liabilities and anticipated expenses.
March	Received $146,000 on the sale of all machinery and equipment.
	Paid $5,000 in final liquidation expenses.
	Retained no cash in the business.

Prepare a schedule to compute the safe installment payments made to the partners at the end of each of these three months.

LO1, LO3

28. Following is a series of *independent cases*. In each situation, indicate the cash distribution to be made at the end of the liquidation process. *Unless otherwise stated, assume that all solvent partners will reimburse the partnership for their deficit capital balances.*

Part A

The Simon, Haynes, and Jackson partnership presently reports the following accounts. Jackson is personally insolvent and can contribute only an additional $3,000 to the partnership. Simon is also insolvent and has no available funds.

Cash	$ 30,000
Liabilities	22,000
Haynes, loan	10,000
Simon, capital (40%)	16,000
Haynes, capital (20%)	(6,000)
Jackson, capital (40%)	(12,000)

Part B

Hough, Luck, and Cummings operate a local accounting firm as a partnership. After working together for several years, they have decided to liquidate the partnership's property. The partners have prepared the following balance sheet:

Cash	$ 20,000	Liabilities	$ 40,000
Hough, loan	8,000	Luck, loan	10,000
Noncash assets	162,000	Hough, capital (50%)	90,000
		Luck, capital (40%)	30,000
		Cummings, capital (10%)	20,000
Total assets	$190,000	Total liabilities and capital	$190,000

The firm sells the noncash assets for $80,000; it will use $21,000 of this amount to pay liquidation expenses. All three of these partners are personally insolvent.

Part C

Use the same information as in Part B, but assume that the profits and losses are split 2:4:4 to Hough, Luck, and Cummings, respectively, and that liquidation expenses are only $6,000.

Part D

Following the liquidation of all noncash assets, the partnership of Redmond, Ledbetter, Watson, and Sandridge has the following account balances:

Liabilities	$ 28,000
Redmond, loan	5,000
Redmond, capital (20%)	(21,000)
Ledbetter, capital (10%)	(30,000)
Watson, capital (30%)	3,000
Sandridge, capital (40%)	15,000

Redmond is personally insolvent.

LO1, LO5

29. The partnership of Frick, Wilson, and Clarke has elected to cease all operations and liquidate its business property. A balance sheet drawn up at this time shows the following account balances:

Cash	$ 48,000	Liabilities	$ 35,000
Noncash assets	177,000	Frick, capital (60%)	101,000
		Wilson, capital (20%)	28,000
		Clarke, capital (20%)	61,000
Total assets	$225,000	Total liabilities and capital	$225,000

The following transactions occur in liquidating this business:

- Distributed safe capital balances immediately to the partners. Liquidation expenses of $9,000 are estimated as a basis for this computation.
- Sold noncash assets with a book value of $80,000 for $48,000.
- Paid all liabilities.
- Distributed safe capital balances again.
- Sold remaining noncash assets for $44,000.

- Paid liquidation expenses of $7,000.
- Distributed remaining cash to the partners and closed the financial records of the business permanently.

Produce a final schedule of liquidation for this partnership.

LO2, LO5

30. **Part A**

The partnership of Wingler, Norris, Rodgers, and Guthrie was formed several years ago as a local architectural firm. Several partners have recently undergone personal financial problems and have decided to terminate operations and liquidate the business. The following balance sheet is drawn up as a guideline for this process:

Cash	$ 15,000	Liabilities	$ 74,000
Accounts receivable	82,000	Rodgers, loan	35,000
Inventory	101,000	Wingler, capital (30%)	120,000
Land	85,000	Norris, capital (10%)	88,000
Building and equipment (net)	168,000	Rodgers, capital (20%)	74,000
		Guthrie, capital (40%)	60,000
Total assets	$451,000	Total liabilities and capital	$451,000

When the liquidation commenced, expenses of $16,000 were anticipated as being necessary to dispose of all property.

Prepare a predistribution plan for this partnership.

Part B

The following transactions transpire during the liquidation of the Wingler, Norris, Rodgers, and Guthrie partnership:

- Collected 80 percent of the total accounts receivable with the rest judged to be uncollectible.
- Sold the land, building, and equipment for $150,000.
- Made safe capital distributions.
- Learned that Guthrie, who has become personally insolvent, will make no further contributions.
- Paid all liabilities.
- Sold all inventory for $71,000.
- Made safe capital distributions again.
- Paid liquidation expenses of $11,000.
- Made final cash disbursements to the partners based on the assumption that all partners other than Guthrie are personally solvent.

Prepare journal entries to record these liquidation transactions.

Develop Your Skills

RESEARCH CASE

A client of the CPA firm of Harston and Mendez is a medical practice of seven local doctors. One doctor has been sued for several million dollars as the result of a recent operation. Because of what appears to be this doctor's very poor judgment, a patient died. Although that doctor was solely involved with the patient in question, the lawsuit names the entire practice as a defendant. Originally, four of these doctors formed this business as a general partnership. However, five years ago, the partners converted the business to a limited liability partnership based on the laws of the state in which they operate.

Read the following articles as well as any other published information that is available on partner and partnership liability:

"Partners Forever? Within Andersen, Personal Liability May Bring Ruin," *The Wall Street Journal,* April 2, 2002, p. C1.

"Collapse: Speed of Andersen's Demise Amazing," *Milwaukee Journal Sentinel,* June 16, 2002, p. D1.

Required

Based on the facts presented in this case, answer these questions:

1. What liability do the other six partners in this medical practice have in connection with this lawsuit?
2. What factors will be important in determining the exact liability (if any) of these six doctors?

ANALYSIS CASE

Go to the website www.napico.com and click on "Partnership Financial Information—Click Here." Then click on "2010 Annual Reports" to access the annual report for National Tax Credit Investors II (NTCI II).

Read the financial statements contained in the 2010 annual report and the accompanying notes, especially any that discuss the partnership form of organization.

Assume that an investor is considering investing in this partnership and has downloaded this report for study and analysis.

Required

1. What differences between NTCI II's financial statements and those of an incorporated entity exist?
2. Assume that this potential investor is not aware of the potential implications of owning a partnership rather than a corporation. What information is available in these statements to advise this individual of the unique characteristics of this legal business form?

COMMUNICATION CASE

Read the following as well as any other published articles on the bankruptcy of the partnership of Laventhol & Horwath:

"Laventhol Says It Plans to File for Chapter 11," *The Wall Street Journal,* November 20, 1990, p. A3.

"Laventhol Partners Face Long Process That Could End in Personal Bankruptcy," *The Wall Street Journal,* November 20, 1990, p. B5.

"Laventhol Bankruptcy Filing Indicates Liabilities May Be as Much as $2 Billion," *The Wall Street Journal,* November 23, 1990, p. A4.

Required

Write a report describing the potential liabilities that the members of a partnership could incur.

EXCEL CASE

The partnership of Wilson, Cho, and Arrington has the following account information:

Partner	Capital Balance	Share of Profits and Losses
Wilson	$200,000	40%
Cho	180,000	20
Arrington	110,000	40

This partnership will be liquidated, and the partners are scheduled to receive cash equal to any ending positive capital balance. If a negative capital balance results, the partner is expected to contribute that amount.

Assume that losses of $50,000 occur during the liquidation followed later by additional and final losses of $100,000.

Required

1. Create a spreadsheet to determine the capital balances that remain for each of the three partners after these two losses are incurred.
2. Modify this spreadsheet so that it can be used for different capital balances, different allocation patterns, and different liquidation gains and losses.

chapter 16

Accounting for State and Local Governments (Part 1)

Learning Objectives

After studying this chapter, you should be able to:

- LO1 Explain the history of and the reasons for the unique characteristics of the financial statements produced by state and local governments.
- LO2 Differentiate between the two sets of financial statements produced by state and local governments.
- LO3 Understand the reason that fund accounting has traditionally been such a prominent factor in the internal recording of state and local governments.
- LO4 Identify the three fund types and the individual fund categories within each.
- LO5 Understand the basic structure of government-wide financial statements and fund financial statements (as produced for the governmental funds).
- LO6 Record the passage of a budget as well as subsequent encumbrances and expenditures.
- LO7 Understand the reporting of capital assets, supplies, and prepaid expenses by a state or local government.
- LO8 Determine the proper timing for the recognition of revenues from nonexchange transactions.
- LO9 Account for the issuance of long-term bonds and the reporting of special assessment projects.
- LO10 Record the various types of monetary transfers that occur within the funds of a state or local government.

To even a seasoned veteran of accounting, the financial statements produced for a state or local government can appear to be written in a complex foreign language.

- The 2010 financial statements for Bismarck, North Dakota, report other financing sources and uses for its governmental funds that include $21.1 million of operating transfers-in and $19.5 million of operating transfers-out.
- The June 30, 2010, balance sheet for the governmental funds of Portland, Maine, reported total fund balances of $74.9 million.
- The 2010 comprehensive annual financial report for Phoenix, Arizona, contains more than 245 pages of data including the dollar amounts of expenditures made in connection with public safety ($812.6 million), community enrichment ($198.0 million), and environmental services ($19.2 million).
- For 2010, Greensboro, North Carolina, reported two complete and distinct sets of financial statements. One disclosed that the city's governmental activities owed more than $247 million in liabilities as of June 30, 2010, whereas the second set indicated that, at the same point in time, the city's governmental funds owed less than $50 million in liabilities.
- For the year ending June 30, 2010, Nashville and Davidson County, Tennessee, reported that operating its public library system resulted in a net financial burden of $27.6 million for the citizens, while its department of water and sewerage services provided a financial benefit of $38.6 million.

Merely a quick perusal of such information points to fundamental differences with the reporting that most people associate with the financial statements of for-profit businesses. One or more underlying causes must be responsible for the uniqueness of the financial statements of state and local governments. This chapter and the next introduce the principles and practices that underlie state and local government accounting and explain the logic behind their application.

These chapters are designed not only to demonstrate reporting procedures but also to explain the evolution that has led state and local governments to produce financial statements that are markedly different in many places from those of for-profit businesses.

Introduction to the Accounting for State and Local Governments

LO1

Explain the history of and the reasons for the unique characteristics of the financial statements produced by state and local governments.

In the United States, thousands of state and local government reporting entities touch the lives of the citizenry on a daily basis. A census is taken every five years to determine the number and types of governments. In addition to the federal and 50 state governments, 89,476 local governments existed as of 2007. Of these, 39,044 were general purpose local governments—3,033 county governments and 36,011 subcounty governments, including 19,492 municipal governments and 16,519 township governments. The remainder, which comprised more than one-half of the total, were special purpose local governments, including 14,561 school districts and school system governments and 37,381 special district governments.[1] Nearly 14.7 million people were employed by state and local governments. Income and sales taxes are collected, property taxes are assessed, schools are operated, fire departments are maintained, garbage is collected, and roads are paved. Actions of one or more governments affect virtually every individual each day.

Despite the huge number of entities, the first question that should be addressed here is whether the creation of a unique set of governmental accounting principles is warranted. Could the financial information of a state or local government be fairly presented by applying the same rules and procedures as a business enterprise such as Microsoft or Google? In response, several major differences have been identified by the Governmental Accounting Standards Board (GASB) that explain the need for an entirely different set of generally accepted accounting principles for a government such as the City of Baltimore.

"The primary purpose of governments is to enhance or maintain the well-being of citizens by providing services in accordance with public policy goals. In contrast, for-profit business enterprises focus primarily on wealth creation, interacting principally with those segments of society that fulfill their mission of generating a financial return on investment for shareholders.

"The white paper cites several other crucial differences that generate user demand for unique information:

- Governments serve a broader group of stakeholders, including taxpayers, citizens, elected representatives, oversight groups, bondholders, and others in the financial community.
- Most government revenues are raised through involuntary taxes rather than a willing exchange of comparable value between two parties in a typical business transaction.
- Monitoring actual compliance with budgeted public policy priorities is central to government public accountability reporting.
- Governments exist longer than for-profit businesses and are not typically subject to bankruptcy and dissolution."[2]

Therefore, accounting for such governments is not merely a matching of expenses with earned revenues so that net income can be determined. The setting of tax rates and allocating of limited financial resources among such worthy causes as education, police protection, welfare, and the environment create heated debates throughout the nation.

Additional questions that should be considered in coming to understand the nature of governmental accounting are: Without a profit motive, what should be reported by a government and who are the potential users of that financial information? Historically, to keep the public informed so that proper decisions are more likely to be made,

[1] www.census.gov/govs/cog/GovOrgTab03ss.html.

[2] "Users of Governmental Financial Reports Require Substantially Different Information than Users of Business Financial Reports," News Release, March 16, 2006, http://www.gasb.org/cs/ContentServer?c=GASBContent_C&pagename=GASB%2FGASBContent_C%2FGASBNewsPage&cid=1176156736250.

government reporting has focused on identifying the methods used to generate financial resources and the uses made of those resources.

Indeed, this approach is appropriate for the short-term decisions necessitated by the gathering and utilizing of financial resources to carry out public policy. For the longer term, though, information to reflect the overall financial stability of the government is also needed, especially by the creditors who provide funding for the government.

Hence, the financial reporting for state and local governments faces a number of unique challenges. Those issues are addressed by GASB which was created in 1984 to serve as the public sector counterpart of the Financial Accounting Standards Board (FASB). GASB holds the primary responsibility in the United States for setting authoritative accounting standards for state and local government units.[3] In the same manner as FASB, GASB is an independent body functioning under the oversight of the Financial Accounting Foundation. Much of this chapter and the next reflect the attempt by GASB to provide relevant information to a wide array of individuals and groups interested in assessing the work and the prospects of a particular government.[4]

Governmental Accounting—User Needs

The unique aspects of any system of accounting should be a direct result of the perceived needs of financial statement users. Identification of these informational requirements is, therefore, a logical introductory step in the study of the accounting principles applied to state and local governments. Specific procedures utilized in the reporting process can be understood best as an outgrowth of these needs.

In *Concepts Statement No. 1,* "Objectives of Financial Reporting," GASB recognized this challenge by identifying three groups of primary users of external state and local governmental financial reports:

> **Citizenry**—Want to evaluate the likelihood of tax or service fee increases, to determine the sources and uses of resources, to forecast revenues in order to influence spending decisions, to ensure that resources were used in accordance with appropriations, to assess financial condition, and to compare budgeted to actual results.
> **Legislative and oversight bodies**—Want to assess the overall financial condition when developing budgets and program recommendations, to monitor operating results to assure compliance with mandates, to determine the reasonableness of fees and the need for tax changes, and to ascertain the ability to finance new programs and capital needs.
> **Investors and creditors**—Want to know the amount of available and likely future financial resources, to measure the debt position and the ability to service that debt, and to review operating results and cash flow data.[5]

Thus, the quest for useful governmental reporting encounters a significant obstacle: User needs are so broad that no one set of financial statements or accounting principles can possibly satisfy all expectations. How can voters, bondholders, city officials, and the other users of the financial statements provided by state and local governments receive the information that they need for decision-making purposes? How can statements that are prepared for citizens also be sufficient for the needs of creditors and investors?

[3] The National Committee on Municipal Accounting held the authority for state and local government accounting from 1934 until 1941. The National Committee on Governmental Accounting, a quasi-independent agency of the Government Finance Officers Association, established government accounting principles from 1949 through 1954 and again from 1967 until 1973 when GASB was formed. During several time periods, no group held primary responsibility for the development of governmental accounting. For an overview of the work of GASB, see Terry K. Patton and Robert J. Freeman, "The GASB Turns 25: A Retrospective," *Government Finance Review*, April 2009.

[4] In 1990, the Director of the Office of Management and Budget, the Secretary of the Treasury, and the Comptroller General created the Federal Accounting Standards Advisory Board (FASAB). FASAB recommends accounting principles and standards for the U.S. federal government and its agencies to use. Information about FASAB can be found at www.fasab.gov. A history of the work of FASAB can be found in "FASAB at 20: Looking Back and Thinking Ahead," by Tom L. Allen, in the Fall 2010 issue of the *Journal of Government Finance Management*.

[5] Government Accounting Standards Board, *Codification of Governmental Accounting and Financial Reporting Standards as of June 30, 2010* (Norwalk, CT, 2010), Appendix B, *Concepts Statement No. 1*, par. 35–37.

LO2

Differentiate between the two sets of financial statements produced by state and local governments.

Two Sets of Financial Statements

Eventually, the desire to provide financial information that could satisfy such broad demands led GASB in 1999 to require the production of two distinct sets of statements by state and local governments, each with its own unique principles and objectives. For a complete understanding of state and local government accounting, nothing is more essential than recognizing the need for these two sets of statements:

1. **Fund financial statements** have more of an interest in the current activities of the government. They report current period revenues and expenditures in connection with individual government functions. These statements also focus on disclosing restrictions that have been placed on the use of any of the resources held by these functions. Citizens interested in the operation of the government are likely to study the fund financial statements.
2. **Government-wide financial statements** have a longer-term focus. They report all revenues and all costs as well as all assets and liabilities. Creditors, especially bondholders, are likely to be most interested in government-wide financial statements as they assess the likelihood of being paid when amounts come due.

Fund Financial Statements

These statements report individual government activities and the amount of financial resources allocated to them each period as well as the use made of those resources. Through these statements citizens are able to assess the government's fiscal accountability in raising and utilizing money. For example, fund financial statements report the amount spent on such services as public safety, education, health and sanitation, and the construction of new roads. The primary measurement focus, at least for the public service activities, is the amount and the changes in *current financial resources* such as cash and receivables. The timing of recognition in most cases is based on *modified accrual accounting*. Modified accrual accounting recognizes (1) revenues when the resulting current financial resources are both measurable and available to be used and (2) expenditures when they cause a reduction in current financial resources.

In applying modified accrual accounting, identifying when financial resources are "available" for current-period expenditures can be quite important. For government accounting, the term "available" means that current financial resources will be received soon enough in the future to be used in paying for current period expenditures. The determination of what is meant by "soon enough" is up to the reporting government.

For example, in 2010, the City of Norfolk, Virginia, disclosed that "the City generally considers revenues, except for grant revenues, to be available if they are collected within 45 days of the end of the fiscal year." For that reason, a 2010 revenue collected within the first 45 days of 2011 is still recognized by this city in 2010 because it was available to pay 2010 expenditures. However, the City of Richmond, Virginia, applies a policy of two months and the City of Raleigh, North Carolina, uses 90 days. In creating fund financial statements, the definition of available can vary from one government to the next. The one exception under modified accrual accounting is the recognition of property taxes where a 60-day maximum period is mandated.

Government-Wide Financial Statements

These statements report a government's financial affairs as a whole. They provide a method of assessing operational accountability, the government's ability to meet its operating objectives. This information helps users make evaluations of the financial decisions and long-term stability of the government by allowing them to:

- Determine whether the government's overall financial position improved or deteriorated during the reporting period.
- Understand the cost of providing services to the citizenry.
- See how the government finances its programs.
- Understand the extent to which the government has invested in capital assets, such as roads, bridges, and other infrastructure assets.

To achieve these reporting goals, the government-wide financial statements' measurement focus is on all *economic resources* (not just current financial resources), and these statements utilize *accrual accounting* for timing purposes much like a for-profit entity. Consequently, these statements report all assets and liabilities and recognize revenues and expenses in a way that is comparable to business-type accounting.

The Need for Two Sets of Financial Statements

One aspect of governmental reporting has remained constant over the years: the goal of making the government accountable to the public. Because of the essential role of democracy within U.S. society, the creators of accounting principles have attempted to provide a vehicle for evaluating governmental actions. Citizens should be aware of the means that officials use to raise money and to allocate scarce resources. Voters must evaluate the wisdom, as well as the honesty, of the members of government. Most voters are also taxpayers; thus they naturally exhibit special interest in the results obtained from their involuntary contributions to the government through taxes and tolls. Because elected and appointed officials hold authority over the public's money, governmental reporting has traditionally stressed this stewardship responsibility.

> Accountability is the cornerstone of all financial reporting in government. . . . Accountability requires governments to answer to the citizenry—to justify the raising of public resources and the purposes for which they are used. Governmental accountability is based on the belief that the citizenry has a "right to know," a right to receive openly declared facts that may lead to public debate by the citizens and their elected representatives.[6]

To promote transparency for users, reporting has historically been directed toward measuring and identifying the current financial resources generated and expended by each of a government's diverse activities. Fund statements allow readers to focus on individual governmental activities. At least in connection with public services, such as the police department and public library, the fund financial statements answer three relevant questions:

- How did the government generate its current financial resources?
- Where did those financial resources go?
- What amount of those financial resources is presently held?

The term *current financial resources* normally encompasses monetary assets available for officials to spend to meet the government's needs this year. Thus, when reporting current financial resources, a government is primarily monitoring cash, investments, and receivables as well as any current claims to those resources. Historically, little reporting emphasis has been placed on accounts such as Buildings, Equipment, and Long-Term Debts that have no direct impact on current financial resources.

Stressing accountability by monitoring the flow of current financial resources is an approach that cannot meet all user needs. Thus, many conventional reporting objectives were long ignored. Does the government have too much long-term debt, for example? As a result, investors and creditors were frequently sharp critics of governmental accounting. "When cities get into financial trouble, few citizens know about it until the day the interest can't be met or the teachers paid. . . . Had the books been kept like any decent corporation's that could never have happened."[7]

Consequently, GASB mandated the inclusion of government-wide financial statements to provide an additional dimension for government reporting. This second set of statements does not focus solely on current financial resources but seeks to report all assets at the disposal of government officials as well as all liabilities that must eventually be paid. Likewise, revenues and expenses are recognized according to accrual accounting and provide a completely different level of financial information.

[6] GASB, *Codification*, Appendix B, *Concepts Statement No. 1,* par 56.

[7] Richard Greene, "You Can't Fight City Hall—If You Can't Understand It," *Forbes,* March 3, 1980, p. 92.

With two sets of financial statements, each user (whether citizen or investor) can select the information considered to be the most relevant. Of course, not everyone believes that additional data will always be helpful. "One of the tougher challenges of the current information age is sorting out the information most relevant for decision making from the vast amounts of data generated by today's state-of-the-art information systems. Financial reports cannot simply keep growing in size indefinitely to encompass every new type of information that becomes available."[8]

	Fund Financial Statements*	**Government-Wide Financial Statements**
Emphasis	Individual activities (during current period)	Government as a whole
Measurement focus	Current financial resources (cash, investments, and receivables and claims to those assets)	All economic resources (all assets and all liabilities)
General information	Inflows and outflows of current financial resources	Overall financial health
Timing of recognition	Modified accrual accounting	Accrual accounting

*The information provided here for fund financial statements only applies to public service activities such as public safety and education. As will be discussed shortly, other activities are reported more in keeping with government-wide financial statements.

LO3

Understand the reason that fund accounting has traditionally been such a prominent factor in the internal recording of state and local governments.

Internal Record-Keeping—Fund Accounting

In gathering financial information, state and local governments have always faced the challenge of reporting a diverse array of activities financed from numerous sources. Accountability and control become special concerns for governments that operate through a multitude of relatively independent departments and functions. Consequently, for internal monitoring purposes, the accounting for each government activity is maintained in a separate quasi-independent bookkeeping system referred to as a *fund*. Hence, separate data are accumulated for every activity (library, school system, fire department, road construction, and the like).

For decades, the internal information gathered in this manner has served as the foundation for fund financial statements. An underlying assumption of government reporting has long been that most statement users prefer to see information segregated by function in order to assess each activity individually. The internal accounting records provided that information and the figures could be transferred directly into fund financial statements for external distribution.

Because no common profit motive exists to tie all of these various functions and services together, consolidated activity balances were historically not presented. Combining operating results from the city zoo, fire department, water system, print shop, and the like would provide figures of questionable utility if accountability and control over the usage of current financial resources are the primary goals. Financial reporting was designed to provide information about the individual activities, not the government as a whole.

The addition of government-wide statements does not affect the use of fund accounting for control purposes. Consequently, the separate funds monitored by a state or local government still serve as the basic foundation for internal reporting. Although a single list of identifiable functions is not possible, the following frequently are included:

Public safety	Judicial system
Highway maintenance	Debt repayment
Sanitation	Bridge construction
Health	Water and sewer system
Welfare	Municipal swimming pool
Culture and recreation	Data processing center
Education	Endowment funds
Parks	Employee pensions

[8] Jeffrey L. Esser, "Standard Setting—How Much Is Enough?" *Government Finance Review,* April 2005, p. 3.

The actual number of funds in use depends on the extent of services that the government offers and the grouping of related activities. For example, separate funds may be set up to account for a high school and its athletic programs, or these activities may be combined into a single fund.

> Only the minimum number of funds consistent with legal and operating requirements should be established, however, because unnecessary funds result in inflexibility, undue complexity, and inefficient financial administration.[9]

The requirement passed in 1999 for government-wide financial statements to be reported along with fund financial statements was a radical departure designed to reflect the overall financial health of the government. One significant outcome for the governments was that they had to start reporting information (the total cost of roads, for example) that had never been accumulated because fund accounting monitors the increases and decreases in current financial resources. As will be seen in this chapter and the next, a considerable amount of additional information was required to create financial statements that reported all of the economic resources of the government as a whole.

LO4

Identify the three fund types and the individual fund categories within each.

Fund Accounting Classifications

For internal record-keeping, all funds (whether for the police department, the municipal golf course, or some other activity) are categorized into one of three distinct groups. This classification system provides clearer reporting of the government's various activities. Furthermore, having separate groups allows for unique accounting principles to be applied to each.

- *Governmental funds*—include all funds that account for activities a government carries out primarily to provide citizens with services that are financed primarily through taxes. For that reason, police and fire departments are reported within the governmental funds.
- *Proprietary funds*—account for a government's ongoing activities that are similar to those conducted by for-profit organizations. This fund type normally encompasses operations that assess a user charge so that determining profitability or cost recovery is important. For example, both a municipal golf course and a toll road are typically reported within the proprietary funds.
- *Fiduciary funds*—account for monies held by the government in a trustee or agency capacity. Such assets must be maintained for others and cannot be used by the government for its own programs. One common example is the monitoring of assets held in a pension plan for government employees.

Governmental Funds

In many state and municipal accounting systems, governmental funds tend to dominate because a service orientation usually prevails. The internal accounting system can maintain individual funds for every distinct service function: public safety, libraries, construction of a town hall, and so on. Each of these governmental funds accumulates and expends current financial resources to achieve one or more desired public goals.

To provide better reported information and control, the governmental funds are subdivided into five categories: the General Fund, Special Revenue Funds, Capital Projects Funds, Debt Service Funds, and Permanent Funds. This classification system forms an overall structure for financial reporting purposes.

The General Fund GASB's definition of the General Fund appears to be somewhat understated: "to account for and report all financial resources not accounted for and reported in another fund."[10] This description seems to imply that the General Fund records only miscellaneous revenues and expenditures when, in actuality, it accounts for many of a government's most important services, a broad range of ongoing functions. For example, the 2010 fund financial statements for the City of Baltimore, Maryland, disclosed 11 major areas of current expenditures within its General Fund:

[9] GASB, *Codification*, Sec. 1100.104.

[10] GASB, *Codification*, Sec. 1300.104.

General government	Recreation and culture
Public safety and regulations	Highways and streets
Conservation of health	Sanitation and waste removal
Social services	Public service
Education	Economic development
Public library	

Expenditures reported for these categories were in excess of $1.25 billion and made up more than 58 percent of the total for all of the city's governmental funds for the year ended June 30, 2010.

Special Revenue Funds Special Revenue Funds account for resource inflows that are restricted or committed for a specific purpose other than debt payments or capital projects. Because of donor stipulations or legislative mandates, these financial resources must be spent in a specified fashion. Saint Paul, Minnesota, for example, reported approximately $150 million of revenues within over 30 individual Special Revenue Funds during the 2008 fiscal year. Sources were as diverse as fees charged for use of the crime laboratory, rent received from the use of Municipal Stadium, administration fees for charitable gambling, money received from solid waste and recycling programs, and parking meter fees. The Special Revenue Funds category accounts for these monies because legal or donor restrictions were attached to the revenue to require that expenditure be limited to specific operating purposes. As an example, according to Saint Paul's annual financial report, receipts from charitable gambling must be administered "in conformance with City Council action for the support of youth athletics or otherwise as legally determined." Thus, the accounting system monitors the receipt and disbursement of any financial resources from this source by including them in the Special Revenue Funds.

Capital Projects Funds As the title implies, this fund type accounts for financial resources restricted, committed, or assigned to be used for capital outlays such as acquiring or constructing bridges, high schools, roads, or municipal office complexes. Funding for these projects normally comes from grants, sale of bonds, or transfers from general revenue. The actual asset being obtained is not reported here; only the money to finance the purchase or construction is recorded. For example, the Lexington-Fayette Urban County Government in Kentucky reported, as of June 30, 2010, that it was holding a total of more than $20.1 million in current financial resources in 19 different Capital Projects Funds to be used in projects such as acquisition or construction in connection with a cultural center, road projects, a golf course, and equipment leasing.

Debt Service Funds These funds record financial resources accumulated to pay long-term liabilities and interest as they come due. However, this fund type does not account for a government's long-term debt. Debt Service Funds are created to monitor the monetary balances currently available to make the eventual payment to satisfy long-term liabilities. Thus, on June 30, 2010, the city of Birmingham, Alabama, reported approximately $40 million of cash and investments in its debt service funds, money being held to pay long-term debt and interest. For the year then ended, this fund had made more than $19.9 million in principal payments and $14.8 million in interest payments.

Permanent Funds The Permanent Funds category accounts for financial resources restricted by external donor, contract, or legislation with the stipulation that the principal cannot be spent but any income can be used by the government, often for a designated purpose to benefit the general citizenry. As an example, the City of Dallas, Texas, reported holding approximately $8 million as of September 30, 2009, that had come almost entirely from private donations whose income was designated to maintain four different parks and to help finance other municipal projects. Such gifts are frequently referred to as *endowments*.

Proprietary Funds

The proprietary funds category accounts for government activities, such as a bus system or subway line, that assess a user charge. Such services resemble those found in the business world. Because the user charge helps the government make a profit or, at least, recover part of its cost, the proprietary funds are reported in much the same way on both the fund financial statements and the government-wide financial statements. The accounting resembles that of a for-profit activity in that accrual accounting is used to recognize all assets and liabilities.

To facilitate financial reporting, the proprietary funds are broken down into two divisions:

Enterprise Funds Any government operation that is open to the public and financed, at least in part, by user charges is likely to be classified as an Enterprise Fund. A municipality, for example, might generate revenues from the use of a public swimming pool, golf course, airport, water and sewage service, and the like. The City of Charlotte, North Carolina, generated $452 million in revenue in 2010 from several Enterprise Funds including its airport, public transit, and water and sewer services.

The number of enterprise funds has increased rather dramatically over recent years as governments have attempted to expand services without raising taxes. This situation requires those citizens utilizing a particular service to shoulder a higher percentage of its costs. "Enterprise funds have become an attractive alternative revenue source for local governments to recover all or part of the cost of goods or services from those directly benefiting from them."[11]

Enterprise Fund activities that collect direct fees from customers resemble business activities. Not surprisingly, even in the fund financial statements, the accounting process for these operations parallels that found in for-profit reporting. These funds use accrual basis accounting with a focus on all economic, not just current financial, resources.

A question arises, though, as to how much revenue an activity must generate before it is viewed as an Enterprise Fund. For example, if a city wants to promote mass transit and charges only a nickel to ride its bus line, should that activity be viewed as part of an Enterprise Fund (a business-type activity) or within the General Fund (a governmental activity)?

Any activity that charges the public a user fee may be classified as an Enterprise Fund. However, this designation is *required* if the activity meets any one of the following criteria. At that point, the amount of revenue is viewed as significant:

- The activity generates net revenues that provide the sole security for the debts of the activity.
- Laws or regulations require recovering the activity's costs (including depreciation and debt service) through fees or charges.
- Fees and charges are set at prices intended to recover costs including depreciation and debt service.

Internal Service Funds This second proprietary fund type accounts for any operation that provides services to another department or agency within the government on a cost-reimbursement basis. As with enterprise funds, internal service funds charge fees but perform their service for the primary benefit of parties within the government rather than for outside users. In the same manner as enterprise funds, internal service funds are accounted for much like a for-profit operation in the private sector.

The City of Lincoln, Nebraska, lists seven operations in its 2010 financial statements that are accounted for as separate internal service funds:

Information services fund—to account for the cost of operating a central data processing facility.

Engineering revolving fund—to account for the cost of operating a central engineering pool.

Insurance revolving fund—to account for the cost of providing several types of self-insurance programs.

[11] Jeffrey Molinari and Charlie Tyer, "Local Government Enterprise Fund Activity: Trends and Implications," *Public Administration Quarterly,* Fall 2003, p. 369.

Fleet services fund—to account for the operations of a centralized maintenance facility for city equipment.

Police garage fund—to account for the operation of a maintenance facility for police and other government vehicles.

Communication services fund—to account for the costs of providing graphic arts and telecommunications services.

Copy services fund—to account for the cost of providing copy services.

Fiduciary Funds

The final classification, fiduciary funds, accounts for assets held in a trustee or agency capacity for external parties so that the money cannot be used to support the government's own programs. Like proprietary funds, fiduciary funds use the economic resources measurement focus and accrual accounting for the timing of revenues and expenses. Because these assets are not available for the benefit of the government, fiduciary funds are omitted entirely from government-wide financial statements although separate statements are included within the fund financial statements.

Four distinct types of fiduciary funds exist:

Investment Trust Funds The first fund type accounts for the outside portion of investment pools when the reporting government has accepted financial resources from other governments in order to have more money to invest and hopefully earn a higher return. For example, the Commonwealth of Virginia held almost $3.3 billion at June 30, 2010, identified as a local government investment pool that "helps local governmental entities maximize their rate of return by commingling their resources for investment purposes."

Private-Purpose Trust Funds The second fund type accounts for monies held in a trustee capacity when both principal and interest are for the benefit of specifically designated external parties such as individuals, private organizations, or other governments. Unclaimed property is usually recorded here, for example. The Commonwealth of Virginia has seven separate Private-Purpose Trust Funds. Notes to the 2010 financial statements describe one common fund: "Education Savings Trust Fund accounts for the activities of the Virginia Education Savings Trust program which is a voluntary, non-guaranteed, higher educational investment program offered by the Virginia College Savings Plan."

Pension Trust Funds The third fund type accounts for an employee retirement system. Because of the need to provide adequate benefits for government workers, this fund type can become quite large. The City of Philadelphia, for example, reported assets of more than $5.1 billion in its pension trust fund as of June 30, 2010.

Agency Funds The fourth type of fiduciary fund records any resources a government holds as an agent for individuals, private organizations, or other government units. For example, one government could collect taxes and tolls on behalf of another. To ensure safety and control, the Agency Fund separately maintains this money until it is transferred to the proper authority.

Overview of State and Local Government Financial Statements

LO5

Understand the basic structure of government-wide financial statements and fund financial statements (as produced for the governmental funds).

Although a complete analysis of the financial statements of a state or local government is presented in the subsequent chapter, an overview of four basic financial statements will be helpful at this point to illustrate how certain events are reported. These examples are not complete but can be used to demonstrate the presentation of various transactions and accounts.

Government-Wide Financial Statements

Only two financial statements make up the government-wide financial statements: *the statement of net assets* and *the statement of activities.* The reporting is separated into governmental activities (all governmental funds and most internal service funds) and business-type activities (all enterprise funds and any remaining internal service funds).[12] As mentioned earlier, government-wide financial statements do not report the transactions and balances of fiduciary funds, which are shown only in separate fund financial statements.

Exhibit 16.1 shows the basic structure of a statement of net assets. Under the economic resources measurement focus used in government-wide financial statements, all assets and liabilities are reported. The final section of this statement, the net assets category, indicates (1) the amount of capital assets being reported less related debt, (2) restrictions on any net assets, and (3) the total amount of unrestricted net assets. For example, in Exhibit 16.1, the Governmental Activities holds $80 of completely unrestricted net assets and the Business-Type Activities has $30 of unrestricted net assets.

The statement of activities in Exhibit 16.2 provides details about revenues and expenses, once again separated into governmental activities and business-type activities. This statement is usually read horizontally first and then vertically. Direct expenses and program revenues are shown for each government function. Program revenues include fines, fees, grants, and the like that the specific activity generates. Thus, a single net revenue or net expense is determined horizontally for each function as a way of indicating its financial burden or financial benefit to the government and its citizens.

Here, for example, at Point A the public safety category shows a net cost to the government of $8,820—expenses of $9,700 that are partially offset by program revenues of $880. Readers of the statements can judge the wisdom of incurring that cost for public safety.

The amounts for all activities are then summed vertically to show the total cost of operating the government, an amount that is offset by general revenues such as property taxes and sales taxes. Here, the governmental activities cost $20,720 (Point B) whereas the business-type activities generated a financial benefit of $1,940 (Point C). At Point D, the reader of the statements can see that the government generated property taxes of $20,400 to cover virtually all of the cost of providing its governmental activities.

Fund Financial Statements

A state or local government produces a number of fund financial statements. However, at this introductory stage, only the two fundamental statements that most parallel the two government-wide statements are included. First, Exhibit 16.3 shows *a balance sheet* for the governmental funds and then Exhibit 16.4 presents *a statement of revenues, expenditures, and changes in fund balances* for the same governmental funds. The balance sheet reports the current financial resources (assets) held by the various funds and the claims to those resources (liabilities). As can be seen in Exhibit 16.4, three categories are present in the second fund statement that will be discussed in detail throughout the remainder of this chapter and the next:

Revenues

Expenditures

Other Financing Sources (Uses)

Note that the figures found in these fund financial statements will not be the same as those presented for the governmental activities in the government-wide statement of net assets (Exhibit 16.1) and statement of activities (Exhibit 16.2). For example, the asset total reported for the governmental activities in Exhibit 16.1 is $4,630, whereas the asset total for all governmental funds in Exhibit 16.3 is only $1,560. These differences result primarily for three reasons:

[12] Government-wide financial statements report internal service funds as governmental activities if their primary purpose is to serve the governmental funds. Conversely, internal service funds are included with business-type activities if they mainly exist to help one or more enterprise funds. For example, a print shop (an internal service fund) should be reported within the governmental activities if its work is primarily for the benefit of a governmental fund such as the public library. However, if its work is to service a bus line (or some other enterprise fund), the print shop is classified within the business-type activities.

EXHIBIT 16.1
Statement of Net Assets—Government-Wide Financial Statements

	Governmental Activities	Business-Type Activities	Total
Assets			
Cash	$ 100	$ 130	$ 230
Investments	900	40	940
Receivables	600	400	1,000
Internal amounts due	50	(50)	–0–
Supplies and materials	30	40	70
Capital assets (net of depreciation)	2,950	2,750	5,700
Total assets	$4,630	$3,310	$7,940
Liabilities			
Accounts payable	$ 750	$ 230	$ 980
Noncurrent liabilities			
Due within one year	400	180	580
Due in more than one year	1,800	700	2,500
Total liabilities	$2,950	$1,110	$4,060
Net Assets			
Invested in capital assets, net of related debt	$1,410	$2,110	$3,520
Restricted for:			
Capital projects	50	–0–	50
Debt service	140	60	200
Unrestricted	80	30	110
Total net assets	$1,680	$2,200	$3,880

EXHIBIT 16.2 Statement of Activities—Government-Wide Financial Statements

			Net (Expense) Revenue		
Function	**Expenses**	**Program Revenues**	**Governmental Activities**	**Business-Type Activities**	**Total**
Governmental activities					
General government	$ 3,200	$ 1,400	$ (1,800)	n/a	$ (1,800)
Public safety	9,700	880	(8,820) Ⓐ	n/a	(8,820)
Public works	2,600	600	(2,000)	n/a	(2,000)
Education	8,400	300	(8,100)	n/a	(8,100)
Total governmental activities	$23,900	$ 3,180	$(20,720)	n/a	$(20,720)
Business-type activities					
Water	$ 3,600	$ 4,030	n/a	$ 430	$ 430
Sewer	4,920	5,610	n/a	690	690
Airport	2,300	3,120	n/a	820	820
Total business-type activities	$10,820	$12,760	n/a	$1,940	$ 1,940
Total government	$34,720	$15,940	$(20,720) Ⓑ	$1,940 Ⓒ	$(18,780)
General revenues:					
Property taxes			$ 20,400 Ⓓ	–0–	$ 20,400
Investment earnings			420	$ 70	490
Transfers			600	(600)	–0–
Total general revenues and transfers			$ 21,420	$ (530)	$ 20,890
Change in net assets			$ 700	$1,410	$ 2,110
Beginning net assets			980	790	1,770
Ending net assets			$ 1,680	$2,200	$ 3,880

EXHIBIT 16.3 **Balance Sheet—Governmental Funds**
Fund Financial Statements

	General Fund	Library Program	Other Governmental Funds	Total Governmental Funds
Assets				
Cash	$ 40	$ 10	$ 50	$ 100
Investments	580	120	200	900
Receivables	120	200	210	530
Supplies and materials	10	10	10	30
Total assets	$750	$340	$470	$1,560
Liabilities				
Accounts payable	$230	$170	$110	$ 510
Notes payable—current	300	–0–	100	400
Total liabilities	$530	$170	$210	$ 910
Fund Balances				
Nonspendable	$ 10	$ 10	$ 10	$ 30
Restricted	100	90	60	250
Committed	30	50	100	180
Assigned	20	20	90	130
Unassigned	60	–	–	60
Total fund balances	$220	$170	$260	$ 650
Total liabilities and fund balances	$750	$340	$470	$1,560

1. In the government-wide statements, internal service funds are grouped with the funds that they primarily benefit. Thus, they are included with the governmental activities if they assist governmental funds and with business-type activities if they assist enterprise funds. However, fund statements report all internal service funds as proprietary funds, not as governmental funds. *Totals will vary because funds are grouped differently.*
2. Governmental activities use the economic resources measurement focus whereas the governmental funds, in the fund statements, use the current financial resources measurement focus. *Different assets and liabilities are being reported.*
3. Governmental activities use accrual accounting in government-wide statements; modified accrual accounting is used in creating fund financial statements for the governmental funds. *The timing of recognition is different.*

Because of these differences, reconciliations between totals presented in Exhibits 16.1 and 16.3 and between Exhibits 16.2 and 16.4 are reported. Those reconciliations are discussed in detail in the following chapter.

Major Funds

In looking at both of the fund financial statements presented (Exhibits 16.3 and 16.4), note that the General Fund and every other individual fund that qualifies as major is shown in a separate column. The assumption here is that the Library Program (probably one of this government's special revenue funds) is the only individual fund outside the General Fund that is considered major. Information for all other funds is then grouped together. Consequently, identification of a "major" fund becomes quite important for disclosure purposes. A major fund is defined as follows:

> The reporting government's main operating fund (the general fund or its equivalent) should always be reported as a major fund. Other individual governmental and enterprise funds should be reported in separate columns as major funds based on these criteria:

EXHIBIT 16.4 Statement of Revenues, Expenditures, and Other Changes in Fund Balances—Governmental Funds Fund Financial Statements

	General Fund	Library Program	Other Governmental Funds	Total Governmental Funds
Revenues				
Property taxes	$17,200	$ 900	$ 2,300	$20,400
Investment earnings	100	200	180	480
Program revenues	500	100	2,500	3,100
Total revenues	$17,800	$1,200	$ 4,980	$23,980
Expenditures				
Current:				
General government	$ 3,400	-0-	$ 100	$ 3,500
Public safety	5,100	-0-	400	5,500
Education	6,700	$ 800	-0-	7,500
Debt service:				
Principal	-0-	-0-	1,000	1,000
Interest	-0-	-0-	600	600
Capital outlay	1,100	300	3,300	4,700
Total expenditures	$16,300	$1,100	$ 5,400	$22,800
Excess (deficiency) of revenues over expenditures	$ 1,500	$ 100	$ (420)	$ 1,180
Other Financing Sources (Uses)				
Bond proceeds	-0-	-0-	$ 1,000	$ 1,000
Transfers in	-0-	$ 20	580	600
Transfers out	$ (1,300)	-0-	$(1,000)	(2,300)
Total other financing sources and uses	$ (1,300)	$ 20	$ 580	$ (700)
Change in fund balances	$ 200	$ 120	$ 160	$ 480
Fund balances—beginning	20	50	100	170
Fund balances—ending	$ 220	$ 170	$ 260	$ 650

a. Total assets, liabilities, revenues, or expenditures/expenses of that individual governmental or enterprise fund are at least 10 percent of the corresponding total (assets, liabilities, and so forth) for all funds of that category or type (that is, total governmental or total enterprise funds), *and*

b. Total assets, liabilities, revenues, or expenditures/expenses of the individual governmental fund or enterprise fund are at least 5 percent of the corresponding total for all governmental and enterprise funds combined.

In addition to funds that meet the major fund criteria, any other governmental or enterprise fund that the government's officials believe is particularly important to financial statement users (for example, because of public interest or consistency) may be reported as a major fund.[13]

Fund Balances

One last unique aspect of the structure of fund financial statements for the governmental funds should be noted. As a government, the balance sheet (Exhibit 16.3) does not need a stockholders' equity section to report contributed capital, retained earnings, and the like for each separate fund. Instead, the term "fund balance" is used to indicate the amount of assets held in excess of liabilities—the net current financial resources at that time. This term has long been used in a rather generic fashion.

[13] GASB, *Codification,* Sec. 2200.153.

Recently, rules have been established to standardize the reporting of the fund balance within five categories. These rules are designed to help statement readers understand the use that will be made of the net current financial resources being held. Much of the asset total that is reported cannot be used by government officials as they please. "Bond investors and rating agencies wish to understand the extent to which the net financial resources of government funds are constrained and how binding those constraints are."[14]

For example, in Exhibit 16.3, the General Fund reports assets of $750 and liabilities of $530 indicating net assets of $220. From a reporting perspective, the most significant question to be answered is: What use can be made of this $220? The purpose of the fund balance classifications, therefore, is to indicate the availability of this excess amount.

Fund-Balance—Nonspendable As the name implies, this amount of the assets reported in a fund cannot be spent by government officials. That typically occurs for two reasons. First, some assets such as supplies and prepaid expenses are simply not in a spendable form. Second, financial resources are occasionally received that cannot be spent because of externally imposed limitations. A gift, for example, is donated by a citizen that must be held with the stipulation that only future income can be used. This fund balance figure indicates that assets are present but not available for government spending.

Fund-Balance—Restricted This figure indicates the amount of assets held by the government that must be spent in a manner designated by an external party. For example, a grant from another government for a specified purpose such as classroom teachers creates an increase in this category as would a bond covenant that requires proceeds to be used in a particular manner.

Fund-Balance—Committed Here, the assets have been designated for a particular purpose, not by an outside party but rather by the highest level of decision-making authority in the government. For example, a state legislature might vote to set aside $100 million for road construction. On the balance sheet, that decision is disclosed by an increase in the reported amount of the "fund balance—committed" total. Of course, the legislature does have the power to reverse its decision so the commitment is not necessarily binding.

Fund-Balance—Assigned Frequently, in the regular operations of a government, money is designated for a specific purpose without formal action by the highest level of decision-making authority. The head of the government's finance committee might designate cash of $1 million to use in a few months to pay off the current installment of a bond. However, if necessary, that money could be switched to some other purpose if needed in the interim. To indicate that its use has been established internally but not by the highest level of authority, the fund balance is labeled as "assigned."

Fund-Balance—Unassigned This category is only found in the General Fund and reflects any amount of net assets where no use has been designated either externally or internally. This money is available to government officials for any purpose viewed as appropriate.

To illustrate the reporting, note how each of the following transactions affects a city government's balance sheet created as part of the fund financial statements for the governmental funds.

- Supplies costing $30,000 that will be used in the future to beautify the local parks are bought on the last day of the fiscal year. The supplies are shown as an asset with an equal amount reported within the "fund-balance—nonspendable" for this fund.
- A citizen dies and leaves investments valued at $1 million to the city with the requirement that only the income can be spent and must be used for park beautification. Reported assets increase by this amount, as does the "fund-balance—restricted" balance for this fund.
- The highest level of decision makers for this city vote unanimously to set aside $90,000 in unassigned cash to be used to beautify the local parks. The "fund-balance—unassigned" drops by $90,000 while the "fund-balance—committed" increases.

[14] Paul A. Copley, *Essentials of Accounting for Governmental and Not-for-Profit Organizations,* 10th edition, published by McGraw-Hill/Irwin, 2011, p. 58.

- The director of finance for the city sets aside $12,000 in previously unassigned cash to be used to buy new benches for the city's parks. Because the decision was not made at the highest level of decision making, the "fund-balance—unassigned" goes down while the "fund-balance—assigned" rises.
- The city government receives property tax revenues of $100,000. City officials might eventually decide to use some or all of this money to complete the beautification of the city's parks, but no decision has yet been made. In the General Fund, assets increase by this amount and the "fund-balance—unassigned" increases. That money is available for use by government officials.

Accounting for Governmental Funds

LO6

Record the passage of a budget as well as subsequent encumbrances and expenditures.

The remainder of this chapter presents many of the unique aspects of the accounting process utilized within the governmental funds: the General Fund, Special Revenue Funds, Capital Projects Funds, Debt Service Funds, and Permanent Funds. It is in these five funds where the distinct approach of governmental accounting can best be seen. Because of the dual nature of the reporting process, most of this accounting must be demonstrated twice, once for fund financial statements and a second time for the government-wide financial statements.

Much discussion has occurred as to whether governments should, for practicality, keep two separate sets of financial records (one for fund statements and another for government-wide statements) or merely one set that must then be adjusted rather significantly at the end of the year to create the second set of financial statements. Many governments have elected to continue maintaining only fund information internally that is transformed into government-wide financial statements at year-end. However, over time, as software programs and computer systems become more sophisticated, governments will likely find that keeping two distinct sets of books is a reasonable approach. Being able to analyze complex transactions completely as they happen seems to be advantageous, and having two sets of records reduces what otherwise could be a massive amount of work at the end of each fiscal year.

Therefore, this textbook examines each transaction from both a fund and a government-wide perspective. Accounting for these events in two different ways seems to be an easier mental process than learning one method now and later attempting to convert that entire set of reported data into figures consistent with the second method.

The Importance of Budgets and the Recording of Budgetary Entries

> Budgeting is an essential element of the financial planning, control, and performance evaluation processes of many governments. In contrast to commercial organizations' planning-oriented budgetary practices, governments usually adopt budgets that have the force of law, are subject to sanctions for overspending budgetary authorizations, and have extensive controls to ensure budgetary compliance.[15]

In a chronological sense, the first significant accounting procedure encountered by a state or locality is the recording of budgetary entries. To enhance accountability, government officials normally are required to adopt an annual budget for each separate activity to anticipate the inflow of financial resources and establish approved expenditure levels. The budget serves several important purposes:

1. *Expresses public policy*. If, for example, more money is budgeted for child care and less for the environment, there are consequences. Through the budget, citizens are made aware of the decision to allocate limited government resources in this manner.
2. *Serves as an expression of financial intent for the upcoming fiscal year*. The budget presents the financial plan for the government for the current period.

[15] American Institute of Certified Public Accountants, *Audit & Accounting Guide, State and Local Governments*, with conforming changes as of March 1, 2010, para. 11.01.

3. *Provides control because it establishes spending limitations for each activity.*
4. *Offers a means of evaluating performance* by allowing a comparison of actual results with the levels found in the budget.
5. *Indicates whether the government anticipates having sufficient revenues to pay for all of the expenditures that have been approved.* In the current economic climate when many governments face declining revenues, the amount and handling of proposed deficits should be of interest to every citizen.

GASB even states that "many believe the budget is the most significant financial document produced by a governmental entity."[16]

Once a budget has been produced and enacted into law, formal accounting recognition is frequently required as a means of enhancing these benefits. In this way, the public has the opportunity to review the amounts of current financial resources expected to be received and expended. By entering budget figures into the accounting records at the start of each fiscal year, comparisons can be made between actual and budgeted figures at any interim point during the period. At the end of the year, all budget entries are reversed and closed.

Budget information must be disclosed for the General Fund and each major fund within the Special Revenue Funds. Governments are also required to report comparisons between the original budget, the final budget, and the actual figures for the period as required supplementary information presented after the notes to its financial statements. As an allowed alternative, a separate statement can be shown within the government's fund financial statements.

To illustrate, assume that a city enacts a motel excise tax with the revenue to be used to promote tourism and conventions. Because the receipts are legally restricted for this specified purpose, the city must establish a separate Special Revenue Fund. Assume that for the 2013 fiscal year, the tax is expected to generate $490,000 in revenues. Based on this projection, the city council authorizes expenditure of $400,000 (referred to as an *appropriation*) for promotional programs during the current year. Of this amount, $200,000 is designated for salaries, $30,000 for utilities, $80,000 for advertising, and $110,000 for supplies. The $70,000 difference between the anticipated revenue inflow and this appropriation is a budgeted surplus to be accumulated by the government for future use or in case actual revenue proves to be too small to support budget plans.

To formally acknowledge the council's action, the accounting records of this fund include the following journal entry. No similar entry is needed for government-wide financial statements.

Fund Financial Statements—Budgetary Entry

Special Revenue Fund—Tourism and Convention Promotions		
Estimated Revenues—Tax Levy	490,000	
Appropriations—Salaries		200,000
Appropriations—Utilities		30,000
Appropriations—Advertising		80,000
Appropriations—Supplies		110,000
Budgetary Fund Balance		70,000
To record annual budget for tourism and convention promotions funded by motel excise tax.		

This entry indicates both the expected level of funding (the tax levy) and the approved amount of expenditures. Each of these figures remains in the records of this Special Revenue Fund for the entire year to allow for planning, disclosure, and control. The Budgetary Fund Balance account indicates an anticipated surplus (or, in some cases, a shortage) projected for the period. Here, the size of this fund is expected to increase by $70,000 during the year.

[16] GASB, *Codification,* Appendix B, *Concepts Statement,* para. 19.

In this way, budgetary entries reflect a government's *interperiod equity.* This term refers to the alignment of revenues and spending for a period and the possible shift of payments to future generations. If a government projects revenues as $10 million but approves expenditures of $11 million, the extra million must be financed in some manner, usually by debt to be repaid in the future. The benefits of the additional expenditures are enjoyed today, but citizens of a later time must bear the cost.

The original budget is not always the final appropriations budget for the year because of later amendments. For example, government officers can vote to change appropriation levels if more or less money becomes available than had been anticipated. Thus, for the year ending June 30, 2010, the City of Greensboro, North Carolina, reported that $29,206,726 had originally been appropriated for culture and recreation. That amount was later increased to $29,847,322, but only $27,432,715 was actually spent.

Assume, to illustrate, that officials in charge of tourism for this city appeal to the council during the year for an additional $50,000 to create a special advertising campaign. If approved, the original budgetary entry is adjusted:

Fund Financial Statements—Budget Amendment

Special Revenue Fund—Tourism and Convention Promotions		
Budgetary Fund Balance.	50,000	
Appropriations—Advertising		50,000
To record additional appropriation for advertising.		

Assume that the city actually received $488,000 in tax revenues during the year and spent $457,000 as follows:

Salaries	$196,000
Utilities	29,000
Advertising	125,000
Supplies.	107,000

This information should be disclosed as follows. The Variance column is recommended but not required:

TOURISM AND CONVENTION PROMOTIONS
Year Ended December 31, 2013
Budget Comparison Schedule

	Budgeted Amounts			
	Original	**Final**	**Actual Amounts (budgetary basis)**	**Variance with Final Budget— Positive (negative)**
Resources (inflows):				
Tax levy	$490,000	$490,000	$488,000	$ (2,000)
Charges to appropriations (outflows):				
Salaries	$200,000	$200,000	$196,000	$ 4,000
Utilities	30,000	30,000	29,000	1,000
Advertising	80,000	130,000	125,000	5,000
Supplies	110,000	110,000	107,000	3,000
Total charges.	$420,000	$470,000	$457,000	$13,000
Change in fund balance	$ 70,000	$ 20,000	$ 31,000	$11,000

Encumbrances

One additional budgetary procedure that plays a central role in government accounting is the recording of financial commitments referred to as *encumbrances.* In contrast to for-profit accounting, purchase commitments and contracts can be recorded in the governmental funds prior to becoming legal liabilities. This recording of encumbrances provides an efficient method for monitoring financial commitments so that officials will not accidentally overspend a fund's appropriated amount. Encumbrance accounting is appropriate (although not required) within any governmental fund. Information on both expended and committed amounts is then available to aid government officials.

To illustrate, assume that a city's police department orders $18,000 in equipment from a vendor. As an ongoing service activity, the police department is accounted for within the General Fund. Because only an order has been placed, no entry is recorded for the government-wide financial statements that tend to follow for-profit accounting. However, this amount of the General Fund's financial resources has been committed even though no formal liability will exist until the equipment is received. To guard against spending more than has been appropriated, an encumbrance is usually recorded any time a governmental fund enters into a purchase order, contract, or other formal commitment.

Fund Financial Statements—Commitment Created by a Governmental Fund

	Debit	Credit
General Fund—Police Department		
Encumbrances Control	18,000	
Fund Balance—Reserved for Encumbrances		18,000
To record an order placed for equipment.		

The Encumbrances account records the commitment that has been incurred. The use of a control account here simply indicates that the government's accounting system includes a subsidiary ledger that maintains more detailed information about this $18,000 amount. Without a subsidiary ledger, the debit entry is made to Encumbrances—Equipment or a similar account.

When the equipment is eventually received, a legal liability for payment replaces the commitment. The encumbrance is removed from the accounting records and an Expenditures account is recognized to reflect the reduction in current financial resources. Often, because of sales taxes, freight costs, or other price adjustments, the actual invoice total will differ from the original estimation. For this reason, the expenditure will not necessarily agree with the corresponding encumbrance. Note that because of the current financial resource focus of fund financial statements, no equipment account entry is recorded for this long-lived asset.

Assume, for illustration purposes, that an invoice for $18,160 accompanies the equipment when it is received.

Fund Financial Statements—Order Received by a Governmental Fund

	Debit	Credit
General Fund		
Fund Balance—Reserved for Encumbrances	18,000	
Encumbrances Control		18,000
To remove encumbrance for equipment that has now been received.		
Expenditures—Equipment	18,160	
Vouchers (or Accounts) Payable		18,160
To record the receipt of equipment and the accompanying liability.		

In contrast, in producing government-wide financial statements, the only entry created by this ordering and receiving of equipment is an increase in the specific asset and the related liability when legal title is conveyed. As in for-profit accounting, the commitment is not recorded.

At the end of the fiscal period, any commitments that remain outstanding are removed from the accounting records by reversing the original entry because no transaction has occurred. The recording of encumbrances is to help prevent spending more money than the amount authorized for the period.

Assuming that the commitment will be honored in the subsequent year, the accounting issue is whether additional reporting is needed on the current balance sheet. If the fund balance has already been reclassified as restricted, committed, or assigned in recognition of this eventual expenditure, then no further change is needed. The labeling of the fund balance reflects the decision to use that portion of the fund's net assets to meet this commitment. However, if no fund balance is reported as restricted, committed, or assigned, then the amount of the encumbrance should be reclassified as a fund balance that is either committed or assigned to denote the anticipated use of the fund's assets.[17]

To illustrate, assume that the general fund of the city that ordered the $18,000 in equipment reports assets of $600,000 and liabilities of $500,000. On the balance sheet, the fund balance shows $40,000 as assigned and $60,000 as unassigned. At the end of the fiscal year, the $18,000 encumbrance is unfulfilled and removed from the records for that period. However, the decision has been made that the government will still pay for the equipment when it arrives in the following year. The reporting of the fund balance figures on the balance sheet can be affected in one of two ways.

- If the $40,000 fund balance—assigned already includes an $18,000 amount reflecting the commitment for this equipment, no change is necessary. The appropriate amount of the fund's net assets is shown as being assigned.
- If the $40,000 fund balance—assigned does not include $18,000 to be spent on this equipment, then the fund balance—unassigned is reduced by that amount and fund balance—assigned (or possibly committed depending on the level of the decision to acquire the equipment) is increased. The assets and liabilities are not affected since the equipment has not been received, but the $18,000 figure is shown as assigned (or committed) to indicate that this amount of the net assets is not freely available to government officials. Per GASB, "Encumbered amounts for specific purposes for which amounts have not been previously restricted, committed, or assigned should not be classified as unassigned but, rather, should be included within committed or assigned fund balance, as appropriate."[18]

Recognition of Expenditures for Operations and Capital Additions

LO6

Record the passage of a budget as well as subsequent encumbrances and expenditures.

Although budgetary and encumbrance entries are unique, their impact on the accounting process is somewhat limited because they do not directly affect a fund's financial results for the period. Conversely, the method by which states and localities record the receipt and disbursement of assets can significantly alter reported data. For example, because a primary emphasis is on measuring changes in current financial resources, *neither expenses nor capital assets are recorded in the fund financial statements of the governmental funds.* Probably no more significant distinction exists between the fund statements and the government-wide statements.

As shown in the previous illustration, governmental funds report an Expenditures account in the fund statements. This balance reflects outflows or other reductions in current financial resources caused by the acquisition of a good or service (or some other utility). The reduction of resources is recorded as an expenditure whether it is for rent, a fire truck, salaries, or a computer. In each case, a good or service is acquired. The statement of revenues, expenditures, and other changes in fund balances (Exhibit 16.4) allows the reader to see the utilization of an activity's current financial resources. Spending $1,000 for electricity for the past three months is an expenditure of a governmental fund's current financial resources in exactly the same way that buying a $70,000 ambulance is:

[17] If not already reported as restricted, a fund balance cannot be internally restricted. The restricted designation is used to indicate that external parties or applicable laws created the restriction.

[18] GASB, *Codification*, Sec. 1800.161.

Fund Financial Statements—Expenditures for Expense and Capital Asset by a Governmental Fund

Expenditures—Electricity	1,000	
Vouchers (or Accounts) Payable.		1,000
To record charges covering the past three months.		
Expenditures—Ambulance	70,000	
Vouchers (or Accounts) Payable.		70,000
To record acquisition of ambulance.		

Within the governmental funds, the timing of the recognition of expenditures (and revenues) follows the *modified accrual basis of accounting.* For expenditures, modified accrual accounting requires recognizing a claim against current financial resources when it is created. If a claim is established in one period to be settled in the subsequent period using year-end financial resources, the expenditure and liability are recorded in the initial year. However, as discussed earlier, the maximum length of time for the change in current financial resources to occur—often 60 days into the subsequent period—should be disclosed. Thus, if equipment is received on the last day of the year but payment will not be made until 60 days later, recording the expenditure is likely to be made in the first year, depending on the recognition period utilized by the government.

The recording by the governmental funds of expenditures for both expenses and capital assets is one of the most distinctive characteristics of traditional governmental accounting. In fund statements, a governmental fund records both operating costs such as salaries and rent and the entire cost of all buildings, machines, and other capital assets as expenditures. No net income figure is calculated for these funds; thus, computing and recording subsequent depreciation is not relevant to the reporting process and is omitted entirely. It has no effect on current financial resources.

For the government-wide financial statements, all economic resources are measured. Consequently, the previous two transactions are recorded in this second set of statements as follows, with depreciation subsequently recorded for the ambulance.

Government-Wide Financial Statements—Recording Expense and Capital Asset

Utilities Expense	1,000	
Vouchers (or Accounts) Payable.		1,000
To record electricity charges for the past three months.		
Ambulance	70,000	
Vouchers (or Accounts) Payable.		70,000
To record acquisition of new ambulance.		

LO7

Understand the reporting of capital assets, supplies, and prepaid expenses by a state or local government.

Capital Assets and Fund Financial Statements

One interesting result of measuring and recording only expenditures within the fund statements of the governmental funds is that virtually no assets other than current financial resources such as cash, receivables, and investments are reported. All capital assets are recorded as expenditures at the time of purchase or construction with that balance closed out at the end of the fiscal period. Note that the statement in Exhibit 16.3 shows no buildings, schools, computers, trucks, or other equipment as assets.

With the creation of government-wide financial statements, a record of all capital assets is available in the statement of net assets (see Exhibit 16.1). Thus, recording only expenditures in the fund financial statements does not leave a gap in the information available to interested parties. In the initial production of government-wide financial statements after they were required by GASB in 1999, one problem was the reporting of "infrastructure" assets including roads, sidewalks, bridges, and the like that are normally stationary and can be preserved for a significant period of time. A bridge, for example, might last for

Discussion Question

IS IT AN ASSET OR A LIABILITY?

During the long evolution of government accounting, many scholars have discussed its unique features. In the August 1989 issue of the *Journal of Accountancy* R.K. Mautz described the reporting needs of governments and not-for-profit organizations (such as charities) in "Not-For-Profit Financial Reporting: Another View."

As an illustration of their accounting challenges, Mautz examined the method by which a city should record a newly constructed high school building. Conventional business wisdom would say that such a property represents an asset of the government. Thus, the cost should be capitalized and then depreciated over an estimated useful life. However, in paragraph 26 of FASB *Concepts Statement No. 6,* an essential characteristic of an asset is "a probable future benefit . . . to contribute directly to future net cash inflows."

Mautz reasoned that the school building cannot be considered an asset because it provides no net contribution to cash inflows. In truth, a high school requires the government to make significant cash outflows for maintenance, repairs, utilities, salaries, and the like. Public educational facilities (as well as many of the other properties of a government such as a fire station or municipal building) are acquired with the understanding that net cash outflows will result for years to come.

Consequently, Mautz considered whether the construction of a high school is not actually the incurrence of a liability because the government is taking on an obligation that will necessitate future cash payments. This idea also is rejected, once again based on the guidance of *Concepts Statement No. 6* (para. 36), because the cash outflow is not required at a "specified or determinable date, on occurrence of a specified event, or on demand."

Is a high school building an asset or is it a liability? If it is neither, how should the cost be recorded? How is the high school reported in fund financial statements? How is the high school reported in government-wide financial statements? Which of these two approaches provides the best portrayal of the decision to acquire or construct this building? Can a government possibly be accounted for in the same manner as a for-profit enterprise?

more than 100 years. Traditionally, the formal recording of such infrastructure assets was optional. To save time and energy, many governments simply did not maintain a record of these assets after the original expenditure. Thus, in creating the initial set of government-wide financial statements, records were often unavailable for some or all of the infrastructure assets that were bought or constructed over the decades.

Because of the potential problem of establishing cost-based balances for all of these infrastructure assets, GASB made an exception in reporting government-wide financial statements. Although a government must now capitalize all new infrastructure assets bought or built, the book value of infrastructure assets acquired before the advent of government-wide financial statements only had to be approximated. GASB suggested methods by which costs incurred for highways, curbing, sidewalks, and the like could be estimated for reporting purposes. For example, current costs for such projects could be determined and then adjusted for both inflation and usage since the dates the assets were originally obtained.

As mentioned previously, fund financial statements do not recognize depreciation expense in connection with governmental funds for two reasons:

1. The entire cost of the asset is reported as an expenditure at the time of the original claim against current financial resources. No cost exists on the balance sheet. Reporting subsequent depreciation would reflect the impact twice: once when acquired and again when depreciated.

2. These funds traditionally do not record expenses. Reporting depreciation expense (rather than an expenditure) is not consistent with measuring the change in current financial resources.

However, the government-wide financial statements (as well as fund statements for proprietary and fiduciary funds) list assets rather than expenditures for such costs, and therefore depreciation is appropriate. Consequently, on these statements, depreciation of all long-lived assets with finite lives is calculated and reported each period.

Supplies and Prepaid Items

In gathering information for government-wide financial statements, the acquisition of supplies and prepaid costs such as rent or insurance is not particularly complicated. An asset is recorded at the time of acquisition and subsequently reclassified to expense as the asset's utility is consumed by use or time. The City of Denver reported $4.3 million for prepaid items and other assets on its statement of net assets as of December 31, 2010.

However, reporting prepaid costs and supplies by the governmental funds within the fund financial statements is not so straightforward. These assets have a relatively short life. Should the cost incurred be reported as an asset until consumed or recorded directly as an expenditure at the time of acquisition?

Traditionally, governmental funds have used the *purchases method,* which simply records such costs as expenditures at the point that a claim to current financial resources is created. No asset is recorded. Thus, the City of Philadelphia discloses that the "supplies of governmental funds are recorded as expenditures when purchased rather than capitalized as inventory." For disclosure purposes, though, any remaining supplies or prepaid items (such as insurance or rent) are entered into the accounting records as assets just prior to production of financial statements. Mechanically, the asset is recorded along with an offsetting amount in fund balance—nonspendable to inform the reader that the fund is reporting assets that are not current financial resources available for spending in the future.

The *purchases method* reflects modified accrual accounting because the entire cost is recognized as an expenditure when current financial resources are initially reduced. However, many governments have chosen to have their governmental funds report supplies and prepaid items using an accepted alternative known as the *consumption method.*

The consumption method parallels the process utilized in creating government-wide financial statements. Supplies or prepayments are recorded as assets when acquired. Subsequently, as the utility is consumed by usage or over time, the cost is reclassified into an expenditures account. As explained by the City of Birmingham, Alabama, "[i]nventory consists of expendable supplies held in the General Fund for consumption. The cost is recorded as an expenditure at the time individual inventory items are used (consumption method)." Under this approach, the expenditure is recognized in the period of specific usage. Because these assets cannot be spent for government programs or other needs, an equal portion of the Fund Balance account should be reclassified as nonspendable as is shown in the balance sheet in Exhibit 16.3.

To illustrate, assume that a municipality purchases $20,000 in supplies for various General Fund activities. During the remainder of the fiscal period, $18,000 of this amount is consumed so that only $2,000 remains at year-end. These events could be recorded through either of the following sets of entries:

Fund Financial Statements—Supplies and Prepaid Expenses—Governmental Funds

Purchases Method		
Expenditures—Supplies	20,000	
Vouchers (or Accounts) Payable		20,000
To record purchase of supplies for various ongoing activities.		
Inventory of Supplies	2,000	
Fund Balance—Nonspendable		2,000
To establish balance for supplies remaining at year's end.		

Consumption Method		
Inventory of Supplies	20,000	
Vouchers (or Accounts) Payable.		20,000
To record purchase of supplies for various ongoing activities.		
Expenditures—Control	18,000	
Inventory of Supplies.		18,000
To record consumption of supplies during period. Because a $2,000 asset that cannot be spent remains, an equal portion of the Fund Balance is reclassified from unassigned to nonspendable. This reclassification is normally done in creating the statements, not through a journal entry.		

LO8

Determine the proper timing for the recognition of revenues from nonexchange transactions.

Recognition of Revenues—Overview

The recognition of some revenues has always posed theoretical issues for state and local governments. For most of their revenues, such as property taxes, income taxes, and grants, no earning process exists as in a for-profit business. These revenues are referred to as nonexchange transactions. Taxes, fines, and the like are assessed or imposed on the citizens to support the government's operations rather than providing the payors with a specific good or service in return for their payments.

To assist in the timing of such revenue recognition, GASB has provided a comprehensive set of guidelines. These rules do not apply to true revenues such as interest or rents for which an earning process does exist. Instead, they concentrate on "nonexchange transactions," including most taxes, fines, grants, gifts, and the like for which the government does not provide a direct and equal benefit for the amount received.

> In a nonexchange transaction, a government (including the federal government, as a provider) either gives value (benefit) to another party without directly receiving equal value in exchange or receives value (benefit) from another party without directly giving equal value in exchange.[19]

For organizational purposes, nonexchange transactions are separated into four distinct classifications, each with its own rules as to proper recognition:

- *Derived tax revenues.* A tax assessment is imposed when an underlying exchange takes place. Income taxes and sales taxes are the best examples of this type of revenue. A sale occurs, for example, and a sales tax is imposed, or income is earned and an income tax is assessed.
- *Imposed nonexchange revenues.* Property taxes and fines and penalties are viewed as imposed nonexchange revenues because the government mandates an assessment, but no underlying transaction occurs. As an example, real estate or other property is owned and a property tax is levied. The government is taxing ownership here, not a specific transaction.
- *Government-mandated nonexchange transactions.* This category includes monies, such as grants conveyed from one government to another, to help cover the costs of required programs. If a state specifies that a city must create a homeless shelter and then provides a grant of $400,000 to help defray the cost, the city records the inflow of money using these prescribed rules. City officials have no choice; the state government has required the shelter to be constructed and is providing part or all of the funding.
- *Voluntary nonexchange transactions.* In this final classification, money has been conveyed willingly to the state or local government by an individual, another government, or an organization, usually for a particular purpose. For example, a state might grant a city $900,000 to help improve reading programs in local schools. Unless the state had mandated an enhancement in these reading programs, this grant is accounted for as a

[19] GASB, *Codification*, Sec., N50,104.

voluntary nonexchange transaction. The decision has been made that the money will provide an important benefit, but no separate government requirement led the state to make the conveyance.

Derived Tax Revenues Such as Income Taxes and Sales Taxes

Accounting for derived tax revenues is relatively straightforward. These revenues are normally recognized in government-wide financial statements when the underlying transaction occurs. Thus, when a taxpayer earns income, the government should record the resulting income tax revenue. Likewise, when a business makes a sale, the government should recognize the sales tax revenue that is created.

Assume, for example, that sales by businesses operating within a locality amount to $10 million for the current year and a sales tax of 4 percent is assessed. In the period in which the sales are made, the following entry is required of the government. The amounts should be reported net of any estimated refunds or uncollectible balances.

Government-Wide Financial Statements—Derived Tax Revenues

Receivable—Sales Taxes	400,000	
Revenue—Sales Taxes		400,000
To recognize amount of sales tax that will be collected in connection with sales for the current period. Same entry is appropriate for the fund financial statements of the governmental fund if the money qualifies as available.		

For fund financial statements, the preceding rules also apply except for one additional requirement. In connection with governmental funds, as mentioned previously, the resources must be available before the revenue can be recognized. That is, the amounts must be received during the year or soon enough thereafter to satisfy current claims to financial resources. In that way, the essence of modified accrual accounting is utilized at the fund level of reporting. Except in the reporting of property taxes, the government selects and must disclose the length of time that serves as the boundary for financial resources to be viewed as available.

Imposed Nonexchange Revenues Such as Property Taxes and Fines

Accounting for imposed nonexchange revenues is a bit more complicated because no underlying transaction exists to guide the timing of the revenue recognition. Interestingly, GASB set up separate rules for recognizing the asset and the related revenue. A receivable is recorded when the government first has an enforceable legal claim as defined in that particular jurisdiction. Cash is recorded rather than a receivable if a prepayment is made. For the revenue side of the transaction, recognition is made in the time period when the resulting resources are required to be used or in the first period in which use is permitted.

To illustrate, assume that on October 1, Year 1, property tax assessments totaling $530,000 are mailed by the City of Alban to its citizens. Assume that according to applicable state law, the city has no enforceable claim until January 1, Year 2 (often called the *lien date*). However, to encourage early payment, the city allows a 5 percent discount on any amount received by December 31, Year 1.

No entry is recorded on October 1, Year 1. Although the assessments have been delivered, no enforceable legal claim yet exists, and the proceeds from the tax cannot be used until Year 2. However, assume that $30,000 of the assessments is collected from citizens during the final three months of Year 1. After reduction for the 5 percent discount, the collection is $28,500.

Government-Wide Financial Statements and Fund Financial Statements—Property Taxes Prepaid for Year Two

Year 1		
Cash	28,500	
Deferred Property Tax Revenues		28,500
To record collection of property tax prior to the start of the levy year after reduction for 5 percent discount.		

Assume that city officials expect to collect 96 percent of the remaining $500,000 in assessments, or $480,000. At the beginning of Year 2, both this receivable and the related revenue can be recognized. The receivable is reported at that time because an enforceable claim comes into existence. For government-wide statements, the revenue is reported in Year 2 because that is the period in which the money can first be used. In the following journal entry, note that the revenue is reduced directly by the estimate of taxes that are expected to be uncollectible. In addition, the previously collected amount is recognized in Year 2 as revenue because, once again, this is the period for which use is allowed.

Government-Wide Financial Statement—Property Taxes for Year Two

January 1, Year 2		
Property Tax Receivable	500,000	
Allowance for Uncollectible Taxes		20,000
Revenues—Property Taxes		480,000
To recognize property tax assessment for Year 2.		
Deferred Property Tax Revenues	28,500	
Revenues—Property Taxes		28,500
To recognize property tax proceeds for Year 2 collected during Year 1.		

The above recording is the same for the fund financial statements unless some portion of the future cash collection is viewed as not being available this period. Because property taxes are such a significant source of revenue for many governments, a specific 60-day maximum period for recognition has been standardized rather than allowing the government to choose.

To illustrate, assume that historical records indicate that $400,000 of this anticipated $480,000 will be collected during Year 2, another $50,000 in the first 60 days of Year 3, and the final $30,000 beyond 60 days into Year 3. This last $30,000 is not viewed as available to pay for Year 2 expenditures. For that amount, recognition is not appropriate until Year 3. Only $450,000 of the financial resources are expected to be available for Year 2 expenditures. For the fund financial statements, the recognition entry must conform to modified accrual accounting. Again, revenues are recorded net of estimated uncollectible taxes.

Fund Financial Statements—Property Taxes for Year Two—Governmental Funds

January 1, Year 2		
Property Tax Receivable	500,000	
Allowance for Uncollectible Taxes		20,000
Revenues—Property Taxes		450,000
Deferred Property Tax Revenues		30,000
To record amount of property taxes measurable and available for Year 2 expenditures. $30,000 is not expected until after 60 days into Year 3.		
Deferred Property Tax Revenues	28,500	
Revenues—Property Taxes		28,500
To recognize property tax proceeds for Year 2 collected during Year 1.		

Government-Mandated Nonexchange Transactions and Voluntary Nonexchange Transactions

Although these two sources of revenues are identified separately, the timing of accounting recognition is the same so they are logically discussed together. Governments recognize these types of revenue (often in the form of a grant) when all eligibility requirements have been met. Until eligibility has been established, the existence of some degree of uncertainty precludes recognition. Thus, revenue reporting occurs at the time of eligibility even if the money was actually received earlier.

Eligibility requirements are divided into four general classifications. Applicable requirements must all be met before revenues can be recorded for either government-mandated nonexchange transactions or voluntary nonexchange transactions.

1. *Required characteristics of the recipients.* In many programs, the government that is scheduled to receive funds is given standards that must be met in advance. For example, assume that a state grant has been awarded to a city to help teach all kindergarten children in its school system to read. However, as part of this program, state law has been changed to mandate that all kindergarten teachers must hold proper certification. Consequently, the state has indicated that it will not convey the grant to the city until all kindergarten teachers have met this standard. The city must conform to state law first. Because of this eligibility requirement, revenue recognition of this grant is delayed until all teachers have become certified.
2. *Time requirements.* Programs can specify when money is to be used. To illustrate, assume that in April, a state provides a grant to a city to buy milk for each child during the subsequent school year starting in September. The grant should be recognized as revenue in the period of use or in the period when the use of the funds is first permitted. Here, the money cannot be used in April so it is not yet revenue.
3. *Reimbursement.* Many grants and other forms of similar support are designed to reimburse a government for amounts spent appropriately. These arrangements are often called *expenditure-driven programs*. Assume that a state informs a locality that it will reimburse the city government for money paid to provide books to schoolchildren who could not otherwise afford them. In such cases, proper spending is the eligibility requirement; the city recognizes no revenue until the city's own money is spent for books.
4. *Contingencies.* In voluntary nonexchange transactions (but not in government-mandated nonexchange transactions), revenue may be withheld until a specified procurement action has been taken. A grant might be given to buy park equipment, for example, but is only available after an appropriate piece of land has been acquired on which to build the park. Until a lot is obtained (or other required action is taken) a contingency exists, and the revenue should not be recognized.

LO9

Account for the issuance of long-term bonds and the reporting of special assessment projects.

Issuance of Bonds

Although not a revenue, the issuance of bonds serves as a major source of financing for many state and local governments. At the end of the first quarter of 2011, the total of all such long-term debt outstanding for state and local governments amounted to the almost unbelievable balance of $2.44 trillion.[20] Proceeds from these debt issuances are used for many purposes, including general financing and a wide variety of construction projects. As of June 30, 2010, the City and County of San Francisco, California, had approximately $9.2 billion of long-term bonds and similar liabilities outstanding. Of that amount, more than $2.1 billion had been issued by governmental activities and nearly $7.1 billion by business-type activities.

Because the proceeds of a bond issuance must be repaid, the government recognizes no revenues under either method of financial reporting. The process for the government-wide financial statements is hardly controversial: Both the cash and the debt are

[20] U.S. Federal Reserve, *Federal Reserve Statistical Release,* "Flow of Funds Accounts of the United States," First Quarter 2011 (Washington, D.C.: Federal Reserve, June 11, 2011), Table L.1, p. 60.

increased to reflect the issuance. Conversely, in the fund financial statements, recording is not so simple. Cash is received, but the debt is not a claim on current financial resources. Thus, from that perspective, the inflow of current financial resources does not create a revenue or a liability that can be reported.

Assume, for example, that the Town of Ruark sells $9 million in general obligation bonds at face value to finance the construction of a new school building. Because of the intended use of this money, the town establishes a Capital Projects Fund to monitor the cash. To emphasize that this inflow of money is not derived from a revenue, Ruark utilizes a special designation, *Other Financing Sources*. Note in Exhibit 16.4 the placement of Other Financing Sources (Uses) at the bottom of the statement of revenues, expenditures, and other changes in fund balance to identify changes in the amount of current financial resources created through transactions other than revenues and expenditures. Issuance of a long-term bond is a prime example.

The following journal entry is created to reflect the sale of these bonds in the fund statements if issued by one of the governmental funds:

Fund Financial Statements—Issuance of Bonds—Governmental Funds

Capital Projects Fund—School Building		
Cash	9,000,000	
Other Financing Sources—Bond Proceeds		9,000,000
To record issuance of bonds to finance construction project.		

Although an inflow of cash into this fund has taken place, no revenue has been generated. However, in the same manner as a revenue, the Other Financing Sources is a measurement account that is closed out at year-end. As the preceding entry shows, the actual $9 million liability is completely omitted from the Capital Projects Fund. Because the governmental funds stress accountability for the inflows and outflows of current financial resources, recognition of long-term debts in fund accounting has traditionally been ignored. For example, the balance sheet in Exhibit 16.3 shows no long-term liabilities for the governmental funds but only claims to current financial resources. Any reader of the financial statements who wants to see the amount of the government's long-term debts must examine the statement of net assets in the government-wide financial statements (see Exhibit 16.1).

Payment of Long-Term Liabilities

The payment of long-term liabilities again demonstrates the fundamental differences between government-wide and fund financial statements. For the government-wide statements, recording the payment of principal and interest is the same as the accounting used by a for-profit organization. For the fund statements, an expenditure is recognized for settlement of the debt and also for the related interest (often paid for and recorded in a Debt Service Fund). Both payments reduce current financial resources.

Assume as an illustration that a government has a $500,000 bond payment coming due along with three months of interest amounting to $10,000. This example assumes that sufficient cash had been set aside previously in the Debt Service Fund to satisfy this obligation. Both sets of entries follow:

Government-Wide Financial Statements—Bond and Interest Payments

Bond Payable	500,000	
Interest Expense	10,000	
Cash		510,000
To record payment of bond and related interest.		

Fund Financial Statements—Bond and Interest Payments—Governmental Funds

Debt Service Funds		
Expenditure—Bond Principal	500,000	
Expenditure—Interest	10,000	
Cash		510,000
To record payment of bond and related interest.		

Tax Anticipation Notes

One type of formal debt is recorded in the same manner for government-wide and fund financial statements. State and local governments often issue short-term debts to provide financing until revenue sources have been collected. For example, if property tax payments are expected at a particular point in time, the government might need to borrow money for operations until that date. These short-term liabilities are often referred to as *tax anticipation notes* because they are only outstanding until a sufficient amount of taxes can be collected. As short-term liabilities, these debts are a claim on current financial resources. Thus, for the fund financial statements, the issuance is not recorded as an other financing source but as a liability in the same manner as in the government-wide financial statements. Amounts paid for interest, though, are still recorded as an expenditure in producing fund statements and as an expense on the government-wide financial statements.

Assume a city borrows \$300,000 on a 60-day note on January 1 and agrees to pay back \$305,000 on March 1. The city expects to repay the debt with receipts from property taxes. For both sets of financial statements, cash is increased as well as the related liability.

At repayment, however, different entries are required as shown below:

Fund Financial Statements—Payment of Tax Anticipation Notes by Governmental Funds

Tax Anticipation Note Payable	300,000	
Expenditure—Interest	5,000	
Cash		305,000
To record payment of short-term debt and interest for two months.		

Government-Wide Financial Statements—Payment of Tax Anticipation Notes

Tax Anticipation Note Payable	300,000	
Interest Expense	5,000	
Cash		305,000
To record payment of short-term debt and interest for two months.		

LO9

Account for the issuance of long-term bonds and the reporting of special assessment projects.

Special Assessments

Governments occasionally provide improvements or services that directly benefit a particular property and assess the costs (in whole or part) to the owner. In some cases, the owners actually petition the government to initiate such projects to enhance property values. Paving streets, installing water and sewage lines, and constructing curbs and sidewalks are typical examples. To finance the work, the government usually issues debt and places a lien on the property being improved to ensure reimbursement. The City of Fargo, North Dakota, reported special assessment receivables of over \$216 million as of December 31, 2009.

Government-wide financial statements handle the debt and subsequent construction project in the manner of a for-profit enterprise. The asset is recorded at cost and assessments are made and collected. Receipts are then used to settle the debt. For example, assume that a sidewalk is to be added to a neighborhood at a cost of $20,000. The city is to sell bonds of this amount to finance the construction with repayment to be made using funds collected from the owners of the property benefited. Total interest to be paid is $2,000. The assessment to the owners is set at $22,000 to cover all costs.

Government-Wide Financial Statements—Special Assessment Project

Account	Debit	Credit
Cash	20,000	
Bond Payable—Special Assessment		20,000
To record debt issued to finance sidewalk construction.		
Infrastructure Asset—Sidewalk	20,000	
Cash		20,000
To record payment to contractor for the cost of building new sidewalk.		
Taxes Receivable—Special Assessment	22,000	
Revenue—Special Assessment		22,000
To record citizens' charges for special assessment project.		
Cash	22,000	
Taxes Receivable—Special Assessment		22,000
To record collection of money from assessment of citizens for sidewalk construction.		
Bond Payable—Special Assessment	20,000	
Interest Expense	2,000	
Cash		22,000
To record payment of debt on special assessment bonds.		

In the fund financial statements, this same series of transactions has a completely different appearance. Neither the infrastructure nor the long-term debt is recorded because the current financial resources measurement basis is used.

Fund Financial Statements—Special Assessment Project—Governmental Funds

Capital Projects Fund—Special Assessment Project	Debit	Credit
Cash	20,000	
Other Financing Sources—Bond Proceeds		20,000
To record issuance of bonds to finance sidewalk construction with payment to be made from a special assessment levy.		
Expenditures—Special Assessment	20,000	
Cash		20,000
To record payment to contractor for the cost of constructing sidewalk.		

Debt Service Fund—Special Assessment Project	Debit	Credit
Taxes Receivable—Special Assessment	22,000	
Revenue—Special Assessment		22,000
To record assessment that will be used to pay bond principal and related interest incurred after construction.		
Cash	22,000	
Taxes Receivable—Special Assessment		22,000
To record collection of assessment paid by citizens to extinguish bond and interest incurred in construction of sidewalk.		
Expenditure—Special Assessment Bond	20,000	
Expenditure—Interest	2,000	
Cash		22,000
To record payment of bonds payable and interest incurred in construction of sidewalk.		

One other aspect of the reporting of special assessment projects should be mentioned. In some cases, the government may facilitate a project but accept no legal obligation for it. The government's role is limited to conveying funds from one party to another. The government assumes no liability (either primary or secondary) for the debt. Normally in such cases, the money goes from citizens to the government and then directly to the contractors. The government merely serves as a conduit.

If the government has no liability for defaults, overruns, or other related problems, the recording of the special assessment assets, liabilities, revenues, expenses, other financing sources, and expenditures is not really relevant to the government's resources. In that situation, all transactions are recorded in an agency fund as increases and decreases in cash, amount due from citizens, and amount due to contractors. As a fiduciary fund, no reportable impact appears within the government-wide statements.

LO10

Record the various types of monetary transfers that occur within the funds of a state or local government.

Interfund Transactions

Interfund transactions are commonly used within government units as a way to direct sufficient resources to all activities and functions. Monetary transfers made from the General Fund are especially prevalent because general tax revenues are initially accumulated in this fund. For example, the General Fund for Houston, Texas, indicated in the fund financial statements for the year ending June 30, 2010, that approximately $285.6 million had been transferred out to other funds while only $43.5 million had been transferred in from other funds. Because of the emphasis on individual funds, transfers are not offset or eliminated in fund statements.

In contrast, the government-wide financial statements do not report many such transfers because they frequently occur solely within the governmental activities. For example, a transfer from the General Fund to the Debt Service Fund is reported in both funds on fund financial statements but would create no net impact in the government-wide financial statements because both funds are classified as governmental activities.

Thus, for government-wide financial reporting, the following distinctions are drawn for transfers:

- *Intra-activity transactions* occur between two governmental funds (so that net totals reported for governmental activities are not affected) or between two enterprise funds (so that totals reported for business-type activities are not affected). Transfers between governmental funds and most Internal Service Funds are also frequently included here because, as discussed previously, Internal Service Funds are usually reported as governmental activities in government-wide statements. Intra-activity transactions are not reported in government-wide financial statements because no overall change is created in either the governmental activities or the business-type activities.
- *Interactivity transactions* occur between governmental funds and enterprise funds. They impact the totals reported for both governmental activities and business-type activities. Government-wide financial statements do report interactivity transactions. In Exhibit 16.1, for example, internal amounts due ($50) are reported within the asset section of the statement of net assets and then offset to arrive at overall government totals. Likewise, in Exhibit 16.2, transfers ($600) between the two activity classifications appear at the very bottom of the general revenues section. Again, individual totals are shown and then eliminated so that no amount is reported for the government as a whole. Although most transfers are intra-activity, interactivity transactions are not uncommon. In its June 30, 2010, government-wide financial statements, the City of St. Louis reported (and then eliminated) internal balances of $8.9 million in its statement of net assets and interactivity transfers of $7.3 million in its statement of activities.

Consequently, in discussing interfund transactions, the reporting for government-wide statements is appropriate only when an interactivity transaction is involved.

Interfund Transfers

The most common interfund transactions are transfers within the governmental funds to ensure adequate financing of budgeted expenditures. For example, a city council could vote to transfer $800,000 from the General Fund to the Capital Projects Funds to cover a portion of the cost of a new school building.

Fund Financial Statements—Intra-Activity Transactions

General Fund		
Other Financing Uses—Transfers Out—Capital Projects Fund	800,000	
Due to Capital Projects Fund		800,000
To record authorization transfer for school construction.		

Capital Projects Funds		
Due from General Fund	800,000	
Other Financing Sources—Transfers In—General Fund.		800,000
To record transfer to be received for school construction.		

The *Other Financing Uses/Sources* designations are appropriate here. Financial resources are being moved into and out of these funds although neither revenues nor expenditures have been earned or incurred. As Exhibit 16.4 shows, these balances are reported by each fund in the statement of revenues, expenditures, and other changes in fund balances. Each figure is shown but is not offset in any way. Both accounts are then closed out at the end of the current year. The *Due to/Due from* accounts are the equivalent of interfund payable and receivable balances. Again no elimination is made in arriving at total figures for the governmental funds.

Because this transfer is an intra-activity transaction, no reporting is made in the government-wide financial statements. Financial resources are simply being shifted within the governmental activities.

Not all monetary transfers are for normal operating purposes; nonrecurring or nonroutine transfers may also take place. For example, money might be transferred from the General Fund to create or expand an enterprise fund such as a bus or subway system. Assume that a city sets aside $1 million of unassigned money to help permanently finance a new subway system that will be open to the public. For convenience, this transaction is recorded as if cash is transferred immediately so that no receivable or payable is necessary:

Fund Financial Statements—Interactivity Transactions

General Fund		
Other Financing Uses—Transfers Out—Subway System	1,000,000	
Cash		1,000,000
To record transfer to help finance subway system.		

Enterprise Fund		
Cash	1,000,000	
Capital Contributions		1,000,000
To record receipt of transfer from unrestricted funds.		

Because this transfer is an interactivity transaction (between governmental activities and business-type activities), entries are also made for the government-wide financial statements. This transfer reduces the assets of the governmental activities but increases the assets in the business-type activities. The transfer balances will be offset in arriving at totals for the government as a whole.

Government-Wide Financial Statements—Interactivity Transactions

Governmental Activities		
Transfers Out—Subway System	1,000,000	
Cash		1,000,000
To record transfer to help finance subway system.		

Business-Type Activities		
Cash	1,000,000	
Transfers In—General Fund		1,000,000
To record receipt of transfer from unrestricted funds.		

Internal Exchange Transactions

Some payments made within a government are actually the same as revenues and expenditures rather than transfers. For example, a city must compensate its own print shop (or any other Internal Service Fund or Enterprise Fund) for services or materials because the transfer is the equivalent of a transaction with an outside party. To avoid confusion in reporting, such transfers are recorded as revenues and expenditures or expenses as if the transaction had occurred with an unrelated party. No differentiation is made; these payments are not designed to shift resources from one fund to another.

The fund financial statements record all such internal exchange transactions. However, because Internal Service Funds are usually reported as governmental activities in the government-wide statements, exchanges between a governmental fund and one of these internal service funds normally has no net impact on the overall figures being reported and is omitted.

To illustrate, assume that a government pays its print shop (an internal service fund) \$8,000 for work done for the police department. In addition, the government pays another \$1,000 to a toll road operated as an enterprise fund to allow fire department vehicles to ride on the highway without having to make individual payments.

Fund Financial Statements—Internal Exchange Transactions

General Fund		
Expenditures—Printing	8,000	
Expenditures—Toll Road Privileges	1,000	
Cash		9,000
To record payment for printing supplies for use by police department and for use of toll road.		

Internal Service Fund—Print Shop		
Cash	8,000	
Revenues		8,000
To record collection of money paid by the police department for printing supplies.		

Enterprise Fund—Toll Road		
Cash	1,000	
Revenues		1,000
To record money collected from government for vehicular use of toll roads.		

The $8,000 transaction with the print shop is not reflected in the government-wide financial statements if this internal service fund is classified within the governmental activities. In that case, the transfer is the equivalent of an intra-activity transaction. However, the $1,000 payment made by the police department (a governmental activity) to the enterprise fund (a business-type activity) is the same as an interactivity transfer and is reported through the following entries.

Government-Wide Financial Statements—Internal Exchange Transactions

Governmental Activities		
Expenses—Toll Road Privileges	1,000	
Cash		1,000
To record payment for use of toll road by fire department's vehicles.		

Business-Type Activities		
Cash	1,000	
Revenues		1,000
To record money collected from government for vehicular use of toll roads.		

Summary

1. Readers of state and local government financial statements have a wide variety of informational needs. No single set of financial statements seems capable of meeting all these user needs, a factor that influenced the requirement that two sets of statements be reported. Accountability of government officials and control over public spending have always been essential elements of traditional government accounting. GASB attempted to keep those priorities in place but to broaden the scope of the financial statements being produced.
2. A state or local government unit produces fund financial statements utilizing fund accounting. In this system, activities are classified into three broad categories (governmental, proprietary, and fiduciary). Governmental funds account for service activities; proprietary funds account for activities for which a user charge is assessed; and fiduciary funds account for assets that the government holds as a trustee or agent for an external party.
3. Governmental funds have several fund types: the General Fund, Special Revenue Funds, Capital Projects Funds, Debt Service Funds, and Permanent Funds. Proprietary funds are comprised of Enterprise Funds and Internal Service Funds. Fiduciary funds encompass Pension Trust Funds, Investment Trust Funds, Private-Purpose Trust Funds, and Agency Funds.
4. Government-wide financial statements are made up of a statement of net assets and a statement of activities that are separated into governmental activities (the governmental funds and usually the Internal Service Funds) and business-type activities (Enterprise Funds and occasionally an Internal Service Fund). These statements measure all economic resources. The timing of recognition is guided by accrual accounting.
5. Fund financial statements include a number of financial statements. This chapter focused on the balance sheet and the statement of revenues, expenditures, and other changes in fund balances for the governmental funds. These statements must show the General Fund and any other individual major fund separately. These statements measure current financial resources. The timing of recognition is guided by modified accrual accounting.
6. "Fund balance" reflects the net asset amount for a particular fund within the governmental funds. To indicate the control over this amount that government officials hold, the fund financial statements must classify the fund balance as nonspendable (the asset cannot be spent), restricted (use has been established by a party outside of the government), committed (use has been established by the highest level of authority within the government), assigned (use has been established within the government but not by the highest level of authority), and unassigned (use has not been designated in any way).
7. To aid in control over financial resources, most governmental funds record their approved budgets each year. This initial budget as well as a final amended budget and actual figures for the period are then reported as required supplementary information along with the financial statements or as a separate statement within the fund financial statements.

8. Commitments for purchase orders and contracts are actually recorded in the individual governmental funds by recognizing encumbrances. These balances are recorded when the commitment is made and removed when an actual claim to current financial resources first exists. This recording is followed to help government officials avoid spending more than the amounts properly appropriated.
9. The fund financial statements recognize expenditures for capital outlay, long-term debt payment, and expense-type costs when a claim to current financial resources comes into existence. Government-wide financial statements capitalize capital outlay, reduce liabilities for debt payments, and record expenses in expense accounts.
10. Revenue recognition for nonexchange transactions such as sales taxes and property taxes is based on a classification system set up by GASB. Recognition depends on whether the revenue is a derived tax revenue, imposed nonexchange revenue, government-mandated nonexchange transaction, or voluntary nonexchange transaction.
11. The issuance of long-term bonds is recorded as an "other financing source" by the governmental funds because the resource inflow is not a revenue. In contrast, it is shown as an increase in a long-term liability by the proprietary funds and in the government-wide financial statements.
12. Transfers between funds are normally reported as an "other financing source" and "other financing use" within the fund financial statements and are not eliminated or offset. The government-wide statements do not report such transactions unless they create an impact in overall governmental activities and business-type activities. If reported, the amounts are offset in deriving figures for the government as a whole. For internal exchange transactions in which payment is made for a good or service, the fund statements recognize a revenue and an expenditure. The government-wide financial statements normally do not reflect such transfers unless they occur between an enterprise fund and a governmental fund.

Comprehensive Illustration

Problem

(*Estimated Time: 50 Minutes*). The Town of Drexel has the following financial transactions.

1. The town council adopts an annual budget for the General Fund estimating general revenues of $1.7 million, approved expenditures of $1.5 million, and approved transfers out of $120,000.
2. The town levies property taxes of $1.3 million. It expects to collect all but 3 percent of these taxes during the year. Of the levied amount, $40,000 will be collected next year but after more than 60 days.
3. The town orders two new police cars at an approximate cost of $110,000.
4. A transfer of $50,000 is made from the General Fund to the Debt Service Fund.
5. The town pays a bond payable of $40,000 along with $10,000 of interest using money previously set aside.
6. The Town of Drexel issues a $2 million bond at face value to acquire a building to convert into a high school.
7. The two police cars are received with an invoice price of $112,000. The voucher has been approved for this amount but not yet been paid.
8. The town acquires the building for the high school for $2 million in cash and immediately begins renovating it.
9. Depreciation on the new police cars is computed as $30,000 for the period.
10. The town borrows $100,000 on a 30-day tax anticipation note.
11. The Town of Drexel begins a special assessment curbing project. The government sells $800,000 in notes at face value to finance this project. The town has pledged to guarantee the debt if the assessments collected do not cover the entire balance.
12. A contractor completes the curbing project and is paid $800,000.
13. The town assesses citizens $850,000 for the completed curbing project.
14. The town collects the special assessments of $850,000 in full and repays the debt plus $50,000 in interest.
15. The town receives a $10,000 cash grant to beautify a local park. The grant must be used to reimburse specific costs that the town incurs.
16. The town spends $4,000 to beautify the park.

Required

a. Prepare journal entries for the town based on the production of fund financial statements.
b. Prepare journal entries in anticipation of preparing government-wide financial statements.

Solution

a. ***Fund Financial Statements***

1. **General Fund**

Estimated Revenues Control	1,700,000	
Appropriations Control		1,500,000
Estimated Other Financing Uses Control		120,000
Budgetary Fund Balance		80,000

2. **General Fund**

Property Tax Receivable	1,300,000	
Allowance for Uncollectible Taxes		39,000
Deferred Revenue		40,000
Revenues—Property Taxes		1,221,000

3. **General Fund**

Encumbrances Control	110,000	
Fund Balance—Reserved for Encumbrances		110,000

4. **General Fund**

Other Financing Uses—Transfers Out	50,000	
Cash		50,000

Debt Service Funds

Cash	50,000	
Other Financing Sources—Transfers In		50,000

5. **Debt Service Funds**

Expenditures—Principal	40,000	
Expenditures—Interest	10,000	
Cash		50,000

6. **Capital Projects Funds**

Cash	2,000,000	
Other Financing Sources—Bond Proceeds		2,000,000

7. **General Fund**

Fund Balance—Reserved for Encumbrances	110,000	
Encumbrances Control		110,000
Expenditures Control	112,000	
Vouchers Payable		112,000

8. **Capital Projects Funds**

Expenditures—Building	2,000,000	
Cash		2,000,000

9. No entry is recorded. Expenditures rather than expenses are recorded by the governmental funds.

10. **General Fund**

Cash	100,000	
Tax Anticipation Note Payable		100,000

11. **Capital Projects Funds**

Cash	800,000	
Other Financing Sources—Special Assessments Note		800,000

12. **Capital Projects Funds**

Expenditures—Curbing	800,000	
Cash		800,000

13. **Debt Service Funds**

Taxes Receivable—Special Assessment	850,000	
Revenues—Special Assessment		850,000

14. **Debt Service Funds**

Cash	850,000	
Taxes Receivable—Special Assessment		850,000
Expenditures—Principal	800,000	
Expenditures—Interest	50,000	
Cash		850,000

15. **Special Revenue Funds**

Cash	10,000	
Deferred Revenues		10,000

16. **Special Revenue Funds**

Expenditures—Park Beautification	4,000	
Cash		4,000
Deferred Revenues	4,000	
Revenues—Grants		4,000

b. ***Government-Wide Financial Statements***

1. Budgetary entries are not reported within the government-wide financial statements. They are recorded in the individual funds and are then shown as required supplementary information.

2. **Governmental Activities**

Property Tax Receivable	1,300,000	
Allowance for Uncollectible Taxes		39,000
Revenues—Property Taxes		1,261,000

3. Commitments are not reported in the government-wide financial statements.

4. This transfer was entirely within the governmental funds and, therefore, had no net effect on the governmental activities. No journal entry is needed.

5. **Governmental Activities**

Bonds Payable	40,000	
Interest Expense	10,000	
Cash		50,000

6. **Governmental Activities**

Cash	2,000,000	
Bonds Payable		2,000,000

7. **Governmental Activities**

Police Cars (or Vehicles)	112,000	
Vouchers (or Accounts) Payable		112,000

8. **Governmental Activities**

Building	2,000,000	
Cash		2,000,000

9. **Governmental Activities**

Depreciation Expense	30,000	
Accumulated Depreciation		30,000

10. **Governmental Activities**

Cash	100,000	
Tax Anticipation Note Payable		100,000

11. **Governmental Activities**

Cash	800,000	
Special Assessment Notes Payable		800,000

12. **Governmental Activities**

Infrastructure Assets—Curbing	800,000	
Cash		800,000

13. **Governmental Activities**

Taxes Receivable—Special Assessment	850,000	
Revenues—Special Assessment		850,000

14. **Governmental Activities**

Cash	850,000	
Taxes Receivable—Special Assessment		850,000
Special Assessment Notes Payable	800,000	
Interest Expense	50,000	
Cash		850,000

15. **Governmental Activities**

Cash	10,000	
Deferred Revenues		10,000

16. **Governmental Activities**

Expenses—Park Beautification	4,000	
Cash		4,000
Deferred Revenues	4,000	
Revenues—Grants		4,000

Questions

1. How have users' needs impacted the development of accounting principles for state and local government units?
2. Why have accountability and control been so important in the traditional accounting for state and local government units?
3. In general, how has the dual system of financial statements impacted the financial reporting of state and local governments?
4. What are the basic financial statements that a state or local government now produces?
5. What measurement focus is used in fund financial statements for governmental funds, and what system is applied to determine the timing of revenue and expenditure recognition?
6. What measurement focus is used in government-wide financial statements, and what system is applied to determine the timing of revenue and expense recognition?
7. What assets are viewed as current financial resources?
8. In applying the current financial resources measurement focus, when are liabilities recognized?
9. What are the three classifications of funds? What funds are included in each of these three?
10. What are the five fund types within the governmental funds? What types of events does each of these report?
11. What are the two fund types within the proprietary funds? What types of events does each report?
12. What are the four fund types within the fiduciary funds? What types of events does each report?
13. What are the two major divisions reported in government-wide financial statements? What funds are *not* reported in these financial statements?
14. Fund financial statements have separate columns for each activity. Which activities are reported in this manner?
15. The General Fund of a city reports assets of $300,000 and liabilities of $200,000 in the fund financial statements. Explain what is meant by each of the following balances: fund balance—nonspendable of $40,000, fund balance—restricted of $28,000, fund balance—committed of $17,000, fund balance—assigned of $4,000, and fund balance—unassigned of $11,000.
16. Why are budgetary entries recorded in the individual funds of a state or local government?
17. How are budget results shown in the financial reporting of a state or local government?
18. When is an encumbrance recorded? What happens to this balance? How are encumbrances reported in government-wide financial statements?
19. What costs cause a governmental fund to report an expenditure?
20. At what point in time does a governmental fund report an expenditure?
21. How do governmental funds report capital outlay in fund financial statements? How do government-wide financial statements report capital expenditures?
22. What are the two different ways that supplies and prepaid items can be recorded on fund financial statements?
23. What are the four classifications of nonexchange revenues that a state or local government can recognize? In each case, when are revenues normally recognized?
24. When is a receivable recognized for property tax assessments? When is the revenue recognized?

25. How is the issuance of a long-term bond reported on fund financial statements? How is the issuance of a long-term bond reported on government-wide financial statements?
26. What is a special assessment project? How are special assessment projects reported?
27. How are interfund transfers reported in fund financial statements?
28. In government-wide financial statements, how do intra-activity and interactivity transactions differ? How is each type of transaction reported?
29. What is an internal exchange transaction, and how is it reported?

Problems

LO4

1. Which of the following is *not* a governmental fund?
   a. Special Revenue Fund.
   b. Internal Service Fund.
   c. Capital Projects Fund.
   d. Debt Service Fund.

LO4

2. What is the purpose of a Special Revenue Fund?
   a. To account for revenues legally or externally restricted as an operating expenditure.
   b. To account for ongoing activities.
   c. To account for gifts when only subsequently earned income can be expended.
   d. To account for the cost of long-lived assets bought with designated funds.

LO4

3. What is the purpose of Enterprise Funds?
   a. To account for operations that provide services to other departments within a government.
   b. To account for asset transfers.
   c. To account for ongoing activities such as the police and fire departments.
   d. To account for operations financed in whole or in part by outside user charges.

LO4

4. Which of the following statements is true?
   a. There are three different types of proprietary funds.
   b. There are three different types of fiduciary funds.
   c. There are five different types of fiduciary funds.
   d. There are five different types of governmental funds.

LO1, LO6

5. A government expects to receive revenues of $400,000 but has approved expenditures of $430,000. The anticipated shortage will have an impact on which of the following terms?
   a. Interperiod equity.
   b. Modified accrual accounting.
   c. Consumption accounting.
   d. Account groups.

LO4

6. A citizen of the City of Townsend gives it a gift of $22,000 in investments. The citizen requires that the investments be held but any resulting income must be used to help maintain the city's cemetery. In which fund should this asset be reported?
   a. Special Revenue Funds.
   b. Capital Projects Funds.
   c. Permanent Funds.
   d. General Fund.

LO2

7. Which of the following statements is correct about the reporting of governmental funds?
   a. Fund financial statements measure economic resources.
   b. Government-wide financial statements measure only current financial resources.
   c. Fund financial statements measure both economic resources and current financial resources.
   d. Government-wide financial statements measure economic resources.

LO2

8. Which of the following statements is correct about the reporting of governmental funds?
   a. Fund financial statements measure revenues and expenditures based on modified accrual accounting.
   b. Government-wide financial statements measure revenues and expenses based on modified accrual accounting.

c. Fund financial statements measure revenues and expenses based on accrual accounting.

d. Government-wide financial statements measure revenues and expenditures based on accrual accounting.

LO2, LO7

9. During the current year, a government buys land for $80,000. Which of the following is *not* true?
   a. The land could be reported as an asset by the business-type activities in the government-wide financial statements.
   b. The land could be reported as an asset by the governmental activities in the government-wide financial statements.
   c. The land could be reported as an asset by the proprietary funds in the fund financial statements.
   d. The land could be reported as an asset by the governmental funds in the fund financial statements.

LO5

10. The City of Bagranoff holds $90,000 in cash that will be used to make a bond payment when it comes due early next year. The assistant treasurer had made that decision. However, just before the end of the current year, the city council formally approved using this money in this way. The city council has been designated as the highest level of decision-making authority for this government. What impact does the council's action have on the reporting of fund financial statements?
    a. Fund balance—unassigned goes down and fund balance—restricted goes up.
    b. Fund balance—assigned goes down and fund balance—committed goes up.
    c. Fund balance—unassigned goes down and fund balance—assigned goes up.
    d. Fund balance—assigned goes down and fund balance—restricted goes up.

LO6

11. Which of the following statements is true concerning the recording of a budget?
    a. At the beginning of the year, debit Appropriations.
    b. A debit to the Budgetary Fund Balance account indicates an expected surplus.
    c. At the beginning of the year, debit Estimated Revenues.
    d. At the end of the year, credit Appropriations.

LO1, LO2, LO7

12. The General Fund pays rent for two months. Which of the following is *not* correct?
    a. Rent expense should be reported in the government-wide financial statements.
    b. Rent expense should be reported in the General Fund.
    c. An expenditure should be reported in the fund financial statements.
    d. If one month of rent is in the first year with the other month in the next year, either the purchases method or the consumption method can be used in fund statements.

LO6, LO7

13. A purchase order for $3,000 is recorded in the General Fund for the purchase of a new computer. The computer is received at an actual cost of $3,020. Which of the following is correct?
    a. Machinery is increased in the General Fund by $3,020.
    b. An encumbrance account is reduced by $3,020.
    c. An expenditure is increased by $3,020.
    d. An expenditure is recorded for the additional $20.

LO5

14. At the end of the current year, a government reports a fund balance—assigned of $9,000 in connection with an encumbrance. What information is being conveyed?
    a. A donor has given the government $9,000 that must be used in a specified fashion.
    b. The government has made $9,000 in commitments in one year that will be honored in the subsequent year.
    c. Encumbrances exceeded expenditures by $9,000 during the current year.
    d. The government spent $9,000 less than was appropriated.

LO2, LO3, LO7

15. A government buys equipment for its police department at a cost of $54,000. Which of the following is *not* true?
    a. Equipment will increase by $54,000 in the government-wide financial statements.
    b. Depreciation in connection with this equipment will be reported in the fund financial statements.
    c. The equipment will not appear within the reported assets in the fund financial statements.
    d. An expenditure for $54,000 will be reported in the fund financial statements.

LO3, LO7

16. A city acquires supplies for its fire department and uses the consumption method of accounting. Which of the following statements is true for the fund statements?
   a. An expenditures account was debited at the time of receipt.
   b. An expense is recorded as the supplies are consumed.
   c. An inventory account is debited at the time of the acquisition.
   d. The supplies are recorded within the General Fixed Assets Account Group.

LO8

17. An income tax is an example of which of the following?
   a. Derived tax revenue.
   b. Imposed nonexchange revenue.
   c. Government-mandated nonexchange revenue.
   d. Voluntary nonexchange transaction.

LO8

18. The state government passes a law requiring localities to upgrade their water treatment facilities. The state then awards a grant of $500,000 to the Town of Midlothian to help pay for this cost. What type of revenue is this grant?
   a. Derived tax revenue.
   b. Imposed nonexchange revenue.
   c. Government-mandated nonexchange revenue.
   d. Voluntary nonexchange transaction.

LO8

19. The state awards a grant of $50,000 to the Town of Glenville. The state will pay the grant money to the town as a reimbursement for money spent on road repair. At the time of the grant, the state pays $8,000 in advance. During the first year of this program, the town spent $14,000 and applied for reimbursement. What amount of revenue should be recognized?
   a. $-0-.
   b. $8,000.
   c. $14,000.
   d. $50,000.

LO5, LO9

20. A city issues a 60-day tax anticipation note to fund operations. What recording should it make?
   a. The liability should be reported in the government-wide financial statements; an other financing source should be shown in the fund financial statements.
   b. A liability should be reported in the government-wide financial statements and in the fund financial statements.
   c. An other financing source should be shown in the government-wide financial statements and in the fund financial statements.
   d. An other financing source should be shown in the government-wide financial statements; a liability is reported in the fund financial statements.

LO5, LO9

21. A city issues five-year bonds payable to finance construction of a new school. What recording should be made?
   a. Report the liability in the government-wide financial statements; show an other financing source in the fund financial statements.
   b. Report a liability in the government-wide financial statements and in the fund financial statements.
   c. Show an other financing source in the government-wide financial statements and in the fund financial statements.
   d. Show an other financing source in the government-wide financial statements; report a liability in the fund financial statements.

LO2, LO9

22. A $110,000 payment is made on a long-term liability. Of this amount, $10,000 represents interest. Which of the following is *not* true?
   a. Reduce liabilities by $100,000 in the government-wide financial statements.
   b. Record a $110,000 expenditure in the fund financial statements.
   c. Reduce liabilities by $100,000 in the fund financial statements.
   d. Recognize $10,000 interest expense in the government-wide financial statements.

LO1, LO9

23. A city constructs a special assessment project (a sidewalk) for which it is secondarily liable. The city issues bonds of $90,000. It authorizes another $10,000 that is transferred out of

the General Fund. The sidewalk is built for $100,000. The citizens are billed for $90,000. They pay this amount and the debt is paid off. Where is the $100,000 expenditure for construction recorded?

a. It is not recorded by the city.
b. It is recorded in the Agency Fund.
c. It is recorded in the General Fund.
d. It is recorded in the Capital Projects Fund.

LO4, LO9

24. A city constructs curbing in a new neighborhood and finances it as a special assessment. Under what condition should this activity be recorded in the Agency Fund?

a. Never; the work is reported in the Capital Projects Funds.
b. Only if the city is secondarily liable for any debt incurred to finance construction costs.
c. Only if the city is in no way liable for the costs of the construction.
d. In all cases.

LO10

25. Which of the following is an example of an interactivity transaction?

a. Money is transferred from the General Fund to the Debt Service Fund.
b. Money is transferred from the Capital Projects Fund to the General Fund.
c. Money is transferred from the Special Revenue Fund to the Debt Service Fund.
d. Money is transferred from the General Fund to the Enterprise Fund.

LO5, LO10

26. Cash of $60,000 is transferred from the General Fund to the Debt Service Fund. What is reported on the government-wide financial statements?

a. No reporting is made.
b. Other Financing Sources increase by $60,000; Other Financing Uses increase by $60,000.
c. Revenues increase by $60,000; Expenditures increase by $60,000.
d. Revenues increase by $60,000; Expenses increase by $60,000.

LO5, LO10

27. Cash of $60,000 is transferred from the General Fund to the Debt Service Fund. What is reported on the fund financial statements?

a. No reporting is made.
b. Other Financing Sources increase by $60,000; Other Financing Uses increase by $60,000.
c. Revenues increase by $60,000; Expenditures increase by $60,000.
d. Revenues increase by $60,000; Expenses increase by $60,000.

LO5, LO10

28. Cash of $20,000 is transferred from the General Fund to the Enterprise Fund to pay for work that was done. What is reported on the government-wide financial statements?

a. No reporting is made.
b. Other Financing Sources increase by $20,000; Other Financing Uses increase by $20,000.
c. Revenues increase by $20,000; Expenditures increase by $20,000.
d. Revenues increase by $20,000; Expenses increase by $20,000.

LO5, LO10

29. Cash of $20,000 is transferred from the General Fund to the Enterprise Fund to pay for work that was done. What is reported on the fund financial statements?

a. No reporting is made.
b. Other Financing Sources increase by $20,000; Other Financing Uses increase by $20,000.
c. Revenues increase by $20,000; Expenditures increase by $20,000.
d. Revenues increase by $20,000; Expenses increase by $20,000.

LO3, LO6

30. The board of commissioners of the City of Hartmoore adopted a General Fund budget for the year ending June 30, 2013, that included revenues of $1,000,000, bond proceeds of $400,000, appropriations of $900,000, and operating transfers out of $300,000. If this budget is formally integrated into the accounting records, what journal entry is required at the beginning of the year? What later entry is required?

LO2, LO6, LO7

31. A city orders a new computer for its General Fund at an anticipated cost of $88,000. Its actual cost when received is $89,400. Payment is subsequently made. Give all required journal entries for fund and government-wide financial statements. What information do the government-wide financial statements present? What information do the fund financial statements present?

LO1, LO2, LO7

32. Cash of $90,000 is transferred from a city's General Fund to start construction on a police station. The city issues a bond at its $1.8 million face value. The police station is built for $1.89 million. Prepare all necessary journal entries for these transactions for fund and government-wide financial statements. Assume that the city does not record the commitment. What information do the government-wide financial statements present? What information do the fund financial statements present?

LO5

33. The governmental funds of the City of Westchester report $445,000 in assets and $140,000 in liabilities. The following are some of the assets reported by this government.

- Prepaid items—$7,000
- Cash from a bond issuance that must be spent within the school system according to the indenture—$80,000
- Supplies—$5,000
- Investments given by a citizen that will be sold with the proceeds used to beautify a public park—$33,000
- Cash that the assistant director of finance has designated for use in upgrading the local roads—$40,000
- Cash from a state grant that must be spent to supplement the pay of local kindergarten teachers—$53,000
- Cash that the city council (the highest level of authority in the government) has voted to use to renovate a school gymnasium—$62,000

On a balance sheet for the governmental funds, what fund balance amounts will be reported by the City of Westchester?

LO5

34. Government officials of Hampstead County ordered a computer near the end of the current fiscal year for $6,400 for the police department. It did not arrive prior to the end of the year. At its final meeting of the year, the city council (the highest decision-making authority for the government) agreed to pay for the computer when it arrived in the subsequent year. In producing a set of government-wide financial statements and a set of fund financial statements for the current year, how will this purchase order be reported?

35. A local government has the following transactions during the current fiscal period. Prepare journal entries without dollar amounts, first for fund financial statements and then for government-wide financial statements.

a. The budget for the police department, ambulance service, and other ongoing activities is passed. Funding is from property taxes, transfers, and bond proceeds. All monetary outflows will be for expenses and fixed assets. A deficit is projected.

b. A bond is issued at face value to fund the construction of a new municipal building.

c. A computer is ordered for the tax department.

d. The computer is received.

e. The invoice for the computer is paid.

f. The city council agrees to transfer money from the General Fund as partial payment for a special assessments project but has not done so. The city will be secondarily liable for any money borrowed for this work.

g. The city council creates a motor pool to service all government vehicles. Money is transferred from the General Fund to permanently finance this facility.

h. Property taxes are levied. Although officials believe that most of these taxes should be collected during the current period, a small percentage is estimated to be uncollectible.

i. The city collects grant money from the state that must be spent as a supplement to the salaries of the police force. No entry has been recorded. Appropriate payment of the supplement is viewed as an eligibility requirement.

j. A portion of the grant money in (*i*) is properly spent.

36. Prepare journal entries for the City of Pudding's governmental funds to record the following transactions, first for fund financial statements and then for government-wide financial statements.

a. A new truck for the sanitation department was ordered at a cost of $94,000.

b. The city print shop did $1,200 worth of work for the school system (but has not yet been paid).

c. An $11 million bond was issued to build a new road.

d. Cash of $140,000 is transferred from the General Fund to provide permanent financing for a municipal swimming pool that will be viewed as an Enterprise Fund.

e. The truck ordered in (*a*) is received at an actual cost of $96,000. Payment is not made at this time.

f. Cash of $32,000 is transferred from the General Fund to the Capital Projects Fund.

g. A state grant of $30,000 is received that must be spent to promote recycling.

h. The first $5,000 of the state grant received in (*g*) is appropriately expended.

LO2, LO5, LO7–LO10

eXcel

37. Prepare journal entries for a local government to record the following transactions, first for fund financial statements and then for government-wide financial statements.

a. The government sells $900,000 in bonds at face value to finance construction of a warehouse.

b. A $1.1 million contract is signed for construction of the warehouse. The commitment is required if allowed.

c. A $130,000 transfer of unrestricted funds was made for the eventual payment of the debt in (*a*).

d. Equipment for the fire department is received with a cost of $12,000. When it was ordered, an anticipated cost of $11,800 had been recorded.

e. Supplies to be used in the schools are bought for $2,000 cash. The consumption method is used.

f. A state grant of $90,000 is awarded to supplement police salaries. The money will be paid to reimburse the government after the supplements have been paid to the police officers.

g. Property tax assessments are mailed to citizens of the government. The total assessment is $600,000, although officials anticipate that 4 percent will never be collected. There is an enforceable legal claim for this money and the government can use it immediately.

LO4–LO10

38. The following unadjusted trial balances are for the governmental funds of the City of Copeland prepared from the current accounting records:

General Fund

	Debit	Credit
Cash	$ 19,000	
Taxes Receivable	202,000	
Allowance for Uncollectible Taxes		$ 2,000
Vouchers Payable		24,000
Due to Debt Service Fund		10,000
Deferred Revenues		16,000
Fund Balance—Reserved for Encumbrances		9,000
Fund Balance—Unassigned		103,000
Revenues Control		176,000
Expenditures Control	110,000	
Encumbrances Control	9,000	
Estimated Revenues Control	190,000	
Appropriations Control		171,000
Budgetary Fund Balance		19,000
Totals	$530,000	$530,000

Debt Service Fund

	Debit	Credit
Cash	$ 8,000	
Investments	51,000	
Taxes Receivable	11,000	
Due from General Fund	10,000	
Fund Balance—Committed		$ 45,000
Revenues Control		20,000
Other Financing Sources—Operating Transfers In		90,000
Expenditures Control	75,000	
Totals	$155,000	$155,000

Capital Projects Fund

	Debit	Credit
Cash	$ 70,000	
Special Assessments Receivable	90,000	
Contracts Payable		$ 50,000
Deferred Revenues		90,000
Fund Balance—Reserved for Encumbrances		16,000
Fund Balance—Unassigned		–0–
Other Financing Sources		150,000
Expenditures Control	130,000	
Encumbrances	16,000	
Estimated Other Financing Sources	150,000	
Appropriations		150,000
Totals	$456,000	$456,000

Special Revenue Fund

	Debit	Credit
Cash	$ 14,000	
Taxes Receivable	41,000	
Inventory of Supplies	4,000	
Vouchers Payable		$ 25,000
Deferred Revenues		3,000
Fund Balance—Nonspendable		4,000
Fund Balance—Reserved for Encumbrances		3,000
Fund Balance—Unassigned		19,000
Revenues Control		56,000
Expenditures Control	48,000	
Encumbrances	3,000	
Estimated Revenues	75,000	
Appropriations		60,000
Budgetary Fund Balance		15,000
Totals	$185,000	$185,000

Based on the information presented for each of these governmental funds, answer the following questions:

a. How much more money can city officials expend or commit from the General Fund during the remainder of the current year without amending the budget?

b. Why does the Capital Projects Fund have no construction or capital asset accounts?

c. What does the $150,000 Appropriations balance found in the Capital Projects Fund represent?

d. Several funds have balances for Encumbrances and Fund Balance—Reserved for Encumbrances. How will these amounts be accounted for at the end of the fiscal year?

e. Why does the Fund Balance—Unassigned account in the Capital Projects Fund have a zero balance?

f. What are possible explanations for the $150,000 Other Financing Sources balance found in the Capital Projects Fund?

g. What does the $75,000 balance in the Expenditures Control account of the Debt Service Fund represent?

h. What is the purpose of the Special Assessments Receivable found in the Capital Projects Fund?

i. In the Special Revenue Fund, what is the purpose of the Fund Balance—Nonspendable account?

j. Why does the Debt Service Fund not have budgetary account balances?

LO2–LO10

39. Following are descriptions of transactions and other financial events for the City of Tetris for the year ending December 2013. Not all transactions have been included here. Only the General Fund formally records a budget. No encumbrances were carried over from 2012.

Paid salary for police officers	$ 21,000
Received government grant to pay ambulance drivers	40,000
Estimated revenues	232,000
Received invoices for rent on equipment used by fire department during last four months of the year	3,000
Paid for newly constructed city hall	1,044,000
Made commitment to acquire ambulance	111,000
Received cash from bonds sold for construction purposes	300,000
Placed order for new sanitation truck	154,000
Paid salary to ambulance drivers—money derived from state government grant given for that purpose	24,000
Paid for supplies for school system	16,000
Made transfer from General Fund to eventually pay off a long-term debt	33,000
Received but did not pay for new ambulance	120,000
Levied property tax receivables for 2013. City anticipates that 95 percent ($190,000) will be collected during the year and 5 percent will be uncollectible	200,000
Acquired and paid for new school bus	40,000
Received cash from business licenses and parking meters (not previously accrued)	14,000
Made appropriations	225,000

The following questions are *independent* although each is based on the preceding information. Assume that the government is preparing information for its fund financial statements.

a. What is the balance in the Budgetary Fund Balance account for the budget for the year? Is it a debit or credit?

b. Assume that 60 percent of the school supplies are used during the year so that 40 percent remain. If the consumption method is being applied, how is this recorded?

c. The sanitation truck that was ordered was not received before the end of the year. The commitment will be honored in the subsequent year when the truck arrives. What reporting is made at the end of 2013?

d. Assume that the ambulance was received on December 31, 2013. Provide all necessary journal entries on that date.

e. Give all journal entries that should have been made when the $33,000 transfer was made for the eventual payment of a long-term debt.

f. What amount of revenue would be recognized for the period? Explain the composition of this total.

g. What are the total expenditures? Explain the makeup of this total. Include (*b*) here.

h. What journal entry or entries were prepared when the bonds were issued?

LO2–LO10

40. Chesterfield County had the following transactions. Prepare the entries first for fund financial statements and then for government-wide financial statements.

a. A budget is passed for all ongoing activities. Revenue is anticipated to be $834,000 with approved spending of $540,000 and operating transfers out of $242,000.

b. A contract is signed with a construction company to build a new central office building for the government at a cost of $8 million. A budget for this project has previously been recorded.

c. Bonds are sold for $8 million (face value) to finance construction of the new office building.

d. The new building is completed. An invoice for $8 million is received and paid.

e. Previously unrestricted cash of $1 million is set aside to begin paying the bonds issued in (*c*).

f. A portion of the bonds comes due and $1 million is paid. Of this total, $100,000 represents interest. The interest had not been previously accrued.

g. Citizens' property tax levies are assessed. Total billing for this tax is $800,000. On this date, the assessment is a legally enforceable claim according to the laws of this state. The money to be received is designated for the current period and 90 percent is assumed to be collectible in this period with receipt of an additional 6 percent during subsequent periods but in time to be available to pay current period claims. The remainder is expected to be uncollectible.

h. Cash of $120,000 is received from a toll road. This money is restricted for highway maintenance.

i. The county received investments valued at $300,000 as a donation from a grateful citizen. Income from these investments must be used to beautify local parks.

LO5

eXcel

41. The following trial balance is taken from the General Fund of the City of Jennings for the year ending December 31, 2013. Prepare a condensed statement of revenues, expenditures, and other changes in fund balance and also prepare a condensed balance sheet.

	Debit	Credit
Accounts Payable		$ 90,000
Cash	$ 30,000	
Contracts Payable		90,000
Deferred Revenues		40,000
Due from Capital Projects Funds	60,000	
Due to Debt Service Funds		40,000
Expenditures	530,000	
Fund Balance—Unassigned		170,000
Investments	410,000	
Revenues		760,000
Other Financing Sources—Bond Proceeds		300,000
Other Financing Sources—Transfers In		50,000
Other Financing Uses—Transfers Out	470,000	
Taxes Receivable	220,000	
Vouchers Payable		180,000
Totals	$1,720,000	$1,720,000

LO2, LO5–LO10

42. A city has only one activity, its school system. The school system is accounted for within the General Fund. For convenience, assume that, at the start of 2013, the school system and the city have no assets. During the year, the city assessed $400,000 in property taxes. Of this amount, it collected $320,000 during the year, received $50,000 within a few weeks after the end of the year, and expected the remainder to be collected about six months later. The city makes the following payments during 2013: salary expense, $100,000; rent expense, $70,000; equipment (received on January 1 with a five-year life and no salvage value), $50,000; land, $30,000; and maintenance expense, $20,000.

In addition, on the last day of the year, the city purchased a $200,000 building by signing a long-term liability. The building has a 20-year life and no salvage value, and the liability accrues interest at a 10 percent annual rate. The city also buys two computers on the last day of the year for $4,000 each. One will be paid for in 30 days and the other in 90 days. The computers should last for four years and have no salvage value. During the year, the school system charged students $3,000 for school fees and collected the entire amount. Any depreciation is recorded using the straight-line method.

a. Produce a statement of net assets and a statement of activities for this city's government-wide financial statements.

b. Produce a balance sheet and a statement of revenues, expenditures, and changes in fund balance for the fund financial statements. Assume that *available* is defined by the city as anything to be received within 60 days.

LO5, LO7–LO10

43. The following transactions relate to the General Fund of the city of Lost Angel for the year ending December 31, 2013. Prepare a statement of revenues, expenditures, and other changes in fund balance for the General Fund for the period to be included in the fund financial statements. Assume that the fund balance at the beginning of the year was $180,000. Assume also that the purchases method is applied to the supplies and that receipt within 60 days is used as the definition of available resources.

a. Collected property tax revenue of $700,000. A remaining assessment of $100,000 will be collected in the subsequent period. Half of that amount should be collected within 30 days, and the remainder will be received in about five months after the end of the year.

b. Spent $200,000 on four new police cars with 10-year lives. A price of $207,000 had been anticipated when the cars were ordered. The city calculates all depreciation using the straight-line method with no salvage value. The half-year convention is used.

c. Transferred $90,000 to a debt service fund.

d. Issued a long-term bond for $200,000 on July 1. Interest at a 10 percent annual rate will be paid each year starting on June 30, 2014.

e. Ordered a new computer with a five-year life for $40,000.

f. Paid salaries of $30,000. Another $10,000 will be owed at the end of the year but will not be paid for 30 days.

g. Received the new computer but at a cost of $41,000; payment is to be made in 45 days.

h. Bought supplies for $10,000 in cash.

i. Used $8,000 of the supplies in (*h*).

LO5, LO7–LO10

44. Use the transactions in problem (43) but prepare a statement of net assets for the government-wide financial statements. Assume that the General Fund had $180,000 in cash on the first day of the year and no other assets or liabilities. No amount was restricted, committed, or assigned.

LO1, LO6

45. Government officials of the City of Jones expect to receive General Fund revenues of $400,000 in 2013 but approve spending only $380,000. Later in the year, as they receive more information, they increase the revenue projection to $420,000. Officials approve the spending of an additional $15,000. For each of the following, indicate whether the statement is true or false and, if false, explain why.

a. In recording this budget, appropriations should be credited initially for $380,000.

b. The city must disclose this budgetary data within the required supplemental information section reported after the notes to the financial statements.

c. When reporting budgetary information for the year, three figures should be reported: amended budget, initial budget, and actual figures.

d. In making the budgetary entry, a debit must be made to some type of Fund Balance account to indicate the projected surplus.

e. The reporting of the budget is reflected in the government-wide financial statements.

LO8

46. On December 1, 2013, a state government awards a city government a grant of $1 million to be used specifically to provide hot lunches for all schoolchildren. No money is received until June 1, 2014. For each of the following, indicate whether the statement is true or false and, if false, explain why.

a. Because the government received no money until June 1, 2014, no amount of revenue can be recognized in 2013 on the government-wide financial statements.

b. If this grant has no eligibility requirements and the money is properly spent in September 2014 for the hot lunches, the revenue should be recognized during that September.

c. Because the money came from the state government and because the government specified the use, this is a government-mandated nonexchange transaction.

d. If the government had received the money on December 1, 2013, but eligibility requirements had not been met yet, a deferred revenue of $1 million would have been recognized on the government-wide financial statements.

LO2, LO5, LO7–LO10

47. Indicate (i) how each of the following transactions impacts the fund balance of the General Fund, and its classifications, for fund financial statements and (ii) what the impact is on the net asset balance of the Government Activities on the government-wide financial statements.

a. Issue a five-year bond for $6 million to finance general operations.

b. Pay cash of $149,000 for a truck to be used by the police department.

c. The fire department pays $17,000 to a government motor pool that services the vehicles of only the police and fire departments. Work was done on several department vehicles.

d. Levy property taxes of $75,000 for the current year that will not be collected until four months into the subsequent year.

e. Receive a grant for $7,000 that must be returned unless the money is spent according to the stipulations of the conveyance. That is expected to happen in the future.

f. Businesses make sales of $20 million during the current year. The government charges a 5 percent sales tax. Half of this amount is to be collected 10 days after the end of the year with the remainder to be collected 14 weeks after the end of the year. "Available" has been defined by this government as 75 days.

g. Order a computer for the school system at an anticipated cost of $23,000.

h. A cash transfer of $18,000 is approved from the General Fund to a Capital Projects Fund.

LO4, LO5, LO10

48. Fund A transfers $20,000 to Fund B. For each of the following, indicate whether the statement is true or false and, if false, explain why.
    a. If Fund A is the General Fund and Fund B is an Enterprise Fund, nothing will be shown for this transfer on the statement of activities within the government-wide financial statements.
    b. If Fund A is the General Fund and Fund B is a Debt Service Fund, nothing will be shown for this transfer on the statement of activities within the government-wide financial statements.
    c. If Fund A is the General Fund and Fund B is an Enterprise Fund, a $20,000 reduction will be reported on the statement of revenues, expenditures, and other changes for the governmental funds within the fund financial statements.
    d. If Fund A is the General Fund and Fund B is a Special Revenue Fund (which is not considered a major fund), no changes will be shown on the statement of revenues, expenditures, and other changes within the fund financial statements.
    e. If Fund A is the General Fund and Fund B is an Internal Service Fund and this is for work done, the General Fund will report an expense of $20,000 within the fund financial statements.

Use the following information for Problems 49–55:

Assume that the City of Coyote has already produced its financial statements for December 31, 2013, and the year then ended. The city's General Fund was only for education and parks. Its Capital Projects Funds worked with each of these functions at times. The city also had established an Enterprise Fund to account for its art museum.

The government-wide financial statements indicated the following figures:

- Education reported net expenses of $600,000.
- Parks reported net expenses of $100,000.
- Art museum reported net revenues of $50,000.
- General government revenues for the year were $800,000 with an overall increase in the city's net assets of $150,000.

The fund financial statements indicated the following for the entire year:

- The General Fund reported a $30,000 increase in its fund balance.
- The Capital Projects Fund reported a $40,000 increase in its fund balance.
- The Enterprise Fund reported a $60,000 increase in its net assets.

The CPA firm of Abernethy and Chapman has been asked to review several transactions that occurred during 2013 and indicate how to correct any erroneous reporting and the impact of each error. View each of the following situations as independent.

LO2, LO5, LO9

49. During 2013, the City of Coyote contracted to build a sidewalk costing $10,000 as a special assessments project for which it collected $10,000 from affected citizens. The government had no obligation in connection with this project. Both a $10,000 revenue and a $10,000 expenditure were recorded in the Capital Projects Fund. In preparing government-wide financial statements, an asset and a general revenue were recorded for $10,000.
    a. In the general information above, the Capital Projects Fund reported a $40,000 increase in its fund balance. What was the correct overall change in the Capital Projects Fund's balance during 2013?
    b. In the general information, a $150,000 overall increase in the city's net assets was found on the government-wide financial statements. What was the correct overall change in the city's net assets on the government-wide financial statements?

LO9

50. On December 30, 2013, the City of Coyote borrowed $20,000 for the General Fund on a 60-day note. In that fund, both Cash and Other Financing Sources were recorded. In the general information above, a $30,000 overall increase was reported in the General Fund balance. What was the correct change in the General Fund's balance for 2013?

LO2, LO4, LO5

51. An art display set up for the City of Coyote was recorded within the General Fund and generated revenues of $9,000 but had expenditures of $45,000 ($15,000 in expenses and $30,000 to buy land for the display). The CPA firm has determined that this program should have been recorded as an Enterprise Fund activity because it was offered in association with the art museum.
    a. Based on the information provided above, what was the correct change in the General Fund's balance for 2013?
    b. What was the correct overall change in the city's net assets on the government-wide financial statements?

c. What was the correct change in the net assets of the Enterprise Fund on the fund financial statements?

LO2, LO5, LO8

52. The City of Coyote mailed property tax bills for 2014 to its citizens during August 2013. Payments could be made early to receive a discount. The levy becomes legally enforceable on February 15, 2014. All money received must be spent during 2014 or later. The total assessment is $300,000; 40 percent of that amount, less a 10 percent discount, is collected in 2013. The city expects to receive all of the remaining money during 2014 with no discount. During 2013, the government increased cash as well as a revenue for the amount received. No change was made in creating the government-wide financial statements.

a. What was the correct overall change in the city's net assets as shown on the government-wide financial statements?

b. What was the correct change for 2013 in the fund balance reported in the General Fund?

LO2, LO5, LO8

53. The City of Coyote mailed property tax bills for 2014 to its citizens during August 2013. Payments could be made early to receive a discount. The levy becomes legally enforceable on February 15, 2014. All money received must be spent during 2014 or later. The total assessment is $300,000, and 40 percent of that amount is collected in 2013 less a 10 percent discount. The city expects to receive all the rest of the money during 2014 with no discount. During 2013, the government increased cash and a revenue for the amount received. In addition, a receivable account and a deferred revenue account for $180,000 were recognized.

a. In the general information above, an overall increase in the city's net assets of $150,000 was found on the government-wide financial statements. What was the correct overall change in the city's net assets as reported on the government-wide financial statements?

b. In the general information above, an overall increase of $30,000 was reported in the General Fund balance. What was the correct change during 2013 in the General Fund's balance?

LO2, LO5, LO7, LO8

54. In 2013, the City of Coyote received a $320,000 cash grant from the state to stop air pollution. Assume that although a special revenue fund could have been set up, the money remained in the General Fund. Cash was received immediately but had to be returned if the city had not lowered air pollution by 25 percent by 2016. On December 31, 2013, Coyote spent $210,000 of this money for a large machine to help begin to reduce pollution. The machine is expected to last for five years and was recorded as an expenditure in the General Fund and as an asset on the government-wide financial statements where it was depreciated based on the straight-line method and the half-year convention. Because the money had been received, all $320,000 was recorded as a revenue on both the fund and the government-wide financial statements.

a. What was the correct change for 2013 in the General Fund's balance?

b. What was the correct overall change in the net assets reported on the government-wide financial statements?

LO2

55. During 2013, the City of Coyote's General Fund received $10,000, which was recorded as a general revenue when it was actually a program revenue earned by its park program.

a. What was the correct overall change for 2013 in the net assets reported on the government-wide financial statements?

b. In the general information above, the parks reported net expenses for the period of $100,000. What was the correct amount of net expenses reported by the parks?

Develop Your Skills

RESEARCH CASE 1

CPA skills

The City of Hampshore is currently preparing financial statements for the past fiscal year. The city manager is concerned because the city encountered some unusual transactions during the current fiscal period and is unsure as to their handling.

Required

Locate a copy (either in hard copy or online) of GASB's *Codification of Governmental Accounting and Reporting Standards*. Either through an online search or a review of the index, answer each of the following questions.

1. For government accounting, what is the definition of an *extraordinary item?*
2. For government accounting, what is the definition of a *special item?*
3. On government-wide financial statements, how should extraordinary items and special items be reported?

RESEARCH CASE 2

The City of Danmark is preparing financial statements. Officials are currently working on the statement of activities within the government-wide financial statements. A question has arisen as to whether a particular revenue should be identified on government-wide statements as a program revenue or a general revenue.

Required

Locate a copy (either in hard copy or online) of GASB's *Codification of Governmental Accounting and Reporting Standards*. Either through an online search or a review of the index, answer each of the following questions.

1. How is a program revenue defined?
2. What are common examples of program revenues?
3. How is a general revenue defined?
4. What are common examples of general revenues?

ANALYSIS CASE

Search the Internet for the official website of one or more state or local governments. After reviewing this website, determine whether the latest comprehensive annual financial report (CAFR) is available on the site. For example, the most recent comprehensive annual financial report for the City of Sacramento can be found at www.cityofsacramento.org/cafr/ and the comprehensive annual financial report for the City of Phoenix can be found at http://phoenix.gov/citygovernment/financial/reports/cafr/index.html. Use the financial statements that you locate to answer the following questions.

Required

1. How does the audit opinion given to this city by its independent auditors differ from the audit opinion rendered on the financial statements for a for-profit business?
2. A reconciliation should be presented to explain the difference between the net changes in fund balances for the governmental funds (fund financial statements) and the change in net assets for the governmental activities (government-wide financial statements). What were several of the largest reasons for the difference?
3. What were the city's largest sources of general revenues?
4. What was the total amount of expenditures recorded by the General Fund during the period? How were those expenditures classified?
5. What assets are reported for the General Fund?
6. Review the notes to the financial statements and then determine the number of days the government uses to define the end-of-year financial resources that are viewed as currently available.
7. Did the size of the General Fund balance increase or decrease during the most recent year and by how much?

COMMUNICATION CASE 1

Go to the website www.gasb.org and click on "Projects" included in the list that runs across the top of the page. Then click on "Current Projects." Click on one of the current projects that is listed. Read the sections that are titled "Project Plan" and "Current Developments."

Required

Write a memo to explain the reason that this issue has been chosen for study by GASB. Describe the progress that has been made to date as well as the potential impact on state and local government accounting.

COMMUNICATION CASE 2

Go to the website www.gasb.org and click on "About GASB" included in the list that runs across the top of the page. Then click on "Mission, Vision, and Core Values." Read the information provided by GASB.

Required

Assume that a financial analyst with whom you are working is interested in knowing more about the purpose of GASB. Write a short memo explaining the work of GASB based on its vision, mission, core values, and goals.

COMMUNICATION CASE 3

Obtain a copy of the original version of GASB *Statement 34*. Read paragraphs 239 through 277.

Required

Write a report describing alternatives that the GASB considered when it created *Statement 34*. Indicate the alternative that you would have viewed as most appropriate, and describe why the GASB did not choose it.

COMMUNICATION CASE 4

Search the Internet for the official website of one or more state or local governments. On this website, determine whether the latest comprehensive annual financial report (CAFR) is available. For example, a recent comprehensive annual financial report for the City of Minneapolis can be found at www.ci.minneapolis.mn.us/financial-reports/ and for the City of Tallahassee, Florida, can be found at www.talgov.com/dma/accounting/annualrprts.cfm. Read the Management's Discussion and Analysis (MD&A) that should be located near the beginning of the annual report.

Required

Write a memo to explain four or five of the most interesting pieces of information that the Management's Discussion and Analysis provides.

EXCEL CASE

The City of Bainland has been undergoing financial difficulties because of a decrease in its tax base caused by corporations leaving the area. On January 1, 2013, the city has a fund balance of only $400,000 in its governmental funds. In 2012, the city had revenues of $1.4 million and expenditures of $1.48 million. The city's treasurer has forecast that, unless something is done, revenues will decrease at 2 percent per year while expenditures will increase at 3 percent per year.

Required

1. Create a spreadsheet to predict in what year the government will have a zero fund balance.
2. One proposal is that the city slash its expenditures by laying off government workers. That will lead to a 3 percent decrease in expenditures each year rather than a 3 percent increase. However, because of the unemployment, the city will receive less tax revenue. Thus, instead of a 2 percent decrease in revenues, the city expects a 5 percent decrease per year. Adapt the spreadsheet created in requirement (1) to predict what year the government will have a zero fund balance if this option is taken.
3. Another proposal is to increase spending to draw new businesses to the area. This action will lead to a 7 percent increase in expenditures every year, but revenues are expected to rise by 4 percent per year. Adapt the spreadsheet created in requirement (1) to predict what year the government will have a zero fund balance under this option.

Accounting for State and Local Governments (Part 2)

chapter 17

Learning Objectives

After studying this chapter, you should be able to:

- LO1 Account for lease contracts where the state or local government finds itself as either lessor or lessee.
- LO2 Recognize the liability caused by the eventual closure and postclosure costs of operating a solid waste landfill as well as for the compensated absences earned by government employees.
- LO3 Record the donation and acquisition of works of art and historical treasures.
- LO4 Explain the reporting and possible depreciation of infrastructure assets.
- LO5 Understand the composition of a state or local government's comprehensive annual financial report (CAFR).
- LO6 Explain the makeup of a primary government and its relationship to component units.
- LO7 Understand the physical structure of a complete set of government-wide financial statements and a complete set of fund financial statements.
- LO8 Prepare financial statements for a public college or university.

The previous chapter introduced many of the unique aspects of financial reporting applicable to state and local governments. Fund accounting, budgets, encumbrances, expenditures, revenue recognition, the issuance of bonds, and the like in connection with both traditional fund financial statements and the newer government-wide financial statements were all presented and analyzed. This initial coverage was designed to explain the rationale underlying the accounting required of these government entities, especially the differences caused by the dual nature of the financial reporting process.

The current chapter carries this analysis further, first by delving into more complex financial situations. Many state and local government units are quite large and face numerous transactions as complicated as any a for-profit business encounters. This chapter examines issues such as capital leases, solid waste landfills, donated artworks, and the depreciation of infrastructure assets to broaden the scope of understanding of state and local government accounting.

Second, the chapter discusses the overall financial reporting model. Within this coverage, the actual composition of a government is examined. Because of the wide variety of agencies, departments, and other activities that operate in connection with a government, determining inclusion within the financial statements is not as easy as in a for-profit business where ownership of more than 50 percent of the voting stock is the primary criterion.

Capital Leases

A note to the 2010 financial statements of the City and County of Denver, Colorado, describes the government in the role of *lessee:*

> The governmental activities capital leases are for various properties including the Wellington Webb Municipal Office Building, 2000 West Third Avenue Wastewater Building, Certain Human Services Facilities, the Blair-Caldwell Research Library, the Buell Theatre, the 5440 Roslyn maintenance facility property, the Central Platte Valley Campus facilities jail dorm building, and portions of three parking garages/facilities. The capital leases also include certain computer software and network equipment, and public works, safety, and parks and recreation equipment.

LO1

Account for lease contracts where the state or local government finds itself as either lessor or lessee.

In contrast, a note to the 2009 financial statements of the City of Dallas, Texas, describes the government as a *lessor:*

> The City is also under several lease agreements as lessor whereby it receives revenues from leasing airport terminal space, hangars, parking spaces, ramps, land, buildings, and office space to air carriers and other tenants. These revenue leases are considered for accounting purposes to be operating leases.

Obviously, state and local governments (in the same manner as for-profit businesses) sometimes lease property rather than purchasing it. For governments such as the City and County of Denver, leasing can provide lower interest rates or reduce the risk of obsolescence and damage. Leasing is an efficient way for many organizations (for-profit or governmental) to acquire needed equipment, machinery, buildings, or other assets. At the same time, a government like the City of Dallas can find itself in the position of lessor. This is particularly true when the city or state holds property that it prefers not to operate itself.

For reporting purposes, such leases must be recorded as either capital leases or operating leases. To guide that decision, GASB has accepted the criteria applied by FASB [FASB ASC (para. 840-10-25-1)] as the method of differentiation. A lease that meets any one of four criteria is classified as a capital lease. If none are met, it is an operating lease.

1. The lease transfers ownership of the property to the lessee by the end of the lease term.
2. The lease contains an option to purchase the leased property at a bargain price.
3. The lease term is equal to or more than 75 percent of the estimated economic life of the leased property.
4. The present value of rental or other minimum lease payments equals or exceeds 90 percent of the fair value of the leased property.

Although the financial reporting for state and local governments is quite unique, many of the basic elements (such as the criteria for identifying a capital lease) are identical whether it is a for-profit enterprise or a government entity.[1]

Leases—Government-Wide Financial Statements

In reporting property obtained through a capital lease, accounting used in constructing the government-wide financial statements is identical to that of a for-profit enterprise. Government-wide statements report both an asset and a liability, initially at the present value of the minimum lease payments, using accounting that is consistent with a debt-financed acquisition. Assume, for example, that a police department signs an 8-year lease on January 1, Year 1, for a truck with a 10-year estimated life. Because this contract meets the third of the preceding criteria, the transaction is recorded as a capital lease.

Assume that the lease calls for annual payments of $10,000 per year with the first payment made at the signing of the lease and that a 10 percent annual interest rate is appropriate for the city. The present value of the minimum lease payments applying a 10 percent annual interest rate to an annuity due for eight years is $58,680 (rounded). The city makes the following entries within the governmental activities because the lease relates to the police department (part of the General Fund). However, the same reporting is appropriate within the business-type activities if an enterprise fund had been involved.

Government-Wide Financial Statements—Capital Lease, Government as Lessee

January 1, Year 1		
Truck—Capital Lease	58,680	
Capital Lease Obligation		58,680
To record capital lease.		

[1] At the time of this writing, FASB is considering a likely change in the rules for leases that will prevent most lease contracts from being reported as operating leases. This will have a probable impact on the reporting by state and local government entities.

Capital Lease Obligation	10,000	
Cash		10,000
To record first payment on leased truck.		

Assuming that the straight-line method is being used, the city should recognize annual depreciation expense of $7,335 ($58,680/8 years). However, if title to the asset will be transferred to the city or if a bargain purchase option exists, the 10-year asset life is appropriate for depreciation purposes because the lessee (the city) expects to get full use of the asset.

At the end of the first year, when the city makes the next payment, part of that $10,000 will be attributed to interest with the remainder viewed as a reduction in the liability principal. Because the initial payment reduced the obligation to $48,680 and the interest rate is 10 percent, interest recorded for the first year is $4,868. The remaining $5,132 ($10,000 less 4,868) decreases the debt to $43,548.

Government-Wide Financial Statements—Capital Lease, Year-End Entries

December 31, Year 1		
Depreciation Expense	7,335	
Accumulated Depreciation—Leased Truck		7,335
To record depreciation of leased truck for first year of use.		
Interest Expense	4,868	
Capital Lease Obligation	5,132	
Cash		10,000
To record payment on capital lease at end of first year.		

Leases—Fund Financial Statements

This truck lease is also recorded in preparation for creating fund financial statements for the governmental funds. As shown in the previous chapter, fund reporting is quite different. However, if a proprietary fund is involved, the handling is the same as in the preceding situation. A difference appears only for the governmental funds.

Using the same eight-year lease in connection with the truck being obtained and payments of $10,000 per year, an amount with a present value of $58,680, the General Fund (or whichever governmental fund is gaining use of the asset) records the following entry:

Fund Financial Statements—Capital Lease, Government Fund as Lessee

January 1, Year 1		
General Fund		
Expenditures—Leased Asset	58,680	
Other Financing Sources—Capital Lease.		58,680
To record signing of an eight-year lease for a truck that meets the requirements of a capital lease.		
Expenditures—Lease Principal	10,000	
Cash		10,000
To record first payment on leased truck.		

Note that the General Fund reports neither the capital asset nor the long-term liability. They are not current financial resources nor are they claims to current financial resources. Instead, an expenditure and an other financing source are established to reflect the transaction.

At the end of this initial year, when the next payment is made, $4,868 (10 percent of the obligation after the first payment) is considered an expenditure for interest; the rest is an expenditure that reduces the principal. Depreciation is ignored.

Fund Financial Statements—Capital Lease, Year-End Entries

December 31, Year 1		
General Fund		
Expenditures—Interest	4,868	
Expenditures—Lease Principal	5,132	
Cash		10,000
To record payment at the end of first year on leased truck recorded as a capital lease.		

At first glance, the fund journal entries appear to be double-counting the expenditures, once when the asset is obtained and again when the periodic payments are made. This approach, though, is consistent with traditional government accounting. The government had an option; it could have either leased the asset or borrowed money and bought the asset. Because the overall result is the same in both cases, the reporting process should not create different pictures.

The preceding entries mirror the presentation that results in the fund statements if the city follows the alternative strategy for acquiring the asset: (1) borrowed money on a long-term liability, (2) used the money to acquire the asset, and (3) subsequently paid the long-term liability and any accrued interest. When the city uses this borrow-and-buy approach, the recording is as follows in the fund statements:

1. To reflect the borrowing, the city reports an other financing source because the money received did not come from a revenue.
2. When the asset is acquired, the city reports an expenditure of that amount in keeping with the goal of presenting the changes in current financial resources.
3. For the same reason, the subsequent payment of debt and interest leads to a second recording of expenditures.

If the city borrows money and buys the asset, one "other financing source" and two separate "expenditures" result. The preceding journal entries created for the capital lease are structured to arrive at that same reporting impact.

The radical differences between fund financial statements and government-wide financial statements are, once again, quite striking. At the end of this first year, the figures found in the two statements are not comparable in any way:

	Fund Financial Statements	Government-Wide Financial Statements
Asset	Not applicable	$58,680
Accumulated depreciation	Not applicable	7,335
Liability	Not applicable	43,548
Expenditures:		
Asset acquisition	$58,680	Not applicable
Debt principal	15,132	Not applicable
Interest	4,868	Not applicable
Other financing sources	58,680	Not applicable
Depreciation expense	Not applicable	7,335
Interest expense	Not applicable	4,868

LO2

Recognize the liability caused by the eventual closure and postclosure costs of operating a solid waste landfill as well as for the compensated absences earned by government employees.

Solid Waste Landfill

Many communities operate landfills. The following information is disclosed in the notes to the financial statements of the City of Greensboro, North Carolina, as of June 30, 2010:

> The City owns and operates a regional landfill site located in the northeast portion of the City. State and federal laws require the City to place a final cover on its White Street landfill site and to perform certain maintenance and monitoring functions at the site for thirty

> years after closure. The City reports a portion of these closure and postclosure care costs as an operating expense in each period based on landfill capacity used as of each June 30. The $22,159,625 reported as landfill closure and postclosure care liability at June 30, 2010, is based on 100% use of the estimated capacity of Phase II and Phase III, Cells 1 and 2. Phase III, Cell 3, is estimated at 46.2% of capacity. . . .
>
> The estimated liability amounts are based on what it would cost to perform all closure and postclosure care in the current year. Actual cost may be higher due to inflation, changes in technology, or changes in regulations. At June 30, 2010, the City had expended $3,876,035 to complete closure for the White Street facility, Phase II. The balance of closure costs, estimated at $13,360,079 and estimated at $8,799,546 for postclosure care will be funded over the remaining life of the landfill.

Thousands of state and local governments operate solid waste landfills to provide a place for citizens and local companies to dispose of trash and other forms of garbage and refuse. Governments frequently report landfill operations within their enterprise funds if these facilities require a user fee. However, some landfills are open to the public without fee so that reporting within the General Fund is appropriate.

Regardless of the type of fund utilized, solid waste landfills can be sources of huge liabilities for these governments. The U.S. Environmental Protection Agency has strict rules on closure requirements as well as groundwater monitoring and other postclosure activities. Satisfying such requirements can be quite costly. Thus, the operation of a landfill can eventually necessitate large payments to ensure that the facility is properly closed and then monitored and maintained for an extended period. Theoretically, the relevant accounting question has always been how to report these eventual costs while the landfill is still in operation.

As an illustration, assume that a city opens a landfill in Year 1 that is expected to take 10 years to fill. To determine the annual amount to be reported, the city must estimate the current costs required to close the landfill. Such costs include the amount to be paid to cover the area and for all postclosure maintenance. As mentioned above by the City of Greensboro, the government uses current—rather than an estimation of future—costs as a better measure of the present obligation. However, such amounts must then be adjusted each period for inflation as well as technology and regulation changes.

Assume, for this example, that the current cost for closure is $1 million and for postclosure maintenance at $400,000. Assume that during Year 1, the city makes an initial payment of $30,000 toward the closure costs. At the end of this first year, city engineers determine that 16 percent of the available space has been filled.

Landfills—Government-Wide Financial Statements

Regardless of whether the city reports this solid waste landfill as a governmental activity (within the General Fund) or as a business-type activity (within an enterprise fund), it must recognize the closure and postclosure costs in the government-wide statements based on accrual accounting and the economic resources measurement basis. Because the government anticipates that the total current cost of cleanup is $1.4 million and the landfill is 16 percent filled, $224,000 should be accrued in this first year ($1.4 million × 16%). The initial payment made this year simply reduces the liability being reported:

Government-Wide Financial Statements—Estimated Landfill Closure Costs

Year 1		
Expense—Landfill Closure	224,000	
Landfill Closure Liability		224,000
To recognize the Year 1 portion of total costs for eventual closure of landfill.		
Landfill Closure Liability	30,000	
Cash		30,000
To record first payment of costs necessitated by eventual closure of the landfill.		

To complete this example, assume that the landfill is judged to be 27 percent filled at the end of Year 2 and the city makes another $30,000 payment toward future closure costs.

However, because of inflation and recent changes in technology, the city now believes that current closure costs are $1.1 million with postclosure costs amounting to $500,000.

Using this new and revised information, the city should now recognize estimated total costs of $432,000 at the end of Year 2 ($1.6 million × 27%). Because it recorded $224,000 in Year 1, the city accrues an additional $208,000 in Year 2 ($432,000 – $224,000):

Government-Wide Financial Statements—Estimated Landfill Closure Costs

Year 2		
Expense—Landfill Closure	208,000	
Landfill Closure Liability		208,000
To recognize Year 2 portion of costs for eventual closure of landfill.		
Landfill Closure Liability	30,000	
Cash		30,000
To record second payment of costs necessitated by eventual closure of the landfill.		

Consequently, in the Year 2 government-wide financial statements, the city reports:

Expense—Landfill closure	$208,000
Landfill closure liability ($224,000 + 208,000 – $30,000 – 30,000)	$372,000

Landfills—Fund Financial Statements

If a government reports a solid waste landfill as an enterprise fund, the reporting is the same in the fund financial statements as just shown above for the government-wide statements. All economic resources are again measured based on accrual accounting.

However, if the landfill is recorded in the General Fund, the city reports only the change in current financial resources. Despite the huge eventual liability, the reduction in current financial resources is limited to the annual payments of $30,000. The actual liability is too far into the future to warrant reporting. Thus, the only entry required each year in this example for the fund financial statements is as follows:

Fund Financial Statements—Payment toward Landfill Closure Costs—Governmental Funds

Year 1 and Year 2		
General Fund		
Expenditures—Closure Costs	30,000	
Cash		30,000
To record annual payment toward the eventual closure costs of the city's solid waste landfill.		

Compensated Absences

LO2

Recognize the liability caused by the eventual closure and postclosure costs of operating a solid waste landfill as well as for the compensated absences earned by government employees.

State and local governments have numerous employees: police officers, school teachers, maintenance workers, and the like. As of June 30, 2010, the City of Baltimore, Maryland, reported having 15,438 full-time-equivalent employees.[2] In the same manner as the

[2] Statistical information listed at the end of a comprehensive annual financial report can provide a wide array of fascinating information about the reporting government. For example, in 2010 the City of Baltimore repaired 15,121 potholes while the police made 82,369 arrests and issued 379,633 parking citations. The city owned 487 marked patrol vehicles, 5,827 acres of parks, 39 fire station buildings, and 34 library buildings (holding 2.6 million library books).

employees of a for-profit organization, government employees earn vacation days, sick leave days, and holidays, collectively known as *compensated absences,* that can amount to a significant amount of money. For example, at June 30, 2010, the City of Baltimore reported a debt of nearly $134 million for such compensated absences ($49.0 million as a current liability and $84.7 million as a long-term liability). This obligation was explained in part through a disclosure note such as: "Employees earn one day of sick leave for each completed month of service, and there is no limitation on the number of sick days that employees can accumulate."

Accounting for such liabilities is much the same as was demonstrated for capital leases and solid waste landfills. In the government-wide financial statements, the city accrues the expense as incurred. Conversely in producing fund financial statements for the governmental funds, only actual payments and claims to current financial resources are included.

For example, assume that a city reaches the end of Year 1 and owes its schoolteachers $400,000 because of compensated absences to be taken in the future for vacation days, holidays, and sick leave that have been earned. However, only $50,000 of these absences are expected to be taken early enough in Year 2 to require the use of current financial resources. Perhaps several employees are scheduled to take vacations in the first two months of the subsequent period.

Consequently, a $400,000 liability exists at the end of Year 1 but only $50,000 of that amount is a claim on the government's current financial resources:

Government-Wide Financial Statements—Compensated Absences

Year 1		
Expenses—Compensated Absences.	400,000	
Liability—Compensated Absences		400,000
To accrue amount owed at the end of Year 1 to schoolteachers for vacations, sick leave, and holidays.		

In the fund financial statements, as the following entry shows, only the $50,000 that will be paid early in the next year is included. The remainder of the debt is not yet reported because it is not a claim to current financial resources. Again, however, if employees work in an area of the government reported as an enterprise fund, fund accounting is the same as in the government-wide statements.

Fund Financial Statements—Compensated Absences—Governmental Funds

Year 1		
General Fund		
Expenditures—Compensated Absences.	50,000	
Liability—Compensated Absences		50,000
To accrue amount of compensated absences that will be taken early in Year 2 so that it requires the use of Year 1 financial resources.		

Works of Art and Historical Treasures

LO3

Record the donation and acquisition of works of art and historical treasures.

As will be discussed in the following chapter, private not-for-profit organizations have long debated the proper reporting of artworks and other museum pieces they buy or receive by gift. Governmental accounting occasionally faces the same issue. How should a government report works of art, museum artifacts, and other historical treasures in its financial statements?

Assume, for example, that a city maintains a small museum in the basement of its main office building. The museum was created to display documents, maps, paintings, and other works of art that depict the history of the city. The government bought several of the displayed items, but local citizens also donated a number of the pieces. Several are quite valuable.

Although optional reporting is allowed, the basic rule for handling such items is clear: "governments should capitalize works of art, historical treasures, and similar assets at their historical cost or fair value at date of donation."[3] Thus, the government-wide statement of net assets will report an antique map bought for $5,000 as an asset at that cost.

In the same manner, a similar map received as a gift is also recorded as a $5,000 asset. Such gifts qualify as voluntary nonexchange transactions. Thus, revenue will be recognized for the value of the gift when all eligibility requirements have been met. Until that time, deferred revenue is recorded.

For fund financial statements, the museum might be viewed as an enterprise fund if an entrance fee is charged. If so, the above reporting is replicated. However, if the museum is reported within the Governmental Funds, any such acquisition is reported as an Expenditure to indicate the decrease occurring in current financial resources. In contrast, no entry is made for gifts of this type because no change took place in the amount of financial resources.

A theoretical problem arises in the recognition of such assets in government-wide financial statements regardless of whether they were purchased or obtained by gift. Unless a user charge is assessed, items such as a map or painting displayed for the public to see will not generate cash flows or any other direct economic benefit. Therefore, do such pieces actually qualify as an asset to be reported by the government?

GASB "encourages" the capitalization of all such artworks and historical treasures. However, if all three of the following criteria are met, recording a work of art or historical treasure as an asset is optional:

1. It is held for public exhibition, education, or research in furtherance of public service rather than for financial gain.
2. It is protected, kept unencumbered, cared for, and preserved.
3. It is subject to an organizational policy that requires the proceeds from sales of collection items to be used to acquire other items for collections.[4]

If these guidelines are met, the artwork or historical treasure will not provide any direct economic benefit to the government. Thus, although the transaction must be recorded, recognition of an asset is not required. Instead, in the entries previously shown for the government-wide statements, an expense rather than an asset can be recorded regardless of whether the item was obtained by purchase or gift. GASB's handling of artwork and historical treasures closely parallels rules established by FASB for private not-for-profit organizations. However, as the next chapter explains, differences do remain.

One other related issue remains to be resolved: depreciation. Does the map on display in the museum actually depreciate in value over time? Does the *Mona Lisa* have a finite life? In connection with such assets, depreciation is required only if the asset is "exhaustible"—that is, if its utility will be used up by display, education, or research. Depreciation is not necessary if the work of art or historical treasure is viewed as being inexhaustible. For example, a bronze statue could well be viewed as an inexhaustible asset according to these guidelines so that depreciation is allowed but not required.

Infrastructure Assets and Depreciation

LO4

Explain the reporting and possible depreciation of infrastructure assets.

Governments often hold significantly more infrastructure assets than other types of entities. Infrastructure is defined as "long-lived capital assets that normally are stationary in nature and normally can be preserved for a significantly greater number of years

[3] Governmental Accounting Standards Board, *Codification of Governmental Accounting and Financial Reporting Standards as of June 30, 2010,* Sec. 1400.109.

[4] Ibid.

than most capital assets."[5] Examples include roads, bridges, tunnels, lighting systems, curbing, and sidewalks. At one time in government accounting the recording of infrastructure items was an optional practice. Now, though, new infrastructure costs must be recorded as assets in the government-wide statements. For the governmental funds, these same costs continue to be recorded as expenditures in the fund statements because both acquisition and construction create a reduction in current financial resources.

Beyond simply recording new infrastructure items as assets, a state or local government also has to capitalize many infrastructure assets acquired prior to the establishment of government-wide financial statements. A major road system constructed 25 years ago, for example, must be shown as an asset in the government-wide statements. Because cost figures for these earlier projects may not be readily available, estimations are allowed. In addition, because approximating the cost of all infrastructure items acquired prior to the initial creation of government-wide statements is virtually impossible, this capitalization requirement is limited to major assets that (1) were acquired in fiscal years ending after June 30, 1980, or (2) had major renovations, restorations, or improvements since that date.

For this reason, a note to the financial statements for the City of St. Louis, Missouri, disclosed:

> General infrastructure assets acquired prior to July 1, 2001, consist of the road network and other infrastructure assets that were acquired or that received substantial improvements subsequent to June 30, 1980, and are reported at estimated historical cost using deflated replacement cost.

As discussed previously, depreciation is required for all capital assets appearing in the government-wide financial statements that have a finite life as well as artworks and historical treasures that are deemed to be exhaustible. The need for depreciation was also debated by GASB in connection with infrastructure items: Is depreciation appropriate for this type of asset? For example, construction of the Brooklyn Bridge was finished in 1883 at a cost of about $15 million. That particular piece of infrastructure has operated now for more than 125 years and, with proper maintenance, might well continue to carry traffic for another 125 years. Much the same can be said of many roads, sidewalks, and the like built today. With appropriate repair and maintenance, such assets could have lives that are almost indefinite. What expected life should New York City use to depreciate the cost incurred in constructing a street such as Fifth Avenue?

Not surprisingly, governments tend to depreciate some of their infrastructure over extended periods. The City of Portland, Oregon, uses lives that range from 20 to 100 years, whereas the City of Portland, Maine, depreciates these assets over periods from 30 to 67 years.

However, a unique alternative to depreciating the cost of eligible infrastructure assets such as the Brooklyn Bridge or Fifth Avenue was created by GASB. This method, known as the *modified approach,* eliminates the need for depreciating infrastructure assets. If specified guidelines are met, a government can choose to expense all maintenance costs each year in lieu of recording depreciation. Additions and improvements must be capitalized, but the cost of maintaining the infrastructure in proper working condition is expensed. Thus, if applied, New York City will directly expense the amount spent on repair and other maintenance of Fifth Avenue so that depreciation of the street's capitalized cost is not recorded. Effectively, proper maintenance of infrastructure assets can extend their lives indefinitely.

Use of the modified approach requires the government to accumulate information about all infrastructure assets within either a network or a subsystem of a network. For example, all roads could be deemed a network while state roads, rural roads, and interstate highways might make up three subsystems of that network.

- For eligible assets, the government must establish a minimum acceptable condition level and then document that this minimum level is being met.
- The government must have an asset management system in place to monitor the eligible assets. This system should assess the ongoing condition to ensure that the eligible assets are, indeed, able to operate at the predetermined level.

[5] Governmental Accounting Standards Board, *Codification of Governmental Accounting and Financial Reporting Standards as of June 30, 2010,* Sec. 1400.103.

The state of Texas has adopted the modified approach in connection with reporting its highway system. In its comprehensive annual financial report, the determination of a minimum acceptable condition level is explained as follows:

> The Texas Department of Transportation (TxDOT) performs yearly condition assessments through its Texas Maintenance Assessment Program (TxMAP). Under this program, visual inspections are conducted on approximately 10 percent of the interstate system and 5 percent of the non-interstate system (national, state and farm-to-market roadways). For each section of highway observed, 21 elements separated into three highway components are assessed scores from 0 to 5 (0 = NA, 1 = Failed, 2 = Poor, 3 = Fair, 4 = Good, 5 = Excellent) in order to determine the condition of the highways. Each element within a component is weighted according to importance and each component is weighted according to importance to determine the overall condition of the highways. The overall score is converted to a percentage measurement for reporting (1 = 20%, 2 = 40%, 3 = 60%, 4 = 80%, 5 = 100%). TxDOT has adopted a minimum condition level of 80 percent for the interstate system, 75 percent for the non-interstate system and 80 percent for the Central Texas Turnpike System based on TxMAP assessments.

The note goes on to indicate that the minimum was met in 2010 with scores of 83.6 percent, 77.9 percent, and 87.9 percent, respectively.

The modified approach provides a method by which governments can avoid depreciating infrastructure assets such as the Brooklyn Bridge that have virtually an unlimited life. The issue is: How many governments will be like the State of Texas and go to the trouble of creating the standards and documentation required by this approach simply to avoid recording depreciation expense? According to a partner at KPMG, "There are relatively few governmental entities that have adopted the modified approach. Airports, transportation authorities and large transportation departments are really the only ones that I've seen that follow the modified approach."[6]

Expanded Financial Reporting

LO5

Understand the composition of a state or local government's comprehensive annual financial report (CAFR).

The financial statements of publicly held for-profit entities are accompanied by a verbal explanation of the reported operations, cash flows, and financial position. This memorandum, known as the *management's discussion and analysis* (MD&A), provides a wealth of vital information for the reader of the financial statements. Thus, in evaluating for-profit organizations, decision makers are accustomed to having a "plain English" explanation of the figures and other critical information disclosed within the statements. For example, the 2010 annual report for The Procter & Gamble Company contained a Management's Discussion and Analysis that covered 20 pages. Consequently, a stockholder, creditor, or other interested party is provided with extensive details to describe and supplement the facts and figures presented within the company's financial statements.

GASB requires state and local governments to provide a similar MD&A. Thus, the general purpose external financial statements of a state or local government are composed of three distinct sections:

1. Management's discussion and analysis.
2. Financial statements:
   a. Government-wide financial statements.
   b. Fund financial statements.
   c. Notes to the financial statements.
3. Required supplementary information (other than the MD&A). For example, the City of Saint Paul, Minnesota, uses this section to compare budgetary figures with actual results for each major fund although a separate statement within the fund financial statements could also have been used.

[6] E-mail from Jack Reagan, partner, KPMG, Washington, DC, June 20, 2011.

GASB explains the benefits of requiring officials to provide readers of the government's financial statements with an MD&A:

> MD&A should provide an objective and easily readable analysis of the government's financial activities based on currently known facts, decisions, or conditions. The financial managers of governments are knowledgeable about the transactions, events, and conditions that are reflected in the government's financial report and of the fiscal policies that govern its operations. MD&A provides financial managers with the opportunity to present both a short- and a long-term analysis of the government's activities. MD&A should discuss current-year results in comparison with the prior year, with emphasis on the current year. This fact-based analysis should discuss the positive and negative aspects of the comparison with the prior year. The use of charts, graphs, and tables is encouraged to enhance the understandability of the information.[7]

As an illustration, the 2010 financial statements for the City of Raleigh, North Carolina, begin with a management's discussion and analysis of 15 pages that present explanations such as the following:

- A property tax base increase resulted in increased property tax revenues of $4.2 million from $180.5 million to $184.7 million. Property taxes represent 47.4% of total governmental revenues. Other taxes, including sales tax, which accounted for 27.1% of total governmental revenues, decreased $7.2 million from 2009.
- The City received $297.7 million in general revenues from taxes and other revenues such as interest and unrestricted grants, which was used to pay for the $267.4 million net cost of governmental activities.
- As of the end of the fiscal year, the City of Raleigh's governmental funds reported combined ending fund balances of $336.2 million, a decrease of $500,000 in comparison with the prior year.

The government-wide and the fund financial statements are presented to the public as part of a comprehensive annual financial report (often referred to as a *CAFR*). The CAFR also includes other extensive information about the reporting government. For example, the 2010 CAFR for the City of Orlando, Florida, with total assets of approximately $2.8 billion, was nearly 300 pages long. In comparison, the 2011 annual report for Walmart, with more than $180 billion in assets, was only 60 pages.

The CAFR of a state or local government must include three broad sections:

1. *Introductory section*—includes a letter of transmittal from appropriate government officials, an organization chart, and a list of principal officers.
2. *Financial section*—presents the general purpose external financial statement (the government-wide and fund statements) and reproduces the auditor's report. The government also presents the MD&A and additional supplementary information such as combining statements to provide financial information for funds that do not qualify as major.
3. *Statistical section*—discloses a wide range of data about the government encompassing both financial and nonfinancial information.

The Primary Government and Component Units

Primary Government

LO6

Explain the makeup of a primary government and its relationship to component units.

> The primary government serves as the nucleus and focus of the financial reporting entity as defined by GAAP. All state governments and general-purpose local governments automatically should be treated as primary governments.[8]

In governmental accounting, every reporting entity prepares a CAFR. However, the components of the reporting entity must be identified. Normally, reporting begins with

[7] Governmental Accounting Standards Board, *Codification of Governmental Accounting and Financial Reporting Standards as of June 30, 2010,* Sec. 2200.106–107.

[8] Stephen J. Gauthier, *Governmental Accounting, Auditing, and Financial Reporting—Using the GASB 34 Model* (Chicago: Government Finance Officers Association, 2005), p. 58.

a primary government such as a town, city, county, or state. The reporting entity also includes activities, organizations, agencies, offices, departments, and the like that are not legally separate from the primary government. However, many entities that interact closely with a government are legally separate. Should they also be included as part of the reporting entity? Except in rare cases, a business enterprise such as IBM or PepsiCo simply consolidates all businesses over which it has control. Should legally separated organizations be reported within the CAFR and, if so, what reporting is appropriate?

The almost unlimited number of activities that can be related to a government raises problems for officials attempting to outline the parameters of the entity being reported. Organizations such as turnpike commissions, port authorities, public housing boards, and downtown development commissions have become commonplace for many cities and counties in recent years. The primary government may have created many of these, but they remain legally separate organizations. Such entities are designed to focus attention on specific issues or problems. They often promise better efficiency because of their corporate-style structure.

As an example, in the notes to the financial statements in its 2010 CAFR, the City of Boston, Massachusetts, lists the following separate organizations related to the government but whose financial information had *not* been included with that of the city. Although the mayor appoints the members of each governing body, city authority does not extend beyond making these appointments:

- Boston Housing Authority.
- Boston Industrial Development Financing Authority.
- Boston Water and Sewer Commission.

Component Units

In contrast, the City of Atlanta, Georgia, at June 30, 2010, indicated a number of activities that were legally separate from the city government but were still presented within that city's financial information because the city is financially accountable:

- Atlanta-Fulton County Recreation Authority.
- Atlanta Development Authority.
- Atlanta CoRA, Inc.

Clearly, the Boston and Atlanta examples show that some legally separated activities are included whereas others are excluded from the CAFR of a primary government. Activities that are included are known as *component units*. The major requirement for inclusion in a CAFR as a component unit is the financial accountability of the primary government. "Financial reporting based on accountability should enable the financial statement reader to focus on the body of organizations that are related by a common thread of accountability to the constituent citizenry."[9]

When elected officials of the primary government are financially accountable for an outside organization, it is labeled a component unit. Such legally separate activities are so closely connected that their omission from the financial statements of a primary government cannot be justified.

That is why the City of Atlanta included the Atlanta-Fulton County Recreation Authority and the other activities mentioned above in its CAFR; they qualified as component units. They are not part of the government but are reported by the government.

Because of the potential impact on the financial statements of the primary government, the determination of component units can be of significant importance. Two sets of criteria have been established. If either is met, the activity qualifies as a component unit to be reported within the CAFR of the primary government. A government can include a legally separate entity even if it does not meet the criteria if it would be misleading to exclude the entity.

[9] Governmental Accounting Standards Board, *Codification of Governmental Accounting and Financial Reporting Standards as of June 30, 2010*, Sec. 2100.102.

Criterion 1

The separate organization (such as the Atlanta-Fulton County Recreation Authority) is viewed as a component unit if it fiscally depends on the primary government (the City of Atlanta). *Fiscal dependency* means that the organization cannot do one or more of the following without approval of the primary government: adopt its own budget, levy taxes or set rates, or issue bonded debt. For fiscal years that begin after June 15, 2012, this criterion also requires that the primary government and the component unit must be financially interdependent (there is a relationship of potential financial benefit or burden between the two of them).

Criterion 2

First, officials of the primary government must appoint a voting majority of the governing board of the separate organization. Second, either the primary government must be able to impose its will on that board or the separate organization provides a financial benefit or imposes a financial burden on the primary government.

For example, a state (the primary government) might establish a legally separate commission to oversee off-track betting. However, if the state appoints a voting majority of the board membership and the financial benefits from revenues generated by the commission accrue to the state, the commission is considered a component unit of the state for reporting purposes.

Because of the importance of this identification process, three aspects of the second criterion should be explained further to ensure proper application.

Voting Majority of the Governing Board The authority to elect a voting majority must be substantive. If, for example, the primary government simply confirms the choices that other parties make, financial accountability is not present. In the same way, financial accountability does not result when the primary government selects the governing board from a limited slate of candidates (such as picking three individuals from an approved list of five). Thus, the primary government must have the actual responsibility of appointing a voting majority of the board before the organization meets this portion of the second criterion.

Imposition of the Primary Government's Will on the Governing Board Such power is indicated if the government can significantly influence the programs, projects, activities, or level of services the separate organization provides. This degree of influence is present if the primary government can remove an appointed board member at will, modify or approve budgets, override decisions of the board, modify or approve rate or fee changes, or hire or dismiss the individuals responsible for day-to-day operations.

Financial Benefit or Financial Burden on the Primary Government A financial connection exists between the separate organization and the primary government if the government is entitled to the organization's resources, the government is legally obligated to finance any deficits or provide support, or the government is responsible for the organization's debts.

Reporting Component Units

Component units are reported in one of two ways: discrete or blended presentation. Many component units are discretely presented at the far right side of the government-wide statements. For example, the June 30, 2010, Statement of Net Assets for the City of Detroit, Michigan, shows that the primary government had total assets of more than $10.3 billion whereas its discretely presented component units shown just to the right of the primary government reported total assets of $563.3 million.

According to the financial statements, these component units were made up of the following separate organizations:

- Detroit Brownfield Redevelopment Authority
- Detroit Public Library
- Detroit Transportation Corporation

Discussion Question

IS IT PART OF THE COUNTY?

Harland County is in a financially distressed area in Missouri. In hopes of enticing business to this county, the state legislature appropriated $3 million to start an industrial development commission. The federal government provided an additional $1 million. The state appointed 15 individuals to a board to oversee the operations of this commission, and county officials named 5 members. The commission began operations by raising funds from local citizens and businesses. It received $700,000 in donations and pledges. The county provided clerical assistance and allowed the commission to use one floor of the county office building for its headquarters. The county government must approve the commission's annual operating budget. The county will also cover any deficits.

During the current period, the commission spent $2.4 million. It achieved notable success. Several large manufacturing companies have recently begun to explore the possibility of opening plants in the county.

Harland County is currently preparing its comprehensive annual financial report. Should the CAFR include the revenues, expenditures, assets, expenses, and liabilities of the industrial development commission? Is it a fund within the county's primary government, a component unit, or a related organization?

Is the industrial development commission a component unit of the State of Missouri? How should its activities be presented in the state's comprehensive annual financial report?

- Downtown Development Authority
- Eastern Market Corporation
- Economic Development Corporation
- Greater Detroit Resource Recovery Authority
- Local Development Finance Authority
- Museum of African American History
- Tax Increment Finance Authority

As an alternative placement, a primary government can include component units as an actual part of the reporting government (a process referred to as *blending*). Although legally separate, the component is so intertwined with the primary government that inclusion is necessary to appropriately present the financial information. A recent change in GASB standards now requires that a component unit will need to be blended if its total debt will be repaid entirely, or almost entirely, from resources of the primary government.

> The City of Detroit has three component units that are blended in with the primary government: Detroit Building Authority, Detroit General Retirement System Service Corporation, and Detroit Police and Fire Retirement System Service Corporation. This placement is justified by the city in the following note: "blended component units, although legally separate entities, are, in substance, part of the City's operations."

One other aspect of the overall reporting process should be noted: the possible existence of *related organizations*. In such cases, the primary government is accountable because it appoints a voting majority of the outside organization's governing board.

However, fiscal dependency as defined earlier is not present, and the primary government cannot impose its will on the board or gather financial benefits or burdens from the relationship. Consequently, the separate organization does not qualify as a component unit to be included in the government's financial reporting. However, the primary government must still disclose the nature of the relationship. The City of Detroit discloses three related organizations: Detroit Historical Society, Detroit Institute of Arts, and Detroit Zoological Society.

Special Purpose Governments

The Chicago Transit Authority and the City of Atlanta School System are independent organizations but they both provide governmental services to the public. What are the reporting requirements for such *special purpose governments*? Cities, counties, states, and the like are known as *general purpose governments.* They provide a wide range of services such as police protection, road repair, and sanitation. They are primary governments, each within its own reporting entity. However, activities that qualify as special purpose governments are also viewed as primary governments for public reporting purposes.

Thousands of special purpose governments exist throughout the country; they carry out only a single function for the public or a limited number of functions. Common examples include public school districts, colleges and universities, utilities, hospitals, transit authorities, and library services. When reporting such operations, the question arises as to whether it is (1) part of a larger government such as a city or county as either a fund or a component unit, (2) a nongovernmental not-for-profit organization, or (3) a special purpose government that produces its own financial statements according to governmental accounting principles.

An activity or function is deemed a special purpose government if it meets the following criteria:

1. Has a separately elected governing body.
2. Is legally independent, which it can demonstrate by having corporate powers such as the right to sue and be sued as well as the right to buy, sell, and lease property in its own name.
3. Is fiscally independent of other state and local governments. As mentioned previously, an activity is normally considered to be fiscally independent if its leadership can determine the activity's budget without having to seek the approval of an outside party, levy taxes or set rates without having to seek outside approval, or issue bonded debt without outside approval.

For example, a school system that satisfies all three is reported as a special purpose government that produces its own financial statements. However, if that same school system fails to meet any one of these, its financial transactions are likely to be maintained within the General Fund or Special Revenue Funds of a city or county government.

The CAFR for the Charlotte-Mecklenburg County, North Carolina, Board of Education shows total expenses for the year ended June 30, 2010, of more than $1.21 billion as a special purpose government. A note to these statements explains why the Board represents a primary government to be reported separately from the local general purpose government:

> The Charlotte-Mecklenburg Board of Education (Board or CMS) is a Local Education Agency empowered by State law [Chapter 115C of the North Carolina General Statutes] with the responsibility to oversee and control the activities related to public school education in Charlotte-Mecklenburg, North Carolina. The Board receives State, Local, and Federal government funding and must adhere to the legal requirements of each funding entity. Although Mecklenburg County (the County) levies all taxes, the Board determines how the school system will spend the funds generated for schools. The County cannot modify the school system's budget, nor is the County entitled to share in any surpluses or required to finance any deficits of the school system. For these reasons, the Board is not fiscally dependent on the County and therefore is recognized as a primary government.

Government-Wide and Fund Financial Statements Illustrated

LO7

Understand the physical structure of a complete set of government-wide financial statements and a complete set of fund financial statements.

At the core of a governmental reporting entity's CAFR are the general purpose financial statements. As described, these statements are made up of government-wide financial statements and fund financial statements. Government-wide statements present financial information for both governmental activities and business-type activities. They measure economic resources and utilize accrual accounting.

The fund statements separately present the governmental funds, the proprietary funds, and the fiduciary funds. The measurement focus and the timing of recognition depend on the fund in question. For governmental funds, the current financial resources measurement focus is used with modified accrual accounting. However, both proprietary funds and fiduciary funds use accrual accounting to report all economic resources.

In the previous chapter, four of these statements were outlined to introduce the basic structure of each. However, now that a deeper understanding of government accounting has been established, government-wide and fund financial statements can be examined in more detail.[10]

Statement of Net Assets—Government-Wide Financial Statements

Exhibit 17.1 presents the June 30, 2010, statement of net assets for the City of Sacramento, California. As a government-wide financial statement, it is designed to report the economic resources of the government as a whole (except for the fiduciary funds, which are not included because those assets must be used for a purpose outside the primary government).

Several aspects of this statement of net assets should be noted specifically:

- The measurement focus is the economic resources controlled by the government. Thus, all assets including capital assets are reported. Long-term liabilities are presented for the same reason.
- Capital assets other than land, land improvements, inexhaustible artworks, and construction in progress (and infrastructure assets if the modified approach is applied) are reported net of accumulated depreciation because depreciation is required on the government-wide statements. (See Point A.)
- The primary government is divided into governmental activities and business-type activities. Governmental funds are reported as governmental activities whereas enterprise funds comprise most, if not all, of the business-type activities. Even though recorded within the proprietary funds, internal service funds are normally included within the governmental activities because those services are rendered primarily for the benefit of activities within the governmental funds. The City of Sacramento reported all of its internal service funds within the governmental activities.
- The internal balances shown in the asset section (Point B) come from receivables and payables between the governmental activities and the business-type activities. The internal balances reported on this statement offset, so that there is no effect on the totals shown for the primary government.
- Discretely presented component units are grouped and shown to the far right side of the statement (Point C) so that the reported amounts do not affect the primary government figures. However, blended component units are included, as appropriate, within either the governmental activities or the business-type activities as if they were individual funds. As can be seen in Exhibit 17.1, the City of Sacramento had only one discretely presented component unit: the Sacramento Regional Arts Facilities Financing Authority. According to the notes to the City of Sacramento's financial statements,

[10] The examples presented here illustrate the government-wide financial statements and the fund financial statements for both governmental funds and proprietary funds. Because they are more specialized, the fund financial statements for the fiduciary funds have been omitted. Those statements can be found at www.cityofsacramento.org/cafr/.

EXHIBIT 17.1 Government-Wide Financial Statements

CITY OF SACRAMENTO
Statement of Net Assets
June 30, 2010
(in thousands)

	Primary Government			Sacramento Regional Arts Facilities Financing Authority ©
	Governmental Activities	**Business-Type Activities**	**Total**	
Assets				
Cash and investments	$ 375,930	$ 110,641	$ 486,571	$ —
Securities lending assets	12,317	5,168	17,485	—
Receivables, net	217,233	78,446	295,679	13,230
Internal balances Ⓑ	11,177	(11,177)	—	—
Inventories	1,465	5,608	7,073	—
Prepaid items	6,183	19	6,202	—
Restricted cash and investments	43,045	31,228	74,273	1,150
Deferred charges	4,641	4,039	8,680	547
Deferred outflow for interest rate swap	12,330	—	12,330	—
Land and other capital assets not being depreciated	378,940	85,059	463,999	—
Other capital assets, net of depreciation Ⓐ	1,433,383	954,457	2,387,840	—
Total assets	2,496,644	1,263,488	3,760,132	14,927
Liabilities				
Securities lending obligations	14,951	6,114	21,065	—
Payables	47,752	21,607	69,359	171
Unearned revenue	7,813	2,810	10,623	—
Long-term liabilities:				
Due within one year	60,432	17,845	78,277	370
Due in more than one year	650,796	391,986	1,042,782	14,031
Total liabilities	781,744	440,362	1,222,106	14,572
Net Assets (Deficit)				
Invested in capital assets, net of related debt	1,411,767	691,197	2,102,964	—
Restricted for:				
Capital projects	186,619	25,781	212,400	—
Debt service	494	—	494	355
Trust and endowments:				
Expendable	4,690	—	4,690	—
Nonexpendable	1,934	—	1,934	—
Other	32,443	—	32,443	—
Unrestricted	76,953	106,148	183,101	—
Total net assets	$1,714,900	$ 823,126	$2,538,026	$ 355

The notes to the financial statements are an integral part of this statement.

there were also two blended component units, the Sacramento City Employee Retirement System and the Sacramento City Financing Authority.

- Because this is a statement of net assets, the format is not structured to stress that assets are equal to liabilities plus equities as is found in a typical balance sheet. Rather, the assets ($3.76 billion for the primary government) less liabilities of $1.22 billion indicated net assets of $2.54 billion.
- As the Net Assets section shows, several amounts have been restricted for capital projects, debt service, and the like. Restrictions are reported in this manner only if usage of the assets has been specified by external parties such as creditors, grantors, or other external party, or because of laws passed through constitutional provisions or enabling legislation.
- Although not restricted, the amount of net assets tied up in capital assets less any related debt is reported as a separate figure within the Net Assets section. Such amounts are not readily available to be spent.

Statement of Activities—Government-Wide Financial Statements

The statement of activities presents a wide array of information about the various functions of a state or local government. As the statement for the City of Sacramento, California, shows in Exhibit 17.2, the same general classification system of governmental activities, business-type activities, and component units used in Exhibit 17.1 provides the structural basis for reporting. However, the format here is more complex and requires close analysis.

- Operating expenses are presented in the first column (Point D). They are not classified according to individual causes such as salaries, rent, depreciation, or insurance. Instead, expenses are shown by function, which is more relevant to readers: general government, police, fire, general services, and the like. According to GASB "as a minimum, governments should report direct expenses for each function. Direct expenses are those that are specifically associated with a service, program, or department and, thus, are clearly identifiable to a particular function."[11] Expenses are shown for governmental activities, business-type activities, and the discretely presented component unit.
- Interest expense on general long-term debt (Point E) is normally viewed as an indirect expense because it benefits many government operations. However, due to its size, informational value, and difficulty of allocation, this expense frequently is shown as in Exhibit 17.2 as a separate "function."
- The second column serves to assign a portion of the general government and general services costs to various business-type activities. Those costs were apparently incurred by the governmental activities for the benefit of the business-type activities.
- After operating and indirect expenses have been determined for each function, related program revenues are reported in the next three columns (Point F). Program revenues are those revenues derived by the function itself or from outsiders seeking to reduce the government's cost for that function. As Exhibit 17.2 shows, program revenues are classified as:

  1. *Charges for services.* For example, a monthly charge is normally assessed for water service; therefore, this first business-type activity shows more than $70.4 million in program revenues. In contrast, most government functions generate only relatively small amounts of revenue from sources such as parking meter revenues, fines for speeding tickets, concessions at parks, and the like.
  2. *Operating grants and contributions.* This column reports amounts received from outside grants and similar sources that were designated for some type of operating purpose. For example, $21.2 million in operating grants and contributions is shown for the Sacramento police.
  3. *Capital grants and contributions.* This column shows outside grants and similar sources where the resources were designated for capital asset additions. For the City of Sacramento, during this year, the largest amount of capital grants and contributions (by far) went to Transportation (Point G).

- After expenses have been assigned along with related program revenues, a net (expense) or revenue can be determined for each function. This figure provides an important measure of the financial cost (or benefit) of the various government functions. For example, in Exhibit 17.2, the police department had more than $152.9 million in operating expenses but was able to generate total program revenues of only $25.4 million from charges for services and operating grants and contributions. Thus, as disclosed at Point H, the Sacramento taxpayers can see that they had to bear a financial burden of over $127.5 million for police protection. That cost is important information to citizens reading these statements. In contrast, the water system reported operating and indirect expenses of $60.9 million, but its charges, grants, and contributions totaled

[11] Governmental Accounting Standards Board, *Codification of Governmental Accounting and Financial Reporting Standards as of June 30, 2010*, Sec. 2200.129.

$80.4 million. Thus, this business-type activity generated net revenues of approximately $19.5 million (see Point I) as a financial benefit for the government during this period.

- Net expenses and revenues can be determined in total for each category of the government. In this example, all of the governmental activities are combined to report net expenses of more than $317 million (see Point J) while the business-type activities generated net revenues of approximately $26 million (see Point K). The component units reported net expenses of $715,000 (see Point L). Notice at Point M that these totals are transferred to the second part of this statement so the impact of general revenues can be included where appropriate.
- General revenues are reported as additions to either the governmental activities, business-type activities, or component units. All taxes are general revenues because they do not reflect a charge for services; they are obtained from the population as a whole. At Point N, property taxes of nearly $124 million are shown as the largest revenue contributing to meet the cost of the governmental activities provided by the City of Sacramento. Utility user taxes are the second biggest.
- Transfers of $19,365,000 during the year between governmental activities and business-type activities are also shown under the general revenues, but they offset for reporting purposes, so that no impact is created on the total for the primary government (see Point O).

Balance Sheet—Governmental Funds—Fund Financial Statements

Switching now to the fund financial statements, Exhibit 17.3 presents the balance sheet for the governmental funds reported by the City of Sacramento. This statement reports only current financial resources and uses modified accrual accounting for timing purposes. No proprietary funds, component units, or fiduciary funds are included; this fund-based statement reflects just the governmental funds. Several parts of this statement should be noted:

- A separate column is shown for the General Fund and any other major fund within the governmental funds. The city has identified six funds as major including the Capital Grants Fund and the Special Revenue Fund associated with the Crocker Art Museum Fund. Government officials can classify any fund as major if they believe it is especially important to statement users. However, as mentioned in the previous chapter, a fund is considered major and must be reported separately if it meets two criteria:

  1. Total assets, liabilities, revenues, or expenses/expenditures of the fund are at least 10 percent of the corresponding total for all such funds.
  2. Total assets, liabilities, revenues, or expenses/expenditures of the fund are at least 5 percent of the corresponding total for all governmental funds and enterprise funds combined.

  All funds that are not considered major are combined and reported as "Other Governmental Funds."

- This balance sheet reports no capital assets or long-term debts because only current financial resources are being measured.
- The Fund Balances figures reported at Point P look significantly different than the nonspendable, restricted, committed, assigned, and unassigned categories discussed in the previous chapter. The City of Sacramento financial statements shown here were produced before the new rules for reporting the Fund Balance were implemented.
- The total Fund Balances figure for the governmental funds of $317.4 million (Point Q) is significantly different from the $1.7 billion in total net assets reported for governmental activities in the statement of net assets (Exhibit 17.1). To explain that large disparity, a reconciliation is presented along with the balance sheet (titled Reconciliation of the Balance Sheet to the Statement of Net Assets—Governmental Funds). According to this reconciliation, the four largest items that create the disparity between the

EXHIBIT 17.2 **Government-Wide Financial Statements**

CITY OF SACRAMENTO
Statement of Activities
For the Fiscal Year Ended June 30, 2010
(in thousands)

Functions/Programs	Operating Expenses (D)	Indirect Expenses Allocation	Program Revenues (F): Charges for Services	Operating Grants and Contributions	Capital Grants and Contributions	Net (Expense) Revenue
Primary government:						
Governmental activities:						
General government	$ 52,060	$(7,782)	$ 6,614	$ 1,970	$ 828	$ (34,866)
Police	152,922	—	4,098	21,214	56	(127,554) (H)
Fire	109,210	—	22,711	2,090	191	(84,218)
General services	31,223	(2,048)	9,964	246	380	(18,585)
Transportation	89,358	—	28,857	13,397	47,137 (G)	33
Economic development	9,815	—	8,497	564	5,445	4,691
Convention, culture & leisure	18,064	—	9,689	1,158	17,611	10,394
Parks and recreation	51,984	—	10,122	13,789	15,205	(12,868)
Code enforcement	10,984	—	5,627	290	—	(5,067)
Community development	18,848	—	8,752	17	1,100	(8,979)
Neighborhood services	1,105	—	166	—	—	(939)
Library	16,827	—	—	4,444	2,935	(9,448)
Interest on long-term debt	29,658 (E)	—	—	—	—	(29,658)
Total governmental activities	592,058	(9,830)	115,097	59,179	90,888	(317,064) (J)
Business-type activities:						
Water	57,972	2,930	70,463	—	9,985	19,546 (I)
Sewer	16,550	839	20,284	—	331	3,226
Storm drainage	35,372	1,668	34,082	578	3,824	1,444
Solid waste	44,168	2,908	58,901	810	8	12,643
Community center	18,721	842	7,020	—	—	(12,543)
Parking	15,863	527	18,784	—	—	2,394
Child development	6,797	—	5,473	993	—	(331)
Marina	1,509	116	1,782	—	—	157
Total business-type activities	196,952	9,830	216,789	2,381	14,148	26,536 (K)
Total primary government	$789,010	$ —	$331,886	$61,560	$105,036	$(290,528)
Component units:						
Sacramento Regional Arts Facilities Financing Authority	$ 715	$ —	$ —	$ —	$ —	$ (715) (L)

(continued from page 764)

CITY OF SACRAMENTO
Statement of Activities
For the Fiscal Year Ended June 30, 2010
(in thousands)

	Primary government			Sacramento Regional Arts Facilities Financial Authority
	Governmental Activities	Business-type Activities	Total	
Change in net assets:				
Net (expense) revenue Ⓜ	$ (317,064)	$ 26,536	$ (290,528)	$(715)
General revenues:				
Taxes:				
Property taxes	123,681 Ⓝ	—	123,681	—
Utility user taxes	58,693	—	58,693	—
Other taxes	18,591	14,233	32,824	—
Unrestricted sales taxes shared state revenue	46,769	—	46,769	—
Unrestricted in lieu sales tax	14,332	—	14,332	—
Grants and other intergovernmental revenue not restricted to specific programs	4,591	—	4,591	—
Unrestricted investment earnings	11,508	4,964	16,472	731
Unrestricted miscellaneous	12,743	—	12,743	—
Gain on disposition of capital assets	—	17	17	—
Transfers	19,365	(19,365)	—Ⓞ	—
Total general revenues and transfers	310,273	(151)	310,122	731
Change in net assets	(6,791)Ⓤ	26,385	19,594	16
Net assets, beginning of year	1,721,691	796,741	2,518,432	339
Net assets, end of year	$1,714,900	$823,126	$2,538,026	$ 355

The notes to the financial statements are an integral part of this statement.

EXHIBIT 17.3 **Fund Financial Statements**

CITY OF SACRAMENTO
Governmental Funds
Balance Sheet
June 30, 2010 (in thousands)

	General Fund	General Fund Projects Fund	Capital Grants Fund	Crocker Art Museum Fund	Financing Plans Fund	1997 Lease Revenue Bond Fund	Transportation and Development Fund	Other Governmental Funds	Total Governmental Funds
Assets									
Cash and investments held by City	$47,273	$ 325	$ —	$ —	$107,033	$ 2,090	$66,910	$ 66,837	$290,468
Cash and investments held by fiscal agent	—	—	—	—	—	—	—	4,601	4,601
Security lending assets	2,086	—	—	—	4,737	—	772	1,539	9,134
Receivables, net:									
Taxes	19,589	—	—	—	—	—	—	—	19,589
Accounts	11,208	—	365	—	1,285	—	605	2,669	16,132
Loans	3,292	—	—	3,846	—	68,655	403	9,357	85,553
Intergovernmental	—	—	20,421	—	—	—	4,953	68,135	93,509
Interest	268	—	—	—	611	761	100	256	1,996
Prepaid items	304	—	—	—	—	—	—	35	339
Restricted assets:									
Cash and investments held by City	—	22,938	27	305	—	—	—	641	23,911
Cash and investments held by fiscal agent	—	—	—	—	—	—	—	19,134	19,134
Total assets	$84,020	$23,263	$20,813	$4,151	$113,666	$71,506	$73,743	$173,204	$564,366
Liabilities:									
Securities lending obligations	$ 2,678	$ 241	$ —	$ 281	$ 5,574	$ —	$ 1,093	$ 1,778	$ 11,645
Accounts payable	19,361	1,924	6,884	—	1,102	—	3,098	3,904	36,273
Due to other funds	—	—	6,698	—	—	—	—	1,443	8,141
Matured bonds and interest payable	—	—	—	—	—	—	—	3,170	3,170
Accrued claims and judgments	—	800	—	—	—	—	1,601	—	2,401

(continued from page 766)

Deposits	158	—	652	—	—	—	532	568	1,910
Deferred revenue	6,716	—	18,468	3,846	2,559	69,416	2,491	72,400	175,896
Advances from other funds	—	—	—	—	—	—	—	7,490	7,490
Total liabilities	28,913	2,965	32,702	4,127	9,235	69,416	8,815	90,753	246,926
Fund Balances (deficit): Ⓟ									
Reserved:									
For noncurrent assets	514	—	—	—	—	—	403	746	1,663
For encumbrances	6,301	4,543	9,855	—	4,601	—	7,037	3,964	36,301
For debt services	—	494	—	—	—	—	—	19,775	20,269
For prepaid items	304	—	—	—	—	—	—	35	339
For trust obligations	—	—	—	—	—	—	—	1,934	1,934
For capital projects	—	—	2,210	—	—	—	—	—	2,210
Unreserved:									
Designated for economic uncertainty	10,540	—	—	—	—	—	—	—	10,540
Designated for capital projects	24,159	9,669	—	—	29,899	—	30,934	—	94,661
Designated for fiscal year 2011 results	3,800	—	—	—	—	—	—	—	3,800
Designated for fiscal year 2011 fire budget	1,000	—	—	—	—	—	—	—	1,000
Designated for subsequent years' expenditures	8,489	400	—	—	2,528	—	9,587	—	21,004
Undesignated	—	5,192	(23,954)	24	67,403	2,090	16,967	—	67,722
Unreserved, reported in:									
Special revenue funds	—	—	—	—	—	—	—	36,095	36,095
Debt service funds	—	—	—	—	—	—	—	7,957	7,957
Capital projects funds	—	—	—	—	—	—	—	9,147	9,147
Permanent funds	—	—	—	—	—	—	—	2,798	2,798
Total fund balances (deficit)	55,107	20,298	(11,889)	24	104,431	2,090	64,928	82,451	317,440 Ⓠ
Total liabilities and fund balances (deficit)	$84,020	$23,263	$20,813	$4,151	$113,666	$71,506	$73,743	$173,204	$564,366

The notes to the financial statements are an integral part of this statement.

totals shown for the governmental activities of the government-wide financial statements and those of the governmental funds of the fund financial statements are:

1. Approximately $1.78 billion of capital assets reported by the governmental activities on the government-wide financial statements (Exhibit 17.1) were omitted on the comparable fund financial statement (Exhibit 17.3).
2. Revenue transactions of $169 million reported on the government-wide statements had not been recognized in the fund statements because the resulting financial resources were not viewed as being available in the current period.
3. The government-wide financial statements reported long-term liabilities (of approximately $642 million), but the fund statement reported none. These debts did not represent claims to current financial resources.
4. Internal service funds with net assets of $99 million were included in the governmental activities although, for fund financial statements, they were classified as proprietary funds rather than governmental funds.

Statement of Revenues, Expenditures, and Changes in Fund Balances—Governmental Funds—Fund Statements

Exhibit 17.4 presents the statement of revenues, expenditures, and changes in fund balances for the governmental funds of the City of Sacramento. Once again, the General Fund is detailed in a separate column along with each of the major funds previously identified. Figures for all remaining nonmajor funds are accumulated and shown together.

In examining Exhibit 17.4, note each of the following:

- Because the current financial resources measurement focus is being utilized, expenditures (Point R) rather than expenses are reported. For example, Capital Outlay is presented here as a reduction in resources rather than the acquisition of an asset. In the same way, Debt Service—Principal is reported on the statement in Exhibit 17.4 as an expenditure instead of a decrease in liabilities.
- Because the modified accrual method of accounting is used for timing purposes, reported amounts will be different than those previously shown under accrual accounting.
- At point S, Exhibit 17.4 presents other financing sources and uses to reflect the issuance of long-term debt, distribution from a component unit, and transfers made between the funds. Because the fund statements are designed to focus on individual activities rather than government-wide figures, no elimination of the transfers is made.
- A reconciliation should be shown between the ending change in governmental fund balances (a decrease at Point T of over $47 million) in Exhibit 17.4 and the ending change in net assets for governmental activities in Exhibit 17.2 (a decrease at Point U of only $6.8 million). For the City of Sacramento, the major differences listed on this reconciliation (not presented in this text) involved the acquisition of capital assets ($146.0 million), the recording of depreciation ($81.2 million), the recording of revenues that did not provide current financial resources ($26.4 million), the recording of expenses that are not claims to current financial resources ($15.0 million), the issuance of long-term debt ($23.0 million), and the repayment of long-term debt ($18.6 million).

Statement of Net Assets—Proprietary Funds—Fund Statements

The assets and liabilities of the City of Sacramento's proprietary funds, as reported in the fund financial statements, are presented in Exhibit 17.5. This statement shows individual information about five major enterprise funds, with a single column for the summation of all other enterprise funds. The statement then provides a total for all of the enterprise funds. Because of their size, specific information is available for the water fund, sewer fund, storm drainage fund, solid waste fund, and the community center fund.

In examining Exhibit 17.5, a considerable amount of information should be noted:

- This fund statement also combines and exhibits the internal service funds (Point W) because they are proprietary funds. However, government-wide financial statements usually report these same internal service funds as part of the governmental activities.
- Because the proprietary funds utilize accrual accounting to measure economic resources, the totals for the enterprise funds in Exhibit 17.5 agree in most ways with the total figures in Exhibit 17.1. The amount of detail, however, is more extensive in the fund financial statements. For example, the statement in Exhibit 17.1 uses only two accounts to describe capital assets whereas Exhibit 17.5 uses seven.
- Restricted assets (Point V) of more than \$31 million (\$19.058 million + \$12.170 million) are listed under noncurrent assets. An external source or specific laws must have designated the use of this money in some manner for it to be reported as noncurrent.
- Note in both the current and noncurrent liabilities that the City of Sacramento discloses amounts owed in connection with accrued compensated absences, liability for landfill closure, and capital lease payable. All three were discussed earlier in this chapter.

Statement of Revenues, Expenses, and Changes in Fund Net Assets—Proprietary Funds—Fund Statements

Just as the statement of net assets in Exhibit 17.5 provides individual information about specific enterprise funds (and totals for the internal service funds), the statement of revenues, expenses, and changes in fund net assets in Exhibit 17.6 gives the revenues and expenses for those same funds in detail.

As an example, in Exhibit 17.2 operating and indirect expenses were listed for each of the business-type functions. Here, in Exhibit 17.6 (Point X), operating expenses are separately listed for employee services, services and supplies, depreciation, insurance premiums, and claims expenses for each major enterprise fund. In addition, several nonoperating items are listed including interest expense and amortization of deferred charges. Finally, because this statement reflects all changes in the net assets of each proprietary activity, capital contributions and transfers in and out are included at the bottom of the statement. Thus, extensive information is available about each of these enterprise funds, which is the objective of the fund financial statements.

Statement of Cash Flows—Proprietary Funds—Fund Statements

One of the most unique aspects of the fund financial statements is the statement of cash flows for the proprietary funds (see Exhibit 17.7). Because a proprietary fund operates in a manner similar to a for-profit business, information about cash flows is considered as vital as it is for Intel and Coca-Cola. However, the physical structure is not entirely the same.

One of the main differences is that the statement of cash flows shown here for the proprietary funds has four sections rather than just three:

1. Cash flows from operating activities.
2. Cash flows from noncapital financing activities.
3. Cash flows from capital and related financing activities.
4. Cash flows from investing activities.

- The presentation of cash flows from operating activities (Point Y) is very similar to that prepared by a for-profit business. However, rather than being an optional method of presentation, as with for-profit accounting, the direct method of reporting operating activities is required. The indirect method that is almost universally used by businesses is not allowed.
- Cash flows from noncapital financing activities includes (1) proceeds and payments on debt *not* attributable to the acquisition or construction of capital assets and (2) grants and subsidies *not* restricted for capital purposes or operating activities.

EXHIBIT 17.4 Fund Financial Statements

CITY OF SACRAMENTO
Governmental Funds
Statement of Revenues, Expenditures and Changes in Fund Balances
For the Fiscal Year Ended June 30, 2010 (in thousands)

	General Fund	General Fund Projects Fund	Capital Grants Fund	Crocker Art Museum Fund	Financing Plans Fund	1997 Lease Revenue Bond Fund	Transportation and Development Fund	Other Governmental Funds	Total Governmental Funds
Revenues:									
Taxes	$260,320	$ —	$ —	$ —	$ —	$ —	$ 429	$ —	$260,749
Intergovernmental	15,294	—	52,174	—	—	—	48,404	58,342	174,214
Charges for services	54,446	—	—	—	—	—	3,084	5,432	62,962
Fines, forfeits, and penalties	11,131	—	—	—	—	—	987	—	12,118
Interest, rents, and concessions	(88)	430	15	(124)	3,358	42	1,527	5,768	10,928
Community service fees	—	—	—	—	3,494	—	350	4,031	7,875
Assessment levies	—	—	—	—	—	—	—	31,970	31,970
Contributions and donations	—	—	1,381	1,449	—	5,100	—	42	7,972
Miscellaneous	142	—	—	—	—	—	—	54	196
Total revenues	341,245	430	53,570	1,325	6,852	5,142	54,781	105,639	568,984
Expenditures: Ⓡ									
Current:									
General government	24,009	—	—	—	491	—	—	2,971	27,471
Police	129,339	—	—	—	—	—	—	17,720	147,059
Fire	100,886	—	—	—	—	—	—	1,544	102,430
General services	11,751	—	—	—	—	—	—	9,274	21,025
Transportation	7,607	—	—	—	—	—	12,453	10,963	31,023
Neighborhood services	941	—	—	—	—	—	—	66	1,007
Convention, culture, and leisure	4,825	365	—	—	—	—	—	8,006	13,196
Economic development	4,044	—	—	—	—	—	—	5,092	9,136
Parks and recreation	16,455	—	—	—	192	—	—	23,665	40,312

(continued from page 770)

Code enforcement	9,833	—	—	—	—	—	—	446	10,279
Community development	12,473	—	—	—	—	—	3,383	17	15,873
Library	7,922	—	—	—	—	—	—	4,444	12,366
Utilities	67	—	—	—	—	—	—	—	67
Nondepartmental	26,330	—	—	—	—	—	—	488	26,818
Capital outlay	4,918	22,912	40,190	22,877	27,933	—	23,326	13,990	156,146
Debt service:									
Principal	918	—	—	—	173	1,215	—	16,271	18,577
Interest and fiscal charges	271	5	—	—	3,760	3,934	299	21,428	29,697
Total expenditures	362,589	23,282	40,190	22,877	32,549	5,149	39,461	136,385	662,482
Excess (deficiency) of revenues over (under) expenditures	(21,344)	(22,852)	13,380	(21,552)	(25,697)	(7)	15,320	(30,746)	(93,498)
Other financing sources (uses): Ⓢ									
Transfers in	23,948	—	—	—	—	—	847	28,826	53,621
Transfers out	(24,136)	(2,621)	(206)	—	(2,575)	—	(246)	(457)	(30,241)
Issuance of long-term debt	4,551	—	—	—	18,412	—	—	—	22,963
Total other financing sources (uses)	4,363	(2,621)	(206)	—	15,837	—	601	28,369	46,343
Net change in fund balances	(16,981)	(25,473)	13,174	(21,552)	(9,860)	(7)	15,921	(2,377)	(47,155) Ⓣ
Fund balances (deficit), beginning of year	72,088	45,771	(25,063)	21,576	114,291	2,097	49,007	84,828	364,595
Fund balances (deficit), end of year	$ 55,107	$20,298	$ (11,889)	$ 24	$104,431	$2,090	$64,928	$ 82,451	$317,440

The notes to the financial statements are an integral part of this statement.

CITY OF SACRAMENTO
Proprietary Funds
Statement of Net Assets
June 30, 2010
(in thousands)

	Business-Type Activities—Enterprise Funds							
	Water Fund	Sewer Fund	Storm Drainage Fund	Solid Waste Fund	Community Center Fund	Other Enterprise Funds	Total	Governmental Activities—Internal Service Funds Ⓦ
Assets								
Current assets:								
Cash and investments held by City	$ 22,425	$ 17,926	$ 21,504	$ —	$ 9,903	$ 35,831	$ 107,589	$ 80,708
Cash and investments held by fiscal agent	—	—	53	—	2,874	125	3,052	153
Securities lending assets	1,679	851	1,038	—	—	1,600	5,168	3,183
Receivables, net:								
Taxes	—	—	—	—	2,202	—	2,202	—
Accounts	11,294	9,722	6,788	13,232	68	1,046	42,150	43
Loans	1,112	126	357	44	—	2	1,641	—
Intergovernmental	13,263	544	1,482	702	—	58	16,049	—
Interest	331	125	185	—	94	221	956	411
Due from other funds	—	—	—	—	—	—	—	11,555
Inventories	5,025	84	499	—	—	—	5,608	1,465
Prepaid items	—	—	—	1	1	17	19	5,844
Total current assets	55,129	29,378	31,906	13,979	15,142	38,900	184,434	103,362
Noncurrent assets:								
Restricted assets: Ⓥ								
Cash and investments held by City	13,641	505	1,128	2,399	12	1,373	19,058	—
Cash and investments held by fiscal agent	—	—	751	—	9,660	1,759	12,170	—
Advances to other funds	—	—	—	—	—	—	—	15,253
Loans receivable	9,326	1,293	3,878	—	221	515	15,233	—
Intergovernmental	—	—	215	—	—	—	215	—
Deferred charges	1,977	—	44	293	1,136	589	4,039	35
Capital assets:								
Land	645	1,138	18,968	1,133	21,739	10,616	54,239	—
Buildings and improvements	37,383	14,906	8,223	31,191	111,201	79,982	282,886	6,610
Machinery and equipment	14,555	4,172	15,345	11,060	3,643	6,282	55,057	1,434
Vehicles	—	—	—	—	—	—	—	107,599
Transmission and distribution system	527,326	134,962	363,560	—	—	—	1,025,848	—
Construction in progress	25,186	2,407	2,324	—	565	338	30,820	926
Software	201	297	584	—	—	—	1,082	—
Less: accumulated depreciation/amortization	(154,027)	(50,456)	(105,765)	(17,072)	(48,337)	(34,759)	(410,416)	(74,706)
Total noncurrent assets	476,213	109,224	309,255	29,004	99,840	66,695	1,090,231	57,151
Total assets	531,342	138,602	341,161	42,983	114,982	105,595	1,274,665	160,513

(*continued from page 772*)

Liabilities								
Current Liabilities:								
Securities lending obligations	2,040	967	1,169	—	93	1,845	6,114	3,306
Accounts payable and accrued expenses	6,707	6,730	1,543	1,264	1,205	1,519	18,968	3,549
Accrued compensated absences	108	16	71	39	24	27	285	67
Due to other funds	329	108	221	2,568	100	88	3,414	—
Interest payable	670	89	372	181	751	454	2,517	12
Liability for landfill closure	—	—	—	895	—	—	895	—
Deposits	—	—	39	—	—	83	122	—
Unearned revenue	—	—	71	—	1,067	1,672	2,810	515
Accrued claims	—	—	—	—	—	—	—	12,957
Capital leases payable, current portion	—	—	—	1,146	—	83	1,229	20
Revenue and other bonds payable, net, current portion	3,423	—	465	716	5,809	1,700	12,113	296
Notes payable, current portion	—	672	2,093	—	—	253	3,018	—
Utility district payable current portion	305	—	—	—	—	—	305	—
Total current liabilities	13,582	8,582	6,044	6,809	9,049	7,724	51,790	20,722
Noncurrent liabilities:								
Accrued compensated absences	2,007	575	2,168	1,199	561	551	7,061	1,140
Advances from other funds	329	107	220	246	6,770	91	7,763	—
Water fee credits	1,699	—	—	—	—	—	1,699	—
OPEB liability	2,690	1,109	1,255	3,531	300	615	9,500	1,256
Accrued claims and judgments	—	—	—	—	—	—	—	34,105
Liability for landfill closure	—	—	—	23,420	—	—	23,420	—
Capital leases payable	—	—	—	5,817	—	1,249	7,066	216
Revenue and other bonds payable, net	161,121	—	6,216	23,353	64,820	34,441	289,951	3,699
Loans payable	7,551	—	—	—	—	—	7,551	—
Notes payable	—	7,424	24,718	—	—	13,596	45,738	—
Total noncurrent liabilities	175,397	9,215	34,577	57,566	72,451	50,543	399,749	40,416
Total liabilities	188,979	17,797	40,621	64,375	81,500	58,267	451,539	61,138
Net Assets (Deficit)								
Invested in capital assets, net of related debt	277,475	99,330	271,626	1,696	27,842	13,228	691,197	37,632
Restricted for:								
Capital projects	24,152	505	—	—	1,124	—	25,781	—
Unrestricted	40,736	20,970	28,914	(23,088)	4,516	34,100	106,148	61,743
Total net assets (deficit)	$342,363	$120,805	$300,540	$(21,392)	$ 33,482	$ 47,328	$ 823,126	$ 99,375

The notes to the financial statements are an integral part of this statement.

EXHIBIT 17.6 Fund Financial Statements

CITY OF SACRAMENTO
Proprietary Funds
Statement of Revenues, Expenses and Changes in Fund Net Assets
For the Fiscal Year Ended June 30, 2010
(in thousands)

	Business-Type Activities—Enterprise Funds							
	Water Fund	Sewer Fund	Storm Drainage Fund	Solid Waste Fund	Community Center Fund	Other Enterprise Funds	Total	Governmental Activities—Internal Service Funds
Operating revenues:								
Charges for services:								
User fees and charges	$ 67,928	$ 19,426	$ 33,786	$ 58,696	$ 2,668	$24,719	$207,223	$66,824
Rents and concessions	—	—	—	—	4,159	1,211	5,370	—
Charge to Regional Sanitation District for operating and maintaining treatment plant	—	837	—	—	—	—	837	—
Miscellaneous	2,535	21	296	205	193	109	3,359	336
Total operating revenues	70,463	20,284	34,082	58,901	7,020	26,039	216,789	67,160
Operating expenses: ⓧ								
Employee services	23,425	7,108	21,102	15,882	6,144	10,593	84,254	12,006
Services and supplies	15,232	6,222	3,778	27,739	5,747	8,549	67,267	24,619
Depreciation/amortization	14,216	3,853	10,981	1,787	2,614	2,671	36,122	8,198
Insurance premiums	—	—	—	—	—	—	—	2,246
Claims and judgments	—	—	—	—	—	—	—	7,250
Total operating expenses	52,873	17,183	35,861	45,408	14,505	21,813	187,643	54,319
Operating income (loss)	17,590	3,101	(1,779)	13,493	(7,485)	4,226	29,146	12,841

(*continued from page 774*)

Nonoperating revenues (expenses):								
Interest and investment revenue	1,662	615	849	—	623	1,215	4,964	3,336
Transient occupancy taxes	—	—	—	—	14,233	—	14,233	—
Revenue from other agencies	—	—	578	810	—	993	2,381	—
Interest expense	(7,910)	(206)	(1,174)	(1,641)	(4,920)	(2,359)	(18,210)	(157)
Amortization of deferred charges	(119)	—	(5)	(27)	(132)	(25)	(308)	(3)
Loan forgiveness	—	—	—	—	(6)	—	(6)	—
Gain (loss) on disposition of capital assets	—	—	—	17	—	(615)	(598)	(539)
Total nonoperating revenues (expenses)	(6,367)	409	248	(841)	9,798	(791)	2,456	2,637
Income (loss) before contributions and transfers	11,223	3,510	(1,531)	12,652	2,313	3,435	31,602	15,478
Capital contributions	9,985	3,678	4,696	8	—	—	18,367	—
Transfers in	10	31	20	55	—	—	116	438
Transfers out	(7,825)	(2,100)	(3,715)	(6,349)	(1,350)	(2,361)	(23,700)	(234)
Changes in net assets	13,393	5,119	(530)	6,366	963	1,074	26,385	15,682
Total net assets (deficit), beginning of year	328,970	115,686	301,070	(27,758)	32,519	46,254	796,741	83,693
Total net assets (deficit), end of year	$342,363	$120,805	$300,540	$(21,392)	$33,482	$47,328	$823,126	$99,375

The notes to the financial statements are an integral part of this statement.

EXHIBIT 17.7 **Fund Financial Statements**

CITY OF SACRAMENTO
Proprietary Funds
Statement of Cash Flows
For the Fiscal Year Ended June 30, 2010
(in thousands)

	Business-Type Activities—Enterprise Funds							
	Water Fund	Sewer Fund	Storm Drainage Fund	Solid Waste Fund	Community Center Fund	Other Enterprise Funds	Total	Governmental Activities—Internal Service Funds
Cash flows from operating activities: Ⓨ								
Receipts from customers and users	$ 68,928	$20,254	$ 34,398	$ 57,726	$ 7,139	$ 26,139	$214,584	$ —
Receipts from interfund services provided	—	—	—	—	—	—	—	120,922
Payments to suppliers	(18,310)	(6,922)	(3,398)	(28,598)	(5,758)	(8,947)	(71,933)	(83,702)
Payments to employees	(23,199)	(7,147)	(21,257)	(15,246)	(6,203)	(10,630)	(83,682)	(11,566)
Claims and judgments paid	—	—	(11)	—	—	—	(11)	(10,426)
Net cash provided by (used for) operating activities	27,419	6,185	9,732	13,882	(4,822)	6,562	58,958	15,228
Cash flows from noncapital financing activities:								
Transient occupancy taxes	—	—	—	—	13,910	—	13,910	—
Transfers in from other funds	10	31	20	55	—	—	116	14
Transfers out to other funds	(7,825)	(2,100)	(3,715)	(6,349)	(1,350)	(2,361)	(23,700)	(234)
Collections on interfund loans	—	—	—	—	—	—	—	42,952
Interfund loan repayments	—	—	—	(5,081)	(700)	(89)	(5,870)	—
Interest payments on interfund borrowings	—	—	—	(79)	—	(5)	(84)	—
Intergovernmental revenue received	—	—	835	810	—	993	2,638	—
Payments for flood control agency	—	—	(1,635)	—	—	—	(1,635)	—
Net cash provided by (used for) noncapital financing activities	(7,815)	(2,069)	(4,495)	(10,644)	11,860	(1,462)	(14,625)	42,732

(continued from page 776)

Cash flows from capital and related financing activities: Ⓩ								
Interfund loan repayments	(329)	(107)	(221)	(245)	—	—	(902)	—
Interest payment on interfund loan repayments	(20)	(6)	(13)	(14)	—	—	(53)	—
Acquisition and construction of capital assets	(25,236)	(1,110)	(420)	(2,697)	(240)	(288)	(29,991)	(2,164)
Proceeds from sale of capital assets	—	—	—	17	—	—	17	336
Proceeds from issuance of debt	1,324	—	2,598	3,065	—	—	6,987	247
Prepayment for capital asset acquisition	—	—	—	—	—	—	—	(5,844)
Principal payments on capital debt	(3,097)	(656)	(2,497)	(1,930)	(6,294)	(1,537)	(16,011)	(287)
Interest payments on capital debt	(8,097)	(203)	(1,083)	(1,481)	(4,033)	(2,199)	(17,096)	(153)
Transfers in from other funds	—	—	—	—	—	—	—	424
Capital contributions received	1,805	28	724	8	—	—	2,565	—
Loan repayments received	1,597	222	665	—	—	—	2,484	—
Net cash provided by (used for) capital and related financing activities	(32,053)	(1,832)	(247)	(3,277)	(10,567)	(4,024)	(52,000)	(7,441)
Cash flows from investing activities:								
Collection of interest and investment revenue	1,583	582	841	—	665	1,114	4,785	2,976
Payments for investments purchased in prior year	(1,323)	(425)	(478)	—	(340)	(898)	(3,464)	(443)
Loans made	(31)	(7)	(9)	(36)	(185)	(200)	(468)	—
Loan repayments received	25	4	24	45	10	200	308	—
Net cash provided by (used for) investing activities	254	154	378	9	150	216	1,161	2,533
Net increase (decrease) in cash and cash equivalents	(12,195)	2,438	5,368	(30)	(3,379)	1,292	(6,506)	53,052
Cash and cash equivalents, beginning of year	48,261	15,993	18,068	2,429	25,828	37,796	148,375	27,809
Cash and cash equivalents, end of year	$ 36,066	$18,431	$ 23,436	$ 2,399	$ 22,449	$ 39,088	$141,869	$ 80,861
Reconciliation of cash and cash equivalents to the Statement of Net Assets:								
Cash and investments held by City	$ 22,425	$17,926	$ 21,504	$ —	$ 9,903	$ 35,831	$107,589	$ 80,708
Cash and investments held by fiscal agent	—	—	53	—	2,874	125	3,052	153
Restricted cash and investments held by City	13,641	505	1,128	2,399	12	1,373	19,058	—
Restricted cash and investments held by fiscal agent	—	—	751	—	9,660	1,759	12,170	—
Total cash and cash equivalents, end of year	$ 36,066	$18,431	$ 23,436	$ 2,399	$ 22,449	$ 39,088	$141,869	$ 80,861

The notes to the financial statements are an integral part of this statement.

- Cash flows from capital and related financing activities focus on the amounts spent on capital assets and the source of that funding. Exhibit 17.7 shows typical examples (Point Z): proceeds from issuance of debt, acquisition and construction of capital assets, and proceeds from disposition of capital assets.
- Cash flows from investing activities disclose amounts paid and received from investments.

Reporting Public Colleges and Universities

LO8

Prepare financial statements for a public college or university.

Private schools such as Harvard, Duke, and Stanford follow the FASB Accounting Standards Codification. Authoritative accounting literature on contributions and the proper form of financial statements has provided a significant amount of official reporting guidance for these private institutions. As will be discussed extensively in the following chapter, generally accepted accounting principles developed for such not-for-profit organizations have progressed greatly over the years.

In contrast, GASB has retained primary authority over the reporting of public colleges and universities. Much of GASB's work, however, has been directed at improving the accounting standards utilized by state and local government units. Consequently, the evolution of financial statements specifically for public schools has lagged behind that for other types of reporting. For that reason public colleges and universities such as The Ohio State University and the University of Kansas historically have been in a somewhat awkward position in terms of financial accounting.

For decades the question of whether the financial statements prepared for public colleges and universities should resemble those of private schools has been the subject of much theoretical discussion. Generally, the operations of public colleges and universities differ in at least two important ways from private schools. First, state or other governments directly provide a significant amount of funding (at least for qualifying students), lessening the reliance on tuition and fees. For example, information provided in the 2010 financial statements of Utah State University disclosed state grants, contracts, and appropriations of $156 million and federal grants, contracts, and appropriations of approximately $127 million in comparison to revenues of only $79 million from tuition and fees (after scholarship allowances).

Second, because of the ability to generate money each year from the government, public schools often raise and accumulate a smaller amount of endowment funds than private colleges and universities. Private schools usually try to build a large endowment to ensure financial security; this is not always necessary at a public school backed by the state or another government. For example, at June 30, 2010, Princeton University, a private school, held investments with a fair value of approximately $13.9 billion, an amount (roughly equal to $1.85 million per student) that is nearly beyond the comprehension of officials at most public colleges.

Do these and other differences warrant unique financial statements for public colleges and universities? In many ways, public and private schools are very much alike. They both educate students, charge tuition and other fees, conduct scholarly research, maintain libraries and sports teams, operate cafeterias and museums, and the like. What should be the measurement basis and what should be the form of the financial statements to reflect the financial activity and position of a public college or university?

Four alternatives have been suggested for properly constructing the financial statements that public colleges and universities prepare and distribute:

1. Adopt FASB's requirements so that all colleges and universities (public and private) prepare comparable financial statements. As the next chapter discusses, the private reporting model is relatively well developed. This suggestion presents some potential problems, however, because FASB, a group that has not had to deal with the intricacies found in governmental entities, might fail to comprehend the unique aspects of public schools. The reporting needs associated with such institutions might go unnoticed. In addition, loss of

authority to FASB could weaken GASB. Politically, reducing the power of this board is not a goal of the organizations that provide much of GASB's support and financing.

2. Apply a more traditional model focusing on fund financial statements and the wide variety of funds that such schools often maintain. However, both private not-for-profit organizations and governments (at least in part) have abandoned the reporting of individual funds. For public schools to continue relying on this approach seems somewhat outdated.

3. Create an entirely new set of financial statements designed specifically to meet the unique needs of a public college or university. If FASB's Accounting Standards Codification is not to be followed, the fundamental differences between private and public schools must be significant. If those differences can be identified, new statements could be developed to satisfy the informational needs of users and properly reflect the events and transactions of these public institutions. Unfortunately, the creation of a new set of financial statements would require an enormous amount of work by GASB. Does the benefit gained from tailor-made financial statements outweigh the cost of producing new standards for reporting public schools?

4. Adopt the same reporting model for public schools that has been created for state and local governments. Because a large amount of funding for public schools comes directly from governments, the financial statement format utilized by a city or county could be applied.

In 1999, GASB officially selected the fourth option by specifying that public colleges and universities are special purpose governments. This pronouncement creates a standard reporting model for schools such as the University of Georgia and Michigan State University.

However, a review of public college and university financial statements shows that many do not prepare both government-wide and fund financial statements. Such schools can logically be viewed as large enterprise funds: They have a user charge (tuition and fees), and they are open to the public. As discussed, accounting for enterprise funds in government-wide statements and fund financial statements is very similar. For these proprietary funds, both statements report all economic resources and use accrual accounting.

Thus, having two sets of almost identical statements was viewed by GASB as redundant. For this reason, most public schools only need to prepare a single set of statements equivalent to those of an enterprise fund. Consequently, a note to the financial statements for Middle Tennessee State University for June 30, 2010, and the year then ending provides a common rationale for the method by which the statements are structured.

> For financial statement purposes, the university is considered a special-purpose government engaged *only in business-type activities.* Accordingly, the financial statements have been prepared using the economic resources measurement focus and the accrual basis of accounting. Revenues are recorded when earned, and expenses are recorded when a liability is incurred, regardless of the timing of related cash flows. Grants and similar items are recognized as revenue as soon as all eligibility requirements imposed by the provider have been met. [Emphasis added.]

Exhibit 17.8 presents the financial statements for June 30, 2010, and the year then ended for James Madison University (a public school) for illustration purposes, although the accompanying notes have been omitted. The component unit that is reported here is identified as follows:

> The James Madison University Foundation, Inc. meets the criteria which qualify it as a component unit of the University. The Foundation is a legally separate, tax-exempt organization formed to promote the achievements and further the aims and purposes of the University.

As would be expected, these statements are quite similar to the fund financial statements presented in this chapter for the proprietary funds of the City of Sacramento, California (Exhibits 17.5, 17.6, and 17.7).

EXHIBIT 17.8

JAMES MADISON UNIVERSITY
Statement of Net Assets
As of June 30, 2010

	2010	
	James Madison University	Component Unit
Assets		
Current assets:		
Cash and cash equivalents (Note 2)	$111,613,999	$ 1,233,323
Securities lending—Cash and cash equivalents (Note 2)	14,788,465	—
Short-term investments (Note 2)	7,970,365	—
Accounts receivable (Net of allowance for doubtful accounts of $486,873 for 2010) (Note 3)	7,201,746	42,795
Contributions receivable (Net of allowance for doubtful contributions of $49,528 for 2010) (Note 3)	—	2,426,869
Due from the Commonwealth (Note 4)	6,797,365	—
Prepaid expenses	6,764,361	18,235
Inventory	743,795	—
Notes receivable (Net of allowance for doubtful accounts of $48,069 for 2010)	413,624	—
Total current assets	156,293,720	3,721,222
Non-current assets:		
Restricted cash and cash equivalents (Note 2)	48,296,607	—
Endowment investments (Note 2)	205,605	40,282,987
Other long-term investments (Note 2)	363,026	25,513,505
Land held for future use	—	2,485,348
Contributions receivable (Net of allowance for doubtful contributions of $114,085 for 2010) (Note 3)	—	5,590,148
Prepaid expenses	372,971	—
Notes receivable (Net of allowance for doubtful accounts of $202,292 for 2010)	1,904,569	—
Capital assets, net: (Note 5)		
Non-depreciable	106,487,583	563,991
Depreciable	557,395,339	1,003,755
Other assets	—	6,282
Total non-current assets	715,025,700	75,446,016
Total assets	871,319,420	79,167,238
Liabilities		
Current liabilities:		
Accounts payable and accrued expenses (Note 6)	48,345,247	156,656
Deferred revenue	12,508,996	—
Obligations under securities lending	22,758,830	—
Deposits held in custody for others	3,800,847	—
Long-term liabilities—current portion (Note 7)	22,868,867	143,564
Advance from the Treasurer of Virginia	50,000	—
Total current liabilities	110,332,787	300,220
Non-current liabilities (Note 7)	198,654,679	840,684
Total liabilities	308,987,466	1,140,904
Net Assets		
Invested in capital assets, Net of related debt	494,182,057	1,567,746
Restricted for:		
Non-expendable:		
Scholarships and fellowships	285,436	28,771,314
Research and public service	—	2,003,679
Other	—	11,524,582
Expendable:		
Scholarships and fellowships	45,839	3,160,812

(continued)

EXHIBIT 17.8
(Continued)

	2010	
	James Madison University	Component Unit
Research and public service	2,117,335	1,133,918
Debt service	3,668	358,123
Capital projects	789,772	10,776,451
Loans	335,156	—
Other	—	12,902,673
Unrestricted	64,572,691	5,827,036
Total net assets	$562,331,954	$78,026,334

The notes to financial statements are an integral part of this statement.

JAMES MADISON UNIVERSITY
Statement of Revenues, Expenses, and Changes in Net Assets
For the Year Ended June 30, 2010

	2010	
	James Madison University	Component Unit
Operating revenues:		
Student tuition and fees (Net of scholarship allowances of $9,654,934 for 2010)	$134,362,802	$ —
Gifts and contributions	—	5,354,277
Federal grants and contracts	15,078,430	—
State grants and contracts	7,576,678	—
Non-governmental grants and contracts	5,203,758	—
Auxiliary enterprises (Net of scholarship allowances of $7,762,059 for 2010) (Note 10)	133,310,463	—
Other operating revenues	1,145,673	148,175
Total operating revenues	296,677,804	5,502,452
Operating expenses (Note 11):		
Instruction	117,952,498	450,450
Research	7,778,217	9,971
Public service	10,636,778	147,696
Academic support	29,831,660	371,020
Student services	12,644,171	78,426
Institutional support	22,863,153	3,917,449
Operation and maintenance—plant	25,172,333	368,231
Depreciation	24,755,766	23,461
Student aid	8,942,184	2,098,553
Auxiliary activities (Note 10)	99,360,569	458,708
Total operating expenses	359,937,329	7,923,965
Operating loss	(63,259,525)	(2,421,513)
Non-operating revenues/(expenses):		
State appropriations (Note 12)	69,185,644	—
Pell grants (Note 1 L.)	8,271,187	—
State fiscal stabilization funds (ARRA) (Note 1 L.)	4,648,818	—
Gifts	1,025,172	—
Investment income (Net of investment expense of $38,189 for the University and $338,251 for the Foundation for 2010)	1,246,947	8,218,054
In-Kind support from James Madison University	—	2,506,494
Interest on capital asset—related debt	(5,907,522)	(22,746)
Loss on disposal of plant assets	(1,272,540)	—
Payment to the Commonwealth	(3,739,118)	—
Net non-operating revenues/(expenses)	73,458,588	10,701,802
Income before other revenues, expenses, gains or losses	10,199,063	8,280,289

(continued)

EXHIBIT 17.8 (Continued)

	2010	
	James Madison University	Component Unit
Capital appropriations and contributions (Note 13)	28,533,586	—
Capital gifts	484,700	—
Additions to permanent endowments	40,000	1,751,321
Net other revenues	29,058,286	1,751,321
Increase/(decrease) in net assets	39,257,349	10,031,610
Net assets—beginning of year, restated (Note 1 P.)	523,074,605	67,994,724
Net assets—end of year	$562,331,954	$78,026,334

The notes to financial statements are an integral part of this statement.

JAMES MADISON UNIVERSITY
Statement of Cash Flows
For the Year Ended June 30, 2010

	2010
Cash flows from operating activities:	
Student tuition and fees	$ 134,902,230
Grants and contracts (Note 1 L.)	26,920,206
Auxiliary enterprises	133,648,505
Other receipts	1,178,052
Payments to employees	(154,141,576)
Payments for fringe benefits	(46,888,999)
Payments for services and supplies	(93,627,527)
Payments for utilities	(13,322,879)
Payments for scholarships and fellowships	(8,942,184)
Payments for non-capitalized plant improvements and equipment	(18,583,242)
Loans issued to students	(444,420)
Collections of loans from students	400,772
Net cash used by operating activities	(38,901,062)
Cash flows from noncapital financing activities:	
State appropriations	69,184,286
Nonoperating grants and contracts (Note 1 L.)	12,920,005
Payment to the Commonwealth	(3,739,118)
Gifts and grants for other than capital purposes	1,025,171
Loans issued to students and employees	(600)
Collections of loans from students and employees	4,946
Agency receipts	97,198,980
Agency payments	(95,104,411)
Additions to permanent endowment	40,000
Net cash provided by noncapital financing activities	81,529,259
Cash flows from capital financing activities:	
Capital appropriations and contributions	33,051,937
Proceeds from capital debt	76,792,509
Proceeds from sale of capital assets	35,540
Purchase of capital assets	(84,669,658)
Principal paid on capital debt, leases, and installments	(8,480,132)
Interest paid on capital debt, leases, and installments	(6,594,932)
Net cash provided/(used) by capital financing activities	10,135,264
Cash flows from investing activities:	
Interest on investments	1,010
Interest on cash management pools	1,389,306
Net cash provided by investing activities	1,390,316
Net increase in cash	54,153,777
Cash and cash equivalents—beginning of the year	105,756,829
Cash and cash equivalents—end of the year	$ 159,910,606

The notes to financial statements are an integral part of this statement.

Summary

1. As with businesses, state and local governments often obtain assets through lease arrangements. Government accounting applies the same criteria for identifying a capital lease as a for-profit organization. Government-wide financial statements initially report the resulting asset and liability at the present value of the minimum lease payments. This asset is depreciated over the time that the government expects to use it. Interest expense on the reported liability is recognized each period. Fund financial statements recognize an expenditure and an other financing source at this same present value when the contract is initiated. Subsequent payments on the debt and interest are then recognized as expenditures.
2. Solid waste landfills create large potential debts for a government because of eventual closure and postclosure costs. Government-wide statements accrue this liability each period based on the latest current cost estimations and the portion of the property that has been filled. Fund financial statements report no expenditures until a claim to current financial resources is made.
3. Government employees often have the right to future compensated absences because of holidays, vacations, sick leave, and the like. In creating government-wide statements, the debts for these absences are estimated and reported as the employees earn them. Fund financial statements do not recognize a liability until the use of current financial resources is expected.
4. A state or local government that obtains a work of art or historical treasure normally records it as a capital asset on the government-wide financial statements. However, if specified guidelines are met, an expense can replace recognition of the asset. A state or local government that receives such a work of art or historical treasure through donation must still recognize revenue according to the rules established for voluntary nonexchange transactions. In contrast, fund financial statements for the governmental funds report no capital assets and, therefore, do not show these items except as expenditures if acquired.
5. Depreciation must be recorded each period for works of art and historical treasures that are capitalized unless they are viewed as inexhaustible.
6. Infrastructure assets are capitalized and depreciated on the government-wide financial statements. However, depreciation is not recorded if the modified approach is applied. Under this method, if a monitoring system is created to ensure that a network of infrastructure is maintained yearly at a predetermined condition, the cost of this care is expensed in lieu of recording depreciation.
7. A state or local government must include a management's discussion and analysis (MD&A) as part of its general purpose external financial reporting. As with for-profit businesses, this MD&A provides a verbal explanation of the government's operations and financial position.
8. A primary government produces a comprehensive annual financial report (CAFR). Both state and local governments as well as any special purpose government that meets certain provisions are viewed as primary governments. A component unit is any function that is legally separate from a primary government but for which financial accountability still exists. In the government-wide statements, component units are either discretely presented to the right of the primary government or blended within the actual funds of the primary government.
9. A statement of net assets and a statement of activities are prepared as government-wide financial statements based on the economic resources measurement focus and accrual accounting. These statements separate governmental activities from business-type activities. Internal service funds are usually included within the governmental activities. The statement of activities reports expenses by function along with related program revenues to determine the net expense or revenue resulting from each function. The government then shows the amount of general revenues as its way of covering the net expenses of the various functions.
10. In fund financial statements reported for the governmental funds, the General Fund and any other major fund are reported in separate columns. These statements are based on measuring current financial resources using modified accrual accounting. Additional statements are presented for proprietary funds and fiduciary funds.
11. Financial statements prepared by public colleges and universities must follow the same reporting guidelines as those created for state and local government units. Those statements will differ from the statements produced by private schools that follow FASB guidelines. Public schools must view themselves as special purpose governments. They often assume that they are engaged only in business-type activities like an enterprise fund. Thus, they only need to present the fund financial statements of a proprietary fund.

Comprehensive Illustration Problem

(*Estimated Time: 40 minutes*) The following is a series of transactions for a city. Indicate how the city reports each transaction within the government-wide financial statements and then on the fund financial statements. Assume that the city follows a policy of considering resources as available if they will be received within 60 days. Incurred liabilities are assumed to be claims to current resources if they will be paid within 60 days.

1. Borrowed money by issuing a 20-year bond for $3 million, its face value. This money is to be used to construct a highway around the city.
2. Transferred cash of $100,000 from the General Fund to the debt service funds to make the first payment of principal and interest on the bond in (1).
3. Paid the cash in (2) on the bond. Of this total, $70,000 represents interest; the remainder reduces the principal of the bond payable.
4. Completed construction of the highway and paid the entire $3 million.
5. The highway is expected to last for 30 years. However, the government qualifies to use the modified approach, which it has adopted for this system. A $350,000 cost is incurred during the year to maintain the highway at an appropriate, predetermined condition. Of this amount, $290,000 was paid immediately but the other $60,000 will not be paid until the sixth month of the subsequent year.
6. Received lights for the new highway donated from a local business. The lights are valued at $200,000 and should last for 20 years. The modified approach is not used for this network of infrastructure, but straight-line depreciation is applied using the half-year convention.
7. Leased a truck to maintain the new highway. The lease qualifies as a capital lease. The present value of the minimum payments is $70,000. Depreciation for this year is $10,000 and interest is $6,000. A single $11,000 payment in cash is made.
8. Recorded cash revenues of $2 million from the local subway system and made salary expense payments of $300,000 to its employees.
9. Opened a solid waste landfill at the beginning of the year that will be used for 20 years. This year an estimated 4 percent of the capacity was filled. The city anticipates closure and postclosure requirements will be $2 million based on current cost figures although no costs have been incurred to date.

Solution

1. *Government-wide financial statements.* On the statement of net assets, under the Governmental Activities column, both Cash and Noncurrent Liabilities increase by $3 million.

   Fund financial statements. The Cash balance increases on the balance sheet by $3 million whereas Other Financing Sources increases by the same amount on the statement of revenues, expenditures, and changes in fund balances. These amounts will be shown in the Other Governmental Funds column unless this particular capital projects fund is judged to be major so that a separate column is required.
2. *Government-wide financial statements.* No recording of this transfer is shown because the amount was an intra-activity transaction entirely carried out within the governmental activities.

   Fund financial statements. The Cash balance of the General Fund on the balance sheet decreases while the cash listed for other governmental funds (or debt service fund) increases. On the statement of revenues, expenditures, and other changes in fund balances, the General Fund shows an Other Financing Use of $100,000 whereas the other governmental funds report an Other Financing Source. These balances will not be offset in arriving at total figures.
3. *Government-wide financial statements.* On the statement of net assets, Cash for the governmental activities decreases by $100,000 and the total reported for Noncurrent Liabilities drops by $30,000 because of the principal payment. The statement of activities then recognizes $70,000 in interest expense as a governmental activity.

   Fund financial statements. First, Cash decreases by $100,000 on the balance sheet under the Other Governmental Funds (or Debt Service Fund) column. Second, on the statement of revenues, expenditures, and changes in fund balances, a $30,000 principal expenditure is reported with a $70,000 interest expenditure. These amounts are shown within other governmental funds (or debt service fund).

4. *Government-wide financial statements.* Under the governmental activities listed on the statement of net assets, Cash decreases by $3 million and Capital Assets increases by the same amount. All new infrastructure costs are capitalized.

   Fund financial statements. On the balance sheet, cash reported for other governmental funds decreases. Again, if this particular capital projects fund qualifies as major, the effects are shown in a separate column rather than in the Other Governmental funds column. The statement of revenues, expenditures, and changes in fund balances reports a $3 million expenditure as a capital outlay.

5. *Government-wide financial statements.* The statement of net assets reports a $290,000 decrease in cash under governmental activities and a $60,000 increase in a current liability. The statement of activities includes the $350,000 expense within an appropriate function such as public works. Because the modified approach is being applied, maintenance expense is recognized instead of depreciation expense.

   Fund financial statements. Because the $60,000 liability will not require the use of current financial resources (it will not be paid within 60 days), it is not recorded at this time at the fund level. Thus, the balance sheet reports only a $290,000 drop in cash, probably under the General Fund. A $290,000 expenditure is recorded on the statement of revenues, expenditures, and changes in fund balances for public works.

6. *Government-wide financial statements.* The lights do not qualify as works of art or historical treasures and must therefore be reported as capital assets on the statement of net assets at the $200,000 value. Based on a 20-year life and the half-year convention, $5,000 in accumulated depreciation must be recognized to reduce the reported net asset to $195,000. For the statement of activities, a $200,000 revenue is appropriate unless eligibility requirements for the donation have not yet been fulfilled. This revenue should be shown as a program revenue (Capital Grants and Contributions) to offset the expenses reported for public works. Depreciation of $5,000 should also be included as an expense for public works ($200,000/20 years × 0.5 year).

   Fund financial statements. No reporting is required because current financial resources were not affected.

7. *Government-wide financial statements.* On the statement of net assets, both the leased truck and the lease liability are reported under the governmental activities, at the present value of $70,000. Then $10,000 in accumulated depreciation reduces the truck's book value. The liability is reduced by $5,000, the amount of the $11,000 payment less the $6,000 attributed to interest. The statement of activities reports interest of $6,000 and depreciation of $10,000 as expenses directly related to the public works function.

   Fund financial statements. The balance sheet, probably under the General Fund, reports an $11,000 reduction in cash. The statement of revenues, expenditures, and changes in fund balances records a $70,000 expenditure as a capital outlay and recognizes an Other Financing Source of the same amount. This statement also shows another $11,000 in expenditures: $6,000 as interest and $5,000 for debt reduction.

8. *Government-wide financial statements.* Cash on the statement of net assets increases under the business-type activities by $1.7 million. The statement of activities reports expenses for the subway system as $300,000 while the related program revenues for charges for services rendered increase by $2 million so that the net revenue resulting from this business-type activity is $1.7 million.

   Fund financial statements. The statement of net assets for the proprietary funds (see Exhibit 17.5) should include a separate column for the subway system, assuming that it qualifies as a major fund. Cash in this column increases by $1.7 million. Likewise, the statement of revenues, expenses, and changes in fund net assets for the proprietary funds (see Exhibit 17.6) reports operating revenues of $2 million for the subway system. The list of operating expenses will include personnel services of $300,000. The statement of cash flows (see Exhibit 17.7) also reports both the inflow and outflow of cash under Cash Flows from Operating Activities.

9. *Government-wide financial statements.* Because the landfill is 4 percent filled and this is its first year, that portion of the overall $2 million ($80,000) cost must be recognized to date. The statement of net assets shows this amount as a noncurrent liability. The balance is presented as either a governmental activity or a business-type activity, depending on the landfill's fund classification. Likewise, the statement of activities reports the same $80,000 expense figure.

   Fund financial statements. This liability does not require the use of current financial resources and is not reported if the landfill is considered a governmental fund. However, if the landfill is viewed as an enterprise fund, the separate statements prepared for the proprietary funds show both the $80,000 expense and liability (see Exhibits 17.5 and 17.6).

Questions

1. What criteria does a state or local government apply to determine whether to capitalize a lease?
2. On January 1, 2013, a city signs a capital lease for new equipment for the police department. How does the city report this transaction on government-wide financial statements? On fund financial statements?
3. On December 31, 2013, the city in question (2) makes its first annual lease payment. How does the city report the payment on government-wide financial statements? On fund financial statements?
4. Why does the operation of a solid waste landfill create reporting concerns for a local government?
5. A landfill is scheduled to be filled to capacity gradually over a 10-year period. However, at the end of the first year of operations, the landfill is only 7 percent filled. How much liability for closure and postclosure costs should be recognized on government-wide financial statements? How much liability should be recognized on fund financial statements assuming that the landfill is recorded in an enterprise fund? How much liability should be recognized on fund financial statements assuming that the landfill is recorded in the General Fund?
6. A city operates a solid waste landfill. This facility is 11 percent full after the first year of operation and 24 percent after the second year. How much expense should be recognized on the government-wide financial statements in the second year for closure costs? Assuming that the landfill is reported in the General Fund, what expenditure should be recognized in the second year on the fund financial statements?
7. A teacher working for the City of Lights earns vacation pay of $2,000 during 2013. However, the vacation will not be taken until near the end of 2014. In the government-wide financial statements for 2013, how is this compensated absence reported? How is this compensated absence reported in the fund financial statements for 2013?
8. Assume in question (7) that the teacher takes the vacation late in 2014 and is paid the entire $2,000. What journal entry is reported in creating each of the two types of financial statements?
9. The City of Salem is given a painting by Picasso to display in its city hall. Under what condition will the city *not* report this painting as a capital asset on its government-wide financial statements? If it does report the painting as a capital asset, must the city report depreciation?
10. Assume in question (9) that the city does not choose to report the painting on the government-wide financial statements as a capital asset. Must the city report a revenue for the gift?
11. Under what condition is the modified approach applied?
12. What impact does the use of the modified approach have on reporting within the government-wide financial statements?
13. What does the management's discussion and analysis (MD&A) normally include? Where does a state or local government present this information?
14. What does a comprehensive annual financial report (known as the CAFR) include?
15. A primary government can be either a general purpose government or a special purpose government. What is the difference in these two? How does an activity qualify as a special purpose government?
16. The Willingham Museum qualifies as a component unit of the City of Willingham. How does an activity or function qualify to be a component unit of a primary government?
17. What is the difference between a blended component unit and a discretely presented component unit?
18. What are the two government-wide financial statements? What does each normally present?
19. What are the two fund financial statements for governmental funds? What information does each normally present?
20. What is the difference in program revenues and general revenues? Why is that distinction important?
21. Why does a government determine the net expenses or revenues for each of the functions within its statement of activities?
22. How are internal service funds reported on government-wide financial statements?
23. How are fiduciary funds reported on government-wide financial statements?
24. What are some of the major differences that exist between private colleges and universities and public colleges and universities that affect financial reporting?
25. What is the most common form for the financial statements prepared by public colleges and universities?

Problems

LO1 1. A city government has obtained an asset through a capital lease. Which of the following is true for the government-wide financial statements?

a. The accounting parallels that used in for-profit accounting.
b. The city must report an other financing source.
c. The city must report an expenditure.
d. Recognition of depreciation is optional.

LO1 2. A city government has a six-year capital lease for property being used within the General Fund. Minimum lease payments total $70,000 starting next year but have a current present value of $49,000. What is the total amount of expenditures to be recognized on the fund financial statements over the six-year period?

a. $-0-.
b. $49,000.
c. $70,000.
d. $119,000.

LO1 3. A city government holds a six-year capital lease for property being used within the General Fund. Minimum lease payments total $70,000 starting next year but have a current present value of $49,000. What is the total amount of other financing sources to be recognized on the fund financial statements over this six-year period?

a. $-0-.
b. $49,000.
c. $70,000.
d. $119,000.

LO1 4. A city government has a nine-year capital lease for property being used within the General Fund. The lease was signed on January 1, 2013. Minimum lease payments total $90,000 starting at the end of the first year but have a current present value of $69,000. Annual payments are $10,000, and the interest rate being applied is 10 percent. When the first payment is made on December 31, 2013, which of the following recordings is made?

Government-Wide Statements	Fund Financial Statements
a. Interest Expense $-0-	Interest Expense $-0-
b. Interest Expense $6,900	Expenditures $6,900
c. Expenditures $10,000	Expenditures $10,000
d. Interest Expense $6,900	Expenditures $10,000

LO1 5. A city government has a nine-year capital lease for property being used within the General Fund. The lease was signed on January 1, 2013. Minimum lease payments total $90,000 starting at the end of the first year but have a current present value of $69,000. Annual payments are $10,000, and the interest rate being applied is 10 percent. What liability is reported on the fund financial statements as of December 31, 2013, after the first payment has been made?

a. $-0-.
b. $59,000.
c. $65,900.
d. $80,000.

LO2 6. A city creates a solid waste landfill. It assesses every person or company that uses the landfill a charge based on the amount of materials contributed. In which of the following will the landfill probably be recorded?

a. General Fund.
b. Special revenues funds.
c. Internal service funds.
d. Enterprise funds.

Use the following information for problems 7, 8, and 9

A city starts a solid waste landfill that it expects to fill to capacity gradually over a 10-year period. At the end of the first year, it is 8 percent filled. At the end of the second year, it is 19 percent filled.

Currently, the cost of closure and postclosure is estimated at $1 million. None of this amount will be paid until the landfill has reached its capacity.

LO2 7. Which of the following is true for the Year 2 government-wide financial statements?
a. Both expense and liability will be zero.
b. Both expense and liability will be $110,000.
c. Expense will be $110,000 and liability will be $190,000.
d. Expense will be $100,000 and liability will be $200,000.

LO2 8. If this landfill is judged to be a proprietary fund, what liability will be reported at the end of the second year on fund financial statements?
a. $-0-.
b. $110,000.
c. $190,000.
d. $200,000.

LO2 9. If this landfill is judged to be a governmental fund, what liability will be reported at the end of the second year on fund financial statements?
a. $-0-.
b. $110,000.
c. $190,000.
d. $200,000.

Use the following information for problems 10 and 11:

The employees of the City of Jones earn vacation time that totals $1,000 per week during the year. Of this amount, $12,000 is actually taken in Year 1 and the remainder is taken in Year 2.

LO2 10. What liability should the city report on government-wide financial statements at the end of Year 1?
a. It depends on whether the employees work at governmental activities or business-type activities.
b. $-0-.
c. $40,000.
d. $52,000.

LO2 11. What amount of liability should the city recognize on fund financial statements at December 31, Year 1? Assume that all remaining vacations will be taken in July.
a. It depends on whether the employees work at governmental activities or business-type activities.
b. $-0-.
c. $40,000.
d. $52,000.

LO3 12. The City of Wilson receives a large sculpture valued at $240,000 as a gift to be placed in front of the municipal building. Which of the following is true for reporting the gift on the government-wide financial statements?
a. A capital asset of $240,000 must be reported.
b. No capital asset will be reported.
c. If conditions are met, recording the sculpture as a capital asset is optional.
d. The sculpture will be recorded but only for the amount paid by the city.

LO3 13. In problem (12), which of the following statements is true about reporting a revenue?
a. A revenue will be reported.
b. Revenue is reported but only if the asset is reported.
c. If the asset is not capitalized, no revenue should be recognized.
d. As a gift, no revenue would ever be reported.

LO3 14. Assume in problem (12) that the city reports the work as a capital asset. Which of the following is true?
a. Depreciation is not recorded because the city has no cost.
b. Depreciation is not required if the asset is viewed as being inexhaustible.

c. Depreciation must be recognized because the asset is capitalized.

d. Because the property was received as a gift, recognition of depreciation is optional.

LO4 15. A city builds sidewalks throughout its various neighborhoods at a cost of $200,000. Which of the following is *not* true?

a. Because the sidewalks qualify as infrastructure, the asset is viewed in the same way as land so that no depreciation is recorded.

b. Depreciation is required unless the modified approach is utilized.

c. The modified approach recognizes maintenance expense in lieu of depreciation expense for qualifying infrastructure assets.

d. The modified approach is allowed only if the city maintains the network of sidewalks at least at a predetermined condition.

LO4 16. Which of the following is true about use of the modified approach?

a. It can be applied to all capital assets of a state or local government.

b. It is used to adjust depreciation expense either up or down based on conditions for the period.

c. It is required for infrastructure assets.

d. For qualified assets, it eliminates the recording of depreciation.

LO5 17. Which of the following is true about the management's discussion and analysis (MD&A)?

a. It is an optional addition to the comprehensive annual financial report, but the GASB encourages its inclusion.

b. It adds a verbal explanation for the numbers and trends presented in the financial statements.

c. It appears at the very end of a government's comprehensive annual financial report.

d. It replaces a portion of the fund financial statements traditionally presented by a state or local government.

LO6 18. Which of the following is *not* necessary for a special purpose local government to be viewed as a primary government for reporting purposes?

a. It must have a separately elected governing body.

b. It must have specifically defined geographic boundaries.

c. It must be fiscally independent.

d. It must have corporate powers to prove that it is legally independent.

LO6 19. An accountant is trying to determine whether the school system of the City of Abraham is fiscally independent. Which of the following is *not* a requirement for being deemed fiscally independent?

a. Holding property in its own name.

b. Issuing bonded debt without outside approval.

c. Passing its own budget without outside approval.

d. Setting taxes or rates without outside approval.

LO6 20. An employment agency for individuals with disabilities works closely with the City of Hanover. The employment agency is legally separate from the city but still depends on it for financial support, which leads to a potential financial burden for the city. How should Hanover report the employment agency in its comprehensive annual financial report?

a. Not at all because the agency is legally separate.

b. As a part of the General Fund.

c. As a component unit.

d. As a related organization.

LO7 21. The City of Bacon holds cash of $820,000 that was received from the issuance of a bond and, according to the contract, must be spent for the construction of a new elementary school. The city also has $60,000 in supplies. How should the fund balance be reported?

a. Restricted—$880,000.

b. Nonspendable—$60,000 and restricted—$820,000.

c. Nonspendable—$60,000 and committed—$820,000.

d. Nonspendable—$60,000 and assigned—$820,000.

LO6

22. For component units, what is the difference in *discrete presentation* and *blending?*
    a. A blended component unit is shown to the left of the statements; a discretely presented component unit is shown to the right.
    b. A blended component unit is shown at the bottom of the statements; a discretely presented component unit is shown within the statements like a fund.
    c. A blended component unit is shown within the statements like a fund; a discretely presented component unit is shown to the right.
    d. A blended component unit is shown to the right of the statements; a discretely presented component unit is shown in completely separate statements.

LO7

23. A government reports that its public safety function had expenses of $900,000 last year and program revenues of $200,000 so that its net expenses were $700,000. On which financial statement is this information presented?
    a. Statement of activities.
    b. Statement of cash flows.
    c. Statement of revenues and expenditures.
    d. Statement of net assets.

LO7

24. Government-wide financial statements make a distinction between program revenues and general revenues. How is that difference shown?
    a. Program revenues are offset against the expenses of a specific function; general revenues are assigned to governmental activities and business-type activities in general.
    b. General revenues are shown at the top of the statement of revenues and expenditures; program revenues are shown at the bottom.
    c. General revenues are labeled as operating revenues; program revenues are shown as miscellaneous income.
    d. General revenues are broken down by type; program revenues are reported as a single figure for the government.

LO7

25. Which of the following is true about the statement of cash flows for the proprietary funds of a state or local government?
    a. The indirect method of reporting cash flows from operating activities is allowed although the direct method is recommended.
    b. The structure of the statement is virtually identical to that of a for-profit business.
    c. The statement is divided into four separate sections of cash flows.
    d. Amounts spent on capital assets are reported in a separate section from amounts raised to finance those capital assets.

LO8

26. Which of the following is most likely to be true about the financial reporting of a public college or university?
    a. It resembles the financial reporting of private colleges and universities.
    b. It will continue to use its own unique style of financial reporting.
    c. It resembles the financial reporting made by a proprietary fund within the fund financial statements for a state or local government.
    d. It will soon be reported using a financial statement format unique to the needs of public colleges and universities that GASB is scheduled to create.

LO1

27. On January 1, 2013, a city entered into the following leases for equipment items. Each of the leases qualifies as a capital lease. Initial payments are on December 31, 2013. An interest rate of 10 percent is viewed as appropriate. No bargain purchase options exist.

Fund	Annual Payments	Total Payments	Present Value of Total Payments
General (5-year life).	$8,000	$40,000	$33,350
Enterprise (6-year life) . . .	6,000	36,000	28,750

    a. What balances should be reported on government-wide financial statements for December 31, 2013, and the year then ended?
    b. What balances should be reported on fund financial statements for December 31, 2013, and the year then ended?

LO1

28. On January 1, 2013, a city entered into the following leases for equipment items. Each of the leases qualifies as a capital lease. Initial payments are on December 31, 2013. An interest rate of 12 percent is viewed as appropriate. No bargain purchase options exist.

Fund	Annual Payments	Total Payments	Present Value of Total Payments
General (10-year life). . . .	$3,000	$30,000	$19,000
Enterprise (4-year life) . . .	9,000	36,000	30,600

a. Prepare journal entries for the year 2013 for both of these leases for government-wide financial statements.

b. Prepare journal entries for the year 2013 for both of these leases for fund financial statements.

LO1

29. On January 1, 2013, the City of Verga leased a large truck for five years and made the initial annual payment of $22,000 immediately. The present value of these five payments based on an 8 percent interest rate is assumed to be $87,800. The truck has an expected useful life of five years.

a. Assuming that the city's fire department will use the truck, what journal entries should be made for 2013 and 2014 on the government-wide financial statements?

b. Assuming that city's fire department will use the truck, what journal entries should be made for 2013 and 2014 on the fund financial statements?

c. Assuming that the airport (an enterprise fund) operated by the city will use the truck, what journal entries should be made for 2013 and 2014 on the fund financial statements?

LO2

30. On January 1, 2013, the City of Hastings created a solid waste landfill that it expects to reach capacity gradually over the next 20 years. If the landfill were to be closed at the current time, closure costs would be approximately $1.2 million plus an additional $700,000 for postclosure work. Of these totals, the city must pay $50,000 on December 31 of each year for preliminary closure work. At the end of 2013, the landfill reached 3 percent of capacity. At the end of 2014, the landfill reached 9 percent of capacity. Also at the end of 2014, a reassessment is made; total closure costs are determined to be $1.4 million rather than $1.2 million.

a. Assuming that the landfill is viewed as an enterprise fund, what journal entries are made in 2013 and 2014 on the government-wide financial statements?

b. Assuming that the landfill is reported within the general fund, what journal entries are made in 2013 and 2014 on the government-wide financial statements?

c. Assuming that the landfill is viewed as an enterprise fund, what journal entries are made in 2013 and 2014 on fund financial statements?

d. Assuming that the landfill is reported within the general fund, what journal entries are made in 2013 and 2014 on fund financial statements?

LO2

31. The City of Lawrence opens a solid waste landfill in 2013 that is at 54 percent of capacity on December 31, 2013. The city had initially anticipated closure costs of $2 million but later that year decided that closure costs would actually be $2.4 million. None of these costs will be incurred until 2017 when the landfill is scheduled to be closed.

a. What will appear on the government-wide financial statements for this landfill for the year ended December 31, 2013?

b. Assuming that the landfill is recorded within the General Fund, what will appear on the fund financial statements for this landfill for the year ended December 31, 2013?

LO2

32. Mary T. Lincoln works for the City of Columbus. She volunteered to work over the 2013 Christmas break to earn a short vacation during the first week of January 2014. She earns three vacation days and will be paid $400 per day. She takes her vacation in January and is paid for those days.

a. Prepare the journal entries on the government-wide financial statements for 2013 and 2014 because of these events.

b. Assume that Lincoln works in an activity reported within the General Fund. Prepare journal entries for the fund financial statements for 2013 and 2014 because of these events.

c. Assume that Lincoln works in an activity reported within the General Fund but that she does not plan to take her three vacation days until near the end of 2014. What journal entries should be made for the fund financial statements in 2013 and 2014?

LO3

33. On January 1, 2013, a rich citizen of the Town of Ristoni donates a painting valued at $300,000 to be displayed to the public in a government building. Although this painting meets the three criteria to qualify as an artwork, town officials choose to record it as an asset. There are no eligibility requirements for the gift. The asset is judged to be inexhaustible so that depreciation will not be reported.
    a. For the year ended December 31, 2013, what will be reported on government-wide financial statements in connection with this gift?
    b. How does the answer to requirement (*a*) change if the government decides to depreciate this asset over a 10-year period using straight-line depreciation?
    c. How does the answer to requirement (*a*) change if the government decides not to capitalize the asset?

LO3

34. On January 1, 2013, a city pays $60,000 for a work of art to display in the local library. The city will take appropriate measures to protect and preserve the piece. However, if the work is ever sold, the money received will go into unrestricted funds. The work is viewed as inexhaustible, but the city has opted to depreciate this cost over 20 years (using the straight-line method).
    a. How is this work to be reported on the government-wide financial statements for the year ended December 31, 2013?
    b. How is this work to be reported in the fund financial statements for the year ended December 31, 2013?

LO4

35. A city government adds street lights within its boundaries at a total cost of $300,000. The lights should burn for at least 10 years but can last significantly longer if maintained properly. The city sets up a system to monitor these lights with the goal that 97 percent will be working at any one time. During the year, the city spends $48,000 to clean and repair the lights so that they are working according to the specified conditions. However, it spends another $78,000 to construct lights for several new streets in the city.

    Describe the various ways these costs could be reported on government-wide statements.

LO5

36. The City of Francois, Texas, has begun the process of producing its current comprehensive annual financial report (CAFR). Several organizations that operate within the city are related in some way to the primary government. The city's accountant is attempting to determine how these organizations should be included in the reporting process.
    a. What is the major criterion for inclusion in a government's CAFR?
    b. How does an activity or function qualify as a special purpose government?
    c. How is the legal separation of a special purpose government evaluated?
    d. How is the fiscal independence of a special purpose government evaluated?
    e. What is a component unit, and how is it normally reported on government-wide financial statements?
    f. How does a primary government prove that it can impose its will on a component unit?
    g. What does the blending of a component unit mean?

LO4, LO5

37. The County of Maxnell decides to create a sanitation department and offer its services to the public for a fee. As a result, county officials plan to account for this activity within the enterprise funds. Make journal entries for this operation for the following 2013 transactions as well as necessary adjusting entries at the end of the year. Assume that the information is being gathered for fund financial statements. Only entries for the sanitation department are required here:

    January 1—Received unrestricted funds of $160,000 from the General Fund as permanent financing.

    February 1—Borrowed an additional $130,000 from a local bank at a 12 percent annual interest rate.

    March 1—Ordered a truck at an expected cost of $108,000.

    April 1—Received the truck and made full payment. The actual cost amounted to $110,000. The truck has a 10-year life and no salvage value. Straight-line depreciation is to be used.

    May 1—Received a $20,000 cash grant from the state to help supplement the pay of the sanitation workers. The money must be used for that purpose.

    June 1—Rented a garage for the truck at a cost of $1,000 per month and paid 12 months of rent in advance.

    July 1—Charged citizens $13,000 for services. Of this amount, $11,000 has been collected.

    August 1—Made a $10,000 cash payment on the 12 percent note of February 1. This payment covers both interest and principal.

September 1—Paid salaries of $18,000 using the grant received on May 1.

October 1—Paid truck maintenance costs of $1,000.

November 1—Paid additional salaries of $10,000, first using the rest of the grant money received May 1.

December 31—Sent invoices totaling $19,000 to customers for services over the past six months. Collected $3,000 cash immediately.

LO2, LO3, LO5, LO7

38. The following information pertains to the City of Williamson for 2013, its first year of legal existence. For convenience, assume that all transactions are for the General Fund, which has three separate functions: general government, public safety, and health and sanitation.

Receipts:	
Property taxes	$320,000
Franchise taxes	42,000
Charges for general government services	5,000
Charges for public safety services	3,000
Charges for health and sanitation services	42,000
Issued long-term note payable	200,000
Receivables at end of year:	
Property taxes (90 percent estimated to be collectible)	90,000
Payments:	
Salary:	
General government	66,000
Public safety	39,000
Health and sanitation	22,000
Rent:	
General government	11,000
Public safety	18,000
Health and sanitation	3,000
Maintenance:	
General government	21,000
Public safety	5,000
Health and sanitation	9,000
Insurance:	
General government	8,000
Public safety ($2,000 still prepaid at end of year)	11,000
Health and sanitation	12,000
Interest on debt	16,000
Principal payment on debt	4,000
Building	120,000
Equipment	80,000
Supplies (20 percent still held) (public safety)	15,000
Investments	90,000
Ordered but not received:	
Equipment	12,000
Due in one month at end of year:	
Salaries:	
General government	4,000
Public safety	7,000
Health and sanitation	8,000

Compensated absences for general government workers at year-end total $13,000. These amounts will not be taken until late in the year 2014.

The city received a piece of art this year valued at $14,000 that it is using for general government purposes. There are no eligibility requirements. The city chose not to capitalize this property.

The general government uses the building that was acquired and is depreciating it over 10 years using the straight-line method with no salvage value. The city uses the equipment for health and sanitation and depreciates it using the straight-line method over five years with no salvage value.

The investments are valued at $103,000 at the end of the year.

For the equipment that has been ordered but not yet received, the City Council (the highest decision-making body in the government) has voted to honor the commitment when the equipment is received.

a. Prepare a statement of activities and a statement of net assets for governmental activities for December 31, 2013, and the year then ended.

b. Prepare a statement of revenues, expenditures, and other changes in fund balances and a balance sheet for the General Fund as of December 31, 2013, and the year then ended. Assume that the city applies the consumption method.

LO1, LO2, LO5, LO7

39. The City of Bernard starts the year of 2013 with the following unrestricted amounts in its General Fund: cash of $20,000 and investments of $70,000. In addition, it holds a building bought on January 1, 2012, for general government purposes for $300,000 and related long-term debt of $240,000. The building is being depreciated on the straight-line method over 10 years. The interest rate is 10 percent. The General Fund has four separate functions: general government, public safety, public works, and health and sanitation. Other information includes the following:

Receipts:	
Property taxes	$510,000
Sales taxes	99,000
Dividend income	20,000
Charges for general government services	15,000
Charges for public safety services	8,000
Charges for public works	4,000
Charges for health and sanitation services	31,000
Charges for landfill	8,000
Grant to be used for salaries for health workers (no eligibility requirements)	25,000
Issued long-term note payable	200,000
Sold above investments	84,000
Receivables at year-end:	
Property taxes ($10,000 is expected to be uncollectible)	130,000
Payments:	
Salary:	
General government	90,000
Public safety	94,000
Public works	69,000
Health and sanitation (all from grant)	22,000
Utilities:	
General government	9,000
Public safety	16,000
Public works	13,000
Health and sanitation	4,000
Insurance:	
General government	25,000
Public safety	12,000
Public works (all prepaid as of the end of the year)	6,000
Health and sanitation	4,000
Miscellaneous:	
General government	12,000
Public safety	10,000
Public works	9,000
Health and sanitation	7,000
Interest on previous debt	24,000
Principal payment on previous debt	10,000
Interest on new debt	18,000
Building (public works)	210,000
Equipment (public safety)	90,000
Public works supplies (30 percent still held)	20,000
Investments	111,000

(continued)

Ordered but not received:	
Equipment	24,000
Supplies	7,000
Due at end of year:	
Salaries:	
General government	14,000
Public safety	17,000
Public works	5,000

The city leased a truck on the last day of the year. The first payment will be made at the end of the next year. Total payments will amount to $90,000 but have a present value of $64,000.

The city started a landfill this year that it is recording within its General Fund. It is included as a public works function. Closure costs today would be $260,000 although the landfill is not expected to be filled for nine more years. The city has incurred no costs to date although the landfill is now 15 percent filled.

For the equipment and supplies that have been ordered but not yet received, the City Council (the highest decision-making body in the government) has voted to honor the commitment when the items are received.

The new building is being depreciated over 20 years using the straight-line method and no salvage value, whereas depreciation of the equipment is similar except that its life is only 10 years. Assume the city records a full year's depreciation in the year of acquisition.

The investments are valued at $116,000 at year-end.

a. Prepare a statement of activities and a statement of net assets for governmental activities for December 31, 2013, and the year then ended.

b. Prepare a statement of revenues, expenditures, and changes in fund balances and a balance sheet for the General Fund as of December 31, 2013, and the year then ended. Assume that the purchases method is being applied.

LO2, LO3, LO5, LO7

40. The City of Pfeiffer starts the year of 2013 with the General Fund and an enterprise fund. The General Fund has two activities: education and parks/recreation. For convenience, assume that the General Fund holds $123,000 cash and a new school building costing $1 million. The city utilizes straight-line depreciation. The building has a 20-year life and no salvage value. The enterprise fund has $62,000 cash and a new $600,000 civic auditorium with a 30-year life and no salvage value. The enterprise fund monitors just one activity, the rental of the civic auditorium for entertainment and other cultural affairs.

The following transactions for the city take place during 2013. Assume that the city's fiscal year ends on December 31.

a. Decides to build a municipal park and transfers $70,000 into a capital projects fund and immediately expends $20,000 for a piece of land. The creation of this fund and this transfer were made by the highest level of government authority.

b. Borrows $110,000 cash on a long-term bond for use in creating the new municipal park.

c. Assesses property taxes on the first day of the year. The assessment, which is immediately enforceable, totals $600,000. Of this amount, $510,000 will be collected during 2013 and another $50,000 is expected in the first month of 2014. The remainder is expected about halfway through 2014.

d. Constructs a building in the park in (*b*) for $80,000 cash for playing basketball and other sports. It is put into service on July 1 and should last 10 years with no salvage value.

e. Builds a sidewalk around the new park for $10,000 cash and puts it into service on July 1. It should last for 10 years, but the city plans to keep it up to a predetermined quality level so that it will last almost indefinitely.

f. Opens the park and charges an entrance fee of only a token amount so that it records the park, therefore, in the General Fund. Collections during this first year total $8,000.

g. Buys a new parking deck for $200,000, paying $20,000 cash and signing a long-term note for the rest. The parking deck, which is to go into operation on July 1, is across the street from the civic auditorium and is considered part of that activity. It has a 20-year life and no salvage value.

h. Receives a $100,000 cash grant for the city school system that must be spent for school lunches for the poor. Appropriate spending of these funds is viewed as an eligibility requirement of this grant. During the current year, $37,000 of the amount received was properly spent.

i. Charges students in the school system a total fee of $6,000 for books and the like. Of this amount, 90 percent is collected during 2013 with the remainder expected to be collected in the first few weeks of 2014.

j. Buys school supplies for $22,000 cash and uses $17,000 of them. The General Fund uses the purchases method.

k. Receives a painting by a local artist to be displayed in the local school. It qualifies as a work of art, and officials have chosen not to capitalize it. The painting has a value of $80,000. It is viewed as inexhaustible.

l. Transfers $20,000 cash from the General Fund to the Enterprise Fund as a capital contribution.

m. Orders a school bus for $99,000.

n. Receives the school bus and pays an actual cost of $102,000. The bus is put into operation on October 1 and should last for five years with no salvage value.

o. Pays salaries of $240,000 to school teachers. In addition, owes and will pay $30,000 during the first two weeks of 2014. Vacations worth $23,000 have also been earned but will not be taken until July 2014.

p. Pays salaries of $42,000 to city auditorium workers. In addition, owes and will pay $3,000 in the first two weeks of 2014. Vacations worth $5,000 have also been earned but will not be taken until July 2014.

q. Charges customers $130,000 for the rental of the civic auditorium. Of this balance, collected $110,000 in cash and will collect the remainder in April 2014.

r. Pays $9,000 maintenance charges for the building and sidewalk in (*d*) and (*e*).

s. Pays $14,000 on the bond in (*b*) on the last day of 2013: $5,000 principal and $9,000 interest.

t. Accrues interest of $13,000 on the note in (*g*) as of the end of 2013, an amount that it will pay in June 2014.

u. Assumes that a museum that operates within the city is a component unit that will be discretely presented. The museum reports to city officials that it had $42,000 of direct expenses this past year and $50,000 in revenues from admission charges. The only assets that it had at year-end were cash of $24,000, building (net of depreciation) of $300,000, and a long-term liability of $210,000.

Prepare the 2013 government-wide financial statements for this city. Assume the use of the modified approach.

LO2, LO3, LO5, LO7

41. Use the information in problem (40) to prepare the 2013 fund financial statements for the governmental funds and the proprietary funds. A statement of cash flows is not required. Assume that "available" is defined as within 60 days and that all funds are major. The General Fund is used for debt repayment.

LO1, LO2, LO5

42. For each of the following, indicate whether the statement is true or false and include a brief explanation for your answer.

a. A pension trust fund appears in the government-wide financial statements but not in the fund financial statements.

b. Permanent funds are included as one of the governmental funds.

c. A fire department placed orders of $20,000 for equipment. The equipment is received but at a cost of $20,800. In compliance with requirements for fund financial statements, an encumbrance of $20,000 was recorded when the order was placed, and an expenditure of $20,800 was recorded when the order was received.

d. The government reported a landfill as an enterprise fund. At the end of Year 1, the government estimated that the landfill will cost $800,000 to clean up when it is eventually full. Currently, it is 12 percent filled. At the end of Year 2, the estimation was changed to $860,000 when it was 20 percent filled. No payments are due for several years. Fund financial statements for Year 2 should report a $76,000 expense.

e. A city reports a landfill in the General Fund. At the end of Year 1, the government anticipated the landfill would cost $900,000 to clean up when it is full and reported that it was 11 percent filled. At the end of Year 2, the estimates were changed to $850,000 and 20 percent filled. No payments are due for several years. Government-wide financial statements for Year 2 should report a $71,000 expense.

f. A lease for a computer (that has a six-year life) is signed on January 1, Year 1, with six annual payments of $10,000. The police department will use the computer. The first payment is to be made immediately. The present value of the $60,000 in cash flows is $39,000 based on a 10 percent rate. Fund financial statements for Year 1 should report total expenditures of $10,000.

g. An agency fund has neither revenues nor expenditures but reports expenses.

h. A lease for a computer (that has a six-year life) is signed on January 1, Year 1, with six annual payments of $10,000. The computer is to be used by the police department. The first payment is to be made immediately. The present value of the $60,000 in cash flows is $39,000 based on a 10 percent rate. Government-wide financial statements for Year 1 should report expenses of $9,400.

For problems 43 through 48, use the following introductory information:

The City of Wolfe has issued its financial statements for Year 4 (assume that the city uses a calendar year). The city maintains the General Fund made up of two functions: (1) education and (2) parks. The city also utilizes capital projects funds for ongoing construction and an enterprise fund to account for its art museum. It also has one discretely presented component unit.

The government-wide financial statements indicated the following Year 4 totals:

Education had net expenses of $710,000.
Parks had net expenses of $130,000.
Art museum had net revenues of $80,000.
General revenues were $900,000; the overall increase in net assets was $140,000.

The fund financial statements issued for Year 4 indicated the following:

The General Fund had an increase of $30,000 in its fund balance.
The Capital Projects Fund had an increase of $40,000 in its fund balance.
The Enterprise Fund had an increase of $60,000 in its net assets.

Officials for Wolfe define "available" as current financial resources to be paid or collected within 60 days.

LO3

43. On the first day of Year 4, the city receives a painting as a gift that qualifies as a work of art. It has a 30-year life, is worth $15,000, and is being displayed at one of the local parks. The accountant accidentally capitalized and depreciated it although officials had wanted to use the allowed alternative.

Respond to the following:

a. According to the information provided above, the General Fund reported a $30,000 increase in its fund balance. If city officials had used proper alternatives in this reporting, what would have been the correct change in the fund balance for the General Fund for the year?

b. According to the information provided above, the parks reported net expenses of $130,000. If city officials had used proper alternatives in this reporting, what was the correct net expense for parks for the year?

c. Assume the same information except that the art was given to the art museum but not recorded at all. What should have been the overall change in net assets for Year 4 on government-wide financial statements, assuming that officials still preferred the allowed alternative?

LO1

44. On January 1, Year 4, the government leased a police car for five years at $20,000 per year with the first payment being made on December 31, Year 4. This is a capitalized lease. Assume that, at a reasonable interest rate of 10 percent, the present value of a five-year annuity due is $62,000. In the government-wide financial statements, the government recorded a $20,000 increase in expense and a $20,000 reduction in cash as its only entry. In the fund financial statements, the government increased Expenditures by $20,000 and reduced Cash for $20,000 as its only entry.

a. According to the information provided above, the overall increase in net assets reported was $140,000. What was the correct overall change in the net assets in the government-wide financial statements?

b. According to the information provided above, the General Fund reported an increase of $30,000 in its fund balance. What was the correct change in the fund balance for the General Fund?

LO6

45. Assume that the one component unit had program revenues of $30,000 and expenses of $42,000 and spent $10,000 for land during Year 4. However, it should have been handled as a blended component unit, not as a discretely presented component unit. According to the information provided above, the overall increase in net assets reported was $140,000. What was the correct overall change in the net assets in the government-wide financial statements?

LO2

46. At the end of Year 4, the city owed teachers $60,000 in vacation pay that had not been recorded. The assumption is that these vacations will be taken evenly over the next year. A 60-day period is used to determine available funds.

    a. What is the correct change in the fund balance of the General Fund for the year?

    b. What is the correct overall change in the net assets in the government-wide financial statements?

LO2

47. The city maintains a landfill that has been recorded during the current year within its parks. The landfill generated program revenues of $4,000 in Year 4 and cash expenses of $15,000. It also paid $3,000 cash for a piece of land. These transactions were recorded as would have been anticipated, but no other recording was made this year. The city assumes that it will have to pay $200,000 to clean up the landfill when it is closed in several years. The landfill was 18 percent filled at the end of Year 3 and is 26 percent filled at the end of Year 4. No payments will be necessary for several more years. For convenience, assume that the entries in all previous years were correctly handled regardless of the situation.

    a. The city believes that the landfill was included correctly in all previous years as one of its Enterprise Funds. According to the information provided, the overall increase in net assets reported was $140,000. What is the correct overall change in the net assets in the government-wide financial statements?

    b. The city believes that the landfill was included correctly in all previous years in one of the Enterprise Funds. According to the information provided, the Enterprise Fund reported an increase in its net assets of $60,000. What is the correct change in the net assets of the Enterprise Fund in the fund financial statements?

    c. The city believes that the landfill was included correctly in all previous years within the General Fund. What is the correct change in the fund balance of the General Fund?

LO4

48. On the first day of the year, the City of Wolfe bought $20,000 of equipment with a five-year life and no salvage value for its school system. It was capitalized but no other entries were ever made. The machine was monitored using the modified approach.

    a. Based on the information provided above, what was the correct overall change in the net assets in the government-wide financial statements?

    b. What was the correct amount of net expenses for education in the government-wide statements?

LO1

49. A police department leases a car on July 1, Year 1, with five annual payments of $20,000 each. It immediately makes the first payment, and the present value of the annuity due is $78,000 based on an assumed rate of 10 percent. The car has a five-year life. Assume that this is a capitalized lease. Indicate whether each of the following *independent* statements is true or false and briefly explain each answer.

    a. The fund financial statements will show a total liability of $3,900 at the end of Year 1.

    b. The government-wide financial statements will show a total liability of $58,000 at the end of Year 1.

    c. The government-wide financial statements will show total interest expense of $2,900 in Year 1.

    d. The fund financial statements will show total expenditures of $20,000 in Year 1.

    e. The government-wide financial statements will show a net leased asset of $70,200 at the end of Year 1.

    f. If this were an ordinary annuity so that the first payment was made in Year 2, no expenditure would be reported in the fund financial statements in Year 1.

    g. If the car had an eight-year useful life, this contract could not be a capitalized lease.

    h. Over the entire life of the car, the amount of expense recognized in the government-wide financial statements will be the same as the amount of expenditures recognized in the fund financial statements.

LO2

50. A city has a solid waste landfill that was filled 12 percent in Year 1 and 26 percent in Year 2. During those periods, the government expected that total closure costs would be $2 million. As a result, it paid $50,000 to an environmental company on July 1 of each of these two years. Such payments will continue for several years to come. Indicate whether each of the following *independent* statements is true or false and briefly explain each answer. The city has a December 31 year-end.
    a. The government-wide financial statements will show a $230,000 expense in Year 2 but only if reported in an enterprise fund.
    b. The fund financial statements will show a $50,000 liability in Year 2 if this landfill is reported in the General Fund.
    c. The fund financial statements will show a $50,000 liability at the end of Year 2 if this landfill is reported in an enterprise fund.
    d. If this landfill is reported in an enterprise fund, the government-wide financial statements and the fund financial statements will basically have the same reporting.
    e. The government-wide financial statements will show a $420,000 liability at the end of Year 2.
    f. Over the landfill's entire life, the amount of expense recognized in the government-wide financial statements will be the same as the amount of expenditures recognized in the fund financial statements. Assume the landfill is reported in the General Fund.

LO2

51. Use the same information as in problem (50) except that, by the end of Year 3, the landfill is 40 percent filled. The city now realizes that the total closure costs will be $3 million. Indicate whether each of the following *independent* statements is true or false and briefly explain each answer.
    a. If the city had known the costs were going to be $3 million from the beginning, the reporting on the fund financial statements would have been different in the past years if the landfill had been reported in an enterprise fund.
    b. If the landfill is monitored in the General Fund, a liability will be reported for the governmental activities in the government-wide financial statements at the end of Year 3.
    c. A $680,000 expense should be recognized in Year 3 in the government-wide financial statements.
    d. Because the closure costs reflect a future flow of cash, any liability reported in the government-wide financial statements must be reported at present value.

LO3

52. A city receives a copy of its original charter from the year 1799 as a gift from a citizen. The document will be put under glass and displayed in the city hall for all to see. The fair value is estimated at $10,000. Indicate whether each of the following *independent* statements is true or false and briefly explain each answer.
    a. If the city government does not have a policy for handling any proceeds if it ever sells the document, the city must report a $10,000 asset within its government-wide financial statements.
    b. Assume that this gift qualifies for optional handling and that the city chooses to report it as an asset. For the government-wide financial statements, depreciation is required.
    c. Assume this gift qualifies for optional handling and the document is deemed to be exhaustible. The city must report an immediate expense of $10,000 in the government-wide financial statements.
    d. Assume that this gift qualifies for optional handling. The city must make a decision as to whether to recognize a revenue of $10,000 in the government-wide financial statements.
    e. Assume that this gift qualifies for optional handling. The city can choose to report the gift in the statement of net activities for the government-wide financial statements in a way so that there is no overall net effect.

LO6

53. A city starts a public library that has separate incorporation and gets some of its money for operations from the state and some from private donations. Indicate whether each of the following *independent* statements is true or false and briefly explain each answer.
    a. If the city appoints 9 of the 10 directors, it must report the library as a component unit.
    b. If the library is a component unit and its financial results are shown as part of the governmental activities of the city, it is known as a *blended component unit.*
    c. If the library appoints its own board but the city must approve its budget, the library must be reported as a blended component unit.

Develop Your Skills

RESEARCH CASE 1

The City of Abernethy has three large bridges built in the later part of the 1980s that were not capitalized at the time. In creating government-wide financial statements, the city's accountant is interested in receiving suggestions as to how to determine a valid amount to report currently for these bridges.

Required

Use a copy of the GASB *Codification of Governmental Accounting and Financial Reporting Standards* as the basis for writing a report to this accountant to indicate various ways to make this calculation. Use the Topical Index or skim Section 1400 which covers "Reporting Capital Assets." Use examples that will help illustrate the process.

RESEARCH CASE 2

Officials for the City of Artichoke, West Virginia, have recently formed a transit authority to create a public transportation system for the community. These same officials are now preparing the city's CAFR for the most recent year. The transit authority has already lost a considerable amount of money and the officials have become interested in its reporting and whether it qualifies as a component unit of the city.

Following are several articles written about the reporting of component units by a state or local government:

"Changes in Component Units," *Government Finance Review,* February 2011.

"GASB Issues Guidance on Financial Reporting Entity, Component Units," *Accounting Policy & Practice Report,* January 7, 2011.

"Financial Reporting for Affiliated Organizations," *The Journal of Government Financial Management,* Winter 2003.

"How to Implement GASB Statement No. 34," *The Journal of Accountancy,* November 2001.

"Accounting for Affiliated Organizations," *Government Finance Review,* December 2002.

"Component Unit Reporting in the New Reporting Model," *The CPA Journal,* October 2001.

Required

Read one or more of the above articles and any others that you may discover about component units. Write a memo to these city officials providing as much detailed information about component units and their reporting as you can to help these individuals understand the challenges and difficulties of this reporting.

ANALYSIS CASE 1

Read the following journal article: "25 Years of State and Local Governmental Financial Reporting—An Accounting Standards Perspective," *The Government Accountants Journal,* Fall 1992.

Or, as a second possibility, do a search of books in the college library for advanced accounting textbooks or government accounting textbooks that were published prior to 2000.

Required

Accounting for state and local governments has changed considerably in just the last 10–20 years. Write a report to highlight some of the differences you noted between the process described before 2000 and that which has been presented in Chapters 16 and 17 of this textbook.

ANALYSIS CASE 2

Go to www.phoenix.gov and do a search for the term "CAFR." Those results should lead to the latest CAFR for the City of Phoenix, Arizona. The financial statements for a state and local government must include a Management's Discussion and Analysis of the information being reported. Read this section of the Phoenix CAFR.

Required

Write a report indicating the types of information found in this government's MD&A.

COMMUNICATION CASE 1

Read the following articles and any other papers that are available on setting governmental accounting standards:

"The Governmental Accounting Standards Board: Factors Influencing Its Operation and Initial Technical Agenda," *Government Accountants Journal,* Spring 2000.

"Governmental Accounting Standards Come of Age: Highlights from the First 20 Years," *Government Finance Review,* April 2005.

"Forward-Looking Information: What It Is and Why It Matters," *Government Accountants Journal,* December 1, 2010.

"Citizen-Centric Reporting," *Journal of Government Financial Management,* Fall 2010.

"GASB Re-Examines Fund Balance Reporting and Definitions of Fund Types," *Government Finance Review,* December 2006.

"A Century of Governmental Accounting and Financial Reporting Leadership," *Government Finance Review,* April 2006.

"The GASB Turns 25: A Retrospective," *Government Finance Review,* April 2009.

Required

Write a short paper discussing the evolution of governmental accounting.

COMMUNICATION CASE 2

The City of Larissa recently opened a solid waste landfill to serve the area's citizens and businesses. The city's accountant has gone to city officials for guidance as to whether to record the landfill within the General Fund or as a separate enterprise fund. Officials have asked for guidance on how to make that decision and how the answer will impact the government's financial reporting.

Required

Write a memo to the government officials describing the factors that should influence the decision as to the fund in which to report the landfill. Describe the impact that this decision will have on the city's future comprehensive annual financial reports.

EXCEL CASE

Prior to the creation of government-wide financial statements, the City of Loveland did not report the cost of its infrastructure assets. Now city officials are attempting to determine reported values for major infrastructure assets that it had obtained prior to the preparation of these statements. The chief concern is determining a value for the city's hundreds of miles of roads that were built at various times over the past 20–25 years. Each road is assumed to last for 50 years (depreciation is 2 percent per year).

As of December 31, 2013, city engineers believed that one mile of new road would cost $2.3 million. For convenience, each road is assumed to have been acquired as of January 1 of the year in which it was put into operation. Officials have done some investigation and believe that the cost of constructing a mile of road has increased by 8 percent each year over the past 30 years.

Required

Build a spreadsheet to determine the value that should now be reported for each mile of road depending on the year it was put into operation. For example, what reported value should be disclosed in the government-wide financial statements for 10 miles of roads put into operation on January 1, 2003?

chapter 18

Accounting and Reporting for Private Not-for-Profit Organizations

Learning Objectives

After studying this chapter, you should be able to:

LO1 Understand the basic composition of the financial statements produced for a private not-for-profit organization.

LO2 Determine the proper classification for assets that are unrestricted, temporarily restricted, or permanently restricted and explain the method of reporting these categories.

LO3 Explain the purpose and the construction of a statement of functional expenses.

LO4 Report the various types of contributions that a private not-for-profit organization can receive.

LO5 Understand the impact of a tax-exempt status.

LO6 Account for both mergers and acquisitions of not-for-profit organizations.

LO7 Describe the unique aspects of accounting for health care organizations.

America loves nonprofits. They represent what is best about the country: generosity, compassion, vision, and the eternal optimism that we can resolve our most serious problems. Unlike the for-profit sector that employs most Americans, nonprofits have a higher calling, a more noble purpose. Each week millions of people volunteer their time to nonprofits, reading to the blind, raising money for the Cancer Society, mentoring adolescents from troubled backgrounds, or doing countless other good deeds. Nonprofits show loving kindness to the most vulnerable and the most wretched in society.[1]

Not-for-profit organizations operate literally throughout the world. Many are well known for their ongoing work to achieve one or more stated missions such as the cure for a particular disease, the eradication of hunger and poverty, or the cleanup of the environment. However, the title of *not-for-profit organization* does not have to be limited to groups with such noble goals; a wide array of entities such as civic organizations, political parties, trade associations, and fraternal organizations also are often formed as not-for-profit organizations. Approximately 1.6 million not-for-profit organizations exist in the United States alone.[2]

Many of these organizations are huge by any standard. In 2010, The Salvation Army held $8.8 billion in net assets. The 10 largest charities alone reported receiving $45 billion in single-year donations.[3] These were led by the organizations listed on the next page. As can be seen, these organizations receive significant revenue beyond pure donations:

[1] Jeffrey M. Berry with David F. Arons, *A Voice for Nonprofits* (Washington, DC: Brookings Institution Press, 2003), p. 1.

[2] http://nccsdataweb.urban.org/PubApps/profile1.php.

[3] William P. Barrett, "America's 200 Largest Charities," November 17, 2010, http://www.forbes.com/2010/11/16/forbes-charity-200-personal-finance-philanthropy-200-largest-charities-charity-10-intro.html.

	2009 Revenues	Largest Revenue Source
YMCA of the United States	$5,843,926,000	Program services: $4,243,097,000
Catholic Charities USA	4,270,309,450	Government: $2,861,107,331
United Way	4,128,778,364	Public support: $3,842,018,486
Goodwill Industries International	3,676,033,245	Program services: $2,590,845,167
American Red Cross	3,301,803,766	Program services: $2,493,347,347[4]

Several general characteristics help to define a not-for-profit organization:

1. They often receive significant amounts of contributed resources from providers who do not expect a commensurate return.
2. They have an operating purpose that is something other than providing goods and services for a profit.
3. They do not have ownership interests like those of a for-profit business enterprise.

Some not-for-profit organizations are viewed as governmental because they receive tax revenues or are controlled by a government. A state-operated hospital, for example, and a public university are both governmental not-for-profit organizations. Most not-for-profit organizations, however, are nongovernmental (or private). The American Cancer Society and Mothers Against Drunk Driving (MADD) are just two examples of not-for-profit organizations that do not qualify as governmental.

The amount of giving to not-for-profit organizations each year is staggering despite the recession. "Total charitable giving by donor source for 2010 is estimated to be $290.89 billion. This is an increase of 3.8 percent (2.1 percent adjusted for inflation) compared with the revised estimate of $280.30 billion for 2009." This generosity comes from a wide sector:

Individuals	$211.77 billion
Foundations	41.00 billion
Bequests	22.83 billion
Corporations	15.29 billion

Recipients of such generosity represent an eclectic assortment of missions:

Religion	$100.63 billion
Education	41.67 billion
Foundations	33.00 billion
Human services	26.49 billion
Public-society benefit	24.24 billion
Health	22.83 billion
International affairs	15.77 billion
Arts, culture, and humanities	13.28 billion
Environment and animals	6.66 billion
Other	6.32 billion[5]

Financial Reporting

LO1

Understand the basic composition of the financial statements produced for a private not-for-profit organization.

With so much money at stake, the need for not-for-profit organizations to provide adequate and fairly presented financial information is understandable. Current and potential contributors and other interested parties want to know how financially stable these organizations are and how they use the monies they receive. Future gifts or grants are often based, at least in part, on the organization's ability to convince donors that it uses its resources wisely to accomplish stated goals. Financial statements are vital to this

[4] Mark Hrywna, "2010 Top 100: An In-Depth Study of America's Largest Nonprofits," *The NonProfit Times,* November 1, 2010, p. 19.

[5] Giving USA Foundation, *Giving USA 2011,* pp. 4–6.

objective because they report both the resources generated and the spending decisions that have been made.

As the previous two chapters discussed, the Governmental Accounting Standards Board (GASB) has the authority to establish accounting standards for state and local governments and any organization that these governments control, such as governmental not-for-profit organizations. In contrast, the Financial Accounting Standards Board (FASB) sets the accounting standards used by for-profit business organizations and private not-for-profit organizations.

Prior to 1993, private not-for-profit organizations utilized a wide array of financial reporting practices. Statements often varied significantly, depending on the specific type of organization. A fund accounting approach was especially common because of all the restrictions added by donors and grantors. In that year, FASB standardized much of the reporting for private not-for-profit organizations with the issuance of two official standards. FASB *Statement (SFAS) 116,* "Accounting for Contributions Received and Contributions Made," established guidelines for determining when and how donations should be recognized and reported. FASB *Statement 117,* "Financial Statements of Not-for-Profit Organizations," specified the required financial statements and the format to be used by these organizations.[6] These requirements are now part of FASB's *Accounting Standards Codification.*

Several basic goals form the framework for the generally accepted accounting principles for private not-for-profit organizations, including:

1. The financial statements should focus on the entity as a whole.
2. Reporting requirements for private not-for-profit organizations should be similar to those for business entities unless critical differences in the informational needs of financial statement users exist.

The first of these goals is important because it asserts that the organization's financial statements should not be structured around the individual funds that these organizations often use for internal record-keeping. Prior to 1993, the reporting of not-for-profit organizations was often patterned after traditional government accounting with a heavy emphasis on separate fund types. For external reporting purposes, FASB wanted to emphasize the operations and financial position of the entire entity.

The second goal is significant because it allows for the application of many of the same accrual basis techniques used by for-profit business entities in reporting transactions. Consequently, existing authoritative literature for capital leases, pensions, contingent liabilities, and similar issues do not have to be rewritten for private not-for-profit organizations.

LO2

Determine the proper classification for assets that are unrestricted, temporarily restricted, or permanently restricted and explain the method of reporting these categories.

Financial Statements for Private Not-for-Profit Organizations

Although private not-for-profit organizations have much in common with for-profit business entities, three critical differences exist. First, the donations that private not-for-profit organizations receive create transactions that have no counterparts in commercial accounting. Second, these contributions often have donor-imposed restrictions that require their use for a specified purpose or not until a specified time. Third, no single reported indicator can describe performance as effectively as net income does for commercial entities; thus, other indicators are necessary.

These differences suggest the need for a somewhat different set of financial statements for not-for-profit organizations. Consequently, three financial statements must be presented:

1. The *statement of financial position* reports the assets, liabilities, and net assets of these private not-for-profits. The final category, net assets, replaces owners' equity or fund

[6] The American Institute of Certified Public Accountants (AICPA) issues an audit and accounting guide, *Not-for-Profit Organizations,* to provide additional guidance in preparing and auditing financial statements by focusing on procedures that are unique or significant to these organizations. This is not part of the FASB *Accounting Standards Codification.*

balance. The amount of net assets the organization holds must be classified as unrestricted, temporarily restricted, or permanently restricted. This distinction is quite significant because it discloses the use that can be made of the assets being held by the organization.

2. The *statement of activities and changes in net assets* reports revenues, expenses, gains, and losses for the period. Revenues and expenses are determined using the accrual basis of accounting and include depreciation of fixed assets. This statement is structured to present the *change in each category of net assets* for the period.
3. The *statement of cash flows* uses the standard classifications of cash flows from operating activities, investing activities, and financing activities. Cash flows from operating activities may be presented by either the direct or indirect method. Because this statement follows the traditional format for a for-profit business, it will not be discussed in this coverage.

In addition to these three statements, voluntary health and welfare organizations are required to prepare a *statement of functional expenses* (see Exhibit 18.3). Other types of not-for-profit organizations can provide this statement but are not required to do so. Voluntary health and welfare organizations are entities that promote humanitarian activities, such as public health clinics, homeless shelters, the cure of a particular disease, and the like. These organizations might receive some revenues from their activities but, in most cases, rely heavily on support from gifts made by individuals, foundations, government grants, United Way allocations, and similar sources to support their work. These not-for-profit organizations are different from other types such as private universities or hospitals that generate a considerable amount of revenue from services rendered. Normally, voluntary health and welfare organizations depend more on donations, so the wise utilization of these resources is of special importance. The statement of functional expenses provides a detailed schedule of expenses by function (such as various programs and administrative activities) and by object (salaries, supplies, depreciation, etc.).

The availability of this statement allows a very important evaluation to be made of the efficient use of funds: "The cost of badly managed cancer charities isn't just wasted money. People are dying while these outfits mishandle funds that could go toward care."[7]

Statement of Financial Position

Exhibit 18.1 presents the 2010 statement of financial position for ChildFund International, USA.[8] The asset and liability sections resemble those of for-profit enterprises. However, unlike such businesses, individuals and organizations often provide resources to not-for-profit organizations without the expectation of earning a return on their investment. As a result, the concept of owners' equity does not apply. In the place of paid-in-capital and retained earnings, the final section of this statement presents total "net assets," which is simply the excess of the organization's assets over liabilities (see Point A).

Importantly, net assets are presented in three categories: *unrestricted, temporarily restricted,* and *permanently restricted.* Specific requirements must be imposed by donors from outside the organization before an asset amount is classified as restricted. For that reason, internally designated assets (often referred to as "board designated") continue to be classified as unrestricted for financial statement purposes. ChildFund International, USA, indicates that the organization holds unrestricted net assets of $16,033,869 (Point B) that can be spent completely at the discretion of the organization's officials.

Temporarily restricted assets are designated by an external party for a particular purpose or for use in a future time period. For example, a private college could receive a

[7] Bill Shapiro, "Check Your Charity!" *Time*, June 13, 2011, p. 81.

[8] With an attitude that seems appropriate for a charity that operates primarily on donations, the website makes the following statement. "Because we are proud of what you help us accomplish: We want you to study our Annual Report and Financial Statements. We want you to know that you can Give with Confidence."

EXHIBIT 18.1

CHILDFUND INTERNATIONAL, USA **Consolidated Statement of Financial Position** **June 30, 2010**	
Assets	**2010**
Cash and cash equivalents	$22,794,361
Receivable from affiliates	2,348,499
Grants receivable	3,703,021
Accounts receivable and other assets	3,339,469
Investments	30,433,241
Beneficial interests in trusts	6,377,558
Property, plant and equipment, net	14,083,289
Total assets	$83,079,438
Liabilities and net assets	
Liabilities:	
Accounts payable and accrued expenses	$13,581,942
Accrued benefit liability	8,474,515
Total liabilities	22,056,457
Net assets: Ⓐ	
Unrestricted	16,033,869 Ⓑ
Temporarily restricted	32,871,076 Ⓒ
Permanently restricted	12,118,036 Ⓓ
Total net assets	61,022,981
Commitments and contingencies	
Total liabilities and net assets	$83,079,483

See notes to consolidated financial statements.

grant to fund medical research. Until properly spent, amounts received from that grant are reported as temporarily restricted for that particular use. Alternatively, the college could be awarded a grant supporting general education programs over the next three years. Because of the time designation, amounts received or promised for use in future periods also are viewed as temporarily restricted.

Assets that are temporarily restricted represent resources that are expected to be released from restriction based on performance of a specific act or the passage of time. The statement of financial position published for ChildFund International, USA, discloses that outside donors had restricted $32,871,076 of its net assets as of June 30, 2010, for a particular purpose or until a specific point in time (Point C). Likewise, the statement of financial position for the University of Notre Dame as of June 30, 2010, indicates temporarily restricted net assets of more than $2.27 billion.

In contrast, permanently restricted assets are those that are expected to remain restricted for as long as the organization exists, although some or all of the income is available for general or specified use. A note to the 2010 financial statements of Yale University explains its permanently restricted net asset total of $2.59 billion: "The University records as permanently restricted net assets the original amount of gifts which donors have given to be maintained in perpetuity ('donor restricted endowment funds')." In the same manner, note disclosure to the financial statements of ChildFund International indicates that the $12,118,036 in permanently restricted net assets (Point D) are "net assets that generally represent contributions and other inflows of assets whose use by ChildFund International is permanently limited by donor-imposed stipulations that neither expire by passage of time nor can be fulfilled or otherwise removed by actions of ChildFund International."

LO2

Determine the proper classification for assets that are unrestricted, temporarily restricted, or permanently restricted and explain the method of reporting these categories.

Statement of Activities and Changes in Net Assets

Exhibit 18.2 presents the statement of activities and changes in net assets for ChildFund International, USA. Note the format adopted here: A separate column is used to present the increases and decreases in each of the three categories of net assets: unrestricted, temporarily restricted, and permanently restricted. The final totals agree with the net asset balances presented on the statement of financial position.

As stated earlier, private not-for-profit organizations receive a significant portion of their resources from contributions. A primary purpose of the statement of activities is to provide a clear picture of those donations and any restrictions that might have been attached. In Exhibit 18.2, public support (sponsorships, contributions, and grants) is reported separately from revenues such as service fees and investment income for which an earning process exists. For the year ended June 30, 2010, ChildFund International, USA, reports (Point E) that it received $43.2 million of public support that was unrestricted, $169.7 million that was temporarily restricted, and only $47,587 that was permanently restricted.

ChildFund reports total earned revenues for the year of only $3.1 million (Point F). Clearly, this charity gets the vast majority of its revenues from donations and grants. In comparison, as shown at the beginning of this chapter, the YMCA of the United States obtains over $4.2 billion (nearly 73 percent of all revenues) from providing program services. That is one aspect that makes this statement interesting—revenues can be generated in a number of ways by a private not-for-profit organization.

Expenses and Release of Temporarily Restricted Net Assets

All expenses are reported in a statement of activities (Point G) solely within the Unrestricted Net Assets column. In that way, this first column can be viewed as a reflection of current operations for the organization. For ChildFund International, USA, unrestricted public support and revenues totaled $214.0 million while the organization's expenses amounted to $212.9 million. Nonoperating gains and losses are then reported separately.

Recording all expenses solely within the unrestricted net assets causes a practical problem in that some expenses are incurred in connection with temporarily restricted net assets. A gift, for example, could be made specifically to support the salaries of the organization's employees. If the contribution is reported as temporarily restricted, how can the eventual salary expense be presented as unrestricted? Mechanically, that does not match.

When a temporary restriction (either time or usage) is fulfilled, that amount is immediately reclassified as unrestricted. Therefore, if an expense is incurred to meet a donor stipulation, both the expense and the contribution appear in the statement of activities in the Unrestricted column in the same time period. As in Exhibit 18.2, this reclassification is reflected in the statement of activities by a line at the bottom of the Public Support and Revenue section that increases unrestricted net assets and decreases temporarily restricted net assets.

ChildFund International, USA, shows approximately $167.8 million (Point H) reclassified as "net assets released from restrictions." Thus, that amount of temporarily restricted net assets was no longer restricted because of one or more of the following:

1. Money was appropriately expended for an expense as designated by the donor.
2. Money was appropriately expended for an asset as designated by the donor.
3. A donor restriction based on time was satisfied.

To illustrate this important concept, assume that in Year 1, a private not-for-profit organization receives three cash gifts of $10,000 each. The donor has specified that the first gift must be used for employee salaries. The second gift is for the purchase of equipment. The third gift must be held until Year 2 before being expended. In Year 1, the statement of activities will show all three gifts as increases in Temporarily Restricted Net Assets.

Assume that this example is extended into Year 2 when the first two gifts are properly spent and the time restriction on the third gift is satisfied. For the first gift, cash is decreased and a salary expense is recorded in the Unrestricted Net Assets column. At the same time, $10,000 is reclassified on the statement of activities from the Temporarily Restricted column to the Unrestricted column in the same manner as the $167.8 million in Exhibit 18.2.

EXHIBIT 18.2

CHILDFUND INTERNATIONAL, USA
Consolidated Statement of Activities
Year Ended June 30, 2010

	Unrestricted	Temporarily Restricted	Permanently Restricted	Total 2010
Public support:				
Sponsorships:				
U.S. sponsors	$ —	$ 89,874,604	$ —	$ 89,874,604
International sponsors	—	54,723,629	—	54,723,629
Special gifts from sponsors for children	—	17,404,318	—	17,404,318
Total sponsorships	—	162,002,551	—	162,002,551
Contributions:				
General contributions	10,726,758	7,079,210	47,587	17,853,555
Major gifts and bequests	2,788,657	621,317	—	3,409,974
Gifts in kind	2,256,854	—	—	2,256,854
Total contributions	15,772,269	7,700,527	47,587	23,520,383
Grants:				
Grants and contracts	27,388,754	—	—	27,388,754
Total public support Ⓔ	43,161,023	169,703,078	47,587	212,911,688
Revenue:				
Investment income and currency transactions	1,203,364	1,859	—	1,205,223
Service fees and other	1,859,144	—	—	1,859,144
Total revenue Ⓕ	3,062,508	1,859	—	3,064,367
Net assets released from restrictions: Ⓗ				
Satisfaction of program and time restrictions	167,767,254	(167,767,254)	—	—
Total public support and revenue	213,990,785	1,937,683	47,587	215,976,055
Expenses: Ⓖ				
Program: Ⓘ				
Basic education	61,535,166	—	—	61,535,166
Health and sanitation	44,145,849	—	—	44,145,849
Nutrition	14,688,825	—	—	14,688,825
Early childhood development	19,958,484	—	—	19,958,484
Micro enterprise	20,408,024	—	—	20,408,024
Emergencies	11,865,159	—	—	11,865,159
Total program	172,601,507	—	—	172,601,507
Supporting services: Ⓙ				
Fund raising	23,420,237	—	—	23,420,237
Management and general	16,849,426	—	—	16,849,426
Total supporting services	40,269,663	—	—	40,269,663
Total expenses from operations	212,871,170	—	—	212,871,170
Change in net assets from operations	1,119,615	1,937,683	47,587	3,104,885
Nonoperating gains (losses):				
Realized loss on investments	(108,273)	(96)	—	(108,369)
Unrealized gain (loss) on investments	2,638,097	10,562	—	2,648,659
Change in value of trusts	—	143,395	344,970	488,365
Change in accrued benefit liability other than net periodic costs	(1,477,893)	—	—	(1,477,893)
Total nonoperating gains (losses)	1,051,931	153,861	344,970	1,550,762
Change in net assets	2,171,546	2,091,544	392,557	4,655,647
Net assets at beginning of year	13,862,323	30,779,532	11,725,479	56,367,334
Net assets at end of year	$16,033,869	$ 32,871,076	$12,118,036	$ 61,022,981

See notes to consolidated financial statements.

For the second gift, equipment (an asset) is increased and cash is decreased, but the same reclassification is made to indicate that this restriction has been met.

A $10,000 reclassification must also be made for the third gift even though it has not been spent. It was restricted only as to time, and the required period has passed. In year 2, the statement of activities will show a total of $30,000 in Net Assets Released from Restriction as an increase in unrestricted net assets with an equal decrease in temporarily restricted net assets.

An alternative in accounting does exist for the long-lived asset bought with the restricted gift. A time restriction can be specified by the donor or assumed by the organization for the use of the asset. For example, the donor might require the organization to hold the equipment for its entire expected life or for a specific number of years. In that case, no immediate reclassification is made from temporarily restricted net assets to unrestricted net assets because use of the asset is not completely at the discretion of the organization. Instead, a gradual reclassification equal to the depreciation of the asset is made each year.

Program Services and Supporting Services

Detailed information about the expenses incurred by a private not-for-profit organization is considered important to contributors. A primary concern of contributors is the extent to which a charity is using the resources provided to fulfill its organizational mission. Is money used, for example, to cure disease or wasted on bloated fund-raising campaigns or executive salaries? For this reason, expenses must be presented in two broad categories: program services and supporting services.

Program services encompass the organization's activities relating to its mission. Within this category, several programs may be reported or only one. ChildFund International, USA (Point I) discloses six program categories: basic education, health and sanitation, nutrition, early childhood development, micro enterprise, and emergencies. *Supporting service* costs (Point J) consist of administrative costs (management and general costs) and fund-raising expenses. These activities are not regarded as directly related to any of the organization's stated missions. Analysts frequently use the ratio of program service expenses to total expenses as one way to evaluate the efficiency of not-for-profits. The Better Business Bureau has suggested that ratio values of less than 65 percent are not desirable.[9] ChildFund International, USA, reports a ratio of 81.1 percent ($172.6 million/$212.9 million) for the year ended June 30, 2010.

As mentioned, below the Expenses and Supporting Services sections in Exhibit 18.2, ChildFund International, USA, reports "Nonoperating gains (losses)" dealing with investment transactions and changes in value and other nonoperating items. Investments in equity securities with readily determinable market values and all debt investments must be adjusted to fair value.[10] A not-for-profit entity reports the resulting unrealized gains and losses in the statement of activities. These entities report all gains and losses on investments, along with dividend and interest income, as increases or decreases in unrestricted net assets unless the donor explicitly restricted this income.

LO3

Explain the purpose and the construction of a statement of functional expenses.

Statement of Functional Expenses

Exhibit 18.3 presents the statement of functional expenses for ChildFund International, USA. Because contributors are concerned with how their gifts are used, this statement provides a detailed analysis of expenses by both function and object. The columns represent functions and include the six previously identified program services followed by the supporting services of fund-raising as well as management and general expenses. These are the same categories reported on the statement of activities, and column totals agree with the operating expenses reported on that statement. The rows list expenses according to their nature—for example, subsidy for children, program grants, professional services, and advertising and public education.

[9] The Better Business Bureau provides an excellent guideline "Implementation Guide to BBB Wise Giving Alliance Standards for Charity Accountability" at www.bbb.org/us/Charity-Evaluation/ to aid interested parties in assessing the efficiency and organizational structure of a charity.

[10] The system of classifying marketable securities into portfolios such as trading securities and available-for-sale securities that for-profit business entities must utilize is not applied to private not-for-profit organizations.

EXHIBIT 18.3

CHILDFUND INTERNATIONAL, USA
Consolidated Statement of Functional Expenses
Year Ended June 30, 2010

	Program Services							Supporting Services			Program and Supporting Services
	Basic Education	Health and Sanitation	Nutrition	Early Childhood Development	Micro Enterprise	Emergencies	Total Program Services	Fund Raising	Management and General	Total Supporting Services	2010
Subsidy for children	$43,196,939	$20,530,568	$ 9,321,761	$14,982,081	$13,574,742	$ 3,759,394	$105,365,485	$ —	$ —	$ —	$105,365,485
Program grants	6,355,043	15,018,444	2,506,605	1,089,745	2,859,082	5,795,178	33,624,097	—	—	—	33,624,097
Supplies	305,458	219,139	72,915	99,073	101,305	58,898	856,788	120,780	428,144	548,924	1,405,712
Occupancy	533,438	382,692	127,335	173,016	176,913	102,857	1,496,251	69,143	364,458	433,601	1,929,852
Professional services	404,271	290,028	96,502	131,122	134,076	77,951	1,133,950	144,780	568,099	712,879	1,846,829
Contract services	653,316	468,695	155,951	211,900	216,671	125,970	1,832,503	1,340,864	1,710,944	3,051,808	4,884,311
Travel	642,228	460,740	153,303	208,302	212,994	123,834	1,801,401	239,775	226,676	466,451	2,267,852
Conferences and meetings	242,880	174,244	57,977	78,777	80,551	46,832	681,261	112,685	158,818	271,503	952,764
Automobile and truck expense	175,852	126,157	41,977	57,036	58,321	33,908	493,251	16,562	—	16,562	509,813
Advertising and public education	86,479	62,040	20,642	28,049	28,680	16,675	242,565	17,126,031	293,156	17,419,187	17,661,752
Equipment purchases and rentals	227,233	163,019	54,242	73,701	75,361	43,815	637,371	55,927	329,423	385,350	1,022,721
Telephone and cables	257,184	184,507	61,391	83,416	85,295	49,590	721,383	81,057	201,372	282,429	1,003,812
Postage and freight	503,881	361,488	120,279	163,430	167,111	97,158	1,413,347	107,744	808,336	916,080	2,329,427
Staff training	161,025	115,520	38,438	52,227	53,403	31,049	451,662	11,776	23,796	35,572	487,234
Miscellaneous expenses	181,285	130,055	43,274	58,798	60,123	34,955	508,490	285,540	1,896,614	2,182,154	2,690,644
Total expenses before personnel costs and other expenses	53,926,512	38,687,336	12,872,592	17,490,673	17,884,628	10,398,064	151,259,805	19,712,664	7,009,836	26,722,500	177,982,305
Personnel costs	7,208,253	5,171,262	1,720,655	2,337,944	2,390,604	1,389,890	20,218,608	3,647,137	8,915,630	12,562,767	32,781,375
Depreciation & interest	400,401	287,251	95,578	129,867	132,792	77,205	1,123,094	60,436	923,960	984,396	2,107,490
Total expenses from operations	$61,535,166	$44,145,849	$14,688,825	$19,958,484	$20,408,024	$11,865,159	$172,601,507	$23,420,237	$16,849,426	$40,269,663	$212,871,170

See accompanying notes to consolidated financial statements.

As a result of the scrutiny placed on the amount that a private not-for-profit organization spends on fund-raising, the allocation of costs is quite important. At one time, joint costs expended for fund-raising appeals that also contained educational literature were routinely divided evenly between fund-raising and program services. Thus, most direct mail solicitations for contributions were accompanied by informational pamphlets and the like so that a significant portion of the cost of the mailing could be reflected as a program service expense such as educating the public.

Now, however, a portion of the costs of such fund-raising campaigns can still be assigned to program service costs but only if several criteria are met.[11] The literature that is mailed or otherwise distributed must include a specific call for action that would have been made even without the fund-raising request. This appeal cannot be directed purely at potential contributors, and the desired action must be specific and help accomplish the entity's overall mission. If all of these criteria are met, some or all of the costs associated with this call for action campaign should be reported under program services rather than fund-raising.

For this reason, the June 30, 2010, financial statements of the American Heart Association, Inc., included the following note:

> The Association conducts joint activities (activities benefiting multiple programs and/or supporting services) that include fund raising appeals. Those activities primarily included direct mail campaigns and special events. The costs of conducting those joint activities were allocated as follows in 2010 and 2009 (in thousands):

	2010	2009
Research	$ —	$ 763
Public health education	90,625	106,569
Professional education and training	4,621	2,840
Community services	4,727	5,809
Management and general	14,814	17,778
Fund-raising	53,236	61,177
Total joint costs	$168,023	$194,936

Accounting for Contributions

LO4

Report the various types of contributions that a private not-for-profit organization can receive.

Contributions are obviously a major source of support for most private not-for-profits. Contributions are unconditional transfers of cash or other resources to an entity in a voluntary nonreciprocal transaction and should be recognized as revenue in the period received at their fair value.

Restricted contributions specify how the donated amounts must be used and are recognized as increases in either temporarily restricted net assets or permanently restricted net assets when the promise is received. However, conditional promises to give are not recognized as revenue until the conditions are met. Conditions are different from restrictions. Conditional promises require some future action on the part of the not-for-profit organization before the asset will be transferred.

Thus, a $1,000 pledge to be paid in eight months that is restricted for the purchase of library books is recorded immediately as follows because it is not conditional. However, a pledge for $90,000 to be made if a famous biology professor is hired is not recorded unless that action is taken.

	Debit	Credit
Pledge Receivable	1,000	
Temporarily Restricted Net Assets—Contributions		1,000
Unconditional pledge of gift made to organization to buy library books.		

Because contribution revenue is recognized at fair value, the estimated uncollectible portion of pledged amounts should be deducted. An allowance account is established to

[11] For more information, see FASB *Accounting Standards Codification*, section 958.720.45.

present the receivable at its expected net realizable value. Furthermore, pledges that are not expected to be collected within one year are discounted to present value using an appropriate interest rate, such as the organization's incremental borrowing rate or the rate of return on its investment portfolio. Over time, the receivable is adjusted toward the face value of the pledge, and the amortization is classified as contribution revenue rather than interest revenue.

For example, as of June 30, 2010, Georgetown University reported gross contributions receivable of $203.1 million. The balance reported was reduced by (1) $7.0 million to arrive at the present value of the expected cash flows and (2) an allowance for doubtful accounts of $31.0 million. Such allowances are often quite high because not-for-profits have very limited ways of forcing a donor to fulfill a pledge. Thus, this school reported a net contribution receivable balance of $165.0 million as a result of its unconditional pledges. A note to the financial statements indicated that the discount rate for determining present value ranged from 2.46 percent to 8.29 percent.

Cash is not the only type of support provided to not-for-profits. Many organizations receive donations of materials intended either to be used by the charity itself (such as vehicles, office furniture, and computers) or to be distributed to needy groups or individuals (food, clothing, and toys). Organizations such as the Salvation Army and Goodwill Industries use these types of donations as a central resource essential to the charity's ongoing operation of its mission.

Because donated supplies and other materials provide resources for the organization, these contributions are reported as support unless the organization cannot use or sell them. Although a value is sometimes apparent (for example, if a new vehicle is given), donations such as used clothing, furniture, and toys can be difficult to assess. In such cases, the use of estimates and averages is allowed provided that they reasonably approximate the results of detailed measurements.

Assume as an illustration that a local voluntary health and welfare organization begins a drive to gather furniture and clothing for needy families living in the area. It receives the following items:

Bed	$ 800 fair value
Tables and chairs	420 fair value
New clothing	960 fair value
Used clothing	190 estimated resale value
Total	$2,370

In addition, one patron donates $32,000 in marketable securities to the charity with the stipulation that the investments are to be held in perpetuity with all income used to support local needy families.

Assuming that the charity distributed the furniture and clothing almost immediately, the not-for-profit organization records the following journal entries:

Account	Debit	Credit
Inventory of Donated Materials	2,370	
Unrestricted Net Assets—Contributions		2,370
To record gifts made to organization to be distributed to needy families.		
Community Service Expenses—Assistance to needy	2,370	
Inventory of Donated Materials		2,370
To record distribution of furniture and clothing to needy families.		
Investments in Marketable Securities	32,000	
Permanently Restricted Net Assets—Contributions		32,000
To record donation of investments to be held by the organization forever with all income used to aid needy families in the local area.		

In connection with the marketable securities, the organization will record income, when it is eventually earned, as an increase in temporarily restricted net assets. That money

Discussion Question

ARE TWO SETS OF GAAP REALLY NEEDED FOR COLLEGES AND UNIVERSITIES?

As this and the previous chapter have discussed, public colleges and universities must follow GASB standards. For that reason, these schools have been directed to use the same reporting model that state and local governments follow, although such schools frequently view themselves as consisting solely of business-type activities so that they only produce fund financial statements.

Private not-for-profit colleges and universities adhere to FASB Accounting Standards Codification requirements and prepare financial statements as illustrated in this chapter. GAAP for public schools comes from GASB; for private schools, it comes from FASB.

Readers of college and university financial statements may want to compare the data presented by various institutions. The use of this information is especially important to potential donors who are attempting to evaluate each school's efficiency and effectiveness in utilizing the funding that it receives.

Does the division between the financial reporting appropriate for public colleges and universities and that utilized by private colleges and universities serve these statement users well? Are these two types of schools so different that they require two separate sets of generally accepted accounting principles created by two official bodies? Should one set of GAAP apply to all schools? Should only one group be in charge of developing GAAP for colleges and universities?

must be used for the purpose designated by the donor. It is reported as temporarily restricted until the purpose is met. Then, it will be released from restriction and reclassified on the statement of activities as unrestricted net assets.

LO4

Report the various types of contributions that a private not-for-profit organization can receive.

Donations of Works of Art and Historical Treasures

In 1990, FASB issued an exposure draft of a proposed official pronouncement that would have required a recipient to record all contributions, including works of art and museum pieces, as assets with a corresponding increase in revenues. Rarely has an accounting proposal created such adverse public reaction. FASB was deluged with more than 1,000 letters, virtually all in opposition to the exposure draft. The argument against recognizing additions to such collections is that works of art and historical pieces do not provide the same types of benefits as contributions of cash or investments. Items held for research or public exhibit create little or no direct increase in cash flows. In fact, most such items require continual outflows of cash for insurance, maintenance, and other preservation expenses. Thus, they are not viewed as assets in the traditional sense. Opponents of the exposure draft argued that recognizing such donations as revenues would mislead potential donors into overrating the organization's financial strength.

This opposition apparently influenced FASB because when the new principle was issued in 1993, gifts of works of art, historical treasures, and the like were handled differently from other donated property. No recognition of these contributions is required if they are (1) added to a collection for public exhibition, education, or research; (2) protected and preserved; and (3) covered by an organization policy whereby any proceeds generated by a sale will be used to acquire other collection items.

For this reason, a note to Georgetown University's 2010 financial statements explains that the school has elected not to capitalize the cost or value of its collection of works of art, historical treasures, and similar assets. However, a note to Princeton University's financial statements for the year ended June 30, 2010, indicates a different approach: "Art objects acquired through June 30, 1973, are carried at insurable values at that date because it is not practicable to determine the historical cost or market value at the date of gift. Art objects acquired subsequent to June 30, 1973, are recorded at cost or fair value at the date of gift."

A subtle difference between private not-for-profit accounting and that utilized for state and local government units is evident here. The criteria for qualifying as a work of art or historical treasure are basically the same. However, the choice for private not-for-profits is between recording the revenue and asset versus no reporting. Governments do not have the same option. Under governmental accounting, the contributed revenue must be recorded. The reporting entity then has the choice of recording either an asset or an expense when the donated item is a work of art or historical treasure.

If a private not-for-profit organization does record art works or historical treasures as assets, the question of recording depreciation is again raised. Private not-for-profit organizations are not required to record depreciation for such assets if the lives are viewed as extraordinarily long. The assumption must be that the organization has the technological and financial ability to preserve an item and that the value is such that the organization has committed to that goal. Thus, Princeton reports $74 million in "fine arts objects" but does not depreciate them.

LO4

Report the various types of contributions that a private not-for-profit organization can receive.

Holding Contributions for Others

Some not-for-profit organizations, such as the United Way, raise donations that will be distributed to other designated charities, or they accept gifts that must be conveyed to other specified beneficiaries. A community group might solicit donations by allowing the donor to identify the charity to be benefited. An independent organization might raise money solely for the use of the athletic programs of a separate college or university.

> When NFPs act as agents, trustees, or intermediaries helping donors to make a contribution to another entity or individual, they do not receive a contribution when they receive the assets, nor do they make a contribution when they disburse the assets to the other entity or individual. Instead, they act as go-betweens, passing the assets from the donor through their organization to the specified entity or individual.[12]

Such conveyances raise questions as to the appropriate recording to be made by the donor, the initial recipient, and the specified beneficiary. For example, assume that Donor A gives $10,000 in cash to Not-for-Profit Organization M (NPO–M) that must then be conveyed to Not-for-Profit Organization Z (NPO–Z).

- Does Donor A record an expense when it initially conveys the cash to NPO–M, or must there be an actual transfer to NPO–Z before Donor A records an expense?
- Upon receipt, does NPO–M report a contribution revenue of $10,000 or a liability to NPO–Z?
- At what point should NPO–Z recognize a contribution revenue as a result of this gift?

For a conveyance of this type, the donor normally records an expense when it conveys the property (to NPO–M) because it has relinquished control over the asset. In this case, Donor A makes the following entry:

Donor A—Relinquishes Control		
Expense—Charitable Contribution	10,000	
Cash		10,000

However, if the donor retains the right to redirect the use of the gift (has variance powers) or if the donation can be revoked, Donor A continues to maintain control over the asset and should not record an expense until it relinquishes that authority. Donor A makes the following entry instead of the previous one:

[12] AICPA, *Audit & Accounting Guide, Not-for-Profit Entities,* March 1, 2010, para. 5.08.

Donor A—Retains Variance Power		
Refundable Advance to NPO–M	10,000	
Cash		10,000

The initial recipient usually records a liability to the eventual beneficiary for such gifts (rather than contribution revenue). The money is simply passing through the not-for-profit organization and is not creating any direct benefit. Thus, normally, NPO–M will make the following journal entry for the money received:

NPO–M—Donation Passing through to Beneficiary		
Cash	10,000	
Liability to NPO–Z		10,000

However, if the donor retains the right to revoke or redirect the gift, NPO–M will not be certain as to whether the money will actually go to the beneficiary or back to the donor. Thus, if the donor retains such rights, the preceding entry must be changed to the following:

NPO–M—Donor Retains Control over Gift		
Cash	10,000	
Refundable Advance from Donor A		10,000

In this type of arrangement, NPO–M records a contribution revenue and a contribution expense in only one situation. If the donor has not retained the right to revoke or redirect the gift and has given the initial charity variance powers that allow it to change the beneficiary, then NPO–M controls the asset. In that case, NPO–M records the following entry rather than either of the previous two. Subsequently, it records an expense when the $10,000 goes to the eventual beneficiary.

NPO–M—Holds Variance Powers		
Cash	10,000	
Temporarily Restricted Net Assets—Contributions		10,000

The beneficiary of such a gift must record contribution revenue at some point. If the donor has retained the right to revoke or redirect the gift or if NPO–M is given variance powers to change the beneficiary, the named beneficiary makes no entry until it receives the gift. Too much uncertainty exists until then. The beneficiary really has no power to control the property's movement until it possesses the item. However, if the donor has not kept the right to revoke or redirect the gift and NPO–M has not received variance powers, the uncertainty is eliminated so that the eventual recipient records the revenue as soon as the donor makes the gift to the first not-for-profit organization:

NPO–Z—Gift to Be Received		
Contribution Receivable	10,000	
Contribution Revenue		10,000

The above entry also needs to indicate whether the donation was unrestricted, temporarily restricted, or permanently restricted.

LO4

Report the various types of contributions that a private not-for-profit organization can receive.

Contributed Services

Donated services are an especially significant means of support for many not-for-profits. The number of volunteers working in some organizations can reach into the thousands. Charities rely heavily on these individuals to fill administrative positions and to serve in fund-raising and program activities. For example, for the year ended June 30, 2010, the American Heart Association recognized more than $5.1 million in contributed services. The notes to its financial statements indicate that nearly 92 percent of this amount related to research.

Not-for-profits recognize contributed services as revenue but only if the service provided meets one of two criteria:

1. Creates or enhances a nonfinancial asset.
2. Requires a specialized skill possessed by the contributor that would typically need to be purchased if not donated.

Examples of the first type include donated labor by carpenters, electricians, and masons. If these services enhance nonfinancial assets, the organization recognizes the fair value of the services as an increase in both fixed assets and contribution revenue.

Examples of the second type of donation include legal or accounting services that are recognized as both an expense and a revenue when contributed. It is a common practice for professionals to bill a not-for-profit entity for the fair value of services rendered and then deduct an amount (or, possibly, the entire charge) from the balance as a contribution to the organization.

Contributed services (such as volunteer servers at a soup kitchen) are not recognized as revenue if they fail to meet either of these criteria. This is not because the services have no value but because of the difficulty in measuring that value. For example, the American Heart Association's financial statements explain,

> The Association receives services from a large number of volunteers who give significant amounts of their time to the Association's programs, fund raising campaigns, and management. No amounts have been reflected for these types of donated services, as they do not meet the criteria for recognition.

To illustrate, assume that a certified public accountant provides accounting services that would cost a local charity $20,000 if not donated. Assume also that a carpenter donated materials ($40,000) and labor ($35,000) to construct an addition to the charity's facilities. The not-for-profit organization records the following journal entries:

General and Administrative Expenses—Accounting Services	20,000	
Unrestricted Net Assets—Contributed Services		20,000
To record contribution of professional services.		
Buildings and Improvements	75,000	
Unrestricted Net Assets—Contributed Services		35,000
Unrestricted Net Assets—Contributed Materials		40,000
To record contribution of professional services and materials.		

Donated services do not have to be limited to work done by individuals. The 2010 financial statements for the Girl Scouts of the USA contained the following note:

> The Organization receives in-kind contributions primarily in the form of donated advertising on television, radio stations and in print. The value of such in-kind contributions, based upon information provided by a third-party advertising service, approximated $6,831,000 and $194,000 for the years ended September 30, 2010 and 2009, respectively, and is reflected in the accompanying consolidated financial statements as contributed advertising revenue and communications expense.

As with the services referred to previously that were provided by the certified public accountant, this donation is recognized as both a contributed service revenue and an appropriate expense. Many charities receive considerable value through such donations.

Exchange Transactions

Exchange transactions are reciprocal transfers when both parties give and receive something of value. Many not-for-profit organizations have regular charges. The local YMCA might have monthly membership dues for exercise classes and locker fees, whereas ChildFund International has monthly sponsorships. The reminders that arrive in the mail each month look very similar, but should the accounting for both be the same?

Dues and fees are frequently considered reciprocal transfers; the member typically receives benefits in the form of newsletters, journals, and use of organization facilities and services. Because these transactions do not meet the definition of a contribution, they follow normal accrual basis accounting and are recognized as revenue when earned.

However, if the individual derives little or no benefit (beyond personal satisfaction) from the monthly payments, the conveyance is viewed (at least in part) as a contribution. Logically, the not-for-profit organization should report the excess amount as a contribution.

Recording membership dues as either earned revenue or contributed revenue causes no net effect on the financial statements but does shift the way in which the organization appears to gain support. For example, assume that a not-for-profit organization receives $5,000 in dues from its membership. These members receive a journal and several other benefits valued at $3,600. The organization reports the receipt of this money as follows:

Cash	5,000	
Unrestricted Net Assets—Revenue from Dues		3,600
Unrestricted Net Assets—Contributions		1,400
To record receipt of membership dues where members receive benefits valued at $3,600.		

LO5

Understand the impact of a tax-exempt status.

Tax-Exempt Status

A note to The Museum of Modern Art's 2010 financial statements explained that this not-for-profit organization is "exempt from tax under Section 501(c)(3) of the Internal Revenue Code." Just as there are many different types of not-for-profit organizations, there are numerous tax-exempt statuses that influence what the entity can and cannot do. Although this is not a taxation textbook, no coverage of not-for-profit organizations is complete without a short overview of tax rules. The following explains three of the most common tax-exempt statuses.

Section 501(c)(3) of the tax code applies to not-for-profit organizations that are charitable, educational, or scientific. At the end of 2009, over 71 percent of nonprofit organizations in the United States (in excess of 1.1 million) held a Section 501(c)(3) tax status.[13] An organization can apply for this status by completing IRS Form 1023, *Application for Recognition of Exemption under Section 501(c)(3) of Internal Revenue Code.* (http://www.irs.gov/pub/irs-pdf/f1023.pdf).

Not surprising, many of the best-known not-for-profit organizations qualify as Section 501(c)(3) entities. They do not pay federal income tax on income (although not-for-profit organizations are generally subject to taxation on any unrelated business income they generate). In most cases, these organizations are also exempt from paying state income tax.

One of the primary benefits of Section 501(c)(3) status is that a donor may take a charitable donation to these organizations as a reduction in his or her taxable income. In addition, such entities qualify for the benefit of a nonprofit postal permit that can reduce mailing charges considerably. Although these organizations may participate in a small amount of lobbying, they cannot engage in political election campaign activity.

Many other types of nonprofit organizations do exist for tax purposes. At the end of 2009, there were 111,849 civic leagues and welfare organizations, 77,811 fraternal beneficiary societies, 72,801 business leagues and chambers of commerce and thousands of others.[14] For example, AARP, Inc., is also a not-for-profit organization, but it is tax exempt based on Section 501(c)(4) of the Internal Revenue Code, which is a status that is

[13] www.nccsdataweb.urban.org/PubApps/profile1.php.

[14] Ibid.

reserved for organizations that function exclusively for the promotion of social welfare. They are often referred to as *advocacy groups* because they operate primarily to further the general welfare of the people of their community. Again, income earned by the organization is not taxed at the federal level although it often is by the states. When individuals or corporations make donations to these organizations, they are not entitled to a tax deduction on their federal income tax return. Likewise, dues or member fees paid to these groups do not qualify as tax deductible. As could be imagined for such advocacy groups, they are allowed to lobby and may engage in political election campaign activity. They do not qualify for a nonprofit postal permit unless they are also an educational organization.

Finally, the website for the Internal Revenue Service (www.irs.gov) indicates that

> Section 501(c)(6) of the Internal Revenue Code provides for the exemption of business leagues, chambers of commerce, real estate boards, boards of trade, and professional football leagues, which are not organized for profit and no part of the net earnings of which inures to the benefit of any private shareholder or individual.

Section 501(c)(6) organizations do not pay federal income taxes but are frequently required to pay state income taxes. Membership dues are tax deductible so long as they are viewed as ordinary and necessary business expenses. Within certain limits, such entities can lobby and engage in political election campaign activity. Like a Section 501(c)(4), 501(c)(6) entities are allowed a nonprofit postal permit but only if they qualify as an educational organization.

Thus, although private not-for-profits are often viewed as a single group, in reality, as just these three categories indicate, the tax laws and regulations include numerous distinctions among the various types of organizations.

Most tax-exempt organizations are required to submit a Form 990 (*Return of Organization Exempt from Income Tax,* http://www.irs.gov/pub/irs-pdf/f990.pdf) or Form 990-EZ along with Schedule A to the Internal Revenue Service each year in order to maintain their tax-exempt status. The Form 990 requires each of these organizations to disclose an extensive amount of information about its operations. For many interested parties, the Form 990 is a better source of information than the entity's financial statements. Groups that study and report on charities and other not-for-profits usually do so by gathering pertinent information from these forms.[15]

The information disclosed in a Form 990 is extensive and available to the public even if financial statements are not issued. A few of the topics included in this document are:

- Part VII—Compensation of Officers, Directors, Trustees, Key Employees, Highest Compensated Employees, and Independent Contractors
- Part VIII—Statement of Revenues
- Part IX—Statement of Functional Expenses
- Part X—Balance Sheet

LO6

Account for both mergers and acquisitions of not-for-profit organizations.

Mergers and Acquisitions

> "The story is the same across the country. The once-booming nonprofit sector is in the midst of a shakeout, leaving many Americans without services and culling weak groups from the strong. Hit by a drop in donations and government funding in the wake of a deep recession, nonprofits—from arts councils to food banks—are undergoing a painful restructuring, including mergers, acquisitions, collaborations, cutbacks and closings."[16]

> "Five United Way chapters in northern New Jersey—Morris County, North Essex, Somerset County, Sussex County and Warren County—will merge Jan. 3 following a year of talks on

[15] The Form 1023 filed by the YMCA of the United States can be viewed at http://www.ymca.net/organizational-profile/form_1023.pdf. It is well over 220 pages long. The Form 990 filed by United Cerebral Palsy can be viewed at www.ucp.org/ucp_generalsub.cfm/1/3/11217. It is 40 pages long although it can extend to many more pages than that (the Form 990 for the University of Richmond is 71 pages, as an example).

[16] Shelly, Banjo, and Mitra Kalita, "Once-Robust Charity Sector Hit with Mergers, Closings," *The Wall Street Journal (online),* January 31, 2010.

> how to increase their fundraising, now a combined $15 million a year, and operate more efficiently in the face of a prolonged economic slowdown that has severely hurt many charities that depend on donations from United Way."[17]

Mergers and acquisitions have become extremely prevalent for not-for-profits. Many reasons exist for two or more of these organizations to come together, such as more efficient use of resources to achieve common goals, cost cutting through efficiencies of size, attempts to rescue charities that are suffering financially because of the recession, and expanding the scope of an organization's outreach.

Accounting for such combinations utilizes many of the same techniques demonstrated in the early chapters of this textbook in connection with the consolidation of for-profit companies. However, several unique situations can be encountered in creating combined statements when two or more not-for-profit organizations come together.

Acquisitions In not-for-profit accounting, an acquisition occurs—as might be suspected—when one not-for-profit organization obtains control over another. As described in earlier chapters, control that leads to the consolidation of for-profit entities is normally based on gaining ownership of a majority of voting stock. However, with not-for-profit organizations, the official definition of control is broader: "the direct or indirect ability to determine the direction of management and policies through ownership, contract, or otherwise."[18]

In most respects, accounting for an acquisition initially parallels the consolidation process demonstrated previously in this textbook. All assets and liabilities of the acquired organization are identified and reported by the acquirer at fair value as of the acquisition date (the date on which control is achieved). If the total acquisition value of the acquired organization is greater than the total of the fair value of all the identifiable assets and liabilities, the excess is reported on the balance sheet as goodwill. That part of the process follows the same basic steps established to consolidate for-profit companies.

However, one important distinction is made at this point. The recognition of goodwill implies the existence of an otherwise unrecorded ability to generate high revenues and profits in the future, higher than should occur based solely on the identifiable assets and liabilities. This reporting is appropriate for organizations such as the YMCA and the Girl Scouts that generate significant amounts of earned revenue. However, what about charities that do not earn revenues from exchange transactions? Does the excess acquisition value truly reflect an asset providing future economic benefits if little or no revenues are to be generated?

As a result of such theoretical questions, in not-for-profit accounting the handling of this excess varies depending on the type of revenues that are anticipated. If the future operations of the acquired organization are expected to be predominantly supported by contributions and returns on investments (rather than dues or other types of earned revenue), any unexplained excess of the acquisition value is reported as a reduction in unrestricted net assets on the statement of activities rather than being recognized as the intangible asset goodwill.[19]

Mergers The most unique aspect of reporting the combination of not-for-profit organizations is the availability of a second method of reporting. All consolidated financial statements produced by for-profit businesses are created by the same set of rules. However, the acquisition method is not the only one utilized in the reporting of not-for-profit organizations and their combinations. If two or more not-for-profit organizations come together to form a new not-for-profit organization and control is turned over to a newly created governing board, then a merger rather than an acquisition has taken place. The two organizations have come together to create a third. An acquirer did not gain control of an acquired organization, but rather two or more of these entities joined together to form an entirely new not-for-profit.

[17] Beth, Fitzgerald, "It's a More United Way as Five Chapters Merge," NJBIZ, December 27, 2010.

[18] FASB ASC Section 958-810-20.

[19] "Predominantly supported" means that significantly more of the revenues to be generated by the acquired company will come from contributions and investment income than from all other sources combined.

In a merger, because neither organization is being acquired, identifiable assets and liabilities are not newly adjusted to fair value. Instead, the carryover method is applied in reporting mergers. The newly formed not-for-profit reports all of the previously recognized assets and liabilities at their book values as of the date of the merger. Fair value adjustments are not made.

Example of Acquisition and Merger Assume that Rather Large NFP is a private not-for-profit organization that is to be joined to Small NFP, another not-for-profit. Small NFP has been struggling financially and this combination has been created to help save the organization and the work that it does.

On the date the combination is created, Small NFP holds just one asset, a building with a net book value of $600,000 but a fair value of $700,000. It has no liabilities. Rather Large NFP has several buildings as well as many other assets. These buildings have a net book value of $3 million and a fair value of $3.9 million.

- Assume that Rather Large NFP pays $820,000 to acquire complete control over Small NFP.

This transaction is an acquisition; control has been gained by one organization over the other. The building owned by the Small NFP will be added at fair value to the book value of Rather Large NFP's building so that this asset will now be reported at $3.7 million ($3 million book value plus $700,000 fair value). If Small NFP's operations will not be predominately supported in the future by contributions and investment income, the remaining excess acquisition value of $120,000 is reported as the intangible asset goodwill ($820,000 acquisition value less $700,000 fair value of the assets and liabilities recognized).

However, if Small NFP will be predominately supported in the future by contributions and investment income, this residual $120,000 figure is reported as a reduction in unrestricted net assets in the statement of activities and not shown as the intangible asset goodwill.

- Assume that, instead of paying money to gain control, Rather Large NFP and Small NFP are joined together to form Huge NFP to be operated by an entirely new governing board.

This event now qualifies as a merger. The carryover method is used and book value is retained. Buildings will be shown at $3.6 million ($3 million book value from Rather Large NFP plus $600,000 book value from Small NFP) with no goodwill or reduction reported. No acquisition value is determined so no excess can result. All assets and liabilities are brought together at book value.

Transactions for a Private Not-for-Profit Organization Illustrated

LO2

Determine the proper classification for assets that are unrestricted, temporarily restricted, or permanently restricted and explain the method of reporting these categories.

The following transactions demonstrate typical journal entries for a private not-for-profit organization. Because financial reporting focuses on the entity as a whole, the organization does not need to record transactions in separate funds. However, not-for-profits can choose to use a fund format for internal management purposes. Reporting by funds as supplemental information is permitted, provided that all interfund transactions have been eliminated.

Assume, for example, that Shenandoah Seminary, a private college, began the year 2013 with unrestricted net assets of $1,250,000 and a permanently restricted endowment of $700,000. During 2013 the seminary received the following contributions from alumni and friends:

Unrestricted pledges due within 12 months.	$130,000
Cash contributions to the endowment.	50,000

Based on past experience, the seminary estimates that it will receive 85 percent of these unrestricted pledges. Because the seminary should be able to collect those pledges within 12 months, it need not compute or record present value.

	Debit	Credit
1. Cash	50,000	
Pledges Receivable	130,000	
Allowance for Uncollectible Pledges ($130,000 × 15%)		19,500
Unrestricted Net Assets—Contributions		110,500
Permanently Restricted Net Assets—Contributions		50,000
To record contributions received.		

Before the end of the fiscal period, the seminary collected $100,000 of the amount pledged and wrote off $5,000 of the remaining pledges.

	Debit	Credit
2. Cash	100,000	
Allowance for Uncollectible Pledges	5,000	
Pledges Receivable		105,000
To record pledges collected and written off.		

Because of the high costs involved in obtaining a college education, many schools distribute a significant amount of financial aid to their students. At one time, schools reported scholarships and other financial assistance as operating expenses separately from revenue. Now, however, to provide a more accurate picture of the impact that these reductions have on tuition and other fees, schools report the amount billed which is then reduced by student aid.

Consequently, for illustration purposes, determination of the impact of such financial assistance can be easily made for private colleges and universities for fiscal years ending during 2010:

School	Student Tuition and Fees	Scholarships and Other Assistance	Net Amount/Percentage
Notre Dame	$419.3 million	$158.3 million	$261.0 million (62.2%)
Wake Forest	244.1 million	74.1 million	170.0 million (69.6)
Colgate	113.0 million	36.8 million	76.2 million (67.4)
Georgetown	575.2 million	113.6 million	461.6 million (80.3)
Vanderbilt	478.8 million	203.6 million	275.2 million (57.5)

Thus, students at these schools directly paid an average of 57.5 to 80.3 percent of the actual tuition and fees that their schools charged.

Returning to the current example, the seminary later receives a $20,000 cash gift that the outside donor has restricted to provide support for a series of lectures by visiting scholars. In addition, the seminary charges its students $800,000 in tuition and other fees. Assume, however, that the seminary awards $200,000 in scholarships and other financial assistance.

The journal entries for the restricted gift and for the tuition charges and scholarships follow:

	Debit	Credit
3. Cash	20,000	
Temporarily Restricted Net Assets—Contributions		20,000
Gift restricted for use in a lecture series.		
Tuition Receivable	800,000	
Unrestricted Net Assets—Tuition Revenue		800,000
Tuition charged for the current period.		
Financial Aid	200,000	
Tuition Receivable		200,000
To record financial aid awards for the current year, an amount that is reported as a reduction in tuition revenue.		

Assume further that the seminary incurred liabilities of $640,000 ($575,000 for operating expenses broken down as the following entry shows and $65,000 for equipment). Of this total, the seminary paid $625,000 before year-end:

4. Instructional Expenses	265,000	
Student Services Expenses	120,000	
Maintenance Expense	75,000	
Administrative Expenses.	115,000	
Accounts Payable		575,000
To record expenses for the year.		
5. Equipment.	65,000	
Accounts Payable		65,000
To record purchases of equipment.		
6. Accounts Payable.	625,000	
Cash.		625,000
To record partial payment of outstanding accounts payable.		

Depreciation on buildings and equipment amounted to $135,000 for the year, as shown in the following journal entry:

7. Depreciation Expense—Instruction.	80,000	
Depreciation Expense—Student Services	20,000	
Depreciation Expense—Administration.	35,000	
Accumulated Depreciation, Buildings, and Equipment.		135,000
To record depreciation on fixed assets.		

Transactions Reported on Statement of Activities

The year-end reporting of this seminary will reflect the changes within each of the three categories of net assets. As mentioned previously, private not-for-profits must also report any temporarily restricted resources that have been released from restriction because the nonprofit performed some activity or the passage of time occurred. Assume here that the instructional expenses shown in entry (4) above include $15,500 of expenses relating to the series of lectures by visiting scholars established in entry (3). The following table summarizes the changes in unrestricted, temporarily restricted, and permanently restricted net assets for the year:

Calculation of Change in Net Assets

Journal Entry	Unrestricted Net Assets	Temporarily Restricted Net Assets	Permanently Restricted Net Assets
1	$110,500		$50,000
3	800,000	$20,000	
	(200,000)		
4	(575,000)		
7	(135,000)		
Net assets released from restriction	15,500	(15,500)	
Increase (decrease) in net assets	$ 16,000	$ 4,500	$50,000

Because all expenses are reflected as decreases in unrestricted net assets, the $15,500 release of the temporarily restricted net assets is added to unrestricted net assets so that this increase and the related expense appear in the same column. The preceding table does not reflect journal entries 2, 5, and 6 because they did not create changes in the seminary's net assets.

Accounting for Health Care Organizations

LO7

Describe the unique aspects of accounting for health care organizations.

Each type of not-for-profit organization tends to retain some unique elements of financial reporting that have evolved over the years. For example, voluntary health and welfare organizations, as mentioned earlier, must report a statement of functional expenses.

Probably the most distinctive version of not-for-profit accounting belongs to health care organizations. From a quantitative perspective, the providers of health care services have many thousands of institutions in operation throughout the United States; virtually every city and town has hospitals, nursing homes, and medical clinics. The large number of these enterprises is not surprising; health care expenditures now make up roughly 16 percent of the gross domestic product in this country.[20] Because of society's focus on the need for health care, a wide array of organizations including for-profit endeavors, governmental operations, and private not-for-profit entities have emerged.

From a financial reporting perspective, a private not-for-profit health care organization has no need to compute and show a net income figure. The presence and size of that amount is not germane to the organization's mission. However, readers of the financial statements need some method for measuring the efficiency of current operations. Just because profit is not a goal does not mean that losses should be ignored. Consequently, FASB requires the reporting of a "performance indicator" to reflect operational success or failure.

> The statement of operations for not-for-profit, business-oriented health care entities shall include a performance indicator. Because of the importance of the performance indicator, it shall be clearly labeled with a descriptive term such as revenues over expenses, revenues and gains over expenses and losses, earned income, or performance earnings.[21]

For example, in the 2010 financial statements of Duke University, the school reports the operating profit generated by its health system (DUHS): "The fiscal 2010 net operating income of $258 million for DUHS represents an increase of $38 million, or 17%, over fiscal 2009."

Accounting for Patient Service Revenues

One major factor influencing the financial reporting of health care organizations is the presence of third-party payors such as insurance companies, Medicare, and Medicaid. These organizations, rather than the individual, pay some or all of the cost of medical services that most patients receive. Because of the significant monetary amounts involved, third-party payors have historically sought reliable financial data, especially concerning the sources of revenue and the costs of patient care.

Not surprisingly, the largest source of health care revenues normally is patient services. For example, The King's Daughters' Hospital and Health Services of Madison, Indiana, reported in 2008 that $114.3 million of its total revenue of $115.0 million came from net patient service revenue. These amounts include fees for surgery, nursing services, medicine, laboratory work, X-rays, blood, housing, food, and so forth.

Reductions in Patient Service Revenues

For a variety of reasons, health care entities often receive much less in total payment than the amount they normally charge for specific patient services. Bad debts and other fee reductions can be significant. However, to provide complete financial data about their operations, these organizations initially record revenues at standard rates. Then they report each of the various reductions in a specified manner to best reflect these activities.

[20] Catherine Rampell, "U.S. Health Spending Breaks from the Pack," July 8, 2009, http://economix.blogs.nytimes.com/2009/07/08/us-health-spending-breaks-from-the-pack/.

[21] FASB ASC para. 954-225-45-4.

Discussion Question

IS THIS REALLY AN ASSET?

Mercy Hospital is located near Springfield, Missouri. A religious organization created the not-for-profit hospital more than 70 years ago to meet the needs of area residents who could not otherwise afford adequate health care. Although the hospital is open to the public in general, its primary mission has always been to provide medical services for the poor.

On December 23, 2013, a gentleman told the hospital's chief administrative officer the following story: "My mother has been in your hospital since October 30. The doctors have just told me that she will soon be well and can go home. I cannot tell you how relieved I am. The doctors, the nurses, and your entire staff have been just wonderful; my mother could not have gotten better care. She owes her life to your hospital.

"I am from Idaho. Now that my mother is on the road to recovery, I must return immediately to my business. I am in the process of finding a buyer for an enormous tract of land. When this acreage is sold, I will receive $15 million in cash. Because of the services that Mercy Hospital has provided my mother, I want to donate $5 million of this money." The gentleman proceeded to write this promise on a piece of stationery that he dated and signed.

Obviously, all of the hospital's officials were overwhelmed by this individual's generosity. This $5 million gift was 50 times larger than any other gift ever received. However, the controller was concerned about preparing financial statements for 2013. "I have a lot of problems with recording this type of donation as an asset. At present, we are having serious cash flow problems; but if we show $5 million in this manner, our normal donors are going to think we have become rich and don't need their support."

What problems are involved in accounting for the $5 million pledge? How should Mercy Hospital report the amount?

Assume, as an illustration, that patient charges for the current month at a small local hospital total $750,000. Of this amount, only $170,000 is due from patients because the remaining $580,000 was billed to third-party payors: Medicare, Medicaid, and various insurance companies. Regardless of expected receipts, the hospital initially records these revenues through the following journal entry:

Accounts Receivable—Third-Party Payors	580,000	
Accounts Receivable—Patients	170,000	
Patient Service Revenues		750,000
To record accrual of patient charges for current month.		

This hospital reports the entire $750,000 as patient service revenue although complete collection is doubtful. This approach is considered the best method of reflecting the health care organization's activities during the period.

Assume that the hospital estimates that $20,000 of the patient receivables will be uncollectible. Furthermore, not-for-profit hospitals and other similar entities often make no serious attempt to collect amounts that indigent patients owe. In many cases, these facilities were originally created to serve the poor. The King's Daughters' Hospital and Health Services explains its policy: "The hospital provides care to patients who meet certain criteria under its charity care policy without charge or at amounts less than its established rates. Amounts determined to qualify as charity care are reported as deductions from revenue." Assume, therefore, that another $18,000 of the accounts receivable will never be collected because several specific patients earn incomes at or below the poverty level.

Thus, to mirror these anticipated reductions, the hospital records two additional entries. As the following shows, the handling of these reductions is not the same. The expected bad debts are reported as an expense in the same manner as a for-profit business, but the revenue and receivable for the charity care are removed entirely so that no financial reporting is shown. If the work was performed with no intention to seek collection, no basis exists for recognizing either a receivable or revenue.

Bad Debt Expense	20,000	
Allowance for Uncollectible and Reduced Accounts		20,000
To record estimation of receivables that will prove to be uncollectible.		
Patient Service Revenues	18,000	
Accounts Receivable—Patients		18,000
To remove accounts that will not be collected because patients' earned income is at the poverty level.		

Contractual Agreements with Third-Party Payors

The adjustments in the preceding entries reflect amounts that the health care entity will not collect from patients. Such organizations make an additional reduction in connection with receivables due from third-party payors. Organizations such as insurance companies and Medicare often establish contractual arrangements with health care providers stipulating that they will pay set rates for specific services. The entity agrees, in effect, to accept as *payment in full* an amount that the third-party payor computes as reasonable (based normally on the average cost within the locality in which the service was rendered).

For example, a note to the 2010 financial statements for Duke University explains that its health system (DUHS)

> has agreements with third-party payors that provide for payments to DUHS at amounts that are generally less than its established rates. Payment arrangements include prospectively determined rates per discharge, reimbursed costs, discounted charges and per diem payments. Accordingly, net patient service revenue is reported at the estimated net realizable amounts from patients, third-party payors, and others. . . .

Thus, although a health care entity charges a patient $30,000, for example, it might collect only $27,000 (or some other total) from a third-party payor if the lower figure is determined to be an appropriate cost. The entity must write off the remaining $3,000, commonly referred to as a *contractual adjustment.*

Because of the current cost of health care, contractual adjustments can be huge. For example, a note to the 2008 financial statements for Parkview Health System reports that the patient charges for the year amounted to $1.49 billion, but contractual adjustments for the same period were $765 million or more than half of the amount charged.

An alternative method of determining the amount to be paid is known as a *prospective payment plan.* Under this system, reimbursement is based not on the cost of the health services being provided but on the diagnosis of the patient's illness or injury. Thus, if a patient suffers a broken leg, for example, the health care entity is entitled to a set reimbursement regardless of the actual expense incurred. Such plans were developed in an attempt to encourage a reduction in medical costs because the facility collects no additional amount if a patient remains longer than necessary or receives more expensive treatment.

For matching purposes, the health care entity should estimate and recognize these reductions in the same period that it earns the patient service revenue. In the example previously presented, the hospital probably does not anticipate collecting the entire $580,000 billed to third-party payors. Assume, for illustration purposes, that this hospital projects receiving only $420,000 of the $580,000 charge. To establish a proper value for the revenues, the entity must record another $160,000 adjustment:

Contractual Adjustments	160,000	
Allowance for Uncollectible and Reduced Accounts		160,000
To recognize estimated reduction in patient billings because of contractual arrangements made with third-party payors.		

Summary

1. Financial statements for not-for-profit organizations are designed to provide users, including contributors, with an overall view of the organization's financial position, results of operations, and cash flows.
2. The required financial statements for private not-for-profit organizations include a statement of financial position, statement of cash flows, and statement of activity and changes in net assets. Voluntary health and welfare organizations are required to issue a statement of functional expenses.
3. The financial statements must distinguish among assets that are permanently restricted, temporarily restricted, and unrestricted. Restrictions are donor imposed. Temporarily restricted assets are expected to be released from restriction after the passage of time or the performance of some act. That release causes an increase in unrestricted net assets and a decrease in temporarily restricted net assets. Permanently restricted net assets are expected to be restricted for as long as the organization exists.
4. Not-for-profit organizations should report expenses as reductions in unrestricted net assets by their functional classification such as major classes of program services and supporting services. Program services are goods or services provided to beneficiaries or customers that fulfill the organization's purpose or mission. Supporting services are general administration and fund-raising.
5. Reporting requirements have been established for contributions, which are unconditional transfers of cash or other resources to an entity in a voluntary nonreciprocal transaction.
6. Not-for-profit organizations recognize contributions, including unconditional promises to give, as revenues in the period received at fair value. Pledges to be received more than one year into the future must be reported at present value and reduced by any expected uncollectible amounts.
7. These private organizations recognize contributed services as revenues if they either create or enhance nonfinancial assets or require a specialized skill (for example, accounting, architecture, or nursing) that would have to be purchased if not provided by donation.
8. Not-for-profit organizations can sometimes receive donations that must be given to a different beneficiary. While such organizations hold the gift, they normally record it as an asset with an accompanying liability. However, if the organization is given variance power to change the beneficiary, then the not-for-profit records a revenue rather than a liability.
9. Not-for-profit organizations can join together by creating either an acquisition or a merger. In an acquisition, one party gains control of the other, and the accounting is much like that used in the consolidation of for-profit businesses with all identifiable assets and liabilities of the acquired organization reported at fair value. As one major exception, goodwill is charged off immediately (rather than capitalized) if the acquired organization is predominantly supported by gifts and investment income. In a merger, the two organizations come together under the control of a newly formed not-for-profit with a different governing body. When a merger occurs, the financial information is combined using the carryover method, which retains the previous book values.
10. Health care organizations frequently receive less than the full amount of patient charges. These entities show contractual adjustments with third-party payors as deductions from revenue in reporting *net patient service revenue.* These entities estimate bad debts and report them as expenses. Charity care charges are not recorded as revenue.

Comprehensive Illustration

Problem

(*Estimated time: 30 to 45 minutes*) Augusta Regional Health Center is a private not-for-profit hospital offering medical care to a variety of patients, including some with no ability to pay for the services received. In addition, the hospital sponsors an educational and research consortium on childhood diseases with the financial support of a private foundation. The hospital also holds an endowment, the principal of which must be maintained permanently. However, the earnings are available to provide charity care. During 2013, the hospital has the financial transactions listed here.

Required:

a. Prepare the journal entries for each of the following:

1. The hospital rendered $950,000 in services to patients, of which it charged $700,000 to third-party payors. The administration estimated that only $800,000 would be collected. Of the $150,000 difference, $85,000 represented estimated contractual allowances with insurance and Medicare providers, $20,000 is for charity care, and $45,000 is estimated for bad debts.
2. A local business donated linens with a $3,000 fair value.
3. Cafeteria sales to nonpatients and gift shop receipts totaled $76,000.
4. The hospital incurred expenses of $12,000 in connection with the annual meeting of the childhood disease consortium. Funding for this series of educational and research events had been received as a restricted donation in 2012.
5. The hospital received unrestricted, unconditional pledges of $12,500. The administration expected to collect only 80 percent of this money. In addition, it received securities with a fair value of $8,000 that the donor designated for the endowment.
6. A computer consultant donated services to upgrade several of the hospital's computer systems. The value of these services was $3,000 and would have been acquired if not donated.
7. The hospital incurred the following liabilities:

   $102,000 for purchase of supplies
   $699,000 for salaries
   $50,000 for purchase of equipment

8. End-of-year adjustment included supplies expense of $99,000 and depreciation expense of $72,000.

b. Prepare a schedule showing the change in unrestricted, temporarily restricted, and permanently restricted net assets.

Solution

a. 1.

Accounts Receivable—Patients	250,000	
Accounts Receivable—Third-Party Payors	700,000	
Patient Service Revenues (Unrestricted)		950,000
To accrue billings for the current period.		
Contractual Adjustments	85,000	
Allowance for Contractual Adjustment		85,000
To recognize estimated amounts not expected to be collected from third-party payors.		
Patient Service Revenues (Unrestricted)	20,000	
Accounts Receivable—Patients		20,000
To remove the amount for charity care for which no expectation to collect exists.		
Bad Debt Expense	45,000	
Allowance for Uncollectible Accounts		45,000
To recognize estimated amounts not expected to be collected from patients.		

2.

Account	Debit	Credit
Inventory of Supplies	3,000	
Unrestricted Net Assets—Contribution of Materials		3,000
To recognize fair value of donated items.		

3.

Account	Debit	Credit
Cash	76,000	
Unrestricted Net Assets—Revenues—Cafeteria and Shops		76,000
To record cafeteria and gift shop revenue.		

4.

Account	Debit	Credit
Consortium Expenses	12,000	
Cash		12,000
To record expenses in connection with the childhood disease consortium.		

5.

Account	Debit	Credit
Pledges Receivable	12,500	
Investments	8,000	
Allowance for Uncollectible Pledges		2,500
Unrestricted Net Assets—Contributions		10,000
Permanently Restricted Net Assets—Contributions		8,000
To record pledges and investments received at estimated fair value.		

6.

Account	Debit	Credit
Expenses for Professional Services	3,000	
Unrestricted Net Assets—Contributed Services		3,000
To record donated services.		

7.

Account	Debit	Credit
Supplies Inventory	102,000	
Equipment	50,000	
Accounts Payable		152,000
To record goods received.		
Salaries Expense	699,000	
Accrued Salaries Payable		699,000
To record salaries payable.		

8.

Account	Debit	Credit
Supplies Expense	99,000	
Supplies Inventory		99,000
To record supplies expense for the period.		
Depreciation Expense	72,000	
Accumulated Depreciation		72,000
To record depreciation expense for the period.		

b.

Calculation of Change in Net Assets

Journal Entry	Unrestricted Net Assets	Temporarily Restricted Net Assets	Permanently Restricted Net Assets
1	$950,000		
	(85,000)		
	(20,000)		
	(45,000)		
2	3,000		
3	76,000		
4	(12,000)		
5	10,000		$8,000
6	(3,000)		
	3,000		
7	(699,000)		
8	(99,000)		
	(72,000)		
Net assets released from restriction—childhood disease consortium	12,000	$(12,000)	
Increase (decrease) in net assets.	$ 19,000	$(12,000)	$8,000

Questions

1. Which organization is responsible for issuing reporting standards for private not-for-profit colleges and universities?
2. What information do financial statement users want to know about a not-for-profit organization?
3. What financial statements are required for private not-for-profit colleges and universities?
4. What are temporarily restricted assets?
5. What are permanently restricted assets?
6. What two general types of expenses do private not-for-profit organizations report?
7. What ratio is frequently used to assess the efficiency of not-for-profit organizations?
8. Why is a statement of functional expenses required of a voluntary health and welfare organization?
9. If a donor gives a charity a gift that this charity must convey to a separate beneficiary, what is the normal method of reporting for each party?
10. If a donor gives a charity a gift that this charity must convey to a separate beneficiary, what is the method of reporting for each party if the donor retains the right to revoke or redirect use of the gift?
11. If a donor gives a charity a gift that the charity must convey to a separate beneficiary, what is the method of reporting for each party if the charity receives variance powers enabling it to change the identity of the beneficiary?
12. When does a not-for-profit organization record donated services?
13. A private not-for-profit organization sends a direct mail solicitation for donations. However, the organization also includes other information with the mailing. Under what conditions can the organization report part of the cost of this mailing as a program service cost rather than a fund-raising cost?
14. A private not-for-profit organization receives numerous pledges of financial support to be conveyed at various times over the next few years. Under what condition should it recognize these pledges as receivables and contribution revenues? At what amount should it report these pledges?
15. What is the difference between an unconditional promise to give and an intention to give?
16. When should membership dues be considered revenue rather than contributions?
17. What are the two methods that can be used to report the combination of two private not-for-profit organizations?

18. Sunshine NFP, a not-for-profit organization, gains control over Dancing Bears NFP, another not-for-profit. The acquisition value of Dancing Bears is $2.3 million, but all of its identifiable assets and liabilities have a total value of only $2.1 million. What recording is made of the $200,000 difference?
19. Helping Hand NFP is a private not-for-profit organization that has equipment with a book value of $1.1 million but a fair value of $1.4 million. Fancy Fingers is a private not-for-profit organization that has equipment with a book value of $1 million and a fair value of $1.2 million. If these two organizations combine, what are the possible amounts that they can report for their equipment?
20. What is a third-party payor, and how does the presence of such payors affect the financial accounting of a health care organization?
21. What is a contractual adjustment? How does a health care organization account for a contractual adjustment?

Problems

LO7

1. A private not-for-profit health care organization has the following account balances:

Revenue from newsstand	$ 50,000
Amounts charged to patients	800,000
Interest income	30,000
Salary expense—nurses	100,000
Bad debts	10,000
Undesignated gifts	80,000
Contractual adjustments	110,000

What is reported as the organization's net patient service revenue?

a. $880,000.
b. $800,000.
c. $690,000.
d. $680,000.

LO1

2. A large private not-for-profit organization's statement of activities should report the net change for net assets that are

	Unrestricted	Permanently Restricted
a.	Yes	Yes
b.	Yes	No
c.	No	No
d.	No	Yes

LO1

3. Which of the following statements is true?

I. Private not-for-profit universities must report depreciation expense.
II. Public universities must report depreciation expense.

a. Neither I nor II is true.
b. Both I and II are true.
c. Only I is true.
d. Only II is true.

LO2

4. A private not-for-profit organization receives three donations:

One gift of $70,000 is unrestricted.

One gift of $90,000 is restricted to pay the salary of the organization's workers.

One gift of $120,000 is restricted forever with the income to be used to provide food for needy families.

Which of the following statements is *not* true?

a. Temporarily restricted net assets have increased by $90,000.
b. Permanently restricted net assets have increased by $210,000.

c. When the donated money is spent for salaries, unrestricted net assets will increase and decrease by the same amount.

d. When the donated money is spent for salaries, temporarily restricted net assets will decrease.

LO4

5. A donor gives Charity 1 $50,000 in cash that it must convey to Charity 2. However, the donor can revoke the gift at any time prior to its conveyance to Charity 2. Which of the following statements is true?

   a. Charity 1 should report a contribution revenue.

   b. The donor continues to report an asset even after it is given to Charity 1.

   c. As soon as the gift is made to Charity 1, Charity 2 should recognize a contribution revenue.

   d. As soon as the gift is made to Charity 1, Charity 2 should recognize an asset.

LO2

6. A private not-for-profit university charges its students tuition of $1 million. However, financial aid grants total $220,000. In addition, the school receives a $100,000 grant restricted for faculty salaries. Of this amount, it spent $30,000 appropriately this year. On the statement of activities, the school reports three categories: (1) revenues and support, (2) net assets reclassified, and (3) expenses. Which of the following is *not* true?

   a. Unrestricted net assets should show an increase of $30,000 for net assets reclassified.

   b. In the unrestricted net assets, the revenues and support should total $1 million.

   c. Unrestricted net assets should recognize expenses of $30,000.

   d. Unrestricted net assets shows the $220,000 as a direct reduction to the tuition revenue balance.

LO4

7. A private not-for-profit organization has the following activities performed by volunteers who work at no charge. In which case should it report *no* amount of contributions?

   a. A carpenter builds a porch on the back of one building so that patients can sit outside.

   b. An accountant does the organization's financial reporting.

   c. A local librarian comes each day to read to the patients.

   d. A computer expert repairs the organization's computer.

LO3

8. To send a mailing, a private not-for-profit charity spends $100,000. The mailing solicits donations and provides educational and other information about the charity. Which of the following is true?

   a. No part of the $100,000 can be reported as a program service expense.

   b. Some part of the $100,000 must be reported as a program service expense.

   c. No authoritative guidance exists, so the organization can allocate the cost as it believes best.

   d. Under certain specified circumstances, the organization should allocate a portion of the $100,000 to program service expenses.

LO1

9. The financial reporting for private not-for-profit organizations primarily focuses on

   a. Basic information for the organization as a whole.

   b. Standardization of fund information reported.

   c. Inherent differences of various not-for-profit organizations that impact reporting presentations.

   d. Distinctions between current fund and noncurrent fund presentations.

LO2

10. On December 30, 2013, Leigh Museum, a not-for-profit organization, received a $7,000,000 donation of Day Co. common stock shares with donor-stipulated requirements as follows:

    The museum is to sell shares valued at $5,000,000 and use the proceeds to erect a public viewing building.

    The museum is to retain shares valued at $2,000,000 and use the dividends to support current operations.

    As a consequence of its receipt of the Day Co. shares, how much should Leigh report as temporarily restricted net assets on its 2013 statement of financial position?

    a. $-0-.

    b. $2,000,000.

    c. $5,000,000.

    d. $7,000,000.

LO4 11. The Jones family lost its home in a fire. On December 25, 2013, a philanthropist sent money to the Amer Benevolent Society, a private not-for-profit organization, specifically to purchase furniture for the Jones family. During January 2014, Amer purchased furniture for the Jones family. How should Amer report the receipt of the money in its 2013 financial statements?

a. As an unrestricted contribution.
b. As a temporarily restricted contribution.
c. As a permanently restricted contribution.
d. As a liability.

LO4 12. Pel Museum is a private not-for-profit organization. If it receives a contribution of historical artifacts, it need not recognize the contribution if the artifacts are to be sold and it will use the proceeds to

a. Support general museum activities.
b. Acquire other items for collections.
c. Repair existing collections.
d. Purchase buildings to house collections.

LO2 13. A private not-for-profit organization receives two gifts. One is $80,000 and is restricted for paying salaries of teachers who help children learn to read. The other is $110,000, which is restricted for purchasing playground equipment. The organization spends both amounts properly at the end of this year. The organization records no depreciation this period. It has elected to view the equipment as having a time restriction. On the statement of activities, what is reported for unrestricted net assets?

a. An increase of $80,000 and a decrease of $80,000.
b. An increase of $190,000 and a decrease of $190,000.
c. An increase of $190,000 and a decrease of $80,000.
d. An increase of $80,000 and no decrease.

LO6 14. AB is a private not-for-profit organization. It acquires YZ, another private not-for-profit organization. The acquisition value is $1 million. YZ has net assets with a book value of $600,000 but a fair value of $700,000. Officials for AB expect that YZ will be predominantly supported by contributions in the future. After the acquisition, what amount of goodwill will be reported on the combined balance sheet?

a. $-0-.
b. $100,000.
c. $300,000.
d. $400,000.

LO6 15. BC and OP are both private not-for-profit organizations. They are combined to create MN, a private not-for-profit organization with an entirely new board of directors. BC has land with a book value of $300,000 and a fair value of $400,000. OP has land with a book value of $500,000 and a fair value of $550,000. After MN has been formed, what is reported for land?

a. $800,000.
b. $850,000.
c. $900,000.
d. $950,000.

LO6 16. Southwest is a private not-for-profit organization. It acquires Northeast, another private not-for-profit organization. The acquisition value is $980,000. Northeast has two assets (and no liabilities): equipment with a book value of $120,000 but a fair value of $150,000 and a building with a book value of $500,000 but a fair value of $800,000. Northeast is expected to receive a lot of support through donations and contributions. However, it is not expected to be predominantly supported by contributions and investment income. After the combination, what should be reported for goodwill?

a. $-0-.
b. $30,000.
c. $60,000.
d. $360,000.

LO7 17. In the accounting for health care providers, what are third-party payors?

a. Doctors who reduce fees for indigent patients.

b. Charities that supply medicines to hospitals and other health care providers.

c. Friends and relatives who pay the medical costs of a patient.

d. Insurance companies and other groups that pay a significant portion of the medical fees in the United States.

LO7 18. Mercy for America, a private not-for-profit health care facility located in Durham, North Carolina, charged a patient $8,600 for services. It actually billed this amount to the patient's third-party payor. The third-party payor submitted a check for $7,900 with a note stating that "the reasonable amount is paid in full per contract." Which of the following statements is true?

a. The patient is responsible for paying the remaining $700.

b. The health care facility will rebill the third-party payor for the remaining $700.

c. The health care facility recorded the $700 as a contractual adjustment that it will not collect.

d. The third-party payor retained the $700 and will convey it to the health care facility at the start of the next fiscal period.

LO7 19. What is a *contractual adjustment*?

a. An increase in a patient's charges caused by revisions in the billing process utilized by a health care entity.

b. A year-end journal entry to recognize all of a health care entity's remaining receivables.

c. A reduction in patient service revenues caused by agreements with third-party payors that allows them to pay a health care entity based on their determination of reasonable costs.

d. The results of a cost allocation system that allows a health care entity to determine a patient's cost by department.

LO7 20. A private not-for-profit health care entity provides its patients with services that would normally be charged at $1 million. However, it estimates a $200,000 reduction because of contractual adjustments. It expects another $100,000 reduction because of bad debts. Finally, the organization does not expect to collect $400,000 because this amount is deemed to be charity care. Which of the following is correct?

a. Patient service revenues = $1 million; net patient service revenues = $300,000.

b. Patient service revenues = $1 million; net patient service revenues = $400,000.

c. Patient service revenues = $600,000; net patient service revenues = $300,000.

d. Patient service revenues = $600,000, net patient service revenues = $400,000.

LO2 21. A local citizen gives a not-for-profit organization a cash donation that is restricted for research activities. The money should be recorded in

a. Unrestricted Net Assets.

b. Temporarily Restricted Net Assets.

c. Permanently Restricted Net Assets.

d. Deferred Revenue.

LO4 22. Theresa Johnson does volunteer work for a local not-for-profit organization as a community service. She replaces without charge an administrator who would have otherwise been paid $31,000. Which of the following statements is true?

a. The organization should recognize a restricted gain of $31,000.

b. The organization should recognize a contribution of $31,000 as an increase in unrestricted net assets as well as salary expense of $31,000.

c. The organization should recognize a reduction in expenses of $31,000.

d. The organization should make no entry.

LO5 23. Which of these forms must most not-for-profit organizations file annually with the Internal Revenue Service?

a. 990.

b. 1203.

c. 501.

d. 501(c)(3).

LO5 24. Belwood University is a private not-for-profit school that has tax-exempt status. Which of the following is most likely to be the type of tax-exempt status that Belwood holds?

a. 501(c)(3)
b. 501(c)(4)
c. 501(c)(5)
d. 501(c)(6)

LO4 25. A group of high school seniors performs volunteer services for patients at a nearby nursing home. The nursing home would not otherwise provide these services, such as wheeling patients in the park and reading to them. At the minimum wage rate, these services would amount to $21,320, but their actual value is estimated to be $27,400. In the nursing home's statement of revenues and expenses, what amount should be reported as public support?

a. $27,400.
b. $21,320.
c. $6,080.
d. $-0-.

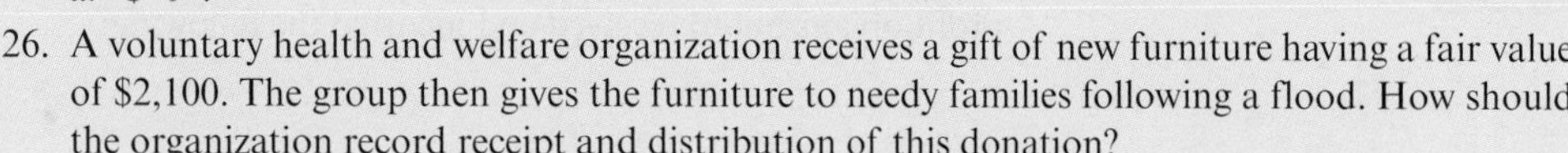

LO4 26. A voluntary health and welfare organization receives a gift of new furniture having a fair value of $2,100. The group then gives the furniture to needy families following a flood. How should the organization record receipt and distribution of this donation?

a. Make no entry.
b. Record a contribution of $2,100 and community assistance expense of $2,100.
c. Recognize revenue of $2,100.
d. Recognize revenue of $2,100 and community expenditures of $2,100.

LO4 27. George H. Ruth takes a leave of absence from his job to work full-time for a voluntary health and welfare organization for six months. Ruth fills the position of finance director, a position that normally pays $88,000 per year. Ruth accepts no remuneration for his work. How should these donated services be recorded?

a. As contribution revenue of $44,000 and an expense of $44,000.
b. As earned revenue of $44,000.
c. As an expense of $44,000.
d. They should not be recorded.

LO3 28. A voluntary health and welfare organization produces a statement of functional expenses. What is the purpose of this statement?

a. Separates current unrestricted and current restricted funds.
b. Separates program service expenses from supporting service expenses.
c. Separates cash expenses from noncash expenses.
d. Separates fixed expenses from variable expenses.

LO3 29. A voluntary health and welfare organization has the following expenditures:

Research to cure disease	$60,000
Fund-raising costs	70,000
Work to help disabled	40,000
Administrative salaries	90,000

How should the organization report these items?

a. Program service expenses of $100,000 and supporting service expenses of $160,000.
b. Program service expenses of $160,000 and supporting service expenses of $100,000.
c. Program service expenses of $170,000 and supporting service expenses of $90,000.
d. Program service expenses of $190,000 and supporting service expenses of $70,000.

LO3 30. A voluntary health and welfare organization sends a mailing to all of its members including those who have donated in the past and others who have never donated. The mailing, which cost $22,000, asks for monetary contributions to help achieve the organization's mission. In addition, 80 percent of the material included in the mailing is educational in nature, providing data about the organization's goals. Which of the following is true?

a. Some part of the $22,000 should be reported as a program service cost because of the educational materials included.

b. No part of the $22,000 should be reported as a program service cost because there is no specific call to action.

c. No part of the $22,000 should be reported as a program service cost because the mailing was sent to both previous donors and individuals who have not made donations.

d. Some part of the $22,000 should be reported as a program service cost because more than 50 percent of the material was educational in nature.

LO4 31. A voluntary health and welfare organization receives $32,000 in cash from solicitations made in the local community. The organization receives an additional $1,500 from members in payment of annual dues. Members are assumed to receive benefits roughly equal in value to the amount of dues paid. How should this money be recorded?

a. Revenues of $33,500.

b. Public support of $33,500.

c. Public support of $32,000 and a $1,500 increase in the fund balance.

d. Public support of $32,000 and revenue of $1,500.

LO7 32. During the year ended December 31, 2013, Anderson Hospital (operated as a private not-for-profit organization) received and incurred the following:

Fair value of donated medicines	$ 54,000
Fair value of donated services (replaced salaried workers)	38,000
Fair value of additional donated services (did not replace salaried workers)	11,000
Interest income	23,000
Regular charges to patients	176,000
Charity care	210,000
Bad debts	66,000

How should this hospital report each of these items?

LO7 33. The following questions concern the appropriate accounting for a private not-for-profit health care entity. Write complete answers for each question.

a. What is a third-party payor, and how have third-party payors affected the development of accounting principles for health care entities?

b. What is a contractual adjustment, and how does a health care entity record this figure?

c. How does a not-for-profit health care entity account for donated materials and services?

LO7 34. Under Lennon Hospital's rate structure, it earned patient service revenue of $9 million for the year ended December 31, 2013. However, Lennon did not expect to collect this entire amount because it deemed $1.4 million to be charity care and estimated contractual adjustments to be $800,000.

During 2013, Lennon purchased medical supplies from Harrison Medical Supply Company at a cost of $4,000. Harrison notified Lennon that it was donating the supplies to the hospital.

At the end of 2013, Lennon had board-designated assets consisting of cash of $60,000 and investments of $800,000.

Lennon is a private not-for-profit organization: How much should Lennon record as patient service revenue and how much as net patient service revenue? How should Lennon record the donation of the supplies? How are the board-designated assets shown on the balance sheet?

LO2, LO4 35. Wilson Center is a private not-for-profit voluntary health and welfare organization. During 2013, it received unrestricted pledges of $600,000, 60 percent of which were payable in 2013, with the remainder payable in 2014 (for use in 2014). Officials estimate that 15 percent of all pledges will be uncollectible.

a. How much should Wilson Center report as contribution revenue for 2013?

b. In addition, a local social worker, earning $20 per hour working for the state government, contributed 600 hours of time to Wilson Center at no charge. Without these donated services, the organization would have hired an additional staff person. How should Wilson Center record the contributed service?

LO1, LO2, LO4 36. A private not-for-profit organization is working to create a cure for a deadly disease. The organization starts the year with cash of $700,000. Of this amount, unrestricted net assets total $400,000, temporarily restricted net assets total $200,000, and permanently restricted net assets total $100,000. Within the temporarily restricted net assets, the organization must use 80 percent for equipment and the rest for salaries. No implied time restriction has been designated for the equipment when purchased. For the permanently restricted net assets, 70 percent of resulting income must be used to cover the purchase of advertising for fund-raising purposes and the rest is unrestricted.

During the current year, the organization has the following transactions:

- Received unrestricted cash gifts of $210,000.
- Paid salaries of $80,000 with $20,000 of that amount coming from restricted funds. Of the total salaries, 40 percent is for administrative personnel and the remainder is evenly divided among individuals working on research to cure the designated disease and individuals employed for fund-raising purposes.
- Bought equipment for $300,000 with a long-term note signed for $250,000 and restricted funds used for the remainder. Of this equipment, 80 percent is used in research, 10 percent is used in administration, and the remainder is used for fund-raising.
- Collected membership dues of $30,000. The members receive a reasonable amount of value in exchange for these dues including a monthly newsletter describing research activities.
- Received $10,000 from a donor that must be conveyed to another organization doing work on a related disease.
- Received investment income of $13,000 generated by the permanently restricted net assets. As mentioned above, the donor has stipulated that 70 percent of the income is to be used for advertising, and the remainder may be used at the organization's discretion.
- Paid advertising of $2,000.
- Received an unrestricted pledge of $100,000 that will be collected in three years. The organization expects to collect the entire amount. The pledge has a present value of $78,000 and related interest (additional contribution revenue) of $3,000 in the year.
- Computed depreciation on the equipment acquired as $20,000.
- Spent $93,000 on research supplies that it utilized during the year.
- Owed salaries of $5,000 at the end of the year. Half of this amount is for individuals doing fund-raising and half for individuals doing research.
- Received a donated painting that qualifies as a museum piece. It has a value of $800,000. Officials do not want to record this gift if possible.

a. Prepare a statement of activities for this organization for this year.

b. Prepare a statement of financial position for this organization for this year.

LO2, LO4

37. A local private not-for-profit health care entity incurred the following transactions during the current year. Record each of these transactions in appropriate journal entry form. Prepare a schedule calculating the change in unrestricted, permanently restricted, and temporarily restricted net assets.

a. The organization's governing board announced that $160,000 in previously unrestricted cash will be used in the future to acquire equipment. The funds are invested until the purchase eventually occurs.

b. Received a donation of $80,000 with the stipulation that all income derived from this money be used to supplement nursing salaries.

c. Expended $25,000 for medicines. Organization received the money the previous year as a restricted gift for this purpose.

d. Charged patients $600,000, 80 percent of which is expected to be covered by third-party payors.

e. Calculated depreciation expense of $38,000.

f. Received interest income of $15,000 on the investments the board acquired in transaction (*a*).

g. Estimated that $20,000 of current accounts receivable from patients will not be collected and that third-party payors will reduce the amounts owed by $30,000 because of contractual adjustments.

h. Consumed the medicines acquired in (*c*).

i. Sold the investments acquired in (*a*) for $172,000. Spent all restricted cash (including [*f*] above) and $25,000 that previously had been given to the organization (with the stipulation that the money be used to acquire plant assets) for new equipment. No time restriction was assumed on this equipment.

j. Received pledges for $126,000 in unrestricted donations. Of the pledges, 10 percent are collected immediately with 90 percent to be received and used in future years. Officials estimate that $9,000 of this money will never be collected. Present value of the receivable is $98,000.

LO1, LO2, LO4

38. The University of Danville is a private not-for-profit university that starts the current year with $700,000 in net assets: $400,000 unrestricted, $200,000 temporarily restricted, and $100,000 permanently restricted. The following transactions occur during the year.

    Make journal entries for each transaction. Then determine the end-of-year balances for unrestricted net assets, temporarily restricted net assets, and permanently restricted net assets by creating a statement of activities.

    a. Charged students $1.2 million in tuition.

    b. Received a donation of investments that had cost the owner $100,000 but was worth $300,000 at the time of the gift. According to the gift's terms, the university must hold the investments forever but can spend the dividends for any purpose. Any changes in the value of these securities must be held forever and cannot be spent.

    c. Received a cash donation of $700,000 that must be used to acquire laboratory equipment.

    d. Gave scholarships in the amount of $100,000 to students.

    e. Paid salary expenses of $310,000 in cash.

    f. Learned that a tenured faculty member is contributing his services in teaching for this year and will not accept his $80,000 salary.

    g. Spent $200,000 of the money in (*c*) on laboratory equipment (no time restriction is assumed on this equipment).

    h. Learned that at the end of the year, the investments in (*b*) are worth $330,000.

    i. Received dividends of $9,000 cash on the investments in (*b*).

    j. Computed depreciation expense for the period of $32,000.

    k. The school's board of trustees decides to set aside $100,000 of previously unrestricted cash for the future purchase of library books.

    l. Received an unconditional promise of $10,000, which the school fully expects to collect in three years although its present value is only $7,000. The school assumes that the money cannot be used until the school receives it.

    m. Received an art object as a gift that is worth $70,000 and that qualifies as a work of art. The school prefers not to record this gift.

    n. Paid utilities and other general expenses of $212,000.

    o. Received free services from alumni who come to campus each week and put books on the shelves in the library. Over the course of the year, the school would have paid $103,000 to have this work done.

LO2, LO3, LO4

39. The following questions concern the accounting principles and procedures applicable to a private not-for-profit organization. Write answers to *each* question.

    a. What is the difference between revenue and public support?

    b. What is the significance of the statement of functional expenses?

    c. What accounting process does the organization use in connection with donated materials?

    d. What is the difference in the two types of restricted net assets found in the financial records of a private not-for-profit organization?

    e. Under what conditions should the organization record donated services?

    f. What is the proper handling of costs associated with direct mail and other solicitations for money that also contain educational materials?

    g. A not-for-profit organization receives a painting. Under what conditions can this painting be judged as a work of art? If it meets the criteria for a work of art, how is the financial reporting of the organization affected?

LO2, LO4

40. The College of Central North (a private school) has the following events and transactions:

    a. On January 1, Year 1, the board of trustees voted to restrict $1.9 million of previously unrestricted investments to construct a new football stadium at some future time.

    b. On April 1, Year 1, Dr. Johnson gives the school $4 million in investments that is to be held forever, but all subsequent cash income is to be used to help pay for construction (and, later, maintenance) of the football stadium.

    c. On December 31, Year 1, the investments in (*b*) generate $500,000 in cash interest revenue. In addition, the investments went up in value by $44,000.

d. On January 1, Year 2, the school builds a football stadium with the restricted $2.4 million in funds. Cash is paid. The stadium has a 20-year life and no salvage value.

e. On January 2, Year 2, Dr. Johnson buys a seat for the current year on the 50-yard line of the stadium for $30,000 in cash when this seat's fair value is actually $12,000.

f. On January 3, Year 2, Dr. Johnson provides free medical services to the school. These services have a $14,000 value and require a specialized skill that the school needed and would have bought otherwise.

g. On January 4, Year 2, Dr. Johnson donated a painting to be displayed in the school library. It is appraised at a value of $30,000.

Unless otherwise noted, assume that the school does *not* have a policy that assumes a time restriction on assets bought with restricted funds.

For each of the following independent situations, indicate whether the statement is true or false and briefly state the reason for your answer.

(1) On January 1, Year 1, unrestricted net assets reported by the school will be reduced.

(2) As of December 31, Year 1, temporarily restricted net assets will have increased by $500,000 during the year.

(3) On December 31, Year 1, permanently restricted net assets went up by $44,000.

(4) On January 1, Year 2, unrestricted net assets increased $500,000.

(5) Unless a time restriction is placed on the use of the football stadium, depreciation expense will not be recorded in Year 2.

(6) If a time restriction is placed on the use of the football stadium, depreciation expense will not be recorded in Year 2.

(7) For reporting purposes, unrestricted net assets increased by $30,000 on January 2, Year 2.

(8) For reporting purposes, contribution revenues increased by $18,000 on January 2, Year 2.

(9) On January 3, Year 2, unrestricted net assets were reported as going both up and down.

(10) On January 3, Year 2, unrestricted net assets might be reported as going both up and down.

(11) On January 3, Year 2, unrestricted net assets will go down and might go up.

(12) On January 4, Year 2, a contribution revenue of $30,000 must be reported.

(13) On January 4, Year 2, a contribution revenue of $30,000 must not be reported.

LO1, LO2, LO4

41. You are preparing a statement of activities for the University of Richland, a private not-for-profit organization. The following questions should be viewed as independent of each other.

Part 1

During the current year, a donor gives $400,000 in cash to the school and stipulates that it must hold this money forever. However, any investment income earned on this money must be used for faculty salaries. During the current year, the investment earned $31,000 and, of that amount, the school has expended $22,000 appropriately to date. As a result of these events, what was the overall change in each of the following for the current year?

a. Unrestricted net assets.

b. Temporarily restricted net assets.

c. Permanently restricted net assets.

Part 2

A donor gives a large machine to the school on January 1 of the current year. It has a value of $200,000, no salvage value, and a 10-year life. The donor requires that the school keep the machine and use it for all 10 years, and the school agrees. It cannot sell or retire the machine in the interim. As a result of these events, what was the overall change in each of the following for the current year?

a. Unrestricted net assets.

b. Temporarily restricted net assets.

c. Operating expenses.

Part 3

Several years ago, a donor gave the school $400,000 in cash to help fund its financial aid program. This year, the school charged $2 million in tuition but granted $700,000 in financial aid.

Collections to date from the students have totaled $1.1 million. The donor's gift has offset $300,000 of the financial aid. As a result of these events, what was the overall change in each of the following for the current year?

a. Unrestricted net assets.

b. Operating expenses.

c. Temporarily restricted net assets.

LO1, LO2, LO4

excel

42. The Watson Foundation, a private not-for-profit organization, starts 2013 with cash of $100,000, pledges receivable (net) of $200,000, investments of $300,000, and land, buildings, and equipment of $200,000. In addition, its unrestricted net assets were $400,000, temporarily restricted net assets were $100,000, and permanently restricted net assets were $300,000. Of the temporarily restricted net assets, 50 percent must be used for a new building; the remainder is restricted for salaries. No implied time restriction was designated for the building when it was purchased. For the permanently restricted net assets, all income is unrestricted.

During the current year, the organization has the following transactions:

- Computed interest of $20,000 on the pledge receivable.
- Received cash of $100,000 on the pledges and wrote off another $4,000 as uncollectible.
- Received unrestricted cash gifts of $180,000.
- Paid salaries of $90,000 with $15,000 of that amount coming from restricted funds.
- Received a cash gift of $12,000 that the organization must convey to another not-for-profit organization. However, Watson has the right to give the money to a different organization if it so chooses.
- Bought a building for $500,000 by signing a long-term note for $450,000 and using restricted funds for the remainder.
- Collected membership dues of $30,000. Individuals receive substantial benefits from the memberships.
- Received income of $30,000 generated by the permanently restricted net assets.
- Paid rent of $12,000, advertising of $15,000, and utilities of $16,000.
- Received an unrestricted pledge of $200,000; it will be collected in five years. The organization expects to collect the entire amount. Present value is $149,000. It then recognized interest of $6,000 for the year.
- Computed depreciation as $40,000.
- Paid $15,000 in interest on the note signed to acquire the building.

a. Prepare a statement of activities for this organization for this year.

b. Prepare a statement of financial position for this organization for this year.

LO6

43. Help & Save is a private not-for-profit organization that operates in Kansas. Swim For Safety is a private not-for-profit organization that operates in Missouri. The leaders of these two organizations have decided to combine forces on January 1, 2013, in order to have a bigger impact from their work. They are currently discussing ways by which this combination can be created. Statements of financial position for both organizations at that date appear below.

HELP & SAVE
Balance Sheet
January 1, 2013

Assets	
Cash	$1,600,000
Pledges Receivable (net)	70,000
Investments	300,000
Buildings & Equipment (net)	700,000
Total Assets	$2,670,000
Liabilities	
Accounts Payable and Accrued Liabilities	$ 110,000
Notes Payable	1,100,000
Total Liabilities	$1,210,000

Net Assets	
Unrestricted	$1,100,000
Temporarily Restricted	250,000
Permanently Restricted	110,000
Total Net Assets	$1,460,000
Total Liabilities and Net Assets	$2,670,000

SWIM FOR SAFETY
Balance Sheet
January 1, 2013

Assets	
Cash	$ 500,000
Pledges Receivable (net)	210,000
Investments	170,000
Buildings & Equipment (net)	590,000
Total Assets	$1,470,000
Liabilities	
Accounts Payable and Accrued Liabilities	$ 70,000
Notes Payable	620,000
Total Liabilities	$ 690,000
Net Assets	
Unrestricted	$ 420,000
Temporarily Restricted	190,000
Permanently Restricted	170,000
Total Net Assets	$ 780,000
Total Liabilities and Net Assets	$1,470,000

The buildings and equipment reported by Help & Save have a fair value of $900,000. The buildings and equipment reported by Swim For Safety have a fair value of $730,000.

a. Assume Help & Save pays $1 million in cash from its unrestricted net assets to gain complete control over Swim For Safety. It is not assumed that Swim For Safety will be predominantly supported by contributions and investment income in the future. What balances will appear on the combined balance sheet immediately after control is gained?

b. Assume Help & Save pays $990,000 in cash from its unrestricted net assets to gain complete control over Swim For Safety. It is assumed that Swim For Safety will be predominantly supported by contributions and investment income in the future. What balances will appear on the combined balance sheet immediately after control is gained?

c. Assume that these two organizations are combined into a new private not-for-profit organization to be known as Help–Swim–Save. A new governing body will be formed to manage and operate this new organization. What balances will appear on the combined balance sheet immediately after control is gained?

The following information relates to problems 44 through 49:

For a number of years, a private not-for-profit organization has been preparing financial statements that do not necessarily follow generally accepted accounting principles. At the end of the most recent year (Year 2), those financial statements show total assets of $900,000, total liabilities of $100,000, total unrestricted net assets of $400,000, total temporarily restricted net assets of $300,000, and total permanently restricted net assets of $100,000. In addition, total expenses for the year were $500,000 (shown in unrestricted net assets).

LO1

44. Assume that this organization is a private college that charged students $600,000 but then provided $140,000 in financial aid. The $600,000 was reported as a revenue; the $140,000 was shown as an expense. Both amounts were included in the unrestricted net assets.

a. What was the correct amount of unrestricted net assets at the end of the year?

b. What was the correct amount of expenses for the year?

LO2, LO4

45. During Year 1, the organization above received a gift of $80,000. The donor specified that this money be invested in government bonds with the interest to be used to pay the salaries of the organization's employees. The gift was recorded as an increase in permanently restricted net assets. It earned interest income of $5,000 during Year 1 and $7,000 during Year 2. The organization reported this interest on the statement of activities as an increase in unrestricted net assets. In both cases, the money was immediately expended for salaries, amounts that were recorded as expenses within unrestricted net assets. No other entries were made in connection with these funds.
    a. What was the correct amount of unrestricted net assets at the end of Year 2?
    b. What was the correct amount of expenses in unrestricted net assets for Year 2?
    c. What was the correct amount of temporarily restricted net assets at the end of Year 2?

LO1, LO2, LO4

46. At the beginning of Year 1, the organization above received $50,000 in cash as a gift with the stipulation that the money be used to buy a bus. The organization made the appropriate entry at that time. On the first day of Year 2, the organization spent the $50,000 for the bus, an asset that will last for 10 years and will have no salvage value. Because the money came from an outside donor, the organization decided that a time restriction on the bus should be assumed for 10 years. In Year 2, it reported $5,000 as depreciation expense in unrestricted net assets. In addition, the organization made a $50,000 reduction in permanently restricted net assets and a $50,000 increase in unrestricted net assets.
    a. What was the correct amount of unrestricted net assets at the end of Year 2?
    b. What was the correct amount of expenses for Year 2?
    c. What was the correct amount of temporarily restricted net assets at the end of Year 2?

LO4

47. Assume that the organization is a charity that charges its "members" monthly dues totaling $100,000 per year (in both Year 1 and Year 2). However, the members get nothing for their dues. The organization has consistently recorded this amount as an increase in Cash along with an increase in revenues within the unrestricted net assets.
    What was the correct amount of unrestricted net assets at the end of Year 2?

LO2, LO4

48. On January 1, Year 2, several supporters of the organization spent their own money to construct a garage for its vehicles that is worth $70,000. It should last for 10 years and will have no salvage value although no time restriction was assumed. The organization increased its contributions within the unrestricted net assets for $70,000 and increased its expenses within unrestricted net assets for $70,000.
    a. What was the correct amount of unrestricted net assets at the end of Year 2?
    b. What was the correct amount of total assets at the end of Year 2?
    c. What was the correct amount of expenses for Year 2?

LO4

49. On December 25 of Year 2, the organization received a $40,000 cash gift. The donor specified that the organization hold the money for four months. If, at the end of four months, the donor still wished to do so, the money was to be given to the local Kidney Fund (a separate not-for-profit organization). However, during these four months, the donor could use the money for any other purpose. The reporting organization recorded the money as an increase in Cash and as contribution revenue within its unrestricted net assets.
    a. What was the correct amount of unrestricted net assets at the end of Year 2?
    b. What was the correct amount of total assets at the end of Year 2?

Develop Your Skills

RESEARCH CASE 1

The law firm of Hackney and Walton has decided to start supporting a worthy charity. The partners want to select an organization that makes good use of its resources to meet its stated mission.

Go to the website www.give.org. Click on "Charity Reports and Standards." Then, click on "List of National BBB Wise Giving Reports" and a list of hundreds of not-for-profit organizations will appear. Select two or more of these charities and read the information available on this website.

Required

Write a report to the partners of Hackney and Walton. Describe the charities you selected and recommend which of these charities they should support. Give adequate justification for this recommendation.

RESEARCH CASE 2

Go to the website www.guidestar.org and enter the name of a private not-for-profit organization. Considerable information will be available about the entity. By registering, it should be possible to find a link to the Form 990 (Return of Organization Exempt from Income Tax) filed with the Internal Revenue Service for informational purposes. Scan through this document and answer the following questions.

Required

1. On line I near the top of the first page, determine the organization's specific type of Section 501 (c) designation.
2. At Part VII, there is a list of officers, directors, trustees, and key employees. List the first three individuals named and their compensation.
3. In Part IX, there is a statement of functional expenses. For this organization, what percentage of its total expenses are labeled as program service expenses?
4. Scan the entire Form 990 for information that would not otherwise be available about this organization.

RESEARCH CASE 3

Go to the following URL for Georgetown University: http://financialaffairs.georgetown.edu/gta/statements.html. Click on the link for the most recent set of financial statements for the university. Scan those statements.

Then, click on the link for the 1987 financial statements. Scan those statements also.

Required

Prepare a list of 3 or 4 of the most obvious structural differences between the 1987 financial statements and the current financial statements.

ANALYSIS CASE 1

Go to the website of a private not-for-profit organization such as United Cerebral Palsy (www.ucp.org), the American Heart Association (www.americanheart.org), or the American Cancer Society (www.cancer.org). Find the charity's latest financial statements, which usually can be found by clicking on a button such as "About Our Charity" and then clicking on "Financial Information" or "Audited Financial Statements." Some financial statements are easy to find while some are quite difficult. Other organizations simply do not include financial statements on their websites.

Required

After examining these financial statements, answer the following questions about the private not-for-profit organization:

1. How many different program services were listed? Name each.
2. What percentage of total expenses went to supporting services?
3. Were any contributed services recognized and, if so, for how much?
4. What dollar amount was spent on fund-raising?
5. What was the year-end total for unrestricted net assets, temporarily restricted net assets, and unrestricted net assets?
6. What amount of net assets was reclassified from temporarily restricted to unrestricted net assets this past year because the external restriction had been satisfied?

ANALYSIS CASE 2

Go to the website of a private not-for-profit college or university such as Duke (www.duke.edu), Vanderbilt (www.vanderbilt.edu), Notre Dame (www.nd.edu), or Georgetown (www.georgetown.edu) and locate the latest set of financial statements for the institution. As an alternative, write to the vice president of finance at your institution and request the most recent financial statements.

Required

Use this report to answer the following questions and document where in the report you located the relevant information:

1. What was the percentage of financial aid to total student tuition and fees? Show your calculation.
2. Did the school report any pledges receivable and, if so, for how much? What amount is *not* to be collected within one year?
3. Looking at the school's expenses, what was the total amount spent on educating the students, and what was spent on research during the period? List the items you include for each category.
4. What was the total amount donated to the school during the previous year?
5. What was the total amount of temporarily restricted net assets and permanently restricted net assets?
6. What was the unrealized gain or loss on the school's investments (caused by changes in fair value) and the realized gain or loss (caused by sales of these investments)?
7. Compare the amount earned in tuition and student fees to the amount of education expenses incurred by the school to determine whether it generated a profit or a loss this past year on educating its students. Support your answer with a schedule of items used to calculate your answer.

COMMUNICATION CASE

Go to the website https://www.independentsector.org/governance_ethics_resource_center and click on Strong Financial Oversight. After registering, the site will provide various topics such as financial records, annual budget, and financial performance. Under each of these topics, click on Core Concepts. Write a short report on the types of policies, actions, and procedures a private not-for-profit organization should take to help ensure proper financial transparency and accountability.

chapter 19

Accounting for Estates and Trusts

From 2004 through 2013, some $10 trillion is going to pass from one generation to another.[1] It is a sum approximating the value of all the companies listed on the stock exchanges.[2]

Individuals labor throughout their lives in part to accumulate property that they eventually can convey for the benefit of spouses, children, relatives, friends, charities, and the like. After amassing wealth, donors typically seek to achieve two goals:

- To minimize the amount of these assets that must be surrendered to the government.
- To ensure that the ultimate disposition of all property is consistent with the donor's wishes.

Therefore, accountants (as well as attorneys and financial planners) often assist individuals who are developing estate plans or creating trust funds to accomplish these goals. At a later date, the accountant may also serve in the actual administration of the estate or trust. In either estate or trust planning, the person's intentions must be spelled out in clear detail so that no misunderstanding arises. All available techniques also should be considered to limit the impact of taxes. To carry out these varied responsibilities properly, it is of paramount importance that the person doing so have a knowledge of the legal and reporting aspects of estates and trusts.

Although many of the complex legal rules and regulations in these areas are beyond the scope of an accounting textbook, an overview of both estates and trusts can introduce the issues that members of the accounting profession frequently encounter.

Learning Objectives

After studying this chapter, you should be able to:

- LO1 Understand the proper methods of accounting for and administering an estate and the corresponding legal terminology.
- LO2 Describe the types of estate distributions and identify the process of asset allocations and distributions from an estate.
- LO3 Understand the federal estate tax and state inheritance tax systems, the corresponding exemptions, and tax planning opportunities.
- LO4 Understand and account for the distinction between principal and income in the context of estate and trust accounting.
- LO5 Describe the financial statements and journal entries utilized to account for estate and trust transactions.
- LO6 Describe various trusts, their proper use, and accounting for activities.

Accounting for an Estate

> While none of us want to contemplate our death, or that of our spouse, we all need an estate plan. If you need motivation to reach this decision, remember that every dollar you keep from the folks in Washington or your state capital goes to someone you like a heck of a lot better—such as your kids, your younger sister, or your alma mater.[3]

The term *estate* simply refers to the property owned by an individual. However, in this chapter, *estate* is more specifically defined as a separate

[1] Experts predict that more than $40 trillion will pass from generation to generation by 2044. John Havens and Paul Schervish, "Why the $41 Trillion Wealth Transfer Estimate Is Still Valid: A Review of Challenges and Comments," *The Journal of Gift Planning*, Vol. 7, No. 1 (March 2003).

[2] Gregory Bresiger, "Prudence Redefined," *Financial Planning*, October 1, 1999, p. 165.

[3] Ellen P. Gunn, "How to Leave the Tax Man Nothing," *Fortune*, March 18, 1996, p. 94.

LO1

Understand the proper methods of accounting for and administering an estate and the corresponding legal terminology.

legal entity holding title to the real and personal assets of a deceased person. *Thus, estate accounting refers to the recording and reporting of financial events from the time of a person's death until the ultimate distribution of all property the estate holds.* To ensure that this disposition is as intended and to avoid disputes, each individual should prepare a *will,* "a person's declaration of how he desires his property to be disposed of after his death."[4] If an individual dies *testate* (having written a valid will), this document serves as the blueprint for settling the estate, disbursing all remaining assets, making various tax elections, and appointing fiduciaries to accomplish these tasks.

When a person dies *intestate* (without a legal will), state laws control the administration of his or her estate. Although these legal rules vary from state to state, they normally correspond with the most common patterns of distribution. When intestacy laws rather than a will apply, real property is conveyed based on the *laws of descent* whereas personal property transfers are made according to the *laws of distribution.*

Each individual state establishes laws governing wills and estates known as *probate laws. The National Conference of Commissioners on Uniform State Laws* developed the Uniform Probate Code in hopes of creating consistent treatment in this area. To date, almost half of the states have officially adopted the Uniform Probate Code.[5] In many of the other states, the rules and regulations applied are somewhat similar to those of the Uniform Probate Code. In practice, however, an accountant must become familiar with the specific laws of the state having jurisdiction over the estate of the specific decedent.

Administration of the Estate

Regardless of the locale, probate laws generally are designed to achieve three goals:

1. Gather, preserve, and account for all of the decedent's property.
2. Administer an orderly and fair settlement of all debts.
3. Discover and implement the decedent's intent for the remaining property held at death.

This process usually begins by filing a will with the probate court or indicating that no will has been discovered. If a will is presented, the probate court must rule on the document's validity. A will must meet specific legal requirements to be accepted. These requirements may vary from state to state. For example, would the following signed and dated statement constitute a valid will?

> "I want my children to have my money."

Because the writer is dead, the intention of this statement cannot be verified. Was this an idle wish made without thought, or did the decedent truly intend for this one sentence to constitute a will conveying all money to these specified individuals upon death? Did the decedent mean for all noncash assets to be liquidated with the proceeds being split among the children? Or did the writer strictly mean that just the cash on hand at the time of death should be transferred to them? Obviously, in some cases, a will's validity (and the decedent's intention) is not easily proven.

If deemed to be both authentic and valid, a will is admitted to probate, and the decedent's specific intentions will be carried to conclusion. All of the decedent's property must be located, debts paid, and distributions appropriately conveyed. Whether a will is present or not, an estate administrator must be chosen to serve in a stewardship capacity. This individual serves in a fiduciary position and is responsible for (1) satisfying all applicable laws and (2) making certain that the decedent's wishes are achieved (if known and if possible).

If a specific person is named in the will to hold this position, the individual is referred to as the *executor* (*executrix* if female; this text will generically use the term *executor*) *of the estate.* If the will does not designate an executor or if the named person is unwilling or unable to serve in this capacity (or if the decedent dies without a will), the courts must select a representative. A court-appointed representative is known legally as the

[4] *Barron's Law Dictionary*, 4th ed. (New York: Barron's Educational Services, Inc. 1996), p. 553.

[5] To see your state's version of the Uniform Probate Code, review the following link: www.law.cornell.edu/uniform/probate.html.

administrator (female: *administratrix*) *of the estate*. An executor/administrator is not forced to serve in this role for free; that person is legally entitled to reasonable compensation for all services rendered.[6]

The executor is normally responsible for fulfilling several tasks:

- Taking possession of all of the decedent's assets and inventorying this property.
- Discovering all claims against the decedent and settling these obligations.
- Filing estate income tax returns, federal estate tax returns, and state inheritance or estate tax returns.
- Distributing property according to the provisions of the will (according to state laws if a valid will is not available) or according to court order if necessary.
- Making a full accounting to the probate court to demonstrate that the executor has properly fulfilled the fiduciary responsibility.

Property Included in the Estate

The basis for all estate accounting is the property the decedent held at death. These assets are used to settle claims and pay taxes. Any property that remains is distributed according to the decedent's will (or applicable state intestacy laws). For estate-reporting purposes, all items are shown at fair value; except for unique situations involving decedents passing in calendar year 2010 (which we explain below), the historical cost paid by the deceased individual is no longer relevant. Fair value is especially important because the sale of some or all properties may be required to obtain enough cash to satisfy claims against the estate. If valuation problems arise, hiring an appraiser could become necessary.

Normally, an estate includes assets such as these:

- Cash.
- Investments in stocks and bonds.
- Interest accrued to the date of death.
- Dividends declared prior to death.
- Investments in businesses.
- Unpaid wages.
- Accrued rents and royalties.
- Valuables such as paintings and jewelry.

At the time of death, the decedent legally owned a certain amount of assets. The executor's task is to locate and value each item belonging to the estate as of that date.

Some state laws specify that real property such as land and buildings (and possibly certain types of personal property) be conveyed directly to the beneficiary or co-owner at the time of death, depending on the type of ownership held. Therefore, in these states, the inventory of the estate property that the executor develops for probate purposes does not include these assets. However, such items must still be listed in the filing of estate and inheritance tax returns because a legal transfer has occurred.

Discovery of Claims against the Decedent

An adequate opportunity should be given to the decedent's creditors to allow them to file claims against the estate. Usually, a public notice must be printed in an appropriate newspaper once a week for three weeks.[7] In many states, all claims must be presented within four months of the first of these notices. The executor must verify the validity of these claims and place them in order of priority. If insufficient funds are available, this ordering becomes quite important in establishing which parties receive payment. Consequently, claims in category 4

[6] To avoid using convoluted terminology, the term *executor* is generally used throughout this chapter to indicate both executors and administrators.

[7] Although many states require three weeks, *Ind. Code* §29-1-7-7(b) requires publication of notice for only two consecutive weeks. The CPA must understand the particular state's requirement(s) because this is a typical statutory variance from state to state.

of the following list, most of which are paid before a beneficiary receives any assets, have the greatest chance of remaining unpaid.

Typical Order of Priority

1. Expenses of administering the estate. Without this preferential treatment, the appointment of an acceptable executor and the hiring of lawyers, accountants, and/or appraisers could become a difficult task in estates with limited funds.
2. Funeral expenses and the medical expenses of any last illness.
3. Debts and taxes given preference under federal and state laws.
4. All other claims, such as unsecured obligations, credit card debts, and the like.

Protection for Remaining Family Members

As indicated, a number of states have adopted the Uniform Probate Code. However, other states have passed a wide variety of individual probate laws that differ in many distinct ways. Thus, no absolute rules about probate laws can be listed. Normally, they provide some amount of protection for a surviving spouse and/or the decedent's minor and dependent children. Small monetary allowances are conveyed to these parties prior to the payment of legal claims. For example, a *homestead allowance* is provided to a surviving spouse[8] and/or minor and dependent children. Even an estate heavily in debt would furnish some amount of financial relief for the members of the decedent's immediate family.

In addition, these same individuals frequently receive a small *family allowance* during a limited period of time while the estate is being administered. Family members are also entitled to a limited amount of exempt property such as automobiles, furniture, and jewelry. All other property is included in the estate to pay claims and be distributed according to the decedent's will or state inheritance laws.

LO2

Describe the types of estate distributions and identify the process of asset allocations and distributions from an estate.

Estate Distributions

If a will has been located and probated, property remaining after all claims are settled is conveyed according to that document's specifications.[9] A gift of real property such as land or a building is referred to as a *devise;* a gift of personal property such as stocks or furniture is a *legacy* or a *bequest*. A devise is frequently specific: "I leave 3 acres of land in Henrico County to my son," or "I leave the apartment building on Monument Avenue to my niece." Unless the estate is unable to pay all claims, a devise is simply conveyed to the intended party. However, if claims cannot be otherwise satisfied, the executor could be forced to sell or otherwise encumber the property despite the will's intention.

In contrast, a legacy may take one of several forms. The identification of the type of legacy becomes especially important if the estate has insufficient resources to meet the specifications of the will.

A *specific legacy* is a gift of personal property that is directly identified. "I leave my collection of pocket watches to my son" is an example of a specific legacy because the property is named.

A *demonstrative legacy* is a cash gift made from a particular source. The statement "I leave $10,000 from my savings account in the First National Bank to my sister" is a demonstrative legacy because the source is identified. If the savings account does not hold $10,000 at the time of death, the beneficiary will receive the amount available. In addition, the decedent may specify alternative sources if sufficient funds are not available. Ultimately, any shortfall usually is considered a general legacy.

A *general legacy* is a cash gift whose source is undesignated. "I leave $8,000 in cash to my nephew" is a gift viewed as a general legacy.

A *residual legacy* is a gift of any remaining estate property. Thus, it includes assets left after all claims, taxes, and other distributions are conveyed according to the residual

[8] Many states provide a $25,000 protective allowance for a surviving spouse. See *Ind. Code* §29-1-4-1.

[9] An exception, however, is that property legally held in joint tenancy with one or more individuals will pass to the surviving joint tenants at death and not be subject to the provisions of a will or intestate distribution.

provisions of the will. "The balance of my estate is to be divided evenly between my brother and the University of Notre Dame" is an example of a residual legacy.

An obvious problem arises if there are not enough assets in the estate to satisfy all legacies the will specified. The necessary reduction of the various gifts is referred to as the *process of abatement.* For illustration purposes, assume that a will lists the following provisions:

I leave 1,000 shares of AT&T to my brother (a specific legacy).

I leave my savings account at Chase Bank of $20,000 to my sister (a demonstrative legacy).

I leave $40,000 cash to my son (a general legacy).

I leave all remaining property to my daughter (a residual legacy).

Example 1

Assume that after paying all claims, the estate holds the shares of AT&T stock, the $20,000 Chase Bank savings account, and $75,000 in other cash. The first three parties (the brother, sister, and son) receive the specific assets stated in the will, and the residual legacy (to the daughter) would be the $35,000 cash balance left after the $40,000 general legacy is paid.

Example 2

Assume that after paying all claims, the estate holds the shares of AT&T stock, the Chase Bank savings account, and only $35,000 in other cash. The first two individuals (the brother and sister) receive the specified assets, but the son can claim only the remaining $35,000 cash rather than the promised $40,000. Based on the process of abatement, the daughter receives nothing; no amount is left as a residual legacy after the other legacies have been distributed.

Example 3

Assume that after paying all claims, the estate holds the shares of AT&T stock, but the Chase Bank savings account has a balance of only $12,000 rather than the promised $20,000. Other cash held by the estate totals $51,000. The stock is distributed to the brother, but the sister gets just the $12,000 cash in the Chase Bank savings account. In most states, the remaining $8,000 is treated as a general legacy. Consequently, in those states the sister receives the additional $8,000 in this manner and the son receives the specified $40,000. The daughter is then left with only the $3,000 in cash that remains. If the decedent resided in a state that did not treat the $8,000 shortfall as a general legacy, then the sister would receive only the $12,000 in the Chase Bank account, and the daughter would receive the $11,000 in cash that remains.

Example 4

Assume that the decedent sold the shares of AT&T stock before death and that after paying all claims, the Chase Bank savings account holds $22,000. Other cash amounts to $30,000. The brother receives nothing from the estate because the specific legacy did not exist at death.[10] The sister collects the promised $20,000 from the Chase Bank savings account, and the remaining $2,000 is added to the general legacy. Therefore, the son receives a total of $32,000 from the two cash sources. Because the general legacy was not fulfilled, no remainder exists as a residual legacy; thus, the daughter collects nothing from the estate.

Insufficient Funds

The debts and expenses of the administration are paid first in settling an estate. If the estate has insufficient available resources to satisfy these claims, the process of abatement

[10] The legal term *ademption* refers to a situation in which a specific bequest or devise fails because the property is not available for distribution. As a different possibility, a bequest or devise is said to *lapse* if the beneficiary cannot be located or dies before the decedent. This property then becomes part of the residual estate. For instance, if Anna Nicole Smith's will leaves her estate to her son, but her son predeceased her, her attempted transfer to her son likely lapses.

is again utilized. Each of the following categories is exhausted completely to pay all debts and expenses before money is taken from the next category:

Residual legacies (first to suffer abatement is the last to receive inheritance).
General legacies.
Demonstrative legacies.
Specific legacies and devises (last to suffer abatement).

LO3

Understand the federal estate tax and state inheritance tax systems, the corresponding exemptions, and tax planning opportunities.

Estate and Inheritance Taxes

Taxes incurred after death can be quite costly. For example, Helen Walton received \$5.1 billion in stock at the death of her husband Sam Walton (founder of Wal-Mart Stores, Inc.). At this value, these shares could eventually have cost her heirs as much as *\$2.8 billion* in taxes at her death: \$2.2 billion to the U.S. government and \$640 million to the State of Arkansas.[11]

Historically, estate taxes have been used as a method for redistributing wealth and raising revenues. According to tax experts, in 2009, estate taxes raised approximately \$21 billion in net revenue.[12] This total amounted to about 1 percent of all tax money generated by the federal government in that year.

The budget surpluses that appeared in the latter part of the 1990s began to cast doubts on the continued need for a federal estate tax. Many arguments can be made both for this tax (to some there is a perceived limit to the amount that a beneficiary should receive without work or effort) and against it (income that has been taxed once when earned should not be taxed again when the resulting assets are conveyed at death).

In 1999 (and again in 2000), the U.S. Congress voted a phased-in repeal of the estate tax, a measure that then-President Bill Clinton vetoed as being too costly. However, in 2001, Congress passed the Economic Growth and Tax Relief Reconciliation Act of 2001, which included provisions to gradually reduce and then abolish this tax by 2010. President George W. Bush signed the measure into law.

Incredibly, Congress failed to reinstate any estate tax for calendar year 2010 until December 2010. The result of this inaction was that taxpayers passing during 2010 did so potentially without the burden of the federal estate tax. Several extremely wealthy individuals managed to transfer hundreds of millions of dollars of additional inheritance to loved ones rather than paying Uncle Sam.[13] Without the federal estate tax scheme, the blanket basis increase at death was also limited—the result being that many wealthy beneficiaries will encounter a sizeable capital gain tax, albeit at a lower rate.

Congress enacted a significant revision to the estate tax in December 2010 that provided limited certitude for planning 2011 and 2012.[14] The provisions sunset at the end of 2012, leaving the potential for reversion to the exemption and rates in effect in 2001.

Federal Estate Taxes

The federal estate tax is an excise tax assessed on the right to convey property. The computation begins by determining the fair value of all property held at death. Therefore, even if real property is transferred immediately to the beneficiary and is not subject to probate, the value must still be included for federal estate tax purposes.[15] In establishing fair value, the

[11] Warren Midgett, "Mrs. Walton's Options," *Forbes*, October 19, 1992, pp. 22–23. Helen Walton passed away in April 2007 with a fortune estimated to exceed \$16 billion. This dramatic increase in Mrs. Walton's net worth reflects the need for, and value of, estate planning.

[12] *IRS Data Book*, 2008, http://www.irs.gov/pub/irs-soi/10esesttaxsnap.pdf (accessed June 2011).

[13] The Probate Lawyer, July 14, 2010, at http://www.probatelawyerblog.com/2010/07/george-steinbrenners-heirs-avoid-estate-tax-or-do-they.html.

[14] Tax Relief, Unemployment Insurance Reauthorization, and Job Creation Act of 2010, P.L. 111-312, December 17, 2010.

[15] Life insurance policies with named beneficiaries are also included in the value of the estate as long as the decedent had the right to change the beneficiary. This rule often results in decedents of modest means having taxable estates. This rule is also one that all estate planning and administration professionals must understand and consider.

executor may choose an alternate valuation date if that tax election will reduce the amount of estate taxes to be paid. This date is six months after death (or the date of disposition for any property disposed of within six months after death). Thus, the federal estate tax process starts by determining all asset values at death or this alternate date. Note that a piecemeal valuation cannot be made; one of these dates must be used for all properties.

Several items then reduce the gross estate figure to arrive at the taxable value of the estate:

- Funeral expenses.
- Estate administration expenses.
- Liabilities.
- Casualties and thefts during the administration of estate.
- Charitable bequests.
- Marital deduction for property conveyed to spouse.
- State inheritance taxes.

Individuals are allowed to deduct a specified amount from the value of the estate in arriving at the federal estate tax. Recent tax legislation has escalated the portion of an estate that is exempted. Any remaining amount is taxed at graduated rates based on the year of death. However, the tax legislation that provided escalating exemptions expired at the end of 2010,[16] as shown in the following chart. The new 2010 legislation renewed an increased exemption.

Date of Death	Estate Tax Exemption at Death	Highest Estate Tax Rate
2009	3.5 million	45
2010	Tax is repealed	N/A
2011	5.0 million	35
2012	5.0 million	35

In the past, individuals have often sought to decrease the size of their estates to reduce estate taxes by making gifts during their lifetimes. Annual gifts of $13,000 per person (an amount that is indexed to change with inflation) can be made tax-free to an unlimited number of donees.[17] The federal gift tax has not been eliminated by tax legislation, but a $5 million lifetime tax-free exclusion has been established over and above the $13,000 exclusion per person per year. Furthermore, instead of having a separate tax rate schedule as in the past, the maximum gift tax rate eventually will be the same as the maximum individual income tax rate.

What is the impact of all these changes? Prognosticators more than a decade ago were correct.

> The death of the estate tax is at best premature, and any planner thinking of abandoning an estate planning practice is missing a large opportunity. In fact, the estate planning provisions within the Economic Growth and Tax Relief Reconciliation Act of 2001 should be a boon for most planners, not a death toll.[18]

Federal Estate Taxes—Example 1 The determination of the taxable estate is obviously an important step in calculating estate taxes. Assume for illustration purposes that a person dies holding assets valued at $14 million and has total debts of $500,000 at death. Funeral expenses cost $100,000, and estate administration expenses amount to

[16] 26 U.S.C. §2001 (c), as amended. The 2010 Tax Relief Act permitted estates to elect to apply the "new" provisions to estates for decedents passing in 2010. The 2010 Tax Relief Act also provided 'portability' for a spouse's exemption, permiting a surviving spouse to increase her $5.0 million ($5.12 million for 2012) exemption by her deceased husband's remaining or unused exemption up to a total combined amount of $10.0 million.

[17] This amount increased from $11,000 to $12,000 in 2006 and to $13,000 in 2009 due to the indexing; Rev. Proc. 2008-66.

[18] Thomas J. Brzezenski, "New Era for Estate Planning," *Financial Planning,* July 1, 2001. The "death" was indeed short-lived as Congress acted in December 2010.

$200,000. This person's will left $5,200,000 to charitable organizations, and the remaining $8,000,000 (after debts and expenses) goes to the surviving spouse.[19] Under this set of circumstances, no taxable estate exists:

Gross estate (fair value)		$14,000,000
Funeral expenses	$ 100,000	
Administration expenses	200,000	
Debts	500,000	
Charity bequests	5,200,000	
Marital deduction	8,000,000	(14,000,000)
Taxable estate		–0–
Estate tax		–0–

Federal Estate Taxes—Example 2 Because of the current exemptions, estate property ($5.12 million in 2012) can be conveyed tax-free to a beneficiary other than a spouse. The ability to shelter this amount of assets from tax has an important impact on estate planning. For example, in the preceding case, if the couple has already identified the recipient of the estate at the eventual death of the second spouse (their children, for example), a conveyance of the tax-free exclusion amount at the time of the first death may be advantageous. The second estate will then be smaller for subsequent taxation purposes, if it exceeds the then-applicable exemption amount. Frequently, individuals establish a trust fund for this purpose as a means of protecting their money and ensuring its proper distribution.

To illustrate, assume that the first spouse died in 2012. Assume also that the will that is written is identical to the preceding example except that only $3,000,000 is conveyed to the surviving spouse and the remaining $5.0 million is placed in a trust fund for the couple's children (a nondeductible amount for estate tax purposes). The estate tax return must now be adjusted to appear as follows:

Gross estate		$14,000,000
Funeral expenses	$ 100,000	
Administration expenses	200,000	
Debts	500,000	
Charity bequests	5,200,000	
Marital deduction	2,880,000	(8,880,000)
Taxable estate (conveyed to trust)		5,120,000
Tax-free amount ($5,120,000 exemption)		(5,120,000)
Taxable estate		–0–

Again, the estate pays no taxes, but only $2,880,000 is added to the surviving spouse's taxable estate rather than $8,000,000 as in the previous example. Thus, an eventual decrease in the couple's *total* estate has been accomplished. This is a particularly important consideration because, while the first spouse's exemption amount of $5.12 million is portable to the surviving spouse, such planning options are presently set to expire at the end of 2012.

To facilitate this type of planning, accountants and estate planners must understand the implications of how assets are titled as well. Legally, if a couple holds property as joint tenants or tenants by the entirety, the property passes automatically to the survivor at the death of the other party. Thus, if all property were held in one of these ways, the decedent would have no estate. However, if property is held by the couple as tenants in common, the portion the decedent owned is included in that person's estate and, up to the set limit, can be conveyed tax-free to a nonspouse beneficiary.

[19] Although not applicable in this case, surviving spouses have the right in many states to renounce the provisions of a will and take an established percentage (normally one-third or one-half) of the decedent's estate. Such laws protect surviving spouses from being disinherited and are referred to as *elective forced share provisions*.

Other Approaches to Reducing Estate Taxes One technique previously used by families with large fortunes to reduce estate taxes was to transfer assets to grandchildren and even great-grandchildren. This manner reduced the number of separate conveyances (each of which would have been subject to taxation at the top rate) from parent to child to grandchild. However, the government effectively eliminated the appeal of this option by establishing a generation-skipping transfer tax. Under this law, after an exemption, a flat tax was assessed on transfers by gift, bequest, or trust distribution to individuals two or more generations younger than the donors or decedents. (However, the exemption was unlimited for a transfer to a grandchild when the grandchild's parent was deceased and she was a lineal descendent of the transferor.)

With its passage of the Tax Relief, Unemployment Insurance Reauthorization, and Jobs Creation Act of 2010, Congress implemented a $5 million exemption per donor from the generation-skipping transfer tax (increased to $5.12 million for 2012).

State Inheritance Taxes

States assess inheritance taxes on the right to receive property with the levy and all other regulations varying, as discussed earlier, based on state laws. However, the specifications of a will determine the actual impact on the individual beneficiaries. Many wills dictate that all inheritance tax payments are to be made from any residual cash amounts that the estate holds. Consequently, individuals receiving residual legacies are forced to bear the entire burden of this tax—although, presumably, that was the testator's desire.

If the will makes no provisions for state inheritance taxes (or if the decedent dies intestate), the amounts conveyed to each party must be reduced proportionately based on the fair value received. Thus, the recipient of land valued at $200,000 would have to contribute twice as much for inheritance taxes as a beneficiary collecting cash of $100,000. Decreasing a cash legacy to cover the cost of inheritance taxes creates little problem for the executor. However, a direct reduction of an estate asset such as land, buildings, or corporate stocks might be virtually impossible. Normally, the beneficiary in such cases is required to pay enough cash to satisfy the applicable inheritance tax. The estate planning process often establishes life insurance policies to provide cash for such payments. However, the ownership of such insurance may in turn result in the proceeds being subjected to the federal estate tax.

Estate and Trust Income Taxes

Although all estates require time to be settled, the period can become quite lengthy if complex matters arise. From the date of death until ultimate resolution, an estate is viewed legally as a taxable entity and must file a federal tax return if gross income is $600 or more. The return is due by the 15th day of the fourth month following the close of the estate's taxable year. The calendar year or any other fiscal year may be chosen as the taxable year. In 2008, the Internal Revenue Service collected $12.3 billion of income taxes from estates and trusts.[20]

Applicable income tax rules for estates and trusts are generally the same as for individual taxpayers. Therefore, dividend, rental, interest, and other income earned by an estate in the period following death is taxable to the estate unless the income is of a type that is specifically nontaxable (such as municipal bond interest).

A $600 personal exemption is provided as a decrease to the taxable balance. In addition, a reduction is allowed for (1) any taxable income donated to charity and (2) any taxable income for the year distributed to a beneficiary. In 2012, federal tax rates were 15 percent on the first $2,400 of taxable income per year with various rates levied on any excess income earned up to $11,650. At a taxable income level more than $11,650, a 35 percent rate was incurred.

As an illustration, assume that in 2012 an estate earned net rental income of $30,000 and dividend income of $10,000. The dividend income was distributed immediately to a

[20] *IRS Data Book,* 2010, p. 3.

beneficiary and was taxable income for that individual, and $7,400 of the rental income was given to charity. Estate income taxes for the year would be computed as follows:

Rental income	$ 30,000
Dividend income	10,000
Total revenue	$ 40,000
Exemption	(600)
Gift to charity	(7,400)
Distributed to beneficiary	(10,000)
Taxable income	$ 22,000
Income tax:	
15% of first $2,400	$ 360.00
25% of next $3,200 ($5,600 − $2,400)	800.00
28% of next $2,900 ($8,500 − $5,600)	812.00
33% of next $3,150 ($11,650 − $8,500)	1,039.50
35% of next $10,350 ($22,000 − $11,650)	3,622.50
	$6,634.00[21]

LO4

Understand and account for the distinction between principal and income in the context of estate and trust accounting.

The Distinction between Income and Principal

In many estates, the executor faces the problem of differentiating between income and principal transactions. For example, a will might state "all income earned on my estate for five years after death is to go to my sister, with the estate then being conveyed to my children." The recipient of the income is known as an *income beneficiary* whereas the party who ultimately receives the principal (also known as the *corpus*) is called a *remainderman.* As the fiduciary for the estate, the executor must ensure that all parties are treated fairly. Thus, if amounts are distributed incorrectly, the court can hold the executor legally liable.

The definitional difference between principal and income appears to pose little problem. The *estate* principal encompasses all of the decedent's assets at death; *income* is the earnings on these assets after death. However, some transactions are not easily categorized as either principal or income. As examples, consider these:

- Are funeral expenses charged to principal or income?
- Is the executor's fee charged to principal or income?
- Are dividends that are declared before death but received after death viewed as principal or income?
- If stocks are sold for a gain, is this gain viewed as income or an increase in principal?
- Are repairs to rental property considered a reduction of principal or of income?

Clearly, the distinction between principal and income is not always obvious. For this reason, in writing a will, an individual may choose (and should be advised) to spell out the procedure by which principal and income are to be calculated. If defined in this manner, the executor merely has to follow these instructions.

In certain cases, the decedent will have provided no guidance as to the method by which transactions are to be classified. The executor must apply state laws to determine these principal and income figures. Many states have adopted the Revised Uniform Principal and Income Act as a standard for this purpose. However, some states have adopted modified versions of the Revised Uniform Principal and Income Act and still others have created their own distinct laws. Generally accepted accounting principles are not applicable; the distinction between principal and income is defined solely by the decedent's intentions or by state laws.

[21] As fiduciary entities, estates and trusts are taxed at the same income tax rates. Note that their top rate of 35 percent becomes applicable at a taxable income level of only $11,650. In comparison, for 2012, this same top income tax rate of 35 percent was not assessed for a single taxpayer, head of household, or joint return until taxable income reached $388,350.

Although differences exist because of unique state laws or the provisions of a will, the following transactions are normally viewed as adjustments (either increases or decreases) to the *principal of the estate:*

- Life insurance proceeds if the estate is named as the beneficiary.
- Dividends declared prior to death and any other income earned prior to death.
- Liquidating dividends even if declared after death.
- Debts incurred prior to death.
- Gains and losses on the sale of corporate securities or rental property.
- Major repairs (improvements) to rental property.
- Investment commissions and other costs.
- Funeral expenses.
- Homestead and family allowances.

The *income of the estate* includes all revenues and expenses recognized after the date of death. Within this calculation, the following items are included as reductions to income:

- Recurring taxes such as real and personal property taxes.
- Ordinary repair expenses.
- Water and other utility expenses.
- Insurance expenses.
- Other ordinary expenses necessary for the management and preservation of the estate.

Several costs such as the executor's fee, court costs, and attorneys' and accountants' charges must be apportioned between principal and interest as required by state law or in some fair manner, if such allocation has not been specified in the decedent's last will and testament.

Recording of the Transactions of an Estate

The accounting process that the executor of an estate uses is quite unique. *Because the probate court has given this individual responsibility over the assets of the estate, the accounting system is designed to demonstrate the proper management and distribution of these properties.* Thus, several features of estate accounting should be noted:

- All estate assets are recorded at fair value to indicate the amount and extent of the executor's accountability. Any assets subsequently discovered are disclosed separately so that these adjustments to the original estate value can be noted when reporting to the probate court. The ultimate disposition of all properties must be recorded to provide evidence that the executor's fiduciary responsibility has been fulfilled.
- Debts, taxes, and other obligations are recorded only at the date of payment. In effect, the system is designed to monitor the disposition of assets. Thus, claims are relevant to the accounting process only at the time that the assets are disbursed. Likewise, distributions of legacies are not entered into the records until actually conveyed. As mentioned earlier, devises of real property are often transferred by operation of law at death so that no accounting is necessary.
- Because of the importance of separately identifying income and principal transactions in many estates, the accounting system must always note whether income or principal is being affected. Quite frequently, the executor maintains two cash balances to assist in this process.

To illustrate, assume that James T. Wilson dies on April 1, 2012. The following valid will has these provisions:

> I name Tim Hernly as executor of my estate.
>
> I leave my house, furnishings, and artwork to my aunt, Ann Wilson.
>
> I leave my investments in stocks to my uncle, Jack E. Wilson.

I leave my automobile and personal effects to my grandmother, Nancy Wilson.

I leave $38,000 in cash to my brother, Brian Wilson.

I leave any income earned on my estate to my niece, Karen Wilson.

All remaining property is to be placed in trust for my children.

Tim Hernly must (1) perform a search to discover all estate assets and (2) allow an adequate opportunity for every possible claim to be filed. The assets should be recorded immediately at fair value with the creation of the Estate Principal account. This total represents the amount of assets for which the executor is initially accountable. The following journal entry establishes the values for the assets owned by James T. Wilson at his death that have been found to date:

Account	Debit	Credit
Cash—Principal	11,000	
Interest Receivable on Bonds	3,000	
Dividends Receivable on Stocks	4,000	
Life Insurance—Payable to Estate	40,000	
Residence	90,000	
Household Furnishings and Artwork	24,000	
Automobile	4,000	
Personal Effects	2,000	
Investment in Bonds	240,000	
Investment in Stocks	50,000	
Estate Principal		468,000

Following is a list of subsequent transactions incurred by this estate with each appropriate journal entry. Because estate income is to be conveyed to one party (Karen Wilson) but the remaining principal is to be placed in trust, careful distinction between these two elements is necessary.

Transaction 1

The executor paid funeral expenses of $4,000.

Account	Debit	Credit
Funeral and Administrative Expenses	4,000	
Cash—Principal		4,000

Transaction 2

The life insurance policy payable to the estate (shown in the initial entry) is collected.

Account	Debit	Credit
Cash—Principal	40,000	
Life Insurance—Payable to Estate		40,000

Transaction 3

The title to 4.0 acres of land is discovered in a safe deposit box. This asset was not included in the original inventory of estate property. An appraiser sets the value of the land at $22,000.

Account	Debit	Credit
Land	22,000	
Assets Subsequently Discovered (Estate Principal)		22,000

Transaction 4

The executor receives claims totaling $24,000 for debts the decedent incurred *prior to death*. This amount includes medical expenses covering the decedent's last illness

($11,000), property taxes ($4,000), utilities ($1,000), personal income taxes ($5,000), and other miscellaneous expenses ($3,000). The executor pays all of these claims.

Debts of the Decedent	24,000	
Cash—Principal		24,000

Transaction 5

Interest of $8,000 is collected on the bonds held by the estate. Of this amount, $3,000 was earned prior to the decedent's death and was included as a receivable in the initial recording of the estate assets.

Cash—Principal	3,000	
Cash—Income	5,000	
Interest Receivable on Bonds		3,000
Estate Income		5,000

Transaction 6

Dividends of $6,000 are collected from the stocks held by the estate. Of this amount, $4,000 was declared prior to the decedent's death and was included as a receivable in the initial recording of the estate assets.

Cash—Principal	4,000	
Cash—Income	2,000	
Dividends Receivable on Stocks		4,000
Estate Income		2,000

Transaction 7

The executor now has a problem. The Cash—Principal balance is currently $30,000:

Beginning balance	$ 11,000
Funeral expenses	(4,000)
Life insurance	40,000
Payment of debts	(24,000)
Interest income	3,000
Dividends	4,000
Current balance	$ 30,000

However, the decedent bequeathed his brother, Brian Wilson, $38,000 in cash. This general legacy cannot be fulfilled without selling some property. Most assets have been promised as specific legacies and cannot, therefore, be used to satisfy a general legacy. Two assets, though, are residual: the investment in bonds and the land that was discovered. The executor must sell enough of these properties to generate the remaining funding needed for the $38,000 conveyance. In this illustration, assume that the executor chooses to dispose of the land and negotiates a price of $24,000. Because a principal asset is being sold, the extra $2,000 received above the recorded value is considered an adjustment to principal rather than an increase in income. Similarly, if the asset sold at an amount below the appraised value of $22,000, this transaction would result in a reduction to principal.

Cash—Principal	24,000	
Land		22,000
Gain on Realization		2,000

Discussion Question

IS THIS REALLY AN ASSET?

Robert Sweingart died during July 2012 at the age of 101. He had outlived many of his relatives, including the person named in his will as executor of his estate. Thus, the probate court selected the decedent's nephew Timothy J. Lee, as administrator. Lee promptly began his duties including reading the will and taking an inventory of Sweingart's properties. Although the will had been written in 1982, Lee could see that most of the provisions would be easy to follow. Sweingart had made a number of specific and demonstrative legacies that could simply be conveyed to the beneficiaries. The will also included a $20,000 general legacy to a local church with a residual legacy to a well-known charity. Unfortunately, after all other legacies were distributed, the estate would have only about $14,000 cash.

One item in the will concerned the administrator. Sweingart had made the following specific legacy: "I leave my collection of my grandfather's letters which are priceless to me, to my cousin, William." Lee discovered the letters in a wall safe in Sweingart's home. About 40 letters existed, all in excellent condition. They were written by Sweingart's grandfather during the Civil War and described in vivid detail the Second Battle of Bull Run and the Battle of Gettysburg. Unfortunately, Lee could find no trace of a cousin named William. He apparently had died or vanished during the thirty-five year period since the will was written.

Lee took the letters to two different antique dealers. One stated, "A museum that maintains a Civil War collection would love to have these. They do a wonderful job of explaining history. But a museum would not pay for them. They have no real value since many letters written during this period still exist. I would recommend donating them to a museum."

The second dealer took a different position: "I think if you can find individuals who specialize in collecting Civil War memorabilia they might be willing to pay a handsome price especially if these letters help to fill out their collections. A lot of people in this country are fascinated by the Civil War. The number seems to grow each day. The letters are in great condition. It would take some investigation on your part, but they could be worth a small fortune."

Lee now has to prepare an inventory of his uncle's property for probate purposes. How should he report these letters? What should Lee do next with the letters in order to meet his fiduciary obligation(s) to the estate and the beneficiaries?

Transaction 8

Fees of $1,000 charged for administering the affairs of the estate are paid. Of this amount, we assume that $200 is considered to be applicable to estate income.

Funeral and Administrative Expenses	800	
Expenses—Income	200	
Cash—Principal		800
Cash—Income		200

Transaction 9

On October 13, 2012, the house, furnishings, and artwork are given to the decedent's aunt (Ann); the stocks are transferred to the uncle (Jack); and the grandmother (Nancy) receives the decedent's automobile and personal effects.

Legacy—Ann Wilson (residence, furnishings, and artwork)	114,000	
Legacy—Jack E. Wilson (stocks)	50,000	
Legacy—Nancy Wilson (automobile and personal effects)	6,000	
Residence		90,000
Household Furnishings and Artwork		24,000
Investment in Stocks		50,000
Automobile		4,000
Personal Effects		2,000

LO5

Describe the financial statements and journal entries utilized to account for estate and trust transactions.

Charge and Discharge Statement

As necessary, the executor files periodic reports with the probate court to disclose the progress being made in settling the estate. This report, which may vary from state to state, is generally referred to as a *charge and discharge statement.* If income and principal must be accounted for separately, the statement is prepared in two parts. For both principal and income, the statement should indicate the following:

1. The assets under the executor's control.
2. Disbursements made to date.
3. Any property still remaining.

Thus, the executor of James T. Wilson's estate can produce Exhibit 19.1 immediately after Transaction 9. (Transaction numbers are included in parentheses for clarification purposes.)

At this point in the illustration, only three transactions remain: distribution of the $38,000 cash to the decedent's brother, conveyance of the $6,800 cash generated as income since death to the niece, and establishment of the trust fund with the remaining principal. The trust fund will receive the $240,000 in bonds and the $15,200 in cash that is left in principal ($53,200 total less $38,000 paid to the brother).

Legacy—Brian Wilson	38,000	
Cash—Principal		38,000
Distribution to Income Beneficiary—Karen Wilson	6,800	
Cash—Income		6,800
Principal Assets Transferred to Trustee	255,200	
Cash—Principal		15,200
Investment in Bonds		240,000

The executor would then prepare a final charge and discharge statement and then closing entries to signal the conclusion of the estate as a reporting entity.

Accounting for a Trust

A trust is created by the conveyance of assets to a fiduciary (or trustee) who manages the assets and ultimately disposes of them to one or more beneficiaries. The trustee may be an individual or an organization such as a bank or other financial institution. Over the years, trust funds have become quite popular in this country for a number of reasons. Often they are established to reduce the size of a person's taxable estate and, thus, the amount of estate taxes that must eventually be paid. As one financial adviser has stated,

EXHIBIT 19.1 Executor's Charge and Discharge Statement

ESTATE OF JAMES T. WILSON
Charge and Discharge Statement
April 1, 2012–October 13, 2012
Tim Hernly, Executor

As to Principal			
I charge myself with:			
Assets per original inventory			$468,000
Assets subsequently discovered: land (Trans. 3)			22,000
Gain on sale of land (Trans. 7)			2,000
Total charges			$492,000
I credit myself with:			
Debts of decedent (Trans. 4):			
Medical expenses	$ 11,000		
Property taxes	4,000		
Utilities	1,000		
Personal income taxes	5,000		
Others	3,000	$ 24,000	
Funeral and administrative expenses (Trans. 1 and 8)		4,800	
Legacies distributed (Trans. 9):			
Ann Wilson (house, furnishings, and artwork)	114,000		
Jack E. Wilson (stocks)	50,000		
Nancy Wilson (automobile and personal effects)	6,000	170,000	
Total credits			198,800
Estate principal			$293,200
Estate principal:			
Cash			$ 53,200
Investment in bonds			240,000
Estate principal			$293,200
As to Income			
I charge myself with:			
Interest income (Trans. 5)			$ 5,000
Dividend income (Trans. 6)			2,000
Total charges			7,000
I credit myself with:			
Administrative expenses charged to income (Trans. 8)			200
Balance as to income			$ 6,800
Balance as to income:			
Cash			$ 6,800

"Who needs to establish a trust? You do, and so does your spouse. There may be several good reasons, but start with this: If you don't set up trusts, your heirs may pay hundreds of thousands of dollars in unnecessary estate taxes."[22]

Estate taxes are not the only reason for establishing a trust. People form trust funds to protect assets and ensure that the eventual use of these assets is as intended. Trusts can also result from the provisions of a will, specified by the decedent as a means of guiding the distribution of estate property. In legal terms, an *inter vivos trust* is one started by a living individual, whereas a *testamentary trust* is created by a will.

[22] Jeff Burger, "Which Trust Is Best for Your Family?" *Medical Economics*, August 1, 1988, p. 141.

Frequently, the *trustor* or *settlor* or *grantor* (the person who funds the trust) will believe that a chosen trustee is simply better suited to manage complicated investments than is the beneficiary. A young child, for example, is not capable of directing the use of a large sum of money. The trustor may have the same opinion of an individual who possesses little business expertise. Likewise, the creation of a trust for the benefit of a person with a mental or severe physical handicap might be considered a wise decision.

During recent years, one specific type of trust, a *revocable living trust,* has become especially popular and controversial. The trustor usually manages the fund and receives most, if not all, of the income until death. After that time, future income and possibly principal payments are made to one or more previously named beneficiaries. Because the trust is revocable, the trustor can change these beneficiaries or other terms of the trust at any time.

> You want to leave knowing your loved ones have the best financial breaks possible. That's why the idea of a revocable living trust may sound so promising. During your lifetime, you turn over all assets to a trust. But you act as your own trustee, so you determine how the assets will be managed and distributed. Then, happy in the knowledge that you can change the trust at any time, you have the joy of knowing you're setting up a financial plan for your life and after death.[23]

Revocable living trusts offer several significant advantages that appeal to certain individuals. First, this type of trust avoids the delay and expense of probate. At the trustor's death, the trust continues and makes future payments as defined in the trust agreement. In some states, this advantage can be quite important, but in others the cost of establishing the trust may be more expensive than the potential probate costs. The taxable income of the revocable living trust is included in the grantor's individual income tax return while that person remains alive. It is not taxed within a fiduciary income tax return until after the grantor's death.

LO6

Describe various trusts, their proper use, and accounting for activities.

Second, conveyance of assets through a trust can be made without publicity whereas a will is a public document. Thus, anyone who values privacy may want to consider the revocable living trust. The entertainer Bing Crosby, for example, set up such a trust so that no outsider would know how his estate was distributed.[24]

Although the number of other types of trusts is quite large,[25] several of the more common that have been utilized and that clients are likely to have established include:

- *Credit shelter trust* (also known as a *bypass trust* or *family trust*). This trust is designed for couples. Each spouse agrees to transfer at death an amount of up to the tax-free exclusion ($5.12 million in 2012) to a trust fund for the benefit of the other. Thus, the income that these funds generate goes to the surviving spouse, but at the time of this second individual's subsequent death, the principal is conveyed to a different beneficiary. As discussed in the previous section, this arrangement can be used to reduce the estate of the surviving spouse and, therefore, the amount of estate taxes paid by the couple. With portability of the $5.12 million exemption, the use of credit shelter trusts will be significantly reduced unless Congress repeals the provision, set to expire at the end of 2012.

  > If your estate is large enough to be threatened by the federal estate tax, you can incorporate provisions to soften the blow. This year [2003], federal law permits each person to leave $1 million in assets tax-free—in addition to the unlimited amount that can go to a surviving spouse. But leaving everything to a spouse can be a costly mistake if it inflates the survivor's estate to the level at which it may be hit by the tax. To avoid this, couples should make sure each owns enough individually to take advantage of the $1 million tax-free allowance, even if it means splitting jointly owned assets. Then, both husband and wife could include in their wills a trust (called a bypass or credit shelter trust) to hold $1 million, from which the survivor would get all

[23] Estelle Jackson, "Living Trust May Sound Promising," *Richmond Times–Dispatch*, October 13, 1991, p. C1.

[24] Ibid., p. C5.

[25] The cost of establishing and maintaining trusts can be significant. Therefore, use of these trusts may be limited to taxpayers of substantial means.

> the income and possibly some principal during his or her lifetime, with the balance going to the children upon the spouse's death. That $1 million would go to the kids tax-free, rather than being included—and possibly taxed—in the surviving spouse's estate.[26]

- *Qualified terminable interest property trust* (known as a *QTIP trust*). Individuals frequently create a QTIP trust to serve as a credit shelter trust. They convey property to the trust and specify that the income, and possibly a portion of the principal, be paid to the surviving spouse (or other beneficiary). At a specified time, the trust conveys the remainder to a designated party. Such trusts are popular because they provide the spouse a steady income but the trustee can guard the principal and then convey it at a later date to the individual's children or other designated parties. However, no trust exists without some potential problems:

> During the spouse's lifetime, no one else—not even the children—can benefit from the QTIP trust. However, this can mean years of potential conflict as the children wait for their inheritance. To minimize this potential problem, it often makes sense to set up another trust for the benefit of the children. This is particularly so if a new spouse (stepparent) is close in age to your children.[27]

- *Charitable remainder trust.* All income is paid to one or more beneficiaries identified by the trustor. After a period of time (or at the death of the beneficiaries), the principal is given to a stated charity. Thus, the trustor is guaranteeing a steady income to the intended parties while still making a gift to a charitable organization. These trusts are especially popular if a taxpayer holds property that has appreciated greatly (such as real estate or stocks) that is to be liquidated. By conveying it to the trust prior to liquidation, the sale is viewed as that of the charity and is, hence, nontaxable. Thus, tax on the gain is avoided and significantly more money remains available to generate future income for the beneficiaries (possibly the original donor). "This trust lets you leave assets to your favored charity, get a tax break, but retain income for life."[28]
- *Charitable lead trust.* This trust is the reverse of a charitable remainder trust. Income from the trust fund goes to benefit a charity for a specified time with the remaining principal then going to a different beneficiary. For example, a charity might receive the income from trust assets until the donor's children reach their 21st birthdays.

> Jacqueline Kennedy Onassis used this technique and ended up sheltering roughly 90 percent of the trust assets from estate taxes. Setup and operating costs, however, preclude the use of this type of trust unless the assets involved are substantial. As such this is a vehicle for the very wealthy, allowing them to keep an asset in the family but greatly reducing the cost of passing it on.[29]

- *Grantor retained annuity trusts* (known as *GRATs*). The trustor maintains the right to collect fixed payments from the trust fund while giving the principal to a beneficiary after a stated time or at the trustor's death. For example, the trustor might retain the right to receive an amount equal to 7 percent of the initial investment annually with any remaining balance of the trust fund to go to his or her children at death. Because the beneficiary will not receive the residual amount for years, a current value is computed for gift tax purposes. Depending on (1) the length of time before final distribution to the beneficiary, (2) the assumed rate of income, and (3) the amounts to be distributed periodically to the trustor, this value is often quite small so that the gift tax is reduced or eliminated entirely. However, GRATs can have certain risks.

[26] Josephine Rossi, "Your Will Be Done," *Kiplinger's Personal Finance*, January 2003. By 2009, this $1 million amount had grown to $3.5 million and increased to $5.12 million in 2012.

[27] Philip Maynard, "A QTIP Protects the Family," *CreativeLiving Magazine*, Autumn 2001.

[28] Lynn Asinof, "Estate-Planning Techniques for the Rich," *The Wall Street Journal*, January 11, 1995, p. C1.

[29] Ibid., p. C15.

> When setting up a GRAT, remember that the annuity you establish at its outset could drain the trust if the expected growth doesn't materialize. Then you will have paid taxes and legal costs . . . and will have left little to your heirs. Equally important, the grantor must outlive the trust. If you die before the GRAT ends, the assets will revert to your estate.[30]

- *Minor's Section 2503(c) trust.* Established for a minor, this trust fund usually is designed to receive a tax-free gift of up to $13,000 each year ($26,000 if the transfer is made by a married couple). Over a period of time, especially if enough beneficiaries are available, this trust can remove a significant amount of assets from a person's estate. The change in the gift tax laws and the expansion of the estate exemption may make this trust less attractive.
- *Spendthrift trust.* This trust is established so that the beneficiary cannot transfer or assign any unreceived payments. The purpose of such trusts is to prevent the beneficiary from squandering the assets the trust fund is holding or the beneficiary's creditors from reaching the assets. This type of trust is particularly useful to protect irresponsible beneficiaries, for example, children, and beneficiaries whose former spouses maintain legal actions against them.
- *Irrevocable life insurance trust.* With this trust, the donor contributes money to buy life insurance on the donor. If a married couple is creating the trust, usually the life insurance policy is designed to pay the proceeds only after the second spouse dies. The proceeds are not part of the estate and the beneficiary can use the cash to pay estate and inheritance taxes.
- *Qualified personal resident trust (QPRT).* The donor gives his or her home to the trust but retains the right to live in the house for a period of time rent-free. This removes what is often an individual's most valuable asset from the estate. This type of trust has characteristics similar to a GRAT.

> The term of the trust can be as short or as long as desired. The longer the term the lower the value of the gift. If the grantor dies before the term of the trust expires, however, the property will revert back to the estate of the deceased and be subject to estate taxes at its current value. Therefore, a term should be picked that the grantor believes he or she will outlive for the benefits of the QPRT to be effective.[31]

As these examples indicate, many trust funds generate income for one or more beneficiaries (known as *life tenants* if the income is to be conveyed until the person dies). At death or the end of a specified period, the remaining principal is transferred to a different beneficiary (a *remainderman*). Therefore, as with estates, differentiating between principal and income is ultimately important in accounting for trust funds. This distinction is especially significant because trusts frequently exist for decades and can control and generate enormous amounts of assets.

The reporting function is also important because of the trustee's legal responsibilities. This fiduciary is charged with the wise use of all funds and may be sued by the beneficiaries if actions are considered to be unnecessarily risky or in contradiction to the terms of the trust arrangement. To avoid potential legal problems, the trustee is normally called on to exercise reasonable and prudent care in managing the assets of the fund.

Record-Keeping for a Trust Fund

Trust accounting is quite similar to the procedures demonstrated previously for an estate. However, because many different types of trusts can be created and an extended time period might be involved, the accounting process may become more complex than that for an estate. As an example, an apartment house or a significant portion of a business could be placed in a trust for 20 years or longer. Thus, the possible range of transactions to be recorded becomes quite broad. In such cases, the fiduciary often establishes two separate

[30] Pam Black, "A GRAT Can Be Great for Saving Your Kids a Bundle," *BusinessWeek*, March 1, 1999, p. 116.

[31] Michael Mingione, "Trust Your House," *The CPA Journal*, September 1996, p. 40.

sets of accounts, one for principal and one for income. As an alternative, the fiduciary could utilize a single set of records with the individual accounts identified as to income or principal.

In the same manner as an estate, the trust agreement should specify the distinction between transactions to be recorded as income and those to be recorded as principal. If the agreement is silent or if a transaction that is not covered by the agreement is incurred, state laws apply to delineate the accounting. Generally accepted accounting principles usually are not considered appropriate. For example, trusts utilize the cash method rather than accrual accounting in recording most transactions. Although a definitive set of rules is not possible, the following list indicates the typical division of principal and income transactions:

Adjustments to the Trust's Principal

Investment costs and commissions.
Income taxes on gains added to the principal.
Costs of preparing property for rent or sale.
Extraordinary repairs (improvements).

Adjustments to the Trust's Income

Rent expense.
Lease cancellation fees.
Interest expense.
Insurance expense.
Income taxes on trust income.
Property taxes.

Trustee fees and the cost of periodic reporting (accountant and legal fees) must be allocated between trust income and principal. This allocation is often based on the value of assets within each (principal/income) category.

Accounting for the Activities of a Trust

An *inter vivos* trust reports on an annual basis (often more frequently) to all income and principal beneficiaries. However, testamentary trusts come under the jurisdiction of the courts so that additional reporting regularly becomes necessary. Normally, a statement resembling the charge and discharge statement of an estate is adequate for these purposes. Two accounts, Trust Principal and Trust Income, monitor changes that occur. For a testamentary trust, the opening principal balance is the fair value used by the executor for estate tax purposes.

To illustrate, assume that the following events occur in connection with the creation of a charitable remainder trust. The will of Samuel Statler created a trust with the income earned each year to go to his niece for 10 years and the principal then conveyed to a local university (the charity).

1. Cash of $80,000 and stocks (that originally cost $39,000 but are now worth $47,000) are transferred from the estate to the First National Bank of Michigan because this organization has agreed to serve as trustee for these funds.
2. The trustee invested cash of $76,000 in bonds paying 11 percent annual cash interest.
3. Dividends of $6,000 on the stocks are collected, and interest of $7,000 is received on the bonds. No receivables had been included in the estate for these amounts.
4. At the end of the year, an additional $3,000 in interest is due on the bonds.
5. As trustee, the bank charges $2,000 for services rendered for the year. Statler's will provided that such fees should be allocated equally between principal and income.
6. The niece is paid the appropriate amount of money from the trust fund.

As the trustee, the bank should record these transactions as follows:

Entry	Debit	Credit
1. Cash—Principal	80,000	
Investment in Stocks	47,000	
Trust Principal		127,000
To record trust assets at the fair market value figure used for estate tax purposes.		
2. Investment in Bonds	76,000	
Cash—Principal		76,000
To record acquisition of bonds using cash in trust fund.		
3. Cash—Income	13,000	
Trust—Income		13,000
To record dividends and interest collected.		
4. No entry is recorded. These earnings cannot be paid to the income beneficiary until collected so that accrual provides no benefit. Therefore, the trustee uses a cash basis system rather than accrual accounting.		
5. Trustee Expense—Income	1,000	
Trustee Expense—Principal	1,000	
Cash—Income		1,000
Cash—Principal		1,000
To allocate the trustee's fees evenly between principal and income.		
6. Equity in Income: Beneficiary	12,000	
Cash—Income		12,000
To record yearly payment made to income beneficiary. Amount is computed as the total of the dividends and interest of $13,000 less expenses of $1,000.		

Summary

1. An *estate* is the legal entity that holds title to a decedent's property until a final settlement and distribution can be made. State laws, known as *probate laws,* govern this process. These laws become particularly significant if the decedent has died intestate (without a will).
2. A decedent's will should name an executor to oversee the estate. If it does not, the probate court selects an administrator. The executor or administrator takes possession of all properties, settles valid claims, files tax returns, pays taxes due, and distributes any remaining assets according to the provisions of the decedent's will or state inheritance laws. The executor must issue a public notice so that all creditors have adequate opportunity to file a claim against the estate. Prior to paying these claims, a homestead allowance and a family allowance are provided to the members of the decedent's immediate family. Claims are then ranked in order of priority to indicate the payment schedule if existing funds prove to be insufficient. For example, administrative expenses and funeral expenses are at the top of this priority listing.
3. *Devises* are gifts of real property; *legacies* (or *bequests*) are gifts of personal property. Legacies can be classified legally as specific, demonstrative, general, or residual, depending on the type of property and the identity of the source. If available funds are insufficient to fulfill all legacies, the process of abatement is applied to determine the final allocations. After residual legacies have been reduced to zero, general legacies are decreased if necessary. Demonstrative legacies are reduced next, followed by specific legacies.
4. Federal estate taxes are assessed on the value of nonexempt estate property. Reductions in the total value of an estate are allowed for funeral and administrative expenses as well as for liabilities, charitable gifts, and all property conveyed to a spouse. For estate tax purposes the tax code provides a tax-free exemption amount of $5.0 million in 2011 and $5.12 million in 2012. Any unused exemption may be utilized by a surviving spouse, thus making the exemption portable. The same exemption amount applies to the generation-skipping tax. Individuals in 2012 have a $5.12 million lifetime gift exclusion, in addition to a $13,000 per donee annual exclusion.
5. The distinction between income and principal for both estates and trusts is frequently an important issue. Income may be assigned to one party with the principal eventually going to a different beneficiary. Such arrangements are especially common in trust funds such as charitable remainder trusts. The decedent (for an estate) or the trustor (for a trust) should have identified

the method of classification to be used for complicated transactions. If no guidance is provided, state laws apply. For example, major repairs and investment costs usually are considered reductions in principal, whereas expenses such as property taxes and ordinary repairs are charged to income. The bookkeeping procedures for estates and trusts are designed to separate and then reflect the transactions affecting principal and income.

6. To provide evidence of the proper handling of an estate or trust, the fiduciary produces a charge and discharge statement. This statement reports the assets over which the representative has been given responsibility. The statement also indicates all disbursements of assets and the property remaining at the current time. Separate reports are prepared for income and principal.

Comprehensive Illustration

(Estimated Time: 45 Minutes)

Problem

Part A

Upon her death, Marie Peterson's will contained the following provisions:

1. I leave my home, personal effects, and stock investments to my husband, Erik.
2. I leave my savings account at State Bank, up to a total of $20,000, to my oldest son, Zach.
3. I leave $5,000 to my niece, Nikki.
4. I leave all remaining assets, including my valuable coin collection, to be placed in trust and managed by Kevin Leahy, if he is willing and able to do so. If not, then I request that a financial institution be engaged to manage such assets. The income from these assets shall be utilized for the benefit of my husband, Erik. At his death, the principal of this trust shall be distributed to St. Patrick's Church, Elkhorn, Wisconsin.
5. In the event that it is necessary for a custodian or guardian to be appointed for any of my children, I request that Mary Breese be appointed in this capacity.
6. I appoint my sister Jodie to manage my estate.

Jodie has now paid all taxes and other claims, and the following assets remain; their fair value(s) follow:

Home	$400,000
Personal effects	100,000
Stock investments	50,000
Bond investments	75,000
State Bank savings account	10,000
Cash	60,000
Coin collection	Disposed of prior to death

Required

a. Identify the following:

(1) Testatrix.
(2) Trustor.
(3) Life tenant.
(4) Remainderman.
(5) Beneficiaries.
(6) Devise.
(7) General legacy.
(8) Demonstrative legacy.

(9) Trustee.

(10) Executrix.

b. Answer the following questions:

(1) Is this trust an *inter vivos* trust or a testamentary trust?

(2) What specific type of trust has been created?

(3) How will Marie Peterson's assets be distributed?

Part B

Upon his death on July 4, 2012, Brian Ulvog's will contained the following provisions:

1. I leave my home and personal effects to my wife, Linny.
2. I leave $20,000 cash to my son, Jake.
3. I leave all my investments to Marquette University.
4. I leave all income earned on my investments but not collected prior to death, and all income earned subsequent to death, to Marquette University.
5. I leave the remainder of my estate to Jamie O'Brien.
6. I appoint Jodie Reichel to be the executrix of my estate.

The executrix, Jodie Reichel, prepares an inventory and identifies the assets. Each asset's fair value, as determined by a qualified appraiser, follows:

Cash	$400,000
Home	500,000
Personal effects	75,000
Stock investments	50,000
Bond investments	70,000
Rental building	200,000
Coin collection	90,000
Dividends receivable	1,000
Interest receivable	2,000
Rent receivable	4,000

The executrix paid the following claims against the estate:

Funeral expenses	$ 20,000
Appraisal expenses	15,000
Executor fees	25,000
Medical expenses	10,000
Debts	125,000

The estate received the following cash payments:

Dividends	$ 2,000
Interest	3,000
Rent	7,000
Sale of coin collection	92,000

Assume that today is December 31, 2012, and that the executrix has completed the distributions to Linny and Jake but not to any other beneficiary.

Required

Prepare a charge and discharge statement for Brian's estate.

Solutions

Part A

a. (1) The testatrix, a female dying with a valid will, is Marie Peterson.

(2) The trustor is also Marie Peterson, the person creating the trust.

(3) The life tenant is Erik, the person possessing an interest in assets, or their income, during a measuring life.
(4) The remainderman is St. Patrick's Church, the legal person receiving the *remainder* of assets after the life tenant's interest terminates.
(5) The beneficiaries include all persons receiving *benefits* from the testatrix via her testamentary documents: Erik, Zach, Nikki, and St. Patrick's Church.
(6) The devise includes Ms. Peterson's home, which the executrix will transfer to her husband, Erik.
(7) The general legacy, the transfer not originating from a designated fund, includes the transfer of $5,000 to Nikki.
(8) The demonstrative legacy, the testamentary transfer derived from a specific source, includes Zach's interest in his mother's savings account.
(9) The trustee, Kevin Leahy, is the person or entity managing trust assets for the benefit of the trust beneficiaries. If Kevin is unable or unwilling to serve as the trustee, a court may appoint a financial institution as an alternate or successor trustee.
(10) The executrix is Jodie, the female handling the testatrix's estate.

b. (1) Because she created the trust through the provisions of her will, Marie Peterson's trust is a *testamentary trust*.
(2) Marie Peterson's trust is an example of a *charitable remainder trust*. This type of trust provides earnings for a specific period of time to a specific income beneficiary, the life tenant (Erik). After the specific time, the remainder is transferred to a charitable organization (St. Patrick's Church).
(3) Jodie, the executrix, should distribute the estate assets as follows:

- Erik—Home ($400,000); personal effects ($100,000); and stock investments ($50,000).
- Zach—State Bank savings account ($10,000). Note that because the account is not large enough to satisfy the upper limit of this demonstrative legacy, Zach will not receive the maximum amount specified by his mother.
- Nikki—Cash ($5,000).
- Trustee—Bond Investments ($75,000); and balance of cash ($55,000).

Part B

ESTATE OF BRIAN ULVOG
Charge and Discharge Statement
July 4, 2012–December 31, 2012
Jodie Reichel, Executrix

As to Principal

I charge myself with:			
Assets per original inventory			$1,392,000
Gain on sale of coin collection			2,000
Total charges			1,394,000
I credit myself with:			
Decedent's debts:			
Medical expenses	$ 10,000		
Other debts	125,000	$135,000	
Funeral and administrative expenses (20,000 + 15,000 + 25,000)		60,000	
Devises and legacies distributed:			
Linny (home and personal effects)	575,000		
Jake	20,000	595,000	
Total credits			790,000
Estate principal			604,000
Estate principal:			
Cash			284,000

Investments:	
Stocks	50,000
Bonds	70,000
Rental building	200,000
Estate principal	604,000
Cash balance analysis:	
Beginning cash	400,000
Sale of coin collection	92,000
Collection of interest	2,000
Collection of dividend	1,000
Collection of rent	4,000
Payment of funeral expense	(20,000)
Payment of appraisal expense	(15,000)
Payment of executor fees	(25,000)
Payment of medical expenses	(10,000)
Payment of other debts	(125,000)
Legacy distribution to Jake	(20,000)
Cash balance	$ 284,000

As to Income

I charge myself with:	
Dividend income (gross less receivable amount at date of death)	$ 1,000
Interest income (gross less receivable amount at date of death)	1,000
Rent income (gross less receivable amount at date of death)	3,000
Balance as to income	$ 5,000
Balance as to income	
Cash	$ 5,000

Questions

1. Distinguish between *testate* and *intestate*.
2. If a person dies without leaving a valid will, how is the distribution of property regulated?
3. What are probate laws?
4. What are the objectives of probate laws?
5. What are the responsibilities of the executor of an estate?
6. At what value are the assets within an estate reported?
7. If an asset of an estate has no readily ascertainable fair value, how should it be presented/valued on the charge/discharge statement?
8. How does an executor discover the claims against an estate?
9. What claims against an estate have priority?
10. What are homestead and family allowances?
11. What are the differences among a devise, a legacy, and a bequest?
12. Describe the four types of legacies, and give examples of each.
13. What is the purpose of the process of abatement? How does the executor of an estate utilize this process?
14. How is the federal estate tax computed?
15. What was the impact of the Tax Relief, Unemployment Insurance Reauthorization, and Job Creation Act of 2010 on the conveyance of property?
16. What is a taxable gift?
17. Why is the establishment of a credit shelter trust fund considered a good estate planning technique?
18. What deductions are allowed in computing estate income taxes?
19. Other than financial considerations, why should individuals consider preparing a valid will?
20. In accounting for an estate or trust, how is the distinction between principal and income determined?

21. What transactions are normally viewed as changes in the principal of an estate? What transactions are normally viewed as changes in the income of an estate?
22. What is the alternate date for valuing the assets of an estate? When should this alternate date be used?
23. In the initial accounting for an estate, why does the executor record only the assets?
24. What is the purpose of the charge and discharge statement that the executor of an estate issues?
25. What is a trust fund?
26. Why have trust funds become especially popular in recent years?
27. What is an *inter vivos* trust?
28. What is a testamentary trust?
29. What are QTIP trusts, GRATs, and charitable remainder trusts?
30. Why is the distinction between principal and income so important in accounting for most trusts?

Problems

LO1

1. Which of the following is *not* a true statement?
   a. *Testate* refers to a person having a valid will.
   b. The laws of descent convey personal property if an individual dies without a valid will.
   c. *Intestate* refers to a person having no valid will.
   d. A specific legacy is a gift of personal property that is specifically identified.

LO1

2. Why might real estate be omitted from an inventory of estate property?
   a. Real estate is subject to a separate inheritance tax.
   b. State laws prohibit real property from being conveyed by an estate.
   c. State laws require a separate listing of all real estate.
   d. In some states, depending on the ownership, real estate is considered to be conveyed directly to a beneficiary at the time of death.

LO1

3. What is the purpose of the laws of distribution?
   a. To guide the distribution of personal property when an individual dies without a will.
   b. To verify the legality of a will, especially an oral will.
   c. To guide the distribution of real property when an individual dies without a will.
   d. To outline the functions of the executor of an estate.

LO4

4. A deceased individual owned a bond. Which of the following is included in the estate principal?
   a. All interest collected prior to distributing the bonds to a beneficiary is considered part of the estate principal.
   b. Only the first cash payment after death is included in the estate principal.
   c. Interest that was not collected prior to death is excluded from the estate principal.
   d. Interest earned prior to death is considered part of the estate principal even if received after death.

LO1

5. Which of the following is *not* a goal of probate laws?
   a. To gather and preserve all of the decedent's property.
   b. To ensure that each individual produces a valid will.
   c. To discover the decedent's intent for property held at death and then to follow those wishes.
   d. To carry out an orderly and fair settlement of all debts and distribution of property.

LO1

6. How are claims against a decedent's estate discovered by an executor?
   a. Public notice must be printed in an appropriate newspaper to alert all possible claimants.
   b. The executor waits for nine months until all possible bills have been received.
   c. The executor directly contacts all companies that the decedent did business with.
   d. Claims the estate is to pay are limited to all of the bills received but not paid prior to the date of death.

LO1

7. Why are claims against an estate put into an order of priority?
   a. To help the executor determine the due date for each claim.
   b. To determine which claims are to be paid if funds are insufficient to pay all claims.

c. To assist in determining which specific assets are to be used to satisfy these claims.

d. To list the claims in order of age so that the oldest can be paid first.

LO1

8. Which of the following claims against an estate does *not* have priority?

   a. Funeral expenses because the amounts incurred are usually at the discretion of family members.

   b. Medical expenses associated with the decedent's last illness.

   c. The costs of administering the estate.

   d. Unpaid rent on the decedent's home if not paid for the three months immediately prior to death.

LO2

9. How does a devise differ from a legacy?

   a. A devise is a gift of money and a legacy is a nonmonetary gift.

   b. A devise is a gift to an individual and a legacy is a gift to a charity or other organization.

   c. A devise is a gift of real property and a legacy is a gift of personal property.

   d. A devise is a gift made prior to death and a legacy is a gift made at death.

LO1

10. What is the homestead allowance?

   a. A reduction of $20,000 in estate assets prior to computing the amount of federal estate taxes.

   b. The amount of property conveyed in a will to a surviving spouse.

   c. An allotment from an estate to a surviving spouse and/or minor and dependent children before any claims are paid.

   d. A decrease in the value of property on which state inheritance taxes are assessed. The reduction is equal to the value of property conveyed to a surviving spouse.

LO2

11. Which of the following is a specific legacy?

   a. The gift of all remaining estate property to a charity.

   b. The gift of $44,000 cash from a specified source.

   c. The gift of $44,000 cash.

   d. The gift of 1,000 shares of stock in IBM.

LO2

12. A will has the following statement: "I leave $20,000 cash from my savings account in the Central Fidelity Bank to my sister, Angela." This gift is an example of

   a. A residual legacy.

   b. A general legacy.

   c. A demonstrative legacy.

   d. A specific legacy.

LO2

13. What is the objective of the process of abatement?

   a. To give legal structure to the reductions that must be made if an estate has insufficient assets to satisfy all legacies.

   b. To ensure that all property distributions take place in a timely manner.

   c. To provide adequate compensation for the estate executor and any appraisers or other experts that must be hired.

   d. To ensure that all legacies are distributed to the appropriate party as specified by the decedent's will or state laws.

LO3

14. For estate tax purposes, what date is used for valuation purposes?

   a. Property is always valued at the date of death.

   b. Property is always valued at the date of distribution.

   c. Property is valued at the date of death unless the alternate date, which is the date of distribution or six months after death, whichever comes first, is selected.

   d. Property is valued at the date of death although a reduction is allowed if the value declines within one year of death.

LO3

15. Which of the following is true concerning the Tax Relief, Unemployment Insurance Reauthorization, and Job Creation Act of 2010?

   a. This tax law leads to the immediate elimination of the federal estate tax.

   b. This tax law leads to the immediate elimination of the federal gift tax.

c. This tax law provides for a $5.12 million tax-free exemption for estates created in 2012.

d. This tax law leads to the immediate elimination of the generation-skipping tax.

LO3

16. In computing federal estate taxes, deductions from an estate's value are allowed for all of the following *except*

a. Charitable bequests.

b. Losses on the disposal of investments.

c. Funeral expenses.

d. Debts of the decedent.

LO3

17. The following unmarried individuals died in 2012. The estate of John Lexington has a taxable value of $4,590,000. The estate of Dorothy Alexander has a taxable value of $4.9 million. The estate of Scotty Fitzgerald has a taxable value of $5.6 million. None of these individuals made any taxable gifts during their lifetimes. Which of the following statements is true?

a. Only Fitzgerald's estate will have to pay federal estate taxes.

b. All three of the estates will have to pay federal estate taxes.

c. None of these estates is large enough to necessitate the payment of estate taxes.

d. Only the estates of Alexander and Fitzgerald are large enough to necessitate the payment of estate taxes.

LO3

18. Sally Anne Williams died on January 1, 2012. All of her property was conveyed to several relatives on April 1, 2012. For federal estate tax purposes, the executor chose the alternate valuation date. On what date was the value of the property determined?

a. January 1, 2012.

b. April 1, 2012.

c. July 1, 2012.

d. December 31, 2012.

LO3

19. M. Wilson Waltman died on January 1, 2012. All of his property was conveyed to beneficiaries on October 1, 2012. For federal estate tax purposes, the executor chose the alternate valuation date. On what date was the value of the property determined?

a. January 1, 2012.

b. July 1, 2012.

c. October 1, 2012.

d. December 31, 2012.

LO3

20. Which of the following is *not* true concerning gift taxes?

a. Gift taxes are not abolished but a lifetime exclusion of $5.12 million is available.

b. The Tax Relief, Unemployment Insurance Reauthorization, and Job Creation Act of 2010 will eventually eliminate the federal gift tax.

c. Historically, gift taxes and estate taxes have been linked through a unified transfer credit.

d. Gift taxes are different from generation-skipping taxes.

LO6

21. A married couple has written a will that leaves part of their money to a trust fund. The income from this trust will benefit the surviving spouse until death, with the principal then going to their children. Why was the trust fund created?

a. To reduce the estate of the surviving spouse and, thus, decrease the total amount of estate taxes to be paid by the couple.

b. To ensure that the surviving spouse is protected from lawsuits filed by the couple's children.

c. To give the surviving spouse discretion over the ultimate use of these funds.

d. To maximize the earning potential of the money because trust funds generate more income than other investments.

LO3

22. The executor of an estate is filing an income tax return for the current period. Revenues of $25,000 have been earned. Which of the following is *not* a deduction allowed in computing taxable income?

a. Income distributed to a beneficiary.

b. Funeral expenses.

c. A personal exemption.

d. Charitable donations.

LO4

23. What is a remainderman?
    a. A beneficiary that receives the principal left in an estate or trust after a specified time.
    b. The beneficiary of the decedent's life insurance policy.
    c. An executor or administrator after an estate has been completely settled.
    d. If a legacy is given to a group of people, the remainderman is the last of the individuals to die.

LO4

24. In an estate, which of the following is charged to income rather than to principal?
    a. Funeral expenses.
    b. Investment costs.
    c. Property taxes.
    d. Losses on the sale of investments.

LO5

25. In recording the transactions of an estate, when are liabilities recorded?
    a. When incurred.
    b. At the date of death.
    c. When the executor takes responsibility for the estate.
    d. When paid.

LO6

26. What is the difference between a testamentary trust and an *inter vivos* trust?
    a. A testamentary trust conveys money to a charity; an *inter vivos* trust conveys money to individuals.
    b. A testamentary trust is created by a will; an *inter vivos* trust is created by a living individual.
    c. A testamentary trust conveys income to one party and the principal to another; an *inter vivos* trust conveys all monies to the same party.
    d. A testamentary trust ceases after a specified period of time; an *inter vivos* trust is assumed to be permanent.

LO6

27. Which of the following is a charitable lead trust?
    a. The income of the trust fund goes to an individual until death, at which time the principal is conveyed to a charitable organization.
    b. Charitable gifts are placed into the trust until a certain dollar amount is achieved and is then transferred to a specified charitable organization.
    c. The income of a trust fund goes to a charitable organization for a specified time with the principal then being conveyed to a different beneficiary.
    d. A charity conveys money to a trust that generates income for the charity's use in its various projects.

LO3

28. The estate of Nancy Hanks reports the following information:

Value of estate assets	$1,400,000
Conveyed to spouse	700,000
Conveyed to children	100,000
Conveyed to charities	420,000
Funeral expenses	50,000
Administrative expenses	20,000
Debts	110,000

What is the taxable estate value?
    a. $70,000.
    b. $100,000.
    c. $180,000.
    d. $420,000.

LO3

29. An estate has the following income:

Rental income	$5,000
Interest income	3,000
Dividend income	1,000

The interest income was immediately conveyed to the appropriate beneficiary. The dividends were given to charity as per the decedent's will. What is the taxable income of the estate?

a. \$4,400.
b. \$5,000.
c. \$8,000.
d. \$8,400.

LO1, LO4, LO6

30. Define each of the following terms:
a. Will.
b. Estate.
c. Intestate.
d. Probate laws.
e. Trust.
f. *Inter vivos* trust.
g. Charitable remainder trust.
h. Remainderman.
i. Executor.
j. Homestead allowance.

LO1

31. Answer each of the following questions:
a. What are the objectives of probate laws?
b. What tasks does the executor of an estate perform?
c. What assets are normally included as estate properties?
d. What claims have priority to the distributions made by an estate?

LO1, LO2, LO4–LO6

32. The will of Josh O'Brien has the following stipulations:
Antique collection goes to Ilsa Lunn.
All money in the First Savings Bank goes to Richard Blaine.
Cash of \$9,000 goes to Nelson Tucker.
All remaining assets are put into a trust fund with the income going to Lucy Van Jones. At her death, the principal is to be conveyed to Howard Amadeus.

Identify the following:
a. Remainderman.
b. Trustor.
c. Demonstrative legacy.
d. General legacy.
e. Specific legacy.
f. Life tenant.
g. Testator.

LO2

33. Marie Hardy's will has the following provisions:
"I leave the cash balance deposited in the First National Bank (up to a total of \$50,000) to Jack Abrams. I leave \$18,000 cash to Suzanne Benton. I leave 1,000 shares of Coca-Cola Company stock to Cindy Cheng. I leave my house to Dennis Davis. I leave all of my other assets and properties to Wilbur N. Ed."
a. Assume that the estate has the following assets: \$41,000 cash in the First National Bank, \$16,000 cash in the New Hampshire Savings and Loan, 800 shares of Coca-Cola stock, 1,100 shares of Xerox stock, a house, and other property valued at \$13,000. What distributions will be made from this estate?
b. Assume that the estate has the following assets: \$55,000 cash in the First National Bank, \$6,000 cash in the New Hampshire Savings and Loan, 1,200 shares of Coca-Cola stock, 600 shares of Xerox stock, and other property valued at \$22,000. What distributions will be made from this estate?

LO3

34. Zac Peterson's estate reports the following information:

Value of estate assets	\$2,300,000
Conveyed to spouse	1,000,000
Conveyed to children	230,000

Conveyed to trust fund for benefit of cousin	500,000
Conveyed to charities	260,000
Funeral expenses	23,000
Administrative expenses	41,000
Debts	246,000

What is the taxable estate value?

LO3

35. Donna Stober's estate has the following assets (all figures approximate fair value):

Investments in stocks and bonds	$1,400,000
House	700,000
Cash	70,000
Investment land	60,000
Automobiles (three rare vehicles)	51,000
Other assets	100,000

The house, cash, and other assets are left to the decedent's spouse. The investment land is contributed to a charitable organization. The automobiles are to be given to the decedent's brother. The investments in stocks and bonds are to be put into a trust fund. The income generated by this trust will go to the decedent's spouse annually until all of the couple's children have reached the age of 25. At that time, the trust will be divided evenly among the children.

The following amounts are paid prior to distribution and settlement of the estate: funeral expenses of $20,000 and estate administration expenses of $10,000.

a. What value is to be reported as the taxable estate for federal estate tax purposes?

b. How does the year in which an individual dies affect the estate tax computation? For example, what is the impact of dying on December 30, 2010, versus January 2, 2011?

LO3

36. During 2012, an estate generated income of $20,000:

Rental income	$9,000
Interest income	6,000
Dividend income	5,000

The interest income is conveyed immediately to the beneficiary stated in the decedent's will. The dividends are given to the decedent's church.

What amount of federal income tax must this estate pay?

LO4, LO5

37. The executor of Rose Shield's estate listed the following properties (at fair value):

Cash	$300,000
Life insurance receivable	200,000
Investments in stocks and bonds	100,000
Rental property	90,000
Personal property	130,000

a. Prepare journal entries to record the property held by Ms. Shield's estate and then each of the following transactions that occur in the months following the decedent's death:

(1) Claims of $80,000 are made against the estate for various debts incurred before the decedent's death.

(2) Interest of $12,000 is received from bonds held by the estate. Of this amount, $5,000 had been earned prior to death.

(3) Ordinary repairs costing $6,000 are made to the rental property.

(4) All debts ($80,000) are paid.

(5) Stocks recorded in the estate at $16,000 are sold for $19,000 cash.

(6) Rental income of $14,000 is collected. Of this amount, $2,000 had been earned prior to the decedent's death.

(7) Cash of $6,000 is distributed to Jim Arness, an income beneficiary.

(8) The proceeds from the life insurance policy are collected and the money is immediately distributed to Amanda Blake as specified in the decedent's will.

(9) Funeral expenses of $10,000 are paid.

b. Prepare in proper form a charge and discharge statement.

LO4, LO5

38. The executor of Gina Purcell's estate has recorded the following information:

Assets discovered at death (at fair value):	
Cash	$600,000
Life insurance receivable	200,000
Investments:	
Walt Disney Company	11,000
Polaroid Corporation	27,000
Ford Motor Company	34,000
Dell Computer Corporation	32,000
Rental property	300,000
Cash outflows:	
Funeral expenses	$ 21,000
Executor fees	12,000
Ordinary repairs of rental property	2,000
Debts	81,000
Distribution of income to income beneficiary	4,000
Distribution to charitable remainder trust	300,000
Cash inflows:	
Sale of Polaroid stock	$ 30,000
Rental income ($4,000 earned prior to death)	11,000
Dividend income ($2,000 declared prior to death)	12,000
Life insurance proceeds	200,000

Debts of $17,000 still remain to be paid. The Dell shares have been conveyed to the appropriate beneficiary. Assume that Ms. Purcell's will stated that all executor fees are to be paid from principal.

Prepare an interim charge and discharge statement for this estate.

LO4, LO5

39. Jerry Tasch's will has the following provisions:

- $150,000 in cash goes to Thomas Thorne.
- All shares of Coca-Cola go to Cindy Phillips.
- Residence goes to Kevin Simmons.
- All other estate assets are to be liquidated with the resulting cash going to the First Church of Freedom, Missouri.

Prepare journal entries for the following transactions:

a. Discovered the following assets (at fair value):

Cash	$ 80,000
Interest receivable	6,000
Life insurance policy	300,000
Residence	200,000
Shares of Coca-Cola Company	50,000
Shares of Polaroid Corporation	110,000
Shares of Ford Motor Company	140,000

b. Collected interest of $7,000.

c. Paid funeral expenses of $20,000.

d. Discovered debts of $40,000.

e. Located an additional savings account of $12,000.

f. Conveyed title to the residence to Kevin Simmons.

g. Collected life insurance policy.

h. Discovered additional debts of $60,000. Paid debts totaling $100,000.

i. Conveyed cash of $150,000 to appropriate beneficiary.

j. Sold the shares of Polaroid for $112,000.

k. Paid administrative expenses of $10,000.

LO4, LO5

40. After the death of Lennie Pope, his will was read. It contained the following provisions:

- $110,000 in cash goes to decedent's brother, Ned Pope.
- Residence and other personal property go to his sister, Sue Pope.
- Proceeds from the sale of Ford stock go to uncle, Harwood Pope.
- $300,000 goes into a charitable remainder trust.
- All other estate assets are to be liquidated with the cash going to Victoria Jones.

a. Prepare journal entries for the following transactions that subsequently occur:

(1) Discovered the following assets (at fair value):

Cash	$ 19,000
Certificates of deposit	90,000
Dividends receivable	3,000
Life insurance policy	450,000
Residence and personal effects	470,000
Shares of Ford Motor Company	72,000
Shares of Xerox Corporation	97,000

(2) Collected life insurance policy.

(3) Collected dividends of $4,000.

(4) Discovered debts of $71,000.

(5) Conveyed title to the residence to Sue Pope along with the decedent's personal effects.

(6) Discovered title to land valued at $15,000.

(7) Discovered additional debts of $37,000. Paid all of the debts totaling $108,000.

(8) Paid funeral expenses of $31,000.

(9) Conveyed cash of $110,000 to Ned Pope.

(10) Sold the shares of Ford for $81,000.

(11) Paid administrative expenses of $16,000.

(12) Made the appropriate payment to Harwood Pope.

b. Prepare a charge and discharge statement.

LO4, LO5

41. James Albemarle created a trust fund at the beginning of 2012. The income from this fund will go to his son Edward. When Edward reaches the age of 25, the principal of the fund will be conveyed to United Charities of Cleveland. Mr. Albemarle specified that 75 percent of trustee fees are to be paid from principal. Terry Jones, CPA, is the trustee.

Prepare all necessary journal entries for the trust to record the following transactions:

a. James Albemarle transferred cash of $300,000, stocks worth $200,000, and rental property valued at $150,000 to the trustee of this fund.

b. Immediately invested cash of $260,000 in bonds issued by the U.S. government. Commissions of $3,000 are paid on this transaction.

c. Incurred permanent repairs of $7,000 so that the property can be rented. Payment is made immediately.

d. Received dividends of $4,000. Of this amount, $1,000 had been declared prior to the creation of the trust fund.

e. Paid insurance expense of $2,000 on the rental property.

f. Received rental income of $8,000.

g. Paid $4,000 from the trust for trustee services rendered.

h. Conveyed cash of $5,000 to Edward Albemarle.

LO4, LO5

42. Henry O'Donnell created an *inter vivos* trust fund. He owns a large department store in Higgins, Utah. He also owns a tract of land adjacent to the store used as an extra parking lot when the store is having a sale and during the Christmas season. O'Donnell expects the land to appreciate in value and eventually be sold for an office complex or additional stores.

O'Donnell places this land into a charitable lead trust, which will hold the land for 10 years until O'Donnell's son is 21. At that time, title will transfer to the son. The store will pay rent to use the land during the interim. The income generated each year from this usage will be given to a local church. The land is currently valued at $320,000.

During the first year of this arrangement, the trustee records the following cash transactions:

Cash inflows:	
Rental income	$60,000
Cash outflows:	
Insurance	$ 4,000
Property taxes	6,000
Paving (considered an extraordinary repair).	4,000
Maintenance	8,000
Distribution to income beneficiary	30,000

Prepare all journal entries for this trust fund including the entry to create the trust.

Develop Your Skills

RESEARCH CASE 1

The CPA firm of Simon, Winslow, and Tate has been approached by a client who is interested in information about the possibility of establishing a minor's Section 2503(c) trust.

Go to the website http://www.finaid.org/savings/2503ctrust.phtml. Alternatively, use an Internet search engine to find other analyses of a Section 2503(c) trust.

Required

Based on the results of this search, write a memo for the client outlining the requirements, design, advantages, and disadvantages of a minor's Section 2503(c) trust so the client can make an informed decision.

RESEARCH CASE 2

A staff employee for the CPA firm of O'Brien, Leahy, and Sweeney is currently preparing Form 1041 as an income tax return for an estate. The staff employee knows that the estate is allowed a deduction for income distributions to beneficiaries up to the amount of the estate's distributable net income (DNI) for the period. However, the employee is not certain how to compute the exact amount of this deduction.

Go to the website www.irs.gov. Do a search for "Instruction 1041" to get the instruction information for estate and trust income taxes published by the IRS.

Required

Read the information provided, and write a memo to the employee explaining (in general terms) how to calculate this deduction.

RESEARCH CASE 3

A client, Beth Voga, asks for advice. She tells you that her grandmother, a widowed resident of Montana, has no will. She asks whether any portion of her grandmother's estate will pass to her (Beth's) cousins, whom her grandmother despises.

Required

Use an Internet search engine to locate the Montana version of the Uniform Probate Code. Then briefly advise Ms. Voga, answering her specific question. Also advise her on the necessity of a will for her grandmother.

ANALYSIS CASE 1

CPA skills

Use an Internet search engine to locate an explanation of the benefits of a grantor retained annuity trust.

Required

Write a memo describing the circumstances that would make this type of trust most advantageous.

ANALYSIS CASE 2

CPA skills

A law firm is preparing to file a federal estate tax return (Form 706). The estate's executor has elected to use the alternate valuation date. The partner in charge of filing this return is not certain about all of the ramifications of having chosen to use this alternate date.

Go to the website www.irs.gov. Do a search for "Instruction 706" to get the instruction information published by the IRS for federal estate taxes.

Required

Read the information provided, and write a memo to the partner outlining the information the IRS provides as to the significance of the alternate valuation date.

Index

Page numbers followed by n refer to notes.

D

E